Contracts:
Cases, Notes & Materials,
Seventh Edition

Contracts:
Cases, Notes & Materials,
Seventh Edition

John Swan
Aird & Berlis LLP

Barry J. Reiter
Bennett Jones LLP

Nicholas C. Bala
Professor of Law, Queen's University

LexisNexis®
Butterworths

Contracts: Cases, Notes & Materials, Seventh Edition
© LexisNexis Canada Inc. 2006
August 2006

Members of the LexisNexis Group worldwide

Canada	LexisNexis Canada Inc, 123 Commerce Valley Dr. E. Suite 700, MARKHAM, Ontario
Argentina	Abeledo Perrot, Jurisprudencia Argentina and Depalma, BUENOS AIRES
Australia	Butterworths, a Division of Reed International Books Australia Pty Ltd, CHATSWOOD, New South Wales
Austria	ARD Betriebsdienst and Verlag Orac, VIENNA
Chile	Publitecsa and Conosur Ltda, SANTIAGO DE CHILE
Czech Republic	Orac, sro, PRAGUE
France	Éditions du Juris-Classeur SA, PARIS
Hong Kong	Butterworths Asia (Hong Kong), HONG KONG
Hungary	Hvg Orac, BUDAPEST
India	Butterworths India, NEW DELHI
Ireland	Butterworths (Ireland) Ltd, DUBLIN
Italy	Giuffré, MILAN
Malaysia	Malayan Law Journal Sdn Bhd, KUALA LUMPUR
New Zealand	Butterworths of New Zealand, WELLINGTON
Poland	Wydawnictwa Prawnicze PWN, WARSAW
Singapore	Butterworths Asia, SINGAPORE
South Africa	Butterworth Publishers (Pty) Ltd, DURBAN
Switzerland	Stämpfli Verlag AG, BERNE
United Kingdom	Butterworths Tolley, a Division of Reed Elsevier (UK), LONDON, WC2A
USA	LexisNexis, DAYTON, Ohio

Library and Archives Canada Cataloguing in Publication

Swan, John
    Contracts : cases, notes & materials / John Swan,
Barry J. Reiter, Nicholas C. Bala. — 7th ed.

Includes bibliographical references and index.
ISBN 0-433-44974-8

    1. Contracts—Canada—Cases. I. Reiter, Barry J., 1948-
II. Bala, Nicholas, 1952- III. Title.

KE850.A7S83 2006   346.7102   C2006-903905-4
KF801.A7S93 2006

Printed and bound in Canada.

For

*William, Philippa, Ellen, Amanda, Hilary, Evan,
Elise, Emily, Katie, Andrew and Sarah Elizabeth*

EDITORIAL NOTES AND ACKNOWLEDGMENTS

The cases and materials in this book have numbered paragraphs to facilitate use by law students and professors. Most of the paragraph numbering was added by the authors of this casebook; it is sequential and does not reflect deleted paragraphs. Some recent Supreme Court of Canada cases, however, have numbered paragraphs in print law reports and on computer databases, and for these cases the numbering is as provided by the Court. Much of the material, especially the modern case material, has been extensively edited, with deletions marked by ellipses (...).

A casebook on such a wide subject necessarily contains a great deal of reference to the work of others in the field. The authors and publishers of these articles and textbooks have been most generous in giving permission for the reproduction in this text of work already in print. References, of course, appear where necessary and possible in the text. It is convenient for us to list below, for the assistance of the reader, the publishers and authors for whose courtesy we are most grateful. The following is organized by author in alphabetical order.

Beale and Dugdale, "Contracts Between Businessmen: Planning and the Use of Contractual Remedies" (1975), 2 British Journal of Law and Society 45; reprinted with permission from Basil Blackwell.

L. Fuller, "Consideration and Form" (1941), 41 Columbia L. Rev. 799; reprinted with permission from the Columbia Law Review Association Inc.

Fuller and Eisenberg, *Basic Contract Law*, 3rd ed. (St. Paul: West Publishing Co., 1972), pp. 100, 1008-1009; reprinted with permission of the West Group.

L.L. Fuller and W.R. Purdue, "The Reliance Interest in Contract Damages" (1936), 46 Yale L. Rev. 52 (part 1) and 373 (part 2); reprinted by permission from the Yale Law Journal Company and Fred B. Rothman & Company from *The Yale Law Journal*, Vol. 46, pp. 52-96 and 373-420.

N. Geis, "Residential Private Governments and the Law" (1981), 67 American Bar Association Journal 1418; reprinted by permission of the *American Bar Association Journal*.

Globe and Mail Report on Business, February 21, 1990, p. B4; reprinted with permission from the Globe and Mail.

Goetz and Scott, "Liquidated Damages, Penalties and the Just Compensation Principle" (1977), 77 Col. L. Rev. 554 at 558, 567-68, 572-76; reprinted with permission from the *Columbia Law Review* Association Inc.

H.C. Havighurst, *The Nature of Private Contract* (1961), pp. 115-118; reprinted with permission from Northwestern University Press.

F. Kessler, "Contracts of Adhesion — Some Thoughts about Freedom of Contract" (1943), 43 Col. L. Rev. 629; reprinted with permission from the author.

A.T. Kronman, "Contract Law and Distributive Justice" (1980), 89 Yale L.J. 472 at 472-75; reprinted by permission of The Yale Law Journal Company and Fred B. Rothman & Company from *The Yale Law Journal*, Vol. 89, pp. 472-511.

Law Society of Upper Canada, "Conduct and Ethics: Independent Legal Advice Never Routine", *Ontario Lawyers Gazette,* vol. 1, no.1 (1997), p. 7-9.

K. Llewellyn, *The Common-Law Tradition* (New York: Little Brown and Company, 1960), pp. 362-71); reprinted with permission from Little Brown and Company.

K. Llewellyn, "What Price Contract? An Essay in Perspective" (1931), 40 Yale L.J. 704 at 741-44; reprinted by permission of The Yale Law Journal Company and Fred B. Rothman & Company from *The Yale Law Journal*, Vol. 40, pp. 704-751.

I. Macneil, *The New Social Contract* (New Haven: Yale University Press, 1980), pp. 4-10, 70, 72-77 (New Haven: Yale University Press); reprinted with permission from Yale University Press.

I. Macneil, "Whither Contracts" (1969), 21 J. of Leg. Ed. 403; reprinted with permission from the Journal of Legal Education.

B. Mensch, "Freedom of Contract as Ideology" (1981), 33 Stan. L. Rev. 753 ©1981 by the Board of Trustees of the Leland Stanford Junior University; reprinted with permission.

R.B. Posner, *Economic Analysis of Law*, 6th ed. (New York: Aspen Publishing, 2002), pp. 118-123; reprinted with permission from Aspen Law & Business.

B.J. Reiter, "Courts, Consideration, and Common Sense" (1978), 27 U.T.L.J. 468-71; reprinted with permission from University of Toronto Press.

K. Renner, *The Institutions of Private Law and Their Social Function* (1906) (London: Routledge and Kegan Paul, 1949, translated by Agnes Schwartz-child), p. 48; reprinted with permission from Routledge and Kegan Paul.

Restatement of the Law, Second, Contracts, paras. 90, 161, 355 ©1981 by The American Law Institute; reprinted with permission.

Uniform Commercial Code, paras. 2-306(2) (Comment), 2-609, 2-610, 2-615, 2-716(1) (Comment) ©1995 by The American Law Institute and the National Conference of Commissioners on Uniform State Laws; reprinted with permission.

W.A. Weigers, "Economic Analysis of Law and "Private ordering": A Feminist Critique" (1992), 42 U.T.L.J. 170; reprinted with permission from University of Toronto Press.

   Professor Bala also wishes to acknowledge support from a grant from the Social Sciences and Humanities Research Council.

ABOUT THE AUTHORS

JOHN SWAN is an Associate at Aird & Berlis LLP in Toronto. He taught at the Faculty of Law at the University of Toronto from 1965 to 1988 and at the Faculty of Law of McGill University from 1996 to 2002. He has been in practice since 1987, a partner at Aird & Berlis from 1989 to 1997 and an associate at Stikeman Elliott in Montreal from 1997 to 2002, before returning to Aird & Berlis in 2002, where his role is principally as Counsel to the firm. He has an AV rating from Martindale-Hubbell. He was Lansdowne Visiting Professor at the University of Victoria in 1984. He is currently an Adjunct Professor at Osgoode Hall Law School.

His major teaching and research interests were in Contracts and the Conflict of Laws. He has published extensively on each topic. His practice is mainly in the corporate/commercial area with a significant emphasis on the drafting, administration and interpretation of contracts of all kinds.

NICHOLAS BALA has been a Professor at the Faculty of Law at Queen's University in Kingston, Canada since 1980. He has a B.A. in Economics from the University of Toronto and law degrees from Queen's and Harvard. He specializes in Family and Children's Law, focusing his research on such issues as juvenile justice, spouse and child abuse, child witnesses, parental rights and responsibilities after divorce, the legal definition of the family, and non-adversarial methods of settling family disputes.

Professor Bala also teaches Contracts Law, which is his favourite subject to teach. He has twice won Queen's Law Students Society Teaching awards at Queen's, and served as Associate Dean at Queen's for five years. He has also been a Visiting Professor at McGill in Montreal, Duke in the United States and the University of Calgary.

TABLE OF CONTENTS

TABLE OF CASES

[A page number in boldface type indicates that
a case has been excerpted in the text.]

INTRODUCTION

Ideas about markets and agreements, about the justification for enforcing promises, and about the proper role of contracts and markets have been and are a battleground for competing philosophical and political ideologies. The transformation
into market-based economies of many of the "command" economies of Eastern
Europe and Asia — the economies formerly based on control by a Communist
Party — into economies with markets that are more or less free has forced the
people living in those countries and, indeed, all of us to consider the role of contracts and markets. The rapid and often disappointing results of the introduction of
market economies and "free enterprise" has forced those societies to address explicitly how well different ways of organizing societies and their economies can
meet the population's basic needs.

There continues, however, to be controversy about how much reliance should
be placed on markets and exchange transactions to organize societies and their
economies.

Closely associated with the faith in the economic virtues of markets and market
economies is the belief that markets and people's ability to make contracts are
aspects of individual freedom: the debate on the role of markets in China, again
from the outside, appears to focus as much on this aspect as on the economic one.
At the heart of an exchange or market economy is the idea that individuals — as
consumers, employees and investors, individually or collectively in various forms
of business enterprises — have a fundamental role to play in producing wealth.
("Wealth" means the ability of a society to meet the needs of its people for food,
shelter and clothing and, of course, for all the other things that make human life
other than "solitary, poor, nasty, brutish, and short".) The recognition of this fact
does not mean that the state has no proper or justifiable role to play in regulating
markets, in creating the conditions in which markets can operate fairly and in controlling or preventing the most obvious forms of unfairness or exploitation.

For the purposes of this study, the existence of a market economy in Canada is
a fact. It is not necessary to agree on the political, moral or philosophical bases of
a market-based economy to make the study of the legal regulation of the market
important. The acceptance of the existence of a market economy in Canada does
not mean that the proper role of the market cannot be debated. A recognition of the
need to assert legal control over what are perceived to be abuses of a market economy and debates over the extent and manner of market regulation are important
aspects of the study of contract law.

The role of the market is changing not only in the societies that are now beginning (or returning to) the development of free enterprise, exchange-based economies, but in our own market-based (or market-dominated) society. There remain
important alternatives to exchange-based transactions for distribution of goods and
services in our own society. Government clearly has an important role in the regulation of many markets, and in provision of some goods and services without regard to ability to pay. Families, charities and religious communities also provide
goods and services based on principles other than exchange. The debate over the
proper role of markets and contracts involves issues of economic efficiency and
human freedom, but it also related to views about the nature of human relations

and of society. There are social and environmental costs to a market-based economy, especially if there is not appropriate regulation and some form of redistribution of wealth. As some countries have moved from command towards market
economies, many in those societies have experienced an increase in poverty and
misfortune.

Our society, as a "market economy" is, among other things, characterized by
the ubiquity of exchange relations. Such relations arise from:

    (a) the inevitable scarcity of resources and the need to allocate them among
         competing claimants, and
    (b) the specialization and division of labour.

The law of contracts is about the rules that govern exchange relations. Because
exchange relations are so important in our society, and indeed, in almost every
other modern society — the problems of exchanges have become the stuff of philosophies and moral codes. As a result of this fact, the law is permeated by ideas
that express very deeply held values and moral ideas. Promise-breaking is an act
that often attracts moral condemnation as well as a legal remedy against the prom-
ise-breaker.

The study of contract law is premised on the existence of privately enforceable
agreements in a market economy. Our economic system is based on contracts for
the exchange of goods, services and property. The study of contract law provides
an important perspective on the operation of the economy and the legal system.
Thinking about what fairness, justice and efficiency demand of different types of
exchange relations requires reflection on the nature of our economy and society.
What legal rules will promote a fairer, more just or more efficient society? The
law is a tool for achieving social, economic and political ends. A useful focus for
law students, lawyers and judges is to remember that, to an important extent, "Law
is the science of getting from here to there".

These materials focus on the law governing contractual relations that is applicable in Canada's common law jurisdictions. Most of the case law and statutory
references are Canadian. There are also some English, Commonwealth and American decisions and statutory excerpts, since courts and legislatures in this country
often look to those countries for precedents and solutions to legal problems. There
are also some references to international treaties and conventions that regulate the
increasing number of international transactions.

There are broad similarities in the types of contractual problems that are faced
in different countries — at least in all countries with market economies. A student
with a good understanding of the contract law in Canada will be well placed to
begin to study contractual regulation in other legal systems. The social and legal
culture of a jurisdiction, however, affects attitudes and laws about negotiations,
promises and contracts. Canada's common law rules have been strongly influenced
by our English legal heritage and increasingly one sees the influences of close
economic and legal ties to the United States. There may also be some subtle influences on Canada's common law of contracts from the thinking of those trained in
the Quebec Civil Code, especially through the Supreme Court of Canada. It is apparent that Canada's common law jurisdictions now have a uniquely Canadian
"law of contracts". The focus of this book is on exchange transactions, but this
does not mean that our concern is only with economic interests. Many contracts
deal with vitally important psychological and social interests, most obviously

employment and domestic contracts. Increasingly the law is struggling with questions of how to recognize non-economic interests in exchange transactions.

While this book makes occasional reference to issues related to public agreements, the focus is on private contracts, and on the laws that govern private agreements. Agreements have a broader relevance in a range of public contexts. The treaties between the Crown and Aboriginal nations also constitute an important type of public agreement that is a significant source of rights for Aboriginal peoples. Treaties between countries are the basis of international law and are increasingly relevant for international commerce. In Canada, negotiations and agreements between different levels of government are also an aspect of constitutional law and politics. An understanding of some of the issues and tensions that arise with private contracts is essential for an understanding of these public agreements, though there are also some very important differences between private contracts and public agreements.

CONTRACT AND PROMISE

It is important to explain at the very beginning of this book some of the terminology to be used. Two key words are "contract" and "promise". Before attempting to define these terms, consider three examples.

1. Nigel lived in an apartment in Halifax. He was offered a job in Toronto beginning on September 1. Early in June, Nigel flew to Toronto to find a place to live. He found an apartment which he liked in Toronto and arranged with the rental agent, the superintendent of the apartment block, to rent it from September 1. He completed the application, gave a deposit of the first and last month's rent, and was told that his application was approved and that he could move in on the Labour Day weekend. On his return to Halifax, Nigel searched the Yellow Pages for a mover, phoned a number of advertisers to get expressions of interest and prices, and eventually arranged with Pam's Moving Inc. that a team of three people would come to his Halifax apartment on August 26, pack his things, load them onto a truck and take them to Toronto where they would be unloaded and carried into his new apartment. The agreed price was $4,000. All the arrangements were made with Pam's Moving over the phone.

2. Akiko lived in Toronto. She decided to buy a computer. She went to her local library to investigate online sources for computers. She found a website, "computerseller.com", that appeared to offer the best price for delivery of the exact type of computer she wanted. Akiko specified the type of computer she would like and agreed to pay a surcharge for fast delivery to Toronto. She charged her purchase to her VISA-TD-Canada Trust credit card, and provided the requested information about her address and phone number.

3. In 1961 the Churchill Falls (Labrador) Corporation and Hydro Québec signed a lengthy set of written documents that provided for the construction of a major hydro-electric project on the Upper Churchill River in Labrador and for the sale of electricity to Hydro Québec for 65 years. The government of Newfoundland and a consortium of lenders also signed these documents. Special legislation was enacted in Newfoundland to govern part of this transaction,

and the government of Newfoundland was to receive royalties under this agreement. Hundreds of millions of dollars were spent on the construction of roads, dams, generating stations and transmission lines. The contract with Hydro Québec gave the lenders some security that the money they had advanced would be repaid.

The fact that the agreements between Nigel and his new landlord and Pam's Moving, between Akiko and the computer seller and her credit card issuer, and between Churchill Falls (Labrador) Inc. and Hydro Québec are all "contracts" illustrates the extraordinarily wide range of relations that can be brought under the heading of "contracts", and the range of situations that the law of contracts must respond to. It is obvious that the social and economic importance of the three contracts differs significantly; all, however, have a number of important features in common.

At the heart of any contract is at least one promise, and most contracts are an exchange of promises. (Even the purchase of candy for cash at a convenience store will entail the inference that the store "promised" that the candy is safe to eat.) One definition of a "promise" is that it is "a present communication of a commitment to engage in a reciprocal measured exchange" (Macneil, *The New Social Contract*, 1980, at p. 7). A "contract" is a term used to refer to a group of related promises that are legally enforceable.

Each of the contracts described above has certain features. Each party had, when each contract was made, a present intention to limit future choice. When Pam's Moving made its contract with Nigel, it made a number of promises: a promise to show up on August 26, another promise to pack, move, unpack, *etc*. It expects that it will have to devote part of its resources — its trucks and employees — to moving Nigel's furniture and that it will no longer be free to take a potentially more lucrative contract that would make it unable to meet its undertaking to Nigel. Akiko has chosen to authorize her credit card issuer to pay the price and delivery charge for her computer, and is committed to paying the balance on her credit card as it falls due. The seller commits itself to deliver a computer of the required specifications for transportation to Toronto by the agreed date. For its part, Churchill Falls has committed a large part of the hydro-electric production of the project to Hydro Québec which, in turn, is committed to paying an agreed price in the form of a royalty, *i.e.*, an amount fixed with reference to the amount of electricity bought. Both parties to each contract communicated their intentions to each other.

Each relation involves a measured reciprocity. Nigel agreed to pay a price in return for what Pam's Moving will do for him, and Pam's Moving agreed to supply the service in return for Nigel's money. Akiko's computer was bought with payment of a price considered by both buyer and seller to be fair. Similarly, the contract between Churchill Falls and Hydro Québec expressed, at least when it was made, what must have been regarded as a fair exchange.

The phrase "exchange" used here is almost synonymous with commercial deal or contract. The term "commercial deal" or "commercial contract" emphasizes that many exchanges take place in a context characterized by certain economic facts. The economic or commercial facts usually include the following:

- There are at least two parties (though one or both parties may not be an individual but an aggregation of individuals like a corporation or even the government).

- The exchange involves things — to use the broadest term — that have an approximate commercial equivalence: gifts, *i.e.*, where one person gives another something and expects nothing in return, or relations that arise within groups like families, are outside the realm of exchange.

- At the time that the exchange is made, both parties believe that they will be better off after the exchange than before it.

- The ability of people to make exchanges permits economic planning.

- The ability to plan is an important aspect of individual freedom.

Some comments may be made on these statements:

- The idea of exchange can only operate if there are at least two parties. Although obviously there may be more than two, at some point serious inefficiencies begin to develop with exchange as a method of planning or organization if the number of parties gets too high. Corporations, partnerships and other forms of group organizations are available to deal with large groups. These forms of business organizations have a contractual foundation. They differ from contractual relations in that there is usually some statutorily imposed form of decision-making structure to provide flexibility in responding to changes in the environment in which the group operates. There are nevertheless similarities between organization or planning achieved through a corporation and that which may be achieved by agreement.

- Our concern in these materials is with exchanges that are motivated by the parties' belief that the exchange will increase economic wealth, that is, the exchange will provide an economic benefit to each party.

- The parties' belief that the exchange they are planning will be beneficial to them sometimes turns out to be wrong. They may have made a mistake in forecasting the future or in perceiving the past; they may have misjudged the wealth, intentions or honesty of the other party. Several years after the completion of the Churchill Falls project, energy prices rose dramatically. The agreement is now very profitable for Hydro Québec (which resells the power to American utilities), but Churchill Falls Corporation and the Newfoundland and Labrador government claim that the price is too low. Newfoundland tried to repudiate the agreement and the dispute was carried to the Supreme Court of Canada (which upheld the original contract). The Newfoundland government has made numerous efforts to re-open the agreement, all without success.

EXCHANGE

The notion of reciprocity is central to the notion of contracting. Contracts arise out of the need to provide a mechanism for exchange (particularly for exchanges that occur partially or wholly in the future) and reciprocity is simply the consequence of the fact that contracts are a mechanism for making exchanges. It is worth pausing for a moment to review the process of exchange.

When a buyer purchases groceries, for example, she is exchanging her money for the store's groceries. Economists can demonstrate that an exchange will occur when the buyer wants groceries more than she wants her money and when the store wants money more than it wants the groceries on its shelves. In a simple society, the food that one person might have obtained by hunting could be exchanged for a different kind of food that another had obtained by fishing or farming.

In both the simple society and our own complex society, there are, however, a number of shared characteristics of exchanges. First, the exchange must occur in a setting that makes it likely that one party will engage in an exchange rather than in an act of violence to get what he or she wants. When the first primitive farmers gave up hunting to grow grain, they did so expecting that they could trade with hunters for meat and furs. If the primitive hunter can steal from the farmer all the grain that his family needs, he will have no incentive to offer his meat and furs in exchange.

Second, both parties must believe that they will be better off by virtue of the exchange than either would be without it. The benefits gained from an exchange by one person are not matched by an equal harm suffered by the other. Because the buyer valued the groceries more than she valued her money (which she could have used for something else) and because the store valued her money more than it valued the groceries, both are better off by the sale than without it. Of course, the buyer would make a better deal if she was able to pay less money and still get the same amount of groceries, just as the store would make a better deal if it could get the buyer to pay more. This fact only means that exchange may take place within a range of prices, and that at any price within that range each party will be better off by making the exchange than without the exchange.

It is hard to overemphasize the importance of this point. An exchange is intended to increase the *total benefit that each party enjoys*. This point is amplified in the following quotation.

> [T]he rule must be that you give, so far as possible, what is less valuable to you but more valuable to the receiver; and you receive what is more valuable to you and less valuable to the giver. This is common sense, good business sense, good social sense, good technology, and is the enduring basis of amicable and constructive relations of any kind. This does not mean that you give as little as you can from the receiver's point of view. In terms of money, you give a man dollars for his services which are worth more to you than the dollars. No sane man would admit anything else. If you give services for dollars it must be that the dollars are worth more to you than the services. Unfortunately for simplicity, neither side of the transaction can be confined to or measured completely in dollars, even in commercial enterprises; and in non-commercial enterprises the exchange is extremely intangible. What conceals this simple fact of experience so often is that subsequent evaluation may change, though this is then beside the point. I may pay a man $10 today with pleasure, and may find tomorrow that I need $10 very badly, but cannot use the services I paid for. I am then perhaps disposed to think I made a bad exchange. I read the past into the present. This leads to the false view that what exchanges should be is as little as possible of what the receiver wants, regardless of its value to me. This philosophy of giving as little as possible and getting as much as possible in the other man's values is the root of bad customer relations, bad labour relations, bad credit relations, bad supply relations, bad technology. The possible margins of cooperative success are too limited to survive the destruction of incentives which this philosophy implies.

(Chester Barnard, *The Functions of the Executive* (1942), quoted in Fuller and Eisenberg, *Basic Contract Law*, 3d ed. (St. Paul: West Publishing Co., 1972) at p. 100.)

We will see that many problems arise from the fact that a deal that looked good yesterday looks much less attractive today. An exchange will only take place when both parties believe they will benefit when the exchange is made. If one forgets that both parties must believe that they will benefit from a contract, it is easy to think that exchange transactions are undesirable and expressive of destructive values. But if the existence of exchange transactions is not, by itself, destructive of our desired values, the context within which the exchange takes place may be unacceptable — that is, it may be exploitative and destructive of important values. It will be an important part of this study of the law of contracts to determine how far, within the context of Canadian society, exchanges have to be controlled to prevent them from becoming destructive of values that should be protected.

The need for exchanges arises from the existence of specialization of labour. In modern society the process of specialization has been carried very much further. The primitive farmer decided to farm rather than to hunt because he discovered that he is better off farming than hunting. The same calculation was made by the hunter. If no exchange were possible, the hunting family would have to spend some (or more) of its time growing or gathering cereals and vegetables if it was to have something other than meat to eat, and the farming family would have to hunt to provide itself with meat. Most of those of us who live in cities would starve if we could not buy food.

The discussion of promises and exchanges has been conducted as if they were solely concerned with economic values. To a large extent this fact is true, and these materials will concentrate on the commercial exchange — that is, the exchange that takes place between merchants (and in Canada most merchants are corporations) even though all of us, as individuals, make contracts for the things we need every day. It is important to remember, however, that human beings are involved in all exchanges, even those between corporations. The hopes, fears, and aspirations of the people who are involved are often as central a feature of the exchange process as economic pressures, even in an exchange that is, to all appearances, entirely commercial. In some exchanges the need for concern about the individual involved is great. Such a situation occurs, for example, in the contract of employment. As will be seen, when an exchange is viewed in terms of human values, as for example, a job may be viewed for its contribution to a person's sense of her own values or ability, it becomes much harder to deal adequately with the broadening of the range of factors that must be considered by the law. It is easier to assume that all that is at stake in any exchange are economic issues, and as a result it is tempting to ignore wider and less precise issues. How far the boundaries of any inquiry into the wider implications of certain exchanges or contracts can be pushed will be one of the pervasive themes of these materials.

An important example of the type of challenging problem that the law must face when the human dimension of a contracts dispute is taken into account arises when it is argued that a domestic contract between separated spouses for the division of their property and for support should be reviewed. On the one hand it can be argued that an arrangement made by adults to settle their affairs should be enforced so that the parties' subsequent relations — a new spouse or new family, perhaps — are not threatened. On the other hand, it may be argued that one party

— usually the woman — entered into the contract in the hope that she could become self-sufficient after being disappointed in the loss of what she had expected would be a life-long arrangement. Should she be left destitute because she is no longer able to support herself and her plans to become self-supporting did not materialize? (The rights of the two contracting parties are, in any case, only part of what has to be considered if there are children to be looked after.) Underlying this problem is the need to examine how far rules developed for commercial relations can be pushed or applied in a very different context. This book will raise some of the issues that arise in regard to domestic contracts (and marriage itself can be viewed as a kind of contract), but a detailed consideration of family contracts is beyond the scope of this study.

EXCHANGE, PLANNING AND THE ROLE OF CONTRACT LAW

There is a tendency for lawyers (perhaps more often lawyers who are judges, academics, or law students than solicitors in practice) to think that if there were no law of contracts there would be no exchanges, and that society as it is would collapse. This is a grand and dangerous illusion. People must eat and have somewhere to sleep, and if these needs require that exchanges be made, they will be made, regardless of the law. The existence of thriving black markets in controlled economies and, in our society, of markets for illegal commodities like drugs, is ample proof of the validity of this statement. If it is true that because the law has some particular features, the process of exchange works more efficiently than it otherwise would, the law may be facilitating the process of exchange, but the process of exchange would be carried on in any event and regardless of the law.

The role that the law plays in any society may make the process of exchange more or less efficient. An important aspect of the study of the law of contracts is to consider how far rules help the parties to get the maximum benefit from the process of exchange. The study of how efficiently contract law facilitates transactions is now part of the field of study known as Law and Economics. Some of the materials and commentary in this book draw on Law and Economics scholarship, though detailed study of this approach is beyond the scope of this work.

One of the central challenges for the countries that are moving towards adopting a market-based economy is to develop an effective legal system to regulate and enforce contractual and property rights. The absence of an effective legal system to enforce consensual, commercial obligations (and to permit the planning that they are designed to effect) tempts people in those countries to enforce their claims by non-legal, if not illegal, means, and has, for example, contributed to the rise of the Russian Mafia.

If the model of exchange that has just been examined is applied to the earlier examples that have been mentioned, some other features of the process of exchange appear. The exchanges between a primitive hunter and a farmer will only involve the exchange of things that each already owns. The hunter and farmer exchange things that each has when the agreement is made and the physical exchange takes place as soon as the agreement is made. Such simultaneous exchanges of goods or similar exchanges of a service for money make up a huge number of transactions each day in our society. Akiko's purchase of her computer approaches this kind of exchange but lacks, of course, any physical relation between her and the seller.

Exchanges of things that each party already owns are, however, of less economic importance than ones that are more similar to those of Nigel and Pam's Moving or the Churchill Falls agreement. The principal feature of these exchanges is the temporal element. Pam's Moving will show up at Nigel's apartment after the agreement is made and will be paid by Nigel only after it has performed the contract. Similarly, Nigel will expect the apartment to be ready when he (and the truck from Pam's Moving) arrive. The money that Nigel will use to pay Pam's Moving may come from his new job. The lease on the apartment will probably have an initial term of a year, though Nigel may stay in his new apartment for much longer. The addition of a temporal element has the potential for greatly expanding the economic effect of exchanges. Pam's Moving is better off by being able to count on work at a fixed time in the future. It can plan the use of its trucks and employees with more certainty than if it had not made the arrangement with Nigel and similar ones with other customers. Similarly, Nigel is better off because he can plan his move with some confidence that a truck will show up when he expects it, and because he can count on having a place to stay when he arrives to start his new job. A series of contracts similar to that made with Nigel, but made over even longer periods of time, could help Pam's Moving to determine how many trucks and employees to have. The economic importance of contracts of the types made by Nigel and Pam's Moving and by Nigel and his landlord is considerable.

The arrangements made to exploit the hydro-electric resources of the Upper Churchill River differ dramatically in degree from those made by Nigel, but they raise similar conceptual issues. A large part of this course will be devoted to investigating the problems with contracts that have this temporal element.

The introduction of a temporal element — a period between the time the promises are made by each side and performance — transforms the simple element of exchange into a powerful method of economic planning. At one extreme the planning function of contract is a small component of its overall function as an exchange transaction. Because we have faith in the ready availability in stores of food and other things we need, we are content to "plan" a week's supply of meals by going to the store as we need to. At the other extreme, the planning function of the law of contract may be an important aspect of an exchange: the Upper Churchill River would never have been developed had there not been firm contracts in place to sell the electricity. Sometimes, however, things may not work out quite as planned, and the problems that then arise will be the focus of much of these materials.

An important conceptual distinction which is related to the temporal nature of many contracts is the difference between a "discrete" and a "relational" contract. A discrete contract is a one-time exchange between two parties, such as the sale of goods for a cash payment. Historically, much of the common law of contracts that developed in the eighteenth and nineteenth centuries was premised on contracts being discrete transactions, though that term "discrete contract" was not used at that time. Commentators in the twentieth century, such as Ian Macneil (*The New Social Contract* (London: Yale University Press, 1980)), developed the concept of the relational contract, a contract which establishes a legal and economic relation between two (or more) parties that will go on over a period of time, and that will involve many exchanges. The Churchill Falls agreement is an example of a relational contract, as is an employment contract. Relational contracts are typically legally, economically and socially both more complex and more important than discrete contracts. One of the issues that will be considered in this book is how to modify the legal regime which largely developed based on the model of the discrete contract to deal with the increasingly common relational contract.

In spite of the fact that planning is often not perfect, and that relational contracts can be especially difficult to deal with, relatively few contracts end up causing disputes that lead to litigation or arbitration. A view that the law's role is one of dealing with disputes rather than as a facilitator of agreements and planning is not only wrong, but the source of very serious misconceptions about the function of the law and lawyers in our society. Lawyers in practice spend much more time planning, negotiating and advising clients about the contracts that the clients want to make — doing solicitors' work — than they do in litigating over those contracts — doing barristers' work. Many solicitors spend a good deal of their time helping their clients manage the contractual relations they are in so that the relations run smoothly and disputes are avoided or dealt with before they become serious. Litigation is hugely expensive and is regarded by both lawyers and their clients as something to be avoided if at all possible.

A NOTE ON THESE MATERIALS

The principal sources of the materials in this book are "cases", the records of the decisions of judges in disputes brought before the courts for resolution. While the focus on cases — on the record of judicial decisions — is typical of most law school courses, especially in first year, it tends to introduce an unfortunate bias in developing an understanding of the law of contracts. It encourages students to think that the main concern is about what happened (or might happen) in court: that every problem and issue should be approached as if it were going to be decided by a court.

The law of contracts is about agreements, agreements which, when they were made, were perceived by the parties as improving their welfare and which, as a result, they expected to perform. Any contractual litigation should therefore be regarded not as a common or everyday event, but as an unfortunate aberration. It is a much more important function of lawyers to keep their clients out of court than it is to engage in the process of litigation once the parties have chosen to bring their dispute before a court.

Contract materials based on judicial decisions are in a sense "pathological". Considering only court decisions does not give a good picture of how "healthy" contracts work. The medical analogy is obvious. The pathological specimen produced by the case — the judicial record — is examined to try to determine what factor precipitated the dispute, why one party decided not to perform the promise, and what lesson can be learned from the case so as to avoid such problems in the future. One gets about as much idea of how a healthy contract works from examining a court record of a contractual dispute as one gets about how a healthy living organism works from a pathologist's report. An analogy closer to law is provided by the comparison of a happy marriage and the record of a contested divorce.

Most lawyers who practise what can broadly be described as "contract law" are negotiators and drafters, not litigators. Nevertheless, much of what lawyers do in planning contractual relations and in drafting agreements requires a knowledge of what a court might do were the arrangement to end up in court. Examples of what went wrong in a contract that led to litigation (and to a particular result) make it possible to consider what might have been done to avoid the problem, what advice (or different advice) the parties might have been given, or how the relation between the parties might have been better structured. Without a knowledge of what might go wrong, it is not possible to recommend what should go into a contract.

These materials are divided into two main parts. The first four chapters introduce some of the central concepts and ideas that are regarded as "fundamental" in the law of contracts and in establishing contractual liability. Case reports make up a large proportion of this part of the book, though even here the role of the lawyer as negotiator, advisor and drafter is considered.

Chapters 5 to 8 examine a range of issues that can arise once the contract is formed, and explore the relation of contractual liability to other forms of liability. While cases are important here, the role of the solicitor in drafting contracts and in structuring contractual arrangements will be considered in greater depth in these chapters. There is also explicit consideration of the problems that arise when contract values (for example, the economic idea of efficiency) run counter to other social values, and on the need for society to control the power conferred on parties by their ability to enter into contractual arrangements. The philosophical and political problems that underlie the law of contract are re-examined in these last chapters.

One of the significant developments in the study of law over the past few decades has been the growing body of theoretical literature that can help students, judges and lawyers to better understand the law and its implications. There are a number of different theoretical perspectives, including historical, economic, moral, feminist, and what is called "critical legal studies". Within the field of Contract Law, there are theoretical debates between those who see this area of law as based primarily on protection of reliance and those who regard the protection of rights or the enforcement of promises as central. At various points, this book makes reference to some of these debates and perspectives, and a few of the seminal theoretical works in the contracts field are excerpted. However, those wishing a sustained theoretical study of contract will have to supplement these readings. (See, *e.g.*, Stephen Smith, *Contract Theory* (Oxford UK: Oxford University Press, 2004) and Stephen Waddams, *Dimensions of Private Law: Categories and Concepts in Anglo-American Legal Reasoning* (Cambridge UK: Cambridge University Press, 2003).) In part, the limited explicit treatment of theory in this book reflects the need to keep the materials manageable in size and scope, but it also recognizes that students and teachers will want to undertake their theoretical studies in very different ways. It should also be appreciated that judges and lawyers developed the common law with only limited explicit reference to theories of law, and an understanding of what judges have done is a foundation for more advanced theoretical analysis and criticism.

This book is intended to offer an *introduction* for first-year law students to the broad principles governing contractual relations in Canada's common law provinces. Although there are some references to legislation, the main focus is on the study of the common law, the law as developed by judges over hundreds of years. In upper-year courses, students will have an opportunity to further study the application of these general principles in the specific statutory and economic contexts that apply in a diverse range of settings. A range of upper-year courses deal in a different way with contracts that are used in real estate transactions, e-commerce transactions, sale of goods, formation of businesses, sales of securities, lending relations, employment relations and domestic relations. It is useful to start the study of contract law with a focus on general principles that have some relevance to all contracts, but it is also important to be aware that this is an *introduction* to a very broad and complex study that may consume the rest or your professional life.

It must also be appreciated that while some important principles of common law are well established, the common law is always changing, both in response to new problems, such as those posed by e-commerce, and to reflect changing ideas about social and economic relations. These materials do not purport to resolve controversies, but rather reflect the fact that there are emerging and controversial areas of contract law, such as determining the extent to which there may be duties of good faith that arise during negotiations or after formation of a contract.

THE USE OF CASES

A case or judgment is the record of the court's solution to the problem raised by the dispute before it. (As a technical matter, what is typically referred to as a "judgment" colloquially and in these materials are the Court's *reasons for judgment*: the actual judgment is a (usually very short and formal) document settled by the lawyers for the parties and signed by the judge or a court official.) As a solution to the specific problem that the court faced, the decision can be analyzed from a number of different perspectives, and, depending on one's point of view, may be regarded as either "good" or "bad". If it appears to be a good solution, it can be argued that it should be accepted as the solution in similar cases. If, on the other hand, it appears to be a bad solution, one may want to find ways to avoid using it in the future. It is often an interesting and difficult task to determine whether the solution is good or bad, and to identify the factors and the criteria to be applied that lead to one conclusion or another.

It is important to study carefully the judge's reasons for the decision. Those reasons may be studied as a statement of what the law "is." It is necessary to consider how useful is the judge's statement, how satisfactory it is as a basis for prediction of what the courts will do in similar cases in the future, and, what is most important, how well the statement functions as a guide to lawyers who want to keep their clients out of trouble. One difficulty is that judges do not always do a good job of articulating their reasons for making a particular decision.

The doctrine of precedent, the principle that previous decisions of higher courts are binding on courts lower in the judicial hierarchy, is an important part of the common law. In practice it is, however, a malleable doctrine. In recent years, Canadian courts, especially appeal courts, have demonstrated a willingness to reconsider common law doctrine. The introduction of the *Canadian Charter of Rights and Freedoms* in 1982, while having little direct impact on contract law, has caused judges to reassess their role as lawmakers. Judges are now more willing to consider whether a principle of common law produces socially, economically and legally desirable results. Although courts are still reluctant to overturn precedents, especially if there if there has been reliance on established common law doctrine, there is now a clear willingness to permit incremental change in the common law — though one judge's "incremental change" may be someone else's "radical departure". As a result, the reasons in any single judicial decision are less important than the overall direction of a line of cases, that is, of a series of decisions dealing with the same issues. The underlying imperatives of the process of exchange will eventually tend to force the common law contract rules to conform to a fairly small number of requirements that affect the negotiation and performance of contracts. One of the objectives of this book is to help students understand those requirements.

The common law of contracts was developed by thousands of judges, with the involvement of many lawyers and scholars, over a period of hundreds of years. The common law is found in the judgments of the courts. Every judgment is a product of the times and of the society in which it was given. These materials contain cases from Canada, England, the United States, Australia and elsewhere. Some judgments were written as early as the seventeenth century, but many are from this millennium. The court and date of each judgment appear at the beginning of each report. A judgment can often be understood only when it is realized that it was, for example, given by an English judge in 1854, when certain events were occurring and certain values were widely accepted, at least by the judge and those he — at that time all judges were men — associated with.

Judges and lawyers sometimes use statements of the law from an earlier decision as a precedent, without considering the facts and background out of which it arose, ignoring its historical context. This tendency is unfortunate. A judgment is a product of a particular period in a particular society. A judgment reflects the prevalent political, economic, moral, and social ideas of the time — or at least the ideas that were congenial to the judge. Students with a background in history, economics, political science or English literature may be aware of the historical context of particular decisions.

The law would, however, be useless if a judgment were only valid for a particular time and place. If a judge says that a particular case should be decided in a certain way, there may be good reasons for following that approach when another similar case comes up, even though some of the values existing or accepted at the date of the earlier judgment may no longer be accepted. The balancing of the concern for constancy in the law with the need for the law to reflect current social values is never easy. In each case it will be necessary to consider the balance that must be achieved and the values at stake. Part of the key to understanding this process is to realize that the judge has a special role in the legal system. The requirements of this role, for example, force her to respect her place in the judicial hierarchy, the parties' reasonable expectations of her discretionary power, and the existence of any relevant legislation indicating how the legislature thinks the case should be decided. Just as no case can be properly understood apart from its context, so no judgment can be understood apart from the institutional structure in which the judge functions.

A first-year law school course called "Contracts" is an artificial construct designed to gather in one manageable body of material (and teaching time) a collection of cases, topics and problems. In an important sense, such a collection presents a misleading picture of the law. It is misleading if it suggests that the neat boundaries fixed for a particular course or a casebook like this really do represent neatly separated ideas or topics. As has been emphasized in this introduction, a study of the law of contracts must be situated in a functioning society and its legal system. Functioning systems, particularly one as complex as that found in Canada today, are analytically messy. A feature of this messiness is that there few neat boundaries. Problems that, from one point of view, can be regarded as contracts problems, are, from another, problems of the law of torts, restitution, business associations or, for example, those of interest to the Competition Bureau or a provincial securities commission. This complexity can be confusing but, like any study of the functioning of what can be called an organism, one has to begin by over-simplifying and then show how the various bits and pieces fit together. A full understanding of the law of contracts will emerge only when the connections it has with other areas of the law can be seen and understood.

VALUES AND CONTRACT LAW

The business of judging typically requires the judge to consider a choice between values that compete for application in the case before the court. The judge may, for example, have to consider both the question of fairness between the parties to a contract and the general need to encourage reliance on contractual promises. In many cases it may be easy to accommodate both values. In others, however, one desirable end can only be achieved at the expense of the other. As you read these materials, it will be necessary for you to ask whether or not each case makes sense, given the values that one might expect the court to advance. It may be that the result a judgment reaches is not defensible on the basis that the court has offered, but is valid when alternative bases for the decision are considered. Sometimes judges do not adequately articulate the reasons that underlie their thinking, and you will have to develop the ability to discover and assess the unarticulated reasons for the decisions.

When you are asked whether a decision "makes sense" or is "just", you are being asked to assess the decision or provide some basis for criticism other than the statement: "That is the law". Blind adherence to rules is never an adequate reason for doing anything in the law, especially in our evolving common law system in which judges are continuously re-articulating and developing the law.

To say that a decision is "unfair" or "unjust" is really a conclusion that needs to be explored: by itself, such a statement is neither a valid criticism of nor a basis for a decision. It may be an adequate criticism of a decision to say that it fails to protect the reasonable expectations of the parties, or that the decision will encourage exploitative behaviour. It may be equally valid to suggest that the result is economically expensive and leads to the mis-allocation or waste of resources.

The judgments in this book were chosen because they raise difficult problems of balancing competing values. They are interesting from a pedagogic point of view. Many of the judgments are contentious, and they do not necessarily offer a succinct statement of the law.

It is worth emphasizing that the most important aspect of any study of the law of contracts (or of any area of the law, for that matter) is the ability to retain a sense that the law is part of human life, and that the law must always respect human dignity. Legal professionals and those who study the law should have and hold on to an almost childlike faith that the law *should* be just and fair. Without this faith, law can easily become little more than an impersonal set of rules, divorced from human values, and based on some abstract idea of the need for certainty and predictability.

Do not become cynical; there is too much at stake to risk the dangers of being unconcerned for fairness and decency. Do not fall into the trap of thinking that it is somehow "unlawyerly" to be passionately concerned about justice. Do not believe that to "think like a lawyer" means to ignore concerns about fairness and human decency. One of the objectives of these materials is to foster an understanding of what fairness and justice require in different contractual situations.

You must, however, be careful in saying that a decision is "just" or "fair". These terms are usually conclusions: they are not reasons and, as conclusions, they have to be justified.

THE INSTITUTIONAL STRUCTURE

As mentioned earlier, judges function in the context of an institutional structure that imposes restrictions on their freedom to do what they want. In a sense, law can be seen as the development of restrictions on the power of the person who has to decide questions presented by competing claimants. In primitive legal systems — and "primitive" does not necessarily refer to those that existed a long time ago — disputes would often be resolved by the personal bias of the decision-maker — perhaps someone such as the King or his delegate — or by an appeal to divine revelation, strength or chance — for example, the trial by ordeal. But in our society legal controversies have to be resolved in a way that meets certain constraints. The law is a rational enterprise that helps society to achieve ends that could not be achieved without it. The law must operate in a way that permits decisions to be made on a clearly articulated and appropriate basis. Judicial decisions have to be rationally defended. The legal process must be carried out in a way that permits such a defence.

The law of contracts involves more than judicial decisions, but it is the judgments that set out the general outline of the law within which solicitors must advise their clients and within which legislation must be crafted. It is worth examining the features that provide the context for judicial decision-making.

First, the courts cannot choose what disputes come before them. The courts have to hear and decide whatever disputes the parties choose to bring. The Supreme Court of Canada has power to choose the appeals that it will hear, but that power only permits it to refuse to hear cases that it does not want to hear. While there is some flexibility in how widely a judgment is written, the courts cannot deal with a legal issue just because the court considers that the issue has been inadequately dealt with in the past or that the law is need of revision.

The courts function as adjudicators. The essence of adjudication is the way in which the parties participate in the dispute. The parties have the right to present proof of the events that they allege took place, and to address reasoned arguments to the court. The normal trial of any case involves these two aspects. First, the evidence on both sides is put before the court. It is one of the features of our civil legal system that the responsibility for fact-gathering rests entirely on the parties. The parties have the responsibility of collecting, examining and analyzing the correspondence and other documents, and then of deciding what evidence to place before the court. The second stage is the argument about the law, often known as "making submissions". Counsel for one side may argue that the facts support the application of one rule; counsel for the other side may argue for the application of another rule.

The judgment, when given by the judge, usually summarizes the facts as found by the court. The judge may believe one side and not the other, or may accept some of the facts put forward by one party and some of the facts put forward by the other party. While there are cases in which a judge believes that some of the witnesses are deliberately lying, more frequently in contracts disputes judges are concerned about the accuracy or completeness of the memory of different witnesses. The judge then applies the law, as she sees it, to those facts.

This process of decision-making has a number of important consequences:

- Before counsel can know what facts to put before the court, he has to have some idea of the applicable rules of law. If he wants to argue that a particular rule applies, he has to make sure that he has the facts to support his argument.

- The idea of "reasoned argument" presupposes that there are standards of argument upon which both counsel and the judge agree. For example, there can be no reasoned argument if the decision turns on the toss of a coin or the judge's whim or on rules that the parties (or one of them) do not know.

- The judge in her role as fact-finder can determine the legal result. If fact A is necessary to the application of rule X, there can be no question of the application of that rule if the judge finds that fact A does not exist.

- Counsel must be prepared to argue his case on the basis of the facts as they are found by the judge, and since the appeal court is not normally free to hear new evidence or to review the trial judge's findings of fact, the arguments at that level are almost entirely on points of law. There is no point in suggesting how different the result might have been if only the facts were not as they were found to be. Many of the decisions studied in law school are appellate judgments, where the appeal court is obliged to base its decision on the facts as found by the trial judge.

All these points must be borne in mind as you read the cases in these materials. Did counsel succeed in getting the facts before the judge? How well did he argue the case for his client? (This will often be a main focus of discussion, but you must not think that, from a practical point of view, this aspect of the process is more important than any other.) Did the judge find something to be a "fact" simply to make her job of deciding the case easier? If the fact-finding function is performed by a jury and not by a judge, what question did the judge ask the jury to determine? Did the judge or jury seem to be influenced by their assessment of the "propriety" of one party's conduct?

If the process of adjudication is to operate properly, the parties must be able to rely on the judge's acceptance of the rules of law as the criteria for her decision. This point was mentioned earlier in connection with the need for rules to be constant and recognized by the judge as binding. If the law is out of date and in need of reform, it will often be a difficult question how far an individual judge, consistent with her role in the process, can accommodate the pressures for reform. Will she be undercutting the reasonable reliance of one party on the existing law? (Remember that decisions in contracts cases provide a basis on which people — perhaps with advice from their lawyers — plan their affairs.) Does the judge have the facts necessary to enable her to make the right decision in the case before her? Does the judge know enough about the likely effects of the adoption of one or other of the rules competing for application? These are important and difficult questions. The process of adjudication operates to restrict the judge's freedom to find the facts and her recourse to facts not put before her by the parties. A judge who finds facts simply to justify the application of a particular rule is undercutting the process of adjudication; a judge who attempts to find facts other than those presented by counsel is undermining effective participation by the parties. Independent fact-finding by the judge, no matter how carefully or responsibly done, may impair the integrity of the adversarial nature of the process of adjudication.

All these issues must be considered at both the trial and appellate levels. The appeal courts may not be free to review the facts as found by the trial judge, but they may be more free than the trial judge to reconsider rules of law. The trial judge may properly have regarded herself as bound by a decision of a court of appeal, but that court may be free to reconsider its own previous decision and do what the trial judge could not do. Similarly, the Supreme Court of Canada, as the highest court in Canada, has more scope than any provincial court of appeal to reconsider an area of the law and to decide that the law should be changed or developed.

Again, there are restrictions on how far even the Supreme Court of Canada can go. Should the Court ignore the fact that parties may have relied on the law being what the lower courts believed it to be? Should it limit the change to the narrow facts of the case before it, or should it seek to deal with a wider range of cases? What should the appellate court do if it needs more facts before making its decision? How far should the Supreme Court of Canada go in changing the law? These questions raise one of the basic problems in law reform: should the court or the legislature institute the reform? Does inactivity by one justify activity by the other? What characteristics of each body enable us to decide which should make the changes?

This last point introduces the problem of institutional design. Any institution in our society — a family, a club, a corporation, a church, a city, a province or (as the constitutional disputes in Canada have demonstrated) a country — has to deal with the problem of how decisions are to be made. For the purposes of this course, there are three principal choices for resolving any problem or dispute: the courts, the legislatures, and a consensual arrangement of the parties (for example, arbitration). Each of these choices has benefits and costs that make it more or less appropriate to perform a particular function. It will be an important part of our study to consider which institution is best suited to resolve a particular dispute and why.

This book begins the examination of the law of contracts by considering what happens when a promise is not performed and the person harmed by the breach — the person (the "promisee") who did not get what the other party (the "promisor") had promised — brings this dispute before a court.

PART ONE

CHAPTER ONE

REMEDIES FOR BREACH OF CONTRACT

INTRODUCTION

It is tempting to begin an examination of the law of contracts by looking first at the creation or formation of a contract, often called the Law of Offer and Acceptance. Many contracts texts and casebooks start with this topic. After all, in a sense the making of a contract is what must come first. One difficulty that such a focus creates is that it distorts the relative importance of the topics that make up what is called the "Law of Contracts". Lawyers spend comparatively little time worrying about the process of contract creation. They spend much more of their time worrying either about the risks that the deal creates for their clients and the ways by which those risks may be avoided or controlled, or in negotiating the deal and keeping the arrangement working smoothly when the parties are in the deal.

Thus it makes sense to start the study of contract law by considering what the risks of non-performance might be, where they come from and what one can do about them. Once one understands the rights that a party may have if a contract is not performed and the consequences of non-performance of a contract, one has a better grasp of the problems that making a deal might create.

This book begins the study of the law of contract by looking at the remedies available for breach of contract. Here the focus is on the problems that arise when one party promises to do something for another and does not do what has been promised. What response should a court make when one party comes into court complaining that the other party has not done what he promised to do? It is important to keep in mind the range of things that could be done to one who does not keep a promise. The possible remedies for breach of contract include:

1. Contract-breaching could be a criminal offence. Section 422 of the *Criminal Code*, for example, makes it an offence wilfully to break a contract when the person doing so has reasonable cause to believe that the probable consequences will be to endanger human life, to expose valuable property to destruction or to deprive the inhabitants of a place of electricity, water, etc. In some situations a breach of contract may constitute fraud or some other offence under the *Criminal Code*, but ordinarily breach of contract is not a crime.

2. A person who breaches a contract could forfeit the right to carry on a business or trade. This punishment might be the result of a formal legal decision. For example, a lawyer who breaks a promise to a client or to another lawyer might be disbarred by the provincial law society. A car dealer who tampers with the odometer of a car may well breach a promise made to a customer; the dealer might also find that the government cancels its dealer's licence, forcing it to

stop doing business. A similar consequence can follow in a less formal setting. Forfeiture of the right to carry on business might be the result of being "blackballed" in a particular trade or industry. A subcontractor on a large construction project might lose any chance of getting future work if it defaults in carrying out a contract, because it will be regarded as an unreliable firm and unreliable firms are expensive to deal with. Contracts with the federal government, for example, sometimes contain a clause stating that: "The Department has the right to exclude the use of specified subcontractors or suppliers with whom it has had a poor working experience."

3.   A person could be <u>publicly labelled</u> as one who did not keep promises. Such labelling occurs when a person goes bankrupt. It is sometimes used to supplement the criminal sanctions; for example, stores that are convicted of fraudulent advertising are often mentioned in the press.

4.   A court could make a declaration that a contract has been breached and leave the provision of any <u>other remedy to outside pressure or to the parties themselves.</u>

5.   A person could be ordered by a court or another governmental body to perform the contract as she has promised. Breach of this order for "specific performance" might be punished by imprisonment or fine.

6.   A court could require a "<u>contract-breaker</u>" — there is no handy word to describe the person who does not perform a contract — to pay <u>damages</u> as compensation to the person to whom the promise was made.

The principal remedies that the courts give for breach of a promise are the last two: an order that a party perform its contractual obligations, often called specific performance, and a monetary award for damages to compensate for the breach of contract. For reasons that will be discussed, the award of damages is the most common judicial remedy for a breach of contract.

   Three broad issues need to be considered when studying remedies for breach of contract. First, what does it mean to say that monetary compensation should be paid for a breach, and what is at stake when compensation is awarded? What types of losses that are suffered should be the subject of compensation? When is it appropriate to make an order that the breaching party actually perform as promised, and what might be the consequences of making such an order?

   Second, there are problems of deciding how to limit the award of damages. Like the ripples caused by a stone thrown into water, the consequences of a breach of contract can be serious and can expand endlessly.

   The third issue relates to the existence of other relevant values, principally those associated with the idea that the party harmed by a breach of contract may have to behave in a commercially reasonable way. This idea emphasizes the importance of the fact that the law of contract can only be understood in a context characterized by the parties' expectations of certain behaviour, and of the role to be played by contracts in our society.

   There are important reasons for beginning the study of the law of contracts with a consideration of the remedies for breach of contract.

1.   One way to define a "contract" in a legal sense is to say that it is "a promise (or set of promises) *which the law will enforce*." This definition is circular and not very helpful. It does however, prompt one to ask further questions, such as: what will the law do if it does decide to enforce a promise? Answer-

ing this question will make more intelligible the inquiry in Chapter 2 into the kinds of promises the law will enforce and what one must do to make an enforceable contract.

2. Lawyers and clients, even at the beginning of a contractual relation, need to have a general idea of the risks and consequences of what they are doing, of how far they can go before the risks run by the client become significant, and what might happen if the relation sours.

3. As a practical matter, every lawyer who is asked to consider a contracts dispute will have to decide if the amount likely to be recovered makes it worth starting or defending an action. A consideration of the remedies available for breach of contract can give a lawyer an answer to the critical question: "How much can the client get if we sue?"

4. The cases on breach are among the more easily understood cases that a beginning law student can study. This is not to say that any judgment at the outset of law school is simple. It is, however, possible for a person without a background in law to understand the issues and what is going on in the first case in these materials, *Peevyhouse v. Garland Coal*.

A major challenge, however, for beginning law students is that judgments are not written for those who know nothing about the law. The judge and the lawyers involved in any case are functioning in the context of an existing legal system, and their responsibilities do not permit them to consider the needs of law students. While some of the terminology and the style of writing in a case like *Peevyhouse v. Garland Coal* is not easy for those starting the study of law to understand, the issues presented by the case are readily apparent and anyone may have a valid criticism to make of the result reached by the court or even of the process of getting there.

THE COMPENSATION PRINCIPLE

The most common response to a finding by a court that a contract has been breached is an award of damages in favour of the person injured by the breach. The rule for assessing damages was set out by Lord Atkinson in *Wertheim v. Chicoutimi Pulp Co.*, [1911] A.C. 301 at p. 307 (P.C.):

> And it is the general intention of the law that, in giving damages for breach of contract, the party complaining should, so far as it can be done by money, be placed in the same position as he would have been in if the contract had been performed . . . that is a ruling principle. It is a just principle.

While there are important exceptions to this general "compensation principle", the courts usually say that they will compensate the plaintiff for the loss that has been caused by the defendant's breach of contract. A consequence of this principle is that the courts generally do not penalize a party for breaching a contract, but only require the party in breach to compensate to the extent that there is a loss. It can be argued that the courts should impose sanctions for a breach of contract even if there is no loss, either to punish the party in breach for failing to honour its promise or to deter others who might be tempted not to honour their promises. We shall consider why the courts have developed the compensation principle, whether it is a fair rule, and when the courts apply some other rule to determine damages.

Our first task is to see exactly what the application of the "compensation principle" involves.

PEEVYHOUSE v. GARLAND COAL & MINING CO.

382 P.2d 109 (Okla S.C. 1963)

JACKSON J.: — [1] In the trial court, plaintiffs Willie and Lucille Peevyhouse sued the defendant, Garland Coal and Mining Company, for damages for breach of contract. Judgment was for plaintiffs in an amount considerably less than was sued for. Plaintiffs appeal and defendant cross-appeals.

[2]   In the briefs on appeal, the parties present their argument and contentions under several propositions; however, they all stem from the basic question of whether the trial court properly instructed the jury on the measure of damages.

[3]   Briefly stated, the facts are as follows: plaintiffs owned a farm containing coal deposits, and in November, 1954, leased the premises to defendant for a period of five years for coal mining purposes. A "strip-mining" operation was contemplated in which the coal would be taken from pits on the surface of the ground, instead of from underground mine shafts. In addition to the usual covenants found in a coal mining lease, defendant specifically agreed to perform certain restorative and remedial work at the end of the lease period. It is unnecessary to set out the details of the work to be done, other than to say that it would involve the moving of many thousands of cubic yards of dirt, at a cost estimated by expert witnesses at about $29,000.00. However, plaintiffs sued for only $25,000.00.

[4]   During the trial, it was stipulated that all covenants and agreements in the lease contract had been fully carried out by both parties, except the remedial work mentioned above; defendant conceded that this work had not been done.

[5]   Plaintiffs introduced expert testimony as to the amount and nature of the work to be done, and its estimated cost. Over plaintiffs' objections, defendant thereafter introduced expert testimony as to the diminution in "value" of plaintiffs' farm resulting from the failure of defendant to render performance as agreed in the contract — that is, the difference between the present value of the farm, and what its value would have been if defendant had done what it agreed to do.

[6]   At the conclusion of the trial, the court instructed the jury that it must return a verdict for plaintiffs, and left the amount of damages for jury determination. On the measure of damages, the court instructed the jury that it might consider the cost of performance of the work defendant agreed to do, "together with all of the evidence offered on behalf of either party."

[7]   It thus appears that the jury was at liberty to consider the diminution in "value" of plaintiffs' farm as well as the "cost of repair work" in determining the amount of damages.

[8]   It returned a verdict for plaintiffs for $5000.00 — only a fraction of the "cost of performance," *but more than the total value of the farm even after the remedial work is done*.

[9]   On appeal, the issue is sharply drawn. Plaintiffs contend that the true measure of damages in this case is what it will cost plaintiffs to obtain performance of the work that was not done because of defendant's default. Defendant argues that

the measure of damages is the cost of performance, "limited, however, to the total difference in the market value before and after the work was performed."

[10] It appears that this precise question has not heretofore been presented to this court. In *Ardizonne v. Archer*, 72 Okl. 70, 178 P. 263 (1919), this court held that the measure of damages for breach of a contract to drill an oil well was the reasonable cost of drilling the well, but here a slightly different factual situation exists. The drilling of an oil well will yield valuable geological information, even if no oil or gas is found, and of course if the well is a producer, the value of the premises increases. In the case before us, it is argued by defendant with some force that the performance of the remedial work defendant agreed to do will add at the most only a few hundred dollars to the value of plaintiffs' farm, and that the damages should be limited to that amount because that is all plaintiffs have lost.

[11] Plaintiffs rely on *Groves v. John Wunder Co.*, 205 Minn. 163, 286 N.W. 235, 123 A.L.R. 502 (1939). In that case, the Minnesota court, in a substantially similar situation, adopted the "cost of performance" rule as opposed to the "value" rule. The result was to authorize a jury to give plaintiff damages in the amount of $60,000, where the real estate concerned would have been worth only $12,160, even if the work contracted for had been done.

[12] It may be observed that *Groves v. John Wunder Co.*, *supra*, is the only case which has come to our attention in which the cost of performance rule has been followed under circumstances where the cost of performance greatly exceeded the diminution in value resulting from the breach of contract. Incidentally, it appears that this case was decided by a plurality rather than a majority of the members of the court. Defendant relies principally upon *Sandy Valley & E.R. Co. v. Hughes*, 175 Ky. 320, 194 S.W. 344 (1917) [and others]. These were all cases in which, under similar circumstances, the appellate courts followed the "value" rule instead of the "cost of performance" rule. Plaintiff points out that in the earliest of these cases . . . the court cites as authority on the measure of damages an earlier Pennsylvania tort case, and that the other two cases follow the first, with no explanation as to why a measure of damages ordinarily followed in cases sounding in tort should be used in contract cases. Nevertheless, it is of some significance that three out of four appellate courts have followed the diminution in value rule under circumstances where, as here, the cost of performance greatly exceeds the diminution in value.

[13] The explanation may be found in the fact that the situations presented are artificial ones. It is highly unlikely that the ordinary property owner would agree to pay $29,000 (or its equivalent) for the construction of "improvements" upon his property that would increase its value only about $300. The result is that we are called upon to apply principles of law theoretically based upon reason and reality to a situation which is basically unreasonable and unrealistic.

[14] In *Groves v. John Wunder Co.*, *supra*, in arriving at its conclusions, the Minnesota court apparently considered the contract involved to be analogous to a building and construction contract, and cited authority for the proposition that the cost of performance or completion of the building as contracted is ordinarily the measure of damages in actions for damages for the breach of such a contract.

[15] In an annotation following the Minnesota case beginning at 123 A.L.R. 515, the annotator places the three cases relied on by defendant . . . under the classification of cases involving "grading and excavation contracts."

[16] We do not think either analogy is strictly applicable to the case now before us. The primary purpose of the lease contract between plaintiffs and defendant was neither "building and construction" nor "grading and excavation." It was merely to accomplish the economical recovery and marketing of coal from the premises, to the profit of all parties. The special provisions of the lease contract pertaining to remedial work were incidental to the main object involved.

[17] Even in the case of contracts that are unquestionably building and construction contracts, the authorities are not in agreement as to the factors to be considered in determining whether the cost of performance rule or the value rule should be applied. The American Law Institute's *Restatement of the Law, Contracts*, Volume 1, Sections 346(1)(a)(i) and (ii) submits the proposition that the cost of performance is the proper measure of damages if this is possible and does not involve "*unreasonable economic waste*"; and that the diminution in value caused by the breach is the proper measure "if construction and completion in accordance with the contract would involve *unreasonable economic waste*." (Emphasis supplied.) In an explanatory comment immediately following the text, the *Restatement* makes it clear that the "economic waste" referred to consists of the destruction of a substantially completed building or other structure.

[18] Of course no such destruction is involved in the case now before us. On the other hand, in McCormick, *Damages*, section 168, it is said with regard to building and construction contracts that . . . in cases where the defect is one that can be repaired or cured without "*undue expense*" the cost of performance is the proper measure of damages, but where . . . the defect in material or construction is one that cannot be remedied without "*an expenditure for reconstruction disproportionate to the end to be obtained*" (emphasis supplied) the value rule should be followed. The same idea was expressed in *Jacob & Youngs, Inc. v. Kent*, 230 N.Y. 239, 129 N.E. 889, 23 A.L.R. 1429 (1929), as follows: "The owner is entitled to the money which will permit him to complete, unless the cost of completion is grossly and unfairly out of proportion to the good to be attained. When that is true, the measure is the difference in value."

[19] It thus appears that the prime consideration in the *Restatement* was "economic waste"; and that the prime consideration in McCormick, *Damages*, and in *Jacob & Youngs, Inc. v. Kent, supra*, was the relationship between the expense involved and the "end to be attained" — in other words, the "relative economic benefit". In view of the unrealistic fact situation in the instant case, and certain Oklahoma statutes to be hereinafter noted, we are of the opinion that the "relative economic benefit" is a proper consideration here . . . 23 O.S. 1961, §§ 96 and 97 provide as follows:

> §96 . . . Notwithstanding the provisions of this chapter, no person can recover a greater amount in damages for the breach of an obligation, than he would have gained by the full performance thereof on both sides. . . .

> §97 . . . Damages must, in all cases, be reasonable, and where an obligation of any kind appears to create a right to unconscionable and grossly oppressive damages, contrary to substantial justice, no more than reasonable damages can be recovered.

[20] Although it is true that the above sections of the statute are applied most often in tort cases, they are by their own terms, and the decisions of this court, also applicable in actions for damages for breach of contract. It would seem that they are peculiarly applicable here where, under the "cost of performance" rule, plaintiffs might recover an amount about nine times the total value of their farm. Such would seem to be "unconscionable and grossly oppressive damages, contrary to substantial justice" within the meaning of the statute. Also, it can hardly be denied that if plaintiffs here are permitted to recover under the "cost of performance" rule, they will receive a greater benefit from the breach than could be gained from full performance, contrary to the provisions of Sec. 96.

[21] An analogy may be drawn between the cited sections, and the provisions of 15 O.S. 1961, §§ 214 and 215. These sections tend to render void any provisions of a contract which attempt to fix the amount of stipulated damages to be paid in case of a breach, except where it is impracticable or extremely difficult to determine the actual damages. This results in spite of the agreement of the parties, and the obvious and well known rationale is that insofar as they exceed the actual damages suffered, the stipulated damages amount to a penalty or forfeiture which the law does not favor.

[22] 23 O.S. 1961, §§ 96 and 97 have the same effect in the case now before us. *In spite of the agreement of the parties*, these sections limit the damages recoverable to a reasonable amount not "contrary to substantial justice"; they prevent plaintiffs from recovering a "greater amount in damages for the breach of an obligation" than they would have "gained by the full performance thereof".

[23] We therefore hold that where, in a coal mining lease, lessee agrees to perform certain remedial work on the premises concerned at the end of the lease period, and thereafter the contract is fully performed by both parties except that the remedial work is not done, the measure of damages in an action by lessor against lessee for damages for breach of contract is ordinarily the reasonable cost of performance of the work; however, where the contract provision breached was merely incidental to the main purpose in view, and where the economic benefit which would result to lessor by full performance of the work is grossly disproportionate to the cost of performance, the damages which lessor may recover are limited to the diminution in value resulting to the premises because of the non-performance. We believe the above holding is in conformity with the intention of the Legislature as expressed in the statutes mentioned, and in harmony with the better-reasoned cases from the other jurisdictions where analogous fact situations have been considered. It should be noted that the rule as stated does not interfere with the property owner's right to "do what he will with his own" . . . or his right, if he chooses, to contract for "improvements" which will actually have the effect of reducing his property's value. Where such result is in fact contemplated by the parties, and is a main or principal purpose of those contracting, it would seem that the measure of damages for breach would ordinarily be the cost of performance.

[24] The above holding disposes of all of the arguments raised by the parties on appeal.

[25] Under the most liberal view of the evidence herein, the diminution in value resulting to the premises because of non-performance of the remedial work was $300.00. After a careful search of the record, we have found no evidence of a higher figure, and plaintiffs do not argue in their briefs that a great diminution in value was sustained. It thus appears that the judgment was clearly excessive, and that the amount for which judgment should have been rendered is definitely and satisfactorily shown by the record. We are asked by each party to modify the

judgment in accordance with the respective theories advanced, and it is conceded that we have authority to do so. . . .

[26] We are of the opinion that the judgment of the trial court for plaintiffs should be, and it is hereby, modified and reduced to the sum of $300.00, and as so modified it is affirmed.

[WELCH, DAVISON, HALLEY and JOHNSON JJ. concur. WILLIAMS C.J., BLACKBIRD V.C.J. and IRWIN and BERRY JJ., dissent.]

IRWIN J. (dissenting): — **[27]** By the specific provisions in the coal mining lease under consideration, the defendant agreed as follows:

> 7b   Lessee agrees to make fills in the pits dug on said premises on the property line in such manner that fences can be placed thereon and access had to opposite sides of the pits.
>
> 7c   Lessee agrees to smooth off the top of the spoil banks on the above premises.
>
> 7d   Lessee agrees to leave the creek crossing the above premises in such a condition that it will not interfere with the crossings to be made in pits as set out,
>
> . . .
>
> 7f   Lessee further agrees to leave no shale or dirt on the high wall of said pits.

[28] Following the expiration of the lease, plaintiffs made demand upon defendant that it carry out the provisions of the contract and to perform those covenants contained therein.

[29] Defendant admits that it failed to perform its obligations that it agreed and contracted to perform under the lease contract and there is nothing in the record which indicates that defendant could not perform its obligations. Therefore, in my opinion defendant's breach of the contract was wilful and not in good faith.

[30] Although the contract speaks for itself, there were several negotiations between the plaintiffs and defendant before the contract was executed. Defendant admitted in the trial of the action, that plaintiffs insisted that the above provisions be included in the contract and that they would not agree to the coal mining lease unless the above provisions were included.

[31] In consideration for the lease contract, plaintiffs were to receive a certain amount as royalty for the coal produced and marketed and in addition thereto their land was to be restored as provided in the contract.

[32] Defendant received as consideration for the contract, its proportionate share of the coal produced and marketed and in addition thereto, the *right to use* plaintiffs' land in the furtherance of its mining operations. The cost for performing the contract in question could have been reasonably approximated when the contract was negotiated and executed and there are no conditions now existing which could not have been reasonably anticipated by the parties. Therefore, defendant had knowledge, when it prevailed upon the plaintiffs to execute the lease, that the cost of performance might be disproportionate to the value of benefits received by plaintiff for the performance.

[33] Defendant has received its benefits under the contract and now urges, in substance, that plaintiffs' measure of damages for its failure to perform should be the economic value of performance to the plaintiffs and not the cost of performance.

[34] If a peculiar set of facts should exist where the above rule should be applied as the proper measure of damages (and in my judgment those facts do not exist in the instant case), before such rule should be applied, consideration should be given to the benefits received or contracted for by the party who asserts the application of the rule.

[35] Defendant did not have the right to mine plaintiffs' coal or to use plaintiffs' property for its mining operations without the consent of plaintiffs. Defendant had knowledge of the benefits that it would receive under the contract and the approximate cost of performing the contract. With this knowledge, it must be presumed that defendant thought that it would be to its economic advantage to enter into the contract with plaintiffs and that it would reap benefits from the contract, or it would have not entered into the contract.

[36] Therefore, if the value of the performance of a contract should be considered in determining the measure of damages for breach of a contract, the value of the benefits received under the contract by a party who breaches a contract should also be considered. However, in my judgment, to give consideration to either in the instant action, completely rescinds and holds for naught the solemnity of the contract before us and makes an entirely new contract for the parties.

[37] In *Globe v. Bell Oil & Gas Co.*, 97 Ok. 261, 223 p. 371 (1924), we held:

> Even though the contract contains harsh and burdensome terms which the court does not in all respects approve, it is the province of the parties in relation to lawful subject matter to fix their rights and obligations, and the court will give the contract effect according to its expressed provisions, unless it be shown by competent evidence proof that the written agreement as executed is the result of fraud, mistake, or accident.

[38] In *Cities Service Oil Co. v. Geolograph Co. Inc.*, 208 Ok. 179, 254 P. 2d 775 (1953), we said:

> While we do not agree that the contract as presently written is an onerous one, we think the short answer is that the folly or wisdom of a contract is not for the court to pass on.

[39] In *Great Western Oil & Gas Company v. Mitchell*, 326 P. 2d 794 (1958), we held:

> The law will not make a better contract for parties than they themselves have seen fit to enter into, or alter it for the benefit of one party and to the detriment of the others; the judicial function of a court of law is to enforce a contract as it is written.

[40] I am mindful of Title 23 O.S. 1961, § 96, which provides that no person can recover a greater amount in damages for the breach of an obligation than he could have gained by the full performance thereof on both sides, except in cases not applicable herein. However, in my judgment, the above statutory provision is not applicable here. In my judgment, we should follow the case of *Groves v. John Wunder Company* [*supra*] which defendant agrees "that the fact situation is apparently similar to the one in the case at bar", and where the Supreme Court of Minnesota held:

> The owner's or employer's damages for such a breach . . . are to be measured, not in respect to the value of the land to be improved, but by the reasonable cost of doing that which the contractor promised to do and which he left undone.

[41] The . . . breach referred to states that where the contractor's breach of a contract is wilful, that is, in bad faith, he is not entitled to any benefit of the equitable doctrine of substantial performance. In the instant action defendant has made no attempt to even substantially perform. The contract in question is not immoral, is not tainted with fraud, and was not entered into through mistake or accident and is not contrary to public policy. It is clear and unambiguous and the parties understood the terms thereof, and the approximate cost of fulfilling the obligations could have been approximately ascertained. There are no conditions existing now which could not have been reasonably anticipated when the contract was negotiated and executed. The defendant could have performed the contract if it desired. It has accepted and reaped the benefits of its contract and now urges that plaintiffs' benefits under the contract be denied. If plaintiffs' benefits are denied, such benefits would inure to the direct benefit of the defendant.

[42] Therefore, in my opinion, the plaintiffs were entitled to specific performance of the contract and since defendant has failed to perform, the proper measure of damages should be the cost of performance. Any other measure of damage would be holding for naught the express provisions of the contract; would be taking from the plaintiffs the benefits of the contract and placing those benefits in defendant which has failed to perform its obligations; would be granting benefits to defendant without a resulting obligation; and would be completely rescinding the solemn obligation of the contract for the benefit of the defendant to the detriment of the plaintiffs by making an entirely new contract for the parties. I therefore respectfully dissent to the opinion promulgated by a majority of my associates.

The plaintiffs asked the United States Supreme Court to review the decision of the Oklahoma Court, but the Supreme Court declined to do so: 375 U.S. 906 (1963).

NOTES AND QUESTIONS

In examining a case like *Peevyhouse v. Garland Coal* (or almost any case, for that matter) there are three broad types of questions that must be considered: (1) is the decision consistent with other legal rules? (2) what was the basis for the court's decision? and (3) what are the implications of the decision for future cases?

1.   The first of these questions focuses on the issues resolved by the decision. These issues include the arguments used by the court (or part of the court) to justify the decision reached. What guidance was available to the court to deal with this case? Was it to be found in other cases, in statutes, or elsewhere? Did the majority and the dissent rely on the same sources for guidance? What does the acceptance of any particular source say about the law of contracts? Some more specific questions address the consistency of the decision with previously articulated legal rules.

   (a) Could either the majority or the minority judgment have found useful support in the compensation principle articulated by Lord Atkinson in *Wertheim v. Chicoutimi Pulp, supra?* conservative, no non-econ loss considered

   (b) Suppose that you were a member of the Oklahoma State Legislature when sections 96 and 97 of the statute were passed. Would you have thought that the statute offered support to the arguments of the majority, of the minority, of both, or neither?

   (c) How important is it that the majority of the Oklahoma court did not follow the decision of the Minnesota court in *Groves v. John Wunder Co.?*

2. A second type of question focuses on the way in which the court made the decision. Did the court (as a whole, the majority, or the minority) have the same view of the facts? How well did the court respond to the arguments of the parties? How appropriate was it for the court to do what it did? Should it have deferred to the legislature in respect of the issue that it was asked to or did decide?

   (a) What did the majority think the plaintiff lost because of the defendant's breach of contract?

   (b) What did the minority think the plaintiff lost?

   (c) When it executed the lease, it would seem that Garland Coal intended to perform what it had promised to do. Suppose that the reason it did not perform was that the amount of coal under the lands owned by Mr. and Mrs. Peevyhouse was far less than had been expected and this fact made it uneconomic for Garland to complete the strip-mining they planned and then to carry out the remedial work. Should this fact affect the outcome of the case?

   (d) Conversely, would evidence that Garland Coal never intended to perform the remedial work be relevant?

   (e) What reasons might there have been for Mr. and Mrs. Peevyhouse to insist on the insertion of the clauses regarding remedial work in the contract? Should the reason for the insertion of these clauses say anything about the consequences of breach? As it so happens, the trial judge in *Peevyhouse* ruled that the jury should not be permitted to hear much evidence about the process of contract formation.

   (f) Notice the language — perhaps "rhetoric" would be a better word — that is used in the two judgments. The majority uses language that suggests that the plaintiffs would get an unjustified or windfall gain if they were to get more than $300 in damages. The minority refers to the contract as if its meaning permitted no disagreement over the undertaking of the defendant. How do you think that each party viewed the issue? Is the language used by the judges fair to the parties?

   (g) The trial in *Peevyhouse* was conducted before a judge and jury. Such trials are common in the United States, but much less common in Canada, where most civil cases and almost all contract cases are conducted by a judge sitting alone. It may be that a judge will be more likely to choose a "principled" position like $300 or $29,000. However, a jury might be more likely to compromise and "split the difference" with, for example, a $5,000 award. All of the evidence and argument by the opposing counsel in *Peevyhouse* centred on the cost of doing the remedial work and the diminution in value of the land. As you study the materials in this chapter, consider whether other measures of damages could have been put before the court. One alternative measure could be based on the gains made by Garland Coal. There are at least two amounts that could be based on this measure: (i) the amount Garland Coal saved by not doing what it had promised to do — a saved expense is, from an economic point of view, as much of a gain as an amount received — and (ii) the profit earned from the contract with Mr. and Mrs. Peevyhouse.

   (h) In 1963, when this case was decided, the ecological consequences of strip-mining in Oklahoma were not a concern to either the legislature or the courts. Reclamation of land after strip-mining was not required under Oklahoma law in 1963, though federal and state legislation now requires restoration. Should these "public" concerns affect the outcome of a private dispute? Notice that even the "ecologically correct" solution does not always point in the direction of strict enforcement of a contract, though it usually will in a strip-mining case. The majority refers (¶ 18) to the decision in *Jacob & Youngs v. Kent*, a decision of the New York Court of Appeals. Had performance of the contract in that case been ordered, a builder would have been expected to tear out all the piping installed in a new house and install the exact piping specified by the contract when there was no evidence that the piping actually installed was in any way inferior to that which the contract specified. Such an order would have been ecologically harmful and economically inefficient.

(i) Two of the judges who sided with the majority in *Peevyhouse* were later involved in a serious bribery scandal. There is some suggestion that counsel for Garland Coal could have improperly influenced some of the judges in other cases, but there is no suggestion of a bribe affecting the outcome in *Peevyhouse*, a case of relatively little financial consequence to Garland Goal. Consider whether this should affect the value of the solution put forward by the majority to the problem before the court.

3. A third type of question relates to the value of the court's judgment for the future. Does the decision give useful guidance to subsequent courts? Does the decision give useful guidance to solicitors who are asked for advice by their clients? Would the guidance that subsequent courts might need be the same as the guidance that solicitors might need? Can one draw useful generalizations from the decision so that its value for future cases can be more clearly seen?

(a) Landlord leased building to Tenant to be used as a store. Tenant promised to restore the building to its original state at the end of the lease. Tenant made significant alterations and failed to restore at the end of the lease. Landlord sold building for the same amount it would have got had the restoration been made. Landlord sues for the cost of restoration. What result?

(b) David promised Joan that he would build a model of the Parliament Buildings in her garden for $20,000. David subsequently changed his mind and refused to do the work. It is proved that it would now cost $25,000 to complete the model. It is also proved that the value of Joan's property would be reduced by $10,000 if the model were built. Joan now sues David to recover the extra cost of having the model completed by someone else. Can she recover, and if so, how much? If Joan can recover $25,000 in this case, would this be consistent with the judgments in *Peevyhouse*?

(c) Mrs. Jones, a lonely old widow living in Oklahoma City, has a pussycat named Fiddler who is her only companion. When Fiddler becomes ill, Mrs. Jones takes him to Dr. Vet. Dr. Vet guarantees to cure the cat. He treats Fiddler with medication and Mrs. Jones pays the bill, but Fiddler gets worse. Mrs. Jones takes the cat to another veterinarian and learns that cure is possible, but only by surgery costing $500. The value of a healthy Fiddler on the open market is about $10. Can Mrs. Jones recover $500 from Dr. Vet? Does your answer depend upon whether she has the operation performed or not?

4. In the light of the decision in *Peevyhouse*, what advice would you give to a farmer whose land is about to be strip-mined? Consider two situations: (i) the farmer *really* wants her land levelled or, (ii) the farmer is indifferent to the state of the land after it has been strip-mined but wants to get the maximum value for the coal that might be under it.

One method of dealing with the problem of non-performance is for one party to require that the contract specify the damages that the other will pay in the event of breach. In Oklahoma, the legislative provisions mentioned in ¶ 19 might restrict a court's willingness to give full effect to such a clause. As discussed in Chapter 6, there are also limitations at common law to this potential solution, arising from a general concern to ensure that clauses that stipulate the damages payable on breach do not provide for "excessive" payments that are much larger than any damage award that would be given. If a "penalty clause" provides for "excessive" payments in the event of breach, it may not be enforceable. As a negotiation strategy, however, specifying the damages would at least make the issues clear, though whether the other party would agree to the terms may be another matter altogether.

need to draft better contracts

The unusual fact situation dealt with by the Oklahoma Supreme Court in *Peevy-house*, *i.e.*, the wide discrepancy between two most obvious measures of damages, can arise in other situations that are less dramatic.   non—econ. loss

In *Radford v. De Froberville*, [1977] 1 W.L.R. 1272, [1978] 1 All E.R. 33, (Ch. D.) the plaintiff had agreed to sell part of his land to the defendant. As part of the deal, the purchaser promised that she would build a stone wall of a specified height and construction between the part sold and the part retained by the vendor. The purchaser failed to build the wall and the vendor sued for damages for breach of contract. The purchaser argued that damages should be nominal (no more than a token amount) as there was no evidence that the value of the property retained by the vendor would be reduced if the stone wall were not built. In the alternative, the purchaser tried to argue that damages should be limited to the cost of building a less expensive wall out of wood. The vendor argued that he was entitled to the full cost of building the wall out of stone, and he stated, in court, that if he were awarded the full cost, he would build the stone wall. The trial judge awarded the cost of building the wall out of stone.

Before considering the relationship between the decisions in *Radford* and in *Peevyhouse*, it is useful to introduce some additional analytical tools. It is reasonably clear that the vendor in *Radford* notionally "paid" the full price of the purchaser's promise, in the sense that, when agreeing to sell the land, the purchaser, in determining her cost of entering into the contract, would have deducted the estimated cost of building the stone wall from the amount that she was prepared to pay as the price of the land. As discussed more fully later, consideration of this fact would permit an alternative argument to be made by the promisee, namely, that the defaulting promisor is unjustly enriched by keeping what she would never have had if the promise had not been made. In *Radford* it makes no difference which measure is adopted for giving relief to the vendor: either the cost of building the wall or the amount by which the price of the sale was reduced to cover the cost of the promise probably leads to the same result. (Can you see why the fact that the cost of building the wall had increased from £1,200 when the contract was made to £3,400 at the date of the trial, some 13 years later, is irrelevant?)

A determination of the cost of the promise to the plaintiff-promisee in *Peevy-house* is more complex. It is first necessary to consider the context of a strip-mining lease. The lessor, the farmer, will want at least three things from the arrangement: the maximum price for the minerals under the land; some control over the way in which the work is done so that the land unaffected by the strip-mining will be workable and the upheaval will be as short as possible; and some protection from the long-term effects of the strip-mining. The lessee, Garland Coal, will not want to promise that any specified amount of coal will be mined, but it will expect to pay something for each ton of coal removed from the lessor's land. The party in the position of Garland Coal will invariably have a standard form of strip-mining lease. This lease, though drafted from the lessee's perspective, is likely to acknowledge some of the concerns that lessors will generally have. The problem is that, unlike the situation in *Radford*, where, at least at the time that the contract is made, one can be fairly sure of the cost of the purchaser's promise to build the wall, in a *Peevyhouse* situation it is usually impossible to know at the time that the contract is made what the promise to "level the land" will cost.

Why did this uncertainty exist in *Peevyhouse*? For any strip-mining project, there is likely to be a roughly standard royalty paid on each ton of coal extracted. While Garland Coal had some expectation of how much coal underlay the Peevyhouse land, until the strip-mining was underway, it was not possible to know how much coal was there, how expensive it would be to extract and what it would cost to restore the land.

This situation might be viewed as one in which the parties had a rough expectation about the amount of coal lying beneath the Peevyhouse lands and would have expected that the total royalty payable to Mr. and Mrs. Peevyhouse would be larger if the promise to level the land were not made. If, when the contract was made, the cost of levelling had been known to be $29,000, then the total expected royalties payable could have been reduced by this amount. (For reasons discussed below, the actual cost of levelling the land was undoubtedly much less than this.) If this was the pattern of the negotiations, it is clear that Mr. and Mrs. Peevyhouse made a poor bargain. They "paid" the full price of the levelling, yet were left with what turned out to be an almost empty promise. The language of the minority judgment is consistent with an assumption that the negotiations took this path.

There is another way in which the negotiations could be viewed. Mr. and Mrs. Peevyhouse could have insisted on Garland's promise to level the land, not because they really wanted the land to be levelled, but because that promise allocated to Garland the risk that the work that Garland would do on the land would permanently reduce the value of the land for any other purpose. If the market value of the land as farm-land (or as land for any other purpose) would be reduced because the land had not been levelled after the strip-mining, Garland's promise to level the land could be used to make it pay the amount of the reduction in the price or value. (This type of risk allocation is the purpose of such the clause in Question 3(a) *supra*: the Landlord only wants to be protected from any negative economic consequences of the Tenant's modifications to the building. The Tenant, for its part, does not want to be responsible for paying the cost of doing restoration work that would give the Landlord more than it would have had if the Tenant had not altered the premises in the first place.) If this risk allocation was the purpose of the promise, it is possible that in the negotiations Garland would not have insisted that the total royalty payments be reduced to cover the costs that restoration would entail: the reduction would be an amount that represented the risk that Garland might be called upon to make up the difference in price. The decision of the majority in *Peevyhouse* is consistent with this assumption about the purpose for the promise to restore the land.

Other negotiating strategies and goals can be imagined; the two that have been mentioned are possible (and extreme) examples only.

The decision of the Oklahoma Supreme Court in *Peevyhouse v. Garland Coal* has become one of the most famous cases studied in North American law schools. Because of the academic interest, more than 25 years after the decision, the case was the subject of an unusual retrospective study that undoubtedly consumed more time and energy than were taken by (or available to) counsel for Mr. and Mrs. Peevyhouse in the original case: Professor Judith L. Maute, "*Peevyhouse v. Garland Coal & Mining Co.* Revisited: The Ballad of Willie and Lucille" (1995), 89 *Northwestern University Law Review* 1341. This account makes it clear that factual assumptions of the appeal court decisions were not accurate.

In some critical respects, the appeal court lacked information about the negotiation and context of the contract. The claim of Mr. and Mrs. Peevyhouse was affected by a combination of tactical decisions by their lawyer and the rulings of the trial judge, which meant that no evidence was before the jury (or the appeal court) about the process of contract formation and the context in which the contract was performed. (The extent to which a court or jury can consider all the facts surrounding a contract raises important and difficult questions about trial procedure, the process of the interpretation of contracts, and the responsibilities and ability of the parties to produce the facts the court needs. These issues will be considered later in these materials.)

Professor Maute reports that of the 120 acres that Mr. and Mrs. Peevyhouse owned, only 60 were affected by the strip-mining. Garland Coal had offered Mr. and Mrs. Peevyhouse a contract on its standard form, but they had refused to sign that contract and had insisted on one dealing specifically with their concerns for the land after the strip-mining had been completed. The clauses mentioned in ¶ 27 of the judgment were put into the contract at their insistence after they had discussed their hopes for and fears of what the strip-mining would do to their land. These concerns were "idiosyncratic" in the sense that they were not reflected in the standard terms offered by Garland Coal, but were perfectly rational. The strip-mining made part of the Peevyhouse land effectively inaccessible to the main part of the farm. Moreover, Mr. and Mrs. Peevyhouse waived a payment of $3,000 offered by Garland Coal at the time of signing as part of the standard deal in exchange for Garland's promise to level the land. As soon as Garland got access to the Peevyhouse land, it diverted a creek onto their land that was impeding strip-mining operations on neighbouring property. The coal seam under the Peevyhouse land turned out to be thinner and deeper than expected, so that Garland Coal did less work on the Peevyhouse land than it had expected to do. The fact that the strip mining was effectively abandoned due to higher than expected costs increased the costs of restoration. Total royalties of only about $2,500 were paid by Garland Coal.

Professor Maute's information makes it clear that the conclusions of the majority of the Oklahoma Supreme Court that the levelling of the land was a minor or "incidental" aspect of the contract and that its "main purpose" was the extraction of coal are incorrect. The Peevyhouses were prepared to allow Garland Coal to strip-mine their land, but only on condition that the land was afterwards made usable by them as pasture for their animals. They waived payment of the $3,000 prepayment and, in return, insisted on the promise to level. They wanted to reduce the risks to their livestock and their family from the existence of unfenced banks and deep pits filled with water on their land.

Professor Maute's exhaustive examination of the litigation and its context illustrates the important role played by rules of procedure and the tactics of the lawyers involved in denying the court access to important facts of the expectations of the parties and the context of a contract.

One important factor seems to have been that the lawyer for Mr. and Mrs. Peevyhouse was paid on a contingent fee basis. While this fee arrangement might have been necessary to enable Mr. and Mrs. Peevyhouse to sue Garland, consider what incentives and pressures it creates. Professor Maute suggests that some of the plaintiffs' lawyer's mistakes were due to the fact that he would only be paid if his clients won and he had an incentive to keep the litigation costs (including the time that he spent on the case) low.

The degree to which anyone deciding a dispute — a parent, a teacher, a police officer, an arbitrator or a judge — can deal with *all* the facts that are relevant is always limited. However, it is clear that in *Peevyhouse* important, readily ascertainable facts that should have affected the outcome were not put before the court. The *Peevyhouse* case was of sufficient interest to make it worth Professor Maute's time to investigate what actually happened and to show where the Oklahoma Supreme Court went wrong, but in very many cases decided by courts, facts that one or another of the parties will consider important will have been ignored, misunderstood or simply not presented to the court. This is in part due to the limit that must be imposed on the factual examination that the court can take time to undertake — no one can investigate every aspect of another's life or even a significant part of it — and in part to the relatively formal process of putting facts before a judge. (As will be discussed in Chapter 5, there are also rules that may deliberately deny the court access to facts that may explain why one party to a contract made the deal in question.)

The facts put before an appellate court are those found by the trial judge and contained in the transcript of the evidence presented at the trial and the documents admitted in evidence. A major additional contributor to the limit that is placed on the judge's access to facts is that the cost of informing the judge of what happened is borne by the parties: the court has no independent access to the facts and cannot and must not investigate them for itself. (Do you know why in our adversarial syatem the court must not make an independent investigation?)

It is important to appreciate that "extra" or new knowledge about the actual facts of *Peevyhouse* does not affect the value of the decision as an example of a judicial solution to the problem presented by the parties to the court. In any other case where there is the same problem of valuing what the plaintiff lost by the defendant's breach, the majority judgment of the Oklahoma Supreme Court may still be a guide to what the court might do. One lesson of Professor Maute's examination of what actually happened is that another lawyer in another case may be more aware of the importance of some particular fact that was not made clear to the appeal court judges in *Peevyhouse*.

If one ignores what is now known about *Peevyhouse* and accepts the facts as presented to the Oklahoma Supreme Court, the decision of the majority of that court may be justifiable. If one accepts that the promisee actually wants to have the work done, even if this is more than the economic value of the promisor's promise, one can award the full cost of performance as the court did in *Radford*. If one is unsure of what approach to take, the kind of intermediate award that the jury gave might have been most appropriate. Indeed, Professor Maute shows that the trial judge, through the questions that he asked the jury to consider, left the matter of compensation entirely to them.

There is one way to test the validity of an award of the cost of performance in *Peevyhouse* and *Radford*. Suppose the judge in each of those cases had made an order for "specific performance", *i.e.*, had ordered the promisor to do what it had promised to do and had not simply given judgment for an amount that might have allowed the plaintiff to hire someone else to do the work. (In the dissent at ¶ 42, Irwin J. refers to the plaintiffs as "being entitled to specific performance" but it is clear that this meant that he would award a sum of money that would equal the cost of performance, not that he would order Garland to do the work. Later in this chapter we will examine a judge's power to make such an order for specific performance, and shall see that such a remedy would not normally be available in either of these cases. The reason for this is largely a reflection of judicial reluctance to in effect supervise construction work. We can ignore this limitation on the remedy for the purpose of exploring the consequences of its exercise here.)

In *Radford* one can see that, as the plaintiff-vendor has already promised in court to build the wall if he is awarded the cost of doing so, the plaintiff would be quite happy to have the defendant ordered to build the wall. But now consider *Peevyhouse*. Suppose that Garland were ordered to level the land, would the plaintiffs want it done? On the facts before the Oklahoma Supreme Court, it seems unlikely that the work would be done. The cost of levelling the land would be almost one hundred times the amount by which the value of the land was decreased. Would you have any confidence that the plaintiffs would not bargain with Garland to have the cost (or part of the cost) of levelling paid directly to them, so that they could buy a new farm of equivalent value and have lots of money left over? If the court were to order Garland to perform, it would force the Peevyhouses to make a decision on the real value of the levelled land to them. Such an order would have some of the qualities of the Biblical decision of King Solomon regarding the two women who both claimed to be the mother of the child — proposing to cut the child in two and awarding custody to the woman who responded by renouncing her claim.

On the facts disclosed by Professor Maute about *Peevyhouse v. Garland Coal*, it is clear that the expert testimony introduced by the plaintiffs about the cost of levelling the land ($29,000) was very significantly inflated, perhaps because the lawyer for the Peevyhouses was being paid on a contingent fee basis. The expert evidence from the defendant's real estate appraiser about the diminution in value of the land ($300) probably under-estimated the actual loss in terms of the value of the land.

It is also clear from Professor Maute's study that the Peevyhouses actually wanted the land levelled and otherwise made safe in accordance with the contract. However, when their counsel was asked by a judge in Supreme Court during oral argument if the Peevyhouses would level the land, he apparently stated that they would not (Maute, *supra*, note 243). This statement by the plaintiffs' lawyer may well have affected the approach of the majority.

Notice what happens if Garland is ordered to specifically perform. If the plaintiffs in *Peevyhouse* will bargain for a monetary payment with Garland when it is ordered to level the land, what does this fact say about what they have lost? If one is, as the majority of the court clearly was, sceptical of the motives behind the claim that Garland's breach caused the plaintiff a loss equal to the cost of levelling the land, one can only accept the judgment of the minority with great difficulty. This difficulty primarily comes from a suspicion that the facts necessary to support the dissenting conclusion may not exist. It is implicit in the compensation principle that the plaintiff should be neither worse off nor better off by an award of damages than by performance. Compensation for a loss that did not occur gives the plaintiff too much.

If we deal only with what the court understood of the facts, the judgments illustrate the importance of drafting the contract with great care. (The additional facts provided by Professor Maute suggest that, from the point of view of Mr. and Mrs. Peevyhouse, the very unsatisfactory judgment of the Supreme Court was largely caused by mistakes made by the trial lawyer employed by them. Notice, by way of contrast, how Mr. Radford's counsel made it easy for the court to find for his client.)

The appeal court was not aware that the Peevyhouses had agreed to forego the usual upfront payment of $3,000 in return for the unusual promise to level the land at the end of the contract. Had this fact been made clear to the court, it might have made it possible to establish that the "price" of the promise to level was at least this much, and likely more. It might have been possible, as we shall see, for the plaintiffs have sued for the return of what they gave up for the promise to level the land (*i.e.*, $3,000), or for what the Garland Coal saved by being able to divert the stream onto their land. The fact is that in the litigation their lawyer did not advance such claims.

It is very important to understand that the problems of damages and how they might be resolved have a direct impact on how a contract should be drafted. If a contract is regarded as a collection of promises, at least in theory every promise in that collection will have a notional price or be a component of the price. If Mr. Radford wants his wall, he will have to pay for it, either by paying a contractor directly out of the total price that he receives for the land, or by taking less for the land with the purchaser's promise to build the wall. The important question for the person negotiating the contract is to determine what is the best way to structure the deal from his or her client's point of view. *Peevy needs more weight on rest.*

Professor Maute's study discloses that the plaintiffs did not in fact consult a lawyer about the lease and that, apart from having the standard contract prepared by a lawyer, Garland also did not negotiate through a lawyer. Mr. Peevyhouse negotiated with a Mr. Cumpton, Garland Coal's agent in Stigler, Oklahoma, the small town close to the Peevyhouse land, though the contract was signed in the office of the lawyer for Garland Coal.

In the next decision, *Ruxley Electronics*, the House of Lords dealt with a case similar to both *Peevyhouse* and *Radford*. This decision offers an interesting analysis of the competing arguments and a reason to believe that the jury award in *Peevyhouse* could be justified as more than just a compromise arrived at by lay-persons.

RUXLEY ELECTRONICS AND CONSTRUCTION LTD. v. FORSYTH

[1996] 1 A.C. 344, [1995] 3 All E.R. 268
(H.L., Lords Keith, Bridge, Jauncey, Mustill and Lloyd)

[The defendant-owner contracted with the plaintiff contractors to build a swimming pool in his garden and a building to enclose it for a total price of over £70,000. The contract required the pool to be seven feet six inches deep at the deep end. After some delay (and some very acrimonious exchanges between the parties), the pool was completed but the defendant refused to pay the balance of some £39,000. After the plaintiffs' actions were started, the defendant discovered that the pool was only six feet nine inches deep and counter-claimed for the cost of reconstructing the pool to the contract depth. It was accepted that the failure to provide the required depth was a breach of contract but the trial judge found that the breach had not decreased the value of the pool or the defendant's property. Further, since there was no diving board, swimmers could safely dive in the pool from the edge of the pool, even at its present depth. During the course of the trial, the owner said that, if he were awarded the money to do so, he intended to rebuild the pool to a depth of seven feet six inches. The trial judge doubted that the owner would actually do so.

The trial judge gave judgment for the contractors in the amount claimed by them but awarded the owner £2,500 general damages for "loss of amenity" on his counterclaim. The owner appealed, contending that the judge should have awarded damages for the breach of contract to reflect the cost of reconstructing the swimming pool to conform to the original contractual specification, and that the award of general damages was too low if he received no other compensation for the breach. The Court of Appeal allowed the appeal, holding that it was not unreasonable to award as damages the cost of reconstructing the swimming pool in order to make good the breach of contract, and awarded the owner £21,560 damages against the contractor, to be partially set off against the balance owing. The contractor appealed to the House of Lords. The House of Lords restored the trial judgment, with several concurring opinions.]

LORD JAUNCEY OF TULLICHETTLE: —

[not benefit/profit from breached contract]

. . .

[1]   Damages are designed to compensate for an established loss and not to provide a gratuitous benefit to the aggrieved party, from which it follows that the reasonableness of an award of damages is to be linked directly to the loss sustained. If it is unreasonable in a particular case to award the cost of reinstatement it must be because the loss sustained does not extend to the need to reinstate. A failure to achieve the precise contractual objective does not necessarily result in the loss which is occasioned by a total failure. This was recognised by the High Court of Australia in the passage in *Bellgrove v. Eldridge* [(1954) 90 C.L.R. 613, H.C.A.)] . . . where it was stated that the cost of reinstatement work (subject to the qualification of reasonableness) was the extent of the loss, thereby treating reasonableness as a factor to be considered in determining what was that loss rather than, as the [owner] argued, merely a factor in determining which of two alternative remedies were appropriate for a loss once established. . . .

. . .

[2]   It was submitted that where the objective of a building contract involved satisfaction of a personal preference the only measure of damages available for a breach involving failure to achieve such satisfaction was the cost of reinstatement. In my view this is not the case. Personal preference may well be a factor in reasonableness and hence in determining what loss has been suffered but it cannot per se be determinative of what that loss is.

[3]   My Lords, the trial judge found that it would be unreasonable to incur the cost of demolishing the existing pool and building a new and deeper one. In so doing he implicitly recognised that the respondent's loss did not extend to the cost of reinstatement. He was, in my view, entirely justified in reaching that conclusion. It therefore follows that the appeal must be allowed.

[LORD MUSTILL, after referring to the argument that the only two possible awards of damages were the full cost of reinstatement or the diminution in the market value of the property, continued:]

[4]   The proposition that these two measures of damage represent the only permissible bases of recovery lies at the heart of the employer's [owner's] case. From this he reasons that there is a presumption in favour of the cost of restitution, since this is the only way in which he can be given what the contractor had promised to provide. Finally, he contends that there is nothing in the facts of the present case to rebut this presumption.

[5]   The attraction of this argument is its avoidance of the conclusion that, in a case such as the present, unless the employer can prove that the defects have depreciated the market value of the property the householder can recover nothing at

all. This conclusion would be unacceptable to the average householder, and it is unacceptable to me. It is a common feature of small building works performed on residential property that the cost of the work is not fully reflected by an increase in the market value of the house, and that comparatively minor deviations from speci-fication or sound workmanship may have no direct financial effect at all. Yet the householder must surely be entitled to say that he chose to obtain from the builder a promise to produce a particular result because he wanted to make his house more comfortable, more convenient and more conformable to his own particular tastes; not because he had in mind that the work might increase the amount which he would receive if, contrary to expectation, he thought it expedient in the future to exchange his home for cash. To say that in order to escape unscathed the builder has only to show that to the mind of the average on-looker, or the average potential buyer, the results which he has produced seem just as good as those which he had promised would make a part of the promise illusory and unbalance the bargain. In the valuable analysis contained in *Radford v. De Froberville*, [1978] 1 All E.R. 33 at 42, [1977] 1 W.L.R. 1262 at 1270, Oliver J. emphasised that it was for the plaintiff to judge what performance he required in exchange for the price. The court should honour that choice. *Pacta sunt servanda*. If the appellant's argument leads to the conclusion that in all cases like the present the employer is entitled to no more than nominal damages, the average householder would say that there must be something wrong with the law.

non commercial interest

[6]   In my opinion there would indeed be something wrong if, on the hypothesis that cost of reinstatement and the depreciation in value were the only available measures of recovery, the rejection of the former necessarily entailed the adoption of the latter; and the court might be driven to opt for the cost of reinstatement, absurd as the consequence might often be, simply to escape from the conclusion that the promisor can please himself whether or not to comply with the wishes of the promisee which, as embodied in the contract, formed part of the consideration for the price. Having taken on the job the contractor is morally as well as legally obliged to give the employer what he stipulated to obtain, and this obligation ought not to be devalued. In my opinion, however, the hypothesis is not correct. There are not two alternative measures of damage, at opposite poles, but only one: namely the loss truly suffered by the promisee. In some cases the loss cannot be fairly measured except by reference to the full cost of repairing the deficiency in performance. In others, and in particular those where the contract is designed to fulfil a purely commercial purpose, the loss will very often consist only of the monetary detriment brought about by the breach of contract. But these remedies are not exhaustive, for the law must cater for those occasions where the value of the promise to the promisee exceeds the financial enhancement of his position which full performance will secure. This excess, often referred to in the literature as the "consumer surplus" (see *e.g.*, the valuable discussion by Harris, Ogus and Phillips, "Contract Remedies and the Consumer Surplus" (1979), 95 *Law Q. Rev.* 581) is usually incapable of precise valuation in terms of money, exactly because it represents a personal, subjective and non-monetary gain. Nevertheless, where it exists the law should recognise it and compensate the promisee if the misperfor-mance takes it away. . . . Neither the contractor nor the court has the right to sub-stitute for the employer's individual expectation of performance a criterion derived from what ordinary people would regard as sensible. As my Lords have shown, the test of reasonableness plays a central part in determining the basis of recovery, and will indeed be decisive in a case such as the present when the cost of reinstatement

would be wholly disproportionate to the non-monetary loss suffered by the employer. But it would be equally unreasonable to deny all recovery for such a loss. The amount may be small, and since it cannot be quantified directly there may be room for difference of opinion about what it should be. But in several fields the judges are well accustomed to putting figures to intangibles, and I see no reason why the imprecision of the exercise should be a barrier, if that is what fairness demands.

[7]   My Lords, once this is recognised, the puzzling and paradoxical feature of this case, that it seems to involve a contest of absurdities, simply falls away. There is no need to remedy the injustice of awarding too little by unjustly awarding far too much. The judgment of the trial judge acknowledges that the employer has suffered a true loss and expresses it in terms of money. Since there is no longer any issue about the amount of the award, as distinct from the principle, I would simply restore his judgment by allowing the appeal.

LORD LLOYD OF BERWICK [stated the facts at length and summarized the judgments in the Court of Appeal. He referred to the judgment in *Jacob & Youngs Inc. v. Kent*, 230 N.Y. 239 (1921), (discussed in *Peevyhouse, supra*) in which Cardozo J. had held that for the cost of reinstatement to the awarded as damages, reinstatement must be reasonable. He continued:]

[8]   Cardozo J's judgment is important because it establishes two principles which I believe to be correct and which are directly relevant to the present case: first, the cost of reinstatement is not the appropriate measure of damages if the expenditure would be out of all proportion to the good to be obtained, and secondly, the appropriate measure of damages in such a case is the difference in value, even though it would result in a nominal award. . . .

[9]   In the present case the judge found as a fact that Mr. Forsyth's stated intention of rebuilding the pool would not persist for long after the litigation had been concluded. In these circumstances it would be "mere pretence" to say that the cost of rebuilding the pool is the loss which he has in fact suffered. This is the critical distinction between the present case and the example given by Staughton L.J. [in the Court of Appeal] of a man who has had his watch stolen. In the latter case, the plaintiff is entitled to recover the value of the watch because that is the true measure of his loss. He can do what he wants with the damages. But if, as the judge found, Mr. Forsyth had no intention of rebuilding the pool, he has lost nothing except the difference in value, if any. . . .

[10]   Does Mr. Forsyth's undertaking to spend any damages which he may receive on rebuilding the pool make any difference? Clearly not. He cannot be allowed to create a loss which does not exist in order to punish the defendants for their breach of contract. The basic rule of damages, to which exemplary damages are the only exception, is that they are compensatory not punitive.

[LORD LLOYD concluded by saying that the award of £2,500 made by the trial judge should be upheld on the ground that it represented the loss of "a pleasurable amenity". LORDS KEITH and BRIDGE agreed with LORDS JAUNCEY, MUSTILL and LLOYD.]

QUESTIONS AND NOTES

1.   The acrimony between the parties in *Ruxley* was such that their dispute made it to the English newspapers. Mr. Forsyth's offer (or even undertaking) to have the pool rebuilt, if he were awarded the costs of doing so, was almost certainly, as Lord Lloyd

notes, motivated by his desire for revenge or to make the contractor suffer. How should this fact be dealt with? Should it be relevant or irrelevant? Suppose that the pre-litigation discussions between Mr. Radford and Ms. De Froberville were characterized by acrimony and extreme rudeness on the part of either or both parties. Should this fact have any impact on the court's belief that Mr. Radford really wanted the wall built? How would you advise a client to behave in such a situation? How should you, as the lawyer for either party, behave?

2. It is important to see the decision of the House of Lords as an example of and not as an exception to the compensation principle stated by Lord Atkinson in *Wertheim v. Chicoutimi Pulp*. What has happened is that the scope of the "position" that the plaintiff would have been in had the contract been properly performed has been enlarged to include the concept of "non-pecuniary damages" or "consumer surplus".

3. Note the amount that the trial judge awarded in respect of the owner's "loss of amenity". The amount is low and conventional in the sense that it does not reflect Mr. Forsyth's personal degree of disappointment, but that of some "reasonable" owner or "reasonably stoic owner". In *Farley v. Skinner*, [2002] 2 A.C. 732, [2001] 4 All E.R. 801, the House of Lords set a cap on such an award of £10,000. The cap was set by the judges' stated conclusion that the £10,000 awarded in that case against a property valuer who had negligently failed to inform his client that the house he was buying as a peaceful retirement home was directly beneath the principal flight path to Gatwick airport was the limit of such an award.

Given the importance that carefully drafted contracts have in helping the parties achieve what they want out of any deal, there is clearly value in having legal advice before signing an important contract. There are ethical considerations to be kept in mind if one party has a lawyer and the other does not.

The American Law Institute in its *Restatement Second, Contracts*, § 161, Comment (1979) states:

> An owner is ordinarily expected to disclose a known error in a bid that he has received from a contractor. . . . Nevertheless, a party need not correct all mistakes of the other and is expected only to act in good faith and in accordance with reasonable standards of fair dealing, as reflected in prevailing business ethics. A party may, therefore, reasonably expect the other to take normal steps to inform himself and to draw his own conclusions. If the other is indolent, inexperienced or ignorant, or if his judgment is bad or he lacks adequate information, his adversary is not normally expected to compensate for these deficiencies. A buyer of property, for example, is not ordinarily expected to disclose circumstances that make the property more valuable than the seller supposes.

The *Code of Professional Conduct* (1987) of the Canadian Bar Association states (pp. 69-70):

> The lawyer should avoid sharp practice and not take advantage of or act without fair warning upon slips, irregularities or mistakes on the part of other lawyers not going to the merits or involving any sacrifice of the client's rights.

The *Rules of Professional Conduct* of the Law Society of Upper Canada (2000) state:

> 2.04(14) When a lawyer is dealing on a client's behalf with an unrepresented person, the lawyer shall:

> (a) urge the unrepresented person to obtain independent legal representation;

(b) take care to see that the unrepresented person is not proceeding under the impression that his or her interests will be protected by the lawyer; and

(c) make clear to the unrepresented person that the lawyer is acting exclusively in the interests of the client and accordingly his or her comments may be partisan.

If you were representing Garland when the lease was being negotiated with the Peevyhouses and they were not represented by a lawyer, or had a lawyer who was unfamiliar with the issues involved in a strip-mining lease, what position would you take in the light of these ethical guidelines or your own ethical standards? Professor Maute pointed out that the Peevyhouses were, as one might have expected, unrepresented in the negotiations, and that at trial the Garland Coal Company had much more experienced counsel with more resources to devote to the case. The company lawyer would not, of course, have been paid on a contingent fee basis.

The next case deals with the problems of assessing damages in a situation that is more common than that in *Peevyhouse* or *Ruxley*. A buyer has refused to take delivery of goods purchased by him from a retailer who has, in turn, purchased them from a manufacturer.

VICTORY MOTORS LTD. v. BAYDA

[1973] 3 W.W.R. 747 (Sask. D.C.)

HUGHES D.C.J.: — [1] The plaintiff is a dealer in new and used automobiles carrying on business in the City of North Battleford. It brings this action for damages to, in effect, recover a commission of $700 it alleges is owing to it by the defendant. On 12th February 1972 the defendant contracted to purchase from the plaintiff a 1972 Mustang automobile. Following the arrival of the vehicle in North Battleford in mid-March 1972 the defendant declined to take delivery. Once it was clear that the defendant was not going to accept the vehicle it was sold by the plaintiff to another customer. The plaintiff's position is that, notwithstanding its recovery of a commission from the third party on the ultimate sale of the vehicle, it was deprived of its profit, by way of a commission, on its transaction with the defendant due to the defendant's refusal to accept and pay for the vehicle as ordered by him from the plaintiff. At the close of the trial I made a finding which I now formally record that the defendant did wrongfully refuse to accept and pay for the vehicle that he had ordered. The reasons therefor are a matter of record. I reserved judgment on and because of the far more complicated question of damages.

[2]   Simply stated, the plaintiff's position is that the ultimate sale to and recovery of a commission from the new purchaser who appeared on the scene is irrelevant insofar as its entitlement to recover from the defendant is concerned. The argument is that the ultimate purchaser would have bought another Mustang vehicle from the plaintiff had the one ordered by the defendant not been available for purchase and hence the plaintiff has, because of the defendant's action, made one profit instead of two, and that accordingly it is entitled to recover its profit, by way of damages, on the transaction contracted for by it with the defendant. . . .

[3]   *W.L. Thompson Ltd. v. R. Robinson (Gunmakers) Ltd.*, [1955] Ch. 177, [1955] 1 All E.R. 154. In that case the facts were that on 4th March 1954 the de-

fendants agreed in writing with the plaintiffs, who were motor car suppliers, to purchase from them a Standard Vanguard motor car. On 5th March 1954 the defendants intimated to the plaintiffs that they were not prepared to accept delivery of the motor car. The plaintiffs returned the motor car to their suppliers, who did not seek compensation, and plaintiffs proceeded to claim damages for breach of the agreement against the defendant. The price at which a Standard Vanguard motor car could be sold by the suppliers throughout the country was fixed by the manufacturers and the amount of profit which the plaintiffs would have realized on the sale of the motor car was £61 1s. 9d. . . .

[4]   *Charter v. Sullivan*, [1957] 2 Q.B. 117, [1957] 1 All E.R. 809. In that case the facts were that the plaintiff, a motor car dealer, agreed to sell a Hillman Minx car to the defendant for £773 17s. The retail price of such cars was fixed by the manufacturers. Subsequently the plaintiff received a letter from the defendant refusing to complete the purchase but seven or ten days later the plaintiff sold the car to another purchaser at the same price. He brought an action for damages for breach of contract against the defendant, claiming as damages the loss of profit of £97 15s. which he would have made if he had completed the sale to the defendant in addition to selling a similar car to the second purchaser. . . .

[5]   The question I must now answer is, what is the "estimated loss directly and naturally resulting in the ordinary course of events from the buyer's breach of contract"?. . .

[6]   In *W.L. Thompson Ltd. v. R. Robinson (Gunmakers) Ltd.* . . . it was an admitted fact that in the relevant trading area at the time the contract of sale between the plaintiff and the defendant took place there was no shortage of Vanguard models to meet all immediate demands. . . .

[7]   [In that case, Upjohn J. said at p. 157]:

> Apart altogether from authority and statute, it would seem to me on the facts to be quite plain that the plaintiffs' loss in this case is the loss of their bargain. They have sold one Vanguard less than they otherwise would. The plaintiffs, as the defendants must have known, are in business as dealers in motor cars and make their profit in buying and selling motor cars, and what they have lost is their profit on the sale of this Vanguard.

[8]   [Upjohn J. went on to say at p. 158]:

> It seems to me that in principle that covers this case. True the motor car in question was not sold to another purchaser, but the plaintiffs did what was reasonable, they got out of their bargain with [their supplier] but they sold one less Vanguard, and lost their profit on that transaction.

Judgment was granted to the plaintiff in the amount of £61 1s. 9d.

[9]   In *Charter v. Sullivan* . . . Jenkins L.J. gave great weight to the evidence of the plaintiff's sales manager, Mr. Winter, when he said, "Can sell all Hillman Minx we can get."

[HUGHES D.C.J. again quoted Jenkins L.J. who pointed out that the significance of what the plaintiff's sales manager said was that the plaintiff would not have been able to sell a car to another customer because the demand for cars outstripped the supply.]

[10]   Upjohn J.'s decision in favour of the plaintiff dealers in *W.L. Thompson Ltd. v. R. Robinson (Gunmakers) Ltd.* was essentially based on the admitted fact that

the supply of the cars in question exceeded the demand, and his judgment leaves no room for doubt that, if the demand had exceeded the supply his decision would have been the other way. . . .

[11] It now becomes a matter of my relating the facts in the instant situation to the foregoing English decisions. I have not located a case in this country where the point has received consideration. As I have already intimated, counsels' preoccupation with the question of breach of contract precluded an in-depth consideration of the matter of damages. . . .

[12] Meagre as [the] evidence is, it does indicate to me that, at the relevant time, the existing situation at North Battleford was that the supply of Mustang automobiles, either in the plaintiff's stock or through order from the manufacturer, exceeded the demand for same. That is to say, the plaintiff has given evidence which stands uncontradicted that it had a supply of vehicles at hand and others close at hand, to meet all willing customers presenting themselves at its place of business. The situation in this regard was similar to that found to exist in . . . *W.L. Thompson Ltd. v. R. Robinson (Gunmakers) Ltd.*, *supra*, and opposite as to supply and demand existing in *Charter v. Sullivan*, *supra*. Adopting the consistent reasoning of [these] decisions, however, the plaintiff is entitled to judgment against the defendant for the amount of profit lost as a result of the defendant's breach of contract. That amount, once determined, will be "the estimated loss directly and naturally resulting in the ordinary course of events from the buyer's breach of contract". . . .

[13] The determination of the amount of profit so lost has required the consideration of a number of factors. The plaintiff suggests that it should be the difference between the purchase price paid by it to the factory of $4,075 and the contractual selling price to the defendant of $4,686.40, or $611.40. I do not see it that way for the following reason: the $4,686.40 was to have come from a cash payment of $2,935.78 (excluding provincial sales tax) and a trade-in allowance on a 1966 Dodge two-door hardtop motor vehicle of $1,750.62. Mr. Magnuson conceded, however, that the trade-in might have sold for as little as $1,500. In that event the plaintiff's profit would be reduced by $250.62 or down to $360.78. That is the amount of the judgment ($360.78) that I award to the plaintiff by way of damages and it will have its costs of the action based upon the amount so recovered. . . .

NOTES AND QUESTIONS

1. What did Victory Motors really lose by Mr. Bayda's breach of contract? Is it relevant that the time taken by the salesman to show the car to Mr. Bayda was probably quite trivial?

2. These cases illustrate the responsibility of the lawyer involved with every aspect of the cases, from the negotiation of the contract to the decision on what facts to put before the court and whether or not to appeal. If the Peevyhouses really did want their land restored, irrespective of the economic value of so doing, their lawyer had to get that desire before the court. The court might be justified in drawing an inference adverse to them from the fact that such evidence was not clearly adduced. Notice that the lawyer for the plaintiff in *Radford* was careful to make clear to the court that the plaintiff wanted the wall built, whether or not it increased the value of the property. It is important to consider how far the mistakes of the lawyer should be visited on his or her client. If a lawyer had made a bad bargain for the Peevyhouses, should this cost be borne by them or by Garland? Does it matter if the mistake is made at the negotiating stage or at the trial?

In *Victory Motors* it would appear that little evidence was led about the issue of remedies by either counsel.

The Rationale for the Compensation Principle

A relatively simple idea underlies the ordinary rule governing remedies for breach of contract: the plaintiff should be compensated for the loss suffered. As stated by Lord Atkinson in *Wertheim v. Chicoutimi Pulp*, the party suffering loss as a result of the breach "should . . . be placed in the same position as he would have been in if the contract had been performed". The cases studied illustrate that the problem of applying the compensation principle is often complex, even in relatively simple fact situations. This is not to suggest that Lord Atkinson's principle is unjust or lacking in utility. It is a widely accepted principle, and there are many situations in which it can be relatively easy to apply.

While the examples thus far are not factually complex, they raise difficult conceptual issues. Why are the problems so difficult? To find an answer to the last question and to begin to find ways of dealing with the problems of compensation, it is useful to investigate some widely used analytical concepts. The following extract from Fuller and Perdue is taken from one of the most influential and important articles on the law of contract. Although it was written in 1936 and some of the thinking about the law of contracts has changed, it remains a seminal article. This article is important not only for contract analysis, but also for its influence on the development of modern ideas about law and about legal reasoning. Some of the discussion, however, is challenging, especially for first-year students.

Fuller and Perdue explain why the courts developed the compensation principle as the general rule for the award of contract damages, and develop tools to help analyze situations in which it may not be appropriate to use the compensation principle to assess damages for breach of contract. They also help to explain and justify the outcome in *Victory Motors*, and provide some answers to issues raised in *Peevyhouse* and *Ruxley*.

FULLER AND PERDUE, "THE RELIANCE INTEREST IN CONTRACT DAMAGES"

not case law

(1936), 46 *Yale L.J.* 52 (part 1) and 373 (part 2)

[All footnotes have been omitted. The extract starts at p. 52.]

[1]   The proposition that legal rules can be understood only with reference to the purposes they serve would today scarcely be regarded as an exciting truth. The notion that law exists as a means to an end has been commonplace for at least half a century. There is, however, no justification for assuming, because this attitude has now achieved respectability, and even triteness, that it enjoys a pervasive application in practice. Certainly there are even today few legal treatises of which it may be said that the author has throughout clearly defined the purposes which his definitions and distinctions serve. We are still all too willing to embrace the conceit that it is possible to manipulate legal concepts without the orientation which comes from the simple inquiry: toward what end is this activity directed? Nietzsche's observation, that the most common stupidity consists in forgetting what one is trying to do, retains a discomforting relevance to legal science.

[2]   In no field is this more true than in that of damages. In the assessment of damages the law tends to be conceived, not as a purposive ordering of human affairs, but as a kind of juristic mensuration. The language of the decisions sounds in terms not of command but of discovery. We measure the extent of the injury; we determine whether it was caused by the defendant's act; we ascertain whether the plaintiff has included the same item of damage twice in his complaint. One unfamiliar with the unstated premises which language of this sort conceals might almost be led to suppose that Rochester produces some ingenious instrument by which these calculations are accomplished.

[3]   It is, as a matter of fact, clear that the things which the law of damages purports to "measure" and "determine" — the "injuries", "items of damage" "causal connections", etc. — are in considerable part its own creations, and that the process of "measuring" and "determining" them is really a part of the process of creating them. This is obvious when courts work on the periphery of existing doctrine, but it is no less true of fundamental and established principles. For example, one frequently finds the "normal" rule of contract damages (which awards to the promisee the value of the expectancy, the "lost profit"), treated as a mere corollary of a more fundamental principle, that the purpose of granting damages is to make "compensation" for injury. Yet in this case we "compensate" the plaintiff by giving him something he never had. This seems on the face of things a queer kind of "compensation". We can, to be sure, make the term "compensation" seem appropriate by saying that the defendant's breach "deprived" the plaintiff of the expectancy. But this is in essence only a metaphorical statement of the effect of the legal rule. In actuality the loss which the plaintiff suffers (deprivation of the expectancy) is not a datum of nature but the reflection of a normative order. It appears as a "loss" only by reference to an unstated ought. Consequently, when the law gauges damages by the value of the promised performance it is not merely measuring a quantum, but is seeking an end, however vaguely conceived this end may be.

[4]   It is for this reason that it is impossible to separate the law of contract damages from the larger body of motives and policies which constitutes the general law of contracts. It is, unfortunately for the simplicity of our subject, impossible to assume that the purposive and policy-directed element of contract law has been exhausted in the rules which define contract and breach. If this were possible the law of contract damages would indeed be simple, and we would have but one measure of recovery for all contracts. Of course this is not the case. What considerations influence the setting up of different measures of recovery for different kinds of contracts? What factors explain the rather numerous exceptions to the normal rule which measures damages by the value of the expectancy? It is clear that these questions cannot be answered without an inquiry into the reasons which underlie (or may underlie) the enforcement of promises generally.

[5]   In our own discussion we shall attempt first an analysis of the purposes which may be pursued in awarding contract damages or in "enforcing" contracts generally; then we shall attempt to inquire to what extent, and under what circumstances, these purposes have found expression in the decisions and doctrinal discussions. As the title suggests, the primary emphasis will be on what we call the "reliance interest" as a possible measure of recovery in suits for breach of contract.

[6]   *The Purposes Pursued in Awarding Contract Damages*: It is convenient to distinguish three principal purposes which may be pursued in awarding contract damages. These purposes, and the situations in which they become appropriate, may be stated briefly as follows: *First*, the plaintiff has in reliance on the promise of the defendant conferred some value on the defendant. The defendant fails to perform his promise. The court may force the defendant to disgorge the value he received from the plaintiff. The object here may be termed the prevention of gain by the defaulting promisor at the expense of the promisee; more briefly, the prevention of unjust enrichment. The interest protected may be called the *restitution interest*. For our present purposes it is quite immaterial how the suit in such a case be classified, whether as contractual or quasi-contractual, whether as a suit to enforce the contract or as a suit based upon a rescission of the contract. These questions relate to the superstructure of the law, not to the basic policies with which we are concerned.

[7]   *Secondly*, the plaintiff has in reliance on the promise of the defendant changed his position. For example, the buyer under a contract for the sale of land has incurred expense in the investigation of the seller's title, or has neglected the opportunity to enter other contracts. We may award damages to the plaintiff for the purpose of undoing the harm which his reliance on the defendant's promise has caused him. Our object is to put him in as good a position as he was in before the promise was made. The interest protected in this case may be called the *reliance interest*.

[8]   *Thirdly*, without insisting on reliance by the promisee or enrichment of the promisor, we may seek to give the promisee the value of the expectancy which the promise created. We may in a suit for specific performance actually compel the defendant to render the promised performance to the plaintiff, or, in a suit for damages, we may make the defendant pay the money value of this performance. Here our object is to put the plaintiff in as good a position as he would have occupied had the defendant performed his promise. The interest protected in this case we may call the *expectation interest*.

[9]   It will be observed that what we have called the *restitution interest* unites two elements: (1) reliance by the promisee, (2) a resultant gain to the promisor. It may for some purposes be necessary to separate these elements. In some cases a defaulting promisor may after his breach be left with an unjust gain which was not taken from the promisee (a third party furnished the consideration), or which was not the result of reliance by the promisee (the promisor violated a promise not to appropriate the promisee's goods). Even in those cases where the promisor's gain results from the promisee's reliance it may happen that damages will be assessed somewhat differently, depending on whether we take the promisor's gain or the promisee's loss as the standard of measurement. Generally, however, in the cases we shall be discussing, gain by the promisor will be accompanied by a corresponding and, so far as its legal measurement is concerned, identical loss to the promisee, so that for our purposes the most workable classification is one which presupposes in the restitution interest a correlation of promisor's gain and promisee's loss. If, as we shall assume, the gain involved in the restitution interest results from and is identical with the plaintiff's loss through reliance, then the restitution interest is merely a special case of the reliance interest; all of the cases coming under the restitution interest will be covered by the reliance interest, and the reliance interest will be broader than the restitution interest only to the extent that it includes cases where the plaintiff has relied on the defendant's promise without enriching the defendant.

[10] It should not be supposed that the distinction here taken between the reliance and expectation interests coincides with that sometimes taken between "losses caused" (*damnum emergens*) and "gains prevented" (*lucrum cessans*). In the first place, though reliance ordinarily results in "losses" of an affirmative nature (expenditures of labor and money) it is also true that opportunities for gain may be forgone in reliance on a promise. Hence the reliance interest must be interpreted as a least potentially covering "gains prevented" as well as "losses caused". (Whether "gains prevented" through reliance on a promise are properly compensable in damages is a question not here determined. Obviously, certain scruples concerning "causality" and "foreseeability" are suggested. It is enough for our present purpose to note that there is nothing in the definition of the reliance interest itself which would exclude items of this sort from consideration.) On the other hand, it is not possible to make the expectation interest entirely synonymous with "gains prevented". The disappointment of an expectancy often entails losses of a positive character.

[11] It is obvious that the three "interests" we have distinguished do not present equal claims to judicial intervention. It may be assumed that ordinary standards of justice would regard the need for judicial intervention as decreasing in the order in which we have listed the three interests. The "restitution interest", involving a combination of unjust impoverishment with unjust gain, presents the strongest case for relief. If, following Aristotle, we regard the purpose of justice as the maintenance of an equilibrium of goods among members of society, the restitution interest presents twice as strong a claim to judicial intervention as the reliance interest, since if A not only causes B to lose one unit but appropriates that unit to himself, the resulting discrepancy between A and B is not one unit but two.

[12] On the other hand, the promisee who has actually relied on the promise, even though he may not thereby have enriched the promisor, certainly presents a more pressing case for relief than the promisee who merely demands satisfaction for his disappointment in not getting what was promised him. In passing from compensation for change of position to compensation for loss of expectancy we pass, to use Aristotle's terms again, from the realm of corrective justice to that of distributive justice. The law no longer seeks merely to heal a disturbed status quo, but to bring into being a new situation. It ceases to act defensively or restoratively, and assumes a more active role. With the transition, the justification for legal relief loses its self-evident quality. It is as a matter of fact no easy thing to explain why the normal rule of contract recovery should be that which measures damages by the value of the promised performance. Since this "normal rule" throws its shadow across our whole subject it will be necessary to examine the possible reasons for its existence. It may be said parenthetically that the discussion which follows, though directed primarily to the normal measure of recovery where damages are sought, also has relevance to the more general question, why should a promise which has not been relied on ever be enforced at all, whether by a decree of specific performance or by an award of damages?

[13] It should also be said that our discussion of "reasons" does not claim to coincide in all particulars with the actual workings of the judicial mind, certainly not with those of any single judicial mind. It is unfortunately very difficult to discuss the possible reasons for rules of law without unwittingly conveying the impression that these "reasons" are the things which control the daily operations of the judicial process. This has had the consequence, at a time when men stand in dread of being labelled "unrealistic", that we have almost ceased to talk about reasons altogether. Those who find unpalatable the rationalistic flavor of what follows are invited to view what they read not as law but as an excursus into legal philosophy, and to make whatever discount that distinction may seem to them to dictate.

[14] *Why Should the Law Ever Protect the Expectation Interest?* Perhaps the most obvious answer to this question is one which we may label "psychological". This answer would run something as follows: The breach of a promise arouses in the promisee a sense of injury. This feeling is not confined to cases where the promisee has relied on the promise. Whether or not he has actually changed his position because of the promise, the promisee has formed an attitude of expectancy such that a breach of the promise causes him to feel that he has been "deprived" of something which was "his". Since this sentiment is a relatively uniform one, the law has no occasion to go back of it. It accepts it as a datum and builds its rule about it.

[15] The difficulty with this explanation is that the law does in fact go back of the sense of injury which the breach of a promise engenders. No legal system attempts to invest with juristic sanction all promises. Some rule or combination of rules effects a sifting out for enforcement of those promises deemed important enough to society to justify the law's concern with them. Whatever the principles which control this sifting out process may be, they are not convertible into terms of the degree of resentment which the breach of a particular kind of promise arouses. Therefore, though it may be assumed that the impulse to assuage disappointment is one shared by those who make and influence the law, this impulse can hardly be regarded as the key which solves the whole problem of the protection accorded by the law to the expectation interest.

[16] A second possible explanation for the rule protecting the expectancy may be found in the much-discussed "will theory" of contract law. This theory views the contracting parties as exercising, so to speak, a legislative power, so that the legal enforcement of a contract becomes merely an implementing by the state of a kind of private law already established by the parties. If A has made, in proper form, a promise to pay B one thousand dollars, we compel A to pay this sum simply because the rule or lex set up by the parties calls for this payment. . . .

[17] It is not necessary to discuss here the contribution which the will theory is capable of making to a philosophy of contract law. Certainly some borrowings from the theory are discernable in most attempts to rationalize the bases of contract liability. It is enough to note here that while the will theory undoubtedly has some bearing on the problem of contract damages, it cannot be regarded as dictating in all cases a recovery of the expectancy. If a contract represents a kind of private law, it is a law which usually says nothing at all about what shall be done when it is violated. A contract is in this respect like an imperfect statute which provides no penalties, and which leaves it to the courts to find a way to effectuate its purposes. There would, therefore, be no necessary contradiction between the will theory and a rule which limited damages to the reliance interest. Under such a rule the penalty for violating the norm established by the contract would simply consist in being compelled to compensate the other party for detrimental reliance. Of course there may be cases where the parties have so obviously anticipated that a certain form of judicial relief will be given that we can, without stretching things, say that by implication they have "willed" that this relief should be given. This attitude finds a natural application to promises to pay a definite sum of money. But certainly as to most types of contracts it is vain to expect from the will theory a ready-made solution for the problem of damages.

[18]   A third and more promising solution of our difficulty lies in an economic or institutional approach. The essence of a credit economy lies in the fact that it tends to eliminate the distinction between present and future (promised) goods. Expectations of future values become, for purposes of trade, present values. In a society in which credit has become a significant and pervasive institution, it is inevitable that the expectancy created by an enforceable promise should be regarded as a kind of property, and breach of the promise as an injury to that property. In such a society the breach of a promise works an "actual" diminution of the promisee's assets — "actual" in the sense that it would be so appraised according to modes of thought which enter into the very fiber of our economic system. That the promisee had not "used" the property which the promise represents (had not relied on the promise) is as immaterial as the question whether the plaintiff in trespass *quare clausum fregit* was using his property at the time it was encroached upon. The analogy to ordinary forms of property goes further, for even in a suit for trespass the recovery is really for an expectancy, an expectancy of possible future uses. Where the property expectancy is limited (as where the plaintiff has only an estate for years) the recovery is reduced accordingly. Ordinary property differs from a contract right chiefly in the fact that it lies within the power of more persons to work a direct injury to the expectancy it represents. It is generally only the promisor or some one working through or upon him who is able to injure the contract expectancy in a direct enough manner to make expedient legal intervention.

[19]   The most obvious objection which can be made to the economic or institutional explanation is that it involves a *petitio principii*. A promise has present value, why? Because the law enforces it. The "expectancy", regarded as a present value, is not the cause of legal intervention but the consequence of it. This objection may be reinforced by a reference to legal history. Promises were enforced long before there was anything corresponding to a general system of "credit", and recovery was from the beginning measured by the value of the promised performance, the "agreed price". It may therefore be argued that the "credit system" when it finally emerged was itself in large part built on the foundations of a juristic development which preceded it.

[20]   The view just suggested asserts the primacy of law over economics; it sees law not as the creature but as the creator of social institutions. The shift of emphasis thus implied suggests the possibility of a fourth explanation for the law's protection of the unrelied-on expectancy, which we may call *juristic*. This explanation would seek a justification for the normal rule of recovery in some policy consciously pursued by courts and other lawmakers. It would assume that courts have protected the expectation interest because they have considered it wise to do so, not through a blind acquiescence in habitual ways of thinking and feeling, or through an equally blind deference to the individual will. Approaching the problem from this point of view, we are forced to find not a mere explanation for the rule in the form of some sentimental, volitional, or institutional datum, but articulate reasons for its existence.

[21]   What reasons can be advanced? In the first place, even if our interest were confined to protecting promisees against an out-of-pocket loss, it would still be possible to justify the rule granting the value of the expectancy, both as a cure for, and as a prophylaxis against, losses of this sort.

[22] It is a cure for these losses in the sense that it offers the measure of recovery most likely to reimburse the plaintiff for the (often very numerous and very difficult to prove) individual acts and forbearances which make up his total reliance on the contract. If we take into account "gains prevented" by reliance, that is, losses involved in forgoing the opportunity to enter other contracts, the notion that the rule protecting the expectancy is adopted as the most effective means of compensating for detrimental reliance seems not at all far-fetched. Physicians with an extensive practice often charge their patients the full office call fee for broken appointments. Such a charge looks on the face of things like a claim to the promised fee; it seems to be based on the "expectation interest". Yet the physician making the charge will quite justifiably regard it as compensation for the loss of the opportunity to gain a similar fee from a different patient. This forgoing of other opportunities is involved to some extent in entering most contracts, and the impossibility of subjecting this type of reliance to any kind of measurement may justify a categorical rule granting the value of the expectancy as the most effective way of compensating for such losses.

[23] The rule that the plaintiff must after the defendant's breach take steps to mitigate damages tends to corroborate the suspicion that there lies hidden behind the protection of the expectancy a concern to compensate the plaintiff for the loss of the opportunity to enter other contracts. Where after the defendant's breach the opportunity remains open to the plaintiff to sell his services or goods elsewhere, or to fill his needs from another source, he is bound to embrace that opportunity. Viewed in this way the rule of "avoidable harms" is a qualification on the protection accorded the expectancy, since it means that the plaintiff, in those cases where it is applied, is protected only to the extent that he has in reliance on the contract forgone other equally advantageous opportunities for accomplishing the same end.

[24] But, as we have suggested, the rule measuring damages by the expectancy may also be regarded as a prophylaxis against the losses resulting from detrimental reliance. Whatever tends to discourage breach of contract tends to prevent the losses occasioned through reliance. Since the expectation interest furnishes a more easily administered measure of recovery than the reliance interest, it will in practice offer a more effective sanction against contract breach. It is therefore possible to view the rule measuring damages by the expectancy in a quasi-criminal aspect, its purpose being not so much to compensate the promisee as to penalize breach of promise by the promisor. The rule enforcing the unrelied-on promise finds the same justification, on this theory, as an ordinance which fines a man for driving through a stop-light when no other vehicle is in sight.

[25] In seeking justification for the rule granting the value of the expectancy there is no need, however, to restrict ourselves by the assumption, hitherto made, that the rule can only be intended to cure or prevent the losses caused by reliance. A justification can be developed from a less negative point of view. It may be said that there is not only a policy in favor of preventing and undoing the harms resulting from reliance, but also a policy in favor of promoting and facilitating reliance on business agreements. As in the case of the stop-light ordinance we are interested not only in preventing collisions but in speeding traffic. Agreements can accomplish little, either for their makers or for society, unless they are made the basis for action. When business agreements are not only made but are also acted on, the division of labor is facilitated, goods find their way to the places where they are most needed, and economic activity is generally stimulated. These advan-

tages would be threatened by any rule which limited legal protection to the reliance interest. Such a rule would in practice tend to discourage reliance. The difficulties in proving reliance and subjecting it to pecuniary measurement are such that the business man knowing, or sensing, that these obstacles stood in the way of judicial relief would hesitate to rely on a promise in any case where the legal sanction was of significance to him. To encourage reliance we must therefore dispense with its proof. For this reason it has been found wise to make recovery on a promise independent of reliance, both in the sense that in some cases the promise is enforced though not relied on (as in the bilateral business agreement) and in the sense that recovery is not limited to the detriment incurred in reliance.

[26] The juristic explanation in its final form is then twofold. It rests the protection accorded the expectancy on (1) the need for curing and preventing the harms occasioned by reliance, and (2) on the need for facilitating reliance on business agreements. From this spelling out of a possible juristic explanation, it is clear that there is no incompatibility between it and the economic or institutional explanation. They view the same phenomenon from two different aspects. The essence of both of them lies in the word "credit". The economic explanation views credit from its institutional side; the juristic explanation views it from its rational side. The economic view sees credit as an accepted way of living; the juristic view invites us to explore the considerations of utility which underlie this way of living, and the part which conscious human direction has played in bringing it into being.

[27] The way in which these two points of view supplement one another becomes clearer when we examine separately the economic implications of the two aspects of the juristic explanation. If we rest the legal argument for measuring damages by the expectancy on the ground that this procedure offers the most satisfactory means of compensating the plaintiff for the loss of other opportunities to contract, it is clear that the force of the argument will depend entirely upon the existing economic environment. It would be most forceful in a hypothetical society in which all values were available on the market and where all markets were "perfect" in the economic sense. In such a society there would be no difference between the reliance interest and the expectation interest. The plaintiff's loss in forgoing to enter another contract would be identical with the expectation value of the contract he did make. The argument that granting the value of the expectancy merely compensates for that loss, loses force to the extent that actual conditions depart from those of such a hypothetical society. These observations make it clear why the development of open markets for goods tends to carry in its wake the view that a contract claim is a kind of property. . . He who by entering one contract passes by the opportunity to accomplish the same end elsewhere will not be inclined to regard contract breach lightly or as a mere matter of private morality. The consciousness of what is forgone reinforces the notion that the contract creates a "right" and that the contract claim is itself a species of property.

[28] If, on the other hand, we found the juristic explanation on the desire to promote reliance on contracts, it is not difficult again to trace a correspondence between the legal view and the actual conditions of economic life. In general our courts and our economic institutions attribute special significance to the same types of promises. The bilateral business agreement is, generally speaking, the only type of informal contract our courts are willing to enforce without proof that reliance has occurred — simply for the sake of facilitating reliance. This is, by no accident, precisely the kind of contract (the "exchange", "bargain", "trade",

"deal") which furnishes the indispensable and pervasive framework for the "unmanaged" portions of our economic activity.

[29]   The inference is therefore justified that the ends of the law of contracts and those of our economic system show an essential correspondence. One may explain this either on the ground that the law (mere superstructure and ideology) reflects inertly the conditions of economic life, or on the ground that economic activity has fitted itself into the rational framework of the law. Neither explanation would be true. In fact we are dealing with a situation in which law and society have interacted. The law measures damages by the expectancy in part because society views the expectancy as a present value; society views the expectancy as a present value in part because the law (for reasons more or less consciously articulated) gives protection to the expectancy. . . .

NOTES

1.   The Fuller and Perdue article developed some very important concepts which will be used throughout this book. Reasons for judgment and law review articles are, however, not written for those beginning their study of the law. What is important to understand at this point is that the notion of compensation can be seen as involving a choice between three different measures — the restitution, reliance, and expectation measures. The choice of the measure that is adopted in a particular case should be justified on some ground that is not circular or based on blind acceptance of existing rules. Fuller and Perdue argue that, depending on the facts in any particular case and on what values the court considers important, one can justify a decision to award damages on any one of these measures. They are also saying that there are a number of practical concerns that have an important bearing on the extent to which any justification can be accepted or applied. The logical result in any case will sometimes be rejected in favour of one that is in some respect a compromise of logic and expediency.

   Because Fuller and Perdue are concerned to find an acceptable reason to support the legal results in the cases, they emphasize what must never be forgotten: every rule must be justified in terms of its contribution to the effort to forward certain social values. As they observe, a common error consists in forgetting what one is trying to do. Because of this focus the article, even though it is slightly dated and less clear than it might be, it is well worth careful study. The three fundamental measures of damages are still used by judges and scholars. There is, however, a large body of scholarship that has been written since 1936 that qualifies, expands on and criticizes the work of Fuller and Perdue; see, *e.g.*, T. Rakoff, "Fuller and Perdue's The Reliance Interest as a Work of Legal Scholarship" (1991), *Wis. L. Rev.* 203, and R. Craswell, "Against Fuller and Perdue" (2000), 67 *U. Chi. L. Rev.* 99.

   It is important to an analysis of the problems of contracts to have a good understanding of terms such as "expectation interest", "reliance interest" and "restitution interest". While there are cases where the distinctions between these measures become blurred, nevertheless these terms refer to substantially different ways of determining how to assess damages and of justifying different results that are reached. As an interesting jurisprudential observation, while American courts adopted these concepts more than 50 years ago, Canadian courts for many years resisted using these terms directly, but more recently, as a result of the writing of Canadian scholars, the concepts developed by the Fuller and Perdue analysis are now regularly employed by Canadian judges. Unfortunately, however, there is some inconsistency in how these terms and concepts are used.

2.   A point of terminology should be noticed. Cases like *Ruxley* and *Radford* illustrate that one can have an economic interest in the performance of a contract and some other kind of interest, aesthetic or emotional, in it as well. In terms of economic theory, any interest can be conceived as economic in the sense that, as in *Radford*, the plaintiff was prepared to pay money (the money that he would receive from the defendant if he got a judgment) to obtain aesthetic or emotional satisfaction from the wall.

Such an interest was referred to as a "consumer surplus", *i.e.*, an interest that exists above those reflected in purely commercial considerations or reflected in market prices, by Lord Mustill in *Ruxley*. An alternative and increasingly common phrase, which has been borrowed from the law of torts, is to refer to such interests as "non-pecuniary" and to an award based in such an interest as "non-pecuniary damages".

While one can analyze non-market interests in economic terms, using the concept of the consumer surplus, it is more common to refer to an "economic interest" as reflected in, say, market values. "Economic interests" commonly refer to only those interests that are reflected in market prices, or that can be measured by an accountant's statement of income and expense. A non-economic "interest" is one that might be referred to as a "consumer surplus", or simply as some kind of psychological or emotional interest in the performance of the contract, or as an aesthetic interest that is not reflected in market prices. The law does not treat the two interests in the same way. While such disparate treatment may be inappropriate from the perspective of a purely theoretical analysis, courts generally distinguish between "economic" and "non-economic" losses. In practice, the distinction between the two types of losses is sometimes difficult to make, and care should be exercised to use precise language.

3. As Fuller and Perdue point out, the most commonly applied rule in a breach of contract situation is to award "expectancy based" damages; this is the compensation principle of *Wertheim v. Chicoutimi Pulp*. The cases of *Peevyhouse*, *Radford* and *Victory Motors* illustrate that what a party may expect from a contract may be just the monetary benefit that the contract's performance would have provided, or it may be the psychological satisfaction of having a wall at the end of one's property. In theory or indeed, as Professor Maute illustrated, in fact, one might argue that for Mr. and Mrs. Peevyhouse, the aesthetic satisfaction of levelled land was within their expectation interest. As the case was presented in the Oklahoma Supreme Court, there was, however, no clear evidence what their expectations were when the contract was formed, so that the Court would have had no justification for awarding damages to compensate for this type of loss.

   Much of modern advertising is based on the message that, if only one buys this car or this perfume, or drinks this beer, personal happiness will be assured. While it might be satisfying to see an advertiser sued for breach of the promise implicit in an advertisement, a court will, for a number of reasons, be very cautious in giving any remedy. As we shall see, while courts now do award damages for certain types of psychological losses arising from breach of contract, they are cautious in doing so. "gains made"

4. What about the other interests that Fuller and Perdue discuss? How can their analysis help to deal with the other problems studied already? If Mr. and Mrs. Peevyhouse or Mr. Radford were to claim, not damages measured by Lord Atkinson's principle, but the return of what the other party had gained, they would be seeking not protection of their *expectation* interests, but protection of their *restitution* interests, *i.e.*, they would be arguing that Garland Coal or the purchaser had made a gain at their expense and, as a result, was unjustly enriched. Until very recently, a "gains-made" basis for recovery for breach of contract was very rarely used, and it is still an exceptional remedy. As discussed later in this chapter, however, courts, particularly the English courts, have begun to explore situations where it may be proper to make the defendant pay an amount based, not on the plaintiff's loss, but on its gain.

   As we will see in Chapter 4, a benefit received by a person who has breached a contract generally cannot be kept. It is said, somewhat mysteriously, that the person in such a situation has been "unjustly enriched". The mystery arises because it is not always clear what is meant by "unjustly". Sometimes the word expresses a simple conclusion that (for reasons which may not be fully specified) the benefit must be paid back. At other times, it means that the transaction falls into one of a number of specific categories in which the law generally holds that a payment received must be returned.

   If one says on the facts of *Radford v. De Froberville*, that the purchaser would be "unjustly enriched" by what she saved by breaching the contract, this means that as between the purchaser and the seller, the latter has the better claim to the price paid for the promise to build the wall. Any other conclusion would run counter to the general purpose of awarding compensation outlined by Fuller and Perdue, and would undercut the reliance on contracts (notice that the seller's claim for the cost of building the wall is a special case of the reliance interest), and thereby make the institution of contracts less capable of fulfilling the purposes for which it exists.

An Economic Analysis of the Law of Damages

The following extract by Richard Posner, comes to a similar conclusion to Fuller and Perdue, supporting the principle of ordinarily awarding expectation damages for a breach of contract, but he has a very different perspective. Posner was one of the early proponents of an economic analysis of the law. At different points in this book, reference is made to an economic analysis of the issue under consideration. It is important to be aware of economic ways of looking at contracts problems, just as one must be aware of ethical and moral points of view.

An economic analysis of law uses economic concepts to analyze the effects of legal rules. A central tenet of the economic analysis of law is that the evolution of the common law is implicitly influenced by concerns of economic efficiency, even if they are not directly acknowledged or addressed. The "efficiency theory of the common law" posits that the common law is best understood as a system for maximizing the wealth of society, and that courts will generally tend to adopt rules that are economically efficient. Most proponents of economic analysis of law, however, recognize that there is more to justice than economics. (See Posner, *infra,* 26-28.)Richard Posner taught law at the University of Chicago until he was appointed a judge of the Circuit Court of Appeals of the Seventh Circuit in Chicago. The volume of writing on economics and contracts is immense. This extract offers a small sampling of the flavour of the work done in this field.

RICHARD B. POSNER, ECONOMIC ANALYSIS OF LAW

6th ed. (2002), pp. 118–123

[Some footnotes have been omitted.]

§4.9   Fundamental Principles of Contract Damages

[1]   When a breach of contract is established, the issue becomes one of the proper remedy. There are a bewildering variety of possibilities, which in rough order of increasing severity can be arrayed as follows:

(1)   the promisee's reliance loss (the costs he incurred in reasonable reliance on the promisor's performing the contract);

(2)   the expectation loss (loss of the anticipated profit of the contract);

(3)   liquidated damages (damages actually specified in the contract as the money remedy for a breach);

(4)   consequential damages (ripple effects on the promisee's business from the breach);

(5)   restitution (to the promisee of the promisor's profits from the breach);

(6) specific performance (ordering the promisor to perform on penalty of being found in contempt of court);

(7) a money penalty specified in the contract, or other punitive damages.

[2] It makes a difference in deciding which remedy to grant whether the breach was opportunistic. If a promisor breaks his promise merely to take advantage of the vulnerability of the promisee in a setting (the normal contract setting) where performance is sequential rather than simultaneous, we might as well throw the book at the promisor. An example would be where A pays B in advance for goods and instead of delivering them B uses the money in another venture. Such conduct has no economic justification and ought simply to be deterred. An attractive remedy in such a case is restitution. The promisor broke his promise in order to make money — there can be no other reason in the case of such a breach. We can deter this kind of behavior by making it worthless to the promisor, which we do by making him hand over all his profits from the breach to the promisee; no lighter sanction would deter.

[3] Most breaches of contract, however, are not opportunistic. Many are involuntary; performance is impossible at a reasonable cost. Others are voluntary but (as we are about to see) efficient — which from an economic standpoint is the same case as that of an involuntary breach. These observations both explain the centrality of remedies to the law of contracts (can you see why?) and give point to Holmes' dictum that it is not the policy of the law to compel adherence to contracts but only to require each party to choose between performing in accordance with the contract and compensating the other party for any injury resulting from a failure to perform.[1] This dictum, though overbroad, contains an important economic insight. In many cases it is uneconomical to induce completion of performance of a contract after it has been broken. I agree to purchase 100,000 widgets custom-ground for use as components in a machine that I manufacture. After I have taken delivery of 10,000, the market for my machine collapses. I promptly notify my supplier that I am terminating the contract, and admit that my termination is a breach. When notified of the termination he has not yet begun the custom grinding of the other 90,000 widgets, but he informs me that he intends to complete his performance under the contract and bill me accordingly. The custom-ground widgets have no use other than in my machine, and a negligible scrap value. To give the supplier a remedy that induced him to complete the contract after the breach would waste resources. The law is alert to this danger and, under the doctrine of mitigation of damages, would not give the supplier damages for any costs he incurred in continuing production after notice of termination.

[4] But isn't the danger unreal if the Coase Theorem[2] is true? There are only two parties, and there is a price for the supplier's forbearing to stand on his contract rights — indeed a range of prices — that will make both parties better off. But this is just another example of bilateral monopoly; transaction costs will be

---

[1] Oliver Wendell Holmes, "The Path of the Law", 10 *Harv. L. Rev.* 457, 462 (1897) ("The duty to keep a contract at common law means a prediction that you must pay damages if you do not keep it — and nothing else").

[2] The Coase Theorem states that, if transactions are costless, the initial assignment of a property right will not affect the ultimate use of the property as parties will negotiate to achieve the most efficient use. Ronald H. Coase, "The Problem of Social Cost" (1960), 3 *J. Law & Econ.* 1. [Note added by editors.]

high even though (in a sense, because) there are only two parties. It is true that the cost of determining damages would be reduced (to zero, in fact) if the seller were entitled to complete the contract and sue for the price. The buyer would be desperate to avoid having to pay for all those unwanted widgets and so would offer a generous settlement. If settlement negotiations failed, performance of the contract was completed, and the seller sued for the price, the determination of damages would be mechanical — it would be the price times the number of widgets. As we saw in discussing the parallel issue of protecting property rights by injunction . . . the decision whether to adopt a remedy that will force the parties to a dispute to negotiate the terms of an exchange requires trading off the costs of bilateral monopoly against the costs (both the error costs and the administrative costs) of having the court determine damages. In the example of the buyer's breach of the widget contract, the costs of measuring damages were low. This is not always true; and in contract law as in property law, it is possible to obtain injunctive relief upon a showing that your damages remedy would be inadequate, for example because your damages cannot be computed with reasonable accuracy.

[5]   The law's sensitivity to the costs of the damages remedy is shown in the distinction it makes between the situation in which the goods (already manufactured, unlike our widget case) are still in the hands of the seller and the situation in which they have been delivered. In the first instance the seller is allowed to sue only for his damages, but in the second he is allowed to sue for the contract price. Once the buyer has the goods, it is probably cheaper for him to resell them than for the seller to do so, so the law makes him accept and pay for them. If the seller still has the goods, it is probably cheaper for him to resell them, which he will do if his only entitlement is to sue for damages — the difference between the contract price and what he can sell the goods for to another buyer.

[6]   Now suppose that the widget contract is broken by the seller rather than the buyer. I really need those 100,000 custom-ground widgets for my machine but the supplier, after producing 50,000, is forced to suspend production because of a mechanical failure. Other suppliers are in a position to supply the remaining widgets that I need but I insist that the original supplier complete his performance of the contract. If the law compels completion (by ordering specific performance, a form of injunction), the supplier will have to make arrangements with other producers to complete his contract with me. Probably it will be more costly for him to procure an alternative supplier than for me to do so directly (after all, I know my own needs best); otherwise he would have done it voluntarily, to minimize his liability for the breach. To compel completion of the contract (or costly negotiations to discharge the promisor) would again result in a waste of resources, and again the law does not compel completion but confines the victim to simple damages.

[7]   But what are simple contract damages? Usually the objective of giving the promisor an incentive to fulfill his promise unless the result would be an inefficient use of resources (the production of the unwanted widgets in the first example, the roundabout procurement of a substitute supplier in the second) can be achieved by giving the promisee his expected profit on the transaction. If the supplier in the first example receives his expected profit from making 10,000 widgets, he will have no incentive to make the unwanted 90,000. We do not want him to make them; no one wants them. In the second example, if I receive my expected

profit from dealing with the original supplier, I become indifferent to whether he completes his performance.

[8]   In these examples the breach was committed only to avert a large loss, but in some cases a party is tempted to break his contract simply because his profit from breach would exceed his profit from completion of the contract. If it would also exceed the expected profit to the other party from completion of the contract, and if damages are limited to the loss of that profit, there will be an incentive to commit a breach. But there should be. Suppose I sign a contract to deliver 100,000 custom-ground widgets at 10¢ apiece to A for use in his boiler factory. After I have delivered 10,000, B comes to me, explains that he desperately needs 25,000 custom-ground widgets at once since otherwise he will be forced to close his pianola factory at great cost, and offers me 15¢ apiece for them. I sell him the widgets and as a result do not complete timely delivery to A, causing him to lose $1,000 in profits. Having obtained an additional profit of $1,250 on the sale to B, I am better off even after reimbursing A for his loss, and B is also better off. The breach is Pareto superior. True, had I refused to sell to B he could have gone to A and negotiated an assignment to him of part of A's contract with me. But this would have introduced an additional step, with additional transaction costs — and high ones, because it would be a bilateral-monopoly negotiation. On the other hand, litigation costs would be reduced.

[9]   Could not the danger of overdeterring breaches of contract by heavy penalties be avoided simply by redefining the legal concept of breach of contract so that only inefficient terminations counted as breaches? No. Remember that an important function of contracts is to assign risks to superior risk bearers. If the risk materializes, the party to whom it was assigned must pay. It is no more relevant that he could not have prevented the risk from occurring at a reasonable, perhaps at any, cost than that an insurance company could not have prevented the fire that destroyed the building it insured. The breach of contract corresponds to the occurrence of the event that is insured against.

[10]   Let us consider the case in which the expectation loss, *i.e.*, the loss of the expected profit of the contract, exceeds the reliance loss. A manufacturer agrees to sell a machine for $100,000, delivery to be made in six months. The day after the contract is signed he defaults, realizing that he would lose $5,000 at the contract price. The buyer's reliance loss — the sum of the costs he has irretrievably incurred as a result of the contract — is zero, but it would cost him $112,000 to obtain a substitute machine. Why should he be allowed to insist on a measure of damages that gives him more (by $12,000) than he has actually lost? Isn't that a windfall? Whether it is or not, awarding the reliance loss in this case would encourage inefficient breaches. The net gain to the buyer from contractual performance is greater (by $7,000, the difference between $12,000 and $5,000) than the net loss ($5,000) to the seller, and we make that net gain a cost of breach to the seller, by giving the buyer his profit on the deal if the seller breaks the contract, in order to discourage an inefficient breach.

[11]   What if the reliance loss exceeds the expectation loss? In *Groves v. John Wunder Co.*,[3] the defendant, as part of a larger deal, had agreed to level some land owned by the plaintiff, and willfully failed to carry out his agreement. The cost of

---

[3]   205 Minn. 163, 286 N.W. 235 (1939).

leveling would have been $60,000 and the value of the land, after leveling, no more than $12,000 — the Depression of the 1930s having supervened after the contract was signed. The court awarded the plaintiff $60,000, reasoning that he was entitled to get the performance he had contracted for and that it was no business of the defendant whether, or how much, his performance would have made the plaintiff's property more valuable. The result is questionable. It was not a case where value and market price were different. The land in question was a commercial parcel, and if the plaintiff had wanted the performance rather than the $60,000 he would have brought an action for specific performance. He did not bring such an action and, even more telling, did not use the money he won from the defendant to level the land. The measure of damages was incorrect from an economic standpoint because, had it been known to the defendant from the start, it would have made him indifferent between breaking his promise to level the land and performing it, whereas efficiency dictated breach; the $60,000 worth of labor and materials that would have been consumed in leveling the land would have bought less than a $12,000 increase in value.[4]

[12] It is true that not enforcing the contract would have given the defendant a windfall. But enforcing the contract gave the plaintiff an equal and opposite windfall: a cushion, which almost certainly the parties had not intended, against the impact of the Depression on land values. Since the plaintiff, as the owner of the land, rather than the defendant, a contractor, would have enjoyed the benefit of any unexpected increase in the value of the land, the parties, if they had thought about the matter, would probably have wanted the plaintiff to bear the burden of any unexpected fall in that value as well.

[13] The expectation measure of damages focuses on the gain that the victim of the breach anticipated from performance of the contract, the reliance measure on the victim's loss from the breach. If the victim "relied" by forgoing an equally profitable contract, the two measures merge. If not, the expectation measure may be a better approximation of the victim's real economic loss than the reliance measure, as well as produce better incentives. In long-run competitive equilibrium, the total revenues of the sellers in a market are just equal to their total costs; there is no "profit" in an economic sense but merely reimbursement of the costs of capital, of entrepreneurial effort, and of other inputs, including the marketing efforts that led up to the contract. All these items of cost are excluded by the reliance measure of damages, which will tend, therefore, to understate the social costs of breach. Even if the breach occurs before the victim has begun to perform, the victim may have incurred costs (especially pre-contractual search costs). Suppose the victim has not, so that until performance begins the reliance cost is zero. If reliance costs were the exclusive measure of damages, it would follow that parties could walk away from their contracts whenever the contracts were still purely executory. Except in special situations, it is unclear what the social gain would be from such a "cooling off" period and there may be a social loss as a result of un-

---

[4]   Would the defendant in fact have leveled the land pursuant to the contract had he known in advance what the measure of damages would be if he did not? Why not? Does it follow that the economist should be indifferent to the measure of damages in the case? A result opposite to *Groves* was reached in *Peevyhouse v. Garland Coal & Mining Co.*, 382 P. 2d 109 (Okla. 1963).

certainty and the need to make additional transactions.[5] Moreover, reliance costs incurred during the executory period are difficult to compute. Having signed a contract, a party will immediately begin to make plans both for performing the contract and for making whatever adjustments in the rest of his business are necessary to accommodate the new obligation; but the costs of this planning, and the costs resulting from the change of plans when he finds out that the contract will not be performed, will be hard to estimate.

[14] We should not suppose that the expectation measure is economically perfect. By giving the performing party a guaranteed profit, as it were, on what in the usual case will be a more or less risky venture — guaranteed, that is, should the other party break the contract — the expectation measure can induce over reliance by the performing party, just as any other form of business insurance will tend to induce the insured to relax his efforts to avoid the hazard insured against. ...

[15] The application of the expectation measure involves other subtle problems as well. Compare the following cases: (1) A tenant defaults, and the landlord promptly rents the property to another tenant at a rental only slightly below that of the defaulting tenant. In a suit against the defaulting tenant for the rental due on the balance of the tenant's lease, should the landlord be required to deduct the rental of the substitute tenant? (2) A manufacturer receives an order for 1,000 widgets from X, but X refuses to accept delivery and the manufacturer resells the widgets to Y at a price only slightly lower than what X had agreed to pay. In a suit against X for the profits that were lost on the sale, should the manufacturer be required to deduct the profits he received on the substitute sale to Y?

[16] The law answers yes in the first case and no in the second, and these answers are correct from an economic standpoint. The landlord's output is fixed in the short run; he cannot add a room because one more family wants to lease from him. The rental that he receives from the substitute tenant in the first case is thus a gain *enabled* by the breach of contract by the first tenant and his true loss is therefore the difference between the two rentals. But a manufacturer can usually vary his output even in the short run. X's default did not enable the manufacturer to obtain a profit from selling to Y; for if X had not defaulted, the manufacturer could still have supplied Y with 1,000 widgets. The profit on the sale to Y is a gain that the manufacturer would have obtained regardless of the default, so his true loss is the entire expected profit from the sale to X.

NOTES

1. This excerpt is from the sixth edition of Posner's book, and his views have considerably modified since the first edition was written more than 30 years earlier. While he does not suggest that there should be limits on his idea of efficient breach, he no longer says that "society is better off" if such breaches are encouraged: he simply observes that an efficient breach is a situation that is "Pareto superior", that is, a position in which no one can be made better off without someone else being worse off. Posner does not deal with the criticisms that have been levelled at the idea of efficient breach. However, his discussion now starts with the recognition that, in some circumstances, the proper remedy where "the promisor breaks his promise merely to take advantage of the vulnerability of the promisor where performance is sequential rather than simul-

---

5   If breaches of executory contracts were costless, business people would not enter into binding executory contracts. Instead they would provide that their contracts would become binding upon the commencement of reliance or performance.

taneous", is to make the promisor pay to the promisee the gains that the promisor makes from the breach. Posner recognizes that in some situations of vulnerability or exploitative breach, it may be appropriate to award restitution-based damages, requiring the defendant to give up any gains received from the breach of contract. Consider what remains of the argument that efficient breach is a "good thing". The questions that this argument raises will be examined later in the context of *Attorney-General v. Blake*, [2001] 1 A.C. 268, [2000] 4 All E.R. 385, reproduced below.

2. In *Bank of America Canada v. Mutual Trust Co.*, [2002] S.C.J. No. 44, [2002] 2 S.C.R. 601, 211 D.L.R. (4th) 385, the Supreme Court of Canada had to deal with the question of damages for breach of contract when the defendant failed to pay amounts due under a construction financing arrangement. The appellant had advanced money to a developer and the respondent had undertaken to advance money to the purchasers of the houses being built by the developer, which funds would have discharged the loan made by the appellant. The respondent had backed out of the deal when the real estate market collapsed in the early 1990's. The amount of the appellant's loss was the difference between what it was owed and what it recovered when it sold the development after the respondent's default, some $10 million. The trial judge had awarded interest on this amount at a compound rate which reflected the interest rate charged in the agreement between the parties. The Supreme Court employed both the Fuller and Perdue terminology and the idea of "efficient breach" (though without referring to the authors who originally developed these terms). In dealing with the breach of a complex loan agreement, the Court upheld the decision of the trial judge to conclude that it should award compound interest on the sum owing from the date of breach. Major J. commented:

> (2) Contract Damages
>
> [25] Contract damages are determined in one of two ways. Expectation damages, the usual measure of contract damages, focus on the value which the plaintiff would have received if the contract had been performed. Restitution damages, which are infrequently employed, focus on the advantage gained by the defendant as a result of his or her breach of contract.
>
> (a) *Expectation Damages*
>
> [26] Generally, courts employ expectation damages where, if breach is proved, the plaintiff will be entitled to the value of the promised performance (S. M. Waddams, *The Law of Damages* (3rd ed. 1997), at p. 267).
>
> [28] Since the value of money decreases with the passage of time, an award, at trial, to a plaintiff of the dollar amount he or she expected to receive had the contract been performed on time would not put the plaintiff in the same position as if the contract had been performed. The party would receive less than his or her expectation damages because of the (i) opportunity cost, (ii) risk and (iii) inflation. The plaintiff would fail to receive the benefit of the bargain.
>
> . . .
>
> [29] To award the plaintiff damages equal to the value of the contract as if it had been performed on time, the court must first determine the dollar value of the promise to the plaintiff at the time the obligation was to have been performed, and then apply the appropriate interest rate and method of calculation to account for the time during which the plaintiff was not paid what was rightfully due.
>
> (b) *Restitution Damages*
>
> [30] The other side of the coin is to examine the effect of the breach on the defendant. In contract, restitution damages can be invoked when a defendant has, as a result of his or her own breach, profited in excess of his or her expected profit had the contract been performed but the plaintiff's loss is less than the defendant's gain. So the plaintiff can be fully paid his damages with a surplus

left in the hands of the defendant. This occurs with what has been described as an efficient breach of contract. In some but not all cases, the defendant may be required to pay such profits to the plaintiff as restitution damages (Waddams, *supra*, at p. 474).

[31] Courts generally avoid this measure of damages so as not to discourage efficient breach (i.e., where the plaintiff is fully compensated and the defendant is better off than if he or she had performed the contract) (Waddams, *supra*, at p. 473). Efficient breach is what economists describe as a Pareto optimal outcome where one party may be better off but no one is worse off, or expressed differently, nobody loses. Efficient breach should not be discouraged by the courts. This lack of disapproval emphasizes that a court will usually award money damages for breach of contract equal to the value of the bargain to the plaintiff.

[32] However, where a sum of money is required to be paid as of a certain date, the benefit to the defendant of the money during the interval between when the money is owed and when the money is paid is, all other things being equal, exactly the same as the detriment to the plaintiff of not having that money during the same interval. This is not a Pareto optimal outcome, but, rather, a zero-sum outcome. The defendant's gain is the plaintiff's loss, the value of which, but for the defendant's breach, would have belonged to the plaintiff.

[33] To prevent defendants from exploiting the time-value of money to their advantage, by delaying payment of damages so as to capitalize on the time-value of money in the interim, courts must be able to award damages which include an interest component that returns the value acquired by a defendant between breach and payment to the plaintiff.

. . .

[45] If the court was unable to award compound interest on the breach of a loan which itself bore compound interest, it would be unable to adequately award the plaintiff the value he or she would have received had the contract been performed. To keep the common law current with the evolution of society and to resolve the inconsistency between awarding expectation damages and the courts' past unwillingness to award compound interest, that unwillingness should be discarded in cases requiring that remedy for the plaintiff to realize the benefit of his or her contract.

[46] A contrary rule would lead to inequity and provide incentives to breach contracts. If courts were restricted to simple interest in assessing damages for breach of contract, an apparent abuse could occur in the following way. Money lent at compound interest would accrue compound interest until there was a breach of contract by the borrower. The lender would then sue and only be entitled to simple interest on the judgment. This would encourage borrowers not to repay loans. Contract law is not the enemy of parties to an agreement but, rather, their servant. It should not frustrate their mutually agreed intentions but, instead, absent overriding policy concerns, should permit those parties to obtain the benefit of their intended agreement.

. . .

[60] If required to pay damages at only simple interest, the respondent would have earned compound interest on the appellant's money while paying only simple interest. By breaching the contract, the respondent would have conferred on itself a profit which the contract envisaged for the appellant.

[61] This is not a case of efficient breach. The respondent's gains have come at the appellant's expense. An award of compound interest will prevent the respondent from profiting by its breach at the expense of the appellant. The

award of the trial judge yields a satisfactory result with respect to both expectation damages and restitution damages.

In making an award of compound interest, was the Court awarding expectation-based damages or restitutionary damages? What did the Court mean when it stated that this was not a case of "efficient breach"?

3. Posner suggests that the award of expectation damages to the promisee will result in an efficient allocation of resources. Posner does not consider that, from the point of view of any reasonable person, litigation is a disaster and that an award of damages comes with almost the highest transaction costs imaginable. To the extent, of course, that a party forced to breach its contract could know the other's loss, cheaper methods of providing compensation would be available. An important point to keep in mind is whether the rules for damages encourage or discourage low transaction cost settlements. People in business are likely to expect that a considerable degree of tolerance and good faith will exist on both sides. The transaction costs involved in achieving the (theoretically most economically) efficient result are likely to be so high as to provide strong incentives to reasonable behaviour, at least on the part of the promisee. No one who is in business for the long term can count on always being the promisor; no one knows when he or she might be the promisee whose expectations have been disappointed.

4. Even the threat of deliberately breaching a contract would cause great ill-will and damage to the party's reputation. Other parties would be very reluctant to deal with anyone who engaged in "efficient breaches". As a result, deliberate "efficient breach" conduct is rare.

5. The analysis of Posner also assumes that individuals considering a breach of contract know the costs associated with breach. In practice it is often difficult if not impossible to know the costs of breach at the time of breach.

6. There are a number of important assumptions hidden in Posner's argument. He suggests that there should sometimes be an incentive to breach, where, for example, the seller can, after payment of full compensation to the buyer, still make a profit by selling to someone who really needs the widgets. If there is a person willing to pay more for the widgets than the buyer was prepared to pay, someone may sell the widgets for a profit. Presumably, from an economic point of view, the most efficient result will be achieved if the person who can appropriate the gain — and someone *must* stand to make a gain in these circumstances — can do so with the lowest transaction costs, that is, the lowest cost of finding out where the chance of gain is and how to take advantage of it. We have no *a priori* reasons for assuming that the seller or the buyer has lower transaction costs. Posner assumes that making the new (desperate) buyer go to the original buyer will cost more than permitting him to buy from the original seller. Whether that is true, and whether the desperate buyer may be able to make a better deal from the original buyer, all become irrelevant if the law regards the original buyer as "owning" the widgets that the seller has allocated to the contract. The importance of the concept of the buyer's ownership of the thing to be sold, even before delivery has taken place, is that the buyer, not the seller, may appropriate the chance of gain. As we shall see, when the thing to be sold is land, the normal rules for damages are displaced and the prospective buyer can generally require actual performance with the result that factors other than efficiency become important. This is an issue to which we shall return.

7. A focus on the question of ownership makes clear that the law must allocate a chance of gain between two parties, either one of which might reasonably claim to be entitled to it. Remembering that may help to avoid assuming that the original seller, for example should always be entitled to the chance of gain arising from breach, as Posner argues.

8. The extracts from Fuller and Perdue and from Posner both provide an analytic framework for thinking about contracts issues. They are useful and important, but do not provide easy or complete answers. It is simply not possible to say what the remedy in any particular case *should* be, using only the terms and concepts developed by those writers. In every case, one needs more facts about the specific agreement, the parties and the context before deciding what should be done about the problem presented by the dispute. In essence the problem always is: "Given what we know about the dispute, the parties and the deal that they made, what do we *want* to do?" If this question is the only one that it makes any sense to ask and if we remember that we are asking it in the context of a process of adjudication, we have to be prepared to answer the consequential question: "What reasons can we give for doing what we did? Why did we award one remedy rather than the other?"

9. Even though there may be no easy answers to the problems of contract breach, an analysis of the issues raised provides lawyers with two useful tools:

    (a) The analysis helps the litigator to know what facts will be important in determining the result in court. The result in *Peevyhouse* was, at least in part, determined by the failure (or inability) of the lawyer for the plaintiffs to convince the court that they had some interest in the land that would justify an award of more than (what the court assumed was) the economic benefit of levelling. The issue of what a party has to prove to get the remedy it seeks and the difficulties of proving those facts are often more important in justifying a decision than the principles involved.

    (b) The analysis also speaks to the solicitor, the lawyer who is negotiating on behalf of a client or drafting an agreement. The negotiator has to know the effect of a simple promise to level the land on the client's bargaining position, and the risks to which the client is exposed from such a clause. The large risk faced by the plaintiffs in *Peevyhouse* or by the plaintiff in *Radford* is that the promise that has been breached has in effect been fully paid for, yet the benefit might not be obtainable on the expectation measure, while the price paid cannot be recovered on the restitution measure.

10. The value of an economic analysis is not the answers that it might produce in a situation where one assumes that the parties' transaction costs are zero; transactions costs are usually significant. Nevertheless, an economic analysis can be useful for understanding and analyzing the bargaining process. If delivery of the widgets ("ownership" of the chance of gain) is very important to the original buyer, that fact may have to be disclosed to the seller and an explicit agreement made as to the allocation of that risk. Given the "default" assumption of the law, the buyer may have to pay more to get that benefit than it would otherwise have to if the benefit was with the original seller. In the absence of legal advice, those making a contract seldom think very much about the problems that might arise on breach.

11. It is fundamental to all the arguments of Posner that damages will provide the promisee with adequate compensation. As we have seen, "compensation" is not an easy concept to deal with. To the extent that there are systematic risks of under- or overcompensation, we may have to consider alternative means of allocating the chance of gain or the risk of loss. The substitution of a rule based on notions of "ownership" or "title", so that in the example of the desperate second buyer discussed by Posner, the original buyer can claim the gain, operates to shift the risk of under-compensation from the buyer.

12. Finally, one also has to keep in mind the need for the law to provide a basis for the settlement of disputes. A rule or a starting position for reasoning about a problem may be justified on the ground that it is simple and provides the parties with useful guidance for their settlement negotiations; it reduces the chance that one party will decide that the law is so uncertain that an action is worth the risk that it will not succeed.

Rules that increase the "unreckonability" of the result cause much litigation that might have been avoided if the result were more easily foreseen.

13. The economic analysis of law put forward by Posner and other scholars is not without its critics. It tends to produce a market-oriented, socially conservative analysis of many problems. We will return to issues raised by the economic analysis of law at several points in this book, and, especially in Chapter 6, we will consider some critiques of this perspective (see the excerpt from Wanda Weigers, *infra*, Chapter 6).

14. Other disciplines such as history, philosophy, sociology, women's studies and psychology offer important perspectives on the study and analysis of law. See for example J.J. Rachlinski, "The 'New' Law and Psychology: A Reply to Critics, Skeptics and Cautious Supporters" (2000), 85 *Cornell L. Rev.* 739-66, for a discussion of the relevance of psychology to the study of contract law, focusing on the issue of the enforceability of liquidated damage clauses. For a discussion of some of the insights of the discipline of philosophy on why promises should be enforced, see M. Pratt, "Scanlon on Promising" (2001), 14 *Can. J. L. & Jur.* 143-54; and Stephen Smith, *Contract Theory* (Oxford University Press, 2004).

WHEN TO STOP AN AWARD OF DAMAGES

Lord Atkinson's principle in *Wertheim v. Chicoutimi Pulp*, and the analyses of Fuller and Perdue and of Posner give reasons that justify awarding damages, starting from the principle that the party in breach should compensate the promisee for the "loss" of the benefit of the bargain. Inherent in each justification, however, is an idea that the amount of compensation should be limited. Posner is explicit in stating that the promisee must get no more than compensation for its loss if the notion of efficient breach is to be pursued. The court in *Peevyhouse* assumed that Peevyhouses would be fairly compensated by payment of an amount tied to the failure of Garland to level the land. While the restitution and reliance interests have built-in limits (though as we shall see those limits are not always easy to discover), the expectation interest may have no such obvious limits.

It is not hard to imagine that a breach of contract could start a chain of events that would be a cascade of misfortunes for the plaintiff. Suppose that Julie is in Toronto and hires a limousine to take her to the airport. Richard, the driver of the limousine, decides that since he has not had anything to eat all day he will stop on the way to get a sandwich, and he arrives late to pick Julie up. Julie arrives late at the airport and misses her flight, which was to have taken her to Vancouver for a job interview. As a result of missing the flight, she fails to attend the interview and fails to get the job that, had she been in time for the interview, she would have got; a job that not only would have paid her $50,000 more per year than her present job, but would have given her a good chance at becoming a senior executive in a major Canadian corporation; as a result of not getting the new job she goes into a deep depression and is then fired from her old job; as a result of that, her kids cannot go to university and . . . The sad story could go on and on.

Lord Atkinson says that the plaintiff should "be placed in the same position as [s]he would have been in if the contract had been performed". Had Richard done what he should have done, Julie's misfortunes would not have occurred: she would have had the new job and a chance at the good things it might have offered her, and she (and her family) might have avoided all the other things that went wrong. Assume that what Richard did was a breach of contract: he had promised to pick Julie up at a certain time and drive her to the airport with reasonable promptness. As a result of Richard's actions, a literal application of Lord Atkinson's principle could support an argument that Richard should be liable for all the harm that his breach of contract caused Julie.

If Lord Atkinson's principle were to entail large damages in the case of Julie and Richard we would have concerns about the application of the principle. Some of these concerns might be based on a feeling that, for the price of a limousine ride fare to the airport, Richard should not be exposed to such a large risk. Other concerns might be based on the thought that, for all that Richard knew when he made the contract to pick Julie up (and also perhaps when he stopped for lunch), her flight was not that important to her and he may reasonably have assumed that the sad consequences that followed were highly unlikely to occur. It might make a difference to what we feel about the appropriate resolution if when Richard arrived on time Julie had told him that she was worried about missing her very important flight and as a consequence Richard drove quickly and caused a minor accident that, in turn, caused the delay. All kinds of other variables can easily be imagined.

The practical problem is that, while the justifications for starting to award damages to protect the expectation interest may entail some kind of implicit limit on the amount of damages that should be awarded, stating that limit in terms that can lead to some kind of limiting rule is extraordinarily difficult. Take the case of Julie and Richard. What would an appropriate award for Julie be? Should she only get her limousine fare refunded? Should she get the cost of having to stay overnight at an airport hotel? What about a charge levied by the airline because she had to change her flight? If we think that she should get some of these costs, where do we stop and why?

The next case has been taken as establishing the limit on the recovery of damages. It is one of the most famous judgments ever decided in the sense that every student of common law is likely to have studied it, and it is still regularly cited in the courts.

HADLEY v. BAXENDALE

(1854), 9 Exch. 341, 156 E.R. 145 (Court of Exchequer)

[The headnote to the report stated:] At the trial before Crompton J., at the last Gloucester Assizes, it appeared that the plaintiffs carried on an extensive business as millers at Gloucester; and that, on the 11th of May, their mill was stopped by a breakage of the crank shaft by which the mill was worked. The steam engine was manufactured by Messrs. Joyce & Co., the engineers, at Greenwich, and it became necessary to send the shaft as a pattern for a new one to Greenwich. The fracture was discovered on the 12th, and on the 13th the plaintiffs sent one of their servants to the office of the defendants, who are the well-known carriers trading under the name of Pickford & Co., for the purpose of having the shaft carried to Greenwich. The plaintiffs' servant told the clerk that the mill was stopped, and that the shaft must be sent immediately; and in answer to the inquiry when the shaft would be taken, the answer was, that if it was sent up by twelve o'clock any day, it would be delivered at Greenwich on the following day. On the following day the shaft was taken by the defendants, before noon, for the purpose of being conveyed to Greenwich, and the sum of £2 4s 0d was paid for its carriage for the whole distance; at the same time the defendants' clerk was told that a special entry, if required, should be made to hasten its delivery. The delivery of the shaft at Greenwich was delayed by some neglect; and the consequence was that the plaintiffs did not receive the new shaft for several days after they would otherwise have done, and the working of their mill was thereby delayed, and they thereby lost the profits they would otherwise have received. On the part of the defendants, it was objected that these damages were too remote, and that the defendants were not liable with respect to them. The learned Judge left the case generally to the jury, who found a verdict with £25 damages beyond the amount paid into Court [which was £25, so the total jury judgment was £50].

The argument of counsel and the responses of the judges are extensively set out in the report. Parke B, in response to the plaintiff's argument that the damages awarded were not too remote, referred to the French Civil Code and to a passage that stated: "The debtor is only liable for the damages foreseen, or which might have been foreseen, at the time of the execution of the contract." One counsel for the defendant was Willes, who was regarded as one of the most learned of nine-teenth-century lawyers and later became a judge. (He was also the editor of *Smith's Leading Cases*, where the judgment subsequently appeared, a fact which might account in part for the case's becoming a leading case.) Willes, quoting the Civilian, Domat, argued that the "object is to discriminate between that portion of the loss which must be borne by the offending party and that which must be borne by the sufferer."

ALDERSON B.: — [NOTE: The judgment has been broken into paragraphs by the editors for ease of reference.]

[1]   We think that there ought to be a new trial in this case; but, in so doing, we deem it to be expedient and necessary to state explicitly the rule which the Judge, at the next trial, ought, in our opinion, to direct the jury to be governed by when they estimate the damages.

[2]   It is, indeed, of the last importance that we should do this; for, if the jury are left without any definite rule to guide them, it will, in such cases as these, mani-festly lead to the greatest injustice. . . . "There are certain established rules," this Court says, in *Alder v. Keighley* (15 M. & W. 117, 153 E.R. 785) "according to which the jury ought to find." And the Court, in that case, adds "and here there is a clear rule, that the amount which would have been received if the contract had been kept, is the measure of damages if the contract is broken."

[3]   Now we think the proper rule in such a case as the present is this: — Where two parties have made a contract which one of them has broken, the damages which the other party ought to receive in respect of such breach of contract should be such as may fairly and reasonably be considered either arising naturally, *i.e.*, according to the usual course of things, from such breach of contract itself, or such as may reasonably be supposed to have been in the contemplation of both parties, at the time they made the contract, as the probable result of the breach of it.

[4]   Now, if the special circumstances under which the contract was actually made were communicated by the plaintiffs to the defendants, and thus known to both parties, the damages resulting from the breach of such a contract, which they would reasonably contemplate, would be the amount of injury which would ordi-narily follow from a breach of contract under these special circumstances so known and communicated. But, on the other hand, if these special circumstances were wholly unknown to the party breaking the contract, he, at the most, could only be supposed to have had in his contemplation the amount of injury which would arise generally, and in the great multitude of cases not affected by any spe-

cial circumstances, from such a breach of contract. For, had the special circumstances been known, the parties might have specially provided for the breach of contract by special terms as to the damages in that case; and of this advantage it would be very unjust to deprive them.

[5]   Now the above principles are those by which we think the jury ought to be guided in estimating the damages arising out of any breach of contract.

[6]   It is said, that other cases such as breaches of contract in the non-payment of money, or in the not making a good title to land, are to be treated as exceptions from this, and as governed by a conventional rule. But as, in such cases, both parties must be supposed to be cognisant of that well-known rule, these cases may, we think, be more properly classed under the rule above enunciated as to cases under known special circumstances, because there both parties may reasonably be presumed to contemplate the estimation of the amount of damages according to the conventional rule.

[7]   Now, in the present case, if we are to apply the principles above laid down, we find that the only circumstances here communicated by the plaintiffs to the defendants at the time the contract was made, were, that the article to be carried was the broken shaft of a mill, and that the plaintiffs were the millers of that mill. But how do these circumstances shew reasonably that the profits of the mill must be stopped by an unreasonable delay in the delivery of the broken shaft by the carrier to the third person? Suppose the plaintiffs had another shaft in their possession put up or putting up at the time, and that they only wished to send back the broken shaft to the engineer who made it; it is clear that this would be quite consistent with the above circumstances, and yet the unreasonable delay in the delivery would have no effect upon the intermediate profits of the mill. Or, again, suppose that, at the time of the delivery to the carrier, the machinery of the mill had been in other respects defective, then, also, the same results would follow. Here it is true that the shaft was actually sent back to serve as a model for a new one, and that the want of a new one was the only cause of the stoppage of the mill, and that the loss of profits really arose from not sending down the new shaft in proper time, and that this arose from the delay in delivering the broken one to serve as a model. But it is obvious that, in the great multitude of cases of millers sending off broken shafts to third persons by a carrier under ordinary circumstances, such consequences would not, in all probability, have occurred; and these special circumstances were here never communicated by the plaintiffs to the defendants.

[8]   It follows, therefore, that the loss of profits here cannot reasonably be considered such a consequence of the breach of contract as could have been fairly and reasonably contemplated by both the parties when they made this contract. For such loss would neither have flowed naturally from the breach of this contract in the great multitude of such cases occurring under ordinary circumstances, nor were the special circumstances, which, perhaps, would have made it a reasonable and natural consequence of such breach of contract, communicated to or known by the defendants. The Judge ought, therefore, to have told the jury, that, upon the facts then before them, they ought not to take the loss of profits into consideration at all in estimating the damages. There must therefore be a new trial in this case. *Rule absolute.*

NOTES AND QUESTIONS

1.　In England, before the *Judicature Acts* of 1873 and 1875, there was no Court of Appeal. The equivalent of an appeal could, however, be taken from the judgment of a single trial judge at first instance to one of the common law courts. The trial judge, Crompton J., sitting with a jury, heard the case on assize at Gloucester.

　　The "appeal" was heard by the Court of Exchequer in London. The judges of this court were not "Mr. Justice" but "Baron", so that the judgment in *Hadley v. Baxendale* is by Baron Alderson or "Alderson B." An "appeal" from the decision of the trial judge was started when the losing party obtained a "rule *nisi*". That is, the appellant obtained an order that *unless* ("*nisi*" is the Latin word for "unless") the respondent could successfully defend the judgment, it would be set aside. If the appeal was dismissed, the judgment would usually state that the rule was "denied", and if the appeal was allowed, the rule would be made "absolute". Note at the end of Alderson B.'s judgment the phrase, "Rule Absolute", indicating that the appeal was allowed. The effect of this was to send the case back to a new trial before a different judge and jury. The focus of the judgment is on the instructions that were given to the original jury, and on what instruction should be given to the jury on the new trial.

2.　The headnote refers to the fact that the shaft was taken to the "well-known carriers", Pickford & Co. This firm (which is still in existence, though now a large corporation) was then an unincorporated partnership of which Baxendale was the managing partner, and the person who would represent the firm in the litigation. Baxendale and his partners would have been personally liable for any damages awarded against the firm. Baxendale was one of the leading figures in the development of the nineteenth-century transportation system in England, and it is possible that the case was seen by Baxendale, his partners, counsel and the court, as important to that industry. The case and its background are discussed in Danzig, "*Hadley v. Baxendale*: A Study in the Industrialization of the Law" (1975), 4 *Journal of Legal Studies* 249.

3.　The jury, who were from Gloucester where the trial was held, would have known that the mill had been stopped. The apparent discrepancy between the statement of the facts in the first paragraph of the headnote, *viz.*, that the plaintiff's employee told the defendant's clerk that the mill was stopped, and the statement by Alderson B. that the defendants had not had notice that the mill was stopped is explicable by reference to the law governing masters and servants (or principals and agents). Under the law of agency then (and now), notice to an agent would only be treated as notice to the principal if the agent was authorized to receive the notice. (For example, even today for some purposes, notice to a bank teller or a supermarket cashier would not be a legally valid notice to a bank or supermarket.) In other words, the defendant was not in fact informed of the stoppage of Hadley's mill, and as the law stood in 1854, the notice to the clerk was not legally sufficient to constitute notice to the employer.

　　As we shall see in Chapter 5, there are important issues to be decided before we can treat a business enterprise such as a corporation (which can only act through agents or employees) as if it was in all respects like an individual. A related issue is whether the defendant's employee was regarded as having authority from his employer to receive the information that Hadley's employee gave him, at least if that information would increase the risk that the defendant undertook by accepting the shaft. While modern cases have not fully resolved this problem, there is a much greater tendency today to regard communication with an agent as communication with the corporate employer. See, *e.g.*, the more recent Canadian case of *Cornwall Gravel v. Purolator Courier*, *infra*.

4.　The language of the judgment in *Hadley v. Baxendale* suggests that there are two tests or one test that has two parts. Alderson B. says (¶ 3):

> Where two parties have made a contract which one of them has broken, the damages which the other party ought to receive in respect of such breach of contract should be such as may fairly and reasonably be considered either arising naturally, *i.e.*, according to the usual course of things, from such breach of

contract itself, or such as may reasonably be supposed to have been in the contemplation of both parties, at the time they made the contract, as the probable result of the breach of it.

The first rule of *Hadley v. Baxendale* — it is more common to speak of there being two rules than two aspects of one rule — deals with what would follow "naturally" from the breach. The second rule deals with any "special circumstances" that might apply in the particular situation of this plaintiff and this defendant. The judgment concludes that the "special circumstances" were not sufficiently communicated to the defendant so that the second rule is inapplicable. The decision is that the losses the plaintiff actually suffered would not occur "in the usual course of things". Alderson B. said, "But it is obvious that, in the great multitude of cases of millers sending off broken shafts to third persons by a carrier under ordinary circumstances, such consequences would not, in all probability, have occurred." The basis for such a judicial finding is not made clear in the judgment. It is very rare for evidence to be introduced about this type of assertion. Judges rely on their own experience for this type of judicial "fact finding". As we shall see throughout these materials, this type of "judicial notice" raises difficult problems.

5. The language in ¶ 3 suggests that whether the "special circumstances" were communicated or not, so that the damages that would follow from a breach would have been "in the contemplation of both parties", is a question of fact. It may, however, be wrong to draw this inference from the judgment.

    Suppose that Hadley's employee had told the defendant's clerk that the mill had shut down, and the defendant's employee responded: "It may well be that the mill is shut down, but so what? What am I to do about that?" It is safe to assume that Hadley's employee did *not* ask the defendant's employee to make sure that the shaft was promptly carried to Greenwich *and offer to pay a surcharge if the defendant promised prompt delivery*. In other words, communication of the importance of prompt delivery is arguably irrelevant to the risks assumed by the defendant, unless the defendant agreed to assume those risks. It may well be assumed that without communication of the special circumstances there would be no possible basis for making the defendant liable for the extra losses that the plaintiff suffered, but communication by itself may not be sufficient to increase the risks upon the defendant.

    The argument that communication by itself is insufficient gets strong support from what Alderson B. goes on to say in ¶ 4:

    > For, had the special circumstances been known, the parties might have specially provided for the breach of contract by special terms as to the damages in that case; and of this advantage it would be very unjust to deprive them.

    In other words, the communication of the "special circumstances" permits the parties to bargain over the allocation of the risk that may now be "contemplated" or foreseen but, unless the defendant undertakes to be responsible for the increased risk, the defendant is not liable for this risk. In this view of the case, there is no discrepancy between the facts and the judgement: what the plaintiff's employee said about the mill being stopped was simply irrelevant, for the existence of the "special circumstances" made no difference to the outcome as the defendant had not accepted the risk that those circumstances created. In this context it would be extremely important to know if the defendant's employee had any authority to alter the terms of the standard contract of carriage used by the firm. A communication to one of the partners of the firm might have had very different consequences for the defendant than communication to an employee, for not only would the partner likely have authority to bind the firm to a more onerous contract, but perhaps his failure to tell Hadley's employee that the firm would not assume all the risks of late delivery might have been sufficient to impose liability on it.

6. The rule derived from *Hadley v. Baxendale* is often stated in the form: "damages that are too remote are not recoverable". It should be appreciated that saying that damages are "too remote" is itself a conclusion; it is not a reason for limiting the damages re-

coverable. In this sense the rules in *Hadley v. Baxendale* operate like a coded language.

If we apply that rule to the facts of the dispute between Richard, the limousine driver, and Julie, the disappointed traveller, we could decide it by saying that at some point Julie's damages are too remote and may not be recovered from Richard. By saying so, we could mean one of two things. The first might be that no one would or should expect Richard to be responsible for all the losses suffered by Julie and her family in the circumstances. We might point out that limousine drivers are not well paid, may not charge more than the licensing commission allows, have to take whoever hires them, may have no idea what demands are upon the person they carry and should not be responsible for all the consequences of even a deliberate breach of contract. The second thing we might mean would be that at some point we believe that the causal connection between the breach and the losses becomes so attenuated as to justify breaking the connection and the responsibility: we might find it hard to believe that, even if Julie had not missed her plane, it was certain that she and her family would have had what, on the assumptions, they ended up losing.

7.   In many respects, the rule in *Hadley v. Baxendale* is similar to the principle that Lord Atkinson stated in *Wertheim v. Chicoutimi Pulp*. It is regarded as a basic or fundamental rule of contract law. It appears to indicate that all that has to be done to apply it is to make a simple factual inquiry into what was "foreseeable". Yet, as Fuller and Perdue recognize (46 *Yale L.J.* 52, at 84), it is at least as difficult to know where to stop as it is to know where to start in awarding damages. We have already seen that the apparent simplicity of Lord Atkinson's rule is an illusion: the simplicity of the rule in *Hadley v. Baxendale* is equally so.

8.   The judgment in *Hadley v. Baxendale* can be seen as saying no more than that it is not wise to visit all the consequences of breach on the defaulting promisor, leaving the determination of what consequences the defendant should be responsible for to the particular circumstances of each case. Such a view of the case would be consistent with the argument of Willes, counsel for the defendant, that the "object is to discriminate between that portion of the loss which must be borne by the offending party and that which must be borne by the sufferer".

9.   In *Bank of America Canada v. Mutual Trust Co.*, [2002] S.C.J. No. 44, [2002] 2 S.C.R. 601, 211 D.L.R. (4th) 385 (*supra*), the Supreme Court of Canada ruled that when the defendant breached its agreement to repay a loan, compound interest should be payable from the date of breach. Justice Major relied, in part on *Hadley*:

> [46] …If courts were restricted to simple interest in assessing damages for breach of contract, an apparent abuse could occur in the following way. Money lent at compound interest would accrue compound interest until there was a breach of contract by the borrower. The lender would then sue and only be entitled to simple interest on the judgment. This would encourage borrowers not to repay loans. Contract law is not the enemy of parties to an agreement but, rather, their servant. It should not frustrate their mutually agreed intentions but, instead, absent overriding policy concerns, should permit those parties to obtain the benefit of their intended agreement.

> [47] I find support for these conclusions in *Hadley v. Baxendale*. [Major J. then summarized the facts of *Hadley* and quoted the "general rule of contract damages" in ¶ 3, and concluded:]

> [48] The court held that the unreasonable delay of delivery of the shaft to the engineer would not necessarily lead to the cessation of operations of the mill. The plaintiffs might have had a substitute shaft which could have been used in the interim. The court found for the defendants, holding that the stoppage of milling did not naturally arise from the delay in delivery nor was this result and the concomitant cost to the plaintiff in the contemplation of both parties at the time they made the contract.

[contracts are mutually beneficial]

[49] With respect to the failure to repay the loan in this appeal when due, it cannot be said that the cost of such delay was not in the contemplation of both parties at the time they made the contract, particularly as both parties were in the business of lending. A loan agreement with a specified interest rate is an agreement between parties on the cost of borrowing money over a period of time. Absent exceptional circumstances, the interest rate which had governed the loan prior to breach would be the appropriate rate to govern the post-breach loan. The application of a lower interest rate would be unjust to the lender.

We have examined the justifications for starting and limiting an award of damages, and some of the situations that may justify an award that does not try to put the innocent party in "the same position as . . . if the contract had been performed" insofar "as it can be done by money". The next group of cases returns to some of the problems of *Hadley v. Baxendale* and presents some fairly common situations.

One of the serious problems raised by *Hadley v. Baxendale* is the extent to which communication to the defendant of the consequences of breach changes the extent of liability. As you read the next two cases, consider how the court should deal with the issue of communication by the plaintiff at the time that a contract is made about the potential losses if there is a breach. Consider the form of the inquiry envisaged by the judgments that follow. What do they suggest is important to the application of the rule?

VICTORIA LAUNDRY (WINDSOR) LTD. v. NEWMAN INDUSTRIES LTD.

[1949] 2 K.B. 528, [1949] 1 All E.R. 997
(C.A., Tucker, Asquith and Singleton L.JJ.)

[The plaintiffs carried on business as launderers and dyers. In April 1946 they agreed to purchase a large boiler from the defendant, an engineering company, for £2,150. The plaintiffs had made it clear to the defendants that they required the boiler "in the shortest possible space of time". The defendants promised to deliver it on 5 June 1946. However, on 1 June the boiler was damaged by the contractors who were dismantling it in preparation for shipping. The boiler was not repaired for 20 weeks. The plaintiffs sought to recover from the defendants their loss of profits during this delay. They proved that they had available extremely lucrative dyeing contracts as well as the normal business of launderers and dyers. The trial judge gave judgment for the plaintiffs for the costs incurred in a futile trip by the plaintiff to pick up the boiler on 1 June, but disallowed any claim for profits. The plaintiffs appealed.]

The judgment of the court was given by **ASQUITH L.J.**: — **[1]** . . . What propositions applicable to the present case emerge from the authorities as a whole, including those analyzed above? We think they include the following:

(1) It is well settled that the governing purpose of damages is to put the party whose rights have been violated in the same position, so far as money can do so, as if his rights had been observed . . . This purpose, if relentlessly pursued, would provide him with a complete indemnity for all loss *de facto* resulting from a particular breach, however improbable, however unpredictable. This, in contract at least, is recognised as too harsh a rule. Hence,

(2) In cases of breach of contract the aggrieved party is only entitled to recover such part of the loss actually resulting as was at the time of the contract reasonably foreseeable as liable to result from the breach.

(3) What was at that time reasonably foreseeable depends on the knowledge then possessed by the parties, or, at all events, by the party who later commits the breach.

(4) For this purpose, knowledge "possessed" is of two kinds — one imputed, the other actual. Everyone, as a reasonable person, is taken to know the "ordinary course of things" and consequently what loss is liable to result from a breach of that ordinary course. This is the subject-matter of the "first rule" in *Hadley v. Baxendale*, but to this knowledge, which a contract- breaker is assumed to possess whether he actually possesses it or not, there may have to be added in a particular case knowledge which he actually possesses of special circumstances outside the "ordinary course of things" of such a kind that a breach in those special circumstances would be liable to cause more loss. Such a case attracts the operation of the "second rule" so as to make additional loss also recoverable.

(5) In order to make the contract-breaker liable under either rule it is not necessary that he should actually have asked himself what loss is liable to result from a breach. As has often been pointed out, parties at the time of contracting contemplate, not the breach of the contract, but its performance. It suffices that, if he had considered the question, he would as a reasonable man have concluded that the loss in question was liable to result. . . .

(6) Nor, finally, to make a particular loss recoverable, need it be proved that on a given state of knowledge the defendant could, as a reasonable man, foresee that a breach must necessarily result in that loss. It is enough if he could foresee it was likely so to result. It is enough . . . if the loss (or some factor without which it would not have occurred) is a "serious possibility" or a "real danger." For short, we have used the word "liable" to result. Possibly the colloquialism "on the cards" indicates the shade of meaning with some approach to accuracy.

[2]   If these, indeed, are the principles applicable, what is [their] effect . . . ? We have, at the beginning of this judgment, summarised the main relevant facts. The defendants were an engineering company supplying a boiler to a laundry. We reject the submission for the defendants that an engineering company knows no more than the plain man about boilers or the purposes to which they are commonly put by different classes of purchasers, including laundries. The defendant company were not, it is true, manufacturers of this boiler or dealers in boilers, but they gave a highly technical and comprehensive description of this boiler to the plaintiffs . . . and offered both to dismantle the boiler . . . and to re-erect it on the plaintiffs' premises. Of the uses or purposes to which boilers are put, they would clearly know more than the uninstructed layman. Again, they knew they were supplying the boiler to a company carrying on the business of laundrymen and dyers, for use in that business. The obvious use of a boiler, in such a business, is surely to boil water for the purpose of washing or dyeing. A laundry might conceivably buy a boiler for some other purpose, for instance, to work radiators or warm bath water for the comfort of its employees or directors, or to use for research, or to exhibit in a museum. All these purposes are possible, but the first is the obvious purpose

which, in the case of a laundry, leaps to the average eye. If the purpose then be to wash or dye, why does the company want to wash or dye, unless for purposes of business advantage.

[ASQUITH L.J. went on to hold that the defendants would be liable for loss of profits as might reasonably have been expected to be earned in the normal course of their laundry business. But in regard to the particularly lucrative dyeing contracts, he said:]

[3]   We agree [with the trial judge] that in order that the plaintiffs should recover specifically and as such the profits expected on these contracts, the defendants would have had to know, at the time of their agreement with the plaintiffs, of the prospect and terms of such contracts. We also agree that they did not, in fact, know these things. It does not, however, follow that the plaintiffs are precluded from recovering some general (and perhaps conjectural) sum for loss of business in respect of dyeing contracts to be reasonably expected any more than in respect of laundering contracts to be reasonably expected.

[The appeal was therefore allowed. The plaintiff had claimed "ordinary" laundry profits of £320 and about £5,240 for the loss of the very lucrative dyeing contracts. A reference to the official referee was ordered for the purposes of determining the exact amount of lost profits.]

QUESTION

Is the result in *Victoria Laundry* consistent with *Hadley v. Baxendale*? Is the difference in outcome in terms of liability of the defendant for loss of profits on other contracts (so called consequential losses) due to a different view of the law, or due to factual differences? If the differences are factual, were the critical findings based on evidence that was called by the parties, or due to a judicial assessment based on "judicial notice" (a factual finding based on a judge's knowledge or assumptions about the world rather than an issue on which evidence is called)?

The next case is regarded as one of the leading cases on the issue of "remoteness". To what extent is it an improvement on the statements in either *Hadley v. Baxendale* or *Victoria Laundry*?

KOUFOS v. C. CZARNIKOW LTD. ("THE HERON II")

[1969] 1 A.C. 350, [1967] 3 All E.R. 686
(H.L., Lords Reid, Morris, Hodson, Pearce and Upjohn)

LORD REID: — [1] My Lords, by charterparty of October 15, 1960, the respondents chartered the appellant's vessel, *Heron II*, to proceed to Constanza [a port in Rumania on the Black Sea], there to load a cargo of 3,000 tons of sugar; and to carry it to Basrah [in Iraq], or, in the charterer's option, to Jeddah. The vessel left Constanza on November 1, 1960. The option was not exercised and the vessel arrived at Basrah on December 2, 1960. The umpire has found that a "reasonably accurate prediction of the length of the voyage was twenty days." But the vessel had in breach of contract made deviations which caused a delay of nine days. [The "deviations" were a result of the decision of the captain to carry extra cargo on deck, as well as the charterers' sugar in the ship's hold, and to deliver the cargo on deck to a port off the shortest route between Constanza and Basrah.]

[2]   It was the intention of the respondents to sell the sugar "promptly after arrival at Basrah and after inspection by merchants." The appellant did not know this, but he was aware of the fact that there was a market for sugar at Basrah. The sugar was in fact sold at Basrah in lots between December 12 and 22, 1960, but shortly before that time the market price had fallen, partly by reason of the arrival of another cargo of sugar. It was found by the umpire that if there had not been this delay of nine days the sugar would have fetched £32 10s 0d per ton. The actual price realised was only £31 2s 9d per ton. The respondents claim that they are entitled to recover the difference as damage for breach of contract. The appellant admits that he is liable to pay interest for nine days on the value of the sugar and certain minor expenses but denies that the fall in market value can be taken into account in assessing damages in this case.

[3]   [The umpire decided in favour of the charterers, allowing £4,183 for loss of profits, and the ship owner appealed. At this first level of appeal], McNair J. . . . decided this question in favour of the appellant. He said: "In those circumstances, it seems to me almost impossible to say that the shipowner must have known that the delay in prosecuting the voyage would probably result, or be likely to result, in this kind of loss."

[4]   The Court of Appeal by a majority (Diplock and Salmon L.JJ., Sellers L.J., dissenting) reversed the decision of the trial judge. The majority held . . . applying the rule (or rules) in *Hadley v. Baxendale* as explained in *Victoria Laundry* . . . that the loss due to fall in market price was not too remote to be recoverable as damages.

[5]   It may be well first to set out the knowledge and intention of the parties at the time of making the contract so far as relevant or argued to be relevant. The charterers intended to sell the sugar in the market at Basrah on arrival of the vessel. They could have changed their mind and exercised their option to have the sugar delivered at Jeddah but they did not do so. There is no finding that they had in mind any particular date as the likely date of arrival at Basrah or that they had any knowledge or expectation that in late November or December there would be a rising or a falling market. The ship owner was given no information about these matters by the charterers. He did not know what the charterers intended to do with the sugar. But he knew there was a market in sugar at Basrah, and it appears to me that, if he had thought about the matter, he must have realised that at least it was not unlikely that the sugar would be sold in the market at market price on arrival. And he must be held to have known that in any ordinary market prices are apt to fluctuate from day to day: but he had no reason to suppose it more probable that during the relevant period such fluctuation would be downwards rather than upwards — it was an even chance that the fluctuation would be downwards.

[6]   So the question for decision is whether a plaintiff can recover as damages for breach of contract a loss of a kind which the defendant, when he made the contract, ought to have realised was not unlikely to result from a breach of contract causing delay in delivery. I use the words "not unlikely" as denoting a degree of probability considerably less than an even chance but nevertheless not very unusual and easily foreseeable.

[7]   For over a century everyone has agreed that remoteness of damage in contract must be determined by applying the rule (or rules) laid down by the court including Lord Wensleydale (then Parke B.), Martin B. and Alderson B. in *Hadley* *v. Baxendale*. But many different interpretations of that rule have been adopted by judges at different times. So I think that one ought first to see just what was decided in that case, because it would seem wrong to attribute to that rule a meaning which, if it had been adopted in that case, would have resulted in a contrary decision of that case. . . .

[**LORD REID** here set out the facts of that case and quoted from the judgment of Alderson B. *supra* (¶ 7).]

[8]   Alderson B. clearly did not and could not mean that it was not reasonably foreseeable that delay might stop the resumption of work in the mill. He merely said that in the great multitude — which I take to mean the great majority — of cases this would not happen. He was not distinguishing between results which were foreseeable or unforeseeable, but between results which were likely because they would happen in the great majority of cases, and results which were unlikely because they would only happen in a small minority of cases. He continued: "It follows, therefore, that the loss of profits here cannot reasonably be considered such a consequence of the breach of contract as could have been fairly and reasonably contemplated by both the parties when they made this contract." He clearly meant that a result which will happen in the great majority of cases should fairly and reasonably be regarded as having been in the contemplation of the parties, but that a result which, though foreseeable as a substantial possibility, would only happen in a small minority of cases should not be regarded as having been in their contemplation. He was referring to such a result when he continued:

> For such loss would neither have flowed naturally from the breach of this contract in the great multitude of such cases occurring under ordinary circumstances, nor were the special circumstances, which perhaps, would have made it a reasonable and natural consequence of such breach of contract, communicated to or known by the defendants.

[9]   I have dealt with the latter part of the judgment before coming to the well known rule because the court were there applying the rule and the language which was used in the latter part appears to me to throw considerable light on the meaning which they must have attached to the rather vague expression used in the rule itself. The rule is that the damages "should be such as may fairly and reasonably be considered either arising naturally, *i.e.*, according to the usual course of things, from such breach of contract itself, or such as may reasonably be supposed to have been in the contemplation of both parties, at the time they made the contract, as the probable result of the breach of it." *naturally arising breach*

[10]   I do not think that it was intended that there were to be two rules or that two different standards or tests were to be applied. The last two passages which I quoted from the end of the judgment applied to the facts before the court which did not include any special circumstances communicated to the defendants; and the line of reasoning there is that because in the great majority of cases loss of profit would not in all probability have occurred, it followed that this could not reasonably be considered as having been fairly and reasonably contemplated by both the parties, for it would not have flowed naturally from the breach in the great majority of cases.

[11]   I am satisfied that the court did not intend that every type of damage which was reasonably foreseeable by the parties when the contract was made should either be considered as arising naturally, *i.e.*, in the usual course of things, or be supposed to have been in the contemplation of the parties. Indeed the decision

makes it clear that a type of damage which was plainly foreseeable as a real possibility but which would only occur in a small minority of cases cannot be regarded as arising in the usual course of things or be supposed to have been in the contemplation of the parties: the parties are not supposed to contemplate as grounds for the recovery of damage any type of loss or damage which on the knowledge available to the defendant would appear to him as only likely to occur in a small minority of cases.

[12] In cases like *Hadley v. Baxendale* or the present case it is not enough that in fact the plaintiff's loss was directly caused by the defendant's breach of contract. It clearly was so caused in both. The crucial question is whether, on the information available to the defendant when the contract was made, he should, or the reasonable man in his position would, have realised that such loss was sufficiently likely to result from the breach of contract to make it proper to hold that the loss flowed naturally from the breach or that loss of that kind should have been within his contemplation . . . But then it has been said that the liability of defendants has been further extended by *Victoria Laundry*. I do not think so. . . .

[13] But what is said to create a "landmark" is the statement of principles by Asquith L.J. This does to some extent go beyond the older authorities and in so far as it does so, I do not agree with it. In paragraph (2) it is said that the plaintiff is entitled to recover "such part of the loss actually resulting as was at the time of the contract reasonably foreseeable as liable to result from the breach." To bring in reasonable foreseeability appears to me to be confusing measure of damages in contract with measure of damages in tort. A great many extremely unlikely results are reasonably foreseeable: it is true that Asquith L.J. may have meant foreseeable as a likely result, and if that is all he meant I would not object further than to say that I think that the phrase is liable to be misunderstood. For the same reason I would take exception to the phrase "liable to result" in paragraph (5). Liable is a very vague word but I think that one would usually say that when a person foresees a very improbable result he foresees that it is liable to happen.

[14] I agree with the first half of paragraph (6). For the best part of a century it has not been required that the defendant could have foreseen that a breach of contract must necessarily result in the loss which has occurred. But I cannot agree with the second half of that paragraph. It has never been held to be sufficient in contract that the loss was foreseeable as a "serious possibility" or a "real danger" or as being "on the cards." It is on the cards that one can win £100,000 or more for a stake of a few pence — several people have done that. And anyone who backs a hundred to one chance regards a win as a serious possibility — many people have won on such a chance. . . .

[15] It appears to me that in the ordinary use of language there is wide gulf between saying that some event is not unlikely or quite likely to happen and saying merely that it is a serious possibility, a real danger, or on the cards. Suppose one takes a well-shuffled pack of cards, it is quite likely or not unlikely that the top card will prove to be a diamond: the odds are only 3 to 1 against. But most people would not say that it is quite likely to be the nine of diamonds for the odds are then 51 to 1 against. On the other hand I think that most people would say that there is a serious possibility or a real danger of its being turned up first and of course it is on the cards. If the tests "real danger" or "serious possibility" are in future to be authoritative then the *Victoria Laundry* case would indeed be a landmark because it would mean that *Hadley v. Baxendale* would be differently decided today. I cer-

tainly could not understand any court deciding that, on the information available to the carrier in that case, the stoppage of the mill was neither a serious possibility nor a real danger. If those tests are to prevail in future then let us cease to pay lip service to the rule in *Hadley v. Baxendale*. But in my judgment to adopt these tests would extend liability for breach of contract beyond what is reasonable or desirable. From the limited knowledge which I have of commercial affairs I would not expect such an extension to be welcomed by the business community and from the legal point of view I can find little or nothing to recommend it. . . .

[16] It appears to me that, without relying in any way on the *Victoria Laundry* case, and taking the principle that had already been established, the loss of profit claimed in this case was not too remote to be recoverable as damages.

[All the judges agreed in the result. Short excerpts from the other judgments follow. The references are to the report in the Appeal Cases.]

LORD MORRIS: — [17] I regard the illuminating judgment of the Court of Appeal in *Victoria Laundry* as a most valuable analysis of the rule. It was there pointed out that in order to make a contract-breaker liable under what was called "either rule" in *Hadley v. Baxendale* it is not necessary that he should actually have asked himself what loss is liable to result from a breach but that it suffices that if he had considered the question he would as a reasonable man have concluded that the loss in question was liable to result. Nor need it be proved, in order to recover a particular loss, that upon a given state of knowledge he could, as a reasonable man, foresee that a breach must necessarily result in that loss. Certain illustrative phrases are employed in that case. They are valuable by way of exposition but for my part I doubt whether the phrase "on the cards" has a sufficiently clear meaning or possesses such a comparable shade of meaning as to qualify it to take its place with the various other phrases which line up as expositions of the rule.

LORD HODSON: — [18] The word "probable" in *Hadley v. Baxendale* covers both parts of the rule and it is of vital importance in applying the rule to consider what the court meant by using this word in its context. The common use of this word is no doubt to imply that something is more likely to happen than not. In conversation, if one says to another, "If you go out in this weather you will probably catch a cold," this is, I think, equivalent to saying that one believes there is an odds-on chance that the other will catch a cold. The word "probable" need not, however, bear this narrow meaning.

[19] Asquith L.J. . . . suggested the phrase "liable to result" as appropriate to describe the degree of probability required. This may be a colourless expression but I do not find it possible to improve on it. If the word "likelihood" is used it may convey the impression that the chances are all in favour of the thing happening, an idea which I would reject.

[20] I find guidance in the use of the expression "in the great multitude of cases" which . . . indicates that the damages recoverable for breach of contract are such as flow naturally in most cases from the breach, whether under ordinary circumstances or from special circumstances due to the knowledge either in the possession of or communicated to the defendants. This expression throws light on the whole field of damages for breach of contract and points to a different approach from that taken in tort cases.

LORD PEARCE: — [21] In my opinion the expressions used in the *Victoria Laundry* case were right. I do not however accept the colloquialism "on the cards" as being a useful test because I am not sure just what nuance it has either in my own personal vocabulary or in that of others. I suspect that it owes its attraction, like many other colloquialisms, to the fact that one may utter it without having the trouble of really thinking out with precision what one means oneself or what others will understand by it, a spurious attraction which in general makes colloquialism unsuitable for definition, though it is often useful as shorthand for a collection of definable ideas. It was in this latter convenient sense that the judgment uses the ambiguous words "liable to result." They were not intended as a further or different test from "serious possibility" or "real danger."

LORD UPJOHN: — [22] It is clear that . . . the loser [need not] establish that the loss was a near certainty or an odds-on probability. I am content to adopt as the test a "real danger" or a "serious possibility." There may be a shade of difference between these two phrases but the assessment of damages is not an exact science and what to one judge or jury will appear a real danger may appear to another judge or jury to be a serious possibility. I do not think that the application of that test would have led to a different result in *Hadley v. Baxendale*.

NOTES

1. The judgments in *The Heron II* appear to reinforce the view that when remoteness is at issue, the major issue is a factual inquiry into the probability of a certain consequence arising. We shall examine in more detail later some of the problems that arise from such a focus. For the moment, note the following issues and consider whether a focus on them would suggest different ways of dealing with the problem of stopping an award of damages:

    (a) The time at which what is in the defendant's "contemplation" is relevant is the time when the contract is "made". In other words, it would not, on this basis, affect the liability of Richard, the limousine driver, if Julie, after getting in the car, told him precisely what the consequences of any delay might be. Would that notice be too late as the contract was already formed?

    (b) The House of Lords in *The Heron II* did not explicitly draw an inference adverse to the defendant from the fact that the delay due to the "deviation", that is, the breach of contract, was deliberate and the defendant sought to make more money for itself by making a detour. While the court did not mention this fact in coming to its conclusion, do you think that this is a relevant fact that might influence how problems of remoteness should be dealt with?

    (c) In *Hadley v. Baxendale* and *The Heron II*, the defendant was a carrier, transporting things belonging to someone else. In *Victoria Laundry*, on the other hand, the defendant was the seller of the goods. It is probably reasonable to assume that, in general, sellers know more about the risks associated with a breach of a contract of sale than a carrier does about the risks of non-delivery or late delivery.

    (d) In *Hadley v. Baxendale* and *The Heron II*, the defendants would have had strong reasons to do what they could to protect themselves in the future. These defendants could see that the resolution of the dispute might have an important effect on future transactions with other shippers or charterers. The plaintiff in *The Heron II* might have had a similar concern, for it too may have had strong reasons to prevent (or, at least, to discourage) shipowners that it might use in the future from doing what the defendant did. (In contrast, the parties in *Victoria Laundry* almost certainly have no such interest in the development of the law.) Carriers and charterers (and of course the insurance companies that are often in the background) have a stake in the litigation that transcends the particular facts; they are sometimes referred to as "institutional" litigants.

2. In *The Heron II* the dispute was initially dealt with by an "umpire". In commercial matters, disputes may be dealt with by an umpire (or arbitrator) because this is required by the contract, or by legislation dealing with a particular type of contract. An umpire generally holds a hearing, and makes findings of fact. The umpire makes an initial ruling which, like a trial decision, may be appealed to the courts if there is an error of law. An umpire (like an arbitrator) will usually be an expert in the trade out of which the litigation has arisen, and should be able to make a determination consistent with the expectations and understandings of those in the trade. This expertise is important for two reasons: (i) the costs of fact-finding are lower because an umpire or arbitrator, unlike a judge, does not have to be educated in the trade practices; and (ii) the risk of the court making a decision on a bizarre or mistaken assumption of fact is reduced.

   In this case the umpire made the important finding of fact which the courts relied upon, *viz.*, how much longer the voyage took because of the detour. But the umpire did not make the crucial finding (or assumption) about the likelihood of the loss arising from the detour on the voyage: that finding was made by the judges without any direct evidence, but rather based on the inferences that the judges drew from the umpire's findings of fact and their own knowledge (or assumptions) about the marketplace.

   In some situations, such as in *Victoria Laundry*, after the court makes a ruling of law, it may refer a case to a Referee or Master, who will conduct an inquiry, make findings of fact and report to the court, for example to determine the exact amount of damages. Often the Referee or Master is a full-time lower level judicial position, though sometimes a referee with particular knowledge is specially appointed to deal with a particular case. While a reference may involve a hearing with witnesses, often the matter is resolved simply by reviewing documents and receiving submissions from counsel.

3. The fact that both parties in *The Heron II* were likely institutional litigants with an interest in the litigation that transcended the particular case makes the resolution of the dispute important for future disputes with other parties similarly situated. Such a decision is certain to become widely known among carriers and shippers through trade journals. It thus especially important that the court understand the commercial context and make correct findings of fact, for if the findings do not coincide with trade expectations, the judgment will be very problematic for those in the trade.

4. The members of the House of Lords in *The Heron II* may have misunderstood what Asquith L.J. in *Victoria Laundry* had in mind when he used the expression, "on the cards". The expression "on the cards" generally refers to tarot cards and their use in fortune-telling and means "predestined to happen". The use of colloquial language in judgments is not without risks.

Note on Legislation and Law Reform

common vs civil law

Thus far we have largely focussed on judge-made rules, that is, the "common law". The term "common law" may refer to judge-made law as opposed to legislation enacted by Parliament or a provincial legislature. The term "common law" may also be used to distinguish a system of legal rules developed and modified by judges, from a "civil law" system, where the fundamental principles of law are set out in a Civil Code. Most of Canada's provinces and territories have a common law tradition, with its roots in the English common law, while the legal system in Quebec is based on the *Civil Code*, which can be traced back through French Civil Law to the Code of Roman Law. This book focuses on the law of contracts in the common law system, particularly as found in the common law jurisdictions of Canada. While it is beyond the scope of this introductory book, an examination of the similarities and differences between the civil and common law systems can be interesting and illuminating.

Our examination of the law of contracts has so far (and will) focus principally on the role of the courts in developing the law, but legislation is frequently relevant to contract issues. Indeed, for the practising lawyer and judge, legislation that governs specific types of transactions is often more important than the common law rules. Generally speaking, legislation deals with the application of general common law contracts principles in specific transactional contexts (such as residential landlord-tenant contracts or purchases of securities). The common law establishes the "fundamental" principles of contract law, and deals with contractual relationships that are not the subject of specific legislation, which may modify or codify the common law.

The *Sale of Goods Act*, R.S.O. 1990, c. S.1, for example, deals with the measure of damages recoverable for breach of contract *for the sale of goods*, providing:

> 49(1) Where the seller wrongfully neglects or refuses to deliver the goods to the buyer, the buyer may maintain an action against the seller for damages for non-delivery.
>
>   → Hadley v Baxendale (mill shaft)
>
> (2) The measure of damages is the estimated loss directly and naturally resulting in the ordinary course of events from the seller's breach of contract.

The origin of the language in this section is obviously *Hadley v. Baxendale*. The *Sale of Goods Acts* of the Canadian common law provinces are based on the English Act of 1893, which was part of an attempt to codify large parts of the law relating to common commercial transactions. Unlike much legislation, the *Sale of Goods Acts* were not reforming acts; their purpose was to codify the common law — to express in statutory form the existing law found in the cases and in so doing to remove inconsistencies and make the law clearer.

Canada has ratified the *United Nations Convention on International Sale of Goods*, or *Vienna Sales Convention*, and the Parliament of Canada and all Canadian provinces have enacted legislation to make it effective in Canada. This legislation applies only to "international sales of goods", making some modification for those transactions in both the common law and in the law under the *Sale of Goods Acts* of the provinces. We shall refer to provisions of these treaties at some points in these materials.

There have been efforts to statutorily reform the common law rules to make them more suitable to modern conditions, and these efforts are continuing. Before we turn to the Canadian schemes for reform, we can examine the way in which reform of the law of contract was implemented in the United States, for reform there has gone further than in Canada, and as we shall see, those American reforms are the models for much recent Canadian legislation.

The impetus for reform in the United States arose from two separate but related concerns. The first was a desire to encourage uniformity across the country. The second was a desire to reduce the complexity of legal regulation of transactions that are governed by the many different state legal systems. These concerns led in 1892 to proposals for the establishment of a body that would promote uniformity of laws, the National Conference on Uniform State Laws. The first result of the Conference was the publication of the *Uniform Negotiable Instruments Law* in 1896. This was eventually adopted by all the states. In 1906 a *Uniform Sales Law* was published. The hope was to produce ultimately a single comprehensive code covering all aspects of commercial law. The drafting of what was to become the *Uniform Commercial Code* (UCC) began in 1942 under the direction of the famous American scholar, Karl Llewellyn. It has undergone several revisions. The UCC has now been adopted in every state. (Louisiana has not adopted the complete Code, since, like Quebec, it has a legal system partially based on the civil law.)

The American UCC is organized in 10 articles. Article 1 contains general provisions applicable in each article. Article 2, with which we shall be most concerned, deals with sales and roughly corresponds to our *Sale of Goods Act*. Article 9, dealing with security interests in chattels, has been adopted (though not in quite identical terms) in Alberta, British Columbia, Manitoba, Ontario, New Brunswick, Nova Scotia and Saskatchewan as the *Personal Property Security Act*. Article 8, which deals with the question of the negotiability of shares, has become part of the *Canada Business Corporations Act*, R.S.C. 1985, c. C-44 and of the business corporations acts of most of the provinces. The UCC has been supplemented by other uniform acts, and legislation similar to these acts has been adopted in various Canadian provinces. The Ontario *Business Practices Act*, R.S.O. 1990, c. B.18, and the British Columbia *Trade Practice Act*, R.S.B.C. 1996, c. 457, are, for example, largely based on the *Uniform Consumer Sales Practices Act* in the United States.

The desire to reduce complexity and uncertainty also led to the production in 1932 of the American *Restatement of the Law, Contracts*. The *Restatement* (referred to in the judgment of the majority in *Peevyhouse*, ¶ 17) was a project of the American Law Institute ("ALI"). The ALI engages in three functions: (i) the preparation of model codes and acts; (ii) continuing legal education; and (iii) the preparation of *Restatements* in various areas of the common law. These *Restatements* are important for various areas of law, with different works for contracts, torts, property and other areas of law.

The *Restatement* is an attempt to reduce the law to the form of "propositions of law". It has no direct legal force, but it has had a significant influence on American judgments. While less commonly cited in Canada, the *Restatement* is increasingly referred to in judgments in this country. The work of producing a *Restatement* of any area of the law is under the direction of a Reporter, who is the principal drafter of the text. The Reporter for the original *Restatement, Contracts* was Samuel Williston, who was assisted by Arthur Corbin (the author of one of the best textbooks on the law of contracts, *Corbin on Contracts*). The *Restatement* was well received by the courts and is regarded as having considerable authority. In 1960 work was begun on a revision of the *First Restatement*. The process of revision is very time-consuming. The full text of the *Restatement, Second, Contracts* was published in 1969, and published in revised version in 1981. The Reporter for the *Restatement, Second* was Robert Braucher, a Harvard Law professor and later a Massachusetts judge.

The notes in this book include extracts from the UCC and the *Restatement*, either as propositions of law that might be applicable in Canada or as different ways of solving problems that we share with the United States. Remember that neither the UCC nor the *Restatement* is of any binding authority in Canada: neither operates to guide a court to a decision in the way that, for example, the *Sale of Goods Act* does. But this does not mean that they are irrelevant.

There is no Canadian equivalent of the American Law Institute, though some of its functions are carried out in different ways. The Canadian Bar Association and the various provincial law societies have extensive programs of continuing education. A number of provinces and the federal government have law reform commissions. These commissions produce recommendations for changes in the law and frequently produce model acts. There are references in this book to some of the recommendations of the Ontario and British Columbia Law Reform Commissions.

In 1987 the Ontario Law Reform Commission published its *Report on Amendment of the Law of Contract*. This Report discussed many of the rules that we shall be dealing with in this course and we shall examine some of the recommendations of the Commission. The Ontario Commission did not directly address any of the issues in damages that we have looked at. Nothing has yet been done to implement any of the Report's recommendations in the Contracts area, and the Commission has been disbanded by the government.

The Canadian equivalent of the American National Conference of Commissioners on Uniform State Laws is the Uniform Law Conference of Canada. This body has produced drafts of acts, many of which have been adopted in several provinces. However, for a variety of political and institutional reasons, very few have had anything like universal acceptance. The history of the Uniform Law Conference of Canada and a summary of its work to date are available in the annual proceedings of the conference that are published each year. The Conference has a project to develop a common legislative framework for commercial law in Canada, but its work is not as well known as it should be (see www.ulcc.ca).

In 1981 the Canadian Conference proposed a model Uniform Act to replace the *Sale of Goods Act*. It was largely based on the Ontario Law Reform Commission's *Report on Sale of Goods*. The proposals of the Commission were in turn substantially based on the provisions of Article 2 of the American UCC. As has been mentioned, the *Sale of Goods Act* made very few changes in the common law. It was an attempt to codify the common law as it was thought to exist in 1893 in England. The 1981 proposals, however, contain provisions that if enacted would change the law considerably in some areas. Some of these proposals are examined in the notes in this book. It seems unlikely that any province will bring the *Uniform Sale of Goods Act* into force in the near future.

The provisions of the proposed *Uniform Sale of Goods Act* that correspond to s. 49 of the present *Sale of Goods Act* are as follows:

9.18(1) Where the seller or buyer breaches the contract, the other party may maintain an action against him for damages.

(2) The measure of damages is the estimated loss which the party in breach ought to have foreseen at the time of the contract as not unlikely to result from his breach of contract.

(3) An aggrieved party must take reasonable steps to mitigate his damages.

(4) Where at the agreed time for performance,

(a)   the buyer wrongfully fails to accept and pay for the goods;

(b)   the seller wrongfully fails to deliver the goods or the goods are rightfully rejected; or

(c)   the buyer wrongfully rejects the goods,

the measure of damages is prima facie to be ascertained by the difference between the contract price and the price that could have been obtained by a commercially reasonable disposition or purchase of the goods within or at a reasonable time and place after the aggrieved party learned of the breach, less any expenses saved in consequence of the breach.

(5) Subsection 4 does not apply where,

(a) the measure of damages would be inadequate to put the seller in as good a position as performance by the buyer would have done;

(b) the seller has resold the goods as provided in section 9.10; or

(c) the buyer has bought substitutional goods as provided in section 9.16.

(6) A seller's or buyer's claim for damages may include a claim for incidental or consequential damages.

NOTES AND QUESTIONS

1. Do the provisions of s. 9.18 offer a better basis for dealing with any of the problems we have encountered? If you were drafting a section to codify the common law rules regarding damages for breach of contract, what would you say? Could you be any more specific than the drafters of either the *Sale of Goods Act* or the *Uniform Sale of Goods Act*?

2. A much larger issue is whether any more precision is desirable.

3. Section 9.18(2) of the proposed *Uniform Sale of Goods Act* provides:

> The measure of damages is the estimated loss which the party in breach ought to have foreseen at the time of the contract as not unlikely to result from his breach of contract.

The Official Comment of the Commissioners to this section states, "Subsection (2) adopts the formula for measuring damages approved in *The Heron II* . . . refining the rules set out in *Hadley v. Baxendale.*"

(a) Is the *Uniform Sale of Goods Act* provision an accurate summary of *The Heron II*?

(b) Is the focus of the court's inquiry the same under s. 9.18(2) as under *Hadley v. Baxendale*?

4. The test as developed by *The Heron II* or s. 9.18(2) suggests a simple factual inquiry of a statistical nature. One asks what the chances were of the loss occurring. Perhaps one might say that if the probability of loss A is greater than 50 per cent, then the defendant is responsible for that loss, but if it is less than 50 per cent, the opposite result is reached. (Does the phrase "not unlikely" suggest that a probability of .3 or .8 might be sufficient or necessary?) Notice, however, that Lord Reid (¶ 12) uses the crucial word "proper": "to make it *proper* to hold that the loss flowed naturally from the breach". Does this mean that the inquiry is not entirely factual? If it is not, what factors are important?

We have now investigated some of the principal problems in dealing with breach of contract where the plaintiff seeks an award of damages from the defendant. We have examined the justifications for making an award of damages, and what might provide a basis for limiting the amount of an award. We shall now explore some further examples that will test these analyses.

SOME PROBLEMS IN AWARDING DAMAGES

The next cases are examples of the courts struggling with the appropriate measure of damages for breach of contract, either in determining what sum of money will put the innocent party in the "same position as . . . if the contract had been performed", or in deciding that there should be some other basis for recovery than an award of expectation-based measure of damages. The cases are important examples of the difficulties of finding satisfactory solutions to the problem of providing an appropriate remedy for breach of contract. As you read them, consider how well they provide a solution to the particular case and in giving guidance to a lawyer who may have to draft an agreement to deal with or avoid a similar problem.

The first case has been considered as making a significant change in the law. To what extent is it consistent with the analysis of either Fuller and Perdue or Posner?

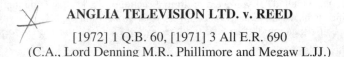

ANGLIA TELEVISION LTD. v. REED

[1972] 1 Q.B. 60, [1971] 3 All E.R. 690
(C.A., Lord Denning M.R., Phillimore and Megaw L.JJ.)

LORD DENNING M.R.: — **[1]** Anglia Television Ltd. were minded in 1968 to make a film of a play for television entitled "The Man in the Wood." It portrayed an American married to an English woman. The American has an adventure in an English wood. The film was to last for 90 minutes. Anglia Television made many arrangements in advance. They arranged for a place where the play was to be filmed. They employed a director, a designer and a stage manager, and so forth. They involved themselves in much expense. All this was done before they got the leading man. They required a strong actor capable of holding the play together. He was to be on the scene the whole time. Anglia Television eventually found the man. He was Mr. Robert Reed, an American who has a very high reputation as an actor. He was very suitable for this part. By telephone conversation on 30th August 1968 it was agreed by Mr. Reed through his agent that he would come to England and be available between 9th September and 11th October 1968 to rehearse and play in this film. He was to get a performance fee of £1,050, living expenses of £100 a week, his first class fares to and from the United States, and so forth. It was all subject to the permit of the Ministry of Labour for him to come here. That was duly given on 2nd September 1968. So the contract was concluded. But unfortunately there was some muddle with the bookings. It appears that Mr. Reed's agent had already booked him in America for some other play. So on 3rd September 1968 the agent said that Mr. Reed would not come to England to perform in this play. He repudiated his contract. Anglia Television tried hard to find a substitute but could not do so. So on 11th September they accepted his repudiation. They abandoned the proposed film. They gave notice to the people whom they had engaged and so forth.

[2]   Anglia Television then sued Mr. Reed for damages. He did not dispute his liability, but a question arose as to the damages. Anglia Television do not claim their profit. They cannot say what their profit would have been on this contract if Mr. Reed had come here and performed it. So, instead of claiming for loss of profits, they claim for the wasted expenditure. They had incurred the director's fees, the designer's fees, the stage manager's and assistant manager's fees, and so on. It comes in all to £2,750. Anglia Television say that all that money was wasted because Mr. Reed did not perform his contract. Mr. Reed's advisers take a point of law. They submit that Anglia Television cannot recover for expenditure incurred before the contract was concluded with Mr. Reed. They can only recover the expenditure after the contract was concluded. They say that the expenditure after the contract was only £854.65, and that is all that Anglia Television can recover. The Master rejected that contention; he held that Anglia Television could recover the whole £2,750; and now Mr. Reed appeals to this court.

[3]   Counsel for Mr. Reed has referred us to the recent unreported case of *Perestrello & Compania Limitada v. United Paint Co. Ltd. (No. 2)* [(1969), 113 Sol. Jo. 324] in which Thesiger J. quoted the words of Lord Tindal C.J. in 1835 in *Hodges v. Earl of Litchfield* [(1835), 1 Bing. (N.C.) 492 at 498, 131 E.R. 1207]: "The expenses preliminary to the contract ought not to be allowed. The party enters into them for his own benefit at a time when it is uncertain whether there will be any contract or not." Thesiger J. applied those words, saying: "In my judgment precontract expenditure, though thrown away, is not recoverable . . ." I cannot accept the proposition as stated. It seems to me that a plaintiff in such a case as this had an election: he can either claim for his loss of profits; or for his wasted expenditure. But he must elect between them. He cannot claim both. If he has not suffered any loss of profits — or if he cannot prove what his profits would have been — he can claim in the alternative the expenditure which has been thrown away, that is, wasted, by reason of the breach. . . .

[4]   If the plaintiff claims the wasted expenditure, he is not limited to the expenditure incurred *after* the contract was concluded. He can claim also the expenditure incurred *before* the contract, provided that it was such as would reasonably be in the contemplation of the parties as likely to be wasted if the contract was broken. Applying that principle here, it is plain that, when Mr. Reed entered into this contract, he must have known perfectly well that much expenditure had already been incurred on director's fees and the like. He must have contemplated — or, at any rate, it is reasonably to be imputed to him — that if he broke his contract, all that expenditure would be wasted, whether or not it was incurred before or after the contract. He must pay damages for all the expenditure so wasted and thrown away. This view is supported by the recent decision of Brightman J. in *Lloyd v. Stanbury* [[1971] 2 All E.R. 267]. There was a contract for the sale of land. In anticipation of the contract — and before it was concluded — the purchaser went to much expense in moving a caravan to the site and in getting his furniture there. The seller afterwards entered into a contract to sell the land to the purchaser, but afterwards broke his contract. The land had not increased in value, so the purchaser could not claim for any loss of profit. But Brightman J. held that he could recover the cost of moving the caravan and furniture, because it was "within the contemplation of the parties when the contract was signed." That decision is in accord with correct principle, namely, that wasted expenditure can be recovered when it is wasted by reason of the defendant's breach of contract. It is true that, if the defendant had never entered into the contract, he would not be liable, and the expenditure would have been incurred by the plaintiff without redress; but, the defendant having made his contract and broken it, it does not lie in his mouth to say he is not liable, when it was because of his breach that the expenditure has been wasted.

[5]   I think the Master was quite right and this appeal should be dismissed.

[**PHILLIMORE** and **MEGAW L.JJ.** agreed with **LORD DENNING M.R.**]

NOTES, QUESTIONS AND PROBLEMS

1.   Lord Denning refers (¶ 4) to the case of *Lloyd v. Stanbury*. In that case, the defendant had offered his farm for sale. The plaintiff wanted to buy it. The defendant would have had no place in which to live after selling his farm until he had built a house for himself and his family on neighbouring land. In order to help the sale, the plaintiff offered to lend his caravan (a small mobile home) to the defendant to live in while the new house was being built. In furtherance of this arrangement, but before a contract for the sale of the land was signed, the plaintiff had the caravan moved to the defendant's farm and incurred expenses in so doing. The contract for the sale of the land was later signed, but the transaction was not completed as the defendant backed out at the last minute. The plaintiff sued for damages for breach of the contract of sale of the land, and included in his claim the costs of moving the camper to the defendant's land. These expenses had been incurred before the date on which the formal contract to sell had been signed by the defendant, but after the parties had arranged all the terms of the deal. Brightman J. allowed the plaintiff to recover the costs of moving the caravan.

     The land contract in *Lloyd v. Stanbury* was made in the standard pattern for contracts for the sale of land in England. In England, the principal terms of a land contract are generally established by the parties in negotiations but the written record of the parties' agreement on the terms of the deal is usually expressed to be "subject to contract", *i.e.*, the terms are not to be binding until a formal contract has been negotiated by the parties' solicitors and signed by the parties. This formal written contract is the only contract for the sale of the land that can be sued upon, since there is an express statement that the initial negotiations were "subject to contract".

     The claim of the plaintiff in *Lloyd v. Stanbury* for the expenses of moving the caravan was "pre-contractual" only in a somewhat technical sense: these expenses were "post-negotiation" in a way that the "pre-contract" expenses in *Anglia Television* were not. It would be perfectly consistent with the result in *Lloyd v. Stanbury* to regard the parties as having made one contract for the moving of the caravan and another later contract for the sale of the land. Giving damages for the losses arising from breach of the first contract would be the normal enforcement of that contract and would have nothing to do with the second contract. The claims of the plaintiffs in *Lloyd v. Stanbury* and *Anglia Television* are for the protection of quite different interests.

     The Canadian practice of selling land is quite different. The first agreement in Canada is usually a binding written "agreement of purchase and sale". In the re-sale market for homes, this agreement will usually be on a standard form prepared by the local real estate board and will set out the terms on which the sale will take place. While in the residential market lawyers are rarely involved in drafting the initial contract — the agreement of purchase and sale — it is very common for purchasers and vendors to employ a lawyer to make sure that the vendor has title to the land being sold and that the transaction is properly "closed". It is also common for the sale of large commercial or industrial properties to involve lawyers in drafting and negotiating initial agreements for the particular transaction, as well as in the "closing".

2.   To return to the option that Lord Denning says the plaintiff has: (¶ 3) "he can either claim for his loss of profits; or for his wasted expenditure". To what extent can this proposition be taken as a correct or defensible statement of the law?

     To explore this question, suppose that Anglia Television could have produced the following statements of income and expense for its position if Reed had performed as he had promised. Assume three different results:

	A	B	C
Sales (£000s)	100	80	50
Cost of sales	60	60	60
Gross Profit	40	20	(10)

Fixed Costs	20	20	20
Net Profit	20	0	(30)

(a) Does Lord Denning mean that if Reed breached his contract and if Anglia could have proved that it would have had result C, Reed would be liable for £60,000 (costs of sales), £80,000 (total of all costs, variable and fixed, *i.e.*, £60,000 + £20,000) or some other amount?

(b) If the results could be proved to have been as in A, does Lord Denning expect that Anglia Television might only recover £20,000? Why would the plaintiff ever sue only for its net profit (£20,000) if its expenses (at least £60,000) are greater? *compensation principle*

(c) The application of Lord Atkinson's principle in *Wertheim v. Chicoutimi Pulp* suggests that the plaintiff should be in as good a position as it would have been in had the contract been performed. Is it consistent with what we are doing when we enforce a contract to say that the plaintiff should be in as good as *but no better* a position than if the contract had been performed?

(d) If the basis for the choice that Lord Denning gives Anglia Television is the fact that it cannot prove that it would have made a profit, then result A can be regarded as eliminated as a possible factual basis for the award of damages. When would a court be justified in assuming that either result C or result B is the more likely one? Is it satisfactory that the result in a case should depend on the fact that the court simply does not know what might have happened? What effect does the fact that we have to live with ignorance have on the rationality and acceptability of the process of adjudication? Are there any obvious alternative ways of dealing with the problem of ignorance that might be more satisfactory?

3. Is it relevant that the inability of Anglia Television to prove any loss was due to the fact that (i) the defendant's breach prevented the film from being made; and (ii) only very speculative estimates of what profits might have been made had the film been produced were possible?

4. The decision of Lord Denning in *Anglia Television* is sometimes characterized as offering the plaintiff a choice between the expectation and reliance measure of damages. After all, the expectation measure is typically associated with profits lost, and the reliance measure with expenses incurred. It is, however, a little odd to include pre-contract expenditures in *reliance* losses. When they were incurred, what did Anglia Television rely on? If such expenditures cannot be called reliance losses and so cannot be seen as recoverable if the reliance interest is being protected, on what basis are they recoverable? Is the clue to a satisfactory statement of the issue presented by *Anglia Television v. Reed* a realization that the word "profit" is ambiguous or misleading?

5. A party who incurs expenses in the hope that a contract will be entered into, whether in anticipation or negotiation of the contract, is usually not entitled to anything if the parties do not enter into a contract.

6. Some commentators have criticized the decision in *Anglia Television*, arguing that the award for pre-contract expenditures is excessive, since these expenditures were not made in reliance on the contract with Reed. (A.I. Ogus, "Note" (1972), 35 *Mod. L. Rev.* 423). It can, however, be argued that the concept of "foregone opportunity", discussed by Fuller and Perdue, justifies the result. Although it is not stated in the report, it seems safe to assume that Anglia Television was considering a number of actors for the lead role. In reliance on the making the contract with Reed, Anglia stopped discussions with other actors, and gave up the opportunity to enter into a contract with another actor that might have allowed them to make a profitable film that would have covered the pre-contract expenditures.

7. Once the proper basis for considering the claim of Anglia Television has been determined, the problems of this case are not resolved. The more basic issues are raised by the following questions:

   (a)   What is the assumption underlying the award of any damages in the case?

   (b)   Suppose that the representative of Anglia Television who made the arrangements with Reed had said to him, "Oh, by the way, you do understand, don't you, that by agreeing to perform, you are guaranteeing that we shall recover all our expenses if you walk out on us at any time before completion of production." What might Reed have said? Should this kind of fact be relevant?

   (c)   Would your answers to these questions be the same if the amount of damages for which Reed might be responsible on the basis of an analysis based on Fuller and Perdue was greater than the amount actually awarded (or awarded on the basis of results of the figures in columns A, B, or C, *supra*) by a factor of 10, 100, or 1,000?

8.   The argument here is not that the questions asked above might have been easily answered in *Anglia Television* itself — though it seems unlikely that Reed would have made a contract in situation 7(b) — but that such questions are the heart of the inquiry. No damages should be imposed on Reed unless the court is prepared to hold that he assumed the risk of that liability. Question 7(c) raises the problem of *Hadley v. Baxendale*. Reed's counsel would certainly raise the argument that damages larger than the amount awarded by, perhaps, a factor of two or 10, let alone 100 or 1,000, would be "too remote". A difficulty with Lord Denning's analysis is that he fails to provide a clear basis for the award, so it is difficult to be certain of the basis for limiting it.

9.   If we assume that the only question relevant under *Hadley v. Baxendale* (as interpreted by *The Heron II*) is the factual one of deciding whether Anglia's losses were or were not "not unlikely", are we any further ahead? Note that it is accepted that *Hadley v. Baxendale* and cases like *The Heron II* speak to what is or is not reasonably contemplated as a loss *when* the contract is made. When the contract was made in *Anglia Television v. Reed*, what was reasonably contemplated as the loss?

10.   As we shall see in Chapter 5, if Reed were unable to perform because of illness or accident, the contract would be said to be frustrated, and he would be discharged without liability.

11.   Does it matter that Reed was unable to perform because he chose to do other, presumably more lucrative, work instead of working for Anglia Television? Should he be asked to account for the money, or the extra money, that he made on this job? Is the outcome of *Anglia Television* an example of Posner's "efficient breach"?

BOWLAY LOGGING LTD. v. DOMTAR LTD.

[1978] 4 W.W.R. 105
(B.C.S.C., Berger J.)

[The plaintiff agreed to log timber for the defendant on land to which the defendant had the timber rights. Under the contract, the defendant was to provide trucks to carry the logged timber. After the contract was partially performed, the defendant stopped providing the trucks, and the plaintiff stopped cutting timber. The plaintiff took the position that the contract was terminated by the defendant's breach. The plaintiff sued the defendant for damages for breach of contract. There were a number of issues at trial; the discussion here focuses one of the central issues the measure of damages.

The contract was very unprofitable for the plaintiff, as it had much higher start-up costs than it had anticipated. At the time of the breach, the plaintiff had been paid pursuant to the contract $108,000 for the wood it had cut, but the plaintiff claimed that it had spent about $232,000. If the contract had been fully performed, the plaintiff would have received a total of $120,000, *i.e.*, only $12,000 more than it was already paid. The evidence established that, if the plaintiff had fully performed, it would have had total expenses of $245,000 and hence lost $125,000. Relying on *Anglia Television*, the plaintiff claimed as "wasted expenditure" $124,000, being the $232,000 of expenses less the $108,000 received.]

BERGER J.: — **[1]** . . . In *Anglia Television Ltd. v. Reed*, [1972] 1 Q.B. 60, Lord Denning M.R. held that a plaintiff had the right to sue for expenditures made in part performance. He said, at p. 64: "If he has not suffered any loss of profits — or if he cannot prove what his profits would have been — he can claim in the alternative the expenditure which has been thrown away, that is, wasted, by reason of the breach. . . .

[2] But Domtar has raised an issue not reached by these cases. Mr. Harvey says that even if there was a breach of contract Domtar is not bound to compensate Bowlay for their expenses — at any rate certainly not the full measure of those expenses — because the operation was losing money. If it had continued it would have lost more money. Domtar says that in fact Bowlay's losses on full performance would have exceeded its losses in expenses "thrown away." It is said that in these circumstances Bowlay cannot recover any damages.

[3] May a claim for expenses made in part performance be sustained where the defendant shows that the plaintiff was engaged in a losing operation and, even if there had been no breach and the contract had been fully performed, would inevitably have suffered a loss on the contract? Should the defendant be entitled to have the losses that would have been incurred deducted from the plaintiff's claim for compensation for expenses made in part performance? What if the plaintiff's losses, in the event the contract had been fully performed, would have exceeded the claim for expenses? To what extent should the plaintiff be entitled to recover in such a case? . . . Mr. Shaw says that the plaintiff should be entitled to recover all of its expenses by way of outlay, and that no deduction should be made even if the plaintiff would have suffered a net loss if the contract had been fully performed. He relies on a judgment of the United States Supreme Court: *United States v. Behan* (1884), 110 U.S. 338. . . .

[4] Professor L.L. Fuller and W.R. Perduc, Jr., writing in "Reliance Interest in Contract Damages", 46 *Yale Law J.* 52 (1937) concluded that the principle enunciated in the *Behan* case compromised the basic notion of *restitutio in integrum*. They urged, at p. 79, that the law ought to reflect the following proposition: "We will not in a suit for reimbursement for losses incurred in reliance on a contract knowingly put the plaintiff in a better position than he would have occupied had the contract been fully performed."

[5] In *L. Albert & Son v. Armstrong Rubber Co.* (1949), 178 F. 2d 182 (U.S.C.A. 2d Cir.), Chief Justice Learned Hand . . . held that on a claim for compensation for expenses in part performance the defendant was entitled to deduct whatever he can prove the plaintiff would have lost if the contract had been fully performed. Chief Justice Learned Hand expressed his concurrence with the formula laid down by Professor Fuller. . . .

[6] It has been said by the United States Circuit Court of Appeals in *Dade County, Florida v. Palmer & Baker Engineers, Inc.* (1965), 339 F. 2d 208 (U.S.C.A. 5th Cir.) that where the defendant alleges that full performance by the plaintiff would have resulted in a net loss to the plaintiff, the burden of proof is on the defendant. Accepting then that the onus is on the defendant, what has the defendant been able to prove in the case at bar? . . .

[7] The law of contract compensates a plaintiff for damages resulting from the defendant's breach; it does not compensate a plaintiff for damages resulting from his making a bad bargain. Where it can be seen that the plaintiff would have incurred a loss on the contract as a whole, the expenses he has incurred are losses flowing from entering into the contract, not losses flowing from the defendant's breach. In these circumstances, the true consequence of the defendant's breach is that the plaintiff is released from his obligation to complete the contract — or in other words, he is saved from incurring further losses.

[8] If the law of contract were to move from compensating for the consequences of breach to compensating for the consequences of entering into contracts, the law would run contrary to the normal expectations of the world of commerce. The burden of risk would be shifted from the plaintiff to the defendant. The defendant would become the insurer of the plaintiff's enterprise. Moreover, the amount of the damages would increase not in relation to the gravity or consequences of the breach but in relation to the inefficiency with which the plaintiff carried out the contract. The greater his expenses owing to inefficiency, the greater the damages.

[9] The fundamental principle upon which damages are measured under the law of contract is *restitutio in integrum*. The principle contended for here by the plaintiff would entail the award of damages not to compensate the plaintiff but to punish the defendant. So it has been argued that a defendant ought to be able to insist that the plaintiff's damages should not include any losses that would have been incurred if the contract had been fully performed. According to Treitel *Law of Contract* 3d ed. (1970) at p. 798: "It is uncertain whether the plaintiff can recover his entire expenses if those exceed the benefit which he would have derived from the contract, had there been no breach." Ogus, in *The Law of Damages* (1973) has said at p. 347 that "it is not yet clear whether English law imposes this limitation."

[10] The tendency in American law is to impose such a limitation. And I think Canadian law ought to impose it too.

[11] The onus is on the defendant. But the onus has been met. The only conclusion that I can reach on the evidence is that if the plaintiff had fully performed the contract its losses would have continued at the rate that the figures show they were running at up to the time when the logging operation was closed down.

[12] The case at bar takes the matter farther than any of the cases cited, because here the defendant has shown that the losses the plaintiff would have incurred on full performance exceed the expenditures actually made in part performance. No award for loss of outlay can therefore be made. There is no escaping the logic of this: see *Corbin on Contracts* (1964) pp. 205-6: "If, on the other hand, it is proved that full performance would have resulted in a net loss to the plaintiff, the recoverable damages should not include the amount of this loss. *If the amount of his expenditure at the date of breach is less than the expected net loss, he should be given judgment for nominal damages only*. If the expenditures exceed this loss, he should be given judgment for the excess."

[In the result, **BERGER J.** awarded only nominal damages to the plaintiff. An appeal to the British Columbia Court of Appeal was dismissed: [1982] 6 W.W.R. 528, 135 D.L.R. (3d) 179.]

NOTES

1. *Bowlay Logging* was apparently the first reported Canadian case to mention Fuller and Perdue's article.

2. By awarding the wasted expenditure minus the loss on full performance on a money-losing contract, *Bowlay Logging* actually puts the plaintiff in the same position as it would have been in if the contract had been fully performed. This point may be illustrated by a simple set of examples:

   Suppose the plaintiff agrees to build a bridge for the defendant-owner for $90,000. The defendant orders the plaintiff to stop work, and the defendant has at the time of breach paid nothing. Assume for the following situations that the costs increase in direct proportion to the amount of work done, so that two-thirds of the bridge costs two-thirds of the full cost.

   (i) If the cost to the builder for the complete bridge would be $70,000, what damages would the builder get if the owner stopped the project before any work was done?

   (ii) If the complete bridge would cost the builder $75,000 and the contract is cancelled by the owner when the job is two-thirds complete, what damages would the builder recover?

   (iii) If the complete bridge would cost the builder $105,000 and the contract is cancelled by the owner when the job is two-thirds done, what damages would the builder recover?

   Situation (i) is like *Victory Motors*, in that the builder will get the loss of profits. Situation (ii) also involves a profitable contract and can be simply solved by applying *Wertheim v. Chicoutimi Pulp*, giving wasted expenditure to the time of breach *plus* loss of profit on full performance. Situation (iii) is an unprofitable contract as in *Bowlay Logging*, in which the builder should get wasted expenditure to the time of breach minus the loss on full performance.

3. Conceptually, the approach in each of these three situations is the same: determine the wasted expenditure (if any) and add the profit (or deduct the loss) that the builder would have had if allowed to finish the job. In each example the builder is to be put in the same position as if the contract were fully performed.

4. These examples illustrate the care that must be taken in determining what constitutes "loss of profits" or expectation-based measure of damages in different factual situations.

5. *Bowlay Logging* and *Anglia Television* raise the question of when courts will not follow the normal rule of awarding expectation-based damages. This is a question to which we shall return repeatedly in these materials.

HORNE v. MIDLAND RAILWAY COMPANY

(1873), L.R. 8 C.P. 131
(Exch. Ch., Kelly C.B., Martin B., Blackburn and Mellor JJ.,
Pigott B., Lush J. and Cleasby B.)

[The plaintiffs, boot manufacturers, were under contract to supply a quantity of boots for the eventual use of the French army. The price was 4s per pair — an unusually high price reflecting the demand caused by the Franco-Prussian war. The boots were to be delivered by 3 February 1871. An armistice was signed on 28 January 1871, ending the war and the French army's need for boots, and causing boot prices to fall. The plaintiffs sent the boots to the defendant's railway station in time for delivery as required by the contract of sale. When the contract of carriage was made, the plaintiff's employee told the defendant's employee that the boots had to be delivered by 3 February 1871 or they would be "thrown on the plaintiffs' hands", *i.e.*, the buyer could refuse delivery after that date. The defendant's employee was not told that the plaintiffs had an exceptionally profitable contract. The boots were not delivered until 4 February and were, consequently, refused by the buyer. The plaintiffs sold them at 2s 9d per pair — the best price obtainable (and the market price on 3 and 4 February) — and sued the defendant for the difference. The defendants paid enough into court to cover any ordinary losses, but the plaintiffs claimed a further £2,600 for the whole loss. The Court of Common Pleas gave judgment for the defendants and error was brought from that judgment. The Court of Exchequer Chamber held, 5-2, that the plaintiffs could not recover more than their "ordinary losses". The defendants had not had notice of the exceptional nature of the plaintiffs' contract. Three judges also held that no notice would have been sufficient unless the defendants had contracted to be liable for the greater amount. Blackburn J. said during argument:

> It is clear the plaintiff gave notice that it was important that goods should be delivered on the 3rd, but he gave no notice of the extraordinary nature of the contract. There is a substantial consideration involved; if the carrier has notice of an extraordinary risk he may perhaps charge a higher rate of carriage to cover it. The real meaning of the limitation as to damages is that the defendant shall not be bound to pay more than he received a reasonable consideration for undertaking the risk of at the time of making the contract.

And in his judgment he said:

> It does not appear that there has been any case in which it has been affirmatively held that in consequence of such a notice the plaintiff could recover exceptional damages. The counsel for the plaintiffs could not refer to any such case, and I know of none. If it were necessary to decide the point, I . . . agree . . . that in order that the notice may have any effect, it must be given under such circumstances, as that an actual contract arises on the part of the defendant to bear the exceptional loss.]

KELLY C.B.: — [1] I am of opinion that the judgment of the court below must be affirmed. The rules by which this case must be determined are the creatures of authority, and we have not so much to consider in determining it what might be just or unjust, reasonable or unreasonable, under the circumstances of the case, in the absence of previous decisions, as to consider the cases that have been decided on the subject and deduce from them the general principles that must govern our judgment. It must, in the first place, be noticed that this is the case of a railway company, though it does not seem to have occurred to the court below, or to the counsel in arguing the case there, that there was any material difference between the case of a railway company and that of any ordinary person who had contracted for the delivery of goods. It therefore becomes incumbent upon us to consider what is the nature of the ordinary contract between the consignor of goods and the carrier, and what is the obligation imposed upon a railway company in respect of the carriage of goods of an ordinary character such as those in the present case . . .

[2]   A question of very great importance has been raised in the course of the argument, to which it is proper to refer, though, for reasons I shall presently state, I do not think it will ultimately become necessary to decide it — that is to say, the question what the position of a railway company is when goods are entrusted to it

for carriage with an intimation of the consequences of non-delivery, such as it was argued on behalf of the plaintiffs existed in the present case. . . .

[3] It does not appear to me that the railway company has any power, such as was suggested, to decline to receive the goods after such a notice, unless an extraordinary rate of carriage be paid. Of course they may enter into a contract, if they will, to pay any amount of damages for non-performance of their contract in consideration of an increased rate of carriage, if the consignors be willing to pay it; but in the absence of any such contract expressly entered into, there being no power on the part of the company to refuse to accept the goods, or to compel payment of an extraordinary rate of carriage by the consignor, it does not appear to me any contract to be liable to more than the ordinary amount of damages can be implied from mere receipt of the goods after such a notice as before mentioned.

[4] For these reasons, even if the notice given in the present case could be taken as having the effect contended for by [counsel for the plaintiff], I do not think, in the absence of any expressed or implied contract by the company to be liable to these damages, that there could be any such liability imposed upon them. . . .

[5] Under those circumstances, in the absence of any notice to the defendants of the exceptional nature of the contract into which the plaintiffs had entered, I think the plaintiffs are only entitled to nominal damages, unless, perhaps, in respect of expenses, if any, that were incurred, which would be amply covered by the amount paid into court. It appears to me that very serious consequences might result from making a railway company liable upon a mere notice that the consignor is under contract to deliver, such as that in the present case, for an indefinite amount of damages arising out of a contract of a highly exceptional nature, entered into under very special circumstances.

MARTIN B.: — [6] . . . If some other person had delivered a similar quantity of shoes to the defendants for carriage on the same day as the plaintiffs, not being under contract to deliver them, it is admitted he could only recover £20. How can it be, in the absence of an express contract to that effect, that by reason of a mere communication to the defendants that the goods would be thrown on the plaintiffs' hands if not delivered in time, so widely a different liability can arise upon contracts for which the consideration is the same, and in all other respects precisely similar?

BLACKBURN and **MELLOR JJ.** agreed with **KELLY C.B.** and **MARTIN B.**; **PIGOTT B.** and **LUSH J.** dissented.

NOTES

1. Kelly C.B. refers to the fact that the defendant, the railway company, as a common carrier, may have had no power to refuse to take the goods of the plaintiff. At common law there were a number of "common callings" of which the innkeeper and the carrier were the most prominent. A common carrier was a person who was bound to carry the goods of anybody who requested him to do so, with the price of carriage generally determined by the weight of the goods and the distance to be travelled. Kelly C.B. is concerned that in this situation — where the price charged is not varied merely on receiving notice of higher potential liability — it would be unfair to force the carrier to assume greater risks with no right to demand extra payment merely by giving notice of potentially greater losses arising from a breach of contract. Blackburn J. makes a similar point, that "the defendant shall not be bound to pay more than he received a reasonable consideration for undertaking the risk of at the time of making the contract."

2. Common carriers like the railways were among the first industries to be closely regulated by the state. The amounts they could charge were often regulated by legislatively imposed tariffs. As the next case indicates, for some carriers standard terms can also be fixed by government regulation (though since that case was decided, de-regulation has removed some of the statutory restrictions). While the decision in *Horne* is that the notice the defendant received was insufficient to impose the "extra" liability on it, the court's concerns for the effect of notice reflect the need to keep the risk allocation aspect of *Hadley v. Baxendale* clearly in mind. If one makes the assumption that, either through regulation or competition, rates for the carriage of goods will reflect the normal risks inherent in the activity, the mere giving of notice, if it should change the normal risks without permitting the carrier to charge more, affects the underlying pricing structure of the industry.

3. Kelly C.B. also raises concerns about the "very serious consequences" that might result from making a railway company liable. Railway companies were the largest and most important companies of the nineteenth century. The economic concerns of railway companies affected the development of significant parts of tort, contract and property law in that era. See Morton Horwitz, *The Transformation of American Law 1780 – 1860* (Cambridge, MA: Harvard University Press, 1977).

    Do you think that owners of railway companies would have supported the decision in *Horne*? If the court came to the contrary decision and imposed liability merely because notice was received, how would the lawyers for the railway company have responded in terms of drafting their standard form contracts for the carriage of goods?

CORNWALL GRAVEL CO. LTD. v. PUROLATOR COURIER LTD.

(1978), 18 O.R. (2d) 551, 83 D.L.R. (3d) 267 (H.C.J.)

R.E. HOLLAND J.: — **[1]** This is an action for damages for breach of contract and negligence brought by Cornwall Gravel against Purolator and Bernard Levert and Rheal Boisvenue who, at the material time, were employees of Purolator, arising out of the late delivery of a tender prepared by the plaintiff for submission to the Ontario Ministry of the Environment.

[2]   It is admitted that had the tender been delivered in time Cornwall Gravel would have been awarded a contract for $698,246.79 and would have made a profit on the contract of $70,000.

[3]   The information for tenderers which governed the submission of the tender provided that tenders were to be delivered on or before 3 p.m. Toronto time on October 2, 1973, at the office of the contracts officer of the Ministry in Toronto and further that under no circumstances would any tender be considered which was received after that time. The tender in question was delivered by Purolator at 3:17 p.m. on October 2, 1973, and was therefore rejected.

[4]   The tender was ready for delivery at Cornwall shortly after 6 p.m. on October 1, 1973. Cornwall Gravel had used the services of Purolator to deliver tenders on prior occasions. Ronald Paymemp, who was at the time the controller of Cornwall Gravel, telephoned the office of Purolator around noon on October 1 to advise that there was a pick-up for Toronto that evening. Cornwall Gravel had been supplied by Purolator with bill of lading forms. The bill of lading for the tender was written up by Cornwall Gravel and reads, on its face, in part, as follows:

[The judgment reproduces the writing on the bill of lading. The document stated that the goods are received by the carrier, specified the point of origin and destination, and contained a clause that read, "Maximum liability $1.50 per pound unless declared valuation states otherwise. If a value is declared see conditions on reverse hereof." The bill of lading also noted the required time of delivery and the signatures of the shipper and the agent of the carrier were added to it.]

[5]   On the reverse the bill reads, in part, as follows:

VALUE

Unless otherwise specifically agreed to in writing the carrier will not transport any goods declared to have a value in excess of $250. Enquiries for such service should be directed to the carrier's closest regional office.

When the tender was picked up by Boisvenue [the driver employed by Purolator to make pickups], there was a conversation between Paymemp, John Fleming, who was an engineer employed by Cornwall Gravel and who had worked on the tender, and Boisvenue. Paymemp and Fleming wished to make sure that the tender would be delivered on time. If there was any question about late delivery one or the other of them would have driven with the tender to Toronto. They were assured by Boisvenue that there would be no problem with delivery. Paymemp had inserted the time [on the front of the bill of lading] as 12 noon rather than 3 p.m. to make the time consistent with other tenders that had previously been delivered to Toronto for other departments where the time for delivery was 12 noon. There was no conversation with Boisvenue or anyone from Purolator as to the amount of the tender.

[6]   Boisvenue . . . admitted on discovery that he was told that the document was very important, . . . and that he knew that a tender was "fairly important" and that it had to be delivered by a certain time.

[7]   [Due to the breakdown of a truck, the] envelope finally arrived in Toronto about 10 o'clock in the morning but by that time routine deliveries had already started in Toronto and the envelope was not delivered until 3:17 p.m. . . .

[8]   There are a number of sections of the Schedule that are important to a decision and to an interpretation of the words "maximum liability $1.50 per pound unless declared valuation states otherwise".

SCHEDULE A

1. The carrier of the goods herein described is liable for any loss thereof or damage or injury thereto, except as herein provided.

. . .

5. The carrier is not liable for loss, damage or delay to any of the goods described in the bill of lading caused by an act of God, the Queen's or public enemies, riots, strikes, defect or inherent vice in the goods, the act or default of the shipper or owner, the authority of law, quarantine or differences in weights of grain, seed, live stock or other commodities caused by natural shrinkage.

. . .

9. Subject to paragraph 10, the amount of any loss, damage or injury for which the carrier is liable, whether or not the loss, damage or injury results from negligence, shall be computed on the basis of,

    (a) the value of the goods at the place and time of shipment including the freight and other charges if paid; or

    (b) where a value lower than that referred to in clause *a* has been represented in writing by the consignor or has been agreed upon, such lower value.

10. Subject to paragraph 11, the amount of any loss or damage computed under clause *a* or *b* of paragraph 9 shall not exceed $1.50 per pound unless a higher value is declared on the face of the bill of lading by the consignor.

. . .

13. The carrier is not liable for loss, damage, injury or delay to any goods carried under the bill of lading unless notice thereof setting out particulars of the origin, destination and date of shipment of the goods and the estimated amount claimed in respect of such loss, damage, injury or delay is given in writing to the carrier at the point of delivery or at the point or origin within ninety days after the delivery of the goods, or, in the case of failure to make delivery, within ninety days after a reasonable time for delivery has elapsed.

. . .

15. No carrier is bound to carry any documents, specie or any articles of extraordinary value unless by a special agreement to do so and, where the nature and stipulated value of the goods is disclosed to him, the duty of obtaining such special agreement is on the carrier.

[9] It seems to me looking at the sections as set out above as a whole that there is a distinction between loss, damage or injury on the one hand and delay on the other and that the limitation of liability of $1.50 per pound applies only to loss, damage or injury to the goods themselves. The word "injury" may seem strange but I suppose could well apply to a shipment of livestock. Liability is excluded for delay under para. 5 in certain circumstances set out therein. None of these circumstances existed in the present case. I therefore conclude on the wording of the sections of the Schedule itself that a limitation of liability in this case only applied to the goods being transported and did not cover consequential loss due to delay. In coming to this conclusion I have not construed any of the provisions *contra proferentem*. . .

[10] There remains the question whether or not this loss was in the contemplation of the parties and this takes us back to *Hadley v. Baxendale* [*supra*] . . . [The judge here set out the statement of the rule in that case.]

[11] In the present case Purolator, through its employee, Boisvenue, knew that the item to be transported was a tender and that it was required to be delivered by 12 noon on October 2, 1973. Boisvenue was told of the importance of the document and must have realized that if delivered late the tender would be worthless and a contract could well be lost. In these particular circumstances it is my opinion that "the special circumstances under which the contract was actually made were communicated by the plaintiff to the defendant" and the damage which in fact flowed from the breach of such contract was damage "which they would reasonably contemplate . . . which would ordinarily follow from a breach of contract under those special circumstances, so known and communicated". . . .

[12] For the above reasons there will be judgment for the plaintiff for $70,000, with interest . . .

[Appeals to the Court of Appeal and Supreme Court of Canada were dismissed without written reasons. Laskin C.J.C., in the latter court, after hearing counsel for the appellant, said, "We are not persuaded that there was any error in the disposition made by the Courts below": [1980] 2 S.C.R. 118*n*, 120 D.L.R. (3d) 575*n*, affirming (1979), 28 O.R. (2d) 704*n*, 115 D.L.R. (3d) 511*n*.]

NOTES AND QUESTIONS

1. Carriers, including couriers, have usually been held responsible for a narrower range of losses than vendors under the rule in *Hadley v. Baxendale*. This difference can be justified on the ground that carriers generally have less knowledge of the plaintiff's business — there was no evidence, for example, that Boisvenue (let alone his employer Purolator Courier) had any idea of the amount of the tender of Cornwall Gravel. It turned out that the tender was not just "important", but *really important*, to the tune of $70,000.

   A strong argument can be made that carriers should not normally be responsible for such a loss. On the other hand, putting the loss on the shipper is likely to put the loss on the party who can most clearly see its extent and take steps to protect itself. Many firms faced with the need to deliver an important document in time, send it with an employee rather than entrust it to the mail or to anyone else.

   In a subsequent decision, *B.D.C. Ltd. v. Hofstrand Farms*, [1986] 1 S.C.R. 228, 26 D.L.R. (4th) 1, the Supreme Court of Canada refused to hold a courier liable for loss resulting from delayed delivery, distinguishing *Cornwall Gravel* as a case where the courier had "actual knowledge of 'special circumstances'". In *B.D.C. v. Hofstrand Farms* the Supreme Court emphasized that Cornwall Gravel, unlike Hofstrand Farms, had communicated to the courier its reliance and the nature of the loss that would result from late delivery. In dismissing the claims, Estey J. wrote (pp. 245-46 S.C.R.):

   > In . . . *Cornwall Gravel Co. v. Purolator Courier Ltd.* (1978), 83 D.L.R. (3d) 267, affirmed [1980] 2 S.C.R. 118, the defendant courier was held liable for profits lost when it failed to deliver the plaintiff's tender on time. There, the courier had been told that the package contained a tender and that delivery had to be made before a certain time. In the ordinary course of events, it would be obvious that unless the tender arrived before the deadline, a contract could be lost. Therefore, the defendant had actual knowledge of "special circumstances", and this fact justified holding it liable for the plaintiff's lost profits.
   >
   > This appeal, however, involves very different circumstances. The . . . courier had no knowledge of the fact that the envelope contained a Crown grant, and even if it had, unlike a tender there is nothing about a Crown grant which would suggest to the reasonable person in the position of the courier that its failure to effect timely delivery could result in consequential lost profits to anyone. Assuming even that the [courier] had had notice both of the nature of the contents of the package and of the existence of a contract between the Crown grantee and a third party whose performance depended on timely delivery, in this case the terms of that "improvident" contract . . . from which the economic loss flowed were so extraordinary that they must fall within the category of "special circumstances" requiring communication to the defendant under the rule in *Hadley v. Baxendale*. . . . It is clear, therefore (there being no such communication), that if the parties had been in a relationship of contractual privity, the losses complained of would not have been foreseeable. They are no more foreseeable because the respondent sued in tort.

   Prof :

2. It is clear that Purolator Courier believed that the terms of the contract, set out in the bill of lading and the Schedule, protected it from this type of liability for consequential loss. While Holland J. denied that he was taking a *contra proferentem* interpretation of the contract (a narrow interpretation "against the drafter"), it is apparent that he was determined to hold Purolator Courier liable, despite the wording of the exemption clauses. (Note: many lawyers, judges and even spell-check programs spell "proferentem" as "proferentum" or "proferuntum" and (who knows) in even more exotic ways. The word comes from the Latin word for the person who proffers something to another, *i.e.*, the "proferens"; "proferentem" is the accusative case of this word.)

   One consequence of the decision in *Cornwall Gravel* is that Purolator (and other couriers) changed the terms of the bill of lading to attempt make it absolutely clear that it excluded by the contract the risk of liability it incurred in that case. The terms used by Purolator in 1995, after the decision of the Supreme Court, were redrafted to include the following:

CONDITION 3   **APPLICABLE LAW**

The contract for the carriage of goods listed in the bill of lading shall be deemed to include and be subject to the terms and conditions prescribed by law for the jurisdiction where the goods originate which, if Newfoundland, Nova Scotia, New Brunswick, Prince Edward Island, Saskatchewan and British Columbia, the regulations made pursuant to the Motor Carrier Act of each province; Quebec, the bill of lading form and terms and conditions approved by the Quebec Transport Commission; Ontario, the Truck Transportation Act and Regulations thereto; Manitoba, The Highway Traffic Act and Regulations thereto; Alberta, the Motor Transport Act and Regulations thereto.

CONDITION 4   **SPECIAL AGREEMENT**

The parties agree that notwithstanding any disclosure of nature or value of the goods, the amount of any loss or damage, including consequential, incidental or indirect damages, loss of earnings or profits, resulting from the loss of or damage to the goods and/or misdelivery, failure to deliver or delay in delivery of the goods, shall not exceed the maximum liability of the carrier aforesaid.

CONDITION 6   **MODIFICATION OF CONTRACT**

This bill of lading constitutes the entire contract between the carrier and the shipper, and no agent, servant, or representative of the carrier has authority to alter, modify or waive any provision of this contract.

This redrafted clause has provided couriers with some protection in situations of failure to deliver tender documents, at least in situations where there is no specific discussion with the driver picking up the package; see *Cathcart Inspection Services v. Purolator Courier* (1981), 34 O.R. (2d) 187, 128 D.L.R. (3d) 227 (H.C.J.), affirmed (1982), 39 O.R. (2d) 656, 139 D.L.R. (3d) 371 (C.A.). We shall spend a considerable amount of time investigating such clauses later in the materials, especially in Chapter 6.

Ontario regulations also govern this type of transaction; Schedule 1, *Carriage of Goods Regulation*, O. Reg. 643/05, made under the *Highway Traffic Act*, R.S.O. 1990, c. H.8 provides:

9. Valuation

Subject to Article 10 [which deals with the situation where the shipper declares a value], the amount of any loss or damage for which the carrier is liable, whether or not the loss or damage results from negligence, shall be the lesser of,

i.   the value of the goods at the place and time of shipment, including the freight and other charges if paid, and

ii. $4.41 per kilogram computed on the total weight of the shipment.

Does the solution adopted by the legislature and the industry make it at all likely that any customer will have the slightest idea of the limit of Purolator's liability? Is this costly type of contractual revision, assuming it is effective, a socially useful expenditure of resources?

For the moment it is sufficient to consider the following questions:

(a)   If the focus of our inquiry is at least in part on what Cornwall Gravel reasonably expected from Purolator, is it likely, given the way in which contracts of this type are usually made, that such expectations would be changed if the contract contained the clauses now in effect rather than those in effect in 1973?

(b) Couriers engage in extensive advertising. Purolator, for example, in advertising at the time that the litigation was being conducted, prominently featured the phrase: "When it's just *got* to get there." The plain and intended inference is that in such circumstances one can safely trust Purolator. What is the more important determinant of the expectations of a customer, an advertising campaign or a fine-print clause in an unread and in any case incomprehensible contract? The carrier may be inviting special reliance by its claim to be completely reliable.

It would seem couriers have become more cautious in the claims that they make in their advertisements. In 1995, a Purolator advertisement stated: "The 10:30 a.m. Quicker Sticker Guarantee*: We promise. Now, we'll deliver by 10:30 a.m. the very next business day or your money back. . .". A footnote appears in very small print at the bottom of the advertisement: "*Contact your Purolator Customer Service Representative for service points, terms and conditions."

This catchy slogan may have the legal advantage of containing an apparent limitation of liability, as well as advertising the service.

(c) Notice the 1995 terms set out above: "Condition 6, Modification of Contract". One of the most difficult problems in contractual planning in business is the near impossibility of controlling employees like Purolator's driver, Boisvenue. If you were employed by Purolator to advise it on the legal aspects of the conduct of its business, what would you advise Purolator to tell its drivers to say? Consider the possibility that an employee like Boisvenue may be compensated by receiving a small commission for all the business he brings in, and that he is likely trained to be "customer friendly".

3. The courier industry in Canada handles over 2 million packages of all kinds every day. Any of the large courier companies will accept several hundred thousand packages a day. While recent figures are not available, it was estimated in 1984 that about two per cent of these packages are delivered late or lost. See McTavish, "Exemption Clauses: Are Couriers Fair Game?" in *Law in Transition: Contracts*, Special Lectures (1984) Law Society of Upper Canada, 65 at 77. Does this fact help you to decide what liability to impose on Purolator?

4. There are two principal ways of covering the risks of loss arising from delays and the loss of goods during shipment. One way is for the shipper to purchase insurance (or assume the risk of loss itself); another is for the carrier to assume the risk. If we ignore for the moment the fact that some kinds of insurance coverage simply are not available, it is generally cheaper for the shipper to purchase "first party" insurance — the first type — rather than for the carrier to purchase "third party" insurance. You can understand this if you think about insurance as the buying of risks. It will cost more to buy insurance for an unknown and possibly large risk than to buy insurance for a known risk. The shipper has the best information on the risk, so its insurance will be cheaper than the carrier's. (If the carrier offers insurance to the shipper — as many couriers and Canada Post do to the person who mails a parcel — that is first party insurance, not third party insurance.) In light of this point, consider the following questions:

(a) Should the court encourage or discourage one or another form of insurance?

(b) What kind of insurance does the judgment in *Horne* encourage the shipper to take out?

(c) What kind of insurance does the judgment in *Cornwall Gravel* encourage?

(d) The contractual provisions introduced by Purolator are a direct response to the insurance problem. If, as they do, courts express concern about the enforceability of clauses like those in the Purolator contract, are they being entirely consistent in the messages they are sending to contracting parties?

(e) In light of the judgment in *Cornwall Gravel*, would it have mattered if the damages that the shipper suffered were $700,000 or $7,000,000?

5. The decision in *Horne v. Midland Railway* suggests that the issue of how far to go in awarding damages is not to be determined simply by asking how much the defendant knows or ought to know. Kelly C.B., for example, mentions the fact that the defendant was bound to receive the goods. What bothered Kelly C.B. was the idea that the obligation of the railway could be increased (if knowledge sufficed to make it liable for the full loss suffered by the plaintiff), yet the railway could neither refuse to carry the goods nor charge more for the increased risk. If the railway is to be liable for more than the normal loss for late delivery, then, in accordance with the analysis of Kelly C.B., the plaintiff will have to show that the railway accepted the risk. The best evidence will be a second contract to pay the increased damages: that is, an express contract to run the increased risk for late delivery.

Returning to *Hadley v. Baxendale*, one can begin to see where the modern problems arose. The actual test stated by Alderson B. uses the word "reasonable". The damages that are "reasonably contemplated" are recoverable by the plaintiff. The word "reasonable" crops up repeatedly in the law, and caution is called for in determining its meaning. It is possible to see him as saying much the same as Kelly C.B in *Horne v. Midland Railway*. A few lines below the famous passage, Alderson B. is dealing with the problem of the communication of the knowledge of the "special circumstances", exactly the problem of *Cornwall Gravel*; he says: "For, had the special circumstances been known, the parties might have specially provided for the breach of contract by special terms as to the damages in that case; and of this advantage it would be very unjust to deprive them."

If one accepts the analysis of *Horne v. Midland Railway* and the latter passage from the judgment of Alderson B as the general response to the problem, the issue is transformed. What becomes important is not the factual knowledge of the defendant, but the extent to which it is *"proper"* (to use the term in *The Heron II*) to hold the defendant responsible. *Horne* suggests that there is a general sense that a railway should not have responsibility for delivering goods late unless, as in the words of Alderson B., the parties "specially provided for the breach," that is, had a chance to bargain about it.

The focus then is not just on a factual enquiry, but the extent to which it is "appropriate", "proper", "fair", "just" or "reasonable", for any particular promisor to be made responsible for the losses caused by its breach. In dealing with the problems of *Cornwall Gravel*, the issue is not just the knowledge of Purolator, but the extent to which it is appropriate to impose liability on the courier in the circumstances of that case. The factors that we might consider to resolve that question include:

(a) the extent to which Cornwall Gravel reasonably relied on Purolator to get the tender there on time;

(b) the extent to which it would be reasonable for Cornwall Gravel to assume that Purolator was *guaranteeing* prompt delivery when the same charge was made as for an ordinary delivery of, so far as we can tell, birthday greetings to one's grandfather; and

(c) the extent to which Purolator could be said to be caught by surprise by being held liable.

6. In *Kienzle v. Stringer* (1981), 35 O.R. (2d) 85 (C.A.) (leave to appeal to S.C.C. refused (1982), 130 D.L.R. (3d) 272, 42 N.R. 352) the Ontario Court of Appeal, in a judgment written by Zuber J.A., said (p. 90 O.R.) [emphasis added]:

It may be helpful to recognize that in using the terms "reasonably foreseeable" or "within the reasonable contemplation of the parties" courts are not often concerned with what the parties in fact foresaw or contemplated. (I leave aside those cases where the disclosure of special facts may lead to the conclusion that a party has assumed an extraordinary risk.) The governing term is "reasonable" and what is reasonably foreseen or reasonably contemplated is a matter to be determined by a court. *These terms necessarily include more policy than fact as courts attempt to find some fair measure of compensation to be paid to those who suffer damages by those who cause them.*

Do you agree that the express recognition of the policy element of the rule in *Hadley v. Baxendale* is a welcome development? Are such policy decisions appropriate for courts? Could they conceivably be more appropriate for anybody else?

7. There are a number of situations in which identifiable problems of remoteness recur. One of these is the position of carriers, which has already been discussed. Another is the case where the plaintiff's losses are large because the plaintiff lacks the financial resources to protect itself from further losses, and is, for example, forced into bankruptcy. Thus, in *Freedhof v. Pomalift Industries Ltd.*, [1971] 2 O.R. 773, 19 D.L.R. (3d) 153 (C.A.), the plaintiff's ski business was sold by a mortgagee because the plaintiff could not meet the mortgage payments. This consequence was the result of the defendant's failure to install an operating ski-lift in breach of a contract to do so. The trial judge awarded the plaintiff compensation for the revenue lost because the ski-lift was not operating, but refused to award anything in respect of the loss caused by the plaintiff's inability to meet the mortgage payments. The Court of Appeal held that the losses arising from the plaintiff's impecuniosity were unrecoverable. In giving the judgment of the court, Kelly J.A. said:

    > In the instant case, even if the plaintiff be entitled to be compensated for damages in the amount of the lost revenue, the loss of property through the sale by the [mortgagee] because of the plaintiff's failure to keep the mortgage in good standing, does not entitle him to damages measured by the loss he alleges that he suffered in the sale of the property. It does not meet the test of foreseeability.

    The courts generally deny claims that arise because a plaintiff's losses are increased by its financial inability to protect itself from some of the consequences of the defendant's breach.

    There is a concern that if defendants who were sued for breach of contract were ordinarily liable for the consequences arising from the plaintiff's impecuniosity, this might cause those who are financially strong to be more reluctant to deal with businesses that are financially weak. See K. Swinton, "Foreseeability: Where Should the Award of Contracts Damages Cease?" in B. Reiter and & J. Swan, eds., *Studies in Contract Law* (Toronto: Butterworths, 1980), 61 at 77.

8. It is usually said that the knowledge of the consequences of breach must be that of the promisor at the date that the contract is made. In *Murano v. Bank of Montreal* (1995), 31 C.B.R. (3d) 1 (Gen. Div.), a bank appointed a receiver and took possession of the plaintiff's business without giving the plaintiff adequate notice. The failure to give notice was a breach of the contract between the bank and the plaintiff, and made the bank's actions in taking possession wrongful. One question before the trial judge was the application of the rule in *Hadley v. Baxendale* in the circumstances. Adams J. said, with regard to this issue:

    > But this case severely tests the reasonableness of this ancient rule because of the "at will" nature of the contractual relationships [*i.e.*, the standard demand loan that is used by all Canadian banks]. Where a party can demand full payment of a loan at will, that party can assess daily whether to break off its contractual relationship. In the case of a demand loan, it can do so without breaching its contract provided it gives reasonable notice. In that particular context, it seems strange to be thrown back to the original date of contract for the purposes of foreseeability. In fact, confining loss assessment to the formation of a long standing "at will" banking relationship seems artificial and may be inconsistent with the general trend of authority harmonizing rules in tort

and contract. Indeed, in this case, judging the foreseeability of loss in light of the Bank's knowledge closer to the date of breach is not likely to upset contractual intentions given the expectations of the parties at the date of contract formation that the plaintiffs' changing conditions would be closely monitored.

The trial decision was affirmed by the Ontario Court of Appeal, though that court specifically declined to rule on the question of whether it was sufficient if the defendant could "reasonably foresee" the damages at the time of breach, rather than at the date when the contract was made. That Court, however, concluded on the facts of the case that the losses in question were reasonably foreseeable at the time of formation of the contract: (1998), 41 O.R. (3d) 222, 163 D.L.R. (4th) 21.

Murano illustrates how the courts can use a variety of remedies to protect the plaintiff's interests. The effect of the bank's breach of contract was to deprive it of the benefit of the credit agreement, with the result that the bank committed the torts of trespass and conversion when it took possession of the plaintiff's business. One effect of this basis for liability was that the plaintiff's damages were determined only by the question of whether they were direct and immediate. Had the bank only breached the contract by, for example, suing without taking possession, the plaintiff's damages would have been minimal. The effect of the bank's torts was to make it liable for almost $4 million. The plaintiff was also able to sue the bank for breach of the obligations of confidentiality that it owed to its customer. The Court of Appeal suggested that the latter breach and the bank's actions in spreading false information about the plaintiff might have been defamatory, but noted that the point was not pleaded or argued. Because the case became a tort case, the relevant date for the calculation of damages was the date when the tort was committed so that the issue of remoteness in a contractual setting did not arise

In *Jackson v. Royal Bank of Scotland*, [2005] U.K.H.L. 3 the House of Lords reaffirmed the significance of assessing foreseeability of loss at the date of contract formation, with Lord Hope of Craighead stating (at para. 36):

> ... it is the date of the making of the contract, not the date of the breach, that was identified as the relevant date in *Hadley v Baxendale*. ... It may appear to be somewhat technical because in this case the date of the making of the contract and the date of the breach were only about two months apart. There is no evidence that the facts that were relevant to what the Bank had in reasonable contemplation changed to any significant extent between [the two dates]... But the error was an error of principle. The choice of dates is more important than the differences, if any, in those facts. The parties have the opportunity to limit their liability in damages when they are making their contract. They have the opportunity at that stage to draw attention to any special circumstances outside the ordinary course of things which they ought to have in contemplation when entering into the contract. If no cut-off point is provided by the contract, there is no arbitrary limit that can be set to the amount of the damages once the test of remoteness according to one or other of the rules in *Hadley v Baxendale* has been satisfied.

What do you think of the Ontario decision in *Murano* in light of the House of Lords decision in *Jackson*?

9.   The problem we face in contracts is faced equally in torts where language that is similar to that in the traditional *Hadley v. Baxendale* rule is also used. In *Smith v. Littlewoods Organization Ltd.*, [1987] 1 All E.R. 710 (H.L.) Lord Goff said (pp. 735-36):

> I wish to emphasize that I do not think that the problem in these cases can be solved simply through the mechanism of foreseeability. . . . It is very tempting to try to solve all problems of negligence by reference to an all-embracing criterion of foreseeability, thereby effectively reducing all decisions in this field

to questions of fact. But this comfortable solution is, alas, not open to us. The law has to accommodate all the untidy complexity of life. . . .

The following case outlines an analysis that puts the issue of remoteness in its commercial context.

CANLIN LTD. v. THIOKOL FIBRES CANADA LTD.

(1983), 40 O.R. (2d) 687, 22 B.L.R. 193
(C.A., Lacourcière, Thorson and Cory JJ.A.)

[The plaintiff, a Canadian corporation, saw a business opportunity in manufacturing and selling mesh swimming pool covers in the United States. It approached the defendant, from which it already bought synthetic fibre material, and asked if it could supply the raw material for the covers. The plaintiff told the defendant that it would be offering its customers a three-year guarantee on the pool covers and specified that the material had to: be similar in appearance and colour to that used by a competitor of the plaintiff; have a minimum life of two winter seasons; be resistant to ultraviolet radiation; and be available for the selling season in the fall of 1975. The defendant undertook to supply the material and to meet the plaintiff's requirements. The defendant delivered the material and it was used in the pool covers manufactured and sold by the plaintiff. The venture was a disaster as the material disintegrated when exposed to sunlight. The plaintiff was flooded with complaints and had to withdraw from the U.S. market.

The plaintiff sued for the losses it had suffered and included a claim for loss of future business. The trial judge held that the defendant had breached a warranty implied by the *Sale of Goods Act* s. 15(1) that the goods supplied would be "reasonably fit for their known and intended purpose." In addition to $93,000 for losses on the covers actually manufactured and sold in 1975, the trial judge included an award of $100,000 in respect of the loss of profits on expected future business for the 1976 to 1980 period. The defendant appealed the decision to allow recovery for loss of future profit.]

CORY J.A.: — [1] It is the position of the appellant Thiokol that the loss of future business profits was not a foreseeable consequence of the breach of warranty. Alternatively it is said that such a loss is not a consequence directly and naturally resulting from the breach of warranty.

Some general comments on the appellant's position

[2]   The appellant's position appears to me to be one that flies in the face of reason and common sense. Most commercial contracts pertaining to the sale and delivery of material or goods must, of necessity, be entered into with a view to making a profit in the future. To say otherwise amounts to a denial of the profit motive in the free enterprise system. The case at bar is a prime example. The plaintiff made known to the defendant that it was in business selling to distributors in the United States and that it wished to manufacture and sell a specific type of pool cover. It had determined that there was a profit to be made. It was to secure such a profit that it entered into the contract with Thiokol to supply the material for the manufacture of the pool covers.

[3]   Let us consider the unlikely scenario wherein the executive or board of directors of Thiokol sat down and discussed what was likely to happen if they supplied defective material to Tarpoly. In my view, the result would be the same in this case and should be the same in all cases whether the question the executives of Thiokol posed was framed as it would be for a tort case or one involving breach of contract. If these executives asked the "tort" question, what can we reasonably "foresee" as likely to befall Tarpoly if we supply inadequate material, the answer of reasonable men of business would be to the effect that Tarpoly would lose the profits it might expect to make on the sale of poolcovers. If the "contract" question was phrased, what can we reasonably "contemplate" as a result directly flowing from our breach of warranty, the answer would be to precisely the same effect. The Thiokol executives would have foreseen or contemplated the very effects that befell Tarpoly.

[4]   Why should not damages be awarded for the loss of that contemplated future profit? The court, I believe, would be shirking its duty if it were to say that no damages should flow because of the difficulty of calculating and assessing such damages and that they are therefore too remote. An assessment of future loss of profits must, of necessity, be an estimate. Whether such damages are awarded will depend entirely upon the court's assessment of the evidence put forward. The clearest case might base the loss of future profits upon past history of sales to the same or similar customers for same or similar items. It may be developed from evidence given by customers of a plaintiff as to what orders they would have given had the product not been defective over a period of time in the future which is deemed by the court to be reasonable and proper. The task will always be difficult but not insurmountable. It poses no greater obstacle to a court than the assessment of general damages in a serious personal injury claim.

[5]   Are there then any obstacles to the court proceeding in this way?

[**Cory J.A.** then considered the authorities relied on by the appellant and the provisions of the *Sale of Goods Act*. The Act provided:

> 51(2) The measure of damages for breach of warranty is the estimated loss directly and naturally resulting in the ordinary course of events from the breach of warranty.   *(Hadley)*

He stated his conclusion:]

[6]   There is then strong and binding authority to the effect that damages for loss of future profits may, in proper cases, be awarded as damages to be included in "the estimated loss directly and naturally resulting in the ordinary course from a breach of warranty".

[**Cory J.A.** then referred to American authorities, including *Williston on Contracts*, Vol. 11, §§ 1345, 1346, and to the *Restatement Second, Contracts*:

§ 351 Unforeseeability and Related Limitations on Damages

(1) Damages are not recoverable for loss that the party in breach did not have reason to foresee as a probable result of the breach when the contract was made.

(2) Loss may be foreseeable as a probable result of a breach because it flows from the breach

    (a)   in the ordinary course of events, or

(b) as a result of special circumstances, beyond the ordinary course of events that the party had reason to know. . . .

and concluded:]

Conclusions

[7]   In earlier times, the view of the courts, at least in the United Kingdom, seems to have been that damages for expected loss of profits arising out of a breach of contract could not be recovered on the ground that they were too remote or speculative. There is now binding authority that such damages are recoverable. The following principles can be gathered from the more recent authorities:

(1) Section 51(2) of the *Sale of Goods Act*, R.S.O. 1980, c. 462, is a legislative codification of the common law. . . .

(2) The test for determining what is a loss that directly and naturally results in the ordinary course of events from the breach of warranty may be phrased in the classical contract question, namely, are the consequences of the breach of contract such that a reasonable man at the time of the making of the contract would contemplate them as being liable to result or to be a serious possibility; or, in the classical tort question, namely, are the consequences of the act such that a reasonable man at the time the tort was committed would foresee that damages are likely to result. The questions are in reality the same. The affirmative answer to either question should lead to the same result. There is no difference between what a reasonable man might reasonably contemplate and what a reasonable man might reasonably foresee. . . . This conclusion would not apply if the contracting parties were specifically aware of certain conditions or if precise contractual provisions fixed the quantum of damages in case of a breach.

(3) Most commercial contracts are entered into with a view to making future profits. The loss of future profits arising from a breach of such a contract are recoverable if they should have been within the contemplation of the parties or ought reasonably to have been foreseen by the parties.

(4) The proof of the loss of the respective profits rests, of course, upon the plaintiff. The amount of future profits and the period for which they should be allowed will depend upon the facts of each individual case. Although such damages may be difficult to assess, it must be remembered that they arise as a result of the breach of the defendant and the court should make all reasonable efforts to assess those damages.

Application of principles to the present case

[8]   There can be no doubt that Thiokol could and should reasonably have contemplated that damages would flow from a breach of the contract. Those damages would include loss of future or prospective profits. *remoteness test*

NOTES

1.   The Supreme Court of Canada has accepted that in terms of verbal formula, the test for remoteness is the same in tort and contract, but also recognized that it is often applied in different ways because the tort context typically differs from the contractual

context. In *Asamera Oil Corp. Ltd. v. Sea Oil & General Corp.*, [1979] 1 S.C.R. 633, 89 D.L.R. (3d) 1, the Court held (at p. 673):

> We therefore approach the matter of the proper appraisal of the damages assessable in the peculiar circumstances of this case on the following basis: that the same principles of remoteness will apply to the claims made whether they sound in tort or contract subject only to special knowledge, understanding or relationship of the contracting parties or to any terms express or implied of the contractual arrangement relating to damages recoverable on breach. ...

2. In *Hamilton v. Open Window Bakery*, [2003] S.C.J. No. 72, [2004] 1 S.C.R. 303, 235 D.L.R. (4th) 193, the defendant wrongfully repudiated a contract with the plaintiff that had a 36-month term, but which allowed the defendant to terminate it on three months' notice after 18 months. In assessing damages, the trial judge considered that but for the wrongful repudiation, it was likely that contract would have lasted much longer, though his actual award of damages discounted the chance that it would last to the end of the 36-month term by 25 per cent. The Supreme Court upheld the decision of the Ontario Court of Appeal to award damages based only on the three-month notice period, concluding that where a contract might be performed in several ways, the mode which is the least burdensome to the defendant is to be used. The test is not how the defendant would most likely have performed its obligations under the contract but for its repudiation. The non-breaching party need not be restored to the position it would likely have been in but for the repudiation, but rather to the position it would have been in had the contract been performed. While the test for remoteness may be similar in both contract and tort, ordinarily the measure of damages is quite different, with tort cases generally based on restoring the plaintiff to the position it would have been in but for the tort — a reliance-like measure — while contracts-based damages are expectation-based. *damages based on expectation*

> [15] This tort-like analysis proposed by [the plaintiff] ... is not an established part of Canadian law. There are compelling reasons for this. Contractual obligations are voluntarily assumed by parties and given effect to by the courts. The failure to perform certain promised positive contractual obligations in contract law is conceptually distinct from the breach of unpromised negative obligations to not harm another's interests in tort law...

> [16] In a successful tort claim for damages, unliquidated damages are awarded to a plaintiff on the basis that the plaintiff has suffered a loss through some wrongful interference by the defendant. The plaintiff in such cases has legally protected interests that have been found by a court to be unduly compromised. In tort cases, it is widely recognized that the inquiry into what would have been but for the tort is appropriate, since the plaintiff's interest is in being restored to (or at least awarded compensation in respect of) the position the plaintiff would otherwise be in. ...

> [17] However, under the general principle applicable in breach of contracts with alternative performances enunciated above, it is not necessary that the non-breaching party be restored to the position they would likely, as a matter of fact, have been in but for the repudiation. Rather, the non-breaching party is entitled to be restored to the position they would have been in had the contract been performed.

> ...

> [19] The trial judge erred in this case in engaging in a tort-like inquiry as to what would have happened if OWB had not breached its contractual obligations to Hamilton, and in concluding that OWB would not have terminated at the earliest opportunity.

> [20] The assessment of damages required only a determination of the minimum performance the plaintiff was entitled to under the contract, i.e., the performance which was least burdensome for the defendant. The plaintiff agreed

at the outset that she was entitled to no more by contracting for a contractual term that could be truncated with notice entirely at the discretion of the defendant.

3.   In a long line of cases going back to *Central Trust Co. v. Rafuse*, [1986] S.C.J. No. 52, [1986] 2 S.C.R. 147, *sub nom. Central & Eastern Trust Co. v. Rafuse*, 31 D.L.R. (4th) 481, 42 R.P.R. 161, varied, [1988] 1 S.C.R. 1206, the Supreme Court has repeatedly said that a plaintiff can sue in either contract or tort. (As we shall see in Chapter 5, there are serious problems in giving effect to this choice.) Arbour J. mentions none of these cases. If she had noticed those cases, what should the plaintiff's damages be? If the "rule" applied by Arbour J. is a rule of law where what might have happened is, in spite of what the trial judge held to be probable course of the parties' relation, irrelevant, what about the rule, as stated in *Central Trust v. Rafuse*, that a plaintiff has a choice?

4.   If you had been present as corporate counsel for Thiokol Fibres at the meeting of the board imagined by Cory J.A., what advice would you have offered at the end of the discussion?

Lost Enjoyment and Non-Economic Interests

We now return to the issue of non-economic or non-pecuniary interests that was the focus of the decision of the House of Lords in *Ruxley*, above, and consider some of the background to that case.

In dealing with damages for breach of contract, the courts have tended, as *Peevyhouse v. Garland Coal* illustrated, to ignore what is often referred to as "non-economic" or "non-pecuniary" losses. The traditional unwillingness of the courts to award damages in contract cases for what is variously described as "non-economic" or "non-pecuniary" loss, "mental suffering" or "distress", or "inconvenience" or "loss of enjoyment", has been reduced, but objections to such awards are often heard and the basis for this type of award is by no means clear. The courts continue to express concerns about not "opening the floodgates" and keeping narrow the range of cases in which such interests may be recognized.

Any contract can provide the promisee with the prospect of benefits that cannot easily be measured in purely monetary terms. Mr. and Mrs. Peevyhouse might, for example, have wanted the land that was strip-mined by Garland Coal to be restored because that would give them enjoyment or aesthetic pleasure. The majority decision in that case is consistent with the inference (i) that Mr. and Mrs. Peevyhouse did not have this goal in mind when they insisted that the contract contain the clause obliging Garland to level the land; (ii) that their counsel was unable to convince the court that they had it in mind; or (iii) that the court assessed their loss of this goal as not worthy of protection. That case was decided in 1963.

Courts are increasingly ready to accept that people have a significant non-economic or "enjoyment" concerns arising out of the performance of contracts. The breach of contract that promises enjoyment can now lead to an award of damages for this loss, and the breach of a contract that causes the promisee "mental distress" — negative "enjoyment" — can lead to an increased award. We have already seen cases that reflect the willingness of courts to recognize non-economic interests, like *Radford v. De Froberville*, where the seller of part of the land recovered the cost of building the promised wall, even though construction of the wall had no effect on the market price.

A range of issues arise when trying to determine whether and how to compensate for non-economic losses. Some of these issues reflect one of the perennial problems in the law of contracts: the tendency of litigants — really their lawyers — to use the law of contracts when no other obvious legal basis for a claim exists. Although the courts may in some cases now use a contractual analysis to protect non-economic interests, sometimes it is a "rough fit" since most contractual doctrines were developed to protect economic or commercial interests. Further, while the courts are now prepared to protect non-economic interests is *some* cases arising out of a breach of contract or disappointed expectations, there is a clear reluctance to award such damages. In "ordinary" contract cases judges do not want to "compensate" for the disappointed expectations, anger and frustration that inevitably accompany any breach of contract.

Until the latter part of the twentieth century the courts generally refused to give compensation for what we have called non-economic losses arising out of a breach of contract. The courts would not award damages for the "inconvenience ... annoyance, loss of temper or vexation" that are a common feature of a breach of contract situation. The 1973 English case of *Jarvis v. Swan's Tours Ltd.* is usually regarded as opening the door to a more generous approach to claims for "lost enjoyment". The decision is a classic example of Lord Denning's literary style, and the plaintiff's sad story had a worthy recorder.

JARVIS v. SWAN'S TOURS LTD.

[1973] Q.B. 233, [1973] 1 All E.R. 71
(C.A., Lord Denning M.R., Edmund Davies and Stephenson L.JJ.)

[Mr. Jarvis, a solicitor working in London, booked a Swiss holiday tour with the defendant. The brochure prepared by the defendant promised that there would be a "House Party Centre with a special resident host" and that the holiday would be spent in Mörlialp, "a most wonderful little resort on a sunny plateau" where the brochure stated there were several ski runs, a skating rink and a toboggan run. The brochure further promised an "Alphütte Bar" which would be open several evenings a week, that Mr. Weibel, the owner, spoke English and that there would be a welcome party, afternoon tea and cake, a Swiss dinner by candlelight, a yodler evening and a farewell party. The plaintiff booked his holiday in August and was to be away over Christmas and the New Year.]

LORD DENNING: — [1] The plaintiff went on the holiday, but he was very disappointed. He was a man of about 35 and he expected to be one of a house party of some 30 or so people. Instead, he found that there were only 13 during the first week. In the second week there was no house party at all. He was the only person there. Mr. Weibel could not speak English. So there was Mr. Jarvis, in the second week, in this hotel with no house party at all, and no one could speak English, except himself. He was very disappointed, too, with the skiing. It was some distance away at Giswil. There were no ordinary length skis. There were only mini-skis, about 3 ft. long. So he did not get his skiing as he wanted to. In the second week he did get some longer skis for a couple of days, but then, because of his boots, his feet got rubbed and he could not continue even with the long skis. So his skiing holiday, from his point of view, was pretty well ruined.

[2]   There were many other matters, too. They appear trivial when they are set down in writing, but I have no doubt that they loomed large in Mr. Jarvis's mind, when coupled with the other disappointments. He did not have the nice Swiss cakes which he was hoping for. The only cakes for tea were potato crisps and little

dry nut cakes. The yodler evening consisted of one man from the locality who came in his working clothes for little while, and sang four or five songs very quickly. The "Alphütte Bar" was an unoccupied annexe which was only open one evening. There was a representative, Mrs. Storr, there during the first week, but she was not there during the second week.

[3]   The matter was summed up by the judge: "During the first week he got a holiday in Switzerland which was to some extent inferior . . . and, as to the second week, he got a holiday which was very largely inferior" to what he was led to expect.

[LORD DENNING held that the statements in the brochure were representations or warranties and the defendant's breach of them gave Mr. Jarvis a right to damages. LORD DENNING referred to two cases, *Hamlin v. Great Northern Railway Co.* (1856), 1 H. & N. 408, and *Hobbs v. London & South Western Railway Co.* (1875), L.R. 10 Q.B. 111, where courts had declined to award damages for mental distress or for "mere inconvenience, such as annoyance or loss of temper, or vexation, or for being disappointed in a particular thing which you have set your mind upon". He continued:]

[4]   I think those limitations are out of date. In a proper case damages for mental distress can be recovered in contract, just as damages for shock can be recovered in tort. One such case is a contract for a holiday, or any other contract to provide entertainment and enjoyment. If the contracting party breaks his contract, damages can be given for the disappointment, the distress, the upset and frustration caused by the breach. I know that it is difficult to assess in terms of money, but it is no more difficult than the assessment which the courts have to make every day in personal injury cases for loss of amenities. Take the present case. Mr. Jarvis has only a fortnight's holiday in the year. He books it far ahead, and looks forward to it all that time. He ought to be compensated for the loss of it. . .

[5]   Here, Mr. Jarvis's fortnight's winter holiday has been a grave disappointment. It is true that he was conveyed to Switzerland and back and had meals and bed in the hotel. But that is not what he went for. He went to enjoy himself with all the facilities which the defendants said he would have. He is entitled to damages for the lack of those facilities, and for the loss of enjoyment.

[LORD DENNING referred to the trial judge's award of £31.23, half the cost of the tour, and concluded:]

[6]   I think the judge was in error in taking the sum paid for the holiday £63.45 and halving it. The right measure of damages is to compensate him for the loss of entertainment and enjoyment which he was promised, and which he did not get. Looking at the matter quite broadly, I think that the damages in this case should be the sum of £125. I would allow the appeal, accordingly.

[EDMUND DAVIES and STEPHENSON L.JJ. agreed.]

NOTES AND QUESTIONS

1.   Lord Denning gave no reason for the award of £125. The plaintiff's claim for his earnings (£93.27) for the two weeks as well as a refund of what he had paid (£63.45) was rejected. It may be coincidental, but (i) twice the cost of the holiday is £126.90 and (ii) half the cost of the holiday (£31.72) plus Mr. Jarvis's earnings for two weeks is £124.99.

2.   Jarvis did get his plane trip and accommodation as promised. Does it matter that someone else might have taken exactly the same trip and been delighted at the extra

solitude from having so few other guests? Does it matter that Jarvis himself might have happened to meet someone in the village and developed a romantic interest that would have made this a memorable vacation for him, or that he might have been so depressed at being alone as to need medical treatment upon his return?

3.   The judgment in *Jarvis v. Swan's Tours* has been the basis for many claims against tour operators and others engaged in the holiday business, and the case establishes the right of the disappointed vacationer to damages that allow something for the loss of enjoyment.

4.   In *Kent v. Conquest Vacations*, [2005] O.J. No. 312 (Div. Ct.), the plaintiffs sued for damages when their package tour holiday resulted in them staying in a hotel with a "deplorable lack of facilities". Beach, tennis courts and diving opportunities described in the tour brochure were not available. While the plaintiffs had good warm weather and missed some of the Canadian winter, and as promised got flights, "some good food", and accommodation (albeit inferior to what was described in the brochure), the trial judge concluded that they lost "the whole purpose of the vacation ... the loss of the opportunity for family relaxation and time together". The trial judge awarded a sum equal to three times the cost of the tour package. In upholding this award, Lane J. noted that it "might have been better [for the trial judge] to steer clear of any language that might be regarded as formulaic". The appeal court judge observed that "[r]elating the award in a general sense to the cost of the travel is not an unreasonable approach, for the higher cost is not unrelated to the legitimate expectations of enjoyment."

5.   In practice, if a disgruntled customer makes a justifiable complaint, most tour operators are prepared to pay some amount, or more commonly to offer a credit for another vacation, as a gesture of goodwill to someone who has had a bad experience on a vacation booked through them. However, *Jarvis v. Swan's Tours* is not a ticket to fortune for someone whose holiday is ruined. The point at which a disappointed vacationer may expect serious opposition to a claim will be where the amount claimed is higher than the amount that the tour operator is prepared to meet out of its own pocket. At that point the operator's insurer will be involved, and insurers do not share the operator's desire to maintain good customer relations and are very likely to resist strongly claims that they think are excessive.

6.   What effect is *Jarvis* likely to have on the travel industry? Assuming that tour operators are forced to raise rates to cover the costs of this type of liability, are you willing to in effect have a portion of the price of your tour package go to providing a pool of money to compensate those whose vacation hopes are not met?

7.   Following *Jarvis*, the first Canadian cases to award damages for non-economic interests arose out of similar situations, ones where the contract itself was clearly for enjoyment, such as when a photographer or disc jockey failed to honour a contract to provide services at a wedding: *Dunn v. Disc Jockey Unlimited Co.* (1978), 87 D.L.R. (3d) 408, 20 O.R. (2d) 309 (Prov. Ct.). A number of contracts cases that allowed claims for mental distress involved pets. In *Newell v. Canadian Pacific Airlines, Ltd.* (1976), 14 O.R. (2d) 752, 74 D.L.R. (3d) 574 (Co. Ct.), a wealthy elderly couple was flying from Toronto to Mexico for a recuperative vacation, taking their two dogs with them. They indicated great concern for the welfare of their pets, offering to purchase the entire first-class section of the aircraft so that their dogs could accompany them for the flight. The airline found this offer to be unacceptable, but reassured the plaintiffs that the dogs would be safe in the cargo compartment. Unfortunately, the dogs were poisoned by dry ice, which was also in the cargo compartment, and one of the dogs died. In addition to awarding the couple damages for the cost of one dog and the price of veterinary services to save the other dog, Borins Co. Ct. J. awarded $500 for mental distress. He concluded that in light of the discussion that the plaintiffs had with the airline representatives, there was communication of "special circumstances" making this distress a "reasonably foreseeable consequence of the contractual breach" within the second rule of *Hadley v. Baxendale*.

8. In *Ferguson v. Birchmont Boarding Kennels*, [2006] O.J. No. 300 (Div. Ct.), Chapnik J. affirmed the decision of the Small Claims Court to award a pet owner the monetary value of her dog plus about $1,400 for "pain and suffering", arising from the breach of contract by a kennel operator that resulted in the escape and disappearance of a pet during the dog's boarding at the kennel. The plaintiff was distressed at the dog's disappearance, and returned from her vacation to search for the dog. Chapnik J., in affirming the lower court decision, wrote (at paras. 23-25):

> In that regard, the [trial] court stated: "... as for recovering damages for emotional trauma or mental distress, our courts regularly compensate victims in this respect without the victim having to establish that he or she experienced nervous shock. One needs only look to the many decisions in the field of damages for wrongful dismissal to see that mental distress is a proper head of damage when the circumstances are proven to exist".

> ... Deputy Judge Yee detailed the effects the loss of the dog had on the plaintiff Susan Ferguson: her emotionally distraught and hysterical state; ... the search efforts to locate [the pet dog]; the relationship Ms. Ferguson and her husband had with the dog for 7½ years; her inability to work; and the insomnia and nightmares she experienced upon his loss. ...

> I am satisfied that the trial judge did not err in law or in fact in making findings and in awarding general damages in this case. Mental distress is a proper head of damages when the appropriate underlying circumstances are proven to exist. The court made no palpable or overriding error in that regard; that is, the findings of the trial judge were well supported by the evidence.

In *Pezzente v. McClain*, [2005] B.C.J. No. 1800 (Prov. Ct.) the plaintiff purchased a puppy for $350 from a breeder who gave a "verbal guarantee" that the dog was healthy. It turned out that the dog had significant health problems. The plaintiff spent in excess of $10,000 on veterinary fees to treat the dog, and suffered from the "stress and strain of coping with an animal" with so many "special needs". Auxier Prov. Ct. J. accepted that there was a breach of warranty, but only awarded $350 in damages and no costs (after a day and a half of trial), writing (at para. 11):

> [The law] limits the measure of damages to those that can reasonably be seen to have resulted from the breach of the warranty. The decision by Ms. Pezzente [the plaintiff] to have the surgery done was an emotional decision, not a reasonable economic one. The money she spent far exceeds the commercial value of the dog. As [counsel for the defendant] put it, "You don't spend $10,000 to repair a $350 stereo". And if you do, the costs of that decision shouldn't have to be borne by the vendor. Ms. Pezzente had a duty to mitigate in the legal sense. That might mean declining to have the surgery done. Cruelly, it might even mean euthanizing the dog.

Which approach is preferable, that of *Ferguson* or *Pezzente*?

9. These and other cases have made similar awards and it is now clear that, in appropriate cases, courts will award damages for loss of enjoyment or mental distress arising from a breach of contract. There remains the problem of justifying any such award. Is *Hadley v. Baxendale* used to start the award or to find a place to stop the award that has been started on some other basis?

10. As in *Ruxley*, the awards for lost enjoyment after *Jarvis* have tended to be modest and conventional in the same sense that the £2,500 awarded in *Ruxley* was conventional, *i.e.*, fixed by the court at a relatively low level and taking little or no account of the subjective unhappiness suffered by the particular plaintiff. Is such a position on such claims inevitable?

11. In *Farley v. Skinner*, [2002] 2 A.C. 732, [2001] 4 All E.R. 801, the House of Lords awarded £10,000 against a property valuer who had negligently failed to inform his client that the house he was buying as a peaceful retirement home was directly beneath

a busy airplane landing path. The court suggested that there should be a cap of £10,000 for awards for non-pecuniary losses arising out of a breach of contract. Lord Steyn dealt with this basis for such an award for breach of contract. He said: (at para. 16):

> . . . In the law of obligations the rules governing the recovery of compensation necessarily distinguish between different kinds of harm. In tort the requirement of reasonable foreseeability is a sufficient touchstone of liability for causing death or physical injury; it is an inadequate tool for the disposal of claims in respect of psychiatric injury. Tort law approaches compensation for physical damage and pure economic loss differently. In contract law distinctions are made about the kind of harm which resulted from the breach of contract. The general principle is that compensation is only awarded for financial loss resulting from the breach of contract: *Livingstone v. Rawyards Coal Co.* (1880), 5 App. Cas. 25, 39, per Lord Blackburn. In the words of Bingham L.J. in [*Watts v. Morrow*, [1991] 1 W.L.R. 1421] as a matter of legal policy "a contract breaker is not *in general* liable for any distress, frustration, anxiety, displeasure, vexation, tension or aggravation which his breach of contract may cause to the innocent party" (my emphasis). There are, however, limited exceptions to this rule. . . . But the two exceptions mentioned by Bingham L.J., namely where the very object of the contract is to provide pleasure . . . and recovery for physical inconvenience caused by the breach . . . are pertinent. . . . It is, however, correct . . . that the entitlement to damages for mental distress caused by a breach of contract is not established by mere foreseeability: the right to recovery is dependent on the case falling fairly within the principles governing the special exceptions. ...

12. In *Turczinski Estate v. Dupont Heating & Air Conditioning Ltd.*, [2004] O.J. No. 4510, 246 D.L.R. (4th) 95, 38 C.L.R. (3d) 123, the Ontario Court of Appeal had to deal with a case in which the trial judge had awarded substantial damages for mental distress. The defendant undertook to renovate a house belonging to the deceased. The defendant dealt with the deceased's daughter who, though the condition had not then been diagnosed, suffered from bipolar disease and obsessive disorder. The defendant breached the contract. The trial judge had awarded the daughter damages for the mental distress she suffered from the defendant's breach. On appeal, the trial judge's award under that head was set aside. The Court of Appeal held that the "thin skull" rule does not apply in contracts. (This rule states that the defendant in a tort action takes the consequences of the fact that the plaintiff may be particularly prone to suffer injury because, to take the classic example, he or she has a thin skull so that an accident that might cause the ordinary person little or no injury, causes the particular plaintiff very serious injury.) The defendant had and could have had no knowledge that the daughter might respond as she did. Moreover, a contract to renovate a house is not a contract that can be regarded as one promising peace of mind so that no damages can be recovered for the fact that mental distress follows from the breach. Feldman J.A. said:

> [38] Before leaving [the issue of damages for mental distress], I observe that there are persuasive reasons to confine within narrow limits the circumstances when damages will be awarded for exacerbation of mental illness for breach of a consumer contract. As in this case, it is very difficult for a lay person to assess the mental state of a stranger, particularly to the extent of predicting with any degree of certainty how a breach of contract might affect the person. An extension of the circumstances when such damages are awarded could cause businesspeople to be wary of dealing with persons with mental disabilities for fear of exposure to claims for damages much higher than the value of the contract.

The Ontario Court of Appeal did not mention *Farley v. Skinner*. The attitude expressed by Feldman J.A. in the quotation just set out would suggest that the Court of

Appeal and the House of Lords do not have the same view of consumer contracts. Notice that, as always with questions of damages, the issue is not some mathematical calculation but what the courts (or we as a society) *want to do*. If we assume that there is some cost to be borne by someone from the mental distress caused by a breach of contract, there are, speaking generally, three choices: we can put the risk of loss on the defendant; we can leave it with the plaintiff; or if the distress is sufficiently severe, the cost may be passed on to society in the hospital or medical costs incurred in dealing with the plaintiff. The existence of insurance does not fundamentally change the nature of the choices.

13. The issues raised by *Farley v. Skinner* and "loss of enjoyment" contracts were considered by the Supreme Court of Canada in *Fidler v. Sun Life Assurance Co. of Canada*, [2006] S.C.J. No. 30. In that case, the Supreme Court held that damages for mental distress are recoverable where such damages "were in the reasonable contemplation of the parties [as a consequence of breach] when the contract was made". The Court held that the "loss of enjoyment" cases are "an expression of the general principle of compensatory damages". Before considering *Fidler*, it is useful to study some other issues related to non-economic losses, including issues related to employment contracts and punitive damages.

Employment Contracts

Employment contracts are an important category of agreements that give rise to conceptual and practical difficulties in regard to the assessment of damages. The attitude of the courts to this type of contract and the various methods for dealing with the employment relationship illustrate a number of significant things about the law. In Canada, many of the most important decisions about the awarding of damages for non-economic losses have concerned employment contracts. This is not surprising as employment relationships are often central to individual feelings of self-worth, and the loss of employment inevitably causes an employee very significant distress, as well as having serious economic implications.

The common law implies a term in employment contracts of indefinite duration that the employer has the right to terminate the employment of an employee either "for cause" or, if there is no cause, on giving "reasonable notice". A contract of indefinite duration is distinguished from a contract of fixed length like, for example, a one-year or five-year contract.

Over the past quarter-century, the courts have made it increasingly difficult for an employer to establish "cause". For the employer to establish "cause", the employee must have done something that is fundamentally inconsistent with the continuance of the employment relation. Theft or fraud by the employee may be sufficient, and courts have more recently accepted that sexual harassment of other employees in contravention of the employer's harassment policy may be cause for termination. In cases of less serious breaches of an employee's obligations, an employer will usually be expected to warn an employee of unsatisfactory performance and give the employee an opportunity to improve before the employer will have "cause" for termination. Recent cases have held that the courts should consider the "context" of a wrongful act and the employment relationship. Some acts of misconduct or dishonesty (without a prior record and warning), may only merit sanction like a reprimand or suspension, but not dismissal; the court must determine whether the misconduct or dishonesty was of a degree that it was incompatible with the employment relationship: *McKinley v. BC Tel*, [2001] 2 S.C.R. 161, 200 D.L.R. (4th) 385.

A business downturn or the redundancy of a specific employee or group of employees is not sufficient to constitute "cause" for dismissal without reasonable notice.

An employee who is not dismissed for legally sufficient cause is entitled, at the employer's option, to either reasonable notice — "We will be terminating your employment in two months" — or the salary payable for the notice period. If an employer wants to terminate an individual employee, and (often after obtaining legal advice) concludes that there is no legally sufficient "cause", the employer will often prefer to pay the employee's salary for the notice period rather than have the employee work to the end of the notice period. Once the employee receives notice, there may be little incentive to do a good job; the employee may be angry or even vindictive as a result of the termination, so monetary compensation is often offered instead of the opportunity to work out the notice. The employee who is only given notice, not compensation, may forfeit the right to compensation if she or he refuses to work out the period of notice. Employment standards legislation in each province establishes minimum periods of notice, with longer periods of notice for employees with longer service. Employers may require employees to enter into written employment contracts that establish periods of notice, which must be at least equal to the statutory periods. In the absence of express contractual provision, courts generally establish a "reasonable notice" period based on common law notions, with the statute establishing a minimum notice period that is usually exceeded by the case law.

An employee who quits is also, in theory, obliged to give an employer "reasonable notice" of the planned termination, or pay damages. However, the courts have held that the requisite notice that an employee must provide is much shorter than what an employer must give. Given the state of the labour market, employers will often have difficulty in proving damages from an employee's failure to give adequate notice. See *RBC Dominion Securities Inc. v. Merrill Lynch Canada Inc.*, [2004] B.C.J. No. 2337 (S.C.) for a case dealing with the obligation of departing employees to give their employers reasonable notice of their departure.

Actions for wrongful dismissal are, for obvious reasons, related to the economic cycle. (There is about a two-year delay before the cases appear in judgments.) Employers are becoming more aware of the need either for employment contracts to deal with termination or of their obligation to make reasonable termination offers. Even in relatively prosperous times, a significant number of lawyers are involved in providing advice and representation in wrongful dismissal cases.

Until the last quarter of the twentieth century, damages for wrongful dismissal were not large, except where the employee had a fixed-term contract, and only senior employees were likely to have such a contract. Severance payments are, however, now large enough to be a significant obligation of corporations. Transactions in which corporations are bought and sold have to be carefully designed to reduce and allocate the risks that the old or new employer may be sued for wrongful dismissal by employees of the business. (When corporations announce a merger or "downsizing", they also announce that they are taking a very large "charge" against their profits to allow for the costs of terminating employment contracts.) By the same token, employment contracts are more important to both the employer and the employee, and are increasingly frequently negotiated with the help of lawyers on both sides.

We shall return to the employment contract a number of times in these materials, for the relation created by that contract is central to the lives of very many people and its legal treatment requires careful analysis. Here we are dealing only with the aspect of the proper measure of damages for wrongful dismissal at common law, especially in the context of claims for increased damages for "mental distress".

As in the nineteenth-century cases referred to by Lord Denning in *Jarvis v. Swan's Tours*, the common law took the position that an employee who was dismissed without legally sufficient cause was only entitled to compensation for lost wages during the period of "reasonable notice": the equivalent in the employment relation of lost profits and the narrow application of the principle stated in *Wertheim v. Chicoutimi Pulp*.

The classic Canadian statement of the test to determine the length of notice is that of McRuer C.J.H.C. in *Bardal v. Globe & Mail Ltd.*, [1960] O.W.N. 253 at p. 255:

> There can be no catalogue laid down as to what was reasonable notice in particular classes of cases. The reasonableness of the notice must be decided with reference to each particular case, having regard to the character of the employment, the length of service of the servant, the age of the servant and the availability of similar employment, having regard to the experience, training and qualifications of the servant.

It was held in *Addis v. Gramophone Co.*, [1909] A.C. 488 (H.L.) that an employee who had been wrongfully dismissed was entitled to compensation for the loss of any contractual expectation, but not to anything in respect of his or her "pain and suffering", mental distress or damage to his or her reputation. *Addis* was followed in *Peso Silver Mines Ltd. (N.P.L) v. Cropper*, [1966] S.C.R. 673, 58 D.L.R. (2d) 1.

After the decision in *Jarvis v. Swan's Tours* in 1973, courts began to develop the idea that damages for "mental distress" and humiliation might be awarded for wrongful dismissal. Beginning in the early 1980's, evidence was sometimes led to show that an employee who was wrongfully dismissed was harmed in psychological ways, in having his or her sense of self-worth damaged and in prolonged depression. The courts responded to this evidence and in a number of cases that arose out of the recession in 1981 and 1982, trial judges gave as much as $25,000 (*Pilato v. Hamilton Place Convention Centre Inc.* (1984), 45 O.R. (2d) 652 (H.C.J.)) on this head. Other cases raised the problem of finding a basis for an award of mental suffering when it could only be "piggy-backed" onto an award of damages for wrongful dismissal. Some judges pointed out that the mental distress might be suffered whether or not the employee was given adequate notice, yet would only be recoverable if the notice period was too short.

In 1989, in *Vorvis v. Insurance Corp. of British Columbia*, [1989] 1 S.C.R. 1085, 58 D.L.R. (4th) 193, the Supreme Court of Canada considered whether a court could award damages for non-economic losses in a wrongful dismissal action. The plaintiff had been badly treated by his supervisor in the months leading up to his dismissal and he claimed not only damages for mental distress but also punitive damages. Damages for mental distress are the converse of damages for lost enjoyment: the plaintiff seeks compensation for the positive misery inflicted on him by the defendant. Punitive damages are, as the phrase suggests, intended to punish the defendant. They raise difficult and important issues which will be dealt with later.

Damages for mental distress are now often referred to as "aggravated damages". As such, they are, like non-pecuniary damages or damages for lost enjoyment, in theory compensatory, *i.e.*, they are intended to compensate the plaintiff for a loss. McIntyre J., giving the judgment of the majority of the Court in *Vorvis*, drew an important distinction between aggravated and punitive damages:

> It will be well to make clear the distinction between punitive and aggravated damages, for in the argument before us and in some of the materials filed there appeared some confusion as to the distinction. Punitive damages, as the name would indicate, are designed to punish. In this, they constitute an exception to the general common law rule that damages are designed to compensate the injured, not to punish the wrongdoer. Aggravated damages will frequently cover conduct which could also be the subject of punitive damages, but the role of aggravated damages remains compensatory. The distinction is clearly set out in Waddams, *The Law of Damages* (2nd ed. 1983), at p. 562, para. 979, in these words:

>> An exception exists to the general rule that damages are compensatory. This is the case of an award made for the purpose, not of compensating the plaintiff, but of punishing the defendant. Such awards have been called exemplary, vindictive, penal, punitive, aggravated and retributory, but the expressions in common modern use to describe damages going beyond compensatory are exemplary and punitive damages. "Exemplary" was preferred by the House of Lords in *Cassell & Co. Ltd. v. Broome* but "punitive" has also been used in many Canadian courts including the Supreme Court of Canada in *H.L. Weiss Forwarding Ltd. v. Omnus*. The expression "aggravated damages", though it has sometimes been used interchangeably with punitive or exemplary damages, has more frequently in recent times been contrasted with exemplary damages. In this contrasting sense, aggravated damages describes an award that aims at compensation, but takes full account of the intangible injuries, such as distress and humiliation, that may have been caused by the defendant's insulting behaviour. The expressions vindictive, penal and retributory have dropped out of common use.

>> Aggravated damages are awarded to compensate for aggravated damage. As explained by Waddams, they take account of intangible injuries and by definition will generally augment damages assessed under the general rules relating to the assessment of damages. Aggravated damages are compensatory in nature and may only be awarded for that purpose. Punitive damages, on the other hand, are punitive in nature and may only be employed in circumstances where the conduct giving the cause for complaint is of such nature that it merits punishment.

While the entire Court accepted this distinction between aggravated and punitive damages, there was a three to two split in *Vorvis* on whether such damages should be awarded in this case. Writing for the majority, McIntyre J. took a narrow approach to the awarding of damages for intangible injuries in wrongful dismissal cases, saying:

> I would conclude that while aggravated damages may be awarded in actions for breach of contract in appropriate cases, this is not a case where they should be given. The rule long established in the *Addis* and *Peso Silver Mines* [*Peso Silver Mines Ltd. (N.P.L.) v. Cropper*, [1966] S.C.R. 673, 58 D.L.R. (2d) 1, 56 W.W.R. 641] cases has generally been applied to deny such damages, and the employer/employee relationship (in the absence of collective agreements which involve consideration of the modern labour law regime) has always been one where either party could terminate the contract of employment by due notice, and therefore the only damage which could arise would result from a failure to give such notice.

> I would not wish to be taken as saying that aggravated damages could never be awarded in a case of wrongful dismissal, particularly where the acts complained of were also independently actionable, a factor not present here.

McIntyre J. rejected any claim for aggravated damages in this case, and further ruled that punitive damages should not be awarded:

The only basis for the imposition of such punishment must be a finding of the commission of an actionable wrong which caused the injury complained of by the plaintiff. This would be consistent with the approach of . . . the *Restatement Second, Contracts* in the United States. . . . § 355, which provides:

> Punitive damages are not recoverable for breach of contract unless the con-
> duct constituting the breach is also a tort for which punitive damages are re-
> coverable.

Wilson J. took a different approach, one which recognized the special nature of the
employment contract. She quoted G.H.L. Fridman, *The Law of Contract in Canada*, 2nd ed. (Toronto: Carswell, 1986), who stated that the most important type of
contract in which damages for mental distress have been awarded is the employment contract and suggested that "this is because of the nature of the relationship it
creates which is one of trust and confidence". She herself said that "it may also be
because of the vulnerability of the employee to the superior authority of the employer". She disagreed with the narrow approach of McIntyre J. to the award of
aggravated damages in wrongful dismissal cases, concluding:

> I must respectfully disagree with my colleague's view that conduct advanced in
> support of a claim for damages for mental suffering must constitute a separate
> "actionable wrong" from the breach itself. I disagree also that because the con-
> duct complained of preceded the wrongful dismissal it cannot aggravate the dam-
> ages resulting from that dismissal. Rather than relying on a characterization of the
> conduct as an independent wrong, I think the proper approach is to apply the basic
> principles of contract law relating to remoteness of damage.

She also took a broader view of the jurisdiction of courts to award punitive damages in wrongful dismissal cases, writing:

> I do not share my colleague's view that punitive damages can only be awarded when
> the misconduct is in itself an "actionable wrong". In my view, the correct approach
> is to assess the conduct in the context of all the circumstances and determine
> whether it is deserving of punishment because of its shockingly harsh, vindictive,
> reprehensible or malicious nature. Undoubtedly some conduct found to be deserving
> of punishment will constitute an actionable wrong but other conduct might not. . . .

While Wilson J. would not have awarded any aggravated damages on the facts of
Vorvis, she would have affirmed the award of one of the judges in the British Columbia Court of Appeal of $5,000 as punitive damages.

Some lawyers and judges interpreted the majority decision in *Vorvis* as precluding the award of damages for mental suffering in cases of wrongful dismissal.
However, even after *Vorvis* sympathetic judges awarded fairly large amounts for
non-economic loses in wrongful dismissal cases where the employer acted in a
reprehensible fashion. See, *e.g.*, *Ribeiro v. Canadian Imperial Bank of Commerce*
(1992), 13 O.R. (3d) 278, 44 C.C.E.L. 165 (C.A.), which involved unfounded allegations of fraud resulting from an incompetent investigation into alleged employee wrong-doing by a bank investigator and a callous termination. In *Ribeiro*
$50,000 punitive damages and $20,000 damages for mental distress were awarded.
The court characterized the dismissal as "harsh, vindictive and reprehensible" and
found that it caused the plaintiff a "reactive depression".

Wilson J.'s use of "remoteness" in *Vorvis* as the basis for the obligation to pay
damages for mental distress for wrongful dismissal causes serious problems of
analysis for all the reasons outlined by Lord Steyn in *Farley v. Skinner*, discussed
above. As noted in that case, liability for damages for mental distress in a case of

breach of contract is "not established by mere foreseeability"; the plaintiff must show that the case is one which is "falling fairly within the principles governing the special exceptions". *Hadley v. Baxendale* was concerned, not with providing a justification for an award or an *increased* award, but with finding a place (or a justification) for *stopping* an award that is justified under the compensation principle. The mere fact that a loss or injury can be foreseen is no justification for making the plaintiff liable unless there is a basis on which the compensation principle can operate. In other words, only if the employer has an obligation not to cause mental distress can an award for such distress be given. The next case explores this issue.

WALLACE v. UNITED GRAIN GROWERS LTD.

[1997] S.C.J. No. 94, [1997] 3 S.C.R. 701, 152 D.L.R. (4th) 1
(Lamer C.J.C., La Forest, L'Heureux-Dubé, Sopinka, Gonthier, Cory, McLachlin, Iacobucci and Major JJ.)

[In 1972 Jack Wallace was 45 years old and had a secure job with his employer. He was induced to leave that job by an offer of employment made by the defendant, United Grain Growers ("UGG"). At that time the defendant said that Mr. Wallace could expect to remain with it until he retired. Mr. Wallace went to work for the defendant and over the next 14 years he was a very successful salesman. He was suddenly dismissed in August 1986. A few days before he was dismissed, he had been complimented on his work by his manager. The dismissal caused Mr. Wallace great distress. Allegations that he had been dismissed for cause were made and persisted in until the trial, when they were abandoned. Mr. Wallace was largely unsuccessful in seeking alternative employment. He started an action for wrongful dismissal about two months after he was dismissed. (An issue of Mr. Wallace's competence, as an undischarged bankrupt, to bring the action was raised by the defendant. The Supreme Court held that Mr. Wallace could bring the claim as it fell within the class of claims for "salary, wages and other remuneration", that, under the *Bankruptcy and Insolvency Act*, R.S.C. 1985, c. B-3, s. 68, could be brought by the bankrupt himself.) He claimed damages for wrongful dismissal, mental distress and punitive damages.

Lockwood J. of the Manitoba Court of Queen's Bench ((1993), 87 Man. R. (2d) 161) held that whatever statements had been made to Mr. Wallace when he was hired by the defendant did not amount to a promise that he would be employed until he retired. Lockwood J. held that 24 months' notice would have been reasonable in the circumstances. Lockwood J. based this decision on (i) Mr. Wallace's length of service, his age, the nature and history of his employment, (ii) his qualifications and the availability of similar employment, and (iii) the effect the allegations that he had been dismissed for cause had on his efforts to find alternative employment.

Lockwood J. further held that Mr. Wallace was entitled to damages of $15,000 for mental distress. He based this award on both contract and tort. He found a contractual basis for the damages by holding that, while Mr. Wallace did not have a fixed-term contract, he "had been given a guarantee of security, provided that he gave UGG no cause to dismiss him" and "that it must have been in the contemplation of UGG that if Wallace was dismissed without cause or warning, he would probably suffer mental distress". Lockwood J. also held, carefully distinguishing the judgment of the Supreme Court in *Vorvis v. Insurance Corp. of British Columbia*, [1989] 1 S.C.R. 1085; that Mr. Wallace could maintain a separate action in tort. He said (p. 177. Quoted by Iacobucci J., ¶ 187):

> I find that it was reasonably foreseeable that mental distress would result from the manner in which the dismissal was handled and also by the decision to play hardball with the plaintiff. That decision resulted in the defendant maintaining the plea of just cause for some two years and four months, during which time the plaintiff undoubtedly suffered further mental distress. There was, consequently, a negligent breach of the duty of care warranting compensation by way of aggravated damages.

Lockwood J. dismissed Mr. Wallace's claim for punitive damages on the ground that the defendant's conduct had not been bad enough; it was not of a "harsh, vindictive, reprehensible and malicious nature" (p. 179, quoted by Iacobucci J., ¶ 20).

The Manitoba Court of Appeal, in a judgment by Scott C.J.M. ((1995), 102 Man. R. (2d) 161), held that Lockwood J.'s award of 24 months was too high and must have reflected an element of aggravated damages. Scott C.J.M. substituted an award of 15 months. He rejected the claim for mental distress on the grounds that (i) the requirement in *Vorvis* that there be an independently actionable claim made the foreseeability of such damages irrelevant and (ii) there was, on the facts, no basis for such a claim. Scott C.J.M. also rejected the plaintiff's argument that there was a tort of "bad faith discharge". He agreed with Lockwood J. that there was no basis for an award of damages for mental suffering.]

IACOBUCCI J. gave the judgment of himself and **LAMER C.J., SOPINKA, GONTHIER, CORY** and .**MAJOR JJ.** After summarizing the facts and the proceedings in the Manitoba courts, and dealing with the issue of the plaintiff's status as an undischarged bankrupt, he continued:]

B. Fixed-Term Contract

[72] The appellant submitted that the courts below erred in rejecting his claim that he had a fixed-term contract for employment until retirement. The learned trial judge exhaustively reviewed all of the circumstances surrounding Wallace's hiring and concluded that there was insufficient evidence to support this claim. The Court of Appeal accepted the facts as they were found by the trial judge and agreed with his conclusion. In light of these concurrent findings of fact, I see no palpable error or other reason to interfere with the conclusion of the courts below.

C. Damages for Mental Distress

[73] Relying upon the principles enunciated in *Vorvis*, *supra*, the Court of Appeal held that any award of damages beyond compensation for breach of contract for failure to give reasonable notice of termination "must be founded on a separately actionable course of conduct" (p. 184). Although there has been criticism of *Vorvis* . . . this is an accurate statement of the law. The Court of Appeal also noted that this requirement necessarily negates the trial judge's reliance on concepts of foreseeability and matters in the contemplation of the parties. An employment contract is not one in which peace of mind is the very matter contracted for (see *e.g.*, *Jarvis v. Swans Tours Ltd.*, [1973] 1 Q.B. 233 (C.A.)) and so, absent an independently actionable wrong, the foreseeability of mental distress or the fact that the parties

contemplated its occurrence is of no consequence, subject to what I say on employer conduct below.

[74] The Court of Appeal concluded that there was insufficient evidence to support a finding that the actions of UGG constituted a separate actionable wrong either in tort or in contract. I agree with these findings and see no reason to disturb them. I note, however, that in circumstances where the manner of dismissal has caused mental distress but falls short of an independent actionable wrong, the employee is not without recourse. Rather, the trial judge has discretion in these circumstances to extend the period of reasonable notice to which an employee is entitled. Thus, although recovery for mental distress might not be available under a separate head of damages, the possibility of recovery still remains. I will be returning to this point in my discussion of reasonable notice below.

D. Bad Faith Discharge

[75] The appellant urged this Court to find that he could sue UGG either in contract or in tort for "bad faith discharge". With respect to the action in contract, he submitted that the Court should imply into the employment contract a term that the employee would not be fired except for cause or legitimate business reasons. I cannot accede to this submission. The law has long recognized the mutual right of both employers and employees to terminate an employment contract at any time provided there are no express provisions to the contrary. In *Farber v. Royal Trust Co.*, [1997] 1 S.C.R. 846, Gonthier J., speaking for the Court, summarized the general contractual principles applicable to contracts of employment as follows, at p. 858:

> In the context of an indeterminate employment contract, one party can resiliate the contract unilaterally. The resiliation is considered a dismissal if it originates with the employer and a resignation if it originates with the employee. If an employer dismisses an employee without cause, the employer must give the employee reasonable notice that the contract is about to be terminated or compensation in lieu thereof.

[76] A requirement of "good faith" reasons for dismissal would, in effect, contravene these principles and deprive employers of the ability to determine the composition of their workforce. In the context of the accepted theories on the employment relationship, such a law would, in my opinion, be overly intrusive and inconsistent with established principles of employment law, and more appropriately, should be left to legislative enactment rather than judicial pronouncement.

[77] I must also reject the appellant's claim that he can sue in tort for breach of a good faith and fair dealing obligation with regard to dismissals. The Court of Appeal noted the absence of persuasive authority on this point and concluded that such a tort has not yet been recognized by Canadian courts. I agree with these findings. To create such a tort in this case would therefore constitute a radical shift in the law, again a step better left to be taken by the legislatures.

[78] For these reasons I conclude that the appellant is unable to sue in either tort or contract for "bad faith discharge". However, I will be returning to the subject of good faith and fair dealing in my discussion of reasonable notice below.

[**IACOBUCCI J.** rejected the appellant's claim that he was entitled to punitive damages. He continued:]

F. Reasonable Notice

[80] The Court of Appeal upheld the trial judge's findings of fact and agreed that in the circumstances of this case damages for failure to give notice ought to be at the high end of the scale. However, the court found the trial judge's award of 24 months' salary in lieu of notice to be excessive and reflective of an element of aggravated damages having crept into his determination. It overturned his award and substituted the equivalent of 15 months' salary. For the reasons which follow, I would restore the trial judge's award of damages in the amount of 24 months' salary in lieu of notice.

[81] In determining what constitutes reasonable notice of termination, the courts have generally applied the principles articulated by McRuer C.J.H.C. in *Bardal v. Globe & Mail Ltd.* (1960), 24 D.L.R. (2d) 140 (Ont. H.C.), at p. 145:

> There can be no catalogue laid down as to what is reasonable notice in particular classes of cases. The reasonableness of the notice must be decided with reference to each particular case, having regard to the character of the employment, the length of service of the servant, the age of the servant and the availability of similar employment, having regard to the experience, training and qualifications of the servant.

[82] This Court adopted the foregoing list of factors in *Machtinger v. HOJ Industries Ltd.*, [1992] 1 S.C.R. 986, at p. 998. Applying these factors in the instant case, I concur with the trial judge's finding that in light of the appellant's advanced age, his 14-year tenure as the company's top salesman and his limited prospects for re-employment, a lengthy period of notice is warranted. I note, however, that *Bardal, supra*, does not state, nor has it been interpreted to imply, that the factors it enumerated were exhaustive. . . . Canadian courts have added several additional factors to the *Bardal* list. The application of these factors to the assessment of a dismissed employee's notice period will depend upon the particular circumstances of the case.

[83] One such factor that has often been considered is whether the dismissed employee had been induced to leave previous secure employment. . . . According to one authority, many courts have sought to compensate the reliance and expectation interests of terminated employees by increasing the period of reasonable notice where the employer has induced the employee to "quit a secure, well-paying job . . . on the strength of promises of career advancement and greater responsibility, security and compensation with the new organization" (I. Christie et al., [*Employment Law in Canada*, 2nd ed. (Toronto: Butterworths, 1993)], at p. 623).

. . .

[85] In my opinion, such inducements are properly included among the considerations which tend to lengthen the amount of notice required. I concur with the comments of Christie et al., *supra*, and recognize that there is a need to safeguard the employee's reliance and expectation interests in inducement situations. I note, however, that not all inducements will carry equal weight when determining the appropriate period of notice. The significance of the inducement in question will vary with the circumstances of the particular case and its effect, if any, on the notice period is a matter best left to the discretion of the trial judge.

[86] In the instant case, the trial judge found that UGG went to great lengths to relieve Wallace's fears about jeopardizing his existing secure employment and to entice him into joining their company. At p. 172 the trial judge stated:

The [respondent] wanted a man with the skills of the [appellant] and to get him was prepared to accommodate his demands. . . . I have found that there was no fixed-term contract. However, there was, in the assurance given to him, a *guarantee of security*, provided he gave the [respondent] no cause to dismiss him. [Emphasis added.]

[87] In addition to the promise that he could continue to work for the company until retirement, UGG also offered several assurances with respect to fair treatment. Further, despite the fact that the company only had salary arrangements with their existing employees, they assured Wallace that they would implement a commission basis for him. Although the trial judge did not make specific reference to the inducement factor in his analysis of reasonable notice, I believe that, in the circumstances of this case, these inducements, in particular the guarantee of job security, are factors which support his decision to award damages at the high end of the scale.

[88] The appellant urged this Court to recognize the ability of a dismissed employee to sue in contract or alternatively in tort for "bad faith discharge". Although I have rejected both as avenues for recovery, by no means do I condone the behaviour of employers who subject employees to callous and insensitive treatment in their dismissal, showing no regard for their welfare. Rather, I believe that such bad faith conduct in the manner of dismissal is another factor that is properly compensated for by an addition to the notice period.

[89] In *Lojstrup v. British Columbia Buildings Corp.* (1989), 34 B.C.L.R. (2d) 357, the British Columbia Court of Appeal found that *Addis v. Gramophone Co.*, [1909] A.C. 488, *Peso Silver Mines Ltd. (N.P.L.) v. Cropper*, [1966] S.C.R. 673, *Ansari v. British Columbia Hydro and Power Authority* (1986), 2 B.C.L.R. (2d) 33 (S.C.), and *Wadden v. Guaranty Trust Co. of Canada*, [1987] 2 W.W.R. 739 (Alta. Q.B.), preclude extending the notice period to account for manner of dismissal. Generally speaking, these cases have found that claims relating to the manner in which the discharge took place are not properly considered in an action for damages for breach of contract. Rather, it is said, damages are limited to injuries that flow from the breach itself, which in the employment context is the failure to give reasonable notice. The manner of dismissal was found not to affect these damages.

[90] Although these decisions are grounded in general principles of contract law, I believe, with respect, that they have all failed to take into account the unique characteristics of the particular type of contract with which they were concerned, namely, a contract of employment. Similarly, there was not an appropriate recognition of the special relationship which these contracts govern. In my view, both are relevant considerations.

[91] The contract of employment has many characteristics that set it apart from the ordinary commercial contract. Some of the views on this subject that have already been approved of in previous decisions of this Court (see *e.g.*, *Machtinger*, *supra*) bear repeating. As K. Swinton noted in "Contract Law and the Employment Relationship: The Proper Forum for Reform" in B.J. Reiter and J. Swan, eds., *Studies in Contract Law* (1980), 357, at p. 363:

. . . the terms of the employment contract rarely result from an exercise of free bargaining power in the way that the paradigm commercial exchange between two traders does. Individual employees on the whole lack both the bargaining power and the information necessary to achieve more favourable contract provisions than those offered by the employer, particularly with regard to tenure.

[92] This power imbalance is not limited to the employment contract itself. Rather, it informs virtually all facets of the employment relationship. In *Slaight Communications Inc. v. Davidson*, [1989] 1 S.C.R. 1038, Dickson C.J., writing for the majority of the Court, had occasion to comment on the nature of this relationship. At pp. 1051-52 he quoted with approval from P. Davies and M. Freedland, *Kahn-Freund's Labour and the Law* (3rd ed. 1983), at p. 18:

> [T]he relation between an employer and an isolated employee or worker is typically a relation between a bearer of power and one who is not a bearer of power. In its inception it is an act of submission, in its operation it is a condition of subordination. . . .

[93] This unequal balance of power led the majority of the Court in *Slaight Communications*, *supra*, to describe employees as a vulnerable group in society: see p. 1051. The vulnerability of employees is underscored by the level of importance which our society attaches to employment. As Dickson C.J. noted in *Reference Re Public Service Employee Relations Act (Alta.)*, [1987] 1 S.C.R. 313, at p. 368:

> Work is one of the most fundamental aspects in a person's life, providing the individual with a means of financial support and, as importantly, a contributory role in society. A person's employment is an essential component of his or her sense of identity, self-worth and emotional well-being.

[94] Thus, for most people, work is one of the defining features of their lives. Accordingly, any change in a person's employment status is bound to have far-reaching repercussions. In "Aggravated Damages and the Employment Contract", *supra*, Schai noted at p. 346 that, "[w]hen this change is involuntary, the extent of our 'personal dislocation' is even greater."

[95] The point at which the employment relationship ruptures is the time when the employee is most vulnerable and hence, most in need of protection. In recognition of this need, the law ought to encourage conduct that minimizes the damage and dislocation (both economic and personal) that result from dismissal. In *Machtinger*, *supra*, it was noted that the manner in which employment can be terminated is equally important to an individual's identity as the work itself (at p. 1002). By way of expanding upon this statement, I note that the loss of one's job is always a traumatic event. However, when termination is accompanied by acts of bad faith in the manner of discharge, the results can be especially devastating. In my opinion, to ensure that employees receive adequate protection, employers ought to be held to an obligation of good faith and fair dealing in the manner of dismissal, the breach of which will be compensated for by adding to the length of the notice period. *Wallace damages*

. . .

[97] I find further support for this approach in the decisions of several cases wherein the manner of dismissal was among the factors considered in determining the notice period: [Cases omitted.]

[98] The obligation of good faith and fair dealing is incapable of precise definition. However, at a minimum, I believe that in the course of dismissal employers ought to be candid, reasonable, honest and forthright with their employees and should refrain from engaging in conduct that is unfair or is in bad faith by being, for example, untruthful, misleading or unduly insensitive. In order to illustrate possible breaches of this obligation, I refer now to some examples of the conduct over which the courts expressed their disapproval in the cases cited above.

[99] In *Trask* [(1995), 9 C.C.E.L. (2d) 157 (Nfld. C.A.)], an employer maintained a wrongful accusation of involvement in a theft and communicated this accusation to other potential employers of the dismissed employee. ... In *Dunning* [(1996), 23 C.C.E.L. (2d) 71 (Ont. Ct. (Gen. Div.))], bad faith conduct was clearly present. Although the plaintiff's position had been eliminated, he was told by several senior executives that another position would probably be found for him and that the new assignment would necessitate a transfer. However, at the same time that the plaintiff was being reassured about his future, a senior representative of the company was contemplating his termination. When a position could not be found, the decision was made to terminate the plaintiff. This decision was not communicated to the plaintiff for over a month despite the fact that his employers knew he was in the process of selling his home in anticipation of the transfer. News of his termination was communicated to the plaintiff abruptly following the sale of his home.

[100] ... The facts in *MacDonald* [(1995), 12 C.C.E.L. (2d) 211 (N.S.S.C.)] are also illustrative of bad faith conduct. In that case, the defendant employer closed its bar for three months and laid off the plaintiff bartender. While the bar was closed, the executive committee was replaced and the new officers decided to implement a different salary structure for bartenders when the bar reopened. The employer advertised for a bartender at a rate of almost half of the plaintiff's hourly rate. The plaintiff was unaware of any change in his status, and it was only when he saw the advertisement in the newspaper that he learned that he had been dismissed and was not to be offered reinstatement.

[101] These examples by no means exhaust the list of possible types of bad faith or unfair dealing in the manner of dismissal. However, all are indicative of the type of conduct that ought to merit compensation by way of an addition to the notice period. I note that, depending upon the circumstances of the individual case, not all acts of bad faith or unfair dealing will be equally injurious and thus, the amount by which the notice period is extended will vary. Furthermore, I do not intend to advocate anything akin to an automatic claim for damages under this heading in every case of dismissal. In each case, the trial judge must examine the nature of the bad faith conduct and its impact in the circumstances.

[102] The Court of Appeal in the instant case recognized the relevance of manner of dismissal in the determination of the appropriate period of reasonable notice. However, relying on Trask, *supra*, ... the court found that this factor could only be considered "where it impacts on the future employment prospects of the dismissed employee" (p. 180). With respect, I believe that this is an overly restrictive view. In my opinion, the law must recognize a more expansive list of injuries which may flow from unfair treatment or bad faith in the manner of dismissal.

[103] It has long been accepted that a dismissed employee is not entitled to compensation for injuries flowing from the fact of the dismissal itself: see *e.g.*, *Addis*, *supra*. Thus, although the loss of a job is very often the cause of injured feelings and emotional upset, the law does not recognize these as compensable losses. However, where an employee can establish that an employer engaged in bad faith conduct or unfair dealing in the course of dismissal, injuries such as humiliation, embarrassment and damage to one's sense of self-worth and self-esteem might all be worthy of compensation depending upon the circumstances of the case. In these situations, compensation does not flow from the fact of dismissal itself, but rather from the manner in which the dismissal was effected by the employer.

[104] Often the intangible injuries caused by bad faith conduct or unfair dealing on dismissal will lead to difficulties in finding alternative employment, a tangible loss which the Court of Appeal rightly recognized as warranting an addition to the notice period. It is likely that the more unfair or in bad faith the manner of dismissal is the more this will have an effect on the ability of the dismissed employee to find new employment. However, in my view the intangible injuries are sufficient to merit compensation in and of themselves. I recognize that bad faith conduct which affects employment prospects may be worthy of considerably more compensation than that which does not, but in both cases damage has resulted that should be compensable.

[IACOBUCCI J. referred to cases of defamation where damages were awarded to reflect the fact that there had been an injury to the plaintiff's feelings.]

[107] In my view, there is no valid reason why the scope of compensable injuries in defamation situations should not be equally recognized in the context of wrongful dismissal from employment. The law should be mindful of the acute vulnerability of terminated employees and ensure their protection by encouraging proper conduct and preventing all injurious losses which might flow from acts of bad faith or unfair dealing on dismissal, both tangible and intangible. I note that there may be those who would say that this approach imposes an onerous obligation on employers. I would respond simply by saying that I fail to see how it can be onerous to treat people fairly, reasonably, and decently at a time of trauma and despair. In my view, the reasonable person would expect such treatment. So should the law.

[108] In the case before this Court, the trial judge documented several examples of bad faith conduct on the part of UGG. He noted the abrupt manner in which Wallace was dismissed despite having received compliments on his work from his superiors only days before. He found that UGG made a conscious decision to "play hardball" with Wallace and maintained unfounded allegations of cause until the day the trial began. Further, as a result of UGG's persistence in maintaining these allegations, "[w]ord got around, and it was rumoured in the trade that he had been involved in some wrongdoing" (p. 173). Finally, he found that the dismissal and subsequent events were largely responsible for causing Wallace's depression. Having considered the *Bardal* list of factors, he stated at p. 170:

> Taking [these] factors into account, and particularly the fact that the peremptory dismissal and the subsequent actions of the defendant made other employment in his field virtually unavailable, I conclude that an award at the top of the scale in such cases is warranted.

[109] I agree with the trial judge's conclusion that the actions of UGG seriously diminished Wallace's prospects of finding similar employment. In light of this fact, and the other circumstances of this case, I am not persuaded that the trial judge erred in awarding the equivalent of 24 months' salary in lieu of notice. It may be that such an award is at the high end of the scale; however, taking into account all of the relevant factors, this award is not unreasonable and accordingly, I can see no reason to interfere. Therefore, for the reasons above, I would restore the order of the trial judge with respect to the appropriate period of reasonable notice and allow the appeal on this ground.

6. Conclusions and Disposition

[110] I would dismiss the cross-appeal with costs and allow the appeal in part with costs here and in the courts below. I would set aside the judgment of the Manitoba Court of Appeal and restore the trial judge's award of 24 months' salary in lieu of notice. As explained above, the other aspects of the appellant's claim are rejected.

MCLACHLIN J., with whom LA FOREST and L'HEUREUX-DUBÉ JJ. agreed, said:

[111] I have read the reasons of Justice Iacobucci. While I agree with much of his reasons, my view of the law leads me to differ both in method and in result.

[112] As to method, I differ from Iacobucci J. in two respects. First, I am of the view that an award of damages for wrongful dismissal should be confined to factors relevant to the prospect of finding replacement employment. It follows that the notice period upon which such damages are based should only be increased for manner of dismissal if this impacts on the employee's prospects of re-employment. Secondly, I am of the view the law has evolved to permit recognition of an implied duty of good faith in termination of the employment.

[113] These differences lead me to a different result than my colleague. I would uphold the trial judge's award of damages for wrongful dismissal based on a 24-month notice period. I would also uphold the trial judge's award of $15,000 for mental distress on the basis of breach of the contractual obligation of good faith in dismissing an employee.

. . .

The Law

. . .

[118] My colleague, Iacobucci J., holds that the manner of dismissal may be considered generally in defining the notice period for wrongful dismissal. An alternative view is that the manner of dismissal should only be considered in defining the notice period where the manner of dismissal impacts on the difficulty of finding replacement employment, and that absent this connection, damages for the manner of termination must be based on some other cause of action.

[119] I prefer the second approach for the following reasons. First, this solution seems to me more consistent with the nature of the action for wrongful dismissal. Second, this approach, unlike the alternative, honours the principle that damages must be grounded in a cause of action. Third, this approach seems to me more consistent with the authorities, notably *Vorvis v. Insurance Corporation of British Columbia*, [1989] 1 S.C.R. 1085, *per* McIntyre J. Fourth, this approach will better aid certainty and predictability in the law governing damages for termination of employment. Finally, there are other equally effective ways to remedy wrongs related to the manner of dismissal which do not affect the prospect of finding replacement work. I will discuss in turn each of these reasons for preferring the second alternative.

1.   *Consistency with the Nature of the Action for Wrongful Dismissal*

[120] As already stated, the action for wrongful dismissal is an action for breach of an implied term in the contract of employment to give reasonable notice of termination. Reasonable notice, in turn, represents the time that may reasonably be re-

quired to find replacement employment. It follows that only factors relevant to the prospects of re-employment should be considered in determining the notice period. To include other factors is to consider matters unrelated to the breach of contract for which damages are ostensibly being awarded.

2. *Consistency with the Principle That Damages Must Be Grounded in a Cause of Action*

[121] Damages, to be recoverable, must flow from an actionable and hence compensable wrong ... Since the compensable wrong in wrongful dismissal actions is the failure to give reasonable notice so that the employee can find replacement employment, a successful plaintiff will only be entitled to damages flowing from that wrong.

[122] It follows that the only damages recoverable in an action based on breach of the contractual duty to give reasonable notice are those related to the prospect of re-employment. Other wrongs must find their remedy elsewhere.

3. *Consistency with the Authorities*

[123] This is not the first time this Court has considered the issue of whether damages related to the manner of dismissal can increase the notice period upon which damages for wrongful dismissal are based. In *Vorvis*, *supra*, this Court declined an invitation to do just this.

[124] As in the case at bar, the plaintiff in *Vorvis* claimed damages for wrongful dismissal as well as damages for mental distress suffered by him as a result of his employer's callous treatment of him around the time of dismissal. The Court affirmed the long-standing principle that damages for wrongful dismissal (as opposed to other wrongs) were confined to loss flowing from the absence of reasonable notice of termination. McIntyre J. for the majority, citing *Addis v. Gramophone Co.*, [1909] A.C. 488 (H.L.), and *Peso Silver Mines Ltd. (N.P.L.) v. Cropper*, [1966] S.C.R. 673, aff'g (1965), 56 D.L.R. (2d) 117 (B.C.C.A.), stated (at p. 1103):

> The rule long established in the *Addis* and *Peso Silver Mines* cases has generally been applied to deny [aggravated] damages, and the employer/employee relationship . . . has always been one where either party could terminate the contract of employment by due notice, and therefore the only damage which could arise would result from a failure to give such notice.

[125] This said, McIntyre J. left open the possibility that aggravated damages could be awarded in a case of wrongful dismissal, "particularly where the acts complained of were also independently actionable" (p. 1103).

[126] It is argued that this phrase means that the notice period on which damages for wrongful dismissal are predicated may be increased to reflect the manner of dismissal, even where it did not affect the prospects of re-employment. This submission seems to me to read a great deal into the phrase. It seems to me more likely that McIntyre J., without closing the door on the possibility of aggravated damages in a contractual action for wrongful dismissal (for example, in a case where manner of dismissal impacts on prospects of re-employment), was of the view that generally, aggravated damages would arise only where the acts were independently actionable. This is consistent with the long-standing distinction affirmed in *Vorvis* between damages for breach of the contractual duty to give reasonable notice of termination and other independent causes of action which may give rise more generally to damages for manner of dismissal. On this view, the first source of damages is the traditional wrongful dismissal action compensating for the failure to give reasonable notice. The second source of damages are actions for independently actionable wrongs. The manner of dismissal may figure in both types of action: in the former, where it impacts on prospects of re-employment; in the latter more generally. When it does so, additional aggravated damages may be awarded if the employer's conduct was so "harsh, vindictive, reprehensible and malicious" that damages representing punishment in addition to compensation should be awarded.

[127] In conclusion, it seems to me that the general principle underlying *Vorvis* is that damages for wrongful dismissal are confined to damages for breach of the implied obligation on the employer to give reasonable notice. Unless the manner of termination increased the time required to find new employment and hence the notice period, damages for manner of dismissal must be grounded in an independent cause of action.

[128] The view I propose is also consistent with the language and spirit of *Bardal*, *supra*. Each of the *Bardal* factors indicate something about the future employment prospects of the particular employee: Christie et al., *supra*, at pp. 611-20. The factor "availability of other employment" clearly relates to the extent of difficulty the employee can expect to confront when searching for new employment. The "characteristics of the job" are considered because of the hypothesis that employees in the higher echelon of employment positions will be less able to find alternative employment because there are fewer job openings available in these positions. Although the "length of service" is potentially considered for a number of reasons, one rationale for considering this factor is that "longer seniority-rated employees are likely to be older and therefore less able to find alternative employment" (Christie et al., *supra*, at p. 618). This also explains why the "age of the employee" is considered.

[129] Finally, the view I endorse is consistent with *Vorvis* and *Bardal* read together. To extend the factors in Bardal to include matters unrelated to prospects of re-employment is to effectively collapse the distinction affirmed in *Vorvis* between the cause of action for breach of the contractual duty to give reasonable notice of termination and independent causes of action for other employer wrongs.

[130] I conclude that the authorities support the following position. If the employer dismisses an employee in a manner that negatively affects the employee's chances of finding alternative employment, a court may properly increase the employee's period of reasonable notice to reflect that increased difficulty. Otherwise, the reasonable notice assessment should not be increased to compensate for employer misconduct in the manner of dismissal. Compensation for such injuries must be founded on an independent cause of action.

4.   *Certainty and Predictability*

[131] As earlier noted, the fact that some courts in the past have considered factors unrelated to prospects of re-employment in determining the notice period upon which damages for wrongful dismissal are based, has rendered the law "uncertain and unpredictable": Christie et al., *supra*, at p. 611. To continue on this path by allowing conduct unrelated to the prospects of employment to affect the notice period would only increase that uncertainty and unpredictability. It would confront employers and judges seeking to establish the reasonable notice period under the contract with new and difficult questions unrelated to the wrong of failure to give reasonable notice. What sort of employer conduct is capable of increasing the notice period? How much time should be added for a particular sort of misconduct? The absence of a legal basis in the action for wrongful dismissal for the increased damages on account of manner of dismissal would make it difficult to provide principled and consistent answers to these questions.

[132] Confining the factors considered in determining reasonable notice to matters impacting on the prospect of finding replacement employment will increase the predictability of wrongful dismissal law, making it easier for employers to anticipate the length of notice a particular employee is likely to receive. To require the employer to take into account undefined conduct not related to these factors in determining the length of notice is to complicate and render less precise the inquiry into the appropriate notice period.

5.   *The Availability of Other Remedies*

[133] It is argued that employer misconduct in the manner of dismissal not affecting prospects of re-employment must be taken into account in calculating the notice period in order to avoid injustice and provide an adequate remedy to the employee in a case such as this. The answer to this argument is that the law affords other remedies for employer misconduct in these circumstances.

[134] The law of tort and contract recognizes a number of independent causes of action for misconduct in dismissing an employee. If the employer defames the employee or wilfully inflicts mental distress, the employee can sue in tort. If the employer has lured the employee from a secure position with promises of better terms, the employee may be able to sue in tort for negligent misrepresentation or for breach of an express contractual term. Finally, unfair treatment at the time of dismissal may give rise to an action for breach of an implied term in the contract of employment.

[135] The law has now developed to the point that to these traditional actions may now be added another: breach of an implied contractual term to act in good faith in dismissing an employee. I agree with Iacobucci J. that an employer must act in good faith and in fair dealing when dismissing employees, and more particularly that "employers ought to be candid, reasonable, honest and forthright with their employees and should refrain from engaging in conduct that is unfair or is in bad faith by being, for example, untruthful, misleading or unduly insensitive" (para. 98). I also agree that this obligation does not extend to prohibiting employers from dismissing employees without "good faith" reasons; such an extension of employment law would be "overly intrusive and inconsistent with established principles of employment law" (para. 76). Both employer and employee remain free to terminate the contract of employment without cause. This is not inconsistent with the duty of good faith. While some courts have recognized employer obligations of good faith outside of the dismissal context (see below), this case does not require us to go beyond the context of dismissal.

[136] I differ from my colleague, however, in that I see no reason why the expectation of good faith in dismissing employees that he accepts should not be viewed as an implied term of the contract of employment. To assert the duty of good faith in dismissing employees as a proposition of law, as does my colleague, is tantamount to saying that it is an obligation implied by law into the contractual relationship between employer and employee. In other words, it is an implied term of the contract.

[137] Implication of this term meets the test set out by this Court in *Canadian Pacific Hotels Ltd. v. Bank of Montreal*, [1987] 1 S.C.R. 711. Le Dain J., for the majority, held that terms may be implied on the basis of custom or usage, presumed intention, and as legal incidents of a particular class or kind of contract, the nature and content of which have to be largely determined by implication. . . .

[138] This is the type of implication that is involved in the proposed obligation of good faith. As Iacobucci J. points out, employment contracts have characteristics quite distinct from other types of contracts as a result of the often unequal bargaining power typically involved in the relationship. This results in employee vulnerability — a vulnerability that is especially acute at the time of dismissal. The nature of the relationship thereby necessitates some measure of protection for the vulnerable party. Requiring employers to treat their employees with good faith at the time of dismissal provides this special measure of protection. It follows that an implied term is necessary in the sense required to justify implication of a contractual term by law.

[139] Recognition of an implied term in the employment contract of good faith in relation to the dismissal of employees is supported by previous decisions, academic commentary and related developments in other areas of contract law.

. . .

[142] The weight of academic commentary supports the judicial imposition of a duty of good faith in dismissing employees. Christie et al., *supra*, suggest that "[t]he implied promise to treat the employee with decency and dignity in job exit situations offers the greatest potential in compensating for mental distress" (p. 750).

. . .

[145] Finally, implication of an implied contractual obligation of good faith in dismissing an employee is consistent with the recognition of an implied obligation of good faith and fair dealing in other areas of contract law, such as commercial contracts, insurance contracts and real estate contracts. . . .

[146] In summary, it is my view that the law has evolved to the point of recognition of an implied contractual obligation of good faith in the contract of employment to treat the employee with good faith in dismissing him or her. To the extent that recognition of such a term may be seen as a new development, it falls within the scope of the incremental step-by-step revision approved in *Watkins v. Olafson*, [1989] 2 S.C.R. 750, at pp. 760-61, and *R. v. Salituro*, [1991] 3 S.C.R. 654, at p. 668. The action for breach of this duty supplements the independent causes of action in contract and tort previously recognized to provide ample redress for wrongs such as those raised by the appellant without altering the traditional notice-based action for wrongful dismissal.

Application of the Law

[147] After taking into account the enumerated *Bardal* factors and the fact that "the peremptory dismissal and the subsequent actions of the defendant made other employment in his field virtually unavailable" (p. 170), the trial judge fixed the period of reasonable notice at 24 months. The Court of Appeal reduced the notice period from 24 to 15 months on the basis that the trial judge may have allowed an element of aggravated damages to creep into his assessment and that recent awards in such cases had been getting too high. I do not agree. The trial judge proceeded on the basis of a careful assessment of the appellant's prospects of re-employment. He considered no other factors. I see no reason to interfere in his assessment.

[148] The appellant also claimed damages for mental distress, loss of reputation and prestige, and punitive damages. The trial judge concluded that it was the dismissal and events following thereafter that were mostly responsible for the mental anguish suffered by Mr. Wallace. These damages are compensable providing they flow from the employer's failure to treat Mr. Wallace in good faith at the time of dismissal. The trial judge found bad faith conduct on the part of UGG in: (1) terminating Mr. Wallace in an abrupt manner after having complimented him numerous times prior to the dismissal; and (2) UGG's decision to play hardball with Mr. Wallace by maintaining completely unfounded allegations of just cause up until the start of the trial which resulted in Mr. Wallace being essentially ostracized from the printing business. UGG thus breached the implied term of good faith and fair dealing by acting as it did at the time of dismissal. The damages claimed under the heading mental distress and loss of reputation are general damages flowing directly from the employer's breach of the implied term and are therefore compensable. Accordingly, I would uphold the trial judge's award of $15,000 representing compensation for those additional damages.

[149] I see no reason to interfere with the trial judge's conclusion that UGG did not engage in sufficiently "harsh, vindictive, reprehensible and malicious" conduct to merit an award representing punitive damages.

. . .

[151] I would dismiss the cross-appeal and allow the appeal with costs here and in the courts below and restore the trial judge's award of 24 months' salary representing damages for wrongful dismissal and $15,000 representing compensation for mental distress and loss of reputation.

NOTES AND QUESTIONS

1. The test of what constitutes reasonable notice stated in *Bardal v. Globe & Mail Ltd.*, [1960] O.W.N. 253, makes certain facts relevant, but does not determine or limit the award that will follow from the test. In *Foster v. Kockums Cancar Division Hawker Siddeley Canada Inc.*, [1993] 8 W.W.R. 477, 83 B.C.L.R. (2d) 207 (C.A.), Southin J.A. considered that the steady increase in the length of notice periods in cases of wrongful dismissal could not be justified on the basis of *Bardal*. She asked (p. 486 W.W.R.): "What, if anything, happened from 1960 to 1987 to leave the oft-quoted passage from *Bardal v. Globe & Mail Ltd.* intact as a guide, but the conclusion of McRuer C.J.H.C. in tatters?" How would you answer Southin J.A.?

2. The traditional approach of *Bardal* gave a longer notice period to employees in more senior and responsible positions, based on the assumption that these employees have more specialized jobs and would take longer to find alternative employment. Thus a company president would get longer notice than a middle manager, and the latter would get more than a clerk or salesperson, all having the same length of service with

the employer. The most senior employees therefore had much larger awards, reflecting both the longer notice period and their higher rate of pay.

3.   This approach was challenged by MacPherson J. in *Cronk v. Canadian General Insurance Co.* (1994), 19 O.R. (3d) 515, 6 C.C.E.L. (2d) 15 (Gen. Div.) In granting a motion for summary judgment brought by the plaintiff employee, MacPherson J. held that she was entitled to 20 months' notice rather than the approximately nine months' notice offered by the defendant employer. MacPherson J. observed that a person with less education would have as much or greater difficulty in getting a new job than a person with more education, so the traditional practice of giving junior employees less than senior ones as damages for wrongful dismissal could no longer be justified. To support his view of the effect of education, MacPherson J. referred to studies done by the Council of Ontario Universities and an article in the *Economist* magazine. MacPherson J. also pointed out that a rule favouring senior employees tended to discriminate against women.

On appeal to the Ontario Court of Appeal (1995), 25 O.R. (3d) 505, 128 D.L.R. (4th) 147, the majority of that court, Morden A.C.J.O. and Lacourcière J.A., held that, on traditional principles, the plaintiff should have received 12 months' notice rather than nine. They rejected the 20 months awarded by MacPherson J. Weiler J.A., in dissent, would have ordered a trial to determine the damages to be awarded to the plaintiff. She pointed out that *Bardal* established a standard, not a rule, and that under *Bardal*, it was appropriate to consider giving a person in a clerical position as much as a person in a senior management position, whether one came at this result by increasing the clerk's damages or reducing the executive's damages. Is this the answer to the question posed by Southin J.A. in *Foster*?

The Ontario Court of Appeal dealt with the fact that MacPherson J. had relied on published material which counsel had not had an opportunity to comment on or rebut about the effects of unemployment on less-educated employees. The Court of Appeal held that a trial judge should not use material that the parties did not have a chance to consider and on which they could have based arguments.

4.   Despite the decision of the Ontario Court of Appeal in *Cronk,* the New Brunswick Court of Appeal in *Bramble v. Medis Health and Pharmaceutical Services Inc.* (1999), 175 D.L.R. (4th) 385, 214 N.B.R. (2d) 111 approved of the approach of MacPherson J. in *Cronk*. Drapeau J.A. said (pp. 398-400 D.L.R.):

> [51] Criticism of the role that character of employment *simpliciter* has been allowed to play in the determination of notice has spread beyond judicial circles to the point that it now emanates not only from academics but from employment law practitioners as well.
>
> [52] In "Employment Law, Recent Developments in Employment and Labour Law", a paper delivered as part of the May 1998 civil law seminar hosted by the National Judicial Institute, Ronald A. Pink, Q.C., an employment law practitioner whose experience is undoubted, questions the role that character of employment has been allowed to play in the determination of notice:
>
>> One issue which must be considered is whether or not the [Ontario] Court of Appeal decision in *Cronk* accurately reflects social reality. *Mr. Justice MacPherson referred to research which indicated that lower level employees actually have a more difficult time in finding employment than more highly educated employees. If this is correct, should courts be perpetuating the hardship of these dismissed employees by failing to acknowledge the social reality that lower level employees have a more difficult time finding adequate replacement employment?* Should Canadian courts continue to award less adequate compensation in dismissal situations by virtue of the fact that the employee in question is less educated than other employees? . . . Simply put, is the decision of the Court of Appeal [in *Cronk*] elitist?

> . . . If justice is blind, why does it see rich businessmen as more needy than clerks? Is one more valuable than the other? Value is measured in the salary of the employee, and the salary equalizes the differences between employees, Bardal must be refined accordingly.

[Emphasis added by Drapeau J.A.]

[53] Other commentators have observed that the traditional approach expresses "class prejudice". Having noted as well the existence of empirical data that contradicts the traditional approach's factual underpinning, namely that senior employees have a greater difficulty in finding new employment, some commentators have described the perfunctory justifications occasionally offered for the traditional approach as having a hollow ring "both empirically and ethically". See Innis Christie, Geoffrey England and Brent Cotter, *Employment Law in Canada*, 2nd ed. (Markham, Ont.: Butterworths, 1993) at pp. 615-17. While it is true that, in the most recent edition of their work, these authors no longer expressly challenge the ethical propriety of the traditional approach, they do nonetheless acknowledge that "the empirical question whether high status occupations in Canada face greater difficulties in obtaining alternate work than low status groups unfortunately has not yet been conclusively answered". See Geoffrey England *et al.*, *Employment Law in Canada*, 3rd ed., vol. 2, looseleaf (Markham, Ont.: Butterworths, 1998) at p. 14.83.4, para. #14.120.

[54] In "Character of Employment and Wrongful Dismissal Notice: *Cronk v. Canadian General Insurance Co.*" (1995), 4 Dal. J. Leg. Studies 271, Griffith Roberts refers to a number of publications that have emphasized how higher employability accompanies higher training and education and he concludes that at pp. 279-80:

> Studies based upon Statistics Canada data also suggest that the skilled and the educated are not disadvantaged when it comes to finding alternative employment. Those on long term unemployment have, on average, lower levels of unemployment than the work force in general. . . . [S]tatistically there is no simple relationship between education and length of unemployment, particularly during a severe economic downturn. A higher level of education would in some circumstances imply a longer duration of unemployment, and in other circumstances, a shorter duration of unemployment. During periods of .economic recovery, however, the better educated were the first to find new jobs. . . .

> The assumption made by the courts that the educated or skilled worker will have a more difficult time finding suitable alternative employment, if not wrong, is clearly unfounded.

Drapeau J.A., after referring to some cases in New Brunswick, commented (at para. 74), ". . . they nonetheless reflect a long-overdue upward trend in the length of notice periods that is in accord with the reasonable expectations of terminated employees in general". The British Columbia Court of Appeal took a similar approach to *Bramble* in *Byers v. Prince George (City)*, [1998] B.C.J. No. 1757, [1999] 2 W.W.R. 335 (C.A.).

Which approach do you prefer, that of the Ontario Court of Appeal in *Cronk*, or that of the New Brunswick Court of Appeal in *Bramble*?

5. It is important to be clear about the decision of the Ontario Court of Appeal. It is unfair to characterize the decision in *Cronk* as "elitist" or insensitive to the needs of less-educated workers. That Court was applying the law as it was at the date of the judgment. The evidence relied on by MacPherson J. could not be considered by the Court: it had been discovered by the trial judge himself and he had given neither counsel and particularly the defendant's counsel any opportunity to deal with it, either by challenging its relevance in the light of the law or by producing evidence to rebut it. The es-

sence of adjudication is the right of the parties to put the facts and their arguments before the judge. The judge who considers evidence that the parties have not put before him or who denies them an opportunity to present arguments on it has undercut the process of adjudication. (What the judge may properly consider by way of "judicial notice" or as notorious facts slightly expands the scope of the facts the judge may look at.) It is also implicit in the process of adjudication that there are agreed standards of adjudication, *i.e.*, that there is a general consensus on the part of counsel and the court on what arguments may be made. A judge who radically changes the standards by considering arguments that, up to that point, had not been part of the consensus again threatens the process of adjudication. These constraints impose real limits on the scope of the courts to make radical reforms of the law and it is an important aspect of any examination of the law to reflect on those limits and to articulate their scope and effect.

6.   In *Wallace v. United Grain Growers Ltd.*, the majority also fashioned a remedy for an employee who was a victim of harsh conduct by an employer by lengthening the notice period, rather than having a purely monetary award for aggravated damages. Each extra month is "worth" more to employees who are more highly paid. Is this fair? No

7.   If an employee who is wrongfully dismissed obtains new employment during the notice period, however long that is, whatever is earned in the new job is deducted from any award. If an employer can establish that a wrongfully dismissed employee failed to take reasonable steps to find another job (and thereby mitigate damages), there may be a reduction in the notice period to reflect this: see, *e.g.*, *Belton v. Liberty Insurance Co. of Canada*, [2004] O.J. No. 3358, 72 O.R. (3d) 81 (C.A.).

8.   It is becoming increasingly common for employers who are hiring employees to have written employment contracts that, among other things, specify the amount of notice that an employee is to receive on termination. If the clause is "clear and conspicuous" then the courts are likely to give effect to such a clause: *Wallace v. Toronto Dominion Bank* (1983), 41 O.R. (2d) 161, 145 D.L.R. (3d) 431 (C.A.). However, if the clause is not clearly written or appears unconscionable, for example by offering less notice than required by legislation, it may be ignored by the courts: *Machtinger v. HOJ Industries Ltd.*, [1992] 1 S.C.R. 986, 91 D.L.R. (4th) 491.

9.   Much feminist literature draws attention to the fact that women are often more concerned with relations and less concerned with abstract rights than men are. Madam Justice Bertha Wilson, at that time a judge of the Supreme Court of Canada, argued that women have a significantly different attitude to law, especially family and criminal law: "Will Women Judges Really Make a Difference" (1990), 24 *L. Soc. Gaz.* 261. She questioned, however, whether gender makes a significant difference to the analysis of contract law, writing (at p. 268):

> Taking from my own experience as a judge of fourteen years' standing, working closely with my male colleagues on the bench, there are probably whole areas of the law on which there is no uniquely feminine perspective. This is not to say that the development in these areas has not been influenced by the fact that lawyers and judges have all been men. Rather, the principles and the underlying premises are so firmly entrenched and so fundamentally sound that no good would be achieved by attempting the re-invent the wheel, even if the revised version did have a few more spokes in it. I have in mind areas such as the law of contract, the law of property and the law applicable to corporations.

Notwithstanding her disclaimer, it is interesting to observe that in *Vorvis* and *Wallace v. United Grain Growers Ltd.* the dissents were written by women. It might be argued that they adopted an approach that attached more importance to the human relations and vulnerability of employees than the majority decisions. You may consider whether the approach of Wilson and McLachlin JJ. to contract law is affected by their sex. It may also be worth noting that the approach of the "male majority" in *Wallace* was quite different from the approach of the "male majority" in *Vorvis*.

10. For a feminist critique of traditional contracts casebooks, see Mary Joe Frug, "Re-Reading Contracts: A Feminist Analysis of a Contracts Casebook" (1985), 34 *Am. U. Law Rev.* 1065-1140.

11. Underlying the whole issue of damages for wrongful dismissal is the fact that most employees would rather have their jobs back than an award of damages. (Paradoxically, of course, those who are employable often do very well with a generous severance allowance, while for those who are not easily employable, even a generous allowance may not make up for what they have lost.) We shall see later in this chapter that courts are generally unwilling to order "specific performance" of employment contracts by ordering reinstatement. However, legislation provides that for unionized workers with a collective agreement, an arbitrator can order reinstatement where the employee has been wrongfully dismissed. Non-unionized employees governed by legislation in Nova Scotia, Quebec and the *Canada Labour Code* may also be able to seek an order for reinstatement.

12. The common law was historically characterized by the fact that its rules were stated not as principles derived from some ultimate values, but as remedies provided for some wrong. (The rules could, of course, be justified by reference to some values, but that is a different matter.) In other words, if there was a remedy for a wrong, then it could be said that there was a law, a rule, that the act that was the wrong should not be done or that the plaintiff who had a remedy had a right not to have the wrong done. While this remedies-based view of the law has been to a large extent replaced by one that states the law in terms of rules, principles and standards, it remains true that, if the plaintiff is to be awarded damages, the defendant must have done something wrong, *i.e.*, something that he or she should not have done. If Mr. Wallace gets a remedy for the bad behaviour of the plaintiff, what is it exactly that the defendant did wrong? You will remember that Iacobucci J. goes out of his way to deny that there is either a contractual obligation on an employer to treat employees in good faith or a tort of "bad faith discharge".

13. It has been said in many cases that an obligation of good faith underlies all contractual relations. For example, in *GATX Corp. v. Hawker Siddeley Canada Inc.* (1996), 27 B.L.R. (2d) 251 (Ont. Ct. (Gen. Div.) [Commercial List]), Blair J. said (p. 276):

> There is, however, another basis upon which I am equally convinced that the Procor transaction cannot proceed except on the foregoing basis. It is well established that the grantor of a right of first refusal must act reasonably and in good faith in relation to that right, and must not act in a fashion designed to eviscerate the very right which has been given. *This is an illustration of the application of the good faith doctrine of contractual performance, which in my view is a part of the law of Ontario.* [Emphasis added.]

In *Wallace* Iacobucci J. says:

> [76] A requirement of "good faith" reasons for dismissal would, in effect, contravene these principles and deprive employers of the ability to determine the composition of their workforce. In the context of the accepted theories on the employment relationship, such a law would, in my opinion, be overly intrusive and inconsistent with established principles of employment law, and more appropriately, should be left to legislative enactment rather than judicial pronouncement.

As will become apparent throughout these materials, the Supreme Court has a very curious attitude to the concept of good faith in contractual relations and this paragraph from Iacobucci J.'s judgment illustrates some of the issues. There seem to be several bases for his conclusion that the obligation of good faith has no place in the employment relation: (i) it would contravene the principle that the employer can determine the size and composition of its workforce; (ii) it would be contrary to some established principle of employment law; or (iii) it would give the courts some unjustified excuse to interfere in the relation.

The requirement that an employer behave in good faith, *i.e.*, decently, does not mean that it cannot dismiss employees without cause: it means only that if it wants to do so, it must do it in the proper way *and with due concern for the employee's dignity and feelings*. The fact that the imposition of punishment under the criminal law must meet the standards of a fair trial does not mean that no one can be convicted of a crime; it means only that the police and the prosecutor have to meet certain standards of conduct and, as a society, we would not have it otherwise. It is hard to understand why anyone would think that the imposition of a requirement that an employer behave decently would have anything but beneficial results. Requirements of decent behaviour do not make contractual obligations vague or imprecise; they simply recognize what everyone would expect to be part of the parties' obligations.

Moreover, if the Supreme Court states that the employment relation is an important aspect of a person's life and well-being, why would it not consider that it is permeated by an obligation of good faith as in any other ordinary commercial relation, like the grant of a right of first refusal?

14. One interesting development is the increasing willingness of courts to impose on employers an obligation of fairness and decency if they are going to allege that there was cause for the employee's dismissal. An employer may, for example, have to give the employee notice of the allegations against him or her and an opportunity to answer them. See, *e.g.*, *Robinson v. Fraser Wharves Ltd.* (2000), 5 C.C.E.L. (3d) 81 (B.C.S.C.).

A similar development is taking place in the law of constructive dismissal. Constructive dismissal is the recognition that an employee who resigns may have been driven to that point by the employer's breach of the employment contract. In other words, the employer's breach will have excused the employee from his or her obligation to work, entitling the employee to resign. In *Shah v. Xerox Canada Ltd.* (2000), 49 C.C.E.L. (2d) 166, 2000 C.L.L.C. ¶ 210-022 (Ont. C.A.), the court held that an employee who had resigned was able to show that he had been constructively dismissed by his employer's failures to do things in the right way. The employee had been subjected to unjustified assessments and was the victim of poorly communicated expectations. These developments can be seen imposing a requirement that the employer behave decently in spite of what the Supreme Court said in *Wallace*.

15. The Supreme Court's decision in *Wallace* appears to allow for an award for damages for mental distress in the employment context only if there has been an "independent actionable wrong". However, in *Prinzo v. Baycrest Centre for Geriatric Care*, [2002] O.J. No. 2712, 60 O.R. (3d) 474 (C.A.) the Ontario Court of Appeal upheld a decision that awarded a wrongfully dismissed employee $15,000 for mental distress suffered as a result of treatment by the employer prior to and at the time of termination. The Court of Appeal characterized the employer's conduct as "flagrant and outrageous", noting that it resulted in stress-related illness, but observed that the damages should be based on the tort of intentional infliction of mental suffering rather than characterized as aggravated damages for wrongful dismissal. The employer's conduct included a false representation that her doctor had said that she was well enough to return to work, and a two-hour meeting at which four supervisors pressured her about termination.

16. Some of the comments of Iacobucci J. at para. 73 appear to have application to all types of contracts, and indicate that "foreseeability of mental distress ... is of no consequence" for determining liability for this type of injury. While much of *Wallace* is clearly still "good law", some of the general statements that he made about the law of contracts may have to be reassessed in light of the Supreme Court of Canada decision in *Fidler v. Sun Life Assurance Co. of Canada*, [2006] S.C.J. No.

30, which is set out below. Before considering that decision, however, it is useful to consider a category of contracts referred to as "peace of mind contracts".

Contracts Promising Peace of Mind

Closely related to the cases, like *Jarvis*, that awarded damages for lost enjoyment are cases where the courts have held that a contract contains, as one aspect of the bundle of benefits promised to a promisee, a promise to provide "peace of mind". In *Wallace* (at ¶ 73) the Supreme Court recognized the special status of such contracts. The principal class of such contracts are those of insurance, principally contracts of disability insurance. If the court decides that an insurer was offering "peace of mind" — and all insurance contracts can be seen as either implicitly or explicitly (often in advertising) offering such reassurance — the actions of the insurer who, by unreasonably disputing a claim, exacerbates the stress and worry suffered by the insured may find itself exposed to a claim for damages for lost peace of mind.

In *Warrington v. Great-West Life Assurance Co.* (1996), 139 D.L.R. (4th) 18, 24 B.C.L.R. (3d) 1 (C.A.), the plaintiff was unemployed as a result of having to quit his job due to "chronic fatigue syndrome" and claimed under his disability policy. While there was (in the words of the trial judge) "overwhelming" medical evidence that this was a genuine medical condition, albeit one that is difficult to diagnose, the insurance company claimed that he was in effect malingering and refused to pay. The insured's wife was pregnant at the time, and he was obliged to seek social assistance. His medical condition was exacerbated by the financial and psychological stress and he was forced to sue the insurance company. Just before trial the company agreed to honour the policy, but the trial judge ruled that the defendant's conduct and its "hard nosed and burdensome tactics" were a breach of its duty of good faith to its insured and justified an award of aggravated damages of $10,000. A claim for punitive damages was dismissed. In affirming the trial judgment, Newbury J.A. said (pp. 29-31 D.L.R.):

> . . . At least one Canadian court has held that parties to a contract of disability insurance should be taken to have contemplated as an important benefit, and indeed a purpose, of their contract the "peace of mind" implicit in the insured's receipt of timely and reliable benefit payments in substitution for his or her wages . . . *Thompson v. Zurich Insurance Co.* (1984), 7 D.L.R. (4th) 664 (Ont. H.C.J.) . . . There, Pennell J. noted that the "rigidity of the rule that no damages could be received in contract for injury to the feelings has yielded . . . to the spirit of the times", and that the parties' contemplation and the scope of the contract have now become the "basic criterion".
>
> . . .
>
> Few contracts could affect one's personal interests more than a contract for medical and rehabilitation benefits. In my judgment, both insured and insurer would contemplate that a failure of the insurer to pay medical and rehabilitation accounts in a timely fashion will foreseeably occasion mental distress and emotional upset. The predominant, if not the sole object of the contract was to provide ease of mind to the insured that his medical accounts would be taken care of by timely payments during the period of rehabilitation.
>
> . . .
>
> [Mr. Warrington's] illness was one that is likely exacerbated by stress. It seems to me that this is exactly the type of mental distress and inconvenience one buys disability insurance to avoid — in other words, that the *object* of this contract was Mr.

Warrington's comfort or peace of mind. I cannot accept that by paying "what was owed" to Mr. Warrington just before trial, Great-West made him whole in any sense of the word.

In summary, I conclude that a disability insurance policy is one of the few contracts in which damages for mental distress are recoverable when they are proven to result from the breach of contract. . . . The effect on him would have been the same whether the insurer had been well-motivated, reasonable, unreasonable, or even malicious in that delay. Thus in my view it was erroneous to find that an independent tort had been proven that resulted in injury in the form of mental distress to Mr. Warrington.

Before concluding consideration of issues raised by *Warrington* and "peace of mind" contracts, it is useful to consider the general topic of punitive damages. The Supreme Court of Canada decision in *Fidler v. Sun Life Assurance Co. of Canada*, [2006] S.C.J. No. 30, which is set out below, considered both aggravated damages and punitive damages in the context of dealing with a case that was quite similar to *Warrington*, and in doing so accepted the outcome in *Warrington*.

Punitive Damages

The decisions in *Vorvis* and *Wallace* appeared to leave little room for punitive damages in contracts cases. However, since those decisions there have been cases in which the courts have wanted to be able to discourage certain kinds of conduct and to afford relief to those who may have been victimized by such conduct. Recent Supreme Court decisions have made clear that, in appropriate cases, punitive damages may be awarded for breach of contract.

The most common method that courts have traditionally used to express their disapproval of what a party (or counsel) has done is to award the successful party "solicitor and client costs" or "substantial indemnity costs". While "solicitor and client" costs might not cover all of the fees that a client might have to pay (giving about 80 per cent to 90 per cent of the client's actual payment to his or her lawyer), it was more generous than the usual award for a successful litigant of "party and party costs" (or "partial indemnity costs"), which might amount to about half, often less, of a client's actual costs. Punitive damages for breach of contract were, until very recently, rare, and if awarded were modest ($5,000 to $25,000); a plaintiff might be significantly financially better off with an award of solicitor and client costs than with punitive damages. The law governing the issue of punitive damages in breach of contract cases, when they can be awarded and how much they should be, was dramatically changed by two Supreme Court of Canada decisions.

In *Royal Bank of Canada v. W. Got & Associates Electric Ltd.* [1999] 3 S.C.R. 408, 178 D.L.R. (4th) 385, the Supreme Court, in a judgment by McLachlin and Bastarache JJ., upheld an award of punitive damages of $100,000 against the bank, which had improperly appointed a receiver for the plaintiff's property, thereby putting it out of business. The punitive damage award in *Got* was relatively small, only about 10 per cent of the value of the compensatory award. A particular judicial concern about the "wrongful conduct" of the bank was that it had filed a misleading affidavit in support of its application for the appointment of the receiver, and hence undermined the justice system. The Supreme Court said (at para. 28):

... this is a case where the conduct of the bank "seriously affronts the administration of justice", as stated by the trial judge. We agree that the bank's conduct did not have to rise to the level of fraud, malicious prosecution, or abuse of process to justify an award of exemplary damages.

It is important to note that the decision to award punitive damages in *Royal Bank* was *not* based on the bank's breach of contract. It did breach its contract with its debtor by not giving the debtor adequate notice of its intention to appoint the receiver — an application of the concept of good faith in commercial dealings — but that breach was not the basis for the award of punitive damages. Punitive damages were awarded for a breach of the Alberta *Rules of Court*. Given the fact that at the time of the award it was unprecedented for a breach of those rules to have that consequence, the bank can have had little expectation that its bad behaviour in the process of getting the receiver appointed would lead to a fine of $100,000: the more usual penalty is the invalidity of the appointment (opening the way for the debtor to recover its damages) and an award of costs. The award of punitive damages in this case should be regarded as the retrospective imposition of what was, in effect, a quasi-criminal or criminal sanction. It is absurd to impose a sanction on a party who could not have known that it was running the risk of the sanction for its conduct.

The next case deals more extensively with the issue of punitive damages and radically changed Canadian law on the award of punitive damages for breach of contract.

WHITEN v. PILOT INSURANCE CO.

[2002] S.C.J. No. 19, [2002] 1 S.C.R. 595
(S.C.C., McLachlin C.J.C., L'Heureux-Dubé, Gonthier, Major, Binnie, Arbour and LeBel JJ.)

[The plaintiff's house caught fire one night in January 1994. She, her husband and their daughter fled the house wearing only their nightclothes. It was minus 18°C outside and Mr. Whiten suffered serious frostbite to his feet. The fire completely destroyed the home and its contents, and killed the family's three cats. Mrs. Whiten was able to rent a small winterized cottage nearby for $650 per month. The respondent insurer made a single payment of $5,000 for living expenses and covered the rent for a couple of months or so, then cut off the rent without telling the family, and thereafter pursued a confrontational policy. The plaintiff had limited financial resources.

The local fire chief, the independent adjuster and an expert initially retained by the defendant all said there was no evidence whatsoever of arson. In addition, the defendant received a report from the Insurance Crime Prevention Bureau that there was no evidence of arson and advice that the claim should be paid.

In spite of the evidence to the contrary, the defendant insurer decided to fight the claim. Counsel for the defendant, Donald Crabbe, made assiduous efforts to find some evidence to support his belief that there had been arson. Another independent expert was retained; he initially also concluded that the fire was accidental but was eventually "influenced" by Crabbe into expressing an opinion that the fire was "suspicious". Crabbe also told his client that if the plaintiff made a claim for punitive damages, evidence about two other fires would become admissible. In fact, there was no connection between those fires and the plaintiff. Crabbe appeared to regard the prospect of a trial (in the light of the family's financial situation) as providing a strong incentive for the plaintiff (and her counsel) to settle.

The defendant conceded before the Supreme Court that, in addition to the Senior Claims Examiner and the Branch Manager, the latter's "superior, George Hamilton (assistant to the Vice-President in charge of claims), [was] copied with all of the material on the file. Mr. Hamilton reported to Clifford Jones, Executive Vice President and Secretary". (It is not disclosed whether the latter officer received copies of Crabbe's reports.) Binnie J. said (at para. 16): "The misconduct was therefore not restricted to middle level management but was made known to the directing minds of the respondent company."

Binnie J. observed (at para. 20):

> It was never explained how the Whitens stood to profit from torching their own home. The fair market value of their house was $157,000. The jury allowed $160,000. The mortgage still had to be paid out of the proceeds, leaving the appellant with only the existing equity in her home. Had the claim been paid promptly, the only financial effect on the appellant would have been to convert the roof over her family's head into cash and oblige them to become renters. Selling the house would have had more or less the same financial impact. It defies common sense to think they would have risked so much — including their daughter's safety, all of their possessions and their cats — for so little. . . .

The trial judge commented unfavourably on Crabbe's role in the litigation. He felt that his "enthusiasm for his client's case appears to have caused him to exceed the permissible limits which ought to confine a lawyer in the preparation of witnesses".

The insurer's position was wholly discredited at trial and, before the Court of Appeal, its counsel conceded that there was no basis for the allegation of arson. The jury awarded compensatory damages of about $345,000 and $1 million in punitive damages. The trial judge also awarded solicitor and client costs, which were ultimately fixed at $317,000. A majority of the Ontario Court of Appeal (1999), 42 O.R. (3d) 641, 170 D.L.R. (4th) 280, allowed the appeal in part and reduced the punitive damages award to $100,000.

The Whitens appealed, seeking to restore the $1 million punitive damages award, while the insurer cross-appealed, arguing that there should be no punitive damages.]

The judgment of MCLACHLIN C.J.C., L'HEUREUX-DUBÉ, GONTHIER, MAJOR, BINNIE and ARBOUR JJ. was delivered by

[1]   BINNIE J.: — This case raises once again the spectre of uncontrolled and uncontrollable awards of punitive damages in civil actions. The jury was clearly outraged by the high-handed tactics employed by the respondent, Pilot Insurance Company, following its unjustified refusal to pay the appellant's claim under a fire insurance policy (ultimately quantified at approximately $345,000). Pilot forced an eight-week trial on an allegation of arson that the jury obviously considered trumped up. It forced her to put at risk her only remaining asset (the insurance claim) plus approximately $320,000 in legal costs that she did not have. The denial of the claim was designed to force her to make an unfair settlement for less than she was entitled to. The conduct was planned and deliberate and continued for over two years, while the financial situation of the appellant grew increasingly desperate. Evidently concluding that the arson defence

from the outset was unsustainable and made in bad faith, the jury added an award of punitive damages of $1 million, in effect providing the appellant with a "windfall" that added something less than treble damages to her actual out-of-pocket loss. The respondent argues that the award of punitive damages is itself outrageous.

. . .

[4] A majority of the Ontario Court of Appeal allowed the appeal in part and reduced the punitive damage award to $100,000. In my view, on the exceptional facts of this case, there was no basis on which to interfere with the jury award. The award, though very high, was rational in the specific circumstances disclosed in the evidence and within the limits that a jury is allowed to operate. The appellant was faced with harsh and unreasoning opposition from an insurer whose policy she had purchased for peace of mind and protection in just such an emergency. The jury obviously concluded that people who sell peace of mind should not try to exploit a family in crisis. Pilot, as stated, required the appellant to spend $320,000 in legal costs to collect the $345,000 that was owed to her. The combined total of $665,000 at risk puts the punitive damage awards in perspective. An award of $1 million in punitive damages is certainly at the upper end of a sustainable award on these facts but not beyond it. I would allow the appeal and restore the jury award of $1 million punitive damages.

[**BINNIE J.** set out the facts and recounted the proceedings and judgments in the Ontario courts.]

III. *Analysis*

[36] Punitive damages are awarded against a defendant in exceptional cases for "malicious, oppressive and high-handed" misconduct that "offends the court's sense of decency": *Hill v. Church of Scientology of Toronto*, [1995] 2 S.C.R. 1130, at para. 196. The test thus limits the award to misconduct that represents a marked departure from ordinary standards of decent behaviour. Because their objective is to punish the defendant rather than compensate a plaintiff (whose just compensation will already have been assessed), punitive damages straddle the frontier between civil law (compensation) and criminal law (punishment).

[37] Punishment is a legitimate objective not only of the criminal law but of the civil law as well. Punitive damages serve a need that is not met either by the pure civil law or the pure criminal law. In the present case, for example, no one other than the appellant could rationally be expected to invest legal costs of $320,000 in lengthy proceedings to establish that on this particular file the insurer had behaved abominably. Over-compensation of a plaintiff is given in exchange for this socially useful service.

[38] Nevertheless, the hybrid nature of punitive damages offends some jurists who insist that legal remedies should belong to one jurisprudential field or the other. That is one major aspect of the controversy, often framed in the words of Lord Wilberforce's comments, dissenting, in *Cassell v. Broome*, [1972] A.C. 1027 (H.L.), at p. 1114:

> It cannot lightly be taken for granted, even as a matter of theory, that the purpose of the law of tort is compensation, still less that it ought to be, an issue of large social import, or that there is something inappropriate or illogical or anomalous (a ques-

tion-begging word) in including a punitive element in civil damages, or, conversely, that the criminal law, rather than the civil law, is in these cases the better instrument for conveying social disapproval, or for redressing a wrong to the social fabric, or that damages in any case can be broken down into the two separate elements. As a matter of practice English law has not committed itself to any of these theories: it may have been wiser than it knew.

[39] A second major aspect of the controversy surrounding punitive damages is related to the quantum. Substantial awards are occasionally assessed at figures seemingly plucked out of the air. The usual procedural protections for an individual faced with potential punishment in a criminal case are not available. Plaintiffs, it is said, recover punitive awards out of all proportion to just compensation. They are subjected, it is said, to "palm tree justice": *Cassell, supra*, at p. 1078. They are handed a financial windfall serendipitously just because, coincidentally with their claim, the court desires to punish the defendant and deter others from similar outrageous conduct. Defendants on the other hand say they suffer out of all proportion to the actual wrongs they have committed. Because the punishment is tailored to fit not only the "crime" but the financial circumstances of the defendant (*i.e.*, to ensure that it is big enough to "sting"), defendants complain that they are being punished for who they are rather than for what they have done. The critics of punitive awards refer *in terrorem* to the United States experience where, for example, an Alabama jury awarded $4 million in punitive damages against a BMW dealership for failure to disclose a minor paint job to fix a cosmetic blemish on a new vehicle in *BMW of North America, Inc. v. Gore*, 517 U.S. 559 (1996). In 1994, a jury in New Mexico awarded 81-year-old Stella Liebeck $160,000 in compensatory damages and $2.7 million in punitive damages against McDonald's Restaurants for burns resulting from a spilled cup of coffee, notwithstanding that she tried to open the cup while balancing it on her lap in the passenger seat of a car (*Liebeck v. McDonald's Restaurants, P.T.S. Inc.*, 1995 WL 360309 (N.M. Dist.)). Critics of punitive damages warn against an "Americanization" of our law that, if adopted, would bring the administration of justice in this country into disrepute.

[40] These are serious concerns, but in fact, the punitive damage controversies have little if anything to do with Americanization of our law. Jury awards of punitive damages in civil actions have a long and important history in Anglo-Canadian jurisprudence. They defy modern attempts at neat classification of remedies. The jury is invited to treat a plaintiff as a public interest enforcer as well as a private interest claimant. Almost 240 years ago, government agents broke into the premises of a Whig member of Parliament and pamphleteer, John Wilkes, to seize copies of a publication entitled *The North Briton*, No. 45, which the Secretary of State regarded as libellous. Lord Chief Justice Pratt (later Lord Camden L.C.) on that occasion swept aside the government's defence. "If such a [search] power is truly invested in a Secretary of State", he held, "and he can delegate this power, it certainly may affect the person and property of every man in this kingdom, and is totally subversive of the liberty of the subject". As to punitive damages, he affirmed that:

[A] jury have it in their power to give damages for more than the injury received. Damages are designed not only as a satisfaction to the injured person, but likewise as a punishment to the guilty, to deter from any such proceeding for the future, and as a proof of the detestation of the jury to the action itself.

(*Wilkes v. Wood* (1763), Lofft. 1, 98 E.R. 489 (K.B.), at pp. 498-99)

[41] Long before the days of Lord Pratt C.J., the related idea of condemning a defendant to a multiple of what is required for compensation (in the present appeal, as stated, the punitive damages were roughly triple the award of compensatory damages) reached back to the Code of Hammurabi, Babylonian law, Hittite law (1400 B.C.), the Hindu Code of Manu (200 B.C.), ancient Greek codes, the Ptolemaic law in Egypt and the Hebrew Covenant Code of Mosaic law (see *Exodus* 22:1 "If a man shall steal an ox, or a sheep, and kill it, or sell it; he shall restore five oxen for an ox, and four sheep for a sheep"). Roman law also included provisions for multiple damages. Admittedly, in these early systems, criminal law and civil law were not always clearly differentiated. The United States Supreme Court in *BMW*, *supra*, referred at p. 581 to "65 different enactments [in English statutes] during the period between 1275 and 1753 [that] provided for double, treble, or quadruple damages".

. . .

[43] The three objectives identified by Lord Chief Justice Pratt, in *Wilkes*, *supra* — punishment, deterrence and denunciation ("proof of the detestation") — are with us still, even though some scholarly critics have argued that these rationales "have very particular and divergent implications" that occasionally wind up undermining each other: B. Chapman and M. Trebilcock, "Punitive Damages: Divergence in Search of a Rationale" (1989), 40 *Ala. L. Rev.* 741, at p. 744. No doubt, as a matter of language, the word "punishment" includes both retribution and denunciation, and the three objectives should perhaps better be referred to as retribution, deterrence and denunciation.

[44] The notion of private enforcers (or "private Attorneys General"), particularly where they act for personal gain, is worrisome unless strictly controlled. Thus, while the availability of punitive damages in Canada was affirmed early on by this Court in *Collette v. Lasnier* (1886), 13 S.C.R. 563, a patent case, they were not widely awarded until the 1970s. Since then the awards have multiplied in number and escalated in amount. A report on punitive damages by the Ontario Law Reform Commission, issued in 1991, which examined research begun in 1989, predicted limited and principled development in the law of punitive damages in Canada: Ontario Law Reform Commission, *Report on Exemplary Damages*, June 1, 1991, at pp. 93 and 98. By 1998, the report's research director, Dean Bruce Feldthusen, conceded that the law was "certainly developing quite differently in Canada than one would have predicted only a short time ago" and that "many of the doctrinal pillars on which the Report's predictions of limited and principled development in the law governing punitive damages were based have since cracked or collapsed": B. Feldthusen, "Punitive Damages: Hard Choices and High Stakes", [1998] *N.Z. L. Rev.* 741, at p. 742. Contrary to expectations, the awards were much larger, more frequent, appeared to rely more often on the defendant's wealth in support, and included more high profile jury awards. The kinds of causes of action had expanded; punitive damages were the "norm" and had "proliferated" in actions in sexual battery, were now "clearly available" for breach of fiduciary duty, and "persisted" in contract actions. Prior criminal convictions, he concluded, no longer automatically barred punitive awards. He added, "[p]erhaps most significantly, the courts seem to have accepted general deterrence, not retributive punishment, as the dominant purpose behind punitive damage awards in a number of important decisions" (p. 742).

[45] This Court more recently affirmed a punitive damage award of $800,000 in *Hill*, *supra*. On that occasion some guidelines were set out to keep this remedy within reasonable limits. The Court on this occasion has an opportunity to clarify further the rules governing whether an award of punitive damages ought to be made and if so, the assessment of a quantum that is fair to all parties.

[46] It is convenient at this point to note how other common law jurisdictions have addressed the problem of disproportionate awards of punitive damages.

[The examination of the law in England, Australia, New Zealand, Ireland and the United States is omitted.]

F.   *Conclusions from the Comparative Survey*

[66] For present purposes, I draw the following assistance from the experience in other common law jurisdictions which I believe is consistent with Canadian practice and precedent.

[67] First, the attempt to limit punitive damages by "categories" does not work and was rightly rejected in Canada in *Vorvis* [*v. Insurance Corporation of British Columbia*, [1989] 1 S.C.R. 1085], at pp. 1104-6. The control mechanism lies not in restricting the category of case but in rationally determining circumstances that warrant the addition of punishment to compensation in a civil action. It is in the nature of the remedy that punitive damages will largely be restricted to intentional torts, as in *Hill*, *supra*, or breach of fiduciary duty as in *M. (K.) v. M. (H.)*, [1992] 3 S.C.R. 6, but *Vorvis* itself affirmed the availability of punitive damages in the exceptional case in contract. In *Denison v. Fawcett*, [1958] O.R. 312, the Ontario Court of Appeal asserted in *obiter* that on proper facts punitive damages would be available in negligence and nuisance as well. In *Robitaille v. Vancouver Hockey Club Ltd.* (1981), 124 D.L.R. (3d) 228), the British Columbia Court of Appeal awarded punitive damages in a negligence case on the principle that they ought to be available whenever "the conduct of the defendant [w]as such as to merit condemnation by the [c]ourt" (p. 250). This broader approach seems to be in line with most common law jurisdictions apart from England.

[68] Second, there is a substantial consensus that coincides with Lord Pratt C.J.'s view in 1763 that the general objectives of punitive damages are punishment (in the sense of retribution), deterrence of the wrongdoer and others, and denunciation (or, as Cory J. put it in *Hill*, *supra*, at para. 196, they are "the means by which the jury or judge expresses its outrage at the egregious conduct").

[69] Third, there is recognition that the primary vehicle of punishment is the criminal law (and regulatory offences) and that punitive damages should be resorted to only in exceptional cases and with restraint. Where punishment has actually been imposed by a criminal court for an offence arising out of substantially the same facts, some jurisdictions, such as Australia and New Zealand, bar punitive damages in certain contexts . . ., but the dominant approach in other jurisdictions, including Canada, is to treat it as another factor, albeit a factor of potentially great importance. . . . The Ontario Law Reform Commission, *supra*, recommended that the "court should be entitled to consider the fact and adequacy of any prior penalty imposed in any criminal or other similar proceeding brought against the defendant" (p. 46).

[70] Fourth, the incantation of the time-honoured pejoratives ("high-handed", "oppressive", "vindictive", etc.) provides insufficient guidance (or discipline) to the judge or jury setting the amount. Lord Diplock in *Cassell, supra*, at p. 1129, called these the "whole gamut of dyslogistic judicial epithets". A more principled and less exhortatory approach is desirable.

[71] Fifth, all jurisdictions seek to promote rationality. In directing itself to the punitive damages, the court should relate the facts of the particular case to the underlying purposes of punitive damages and ask itself how, *in particular*, an award would further one or other of the objectives of the law, and what is the lowest award that would serve the purpose, i.e., because any higher award would be irrational.

[72] Sixth, it is rational to use punitive damages to relieve a wrongdoer of its profit where compensatory damages would amount to nothing more than a licence fee to earn greater profits through outrageous disregard of the legal or equitable rights of others. *focus on defendant misconduct*

[73] Seventh, none of the common law jurisdictions has adopted (except by statute) a formulaic approach, as advocated by the intervener the Insurance Council of Canada in this appeal, such as a fixed cap or fixed ratio between compensatory and punitive damages. The proper focus is not on the plaintiff's loss but on the defendant's misconduct. A mechanical or formulaic approach does not allow sufficiently for the many variables that ought to be taken into account in arriving at a just award.

[74] Eighth, the governing rule for quantum is *proportionality*. The overall award, that is to say compensatory damages plus punitive damages plus any other punishment related to the same misconduct, should be rationally related to the objectives for which the punitive damages are awarded (retribution, deterrence and denunciation). Thus there is broad support for the "if, but only if" test formulated, as mentioned, in *Rookes* [*v. Barnard*, [1964] A.C. 1129, [1964] 1 All E.R. 367], and affirmed here in *Hill, supra*.

[75] Ninth, it has become evident that juries can and should receive more guidance and help from the judges in terms of their mandate. They should be told in some detail about the function of punitive damages and the factors that govern both the award and the assessment of a proper amount. Juries should not be thrown into their assignment without any help, then afterwards be criticized for the result.

[76] Tenth, and finally, there is substantial consensus (even the United States is moving in this direction) that punitive damages are not at large (as pointed out by Cory J. in *Hill, supra*) and that an appellate court is entitled to intervene if the award exceeds the outer boundaries of a rational and measured response to the facts of the case.

[77] With the benefit of these general principles, I now turn to the specific issues raised by this appeal.

(1) *Punitive Damages for Breach of Contract*

[78] This, as noted, is a breach of contract case. In *Vorvis, supra*, this Court held that punitive damages are recoverable in such cases provided the defendant's conduct said to give rise to the claim is itself "an actionable wrong" (p. 1106). The scope to be given this expression is the threshold question in this case, i.e., is a breach of an insurer's duty to act in good faith an actionable wrong independent of the loss claim under the fire insurance policy? *Vorvis* itself was a case about the employer's breach of an employment contract. This is how McIntyre J. framed the rule at pp. 1105-6:

> When then can punitive damages be awarded? It must never be forgotten that when awarded by a judge or jury, a punishment is imposed upon a person by a Court by the operation of the judicial process. What is it that is punished? It surely cannot be merely conduct of which the Court disapproves, however strongly the judge may feel. Punishment may not be imposed in a civilized community without a justification in law. *The only basis for the imposition of such punishment must be a finding of the commission of an actionable wrong which caused the injury complained of by the plaintiff.* [Emphasis added.]

This view, McIntyre J. said (at p. 1106), "has found approval in the *Restatement on the Law of Contracts 2d* in the United States", which reads as follows:

> [§ 355] Punitive damages are not recoverable for a breach of contract unless the conduct constituting the breach is also a *tort* for which punitive damages are recoverable. [Emphasis added.]

Applying these principles in *Vorvis*, McIntyre J. stated, at p. 1109:

> Each party had the right to terminate the contract without the consent of the other, and where the employment contract was terminated by the employer, the appellant was entitled to reasonable notice of such termination or payment of salary and benefits for the period of reasonable notice. The termination of the contract on this basis by the employer is not a *wrong in law* and, where the reasonable notice is given or payment in lieu thereof is made, the plaintiff — subject to a consideration of aggravated damages which have been allowed in some cases but which were denied in this case — is entitled to no further remedy. . . . [Emphasis added.]

Wilson J., with whom L'Heureux-Dubé J. concurred, dissented. She did not agree "that punitive damages can only be awarded when the misconduct is in itself an 'actionable wrong'". She stated, at p. 1130:

> In my view, the correct approach is to assess the conduct in the context of all the circumstances and determine whether it is deserving of punishment because of its shockingly harsh, vindictive, reprehensible or malicious nature. Undoubtedly some conduct found to be deserving of punishment will constitute an actionable wrong but other conduct might not.

[79] In the case at bar, Pilot acknowledges that an insurer is under a duty of good faith and fair dealing. Pilot says that this is a contractual duty. *Vorvis*, it says, requires a tort. However, in my view, a breach of the contractual duty of good faith is independent of and in addition to the breach of contractual duty to pay the loss. It constitutes an "actionable wrong" within the *Vorvis* rule, which does not require an independent tort. I say this for several reasons.

[80] First, McIntyre J. chose to use the expression "actionable wrong" instead of "tort" even though he had just reproduced an extract from the *Restatement* which *does* use the word tort. It cannot be an accident that McIntyre J. chose to employ a much broader expression when formulating the Canadian test.

[81] Second, in *Royal Bank of Canada v. W. Got & Associates Electric Ltd.*, [1999] 3 S.C.R. 408, at para. 26, this Court, referring to McIntyre J.'s holding in Vorvis, said "the circumstances that would justify punitive damages for breach of contract *in the absence* of actions also constituting a *tort* are rare" (emphasis added). Rare they may be, but the clear message is that such cases do exist. The Court has thus confirmed that punitive damages can be awarded in the absence of an accompanying tort.

[82] Third, the requirement of an independent tort would unnecessarily complicate the pleadings, without in most cases adding anything of substance. *Central Trust Co. v. Rafuse*, [1986] 2 S.C.R. 147, held that a common law duty of care sufficient to found an action in tort can arise within a contractual relationship, and in that case proceeded with the analysis in tort instead of contract to deprive an allegedly negligent solicitor of the benefit of a limitation defence. To require a plaintiff to formulate a tort in a case such as the present is pure formalism. An independent actionable wrong is required, but it can be found in breach of a distinct and separate contractual provision or other duty such as a fiduciary obligation.

[83] I should add that insurance companies have also asserted claims for punitive damages against their insured for breach of the mutual "good faith" obligation in insurance contracts. In *Andrusiw v. Aetna Life Insurance Co. of Canada*, [2001] A.J. No. 789 (Q.B.) (QL), the court awarded $20,000 in punitive damages against an Aetna policy holder in addition to an order for the repayment of $260,000 in disability payments. The insurance company was not required to identify a separate tort to ground its claim for punitive damages. In that case it was the misconduct of the policy holder, not the insurance company, that was seen as such a marked departure from ordinary standards of decent behaviour as to invite the censure of punitive damages, *per* Murray J. at paras. 84-85:

> This leaves the question of whether or not the Plaintiff's conduct was so reprehensible and high-handed that he should be punished for his behaviour. Counsel for the Defendant makes the point that the Plaintiff embarked on a deliberate course of conduct to misrepresent facts to the Defendant in order to continue to collect disability benefits. If the only consequence of this behaviour is forfeiture of his claim then in effect he is no worse off than if he had been truthful in the first place and deterrence which is one of the objects of granting punitive damages is given no effect.
>
> A great deal has been made in the case law, to which this Court was referred, of the fact that insurers *vis-à-vis* their insureds are in a superior bargaining position and one which places the insureds in positions of dependency and vulnerability. Equally, insurers must not be looked upon as fair game. It is a two-way street founded upon the principle of utmost good faith arising from the very nature of the contract. Thus, it is appropriate that punitive damages be awarded and I do so in the sum of $20,000.00.

I refrain from any comment on the correctness of this award, but to those who subscribe to "the sting" approach to punitive damages, I pose the question whether an award of $20,000 against a cheating policy holder in the Aetna case has at least as much "sting", or possibly more, than the award of $1 million against Pilot in this case.

[BINNIE J. held that the plaintiff's claim for punitive damages was properly pleaded and that the defendant had adequate notice of the allegations that it would have to meet.]

(3)   *Was the Jury Charge Adequate?*

[93] The respondent argues that the trial judge did not give the jury adequate guidance on how to assess punitive damages. There is considerable merit in this submission. The judge's charge on this point was skeletal. It is my view, for the reasons already discussed, that the charge on punitive damages should not be given almost as an afterthought but should be understood as an important source of control and discipline. The jurors should not be left to guess what their role and function is.

[94] To this end, not only should the pleadings of punitive damages be more rigorous in the future than in the past . . ., but it would be helpful if the trial judge's charge to the jury included words to convey an understanding of the following points, even at the risk of some repetition for emphasis. (1) Punitive damages are very much the exception rather than the rule, (2) imposed *only* if there has been high-handed, malicious, arbitrary or highly reprehensible misconduct that departs to a marked degree from ordinary standards of decent behaviour. (3) Where they are awarded, punitive damages should be assessed in an amount reasonably proportionate to such factors as the harm caused, the degree of the misconduct, the relative vulnerability of the plaintiff and any advantage or profit gained by the defendant, (4) having regard to any other fines or penalties suffered by the defendant for the misconduct in question. (5) Punitive damages are generally given only where the misconduct would otherwise be unpunished or where other penalties are or are likely to be inadequate to achieve the objectives of retribution, deterrence and denunciation. (6) Their purpose is not to compensate the plaintiff, but (7) to give a defendant his or her just dessert (retribution), to deter the defendant and others from similar misconduct in the future (deterrence), and to mark the community's collective condemnation (denunciation) of what has happened. (8) Punitive damages are awarded *only* where compensatory damages, which to some extent are punitive, are insufficient to accomplish these objectives, and (9) they are given in an amount that is no greater than necessary to rationally accomplish their purpose. (10) While normally the state would be the recipient of any fine or penalty for misconduct, the plaintiff will keep punitive damages as a "windfall" in addition to compensatory damages. (11) Judges and juries in our system have usually found that moderate awards of punitive damages, which inevitably carry a stigma in the broader community, are generally sufficient.

[95] These particular expressions are not, of course, obligatory. What is essential in a particular case will be a function of its particular circumstances, the need to emphasize the nature, scope and exceptional nature of the remedy, and fairness to both sides.

[96] The trial judge should keep in mind that the standard of appellate review applicable to punitive damages ultimately awarded, is that a reasonable jury, properly instructed, could have concluded that an award in that amount, *and no less*, was rationally required to punish the defendant's misconduct, as discussed below.

[97] If counsel can agree on a "bracket" or "range" of an appropriate award, the trial judge should convey these figures to the jury, but at the present time specific figures should not be mentioned in the absence of such agreement (*Hill, supra, per* Cory J., at paras. 162-63. This prohibition may have to be reexamined in future, based on further experience). Counsel should also consider the desirability of asking the trial judge to advise the jury of awards of punitive damages made in comparable circumstances that have been sustained on appeal.

[98] The foregoing suggestions are put forward in an effort to be helpful rather than dogmatic. They grow out of the observation in *Hill* that punitive damages are not "at large" (para. 197). Unless punitive damages can be approached rationally they ought not to be awarded at all. To the extent these suggestions are considered useful, they will obviously have to be both modified and elaborated to assist the jury on the facts of a particular case. The point, simply, is that jurors should not be left in any doubt about what they are to do and how they are to go about it.

[99] It is evident that I am suggesting a more ample charge on the issue of punitive damages than was given in this case. Finlayson J.A. said that he was "not entirely happy with the trial judge's charge to the jury on the issue of punitive damages" (p. 661), and Laskin J.A. agreed that "[t]he trial judge might have given the jury more help than he did" (p. 656). However, both Finlayson and Laskin JJ.A. agreed that the jury charge covered the essentials, however lightly. This conclusion is reinforced by the fact that no objection was made by either counsel. With some hesitation, I agree with the Court of Appeal, unanimous on this point, that in the circumstances this ground of appeal should be rejected.

(4)   *Reviewing the Jury Award*

(a)   Whether the Award of Punitive Damages in This Case was a Rational
        Response to the Respondent's Misconduct

[100] The applicable standard of review for "rationality" was articulated by Cory J. in *Hill, supra*, at para. 197:

> Unlike compensatory damages, punitive damages are not at large. Consequently, courts have a much greater scope and discretion on appeal. The appellate review should be based upon the court's estimation as to whether the punitive damages serve a rational purpose. In other words, was the misconduct of the defendant so outrageous that punitive damages were rationally required to act as deterrence?

[101] The "rationality" test applies both to the question of whether an award of punitive damages should be made at all, as well as to the question of its quantum.

[102] The respondent claims that an insurer is entirely within its rights to thoroughly investigate a claim and exercise caution in evaluating the circumstances. It is not required to accept the initial views of its investigators. It is perfectly entitled to pursue further inquiries. I agree with these points. The problem here is that Pilot embarked on a "train of thought" as early as February 25, 1994 . . . that led to the arson trial, with nothing to go on except the fact that its policy holder had money problems.

[103] The "train of thought" . . . kept going long after the requirements of due diligence or prudent practice had been exhausted. There is a difference between due diligence and wilful tunnel vision. The jury obviously considered this case to be an outrageous example of the latter. In my view, an award of punitive damages (leaving aside the issue of quantum for the moment) was a rational response on the jury's part to the evidence. It was not an inevitable or unavoidable response, but it was a *rational* response to what the jury had seen and heard. The jury was obviously incensed at the idea that the respondent would get away with paying no more than it ought to have paid after its initial investigation in 1994 (plus costs). It obviously felt that something more was required to demonstrate to Pilot that its bad faith dealing with this loss claim was not a wise or profitable course of action. The award answered a perceived need for retribution, denunciation and deterrence.

[104] The intervener, the Insurance Council of Canada, argues that the award of punitive damages will over-deter insurers from reviewing claims with due diligence, thus lead to the payment of unmeritorious claims, and in the end drive up insurance premiums. This would only be true if the respondent's treatment of the appellant is not an isolated case but is widespread in the industry. If, as I prefer to believe, insurers generally take seriously their duty to act in good faith, it will only be rogue insurers or rogue files that will incur such a financial penalty, and the extra economic cost inflicted by punitive damages will either cause the delinquents to mend their ways or, ultimately, move them on to lines of work that do not call for a good faith standard of behaviour.

[105] The Ontario Court of Appeal was unanimous that punitive damages in some amount were justified and I agree with that conclusion. This was an exceptional case that justified an exceptional remedy. The respondent's cross-appeal will therefore be dismissed.

[106] We now come to the issue of quantum.

(b)　Whether the Jury's Award of $1 Million in Punitive Damages Should Be Restored

[107] In *Hill*, *supra*, Cory J., while emphasizing the overriding obligation of rationality, also recognized that the jury must be given some leeway to do its job. The issue of punitive damages, after all, is a matter that has been confided in the first instance to their discretion. Thus, to be reversed, their award of punitive damages must be "so inordinately large as obviously to exceed the maximum limit of a reasonable range within which the jury may properly operate" (para. 159). Putting these two notions together, the test is whether a reasonable jury, properly instructed, could have concluded that an award in that amount, and no less, was rationally required to punish the defendant's misconduct.

[108] This test provides an appellate court with supervisory powers over punitive damages that are more interventionist than in the case of other jury awards of general damages, where the courts may only intervene if the award is "so exorbitant or so grossly out of proportion [to the injury] as to shock the court's conscience and sense of justice" (*Hill*, *supra*, at para. 159; *Walker v. CFTO Ltd.* (1987), 59 O.R. (2d) 104 (C.A.)). In the case of punitive damages, the emphasis is on the appellate court's obligation to ensure that the award is the product of reason and rationality. The focus is on whether the Court's sense of reason is offended rather than on whether its conscience is shocked.

[109] If the award of punitive damages, when added to the compensatory damages, produces a total sum that is so "inordinately large" that it exceeds what is "rationally" required to punish the defendant, it will be reduced or set aside on appeal.

[110] An award that is higher than required to fulfil its purpose is, by definition, irrational. The more difficult task is to determine what is "inordinate". Here, I think, the Court must come to grips with the issue of proportionality.

[111] I earlier referred to proportionality as the key to the permissible quantum of punitive damages. Retribution, denunciation and deterrence are the recognized justification for punitive damages, and the means must be rationally proportionate to the end sought to be achieved. A disproportionate award overshoots its purpose and becomes irrational. A less than proportionate award fails to achieve its purpose. Thus a proper award must look at proportionality in several dimensions, including:

(i) *Proportionate to the Blameworthiness of the Defendant's Conduct*

[112] The more reprehensible the conduct, the higher the rational limits to the potential award. The need for denunciation is aggravated where, as in this case, the conduct is persisted in over a lengthy period of time (two years to trial) without any rational justification, and despite the defendant's awareness of the hardship it knew it was inflicting (indeed, the respondent anticipated that the greater the hardship to the appellant, the lower the settlement she would ultimately be forced to accept).

[113] The level of blameworthiness may be influenced by many factors, but some of the factors . . . include:

(1) whether the misconduct was planned and deliberate. . .;

(2) the intent and motive of the defendant. . .;

(3) whether the defendant persisted in the outrageous conduct over a lengthy period of time. . .;

(4) whether the defendant conceded or attempted to cover up its misconduct. . .;

(5) the defendant's awareness that what he or she was doing was wrong. . .;

(6) whether the defendant profited from its misconduct. . .;

(7) whether the interest violated by the misconduct was known to be deeply personal to the plaintiff . . . or a thing that was irreplaceable . . . Special interests have included the reproductive capacity of the plaintiff deliberately sterilized by an irreversible surgical procedure while the plaintiff was confined in a provincial mental institution, . . . the deliberate publication of an informant's identity . . . [The shooting and killing of the] plaintiffs' three companion and breeding German Shepherds who had merely wandered onto the defendant's property from a neighbouring yard. Here the "property" was sentimental, not replaceable, and, unlike the trees, themselves sentient beings.

(ii) *Proportionate to the Degree of Vulnerability of the Plaintiff*

[114] The financial or other vulnerability of the plaintiff, and the consequent abuse of power by a defendant, is highly relevant where there is a power imbalance. . . .

[115] I add two cautionary notes on the issue of vulnerability. First, this factor mitigates [*sic*] *against* the award of punitive damages in most commercial situations, particularly where the cause of action is contractual and the problem for the Court is to sort out the bargain the parties have made. Most participants enter the marketplace knowing it is fuelled by the aggressive pursuit of self-interest. Here, on the other hand, we are dealing with a homeowner's "peace of mind" contract.

[116] Second, it must be kept in mind that punitive damages are not compensatory. Thus the appellant's pleading of emotional distress in this case is only relevant insofar as it helps to assess the oppressive character of the respondent's conduct. Aggravated damages are the proper vehicle to take into account the additional harm caused to the plaintiff's feelings by reprehensible or outrageous conduct on the part of the defendant. Otherwise there is a danger of "double recovery" for the plaintiff's emotional stress, once under the heading of compensation and secondly under the heading of punishment.

(iii)   Proportionate to the Harm or Potential Harm Directed Specifically at the Plaintiff

[117] The jury is not a general ombudsman or roving Royal Commission. There is a limited role for the plaintiff as private attorney general. It would be irrational to provide the plaintiff with an excessive windfall arising out of a defendant's scam of which the plaintiff was but a minor or peripheral victim. On the other hand, malicious and high-handed conduct which could be expected to cause severe injury to the plaintiff is not necessarily excused because fortuitously it results in little damage.

(iv)   Proportionate to the Need for Deterrence

[118] The theory is that it takes a large whack to wake up a wealthy and powerful defendant to its responsibilities. The appellant's argument is that the punitive damages award of $1 million represents less than one half of one percent of Pilot's net worth. This is a factor, but it is a factor of limited importance.

[119] A defendant's financial power may become relevant (1) if the defendant chooses to argue financial hardship, or (2) it is *directly* relevant to the defendant's misconduct (e.g., financial power is what enabled the defendant Church of Scientology to sustain such an outrageous campaign for so long against the plaintiff in *Hill, supra*), or (3) other circumstances where it may *rationally* be concluded that a lesser award against a moneyed defendant would fail to achieve deterrence.

[120] Deterrence is an important justification for punitive damages. It would play an even greater role in this case if there had been evidence that what happened on this file were typical of Pilot's conduct towards policyholders. There was no such evidence. The deterrence factor is still important, however, because the egregious misconduct of middle management was known at the time to top management, who took no corrective action.

[121] The fact the respondent's assets of $231 million were mentioned to the jury in this case was unhelpful. . . . In any event, the court should hesitate to attribute anthropomorphic qualities to large corporations (i.e., the punishment should "sting").

. . .

(v)   Proportionate, Even After Taking Into Account the Other Penalties, Both Civil and Criminal, Which Have Been or Are Likely to be Inflicted on the Defendant for the Same Misconduct

[123] Compensatory damages also punish. In many cases they will be all the "punishment" required. To the extent a defendant has suffered other retribution, denunciation or deterrence, either civil or criminal, for the misconduct in question, the need for *additional* punishment in the case before the court is lessened and may be eliminated. In Canada, unlike some other common law jurisdictions, such "other" punishment is relevant but it is not necessarily a bar to the award of punitive damages. The prescribed fine, for example, may be disproportionately small to the level of outrage the jury wishes to express. The misconduct in question may be broader than the misconduct proven in evidence in the criminal or regulatory proceeding. The legislative judgment fixing the amount of the potential fine may be based on policy considerations other than pure punishment. The key point is that punitive damages are awarded "if, but only if" *all* other penalties have been taken into account and found to be inadequate to accomplish the objectives of retribution, deterrence, and denunciation. The intervener, the Insurance Council of Canada, argues that the discipline of insurance companies should be left to the regulator. Nothing in the appeal record indicates that the Registrar of Insurance (now the Superintendent of Financial Services) took an interest in this case prior to the jury's unexpectedly high award of punitive damages.

(vi)   Proportionate to the Advantage Wrongfully Gained by a Defendant from the Misconduct

[124] A traditional function of punitive damages is to ensure that the defendant does not treat compensatory damages merely as a licence to get its way irrespective of the legal or other rights of the plaintiff. Thus in *Horseshoe Bay Retirement Society* [*v. S.I.F. Development Corp.* (1990), 66 D.L.R. (4th) 42], a real estate developer cut down mature trees on the plaintiff's property to improve the view from neighbouring lots which it was developing for sale. The defendant appeared to have calculated that enhanced prices for its properties would exceed any "compensation" that it might be required to pay to the plaintiff. Punitive damages of $100,000 were awarded to reduce the profits and deter "like-minded" developers (p. 50). For a similar case, see *Nantel v. Parisien* (1981), 18 C.C.L.T. 79 (Ont. H.C.), *per* Galligan J., at p. 87, ". . . the law would say to the rich and powerful, 'Do what you like, you will only have to make good the plaintiff's actual financial loss, which compared to your budget is negligible'". In *Claiborne Industries Ltd.* [*v. National Bank of Canada* (1989), 69 O.R. (2d) 65], an award of punitive damages was made against the defendant bank in an amount sufficient to ensure that it did not profit from its outrageous conduct (p. 106).

[125] On the other hand, care must be taken not to employ the "wrongful profit" factor irrationally. . . .

[126] In the present case, the effort to force the appellant into a disadvantageous settlement having failed, it is not alleged that the respondent profited from its misconduct.

(5)   The Usefulness of Ratios

[127] The respondent and its supporting intervener suggest that an award of $1 million in punitive damages is out of line because compensatory damages were ultimately assessed only at about $345,000. The result, they argue, is an improper ratio. It is apparent from what has already been said, however, that proportionality is a much broader concept than the simple relationship between punitive damages and compensatory damages. That relationship, moreover, is not even the most relevant because it puts the focus on the plaintiff's loss rather than where it should be, on the defendant's misconduct. If a ratio is to be used what should the ratio measure? The fact that compensatory damages are quantified in dollars and cents is temptingly useful, but wholly inadequate, for example, in a case where outrageous misconduct has fortuitously (and fortunately) resulted in a small financial loss. Potential, as well as actual, harm is a reasonable measure of misconduct, and so are the other factors, already mentioned, such as motive, planning, vulnerability, abuse of dominance, other fines or penalties, and so on. None of these features are captured by the ratio of punitive damages to compensatory damages. Adoption of such a ratio, while easy to supervise, would do a disservice to the unavoidable complexity of the analysis. It would in fact undermine the nuanced principles on which the concept of punitive damages has been justified. There is no doubt at all that evaluation of outrageous conduct in terms of dollars and cents is a difficult and imprecise task, but so is evaluating the worth of a cracked skull, a lost business opportunity or a shattered reputation. Yet all these things are done every day in the courts in the calculation of compensatory damages without resort to formulae or arbitrary rules such as ratios.

(6)   *Conclusion on "Rationality"*

[128] I would not have awarded $1 million in punitive damages in this case but in my judgment the award is within the rational limits within which a jury must be allowed to operate. The award was not so disproportionate as to exceed the bounds of rationality. It did not overshoot its purpose. I have already outlined the reasons why I believe this to be the case.

[129] The jury followed the "if but only if" model, i.e., punitive damages should be awarded "if but only if" the compensatory award is insufficient. The form and order of the questions put to the jury required them first of all to deal with compensation for the loss of the plaintiff's house (replacement or cash value), its contents, and any increase in her living and moving expenses. Only after those matters had been dealt with was the jury instructed to turn their minds to a final question on punitive damages. They were clearly aware that compensatory damages might well be sufficient punishment to avoid a repetition of the offence and a deterrent to others. In this case, the jury obviously concluded that the compensatory damages ($345,000) were not sufficient for those purposes. It was no more than the respondent had contractually obligated itself to pay under the insurance policy. In this case, the power imbalance was highly relevant. Pilot holds itself out to the public as a sure guide to a "safe harbour". In its advertising material it refers to itself as "*Your* Pilot" and makes such statements as:

> At Pilot Insurance Company, guiding people like you into safe harbours has been our mission for nearly 75 years.

Insurance contracts, as Pilot's self-description shows, are sold by the insurance industry and purchased by members of the public for peace of mind. The more devastating the loss, the more the insured may be at the financial mercy of the insurer, and the more difficult it may be to challenge a wrongful refusal to pay the claim. Deterrence is required. The obligation of good faith dealing means that the appellant's peace of mind should have been Pilot's objective, and her vulnerability ought not to have been aggravated as a negotiating tactic. It is this relationship of reliance and vulnerability that was outrageously exploited by Pilot in this case. The jury, it appears, decided a powerful message of retribution, deterrence and denunciation had to be sent to the respondent and they sent it.

[130] The respondent points out that there is no evidence this case represents a deliberate corporate strategy as opposed to an isolated, mishandled file that ran amok. This is true, but it is also true that Pilot declined to call evidence to explain *why* this file ran amok, and what steps, if any, have been taken to prevent a recurrence.

[131] The respondent also argues that at the end of the day, it did not profit financially from its misbehaviour. This may also be true, but if so, that result was not for want of trying. The respondent clearly hoped to starve the appellant into a cheap settlement. Crabbe's letter of June 9, 1994 . . . suggests as much. That it failed to do so is due in no small part to appellant's counsel who took a hotly contested claim into an eight-week jury trial on behalf of a client who was effectively without resources of her own; and who obviously *could* have been starved into submission but for his firm's intervention on her behalf.

[132] While, as stated, I do not consider the "ratio" test to be an appropriate indicator of rationality, the ratio of punitive damages to compensatory damages in the present case would be either a multiple of three (if only the insurance claim of $345,000 is considered) or a multiple of less than two (if the claim plus the award of solicitor-client costs is thought to be the total compensation). Either way, the ratio is well within what has been considered "rational" in decided cases.

. . .

IV.   CONCLUSION

[141] I would allow the appeal and restore the jury award of $1 million in punitive damages, with costs in this Court on a party and party basis.

[142] The respondent's cross-appeal against the award of any punitive damages is dismissed with costs to the appellant, also on a party and party basis.

[LEBEL J. dissented on the ground that the quantum of punitive damages in this case was excessive. He argued that in the absence of evidence that this was a systemic abuse by the insurer, the punitive damages should have been more closely related to the economic loss.]

NOTES AND QUESTIONS

1.   Of what use in a contracts case decided in 2002 are the eighteenth-century cases dealing with a citizen's battles with a government's attempts to control peaceful political dissent?

2.   What was the obligation that Pilot breached? Was the breach, a breach of a contractual obligation, a tort or some vague obligation to behave properly? If what Pilot did is, as Laskin J.A. and the other judges in the Ontario Court of Appeal thought, a breach of its obligations of good faith towards its insured, has the Supreme Court now recognized (i) a general duty of good faith in the performance of contracts; (ii) a special duty applicable only to insurers and insurance contracts; or (iii) some kind of non-contractual obligation? Binnie J. does not explore the issue and, in particular, he does not consider the nature of the insurer's obligations to its insured. What was most important, the failure to pay the claim promptly, the unfounded allegations of arson or

the attempt to force an advantageous settlement? It is important for those exposed to
the risk of punitive damages that these questions be answered.

Can you think of things that an insurer might do to minimize the risk of being
found liable for aggravated or punitive damages if its denial of a claim is later shown
to be wrong? Keep in mind that (i) the initial decisions on what claims are to be accepted or denied are made at a junior level; (ii) not all claims are genuine; and (iii)
some claims, like the insured's claim in *Warrington*, are very hard to assess.

3.   Bearing in mind the concerns expressed above with the decision of the Supreme Court
      in *Royal Bank of Canada v. W. Got & Associates Electric Ltd.*, it is not clear that the
      bank had any idea that it — and in using this pronoun its referent may have to be care-
      fully spelled out: is it the board of directors, the bank president, the branch manager,
      its counsel? — was exposed to the risk of liability to its customer from what it did. Is
      it sufficient that Pilot knew — and again what the corporation "knew" may not be
      clear — that it had some risk of liability to punitive damages, even if it had no idea
      that the damages might be as high as $1 million?

4.   The Supreme Court rejects what it calls the restriction of punitive damages to "catego-
      ries" of the law. But categories in the law exist only because the relations that people
      have depend on different things: Mrs. Whiten only had a claim against Pilot Insurance
      because she bought an insurance policy from it; Mr. Hill only had a claim against the
      Church of Scientology because it defamed him; and the victim of a sexual assault only
      has a claim against the aggressor because what the latter did is both a crime and a tort.
      While it does not have to follow that the existence of a claim for punitive damages
      should be confined to certain categories of claims, an award of punitive damages
      should reflect (i) the nature of the relation (and its associated obligations); and (ii) the
      fact that the existence of categories has an important effect on the range of remedies
      available.

5.   Binnie J., while obviously aware of the possibility that the plaintiff could have made a
      claim for aggravated damages for loss of peace of mind (he makes reference to that is-
      sue in paras. 4, 115 and 129), does not consider the relation between damages for that
      loss — he makes no reference to *Warrington* — and punitive damages. In other
      words, if Mrs. Whiten had made a claim for damages for the loss of her peace of mind
      (or for mental distress), to what extent would that claim — a purely compensatory
      claim — have met the goals that Binnie J. sees for punitive damages? Binnie J. does
      acknowledge the need to avoid "double recovery" (in para. 116), but the failure of the
      Supreme Court to deal explicitly with the relation between damages for economic loss,
      mental distress and punishment may cause difficulty.

6.   Binnie J. constantly refers to the plaintiff's claim as a claim for damages. The plain-
      tiff's claim was *not* a claim for damages; it was a claim to be paid the amount of the
      indemnity promised by the defendant under the terms of the fire insurance policy it
      had issued to Mrs. Whiten and the jury awarded her that amount, reduced by the fact
      that her claim exceeded the policy limit, down to the cent. The importance of this fact
      is that there is no claim for damages on which the claim for *punitive damages* or, in-
      deed, any claim for damages for mental distress or loss of peace of mind, can, so to
      speak, catch a ride piggy-back. It is at this point that the concept of the "independently
      actionable wrong" stated by McIntyre J. in *Vorvis* to be a requirement for a claim for
      punitive or extended damages becomes important. The existence of such a wrong
      might then provide a basis for a claim for compensatory damages and such a claim
      might then further support a claim for punitive damages. There is, however, a serious
      problem if the concept of the "independently actionable wrong" is, so to speak, a free-
      standing claim, the only consequence of which is that Mrs. Whiten can get punitive
      damages. The obvious question to ask is that if there is an "independently actionable
      wrong", why couldn't Mrs. Whiten get damages, *i.e.*, compensatory damages, for that
      wrong? These issues are obscured by what Binnie J. says and, perhaps as a result, ig-
      nored by him. While the approach of Newbury J.A. in *Warrington* did not build on the
      concept of the "independently actionable wrong", her approach to compensation for

bad treatment could have been used by the Supreme Court, not only to clarify the concept of the "independently actionable wrong" but to provide a far preferable basis for giving Mrs. Whiten compensation for the distress she suffered. When Binnie J. says (para. 129) that the jury had no alternative but to award punitive damages in order to give Mrs. Whiten more, he is ignoring the example in *Warrington* of a court giving more without awarding punitive damages. There is no reason that such an award has to be modest, though there are arguments that it should not be very large.

7. On the facts, the punitive damages were about three times the amount of the plaintiff's claim on the policy (though that amount has to have been considerably increased by pre-judgment interest — the jury awarded Mrs. Whiten about $320,000 for the value of her home and contents). If Mrs. Whiten had sued for damages for lost peace of mind and if, given the egregious conduct of the defendant, an award on that basis would have been, say, $50,000 — it would be hard to justify more, given the level of awards in tort cases for the pain and suffering caused by truly horrific injuries — does the multiplier operate on that figure? If it does, then, to the extent that punitive damages are in some sense at least to provide solace to the plaintiff, the plaintiff will be compensated twice (or, perhaps, four times) for the same loss. A similar problem arises with any costs award, though Binnie J. refers to this issue and refuses to award Mrs. Whiten more than partial indemnity costs. (Note that the use of United States authority in relation to "multiples" may be misleading since most of the American cases that the Supreme Court referred to would have been brought on a contingency basis, with the successful lawyer being compensated by taking as much as one-third to one-half of the punitive damages award. Binnie J. does not discuss the implications of his decision in the light of the existence of contingency fees.) Would you advise a person in the position of Mrs. Whiten to make a claim for defamation or intentional infliction of mental suffering?

8. The Supreme Court standardized and limited recovery for pain and suffering in tort cases — LeBel J. in his dissent refers to the 1978 trilogy of *Andrews v. Grand & Toy Alberta Ltd.*, [1978] 2 S.C.R. 229, *Thornton v. Board of School Trustees of School District No. 57 (Prince George)*, [1978] 2 S.C.R. 267, and *Arnold v. Teno*, [1978] 2 S.C.R. 287, in which the Court set a cap of $100,000 for non-pecuniary damages in tort (the cap has been adjusted for inflation since then and is now in the order of $300,000). Can one justify an award of $1 million for the temporary suffering of Mrs. Whiten, while the victim of a tort — perhaps caused by drunken driving or a sexual assault — would get far less for his or her lifetime suffering?

9. Binnie J. refers (para. 124) to three cases, *Horseshoe Bay Retirement Society v. S.I.F. Development Corp.* (1990), 66 D.L.R. (4th) 42, 3 C.C.L.T. (2d) 75, *Nantel v. Parisien* (1981), 22 R.P.R. 1, 18 C.C.L.T. 79 (Ont. H.C.J.) and *Claiborne Industries Ltd. v. National Bank of Canada* (1989), 69 O.R. (2d) 65, 59 D.L.R. (4th) 533 (C.A.), where the court justified the award of punitive damages on the ground that it would prevent the defendant from benefiting from its wrongful act. In the first case there was evidence of the amount by which the value of the tortfeasor's property was enhanced by the wrongful act (though the court awarded far more). In the second case no evidence was led as to the profit that the defendant had made by wrongfully evicting the tenant, though it probably significantly exceeded the amount awarded as punitive damages. In the third case evidence that the defendant had actually profited from what it had done did not exist. Is it "rational" (in the sense that Binnie J. claims that punitive damages have to be *rational*) to say that punitive damages are justified because they deprive the wrongdoer of its profits if there is no evidence what profit was made or if little notice is taken of what the actual profit may be?

   The decision of the House of Lords in *Attorney-General v. Blake*, [2001] 1 A.C. 268, [2000] 4 All E.R. 385, measured the damages that the plaintiff was entitled to by the defendant's gain, even though the plaintiff had suffered no loss. Such an award can also fulfil some of the goals that the Supreme Court sees for punitive damages. *Attorney-General v. Blake* is reproduced and examined in the section of this chapter dealing with equitable remedies.

10. The judgment of the Supreme Court makes reference to the possibility that other plaintiffs might have been badly treated by the defendant in *Whiten*. If there had been evidence of this fact, what should be done about it? If the purpose of the award is denunciation, deterrence and retribution, what happens if there is more than one plaintiff? Do they share in the award? Does each get the same (large) amount? Might a preferable solution be to certify the plaintiffs as a class for a class action? How is giving one plaintiff what is admitted to be a windfall a rational response to whatever problems the defendant's conduct discloses?

11. While the judgment in *Whiten* might not (because of what the Supreme Court says about the instructions that the jury should get and the power of courts of appeal to review the award) lead to huge awards of punitive damages, the judgment has clearly made litigation more unreckonable and in some sense more attractive for plaintiffs. Plaintiffs now have a strong incentive to sue because the chances of gain have been vastly improved. This development is regarded with a sense of foreboding by the insurance defence bar, and more generally by corporate defendants. See, for example, Rudy Buller, "*Whiten v. Pilot*: Controlling Jury Awards of Punitive Damages" (2003), 36 *U.B.C. L. Rev.* 357.

    Plaintiffs may now have a much reduced incentive to make claims for compensation for mental distress because such a claim is likely to lead to a far smaller award than any punitive damages award would be, even with all the disclaimers the Supreme Court has made. The history of the Anglo-Canadian common law has been characterized by, *inter alia*, adherence to the principle that litigation is always to be discouraged. The Anglo-Canadian costs regime, as illustrated by the terms now used in Ontario, *viz.*, "*partial* indemnity costs" or "*substantial* indemnity costs", is and has always been designed *not* to give the plaintiff a full indemnity and thereby to provide an incentive not to go to court. (The heads of compensable claims under the compensation principle and the operation of that principle are also very effective in denying the plaintiff a complete indemnity.) It may be an important social question whether or not plaintiffs should be denied full compensation for their losses; one may ask, however, whether that question should be answered indirectly by a radical change in the calculations that a prospective plaintiff will now make in considering whether or not to litigate.

    The startling disparity between the amount of punitive damages awarded to Mrs. Whiten and those, for example, awarded to a victim of sexual assault can perhaps be justified on the ground that the richer the defendant, the higher the award. (In this context, Binnie J.'s objection (para. 21) to the desire to make the award "sting" is very hard to understand: the shareholders of the corporation are certainly "stung".) That principle is recognized in the criminal law, particularly with regard to things like environmental offences, where the fines that a corporation may be exposed to are larger than those facing an individual. Nevertheless, this factor adds to the uncertainty: corporations, after all, come in all sizes. Will shareholders and employees be able to argue that too large an award will threaten their investment or livelihood?

12. Under the *Canadian Charter of Rights and Freedoms*, an accused person facing a sentence of five years or longer has the right to a jury trial. The jury trial is an accepted part of the criminal process in our democracy, with juries reflecting community values. Further, the fact that the Crown must convince 12 persons of the guilt of the accused, beyond a reasonable doubt, serves to provide some protection against wrongful convictions. While civil jury trials are common in the United States, in Canada civil jury trials are less common and more controversial. Outside Ontario and British Columbia, civil jury trials are very rare, and even in those two provinces they are not common. Jury trials are expensive for litigants and the state. There are also concerns that they may be "irrational", biased or at least unpredictable. However, others argue that civil juries can be sophisticated decision-makers who keep the justice system "close to the people". See Lynee Cohen, "The Endangered Civil Jury", *Canadian Lawyer* (June 2002) 32. Do you think that cases like *Whiten* should be tried by a jury?

13. The same day that the Supreme Court rendered its decision in *Whiten*, it gave a decision in *Performance Industries Ltd. v. Sylvan Lake Golf & Tennis Club Ltd.*, [2002], S.C.J. No. 20, 2002 SCC 19, concluding that the trial judge had erred in awarding $200,000 damages in a breach of contract case where the defendant had made a "fraudulent misrepresentation." While the Court characterized the defendant's conduct as "reprehensible", it felt that a punitive damage award would serve no "rational purpose". Binnie J. commented (at para. 88): "This was a commercial relationship between two businessmen. One tried to pull a fast one on the other. There was no abuse of a dominant position." Do you agree that punitive damages are more appropriate as a response to "abuse of a dominant position" than as a response to fraud?

14. In *Keays v. Honda Canada Inc.*, [2005] O.J. No. 1145 (S.C.J.) McIsaac J. awarded an employee in a wrongful dismissal case $500,000 in punitive damages, in addition to an extra nine months that the judge added to the 15-month notice period for *Wallace* factors arising from the dismissal. The employee had an excellent work record at a Honda automobile plant for 10 years before going on long-term disability due to chronic fatigue syndrome. After his benefits were terminated by the insurer, he returned to work, but was frequently absent. The employee's physician supported accommodation of his condition, but the employer's physicians were sceptical of the employee's claim that he was unable to work. Relations between the employee and his supervisors deteriorated, and the employee sought legal advice before being sent for another consultation with a company physician. The employer had an "unwritten policy" against involvement of "third party advocates" (like lawyers). After receiving a "conciliatory" letter from the employee's lawyer, inquiring about a proposed medical examination by a company doctor, the employer terminated the employee. The judge characterized various meetings between the supervisors and the employee as "acts of discrimination and harassment", and concluded that the employer failed in its duty under the Ontario *Human Rights Code* to provide reasonable accommodation for an employee with a disability. The judge was also scathing in his commentary on the lack of understanding of the company physicians about chronic fatigue syndrome, while noting that there is no diagnostic test for this condition. Do you think that this decision is consistent with *Wallace*? What effect might this type of decision have on employers? What effect might this decision have on investment by major foreign corporations like Honda in Canada?

FIDLER v. SUN LIFE ASSURANCE CO. OF CANADA

[2006] S.C.J. No. 30

(McLachlin C.J.C., Bastarache, Binnie, LeBel, Deschamps, Fish, Abella and Charron JJ.)

[The plaintiff Fidler worked as a bank receptionist and was covered by a group policy that included long-term disability benefits. At the age of 36, she became ill; she was eventually diagnosed with chronic fatigue syndrome and fibromyalgia, and began receiving long-term disability benefits in January 1991. Under the terms of the policy with the defendant insurer, she was entitled to coverage for two years if she was unable to do her job; after two years on disability, she was only entitled to continued benefits if she was unable to do any job. In May 1997, the insurer informed her that her benefit payments would be terminated. According to the insurer, its video surveillance detailed activities inconsistent with Fidler's claim that she was incapable of performing light or sedentary work. The insurer's denial of benefits was followed by almost two years of correspondence with Fidler and medical professionals. Despite the medical evidence in its possession to the effect that Fidler was not yet capable of doing any work, the insurer, relying on its own consultants and experts, confirmed its decision to terminate benefits in December

1998. In February 1999 Fidler commenced an action and, one week before the trial was scheduled to start, the insurer offered to reinstate her benefits and to pay all arrears with interest. As a result, the only issue at trial was Fidler's entitlement to aggravated and punitive damages. The trial judge, Ralph J., [2002] B.C.J. No. 2209, [2002] 11 W.W.R. 352 (S.C.) awarded her $20,000 in aggravated damages for mental distress but, concluding that the insurer had not acted in bad faith, dismissed her claim for punitive damages. The British Columbia Court of Appeal, [2004] B.C.J. No. 982, 239 D.L.R. (4th) 547, unanimously upheld the award for mental distress, and a majority of the court awarded Fidler an additional $100,000 in punitive damages, finding palpable and overriding error on the question of bad faith. In a unanimous decision, the Supreme Court of Canada allowed the appeal in part, restoring the decision of the trial judge that Fidler was entitled to aggravated damages of $20,000, but not to punitive damages.]

McLACHLIN C.J.C. AND **ABELLA J.**: —

II. *Analysis*

(a) *Damages for Mental Distress for Breach of Contract*   compensation principle

[27] Damages for breach of contract should, as far as money can do it, place the plaintiff in the same position as if the contract had been performed. However, at least since the 1854 decision of the Court of Exchequer Chamber in *Hadley v. Baxendale* (1854), 9 Ex. 341, 156 E.R. 145, at p. 151, it has been the law that these damages must be "such as may fairly and reasonably be considered either arising naturally ... from such breach of contract itself, or such as may reasonably be supposed to have been in the contemplation of both parties".

[28] Until now, damages for mental distress have not been welcome in the family of remedies spawned by this principle. The issue in this appeal is whether that remedial ostracization continues to be warranted. ...

[29] In *Hadley v. Baxendale*, the court explained the principle of reasonable expectation as follows:

> Where two parties have made a contract which one of them has broken, the damages which the other party ought to receive in respect of such breach of contract should be such as may fairly and reasonably be considered either arising naturally, i.e., according to the usual course of things, *from such breach of contract itself, or such as may reasonably be supposed to have been in the contemplation of both parties, at the time they made the contract, as the probable result of the breach of it* ... [Emphasis added by Supreme Court.]

[30] *Hadley v. Baxendale* makes no distinction between the types of loss that are recoverable for breach of contract. The principle of reasonable expectation is stated as a general principle. Nevertheless, subsequent cases purported to rule out damages for mental distress for breach of contract except in certain defined situations.

[31] While courts have always accepted that some non-pecuniary losses arising from breach of contract are compensable, including physical inconvenience and discomfort, they have traditionally shied away from awarding damages for mental suffering caused by the contract breach.

[32] This tradition of refusing to award damages for mental distress was launched in *Hobbs v. London and South Western Rail. Co.* (1875), L.R. 10 Q.B. 111, and

Hamlin v. Great Northern Railway Co. (1856), 1 H. & N. 408, 156 E.R. 1261 (Ex.). In 1909, in the case of *Addis v. Gramophone Co.*, [1909] A.C. 488, the House of Lords "cast a long shadow over the common law" when it rejected a claim for mental distress because the conduct said to cause the distress was not actionable: *Eastwood v. Magnox Electric plc*, [2004] 3 All E.R. 991, 2004 UKHL 35, at para. 1.

[33] To this day, *Addis* is cited for the proposition that mental distress damages are not generally recoverable for breach of contract …

[34] In short, the foundational concepts of reasonable expectations had a ceiling: mental distress. As Bingham L.J. said in *Watts v. Morrow*, [1991] 1 W.L.R. 1421 (C.A.), at p. 1445:

> A contract-breaker is not in general liable for any distress, frustration, anxiety, displeasure, vexation, tension or aggravation which his breach of contract may cause to the innocent party. *This rule is not, I think, founded on the assumption that such reactions are not foreseeable, which they surely are or may be, but on considerations of policy.* [Emphasis added by Supreme Court.]

[35] A number of policy considerations have been cited in support of this restriction. One is the perceived minimal nature of mental suffering:

> [A]s a matter of ordinary experience, it is evident that, while the innocent party to a contract will generally be disappointed if the defendant does not perform the contract, the innocent party's disappointment and distress are seldom so significant as to attract an award of damages on that score.

(*Baltic Shipping Co. v. Dillon* (1993), 176 C.L.R. 344 (Austl. H.C.), at p. 365, *per* Mason C.J.)

[36] Others have suggested that a "stiff upper lip" expectation in commercial life is the source of the prohibition. In *McGregor on Damages* (17th ed. 2003), the author explains:

> The reason for the general rule is that contracts normally concern commercial matters and that mental suffering on breach is not in the contemplation of the parties as part of the business risk of the transaction. [p. 63]

This resonated in *Johnson v. Gore Wood & Co.*, [2001] 2 W.L.R. 72 (H.L.), at p. 108, where Lord Cooke observed: "Contract-breaking is treated as an incident of commercial life which players in the game are expected to meet with mental fortitude".

[37] This Court's jurisprudence has followed the restrictive interpretation of *Addis*, generally requiring that a claim for compensation for mental distress be grounded in independently actionable conduct. The general rule that damages for mental distress should not be awarded for breach of contract was thus preserved: *Peso Silver Mines Ltd. (N.P.L.) v. Cropper*, [1966] S.C.R. 673.

[38] Without resiling from the general rule that damages for mental suffering could not be awarded at contract, the courts in the 1970s acknowledged that the reasons of principle and policy for the rule did not always apply, and began to award such damages where the contract was one for pleasure, relaxation or peace of mind. The charge was led, as so many were, by Lord Denning. In *Jarvis v. Swans Tours Ltd.*, [1973] 1 All E.R. 71 (C.A.), the plaintiff had contracted with the defendant to arrange a holiday. The defendant breached the contract by pro-

viding a terrible vacation. Acknowledging but declining to follow what he referred to as the "out of date" decisions in *Hamlin* and *Hobbs*, which had sired *Addis*, Lord Denning held that mental distress damages could be recovered for certain kinds of contracts:

> In a proper case damages for mental distress can be recovered in contract, just as damages for shock can be recovered in tort. One such case is a contract for a holiday, or any other contract to provide entertainment and enjoyment. If the contracting party breaks his contract, damages can be given for the disappointment, the distress, the upset and frustration caused by the breach. [p. 74]

[39] This holding in *Jarvis* emerged from the common law chrysalis as the "peace of mind exception" to the general rule against recovery for mental distress in contract breaches. This exception was confined to contracts which had as their object the peace of mind of a contracting party. Bingham L.J. in *Watts v. Morrow* stated: "Where the very object of [the] contract is to provide pleasure, relaxation, peace of mind or freedom from molestation, damages will be awarded" (para. 1445).

[40] More recently, the House of Lords in *Farley v. Skinner*, [2001] 4 All E.R. 801, 2001 UKHL 49, loosened the peace of mind exception so as to permit recovery of mental distress not only when pleasure, relaxation, or peace of mind is "the very object of the contract", but also when it is a "major or important object of the contract" (para. 24).

[41] The right to obtain damages for mental distress for breach of contracts that promise pleasure, relaxation or peace of mind has found wide acceptance in Canada. Mental distress damages have been awarded not only for breach of vacation contracts, but also for breaches of contracts for wedding services (*Wilson v. Sooter Studios Ltd.* (1988), 33 B.C.L.R. (2d) 241 (C.A.)), and for luxury chattels (*Wharton v. Tom Harris Chevrolet Oldsmobile Cadillac Ltd.* (2002), 97 B.C.L.R. (3d) 307 (C.A.)). Some courts have included disability insurance contracts: see *Warrington* and *Thompson v. Zurich Insurance Co.* (1984), 7 D.L.R. (4th) 664 (Ont. H.C.J.). The Ontario Court of Appeal has endorsed contractual damages for mental distress where peace of mind is the "very essence" of the promise: see *Prinzo v. Baycrest Centre for Geriatric Care* (2002), 60 O.R. (3d) 474, at para. 34.

[42] In *Vorvis v. Insurance Corporation of British Columbia*, [1989] 1 S.C.R. 1085, this Court described the line of cases awarding mental distress damages as standing for the proposition that "in some contracts the parties may well have contemplated at the time of the contract that a breach in certain circumstances would cause a plaintiff mental distress" (p. 1102). It is thus clear that an independent actionable wrong has not always been required, contrary to Sun Life's arguments before us.

[43] The view taken by this Court in *Vorvis* that damages for mental distress in "peace of mind" contracts should be seen as an expression of the general principle of compensatory damages of *Hadley v. Baxendale*, rather than as an exception to that principle, is shared by others. In *Baltic Shipping*, Mason C.J. of the High Court of Australia questioned whether one should confine mental distress claims for breach of contract to particular categories, noting:

> ... the fundamental principle on which damages are awarded at common law is that the injured party is to be restored to the position (not merely the financial position)

in which the party would have been had the actionable wrong not have taken place. Add to that the fact that anxiety and injured feelings are recognized as heads of compensable damage, at least outside the realm of the law of contract. Add as well the circumstance that the general rule has been undermined by the exceptions which have been engrafted upon it. We are then left with a rule which rests on flimsy policy foundations and conceptually is at odds with the fundamental principle governing the recovery of damages, the more so now that the approaches in tort and contract are converging. [p. 362]

Similarly, Professor J. D. McCamus in *The Law of Contracts* (2005) argues at p. 877 that once peace of mind is understood as a reflection of, or "proxy" for the reasonable contemplation of the contracting parties, "there is no compelling reason not to simply apply the foreseeability test itself". At this point, the apparent inconsistency between the general rule in *Hadley v. Baxendale* and the exception vanishes. See also: S. K. O'Byrne, "Damages for Mental Distress and Other Intangible Loss in a Breach of Contract Action" (2005), 28 *Dal. L.J.* (forthcoming), at pp. 36-37 of manuscript, and R. Cohen and S. O'Byrne, "Cry Me a River: Recovery of Mental Distress Damages in a Breach of Contract Action — A North American Perspective" (2005), 42 *Am. Bus. L.J.* 97.

[44] We conclude that damages for mental distress for breach of contract may, in appropriate cases, be awarded as an application of the principle in *Hadley v. Baxendale*: see *Vorvis*. The court should ask "what did the contract promise?" and provide compensation for those promises. The aim of compensatory damages is to restore the wronged party to the position he or she would have been in had the contract not been broken. As the Privy Council stated in *Wertheim v. Chicoutimi Pulp Co.*, [1911] A.C. 301, at p. 307: "the party complaining should, so far as it can be done by money, be placed in the same position as he would have been in if the contract had been performed". The measure of these damages is, of course, subject to remoteness principles. There is no reason why this should not include damages for mental distress, where such damages were in the reasonable contemplation of the parties at the time the contract was made. This conclusion follows from the basic principle of compensatory contractual damages: that the parties are to be restored to the position they contracted for, whether tangible or intangible. The law's task is simply to provide the benefits contracted for, whatever their nature, if they were in the reasonable contemplation of the parties.

[45] It does not follow, however, that all mental distress associated with a breach of contract is compensable. In normal commercial contracts, the likelihood of a breach of contract causing mental distress is not ordinarily within the reasonable contemplation of the parties. It is not unusual that a breach of contract will leave the wronged party feeling frustrated or angry. The law does not award damages for such incidental frustration. The matter is otherwise, however, when the parties enter into a contract, an object of which is to secure a particular psychological benefit. In such a case, damages arising from such mental distress should in principle be recoverable where they are established on the evidence and shown to have been within the reasonable contemplation of the parties at the time the contract was made. The basic principles of contract damages do not cease to operate merely because what is promised is an intangible, like mental security. ✓

[46] This conclusion is supported by the policy considerations that have led the law to eschew damages for mental suffering in commercial contracts. As discussed above, this reluctance rests on two policy considerations — the minimal nature of the mental suffering and the fact that in commercial matters, mental suffering on breach is "not in the contemplation of the parties as part of the business risk of the transaction": *McGregor on Damages*, at p. 63. Neither applies to contracts where promised mental security or satisfaction is part of the risk for which the parties contracted.

[47] This does not obviate the requirement that a plaintiff prove his or her loss. The court must be satisfied: (1) that an object of the contract was to secure a psychological benefit that brings mental distress upon breach within the reasonable contemplation of the parties; and (2) that the degree of mental suffering caused by the breach was of a degree sufficient to warrant compensation. These questions require sensitivity to the particular facts of each case.

[48] While the mental distress as a consequence of breach must reasonably be contemplated by the parties to attract damages, we see no basis for requiring it to be the dominant aspect or the "very essence" of the bargain. As the House of Lords noted in *Farley*, the law of contract protects all significant parts of the bargain, not merely those that are "dominant" or "essential". Lord Steyn rejected this kind of distinction as "a matter of form and not substance" (para. 24). Lord Hutton added:

> I can see no reason in principle why, if a plaintiff who has suffered no financial loss can recover damages in some cases if there has been a breach of the principal obligation of the contract, he should be denied damages for breach of an obligation which, whilst not the principal obligation of the contract, is nevertheless one which he has made clear to the other party is of importance to him. [para. 51]

Principle suggests that as long as the promise in relation to state of mind is a part of the bargain in the reasonable contemplation of the contracting parties, mental distress damages arising from its breach are recoverable. This is to state neither more nor less than the rule in *Hadley v. Baxendale*.

[49] We conclude that the "peace of mind" class of cases should not be viewed as an exception to the general rule of the non-availability of damages for mental distress in contract law, but rather as an application of the reasonable contemplation or foreseeability principle that applies generally to determine the availability of damages for breach of contract.

[50] One further point should be added.

[51] It may be useful to clarify the use of the term "aggravated damages" in the context of damages for mental distress arising from breach of contract. "Aggravated damages", as defined by Waddams (*The Law of Damages* (2nd ed. 1983), at pp. 562-63), and adopted in *Vorvis*, at p. 1099

> describ[e] an award that aims at compensation, but takes full account of the intangible injuries, such as distress and humiliation, that may have been caused by the defendant's insulting behaviour.

As many writers have observed, the term is used ambiguously. The cases speak of two different types of "aggravated" damages.

[52] The first are true aggravated damages, which arise out of aggravating circumstances. They are not awarded under the general principle of *Hadley v. Baxendale*, but rest on a separate cause of action — usually in tort — like defamation, oppression or fraud. The idea that damages for mental distress for breach of contract may be awarded where an object of a contract was to secure a particular psychological benefit has no effect on the availability of such damages. If a plaintiff can establish mental distress as a result of the breach of an independent cause of action, then he or she may be able to recover accordingly. The award of damages in such a case arises from the separate cause of action. It does not arise out of the contractual breach itself, and it has nothing to do with contractual damages under the rule in *Hadley v. Baxendale*.

[53] The second are mental distress damages which do arise out of the contractual breach itself. These are awarded under the principles of *Hadley v. Baxendale*, as discussed above. They exist independent of any aggravating circumstances and are based completely on the parties' expectations at the time of contract formation. With respect to this category of damages, the term "aggravated damages" becomes unnecessary and, indeed, a source of possible confusion.

[54] It follows that there is only one rule by which compensatory damages *for breach of contract* should be assessed: the rule in *Hadley v. Baxendale*. The *Hadley* test unites all forms of contractual damages under a single principle. It explains why damages may be awarded where an object of the contract is to secure a psychological benefit, just as they may be awarded where an object of the contract is to secure a material one. It also explains why an extended period of notice may have been awarded upon wrongful dismissal in employment law: see *Wallace v. United Grain Growers Ltd.*, [1997] 3 S.C.R. 701. In all cases, these results are based on what was in the reasonable contemplation of the parties at the time of contract formation. They are not true aggravated damages awards.

[55] The recognition that *Hadley* is the single and controlling test for compensatory damages in cases of breach of contract therefore refutes any argument that an "independent actionable wrong" is a prerequisite for the recovery of mental distress damages. Where losses arise from the breach of contract itself, damages will be determined according to what was in the reasonable contemplation of the parties at the time of contract formation. An independent cause of action will only need to be proved where damages are of a different sort entirely: where they are being sought on the basis of aggravating circumstances that extend beyond what the parties expected when they concluded the contract. remoteness test not: proof

[56] Turning to the case before us, the first question is whether an object of this disability insurance contract was to secure a psychological benefit that brought the prospect of mental distress upon breach within the reasonable contemplation of the parties at the time the contract was made? In our view it was. The bargain was that in return for the payment of premiums, the insurer would pay the plaintiff benefits in the case of disability. This is not a mere commercial contract. It is rather a contract for benefits that are both tangible, such as payments, and intangible, such as knowledge of income security in the event of disability. If disability occurs and the insurer does not pay when it ought to have done so in accordance with the terms of the policy, the insurer has breached this reasonable expectation of security. ie.

[57] Mental distress is an effect which parties to a disability insurance contract may reasonably contemplate may flow from a failure to pay the required benefits. The intangible benefit provided by such a contract is the prospect of continued financial security when a person's disability makes working, and therefore receiving an income, no longer possible. If benefits are unfairly denied, it may not be possible to meet ordinary living expenses. This financial pressure, on top of the loss of work and the existence of a disability, is likely to heighten an insured's

anxiety and stress. Moreover, once disabled, an insured faces the difficulty of finding an economic substitute for the loss of income caused by the denial of benefits. See D. Tartaglio, "The Expectation of Peace of Mind: A Basis for Recovery of Damages for Mental Suffering Resulting from the Breach of First Party Insurance Contracts" (1983), 56 *S. Cal. L. Rev.* 1345, at pp. 1365-66.

[58] People enter into disability insurance contracts to protect themselves from this very financial and emotional stress and insecurity. An unwarranted delay in receiving this protection can be extremely stressful. Ms. Fidler's damages for mental distress flowed from Sun Life's breach of contract. To accept Sun Life's argument that an independent actionable wrong is a precondition would be to sanction the "conceptual incongruity of asking a plaintiff to show *more* than just that mental distress damages were a reasonably foreseeable consequence of breach" (O'Byrne, at p. 24 of manuscript (emphasis in original)).

[59] The second question is whether the mental distress here at issue was of a degree sufficient to warrant compensation. Again, we conclude that the answer is yes. The trial judge found that Sun Life's breach caused Ms. Fidler a substantial loss which she suffered over a five-year period. He found as a fact that Ms. Fidler "genuinely suffered significant additional distress and discomfort *arising out of the loss of the disability coverage*" (para. 30 (emphasis added by Court)). This finding was amply supported in the evidence, which included extensive medical evidence documenting the stress and anxiety that Ms. Fidler experienced. He concluded that merely paying the arrears and interest did not compensate for the years Ms. Fidler was without her benefits. His award of $20,000 seeks to compensate her for the psychological consequences of Sun Life's breach, consequences which are reasonably in the contemplation of parties to a contract for personal services and benefits such as this one. We agree with the Court of Appeal's decision not to disturb it.

(b) *Punitive Damages*

[60] Ms. Fidler also seeks punitive damages. The trial judge declined to award them, citing no bad faith, but the Court of Appeal reversed this aspect of his judgment and awarded Ms. Fidler an additional $100,000 as punitive damages.

[61] While compensatory damages are awarded primarily for the purpose of compensating a plaintiff for pecuniary and non-pecuniary losses suffered as a result of a defendant's conduct, punitive damages are designed to address the purposes of retribution, deterrence and denunciation: *Whiten v. Pilot Insurance Co.*, [2002] 1 S.C.R. 595, 2002 SCC 18, at para. 43.

[62] By their nature, contract breaches will sometimes give rise to censure. But to attract punitive damages, the impugned conduct must depart markedly from ordinary standards of decency — the exceptional case that can be described as malicious, oppressive or high-handed and that offends the court's sense of decency: *Hill v. Church of Scientology of Toronto*, [1995] 2 S.C.R. 1130, at para. 196; *Whiten*, at para. 36. The misconduct must be of a nature as to take it beyond the usual opprobrium that surrounds breaking a contract. As stated in *Whiten*, at para. 36, "punitive damages straddle the frontier between civil law (compensation) and criminal law (punishment)". Criminal law and quasi-criminal regulatory

schemes are recognized as the primary vehicles for punishment. It is important that punitive damages be resorted to only in exceptional cases, and with restraint.

[63]   In *Whiten*, this Court set out the principles that govern the award of punitive damages and affirmed that in breach of contract cases, in addition to the requirement that the conduct constitute a marked departure from ordinary standards of decency, it must be independently actionable. Where the breach in question is a denial of insurance benefits, a breach by the insurer of the contractual duty to act in good faith will meet this requirement. The threshold issue that arises, therefore, is whether the appellant breached not only its contractual obligation to pay the long-term disability benefit, but also the independent contractual obligation to deal with the respondent's claim in good faith. On this threshold issue, the legal standard to which Sun Life and other insurers are held is correctly described by O'Connor J.A. in *702535 Ontario Inc. v. Lloyd's London, Non-Marine Underwriters* (2000), 184 D.L.R. (4th) 687 (Ont. C.A.), at para. 29:

> The duty of good faith also requires an insurer to deal with its insured's claim fairly. The duty to act fairly applies both to the manner in which the insurer investigates and assesses the claim and to the decision whether or not to pay the claim. In making a decision whether to refuse payment of a claim from its insured, an insurer must assess the merits of the claim in a balanced and reasonable manner. It must not deny coverage or delay payment in order to take advantage of the insured's economic vulnerability or to gain bargaining leverage in negotiating a settlement. A decision by an insurer to refuse payment should be based on a reasonable interpretation of its obligations under the policy. This duty of fairness, however, does not require that an insurer necessarily be correct in making a decision to dispute its obligation to pay a claim. Mere denial of a claim that ultimately succeeds is not, in itself, an act of bad faith.

[64]   The proper characterization of Sun Life's conduct on the "good faith" issue requires a careful consideration of the evidence. The trial judge concluded that Sun Life did not act in bad faith. He heard the evidence over nine days. He had an opportunity to observe the witnesses, who included James Craig, a representative of Sun Life's disability management unit, and Ms. Fidler herself. Bearing in mind the subjective element of the duty of good faith, the trial judge's assessment of Mr. Craig's credibility in particular takes on some significance in determining whether Sun Life acted with an improper purpose in denying Ms. Fidler's claim.

[65]   Having heard and considered the evidence, the trial judge rejected Ms. Fidler's punitive damages claim. In his reasons, the trial judge noted the following evidence: Sun Life's surveillance recorded activities that were not inconsistent with Ms. Fidler's self-reporting; an internal memorandum exaggerated the nature of Ms. Fidler's activities; a claims administrator with Sun Life had written a memorandum contemplating the successful denial of Ms. Fidler's claim in the event of litigation; and Sun Life's medical consultant was wrong in concluding that there was no medical or non-medical evidence that Ms. Fidler could not perform light work.

[66]   On the other hand, he took into consideration that the medical reports about Ms. Fidler's condition were inconclusive; that Sun Life acted in reliance on its own consultants and experts; that Ms. Fidler's condition was contracted at a young age; and that her previous experience was in sedentary work. He summarized his considerations and conclusions as follows:

I must recognize, however, that after two years of benefits had been paid to Ms. Fidler, the test for continued coverage was whether Ms. Fidler could perform any work at all. Given the fact that the nature of Ms. Fidler's illness is of a type that is not demonstrated by indicators such as an x-ray or MRI, I do not think that Sun Life's conduct should be characterized as an act of bad faith. I say this even though Sun Life carried out what would appear to be at times a rather zealous approach to refuting Ms. Fidler's entitlement to the long term disability benefits despite strong medical evidence that she continued to be disabled. [para. 38]

[67] The majority of the Court of Appeal, *per* Finch C.J.B.C., found palpable and overriding error on the question of bad faith. Finch C.J.B.C. relied in particular on three aspects of the record: first, the absence of medical evidence to justify a denial of Ms. Fidler's claim; second, Sun Life's internal memoranda exaggerating the surveillance results and indicating an intention to avoid looking "bad" in the event of litigation; and third, Sun Life's failure to disclose to Ms. Fidler the surveillance video on which it relied in denying her claim.

[68] The surveillance team's observations were, arguably, consistent with the information provided by Ms. Fidler in her supplementary answers to the questionnaire. Moreover, Sun Life's internal memoranda, such as the surveillance summary and the medical consultant's report, reveal bald factual misstatements that weigh against a finding that Sun Life fairly and carefully considered the insured's claim.

[69] On the other hand, the fact that Ms. Fidler's behaviour in the course of the surveillance seemed to demonstrate an ability to engage in some activities, taken with the ambiguity of the IME assessment, helps reduce the force of a conclusion that Sun Life had an improper purpose in denying Ms. Fidler's claim.

[70] Except for the matter of disclosure, this evidence was expressly considered by the trial judge. And the disclosure issue is significantly tempered by the fact that Sun Life set out in a letter to Ms. Fidler the specific activities observed in the surveillance and the conclusions Sun Life drew as a consequence.

[71] We share Finch C.J.B.C.'s concerns about Sun Life's decision to terminate benefits relating to an unobservable disability in the absence of any medical evidence indicating an ability to return to work. And we appreciate that the facts in this case represent conduct that is extremely troubling — the five-year denial by Sun Life of disability benefits without medical support for the denial is, to say the least, inappropriate. But an insurer will not necessarily be in breach of the duty of good faith by incorrectly denying a claim that is eventually conceded, or judicially determined, to be legitimate. In this respect, we respectfully part company with Finch C.J.B.C. who, in awarding punitive damages, characterized Sun Life's concession that Ms. Fidler was entitled to benefits as "the civil equivalent of [a] 'guilty plea'" (para. 78). The question instead is whether the denial was the result of the overwhelmingly inadequate handling of the claim, or the introduction of improper considerations into the claims process.

[72] Ultimately, each case revolves around its own facts. As O'Connor J.A. stated in *702535 Ontario*:

> What constitutes bad faith will depend on the circumstances in each case. A court considering whether the duty has been breached will look at the conduct of the insurer throughout the claims process to determine whether in light of the circumstances, as they then existed, the insurer acted fairly and promptly in responding to the claim. [para. 30]

[73] The trial judge's conclusion that Sun Life did not act in bad faith was the product of a thorough review of the relevant evidence, and depended heavily on his appreciation of the basis on which Sun Life denied Ms. Fidler's claim. He considered every salient aspect of how Sun Life handled Ms. Fidler's claim, including those features that might be relied upon to suggest that Sun Life approached the claim obstructively or dismissively, but made no such finding.

[74] Nor did the trial judge find an improper purpose on the part of Sun Life. The trial judge's reliance, in particular, on the difficulty Sun Life had in ascertaining whether Ms. Fidler was actually disabled supported his conclusion that Sun Life did not act in bad faith and that, instead, its denial of benefits was the product of a real, albeit incorrect, doubt as to whether Ms. Fidler was incapable of performing *any* work, as required under the terms of the policy.

[75] Sun Life's conduct was troubling, but not sufficiently so as to justify interfering with the trial judge's conclusion that there was no bad faith. The trial judge's reasons disclose no error of law, and his eventual conclusion that Sun Life did not act in bad faith is inextricable from his findings of fact and his consideration of the evidence. As Ryan J.A. concluded in dissent:

> The trial judge saw and heard the witnesses. He examined the written material filed as exhibits. It was for him to assess the evidence and to determine its weight and effect. In my view Ms. Fidler has not been able to demonstrate that the conclusions of the trial judge were unreasonable or palpably wrong. [para. 104]

The award of punitive damages, of course, does not depend exclusively on the existence of an actionable wrong. In *Whiten*, the Court clearly established the relevant factors to consider in determining whether or not an award of punitive damages is warranted. Absent bad faith in this case, however, there is no need to go further.   *no punitive damages*

[76] Ms. Fidler is entitled to $20,000 for mental distress, but her claim for punitive damages is dismissed. Accordingly, we would allow the appeal in part, set aside the Court of Appeal's award of punitive damages and restore the order of Ralph J., with costs to Ms. Fidler throughout.

NOTES AND QUESTIONS

1. In articulating a foreseeability test for aggravated damages for mental distress, was the Supreme Court in *Fidler* consistent with the approach which that Court adopted in *Vorvis*, *Wallace* and *Whiten*?

    The Court in *Hadley v. Baxendale* did not purport to articulate a test for deciding when damages should be awarded in breach of contract cases, but only developed a test for deciding when damages, *i.e.*, damages in fact caused by the defendant's breach, should not be recoverable. Given the unanimity of the Supreme Court in *Fidler*, however, it is apparent that foreseeability is now a primary test for determining whether there should be liability for mental distress damages for breach of contract cases, provided that such a damage award fits within a compensatory claim consistent with *Wertheim v. Chicoutimi Pulp Co*.

    In many cases there will likely be real difficulties in determining whether to compensate for emotional distress. Many of the precedents cited by the Supreme Court were very different cases from *Fidler*. In both *Jarvis v. Swan's Tours* and *Ruxley*, the plaintiff's awards for lost enjoyment or amenity were based on the recognition that a psychological element could be found in the concept of position in the compensation principle. In other words, putting the plaintiffs in the positions that they would have been in had the respective contracts been performed, justified the recognition of and compensation for their lost enjoyment or disappointment. It is also important to remember that the £125 awarded to Mr. Jarvis, the £2,500 awarded to Mr. Forsyth and the £10,000 awarded to Mr. Farley are conventional in the sense that the actual disappointment or anger experienced by each plaintiff is irrelevant; what is important is a compensatory measure to compensate the reasonable plaintiff in the circumstances.

In both *Whiten* and *Fidler*, the plaintiff's basic claims were not for damages; they were for the amounts promised them under the insurance policies each plaintiff had with the respective defendants. Once judgment has been given on the plaintiff's claim in *Whiten* or the defendant has conceded that Ms. Fidler is entitled to the disability payments she claims, there is nothing on which either plaintiff can then sue the defendant unless there is an independently actionable wrong, because there remains no contractual obligation unpaid: *transit in rem judicatam* (Latin expression for a cause of action that has no legal existence because it has been adjudicated). The statement in *Fidler* that there is no need for an independently actionable wrong as the basis for an award of aggravated damages and an award of compensatory damages undercuts the basis on which Binnie J. justified giving Mrs. Whiten punitive damages; he said that she would not otherwise be adequately compensated if she did not receive an award of punitive damages. This point is perhaps the most important one that will have to be elucidated in order to understand the effect of *Fidler v. Sun Life* on claims for punitive damages in general.

It is now probable that it will take years of litigation before it is clear (i) what the basis is for such compensation for aggravated damages; and (ii) how much such awards should be.

Does the recognition of Ms. Fidler's claim suggest that a similar claim might now be recognized in *Wallace v. United Grain Growers Ltd.*? It may be hard to now argue that mental distress arising from the manner of an employee's dismissal is not foreseeable and, if that is all that is required to support a claim for compensation, has the Supreme Court now imposed a new set of duties on the employer? It is worth noting that at para. 41 the Supreme Court in *Fidler* seemed to endorse the Ontario Court of Appeal decision in *Prinzo v. Baycrest*, where aggravated damages were awarded in a wrongful dismissal case.

2.   In dealing with the issue of punitive damages, do you think that the Supreme Court was heavily influenced by the conclusion of the trial judge, *viz.* that the defendant had not acted in bad faith? Or do you think that the Supreme Court actually intended to narrow the effect of its own decision in *Whiten*, limiting the range of cases in which insurers and other defendants should be liable for punitive damages?

3.   If you were corporate counsel for an insurer, overall would you be pleased with *Fidler* or concerned? If you were a plaintiff's counsel, would you be concerned about *Fidler*? What effect do you think that *Whiten* had on the practices or premiums of insurance companies? What effect do you think that *Fidler* will have on the practices or premiums of insurance companies?

Uncertainty and Damages

Two seemingly contradictory statements are often made by courts. The first is that if the plaintiff has shown a loss arising from the defendant's breach of contract, the mere fact that damages are uncertain or hard to determine will not stop the court from making the effort: *Carson v. Willitts* (1930), 65 O.L.R. 456, [1930] 4 D.L.R. 977 (S.C. App. Div.). But it is also sometimes said that the court will refuse to enforce a contract if the damages recoverable would be too uncertain or too hard to determine: *Courtney and Fairbairn Ltd. v. Tolaini Brothers (Hotels) Ltd.*, [1975] 1 All E.R. 716. (We will look at this case in more detail in Chapter 3.)

The problem of uncertainty in assessing damages is endemic. An important aspect of the uncertainty arises because damages have to be awarded in one lump sum; the court cannot order periodic payments or permit the plaintiff to come back to court to have the damages assessed on an interim basis. While making a decision in this way has obvious advantages in terms of efficiency and finality, in many cases future events have to be taken into consideration at the date of the trial. The actual course of events may make it clear that a particular award is either too high or too low. In spite of these difficulties, courts usually do their best in assessing damages. The mere fact that damages are hard to calculate will not justify the conclusion that no damages should be awarded.

In other cases, difficulties arise because the breach of promise makes any determination of loss of profits an inherently speculative exercise. We saw one response to this in *Anglia Television v. Reed*; although courts will struggle to assess damages, in some cases the exercise may be so speculative that the court (or plaintiff) will look to wasted expenditure rather than loss of profits.

One particular problem requires special mention. In some cases the loss that the plaintiff suffers as a result of the breach of contract is only the loss of a chance of benefiting. That is, whether the contract were breached or not, the plaintiff never had more than a chance that it would gain from performance.

The classic case on loss of an opportunity (or loss of a chance of gain) arising from a breach is the English case of *Chaplin v. Hicks*, [1911] 2 K.B. 786 (C.A.). The defendant's breach of contract caused the plaintiff to lose the chance to be one of 50 women in a beauty contest, 12 of whom were to be chosen for lucrative employment as actresses. If the plaintiff had been one of the 12 finalists she would have been offered a job that would have paid her several hundred pounds more over the life of the contract than her employment at that time, but she could also have ended up as one of the other 38 contestants who received nothing. The jury, which had the benefit of seeing the plaintiff, awarded her £100. The English Court of Appeal upheld the jury award. The Court rejected the defendant's argument that only nominal damages were payable since the plaintiff lost only the chance to be a winner, and might have had no gain had the contract been fully performed. Vaughan Williams L.J. said (pp. 791-92):

> . . . Then it is said that the questions which might arise in the minds of the judges [in selecting the winners] are so numerous that it is impossible to say that the case is one in which it is possible to apply the doctrine of averages at all. I do not agree with the contention that, if certainty is impossible of attainment, the damages for a breach of contract are unassessable.

> . . . In such a case the jury must do the best they can, and it may be that the amount of their verdict will be a matter of guesswork. But the fact that the damages cannot be assessed with certainty does not relieve the wrong-doer of the necessity of paying damages for his breach of contract.

Vaughan Williams L.J. went on to say that, while the plaintiff's chance to win the competition had no market value and could not have been sold by her, the "jury might well take the view that such a right, if it could have been transferred, would have been of such value that every one would recognize that a good price could be obtained for it". He concluded by saying (p. 793):

> My view is that under such circumstances as those in this case the assessment of damages was unquestionably for the jury. The jury came to the conclusion that the taking away from the plaintiff of the opportunity of competition, as one of a body of

fifty, when twelve prizes were to be distributed, deprived the plaintiff of something which had a monetary value. I think that they were right and this appeal fails.

In *Carson v. Willitts*, *supra*, the plaintiff sued the defendant for breach of a contract to drill oil wells. The deal was that the wells would be drilled (on land owned by the plaintiff) at the expense of the defendant, who after drilling would have a share in any profits obtained from the wells. The defendant drilled one well but refused to drill any more. Masten J.A., giving judgment for the court, said (at pp. 458-59 O.L.R.):

> Then what is the basis on which this Court should now direct the damages to be assessed? In my opinion, what the plaintiff lost by the refusal of the defendant to bore two more wells was a sporting or gambling chance that valuable oil or gas would be found when the two further wells were bored. If the wells had been bored and no oil or gas had been found, the effect would be that the plaintiff has lost nothing by the refusal of the defendant to go on boring. On the other hand, if valuable or gas had been discovered, by the boring of these two wells, he has lost substantially. It may not be easy to compute what that chance was worth to the plaintiff, but the difficulty in estimating the quantum is no reason for refusing to award any damages.

> In *Mayne on Damages*, 10th ed., p. 6, it is said: "A distinction must be drawn between cases where absence of evidence makes it impossible to assess damages, and cases where the assessment is difficult because of the nature of the damage proved. In the former case only nominal damages can be recovered. In the latter case, however, the difficulty of assessment is no ground for refusing substantial damages".

In the Supreme Court of Canada decision in *Kinkel v. Hyman*, [1939] S.C.R. 364, [1939] 4 D.L.R. 1, the Court considered the consequences of a breach of contract by the defendant that deprived the plaintiff of the opportunity to seek ratification at a meeting of shareholders of a transaction that would have been profitable to the plaintiff. The Court concluded that even if the contract had not been breached and the meeting had been called, it was unlikely that the transaction would have been approved, and awarded only nominal damages. Crockett J. wrote (p. 383 S.C.R.):

> For my part, I can find no authority in either *Chaplin v. Hicks* (1) or *Carson v. Willitts* (2) justifying any court in awarding any more than a nominal sum as damages for the loss of a mere chance of possible benefit except upon evidence proving that there was some reasonable probability of the plaintiff realizing therefrom an advantage of some real substantial monetary value. Indeed . . . *Chaplin v. Hicks* (1) and the decision in *Carson v. Willitts* (2) seem to me to point to the contrary.

If a litigation lawyer breaches his or her obligation to a client by, for example, failing to begin an action within the limitation period, the measure of damages to which the client will be entitled in a negligence action against the lawyer is what would have been obtained had the action been brought in time and been successful, discounted by the chance that the action might have failed. The action against the lawyer involves a kind of trial of the action that would, had the lawyer done what he or she should have done, have been brought against the tortfeasor. If the lawyer negligently failed to begin an action against a doctor, the client's damages against the lawyer would be the amount that the client might have recovered from the doctor, discounted to reflect the chance that the client might not have been successful. Mathematically this could be represented by:

Expected Loss = (amount of damage award) multiplied by (probability of success)

Of course these numbers are likely to be, at best, rough approximations. If the client's claim against the doctor had no chance of success, the client will recover no damages from the negligent lawyer. In *Fisher v. Knibbe*, [1992] 5 W.W.R. 385 (Alta. C.A.) the court assessed the client's chance of successfully suing a doctor at zero and awarded no damages in the client's action against the lawyer who had negligently failed to sue the doctor within the limitation period.

A number of cases have dealt with breach of a contract to sell land which is conditional upon the owner obtaining the required permission from planning authorities to allow development or sale of the land, and which requires the owner to use "best efforts" to obtain the permission. The owner has breached the contract by failing to seek the permission, or by making insufficient effort to obtain the permission. The plaintiff-buyer can usually show that it would have made a substantial profit if permission had been obtained. However, even if the defendant had assiduously sought permission, there was a chance that permission would not have been obtained. In these cases the courts have taken the estimate of the profit that would have been obtained and have then discounted this figure by a factor representing the chance that permission would have been refused.

Thus, in *Multi-Malls Inc. v. Tex-Mall Properties Inc.* (1980), 28 O.R. (2d) 6, 108 D.L.R. (3d) 399 (H.C.), affirmed (1981), 37 O.R. (2d) 133, 128 D.L.R. (3d) 192 (C.A.), the defendant failed to seek the permission of the Ontario Municipal Board to develop a shopping centre. Damages were determined by taking the gross profit that the defendant would have earned and reducing that figure by 80 per cent, which was the court's estimate of the chance of the application's being refused even if the defendant had done what it should have.

In *Eastwalsh Homes Ltd. v. Anatal Developments Ltd.* (1993), 12 O.R. (3d) 675, 100 D.L.R. (4th) 469 (C.A.), reversing 72 O.R. (2d) 661, 68 D.L.R. (4th) 46 (H.C.J.), one planning expert called by the plaintiff testified that there was an 80 per cent chance of the necessary permission being obtained within the time required under the contract, and another expert called by the plaintiff suggested that there was a 20 per cent chance. The trial judge, apparently averaged these two estimates, discounted the approximately $4 million loss of profit by 50 per cent and awarded about $2 million. However, the Court of Appeal concluded that the evidence of the plaintiff's experts was based on erroneous assumptions, and accepted the evidence of an expert called by the defendant that there was "no reasonable prospect" of the permission being obtained in the time required. Accordingly, the Court of Appeal awarded only nominal damages. Griffith J.A. wrote (p. 689 O.R.):

> The burden rests on the plaintiff alleging breach of contract to prove on the balance of probabilities that the breach and not some intervening factor or factors has caused loss to the plaintiff. In this respect the courts have not relaxed the basic standard of proof. Where it is clear that the defendant's breach has caused loss to the plaintiff it is no answer to the claim that the loss is difficult to assess or calculate. The concept of the loss of a chance then begins to operate and the court will estimate the plaintiff's chance of obtaining a benefit had the contract been performed. But even in this situation, the Supreme Court of Canada has said in *Kinkel v. Hyman, supra*, that proof of the loss of a mere chance is not enough; the plaintiff must prove that the chance constitutes "some reasonable probability" of realizing "an advantage of some real substantial monetary value".

In *Kinbauri Gold Corp. v. IAMGOLD International African Mining Gold Corp.*, [2004] O.J. No. 4568, 246 D.L.R. (4th) 595 (C.A.), the Ontario Court of Appeal cited *Chaplin v. Hicks* and Cronk J.A. wrote (at para. 93):

> The courts have recognized the application of a contingency allowance to the calculation of damages in breach of contract cases where performance of the contract may have been prevented, notwithstanding the wrongdoer's breach, by some other intervening factor. Where the plaintiff establishes that its loss was caused by the defendant's breach of contract, but is unable to prove loss of a definite benefit, demonstrating only the "chance" of receiving a benefit had the contract been performed, the courts will discount the value of the chance by the improbability of its occurrence ...

In *Kinbauri,* the Court of Appeal agreed with the assessment of the trial judge that the award should only be reduced by 10 per cent, as the probability of obtaining necessary consent was "high but not absolute."

In Chapter 4, we will return to some of the problems that arise when a contract is conditional upon obtaining permission from a government body.

Do People Expect Expectation Damages?

There are a number of fundamental questions about the rule that the normal measure of damages is based on an award of expectation-based damages. A central but unstated premise of this rule is that it is what people normally expect. The premise is, as we have seen, widely accepted by judges and academics and therefore by lawyers. There are, for example, statements by academics implicitly criticizing businesspeople for their ignorance in not knowing that they can get expectation damages for breach of contract. (See M.P. Furmston, "Ignorance of the Law" (1981), 1 *Legal Studies* 37.) Such criticism may be unfounded. Indeed, one can ask whether it is justifiable to award expectation damages if those most affected by the breach do not expect such an award.

Lord Atkinson's principle in *Wertheim v. Chicoutimi Pulp* may be problematic if one sees the purpose of the law of contract as the protection of the parties' reasonable expectations. It may not be appropriate to protect expectations that few people have. Is there anything illogical in an attitude to contracts that does *not* regard them as guaranteeing that, come what may, the promisee will be in as good a position as if the promise were performed?

One would like to know a lot more about the expectations that people actually have when they make contracts. Even with contracts for the sale of residential homes, a major class of contracts, it would seem that at the time of entering into the agreement, most individuals (whether buyers or sellers) do *not* have the "expectation" that in the event of breach they will be put in the "same position as if the contract had been fully performed, in so far as money can do". Developers and speculators are, of course, more likely to be aware of their legal rights and obligations, and usually have the knowledge and hence an expectation that in the event of breach expectation damages are likely to be awarded. Individuals who are buying or selling a home will usually consult a lawyer after, if not before, entering into the agreement. By the time that breach is a possibility, they are likely to be aware of the chance that expectation damages will be awarded by a court.

The casual assumption of many law students and academics, and even some lawyers, that those involved in commercial transactions see the law and an action for breach of contract as a generally accepted remedy for breach of contract, is very likely false.

Generally speaking, litigation is avoided like the plague and is only likely to be resorted to in special situations. These special situations include the bankruptcy of one party; a serious and unexpected change in the context in which the deal was made, for example, a sudden and drastic change in price; or a situation where the parties lack any incentive to work things out on their own. This last factor is often the most important. Almost all contracts are made in a context that provides some incentive for the parties to work things out for themselves in the event of breach by one party. This incentive may arise because of the need to preserve good customer relations, because a lack of co-operativeness leads sooner or later to costly litigation, or for any one of a number of reasons.

Most of the cases to this point in the book are "transactional", in that they involve a discrete contract, with no expectation of future dealings between the parties. However, many contractual situations are "relational", with any single contract being part of an ongoing commercial relationship. In some cases a relational contract itself creates a long-term legal relationship, while in other situations the legal contract is discrete, but there is expected to be a long-term commercial relationship; in either situation the relationship is likely to be characterized by a high degree of co-operativeness. Each side will be very reluctant to jeopardize future relations because one transaction has not turned out as expected. A tendency on the part of one firm to stand on its strict legal rights is likely to be highly unpopular and to lead to a refusal or, at least, caution on the part of other firms before they will agree to engage in further deals.

Throughout these materials we will confront the failure of the law to take into account the context of the contract that is being considered. Contract law tends to be premised on a "transactional" model of contracting, whereas the commercial reality is often "relational". The failure to consider commercial context may give one party an unexpected and unjustified opportunity to extract far greater damages than *either* party may have expected before things went sour in the relation. If there is no incentive to work things out, for example because one party is going out of business, the party who is told by its lawyer that it can get lost profits will, of course, try to do so, even though it might never have expected this "compensation" while the relation remained friendly and co-operative. We will see statements and the actions of individuals being interpreted in one way, when it is likely that if they were seen against a more realistic and accurate background, they might be understood in a different way.

A failure on the part of the courts to consider the background to the contract can lead to a significant reduction in the pressure that is exerted on parties to work things out for themselves. The assumption that expectation damages are the normal measure of damages may offer one side a good chance of getting more by litigating than by settling the dispute. The existence of this chance creates the same risk of catching the other party by surprise when expectation damages are awarded.

This is not to suggest that courts and the law usually get things wrong: they are very often right, though unfortunately the reasons for judgment may not adequately explain why the judges made the decisions that they did. Judges are usually sensitive to the commercial context of cases, even if they do not state this in their reasons. What needs to be emphasized is the recurrent theme of the importance of the context of any transaction. An award of damages should only be justified if it can be seen as protecting the plaintiff's reasonable expectations without doing too much violence to the expectations of the defendant, if they are different.

Such a justification requires one to be aware of the possibility, at least, that an award to protect a particular interest may not be justifiable on the facts.

One more complication: an argument can be made for treating the remedy in those situations where things go badly wrong differently from what the actual expectations of the parties in a functioning relation would indicate. In other words, once the courts are dealing with a situation of breach, what the parties expect in the ordinary case may not be relevant. This argument can be supported by pointing out that the parties rarely think about what might go wrong until something does, and may justify the general approach of the courts in awarding expectation damages.

EQUITABLE REMEDIES

Reference was made earlier to the question of when the courts have power to order promisors actually to perform what they have promised to do. It was, for example, stated that the courts would not make such an order on the facts of *Peevyhouse* or *Radford v. De Froberville*. It is now necessary to consider the reason for this statement, and consider situations in which the courts will order that the contract be actually be performed, *i.e.*, make an order for "specific performance".

The Canadian law that was received from England is based on two major jurisprudential systems. The first is known as the common law. The term "common law" has several meanings, but it is used here to refer to the law applied by the common law courts in England, such as the Court of King's Bench and the Court of Common Pleas. These courts owe their origin to the administrative reforms of Henry II (1154-89). The word "common" signifies that the law applied in these courts was administered by judges appointed by the King and was common to the whole of England. Much of the early history of the common law courts involved the struggle of the central administration (represented by the King) against the decentralizing pressure of the local barons. The King eventually won and, as a consequence, his courts, the courts applying a law common to all parts of the kingdom, were established as the principal judicial authority.

The second jurisprudential system, known as "equity", developed in response to the limitations of the common law. Litigants who were disappointed by the decisions and remedies in the common law courts would petition the King for relief that the common law courts would not grant. Medieval kings were too busy to examine each petition that came to them, so they passed these petitions on to the chancellor. The medieval chancellor was one of the great officers of state. He originally sat in the King's court behind a "chancel", or latticework screen, hence the name chancellor. Originally he was a cleric — a bishop — and in addition to his duties as a member of the King's council, he carried a heavy administrative burden. By the end of the twelfth century the volume of petitions coming before the chancellor was already large.

When a petition came to the chancellor he would call the defendant before him by subpoena (Latin for "under (threat of) punishment", suggesting the consequence if the person failed to attend) to answer, on oath, the allegation that had been made by the plaintiff. This procedure was different from that of the common law courts where, by means of a writ, the defendant was called upon to answer, not under oath, since parties could not be witnesses, but at trial before a jury governed by formalistic and (historically) rigid rules.

Initially the rulings of the chancellor depended on his assessment of individual cases. Such single instances developed into a body of rules and the chancellors began the creation of a body of jurisprudence — known as "equity" — that they applied to the cases coming before them. Equity and common law continued as two distinct bodies of jurisprudence applied by different courts until the nineteenth century. The chancellor's power could not directly overrule the decisions of the common law courts, but he could often remedy the deficiencies in the common law rules, as he saw them. The power of the chancellor was corrective or supplemental to the common law.

At common law, it was, for example, at one time impossible for a person sued for breach of certain formal contracts — known as "deeds" (*i.e.*, written contracts under seal) to raise as a defence that he had been induced by fraud to enter into the deed. In some cases, a fraudulent person might have secured a judgment on the deed in a common law court. A person who claimed that he was the victim of fraud might go to the chancellor after the common law judgment was obtained and seek relief "in equity". If the chancellor found that there had been fraud, he would "rescind" the deed; that is, he would declare that the contract had never or no longer had any binding force, and might issue an order that the fraudulent person not seek to enforce the common law judgment.

It is said that the rules applied by the chancellor *supplemented* rather than *changed* the rules of the common law. While in a modern sense one might regard the chancellor as being a form of "appeal" or "review" judge from the common law judges, this is a more coherent explanation than was the situation in medieval times. Two distinct bodies of jurisprudence co-existed — equity and common law — and had different rules of evidence, procedure and substantive law. Individuals sometimes had to litigate in both the courts of common law and equity (or chancery) to be able to obtain the relief that they sought.

There were a number of important areas of the common law where the chancellor intervened. Equity made a large contribution to the law governing mortgages by tempering the harshness of the common law with some concern for the unfortunate mortgagor in default, providing that even if the mortgage called for forfeiture of all payments in the event of a default, the mortgagor might get some protection. The law of trusts was also created by the Court of Chancery.

For present purposes, the most important contribution of the chancellor was his power to order a promisor to perform his contract as he had promised. This remedy is known as an order for specific performance, and had a number of important features that made it attractive to plaintiffs. For a variety of reasons the remedies that the common law courts could offer to litigants were limited. The limitation that most concerns us here is that the common law courts would only give a remedy expressed as a monetary damage award. The form of the judgment of a common law court in favour of a plaintiff was not, as one might have expected, an order that the defendant pay a sum of money to the plaintiff. Rather, it was an order directed to the sheriff, commanding him to seize the goods of the defendant and sell them to obtain proceeds to pay the plaintiff. (This is still the method of enforcement most typically used in the common law provinces of Canada, though there are other methods of direct enforcement, such as garnishment of wages.)

In contrast to the method of enforcement of a common law judgment, the method of enforcement by the chancellor was more direct. A defendant who, for example, disobeyed an order of the chancellor was guilty of contempt of court. The penalty for contempt was (as it can still be) imprisonment. A recalcitrant defendant would then stay in prison until he obeyed, or (since the chancellor would only make those orders that it was in good conscience to make) until the defendant agreed that the chancellor was correct and that he should do what he had promised to do. The prospect of a stay in a medieval prison usually did much to induce a defendant to find that his idea of proper conduct was similar to that of the chancellor, so that compliance with the chancellor's order would follow. Today the historic power of the chancellor to imprison is now supplemented by the power to seize property and to hold it until the defendant submits to the power of the court. This power is obviously more effective if a corporation or a body like a trade union has to have pressure brought upon it. These powers are set out in the Rules of Court or equivalent sources. See, for example, the Ontario *Rules of Civil Procedure*, rules 60.05 and 60.11.

The power of the chancellor extended to those cases where the defendant could be ordered not to do something that would be in breach of his contract. This power is sometimes referred to as the power to issue an "injunction." Then, as now, breach of an injunction may be a contempt of court and renders a person liable to punishment which may include a fine or imprisonment. The method of enforcement made the chancellor's remedies popular with plaintiffs, and some care had to be taken not to prejudice defendants unfairly.

Since the plaintiff who came before the chancellor was seeking justice, he had to be prepared "to do justice". This view led to the development of limitations on the right of a plaintiff to get an equitable remedy when he had behaved improperly. It was said that the defendant had to "come to equity with clean hands". As a further result of the origin of the equitable remedies, those remedies were always discretionary. No plaintiff could ever demand as of right that the defendant be compelled to perform a contract specifically: no matter how meritorious the claim and upright the conduct of the defendant, the chancellor would always compare the conduct of the two parties and consider the "equities" of a case as well as the legal effect of the contract between the parties. By way of contrast, at common law, a plaintiff could not be denied his remedy if he could show breach of contract and damages. Even if the latter could not be shown, the plaintiff was entitled to judgment for nominal damages. Such relief might be important to an institutional litigant seeking to establish a precedent in a test case.

One very important limitation was from the beginning recognized by the Court of Chancery on its remedies. Equitable remedies were "personal" in the sense that only a person bound in "conscience" to do what the court said had to be done was bound by them. For example, an equitable remedy was not available against a person who, as *bona fide* third party purchaser without notice, bought trust property from a trustee who was in breach of his trust obligations. This limit remains a practical problem for anyone seeking equitable relief.

It is now some 700 years since the power of the chancellor was established. During that time the jurisdiction of the chancellor became formalized and reduced to rules. In the Middle Ages a regular court developed to supplement the work of the individual chancellor. As was inevitable, friction developed between the jurisdiction of the chancellor and the common law courts, and complex, bitter disputes occurred. These disputes came to a head early in the seventeenth century in a case that found its way before King James I. The cantankerous Sir Edward Coke presented the claims of the common law courts. The chancellor's side was taken by Coke's arch-enemy, Sir Francis Bacon. The dispute was resolved by the king, who determined the dispute in favour of the court of equity. While there was a tendency thereafter for the rules of equity to prevail over the rules of common law, jurisdictional disputes and complexity caused by the existence of two court systems continued until the nineteenth century.

The Court of Chancery existed as a separate court in England until the *Judicature Act* of 1873 and in Ontario until the *Judicature Act* of 1881. From that time, the Superior Court exercised the jurisdiction of both common law and equity, and could give either equitable or legal remedies. The historical origin of the separate systems still determines which remedies we call equitable and which we call legal. The distinctions are still important in some situations. In *Peachtree II Associates - Dallas, L.P. v. 857486 Ontario Ltd.*, [2005] O.J. No. 2749, 76 O.R. (3d) 362, the Ontario Court of Appeal had to consider the treatment of "stipulated remedy clauses" (or "penalty clauses") at common law and in equity. Justice Sharpe wrote:

> [21] To understand the law's treatment of stipulated remedy clauses as it pertains to this case, we must turn to history and to the two great streams of our legal tradition, common law and equity. Although those two streams were joined well over a century ago, as this case demonstrates, we continue to encounter issues of confluence and the reconciliation of doctrines derived from one tradition with those derived from the other.

> [29] … I pause here to note that it is with some reluctance that I frame the issue in terms of a choice between common law and equity. In doing so, I do not wish to be taken as encouraging the perpetuation of what very well may amount to an outdated distinction between the common law's treatment of penalty clauses and the equitable doctrine of relief from forfeiture. … Moreover, as I will explain, my analysis is driven in large part by considerations that would tend to favour, whenever possible, the equitable approach as the dominant one.

Today the term "equitable remedy" refers to a remedy historically administered by a court of equity according to the legal principles developed by that court, and which, were it not for the operation of the *Judicature Acts*, would be administered only by that court. Although common law and equity have merged, for some purposes this historical division remains significant.

Implicit in the preceding discussion is the idea that the jurisdiction of equity is limited. If a common law remedy provided adequate relief, the court of equity would not intervene. The basic test to determine the plaintiff's entitlement to an equitable remedy is that the common law remedy of an award of monetary damages must be "inadequate". Before we explore the meaning of the term "inadequate", it must be remembered that in many cases the plaintiff would be quite content with the monetary remedy available at common law. The owner of a house damaged by the bad workmanship of a contractor employed to fix the roof would only want money in compensation. The last thing the owner wants is to have the bad contractor ordered to fix the damage.

As a test of the jurisdiction of the Court of Chancery, the requirement that the common law remedies available to the plaintiff be "inadequate" is less than fully satisfactory. A word like "inadequate" can be very confusing. There are a great many ways in which damages could be considered "inadequate." They might be inadequate if the court awards too little, and, as we have seen, there are many reasons why the court may award too little. Damages might also be inadequate if, apart from the problem of quantification, the defendant has insufficient assets to meet the monetary judgment.

The legal test for the "inadequacy", as developed by the court of equity, had a particular meaning. There was a range of cases in which the court of equity considered the damage award that a court of common law was likely to give was "inadequate", in particular, situations where damages may not have reflected important non-market interests. For a variety of institutional and historical reasons, the courts of equity were especially concerned about contracts for the sale of land and "unique" personal property, where there was a sense that damages might be "inadequate". Other situations that may have involved an "inadequate" damage award, such as where an employee was wrongfully dismissed, were ignored by the court of equity.

The principal area where the remedy of damages was historically regarded as inadequate, and where the remedy of specific performance was most often granted, was for contracts for the sale of land. Damages were said to be inadequate in such a case because each piece of land is unique (in that it occupies a unique position on the earth's surface). Because land can have some special aesthetic, emotional, or psychic value to the purchaser, a value that cannot be easily quantified, a damage award based on market values might not reflect these non-economic interests. A disappointed purchaser cannot buy a piece of land identical to the one that was the subject of a breached contract in the marketplace. This justification for the remedy in land cases gains some support from the fact that the remedy is also available in sales of unique chattels (for example, a Ming vase or a portrait by Rubens), but is generally not available for a contract for the sale of commodities that are readily available in the marketplace.

The court of equity's granting of specific performance for contracts for the sale of land may also have been a reflection of the political power inherent in the ownership of land (Cohen, "The Relationship of Contractual Remedies to Political and Social Status: A Preliminary Inquiry" (1982), 32 *U.T.L.J.* 31). At one time, a person who was denied the opportunity to buy land might suffer a political as much as an economic loss. A justification for specific performance on the basis that the ownership of land confers political power is clearly not relevant today.

Whatever the justification, recognition of aesthetic or emotional interests, or protection of political power, the general availability of the remedy of specific performance for breach of a contract for the purchase of land was well established, though as we shall see judicial attitudes to land contracts have changed in the past few years.

Another important example of a situation where the equitable remedy of specific performance is available is for the breach of a contract to sell "unique" goods. Legislation such as Ontario's *Sale of Goods Act* provides:

> 50. In an action for breach of contract to deliver specific or ascertained goods, the court may, if it thinks fit, direct that the contract be performed specifically, without giving the defendant the option of retaining the goods on payment of damages, and may impose such terms and conditions as to damages, payment of the price, and otherwise, as to the court seems just.

While this section appears to give courts an unfettered discretion to do what is "fit", specific performance for the sale of goods is typically only ordered for chattels that are in some way "unique" or not readily available in the market place, *i.e.*, cases in which an award of damages would be "inadequate" since a disappointed buyer cannot go into the marketplace to purchase goods that would satisfy the contract.

An early example of the section in operation is provided by *Behnke v. Bede Shipping Co.*, [1927] 1 K.B. 649. The plaintiff, the buyer, sought a decree of specific performance of a contract to sell a reconditioned ship. The court found that the ship was "of peculiar and practically unique value to the plaintiff". On the basis of this finding, an award of common law damages was regarded as inadequate, and an order of specific performance was made. This case is a good illustration of the meaning of the "inadequacy" of damages. While the ship was unique, in that it was not "mass produced", it was used for commercial purposes. There was doubtless a sum of money that would have fully compensated the plaintiff for his loss; it would only be a question of finding it. Given the uniqueness of the ship, that may be more difficult than the usual problem of determining damages, and given the market-based approach of the courts to assessing monetary damages, there may be a significant risk of undercompensation. The desire to remove this risk of undercompensation from the plaintiff may be a sufficient reason to award specific performance. Further, given the unique nature of the subject of the sale, the "market price" would be virtually impossible to establish without selling the vessel. Understanding of what is behind the decision is obscured by the statement that common law damages are "inadequate".

The UCC provision equivalent to the *Sale of Goods Act* is broader, though not much more specific (§2-716(1)):

> Specific performance may be decreed when the goods are unique or in other proper circumstances.

The Official Comment to this section states:

> In view of this Article's emphasis on the commercial feasibility of replacement, a new concept of what are "unique" goods is introduced under this section. Specific performance is no longer limited to goods which are already specific or ascertained at the time of contracting. The test of uniqueness under this section must be made in terms of the total situation which characterizes the contract. Output and requirements contracts involving a particular or peculiarly available source or market present today the typical commercial specific performance situation, as contrasted with contracts for the sale of heirlooms or priceless works of art which were usually involved in the older cases. However, uniqueness is not the sole basis of the remedy under this section for the relief may also be granted "in other proper circumstances" and inability to cover is strong evidence of "other proper circumstances."

The UCC provides in §2-716(3) that the buyer may claim the goods from the seller if he is unable or likely to be unable to "effect cover", that is, to obtain the goods that were the subject of the contract elsewhere.

A justification of the remedy of specific performance based on the uniqueness of the subject matter of the contract of sale or on the need to protect aesthetic interests is not very persuasive, especially when consideration is given to recent developments in the law. The argument is too broad as it would justify an award of specific performance in cases like *Peevyhouse v. Garland Coal* or *Radford v. De Froberville* (when the claim might provide a basis for the plaintiff's extracting too much compensation from the defendant).

The justification could be considered obsolete if the developments that began with *Jarvis v. Swan's Tours* would permit monetary compensation whenever there are intangible, psychic or emotional losses. In other words, it might be argued that although historically the limited nature of damage awards did justify the development of the remedy of specific performance, the remedy of specific performance is no longer necessary to protect interests as aesthetic and non-economic interests can be protected in damage awards.

A simple example may help to explain the limitations of a justification for specific performance based on uniqueness. Suppose that Eleanor agrees to sell Blackacre to William and subsequently refuses to complete the transaction. This situation was a historically paradigmatic example of a case where specific performance would be granted. In theory, there is nothing to prevent an award to William of damages for economic loss (for example, loss of profit on a projected resale), and non-economic losses (loss of emotional or aesthetic satisfaction). In theory there is some amount of money that is sufficiently large that William would not care whether the contract was performed or he was paid the money — that is, an economist would say that William would be "indifferent" whether he would get the money or the land. In other words, *in theory* there is no reason to assume that an award of money damages is *necessarily* inadequate. Such an award may be inadequate in the sense that William regards himself as less well off with an award of money rather than performance, only if the method by which damages are determined fails to take into account all the items that go to make up William's loss from Eleanor's breach. In theory, the development of aggravated damages could be extended to cover all types of non-economic losses. However, as discussed earlier, in many situations plaintiffs are still restricted to economic losses (and even then to economic losses that are often quite narrowly defined), and hence there continues to be a justification for the award of specific performance in appropriate cases.

Beyond the justification based on "uniqueness," an award of specific performance functions as a device for removing from the promisee the risk of undercompensation. An order for specific performance ensures that the promisee gets *all* the benefits that the promise was intended to provide, or which it was hoped that the promise would provide.

An order for specific performance also absolves the promisee from having to take steps to mitigate losses arising from breach. The remedy of specific performance provides the same allocative function in the case of the sale of land as it does in the context of "efficient breach" discussed by Posner; it allocates to the promisee the chance of gain due to an increase in the value of the subject matter of the contract that the contract's performance would have provided. Posner argues that the promisee should bear the risk that the promisor may make an "efficient breach" and gain the advantage of an increase in the value of the subject matter of the sale. That argument assumes that the promisee should only get compensation that gives it what it lost from the breach. While an award of expectation damages based on *Wertheim v. Chicoutimi Pulp* is usually limited in this way, this argument ignores the question of which party should benefit from the increase in value of the subject matter of the sale, and which party should mitigate its losses. If the court grants specific performance, the buyer has no obligation to mitigate, and gets the advantage of any increase in value until the date of trial. In practice, therefore, buyers tend to want at least to have the option of specific performance.

A justification for an award of specific performance might, therefore, be found in considering the risks inherent in an award of damages, and by deciding that in all the circumstances of the case these should not be borne by the promisee. The question of whether to protect this interest may not be easy to decide. An answer that the risks should not be on the promisee would *prima facie* be as applicable in any contract of sale; it is not clear why it should be restricted to cases involving

specific perf.
restrict to land

land or the contract for the sale of a unique chattel. The question is, as always, what values and interests should the law support? What is the purpose of the legal rules about remedies?

There is, in addition, an important practical reason for the disappointed purchaser of land to seek the remedy of specific performance. Equity will not make its remedies available if the vendor, in breach of contract, sells the property to a purchaser for value without notice of the prior claim, as that person would not be bound "in conscience" to obey the Chancellor's order. However, as soon as an action is commenced, a plaintiff who is seeking specific performance may be able to register the existence of its claim in the Land Registry Office. Registration is deemed to be "notice to the world". Registration of a pending claim effectively prevents the vendor from selling the land, as any prospective purchaser will check for outstanding claims and will likely be most unwilling to complete a transaction knowing that the claimant may recover the land.

The issue of what the law of equitable remedies is trying to achieve cannot be answered solely by considering theoretical justifications; one must also take into account the historical evolution of the law. In other words, while one can question whether there are still sound rationales for giving equitable relief to purchasers of land or unique chattels, the courts continue to say that damages — in the amounts that they are actually likely to award — are "inadequate", and hence will order specific performance, at least in some cases. The historical reasons for awarding specific performance are still relevant. However, the courts are slowly developing a more rational approach to the law governing equitable remedies, so it is necessary both to understand the historical rationales for determining that an award of damages is "inadequate", and to appreciate the limitations of the historical approaches.

For example, historically it was thought to be unfair that only one party (the buyer) could get equitable relief — an order of specific performance — while the other might be limited to common law remedies. Thus the equitable rule developed that if the purchaser of land could get equitable relief, so too could the vendor. This concern that both parties have the same rights to equitable relief was referred to as the "doctrine of mutuality". In a suit by the vendor such an order would be an order to pay the full purchase price. It is now logically difficult to justify an award of specific performance in favour of a vendor of land, even if the land is unique, as the land can always be sold to another purchaser, albeit at a lower price that would be reflected in a damage award. A vendor can only want money, and a judgment for damages at common law would give that. As we shall see, the right of a vendor (or any other person who wants only money, as opposed to the person who wants something other than money) to an order of specific performance causes some problems that have forced the courts to treat this right much as if it were a common law right. The doctrine of mutuality had little justification, apart from a spurious concern for symmetry. Indeed, the effect of the doctrine of mutuality was that a vendor of land would be absolved from the need to mitigate — to sell the land to another, even in a falling market. As a result, courts have effectively ceased to grant a vendor specific performance.

Historically, land was always regarded as unique, giving a purchaser the opportunity of seeking specific performance. As late as 1995, the Ontario Court of Appeal in *Landmark of Thornhill Ltd. v. Jacobson* (1995), 25 O.R. (3d) 628, upheld the rule that a purchaser of land is *prima facie* entitled to a decree of specific performance, and did not have to prove either that the land had some special value or

unique quality, or that damages would be in some sense inadequate. The right of
the purchaser to the remedy of specific performance for land contracts was simply
based on the historical notion that all land is unique, and by definition damages
would be an inadequate remedy.

prof : However, the 1996 decision of the Supreme Court of Canada in *Semelhago v.
Paramadevan,* [1996] 2 S.C.R. 415, 136 D.L.R. (4th) 1, in *obiter dicta,* on a point
without argument by counsel, stated that the general rule that specific performance
is available for purchasers in contracts for the sale of land was no longer to be
accepted, unless the land is "unique". Sopinka J. wrote (pp. 428-30 S.C.R.):

> [21] It is no longer appropriate, therefore, to maintain a distinction in the approach
> to specific performance as between realty and personalty. It cannot be assumed that
> damages for breach of contract for the purchase and sale of real estate will be an in-
> adequate remedy in all cases. The common law recognized that the distinction might
> not be valid when the land had no peculiar or special value. In *Adderley v. Dixon*
> (1824), 1 Sim. & St. 607, 57 E.R. 239, Sir John Leach, V.C., stated (at p. 240):
>
>> Courts of Equity decree the specific performance of contracts, not upon any
>> distinction between realty and personalty, but because damages at law may
>> not, in the particular case, afford a complete remedy. Thus a Court of Equity
>> decrees performance of a contract for land, not because of the real nature of
>> the land, but because damages at law, which must be calculated upon the
>> general money value of land, may not be a complete remedy to the purchaser,
>> to whom the land may have a peculiar and special value.
>
> [22] Courts have tended, however, to simply treat all real estate as being unique and
> to decree specific performance unless there was some other reason for refusing equi-
> table relief. . . . Some courts, however, have begun to question the assumption that
> damages will afford an inadequate remedy for breach of contract for the purchase of
> land. In *Chaulk v. Fairview Construction Ltd.* (1977), 14 Nfld. & P.E.I.R. 13, the
> Newfoundland Court of Appeal (*per* Gushue J.A.), after quoting the above passage
> from *Adderley v. Dixon,* stated, at p. 21:
>
>> The question here is whether damages would have afforded Chaulk an ade-
>> quate remedy, and I have no doubt that they could, and would, have. There
>> was nothing whatever unique or irreplaceable about the houses and lots bar-
>> gained for. They were merely subdivision lots with houses, all of the same
>> general design, built on them, which the respondent was purchasing for in-
>> vestment or re-sale purposes only. He had sold the first two almost immedi-
>> ately at a profit, and intended to do the same with the remainder. It would be
>> quite different if we were dealing with a house or houses which were of a par-
>> ticular architectural design, or were situated in a particularly desirable loca-
>> tion, but this was certainly not the case.
>
> Specific performance should, therefore, not be granted as a matter of course absent
> evidence that the property is unique to the extent that its substitute would not be
> readily available. The guideline proposed by Estey J. in *Asamera Oil Corp. v. Seal
> Oil & General Corp.,* [1979] 1 S.C.R. 633, with respect to contracts involving chat-
> tels is equally applicable to real property. At p. 668, Estey J. stated:
>
>> Before a plaintiff can rely on a claim to specific performance so as to insulate
>> himself from the consequences of failing to procure alternate property in
>> mitigation of his losses, some fair, real and substantial justification for his
>> claim to performance must be found.

. . .

[23] The trial judge was of the view in this case that the property was not unique. She stated that, "It was a building lot under construction which would be interchangeable in all likelihood with any number of others". Notwithstanding this observation, she felt constrained by authority to find that specific performance was an appropriate remedy. While I would be inclined to agree with the trial judge as to the inappropriateness of an order for specific performance, both parties were content to present the case on the basis that the respondent was entitled to specific performance. The case was dealt with on this basis by the Court of Appeal. In the circumstances, this Court should abide by the manner in which the case has been presented by the parties and decided in the courts below. In future cases, under similar circumstances, a trial judge will not be constrained to find that specific performance is an appropriate remedy.

The Supreme Court gave little indication of the factors that are relevant in deciding when land or a house is sufficiently "unique" so as to entitle the purchaser to specific performance, though the Court seemed to indicate that the purchaser of a house in a subdivision would not normally be entitled to specific performance.

In some cases the courts will order specific performance or an equivalent restitutionary remedy in order to ensure that a defendant does not gain as a result of a breach of contractual or other duty. In *Soulos v. Korkontzilas*, [1997] 2 S.C.R. 217, 146 D.L.R. (4th) 214, a client of a real estate agent wanted to purchase a commercial property that had a bank branch as a tenant. Although the agent knew of the client's interest, he failed to communicate an offer from the owner to the client, and instead arranged for his wife to buy the building. The client sued the agent, seeking a conveyance of the property, claiming that the property had special value to him because its tenant was his banker, and "being one's banker's landlord was a source of prestige in the [Toronto] Greek community of which he was a member". The trial court found that there was no financial loss to the client from the failure to purchase the building (indeed the building had declined in value), and dismissed the action. While there was no "unjust enrichment", the Supreme Court of Canada concluded that this was a proper case for the imposition of a constructive trust, so that the agent's wife would have to convey the building to the client. McLachlin J. wrote (pp. 242-43 S.C.R.):

> [W]hile Mr. Korkontzilas [the real estate agent] was not monetarily enriched by his wrongful acquisition of the property, ample reasons exist for equity to impose a constructive trust. Mr. Soulos [the client] argues that a constructive trust is required to remedy the deprivation he suffered because of his continuing desire, albeit for non-monetary reasons, to own the particular property in question. No less is required, he asserts, to return the parties to the position they would have been in had the breach not occurred. That alone, in my opinion, would be sufficient to persuade a court of equity that the proper remedy for Mr. Korkontzilas' wrongful acquisition of the property is an order that he is bound as a constructive trustee to convey the property to Mr. Soulos.

> But there is more . . . a constructive trust is required in cases such as this to ensure that agents and others in positions of trust remain faithful to their duty of loyalty. . . . If real estate agents are permitted to retain properties which they acquire for themselves in breach of a duty of loyalty to their clients provided they pay market value, the trust and confidence which underpin the institution of real estate brokerage will be undermined. The message will be clear: real estate agents may breach their duties to their clients and the courts will do nothing about it, unless the client can show that the real estate agent made a profit. This will not do. Courts of equity have always been concerned to keep the person who acts on behalf of others to his ethical mark; this Court should continue in the same path.

As the law was understood until *Semelhago v. Paramadevan* was decided by the Supreme Court in 1996, a lawyer could safely advise a client that if the vendor of land did not complete the deal, the purchaser would almost certainly be entitled to an order for specific performance. If the land increased in value, the purchaser who sought specific performance stood to gain if the decree was granted. If the value of the land did not increase, or if, having perhaps increased, it then fell, the purchaser would almost always elect damages at trial or before. In this situation, it was comparatively easy to advise clients. After *Semelhago v. Paramadevan*, it has become more difficult for solicitors to advise their clients about real estate contracts. In *John E. Dodge Holdings Ltd. v. 805062 Ontario Ltd.*, [2003] O.J. No. 350, 63 O.R. (3d) 304 (C.A.), Weiler J.A. wrote (at paras. 39-40) [emphasis added]:

> ... in order to establish that a property is unique the person seeking the remedy of specific performance must show that the property in question has a quality that cannot be *readily duplicated* elsewhere. This quality should relate to the proposed use of the property and be a quality that makes it particularly suitable for the purpose for which it was intended. ...
>
> The time when a determination is to be made as to whether a property is unique is the date when an actionable act takes place and the wronged party must decide whether to keep the agreement alive by seeking specific performance or accept the breach and sue for damages. ... It may also be that in certain cases the date chosen for determining the issue of whether specific performance is appropriate is a later date but the date will not, in any event, occur before the breach has taken place.

Must the purchaser now make a "paper trail" to establish that the land is unique to him or her? Is uniqueness an objective or subjective quality?

Relational Contracts and Equitable Remedies

In cases involving the sale of land and chattels, the courts tend to focus on the issue of "uniqueness" to determine whether damages are "inadequate", and hence an equitable remedy is appropriate. This type of analysis focuses on discrete contracts, and creates special problems when applied to contracts which create a relation for future co-operation, *i.e.*, relational contracts.

The issue of specific performance should be understood not as a simply as a question of whether or not damages are "adequate", but as an aspect of the allocation of the risks inherent in an award of damages or of the chance of gain from performance or breach (as in the issue of "efficient breach"). The extent of the risks of loss or chances of gain involved in a contractual situation will largely depend on the extent to which the contract is at the relational end as opposed to the transactional end of the spectrum. There are major difference between the two kinds of contracts. In a discrete transaction, the benefits of the arrangement are fully planned so that it is possible to regard an award of damages as representing what the promisee would have had if the contract had been fully performed. A relational contract is a framework for future co-operation in which the benefits are subject to a large number of variables. The concept of the relational contract is discussed in David Campbell, Hugh Collins & John Wightman, eds., *Implicit Dimensions of Contract: Discrete, Relational and Network Contracts* (Oxford: Hart, 2003); for a review which argues that it is also important to consider the race, class, gender and ethnic context of a contract, see Alberto Valle, "Review Essay: The Complex Context of Contract Law" (2004), 42 *Osgoode Hall L.J.* 515.

The problems of providing a satisfactory monetary remedy for breach of a relational contract are complex, suggesting that equitable remedies may be appropriate for some of these cases. The remedy of specific performance might seem to be better adapted to relational contracts, though as we shall see there are some relationships where concerns about judicial supervision of performance make this remedy inappropriate.

The law is developing new approaches that recognize the need for different approaches to equitable remedies for relational contracts. Some of these developments will be examined later in these materials, especially in Chapters 3 and 6. These developments include imposing an obligation of good faith in many contracts that establish relations of trust using two important equitable remedies: the injunction — to prevent a former employee from competing unfairly with her former employer — and the constructive trust. The constructive trust provides an alternative method for measuring compensation that focuses on the gains made from breach of the obligations of the relation rather than on damages caused by the breach.

A second development is the use of the order of reinstatement for wrongfully dismissed employees. As noted earlier, most employees who lose their job would generally prefer restoration of the employment relationship to a claim for damages. However, while reinstatement is not available in a wrongful dismissal suit in a court of law, when a unionized employee is wrongfully dismissed and the relation between the employer and the employee is governed by a collective agreement, legislation allows labour arbitrators to order reinstatement; further, legislation in Quebec and Nova Scotia and for employees governed by the federal *Canada Labour Code* also allows for reinstatement of non-unionized employees in some situations. This book does not deal with the nature of either a collective agreement or arbitration under it, but it is important to note that arbitrators are generally willing to order the resumption of the employment relationship if they find that the employer had no right to dismiss.

There are wide ramifications to making a distinction between relational and discrete contracts. Many of the attitudes about law in our society are premised on the notion that law is a forum (perhaps the word "arena" might be better) for a confrontation between parties with "rights-based" claims. This, however, is a restricted idea of the nature and scope of the relationship that the law governs and supports. There are other ways of looking at law. If one focuses less on the idea of rights and more on the ideas of mutual duties and good faith, one may appreciate that ideas like "efficient breach" and judgments for damages sometimes do a great disservice to what is actually present in many contractual relationships. Similarly, if one focuses less on the limited bounds of the relation created by a contract and more on the expectations that the relation has encouraged, one may have greater appreciation of the value of a range of equitable remedies.

As we shall see repeatedly in this book, the rules that govern contract law are generally based on the paradigm of the discrete transaction. In reality, many important contractual relationships are relational in nature. Gradually courts have been prepared to "stretch" the law to fairly govern the contractual context, though frequently they do so without fully recognizing what they are doing.

The following excerpt by Rick Brown, a labour law specialist, illustrates that there are alternative ways of looking at contract problems than those of the traditional common law, ways that put more emphasis on relations and less on transactions. He compares approaches in situations governed by collective agreements, where legislation gives arbitrators special powers, to the evolving commercial jurisprudence. He also addresses the problem of supervision, which limits the use of specific performance by the courts and even the use of reinstatement by arbitrators.

BROWN, "CONTRACT REMEDIES IN A PLANNED ECONOMY: LABOUR ARBITRATION LEADS THE WAY"

Reiter and Swan (eds.), *Studies in Contract Law* (Toronto: Butterworths, 1980) pp. 102-107

(Most footnotes have been omitted.)

[1]   *Specific Performance and Damages* . . . [W]hen a transactional performance is not carried out, a replacement exchange can usually be obtained and associated expenses can be recovered. Should no substitute be available, damages for lost profits are generally awarded, although a loss of goodwill is not compensable. Both the cost of a replacement and the quantum of lost profits can be assessed with substantial certainty because performance is fully described by the agreement. Damages provide substantial, although not complete, compensation for the losses suffered when a transaction breaks down.

[2]   Monetary compensation offers far less adequate protection in relational settings than in transactional contexts. The reason is simple. Relational agreements do not detail contractual performance fully so that the injury suffered when the contract is breached is indeterminate. Consider an action against a supplier who wrongfully terminates a contract to supply all of a purchaser's requirements. Could a damage remedy be fashioned which would adequately safeguard the buyer's interests? The answer depends upon whether another supplier who will furnish the buyer's needs can be found. If another requirements contract can be secured, the purchaser would be adequately protected by an award of the additional cost of the second arrangement.

[3]   However, another contract of this type will often not be readily available. The buyer might then resort to the market to buy goods as needs arise. How are damages to be assessed in this situation? If suit is brought before the contract's term has run, the exact dimensions of contractual performance will be unknown. The buyer's needs can be determined in advance only by predicting future conditions, a task so difficult that a flexible contract was devised to avoid resolving the uncertainty. This difficulty can be overcome by postponing the action until the end of the term of the contract. However, a purchaser who negotiates a requirements contract does so to ensure the delivery of precisely the quantity needed at exactly the right time. A substitute arrangement for the delivery of fixed quantities at predetermined times will usually produce shortfalls in supply or lead to an accumulation of inventory, reducing revenues or increasing costs. The extent of these injuries will be difficult to determine, especially in the case of an undersupply. When an arrangement to supply a fixed quantity of goods at a particular time is breached, the terms of the contract serve to quantify the profit that would have been earned upon resale. No such guidance exists for a contract which describes the quantity of goods as the buyer's requirements and the date of delivery as the time at which the goods are needed. A failure to perform under this contract interrupts the buyer's business and disrupts the process that would have determined resale profits.

[4]   Similar problems arise upon the breach of contract to deliver a buyer's requirements of a commodity for which there is no market. The buyer may be unable to obtain true replacement goods if the product is highly differentiated as products distributed through franchises and other similar arrangements often are. The distinctive character of the product is a central part of the exchange between the supplier and distributor. A retailer whose source of supply is terminated may be able to obtain a functionally similar good but the benefits of consumer loyalty to the first product will be lost. The success which would have been enjoyed in marketing that product cannot be determined readily.

[5]   The injury suffered when a requirements contract is wrongfully terminated is hard to measure because the aggrieved party retains the discretion to determine contractual performance. A similar problem arises when obligations are defined at the discretion of the party in breach. The discharge of an employee [governed by a collective agreement] for misconduct in violation of a contractual provision which requires just cause raises both kinds of problems. Either party may terminate their relationship. Management may not fire without cause but may lay off, in accord with seniority, to reduce the work force. The employee is free to quit. Alternative employment is not usually available immediately and the injury caused by a wrongful discharge is difficult to assess. Should a prediction be made as to whether, at some future time, the employee might have been properly terminated or might have quit? Labour market imperfections may leave the worker unemployed for a substantial period of time. Should an attempt be made to predict when another job will be found? If the employee finds work at a lower rate of remuneration, ought a claim for the differential be allowed? The improper termination of employment under a collective agreement raises other problems. A discharged worker loses seniority rights as well as wages. These invaluable rights entitle the employee to vacations and other benefits, to preference when promotions are made and to protection against layoffs. Finally, self-respect and life-style are closely related to employment. The parties to commercial arrangements are often not individuals, and even when they are, their personal life is usually only remotely linked to the exchange. On the other hand, workers, like consumers, have interests in their dealings which are not strictly economic. The courts have [also] recently recognized that these interests are deserving of protection and have awarded damages for injury to them. Obviously, the loss cannot be measured readily and no sound basis has been offered for the amounts awarded.

[6]   The injury suffered when an employer violates the [collective] agreement in a manner that reduces the level of employment is also problematic. It will be recalled that collective agreements usually do not define the level of employment. Instead, they address employer initiatives which will affect manpower needs, permitting some, prohibiting others and allowing still others only after prescribed procedures are followed. Consider a situation in which subcontracts are forbidden. When the employer violates the agreement by sending work out to another firm, the union may launch a grievance on behalf of the workers who are displaced from their jobs. If the contract had not been contravened the employer might have not done the work so that the number of jobs would have been no greater than it was after the breach. How is the level of employment that would have resulted from compliance with the agreement to be known?

[7]   Collective agreements often require that the union be consulted before work is subcontracted, allowing the employer to act unilaterally if an accord is not

reached with the union. The injury caused when the obligation to consult is con-travened is obviously very speculative, since management may properly reject the position taken by the union during consultations.

[8] Damages for the losses incurred when the performance due under a rela-tional contract is not rendered are very difficult to assess and will often be highly inexact compensation. Most likely adjudicators will err on the side of insufficient recovery. The groundwork for an argument in favour of specific relief has been laid. In cases in which compliance with the contract is feasible and can be under-taken in a timely manner, relief in specie will protect the promisee's interests while avoiding all of the tangles of uncertainty that arise in measuring the value of a lost performance.

[9] A review of [court] cases suggests that specific performance is becoming more readily available when relational contracts are breached. A petroleum sup-plier has been ordered to continue to deliver a customer's requirements.[6] Pepsi-Cola and American Motors have been required to continue to deal with their distribution agents.[7] In the case of output contracts, a poultry processor has been instructed to carry out its obligations. Although relief was of an interim nature in all cases but one, the signs of change are clear. . . .

[10] Labour arbitrators frequently direct management to fulfil contractual obliga-tions. The union's only obligation is usually not to strike. In all jurisdictions ex-cept Saskatchewan this obligation is imposed by statute. The courts will order striking employees back to work . . . Recently labour relations boards have been given this power . . . Arbitrators have long ordered that employees discharged without just cause be reinstated. A review of over 600 discharge awards did not disclose a single instance where damages were awarded instead of specific per-formance. However, several arbitration awards in British Columbia have departed from this pattern and, on the employers' motion, denied reinstatement of an em-ployee discharged without just cause.

[11] Labour arbitrators have also ordered employers to adhere to the terms of collective agreements which regulate subcontracting, technological change, layoffs and recalls. Management has been ordered to comply with an obligation to consult the union before implementing changes. The courts refuse to enforce a promise to negotiate because the freedom to disagree is as basic to a transactional economy as is the freedom to agree. Unless an option or right of refusal has been purchased, the interest in being consulted is treated as not deserving of protection and indi-viduals are free to deal with whom they wish on the terms which are most profit-able. Once the parties have entered into a long-term arrangement, the obligation to discuss takes on a different hue. It is one of the benefits for which the others' par-ticipation in the larger enterprise is traded. Although one party may do as it pleases if consultation fails to produce a mutually acceptable compromise, discussions ensure that the interests of other participants are considered.

[12] Some arbitrators have even gone so far as to order specific performance in anticipation of future violations of the agreement. Orders of this nature are only

6   In *Sky Petroleum Ltd. v. VIP Petroleum Ltd.*, [1974] 1 W.L.R. 576, [1974] 1 All E.R. 954, *infra*.
7   *North West Beverages Ltd. v. Pepsi-Cola (Canada)* (1971), 20 D.L.R. (3d) 341 (Man.); *Baxter Motors Ltd. v. American Motors (Canada) Ltd.* (1973), 40 D.L.R. (3d) 450 (B.C.).

granted where the employer has flagrantly violated the agreement or has otherwise raised an apprehension of further contraventions.

[13] The uncertainty of losses is not the only reason for granting specific relief more readily in relational situations than in transactional settings. When a simple exchange breaks down the effort required to resurrect it may be greater than the relative benefit of specific performance over damages. Monetary compensation can be more easily administered than relief in specie since the former does not require further supervision to ensure compliance. Relations have a much longer life and will inevitably suffer minor breakdowns. Their future promises much benefit and the energy required to ensure their completion is well spent. It might be thought that it would be impossible to officially supervise specific performance of complex relational obligations. The courts refuse to grant specific enforcement of building and employment contracts for this reason. The problem is not insurmountable. The mere existence of a formal decree in many cases may, by clarifying obligations, ensure compliance with them. Intransigence by the party in breach or further disputes over the details of performance could be dealt with by a receiver appointed to supervise the exchange. In this way it will generally be possible to ensure that the party in breach obeys an order for specific performance. Compliance with an order to rehire a worker, to terminate a subcontract or to deliver a purchaser's needs is easily determined. Some situations may be more problematical. It would, for example, be almost impossible to supervise an employee's job performance because the precise obligations of employment are most difficult to define and, even if they could be determined, constant vigilance would be required to ensure that they were met.

[14] Coercion is another ground upon which the courts have refused specific relief of employment contracts. This objection loses force in an age when many contracting parties are not individuals, but corporate and commercial entities. It is difficult to identify a person who is unjustifiably coerced when a large corporation is ordered to reinstate an employee. The liberty of supervisors and managers may be infringed but their interest in the operation of the enterprise is quite different than that of a sole proprietor and may be no greater than the worker's interest.

In some cases where the parties have a relational contract, the courts have recognized the need to protect the *relation* by the granting of an injunction that restrains a breach of contract.

In *Sky Petroleum Ltd. v. VIP Petroleum Ltd.*, [1974] 1 All E.R. 954 (Ch. D.), the plaintiff was an independent gas retailer that had a 10-year "requirements contract" under which it agreed to purchase all its supplies of gasoline from the defendant at stipulated prices. After three years of performance, the Arab oil embargo of 1973 resulted in a dramatic increase in the price of gasoline, and supplies became scarce. The contract price was far less than that which the seller could get on the open market. A dispute arose between the parties, with the seller alleging that the buyer had breached some terms of the contract, though there was a suspicion that the seller was looking for an excuse to end its contractual obligations on a contract that had become unprofitable for it. On 16 November 1973, the seller claimed that the plaintiff was in breach and refused to sell any more gasoline to the buyer. On 20 November 1973, the buyer brought a motion for an interim injunction to prevent the seller from refusing to sell gas pursuant to the contract.

The defendant argued that the subject matter of the contract — gasoline — was not a "unique" good. But Goulding J. rejected this argument and granted the interim injunction. He accepted evidence that the plaintiff had no likely prospect of finding any alternative source of supply at a commercially viable price. If the plaintiff was forced to try to cover the contract by buying gas in the marketplace, there was a serious danger that unless the court interfered the plaintiff would be forced out of business before a trial. The injunction was limited in time until the expected date of the trial, and required the defendant only to supply as much gas as it had formerly supplied.

prot: In *Sky Petroleum* the court only made an order for an *interim* injunction, *i.e.,* an injunction pending trial or the settlement of the action. There is no report of a trial in this case and this suggests that the parties settled the dispute on some basis that likely would have included a renegotiation of the supply contract. As a condition of getting an interim injunction, the plaintiff had to give an undertaking to pay damages to the defendant should the court later hold that the plaintiff was in breach of its contractual obligations not entitled to an injunction and the grant of the interim injunction had caused the defendant loss. It is very unlikely that a court would grant a permanent injunction at a trial in a case involving a long-term supply contract, like *Sky Petroleum*. Concerns about supervision and forcing parties into a continuing relationship would preclude this. However, an interim injunction will usually allow the wronged party enough time to adjust to the new situation and make new arrangements, seeking financial compensation for future losses arising from the breach of the contract.   *shares sig. unique*

In *Gilbert v. Barron*, [1958] O.W.N. 98 (H.C.J.), an agreement among shareholders establishing an arrangement for the control of the corporation was specifically enforced when one shareholder obtained control in breach of the agreement. Many cases since then have enforced agreements dealing with shares by decrees of specific performance when these shares are not readily obtainable in the market, for example shares that are either not traded or very thinly traded.

The need for equitable relief in cases like *Sky Petroleum* and *Gilbert v. Barron* can be easily demonstrated. In each case, the arrangement in issue was not a one-shot deal, a fully planned exchange, but a relation that was to be a framework for future co-operation. On breach by one side, the damages would be very hard to calculate. Further, the rules of remoteness might preclude full recovery for all losses; in particular, in a case like *Sky Petroleum* the courts' approaches to remoteness would typically preclude recovery for costs associated with going out of business due to "impecuniosity". In each case, it would be appropriate to remove from the promisee the risk of undercompensation and retain, if only for a time, the framework established by the parties, leaving that to provide whatever benefits might accrue to the promisee, and to establish an orderly and fair way for the arrangement to be terminated.

The next case, a famous one, raises the issue of equitable remedies in a wide context.

WARNER BROS. PICTURES INC. v. NELSON

[1937] 1 K.B. 209 (Ch. D.)

BRANSON J.: — **[1]** The facts of this case are few and simple. The plaintiffs are a firm of film producers in the United States of America. In 1931 the defendant, then not well known as a film actress, entered into a contract with the plaintiffs. Before the expiration of that contract the present contract was entered into between the parties. Under it the defendant received a considerably enhanced salary, the other conditions being substantially the same. This contract was for fifty-two weeks and contains options to the plaintiffs to extend it for further periods of fifty-two weeks at ever-increasing amounts of salary to the defendant. No question of construction arises upon the contract, and it is not necessary to refer to it in any great detail; but in view of some of the contentions raised it is desirable to call attention quite generally to some of the provisions contained in it. It is a stringent contract, under which the defendant agrees "to render her exclusive services as a motion picture and/or legitimate stage actress" to the plaintiffs, and agrees to perform solely and exclusively for them. She also agrees, by way of negative stipulation, that "she will not, during such time" — that is to say, during the term of the contract — "render any services for or in any other phonographic, stage or motion picture production or productions or business of any other person . . . or engage in any other occupation without the written consent of the producer being first had and obtained."

[2]   With regard to the term of the contract there is a further clause, clause 23, under which, if the defendant fails, refuses or neglects to perform her services under the contract, the plaintiffs "have the right to extend the term of this agreement and all of its provisions for a period equivalent to the period during which such failure, refusal or neglect shall be continued."

[3]   In June of this year the defendant, for no discoverable reasons except that she wanted more money, declined to be further bound by the agreement, left the United States and, in September, entered into an agreement in this country with a third person. This was a breach of contract on her part, and the plaintiffs on September 9 commenced this action claiming a declaration that the contract was valid and binding, an injunction to restrain the defendant from acting in breach of it, and damages. The defence alleged that the plaintiffs had committed breaches of the contract which entitled the defendant to treat it as at an end; but at the trial this contention was abandoned and the defendant admitted that the plaintiffs had not broken the contract and that she had; but it was contended on her behalf that no injunction could as a matter of law be granted in the circumstances of the case. . . .

[4]   I turn then to the consideration of the law applicable to this case on the basis that the contract is a valid and enforceable one. It is conceded that our Courts will not enforce a positive covenant of personal service; and specific performance of the positive covenants by the defendant to serve the plaintiffs is not asked in the present case. The practice of the Court of Chancery in relation to the enforcement of negative covenants is stated on the highest authority by Lord Cairns in the House of Lords in *Doherty v. Allman* (1877), 3 App. Cas. 709, 719. His Lordship says:

> My Lords, if there had been a negative covenant, I apprehend, according to well-settled practice, a Court of Equity would have had no discretion to exercise. If parties, for valuable consideration, with their eyes open, contract that a particular thing shall not be done, all that a Court of Equity has to do is to say, by way of injunction, that which the parties have already said by way of covenant, that the thing shall not be done; and in such case the injunction does nothing more than give the sanction of the process of the Court to that which already is the contract between the parties. It is not then a question of the balance of convenience or inconvenience or of the amount of damage or of injury — it is the specific performance, by the Court, of that

negative bargain which the parties have made, with their eyes open, between themselves.

[5]   That was not a case of a contract of personal service; but the same principle had already been applied to such a contract by Lord St. Leonards in *Lumley v. Wagner* (1852), 42 E.R. 687. . . .

[6]   The defendant, having broken her positive undertakings in the contract without any cause or excuse which she was prepared to support in the witness-box, contends that she cannot be enjoined from breaking the negative covenants also. The mere fact that a covenant which the court would not enforce, if expressed in positive form, is expressed in the negative instead, will not induce the court to enforce it. . . .

[7]   The conclusion to be drawn from the authorities is that, where a contract of personal service contains negative covenants the enforcement of which will not amount either to a decree of specific performance of the positive covenants of the contract or to the giving of a decree under which the defendant must either remain idle or perform those positive covenants, the Court will enforce those negative covenants; but this is subject to a further consideration. An injunction is a discretionary remedy, and the Court in granting it may limit it to what the Court considers reasonable in all the circumstances of the case . . .

[8]   The case before me is, therefore, one in which it would be proper to grant an injunction unless to do so would in the circumstances be tantamount to ordering the defendant to perform her contract or remain idle or unless damages would be the more appropriate remedy.

[9]   With regard to the first of these considerations, it would, of course, be impossible to grant an injunction covering all the negative covenants in the contract. That would, indeed, force the defendant to perform her contract or remain idle; but this objection is removed by the restricted form in which the injunction is sought. It is confined to forbidding the defendant, without the consent of the plaintiffs, to render any services for or in any motion picture or stage production for any one other than the plaintiffs.

[10]   It was also urged that the difference between what the defendant can earn as a film artiste and what she might expect to earn by any other form of activity is so great that she will in effect be driven to perform her contract. That is not the criterion adopted in any of the decided cases. The defendant is stated to be a person of intelligence, capacity and means, and no evidence was adduced to show that, if enjoined from doing the specified acts otherwise than for the plaintiffs, she will not be able to employ herself both usefully and remuneratively in other spheres of activity, though not as remuneratively as in her special line. She will not be driven, although she may be tempted, to perform the contract, and the fact that she may be so tempted is no objection to the grant of an injunction. . . .

[11]   With regard to the question whether damages is not the more appropriate remedy, I have the uncontradicted evidence of the plaintiffs as to the difficulty of estimating the damages which they may suffer from the breach by the defendant of her contract. I think it is not inappropriate to refer to the fact that, in the contract between the parties, in clause 22, there is a formal admission by the defendant that her services, "being of a special, unique, extraordinary and intellectual character" gives them a particular value "the loss of which cannot be reasonably or adequately compensated in damages" and that a breach may "cost the producer great

and irreparable injury and damage," and the artiste expressly agrees that the producer shall be entitled to the remedy of injunction. Of course, parties cannot contract themselves out of the law; but it assists, at all events, on the question of evidence as to the applicability of an injunction in the present case, to find the parties formally recognizing that in cases of this kind injunction is a more appropriate remedy than damages.

[12] Furthermore, in the case of *Grimston v. Cunningham*, [1894] 1 Q.B. 125, which was also a case in which a theatrical manager was attempting to enforce against an actor a negative stipulation against going elsewhere, Wills J. granted an injunction, and used the following language:

> This is an agreement of a kind which is pre-eminently subject to the interference of the Court by injunction, for in cases of this nature it very often happens that the injury suffered in consequence of the breach of the agreement would be out of all proportion to any pecuniary damages which could be proved or assessed by a jury. This circumstance affords a strong reason in favour of exercising the discretion of the Court by granting an injunction.

[13] I think that applies to the present case also, and that an injunction should be granted in regard to the specified services.

[14] Then comes the question as to the period for which the injunction should operate. The period of the contract, now that the plaintiffs have undertaken not as from October 16, 1936, to exercise the rights of suspension conferred upon them by clause 23 thereof, will, if they exercise their options to prolong it, extend to about May, 1942 . . . the Court should make the period such as to give reasonable protection and no more to the plaintiffs against the ill effects to them of the defendant's breach of contract. The evidence as to that was perhaps necessarily somewhat vague. The main difficulty that the plaintiffs apprehend is that the defendant might appear in other films whilst the films already made by them and not yet shown are in the market for sale or hire and thus depreciate their value. I think that if the injunction is in force during the continuance of the contract or for three years from now, whichever period is the shorter, that will substantially meet the case.

[15] The other matter is as to the area within which the injunction is to operate. The contract is not an English contract and the parties are not British subjects. In my opinion all that properly concerns this Court is to prevent the defendant from committing the prohibited acts within the jurisdiction of this Court, and the injunction will be limited accordingly.

NOTES AND QUESTIONS

1. The defendant in *Warner Bros. v. Nelson* was better known as Bette Davis. At the date of the case, she had already won one Oscar for her performance in *Dangerous* (1935). The basis for the dispute was her feeling that Warner Brothers Studios refused to give her the kind of roles that she wanted to play. The very strong position of the major film studios in their relations with their stars is well documented in a large number of biographies.

    (a) What effect would the decision have on the contracts that Warner Brothers had with all their stars?

    (b) What are the features of this case that support the argument that common law damages would be inadequate?

    (c) What are the issues that underlie the decision to grant an injunction against a person like Bette Davis? How relevant would it be if Bette Davis were correct in her perception that the studio, for its own reasons, wanted to frustrate her career? What is the social value in allowing an employee to achieve the fullest possible personal and professional development that she can?

2. The contract between Bette Davis and Warner Brothers was a relational one. It has a long term and the benefits that each side will get cannot be planned for at the beginning. If the contract is of this type, it is interesting to consider in more detail what each party expected from the deal at the time it was made. A person like Bette Davis would often sign the studio's standard contract at a relatively young age. For a struggling young actress the offer of a contract from a major studio must have seemed a fantastic piece of good fortune. But now suppose that the studio representative had said: "Of course you realize that by signing this contract, we have the right to keep you 'on ice'. You can only work in the movie business or on stage if we allow you to do so, and we could well have reasons to prevent you from acting for many years to come, or at least, for long enough to eliminate any possibility of your resurrecting your career."

(a) Do you think that even a stage-struck young actress would agree to such a contract?

(b) Should an employer be able to use such a contract?

(c) Should a court grant an injunction to enforce in any way a contract of this type?

(d) Would the problems of the contract be avoided or lessened if the court could regard the employer as having a duty to behave in good faith towards its employees and to respond reasonably to suggestions and requests from employees who are seeking to advance their careers?

As we shall see in Chapter 6, the courts are now more willing than they were in 1937 to interfere in contractual disputes to protect performers who have signed long-term contracts that are disadvantageous to them. See, for example, *Schroeder Music Publishing v. Macaulay, infra*, Chapter 6. The courts are more willing to declare that such a long-term one-sided contract is a "restraint on trade" and unenforceable. However, if an agreement (now generally one of shorter duration) is regarded as valid, the approach of *Warner Bros. v. Nelson* is likely to be followed in regard to issues of equitable relief.

After this decision, Bette Davis returned to work for Warner Brothers, and they gave her better roles, which resulted in her winning another Oscar for *Jezebel* in 1938. While Warner Brothers won the case, and in legal terms had full control of the movies in which Bette Davis would appear, can you think of why they might want to accede to some of her demands when she came back?

3. It may be that the courts have too much concern for the confidence and trust that an employer is supposed to lack in a dismissed employee, especially if the employer is a large enterprise. Given the extraordinary importance that a job has for most of us, the remedies available in arbitration for unionized employees *viz.*, that a wrongfully dismissed employee may be entitled to be reinstated, may be socially preferable. This remedy is being increasingly adopted in legal systems around the world, and legislation in Quebec and Nova Scotia allows a judge to order reinstatement for a non-unionized employee; this remedy is also available for employees governed by the federal *Labour Relations Code*.

Restitutionary Remedies

The compensation principle focuses on the loss that the breach of contract has caused to the plaintiff. As has been shown, the remedy for breach may be an award based on the plaintiff's expectation interest or, when that measure is unavailable, on the plaintiff's reliance interest. The plaintiff's restitution interest, *i.e.*, its right perhaps to recover what it paid the defendant, can be regarded as a special case of the reliance interest. Thus, in *Anglia Television v. Reed* there was, for example, no suggestion that Reed ought to pay over what he gained from the (presumably) more lucrative work that he chose to do instead of the English production. While the plaintiff's restitution interest, *i.e.*, its right perhaps to recover what it paid the defendant, can be regarded as a special case of the reliance interest, it has not tra-ditionally been regarded as a contractual remedy.

There is, however, a growing tendency for judges to accept that there are some contractual situations in which it is appropriate not just to focus on the loss of the bargain, but rather to consider the gain of the party in breach. In these cases, the courts may award a remedy that is often referred to as a "restitutionary remedy", though the term is a little confusing since it is not always used in the same way as Fuller and Perdue use the concept of "restitution".

The term "restitutionary remedy" covers a range of situations, some of which involve a defendant giving to the plaintiff what he gained by breaching the con-tract; this is a situation that Fuller and Perdue would also characterize as "restitu-tion", and is sometimes referred to as "disgorgement". In other cases, the courts will give what they call a "restitutionary remedy" which has the effect of requiring compensation for losses even though there is no corresponding gain.

Some argue that the granting of a restitutionary remedy, at least in some cases, lacks intellectual coherence, and runs contrary to fundamental contract principles. However, it is clear that there are contracts cases in which the courts will move away from the award of a purely expectation-based measure of damages, and give what are called "restitutionary awards". Many of these cases involve a breach of fiduciary duty, or some type of exploitative conduct. They may be cases in which the courts are, at least in part, trying to deter reprehensible conduct.

The following case explores some of these issues, admittedly in a case with very special facts.

ATTORNEY-GENERAL v. BLAKE

[2001] 1 A.C. 268, [2000] 4 All E.R. 385
(H.L., Lords Nicholls, Goff, Browne-Wilkinson, Steyn and Hobhouse)

[During the 1950s, Blake, an Englishman, was a "double agent" providing the Soviet Union with important information while in the employ of British intelli-gence. This was at the height of the Cold War. Blake was apparently motivated by a belief in the benefits of communism for the human race, though as a result of his treachery many English agents were killed or imprisoned. Blake's work as a "mole" was discovered by the English and in 1961 he was sentenced to 42 years in prison for violating the *Official Secrets Act.* In 1966 he made a daring escape and ended up in Moscow. After the collapse of the Soviet Union, he de-cided to publish his memoirs. Blake entered into a contract with an English pub-lisher, Jonathan Cape Ltd., under which he was paid an advance on royalties of £60,000 at the time of delivery of the manuscript, with a further £90,000 due after publication.

The book was published in England in 1990 without any prior notice to the British government, which then commenced an action to prevent the payment of the £90,000 still owing under the contract with Jonathan Cape Ltd. The govern-ment obtained an injunction preventing immediate payment but had to convince the courts of the basis for its cause of action. The government primarily relied on breach of fiduciary duty and various public law-based claims, and succeeded at trial before the Vice Chancellor. Blake's appeal was dismissed. The Court of Appeal suggested that a contract-based claim might also succeed. Blake appealed to the House of Lords, which rejected all of the public law and fiduciary-based arguments, but accepted the contract-based claim of the government.]

LORD NICHOLLS OF BIRKENHEAD: —

The private law claim

[1]   In the course of his judgment [in the English Court of Appeal], Lord Woolf made some interesting observations, at [1998] Ch. 439, 455G to 459D, on a matter which had not been the subject of argument either in the Court of Appeal or before the Vice-Chancellor. The point arose out of the amendments made to the statement of claim in the course of the proceedings in the Court of Appeal. On 16 August 1944 Blake signed an *Official Secrets Act* declaration. This declaration included an undertaking:

> . . . I undertake not to divulge any official information gained by me as a result of my employment, either in the press or in book form. I also understand that these provisions apply not only during the period of service but also after employment has ceased.

This undertaking was contractually binding. Had Blake not signed it he would not have been employed. By submitting his manuscript for publication without first obtaining clearance Blake committed a breach of this undertaking. The Court of Appeal suggested that the Crown might have a private law claim to "restitutionary damages for breach of contract" and invited submissions on this issue. The Attorney General decided that the Crown did not wish to advance argument on this point in the Court of Appeal. The Attorney General, however, wished to keep the point open for a higher court. The Court of Appeal expressed the view, necessarily tentative in the circumstances, that the law of contract would be seriously defective if the court were unable to award restitutionary damages for breach of contract. The law is now sufficiently mature to recognise a restitutionary claim for profits made from a breach of contract in appropriate situations. These include cases of "skimped" performance, and cases where the defendant obtained his profit by doing "the very thing" he contracted not to do. The present case fell into the latter category: Blake earned his profit by doing the very thing he had promised not to do.

[2]   This matter was pursued in your Lordships' House. Prompted by an invitation from your Lordships, the Attorney General advanced an argument that restitutionary principles ought to operate to enable the Crown to recover from Blake his profits arising from his breach of contract. It will be convenient to consider this private law claim first.

[3]   This is a subject on which there is a surprising dearth of judicial decision. By way of contrast, over the last 20 years there has been no lack of academic writing. This includes valuable comment on the Court of Appeal dicta in the present case: by Janet O'Sullivan, "Reflections on the Role of Restitutionary Damages to protect contractual expectations" (to be published), and Catherine Mitchell, "Remedial Inadequacy in Contract and the Role of Restitutionary Damages" (1999) 15 *J.C.L.* 133. Most writers have favoured the view that in some circumstances the innocent party to a breach of contract should be able to compel the defendant to disgorge the profits be obtained from his breach of contract. However, there is a noticeable absence of any consensus on what are the circumstances in which this remedy should be available. Professor Burrows has described this as a devilishly difficult topic: see "No Restitutionary Damages for Breach of Contract" [1993] *L.M.C.L.Q.R.* 453. The broad proposition that a wrongdoer should not be allowed to profit from his wrong has an obvious attraction. The corollary is that the person wronged may recover the amount of this profit when he has suffered no financially measurable loss. As Glidewell L.J. observed in *Halifax Building Society v. Thomas*, [1996] Ch. 217, 229, the corollary is not so obviously persuasive. In these choppy waters the common law and equity steered different courses. The effects of this are still being felt.

Interference with rights of property

[4] So I turn to established, basic principles. I shall first set the scene by noting how the court approaches the question of financial recompense for interference with rights of property. As with breaches of contract, so with tort, the general principle regarding assessment of damages is that they are compensatory for loss or injury. The general rule is that, in the oft quoted words of Lord Blackburn, the measure of damages is to be, as far as possible, that amount of money which will put the injured party in the same position he would have been in had he not sustained the wrong: *Livingstone v. Rawyards Coal Co.* (1880), 5 App. Cas. 25, 39. Damages are measured by the plaintiff's loss, not the defendant's gain. But the common law, pragmatic as ever, has long recognised that there are many commonplace situations where a strict application of this principle would not do justice between the parties. Then compensation for the wrong done to the plaintiff is measured by a different yardstick. A trespasser who enters another's land may cause the landowner no financial loss. In such a case damages are measured by the benefit received by the trespasser, namely, by his use of the land. The same principle is applied where the wrong consists of use of another's land for depositing waste, or by using a path across the land or using passages in an underground mine. In this type of case the damages recoverable will be, in short, the price a reasonable person would pay for the right of user: see *Whitwam v. Westminster Brymbo Coal and Coke Co.*, [1896] 2 Ch. 538, and the "wayleave" cases such as *Martin v. Porter* (1839), 5 M. & W. 351, and *Jegon v. Vivian* (1871), L.R. 6 Ch. 742. A more recent example was the non- removal of a floating dock, in *Penarth Dock Engineering Co. Ltd. v. Pounds*, [1963] 1 Lloyd's Rep 359.

[5] The same principle is applied to the wrongful detention of goods. . . . The Earl of Halsbury L.C. famously asked in *The Mediana*, [1900] A.C. 113, 117, that if a person took away a chair from his room and kept it for 12 months, could anybody say you had a right to diminish the damages by showing that I did not usually sit in that chair, or that there were plenty of other chairs in the room? To the same effect was Lord Shaw's telling example in *Watson, Laidlaw & Co. Ltd. v. Pott, Cassels and Williamson* (1914), 31 R.P.C. 104, 119. It bears repetition:

> If A, being a liveryman, keeps his horse standing idle in the stable, and B, against his wish or without his knowledge, rides or drives it out, it is no answer to A for B to

say: "Against what loss do you want to be restored? I restore the horse. There is no loss. The horse is none the worse; it is the better for the exercise."

Lord Shaw prefaced this observation with a statement of general principle:

> wherever an abstraction or invasion of property has occurred, then, unless such abstraction or invasion were to be sanctioned by law, the law ought to yield a recompense under the category or principle . . . either of price or of hire.

That was a patent infringement case. The House of Lords held that damages should be assessed on the footing of a royalty for every infringing article.

[6]   This principle is established and not controversial. More difficult is the alignment of this measure of damages within the basic compensatory measure. Recently there has been a move towards applying the label of restitution to awards of this character. . . . However that may be, these awards cannot be regarded as conforming to the strictly compensatory measure of damage for the injured person's loss unless loss is given a strained and artificial meaning. The reality is that the injured person's rights were invaded but, in financial terms, he suffered no loss. Nevertheless the common law has found a means to award him a sensibly calculated amount of money. Such awards are probably best regarded as an exception to the general rule.

[7]   Courts of equity went further than the common law courts. In some cases equity required the wrongdoer to yield up all his gains. In respect of certain wrongs which originally or ordinarily were the subject of proceedings in the Court of Chancery, the standard remedies were injunction and, incidental thereto, an account of profits. These wrongs included passing off, infringement of trade marks, copyrights and patents, and breach of confidence. Some of these subjects are now embodied in statutory codes. An injunction restrained the continuance of the wrong, and the wrongdoer was required to account for the profits or benefits he had obtained from breaches or infringements which had already occurred. The court always had a discretion regarding the grant of the remedy of an account of profits, and this remains the position. Further, the circumstances in which an account of profits is available under the statutes vary. For instance, an account of profits may not be ordered against a defendant in a patent infringement action who proves that at the date of the infringement he was not aware, and had no reasonable grounds for supposing, that the patent existed: *Patents Act 1977*, section 62(1).

[8]   In these cases the courts of equity appear to have regarded an injunction and account of profits as more appropriate remedies than damages because of the difficulty of assessing the extent of the loss. Thus, in 1803 Lord Eldon L.C. stated, in *Hogg v. Kirby* (1803), 8 Ves. Jun. 215, 223, a passing off case:

> [w]hat is the consequence in Law and in Equity? . . . a Court of Equity in these cases is not content with an action for damages; for it is nearly impossible to know the extent of the damage; and therefore the remedy here, though not compensating the pecuniary damage except by an account of profits, is the best: the remedy by an injunction and account. . . .

[9]   Considered as a matter of principle, it is difficult to see why equity required the wrongdoer to account for all his profits in these cases, whereas the common law's response was to require a wrongdoer merely to pay a reasonable fee for use of another's land or goods. In all these cases rights of property were infringed.

This difference in remedial response appears to have arisen simply as an accident of history.

[10] In some instances the common law itself afforded a wronged party a choice of remedies. A notable example is the wrong of conversion. A person whose goods were wrongfully converted by another had a choice of two remedies against the wrongdoer. He could recover damages, in respect of the loss he had sustained by the conversion. Or he could recover the proceeds of the conversion obtained by the defendant: see *United Australia Ltd. v. Barclays Bank Ltd.*, [1941] A.C. 1, 34, *per* Lord Romer. Historically, the latter alternative was achieved by recourse to an element of legal fiction, whereby the innocent party "waived the tort". The innocent party could suppose that the wrongful sale had been made with his consent and bring an action for money "had and received to his use": see *Lamine v. Dorrell* (1705), 2 Ld. Raym. 1216, 1217. Holt C.J. observed that these actions had "crept in by degrees".

Breach of trust and fiduciary duty

[11] I should refer briefly to breach of trust and breach of fiduciary duty. Equity reinforces the duty of fidelity owed by a trustee or fiduciary by requiring him to account for any profits he derives from his office or position. This ensures that trustees and fiduciaries are financially disinterested in carrying out their duties. They may not put themselves in a position where their duty and interest conflict. To this end they must not make any unauthorised profit. If they do, they are accountable. Whether the beneficiaries or persons to whom the fiduciary duty is owed suffered any loss by the impugned transaction is altogether irrelevant. . . .

. . .

Breach of contract

[12] Against this background I turn to consider the remedies available for breaches of contract. The basic remedy is an award of damages. In the much quoted words of Baron Parke, the rule of the common law is that where a party sustains a loss by reason of a breach of contract, he is, so far as money can do it, to be placed in the same position as if the contract had been performed: *Robinson v. Harman* (1848), 1 Exch. 850, 855. Leaving aside the anomalous exception of punitive damages, damages are compensatory. That is axiomatic. It is equally well established that an award of damages, assessed by reference to financial loss, is not always "adequate" as a remedy for a breach of contract. The law recognises that a party to a contract may have an interest in performance which is not readily measurable in terms of money. On breach the innocent party suffers a loss. He fails to obtain the benefit promised by the other party to the contract. To him the loss may be as important as financially measurable loss, or more so. An award of damages, assessed by reference to financial loss, will not recompense him properly. For him a financially assessed measure of damages is inadequate.

[13] The classic example of this type of case, as every law student knows, is a contract for the sale of land. The buyer of a house may be attracted by features which have little or no impact on the value of the house. An award of damages, based on strictly financial criteria, would fail to recompense a disappointed

buyer for this head of loss. The primary response of the law to this type of case is to ensure, if possible, that the contract is performed in accordance with its terms. The court may make orders compelling the party who has committed a breach of contract, or is threatening to do so, to carry out his contractual obligations. To this end the court has wide powers to grant injunctive relief. The court will, for instance, readily make orders for the specific performance of contracts for the sale of land, and sometimes it will do so in respect of contracts for the sale of goods. In *Beswick v. Beswick*, [1968] A.C. 58, the court made an order for the specific performance of a contract to make payments of money to a third party. The law recognised that the innocent party to the breach of contract had a legitimate interest in having the contract performed even though he himself would suffer no financial loss from its breach. Likewise, the court will compel the observance of negative obligations by granting injunctions. This may include a mandatory order to undo an existing breach, as where the court orders the defendant to pull down building works carried out in breach of covenant.

[14] All this is trite law. In practice, these specific remedies go a long way towards providing suitable protection for innocent parties who will suffer loss from breaches of contract which are not adequately remediable by an award of damages. But these remedies are not always available. For instance, confidential information may be published in breach of a non-disclosure agreement before the innocent party has time to apply to the court for urgent relief. Then the breach is irreversible. Further, these specific remedies are discretionary. Contractual obligations vary infinitely. So do the circumstances in which breaches occur, and the circumstances in which remedies are sought. The court may, for instance, decline to grant specific relief on the ground that this would be oppressive.

[15] An instance of this nature occurred in *Wrotham Park Estate Co. Ltd. v. Parkside Homes Ltd.*, [1974] 1 W.L.R. 798. For social and economic reasons the court refused to make a mandatory order for the demolition of houses built on land burdened with a restrictive covenant. Instead, Brightman J. made an award of damages under the jurisdiction which originated with *Lord Cairns' Act*. The existence of the new houses did not diminish the value of the benefited land by one farthing. The judge considered that if the plaintiffs were given a nominal sum, or no sum, justice would manifestly not have been done. He assessed the damages at five per cent of the developer's anticipated profit, this being the amount of money which could reasonably have been demanded for a relaxation of the covenant.

[16] In reaching his conclusion the judge applied by analogy the cases mentioned above concerning the assessment of damages when a defendant has invaded another's property rights but without diminishing the value of the property. I consider he was right to do so. Property rights are superior to contractual rights in that, unlike contractual rights, property rights may survive against an indefinite class of persons. However, it is not easy to see why, as between the parties to a contract, a violation of a party's contractual rights should attract a lesser degree of remedy than a violation of his property rights. As Lionel D. Smith has pointed out in his article "Disgorgement of the Profits of Breach of Contract: Property, Contract and "Efficient Breach'" (1995), 24 *Can. Bus. L.J.* 121, it is not clear why it

should be any more permissible to expropriate personal rights than it is permissible to expropriate property rights.

[17] I turn to the decision of the Court of Appeal in *Surrey County Council v. Bredero Homes Ltd.*, [1993] 1 W.L.R. 1361. A local authority had sold surplus land to a developer and obtained a covenant that the developer would develop the land in accordance with an existing planning permission. The sole purpose of the local authority in imposing the covenant was to enable it to share in the planning gain if, as happened, planning permission was subsequently granted for the erection of a larger number of houses. The purpose was that the developer would have to apply and pay for a relaxation of the covenant if it wanted to build more houses. In breach of covenant the developer completed the development in accordance with the later planning permission, and the local authority brought a claim for damages. The erection of the larger number of houses had not caused any financial loss to the local authority. The judge awarded nominal damages of £2, and the Court of Appeal dismissed the local authority's appeal.

[18] This is a difficult decision. It has attracted criticism from academic commentators. . . . In the *Bredero* case Dillon L.J. himself noted, at p. 1364, that had the covenant been worded differently, there could have been provision for payment of an increased price if a further planning permission were forthcoming. That would have been enforceable. But, according to the *Bredero* decision, a covenant not to erect any further houses without permission, intended to achieve the same result, may be breached with impunity. That would be a sorry reflection on the law. Suffice to say, in so far as the *Bredero* decision is inconsistent with the approach adopted in the *Wrotham Park* case, the latter approach is to be preferred.

[19] The *Wrotham Park* case, therefore, still shines, rather as a solitary beacon, showing that in contract as well as tort damages are not always narrowly confined to recoupment of financial loss. In a suitable case damages for breach of contract may be measured by the benefit gained by the wrongdoer from the breach. The defendant must make a reasonable payment in respect of the benefit he has gained. In the present case the Crown seeks to go further. The claim is for all the profits of Blake's book which the publisher has not yet paid him. This raises the question whether an account of profits can ever be given as a remedy for breach of contract. The researches of counsel have been unable to discover any case where the court has made such an order on a claim for breach of contract. In *Tito v. Waddell (No. 2)*, [1977] Ch. 106, 332, a decision which has proved controversial, Sir Robert Megarry V.-C. said that, as a matter of fundamental principle, the question of damages was "not one of making the defendant disgorge" his gains, in that case what he had saved by committing the wrong, but "one of compensating the plaintiff." In *Occidental Worldwide Investment Corporation v. Skibs A/S Avanti*, [1976] 1 Lloyd's Rep. 293, 337, Kerr J. summarily rejected a claim for an account of profits when ship owners withdrew ships on a rising market.

[20] There is a light sprinkling of cases where courts have made orders having the same effect as an order for an account of profits, but the courts seem always to have attached a different label. A person who, in breach of contract, sells land twice over must surrender his profits on the second sale to the original buyer. Since courts regularly make orders for the specific performance of contracts for the sale of land, a seller of land is, to an extent, regarded as holding the land on trust for the buyer: *Lake v. Bayliss*, [1974] 1 W.L.R. 1073. In *Reid-Newfoundland Co. v. Anglo-American Telegraph Co. Ltd.*, [1912] A.C. 555 a railway company

agreed not to transmit any commercial messages over a particular telegraph wire except for the benefit and account of the telegraph company. The Privy Council held that the railway company was liable to account as a trustee for the profits it wrongfully made from its use of the wire for commercial purposes. In *British Motor Trade Association v. Gilbert*, [1951] 2 All E.R. 641, the plaintiff suffered no financial loss but the award of damages for breach of contract effectively stripped the wrongdoer of the profit he had made from his wrongful venture into the black market for new cars.

[21]   These cases illustrate that circumstances do arise when the just response to a breach of contract is that the wrongdoer should not be permitted to retain any profit from the breach. In these cases the courts have reached the desired result by straining existing concepts. Professor Peter Birks has deplored the "failure of jurisprudence when the law is forced into this kind of abusive instrumentalism": see "Profits of Breach of Contract" (1993), 109 *Law Q. Rev.* 518, 520. Some years ago Professor Dawson suggested there is no inherent reason why the technique of equity courts in land contracts should not be more widely employed, not by granting remedies as the by-product of a phantom "trust" created by the contract, but as an alternative form of money judgment remedy. That well known ailment of lawyers, a hardening of the categories, ought not to be an obstacle: see "Restitution or Damages" (1959), 20 *Ohio State L.J.* 175.

[22]   My conclusion is that there seems to be no reason, in principle, why the court must in all circumstances rule out an account of profits as a remedy for breach of contract. I prefer to avoid the unhappy expression "restitutionary damages". Remedies are the law's response to a wrong (or, more precisely, to a cause of action). When, exceptionally, a just response to a breach of contract so requires, the court should be able to grant the discretionary remedy of requiring a defendant to account to the plaintiff for the benefits he has received from his breach of contract. In the same way as a plaintiff's interest in performance of a contract may render it just and equitable for the court to make an order for specific performance or grant an injunction, so the plaintiff's interest in performance may make it just and equitable that the defendant should retain no benefit from his breach of contract.

[23]   The state of the authorities encourages me to reach this conclusion, rather than the reverse. The law recognises that damages are not always a sufficient remedy for breach of contract. This is the foundation of the court's jurisdiction to grant the remedies of specific performance and injunction. Even when awarding damages, the law does not adhere slavishly to the concept of compensation for financially measurable loss. When the circumstances require, damages are measured by reference to the benefit obtained by the wrongdoer. This applies to interference with property rights. Recently, the like approach has been adopted to breach of contract. Further, in certain circumstances an account of profits is ordered in preference to an award of damages. Sometimes the injured party is given the choice: either compensatory damages or an account of the wrongdoer's profits. Breach of confidence is an instance of this. If confidential information is wrongfully divulged in breach of a non-disclosure agreement, it would be nothing short of sophistry to say that an account of profits may be ordered in respect of the equitable wrong but not in respect of the breach of contract which governs the relationship between the parties. With the established authorities going thus far, I consider it would be only a modest step for the law to recognise openly that, exceptionally,

an account of profits may be the most appropriate remedy for breach of contract. It is not as though this step would contradict some recognised principle applied consistently throughout the law to the grant or withholding of the remedy of an account of profits. No such principle is discernible.

[24] The main argument against the availability of an account of profits as a remedy for breach of contract is that the circumstances where this remedy may be granted will be uncertain. This will have an unsettling effect on commercial contracts where certainty is important. I do not think these fears are well founded. I see no reason why, in practice, the availability of the remedy of an account of profits need disturb settled expectations in the commercial or consumer world. An account of profits will be appropriate only in exceptional circumstances. Normally the remedies of damages, specific performance and injunction, coupled with the characterisation of some contractual obligations as fiduciary, will provide an adequate response to a breach of contract. It will be only in exceptional cases, where those remedies are inadequate, that any question of accounting for profits will arise. No fixed rules can be prescribed. The court will have regard to all the circumstances, including the subject matter of the contract, the purpose of the contractual provision which has been breached, the circumstances in which the breach occurred, the consequences of the breach and the circumstances in which relief is being sought. A useful general guide, although not exhaustive, is whether the plaintiff had a legitimate interest in preventing the defendant's profit-making activity and, hence, in depriving him of his profit.

[25] It would be difficult, and unwise, to attempt to be more specific. In the Court of Appeal Lord Woolf, M.R. suggested there are at least two situations in which justice requires the award of restitutionary damages where compensatory damages would be inadequate: see [1998] Ch. 439, 458. Lord Woolf was not there addressing the question of when an account of profits, in the conventional sense, should be available. But I should add that, so far as an account of profits is concerned, the suggested categorisation would not assist. The first suggested category was the case of "skimped" performance, where the defendant fails to provide the full extent of services he has contracted to provide. He should be liable to pay back the amount of expenditure he saved by the breach. This is a much discussed problem. But a part refund of the price agreed for services would not fall within the scope of an account of profits as ordinarily understood. Nor does an account of profits seem to be needed in this context. The resolution of the problem of cases of skimped performance, where the plaintiff does not get what was agreed, may best be found elsewhere. If a shopkeeper supplies inferior and cheaper goods than those ordered and paid for, he has to refund the difference in price. That would be the outcome of a claim for damages for breach of contract. That would be so, irrespective of whether the goods in fact served the intended purpose. There must be scope for a similar approach, without any straining of principle, in cases where the defendant provided inferior and cheaper services than those contracted for.

[26] The second suggested category was where the defendant has obtained his profit by doing the very thing he contracted not to do. This category is defined too widely to assist. The category is apt to embrace all express negative obligations. But something more is required than mere breach of such an obligation before an account of profits will be the appropriate remedy.

[27] Lord Woolf, at [1998] Ch. 439, 457, 458, also suggested three facts which should not be a sufficient ground for departing from the normal basis on which damages are awarded: the fact that the breach was cynical and deliberate; the fact that the breach enabled the defendant to enter into a more profitable contract elsewhere; and the fact that by entering into a new and more profitable contract the defendant put it out of his power to perform his contract with the plaintiff. I agree that none of these facts would be, by itself, a good reason for ordering an account of profits.

The present case

[28] The present case is exceptional. The context is employment as a member of the security and intelligence services. Secret information is the lifeblood of these services. In the 1950s Blake deliberately committed repeated breaches of his undertaking not to divulge official information gained as a result of his employment. He caused untold and immeasurable damage to the public interest he had committed himself to serve. In 1990 he published his autobiography, a further breach of his express undertaking. By this time the information disclosed was no longer confidential. In the ordinary course of commercial dealings the disclosure of nonconfidential information might be regarded as venial. In the present case disclosure was also a criminal offence under the *Official Secrets Acts*, even though the information was no longer confidential. . . .

[An argument based on Article 10 of the *Convention for the Protection of Human Rights and Fundamental Freedoms* (European Human Rights Convention) (Rome, 1950; T.S. 71 (1953); Cmd 8969)) was rejected. **LORD NICHOLLS** pointed out that the argument was first made before the House of Lords. He continued:]

[29] In the event this does not matter, because there is in the present case another consideration which is sufficient for the purposes of the Attorney General. When he joined the Secret Intelligence Service, Blake expressly agreed in writing that he would not disclose official information, during or after his service, in book form or otherwise. He was employed on that basis. That was the basis on which he acquired official information. The Crown had and has a legitimate interest in preventing Blake profiting from the disclosure of official information, whether classified or not, while a member of the service and thereafter. Neither he, nor any other member of the service, should have a financial incentive to break his undertaking. It is of paramount importance that members of the service should have complete confidence in all their dealings with each other, and that those recruited as informers should have the like confidence. Undermining the willingness of prospective informers to co-operate with the services, or undermining the morale and trust between members of the services when engaged on secret and dangerous operations, would jeopardise the effectiveness of the service. An absolute rule against disclosure, visible to all, makes good sense.

[30] In considering what would be a just response to a breach of Blake's undertaking the court has to take these considerations into account. The undertaking, if not a fiduciary obligation, was closely akin to a fiduciary obligation, where an account of profits is a standard remedy in the event of breach. Had the information which Blake has now disclosed still been confidential, an account of profits would have been ordered, almost as a matter of course. In the special circumstances of the intelligence services, the same conclusion should follow even though the information is no longer confidential. That would be a just response to the breach. I am reinforced in this view by noting that most of the profits from the book derive

indirectly from the extremely serious and damaging breaches of the same undertaking committed by Blake in the 1950s. As already mentioned, but for his notori-
ety as an infamous spy his autobiography would not have commanded royalties of
the magnitude Jonathan Cape agreed to pay. ...

The form of the order

[31] The Attorney General's entitlement to an account of Blake's profits does
not, in this case, confer on the Crown any proprietary interest in the debt due to
Blake from Jonathan Cape. The Crown is entitled, on the taking of the account, to
a money judgment which can then be enforced by attachment of the debt in the
usual way. These formal steps may be capable of being short-circuited. Despite the
niceties and formalities once associated with taking an account, the amount payable under an account of profits need not be any more elaborately or precisely
calculated than damages. But in this case there is a complication. Blake has
brought third party proceedings against Jonathan Cape, seeking payment of
£90,000 (less tax). In the third party proceedings Jonathan Cape has sought to deduct legal expenses incurred in resisting a defamation claim and in resisting the
Crown's claim. Accordingly, the appropriate form of order on this appeal is a declaration that the Attorney-General is entitled to be paid a sum equal to whatever
amount is due and owing to Blake from Jonathan Cape under the publishing
agreement of 4 May 1989. The injunction granted by the Court of Appeal will
remain in force until Jonathan Cape duly makes payment to the Attorney General.
I would dismiss this appeal.

[**LORD GOFF** and **LORD BROWNE-WILKINSON** agreed with **LORD NICHOLLS**.
LORD STEYN agreed in a separate judgment and **LORD HOBHOUSE** dissented.]

LORD HOBHOUSE OF WOODBOROUGH (dissenting): —

. . .

[32] Blake has now appealed to your Lordships' House against the grant of the
injunction. Like all of your Lordships, I agree that the grant of the injunction was
wrong and should be set aside. But the Crown has, with your Lordships' encouragement and leave, cross-appealed to make the private law claim to restitutionary
damages which it had previously declined to make. Your Lordships have concluded that this claim should be allowed.

[33] I cannot join your Lordships in that conclusion. I have two primary difficulties. The first is the facts of the present case. The speech of my noble and learned
friend [Lord Nicholls] explores what is the "just response" to the defendant's conduct. The "just response" visualised in the present case is, however it is formulated, that Blake should be punished and deprived of any fruits of conduct connected with his former criminal and reprehensible conduct. The Crown have made
no secret of this. It is not a commercial claim in support of any commercial interest. It is a claim relating to past criminal conduct. The way it was put by the Court
of Appeal, [1998] Ch. 439, 464 was:

> The ordinary member of the public would be shocked if the position was that the
> courts were powerless to prevent [Blake] profiting from his criminal conduct.

The answer given by my noble and learned friend does not reflect the essentially
punitive nature of the claim and seeks to apply principles of law which are only

appropriate where commercial or proprietary interests are involved. Blake has made a financial gain but he has not done so at the expense of the Crown or making use of any property of or commercial interest of the Crown either in law or equity.

[34] My second difficulty is that the reasoning of my noble and learned friend depends upon the conclusion that there is some gap in the existing state of the law which requires to be filled by a new remedy. He accepts that the term "restitutionary damages" is unsatisfactory but, with respect, does not fully examine why this is so, drawing the necessary conclusions.

[35] The cross-appeal has to be determined on the basis that the only civil cause of action which the Crown has against Blake is a bare legal cause of action in contract for breach of contract in that he failed in 1989 to observe the negative undertaking which he gave in 1944. As already observed, it is recognised by Blake that the Crown had at the least a good arguable case for the grant of an injunction against him at that time. In other words it was a breach of contract — breach of a negative undertaking — liable to be restrained by injunction, *i.e.*, specifically enforced.

[36] But the Crown did not apply for an injunction at the time it would have done some good and quite probably stopped the publication of the book. This is the source of the problems for the Crown in achieving its purpose in bringing these proceedings. It cannot say that it intends to prosecute Blake because it does not expect that he will ever return to this country; consequently it admits that it cannot say that it will ever be in a position to make use of the provisions of the *Criminal Justice Act 1988* and the *Proceeds of Crime Act 1995*. It does not say that the payment of the £90,000 by Jonathan Cape to Blake would amount to the commission of any criminal offence by either Jonathan Cape or Blake. It accepts that it has no direct right of recourse against Jonathan Cape; it is confined to claiming some public law or private law remedy against Blake. It now accepts that its original claim that it has equitable or fiduciary or proprietary rights against Blake cannot be sustained. It cannot claim compensatory damages for breach of contract because it has suffered no loss as a result of the publication.

[37] What then was left? First there was the public law claim to an interim injunction as awarded by the Court of Appeal. Second there now is the claim not made as such in the Court of Appeal but now fully argued in your Lordships' House as a cross-appeal by the Crown for restitutionary damages.

[**LORD HOBHOUSE**'s discussion of the public law claim is omitted.]

The private law claim: restitutionary damages

[38] It is with some hesitation that I enter upon this field at all in view of your Lordships' so far unanimous opinion save so as to record my dissent. The subject is a profound one which has attracted much attention among the academic writers for some time. Neither the subject nor the opinions of my noble and learned friends, Lord Nicholls and Lord Steyn, could be done justice in many fewer pages than their opinions will occupy. However I do not believe that it is helpful (or courteous to Mr. Clayton [counsel for Blake]) that I should add nothing at all. Exceptional though this case is, courts hereafter will have to consider its relevance to the decisions of other cases which will surely come before them. I will however confine myself to what I regard as the minimum of explanatory comment (with the inevitable consequence of some simplification).

[39] The concepts of restitution and compensation are not the same though they will on occasions fulfil the same need. Restitution is analogous to property: it concerns wealth or advantage which ought to be returned or transferred by the defendant to the plaintiff. It is a form of specific implement. Its clearest form is an order for the return or transfer of property which belongs in law or in equity to the plaintiff. Property includes an interest in property. Then there are rights recognised in equity such as those which arise from a fiduciary relationship. These rights give rise to restitutionary remedies including the remedy of account which, depending on the circumstances, could also derive from a common law relationship such as agency. Then, again, there are the rights now grouped under the heading of the law of restitution or unjust enrichment. These are still truly restitutionary concepts leading to restitutionary remedies. Typically they require the payment of money by the person unjustly enriched to the person at whose expense that enrichment has taken place. Insofar as the appropriate remedy is the payment of money or the delivery up of a chattel or goods is concerned the common law could provide it; insofar as it required some other remedy or the recognition of an equitable right, the chancery jurisdiction had to be invoked.

[40] The essential of such rights and their enforcement was the procuring by the courts of the *performance* by the defendant of his obligations. The plaintiff recovers what he is actually entitled to not some monetary substitute for it. If what the plaintiff is entitled to is wealth expressed in monetary terms, the order will be for the payment of money but this does not alter the character of the remedy or of the right being recognised. He gets the money because it was his property or he was in some other way entitled to it. It is still the enforced performance of an obligation. The same is the case where an injunction is granted or a decree of specific performance or the ordering of an account.

[41] It is this class of rights which the Crown is unable to invoke as a result of the judgment the Vice-Chancellor upheld by the Court of Appeal. There is no obligation of Blake left to perform or which now can be enforced. That time passed with the failure to apply for an injunction in 1989 or 1990. The Crown has no right to an injunction to stop the payment of the royalty to Blake and procure its payment to the Crown instead. The Crown has no right to the royalty and does not now assert one.

[42] The law, including equity, provides extensive and effective remedies for protecting and enforcing property rights. It is no criticism of the law that they are not available now to the Crown. The Crown does not have the substantive rights to support such remedies.

. . .

[43] The Crown has to allege a breach of contract. . . . The claim is for damages in order to put the plaintiff in the same position as if the contract had been performed. It is a *substitute* for performance. That is why it is necessarily compensatory. The error is to describe compensation as relating to a loss as if there has to be some identified physical or monetary loss to the plaintiff. In the vast majority of cases this error does not matter because the plaintiff's claim can be so described without distortion. But in a minority of cases the error does matter and cases of the breach of negative promises typically illustrate this category.

[44]   But, before coming to them, I would like to refer to *Ruxley Electronics and Construction Ltd. v. Forsyth*, [1996] A.C. 344. This was the case of the swimming pool. . . . The *prima facie* measure of damages would have been the cost of increasing the depth of the pool to the stipulated depth — a considerable sum. But this sum was so disproportionate that the courts refused to award it. It would be unreasonable for the plaintiff to incur that expense. His damages must be assessed at a lower figure. The speech of Lord Mustill (at pp. 359-361) is illuminating. The loss is a reasonable valuation of what the plaintiff ought to have had but did not get. It is not just the amount (if any) by which his property has a lower market value than that it would have had if the contract had been performed. In the present case, by 1989, Blake's undertaking had no remaining value to the Crown.

[45]   The question of negative covenants typically arise in relation to land and covenants not to build. A complication is that they usually involve a proprietary right of the plaintiff which he is *prima facie* entitled to enforce as such. Where the plaintiff has failed to obtain or failed to apply for an injunction, he has to be content with a remedy in damages. What has happened in such cases is that there has either actually or in effect been a compulsory purchase of the plaintiff's right of refusal. (The award of damages in tort for the conversion or detinue of goods is also an example of compulsory purchase as is demonstrated by the common law rule that the payment of the damages vests the title in the goods in the defendant.) What the plaintiff has lost is the sum which he could have exacted from the defendant as the price of his consent to the development. This is an example of compensatory damages. They are damages for breach. They do not involve any concept of restitution and so to describe them is an error. The error comes about because of the assumption that the only loss which the plaintiff can have suffered is a reduction in the value of the dominant tenement. It is for this reason that I agree with my noble and learned friend Lord Nicholls that the decision in *Wrotham Park Estate Co. Ltd. v. Parkside Homes Ltd.*, [1974] 1 W.L.R. 798 is to be preferred to that in *Surrey County Council v. Bredero Homes Ltd.*, [1993] 1 W.L.R. 1361: see also *Jaggard v. Sawyer*, [1995] 1 W.L.R. 269. I would however add that the order proposed by your Lordships does not reflect this principle; it goes further. It does not award to the Crown damages for breach of contract assessed by reference to what would be the reasonable price to pay for permission to publish. It awards the Crown damages which equal the whole amount owed by Jonathan Cape to Blake. That is a remedy based on proprietary principles when the necessary proprietary rights are absent.

[46]   The principle of compensation is both intellectually sound as the remedy for breach and provides the just answer. The examples discussed in my noble and learned friend's speech do not on the correct analysis disclose the supposed need to extend the boundaries of remedies for breach of contract. The reason why the Crown should not recover damages in the present case derives from the exceptional public law nature of the undertaking which Blake gave. If the relationship had been a commercial one it is probable that by 1989 the undertaking would be regarded as spent or no longer enforceable, but if still enforceable the breach of it would have supported compensatory damages on the "compulsory purchase" basis.

[47]   The examples given by my noble and learned friend are examples of compensatory damages. Lord Halsbury's dining-room chair is no different unless the error which I have identified is made. He would have lost the use of the chair and it, like other such amenity-value assets, can be assessed by reference to the sum which has been expended on its acquisition and/or maintenance or interest upon its capital value during the period of deprivation. The supposed problem arises from asking the wrong question not from receiving the wrong answer.

[48] I must also sound a further note of warning that if some more extensive principle of awarding non-compensatory damages for breach of contract is to be introduced into our commercial law the consequences will be very far reaching and disruptive. I do not believe that such is the intention of your Lordships but if others are tempted to try to extend the decision of the present exceptional case to commercial situations so as to introduce restitutionary rights beyond those presently recognised by the law of restitution, such a step will require very careful consideration before it is acceded to.

[49] My Lords, Mr. Clayton was right to say that the exceptional facts of this case have been critical to its decision. The policy which is being enforced is that which requires Blake to be punished by depriving him of any benefit from anything connected with his past deplorable criminal conduct. Your Lordships consider that this policy can be given effect to without a departure from principle. I must venture to disagree. I would allow the appeal and dismiss the cross-appeal.

Appeal dismissed with costs.

NOTES AND QUESTIONS

1. Is it proper for a court to express motives of revenge and punishment in a case like that presented by *Blake?*

2. Is the case a good example of the flexibility of the common law of contracts?

3. Does Lord Nicholls satisfactorily deal with the objections raised by Lord Hobhouse?

4. Professor Mitchell McInnes, in "Gain-Based Relief for Breach of Contract: *Attorney General v. Blake*" (2001), 35 *Can. Bus. L.J.* 72, observes that "the issue of disgorgement for breach of contract has proven diabolically difficult". He argues that Canadian courts should resist the temptation to follow *Blake*, as doing so would require "a reconceptualization of the institution of contracts". Do you agree?

   He points out that disgorgement of profits runs counter to Posner's notion of "efficient breach". Prof. McInnes also notes that most of the cases in which this remedy is offered are not simply cases of a breach of contract, but rather of an "outrageous breach".

   While restitutionary relief is clearly not the norm in contracts cases, courts will provide this type of remedy in a wide variety of commercial cases. Some of these cases will be explored later in the materials. One of them, *Lac Minerals Ltd. v. International Corona Resources Ltd.*, [1989] 2 S.C.R. 574, 61 D.L.R. (4th) 14, will be examined in Chapter 3 in the context of the obligations of those involved in negotiations for a contract.

5. In *Bank of America Canada v. Mutual Trust Co.*, [2002] S.C.J. No. 44, [2002] 2 S.C.R. 601, in *obiter dicta*, Major J., after discussing expectation damages, wrote:

   > [30] The other side of the coin is to examine the effect of the breach on the defendant. In contract, restitution damages can be invoked when a defendant has, as a result of his or her own breach, profited in excess of his or her expected profit had the contract been performed but the plaintiff's loss is less than the defendant's gain. So the plaintiff can be fully paid his damages with a surplus left in the hands of the defendant. This occurs with what has been described as an efficient breach of contract. In some but not all cases, the defendant

may be required to pay such profits to the plaintiff as restitution damages.
...

> [31] Courts generally avoid this measure of damages so as not to discourage
> efficient breach (i.e., where the plaintiff is fully compensated and the defen-
> dant is better off than if he or she had performed the contract) ... Efficient
> breach is what economists describe as a Pareto optimal outcome where one
> party may be better off but no one is worse off, or expressed differently, no-
> body loses. Efficient breach should not be discouraged by the courts. This lack
> of disapproval emphasizes that a court will usually award money damages for
> breach of contract equal to the value of the bargain to the plaintiff.

The Supreme Court did not explicitly refer to *Attorney-General v. Blake*. Do
you think that the position of the Supreme Court is consistent with that of the
House of Lords in *Blake*?

REASONABLENESS IN THE FACE OF CONTRACT BREACH

The final theme in this chapter on remedies is the notion that the party who is
faced with a breach of contract by the other party is expected to respond in a way
that is commercially reasonable. This idea is sometimes expressed by saying that
the plaintiff has a "duty to mitigate" its losses. Using the term "duty" is this context may be confusing and can mislead. It may be preferable and more accurate to
say that the plaintiff cannot recover in respect of those losses or harms which, acting reasonably, it could have avoided. For this reason it may be preferable to refer
to the principle of "avoidable harms" rather than the "duty to mitigate", though the
latter expression is commonly used.

A paradigm example of a decision establishing an expectation of commercially
reasonable behaviour in the face of breach is the following case:

PAYZU LIMITED v. SAUNDERS

[1919] 2 K.B. 581
(C.A., Bankes and Scrutton L.JJ. and Eve J.)

[The plaintiffs entered into a contract for the purchase of silk from the defendant,
who was a dealer in silk. The contract was for a nine-month period; the plaintiff
was to receive a quantity of silk each month, was entitled to a 2½ per cent discount
from the list price and was to pay by cheque within 30 days of receipt of each
shipment. A misunderstanding arose over one payment that was received late. The
defendant, mistakenly believing that the plaintiffs could not pay for the order, refused to make another shipment unless she was paid the full price in cash with
each order. The defendant's offer to sell the silk, but only for cash and without a
discount, was contained in an "unfortunately worded" letter from the defendant
which indicated her concern over the solvency of the plaintiff firm. The manager
of the plaintiff firm felt insulted by the suggestion of possible insolvency, and refused to deal further with the defendant. In the exchange of communications, each
party "was ready to accuse the other of conduct unworthy of a high commercial
reputation".

The price of silk was rising, and the plaintiffs sued for damages for breach of
contract, claiming the difference between the contract price of silk and the market
price. The trial judge held that the defendant had breached the contract by her refusal to deliver, but that the plaintiffs should not have refused to accept the defen-

dant's offer. The damages were accordingly limited to compensation for loss of the discount and the loss of interest from having to pay cash instead of getting a 30-day credit period. The plaintiffs appealed to the Court of Appeal, arguing that they should also get the difference between the contract price and the market price. They argued that they were not required to deal further with the defendant after her breach of contract and their receipt of the "unfortunately worded" letter.]

BANKS L.J.: — [1] At the trial of this case the defendant, the present respondent, raised two points: first, that she had committed no breach of the contract of sale, and secondly that, if there was a breach, yet she had offered and was always ready and willing to supply the pieces of silk, the subject of the contract, at the contract price for cash; that it was unreasonable on the part of the appellants not to accept that offer, and that therefore they cannot claim damages beyond what they would have lost by paying cash with each order instead of having a month's credit and a discount of 2½%. We must take it that this was the offer made by the respondent. The case was fought and the learned judge has given judgment on that footing. It is true that the correspondence suggests that the respondent was at one time claiming an increased price. But in this court it must be taken that the offer was to supply the contract goods at the contract price except that payment was to be by cash instead of being on credit.

[2] In these circumstances the only question is whether the appellants can establish that as a matter of law they were not bound to consider any offer made by the respondent because of the attitude she had taken up. . . .

[3] It is plain that the question what is reasonable for a person to do in mitigation of his damages cannot be a question of law but must be one of fact in the circumstances of each particular case. There may be cases where as matter of fact it would be unreasonable to expect a plaintiff to consider any offer made in view of the treatment he had received from the defendant. It he had been rendering personal services and had been dismissed after being accused in presence of others of being a thief, and if after that his employer had offered to take him back into his service, most persons would think he was justified in refusing the offer and that it would be unreasonable to ask him in this way to mitigate the damages in an action of wrongful dismissal. But that is not to state a principle of law, but a conclusion of fact to be arrived at on a consideration of all the circumstances of the case. Mr. Matthews complained that the respondents had treated his clients so badly that it would be unreasonable to expect them to listen to any proposition she might make. I do not agree. In my view each party was ready to accuse the other of conduct unworthy of a high commercial reputation and there was nothing to justify the appellants in refusing to consider the respondent's offer. I think the learned judge came to a proper conclusion on the facts, and that the appeal must be dismissed.

SCRUTTON L.J.: — [4] I am of the same opinion. Whether it be more correct to say that a plaintiff must minimize his damages, or to say that he can recover no more than he would have suffered if he had acted reasonably, because any further damages do not reasonably follow from the defendant's breach, the result is the same. . . . In certain cases of personal service it may be unreasonable to expect a plaintiff to consider an offer from the other party who has grossly injured him; but in commercial contracts it is generally reasonable to accept an offer from the party in default. However, it is always a question of fact. About the law there is no difficulty.

[The concurring judgment of **EVE J.** is omitted.]

NOTES AND QUESTIONS

1. In *Apeco of Canada Ltd. v. Windmill Place*, [1978] 2 S.C.R. 385, the defendant had agreed to lease space in a commercial building owned by the plaintiff. The defendant then refused to take up the lease. The space that the defendant had agreed to rent was four per cent of the available space. After the breach, the plaintiff rented out this space to another tenant at the same rate as that charged the defendant. At the time of this lease with the new tenant the building was not completely leased, and if this space were not available, the new tenant would have taken other space in the same building. The defendant argued that the loss the plaintiff had suffered by its refusal to take the space had been fully made up by the new tenant.

   The Supreme Court rejected this argument: the plaintiff still had space to lease and had it not leased the space that the defendant had originally agreed to take, it would have leased other space that would have suited the new tenant equally well. The conclusion is that the plaintiff had been unable to avoid the harm arising from the defendant's breach, and so the latter was liable for damages for breach.

   How does the result in *Apeco of Canada Ltd. v. Windmill Place* fit with the analysis in *Victory Motors v. Bayda*, *supra*, the case where the buyer who refused to take a new car was liable to the dealer for the loss of commission despite the fact that the dealer sold the car to another person for the same price?

2. The conclusion in *Apeco of Canada Ltd. v. Windmill Place* is similar to that in an earlier Supreme Court case, *Cockburn v. Trusts & Guarantee Co.* (1917), 54 S.C.R. 264, 37 D.L.R. 701. A sales manager, Cockburn, had his five-year employment contract cancelled without legal cause when the firm that employed him went into bankruptcy. Cockburn sued the estate of the person who had guaranteed his salary for five years. After the bankruptcy, Cockburn had bought some of the goods of his former employer and had resold them, making a substantial profit for himself. It was held by the Supreme Court that this profit was to be taken into account and the amount of his damages reduced by the profit that he had made. The reason for this conclusion was that Cockburn could not have made the profit had he been employed, for such a transaction would have been a breach of his employment contract.

   In *Apeco of Canada Ltd. v. Windmill Place*, the gain made from leasing the space did not "arise out of the breach". The gain was not one that would not have been earned had it not been for the breach. In *Cockburn v. Trusts & Guarantee Co.* the plaintiff's gain could only have been made because he was no longer employed by the bankrupt company. Thus, the gain made in the latter case "arose out of the breach" and had to be taken into account in reducing the plaintiff's recovery. By making a profit by trading in his former employer's goods, Cockburn had avoided the harms caused by breach.

   In both *Apeco of Canada Ltd. v. Windmill Place* and *Cockburn v. Trusts & Guarantee Co.* the issue was whether the plaintiff had avoided the harmful consequences of the defendant's breach. There is another question suggested by the principle of avoidable harms: did the plaintiff do what was reasonable to avoid the harmful consequences of the defendant's breach? The next two cases raise this issue.

WHITE AND CARTER (COUNCILS) LTD. v. McGREGOR

[1962] A.C. 413, [1961] 3 All E.R. 1178
(H.L., Lords Reid, Hodson, Tucker, Morton and Keith)

[This case went to the House of Lords on appeal from the Scottish courts. The parties made an agreement under which the appellants, the pursuers,[8] would dis-

---

8   In Scotland the plaintiff is called the "pursuer" and the defendant is called the "defender".

play advertisements for the respondent's, the defender's, business on municipal garbage bins. The original three-year contract was renewed by the defender's sales manager. Almost immediately after the renewal, and before any work was done by the pursuers on the new contract, the defender contacted the pursuer to "cancel" the contract. The pursuers refused to accept this cancellation. They prepared the necessary plates for attachment to the bins and exhibited them on the garbage cans. The pursuers claimed £196 4s, the full sum due under the contract for the period of three years. As noted in the judgment, the contract contained an "acceleration clause", allowing the municipality to claim the full amount for the balance of the contract in the event of a four-week default in payment by the advertiser. The Sheriff-Substitute (the trial judge) dismissed the action. He relied on the decision in *Langford & Co. Ltd. v. Dutch*, 1952 S.C. 15, in holding that the pursuers could not, in the circumstances, claim the full contract amount. The pursuers appealed to the Court of Session (the Scottish Court of Appeal) and the appeal was dismissed. The pursuers appealed to the House of Lords.]

LORD REID: — **[1]** The case for the defender (now the respondent) is that, as he repudiated the contract before anything had been done under it, the appellants were not entitled to go on and carry out the contract and sue for the contract price: he maintains that in the circumstances the appellants' only remedy was damages, and that, as they do not sue for damages, this action was rightly dismissed.

[2] The contract was for the display of advertisements for a period of 156 weeks from the date when the display began. . . . The reason why the appellants sued for the whole sum due for the three years is to be found in clause 8 of the conditions:

> In the event of an instalment or part thereof being due for payment, and remaining unpaid for a period of four weeks or in the event of the advertiser being in any way in breach of this contract then the whole amount due for the 156 weeks or such part of the said 156 weeks as the advertiser shall not yet have paid shall immediately become due and payable.

[3] . . . Accordingly, if the appellants were entitled to carry out their part of the contract notwithstanding the respondent's repudiation, it was hardly disputed that this clause entitled them to sue immediately for the whole price and not merely the first instalment.

[4] The general rule cannot be in doubt. It was settled in Scotland at least as early as 1848 and it has been authoritatively stated time and again in both Scotland and England. If one party to a contract repudiates it in the sense of making it clear to the other party that he refuses or will refuse to carry out his part of the contract, the other party, the innocent party, has an option. He may accept that repudiation and sue for damages for breach of contract, whether or not the time for performance has come; or he may if he chooses disregard or refuse to accept it and then the contract remains in full effect. . . .

[5] I need not refer to the numerous authorities. They are not disputed by the respondent but he points out that in all of them the party who refused to accept the repudiation had no active duties under the contract. The innocent party's option is generally said to be to wait until the date of performance and then to claim damages estimated as at that date. There is no case in which it is said that he may, in face of the repudiation, go on and incur useless expense in performing the contract and then claim the contract price. The option, it is argued, is merely as to the date as at which damages are to be assessed.

[6]   Developing this argument, the respondent points out that in most cases the innocent party cannot complete the contract himself without the other party doing, allowing or accepting something, and that it is purely fortuitous that the appellants can do so in this case. In most cases by refusing co-operation the party in breach can compel the innocent party to restrict his claim to damages. Then it was said that, even where the innocent party can complete the contract without such co-operation, it is against the public interest that he should be allowed to do so. An example was developed in argument. A company might engage an expert to go abroad and prepare an elaborate report and then repudiate the contract before anything was done. To allow such an expert then to waste thousands of pounds in preparing the report cannot be right if a much smaller sum of damages would give him full compensation for his loss. It would merely enable the expert to extort a settlement giving him far more than reasonable compensation.

[7]   The respondent founds on the decision of the First Division in *Langford & Co. Ltd. v. Dutch*. There an advertising contractor agreed to exhibit a film for a year. Four days after this agreement was made the advertiser repudiated it but, as in this present case, the contractor refused to accept the repudiation and proceeded to exhibit the film and sue for the contract price. The Sheriff-Substitute dismissed the action as irrelevant and his decision was affirmed on appeal. In the course of a short opinion Lord President Cooper said:

> It appears to me that, apart from wholly exceptional circumstances of which there is no trace in the averments on this record, the law of Scotland does not afford to a person in the position of the pursuers the remedy which is here sought. The pursuers could not force the defender to accept a year's advertisement which she did not want, though they could of course claim damages for her breach of contract. On the averments the only reasonable and proper course, which the pursuers should have adopted, would have been to treat the defender as having repudiated the contract and as being on that account liable in damages, the measure of which we are, of course, not in a position to discuss.

[8]   The Lord President cited no authority and I am in doubt as to what principle he had in mind. In the earlier part of the passage which I have quoted he speaks of forcing the defender to accept the advertisement. Of course, if it had been necessary for the defender to do or accept anything before the contract could be completed by the pursuers, the pursuers could not and the court would not have compelled the defender to act, the contract would not have been completed and the pursuers' only remedy would have been damages. But the peculiarity in that case, as in the present case, was that the pursuers could completely fulfil the contract without any co-operation of the defender. The Lord President cannot have meant that because of non-acceptance the contract had not been completely carried out, because that in itself would have been a complete answer to an action for the contract price. He went on to say that the only reasonable and proper course which the pursuers should have adopted would have been to treat the defender as having repudiated the contract, which must, I think, mean to have accepted the repudiation. It is this reference to "the only reasonable and proper course" which I find difficult to explain. It might be, but it never has been, the law that a person is only entitled to enforce his contractual rights in a reasonable way, and that a court will not support an attempt to enforce them in an unreasonable way. One reason why that is not the law is, no doubt, because it was thought that it would create too much uncertainty to require the court to decide whether it is reasonable or equitable to allow a party to enforce his full rights under a contract. The Lord President cannot have meant that. . . . *Langford v. Dutch* is indistinguishable from the present case. Quite properly the Second Division followed it in this case as a binding authority and did not develop Lord Cooper's reasoning: they were not asked to send this case to a larger court. We must now decide whether that case was rightly decided. In my judgment it was not. It could only be supported on one or other of two grounds. It might be said that, because in most cases the circumstances are such that an innocent party is unable to complete the contract and earn the contract price without the assent or co-operation of the other party, therefore in cases where he can do so he should not be allowed to do so. I can see no justification for that.

[9]   The other ground would be that there is some general equitable principle or element of public policy which requires this limitation of the contractual rights of the innocent party. It may well be that, if it can be shown that a person has no legitimate interest, financial or otherwise, in performing the contract rather than claiming damages, he ought not to be allowed to saddle the other party with an additional burden with no benefit to himself. If a party has no interest to enforce a stipulation, he cannot in general enforce it: so it might be said that, if a party has no interest to insist on a particular remedy, he ought not to be allowed to insist on it. And, just as a party is not allowed to enforce a penalty, so he ought not to be allowed to penalise the other party by taking one course when another is equally advantageous to him. If I may revert to the example which I gave of a company engaging an expert to prepare an elaborate report and then repudiating before anything was done, it might be that the company could show that the expert had no substantial or legitimate interest in carrying out the work rather than accepting damages: I would think that the *de minimis* principle would apply in determining whether his interest was substantial, and that he might have a legitimate interest other than an immediate financial interest. But if the expert had no such interest then that might be regarded as a proper case for the exercise of the general equitable jurisdiction of the court. But that is not this case. Here the respondent did not set out to prove that the appellants had no legitimate interest in completing the contract and claiming the contract price rather than claiming damages; there is nothing in the findings of fact to support such a case, and it seems improbable that any such case could have been proved. It is, in my judgment, impossible to say that the appellants should be deprived of their right to claim the contract price merely because the benefit to them, as against claiming damages and re-letting their advertising space, might be small in comparison with the loss to the respondent: that is the most that could be said in favour of the respondent. Parliament has on many occasions relieved parties from certain kinds of improvident or oppressive contracts, but the common law can only do that in very limited circumstances. Accordingly, I am unable to avoid the conclusion that this appeal must be allowed and the case remitted so that decree can be pronounced as craved in the initial writ.

LORD KEITH (dissenting): — [10] . . . The party complaining of the breach also has a duty to minimise the damage he has suffered, which is a further reason for saying that after the date of breach he cannot continue to carry on his part of an executory contract. A breach of a contract of employment will serve to illustrate the nature of this duty. A person is engaged to serve for a certain period, say three months, to commence at a future date. When that date arrives the prospective employer wrongfully refuses to honour the engagement. The servant is not entitled to see out the three months and then sue the recalcitrant employer for three months' wages. He must take steps by seeking other employment to minimise his loss. It is true, of course, that a servant cannot invoke a contract to force himself on an unwilling master, any more than a master can enforce the service of an unwilling servant. But if the appellants' contention is sound, it is difficult to see why, by parity of reasoning, it should not apply to a person who keeps himself free to perform the duties of his contract of service during the whole period of the contract and is prevented from doing so by the refusal of the other contracting party. Yet in *Hochster v. De La Tour* [(1853), 118 E.R. 922], from which the whole law about anticipatory repudiation stems, Lord Campbell plainly indicated that if the courier in that case, instead of accepting as he did the repudiation of his engagement as a cause of action, before it was due to commence, had waited till the lapse of the three months of the engagement he could not have sued as for a debt. The jury, he said, would be entitled to look at all that might "increase" or "mitigate the loss of the plaintiff down to the day of trial." There is no difference in this matter between the law of England and the law of Scotland. . . .

[11] This brings me to the case of *Langford v. Dutch*. I took part in the judgment in that case, though the only opinion delivered in the case was given by the Lord President (Lord Cooper), with whom I and the other judges of the Division concurred. . . .

[12] I have reconsidered the decision in *Langford v. Dutch* in the light of the further argument on this appeal. I have come to the conclusion that it was rightly decided and that the Second Division in the present case was bound to follow it.

[13] I find the argument advanced for the appellants a somewhat startling one. If it is right it would seem that a man who has contracted to go to Hongkong at his own expense and make a report, in return for remuneration of £10,000, and who, before the date fixed for the start of the journey and perhaps before he has incurred any expense, is informed by the other contracting party that he has cancelled or repudiates the contract, is entitled to set off for Hongkong and produce his report in order to claim in debt the stipulated sum. Such a result is not, in my opinion, in accordance with principle or authority, and cuts across the rule that where one party is in breach of contract the other must take steps to minimise the loss sustained by the breach.

[**LORD HODSON** and **LORD TUCKER** agreed with **LORD REID** in allowing the appeal. **LORD MORTON** dissented in a separate opinion on much the same grounds as **LORD KEITH**.]

NOTES AND QUESTIONS

1. What is the effect of the judgment in the case on the future conduct of the pursuers' business? Is this conduct something that the court ought to encourage? Is the result consistent with Posner's idea of "efficient breach"?

2. In *White and Carter* the amount that the plaintiff would recover if it were successful was less than £200. It is likely that the plaintiff incurred little or no expense in putting itself into the position to recover this amount for, under the acceleration clause in the contract, it could claim the full contract amount after four weeks' performance. These facts make the case a relatively safe one for the pursuers to litigate. Its maximum risk is its liability for the defender's costs. Keep this fact in mind as you consider what advice you might give a client in the position of the pursuer.

3. Notice the power of words. Lord Reid is bothered by the idea that an "innocent" party can be put under a "duty" to do something by the act of a "guilty" party. This problem may be avoided by avoiding the rhetoric of the "duty to mitigate" and referring, in-

stead, to the principle of avoidable harms, *i.e.*, that the plaintiff cannot recover in respect of those losses, which, acting reasonably, it could have avoided.

4. Laskin J.A., sitting as a single judge on appeal from the Division Court (then equivalent to the Small Claims Court) in *Finelli v. Dee*, [1968] 1 O.R. 676, 67 D.L.R. (2d) 393, dealt with a similar case to *White and Carter*, but developed a different analysis.

In *Finelli* a homeowner signed a contract to have his driveway paved by the plaintiff contractor. The defendant then called the contractor to cancel the contract. The contractor nevertheless went ahead and did the work without giving the homeowner prior notice, doing the work when the homeowner was out. The contractor then sued for the contract price of the work. In dismissing the contractor's claim, Laskin J.A. said that he was "attracted by the arguments of the dissent" in *White and Carter*, but was able to distinguish that case on the ground that in the case before him the contractor should have given notice of his intention to do the work before he did it. Laskin J.A. pointed out that, unlike the situation in *White and Carter*, performance of the contract required the defendant's permission for the plaintiff to enter on the defendant's land, and that permission had not been given. (If permission could have been regarded as given when the agreement was made, it was revoked by the cancellation.) The plaintiff's failure to get permission disentitled him from suing for the contract price.

Do you agree with Laskin J.A. that the approach of Lord Keith in the dissent in *White and Carter* is preferable?

5. The defendants in *White and Carter* and *Finelli v. Dee* had no legal right to cancel the contract. The word "cancel" is not a technical term. "Cancellation" (or an attempt to do so) usually entails repudiation, the technical term for a declaration (either in words or acts) that one party is no longer prepared to perform its obligations under a contract. When one party has repudiated the contract, the other may be prepared to regard the contract as over and, in effect, release the other — as a consumer may cancel an appointment for a haircut — or treat the repudiation as a breach, as the pursuer did in *White and Carter*. If the repudiation is accepted in the sense that the promisee regards the contract as over, there will have been a rescission by the parties' agreement. If the promisee does not end the contract in this way, the promisor's breach entitles the promisee to sue for damages. The House of Lords in *White and Carter* held that the promisee may ignore the attempted cancellation or repudiation, perform its obligations under the contract and sue for the price, in cases where the promisee can perform without the co-operation of the party who has repudiated. The issue raised by the case is whether the promisee should have this option.

The decision in *White and Carter* has never been overruled in the United Kingdom, but as noted in *Ministry of Sound (Ireland) Ltd. v. World Online Ltd.*, [2003] E.W.H.C. 2178 (Ch. Div.), there has been a "degree of judicial reluctance to apply ... *White and Carter* outside the strict limits of its ratio". As noted in *Ministry of Sound*, the effect of the decision has been limited by courts taking a broad view of contracts that require the "co-operation" of both parties, and by using the exception that Lord Reid recognized for cases where there is no "substantial or legitimate reason" for performance.

6. The judgments of Lord Reid and Lord Keith raise the issue of "anticipatory breach". In ¶ 4, Lord Reid said that, when the promisor has repudiated the contract, the promisee has an option either to treat the repudiation as a breach, an "anticipatory breach", by treating its further obligations as discharged and immediately sue for damages, or to ignore the repudiation and treat the contract as still in full force. The existence of this "option" is usually based on the case of *Frost v. Knight* (1872), L.R. 7 Exch. 111, 26 L.T. 77 (Exch. Ch.). *Frost v. Knight* and the general problems of "anticipatory breach" are considered in Chapter 4. We shall have to ask whether the "rule of *Frost v. Knight*" is consistent with the modern approach to mitigation, as illustrated in the next case, *Asamera Oil Corp.*

7.   In an important sense, it is possible to see all of the different sections of this chapter on remedies as merely different aspects of the same basic issue: what Lord Atkinson said in *Wertheim v. Chicoutimi* is the basic rule, and issues of remoteness and mitigation (or avoidable harms) are exceptions or limitations on the amount recoverable under the compensation principle. Such a view underlies judgments like that of Lord Reid in *White and Carter* and in *The Heron II*. There is nothing inevitable about such a view of the law. One can, for example, rephrase the issues by saying that the plaintiff can recover compensation for those losses that in all the circumstances it is proper to charge to the defendant and which could not have been avoided had the plaintiff acted reasonably.

The way which Lord Reid used to articulate the issue suggests that the determination of the damages is a matter of arithmetic: a question only of determining that figure for damages which will compensate. Remoteness issues raise only a question of factual inquiry: what consequences are "not unlikely" to occur? The notion of a duty to mitigate requires a factual determination of the losses that could have been avoided.

The alternative way of considering remedies issues suggests that the assessment of the appropriate amount of damages depends on the context of the transaction and on the expectations of the parties. The use of the word "proper" in the rephrasing incorporates all the aspects of cases such as *Pazyu v. Saunders* (*supra*) and *Cornwall Gravel v. Purolator Courier* (*supra*). These incorporate large aspects of the parties' expectations, both as those have been determined by the particular deal (for example, in *Cornwall Gravel* the effect of Purolator's advertising as well as the oral statements of its employee) and as shaped by the general features of the business that the parties are engaged in. Utilizing this approach, the notion of avoidable harms (the idea that the plaintiff must always act in a commercially reasonable manner) can be seen as one more example of the role played by the parties' reasonable expectations in all the circumstances.

8.   The next case, the Supreme Court decision in *Asamera Oil Corp.*, is factually complex, but doctrinally very important. It offers support for the view that the concept of avoidable harms is a pervasive and basic doctrine of contract law.

ASAMERA OIL CORP. LTD. v. SEA OIL & GENERAL CORP.

[1979] 1 S.C.R. 633, 89 D.L.R. (3d) 1
(S.C.C., Laskin C.J.C., Martland, Spence, Pigeon, Dickson, Estey and Pratte JJ.)

[This was a complex proceeding involving three separate actions extending over a period of 18 years.

In 1957, as part of a larger, complex transaction, Baud Corporation loaned 125,000 shares of Asamera Oil Corp. to Brook, president and chief executive officer of Asamera. The purpose of the loan was to enable Brook to use them as collateral for a loan from his broker that enabled Brook to buy other shares. The shares were in fully negotiable form; that is, they could be sold by the person into whose possession they came. The shares were transferred to the broker's name, and were sold by the broker in 1958 as the value of the shares fell. The contract was complex, and there was a dispute about its interpretation.

Baud Corporation commenced an action in July 1960 against Brook. In another related action that gives this case its style of cause, Asamera Oil launched an action against Sea Oil & General and Baud Corporation alleging that the loan agreement was void. The agreement was complex, and there was a dispute about its interpretation, but it was ultimately held that the agreement required Brook to return the shares in 1960, which was not done. In 1960 the Alberta Supreme Court granted an injunction in favour of Baud Corporation in its action, to prohibit Brook from selling the 125,000 shares. This injunction was interpreted as only requiring Brook to hold 125,000 shares of Asamera, and not necessarily to hold the share certificates that had been loaned by Baud to Brook (which in fact had already been sold). The actions begun in 1960 were dismissed in 1967.

In 1966 Baud commenced another action against Brook for damages for the December 1960 breach of the agreement to return 125,000 shares. The Alberta courts found that Brook was in breach of his obligation to return the shares to Baud. While in the lower courts there were issues about the interpretation of the contracts, by the time the case got to the Supreme Court of Canada, the only contentious issues dealt with remedies. The major issues were whether Baud could get an order for specific performance, and if not what was the appropriate measure of damages for Brook's breach of the agreement to return the 125,000 shares to Baud Corporation in 1960; the shares had fluctuated widely in value over the period between the time that the loan was made in 1957, the initial breach of contract in 1960, and the conclusion of the trial in the action under appeal in 1972. More precise facts are given in the judgment of Estey J.

The trial judge gave judgment for Baud in the third action, and awarded damages of $250,000. The amount of damages was determined by taking the value of each share as $2, an agreed *minimum* price as set out in the original contract. The Alberta Supreme Court, Appellate Division, dismissed Baud's appeal. Baud appealed to the Supreme Court of Canada seeking larger damages.]

ESTEY J. (for the Court): — **[1]** . . . The action in substance is a simple case of breach of contract to return 125,000 Asamera shares and, in my view, the claims made and the issues arising in this action should be disposed of on that basis. That being so, we come to the only real issue in this appeal, namely, to what recovery is the appellant Baud in these circumstances entitled and, if the appropriate relief be a monetary award, the quantum of damages?

[2] Baud has asked this Court to award specific performance of the agreement to return 125,000 Asamera shares, and in particular in its statement of claim has requested an order directing the return or replacement of the shares. The jurisdiction to award specific performance of contractual obligations is ordinarily exercised only where damages would be inadequate to compensate a plaintiff for his losses. As the original 125,000 shares are indistinguishable from all other Asamera shares, and since there has been no suggestion that corporate control is at issue in this case, or that shares were not readily available in the stock market, an order for delivery of shares would merely be another method or form for the payment of any judgment awarded. Asamera shares are listed on the public stock exchanges and consequently some estimate of their market value can be readily ascertained from day to day. The parties themselves therefore throughout the 21 years since these transactions began have had the benefit of the daily assessment by the stock market of the value of these shares. It is obvious that damages are an adequate remedy and that the Courts in such circumstances do not resort to the equitable remedy of specific performance.

[3] The assessment of the quantum of damages for this breach of contract is somewhat complex. The calculation of damages relating to a breach of contract is, of course, governed by well-established principles of common law. Losses recoverable in an action arising out of the non-performance of a contractual obligation are limited to those which will put the injured party in the same position as he would have been in had the wrongdoer performed what he promised.

[4] Not all kinds of losses are recoverable in actions for breach of contract. The limitations on damages recoverable in contract were discussed in *Victoria Laundry* [*supra*], wherein Asquith L.J. . . . went to great lengths to explain such limits. . . .

[5] In any event the damage flowing from the wrongful act of the respondent in this case, that is the loss of the opportunity to resell the shares at a profit, is recoverable under any of the tests set out above.

[6] In cases dealing with the measure of damages for non-delivery of goods under contracts for sale, the application over the years of the above-mentioned principles has given the law some certainty, and it is now accepted that damages will be recoverable in an amount representing what the purchaser would have had to pay for the goods in the market, less the contract price, at the time of the breach. This rule . . . may be seen as a combination of two principles. The first, as stated earlier, is the right of the plaintiff to recover all of his losses which are reasonably contemplated by the parties as liable to result from the breach. The second is the responsibility imposed on a party who has suffered from a breach of contract to take all reasonable steps to avoid losses flowing from the breach. This responsibility to mitigate was explained by Laskin C.J.C., in *Red Deer College v. Michaels*, [1976] 2 S.C.R. 324, 330-1. . .:

> It is, of course, for a wronged plaintiff to prove his damages, and there is therefore a burden upon him to establish on a balance of probabilities what his loss is. The parameters of loss are governed by legal principle. The primary rule in breach of contract cases, that a wronged plaintiff is entitled to be put in as good a position as he would have been in if there had been proper performance by the defendant, is subject to the qualification that the defendant cannot be called upon to pay for avoidable losses which would result in an increase in the quantum of damages payable to the plaintiff. The reference in the case law to a "duty" to mitigate should be understood in this sense.

> In short, a wronged plaintiff is entitled to recover damages for the losses he has suffered but the extent of those losses may depend on whether he has taken reasonable steps to avoid their unreasonable accumulation.

And later in the judgment at p. 331 S.C.R.:

> If it is the defendant's position that the plaintiff could reasonably have avoided some part of the loss claimed, it is for the defendant to carry the burden of that issue, subject to the defendant being content to allow the matter to be disposed of on the trial judge's assessment of the plaintiff's evidence on avoidable consequences.

[7] Thus, if one were to adopt, without reservation, in the settlement of Baud's damage claims, the rules governing recovery for non-delivery of goods in sales contracts, the *prima facie* measure of damages in the case at bar would be the value of the shares on the date of breach, that is, December 31, 1960. The learned trial Judge found the market price on December 31, 1960, to be $0.29 per share. The value of the 125,000 shares wrongfully retained by Brook, and thus the loss to Baud by reason of its not being in possession of those shares on that date therefore was $36,250 assuming, for the purposes of discussion only, the market price to be constant throughout the purchase or sale of such a number of shares. To this must be added other expenses which could reasonably be said to be incidental to steps taken to mitigate the damages flowing from the breach. The most obvious of these are brokerage and commission fees which would have been incurred by Baud in purchasing replacement shares. Of greater importance is the inevitable upward pressure the purchase on the open market of such a large number of Asamera shares would exert on the market price. The impact of forced sales or purchases of shares on market prices has been the subject of judicial comment in the past . . . and must be taken into account in determining the weight to be accorded to mitigation factors in an assessment of damages in circumstances such as exist here. Unhappily, Baud has led no evidence on this problem and one is left to take note of the presence of this factor without being able precisely to quantify it. This point requires more detailed discussion at a later stage.

[8] Assuming for the moment that the breach of contract occurred on December 31, 1960, and that the appellant's right to damages came into being at that time and assuming that it should then have acted to forestall the accumulation of avoidable losses, what action did the law then require of the appellant by way of mitigation of damages? A plaintiff need not take all possible steps to reduce his loss and, accordingly, it is necessary to examine some of the special circumstances here present. The appellant argues that there exist in this case clear circumstances which render the duty to purchase 125,000 Asamera shares an unreasonable one. The first of these has its foundations in the established principle that a plaintiff need not put his money to an unreasonable risk including a risk not present in the initial transaction in endeavouring to mitigate his losses . . . The appellant here was placed in the unusual position where mitigative action would require that it purchase as replacement property, shares of a company engaged in a speculative undertaking under the effective control and under the promotional management of a person in breach of contract, the respondent, Brook, who thereafter was in an adversarial position in relation to the appellant.

[9] On the evidence adduced at trial, the market value of shares in Asamera had fallen from $3.00 shortly before the dates on which Baud first loaned the two blocs of shares to Brook, to between $1.62 and $1.87 in November, 1958, and to $0.29 per share on December 31, 1960. Evidence of share values after that date indicates only that there was a relatively small recovery in value to about $1.21 a share by March, 1965, when the fortunes of the company improved. The appellant argues that it could not have been expected in December, 1960, to purchase shares in mitigation of its losses where the value of these shares had fallen as rapidly as is indicated in the evidence.

[ESTEY J. discussed the significance of the fact that Baud had obtained an injunction restraining the respondent from selling the 125,000 Asamera shares. Baud had argued that it could not be expected to purchase shares when it had obtained the injunction. This argument was rejected because Brook had informed Baud in his pleadings that the shares which were subject to the injunction had been sold. ESTEY J. continued:]

[10] . . . As of [July 1967] the shares were selling at $4.30 to $4.35 and had been rising in value since April, 1965, and at a median price of $4.33 would have cost Baud $541,250. Accordingly, at least by July, 1967, it could not be said that Baud would reasonably be discouraged from replacing the 125,000 shares in the open market because of the low price of an inactive company, nor could it be said that thereafter it could reasonably refrain from prosecuting its claim for damages because of the order enjoining the disposition of the shares by Brook. It remains the case, however, that the market price for such speculative shares as those of an oil-exploration company was subject to wide price fluctuations sometimes inspired by management which itself held, as did Brook, a considerable number of shares.

[11] The learned trial Judge referred to a number of English authorities in support of the proposition that in the case of a loan of shares a plaintiff need not mitigate his losses either by purchasing shares on the market or even by bringing a suit for recovery of damages within a reasonable time. The result under these authorities where the market value of the shares has risen or fallen between breach and trial, has been an award of damages representing the value of the shares at the time of the breach or of the trial at the election of the plaintiff. . . .

[12] A proper analysis of these cases is made difficult by reason of their antiquity, and after serious consideration, I have concluded that they ought not to be followed by this Court. In the first place, they were decided long before modern principles of contractual remedies had been developed. Secondly, they are not in accord with recent decisions of this Court. Thirdly, they ignore the all-important and overriding considerations which have led to the judicial recognition of the desirability and indeed the necessity that a plaintiff mitigate his losses arising on a breach of contract. There is a fourth consideration. This old principle produces an arbitrary, albeit a readily ascertainable result because it lacks the flexibility needed to take into account the infinite range of possible circumstances in which the parties may find themselves at the time of the breach and before a trial can in practice take place. The pace of the market place and the complexities of business have changed radically since this rule or principle was developed in the early 19th century. . . .

[13] The application of the basic principles of remoteness and causality enunciated in the leading cases mentioned earlier points to the conclusion that Baud may have, in the absence of a duty to mitigate, a right of recovery in damages for breach of contract represented by the highest value attained by the shares between the date of breach and the end of trial, that is, $46.50 or $5,812,500. That is the high-water mark attainable under the doctrines which can be gleaned from the older authorities, but as we shall see is not now properly attainable. Such authorities as I have been able to discover suggest that this highest intermediate value is the proper starting point in assessing damages arising on the wrongful detention of another's shares, although the basis therefor is not clearly founded in the concepts of either tort or contract discussed above . . . Before the Courts made a conscious effort to remove the distinctions between recovery in tort and recovery in contract it had been held in the case of a breach of contract that the loss of an opportunity to sell shares at the highest intervening market price was too remote to support recovery. . . .

[14] It is very likely that Brook would have foreseen the probable loss to be suffered by Baud on the nonreturn of its property, particularly bearing in mind his activity as a stock broker and his own dealings in Asamera shares. In the absence of a contrary indication he may be taken to have assumed the risk of its occurrence. Such a loss is not speculative; neither is it so improbable nor so remote as to remove it from the kind of damages recoverable in an action in contract. As to quantum of damages, it is not unreasonable to scale the recovery for the loss suffered by Baud by virtue of its loss of the opportunity to sell the shares [for] a price or prices at least approaching the median point between breach and trial, subject to the varying influences of the many relevant factors to be discussed below.

[15] The application of another basic principle relating to the computation of contract damages, namely, that the plaintiff should be, so far as money may do so, placed in the same position as he would have enjoyed had the breach not occurred,

produces a like result. Had Brook returned the shares when the contract provided, Baud would then have been in a position to dispose of those shares during the period of market appreciation. The range of damages on such a basis would be from $0.29 or, more realistically, $2.00 per share to $46.50 per share. The $2.00 per share is more properly the baseline for computation of value because that is the option price agreed upon between the parties for the period ending at the time the breach of contract occurred. Since it is entirely unrealistic to assume that the peak price was attainable for a block sale of 125,000 Asamera shares, and as it is most unlikely that Baud or anyone else would enjoy such perspicacity, a median range of $20 to $25 for the period from mid-1967 to the end of trial is more appropriate. . . .

[16] This would produce damages of about $3,000,000 before any consideration is given to the required mitigation. . . .

[17] The cases which establish the exceedingly technical rules relating to recovery of damages for the non-return of shares turn on the theory that only where a breach of contract gives rise to an asset in the hands of the plaintiff will the law require him to mitigate his losses by employing that asset in a reasonable manner. Thus if an employer wrongfully dismisses an employee the breach results in the employee obtaining an asset, an ability to work for another employer, or at least the opportunity to offer his services to that end, which he did not enjoy prior to the dismissal. This is no more than a philosophical explanation of the simple test of fairness and reasonableness in establishing the presence and extent of the burden to mitigate in varying circumstances. . . . An analogous situation arises in the breach of a contract for the sale of goods where on the failure of a supplier to deliver goods, the purchaser, because he is relieved of the obligation to pay, has an asset (the financial resource represented by the sums previously committed to the purchase) of which he did not have the free use prior to the breach. This is not the situation of Baud, who might in mitigation of the damage suffered on the non-return of its shares of Asamera, be called upon to lay out substantial assets to replace the shares retained by Brook. . . . There is of course no asset created by the breach of the contract to return shares and if that theory be the law and the creation of an asset be a necessary prerequisite of a duty to mitigate, no such duty arose in the case at hand.

[18] It follows that a contrary result should arise where damages are recoverable for a breach of contract by a vendor on a sale of shares. There the breach would normally allow a buyer the use of his funds formerly committed to the purchase and consequently damages should be calculated on the basis that he ought to have taken steps to avoid his losses by the purchase of shares on the market at the time of the breach. This, in fact, appears to be the law at present. . . .

[19] A different consideration arises where the plaintiff-buyer has prepaid the contract price and has not received delivery. As in the case of non-return of shares, the breach does not give rise to any asset in the hands of the plaintiff since he has already parted with his funds, and on that basis some Courts have held that the injured party need not purchase like goods in the market. . . .

[20] In short, it would appear that the principles of mitigation in respect of contracts for the sale of goods generally may not be applied without reservation to the determination of the duty to mitigate arising in respect of contracts for the sale of shares and, in any case, differ fundamentally from the case of a breach of a contract for the return of shares. It is inappropriate in my view simply to extend the

old principles applied in the detinue and conversion authorities to the non-return of shares with the result that a party whose property has not been returned to him could sit by and await an opportune moment to institute legal proceedings, all the while imposing on a defendant the substantial risk of market fluctuations between breach and trial which might very well drive him into bankruptcy. Damages which could have been avoided by the taking of reasonable steps in all the circumstances should not and, indeed, in the interests of commercial enterprise, must not be thrown onto the shoulders of a defendant by an arbitrary although nearly universal rule for the recovery of damages on breach of the contract for redelivery of property. . . .

[21] It is interesting that in the United States, rules essentially the same as those advanced towards the end of the 19th century in England were jettisoned in 1899 through the adoption of what is now commonly referred to as the "New York rule." This rule has been applied in a variety of situations encompassing both contractual and tortious wrongs, and its justification is not easily disputed. . . .

[22] I have come to the conclusion that the authorities cited from the early 1800s, principally from the Courts of England, which in effect allow recovery of "avoidable losses" ought not to be followed . . . Subject always to the precise circumstances of each case, this will impose on the injured party the obligation to purchase like shares in the market on the date of breach (or knowledge thereof in the plaintiff) or, more frequently, within a period thereafter which is reasonable in all the circumstances. The implementation of this principle must take cognizance of the realities of market operations, including the nature of the shares in question, the strength of the market when called upon to digest large orders to buy or sell, the number of shares qualified for public trading, the recent volatility of the price, the recent volume of trading, the general state of the market at the time, the susceptibility of the price of the shares to the current operation of the corporation and similar considerations.

[23] Some classes of property, including shares, whose value is subject to sudden and constant fluctuations of unpredictable amplitude, and whose purchase is not lightly entered into, call for a modification of the general rule that the value of the property on the "date of breach" be taken as the starting point for the calculation of damages. . . .

[24] There are numerous explanations given by the appellant and indeed not seriously disputed in this Court by the respondent for these protracted proceedings. At one stage, for example, Brook asked Baud some time prior to 1966 to "abstain from following up the lawsuit." Baud, on the other hand, expressed no desire for very practical reasons either to press its suit until the end of 1966, when Asamera finally managed to produce its first oil in Sumatra "and the shares began to slowly get up in value" and, as the appellant put it, "we had to renew the case against him." In my view the law required more of Baud. It placed upon Baud the duty in the sense referred to in *Red Deer College (supra)* to mitigate its losses by acquiring shares in a company known by Baud to be far from financially sound. It might therefore be said that Baud would have hung back from any action (either the purchase of shares or the pressing of its claims in Court) until Asamera struck oil, whether or not Brook had requested it to do so.

[25] One must not become so lost in the technicalities of damages in the law of contract as to lose sight of the practical consideration of the cost of money and of

the reality of the risks to be imposed on a plaintiff by a requirement of complete mitigating measures. In this case the magnitude of the operation, in the range of $800,000 to $1,000,000 if the shares were to cost $7 to $8 each, leads one to conclude that a "reasonable" time for mitigative action must be allowed after the appropriate point of time in law has been isolated.

[26] The appellant bases its contention that it has no obligation to purchase shares in the market in part on the ground that it ought to be allowed to seek specific performance of the contract to return the shares, and while relying on an injunction restraining their disposition it need not have any concern with losses occasioned by its inaction. Counsel for the appellant did not refer this Court to any cases in which the principle of mitigation has interacted and conflicted with recovery by way of specific performance, and such authority as I have been able to discover supports the common sense view that the principle of mitigation should, unless there is a substantial and legitimate interest represented by specific performance, prevail in such a case. . . .

[27] On principle it is clear that a plaintiff may not merely by instituting proceedings in which a request is made for specific performance and/or damages, thereby shield himself and block the Court from taking into account the accumulation of losses which the plaintiff by acting with reasonable promptness in processing his claim could have avoided. Similarly, the bare institution of judicial process in circumstances where a reasonable response by the injured plaintiff would include mitigative replacement of property, will not entitle the plaintiff to the relief which would be achieved by such replacement purchase and prompt prosecution of the claim. Before a plaintiff can rely on a claim to specific performance so as to insulate himself from the consequences of failing to procure alternate property in mitigation of his losses, some fair, real and substantial justification for his claim to performance must be found. Otherwise its effect will be to cast upon the defendant all the risk of aggravated loss by reason of delay in bringing the issue to trial. The appellant in this case contends that it ought to be allowed to rely on its claim for specific performance and the injunction issued in support of it, and thus recover avoidable losses. After serious consideration, I have concluded that this argument must fail.

[28] It is, of course, an eminently reasonable position to take if, as Lord Reid suggests in *White and Carter* [*supra*] in the case of anticipatory breach, there is a substantial and legitimate interest in looking to performance of a contractual obligation. So a plaintiff who has agreed to purchase a particular piece of real estate, or a block of shares which represent control of a company, or has entered into performance of his own obligations, and where to discontinue performance might aggravate his losses, might well have sustained the position that the issuance of a writ for specific performance would hold in abeyance the obligation to avoid or reduce losses by acquisition of replacement property. Yet, even in these cases, the action for performance must be instituted and carried on with due diligence. This is but another application of the ordinary rule of mitigation which insists that the injured party act reasonably in all of the circumstances. Where those circumstances reveal a substantial and legitimate interest in seeking performance as opposed to damages, then a plaintiff will be able to justify his inaction and on failing in his plea for specific performance might then recover losses which in other circumstances might be classified as avoidable and thus unrecoverable; but such is not the case here. . . .

[29] It seems to me that the motives or unjust enrichment of the defendant on breach are generally of no concern in the assessment of contractual damages. . . .

[30] . . . Having regard to all the above-noted special circumstances, the time for purchase in my opinion was the fall of 1966, when Baud was, by its own admission, free from any agreed restraint not to press its claim against Brook. . . . It would be unreasonable to impose on Baud the burden of going into the market and acquiring replacement shares at a time when the litigation of its claims was in a dormant state at Brook's request. Furthermore, Baud acknowledged that by the fall of 1966 the fortunes of Asamera had improved and this had begun to be reflected in the market price of its shares. In short, the appellant is not, in my view, entitled in law to any compensation for the loss of opportunity to sell its shares after that date. Thereafter its loss of this opportunity is of its own making. The theory of such a damage award is to provide the funds needed to replace the shares at the time the law required it to do so in order to avoid an accumulating claim. There should be an allowance of a reasonable time to permit the organization of the finances and the mechanics required for the careful acquisition of 125,000 shares either by a series of relatively small purchases or by negotiated block purchases. This would carry the matter into the fall of 1967. By this time the price had risen to a range of $5 to $6. Making allowance for the upward pressure on the market price which would be generated by the purchase of such a large number of shares on a relatively low-volume stock, the purchase price would surely have exceeded the $6 price reached in mid-1967 without any market intervention by Baud. For this factor, in my best consideration, an allowance of $1 per share should be made. Taking into account the effect of market intervention by Baud, the median price during the period from late 1966 to mid-1967, adjusted accordingly, would be about $6.50, and in my view, the damages should be awarded to Baud on that basis, that is, the total damages for breach of agreement to return the Asamera shares should amount to $812,500. In weighing the magnitude of this award one should not lose sight of the essential fact that Brook at any time right down to trial could, if he had remained in compliance with the injunction of July, 1960, have avoided this result or the risk of this award by delivering from any source 125,000 Asamera shares.

QUESTIONS AND NOTES

1. It is apparent from the Supreme Court judgment in *Asamera Oil* that the trial court in the first action erred in granting an injunction. Why?

2. Estey J. at ¶ 28 cites the judgment of Lord Reid in *White and Carter*. Does Estey J. agree with the decision of Lord Reid?

3. An aspect of the doctrine of mitigation, as revealed in *Asamera Oil*, is that the innocent party may add any expenses that are reasonably incurred to reduce losses to the damage award. The courts have gone so far as to suggest that if a plaintiff can show that expenses were reasonably incurred to reduce losses, they are recoverable even if the plaintiff has not actually managed to reduce the losses arising from the breach of contract: *Banco De Portugal v. Waterlow & Sons Ltd.*, [1932] A.C. 452, 147 L.T. 101 (H.L.). Why have the courts taken this "generous" approach to plaintiffs?

4. In *Hunt v. TD Securities Inc.*, [2003] O.J. No. 3245, 66 O.R. (3d) 481 (C.A.), the Ontario Court of Appeal dealt with a case where a broker sold shares of the plaintiffs without their authorization. One of the issues in the case was the date of assessment of damages. The Court held that the plaintiffs should reasonably have repurchased the

shares within two months of discovering the sale, and that their failure to do so should be taken into account. Gillese J.A. wrote:

> [95] Turning then to a determination of the mitigation period in the instant appeal, the starting point, according to *Asamera*, is that the obligation to purchase like shares arises on the date of breach or knowledge thereof in the injured party. This appropriately reflects the principle that underlies the duty to mitigate; namely, that the injured party may not recover losses that could have been avoided by him or her taking reasonable steps after the wrong.
>
> [96] But the process of determining the mitigation period is not a mechanical one; the period must be a reasonable one, in light of all of the circumstances.
>
> [97] In determining what is reasonable, the case law suggests that the following factors warrant consideration:
>
> 1. ease of purchase of replacement shares — which involves considering the number of shares to be purchased, whether they are readily available in the market, and the time and risk involved in their purchase,
>
> 2. the degree of sophistication and experience of the investor,
>
> 3. the degree of trust reposed in the broker,
>
> 4. whether the broker was obliged to follow the investor's instructions in making transactions, and
>
> 5. whether the relationship between the investor and broker has broken down to the point that the client has lost confidence in the broker.
>
> [98] In my view, application of these factors leads to the conclusion that, in the instant appeal, a brief mitigation period is reasonable.

One argument of the plaintiffs in *Hunt* was that they should not have been expected to mitigate as they lacked the funds to repurchase the shares. The Court accepted that in principle "lack of funds" could be a reason not to mitigate, but in this case their lack of funds arose from their decision to use the proceeds of the sale to make other purchases and hence should not be taken into account. In *Asamera* the Supreme Court indicated that a commercial party would be expected to use reasonable efforts to borrow funds to mitigate.

INTEREST AND THE DATE FOR ASSESSING DAMAGES

If an award of damages is to fully compensate a plaintiff for the loss arising from the breach of a contract, interest must be taken into account. Until quite recently, interest was not awarded on any amounts found due by the court until judgment. (Interest payable under, for example, a loan agreement would, of course, run from the date of breach to final payment, in accordance with the contract.)

At common law, interest was allowed from the date of judgment on the amount of a judgment and was set at five per cent. It is obvious that a plaintiff who, after litigation, is paid an amount that is based on the state of affairs at the date of breach will be undercompensated if no account is taken of the time value of money. The rules regarding both pre- and post-judgment interest were changed by legislation, much of it enacted in the 1970s and 1980s. Sections 128-130 of the Ontario *Courts of Justice Act*, R.S.O. 1990, c. C.43 provide that a plaintiff is, subject to the court's discretion, entitled to pre-judgment interest from the date that the cause of action arose and this date will usually be the date of the breach of the contract; post-judgment interest will run from the date of judgment. The interest is presumptively set by reference to the bank rate, but as discussed in the next case, the court has a discretion to award a higher or lower rate in either situation. The next decision deals with the interpretation of the provisions of the Ontario *Courts of Justice Act* dealing with the award of interest, and more generally with questions related to the awarding of interest.

BANK OF AMERICA CANADA v. MUTUAL TRUST CO.

[2002] S.C.J. No. 44, [2002] 2 S.C.R. 601, 211 D.L.R. (4th) 385

(S.C.C., McLachlin C.J.C. and L'Heureux-Dubé, Gonthier, Iacobucci, Major, Bastarache, Binnie, Arbour and LeBel JJ.)

[This case arose out of a financing and construction transaction for a condominium project, involving a number of parties. Under the terms of the agreement, the appellant (plaintiff) was to provide financing on a loan that required compound interest to be paid. After the collapse of the real estate market, litigation arose. At trial, the judge found that the respondent had liability for the loan, and awarded the amount outstanding plus pre-judgment and post-judgment compound interest. The Ontario Court of Appeal upheld the trial decision on the issue of liability, but held that only simple interest could be awarded under s. 128 of the *Courts of Justice Act*. The appellant lender appealed to the Supreme Court on the question of whether compound interest could be awarded; by the time that the case was argued in the Supreme Court, the difference between simple and compound interest was more than $5 million. The Supreme Court reversed the Court of Appeal decision, holding that pre- and post-judgment compound interest could be awarded.]

MAJOR J. (for the Court): —

. . .

VI. *Analysis*

A. *Jurisdiction*

(1) *The Time-Value of Money*

[21] The value of money decreases with the passage of time. A dollar today is worth more than the same dollar tomorrow. Three factors account for the depreciation of the value of money: (i) opportunity cost (ii) risk, and (iii) inflation.

[22] The first factor, opportunity cost, reflects the uses of the dollar which are foregone while waiting for it. The value of the dollar is reduced because the opportunity to use it is absent. The second factor, risk, reflects the uncertainty inherent in delaying possession. Possession of a dollar today is certain but the expectation of the same dollar in the future involves uncertainty. Perhaps the future dollar will never be paid. The third factor, inflation, reflects the fluctuation in price levels. With inflation, a dollar will not buy as much goods or services tomorrow as it does today (G. H. Sorter, M. J. Ingberman and H. M. Maximon, *Financial Accounting: An Events and Cash Flow Approach* (1990), at p. 14). The time-value of money is common knowledge and is one of the cornerstones of all banking and financial systems.

[23] Simple interest and compound interest each measure the time value of the initial sum of money, the principal. The difference is that compound interest reflects the time-value component to interest payments while simple interest does not. Interest owed today but paid in the future will have decreased in value in the interim just as the dollar example described in paras. 21-22. Compound interest compensates a lender for the decrease in value of all money which is due but as yet unpaid because unpaid interest is treated as unpaid principal.

[24] Simple interest makes an artificial distinction between money owed as principal and money owed as interest. Compound interest treats a dollar as a dollar and is therefore a more precise measure of the value of possessing money for a period of time. Compound interest is the norm in the banking and financial systems in Canada and the western world and is the standard practice of both the appellant and respondent.

(2) *Contract Damages*

[25] Contract damages are determined in one of two ways. Expectation damages, the usual measure of contract damages, focus on the value which the plaintiff would have received if the contract had been performed. Restitution damages, which are infrequently employed, focus on the advantage gained by the defendant as a result of his or her breach of contract.

(a) *Expectation Damages*

[26] Generally, courts employ expectation damages where, if breach is proved, the plaintiff will be entitled to the value of the promised performance (S. M. Waddams, *The Law of Damages* (3rd ed. 1997), at p. 267).

. . .

[28] Since the value of money decreases with the passage of time, an award, at trial, to a plaintiff of the dollar amount he or she expected to receive had the contract been performed on time would not put the plaintiff in the same position as if the contract had been performed. The party would receive less than his or her expectation damages because of the (i) opportunity cost, (ii) risk and (iii) inflation. The plaintiff would fail to receive the benefit of the bargain.

[29] To award the plaintiff damages equal to the value of the contract as if it had been performed on time, the court must first determine the dollar value of the promise to the plaintiff *at the time the obligation was to have been performed,* and then apply the appropriate interest rate and method of calculation to account for the time during which the plaintiff was not paid what was rightfully due.

. . .

[32] ... where a sum of money is required to be paid as of a certain date, the benefit to the defendant of the money during the interval between when the money is owed and when the money is paid is, all other things being equal, exactly the same as the detriment to the plaintiff of not having that money during the same interval. This is not a Pareto optimal outcome, but, rather, a zero-sum outcome. The defendant's gain is the plaintiff's loss, the value of which, but for the defendant's breach, would have belonged to the plaintiff.

[33] To prevent defendants from exploiting the time-value of money to their advantage, by delaying payment of damages so as to capitalize on the time-value of money in the interim, courts must be able to award damages which include an interest component that returns the value acquired by a defendant between breach and payment to the plaintiff.

(3) *Judgment Interest in Canada*

[34] The history of interest at law was identified in *Costello v. Calgary (City)* (1997), 152 D.L.R. (4th) 453 (Alta. C.A.), by Picard J.A., at pp. 492-94:

> The history of interest at law is long and miserly. Traditionally, pre-judgment interest generally was denied because it was thought usurious and the case against compound interest was considered particularly strong because of the (supposed) difficulty of calculation: M.A. Waldron, *The Law of Interest in Canada* (Scarborough, Ont.: Carswell, 1992) at pp. 1-10, 142. In time, at least the former rationale was abandoned and the harshness of the law's position was recognized. The legislative response, however, initially was limited. Section 28 of the *Civil Procedure Act, 1833* (U.K.), 3 & 4 Will. 4, c. 42 (better known as Lord Tenterden's Act), merely provided for the availability of interest upon "Debts or Sums certain". ...

> Of course, that is not to say that non-statutory, pre-judgment interest was entirely foreign to the common law. Exceptions have always existed. Most obviously, interest has long been granted when provided for by agreement of the parties or when implied by usage of trade: *Page v. Newman* (1829), 9 B. & C. 378, 109 E.R. 140.

[35] Judgment interest in Canada has had statutory authorization since 1837 ... Today in Ontario, each of pre-judgment and post-judgment interest is governed by ss. 128 to 130 [*Courts of Justice Act*].

(4) *Interest as Compensation*

[36] In *The Law of Interest in Canada* (1992), at pp. 127-28, M. A. Waldron explained that the initial theory underpinning an award of judgment interest was that the defendant's conduct was such that he or she deserved additional punishment. The modern theory is that judgment interest is more appropriately used to compensate rather than punish. At pp. 127-28, she wrote:

> Compensation is one of the chief aims of the law of damages, but a plaintiff who is successful in his action and is awarded a sum for damages assessed perhaps years before but now payable in less valuable dollars finds it quite obvious that he has been short-changed. Equally obviously, payment of interest on his damage award from some relevant date is one way of redressing this problem.

> The overwhelming opinion today of Law Reform Commissions and the academic community is that interest on a claim prior to judgment is properly part of the compensatory process. [Citations omitted.]

[37] After acknowledging that historically compound interest was not available at common law, Waddams [*The Law of Damages*, 1997], at p. 437, concludes that an award of compound interest should be available to courts so as to allow them to award full compensation to a plaintiff.

> [T]here seems in principle no reason why compound interest should not be awarded. Had prompt recompense been made at the date of the wrong the plaintiff would have had a capital sum to invest; the plaintiff would have received interest on it at regular intervals and would have invested those sums also. By the same token the defendant will have had the benefit of compound interest.

[38] Although not historically available, compound interest is well suited to compensate a plaintiff for the interval between when damages initially arise and when they are finally paid.

(5) *Sections 128 to 130 of the Courts of Justice Act*

[39] Sections 128 to 130 *CJA* entitle a person with an award for damages to interest on the damages for the period between the date that the cause of action arose and the judgment ("pre-judgment interest") as well as for the period between the judgment and the time when payment is made in full ("post-judgment interest"). The legislation recognizes the unfairness of awarding a plaintiff damages, *at trial*, in the amount to which he or she was entitled as of the date that the cause of action arose, and no more for the period in between which is frequently years. Sections 128 and 129 *CJA*, therefore, contain interest rates and methods of calculation to serve for pre-judgment and post-judgment interest, respectively, in those cases for which there is no evidence of a more appropriate interest rate and/or method of calculation.

[40] Sections 128(4)(g), 129(5) and 130 CJA, each of which allows the judge to award interest other than as specifically set out in ss. 128 and 129, clearly indicate that the rates and calculation methods of interest provided in ss. 128 and 129 are applicable in the absence of more appropriate rates and methods of calculation. Section 130 allows a court, where it considers it just, to vary the interest rate or the time for which interest may be awarded. Sections 128(4)(g) and 129(5) allow a court to award pre-judgment and post-judgment interest, respectively, where interest is payable by another right.

(6) *Interest Payable by Another Right*

[41] Equity has been recognized as one right by which interest may be awarded other than as specifically stated in ss. 128 and 129 *CJA*, including an award of compound interest. ... It is of some interest that in *Air Canada v. Ontario (Liquor Control Board)*, [1997] 2 S.C.R. 581, at para. 85, ... Iacobucci J. emphasized that in equity the awarding of compound interest is a discretionary matter. Simple breach of contract does not require moral sanction and is usually governed by common law, not equity.

[42] In this case, the Court of Appeal recognized that the court has the jurisdiction to award compound interest under the court's general equitable jurisdiction and that an award of compound interest grounded in equity is, in the language of ss. 128(4)(g) and 129(5) "payable by a right other than under this section". The Court of Appeal found that equity did not apply and therefore the court had no jurisdiction to award compound interest. Implicit in their holding was that the only "right other than under this section" was the right to receive compound interest in equity. This is not so, as a common law right of interest can be an "other right".

[43] The common law right in contract law to be awarded expectation damages is another such other right. As noted in *Westdeutsche Landesbank Girozentrale v. Islington London Borough Council*, [1996] 2 All E.R. 961 (H.L.), at p. 969, the power to award compound interest was not traditionally available at common law, although it is now. This is so because, as our jurisprudence demonstrates, the common law has been able to grow and adapt to changing conditions. In *Friedmann Equity Developments Inc. v. Final Note Ltd.*, [2000] 1 S.C.R. 842, 2000

SCC 34, at para. 42, this Court outlined the following conditions where the rules of common law may be changed if necessary:

(1) to keep the common law in step with the evolution of society,

(2) to clarify a legal principle, or

(3) to resolve an inconsistency.

It warned that the changes should be incremental, and their consequences capable of assessment.

[44] Compound interest is no longer commonly thought to be, in the language quoted in *Costello*, *supra*, at pp. 492-93, usurious or to involve prohibitively complex calculations. Compound interest is now commonplace. Mortgages are calculated using compound interest, as are most other loans, including such worthy endeavours as student loans. The growth of a company or a country's gross domestic product over a period of years is often stated in terms of an annually compounded rate. The bank rate, which garners much attention as an indicator of the health and direction of the economy, is a compound interest rate. It is for reasons such as these that the common law now incorporates the economic reality of compound interest. The restrictions of the past should not be used today to separate the legal system from the world at large.

[45] If the court was unable to award compound interest on the breach of a loan which itself bore compound interest, it would be unable to adequately award the plaintiff the value he or she would have received had the contract been performed. To keep the common law current with the evolution of society and to resolve the inconsistency between awarding expectation damages and the courts' past unwillingness to award compound interest, that unwillingness should be discarded in cases requiring that remedy for the plaintiff to realize the benefit of his or her contract.

[46] A contrary rule would lead to inequity and provide incentives to breach contracts. If courts were restricted to simple interest in assessing damages for breach of contract, an apparent abuse could occur in the following way. Money lent at compound interest would accrue compound interest until there was a breach of contract by the borrower. The lender would then sue and only be entitled to simple interest on the judgment. This would encourage borrowers not to repay loans. Contract law is not the enemy of parties to an agreement but, rather, their servant. It should not frustrate their mutually agreed intentions but, instead, absent overriding policy concerns, should permit those parties to obtain the benefit of their intended agreement.

[47] I find support for these conclusions in *Hadley v. Baxendale* (1854), 9 Ex. 341, 156 E.R. 145. In *Hadley* the Court of Exchequer was confronted with the issue of the proper measure of damages for a breach of contract. ...

[48] The court [in *Hadley*] held that the unreasonable delay of delivery of the shaft to the engineer would not necessarily lead to the cessation of operations of the mill. The plaintiffs might have had a substitute shaft which could have been used in the interim. The court found for the defendants, holding that the stoppage of milling did not naturally arise from the delay in delivery nor was this result and the concomitant cost to the plaintiff in the contemplation of both parties at the time they made the contract.

[49] With respect to the failure to repay the loan in this appeal when due, it cannot be said that the cost of such delay was not in the contemplation of both parties at the time they made the contract, particularly as both parties were in the business of lending. A loan agreement with a specified interest rate is an agreement between parties on the cost of borrowing money over a period of time. Absent exceptional circumstances, the interest rate which had governed the loan prior to breach would be the appropriate rate to govern the post-breach loan. The application of a lower interest rate would be unjust to the lender.

[50] This analysis applies equally to pre-judgment interest and post-judgment interest. Pre-judgment interest is necessary to compensate a plaintiff for the period from when the money was initially owed until the date of the judgment. Contract law principles may require such interest to be compounded so as to award the plaintiff the benefit of the bargain. Damage awards, however, are not necessarily paid at the date judgment is rendered. Contract law entitles the plaintiff to the full value of the benefit of the bargain at the time payment is finally made. Where the parties have earlier agreed on a compound rate of interest, or there are circumstances warranting it, it seems fair that a court have the power to award compound post-judgment interest as damages to enable the plaintiff to be fully compensated when the award is finally paid.

[51] Additionally, it would be illogical and unfair to the plaintiff to change to a simple rate of interest charged upon the judgment at the post-judgment phase. This would delay but not eliminate the period when the defendant gains a benefit that belongs to the plaintiff by not paying compound interest. It would encourage the defendant to delay paying the judgment award. As noted above, equity is another jurisdiction under which compound interest may be ordered in accordance with s. 129(5) *CJA*. In light of the illogical and inequitable result that would be occasioned by refusing to extend an award of compound interest to the post-judgment phase, in addition to common law remedies, it may be appropriate to extend that award on equitable grounds where it has been already determined that compound interest was part of the damages for breach in the pre-judgment phase.

[52] The court's common law power to award damages flows from the application of contract law. In addition, ss. 128(4)(g) and 129(5) *CJA*, provide statutory authority to award compound pre-judgment and post-judgment interest according to this common law power. The court also has an equitable power to award compound interest, as has traditionally been done in cases of, *inter alia*, wrongful retention of funds and s. 129(5) *CJA* provides statutory authority to award compound post-judgment interest according to this equitable power.

B. *Was the Court Below Correct to Award Compound Interest?*

[53] At trial, Farley J. found that the respondent had breached the ... [agreement, which had terms that] ... incorporated by reference [documents that provided for] the compound interest rate.

[54] The respondent submitted that the appellant had not pleaded damages at compound interest, this was raised at the trial where the trial judge determined that there was no prejudice to the respondent by raising that issue as the appellant at the time had the ability if requested by the respondent to call evidence on the question of what the interest component of the damages should be. The manner in which a trial should proceed is properly left to the discretion of the trial judge, and, absent prejudice or error, an appellate court should not lightly interfere.

[55] An award of compound pre- and post-judgment interest will generally be limited to breach of contract cases where there is evidence that the parties agreed, knew, or should have known, that the money which is the subject of the dispute would bear compound interest as damages. It may be awarded as consequential damages in other cases but there would be the usual requirement of proving that damage component.

. . .

[60] If required to pay damages at only simple interest, the respondent would have earned compound interest on the appellant's money while paying only simple interest. By breaching the contract, the respondent would have conferred on itself a profit which the contract envisaged for the appellant.

[61] This is not a case of efficient breach. The respondent's gains have come at the appellant's expense. An award of compound interest will prevent the respondent from profiting by its breach at the expense of the appellant. The award of the trial judge yields a satisfactory result with respect to both expectation damages and restitution damages.

QUESTION

Did the Supreme Court give a good indication of when the courts should award pre- or post-judgment compound interest?

One of the significant features of the judgment in *Asamera Oil* is the discretion that the Supreme Court has given trial judges to determine the date on which damages will be assessed, reversing the traditional approach that damages are to be assessed at the date of breach. Since Brook's obligation to return the shares was held to have been breached on 31 December 1960, the traditional view would have been that damages should have been measured by the value of the shares on that date. (The lower courts had accepted this traditional rule but had determined that, because the parties had agreed in their contract on a minimum value of $2 per share, this was the appropriate value, and not $0.29 per share, the actual value on 31 December 1960.)

While the general rule is still that damages are assessed as of the date of breach, some cases have also recognized a judicial discretion to chose another date.

The traditional breach-date rule for the assessment of damages was not followed in *Wroth v. Tyler*, [1973] 1 All E.R. 897 (Ch. D., Megarry J.). The facts of that case are a good illustration of the potential unfairness of the breach-date rule and of the danger of an unthinking replacement of it by the judgment-date rule. Tyler agreed in May 1971 to sell the house occupied by himself and his wife to the Wroths for £6,000. According to the law of England at that time (and similar laws in effect in Canada today), an agreement to sell a family home might be valid as a contract if entered into by the owner of the home, in this case Mr. Tyler alone. However, the actual conveyance of title (and the right of the purchasers to obtain possession) could only be completed with the consent of both spouses or by a court order dispensing with consent, obtained in the context of matrimonial proceedings. When the agreement was signed by Mr. Tyler, the Tylers' marriage was under stress; he signed the agreement with the Wroths without his wife's approval, and she then refused to agree to the conveyance. (Her refusal may have been a strategic move to avoid the sale, the sale price being far less than the market price at the date of closing: if so, the strategy was badly misguided.)

The Wroths brought an action for breach of contract against Mr. Tyler, seeking specific performance or damages. Land values were increasing dramatically; at the date scheduled for closing, October 1971, the price of the house had risen to £7,500. By the date of trial, January 1973, the property was worth £11,500. Megarry J. denied the plaintiffs' claim for specific performance. (Mr. Tyler could not force his wife to consent, and so a specific performance order would only put Mr. Tyler in contempt of court with no guarantee that Mrs. Tyler would be moved by his plight to agree to the conveyance. Mr. Tyler would have had to bring a matrimonial action against his wife to dispense with her consent but that action might not have been successful.) Damages were, however, assessed at £5,500 — the difference between the contract price and the market price at the date of trial.

The rate of increase in the value of the land in England during the period between May 1971 and January 1973 was high — about 40 per cent per annum. Further, the Wroths lacked the resources at the date of breach to buy another equivalent house; their finances were stretched in making the original offer of £6,000. Breach-date damages (even with an adjustment for interest) would be inadequate in the sense that, at the date of the trial, the plaintiff could not, with such damages, go out and buy an equivalent house. Judgment-date damages were a fairer alternative. The court in effect accepted that there was a "real and legitimate" reason not to expect the Wroths to mitigate their damages — they lacked the resources to do so. (Mr. Tyler may have added to his problems by not promptly returning the Wroths' deposit when he first encountered problems in completing the transaction.)

The trial (or judgment) date rule as an alternative to the breach date rule for the assessment of damage is now well established. See *Johnson v. Agnew*, [1980] A.C. 367, [1979] 1 All E.R. 883 (H.L.); *Metropolitan Trust Co. of Canada v. Pressure Concrete Services Ltd.*, [1973] 3 O.R. 629, 37 D.L.R. (3d) 649 (H.C.J.) affirmed (1975), 9 O.R. (2d) 375, 60 D.L.R. (3d) 431 (C.A.).

A judgment for damages assessed as of the date of trial is sometimes referred as an award of "equitable damages", since it is a monetary award that allows the plaintiff to go into the market after the judgment to buy land of equivalent value — the monetary equivalent to specific performance. Note, however, that the court in *Wroth* made its award purely on the basis of an economic measure of the plaintiffs' loss, and made no effort to compensate for any aesthetic or emotional (or non-economic) value that they might have had in the particular house that was the subject of the contract.

If the date for the calculation of damages depends on the election of the purchaser, the vendor faces very serious risks, for the purchaser may be able to speculate on a gain in value, entirely at the vendor's risk. The inherent unfairness in this result is limited by the ruling of Sopinka J. in *Semelhago v. Paramadevan* that a purchaser of land is not, as a matter of course, entitled to specific performance unless the land is unique, but that argument postpones important questions to the trial. Neither purchaser nor vendor can know with certainty what risks each faces in the period between breach and trial. Uncertainty of this type may encourage litigation because each party has less incentive to be reasonable when being unreasonable brings a chance of making a large gain.

There are many complex issues that have to be considered before the difficulties of interest rates, damages, specific performance and other related problems are fully solved. Under the historical rules, the courts applied a date-of-breach approach to damage assessment and were unable to award pre-judgment interest;

these rules treated plaintiffs unfairly. In the 1970s and 1980s this unfairness was treated from two directions: first, the courts were given power to award pre-judgment interest; second, the breach-date rule was relaxed. Now, however, a defendant runs the risk of being unfairly treated if the plaintiff gets the benefit of both rules, or if the notion of mitigation or avoidable harms is not rigorously applied. In either of these cases the plaintiff is better off than he would have been had the contract been performed. Such a result appears to be contrary to the principles on which damages are awarded. For a critical discussion of some of the issues raised here, see Donald Clark, "'Will that be Performance . . . or Cash?': *Semelhago v. Paramadevan* and the Notion of Equivalence" (1999), 37 *Alta. L. Rev.* 589-619.

REVIEW PROBLEMS

1. Canner carries on the business of canning tomatoes. The season for tomatoes lasts about six weeks and during this time enough tomatoes must be harvested and delivered to Canner to keep Canner's plant operating at capacity. To ensure adequate supplies of tomatoes, Canner makes agreements with local farmers under which each farmer agrees to sell his entire crop of tomatoes to Canner at a fixed price. It is never clear at the time that these agreements are made whether the fixed price for the tomatoes will be higher or lower than the market price at the date of delivery. At the time when the fixed price is less than the market price, Farmer refuses to sell to Canner and instead sells to Wholesaler for the market price. Canner sues for specific performance and an injunction. What result?

2. Frank is an expert in tying fancy knots in string, though he works as a used-car salesman. He feels that if he could only get some attention from the world for his hobby he could make a fortune. His hobby is finally noticed by Susan, a CBC producer. She offers him a 15-minute TV show during which time he can demonstrate his skill. Frank eagerly accepts the offer. One week before the show is to be taped Susan calls to say that the show has been cancelled. She refuses to give any reasons. Frank is absolutely crushed by this, and foresees a lifetime spent selling broken-down used cars.

    Frank has started an action against the CBC claiming specific performance of the contract and damages for breach in the alternative. You have been asked to draft the arguments that each side might use in the case.

    You have found out the following additional facts: two weeks before the show, Frank took three days off work to practise his skill. This cost him $200 in lost wages and commission. He also bought a $500 suit for the occasion. Frank would have appeared on a weekly program devoted to the exhibition of novel or unusual artistic skill that has a fairly large audience.

3. Garth booked a holiday with "Sea-Breeze" Holidays for a two-week coach tour of Vancouver Island. On his first night in his hotel, he encountered a large and very lively spider in his bed. This so unnerved him that he does not feel that he can continue his holiday. He meets you next morning for breakfast and asks you what he should do. What advice would you give him? On the assumption that you advise him that he may claim against "Sea-Breeze", draft a letter from "Sea-Breeze" in response to his claim. Consider carefully the arguments that you should make.

4. You act for a client that makes special materials handling equipment. The equipment is manufactured at your client's plant and then taken for assembly to the customer's premises. A customer has just informed your client that it does not want some equipment that it had ordered. The customer has paid 20 per cent of the $1,250,000 purchase price and about 15 per cent of the equipment has been manufactured. Your client would like to keep working on the equipment and be able to recover from the customer as much of the price as possible. What advice do you give your client? What do you recommend that it do now?

CHAPTER TWO

THE KINDS OF PROMISES
THE LAW WILL ENFORCE

INTRODUCTION

Chapter 1 considered what it means to say that a promise is legally enforceable, discussing the remedies that the law provides for the promisor's failure to do what it had promised to do. No legal system, however, will enforce all promises. This chapter focuses on determining which promises the law will enforce.

Some of the law's concerns about the enforcement of promises are almost intuitively obvious. If you had promised to meet a friend for lunch, or to pick up your spouse's dry-cleaning, you would be surprised if breach of these promises led to legal liability. Your intuition is correct in that no one ever sues for breach of a promise like the ones that have just been mentioned — and not just because damages would be limited. The fact that people would be surprised by enforcement may be in itself a good reason why such promises should not be enforced. Conversely, if the person who has made a promise that he or she has not kept would *not* be surprised by enforcement, that fact by itself may go a long way to justify enforcement. There is a kind of circular argument. What promises does the law enforce? The law enforces promises that people expect to be enforced. Why do people expect a particular kind of promise to be enforced? Because those are the ones the courts have always enforced.

The importance of this argument is not that it illustrates a serious limitation in the reasons that the law does or does not enforce some promises, but that it emphasizes a far more important point: one cannot consider what promises to enforce without taking into account people's common expectations. In other words, we should not ask the question, "What promises should the law enforce?" and answer it by having regard only to some legal concept of contracting or to some theory of promise-keeping. We should consider the question in the context of social and economic relations that presently exist. It must, however, be recognized that too often courts dealing with questions of enforceability focus exclusively on fairly narrow doctrinal issues, and not on the underlying rationales that explain why the doctrines developed.

Chapter 1, and indeed much of this book, focuses on promises made in the context of commercial or economic exchanges. The paradigmatic legal contract is the discrete commercial transaction, such as the promise to sell goods in exchange for the promise to pay for them. There are, however, many important promises that are not strictly part of economic exchange transactions. Some of the promises that are not made in the context of economic exchange are familial or social. There are also promises made in a commercial setting that do not involve an exchange, but

that may be made to obtain goodwill. As we move away from the economic exchange, the law struggles to decide whether to enforce a promise.

One can identify four factors that indicate the existence of strong pressures to
enforce a promise:

1. the promise arises out of a commercial exchange;

2. one party has performed its obligation and is asking for the court's support
   either to provide compensation for the other's failure to perform or to make
   the other perform its obligation;

3. there is strong evidence that the promise was made with deliberation; or

4. one party has relied on an undertaking given by the other in circumstances
   where this reliance requires protection.

The first factor — commercial exchange — is by far the most important, and
also conceptually the easiest to deal with. The second and third concerns may offer
a party a way to enforce a promise even when it does not arise in a commercial
setting, or when, as we shall see, there are particular problems in enforcement. The
fourth factor — protection of reliance — is of increasing importance and is becoming a dominant basis for enforcement in some situations. As we shall see, this
development has important consequences for the law of contract.

In many situations there may be more than one factor suggesting that the contract should be enforced. An action for the repayment of a commercial loan, for
example, will usually offer at least three reasons for enforcement. Ideas of reliance
and restitution are reasons for the enforcement of a promise, as they were considered in the previous chapter as a way of measuring the loss suffered by the promisee on the other's breach. If a promise does not fit any one of these situations
(or as it moves away from one of these situations), the pressure to enforce it is
attenuated.

The cases in this chapter reflect some perennial legal problems. The legal rules
that developed to deal with enforceability questions had some economic and social
logic. However, the application of some of the rules may, today, seem unfair or
inappropriate. To what extent should the courts follow the rules, and to what extent should they change the rules? To what extent should the courts consider underlying social and economic concerns? If we are forced to change the basis for
enforcement in order to respond to some strong pressure to enforce, what happens
if we pursue the logical consequences of a new basis for enforcement and discover, for example, that setting limits on the recovery of damages is no longer so
easily justifiable? How should the law respond to changing technology? Should
rules that developed about the enforceability of promises in an age when few people could read and it took months for a letter to travel from England to Canada
apply in the era of the Internet?

The cases illustrate that judges tend to want to give a remedy simply because it
seems "just" to do so on the facts of a particular case. A general lesson is that one
has to be aware of the importance of such pressures, and that the effort to respond
to them may result in ignoring some theory of contract enforcement. The cases in
this chapter introduce a problem that will be with you throughout your legal studies. How should the courts respond if the legal theory used to determine what contracts to enforce appears to prevent reaching results that are clearly desirable from
a moral, social or economic perspective?

Another issue raised in these cases is the problem caused by the fact that there may be a good reason not to enforce a particular contract. One party has behaved badly, and it may be unfair to enforce the contract at its request. Historically the courts were reluctant to address directly this type of concern and sometimes stretched the rules to achieve the desired result. The law cannot develop properly if the reasons why a contract should not be enforced are not directly addressed. And, of course, when the courts do so, they have a useful device for limiting the logical consequences of any theory of enforcement.

The general picture that emerges in regard to enforceability questions is similar to that which developed in the first chapter: the law is moving away from being governed by strict legal rules developed to deal with relatively simple discrete exchange transactions to achieve results that accord with modern reality and that seem just. It should come as no surprise that the law evolves, the process is uneven and there are some hard cases where the correct thing to do is not clear.

In this chapter, we will study the principal doctrinal requirements for the enforcement of contracts:

1. *Writing*: Legislation such as the *Statute of Frauds* requires that some kinds of contracts be in writing to be enforceable. The requirement of writing is intended to ensure deliberation, as well as to provide clear evidence of the terms of the contract. The statutory requirement for writing only applies to a limited range of contracts, such as contracts for the sale of land and guarantees for the debt of another.

2. *Consideration or the Equivalent*: The principal scope for the law of contracts is the commercial exchange. This fact has led to the rule that the person seeking to enforce a promise must generally have given value to the other party, *i.e.* that there must have been an exchange of "commercial equivalents". This requirement that value must have been given is expressed in the rule that a promise, to be enforceable, must be "bought" with "consideration": courts will not ordinarily enforce gift promises. The courts do not, however, require consideration if the promise is made under seal or if there has been substantial reliance on the promise.

3. *Intention to Create a Legal Relation*: A promise will only be enforced if the court is satisfied that the person who made the promise had a reasonable expectation that it could be enforced in a court of law. The law does not, for example, directly enforce the promises exchanged by those who are getting married, such as: "With all my worldly goods I thee endow." Nor will the law enforce the promise of a politician in order to get elected, even if it is made clearly and in writing, and was intended to be acted upon by voters. (See, *e.g.*, *Canadian Taxpayers Federation v. Ontario (Minister of Finance)*; [2004] O.J. No. 5239, 73 O.R. (3d) 621 (S.C.J.), a case briefly examined further below).

4. *Privity of Contract*: A person must be a party to a contract to have the benefit of it. Third parties generally cannot enforce contracts.

The following extract from an article by Lon Fuller is an attempt to offer a basis for understanding what is important in the decision to enforce a contract. Most of the specific legal rules that he mentions will be examined in this chapter. Like much that is written on the law, no concession is made to the special problems of those who are not familiar with the law. The extract is offered as an important but challenging introduction. It may also be useful to reread it as a summary and conclusion to the chapter.

FULLER, "CONSIDERATION AND FORM"

(1941), 41 *Colum. L. Rev.* 799

[Most footnotes have been omitted.]

Introduction

[1]   What is attempted in this article is an inquiry into the rationale of legal formalities, and an examination of the common-law doctrine of consideration in terms of its underlying policies. That such an investigation will reveal a significant relationship between consideration and form is a proposition not here suggested for the first time; indeed the question has been raised (and sometimes answered affirmatively) whether consideration cannot in the end be reduced entirely to terms of form.

[2]   That consideration may have both a "formal" and a "substantive" aspect is apparent when we reflect on the reasons which have been advanced why promises without consideration are not enforced. It has been said that consideration is for the "sake of evidence" and is intended to remove the hazards of mistaken or perjured testimony which would attend the enforcement of promises for which nothing is given in exchange. Again, it is said that enforcement is denied gratuitous promises because such promises are often made impulsively and without proper deliberation. In both these cases the objection relates, not to the content and effect of the promise, but to the manner in which it is made. Objections of this sort, which touch the form rather than the content of the agreement, will be removed if the making of the promise is attended by some formality or ceremony, as by being under seal. On the other hand, it has been said that the enforcement of gratuitous promises is not an object of sufficient importance to our social and economic order to justify the expenditure of the time and energy necessary to accomplish it. Here the objection is one of "substance" since it touches the significance of the promise made and not merely the circumstances surrounding the making of it.

[3]   The task proposed in this article is that of disentangling the "formal" and "substantive" elements in the doctrine of consideration. Since the policies underlying the doctrine are generally left unexamined in the decisions and doctrinal discussions, it will be necessary to postpone taking up the common-law requirement itself until we have examined in general terms the formal and substantive bases of contract liability.

The Functions Performed by Legal Formalities

[4]   *The Evidentiary Function*: The most obvious function of a legal formality is, to use Austin's words, that of "providing evidence of the existence and purport of the contract, in case of controversy." The need for evidentiary security may be satisfied in a variety of ways: by requiring a writing, or attestation, or the certification of a notary. It may even be satisfied, to some extent, by such a device as the Roman *stipulatio* which compelled an oral spelling out of the promise in a manner

sufficiently ceremonious to impress its terms on participants and possible by-standers.

[5] *The Cautionary Function*: A formality may also perform a cautionary or deterrent function by acting as a check against inconsiderate action. The seal in its original form fulfilled this purpose remarkably well. The affixing and impressing of a wax wafer — symbol in the popular mind of legalism and weightiness — was an excellent device for inducing the circumspective frame of mind appropriate in one pledging his future. To a less extent any requirement of a writing, of course, serves the same purpose, as do requirements of attestation, notarization, etc.

[6] *The Channelling Function*: Though most discussions of the purposes served by formalities go no further than the analysis just presented, this analysis stops short of recognizing one of the most important functions of form. That a legal formality may perform a function not yet described can be shown by the seal. The seal not only insures a satisfactory memorial of the promise and induces deliberation in the making of it. It serves also to mark or signalize the enforceable promise; it furnishes a simple and external test of enforceability. This function of form Ihering described as the "facilitation of judicial diagnosis," and he employed the analogy of coinage in explaining it.

> Form is for a legal transaction what the stamp is for a coin. Just as the stamp of the coin relieves us from the necessity of testing the metallic content and weight — in short, the value of the coin (a test which we could not avoid if uncoined metal were offered to us in payment), in the same way legal formalities relieve the judge of an inquiry *whether* a legal transaction was intended, and — in case different forms are fixed for different legal transactions — *which* was intended.[1]

[7] In this passage it is apparent that Ihering has placed an undue emphasis on the utility of form for the judge, to the neglect of its significance for those transacting business out of court. If we look at the matter purely from the standpoint of the convenience of the judge, there is nothing to distinguish the forms used in legal transactions from the "formal" element which to some degree permeates all legal thinking. Even in the field of criminal law "judicial diagnosis" is "facilitated" by formal definitions, presumptions, and artificial constructions of fact. The thing which characterizes the law of contracts and conveyances is that in this field forms are deliberately used, and are intended to be so used, by the parties whose acts are to be judged by the law. To the business man who wishes to make his own or another's promise binding, the seal was at common law available as a device for the accomplishment of his objective. In this aspect form offers a legal framework into which the party may fit his actions, or, to change the figure, it offers channels for the legally effective expression of intention. It is with this aspect of form in mind that I have described the third function of legal formalities as the "channelling function."

[8] In seeking to understand this channelling function of form, perhaps the most useful analogy is that of language, which illustrates both the advantages and dangers of form in the aspect we are now considering. One who wishes to communicate his thoughts to others must force the raw material of meaning into defined and

---

[1] *Geist Des Romischen Rechts* (8th ed. 1923) 494. In all legal systems the effort is to find definite marks which shall at once include the promises which ought to be enforceable, exclude those which ought not to be, and signalize those which will be. Llewellyn, "What Price Contract?" (1931), 40 *Yale L.J.* 704, 738.

recognizable channels; he must reduce the fleeting entities of wordless thought to the patterns of conventional speech. One planning to enter a legal transaction faces a similar problem. His mind first conceives an economic or sentimental objective, or, more usually a set of overlapping objectives. He must then, with or without the aid of a lawyer, cast about for the legal transaction (written memorandum, sealed contract, lease, conveyance of the fee, etc.) which will most nearly accomplish these objectives. Just as the use of language contains dangers for the uninitiated, so legal forms are safe only in the hands of those who are familiar with their effects. Ihering explains that the extreme formalism of Roman law was supportable in practice only because of the constant availability of legal advice, *gratis*.

[9]   The ideal of language would be the word whose significance remained constant and unaffected by the context in which it was used. Actually there are few words, even in scientific language, which are not capable of taking on a nuance of meaning because of the context in which they occur. So in the law, the ideal type of formal transaction would be the transaction described on the Continent as "abstract," that is, the transaction which is abstracted from the causes which gave rise to it and which has the same legal effect no matter what the context of motives and lay practices in which it occurs. The seal in its original form represented an approach to this ideal, for it will be recalled that extra-formal factors, including even fraud and mistake, were originally without effect on the sealed promise. Most of the formal transactions familiar to modern law, however, fall short of the abstract transaction; the channels they cut are not sharply and simply defined. The *Statute of Frauds* [legislation that requires some contracts, such as those involving the sale of land to be in writing], for example, has only a kind of negative canalizing effect in the sense that it indicates a way by which one may be sure of *not* being bound. On the positive side, the outlines of the channel are blurred because too many factors, including consideration, remain unassimilated into the form.

[10]   As a final and very obvious point of comparison between the forms of law and those of language, we may observe that in both fields the actual course of history is determined by a continuous process of compromise between those who wish to preserve the existing patterns and those who wish to rearrange them. Those who are responsible for what Ihering called the "legal alphabet" — our judges, legislators, and text writers — exercise a certain control over the usages of business, but there are times when they, like the lexicographer, must acquiesce in the innovations of the layman. The mere fact that the forms of law and language are set by a balance of opposing tensions does not, of course, insure the soundness of the developments which actually occur. If language sometimes loses valuable distinctions by being too tolerant, the law has lost valuable institutions, like the seal, by being too liberal in interpreting them. On the other hand, in law, as in language, forms have at times been allowed to crystallize to the point where needed innovation has been impeded.

[11]   *Interrelations of the Three Functions*: Though I have stated the three functions of legal form separately, it is obvious that there is an intimate connection between them. Generally speaking, whatever tends to accomplish one of these purposes will also tend to accomplish the other two. He who is compelled to do something which will furnish a satisfactory memorial of his intention will be induced to deliberate. Conversely, devices which induce deliberation will usually have an evidentiary value. Devices which insure evidence or prevent inconsiderateness will normally advance the desideratum of channelling, in two different

ways. In the first place, he who is compelled to formulate his intention carefully will tend to fit it into legal and business categories. In this way the party is induced to canalize his own intention. In the second place, wherever the requirement of a formality is backed by the sanction of the invalidity of the informal transaction (and this is the means by which requirements of form are normally made effective), a degree of channelling results automatically. Whatever may be its legislative motive, the formality in such a case tends to effect a categorization of transactions into legal and non-legal.

[12] Just as channelling may result unintentionally from formalities directed toward other ends, so these other ends tend to be satisfied by any device which accomplishes a channelling of expression. There is an evidentiary value in the clarity and definiteness of contour which such a device accomplishes. Anything which effects a neat division between the legal and the non-legal, or between different kinds of legal transactions, will tend also to make apparent to the party the consequences of his action and will suggest deliberation where deliberation is needed. Indeed, we may go further and say that some minimum satisfaction of the desideratum of channelling is necessary before measures designed to prevent inconsiderateness can be effective. This may be illustrated in the holographic will. The necessity of reducing the testator's intention to his own handwriting would seem superficially to offer, not only evidentiary safeguards, but excellent protection against inconsiderateness as well. Where the holographic will fails, however, is as a device for separating the legal wheat from the legally irrelevant chaff. The courts are frequently faced with the difficulty of determining whether a particular document — it may be an informal family letter which happens to be entirely in the handwriting of the sender — reveals the requisite "testamentary intention." This difficulty can only be eliminated by a formality which performs adequately the channelling function, by some external mark which will signalize the testament and distinguish it from non-testamentary expressions of intention. It is obvious that by a kind of reflex action the deficiency of the holographic will from the standpoint of channelling operates to impair its efficacy as a device for inducing deliberation.

[13] Despite the close interrelationship of the three functions of form, it is necessary to keep the distinctions between them in mind since the disposition of borderline cases of compliance may turn on our assumptions as to the end primarily sought by a particular formality. Much of the discussion about the parol evidence rule [which excludes oral evidence to modify a written contract], for example, hinges on the question whether its primary objective is channelling or evidentiary. Furthermore, one or more of the ends described may enter in a subsidiary way into the application of requirements primarily directed to another end. Thus there is reason to think that a good deal of the law concerning the suretyship section of the *Statute of Frauds* is explainable on the ground that courts have, with varying degrees of explicitness, supposed that this section served a cautionary and channelling purpose in addition to the evidentiary purpose assumed to be primarily involved in the *Statute* as a whole.

[14] *When Are Formalities Needed? The Effect of an Informal Satisfaction of the Desiderata Underlying the Use of Formalities*: The analysis of the functions of legal form which has just been presented is useful in answering a question which will assume importance in the later portion of this discussion when a detailed treatment of consideration is undertaken. That question is: In what situations does

good legislative policy demand the use of a legal formality? One part of the answer to the question is clear at the outset. Forms must be reserved for relatively
important transactions. We must preserve a proportion between means and end; it
will scarcely do to require a sealed and witnessed document for the effective sale
of a loaf of bread.

[15] But assuming that the transaction in question is of sufficient importance to
support the use of a form if a form is needed, how is the existence of this need to
be determined? A general answer would run somewhat as follows: *The need for
investing a particular transaction with some legal formality will depend upon the
extent to which the guaranties that the formality would afford are rendered superfluous by forces native to the situation out of which the transaction arises* — including in these "forces" the habits and conceptions of the transacting parties.

[16] Whether there is any need, for example, to set up a formality designed to
induce deliberation will depend upon the degree to which the factual situation,
innocent of any legal remoulding, tends to bring about the desired circumspective
frame of mind. An example from the law of gifts will make this point clear. To
accomplish an effective gift of a chattel without resort to the use of documents,
delivery of the chattel is ordinarily required and mere donative words are ineffective. It is thought, among other things, that mere words do not sufficiently impress
on the donor the significance and seriousness of his act. In an Oregon case, however, the donor declared his intention to give a sum of money to the donee and at
the same time disclosed to the donee the secret hiding place where he had placed
the money. Though the whole donative act consisted merely of words, the court
held the gift to effective. The words which gave access to the money which the
donor had so carefully concealed would presumably be accompanied by the same
sense of present deprivation which the act of handing over the money would have
produced. The situation contained its own guaranty against inconsiderateness.

[17] So far as the channelling function of a formality is concerned it has no place
where men's activities are already divided into definite, clear-cut business categories. Where life has already organized itself effectively, there is no need for the
law to intervene. It is for this reason that important transactions on the stock and
produce markets can safely be carried on in "the most informal" manner. At the
other extreme we may cite the negotiations between a house-to-house book salesman and the housewife. Here the situation may be such that the housewife is not
certain whether she is being presented with a set of books as a gift, whether she is
being asked to trade her letter of recommendation for the books, whether the
books are being offered to her on approval, or whether — what is, alas, the fact —
a simple sale of the books is being proposed. The ambiguity of the situation is, of
course, carefully cultivated and exploited by the canvasser. Some channelling"
here would be highly desirable, though whether a legal form is the most practicable means of bringing it about is, of course, another question.

[18] What has been said in this section demonstrates, I believe, that the problem
of form, "when reduced to its underlying policies, extends not merely to formal"
transactions in the usual sense, but to the whole law of contracts and conveyances.
Demogue has suggested that even the requirement, imposed in certain cases, that
the intention of the parties be express, rather than implied or tacit, is in essence a
requirement of form. If our object is to avoid giving sanction to inconsiderate engagements, surely the case for legal redress is stronger against the man who has

spelled out his promise than it is against the man who has merely drifted into a situation where he appears to hold out an assurance for the future.

NOTE

It is interesting to observe that since Fuller wrote this article, many jurisdictions have enacted legislation to give consumers a "cooling off period" if they enter into contracts in their homes. These contracts can be the result of consumers being pressured into making making contracts in their homes by unsolicited, aggressive and perhaps misleading sellers. When Fuller was writing in 1941, he described the concern of that time — the door-to-door salesman. To this has been added the problem of unsolicited e-mails and telemarketers. In Ontario, the *Consumer Protection Act, 2002*, S.O. 2002, c. 30, Sched. A, s. 43, provides that a consumer who has purchased goods or services under a "direct contract" (a contract made at a place other than the seller's place of business or a trade fair or market place) may be cancelled *by the consumer* "without any reason" within 10 days of receiving a copy of the agreement.

THE REQUIREMENT OF WRITING — THE STATUTE OF FRAUDS

While it may, as a practical matter, be more difficult to prove that an oral contract was made, in most situations, an oral contract is as enforceable as a written one. There is, however, an important statutory requirement, applicable to a limited class of promises, that they will only be enforceable if recorded in a writing, *i.e.*, a written document, signed by the person being sued.

We will focus our study on the *Statute of Frauds*, first enacted in 1677 in England (29 Char. II, c. 3). However, there are other recent legislative examples of requirements for writing, such as those governing domestic contracts and documents dealing with the purchase of securities by investors. While much has changed since 1677, there are still situations in which certainty and deliberation are to be promoted, and contracts have to be in writing. In some cases the application of this legislative requirement is thought by a court to lead to an injustice and judges will stretch their powers of statutory interpretation to avoid it.

When enacted in 1677, the *Statute of Frauds* was aimed at the "prevention of many fraudulent practices which are commonly endeavoured to be upheld by perjury and subornation of perjury". The method of achieving this was the requirement that certain kinds of transactions had to be evidenced by a written document, signed by the person being sued. A similar technique has been widely used by legislatures and authorities, including those in ancient Babylon and Soviet Russia, by African customary law and by the French Civil Code. The English Act of 1677 was almost universally adopted in common law jurisdictions, though all have amended the Statute in some respects, Ontario most recently in 1994. The Ontario Act (R.S.O. 1990, c. S.19, as amended by S.O. 1994, c. 27, s. 55) contains 11 sections, but only a few of these are of concern to most lawyers. The principal sections of the present Act are:

> 4. No action shall be brought to charge any executor or administrator upon any special promise to answer damages out of the executor's or administrator's own estate, or to charge any person upon any special promise to answer for the debt, default or miscarriage of any other person, or to charge any person upon any agreement made upon consideration of marriage, or upon any contract or sale of lands, tenements or hereditaments, or any interest in or concerning them, unless the agreement upon which the action is brought, or some memorandum or note thereof is in writing and signed by the party to be charged therewith or some person thereunto lawfully authorized by the party.

. . .

6. No special promise made by a person to answer for the debt, default or mis-carriage of another person, being in writing and signed by the party to be charged therewith, or by some other person lawfully authorized by the party, shall be deemed invalid to support an action or other proceeding to charge the person by whom the promise was made by reason only that the consideration for the promise does not appear in writing, or by necessary inference from a written document.

7. No action shall be maintained whereby to charge a person upon a promise made after full age to pay a debt contracted during minority or upon a ratification af-ter full age of a promise or simple contract made during minority, unless the promise or ratification is made by a writing signed by the party to be charged therewith or by his or her agent duly authorized to make the promise or ratification.

A statute can only be understood in the context of the ideas, values and character-istics of the society in which it was enacted. To understand the context of the *Stat-ute of Frauds*, it is important to consider the features of the English legal system in 1677. Until *Slade's Case* (1602), 4 Co. Rep. 91a, 76 E.R. 1074, and the triumph of the action of *assumpsit*, the law of contracts had been heavily biased in favour of defendants and liability usually rested on formal, sealed documents and the action of debt; in *Slade's Case* the Court of King's Bench accepted that actions in *as-sumpsit* [Latin for "he has undertaken"] could be based on informal contracts. Prior to *Slade's Case*, a defendant who could, for example, "wage his law" (bring forward witnesses to swear under oath, not what the truth was, but that the defendant was telling the truth) was in a strong position compared with the plaintiff. This bias in favour of the defendant was largely eliminated when plaintiffs were able to sue on informal contracts, *i.e.*, oral contracts and signed contracts not under seal, in the action of *assumpsit*. After 1602, the plaintiff could get his case before the jury, which at that time was far less subject to judicial control than it was later to become.

In addition, the courts in the seventeenth century took the view that anyone who was a party to litigation might be tempted to give perjured evidence and was there-fore not permitted to testify as a witness. As a result, if a fraudulent plaintiff could arrange for another person to testify falsely that he heard the defendant make a promise (*i.e.*, the plaintiff found a witness to commit a fraud on the court), the honest defendant was not even permitted to be a witness and testify that this was false. There was therefore a concern that fraudulent law suits were being brought before the courts. A further complicating factor was the extreme litigiousness of the English during the sixteenth and seventeenth centuries.

While the problem of fraudulent law suits might have been addressed by alter-ing the laws of evidence and permitting parties to testify, there was substantial resistance to changes in fundamental procedural and evidentiary rules at that time. This type of change in the legal system did not occur for almost two hundred years. Parliament was, however, prepared to deal with the problem of fraudulent law suits by enacting the *Statute of Frauds*.

As will be seen, the *Statute of Frauds* is in some respects quite inappropriate now. In fairness to those who drafted it, it is unlikely that any legislation passed more than 300 years ago to deal with problems that existed at that time and in the legal context which created those problems would work well now. It should also be remembered that in 1677 the law of contract looked very different from how it looks now. The law was wholly case law at that time: the *Statute of Frauds* was the first statute dealing with contracts in general.

Section 4 of Ontario's *Statute of Frauds*, edited to emphasize its several points, reads as follows: *prof*

No action shall be brought

[(a)] to charge any executor or administrator upon any special promise to answer damages out of the executor's or administrator's own estate, or

[(b)] to charge any person upon any special promise to answer for the debt, default or miscarriage of any other person, or

[(c)] to charge any person upon any agreement made upon consideration of marriage, or *not relevant*

[(d)] upon any contract or sale of lands, tenements or hereditaments, or any interest in or concerning them,

unless the agreement upon which the action is brought, or some memorandum or note thereof is in writing and signed by the party to be charged therewith or some person thereunto lawfully authorized by the party.

Clauses (a) and (b) can be conveniently dealt with together. Clause (b) is the general clause and is often referred to as the "suretyship section". Clause (a) concerns the special case of suretyship when an executor promises to answer for the debt of the deceased; few cases have come up under clause (a) and we will focus on clause (b). The drafting of clause (b) is not very clear and there are major difficulties in the cases that have come up. The word "special" is used in both clauses (a) and (b), but it has no significance now. The phrase "debt, default or miscarriage" has been held to cover liability under contract and in tort. Thus, a promise to pay for tortious damage done by another person is "within the statute" — the phrase used to describe those cases where a promise may be held to be unenforceable if it is not in writing because of the *Statute*. Because the *Statute of Frauds* can be a trap for the unwary and allows for quite technical defences, there has been a tendency of courts from at least the beginning of the nineteenth century (and probably earlier) to restrict the scope of agreements that come within it. The broadening of the scope of clause (b) by inclusion of tort claims is therefore unusual.

A typical case that illustrates the normal tendency to narrow the scope of the *Statute of Frauds* is the following. Assume that D(ebtor) owes C(reditor) money. S(urety) promises C that if D does not pay him, S will do so. This case would be within the statute, and S's promise would only be enforceable by C if it were in writing. If, however, the promise of S is made to D himself, then the *Statute* does not apply: *Eastwood v. Kenyon* (1840), 113 E.R. 482, 11 A. & E. 438 (K.B.). (*Eastwood v. Kenyon* is reproduced below but on a point other than the *Statute of Frauds*.)

In the famous case of *Mountstephen v. Lakeman* (1871), L.R. 7 Q.B. 196, affirmed (1874), L.R. 7 H.L. 17, the defendant, Lakeman, was chairman of a local board of health, and the plaintiff, Mountstephen, was a builder. Lakeman asked Mountstephen to connect some houses to the main sewer. Mountstephen wanted to know how he would be paid, and the following conversation took place:

Lakeman: What objection have you to make the connection?

Mountstephen: I have none, if you or the board will order the work or become responsible for payment.

> Lakeman: Go on, Mountstephen, and do the work, and I will see you paid.

The board refused to pay, and the plaintiff sued the defendant. The defendant pleaded the *Statute*. The court held that the defendant's promise was not within the *Statute* as there was no other debtor — the board not having authorized the work, it was not liable. The defendant's promise was then not a promise to answer for another's debt, but an oral promise made by the defendant himself on which the plaintiff could sue. It is said that Lakeman did not create a relation of "secondary guarantee", but rather one of "primary indemnity".

These examples are fairly straightforward and the cases can be justified by a close reading of the statute. More difficult problems arise in the following case, which is taken from Fuller and Eisenberg, *Basic Contract Law*, 3d ed. at 1008-09:

> Manley Minus owes Cherie Claim $1,000. Minus gives Claim a mortgage on Black-acre to secure this debt. Thereafter Minus conveys Blackacre to Palfrey Pawn, subject to the mortgage but with a promise by Minus that he will discharge the mortgage and thus release Pawn's land of the mortgage lien. Minus fails to pay the debt and Claim brings a suit to foreclose the mortgage on Blackacre. To save his land, Pawn orally promises Claim that if Claim will give up the suit, he, Pawn, will stand back of Minus's debt. Claim discontinues the suit. Pawn refuses to honor his promise. Claim sues Pawn on the oral agreement. Pawn pleads the Statute of Frauds, asserting that his promise was a promise to answer for the debt of another, namely Minus. A well-established line of authorities would hold the promise not within the Statute and would render judgment for Claim.

The usual way of explaining the result in this case is to say that when Pawn promised to pay the debt owed to Claim, he was only doing so to save his own property and therefore his promise is outside the *Statute*. There is nothing explicit in the words of the section to support this interpretation, but it illustrates the tendency of the courts to restrict the effect of the *Statute*. It could be argued that the purpose of the formal requirements of the *Statute* is concern for the *cautionary* function. When someone in the position of Pawn promises to pay another's debt and does so to protect his own interest, then the cautionary function is already adequately protected and the added protection of the *Statute* is not necessary. A conceptual difficulty with this rationalization is that the *Statute* is generally regarded as serving the *evidentiary* function. (Such a purpose could be inferred from the origin of the statute.) This conclusion is supported by the rule that even if the creditor should give value to the surety for the surety's promise, the promise is within the *Statute* and unenforceable unless in writing. The result in the example with Claim is sometimes referred to as the "main purpose rule". The *Statute* will not apply where the main purpose of the surety's promise is to protect his own property or his own interests.

Clause (c), the "marriage section", is of no real importance today. It does not apply to a person's promise to marry another in the future. Such an exchange of mutual promises could give rise to the common law action of "breach of promise" (of marriage), a cause of an action that was especially important to middle-class women in the nineteenth century and earlier who might find it difficult to find a husband if an engagement were broken off — and as a consequence suffer social and economic losses. Many jurisdictions have now abolished the action of "breach of promise", viewing it as anachronistic. (The need to protect reliance on what might once have been a promise of marriage still exists and courts will sometimes respond to it, even though no longer directly allowing damages for disappointment or loss of reputation as a result of the breach of an engagement. See, *e.g.*, *Dupuis v. Austin* (1998), 168 D.L.R. (4th) 483 (N.B.Q.B).)

Clause (c) does, however, apply to the promise, say, by a father to pay his son $10,000 on the latter's marriage. A promise by both sets of parents to pay the couple $10,000 on their marriage is considered outside the statute, since the parents are each promising to pay and the consideration is then in the mutual promises. The marriage is then the condition for the payment, not the consideration.

Clause (c) does not apply to "marriage contracts", *i.e.* agreements that regulate rights and responsibilities between spouses during marriage and upon divorce, though as discussed below, family law legislation generally requires such "domestic contracts" to be in writing to be enforceable.

Clause (d) brings within the *Statute* all contracts for the sale of land. (The words "contract *or* sale" represent a "fossilized" seventeenth century misprint.) It has been held that this includes promises to give land away by will as well as contracts for the exchange of land for something else. It does not matter what the value of the interest in land might be. (Contracts and conveyances of interests in land are also covered by the first three sections of the Act. Under these sections all conveyances have to be made by written document, subject to certain exceptions, and all leases, except those for less than three years, have to be by written deed. Section 4 is the section that catches most people by surprise.)

The courts have generally regarded as interests in land the kind of rights that would be generally thought to relate to real property. These include the fee simple, life estate and easement, but might not include all cases of licences — for example, an agreement to permit someone to occupy a particular seat in a church for the rest of his or her life is not within the *Statute*.

There is one major exception to the rule requiring contracts for the sale of land to be in writing which has been developed by the courts of equity. This is the doctrine of "part performance". This aspect of the interpretation of the statute was discussed by the Supreme Court of Canada in *Deglman v. Guaranty Trust Co.*, [1954] S.C.R. 725, [1954] 3 D.L.R. 785 (the next case in the materials, *infra*). The position taken by the Supreme Court in that case is consistent with the general view of the courts, and is summed up in the judgment of Rand J. To constitute "part performance" sufficient to avoid the effects of the *Statute*, the acts of part performance must be "uniquely referable" to the contract regarding the land. The most common example is the purchaser's taking possession of the land. This act offers evidence of the contract that is independent of the oral contract.

The *Statute* requires that the "agreement . . . or some memorandum or note thereof" be in writing. What is a sufficient memorandum or note under the statute? The courts have tended to take a broad view of what constitutes a "sufficient note or memorandum" thereby restricting the effect of the *Statute*. A signed offer by one party that has been orally accepted is sufficient to allow the other to enforce the agreement; the *Statute* does not require that the entire agreement be in writing. A document is "signed" within the meaning of the *Statute* even if the party's name appears in printed form. An actual "signature" is not required. The note must be sufficiently precise to enable the court to understand the contract, but it is not necessary for all terms to be recorded. A sufficient "note" may be obtained from more than one piece of paper, provided that it can be shown that the pieces relate to the same agreement.

A memorandum may fail to correctly set out the actual agreement of the parties, but in this case the courts may "rectify" or correct the agreement based on oral evidence. Thus, there is the paradox that oral evidence may be used to correct a memorandum when an oral agreement itself could not be sued upon because of the statute! (Rectification provides relief for certain kinds of mistake and will be examined in Chapter 5.) The general rule is that the contract's coming within the *Statute* does not, of itself, prevent rectification. However, the result in any particular case may depend on what term is sought to be rectified, and on the parties' reliance on the contract. Rectification will not usually be allowed when the only purpose of rectification will be to supply a memorandum satisfying the statute.

Section 6 specifies that in the case of an agreement coming within clause (b) — the suretyship section — the note need not show the consideration for the promise. This is an important concession since in contracts of guarantee the consideration is seldom stated and often challenged.

So far we have largely been discussing the application of the *Statute* when the contract is executory, *i.e.*, when one party is suing to enforce a contract that neither has, at that time, performed. It is one thing to say that because of distrust of oral evidence a contract within the *Statute* is not enforceable when neither party has done anything in reliance on the contract. It is another to say that the oral contract is of absolutely no effect if caught by the *Statute* so that no remedy is available to a party who has significantly changed its position.

As will be seen in *Deglman v. Guaranty Trust Co.* (*infra*) the Supreme Court of Canada, after holding that the agreement was within the *Statute* and unenforceable, went on to allow the plaintiff's claim for the value of the services provided. The justification for this is that the remedy given is not based on the unenforceable contract, but on an obligation implied in law. The difference would be in the measure of the plaintiff's recovery. In an action on the contract, the normal measure of damages would be the expectation interest — the value of the thing promised. The measure in an action in quasi-contract or restitution would be the extent to which the other side would be unjustly enriched. The oral agreement has to be proved to show that the plaintiff's performance was not intended to be a gratuitous act, and the plaintiff will be able to adduce evidence of the value of the property that he was promised. There is a certain logical inconsistency in allowing proof of an oral contract for one purpose but not for another. However, the courts want to provide protection for reliance or to prevent unjust enrichment, and will give a restitutionary remedy to prevent unjust enrichment.

In 1994 the Ontario legislature amended the *Statute of Frauds* (S.O. 1994, c. 27, s. 55) and removed the provisions in s. 4 that had previously required written evidence of contracts that were not be performed within one year. At the same time, a provision that had been in the original *Statute of Frauds* of 1677, *viz.*, that contracts for the sale of goods of a value greater than £10 had to be supported by a memorandum in writing, which had been re-enacted as s. 5 of the *Sale of Goods Act* when that act was brought into Ontario in 1920, was also repealed. The former restriction had never worked as intended and was bizarre and perverse in its operation. The latter was seen as hindering the making of commercial contracts, especially by electronic data interchange.

Under the *Consumer Protection Act, 2002*, S.O. 2002, c. 30, Sched. A., various types of consumer contracts are only enforceable *against* a consumer if in writing. For example, under s. 21, a "future performance agreement" for provision of goods or services to the consumer" in excess of "a prescribed amount" (set at $50 by O. Reg. 17/05) is not binding on the *buyer* unless it is in writing and the consumer is given a copy of the contract. The contract must include all terms relating to price, credit and warranty. A "future performance agreement" is defined in s. 1 as a consumer contract for goods or services for "which delivery, performance or payment in full is not made when the parties enter the agreement". While as a matter of practice, a commercial seller will usually want consumers to sign a copy of such a contract, to establish that they have received a copy, signing is not a requirement, and these contracts may be entered into electronically. If the consumer does not receive a written copy of the agreement, s. 23 allows the consumer to cancel the contract. This Act applies only to individual consumers buying from commercial sellers. A consumer has significantly broader scope for enforcing oral representations *against* a commercial seller (see, *e.g.*, s.18(10)).

Section 39 of the *Consumer Protection Act, 2002* deals with "internet agreements"; while the consumer must receive a written copy of the agreement, it may be sent in electronic form to the consumer, as long as the consumer can print it out.

Similarly, Ontario's *Family Law Act*, R.S.O. 1990, c. F.3, s. 55, provides that a domestic contract is "unenforceable" unless "made in writing and signed by the parties to be bound and witnessed". This provision is intended to provide some assurances of deliberation and understanding of the obligations being undertaken. As with the *Statute of Frauds*, the courts sometimes strain to restrict the effect of s. 55 when it seems unfair to apply it. A good example of such an attitude is *Sanderson v. Sanderson* (1982), 40 O.R. (2d) 82, 141 D.L.R. (3d) 588 (H.C.J.). A written separation agreement between a husband and wife for the support of their child was held to be enforceable by the wife even though the agreement was not witnessed as required by the *Family Law Reform Act*, R.S.O. 1980, c. 152. Walsh J. held that, since the wife was not obliged to make a claim under the legislation but could rely on the agreement as an ordinary contract, the statutory formalities required for a "domestic contract" did not apply.

The Ontario *Electronic Commerce Act, 2000*, S.O. 2000, c. 17, does not deal with the requirement for a written document, but with the requirement that a document be signed. The Act provides in s. 11 that any requirement of signing may be satisfied by an "electronic signature", provided that both parties implicitly or explicitly consent. There are a few specified exclusions in s. 31, such as wills and documents that create an interest in land which, to be effective against third parties, have to be registered. An electronic or digital signature allows the recipient of an electronically transferred document to be assured of the authenticity of the "signer" though use of an "asymmetric cryptosystem". This system also ensures that each document is "unique" and cannot be altered without detection. "Public key certification" agencies are being established to facilitate use of this system. The Ontario legislation is based on the *United Nations Model Law on Electronic Commerce*, which has been endorsed by the Uniform Law Conference of Canada; similar legislation is being or has been enacted in most jurisdictions.

While it is effectively impossible to "forge" an electronic signature, problems may arise if individuals trust others with their pass codes and access to their computers. Such problems are likely to be eliminated in the future as signer verification processes are introduced based on fingerprints, voice prints or other unique biometric identifiers. In the meantime, who should bear the cost of losses that may arise if a person places confidence in a rogue who then "forges" a document?

NOTES AND QUESTIONS

1. What assumptions are made by the legislature in enacting or refusing to repeal the *Statute of Frauds*? To what extent are these assumptions justified? How are the answers to these questions relevant:

    (a) to a lawyer asked to represent one party to a dispute;

    (b) to courts presented with a plea of the *Statute of Frauds* in any particular litigation; or

    (c) to a legislature considering questions of whether and how the *Statute of Frauds* should be reformed?

2. Although the *Statute of Frauds* was originally enacted to deal with evidentiary concerns by requiring certain contracts to be in writing, the fact that there is very convincing evidence that an oral contract was made does not render that contract enforceable if the *Statute* requires it to be in writing. In *Neighbourhoods of Cornell Inc. v. 1440106 Ontario Inc.*, [2003] O.J. No. 2919 (S.C.J.), (affirmed on other grounds, [2004] O.J. No. 2350, 22 R.P.R. (4th) 176 (C.A.), leave to appeal dismissed, [2004] S.C.C.A. 390), one party recorded a phone conversation in which an agreement was made to sell a piece of land. The trial judge accepted that an agreement was made, but held it unenforceable because of the *Statute*. The Court of Appeal in dismissing an appeal did not deal with this issue.

3. The formalities requirements of the *Statute of Frauds* tend to be broadly interpreted to limit the effect of this legislation on contractual obligations, and prevent unjust enrichment or protect reliance. Legislation governing wills also has formality requirements, for example, requiring that the testator's signature is to be witnessed by two persons. While a consideration of this type of legislation is clearly beyond the scope of this book, it is interesting to note that wills legislation is generally interpreted strictly, so that a bequest under a will is only enforceable if there has been strict compliance with the formality requirements. Is this difference in treatment consistent with Fuller's analysis?

Unjust Enrichment and the Doctrine of Part Performance

The next case, *Deglman v. Guaranty Trust*, illustrates how the courts respond to problems that can arise when the *Statute of Frauds* renders a promise unenforceable, but the party to whom it was made has already given value for the promise. There is great pressure to prevent a party from getting a benefit without paying for it. This decision applies a restitutionary remedy to prevent the "unjust enrichment" of the defendant. The general lesson to be drawn from the cases where unjust enrichment is the basis for giving a remedy for breach of contract is the realization that the pressure to give a remedy may sometimes be so strong that even statutory unenforceability will not be sufficient to resist it.

DEGLMAN v. GUARANTY TRUST CO. OF CANADA AND CONSTANTINEAU

[1954] S.C.R. 725, [1954] 3 D.L.R. 785
(S.C.C., Rinfret C.J.C., Taschereau, Rand, Estey, Locke,
Fauteux and Cartwright JJ.)

RAND J.: — **[1]** In this appeal the narrow question is raised as to the nature of part performance which will enable the Court to order specific performance of a contract relating to lands unenforceable at law by reason of s. 4 of the *Statute of*

Frauds, R.S.O. 1950, c. 371. The respondent Constantineau claims the benefit of such a contract and the appellant represents the next-of-kin other than the respondent of the deceased, Laura Brunet, who resist it.

[2]   The respondent was the nephew of the deceased. Both lived in Ottawa. When he was about 20 years of age, and while attending a technical school, for 6 months of the school year 1934-35 he lived with his aunt at No. 550 Besserer St. Both that and the house on the adjoining lot, No. 548, were owned by the aunt and it was during this time that she is claimed to have agreed that if the nephew would be good to her and do such services for her as she might from time to time request during her lifetime she would make adequate provision for him in her will, and in particular that she would leave to him the premises at No. 548. While staying with her the nephew did the chores around both houses which, except for an apartment used by his aunt, were occupied by tenants. When the term ended he returned to the home of his mother on another street. In the autumn of that year he worked on the national highway in the northern part of Ontario. In the spring of 1936 he took a job on a railway at a point outside of Ottawa and at the end of that year, returning to Ottawa, he obtained a position with the city police force. In 1941 he married. At no time did he live at the house No. 548 or, apart from the 6 months, at the house No. 550.

[3]   The performance consisted of taking his aunt about in her own or his automobile on trips to Montreal and elsewhere, and on pleasure drives, of doing odd jobs about the two houses, and of various accommodations such as errands and minor services for her personal needs. These circumstances, Spence J. at trial and the Court of Appeal, finding a contract, have held to be sufficient grounds for disregarding the prohibition of the statute. . . .

[4]   The leading case on this question is *Maddison v. Alderson* (1883), 8 App. Cas. 467. The facts there were much stronger than those before us. The plaintiff, giving up all prospects of any other course of life, spent over 20 years as housekeeper of the intestate until his death, without wages on the strength of his promise to leave her the manor on which they lived. A defectively executed will made her a beneficiary to the extent of a life interest in all his property, real and personal. The House of Lords held that, assuming a contract, there had been no such part performance as would answer s. 4 [of the *Statute of Frauds*]. . . .

[5]   I am quite unable to distinguish that authority from the matter before us. Here, as there, the acts of performance by themselves are wholly neutral and have no more relation to a contract connected with premises No. 548 than with those of No. 550 or than to mere expectation that his aunt would requite his solicitude in her will, or that they were given gratuitously or on terms that the time and outlays would be compensated in money. In relation to specific performance, strict pleading would seem to require a demonstrated connection between the acts of performance and a dealing with the land before evidence of the terms of any agreement is admissible. This exception of part performance is an anomaly; it is based on equities resulting from the acts done; but unless we are to say that, after performance by one party, any refusal to perform by the other gives rise to them, which would in large measure write off the section, we must draw the line where those acts are referable and referable only to the contract alleged. The facts here are almost the classical case against which the statute was aimed: they have been found to be truly stated and I accept that; but it is the nature of the proof that is condemned, not the facts, and their truth at law is irrelevant. Against this, equity intervenes only in circumstances that are not present here.

[6]   There remains the question of recovery for the services rendered on the basis of a *quantum meruit*. On the findings of both Courts below the services were not given gratuitously but on the footing of a contractual relation: they were to be paid for. The statute in such a case does not touch the principle of restitution against what would otherwise be an unjust enrichment of the defendant at the expense of the plaintiff. This is exemplified in the simple case of part or full payment in money as the price under an oral contract; it would be inequitable to allow the promisor to keep both the land and the money and the other party to the bargain is entitled to recover what he has paid. Similarly is it in the case of services given.

[7]   This matter is elaborated exhaustively in the *Restatement of the Law of Contract* issued by the American Law Institute, and Professor Williston's monumental work on *Contracts* (1936), vol. 2, s. 536, deals with the same topic. On the principles there laid down the respondent is entitled to recover for his services and outlays what the deceased would have had to pay for them on a purely business basis to any other person in the position of the respondent. The evidence covers generally and perhaps in the only way possible the particulars, but enough is shown to enable the Court to make a fair determination of the amount called for; and since it would be to the benefit of the other beneficiaries to bring an end to this litigation, I think we should not hesitate to do that by fixing the amount to be allowed. This I place at the sum of $3,000.

[8]   The appeal will therefore be allowed and the judgment modified by declaring the respondent entitled to recover against the respondent administrator the sum of $3,000; all costs will be paid out of the estate, those of the administrator as between solicitor and client.

[**RINFRET C.J.C.** and **TASCHEREAU J.** concurred with **RAND J.**]

CARTWRIGHT J.: — [9] . . . The appeal was argued on the assumption that there was an oral contract made between the respondent and the late Laura Constantineau Brunet under the terms of which the former was to perform certain services in consideration whereof the latter was to devise No. 548 Besserer St. to him, that the contract was fully performed by the respondent and that there was no defence to his claim to have the contract specifically performed other than the fact that there was no memorandum in writing thereof as required by the *Statute of Frauds*, which was duly pleaded.

[10]   It is clear that none of the numerous acts done by the respondent in performance of the contract were in their own nature unequivocally referable to No. 548 Besserer St., or to any dealing with that land. On the other hand there are concurrent findings of fact, which were not questioned before us, that the acts done by the respondent were in their nature referable to some contract existing between the parties. On this view of the facts the learned trial Judge and the Court of Appeal were of opinion that the acts done by the respondent in performance of the agreement were sufficient to take it out of the operation of the *Statute of Frauds* and that it ought to be specifically enforced. . . .

[11]   I have already expressed the view that the acts relied upon by the respondent in the case at bar are not unequivocally and in their own nature referable to any dealing with the land in question and on this point the appellant is entitled to succeed.

[12] It remains to consider the respondent's alternative claim to recover for the value of the services which he performed for the deceased. . . .

[13] I agree with the conclusion of my brother Rand that the respondent is entitled to recover the value of these services from the respondent administrator. This right appears to me to be based, not on the contract, but on an obligation imposed by law.

[14] In *Fibrosa Spolka Akcina v. Fairbairn Lawson Combe Barbour Ltd.*, [1943] A.C. 32 at p. 61, Lord Wright said:

> It is clear that any civilized system of law is bound to provide remedies for cases of what has been called unjust enrichment or unjust benefit, that is to prevent a man from retaining the money of or some benefit derived from another which it is against conscience that he should keep. Such remedies in English law are generically different from remedies in contract or in tort, and are now recognized to fall within a third category of the common law which has been called quasi-contract or restitution.

And at p. 62:

> Lord Mansfield does not say that the law implies a promise. The law implies a debt or obligation which is a different thing. In fact, he denies that there is a contract; the obligation is as efficacious as if it were upon a contract. The obligation is a creation of the law, just as much as an obligation in tort. The obligation belongs to a third class, distinct from either contract or tort, though it resembles contract rather than tort.

Lord Wright's judgment appears to me to be in agreement with the view stated in Williston on *Contracts* referred by my brother Rand . . .

[15] In the case at bar all the acts for which the respondent asks to be paid under his alternative claim were clearly done in performance of the existing but unenforceable contract with the deceased that she would devise 548 Besserer St. to him, and to infer from them a fresh contract to pay the value of the services in money would be . . . to draw an inference contrary to the fact.

[16] In my opinion when the *Statute of Frauds* was pleaded the express contract was thereby rendered unenforceable, but the deceased having received the benefits of the full performance of the contract by the respondent, the law imposed upon her, and so on her estate, the obligation to pay the fair value of the services rendered to her . . .

[17] For the above reasons I would dispose of the appeal as proposed by my brother Rand.

[**ESTEY, LOCKE** and **FAUTEUX JJ.** concurred with **CARTWRIGHT J.**]

NOTES AND QUESTIONS

1.   The courts traditionally held that the payment of money by a buyer to a seller as part or total payment for land pursuant to an oral contract did not constitute part performance, and the buyer could not obtain specific performance. This result followed because the payment of money was considered "an equivocal act", that might be referable to some other type of contract, a loan or a gift perhaps, one not related to the land. Any payment made to the seller pursuant to an unenforceable contract could, however, be recovered on the basis of unjust enrichment.
     The House of Lords in *Steadman v. Steadman*, [1974] 2 All E.R. 977 held that part performance would be available in a wider range of situations than had previously been the case. A husband and wife had orally agreed that the wife would release her

interest in the family home for a promise by the husband to pay her £1,500 and that he would immediately pay £100 in respect of arrears of maintenance. The promise to pay the arrears of maintenance in this way was approved by the magistrates' court. The husband paid £100 in accordance with the agreement, but the wife refused to execute a transfer of her interest in the house. The wife argued that the promise was not in writing, and that there had been no part performance. The House of Lords accepted that the husband's acts were sufficient to constitute part performance, with Lord Reid saying (pp. 981-82):

> The argument for the wife, for which there is a good deal of authority, is that no act can be relied on as an act of part performance unless it relates to the land to be acquired and can only be explained by the existence of a contract relating to the land. But let me suppose a case of an oral contract where the consideration for the transfer of the land was not money but the transfer of some personal property or the performance of some obligation. The personal property is then transferred or the obligation is performed to the knowledge of the owner of the land in circumstances where there can be no *restitutio in integrum*. On what rational principle could it be said that the doctrine of part performance is not to apply? And we were not referred to any case of that kind where the court had refused to apply it. The transfer of the personal property or the performance of the obligation would indicate the existence of a contract but it would not indicate that the contract related to that or any other land.
>
> I think that there has been some confusion between this supposed rule and another perfectly good rule. You must not first look at the oral contract and then see whether the alleged acts or part performance are consistent with it. You must first look at the alleged acts of part performance and see whether they prove that there must have been a contract and it is only if they do so prove that you can bring in the oral contract. . . .
>
> I am aware that it has often been said that the acts relied on must necessarily or unequivocally indicate the existence of a contract. It may well be that we should consider whether any prudent reasonable man would have done those acts if there had not been a contract but many people are neither prudent nor reasonable and they might often spend money or prejudice their position not in reliance on a contract but in the optimistic expectation that a contract would follow. So if there were a rule that acts relied on as part performance must of their own nature unequivocally shew that there was a contract, it would be only in the rarest case that all other possible explanations could be excluded. . . .
>
> In my view, unless the law is to be divorced from reason and principle, the rule must be that you take the whole circumstances, leaving aside evidence about the oral contract, and see whether it is proved that the acts relied on were done in reliance on a contract: that will be proved if it is shewn to be more probable than not.
>
> Authorities which seem to require more than that appear to be based on an idea, never clearly defined, to the effect that the law of part performance is a rule of evidence rather than an application of an equitable principle. I do not know on what ground any court could say that, although you cannot produce the evidence required by the Statute of Frauds, some other kind of evidence will do instead. But I can see that if part performance is simply regarded as evidence then it would be reasonable to hold not only that the acts of part performance must relate to the land but that they must indicate the nature of the oral contract with regard to the land. But that appears to me to be a fundamental departure from the true doctrine of part performance.

Hunter v. Baluke [1998] O.J. No. 6469, 42 O.R. (3d) 553 (Gen. Div.) involved the sale of an expensive cottage property north of Toronto. As is often the case, some terms of the proposed agreement were amended in writing by each party in turn as the negotiations proceeded, with each proposed change being initialled by each of the parties to indicate agreement. At the end of the negotiations, there was an agreement about the price and date of closing, but the vendors wanted the right to store their boats and some furniture in the boathouse for several months after the deal closed. The real estate agent for the vendors orally agreed with the final signed proposal of the purchasers (the hockey star Wayne Gretzky and his wife) that the boats could remain in the boathouse, but that the furniture had to be removed at the time of closing to allow work on renovations to begin immediately after closing. The purchasers then paid the deposit to the agent for the vendors and had a home inspection carried out. The vendors never signed or initialled the final agreement. When the vendors refused to convey the land, the purchasers sued for specific performance. On a motion for summary judgment, Spiegel J. dismissed the action. He found that there was no evidence that the vendors actually agreed to the final changes. The vendor's agent (doubtless eager for the commission on a multimillion-dollar deal) thought that the issue of the storage of the boats was a minor detail, and felt certain that the vendors would agree to the purchasers' proposal on this point to complete the deal. The judge also said (pp. 569-70):

> Mr. Smith [for the plaintiff purchasers] submits that the act of the purchasers in forwarding the deposit in response to the request of the vendors' agent, by conducting the inspection and waiving the conditions with respect thereto, are acts which are unequivocally referrable to the existence of an agreement and constitutes such part performance as to make it inequitable for the defendants to rely on the *Statute of Frauds*. He relies on . . . *Steadman v. Steadman.* . . .

> . . .

> I carefully read the *Deglman* case and although in this case the act of part performance relied upon was not the payment of money, the Court clearly laid down the rule that had been formulated in the House of Lords case of *Maddison v. Alderson* (1883), 8 App. Cas. 467 . . . which held that a plaintiff who relied on part performance to take an oral agreement respecting land out of the operation of the *Statute of Frauds* must show that the act or acts by themselves unequivocally refer to a deal with land of the kind which is alleged to be the subject matter of the agreement sued upon. Only then can the evidence of the oral agreement be admissible for purposes of explaining the acts. It is for this reason that a payment of money alone can never be a sufficient act of part performance within the rule.

> In the case of *Alvi v. Lal* (1990), 13 R.P.R. (2d) 382 (Ont. H.C.J.), Then J., after reviewing the then current jurisprudence, concluded:

> > Whatever may be the current judicial trend, it seems clear that until the Supreme Court of Canada accepts *Steadman, supra,* the payment of money cannot constitute part performance with respect to a contract involving land.

> I have carefully read *Steadman* and if *Steadman* is good law in Canada, it does not stand for the proposition that the payment of money may in some cases be a sufficient act of part performance. What it stands for is that there is no general rule that the payment of money cannot constitute a sufficient act of part performance. However, if the payment of money is to be relied on, it has to be money which the defendant has retained and not repaid and had not offered to repay or cannot repay. This is clear from the decision of, at least two of the law lords, and I would refer to Lord Salmon's judgment at p. 573 in particular. This conclusion is also supported by the passage from Di Castri, *The Law of Vendor and Purchaser,* supra, p. 141, relied upon by Mr. Dizgun [counsel for the vendors], where referring to the doctrine of part performance the author says at p. 4-10:

The doctrine is an invention of the Court of Chancery to ensure equity being done where the defendant had stood by and allowed the plaintiff, to his detriment, to fulfil his part of the oral contract, and where it would be unconscionable for the defendant to set up the statute by asserting that the contract is unenforceable so that he might retain benefits which have accrued to him from the contract.

In the case before me, the deposit was at all material times held in trust by the vendors' real estate agent and at no time did the vendors assert any claim to the money. Indeed, the vendors' agent brought a motion before me to interplead the deposit and I understand that the vendors had not objected to the return of the money to the purchasers. Therefore, even if *Steadman* is considered to be good law in Canada, it would not assist the purchasers on the facts of this case, since paying the deposit could hardly be an act to their detriment so as to make it unconscionable to permit the vendors to rely on the Statute.

With respect to the allegation that conducting the inspection and waiving of the condition are acts of part performance, I find that these acts are clearly not unequivocally referable to the contract alleged and, also, I do not find them so detrimental to the purchasers and to the benefit of the vendors as to make it unequitable for the vendors to rely on the Statute.

While Canadian courts have not adopted the broad view of part performance articulated in *Steadman*, they have tended to interpret the "unequivocally referable" test of *Deglman* in a liberal fashion in cases where there were acts regarding the land. In *Devereux v. Devereux* (1978), 2 E.T.R. (Ont. H.C.J.), (affirmed, unreported, June 1979, Ont. C.A.) the court ruled that a son could enforce his father's oral promise to leave him the family farm after his death in exchange for caring for the farm and father until his death. The acts of past performance were moving onto the farm property with his father, and working for a nominal wage.

In *Starlite Variety Stores v. Cloverlite Investments* (1978), 92 D.L.R. (3d) 270, (Ont. H.C.J.) it was held when a prospective commercial tenant prepared advertising signs and shelving designed to fit the premises, and the defendant landlord made alterations to meet the plans of the prospective tenant, these were sufficient acts to be "part performance".

2. The development of the doctrine of part performance by the court of equity was aimed at preventing the *Statute* being used to permit frauds rather than to prevent them. The equitable doctrine of part performance is a striking example of what one might regard as a purposive interpretation of a piece of legislation. Can a court properly say: "Although the legislature's words appear clear, we cannot believe that they were meant to have the interpretation that they appear to require?" The answer to this question may lie in the fact that the relation of courts and the legislature in seventeenth-century England was not what that relation is in Canada today.

3. The courts developed the doctrine of part performance "to prevent the Court of Equity from giving relief in a case of a plain, clear and deliberate fraud": *Haigh v. Kaye* (1872), L.R. 7 Ch. App. 469, *per* James L.J. at p. 474.

4. Another example of the operation of the principle that "the *Statute of Frauds* cannot be used as an engine of fraud" is *Bannister v. Bannister*, [1948] 2 All E.R. 133 (C.A.). The defendant sold properties to the plaintiff on the plaintiff's oral promise that the defendant could live rent-free in a particular cottage on the land for as long as she liked. After the properties had been conveyed (by a deed containing no reference to the earlier oral agreement), disagreement arose between the parties and the plaintiff claimed possession of the cottage. The defendant pleaded the oral agreement, while the plaintiff relied on the English equivalent of s. 4, which required such an agreement to be in a written and signed form. The Court of Appeal held (*inter alia*) that it was fraudulent on the plaintiff's part to insist on the absolute nature of the conveyance in an attempt to defeat the defendant's beneficial interest. Such "hiding behind the stat-

ute" was not to be permitted: the plaintiff was held to be a constructive trustee of the property for the defendant, and he was required to hold the property on the terms of the oral agreement.

5.   While the restitution interest as developed by Fuller & Perdue (Chapter 1, above) can be seen as a special case of the reliance interest, the remedy of unjust enrichment is restitutionary in nature in the sense that it is based on the gain of the promisor. Although in many cases the gain of the promisor is the amount that the promisee gave up in reliance on the broken promise, the award is not a *reliance*-based measure of damages.

   This fact is illustrated by *Boone v. Coe*, 154 S.W. 900 (1913 Kent C.A.). The defendant orally agreed to a long-term lease of property in Texas to the plaintiffs. In reliance on this promise, the plaintiffs moved from Kentucky to Texas. When the plaintiffs arrived in Texas, the defendant refused to sign the lease or allow the plaintiffs to enter the land. The plaintiffs returned to Kentucky and sued the defendant for the expenses arising out of the abortive move based on the breach of the defendant's oral promise. In dismissing the plaintiff's action, Clay C. said:

   > [I]t must appear that the defendant has actually received, or will receive, some benefit from the acts of part performance. It is immaterial that the plaintiff may have suffered a loss because he is unable to enforce his contract. . . . In the case under consideration the plaintiffs merely sustained a loss. Defendant received no benefit. Had he received a benefit, the law would imply an obligation to pay therefor. Having received no benefit, no obligation to pay is implied. The *Statute* says that the contract of defendant made with plaintiffs is unenforceable. Defendant therefore had the legal right to decline to carry it out. To require him to pay plaintiffs for losses and expenses incurred on the faith of the contract, without any benefit accruing to him, would, in effect, uphold a contract upon which the *Statute* expressly declares no action shall be brought.

   The differing results in *Deglman* and *Boone v. Coe* illustrate the comparative strengths of the restitution and reliance interests. A remedy in *Boone v. Coe* might today be available on the basis that the defendant's words caused the plaintiff economic loss; we shall explore the issue of "negligent misstatement" further in Chapter 5.

6.   Would it have mattered on the facts of *Deglman* that the value of the house (market price less any mortgages or other charges) was (a) $20,000 or (b) $2? Should some notion of the expectation interest set a limit on recovery under any other interest?

   The *Statute of Frauds* makes the promise of the aunt unenforceable *against* her, but if she wants, she (or her estate) can still rely on the promise to give the nephew the house rather than pay *quantum meruit* damages. In what circumstances might she prefer to give the nephew the expectation interest, *i.e.*, the house.

   The nephew in *Deglman* cannot, *ex hypothesi*, have a claim for breach of contract for the promise of his aunt is unenforceable. The claim that his aunt (and, after her death, her estate) is "unjustly enriched" is not just shown by some mathematical calculation that shows a net benefit to the estate and a net loss to the nephew from what he did; there must be something to make it *unjust* for the aunt's estate to keep the benefit. The "unjustness" of the benefit is based on the assumption that the nephew would not have done what his aunt had asked, if she had not made the promise. The promise (and its recognition by the court) is central to the nephew's claim. The nephew's claim is not one for damages for breach of contract and so, in this sense, it is not a contractual claim, but it is clearly not one made completely outside a contractual relation. It is this confusion that makes the question about the relation between the measure of recovery allowed by the court and the expectation interest important.

7.   Lord Wright, in the quotation from *Fibrosa Spolka Akcyjna v. Fairbairn Lawson Combe Barbour Ltd.*, [1943] A.C. 32, reproduced by Cartwright J. in *Deglman* (¶ 14), suggests that the law of restitution is different from both contract and tort. Lord Wright's claim has been accepted by some academic commentators and rejected by

others. What is important is that courts and others justify what they do, and that these justifications respond to the concerns that we might have about fairness and the general issues discussed in Chapter 1.

There is a degree of flexibility in the type of relief that courts give in cases of unjust enrichment. Courts may award monetary relief, based on a *quantum meruit* assessment of the value of the services or property received by the defendant — restitutionary relief in terms of Fuller and Perdue terminology. There may also be cases in which a monetary award is given in a quasi-contract case, but the damages awarded are based on the plaintiff's reliance interest rather than on a restitution interest: see *Brewer Street Investments Ltd. v. Barclay's Woollen Co. Ltd.*, [1954] 1 Q.B. 428, [1953] 2 All E.R. 1330, in Chapter 3. In other cases, a court may recognize a proprietary claim through the imposition of a constructive trust; see *Lac Minerals Ltd. v. International Corona Resources Ltd.*, [1989] 2 S.C.R. 574, 61 D.L.R. (4th) 14, also in Chapter 3.

8. In some cases the right of a plaintiff to recover the defendant's unjust enrichment is an important adjunct to an action for damages for breach of contract. Thus, if a vendor of land breaches a written contract to sell, the purchaser has the right to seek the recovery of the deposit she has paid instead of seeking expectation damages for breach of contract. There may be good reasons for doing so: the price of land may have declined so that the purchaser would get no damages for the loss of the bargain; the purchaser may find it sufficient just to get back the deposit, without the trouble of seeking damages measured by a more complex formula. The vendor is not entitled to claim that the purchaser has suffered no loss, or even that she has been saved some money. The purchaser's claim is not for what she would have had if the contract had been performed, but for what she has paid the vendor, and by which he has been unjustly enriched. The vendor has no answer to this claim because he has no contractual right to keep the deposit. The vendor has no right to the deposit since his breach of contract has discharged the purchaser from her obligation to perform her part of the bargain — to pay the price.

The right to claim on the basis that the plaintiff has enriched the defendant and that this enrichment is unjust is, as we have seen, an alternative remedy when the plaintiff cannot show any true expectation damages.

9. Unjust enrichment is a restitutionary concept courts may use to give relief when there is no enforceable contract. It is sometimes difficult for the courts to decide whether or not a situation is "unjust", and the reasoning of courts about this may, on occasion, appear to be circular. It is sufficient to note that enrichment is not "unjust" if it occurs pursuant to a valid contract or a gift. We shall return to the various issues related to unjust enrichment at various points in this book.

10. Winston, a wealthy investor, has a fervent belief in astrology. He asks Eleanor to learn astrology so that she can assist him in his investments. In return, Winston promises to give Eleanor his cottage on his death. Eleanor attends courses and reads books in order to learn astrology. She gives Winston advice for many years. Winston dies without fulfilling his promise. What remedy does Eleanor have? Does it matter whether Winston made or lost money on the investments purchased on the advice of Eleanor?

PROMISES THAT WILL BE DENIED ENFORCEMENT: UNFAIRNESS

The courts traditionally were reluctant to deal with the argument that a contract should not be enforced on the ground that it is "unfair". Chapter 6 explores some of the reasons for this judicial reluctance. In recent years, however, courts have been more willing to acknowledge directly that they have the power to control objectionable behaviour. The exercise of that power results in the denial of contractual effect to the contract that is found to be objectionable. It is an inherently discretionary function for a court to decide whether or not an agreement is so "unfair" (or "unconscionable" or the product of "economic duress", to use more modern technical terms) that it should not be enforced. A considerable portion of these materials is devoted to examining this issue.

As discussed below, the doctrine of consideration is very technical, and there are some commercial situations in which courts use the doctrine of consideration to declare a promise unenforceable. But in some of the cases it is clear that when the argument is being made that a promise should not be enforced because of a lack of "consideration", the real concern is that the agreement is fundamentally unfair, or the product of overreaching in the bargaining process. Because of the discretionary, vague nature of the power to refuse to enforce agreements that are "unconscionable", judges were reluctant to use this power explicitly. Rather, they tended to make decisions about enforcement that seemed to turn on the application of complex rules about consideration.

Nevertheless judges have always been prepared — in clear cases — to exercise the power to refuse enforcement to unfair agreements. The following case is an example of a court refusing to enforce an "inequitable" contract.

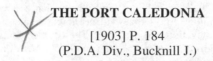

THE PORT CALEDONIA

[1903] P. 184
(P.D.A. Div., Bucknill J.)

[Two large sailing vessels were sheltering in Holyhead Harbour from a gale, when the master of one of them, the *Port Caledonia*, finding that his vessel had floated into dangerous proximity to the *Anna*, signalled for a tug. In response to the signal a tug came up, but her master demanded, "£1,000, or no rope" to pull the vessel away from a likely collision. The master of the *Port Caledonia* initially offered £100, but quickly agreed to pay the sum named, and was towed back to his original berth. The owner of the tug sued for £1,000 on the basis of the promise.]

BUCKNILL J.: — **[1]** . . . I shall not attempt to describe what the Elder Brethren and I think of conduct like that [*viz.*, the demand of the tug captain]. Language could not be too strong. It was most reprehensible conduct, and I will add, cowardly. But the master of the Port Caledonia, finding himself in a difficulty, promised to give a thousand pounds for the tug's services, which I value at very much less. . . .

[2] With the £1000 agreement on one side, and that which I think was the value of the services on the other, I have to ask myself whether the bargain that was made was so inequitable, so unjust, and so unreasonable that the Court cannot allow it to stand?

[3] The first question to consider is, What was the position of the two persons who made the agreement? The position was this. One man was in a position to insist upon his terms, and the other man had to put up with it. He could not help himself. He says in his letter to his owners: "He demanded £1000 to take me away. I offered him £100, or to leave it to the owners; but he would not agree, so I agreed to give £1000 rather than foul the Anna . . .". So he found himself obliged to give way to a person who would not move him, and who would have allowed him and the Anna to drift towards the rocks, and who would, I think, have seen them go there without putting a hawser on board unless he got a promise of £1000.

[4]   I have expressed my opinion about the matter. This opinion is shared by the Elder Brethren, and I hold that this agreement cannot be allowed to stand, and I set it aside.

[5]   I hope that those who perform such grand services in tugs from time to time, in worse weather than this, and, in peril of their own lives, save property around the coast, will note that this Court will keep a firm hand over them if they attempt to do what has been done in this case.

[6]   This was an inequitable, extortionate, and unreasonable agreement, and I think that the services rendered will be well rewarded by the sum of £200, and with county court costs.

NOTES

1.   In an admiralty case like *The Port Caledonia* the judge often sits with two of the "Elder Brethren", who are referred to as the "Masters of The Trinity House" or the "Nautical Assessors". The Trinity House is the name for the organization that supervised buoys, lighthouses and other navigational aids around the shores of the United Kingdom. The Elder Brethren are the senior, retired Royal Navy or merchant marine captains who would sit with the judge, listen to the evidence and then, as Bucknill J. indicates, give their opinion of how that evidence might be assessed by those experienced in the rules of navigation and seafaring. The practice continues to the present day, as noted in *Bow Spring (owners) v. Manzanillo II (owners)*, [2004] EWCA Civ 1007, where Lord Justice Clarke observed:

> In other words, in collision proceedings before the Admiralty Court, a good plot or simulation [of a nautical collision], no matter how well prepared and presented, will be treated with caution. Its true probative value will often be that it will assist the Court to determine not what happened, but rather what could not possibly have happened. What in fact happened in the collision remains, as ever, to be decided by the Admiralty Judge, with assistance from the Nautical Assessors sitting with him, after consideration of all the evidence before them.

2.   The presence of outside assessors like the Elder Brethren of The Trinity House may make the assertion of a wide reviewing power easier to maintain. Judges are not, in general, open to having those who are not legally trained join them as decision-makers.

    The current interest in alternative dispute resolution ("ADR"), *i.e.*, dispute resolution outside the framework of the courts, with their fairly cumbersome rules of procedure and judges, does not, in general, address this problem. Most of those who act as commercial arbitrators are retired judges or lawyers. In Canada, at least, there has not been a move to use people experienced in the business out of which a commercial dispute arose. In London, however, there is extensive use of commercial arbitrators experienced in the business that is the background to the dispute. In family law disputes, especially those involving children, psychologists and other mental health professionals are now sometimes used as arbitrators.

3.   The court in *The Port Caledonia* had no difficulty in setting the contract aside. This power is a dramatic assertion of the court's power to police the fairness of contracts. Outside the admiralty situation, the common law courts were reluctant to assert such a power until after 1950 when, initially with a great deal of circumlocution and with much confusion, they began to review contracts on the ground that their enforcement might be substantively unfair. We shall look at this development at various points in this book, especially in Chapter 6.

    One of the problems in deciding whether to enforce a contract in circumstances where the court is asked to consider the fairness of the deal is to determine what kind of pressure put by one side on the other is justifiable and what kind is not. *The Port*

Caledonia is an easy case — though it is, nevertheless, important to stop and ask why it is easy. There are much more difficult ones. We shall examine some of these cases later in this chapter, and return to this issue in Chapter 6.

The next section discusses a method of making contracts enforceable that does not depend on anything other than the fact that the agreement has been made with certain formalities through use of a sealed document. It is important to know that this method exists and what its requirements are; it offers an alternative basis for the enforcement of a promise if the more usual basis, *i.e.*, consideration, is not available.

FORMAL CONTRACTS: THE PROMISE UNDER SEAL

One of the earliest examples of a contract enforceable at common law was the promise under seal (also called a "deed" or, in a narrower class, a "specialty"). Deeds once played a very important role in the law: they were required for conveyances of land and for certain kinds of formal arrangements. Much of the significance of the deed — the promise that is contained in a document that is "signed, sealed and delivered" — is now gone, but it remains important for some non-commercial situations. As a general rule, considered below in some detail, a promise is only enforceable if given as part of an exchange transaction — that is, the promisee has given "consideration" and, in so doing, has "bought" the promisor's promise. The importance of the promise given under seal — the deed — is that it is enforceable even if there is no consideration. Thus, for example, it is possible to use a deed to make an enforceable promise to make a gift in the future.

A deed is enforceable because it is executed in a way that indicates care and deliberateness by the parties (perhaps now more in theory than in practice). In other words, a deed is enforceable not because it is part of a commercial exchange or because without enforcement the defendant would be unjustly enriched, but because of its *form*. A promise contained in a deed (a document under seal) is enforceable because it satisfies certain formal requirements.

Historically, the elaborate ritual sealing with hot wax and signet rings or hand-engraved seals must have been an impressive formal ceremony in a largely non-literate society. As we shall see, the modern requirements for sealing are not elaborate, and the significance of having a sealed document may not be apparent to a person who has signed it.

It is sometimes stated that a seal "imports" consideration or that the presence of a seal creates the presumption that there is consideration. These statements are not correct: the seal obviates the need for consideration. It is the presence of the seal alone that makes the promise under seal enforceable. There is always a danger in saying that there is "deemed to be" consideration when there is none. Statements that are inaccurate can mislead, so that it is usually better to say what is both accurate and sufficient.

The law regarding sealed instruments was originally special in that many of the rules that we now regard as of the essence of the law of contract were not applicable to deeds. Many of the special features of the old law have now been abolished, though some of the law regarding deeds remains to remind us of their former status. In some jurisdictions, legislation provides that an action on a sealed instrument has a longer limitation period than is applicable to contracts generally. In some important respects deeds have advantages that an ordinary contract does not have. A deed is also the only way of making a valid promise to make a gift. It is, for example, used by lawyers who want to make sure that their clients can take advantage of certain tax rules by making valid promises to make gifts, or otherwise ensure that a gift promise is enforceable: see, e.g., *Romaine v. Romaine*, [2001] B.C.J. No. 1775 (C.A.), 205 D.L.R. (4th) 320.

Deeds were commonly used in transactions concerning land, sometimes because there was a legislative requirement that they be used, but also out of habit: they have always been used, so why bother to change? Many bank forms, especially guarantees, are still executed as sealed instruments, because as guarantees they might be open to a challenge that there was no consideration for the guarantor's promise and, at least where the old law regarding limitation periods, *i.e.*, the time within which a plaintiff must start its action, is still in force, they have a much longer limitation period. One suspects that here too they are often used out of habit as much as for their special features.

At common law a contract under seal was a written document to which the contracting parties had affixed their seals. Seals were originally impressions made in hot wax by the parties' signet rings, or personal seals.

The crucial part of a sealed document is the end, where it is signed, and there is usually something like this:

IN WITNESS WHEREOF I have executed this Agreement this 26th day of July, 2006.

Signed, sealed and delivered in the presence of

_____   _____   (*seal*)
Witness   Name

The seal should be placed over or near the circle. An individual will usually affix a red wafer (taken from a strip purchased from a stationer) but may, if he or she chooses, still use hot sealing wax.

The part of the document that starts, "In witness . . .", is the "testimonium". The "attestation" clause states that the document is "signed, sealed and delivered in the presence of" a witness.

At one time, all the steps of signing, sealing and delivery of the deed were necessary, but the only essential requirement now is that the document be *intended* to be a sealed document, and no individual step is required, though the document must be in writing.

Signing is not strictly necessary (though now deeds are invariably signed by the promisor, and the *Statute of Frauds* requires it for certain documents) since the use of the seal antedated both that statute and the widespread practice of signing documents. Since seals were first used when many people could not sign their names, it was possible to signify assent by making a "mark", such as an "X", or even by placing the imprint of one's tooth on the document. The seal originally had to be wax and imprinted. Now a red wafer or printed blob or circle, usually with the letters "l.s." (*locus signali* — the place of the seal — or legal seal) or "c.s." (corporate seal) in the middle, suffices. Delivery of a sealed instrument, *i.e.*, the transfer of the instrument from the possession of the maker to the other or another person, is not necessary; the document can bind even though it has never left the obligor's possession.

Delivery is still sometimes important. A relatively recent case, *Paul D'Aoust Construction Ltd. v. Markel Insurance Co. of Canada* [1999] O.J. No. 1837, 45 C.L.R. (2d) 65 (C.A.) (affirmed, without reasons, [2001] S.C.J. No. 78) emphasizes the importance of the delivery of a deed. The question was the enforceability of a performance bond, given on behalf of a contractor by a surety company, the defendant in the case. The contractor signed the bond but it was never delivered to the plaintiff owner. When the contractor defaulted, the plaintiff claimed under bond. A majority of the Court of Appeal dismissed the claim as the bond, as a deed, had not been delivered. The Court held that delivery by the surety company to the contractor did not constitute delivery to the owner in the absence of an industry practice that contractors took delivery as agent for the owner. There was a strong dissent by Doherty J.A.

An example of the modern evolution of the old law of sealed documents is provided by *872899 Ontario Inc. v. Iacovoni* [1998] O.J. No. 2797, 40 O.R. (3d) 715, 163 D.L.R. (4th) 263 (C.A.). The plaintiff sought to enforce an agreement in which the defendants agreed to purchase a new home being built by the plaintiff. The issue was the applicable limitation period. At that time in Ontario, if the document was under seal, the period would be 20 years under the *Limitations Act*, R.S.O. 1990, c. L.15, s. 45(1)(c). If the agreement was not a sealed document, the period was six years and the plaintiff would be out of time. The signatures of the defendants followed a standard testimonium clause, stating that the document was "signed, sealed and delivered". There was, however, no physical indication of any kind that the document was sealed. The Ontario Court of Appeal held that this was a "simple contract" and not a "specialty" and hence the action was statute barred. This judgment shows the importance of making sure that a seal or some other physical manifestation of sealing is actually on the document at the time it is signed, so that there is some objective evidence of the parties' intention to make a deed. (The *Limitations Act, 2002*, S.O. 2002, c. 24, Sched. B changed the law in Ontario and abolished the different limitation period for sealed instruments, making it similar to that of most other common law provinces. The following case deals with the legal significance of a seal in the context of the doctrine of consideration, and also indicates what constitutes a seal:

 RE/MAX GARDEN CITY REALTY v. 828294 ONTARIO INC.

(1992), 8 O.R. (3d) 787, 25 R.P.R. (2d) 11
(Ont. Gen. Div., Philp J.)

[As part of an agreement of purchase and sale of land, the defendant vendor, a numbered company, 828294 Ontario Inc. ("828"), signed an irrevocable direction to pay to the plaintiff, its real estate agent, the unpaid balance of the commission. On the agreement, there was printed a black circle that resembled a seal under which was the word "(Seal)". Above the signature on behalf of the numbered company were the printed words "In witness whereof I have hereunto set my hand and seal", and to the left where the witness signed were the words "Signed, sealed and delivered in the presence of . . .".

The commission payment to the plaintiff agent was to be made from the proceeds of the sale. The sale closed, but Fleming, the solicitor for the defendant numbered company, although aware of the "irrevocable" direction, accepted and acted on a new direction from Louras, the president of 828, to pay the proceeds to the numbered company. Louras also gave Fleming an undertaking to indemnify Fleming if he incurred any liability as a result of following the new direction.

The plaintiff sued and moved for summary judgment against Fleming and 828 Ltd. for $35,600 — the outstanding balance of its commission. In its statement of defence, 828 claimed that no commission was owing, since the plaintiff real estate agent breached its obligations in that it had failed to bring forward another potential buyer who would have paid more for the property.]

PHILP J.: — **[1]** There is a question of whether or not proper consideration was given by the plaintiff to 828 and Louras, which would enable him to give the irrevocable direction.

[2]   The case that has come before me from the Divisional Court of Ontario is *Family Trust Corp. v. Morra* (1987), 60 O.R. (2d) 30. In that case Trainor J. held in a similar clause contained in an agreement of purchase and sale that there was no consideration from the agent for the vendor to complete an irrevocable direction to his solicitor and, therefore, in that case the previous decision of the trial judge was reversed and the agent's right to recover under the irrevocable direction from the solicitor was not allowed. In that case, as pointed out by counsel for the plaintiff, there was no seal contained in the agreement signed by the vendor; on the contrary, the instructions in the agreement opposite the signature of the vendor read "affix seal". No such seal was affixed. Without a seal the need for consideration must prevail.

[3]   In the tenth edition of Cheshire and Fifoot's *Law of Contract* (London: Butterworths, 1981), at p. 462, the author states:

> . . . a gratuitous agreement to assign a chose in action, like a gratuitous promise to give any form of property, is nudum pactum unless made under seal, and creates no obligation either legal or equitable.

On the basis of that principle the Divisional Court ruled in the case of *Family Trust Corp. v. Morra*, above, that the agreement could not stand.

[4]   It appears clear to me that the irrevocable direction is, in effect, an assignment by 828 to the plaintiff of monies that would be coming into the possession of its solicitor when the purchase was completed. It was an assignment under seal and, in my view, amounted to an equitable assignment which is enforceable. The agreement of purchase and sale before me has printed opposite the signature of Louras a black circle that resembles a seal, and under that circle is the word "(Seal)". It is clear from the document that the parties intended that that black printed circle be deemed a seal. Above the signature of Louras appears the printed words "In witness whereof I have hereunto set my hand and seal", and to the left where the witness signed are the words "Signed, sealed and delivered in the presence of".

[5]   For the defendant Fleming to pay that money, which is clearly described as the net real estate commission due and owing to Re/Max Garden City Realty Inc., was to breach the equitable assignment made by Louras on behalf of 828 to the plaintiff.

[6]   I should also state that the defendant, Louras, in cross-examination on his affidavit agreed that when he signed the acceptance of the agreement and agreed with the plaintiff to pay him the commission of $60,000 as set out in the listing agreement, he intended that 828 should pay the plaintiff the $60,000 commission after closing. By irrevocably instructing his solicitor to pay directly to the listing broker the unpaid balance he was, indeed, carrying out his intention, as it then was. The transaction was closed, the money was paid but Fleming breached his clear direction under seal to pay the balance of the commission to the plaintiff. . . .

[7]   I am satisfied, having taken a "good hard look", that the plaintiff is entitled to its judgment against Arthur D. Fleming for the sum of $35,600, and that the defendant Fleming is entitled to a summary judgment against 828 and Louras on the basis of the indemnification agreement that he received from them when they instructed him to pay the balance of the commission to them rather than to the plaintiff. Fleming, therefore, will be entitled to be indemnified for any monies paid by him to the plaintiff and to a judgment against 828 and Louras for that purpose.

NOTES

1. The decision in *Re/Max Garden City* allowed the real estate agent to enforce the sealed direction against Fleming, the vendor's lawyer, on a motion for summary judgment. It would not, however, prevent the vendor from bringing an action against the agent to establish that the agent had breached its duty to the vendor; such an action would likely require a trial to resolve.

2. A corporation, being a legal and not a physical person, cannot sign a document. Corporations therefore have to act through agents. For most ordinary contracts, the contract will be made by an officer or an employee who will be authorized to act in accordance with the corporation's hierarchy: the CEO will have been appointed and given his or her authority by the board of directors, and the CEO will have given authority down the line to the person who, for example, makes an individual sale. For many large contracts, especially contracts with banks, corporations had to and are still sometimes required to use a corporate seal. A corporate seal would make an impression on the paper and its use would have been specially authorized by the board of directors. Most modern corporate statutes provide that the use of a seal is no longer necessary to bind the corporation.

   The *Canada Business Corporations Act*, R.S.C. 1985, c. C-44, s. 23, provides that an agreement executed on behalf of a corporation is not invalid "merely because a corporate seal is not affixed to it", but does not change the effect of a document's being unsealed. The Ontario *Business Corporations Act*, R.S.O. 1990, c. B.16, s. 13, also provides that a corporation no longer has to have a seal. Nevertheless, a lender, a bank for instance, may still require that the corporation obtain a seal to execute loan or guarantee agreements. *corporate seal: x seal or signature?*

3. In *Friedmann Equity Developments Inc. v. Final Note Ltd.*, [2000] S.C.J. No. 37, [2000] 1 S.C.R. 842, 188 D.L.R. (4th) 269, the plaintiff was a mortgagee under a mortgage executed by the defendant under seal. The mortgage was registered under the *Land Registration Reform Act, 1984*. The plaintiff sued third parties as alleged undisclosed principals of the defendant. The third parties raised the defence of the "sealed contract rule", which precludes a claim against an undisclosed principal if the document expressing the obligation and signed by the (undisclosed) agent is under seal. The defendants moved for the determination of a point of law and for an order dismissing the claim. The trial judge denied the motion; the Divisional Court reversed him. The Court of Appeal held that the well-established "sealed contract rule" operated to prevent the claim. The fact that the *LRRA* gave any document purporting to convey an interest in land the same effect as if it had been sealed, meant that any registered document was subject to the rule. The rule was admitted to be an exception to general agency principles. A further appeal to the Supreme Court was dismissed.

   Bastarache J., giving the judgment of the Court, commented on the relation between the corporate seal and a sealed document (pp. 867-68 S.C.R.):

   > [37] . . . [T]he affixing of a corporate seal may not in all cases be evidence of an intention to create a sealed instrument, within the meaning of the sealed

contract rule. I agree with the reasoning of Morgan J.A. in *Newfoundland & Labrador Housing Corp.* [(1987), 38 D.L.R. (4th) 150 (Nfld. C.A.), who described the effect of a corporate seal as follows, at p. 152:

> . . . not every document signed by a corporation by the affixing its corporate seal would become a specialty. When the seal of a corporation is affixed to a contract made by the corporation it has the same effect as the signature of an individual. However, any contract which, if made between private persons would by law be required to be under seal, may be made on behalf of a company in writing under its common seal. Whether what would ordinarily be a simple contract is transformed into a contract by specialty by execution under seal can only be determined having regard to the intention of the parties as evidenced and the true construction of the document in question.

In my view, a corporation is certainly capable of creating a sealed instrument and availing itself of the different incidents which flow from such an agreement. However, the attachment of its corporate seal, on its own, may not be sufficient to do so. Courts must examine the instrument itself and the circumstances surrounding its creation to determine whether the corporation intended to create a sealed instrument by affixing its corporate seal.

This passage suggests that when a corporation intends to seal a document there must at least be some form of testimonium clause, indicating that the corporate seal is intended to both manifest the intent to bind the contract and to make the document a deed, a contract under seal.

Bastarache J. defended the "sealed contract rule" as an established rule which should not be disturbed. He said (pp. 854, 856-57, 873-74)

> [14] . . . In my view, there is no evidence that the sealed contract rule creates injustice or that it is inconsistent with commercial reality. The sealed contract rule is part of a system of property and contract rules which provide certainty in commercial relations. To change or abolish one rule within that system would inevitably create uncertainty with regard to the other rules. . . .

> . . .

> [19] The practice of sealing documents is one which is centuries old and which predates much of our modern legal history. Originally, it was used as a means of authenticating a document when most individuals were unable to sign their names. However, as time passed, the seal became a symbol of the solemnity of a promise and began to serve an evidentiary function. The seal rendered the terms of the underlying transaction indisputable, and thus rendered additional evidence unnecessary: see L. Fuller, "Consideration and Form" (1941), 41 *Colum. L. Rev.* 799, at p. 802. A contract under seal derived, and still derives, its validity from the form of the document itself: . . .

> [20] Because a contract under seal derives its validity from its form alone, there are several incidents of such a contract which differ from those of a simple contract. The fundamental difference between contracts under seal and simple contracts is in relation to the doctrine of consideration. The law will enforce a contract under seal even without consideration. Therefore, a gratuitous promise which is expressed in an instrument under seal is enforceable. There are other incidents of a contract under seal, which may be summarized as follows:

1. Where a debtor covenants in a deed to pay a debt antecedently based in simple contract, the right to sue in debt merges in the right to sue on the covenant and is extinguished in law.

2. In an action on a deed, a statement in the deed may operate by way of estoppel against the maker of the statement.

3. At common law, only a person named in an instrument under seal as a party to it could sue on a covenant in the instrument expressed to be for his benefit.

4. The limitation period for an action for a breach of a contract under seal may be longer than for a simple contract in some provinces. . . .

. . .

[45] . . . Scarcely anyone in society today would agree that the affixation of a seal is evidence of the greater solemnity and force of a promise. While the rationale for sealing a document may appear to be no longer socially relevant, it is not evident that the rules relating to sealed documents fall victim to the same critique.

[46] While our common law rules must be in step with the evolution of society as a whole, when examining a proposed change to a rule of property or contract law, we must also examine whether the rule is consistent or inconsistent with commercial reality. A rule may have a rationale which appears to be anachronistic while continuing to serve a useful commercial purpose. Our common law is replete with artificial rules which, although they may appear to have no underlying rationale, promote efficiency or security in commercial transactions. Such rules, in the circumstances where they apply, must be followed to create a legally recognized and enforceable right or obligation. Parties, therefore, structure their relations with these rules in mind and the rules themselves become part of commercial reality. Commercial relations may evolve in such a way that a particular rule may become unjust and cumbersome, and may no longer serve its original purpose. When the hardship which a rule causes becomes so acute and widespread that it outweighs any purpose that it may have once served, it is certainly open to a court to make an incremental change in the law. However, there must be evidence of a change in commercial reality which makes such a change in the common law necessary.

[47] The seal continues to serve a useful purpose in our law. It allows a promise to be enforced without evidence of consideration and, more importantly in the context of this case, grants parties to a contract a simple means of ensuring that they will not be liable to anyone but the parties named therein.

seals still relevent

The "sealed contract rule", like the rule to which it is an exception, is one that neatly illustrates the problems of rules and how they operate. The person who deals with an agent, believing the agent to be at all times a principal, *i.e.*, as a person dealing on his or her own behalf, always has an action against the apparent principal and will be entitled to what can fairly be called a windfall if it turns out the person who appeared to be the principal was, in fact, the agent of an undisclosed principal, because that person can now be sued also. The principal's appearance can never disadvantage the person because he or she has such rights of set-off or defence as the agent, the apparent principal, would have been subject to. *Ex hypothesi*, the person cannot have relied on there being a principal. The "sealed contract rule" therefore does not operate to defeat the person's expectations: all it does is to deny the person a right to sue someone who, when the contract was made, was unknown. In this context it is not clear in what direction "justice" would be found: neither the person nor the principal is entitled to much protection, the person because the existence of the principal was unknown, the principal because it chose to do business as it were in the background. To the extent that the undisclosed principal relied on the "sealed contract rule" to protect itself from liability (at the risk of being unable to enforce the agreement if the agent was unwilling or unable to do so), the abolition of the rule might catch it by surprise. However, abolition of the sealed contract rule would not protect any expectation that the person dealing with the agent might have had. If that person did not wish to trust the agent, he or she was entitled to refuse to do business with it or to require some form of security or protection. In other words, it does not matter that the rule is ar-

chaic, technical, idiosyncratic or even inconsistent with the law of undisclosed principals: its abolition would not serve to protect any reliance or reasonable expectations.
In this situation, it is difficult to see what evidence could be led to show that the rule
operated unjustly or was inconsistent with "commercial reality" — whatever that
might be.

4.   The history of the seal illustrates an important fact about legal formalities. In the hey-
      day of the seal (from about 1300 to 1700, and even later) sealing was a process calcu-
      lated to impress upon the person doing it the solemnity and seriousness of what was
      being done: hot wax was poured over the document and the seal was pressed into it.
      The fact of sealing served an evidentiary and cautionary function. Gradually the so-
      lemnity became reduced until today sealing is a virtually meaningless ritual: at best it
      is the affixing of a little red circle taken from a roll of peel-off labels. The risk is that
      there is now no particular importance attached to the seal, and whatever cautionary
      function it had may be largely gone. It is difficult to know whether someone really in-
      tended to execute a sealed document.

           There are, however, situations in which individuals want to ensure that a promise is
      free from attack on the ground that it did not satisfy the technical requirement of the
      law of consideration. The rules regarding sealed documents still provide a lawyer with
      an important tool that remains necessary even today. It is desirable to have a device
      that serves a channelling function — that ensures that an enforceable promise has been
      made.

5.   The Ontario Law Reform Commission in its *Report on Amendment of the Law of Con-
      tract* (1987), at p. 47, recommended that the "seal should be denied all legal effect in
      the law of contracts" and that a "witnessed and signed writing should take the place of
      the seal for the purposes of contract law".

           A witnessed and signed writing would probably have as much effect as the seal has
      now in bringing the significance of what the signer is doing home to him or her. Seals
      are used in many places outside the law of contracts — a deed of gift must be under
      seal, but such a promise will not be part of a contract — and while most sealed docu-
      ments will be witnessed and signed, why "abolish" the seal? Would this mean that a
      document executed under seal that is not, for example, formally witnessed, is to be of
      no effect?

           The Ontario proposal may be contrasted with the Law Reform Commission of Brit-
      ish Columbia's *Report on Deeds and Seals* (LRC 96, June 1988), which recommends
      retention of the seal.

6.   The Ontario *Electronic Commerce Act, 2000*, S.O. 2000, c. 17, s. 11(6) allows for an
      electronic document to be "deemed" to be sealed by following the "prescribed seal
      equivalency requirements". Other jurisdictions are enacting similar laws.

7.   The power exercised by the court in the *Port Caledonia* to refuse to enforce a contract
      because it is unfair or, to use the modern word, "unconscionable", is available in *all*
      kinds of contracts, including those made by seal: *Chilliback v. Pawliuk* (1956), 1
      D.L.R. (2d) 611 (Alta. S.C.).

CONSIDERATION

The Rationale: Enforcing Bargains and Not Gifts

The doctrine of consideration is traditionally regarded as being at the heart of the
common law rules regarding the enforcement of contracts. Any selection of cases
about consideration is necessarily an examination of contracts where things may
have gone wrong. The rules that can be deduced from cases where things have
gone wrong are often poor indications of the concerns of the courts and, what may
be more important, of the concerns of practising lawyers as they guide their clients
through the thickets of the law. The cases in this section may suggest that prob-

lems with the enforceability of the commercial exchange are common, whereas in practice they are relatively rare.

There are two general types of problems in regard to consideration. The first type occurs where promises are made that are not part of a commercial exchange. The other group of cases are ones where the courts are prepared to deny enforcement of a promise made as part of a commercial exchange for a variety of reasons — some good, some very bad.

In almost all cases of commercial transactions, there is clearly consideration, and enforceability is not an issue. The problem cases occur in a number of fairly well-defined situations. While it is important to understand the law of consideration, in practice consideration problems arise relatively rarely.

In many situations there are very strong reasons for enforcing promises, or providing other relief when necessary to prevent unjust enrichment or to protect reliance. There are also good reasons to enforce promises that are deliberately made and clearly expected to be enforced. As Fuller suggests, three related questions can help determine whether a promise should be enforced:

(1) To what extent is there clear evidence of the promise and of the other factors that would suggest it should be enforced?

(2) To what extent is there evidence that the promisor was aware of the fact that he or she was undertaking a legally enforceable obligation?

(3) To what extent is the promise one that is common or typical of commercial exchange?

As Fuller argues, these three questions are closely related: the more formal the document and the more formality there was when it was signed, the more likely it is that there was deliberateness in its making; the document that results will probably also provide very good evidence of the promise, what it was and what risks each party assumed. A standard transaction in business — ordering supplies, hiring staff, taking orders for goods — similarly brings with it evidence that the individuals making the promises knew what they were doing, and expect that the transaction will have legal consequences. The more certainty that one of these three questions can be answered strongly positively, the more of a rationale there is for enforcement.

For good reasons, courts are ordinarily reluctant to enforce promises to make a gift, though once a gift is executed, it is a valid and generally irrevocable way to transfer property.

One of the problems with gift promises is that they are often vague and made with a lack of deliberation. It may be difficult to distinguish a clear promise to make a gift from an expression of hope that a gift may be made. "I promise to give you $100" may not sound very different from, "I sincerely hope to give you $100". Should courts struggle with trying to make this type of distinction — especially in the absence of reliance or unjust enrichment?

There is also a feeling that perhaps donors should have the right to change their minds about making a gift before it is executed: perhaps the donee turns out to be ungrateful or unworthy. Should a court try to "second guess" the validity of a decision to revoke a gift promise?

Furthermore, enforcing a gift promise as a contract may serve to benefit those who gave nothing of value to the donor to the prejudice of real creditors who have given value. *Dalhousie College v. Boutilier*, [1934] S.C.R. 642, [1934] 3 D.L.R. 593 (*infra*) explores this issue.

For a fuller discussion of some of the reasons courts are reluctant to enforce gift promises, see M.A. Eisenberg, "Donative Promises" (1979), 47 *U. Chi. L. Rev.* 1-33; and R. Kreitner, "The Gift Beyond the Grave: Revisiting the Question of Consideration" (2001), 101 *Colum. L. Rev.* 1876.

The Basic Concept of Consideration

In the nineteenth century the courts began to develop the "bargain theory" of enforceability. Promises could only be enforced if they were part of a bargain, that is if the promisee gave consideration to the promisor. It was said that a plaintiff could establish consideration either by showing that he had conferred a benefit on the defendant, or that he had suffered a detriment. In *Thomas v. Thomas* (1842), 2 Q.B. 851, 144 E.R. 330 (*infra*) Patteson J. said:

> Consideration means something which is of value in the eye of the law, moving from the plaintiff: it may be some benefit to the [defendant] or some detriment to the [plaintiff].

In *Currie v. Misa* (1875), L.R. 10 Exch. 153, 162 (Exch. Ch.), affirmed (1876), 1 App. Cas. 554, Lush J. said:

> A valuable consideration in the sense of the law may consist either in some right, interest, profit or benefit accruing to one party, or some forbearance, detriment, loss or responsibility given, suffered or undertaken by the other.

Another judicially approved version is that of *Pollock on Contracts*, 8th ed., p. 175:

> An act of forbearance of one party, or the promise thereof, is the price for which the promise of the other is bought, and the promise thus given for value is enforceable.

This statement was approved by Lord Dunedin in *Dunlop Pneumatic Tyre Co. Ltd. v. Selfridge and Co. Ltd.*, [1915] A.C. 847 at p. 855.

In the twentieth century, other definitions were developed, such as that of Cheshire, Fifoot and Furmston, *Law of Contract*, 13th ed. (1996):

> [T]he plaintiff must show that he has bought the defendant's promise either by doing some act in return for it or by offering a counter-promise. . . . This definition of consideration as the price paid by the plaintiff for the defendant's promise is preferable to the nineteenth-century terminology of benefit and detriment. It is easier to understand, it corresponds more happily to the normal exchange of promises and it emphasizes the commercial character of the English contract.

Notice that under these definitions, the promisee must have given value in order to be able to enforce the promise of the promisor, but it is *not* necessary for the promisor to have received value. Thus, a creditor-promisee can enforce a guarantee of a loan made to a debtor on condition that the promisor provides the guarantee. The consideration moving from the promisee is the making of the loan — while the benefit goes to debtor from the creditor, it does *not* go *to* the promisor-guarantor.

The following three cases are examples of the courts using the doctrine of consideration to determine whether a promise made in a non-commercial situation is enforceable. Consider how well the doctrine of consideration functions as a useful test for the enforceability of promises. Is there any other test that might be more useful? Remember also that these cases are not commercial cases, and for that reason they offer any test for enforceability its most difficult challenge. These cases are useful in suggesting what the limits of any test might be. How well does the doctrine of consideration function — in any of its formulations — as a predictively useful rule? In other words, after you have read the first case, could you predict the outcome of the second or third? As you read these three cases, consider whether there are facts which the judges do not mention that might influence the decision whether or not to enforce the promises in question.

THOMAS v. THOMAS

(1842), 2 Q.B. 851, 114 E.R. 330
(Q.B., Lord Denman C.J., Patteson and Coleridge JJ.)

[A few hours before his death, John Thomas, wishing to make further provision for his wife beyond that which he had already provided in his will, declared in the presence of several witnesses that he wanted her to have the house in which they lived (which he held under a long lease) for her life. After the death of John Thomas, his executors made an agreement with his widow under which she was to have the house for her life. Under this agreement she was to have the house "provided . . . that [she] shall pay . . . £1 yearly towards the ground rent payable in respect" of the house, and provided that she maintain the premises in a state of good repair. Mrs. Thomas remained in possession of the house until, on the death of one of the executors, the other evicted her. Mrs. Thomas sought to recover possession in these proceedings. Counsel on behalf of the defendant executor argued that there was no consideration for the promise to let Mrs. Thomas remain in the house for her life.]

LORD DENMAN C.J.: — [1] There is nothing in this case but a great deal of ingenuity, and a little wilful blindness to the actual terms of the instrument itself. There is nothing whatever to shew that the ground rent was payable to a superior landlord; and the stipulation for the payment of it is not a mere proviso, but an express agreement.

[2] This is in terms an express agreement, and shews a sufficient legal consideration quite independent of the moral feeling which disposed the executors to enter into such a contract. Mr. Williams's [counsel for the defendant's] definition of consideration is too large; the word *causa* in the passage referred to means one which confers what the law considers a benefit on the party. Then the obligation to repair is one which might impose charges heavier than the value of the life estate.

PATTESON J.: — [3] It would be giving to *causa* too large a construction if we were to adopt the view urged for the defendant: it would be confounding consideration with motive. Motive is not the same thing with consideration. Consideration means something which is of some value in the eye of the law, moving from the plaintiff: it may be some benefit to the [defendant], or some detriment to the [plaintiff]; but at all events it must be moving from the plaintiff. Now that which is suggested as the consideration here, a pious respect for the wishes of the testator, does not in any way move from the plaintiff; it moves from the testator; therefore, legally speaking, it forms no part of the consideration. Then it is said that, if that be so, there is no consideration at all, it is a mere voluntary gift; but when we look at the agreement we find that this is not a mere proviso that the donee shall take the gift with the burthens; but it is an express agreement to pay what seems to be a fresh apportionment of a ground rent, and which is made payable not to a superior landlord but to the executors. So that this rent is clearly not something incident to the assignment of the house; for in that case, instead of being payable to the executors, it would have been payable to the landlord. Then as to the repairs: these houses may very possibly be held under a lease containing covenants to repair; but we know nothing about it: for anything that appears, the liability to repair is first created by this instrument. The proviso certainly struck me at first as Mr. Williams put it, that the rent and repairs were merely attached to the gift by the donors; and, had the instrument been executed by the donors only, there might have been some ground for that construction; but the fact is not so. Then it is suggested that this would be held to be a mere voluntary conveyance as against a subsequent purchaser for value: possibly that might be so: but suppose it would: the plaintiff contracts to take it, and does take it, whatever it is, for better for worse; perhaps a bona fide purchase for a valuable consideration might override it; but that cannot be helped.

[**COLERIDGE J.**'s judgment was to the same effect.]

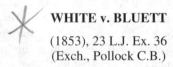

WHITE v. BLUETT

(1853), 23 L.J. Ex. 36
(Exch., Pollock C.B.)

[The action was brought on a promissory note made by the defendant in favour of his father. The father, who was now dead, had lent money to his son and the promissory note acknowledged this debt. The father's executor sued the son on the note. The defence raised by the son was that his father had promised to forgive the debt. The son's evidence was that he had complained to his father that he (the son) had not been given as much as the other children. As a result, the father had agreed that, if the son would not complain any more, he (the father) would forgive the debt. The son claimed that he had kept his part of the bargain up to the death of his father. The form of the action did not put the son's evidence to any test of its accuracy: the plaintiff merely denied that the evidence even if true was a defence to the action on the note. If the father had destroyed the promissory note or given it to the son, it could not have been enforced against the son.]

POLLOCK C.B.: — The plea is clearly bad. By the argument a principle is pressed to an absurdity, as a bubble is blown until it bursts. Looking at the words merely there is some foundation for the argument, and, following the words only, the conclusion may be arrived at. It is said, the son had a right to an equal distribution of his father's property, and did complain to his father because he had not an equal share, and said to him, I will cease to complain if you will not sue upon this note. Whereupon the father said, if you will promise me not to complain I will give up the note. If such a plea as this could be supported, the following would be a binding promise: A man might complain that another person used the public highway more than he ought to do, and that other might say, do not complain, and I will give you five pounds. It is ridiculous to suppose that such promises could be binding. So, if the holder of a bill of exchange were suing the acceptor, and the acceptor were to complain that the holder had treated him hardly, or that the bill ought never to have been circulated, and the holder were to say, Now, if you will not make any more complaints, I will not sue you. Such a promise would be like that now set up. In reality, there was no consideration whatever. The son had no right to complain, for the father might make what distribution of his property he

liked; and the son's abstaining from doing what he had no right to do can be no _vatio_
consideration.

HAMER v. SIDWAY

27 N.E. 256 (1891)
(Court of Appeals New York)

[William Story Sr. had a nephew, William Story II. At the golden wedding anniversary of the nephew's parents the uncle promised that if his nephew (who was then 15 years old) would refrain from using alcohol or tobacco, from swearing, and from playing cards or billiards for money until he was 21, the uncle would pay him $5,000. The nephew agreed to do as his uncle requested, and fulfilled the conditions of his uncle's promise. After the nephew became 21 he wrote to his uncle reminding him of his promise. The uncle replied by letter in which he acknowledged the debt, said that the money was set aside for the nephew, and that it could be regarded as earning interest. The letter was full of good advice, and concluded by saying that the uncle did not want to pay so large a sum to a young man. Nothing further was done by either party until the uncle died. A claim was then made to his executor by a person to whom the nephew had assigned the debt for $5,000. Although it was not mentioned in the judgment, the assignee, who was enforcing the obligation, undoubtedly gave the nephew something of value in return for the assignment, expecting to be able to enforce the obligation.]

PARKER J.: — The defendant contends that the contract was without consideration to support it, and therefore invalid. He asserts that the promisee, by refraining from the use of liquor and tobacco, was not harmed, but benefited; that which he did was best for him to do, independently of his uncle's promise, — and insists that it follows that, unless the promisor was benefited, the contract was without consideration, — a contention which, if well founded, would seem to leave open for controversy in many cases whether that which the promisee did or omitted to do was in fact of such benefit to him as to leave no consideration to support the enforcement of the promisor's agreement. Such a rule could not be tolerated, and is without foundation in the law. The Exchequer Chamber in 1875 [*Currie v. Misa* (1875), L.R. 10 Exch. 153] defined "consideration" as follows: "A valuable consideration, in the sense of the law, may consist either in some right, interest, profit, or benefit accruing to the one party, or some forbearance, detriment, loss, or responsibility given, suffered, or undertaken by the other." Courts "will not ask whether the thing which forms the consideration does in fact benefit the promisee or a third party, or is of any substantial value to any one. It is enough that something is promised, done, forborne, or suffered by the party to whom the promise is made as consideration for the promise made to him." *Anson, Contracts.* 63. "In general a waiver of any legal right at the request of another party is a sufficient consideration for a promise." *Parsons Contracts* 444. "Any damage, or suspension, or forbearance of a right will be sufficient to sustain a promise." 2 Kent, *Commentaries.* (12th ed.) 465. Pollock in his work on *Contracts* (page 166), after citing the definition given by the Exchequer Chamber, already quoted, says: "The second branch of this judicial description is really the most important one. "Consideration" means not so much that one party is profiting as that the other abandons some legal right in the present, or limits his legal freedom of action in the future, as an inducement for the promise of the first." Now, applying this rule to the facts before us, the promisee used tobacco, occasionally drank liquor, and he had a legal right to do so. That right he abandoned for a period of years upon the strength of the promise of the testator that for such forbearance he would give him $5,000. We need not speculate on the effort which may have been required to give up the use of those stimulants. It is sufficient that he restricted his lawful freedom of action within certain prescribed limits upon the faith of his uncle's agreement, and now, having fully performed the conditions imposed, it is of no moment whether such performance actually proved a benefit to the promisor, and the court will not inquire into it; but, were it a proper subject of inquiry, we see nothing in this record that would permit a determination that the uncle was not benefited in a legal sense. . . .

All concur.

NOTES AND QUESTIONS

1. Could an expression of heart-felt gratitude be consideration? While such an expression might not be a detriment to the promisee, it could be a benefit to the promisor.

2. Consideration is premised on there being a bargain or an exchange relation. To what extent does each of these cases present an exchange transaction?

    Each of these cases actually involved an incompleted gift transaction, with a dead donor. The usual way for a person to make a legally valid gift to take effect on death is by means of a will. A will is a signed document, made with evidence of deliberation, for example by having two witnesses other than a beneficiary sign the will to indicate that it was executed by the testator in their presence.

    If the person seeking to enforce the gift in each case could not frame the action as one to enforce a contract in which the promisee gave consideration, the benefit of the promised gift would not be enjoyed by the "donee".

    Forgetting for a moment the whole idea of consideration, focus instead on a number of issues that are discussed at the beginning of this chapter and consider the following questions:

    (a) What evidence is there that the promise being sued on in each case was carefully made? (Try, for example, to imagine the actual conversation between the father and son in *White v. Bluett*.)

    (b) What evidence is there of the terms of the promise made in each case?

    (c) To what extent does each case represent what might be regarded as a common type of arrangement? (In *Thomas v. Thomas*, for example, the ordinary method for the husband to have left a life interest in the house to his wife would be by making a will. To what extent can what happened be seen simply as a means of giving effect to what the husband wanted done with his property on his death, in circumstances where he did not make a will?)

    (d) Each case involved what was, in effect, an uncompleted gift. Are there differences in each case that might justify the different results? What evidence is there of deliberation, reliance or unjust enrichment in each case?

3. What about the following two promises?

    (a) A promises to give B $1,000 on the condition that B will promise to accept it. B promises to accept the money.

    (b) A promises to give B her a car if B will promise to obtain the annual licence sticker.

    Can B sue A for the $1,000 or the car? The transactions are in form an exchange of promises, but in substance they are gifts. Even the second is a gift, for if the car is transferred to B, A has no more responsibility for the licence. Are these the kinds of contracts you would expect the court to enforce? Are there any more reasons to support these promises than to support what may be called an "ordinary" gift promise?

There will inevitably be problems in the transformation of an unenforceable gift promise into an "exchange" promise by arguments or devices such as these. The executor argued, for example, in *Thomas v. Thomas* that the widow's promise to pay £1 a year towards the ground rent of the house was a promise of the type in the second example above. That is, he argued that the widow's undertaking was a mere condition of accepting the gift. Patteson J., however, held that the widow's promise was "not a mere proviso that [she should] take the gift with the burthens".

It is sometimes said that there is no consideration if the return promise turns out on examination to be a promise that obligates the promisor to do nothing, in the sense that a promise to accept a gift is a promise to do nothing. Is this helpful?

4. It is important to notice the context and effect of the court's use of the doctrine of consideration in each of the three cases. The decisions are based on the assumption that if a promise made can be fitted into a bargain structure, it will be enforceable. The court in each case discusses the doctrine of consideration as *the test* for the *enforceability* of promises, and implies that there is really nothing else to be looked at in each case except the extent to which the promise sued on was "bought" by the promisee. While many judges, writers and students make the same assumptions and argue that consideration is the test for enforceability, this may not be the best way to look at the problems raised.

Keep in mind that, while the courts will give a remedy to prevent unjust enrichment without an explicit promise and will enforce the gift promise under seal, the normal situation for enforcement of promises involves commercial exchanges. The significance of this observation is that the doctrine of consideration is, as a matter of practice, only relevant in two classes of promises. The first is the kind of promise we have seen in the three cases above. These were not commercial promises, or more precisely, these were not promises made in a commercial setting. The second class comprises promises made in a commercial setting, but which, as we shall see, are made *unenforceable* because of the operation of the doctrine of consideration.

While the three cases are factually distinguishable, by using the doctrine of consideration the courts did not give much guidance for distinguishing *White v. Bluett* from *Hamer v. Sidway*. It is more likely that the attitude of the court will be to enforce a promise where:

(a) the promisee can show that the promise met some minimum standard of care in its making;

(b) the terms of the promisor's undertaking are fairly clearly proved; and

(c) the promise was made in the course of some readily comprehensible or common arrangement.

The three cases we have looked at are arguably more easily understood in terms of these three factors than by applying the doctrine of consideration.

There is a logical flaw in the conventional view that a promisee must prove that he or she has given consideration to enforce a promise. This view of consideration as a requirement for enforceability holds that since the ordinary commercial contract is enforced because it is a bargain and there is consideration, only those promises where there is consideration should be enforced. The flaw lies in regarding a *sufficient* reason for enforcement as a *necessary* reason. In other words, the enforcement of bargains does not necessarily entail the denial of enforcement to non-bargain promises.

There are other reasons besides the presence of consideration for enforcing commercial promises, and there may be reasons for enforcing some non-commercial promises that should not turn on whether a court can find consideration.

Despite these reservations about the value of the doctrine of consideration, it remains an important legal concept and solicitors worry a lot about it.

5.   As a practical matter, the doctrine of consideration runs into difficulty in a fairly small number of situations. These situations are sometimes non-commercial, but a surprisingly large number are commercial.

In the commercial cases there is a significant risk of harm from the unthinking application of the doctrine of consideration. The effect of the application of the doctrine in these cases is to make unenforceable a contract that should be enforced. The doctrine of consideration can never make enforceable a contract that should not be enforced because it was induced by fraud or duress, or because it is unfair or unconscionable.

In other words, as we saw in *The Port Caledonia*, a court will not enforce a promise made in a grossly unfair exchange transaction, though it may require compensation for any value conferred. "Dressing up" a fraudulent transaction as a deed will not save the promise of the person defrauded and make it enforceable. On the other hand, the conclusion that the promisee was unjustly enriched by what the fraudulent party did may be a reason for allowing even a fraudulent person to obtain some relief.

6.   There are ways by which any lawyer can *always* avoid the problems of the doctrine of consideration. The cases that come up are nearly always those in which the parties did not have legal advice. The problems that arose in the three cases we have just looked at could all have been avoided by appropriately drafted wills or by the use of instruments under seal, and any solicitor should know how to make such promises enforceable, provided, of course, that the donor is prepared to make such a promise in a form that would clearly be enforceable.

A common legal statement is that: "Consideration need not be adequate, but must be sufficient." This opaque statement means that the doctrine of consideration does *not* require that the parties make or agree to make an exchange of commercial equivalents. It is sufficient consideration if the arrangement is cast in the form of an exchange so that, as in *Hamer v. Sidway*, the nephew gave up something at his uncle's request.

The statements about the "adequacy" of consideration in *Westlake v. Adams* (1858), 5 C.B. (N.S.) 248, 141 E.R. 99 at p. 106, *per* Byles J. are still generally accepted as good law:

> It is an elementary principle, that the law will not enter into an inquiry as to the adequacy of the consideration; so that much less consideration than here existed might have sufficed. Lastly, it must be remembered that the defendant in this case has received a full performance of the terms of the indenture at the hands of the plaintiff. The jury have, I think, made an end of the question; for, they have found (as they well might) that the defendant received what he bargained for, and all that he bargained for.

From this quotation comes the proposition that the law will not concern itself with the *adequacy*, *i.e.*, the *amount*, of consideration or the substance of the bargain, but only with the question whether there is any consideration or whether it is of a legally *sufficient nature*. This statement is not, however, entirely accurate. The courts will sometimes examine the substance or fairness of the bargain, as *The Port Caledonia* revealed.

The idea that consideration could be satisfied by a formal exchange of things (not money) has been accepted for a long time — this is the idea of nominal consideration, which is legally sufficient consideration. Among the things that were traditionally regarded as nominal consideration were peppercorns (small kernels of unground pepper). If, therefore, B gave A a peppercorn in each of the situations in question 2, the promises to make the gifts would be enforceable. Yet what distin-

Something must be exchanged

guishes the case in which B promises to accept the gift or pay the licence fee, from that in which he pays (or promises to pay) a peppercorn? It cannot be in the adequacy of the consideration: both promises are equally valueless. To say that the consideration is sufficient in one, but not in the other, avoids the issue because we then need to know what "sufficient" means.

Even though it is accepted in texts that a peppercorn given as the "price" for the other's promise is sufficient to make the promise enforceable, you should be cautious before you carry a supply of peppercorns with you or provide them to your clients. Unless the person given the peppercorn appreciates its significance, a court may be unwilling to enforce the promise so "bought". The courts are likely to want to ensure that a promisor understands that something is truly intended to be "nominal consideration", in the way that people will understand that an agreement to sell a house for "one dollar" is intended to signify that the parties wish to have an enforceable promise.

The existence of nominal "consideration" as a means of making promises enforceable illustrates the fact that it is not totally clear what, in situations outside the commercial exchange, is the true touchstone of enforceability.

Past Consideration

An aspect of the doctrine of consideration is the rule that: "Past consideration is no consideration". That is, if *after* a promisee has already performed an act, the promisor makes a promise to pay for it, *the promise* will generally not be enforceable because the consideration is said to be "past". However, as with gift promises, if the promise to pay for "past consideration" is honoured, the payment that has been made is not recoverable. The rationale behind the rule about past consideration is that the promise was not part of a bargain or exchange, and is too much like a gift or gratuity given in recognition of a fully performed act.

The leading precedent on past consideration is the nineteenth-century decision in *Eastwood v. Kenyon*. It is an important decision, though not easy for modern readers to follow.

EASTWOOD v. KENYON

(1840), 11 A. & E. 438, 113 E.R. 482
(Q.B., Lord Denman C.J., Patteson and Coleridge JJ.)

[The plaintiff was the executor of the will of John Sutcliffe; John Sutcliffe died leaving an infant daughter, Sarah, who later married the defendant. The plaintiff, acting as Sarah's guardian, spent £140 of his own money in looking after Sarah's estate. The plaintiff had to borrow this money from one Blackburn, to whom he gave a promissory note. When Sarah became of full age (21 at that time) she assented to the loan, and she orally promised the plaintiff that she would pay the amount of the loan from Blackburn to the plaintiff. Sarah paid one year's interest on the loan. When Sarah married the defendant, he orally promised the plaintiff that he would pay Blackburn and discharge the loan. The defendant did not pay the loan, and so the plaintiff had to pay it. The plaintiff then sued the defendant on his promise. The defendant argued that he was not liable for his promise to pay Sarah's debt since it was barred by the suretyship provision of the *Statute of Frauds*.

At trial, there was a verdict for the plaintiff, subject, however, to a motion to enter a verdict for the defendant on the ground that the promise was unenforceable under the *Statute of Frauds.* A rule *nisi* was obtained arresting judgment on the ground that the declaration showed no consideration for the promise alleged. Lord Denman delivered the judgment of the court. The portion of the judgment dealing with the *Statute of Frauds* is omitted. The court held on that issue that the promise was outside the *Statute* since the defendant made the promise to repay to the primary debtor, the plaintiff, and not to the creditor, Blackburn, and hence it was not a suretyship.]

LORD DENMAN: — [1] The second point arose in arrest of judgment, namely, whether the declaration showed a sufficient consideration for the promise. . . .

[2]   Upon motion in arrest of judgment, this promise must be taken to have been proved, and to have been an express promise, as indeed it must of necessity have been, for no such implied promise in law was ever heard of. It was then argued for the plaintiff that the declaration disclosed a sufficient moral consideration to support the promise.

[3]   Most of the older cases on this subject are collected in a learned note to the case of *Wennall v. Adney* (1802), 3 B. & P. 249, 127 E.R. 137, and the conclusion there arrived at seems to be correct in general,

> that an express promise can only revive a precedent good consideration, which might have been enforced at law through the medium of an implied promise, had it not been suspended by some positive rule of law; but can give no original cause of action, if the obligation, on which it is founded, never could have been enforced at law, though not barred by any legal maxim or statute provision.

[4]   Instances are given of voidable contracts, as those of infants ratified by an express promise after age, and distinguished from void contracts, as of married women, not capable of ratification by them when widows; *Loyd v. Lee* (1718), 1 Stra. 94; debts of bankrupts revived by subsequent promise after certificate; and similar cases. . . .

[5]   The enforcement of such promises by law, however plausibly reconciled by the desire to effect all conscientious engagements, might be attended with mischievous consequences to society; one of which would be the frequent preference of voluntary undertakings to claims for just debts. Suits would thereby be multiplied, and voluntary undertakings would also be multiplied, to the prejudice of real creditors. The temptations of executors would be much increased by the prevalence of such a doctrine, and the faithful discharge of their duty be rendered more difficult.

[6]   Taking then the promise of the defendant, as stated on this record, to have an express promise, we find that the consideration for it was past and executed long before, and yet it is not said to have been at the request of the defendant, nor even of his wife while sole (though if it had, the case of *Mitchinson v. Hewson* (1797), 7 T.R. 348, shews that it would not have been sufficient), and the declaration really discloses nothing but a benefit voluntarily conferred by the plaintiff and received by the defendant, with an express promise by the defendant to pay money.

[7]   If the subsequent assent of the defendant could have amounted to a *ratihabitio*, the declaration should have stated the money to have been expended at his request, and the ratification should have been relied on as matter of evidence, but this was obviously impossible, because the defendant was in no way connected

with the property or with the plaintiff, when the money was expended. If the ratification of the wife while sole [*i.e.*, while she was unmarried] were relied on, then a debt from her would have been shewn, and the defendant could not have been charged in his own right without some further consideration, as of forbearance after marriage, or something of that sort; and then another point would have arisen upon the *Statute of Frauds* which did not arise as it was, but which might in that case have been available under the plea of *non assumpsit*.

[8]   In holding this declaration bad because it states no consideration but a past benefit not conferred at the request of the defendant, we conceive that we are justified by the old common law of England.

[9]   *Lampleigh v. Brathwait* (1615), Hob. 105, 80 E.R. 255, is selected by Mr. Smith (1 *Smith's Leading Cases* 67), as the leading case on this subject, which was there fully discussed, though not necessary to the decision. Hobart C.J. lays it down that

> a mere voluntary courtesy will not have a consideration to uphold an assumpsit. But if that courtesy were moved by a suit or request of the party that gives the assumpsit, it will bind; for the promise, though it follows, yet it is not naked, but couples itself with the suit before, and the merits of the party procured by that suit; which is the difference;

a difference brought fully out by *Hunt v. Bate* (1568), Dyer 272 (a), there cited from Dyer, where a promise to indemnify the plaintiff against the consequences of having bailed the defendant's servant, which the plaintiff had done without request of the defendant, was held to be made without consideration; but a promise to pay £20 to plaintiff, who had married defendant's cousin, but at defendant's special instance, was held binding.

[10]   The distinction is noted, and was acted upon, in *Townsend v. Hunt* (1635), Cro. Car. 408, and indeed in numerous old books; while the principle of moral obligation does not make its appearance till the days of Lord Mansfield, and then under circumstances not inconsistent with this ancient doctrine when properly explained.

[11]   Upon the whole, we are of opinion that the rule must be made absolute to arrest the judgment.

NOTES AND QUESTIONS

1.   The judgment of Lord Denman is very technical, dealing with fine points of law and procedure. As was the situation in *Hadley v. Baxendale*, this judgment was given, in effect, on an appeal from a trial judgment (after a jury verdict) in favour of the plaintiff. The defendant argued (apart from the *Statute of Frauds* issue) that the plaintiff, in modern terms, had disclosed no cause of action. That is, the issue was: assuming that the facts as alleged by the plaintiff were true, had the plaintiff pleaded a valid cause of action?

      The court ruled that there was no valid cause of action. The plaintiff did not allege (because it was not true, so he could not prove it) that he made the expenditure at the request of the defendant.

2.   The case of *Lampleigh v. Brathwait*, referred to by Lord Denman, provides an important exception to the rule on past consideration. It is a case where the court said that if the plaintiff does something at the request of the defendant without any specific agreement at that time for the amount of payment, a subsequent promise to pay for the original thing will be enforceable if the thing was done at the defendant's request or in

the expectation that there would be some payment. The subsequent promise is the quantification of the original legal obligation, not a new obligation.

If the promisor never made a promise to pay a specific amount in a case like this, the person who performed the obligation could sue for *quantum meruit* relief.

This may be relevant in many situations, such as when a client retains a lawyer without any discussion of fees. It is certainly a preferable professional practice to discuss fees, but the failure to do so does not prevent a lawyer from later enforcing payment.

3. The traditional common law position has been that a person who performs a service for another, without being requested, has no legal right to enforce payment, even if a benefit is conferred. There is no "unjust" enrichment, since the service was provided without request or legal expectation of payment.

    At common law, an exception developed so that a doctor or hospital could enforce a claim for payment for the value of medical services provided to an unconscious or incompetent patient, based on the "implied request" of the patient. The courts went so far as to "imply" a request for the provision of medical services by a man who was taken to a hospital unconscious after a suicide attempt: *Matheson Hospital v. Smiley*, [1932] 2 D.L.R. 787 (Man. C.A.). Why did the courts develop this exception?

4. The problems facing the plaintiff in *Eastwood* arose principally because he had to sue Mr. Kenyon. In 1840 any action against Mrs. Kenyon personally would have been pointless for all of her property vested in her husband, though he was liable for her premarital debts. As the defendant obtained all of his wife's property on his marriage to her, he would have received the ultimate benefit of the expenditure made by the plaintiff. Could you use this fact to strengthen the plaintiff's claim?

5. The common law rules vested the property of a married woman in her husband. As stated in Blackstone's *Commentaries*, written in the mid 1700s (4th edition, 1899, vol. 1, p. 374):

    > The very being or legal existence of the woman is suspended during the marriage, or at least is incorporated and consolidated into that of the husband, under whose wing, protection and cover, she performs everything. . . .

    These common law rules were, of course, formulated by male judges, and were highly discriminatory. Inheritance laws also favoured sons over daughters. Wealthy families sometimes protected the property of married daughters by means of a "marriage settlement", establishing a trust for the benefit of the daughter. Such a settlement would not, however, permit a married woman to make contracts on her own, since the property would be vested in a trustee and, what was most important, would not be available to her husband or his creditors.

    These and other common law rules both reinforced the notion that women were incapable of looking after their own affairs, and made it virtually impossible for them to do so. The common law rules restricting the legal capacities of women were gradually repealed by legislation in the latter part of the nineteenth century and during the twentieth century.

6. Lord Denman refers to a note to the case of *Wennall v. Adney* (1802), 3 B. & P. 249, 127 E.R. 137. That note is a long discussion of the cases of past consideration up to that time. It is an interesting example of the law's being created by a process of doctrinal refinement. The editors do not state why it is preferable that the law should leave promises like those in *Eastwood v. Kenyon* unenforceable. It is presumed to be a sufficient justification that to do so is more consistent with the doctrine of consideration.

7. Notice that Lord Denman does give one reason to support the general refusal to enforce "gift" promises. He points out that the enforcement of such promises might defeat creditors. The concern here is to the fact that a donee who claims under a promise to make a gift cannot have enriched the donor's estate. If the donee were able to claim as a contractual creditor, the claim would disadvantage those, the ordinary trade creditors or lenders, whose claims had enriched the estate. This concern is an important factor

when the enforcement of gift promises is being considered, but the argument does not justify the result in *Eastwood v. Kenyon*. Why not?

8. The rule regarding past consideration has also been applied in the purely commercial context. Two years after *Eastwood v. Kenyon*, Lord Denman relied on his judgment in that case to decide *Roscorla v. Thomas* (1842), 3 Q.B. 234, 114 E.R. 496 (Q.B.).

    The plaintiff entered into a contract to buy a horse from the defendant for £30. Sometime *after the contract was made* (it is possible, drawing an inference from what Lord Denman says in the quotation below, that the promise was made before the delivery of the horse) the seller told the buyer that the horse was "sound and free from vice". The horse was then delivered, and turned out to be in poor condition. The buyer sued for breach of the warranty (promise) that the horse was "sound and free from vice". The court held that since the promise about the horse's quality followed the contract for sale, it was without consideration and unenforceable. Lord Denman said:

    > . . . the precedent executed consideration was insufficient to support the subsequent promise. And we are of the opinion that the object must prevail . . . It may be taken as a general rule, subject to exceptions not applicable to this case, that the promise must be coextensive with the consideration. In the present case, the only promise that would result from the consideration, as stated, and be coextensive with it, would be to deliver the horse upon request.

    A number of recent Canadian cases have dealt with situations where the purchaser of land tried to sue the vendor for untrue statements that were made at the time of closing, but was unsuccessful because of a lack of consideration. For example, in *Melko v. Lloyd Estate*, [2002] O.J. No. 3822, 61 O.R. (3d) 151 (S.C.J.) a relative of the owner of land entered into an agreement to sell the land under a power of attorney, the owner being incapacitated. In the agreement of sale, the attorney warranted that to the "best of his knowledge and belief", the septic system for the house complied with provincial environmental standards, and that this warranty was to survive the closing. At the time of closing of the land sale, at the request of the purchasers, an undertaking was given and a statutory declaration was signed by the vendor's representative, in which he warranted that there was in fact compliance with provincial standards. After the purchasers went into possession, they discovered that the septic system was largely on a neighbour's land, in violation of provincial standards, and that it would cost more than $16,000 to remedy this situation. Fedak J. dismissed the action on the ground that the attorney believed that the statement made at the time of the agreement was true, and "the undertaking [made at the time of closing] cannot support an action, as it was not under seal and there was no fresh consideration for the warranty contained in the undertaking." What could the purchasers have done to protect their interests?

9. The contracts of an infant are, at common law, voidable. (An infant, now called a "minor", is any person under 18 years of age: *Age of Majority and Accountability Act*, R.S.O. 1990, c. A.7, s. 1. Some provinces have set 19 rather than 18 as the age of majority. At common law an infant was any person less than 21 years old.) There is a great deal of law on the general enforceability of contracts made by minors, most of which has been rendered of less importance by the reduction of the age of majority. Here, consideration is given to one aspect of the law, the rule regarding the affirmation by the minor of a contract made when he or she reaches the age of majority.

    The rule is that if a person, on reaching the age of majority, affirmed or "ratified" a contract that he or she had entered into as a minor, the person is liable on that contract even though the consideration was past: the new promise to pay made after the person has come of full age is a promise for which the consideration is past. In this case that feature of the promise is not fatal to an action on it. In most jurisdictions the promise to pay in such circumstances must, however, be in writing: see, *e.g.*, *Statute of Frauds*, R.S.O. 1990, c. S.19, s. 7.

    Recall that in *Eastwood v. Kenyon*, Mrs. Kenyon, then Sarah Sutcliffe, had ratified her promise to pay the loan after becoming an adult. This promise might have been actionable against Mr. Kenyon as a pre-marital debt, but it would have been subject to the *Statute of Frauds*.

10. Under the Ontario *Limitations Act, 2002*, S.O. 2002, c. 24, Sched. B, an action on an ordinary contract has to be commenced within two years after the discovery of the "claim". (Previously in Ontario the limitation period for actions on contracts was six years, and that is still the limitation period in some jurisdictions.) An action brought outside the limitation period is said to be statute-barred. It was, however, well established at common law that the time from which the limitation period runs can be reopened by an acknowledgment by the debtor that the amount is due, a rule reflected in s. 13 of the Ontario Act.

Thus, if P owes money to S for goods purchased on 1 October 2004, S cannot maintain an action on this debt if the Statement of Claim is issued after 1 October 2006. If, however, P acknowledged the debt in May 2006, then the period runs from that date and the action will be barred only in May 2008. It might be thought that the action in the latter case would be on a promise made in May 2006 for which the consideration would be past. An acknowledgment of the debt takes it out of the statute and an action can be brought even though two years may have passed from the original cause of action. The limitation period runs from the last acknowledgment (or promise to pay) the debt. This result is rationalized by saying that the action is still on the original contract, and that the only effect of the later acknowledgment is to take the case out of the statute. Note that an acknowledgment that operates to extend the time for bringing an action must be in writing: *Limitations Act, 2002*, s. 13.

11. The purpose of bankruptcy and the proceedings that "going bankrupt" entail is to permit individuals who cannot meet their financial obligations to make a fresh start with the compulsory discharge of all unpaid debts. The court will be concerned to make sure that the person is not using the procedure to hide assets or income that could be used to pay creditors, and that creditors are fairly treated. The traditional view was that if, after obtaining a discharge as a bankrupt, the person promised to pay one of his former creditors, that promise, like the promise of the infant made after majority, would be enforceable. This too was an exception to the rule of "past consideration" as articulated in *Eastwood v. Kenyon* ¶ 4.

The motives of the courts in developing these exceptions to the rule about past consideration are obvious. Their existence illustrates once again the extent to which courts, strongly moved to reach a result that they believe to be proper, will ignore (or manipulate) the rules of the common law. The situations of infant's debts, debts barred by the limitation period and debts discharged by bankruptcy, are all ones in which the plaintiff originally conferred a benefit with a reasonable expectation of payment, rather than gratuitously in the hope that payment might later be conferred.

One Canadian court, however, has relatively recently held that a debt discharged by bankruptcy cannot be enforced as the consideration is past. In *Tildesley v. Weaver*, [1998] B.C.J. No. 1838, 7 C.B.R. (4th) 313 (B.C.S.C.), Scarth J. said (p. 318):

> Although the notion that a moral obligation arising out of an antecedent event is sufficient consideration for a new promise to pay finds acceptance under the civil law of Quebec . . . the doctrine has been rejected in England: *Eastwood v. Kenyon*. . . . In British Columbia, in order to constitute consideration sufficient to support a simple contract, there must be valuable consideration moving from one party to the other. . . . In my judgment a purely moral obligation does not provide sufficient consideration for the note in question here.

12. The traditional view has been that there is no obligation to pay for an unrequested benefit. More recently, however, it has been argued that there may be situations in which restitutionary principles can be invoked by a court to order payment for an "incontrovertible benefit" that is conferred without request, provided that the plaintiff can show that "he did not act officiously, that the particular defendant has gained a realisable financial benefit or saved an inevitable expense and that it will not be a hardship

to the defendant . . . to make restitution." (Goff and Jones, *The Law of Restitution*, 3d ed., 1998, p. 25). This argument was considered by the Supreme Court in *Peel (Regional Municipality) v. Canada*, [1992] S.C.J. No. 101, [1992] 3 S.C.R. 762, 98 D.L.R. (4th) 140 — though it was not successful in that case.

There is a long line of cases, *Mills v. Wyman*, 20 Mass. (3 Pick.) 207 (1825), being a classic example, where the plaintiff had looked after the defendant's son when the son was seriously ill far from home. When the defendant, the son's father, heard what the plaintiff had done, he wrote a letter expressing his gratitude and promising to reimburse the plaintiff for his expenses. The Supreme Judicial Court of Massachusetts dismissed the plaintiff's claim on the basis that the consideration for the father's promise was "past". The court observed (p. 210) that such promises as that of the father, "the law . . . has left . . . to the interior forum, as the tribunal of conscience has been aptly called".

In *Webb v. McGowin*, 168 So. 196 (Ala. Ct. App. 1935), a claim was made against an estate by a man who, at great risk and seriously injuring himself in the act, had saved the deceased from serious injury in an accident. After the accident, the deceased promised to pay the plaintiff an allowance for the rest of his life and punctually did so for over eight years. After the deceased's death his executors made two payments and then refused to pay any more. The court, relying in part on Lord Mansfield, held the promise enforceable. In *Hawkes v. Saunders* (1782), 1 Cowp. 289, 290, 98 E.R. 1091 (K.B.), Lord Mansfield had said:

> Where a man is under a moral obligation, which no Court of Law or Equity can inforce [*sic*], and promises, the honesty and rectitude of the thing is a consideration. . . . [T]he ties of conscience upon an upright mind are a sufficient consideration.

It was this idea that a moral obligation might support a contract that Lord Denman explicitly rejected in *Eastwood v. Kenyon* (¶ 2, above).

How can *Webb v. McGowin* be distinguished from *Mills v. Wyman*?

If courts accept the principle that a restitutionary remedy may be available to recover the value of unrequested, but "incontrovertible benefit" conferred on the defendant, what effect might this have on the doctrine of past consideration?

PROBLEMS

1. Winston had a badly run-down house that he lent to his daughter Mary to live in. Mary had a friend, Tom, a painter. Mary asked Tom to paint a mural on one of the walls and agreed to pay him $200. Tom painted a beautiful mural that increased the value of the house by $2,000. When Winston saw the mural, he promised to pay Tom the $200 that Mary promised to pay. Would Tom be successful if he were to sue Winston or Mary?

2. Alan and Don are neighbours. When Don was going away on his summer vacation he asked Alan to look after his house, mow his lawn and weed his garden. Alan agreed to do so. Both expected that Don would return the kindness when Alan went on his holiday. Alan, however, could not get away that year. In the fall, Don said to Alan, "Since I could not return the favour you did me, I'll pay you $500 for the work that you did. Is that okay with you?" Alan said that was fine. Don and Alan have now fallen out, and Alan wants to sue Don for the amount he promised to pay.

   If you believe that a court might well hold the work to be worth less than Don has now agreed to pay, what problems might you meet, and how can you overcome them, if you argue Alan's case for the promised amount?

Mutual Promises

The wholly executory contract — that is, an exchange of promises of performance before either side actually performs — was not recognized in English law until the end of the sixteenth century. Gradually the courts developed a bargain model of contract law, and were prepared to award a disappointed promisee expectation damages even if the promisee had taken no steps to perform. With the development of the classical bargain-based model of contract law in the nineteenth century, courts gave little thought to the theoretical problems that arise with the enforcement of the wholly executory contract, *i.e.*, the contract where A promises to do something for B in return for B's promise to pay (or to do something) for A. Academic commentators, however, raised concerns about the absence of consideration in a contract based on mutual promises. If the bargain theory of consideration requires a detriment to the promisee, how can there be any detriment in the simple case where A promises to buy B's car for $1,000 in exchange for B's promise to sell, the sale to take place in one month's time? A has incurred no detriment in return for B's promise unless his promise is enforceable, but to assume that A's promise is enforceable is arguing in a circle, since A's promise is no more enforceable than B's.

A leading English contracts scholar, Sir Frederick Pollock, was moved to write in 1912: "What logical justification is there for holding mutual promises good consideration for each other? None it is submitted." (28 *Law Q. Rev.* 101). Courts have largely ignored this abstract doctrinal problem. The better questions to ask are: "What concerns would justify one in refusing to enforce mutual promises? And if there are no concerns that one party might, for example, be caught by unfair surprise by enforcement, why not enforce them?"

The problem posed by scholars like Pollock — and he was not arguing that mutual promises should not be enforced — is just a curious consequence of some of the definitions of consideration, ones that focus on the promisee incurring a detriment. This kind of problem is avoided by the definition of consideration articulated by Cheshire, Fifoot and Furmston, *Law of Contract*, 13th ed. (above) as "the price paid" by the promisee.

Given the central role that contracts play in economic planning, and given that most planning collapses the distinction between present and future goods, the theoretical problems that "mutual promises" might create are ignored by the courts. There are strong commercial pressures to enforce a contract based on an exchange of promises; by enforcing such contracts, the courts protect and encourage reliance on commercial undertakings.

The courts enforce mutual promises — the wholly executory contract — and regard each promise in an executory contract as legally binding, and hence as a detriment to the promisee. The courts say in support of the enforceability of mutual promises that if doing something would be good consideration, then a promise to do it is good consideration. Several problems remain, however, and these are related to the logical problem of enforcement.

One problem that sometimes causes difficulty has to do with the requirement that both parties must be bound or neither is bound. This is sometimes referred to as the requirement of "mutuality". This issue of mutuality is raised in the cases that follow.

GREAT NORTHERN RAILWAY COMPANY v. WITHAM

(1873), L.R. 9 C.P. 16
(Common Pleas, Keating, Brett and Grove JJ.)

KEATING J.: — **[1]** In this case [counsel for Witham] moved to enter a nonsuit. The circumstances were these: The Great Northern Railway Company advertised for tenders for the supply of stores. The defendant made a tender in these words, "I hereby undertake to supply the Great Northern Railway Company, for twelve months, from &c. to &c., with such quantities of each or any of the several articles named in the attached specifications as the company's store-keeper may order from time to time, at the price set opposite each article respectively," &c. Some orders were given by the company, which were duly executed. But the order now in question was not executed; the defendant seeking to excuse himself from the performance of his agreement, because it was unilateral, the company not being bound to give the order. The ground upon which it was put by Mr. Seymour [counsel for the defendant seller] was, that there was no consideration for the defendant's promise to supply the goods; in other words, that, inasmuch as there was no obligation on the company to give an order, there was no consideration moving from the company, and therefore no obligation on the defendant to supply the goods. . . . If before the order was given the defendant had given notice to the company that he would not perform the agreement, it might be that he would have been justified in so doing. But here the company had given the order, and had consequently done something which amounted to a consideration for the defendant's promise. I see no ground for doubting that the verdict for the plaintiffs ought to stand.

BRETT J.: — **[2]** The company advertised for tenders for the supply of stores, such as they might think fit to order, for one year. The defendant made a tender offering to supply them for that period at certain fixed prices; and the company accepted his tender. If there were no other objection, the contract between the parties would be found in the tender and the letter accepting it. This action is brought for the defendant's refusal to deliver goods ordered by the company; and the objection to the plaintiffs' right to recover is, that the contract is unilateral. I do not, however, understand what objection that is to a contract. Many contracts are obnoxious to the same complaint. If I say to another, "If you will go to York, I will give you £100," that is in a certain sense a unilateral contract. He has not promised to go to York. But, if he goes, it cannot be doubted that he will be entitled to receive the £100. His going to York at my request is a sufficient consideration for my promise. So, if one says to another, "If you will give me an order for iron, or other goods, I will supply it at a given price," if the order is given, there is a complete contract which the seller is bound to perform. There is in such a case ample consideration for the promise. So, here, the company having given the defendant an order at his request, his acceptance of the order would bind them. If any authority could have been found to sustain Mr. Seymour's contention, I should have considered that a rule ought to be granted. But none has been cited. This is matter of every day's practice; and I think it would be wrong to countenance the notion that a man who tenders for the supply of goods in this way is not bound to deliver them when an order is given. I agree that this judgment does not decide the question whether the defendant might have absolved himself from the further performance of the contract by giving notice.

NOTES AND QUESTIONS

prof

1. The arrangement between the parties here is a relational one; it is to exist for at least a
   year. The court does not say that Witham could not terminate his undertaking to stand
   ready to supply the goods to the railway. It says that the railway, having given an order before Witham had withdrawn his undertaking, Witham was bound to supply the
   goods actually ordered.

      The case can be analyzed as one where there are two promises: one (explicit)
   promise to stand ready to supply for the full year, and the other (implicit) promise to
   supply the goods actually ordered. In respect to the promise of Witham to stand ready
   to supply — what can be called the "framework agreement" — Keating J. suggests
   that Witham could have given notice at any time of his refusal to continue with the
   deal and would have incurred no liability in so doing. It is generally accepted that in
   respect of the framework agreement, Witham's promise would be unenforceable because GNR had given no consideration for it. In terms that will be explored in Chapter
   3, Witham's "framework" promise can be looked at as a "standing offer". The common law takes the view that "standing offers" are revocable, unless bought for consideration and transformed into option contracts or put under seal.

prof

2. The framework agreement could have been transformed into an enforceable option
   contract, with GNR giving Witham some consideration for the right (but not the obligation) to buy goods from Witham at specified prices for a specified period.

      Another method to provide for enforceability is an exclusivity contract, with GNR
   promising to purchase specified goods only from Witham, but not having an obligation to purchase any minimum amounts. GNR's undertaking to buy only from Witham
   would be consideration for Witham's promise to stand ready to supply.

3. J.N. Adams, "Consideration for Requirements Contracts" (1978), 94 *Law Q. Rev.* 73,
   points out that, while the view that Witham could withdraw the framework offer before any order is made is standard in the textbooks, judicial support for it is much less
   than the text-writers appear to assume. He discusses a number of cases where the
   courts assume that a contract of the framework type is a valid contract from the moment that the supplier offers to supply and the buyer accepts this offer, even though
   the buyer has not promised to take any minimum amount. Adams concludes by saying
   (at p. 84):

   > . . . it may not be inappropriate to observe that in spite of the prevalence of re-
   > quirements contracts, the question of their legal enforceability may be of less
   > importance than might be thought. The small amount of research which has
   > been done into the making of business agreements . . . seems to suggest that
   > businessmen care little whether or not such agreements have legal effect, since
   > apart from anything else they think primarily in terms of extra-legal sanctions.
   > Whilst however the law of contract may in a sense be irrelevant to much of
   > what goes on in real life, surely courts should not refuse recovery in the name
   > of doctrinal tidiness when occasionally they are resorted to?

   The argument Adams makes for the recognition by courts of the need to respect the
   parties' contractual planning is often denied by the courts. There are many examples
   of this denial in the balance of this chapter and throughout this book. It is an important
   study to determine how far courts should be able to prefer doctrinal tidiness over practical good sense.

4. Agreements of the kind in *GNR v. Witham* are an important part of the efforts of businesses to plan their affairs. What are the likely reasons that both GNR and Witham
   might make the arrangement that they did? What risks does each side run? Are any of
   these risks so serious that the contract should be refused enforcement on the ground
   that it is unfair to one side? What constraints operate on the parties that might prevent
   abuse of the system?

5. Agreements similar to that in *GNR v. Witham* are a common feature of the North American automobile industry. The auto manufacturers make deals with their parts suppliers that are economically identical to that made by the railway company and Witham, though they may be placed under seal at the recommendation of the lawyers involved to create technical enforceability. Under these arrangements the manufacturers have no obligation to buy any quantity of the parts covered by the specifications, and the suppliers bear all the risks associated with this kind of deal. However, despite the apparent one-sidedness of such agreements, it would be wrong to assume that there is consistent unfairness in such arrangements. It is in the manufacturers' long-term interest to make fair arrangements, and there is strong competition to sell to the auto manufacturers.

Some of the auto parts suppliers are very large corporations with sales of billions of dollars annually. There is little pressure to change this system of "just-in-time" manufacturing. (In just-in-time manufacturing, the automobile manufacturer keeps almost no inventory of parts and the supplier constantly delivers parts and components as they are needed on the assembly line.) One of the effects of just-in-time manufacturing is to make both supplier and auto manufacturer more vulnerable to each other. As a result, contracts have a longer term, but failure of the supplier to deliver on time will promptly lead to the end of the relation. Sometimes these contracts provide for annual price reductions or, depending perhaps on the nature of the product, escalation clauses tied to the price of raw materials. A person close to the industry said (*The Globe & Mail*, 21 February 1990, p. B4):

> The supplier-developer relationship is evolving to one of mutual support and trust yet demand for performance. If I'm a purchaser, I don't want to bankrupt my supplier or cause him huge grief. But I want him to be sharp on his toes and [to] be looking for ways to bring his costs down.

Since the early 1990's the integration of North American automobile manufacturers and their suppliers has increased. One aspect of this development is the recognition by the manufacturers that they have to bring their suppliers more fully into the production planning process. When this happens, suppliers will have intimate knowledge of the plans of the manufacturers, information that the manufacturers had previously treated as highly confidential. It may be hard to say if the manufacturers are more dependent on their suppliers than the latter are on the manufacturers. The idea of suing for breach is not seen by either the supplier or the manufacturer as a useful remedy for a breach.

The arrangements that the automobile manufacturers made with their dealers were of a similar type. Here, however, the possibilities for abuse were much greater. The dealer got a franchise to sell a particular manufacturer's cars, but the latter made no promise to make any cars available to the dealer. A dealer who stepped out of line might find that he was out of business because he could get no cars to sell. The difference between the parts supplier and the car dealer was that the manufacturer depended less on any one dealer and dealers had far lower start-up costs, so that, from a manufacturer's point of view, individual dealers became almost a fungible selling device. No dealer could have the influence with an auto manufacturer that a parts supplier the size of Magna International would have with the manufacturer. See Arruñada, Garicano and Vázquez, "Contractual Allocation of Decision Rights and Incentives: The Case of Automobile Distribution" (2001), 17 *J.L. Econ. & Org.* 256-83.

These differences led to frequent abuse by the auto manufacturers of their power over their dealers and there was pressure to reform the law. Legislation has been enacted in some American states to protect auto dealers and other franchisees. In Canada there have been intermittent problems over the refusal of auto manufacturers to supply parts to dealers that they want to control. The *Competition Act*, R.S.C. 1985, c. C-34, s. 61, which makes certain kinds of refusals to sell criminal offences, has been called into use. The criminal law is a very cumbersome tool in this situation.

The problem of unfairness in franchising and other business relations is considered further in Chapter 6.

The financial problems of the major U.S. automobile manufacturers, particularly General Motors and Ford, are forcing their suppliers to revise their relations with them. It's one thing to trust the manufacturers when there is no doubt that invoices will be paid on time, but quite another when there is a not insignificant risk that either GM and Ford, or both, may seek protection from their creditors under Chapter 11 of the U.S. Bankruptcy Code, leaving the suppliers (who would be unsecured creditors) to share in what might be available after the banks (as secured creditors) have been paid.

It is also interesting to note that the general give-and-take which characterizes the relation between the manufacturers and their suppliers was put to the test in the aftermath of Hurricane Katrina in 2005. Significant damage was done to plants, particularly chemical plants, and installations such as refineries along the U.S. Gulf Coast which supplied large amounts of what the suppliers needed to meet their obligations to the manufacturers, and everyone involved, the Gulf Coast chemical plants and refineries, the suppliers to the manufacturers and the manufacturers, had to find some way of accommodating each other. Clauses in the various contracts involved that neither side had ever worried much about before were now anxiously scrutinized by executives and their lawyers. So far as is known, no one resorted to litigation and measures like across-the-board proportionate reductions in supply were adopted. There was concern that such reductions be equitably made and efforts were made to deal with the problems fairly and in good faith. Everyone involved was acutely conscious of the fact that, whatever the temporary problems might be, they were all committed to each other for the long term. The issues raised by a natural disaster like Hurricane Katrina will be dealt with under the heading of "Frustration" in Chapter 5.

6.   The draft Canadian *Uniform Sale of Goods Act* has the following provision for dealing with output and requirements contracts:

> 5.4(1) An agreement that measures the quantity of goods to be bought or sold by the output of the seller or the requirements of the buyer means such reasonable quantity as may be required or supplied by the buyer or seller acting in good faith, having regard to any stated estimates, any previous output or requirements, and all the circumstances of the case.

Does this provision deal adequately with the problem presented by *GNR v. Witham*?

The same problems of apparent lopsidedness (all the risk being on one party) as arose with requirements contracts can also arise in other areas of commercial activity. The following cases are examples of how courts handle the problem.

BERNSTEIN v. W.B. MFG. CO.

131 N.E. 200 (1921)
(Supreme Judicial Court of Massachusetts)

PIERCE J.: — [1] This is an action to recover damages for the alleged breach of a contract, which the plaintiff claims resulted from an order that the defendant admits it placed with the plaintiff for the delivery of certain goods.

[2]   The order so given called for the sale and delivery of one hundred and seventy-four dozen boys' wash suits, and five sets of samples thereof at $16.50 a dozen. The admitted facts and evidence show that the plaintiff delivered to the defendant on August 20, 1918, the five sets of samples called for by the order, and that it was paid therefor by the defendant in September 1918. The evidence also

shows that the plaintiff on December 15, 1918, shipped to the defendant seventy-two dozen wash suits; that they were delivered in the shipping room of the defendant; that the defendant "opened them up" and immediately notified the plaintiff that it would not accept the goods. A memorandum of the order was made by the representative of the plaintiff on a printed order blank of the plaintiff. It was not signed by the defendant, and it contained the following printed clause:

> This order is given and accepted subject to a limit of credit and determination at any time by us.

[3]   At the close of the evidence the defendant excepted to the refusal of the judge to direct a verdict for the defendant.

[4]   Because of the clause above quoted the defendant contends that the agreement was invalid in its inception for want of mutuality of obligation; and rests its defense upon the accepted legal maxim that in a bilateral agreement both of the mutual promises must be binding or neither will be, for if one of the promises is for any reason invalid the other has no consideration and so they both fall. . . . The plaintiff admits the legal force of the rule invoked by the defendant, and replies thereto that the clause does not have the effect of reserving to the plaintiff the right to determine the contract (which otherwise resulted from the placing and acceptance of the order) but is obviously only referable to a determination of "a limit of credit". Giving to the clause a fair construction, we think the right of "determination" was intended to embrace the "order" as well as "a limit of credit".

[5]   The plaintiff next contends that the delivery and acceptance of the five sample suits were such partial performance by the plaintiff as afforded a sufficient consideration for the defendant's promises, even though there was no obligation to support the contract at its inception. We do not think the agreement which was void in its inception for want of mutuality became an agreement which was supported by a sufficient consideration upon the delivery and acceptance of part of the goods called for in the order of the defendant, because the plaintiff was not thereby precluded from exercising his reserved option. He was not bound to fill the balance of the order unless he chose to do so, and the defendant gained thereby no additional contractual right against the plaintiff. . . . The motion to direct a verdict for the defendant should have been granted. . . .

Prof (handwritten margin note)

WOOD v. LUCY, LADY DUFF-GORDON

118 N.E. 214 (1917)
(Court of Appeals of New York)

CARDOZO J.: — [1] The defendant styles herself "a creator of fashions." Her favor helps a sale. Manufacturers of dresses, millinery, and like articles are glad to pay for a certificate of her approval. The things which she designs, fabric, parasols, and what not, have a new value in the public mind when issued in her name. She employed the plaintiff to help her to turn this vogue into money. He was to have the exclusive right, subject always to her approval, to place her endorsements on the designs of others. He was also to have the exclusive right to place her own designs on sale, or to license others to market them. In return she was to have one-half of "all profits and revenues" derived from any contracts he might make. The exclusive right was to last at least one year from April 1, 1915, and thereafter from year to year unless terminated by notice of 90 days. The plaintiff says that he kept the contract on his part, and that the defendant broke it. She placed her endorsement on fabrics, dresses, and millinery without his knowledge, and withheld the profits. He sues her for the damages, and the case comes here on demurrer.

[2]   The agreement of employment is signed by both parties. It has a wealth of recitals. The defendant insists, however, that it lacks the elements of a contract. She says that the plaintiff does not bind himself to anything. It is true that he does not promise in so many words that he will use reasonable efforts to place the defendant's endorsements and market her designs. We think, however, that such a promise is fairly to be implied. The law has outgrown its primitive stage of formalism when the precise word was the sovereign talisman, and every slip was fatal. It takes a broader view to-day. A promise may be lacking, and yet the whole writing may be "instinct with an obligation," imperfectly expressed. . . . If that is so, there is a contract.

[3]   The implication of a promise here finds support in many circumstances. The defendant gave an exclusive privilege. She was to have no right for at least a year to place her own endorsements or market her own designs except through the agency of the plaintiff. The acceptance of the exclusive agency was an assumption of its duties. . . . Many other terms of the agreement point the same way. We are told at the outset by way of recital that: "The said Otis F. Wood possesses a business organization adapted to the placing of such endorsements as the said Lucy, Lady Duff-Gordon, has approved."

[4]   The implication is that the plaintiff's business organization will be used for the purpose for which it is adapted. But the terms of the defendant's compensation are even more significant. His sole compensation for the grant of an exclusive agency is to be one-half of all the profits resulting from the plaintiff's efforts. Unless he gave his efforts, she could never get anything. Without an implied promise, the transaction cannot have such business "efficacy, as both parties must have intended that at all events it should have." Bowen L.J., *Moorcock* (1889), 14 P.D. 64, p. 68. But the contract does not stop there. The plaintiff goes on to promise that he will account monthly for all moneys received by him, and that he will take out all such patents and copyrights and trade-marks as may in his judgment be necessary to protect the rights and articles affected by the agreement. It is true, of course, as the Appellate Division has said, that if he was under no duty to try to market designs or to place certificates of endorsement, his promise to account for profits or take out copyrights would be valueless. But in determining the intention of the parties the promise has a value. It helps to enforce the conclusion that the plaintiff had some duties. His promise to pay the defendant one-half of the profits and revenues resulting from the exclusive agency and to render accounts monthly was a promise to use reasonable efforts to bring profits and revenues into existence. For this conclusion the authorities are ample. . . .

[5]   The judgment of the Appellate Division should be reversed, and the order of the Special Term affirmed, with costs in the Appellate Division and in this court.

QUESTIONS AND NOTES

1.   How can *Bernstein v. W.B. Mfg.* and *Wood v. Lucy, Lady Duff-Gordon* be distinguished?

     The cases are in part distinguishable based on the explicit words of the contract in *Bernstein*, which appear to limit the seller's obligations, in contrast to the absence of any words in *Wood.* But the judicial attitudes to these two particular cases may also have been influenced by judicial attitudes to the types of contracts involved.

It may be significant that *Bernstein* involves a one-time sale of goods where the seller tried to draft the contract so as to minimize (or eliminate) any liability on its part, and then seeks to enforce that contract. Courts often adopt an approach to the interpretation of a contract drafted by a seller which is characterized by an unwillingness to give the seller any benefit of the doubt as to the meaning of the terms it uses (a *contra proferentem* interpretation).

On the other hand, *Wood* involved an exclusive dealing contract, where one party would normally rely heavily on the other. Courts generally try to interpret these relational agreements to protect vulnerability and possible reliance.

2.   The judgment in *Wood* is typical of the style of Benjamin Cardozo (later Chief Justice of New York and then a judge of the United States Supreme Court). Is his notion that a promise may be "instinct with an obligation imperfectly expressed" helpful in deciding what promises should be enforced? What is connoted by the word "instinct"?

3.   Suppose that Wood had identical contracts with three other prominent women and that he gave Lady Duff-Gordon only five per cent of the total business generated by all of them.

   (a)   Would Lady Duff-Gordon have a remedy if she sued Wood for damages for breach?

   (b)   If a court should hold that Wood had breached the contract, what damages would Lady Duff-Gordon get?

   These questions raise the problem of the content of the term implied by Cardozo J.

   It may not be appropriate to use "lack of mutuality" as a basis for failing to protect Lady Duff-Gordon from possible unfair behaviour by Wood. However, if the exchange is very one-sided, or if one party's obligation is very imprecise, there might be other concerns that should be addressed by the court.

4.   The American *Uniform Commercial Code* deals with an analogous problem to *Wood v. Lucy, Lady Duff-Gordon* in sales cases:

   § 2-306(2)   A lawful agreement by either the seller or the buyer for exclusive dealing in the kind of goods concerned imposes unless otherwise agreed an obligation by the seller to use best efforts to supply the goods and by the buyer to use best efforts to promote their sale.

The comment to this provision states:

   Subsection 2-306(2), on exclusive dealing, makes explicit the commercial rule embodied in this Act under which the parties to such contracts are held to have impliedly, even when not expressly, bound themselves to use reasonable diligence as well as good faith in their performance of the contract. Under such contracts the exclusive agent is required, although no express commitment has been made, to use reasonable effort and due diligence in the expansion of the market or the promotion of the product, as the case may be. The principal is expected under such a contract to refrain from supplying any other dealer or agent within the exclusive territory. An exclusive dealing agreement brings into play all the good faith aspects of the output and requirement problems of subsection (1). It also raises questions of insecurity and right to adequate assurance under this Article.

   How would Lady Duff-Gordon fare under the provisions of the U.C.C. (assuming that the relation between her and her agent came within its scope) in her dispute with her agent?

   The language of the U.C.C. has passed into the standard language of lawyers and the agreements that they draft. It is common now to find parties agreeing to make their "best efforts" to do something or to achieve some result. An odd development, at least from a linguistic or grammatical point of view, is the common transformation of a "best efforts" clause into one in which one party undertakes to make "reasonable best efforts". Can you think of a reason that would explain parties' willingness to agree to such a term?

5.   A "Term Sheet" is a document, drafted as a letter from a lender (often a bank) to a prospective borrower, in which the bank will offer to lend money to the borrower. A standard term sheet may say something like the following:

> You have asked that Credit Facilities be made available through and extended on the terms and subject to the conditions set forth in Annexes 1 and 2 (collectively, the "Term Sheets"). We are pleased to confirm that we or our affiliates are willing to provide, on the terms and subject to the conditions set forth in this letter and in the Term Sheets, the Credit Facilities. If we are unable to arrange a syndication on terms and conditions satisfactory to you and us, we reserve the right to reduce the amount or change the maturity of the Senior Credit Facilities, or, in our sole discretion, to suggest alternative financing amounts or structures that will enable us to syndicate the Credit Facilities.
>
> Our commitment is also expressly subject to the absence of any adverse change after this date in the market for syndicated facilities similar in nature to the Credit Facilities and the absence of any [material] disruption of, or a [material] adverse change in, financial, banking or capital markets generally, in each case as determined by us in our sole discretion. Our commitment under the Credit Facilities shall terminate on [date].

The bank and the borrower will regard the bank's commitment as binding. How would such an agreement fare in a court in the light of the requirement of mutuality and, if the agreement is enforceable, what role does the doctrine of mutuality continue to play?

6.   Clauses that operate to prevent a party from throwing good money after bad are very common in business. It is, for example, usual in any long-term agreement to find an exhaustive list of "events of default" which will excuse a party from further performance. Standard terms in a Credit Agreement between a bank and a borrower will contain terms much like the following:

> *Events of Default*: Upon the occurrence of any one or more of the following events:
>
> (a)   the non-payment of any amount due hereunder;
>
> (b)   the commencement of proceedings for the dissolution, liquidation or winding-up of the Borrower or for the suspension of the operations of the Borrower unless such proceedings are being contested in good faith by proper legal proceedings;
>
> (c)   if the Borrower ceases or threatens to cease to carry on its business or is adjudged or declared bankrupt or insolvent or makes an assignment for the general benefit of creditors, petitions or applies to any tribunal for the appointment of a receiver or trustee for it or for any part of its property, or commences any proceedings relating to it under any reorganization, arrangement, readjustment of debt, dissolution or liquidation law or statute of any jurisdiction whether now or hereafter in effect, or by any act indicates its consent to, approval of, or acquiescence in, any such proceeding for it or for any part of its property, or suffers the appointment of any receiver or trustee;
>
> (d)   if any representation or warranty made by the Borrower in this agreement or in any other document, agreement or instrument delivered pursuant hereto or referred to herein or any information furnished in writing to the

Bank by the Borrower proves to have been incorrect in any material respect when made or furnished;

(e) if a writ, execution, attachment or similar process is issued or levied against all or any portion of the property of the Borrower in connection with any judgment against it in any amount which materially affects its ability to satisfy its obligations to the Bank, and such writ, execution, attachment or similar process is not released, bonded, satisfied, discharged, vacated or stayed within thirty days after its entry, commencement or levy;

(f) the breach or failure of due observance or performance by the Borrower of any covenant or provision of this agreement, other than those heretofore dealt with in this Section 13.01, or of any other document, agreement or instrument delivered pursuant hereto or referred to herein which is not remedied within 3 Banking Days after written notice to do so has been given by the Bank to the Borrower;

(g) if an encumbrancer, lienor or landlord takes possession of any part of the property of the Borrower or attempts to enforce its security or other remedies against such property and its claim remains unsatisfied for such period as would permit such property to be sold thereunder and such property which has been repossessed or is capable of being sold has an aggregate fair market value of at least $10,000; or

(h) if expropriation proceedings are instituted against any of the property or assets of the Borrower and, in the opinion of the Bank, such expropriation would materially affect the Borrower's ability to satisfy its obligations hereunder or to carry on its business;

the right of the Borrower to obtain any further credit hereunder and all of the obligations of the Bank hereunder to extend such further credit shall automatically terminate and the Bank may, by notice to the Borrower, declare all indebtedness of the Borrower to the Bank pursuant to this agreement to be immediately due and payable whereupon all such indebtedness shall immediately become and be due and payable without further demand or other notice of any kind, all of which are expressly waived by the Borrower, and any collateral security for such indebtedness shall thereupon become enforceable by the Bank.

It is not hard to imagine the reasons that would lead a bank to insist on this kind of agreement. The agreement may be lopsided in that the bank has ample grounds for either calling the loan or refusing to allow any further draws under it, but no court is likely to regard the bank's powers as so extensive as to make the bank's contractual rights unenforceable.

Loan agreements are quite unlike many other commercial agreements because the lender typically performs all it has to do before the borrower has to do any of what it promises.

7. A more extreme example of one-sided obligations is provided by *Jim Landry Pontiac Buick Ltd. v. Canadian Imperial Bank of Commerce* (1987), 40 D.L.R. (4th) 343 (N.S.T.D.), where the court intervened to prevent what it saw as unfairness. The defendant bank financed the business of the plaintiff automobile dealer. The bank took security in the form of a conditional sales contract and chattel mortgage. The contract permitted the bank to repossess if it felt itself "insecure", providing that the bank could immediately proceed under the mortgage if it "shall feel unsafe or insecure or deem the . . . goods . . . in danger of being sold . . .". The bank repossessed without notice to the debtor. The defendant argued that notice was required. The court held that, as regards the conditional sales contract, the legislation required only that notice be given after repossession, so under the statute no notice *before* repossession was required. Glube C.J.T.D., however, said (p. 356):

To allow a party to say, "I feel insecure", without either communicating that to the debtor or being obliged to prove it should an action be brought, when [it] acted without demand and notice, would be unjust. It is my view that the debtor must know that he is in default whether in the eyes of the creditor only or actually, and know the creditor wants his money. It cannot be a one-sided mental decision left uncommunicated.

In the result, the bank's assertion of an uncontrollable power was not upheld.

The idea of a bank having "feelings of insecurity" raises a conceptual problem. If a corporation has neither soul to be damned nor body to be kicked, it is hard to see how it can have "feelings". Can you think of a way of drafting the agreement to acknowledge the concerns of the bank and the debtor — at least as those were articulated by the court? Remember that the existence of any "feelings" or similar sensations or thoughts that the bank might have may have to be proved in evidence before a judge.

8. The requirement of mutuality is not absolute, for many kinds of promises are enforceable on one side only. A person defrauded by another in a contractual relation may sue on the contract while the fraudulent party may not. An infant (minor) may sue on a contract (through a litigation guardian) while the other party may not.

Many commercial agreements are executed by one party, not both. The standard bank guarantee, for example, is only executed (almost always under seal) by the guarantor, not by the bank; a mortgage is executed by the mortgagor, not by the mortgagee. A loan "commitment" may be drafted to oblige the borrower to accept the loan, but may not oblige the lender to make it.

Going Transaction Adjustments

The problem to be discussed in this section typically arises in situations like the following:

(a) A general contractor, under contract to the owner of land to construct a building, employs a subcontractor to excavate the foundations for an agreed price. The excavation encounters unexpected difficulties. The subcontractor does not have the resources to complete the work. To encourage the subcontractor to stay on the job, the general contractor pays an additional $25,000 and promises to pay a further 15 per cent over the contract price upon completion.

(b) A creditor is owed $10,000 by a debtor. The prospects of the creditor obtaining payment in full are dim. The debtor, on the other hand, would like to be free of the debt. The debtor offers the creditor $7,500 in full settlement and the creditor agrees to accept this offer.

These changes to the original deal that the parties made are "going-transaction adjustments" — the parties agree to modify the terms of their relation so that one party pays the other more (or gets less) than the original contract called for. This change occurs when one or both of the parties still have obligations to fulfil under the contract. In addition, the party benefiting from the change does not do any more for the other than the original contract required; it either did or will do less than it had originally promised to do.

The doctrinal question raised in these cases is whether there is consideration for the modifying promises, the promise to pay more or the promise to take less in full satisfaction. The traditional legal analysis is that if there is no new consideration, the promise to modify the original contract is not enforceable.

The problem posed by going-transaction adjustments remains an important one for the law of contracts, although it is often of more theoretical than practical importance. The practical insignificance is determined by the common practice of

business people in carrying on business in obliviousness of the law, and in performing contracts that the law persists in regarding as unenforceable.

The general form of the argument under the doctrine of consideration in these
cases is that if a person has agreed to do something in return for a certain payment,
any promise to pay more for doing that which he or she promised to do must be
unenforceable as being made without consideration. Thus in Pollock, *Principles of
Contracts* (13th ed., London: Stevens, 1950) p. 143, it was said:

> Neither the promise to do a thing nor the actual doing of it will be a good considera-
> tion if it is a thing which the party is already bound to do either by the general law or
> by a subsisting contract to the other party. It seems obvious that an express promise
> by A to B to do something which B can already call on him to do can in contempla-
> tion of law produce no fresh advantage to B or detriment to A.

Notice the form of this argument. The second sentence begins by saying, "It
seems obvious . . .", which nearly suggests that *as a matter of fact* there can be
neither fresh advantage to one party nor detriment to the other. To the extent that
the commercial reasons for the modifying promises in the two examples above are
obvious and understandable, such a conclusion cannot be a question of fact. Indeed, Pollock does not claim that it is a fact, for the crucial phrase is *"in contemplation of law"*. What we have here is a *deemed* insufficiency of consideration.
The enquiry is not a factual one at all.

To justify Pollock's conclusion that there is neither benefit nor detriment from
making the promises in the two situations outlined, one must assume:

(a) the costs of finding an alternative person to complete the excavation (in the
event that the subcontractor cannot perform and cannot pay a damage claim)
are so low as to make it illogical to pay more to the subcontractor to ensure its
performance of the contract; and

(b) the costs of obtaining a substituted performance — as, for example, through a
claim for damages from the debtor — is so low as to make it illogical for either party to compromise or abandon any of its rights under the contract.

It is true that if the subcontractor breached its contract, the general contractor
could sue it for damages, but what good would that do? The subcontractor's bankruptcy has only been made more certain and the work will not be done. If the general
contractor agrees to pay more, it may be able to pass on these increased costs to the
owner, and even if it cannot, its net costs may be less than the cost of getting another
subcontractor. (The existence of performance bonds, *i.e.*, insurance payable on the
subcontractor's breach, may provide compensation to the general contractor, but if
the general contractor claims under the bond, it will have put the subcontractor out of
business and will probably not get full compensation in any case.)

Moreover, a spirit of co-operation on the general contractor's part may make its
relations with the subcontractor more profitable over the long run. It is false, therefore, to suggest that the general contractor cannot get a benefit *in fact* from agreeing to pay more. It remains to be seen if there is any conceivable advantage in
saying, if one speaks in the coded language required by the doctrine of consideration, that the general contractor gets "no benefit *in law*" so as to justify the refusal
to enforce the promise to pay more made by the general contractor.

A mathematician, J.A. Paulos (*Innumeracy: Mathematical Illiteracy and Its
Consequences*, New York: Hill & Wang, 1990) discussed the strategies open to
two people who agree to do a cash deal for drugs. Paulos argued that, on a mathematical basis, it would be best for them if both parties fulfilled their respective

obligations with worthless substitutes for what they had agreed to exchange; the parties would, in effect, simply exchange bags containing shredded newspaper. Paulos then observes (p. 139):

> A similar situation can arise in legitimate business transactions or, indeed, in almost any sort of exchange.

The only plausible assumption that can justify this statement about "legitimate business transactions" is that the parties meet once in circumstances in which both know that there is no chance of their ever doing business again, and that no one else will ever hear about their behaviour. It is nearly impossible to imagine such a situation, even among two drug dealers, let alone among business people.

Regardless of the fact that such completely discrete transactions hardly ever exist, the traditional bargain model of contracts that is reflected in the doctrine of consideration is, to a large extent, based on an assumption like that underlying Paulos' statement.

The traditional rule about the modification of contracts is that without "fresh consideration" a promise to modify a contract is unenforceable. This rule is based on a model of contracting which is based on various assumptions about contracting:

(a) the original deal expresses the whole relation of the parties — the terms of their relation are entirely "bounded" by the deal;

(b) so complete is the isolation of the deal that neither party shares any acquaintances with the other — there is no one to say to someone who is planning to deal with one of them, "Be careful, that person cheated on an earlier deal like the one you are making"; and

(c) neither party places any value on the chance that careful and exact performance of one deal may make it easier to make other deals with the same person or another person.

It does not take much thought to see how unrealistic these assumptions are. The cases in this section demonstrate some of the consequences of the acceptance of some of these assumptions by the courts.

HARRIS v. WATSON

(1791), Peake 102, 170 E.R. 94.
(Nisi Prius, Lord Kenyon)

In this case the declaration stated, that the plaintiff being a seaman on board the ship "Alexander", of which the defendant was master and commander, and which was bound on a voyage to Lisbon: whilst the ship was on her voyage, the defendant, in consideration that the plaintiff would perform some extra work, in navigating the ship, promised to pay him five guineas over and above his common wages. There were other counts for work and labour, &c.

The plaintiff proved that the ship being in danger, the defendant, to induce the seamen to exert themselves, made the promise stated in the first count.

LORD KENYON: — [1] If this action was to be supported, it would materially affect the navigation of this kingdom. It has been long since determined, that when the freight is lost, the wages are also lost. This rule was founded on a principle of policy, for if sailors were in all events to have their wages, and in times of danger entitled to insist on an extra charge on such a promise as this, they would in many cases suffer a ship to sink, unless the captain would pay any extravagant demand they might think proper to make.

[The plaintiff was nonsuited.]

STILK v. MYRICK

(1809), 2 Camp. 317, 170 E.R. 1168
(Nisi Prius, Lord Ellenborough)

This was an action for seaman's wages, on a voyage from London to the Baltic and back. By the ship's articles, executed before the commencement of the voyage, the plaintiff was to be paid at the rate of £5 a month; and the principal question in the cause was, whether he was entitled to a higher rate of wages?

In the course of the voyage two of the seamen deserted; and the captain having in vain attempted to supply their places at Cronstadt [a port in what is now Finland on the Baltic Sea], there entered into an agreement with the rest of the crew, that they should have the wages of the two who had deserted equally divided among them, if he could not procure two other hands at Gottenburgh. This was found impossible; and the ship was worked back to London by the plaintiff and eight more of the original crew, with whom the agreement had been made at Cronstadt.

Garrow for the defendant insisted, that this agreement was contrary to public policy, and utterly void. In West India voyages, crews are often thinned greatly by death and desertion; and if a promise of advanced wages were valid, exorbitant claims would be set up on all such occasions. This ground was strongly taken by Lord Kenyon in *Harris v. Watson* [above] where that learned Judge held, that no action would lie at the suit of a sailor on a promise of a captain to pay him extra wages, in consideration of his doing more than the ordinary share of duty in navigating the ship; and his Lordship said, that if such a promise could be enforced, sailors would in many cases suffer a ship to sink unless the captain would accede to any extravagant demand they might think proper to make.

The Attorney-General, *contra*, distinguished this case from *Harris v. Watson*, as the agreement here was made on shore, when there was no danger or pressing emergency, and when the captain could not be supposed to be under any constraint or apprehension. The mariners were not to be permitted on any sudden danger to force concessions from the captain; but why should they be deprived of the compensation he voluntarily offers them in perfect security for their extra labour during the remainder of the voyage?

LORD ELLENBOROUGH: — [1] I think *Harris v. Watson* was rightly decided; but I doubt whether the ground of public policy, upon which Lord Kenyon is stated to have proceeded, be the true principle on which the decision is to be supported. Here, I say, the agreement is void for want of consideration. There was no consideration for the ulterior pay promised to the mariners who remained with the ship. Before they sailed from London they had undertaken to do all that they could under all the emergencies of the voyage. They had sold all their services till the voyage should be completed. If they had been at liberty to quit the vessel at Cronstadt, the case would have been quite different; or if the captain had capriciously discharged the two men who were wanting, the others might not have been compellable to take the whole duty upon themselves, and their agreeing to do so might have been a sufficient consideration for the promise of an advance of wages. But the desertion of a part of the crew is to be considered an emergency of the voyage as much as their death; and those who remain are bound by the terms of their original contract to exert themselves to the utmost to bring the ship in safety to her destined port. Therefore, without looking to the policy of this agreement, I think it is void for want of consideration, and that the plaintiff can only recover at the rate of £5 a month.

NOTES

1.   One of the plaintiff's counsel in *Stilk v. Myrick* was Espinasse, who published a different version of report of this case (6 Esp. 129, 170 E.R. 851). In that report Lord Ellenborough made no mention of the problem of consideration and was quite content simply to follow *Harris v. Watson*. Espinasse, however, was not considered to be an accurate reporter (one judge apparently said that he did not want to consider a law report "from Espinasse or any other ass") and it is assumed that Campbell (a future Lord Chancellor, whose entire report is given above) was more accurate. Nevertheless, Espinasse was counsel and, moreover, the arguments of counsel, as reported by Campbell, are based entirely on the applicability of the public policy decision in *Harris v. Watson*. P. Luther's "Campbell, Espinasse and the sailors: text and context in the common law" (1999), 19 *Legal Studies* 526, is a fascinating analysis of law reporting at the beginning of the nineteenth century and the attitude of the common law (and the British Parliament) to seamen. Luther's analysis of the two reports of *Stilk v. Myrick* is considerably more detailed than the one provided here.

It is now impossible to know exactly what Lord Ellenborough said and in an important sense it does not matter, for Campbell's report of the case has been treated as a "leading case" and is now authority for the proposition that a new promise by a person who is already bound to perform for the defendant is unenforceable because of a lack of consideration. See Gilmore, *The Death of Contract* (Columbus: Ohio State University Press, 1974), c. 1.

It is, however, worth keeping in mind that what seem to be no more than the prejudices of reporters have powerfully influenced the development of the doctrine of consideration.

2.   *Harris v. Watson*, decided in 1791, raises a legitimate concern of policy, namely the possibility of inappropriate pressure being brought to bear on a party to a contract to increase the amount of payment promised. The same issue arose in *The Port Caledonia* (above), and such pressure is now referred to as "economic duress". Less than 20 years after *Harris*, early in the nineteenth century, in *Stilk v. Myrick*, the analysis has moved away from policy concerns and the assessment of the factual circumstances of the contractual modification, to the development of a general model of contracting, one that could apply to any contractual modification, regardless of the circumstances. It was during precisely this period, in 1802, that the reporters Bulstrode and Pullen drafted their note to *Wennall v. Adney*, which so influenced Lord Denman in *Eastwood v. Kenyon*, above, at ¶ 3.

What view of the law, of the process of development of the law and of the role of the courts would regard this development as an improvement in any respect?

RAGGOW v. SCOUGALL

(1915), 31 T.L.R. 564
(Div. Ct., Darling and Coleridge JJ.)

This was an appeal by the defendants, Messrs Scougall and Co., who were a firm of mantle-makers, from a decision of Judge Rentoul in the City of London Court, by which the plaintiff, a mantle designer, recovered judgment for £58 . . .

In August 1913, the plaintiff by an agreement in writing agreed to become the defendants' designer for two years at a certain salary. It was provided that if the business should be discontinued during the period the agreement should cease to be of any effect. When [World War I] broke out many customers cancelled orders which they had given to the firm, and the defendants had to consider whether they should close the business altogether. They called their employees together, and most of them agreed to a reduction of wages during the war if the defendants would continue the business. The plaintiff entered into a new agreement in writing, in which he, like other employees of the firm, agreed to accept a smaller salary for the duration of the war, provided that when the war was over the terms of the old agreement should be revived. He went on with his work and accepted the new salary until February last, when the defendants received a solicitor's letter claiming payment in full at the rate fixed in the old agreement; and as they refused to pay the excess this action was brought.

In the Court below judgment was given for the plaintiff on the ground that no consideration had been shown for the new agreement to accept a reduced payment.

Mr. Frampton [for the defendants] now submitted that the new agreement had annulled the old one, and had entirely replaced it.

Mr. Tyfield [for the plaintiff] submitted that the new agreement was merely a variation of the old in one particular, the amount of salary, and that in all other respects the old one remained in force; there was, therefore, no consideration for the promise to accept a less sum and the new agreement was void. . . .

DARLING J.: — **[1]** . . . the appeal must be allowed. It was clear from the provision in the new agreement that the terms of the old one should be revived when the war came to an end, and that until the war ended the old agreement was dead. The parties had in fact torn up the old agreement and made a new one by mutual consent. They could have done it by recitals setting out the existence and rescission of the old agreement, but they had adopted a shorter course. The new agreement was an agreement contemplating employment on certain terms while the war lasted, and on certain other terms, which could be ascertained by reference to the older document, after the war had ended. The point, therefore, as to want of consideration failed and the appeal succeeded. He was the more glad to be able to arrive at this conclusion on the law, for it was evident that the plaintiff was trying to do a very dishonest thing.

QUESTIONS

1. Why is this plaintiff *dishonest*? Is there any suggestion in *Stilk v. Myrick* or in Pollock that the person who wants to argue that there is no consideration for his promise must be acting honestly? If "dishonesty" simply means going back on that what one has promised, why isn't the defendant captain in *Stilk v. Myrick* equally dishonest?

2. While the judge in *Raggow* does not directly address the argument of counsel for the plaintiff about consideration, given that under the terms of the original contract the employer had the right to go out of business, the employer's undertaking to stay in business (and employ the plaintiff) might be consideration for the employee's promise.

3. If there is rescission in *Raggow v. Scougall*, then why not in *Stilk v. Myrick*? What role is rescission playing in *Raggow v. Scougall*?

   It is clear that if parties have legal advice the problems of consideration can be avoided. (Would it have helped the plaintiff in *Stilk v. Myrick* if he had given the ship's captain a peppercorn in return for the captain's promise to pay him more? Should it have helped?)

4.   The problem in dealing with these cases of modification of contracts is similar to the problem in the cases already studied on the doctrine of consideration. The outcome is said to be supported by the application of the doctrine of consideration. There are some cases in which it is easy to see why the promise should not be enforced. We do not want sailors to be able to say: "Oh, Captain! Do you see those rocks there? What is it worth to you to have us work a little bit harder?" (The example is fanciful; even the most greedy sailor would have a very strong incentive to work very hard if the ship were in danger, whether or not the captain offers to pay him more.) Yet when there are no such objections, why should the courts not enforce the promise?

STOTT v. MERIT INVESTMENT CORPORATION

(1988), 63 O.R. (2d) 545, 48 D.L.R. (4th) 288
(C.A., Blair, Finlayson and Krever JJ.A.)

[Stott was a broker with Merit Investment Corporation. Stott purchased gold futures contracts for a customer, Guyenot. Merit Investment was loaning Guyenot most of the money for these purchases, with the futures contracts that he purchased serving as collateral (a "margin account"). The price of gold was falling, and Guyenot failed to "maintain the margin" [provide additional collateral] required by Merit; accordingly Stott, as he was entitled to do, sold two of Guyenot's contracts to protect the position of Merit Investment. Guyenot complained to Douglas, Stott's superior, and Douglas authorized repurchase of the contracts for Guyenot, and acceptance of a post-dated cheque from Guyenot to satisfy the "margin call". The cheque was not honoured, and Guyenot's accounts were sold out. The price of gold having declined further, Guyenot was left owing about $66,000 to Merit, which would not have been owed if the account had been sold out before Douglas's intervention.

On January 30, 1980, Stott met with Kasman, the national sales manager for Merit. It is a term of employment in the securities business that a broker is ordinarily liable to his firm for any losses caused the firm by his client's default on a margin account (giving the broker a strong incentive to closely monitor margin accounts). Stott thought that he should not have to pay for the losses in this case since he felt that the intervention of his superior Douglas caused the loss, while Douglas thought Stott should be liable. After discussion with Kasman, Stott agreed to sign the following document:

REGISTERED REPRESENTATIVE CLIENT LOSS OBLIGATION

This will acknowledge my unconditional responsibility of the debt to Merit Investment Corporation owing by my client, Michael Guyenot, in the amount of $66,308.68 U.S. Funds.

As agreed, interest will be incurred on the said debit balance at the rate of 12% per year and I acknowledge the said interest charge and my corresponding obligation and responsibility to pay the same.

Further, should I for any reason, leave the employment of Merit Investment Corporation, any amount outstanding and owing by me and my clients, to the company will become immediately due and payable.

As he was leaving the meeting, Kasman said: "This document would probably not hold up in court anyways." Thereafter, every month sums were deducted from the commissions due to Stott to repay this obligation, and Stott signed monthly summaries that showed the deductions. On November 25, 1981, Stott signed another document, agreeing that in light of a settlement reached between Merit and Guyenot, $35,000 was owing from him at that time. On July 30, 1982, Stott resigned from Merit and brought an action to recover the amount that had been deducted from commissions. Merit counterclaimed for the balance owing. Stott succeeded at trial.

A crucial issue at trial was whether or not Stott was liable for Guyenot's debt to Merit. While industry custom made brokers liable for losses that were caused by their own fault, the trial judge concluded that the losses were a result of the intervention of Douglas and not Stott's fault. Accordingly, Stott was not obliged under the terms of his employment contract with the broker for the $66,308.68 that Guyenot owed to Merit Investments. Merit appealed.]

FINLAYSON J.A.: — [1] . . . [I]t seems to me that the case turns on the trial judge's determination that there was no consideration for the initial agreement of January 30, 1980, and consequently anything done thereafter was of no legal consequence. I do not regard this determination as a finding of fact but rather a finding that there was no evidence of anything that in law was capable of being consideration. With respect, there was such evidence. It is one thing for a trial judge to say, well after the event, that upon a weighing of all the evidence, including an assessment of the credibility of the principal witnesses, he does not accept that there was any legal obligation on the part of Stott to answer for the debt of his customer, Guyenot. It is quite another, to transpose that finding back in time and postulate it as a fact current to the then discussion. To put it another way, it is not a question of whether the claim of Kasman as to Stott's liability would have stood the test of a court proceeding, but whether it was a bona fide claim at the time it was asserted. It is conceded that forbearance of a non-existing claim is not forbearance at all, but this claim was not in that category in the minds of either Kasman or Stott.

[2] **FINLAYSON J.A.** referred to the case of *Miles v. New Zealand Alford Estate Co.* (1886), 32 Ch. D. 266 (C.A.), and to the judgments of Bowen and Cotton L.JJ. Bowen L.J. said] that forbearance to sue would be good consideration if the claim given up were "a real cause of action . . . one that [was] bona fide and not frivolous or vexatious" even if it might not be ultimately successful were it to be litigated. Cotton L.J. said "that if there is in fact a serious claim honestly made, the abandonment of the claim is a good 'consideration' for a contract". Cotton L.J. explained "honest claim" by saying "that a claim is honest if the claimant does not know that his claim is unsubstantial, or if he does not know facts, to his knowledge unknown to the other party, which shew that his claim is a bad one".

[3] The above covers the situation in the case on appeal. Leaving aside, for the moment, the issue of duress, Stott had clearly acknowledged his indebtedness on January 30, 1980, and reaffirmed it by his subsequent conduct in acknowledging the monthly withdrawals and in signing the agreement of November 25, 1981. The learned trial judge's finding that the consideration for the agreement of January 30th was non-existent is based upon his erroneous conclusion that Stott's contract of employment made him liable only for losses incurred because of error or negligence. He was, in fact, liable in any event for his client's obligations to the firm. Merit certainly believed that Stott was liable despite the effect of the actions of

Douglas as they were ultimately found by the trial judge. Merit's position in asserting the claim never wavered even after the spring of 1981 when Stott started to complain about his treatment. The claim by Merit was clearly a sound one in the minds of its senior officers and I believe in the mind of Stott as well. It is significant that the trial judge made no finding that Merit had acted in bad faith.

[4]   In any event, forbearance is not the only consideration in the case at bar. Stott explicitly stated that he believed his job was on the line, and while the trial judge did not so find, it is clear from those same findings as to what Kasman said, that Stott's future at the firm would have been bleak indeed unless he agreed to the arrangements in question. Stott wanted to remain at the firm and as part of the incentive to sign the acknowledgement of indebtedness, he was given a trading account. Later, as incidents of his employment, he received incentive bonuses and a guarantee for a bank loan.

[5]   Looked at another way, it would be fair to say that his original contract of employment was changed in January of 1980, to adjust for the fiasco of the Guyenot account. He continued on in his employment for two and one-half years. It is difficult to say that there was no mutuality involved in the complained of arrangement.

[6]   Much was said in argument by counsel for the respondent that there was no mention of forbearance to sue (nor any other consideration) in the agreement of January 30, 1980. I think we should adopt the advice of Bowen L.J. and look at this matter as businessmen would. In the first place, absent the intervention of Douglas, there can be no question that Stott would be liable for the default of his customer under the terms of his contract of employment. Even Stott conceded this. The agreement of January 30th, combined with the arrangement for deductions from his earned commissions, clearly implied a forbearance on the part of Merit to sue during the continuation of his employment. A specific request for forbearance for a precise period of time is not necessary where it can be implied from the surrounding circumstances that such a request was made and that forbearance for a reasonable time was extended. . . . The action of Douglas in accepting the post-dated cheque and his extension of credit muddies the waters, but it has the effect only of reducing Stott's liability for Guyenot's account from a certainty to something less than that. His acknowledgements of the debt by his signatures on the monthly statements and the agreement of November 25, 1981, make it clear that he accepted responsibility notwithstanding the actions of Douglas. . . .

BLAIR J.A. (dissenting): — [7] In my view, the intervention of Douglas exonerated Stott from liability on the Guyenot account. Merit, through Douglas, who was not only the compliance officer but also the secretary-treasurer and a director of the company, assumed responsibility for all ensuing losses.

[8]   Since Stott was not liable under his contract of employment to indemnify Merit for Guyenot's loss, Merit had no claim against Stott upon which it could assert forbearance to sue as consideration for the undertaking given by Stott on January 30, 1980. I recognize that forbearance to sue on a non-existent claim made in good faith may, in some circumstances, constitute consideration. Merit, however, is precluded from arguing that its non-existent claim was made in good faith. It is asserted in blatant disregard of the terms of the contract of employment. Moreover, the trial judge's findings on the credibility and motivation of Merit's two witnesses referred to above established that its real purpose was not to affirm

Stott's purported liability under the contract but rather to force him to assume responsibility for the actions of Douglas.

[9] In many respects this case is similar to *Ex p. Banner; Re Blythe* (1881), 17 Ch. D. 480, where the Court of Appeal set aside a bankruptcy claim founded on an alleged compromise agreement. It held that the party making the claim did not act bona fide in bringing the action which was compromised knowing that he had no legal claim but being aware that the defendants would not risk damage to their reputation in defending it. Cotton L.J. said at p. 492:

> . . . it cannot be said that Sheil [the plaintiff] acted bona fide in bringing the action. I will explain what I mean by bona fide. In my opinion, in judging of his bona fides, the question is, not whether he thought he would succeed in the action — very probably he did in consequence of the hold which his knowledge of the Defendants' conduct had given him over them — but whether he really believed that he had a right to claim the money as his.

[10] In *Ex p. Banner* the claim was not bona fide because it was made for purposes of extortion. It resembles this case where Merit's claim was not bona fide because it was made, as the trial judge found, to shift responsibility for the actions of Douglas to Stott. . . .

[11] As a result of the fall-off in market activity in 1981, he was in desperate straits when he signed the agreement of November 25th, which provided for the immediate payment of $3,000, being a portion of a bonus which he had already earned. The payment of the bonus, like the setting-up of a trading account in January, 1980, was made under an ordinary term of Stott's employment and, in my opinion, the manipulation of such employee benefits provides no consideration for the agreement. Since no valid consideration was given for the undertaking exacted from Stott on November 25, 1981, it was without legal effect. It purported to be an affirmation of his alleged obligation under his employment contract to make good losses on the Guyenot account, which, for reasons already given, had no legal foundation.

[**KREVER J.A.** agreed with **FINLAYSON J.A.** Appeal allowed, with Merit awarded judgment on its counterclaim.]

NOTES AND QUESTIONS

1. Both Finlayson and Blair JJ.A. (in dissent) agree on the legal principle that the compromise of a potential claim to cause of action or defence is good consideration, even if it should later turn out that the claim was without legal merit, provided:

    (a) the claim or defence is reasonable, that is, not frivolous or vexatious;

    (b) the person giving up the claim or defence has a *bona fide* belief in its chance of success, that is, the person is not simply "blackmailing" the other; and

    (c) there has been no concealment of material facts.

    The judges in *Stott* disagreed about how to apply this principle to the facts of this case.

    This legal principle is in part premised on a desire to promote settlements and finality. Once a claim is settled, courts ordinarily do not allow the parties to re-litigate the issue. Further, the settlement of a claim or defence is understood to be the purchase of something of contingent value that may ultimately prove worth more or less than when the contract was made.

2. As in many other cases, *Stott* illustrates that issues of economic duress and lack of consideration may both be raised. The portions of the judgments in *Stott* that deal with economic duress have been omitted here.

3. According to the principle articulated in *Stott v. Merit Investments*, if the plaintiff sailors in *Stilk* had thought that they had no obligation to go on, the promise of the captain might have been enforceable. Why should such a state of mind make a difference and what might you, as a solicitor, do to take advantage of the difference? Would you like to argue that there should be some kind of objective standard of belief, so that the plaintiffs should reasonably have thought that they had no obligation to go on?

    It is clear that had anyone given any thought to using a lawyer, the transactions in all of these cases could have been made immune to challenge, subject to the defence of economic duress.

    Does this suggest that the doctrine of consideration is not quite doing what it might be expected to do?

4. In *D.C.B. v. Zellers Inc.*, [1996] M.J. No. 362, 138 D.L.R. (4th) 309 (Q.B.) the mother of a young shoplifter had paid $225 to Zellers in response to a demand letter from the store's lawyer. The letter threatened to bring a civil suit against her for $1,000 to provide "restitution" for the "incremental" costs of this shoplifting incident, even though the items stolen were only worth $60 and were recovered undamaged.

    The woman later sued to recover her payment of $225, arguing that she had no legal obligation to pay for her son's crime. The store argued that even if the mother had no legal obligation to pay any money, this payment constituted a compromise of an action, their forbearance from bringing suit. In ordering the return of the $225 to the plaintiff mother, Jewers J. observed that, at common law, parents are not liable for the acts of their children, unless they have been negligent in supervising them, which was not alleged by the store in this case.

    > In my opinion, the defendant's claim was not merely a doubtful claim — it was an invalid claim. . . . Whatever legal opinion or opinions Zellers might have had regarding their claims generally, I cannot believe that they seriously thought that this claim could succeed or that they seriously intended to pursue it to court if it was not paid. Mr. Arkin [the lawyer who wrote the demand letter] was not called as a witness at the trial and so we do not have the benefit of what his opinion of the claim was. But I assume that as a competent and responsible lawyer, he knew or ought to have known that the claim had no prospect whatsoever of succeeding in court and that it would be futile to pursue it.

    What is the ethical duty imposed on a lawyer who writes a demand letter for a client like Zellers? The *Code of Conduct* (1993) of the Canadian Bar Association, Rule IX, Comment 7, on the Lawyer as Advocate states:

    > In civil matters it is desirable that the lawyer should avoid and discourage the client from resorting to frivolous or vexatious . . . attempts to . . . harass the other side.

    In *Saif Ali v. Sydney Mitchell & Co.*, [1978] Q.B. 95 (C.A.), affirmed [1980] A.C. 198 (H.L.), Lord Denning M.R. said (p. 103):

    > [I]n giving his opinion beforehand [the lawyer] must only advise proceedings if there is a reasonable case to be made — putting away from himself, like the plague, any thought of the extra fees which would come to him if the case was fought — and remembering the hardship on the other side if harassed unfairly.

The next case is an example of a common situation in business relations. What is unusual about this case is that it ever went to court. What factors would you expect to find that would discourage the litigation of such disputes?

GILBERT STEEL LTD. v. UNIVERSITY CONSTRUCTION LTD.

(1976), 12 O.R. (2d) 19, 67 D.L.R. (3d) 606
(C.A., Gale C.J.O., Howland and Wilson JJ.A.)

The judgment of the court was given by **WILSON J.A.**: —

[1]   This is an appeal from the Order of Mr. Justice Pennell [(1973), 36 D.L.R. (3d) 496] dismissing the plaintiff's action for damages for breach of an oral agreement for the supply of fabricated steel bars to be incorporated into apartment buildings being constructed by the defendant. The case raises some fundamental principles of contract law.

[2]   The circumstances giving rise to the action are as follows. On September 4, 1968 the plaintiff entered in to a written contract to deliver to the defendant fabricated steel for apartment buildings to be erected at three separate sites referred to in the contract as the "Flavin, Tectate and University projects." The price fixed by that contract was $153 per ton for "hard grade" and $159 per ton for "grade 60,000." Deliveries for the Flavin and Tectate projects were contemplated in August 1969 and October 1969, respectively, and paid for at the agreed-upon prices.

[3]   Two apartment buildings calling for the supply of 3,000 tons of fabricated steel were to be erected at the University site. However, prior to the defendant's notifying the plaintiff of its intention to commence construction on the first of these two buildings, the owners of the steel mill announced an increase in the price of unfabricated steel. They also gave warning of a further increase to come. The plaintiff approached the defendant about a new contract for the University project and a written contract dated October 22, 1969, was entered into for the supply of fabricated steel for the first building. The new price was $156 per ton for "hard grade" and $165 per ton for "grade 60,000." In fact this increase in price did not reflect the full amount of the initial increase announced by the mill owners.

[4]   On March 1, 1970, while the building under construction was still far from completion, the mill owners announced the second increase in price and a further discussion took place between John Gilbert and his brother Harry representing the plaintiff and Mendel Tenenbaum and Hersz Tenenbaum representing the defendant with respect to the price to be paid for the steel required to complete the first building. It is this discussion which the plaintiff alleges resulted in a binding oral agreement that the defendant would pay $166 per ton for "hard grade" and $178 per ton for "grade 60,000." Although the plaintiff submitted to the defendant a written contract embodying these revised prices following their meeting, the contract was not executed. It contained, in addition to the increased prices, two new clauses which the trial Judge found had not been the subject of any discussion with the defendant but were unilaterally imported into the written document by the plaintiff. The trial Judge also found, however, that the defendant agreed at the meeting to pay the increased price.

[5]   From March 12, 1970, until the completion of the first building the defendant accepted deliveries of the steel against invoices which reflected the revised prices but, in making payments on account, it remitted cheques in rounded amounts which at the date of the issuance of the writ resulted in a balance owing to the plaintiff in accordance with the invoices.

[6]   Having found on the evidence that the defendant had orally agreed to pay the increased prices, the legal issue confronting Mr. Justice Pennell was whether that

agreement was legally binding upon the defendant or whether it failed for want of consideration. Counsel for the defendant submitted at the trial that past consideration is no consideration and that the plaintiff was already obliged before the alleged oral agreement was entered into to deliver the steel at the original prices agreed to in the written contract of October 22, 1969. Where then was the *quid pro quo* for the defendant's promise to pay more?

[7]   Counsel for the plaintiff sought to supply this omission from the evidence of Hersz Tenenbaum who, during the course of discussions which took place in September 1970, with a view to a contract for the supply of steel for the second building at the University site, asked whether the plaintiff would give him "a good price" on steel for this building. Plaintiff's counsel argued that the promise of a good price on the second building was the consideration the defendant received for agreeing to pay the increased price on the first. The trial Judge rejected this submission and found the oral agreement unenforceable for want of consideration. In the course of his reasons for judgment the trial Judge adverted briefly to an alternate submission made by the plaintiff's counsel. He said:

> I should, in conclusion, mention a further point which was argued with ingenuity by Mr. Morphy [counsel for the plaintiff]. His contention was that the consideration for the oral agreement was the mutual abandonment of right under the prior agreement in writing. I must say, with respect, that this argument is not without its attraction for me.

[8]   On the appeal Mr. Morphy picked up and elaborated upon this submission which had intrigued the trial Judge. In launching his main attack on the trial Judge's finding that the oral agreement was unenforceable for want of consideration, he submitted that the facts of this case evidenced not a purported oral variation of a written contract which failed for want of consideration but an implied rescission of the written contract and the creation of a whole new contract, albeit oral, which was subsequently reneged on by the defendant. The consideration for this new oral agreement, submitted by Mr. Morphy, was the mutual agreement to abandon the previous written contract and to assume the obligations under the new oral one. Mr. Morphy submitted to the Court for its consideration two lines of authority, the first line illustrated by the leading case of *Stilk v. Myrick* [above], in which the subsequent agreement was held to be merely a variation of the earlier agreement and accordingly failed for want of consideration and the other line illustrated by *Morris v. Baron & Co.*, [1918] A.C. 1, in which the subsequent agreement was held to have rescinded the former one and was therefore supported by the mutual agreement to abandon the old obligations and substitute the new. Mr. Morphy invited us to find that the oral agreement to pay the increased price for steel fell into the second category. There was, he acknowledged, no express rescission of the written contract but price is such a fundamental term of a contract for the supply of goods that the substitution of a new price must connote a new contract and impliedly rescind the old.

[9]   It is impossible to accept Mr. Morphy's submission in the face of the evidence adduced at the trial. It is clear that the sole reason for the discussions between the parties in March 1970 concerning the supply of steel to complete the first building at the University site was the increase in the price of steel by the mill owners. No changes other than the change in price were discussed. The trial Judge found that the other two changes sought to be introduced into the written document submitted by the plaintiff to the defendant for signature following the discussions

had not even been mentioned at the meeting. Moreover, although repeated references were made at trial by the Gilbert brothers to the fact that the parties had made "a new contract" in March 1970, it seems fairly clear from the evidence when read as a whole that the "new contract" referred to was the agreement to pay the increased price for the steel, *i.e.*, the agreement which effected the variation of the written contract and not a new contract in the sense of a contract replacing in toto the original contract of October 22, 1969.

[10] I am not persuaded that either of the parties intended by their discussions in March 1970 to rescind their original contract and replace it with a new one. Indeed, it is significant that no such plea was made in the statement of claim which confined itself to an allegation that "it was orally agreed in March 1970 that the prices as set forth in the said contract [of October 22, 1969] would be varied . . . Accordingly, consideration for the oral agreement is not to be found in a mutual agreement to abandon the earlier written contract and assume the obligations under the new oral one.

[11] Nor can I find consideration in the vague references in the evidence to the possibility that the plaintiff would give the defendant "a good price" on the steel for the second building if it went along with the increased prices on the first. The plaintiff, in my opinion, fell far short of making any commitment in this regard.

[12] Counsel for the appellant put before us as an alternate source of consideration for the agreement to pay the increased price the increased credit afforded by the plaintiff to the defendant as a result of the increased price. The argument went something like this. Whereas previously the defendant had credit outstanding for 60 days in the amount owed on the original prices, after the oral agreement was made he had credit outstanding for 60 days in the amount owed on the higher prices. Therefore, there was consideration flowing from the promisee and the law does not enquire into its sufficiency. Reliance was placed by counsel on the decision of Chief Justice Meredith in *Kilbuck Coal Co. v. Turner & Robinson* (1915), 7 O.W.N. 673. This case, however, is clearly distinguishable from the case at bar, as Mr. Justice Pennell pointed out in his reasons, on the basis of the *force majeure* clause which had relieved the plaintiff of its obligations under the original contract. In undertaking to supply coal despite the strike the plaintiff was unquestionably providing consideration of real substance in that case. I cannot accept counsel's contention, ingenious as it is, that the increased credit inherent in the increased price constituted consideration flowing from the promisee for the promisor's agreement to pay the increased price.

[13] The final submission put forward by counsel for the appellant was that the defendant, by his conduct in not repudiating the invoices reflecting the increase in price when and as they were received, had in effect acquiesced in such increase and should not subsequently be permitted to repudiate it. There would appear to be two answers to this submission. The first is summed up in the maxim that estoppel can never be used as a sword but only as a shield. A plaintiff cannot found his claim in estoppel. Secondarily, however, it should perhaps be pointed out that in order to found an estoppel the plaintiff must show, not only that the conduct of the defendant was clearly referable to the defendant's having given up its right to insist on the original prices, but also that the plaintiff relied on the defendant's conduct to its detriment. I do not think the plaintiff can discharge either of these burdens on the facts of this case.

[14] In summary, I concur in the findings of the trial Judge that the oral agreement made by the parties in March 1970 was an agreement to vary the written contract of October 22, 1969 and that it must fail for want of consideration . . .

[15] The respondent cross-appealed on the subject of costs. The trial judge made no order as to costs although the defendant was successful in the action. Mr. Starkman submits that, in failing to award costs to his successful client, Mr. Justice Pennell did not exercise his discretion with respect to costs judicially. A review of Mr. Justice Pennell's reasons for judgment indicates that he was motivated to withhold costs by his assessment of the conduct of the defendant which led up to this litigation and, since he was in a better position than this Court to make such an assessment, I see no reason to interfere with his disposition as to the costs at trial.

[16] The cross-appeal should accordingly be dismissed. There will be no order as to costs of the cross-appeal.

Appeal and cross-appeal dismissed.

NOTES, QUESTIONS AND PROBLEMS

1.   If you had been solicitor for Gilbert Steel, what advice would you have given in March 1970 when the oral agreement was being negotiated? Is it likely that Gilbert Steel sought legal advice at that time?
     Assuming that University Construction had sought legal advice in March 1970, what would be the legally appropriate advice? Are there any ethical constraints on a lawyer in this situation — does it depend on whether the other party has legal representation?

2.   What do you think Wilson J.A. means when she says that "the case raises some fundamental principles of contract law"? What is a *fundamental* principle? In particular, what fundamental principle is relevant here? Draft a statement of the principle applied by Wilson J.A. To what extent is your statement consistent with all the cases in this section?

3.   *Raggow v. Scougall* was cited to the Court of Appeal by the plaintiff in the argument in *Gilbert Steel v. University Construction*. The court in *Raggow v. Scougall* was prepared to hold the parties had entered into a new agreement. Why did this principle not apply in *Gilbert Steel*? Why was *Raggow v. Scougall* not mentioned by the Court?

4.   Would you have filed a different statement of claim from the one the plaintiff filed in *Gilbert Steel*?

5.   Throughout this section of these materials, we have suggested that in some cases there may be good reasons that would justify a refusal to enforce a "going-transaction" adjustment. Are there any reasons that would justify the decision of the Court of Appeal in *Gilbert Steel*? What kind of conduct does the decision encourage?

6.   The estoppel argument, discussed by the Court of Appeal in *Gilbert Steel*, is more fully explored later in this chapter. Estoppel is sometimes used by the courts to mitigate the rigours of the doctrine of consideration.

The following excerpt comments on the doctrine of consideration.

BARRY J. REITER, "COURTS, CONSIDERATION, AND COMMON SENSE"

(1978), 27 *U.T.L.J.* 468-71 (footnotes omitted)

[1] The decision in *Gilbert Steel* suggests that the "doctrine of consideration" and its "corollaries" represent the time-tested all-embracing opinion of the common law about which promises are and which are not enforceable. It is as if a theory of enforceability had been carefully built around consideration and that consideration had been carefully developed and defined to be coextensive with the policy reasons underlying the enforcement of promises.

[2] Almost nothing could be farther from the truth. The courts never set out to create any theory to answer decisively questions about the enforceability of particular promises. Rather, they were initially concerned with the much less esoteric and much more practical problem of deciding whether or not it seemed desirable to enforce the particular promise alleged to have been made in the case before them.

[3] No simple and uniform doctrine for the conclusive deductive determination of enforceability ever was evolved by the courts. Though "the doctrine of consideration" has come to be associated with a meaning given it extrajudicially [by contracts scholars like Pollock] during the nineteenth century, the doctrine meant very different things at different times in its history and "the very changes which [it] has undergone are warnings that there is nothing in it more peculiarly fundamental than in many other legal doctrines and that a theory which has changed so much in the past may very well change once again." The doctrine cannot be defended as an exercise in logic and its significance can only be understood in the light of its history and of the society which produced it. The doctrine is a convincing demonstration of the oft-quoted truth that "the life of the law has not been logic, it has been experience". . . .

[4] [*Slade's Case*, decided in 1602, marks the beginning of the development of modern contract law, with the action of *assumpsit* established as the way to enforce contractual undertakings. It] did far more than settle a disputed pleading point. It was quickly recognized as providing a technique that could permit the enforcement of promises generally and could replace the pockets of legal enforcement that had been developing around debt, covenant, and other contract-like actions. Before, the writs in *assumpsit* usually recited the facts said to have made the defendant indebted, and then alleged that, "in consideration of" those facts, defendant had promised to pay plaintiff and had defaulted. During the sixteenth century, it had become customary to refer to the recited facts as "the considerations" for the later express promise, but no technical meaning attached to these words. After *Slade's Case* and the presumption of the later promise, however, these "considerations" were no longer merely reasons sufficient to enforce subsequent express promises but, if they showed defendant "indebted" to plaintiff, were sufficient alone to establish defendant's liability in *assumpsit*. Accordingly, attention in *assumpsit* shifted from the making of the subsequent express promise to the earlier "considerations" as courts began to identify the sorts of "considerations" which would justify imposing liability in *assumpsit*. Certainly, where debt or *assumpsit* lay before, *indebitatus assumpsit* would now be permitted. But it is clear that, immediately after *Slade*, the courts began to experiment and to find new "considerations" that would establish "indebtedness" and therefore *assumpsit* liability.

[5]   The design of the new *assumpsit* as liability was influenced by many views of the appropriate liability for promises. The benefit to the defendant, *quid pro quo*, restitution sentiments of the action of debt were important, as was the protection of detrimental reliance by the plaintiff upon which the older *assumpsit* actions had been founded. From the Chancery came the notion that all promises deliberately made ought to be enforced, particularly where the promises involved exchange of rough equivalents. There was influence from the general theories of obligations of the civilians and from the mercantile law, itself much affected by continental thinking. The pressure that any one or any combination of these factors would exert in a given case would vary with the facts, the judges, and the proximity of the case to one of the "pockets of law" that surrounded the older contract-like actions. However, a definite trend towards the wider enforcement of promises was visible shortly after *Slade* freed juries to decide whether or not, on the facts, the defendant was indebted; the passage of the Statute of Frauds some seventy-five years later was undoubtedly hastened by the ease with which a defendant, incompetent as a witness, could be found liable in *assumpsit* on a promise.

[6]   For two centuries after 1602, courts often referred to the presence or absence of consideration, or considerations, but they were using the term in no technical or unitary sense. A finding of "consideration" or "sufficient considerations" meant no more than that, on the facts, defendant was indebted and *assumpsit* would lie. There was no unitary concept of what were sufficient "considerations" beyond the examples of the cases in which *assumpsit* had been held to lie before, though there was no suggestion that the decided cases were exhaustive of the scope of *assumpsit* liability: indeed, the old cases were frequently referred to in new efforts to broaden the action. During this period the development of the "doctrine of consideration" was almost openly a functional approach, with courts asking if there were good reasons for enforcement (or refusal of enforcement) in each case; what would be the consequences of a decision each way; which answer would produce the "best" result. Wilmot J. was not exercising a fanciful imagination in 1765 when he said that "consideration has been melting down into common sense, of late."

[7]   One would have required an exceptionally vivid imagination to make the same observation one hundred years later. The nineteenth century produced a sharp break with the contracts-assumpsit developments of the then very recent past. The chain-cutting was engineered with a double-edged sword. Within one century, in theory at least, liberal views of what considerations would suffice to found an *assumpsit* were replaced first by the notion that only "bargains" were enforceable then by the oversimplification of requiring benefit to the promisor or detriment to the promisee; and finally by the intensive oversimplification of the requirement of detriment to the promisee. Contemporaneously, a unitary approach to promise enforcement was gaining formal acceptance: the narrowing doctrine of consideration was to be applied equally to all promises; and functional differences between initiating and modifying promises, between promises to pay for benefits already received and wholly gratuitous promises, between promises made in family and commercial settings, and between contracts that might be specifically enforced and those that could not, were wholly ignored.

Note on Relational Contracts and Consideration

As the excerpt from Reiter illustrates, the decision of the Ontario Court of Appeal in *Gilbert Steel* was heavily criticized by legal commentators. Such renegotiated contracts are common and most people who make a promise to pay an increased price pay without complaint. It is possible to see in the Court of Appeal's decision an important problem with traditional contracts doctrine.

The cases in these materials illustrate that in some situations the legal rules being applied by the courts bear little or no relation to what actually goes on between businesses. This statement is corroborated by the research referred to by Adams and Macaulay (above, Notes following *GNR v. Witham*). What concerns business is *not* the legal rules of consideration, but the sense that the parties to any transaction are engaged in a relation that has some permanence. In such a context, it is rare to find a firm standing on its rights and seeking damages or playing consideration games. Instead, what happens is that there is a sense of give-and-take, a sense of the need to co-operate and to keep a relation working smoothly for the benefit, in the long run, of both parties. Litigation is rare and only in a few cases will the parties pay much attention to the problems of planning their legal affairs. The traditional legal rules such as consideration are generally irrelevant to the modification of commercial relations.

Litigation usually occurs when one party has become bankrupt or when problems are too serious to be worked out by negotiation. Before the parties will resort to litigation, they usually have to be in a situation where the normal pressure to work things out is either absent or not strong enough. It is, for example, significant that the price increase that Gilbert Steel tried to pass along to University Construction was triggered not by their sole decision, but by the increase established by the steel mills. There was also evidence found by the trial judge that the effect of the price increase was greater because the building was behind schedule. Further, while the court found that the promise to provide steel at a "good price" for the next project was too vague to be consideration, if the relation had not disintegrated, it is likely that Gilbert Steel would have provided steel for that project and that its promise would have had real commercial value.

When the rules of law and the expectations of those who are governed by them become seriously incongruent, odd things begin to happen. The most serious of these is the risk that people will be caught by surprise, as in *Gilbert Steel*. Renegotiated contracts with price adjustments are common. There are, of course, extralegal sanctions that might be applied against the business that behaves improperly. It may be that Gilbert Steel would never deal with University Construction again regardless of the outcome of the litigation, but that fact does not justify the result.

This case illustrates the importance of the assumptions that are made in developing the law in this area. Gilbert Steel and University Construction both saw the agreement of March 1970 as one in a series of contracts, with the possibility of future contracts. Co-operation in performance of this one could be "rewarded" in the next. The model of contracting developed in the nineteenth century and recognized by the Court of Appeal in *Gilbert Steel* (and the traditional textbooks) is based on a discrete contract between the parties that has neither past nor future. It arises out of negotiations that take place in a vacuum. The contract is not seen as being influenced by the expectations that each party would have from its knowledge of the construction industry. When the contract comes to an end, nothing remains: the parties have no other relation of any kind. The idea behind this view of contracts is that a contract only applies to or governs a single, discrete transaction.

In reality, few contracts fit this model. The cash purchase of gas from a self-serve service centre on a highway is sometimes offered as an example of a highly discrete transaction. It is assumed that the customer goes there for one purchase and never expects to return. But this view is false if it is a sale of brand-name gas, if the customer uses a credit card, or if the customer wants to buy a snack. Then the transaction has a past and a future. Expectations will have been created by advertising, by claims of cleanliness, friendliness and the quality of the gas. The conduct of the seller will be influenced by the gas company's desire to encourage repeat business at other service centres and to keep its good name. It is interesting to note that the inconsistent quality of food at the service centres along the 401 highway between Windsor and Montreal was remedied some years ago when the food concessions were transferred from purely local enterprises to corporations that have a very strong interest in the preservation of good customer relations, corporations like Tim Hortons, Wendy's, Kentucky Fried Chicken, etc.

The view of contracts that sees them as not discrete but as part of a relation suggests that some of the traditional rules are inappropriate. A relational perspective suggests that the issue in *Gilbert Steel* is not one of the doctrine of consideration — the agreement to pay more was part of a bargain — but rather the only concern is whether there was some kind of objectionable economic pressure brought to bear by Gilbert Steel against University Construction. As an "episode" in a relation, the situation is similar to when in an employment relation the employer raises the employee's wages.

At trial, University Construction alleged that there had been economic duress. The Tenenbaums alleged that at the meeting at which they agreed to pay a higher price, John Gilbert said: "You know that we can send you steel whenever we want, not when you need it" and "What does a contract mean? A contract doesn't mean nothing." However, the trial judge did not accept this evidence. Once the trial judge in *Gilbert Steel* concluded that there was no duress, there was no real justification for not holding the defendant to the bargain it made, other than the legal doctrine of consideration.

Whether there was any kind of unfairness in the actions of Gilbert Steel could have been dealt with by examining the expectations of both parties and the general understanding in the construction business in Toronto concerning the allocation of the risk of price increases imposed on the steel supplier. Arguably, it may be significant that at the time of making the second written contract (September 1969), Gilbert Steel was informed by the steel mills which supplied them that further price increases in the price of raw steel could be expected, but Gilbert Steel nevertheless chose to enter a contract without a price escalator clause. One might also have wanted to know whether University Construction would have been able to pass on any increase in costs.

There are a number of areas of law where serious problems arise if contracts are regarded as purely discrete transactions, whereas in reality they are a part of an ongoing commercial relation, but perhaps the most graphic illustration is the rules of consideration and modification.

NOTES

1.   Recall that in *The Port Caledonia*, the Elder Brethren of The Trinity House advised the court about the context of the contract so that the propriety of the plaintiff's con-

duct could be assessed. Such a broadening of the courts' understanding of the commercial context in *Gilbert Steel* might have resulted in a better decision.

2.   The problems of developing a satisfactory rule for modification of contracts, where there is a possibility that one person may use the dependence of the other party to extract a favourable change in the agreement, are explored by Aivazian, Trebilcock and Penney, in "The Law of Contract Modifications: The Uncertain Quest for a Bench-Mark of Enforceability" (1984), 22 *Osgoode Hall L.J.* 173. The authors take the position that the opportunity for what they call "strategic behaviour" (or exploitative conduct by the party seeking to increase the price) is so great that the law faces great difficulty in deciding whether to enforce agreements that modify an existing relation. An economic analysis points up the problems with an analysis based on the doctrine of consideration, but may underestimate the commercial pressure that exists in practice to perform the original contract even if it should prove unprofitable. A concern about the potential for exploitation and economic duress is very legitimate in cases where one party seeks to modify an existing contract. It is unfortunate that Anglo-Canadian courts have often *not* directly addressed this concern, but rather have focused on the narrow, artificial issue of whether or not there is consideration.

3.   The following cases illustrate that there are several available legal tools that judges can use to mitigate the harshness of the doctrine of consideration. The questions to be considered are:

   (a)   Does the use of a device to avoid the doctrine of consideration so materially increase the uncertainty of the law that the cost of providing relief from the doctrine outweighs the benefits?

   (b)   If there exist so many and so readily available devices for avoiding the doctrine of consideration, what purpose does the doctrine serve?

   (c)   Given the unhappy or uneasy co-existence of the doctrine of consideration and the other methods for dealing with the problems of deciding what promises will be enforced, what alternatives to the doctrine are there?

4.   The Ontario Law Reform Commission in its *Report on Amendment of the Law of Contract* (1987) recommended (p. 17) that "an agreement in good faith modifying a contract should not require consideration in order to be binding". Would you support the enactment of legislation to implement this recommendation? Or can the courts be relied upon to modify the doctrine they formulated?

WILLIAMS v. ROFFEY BROS AND NICHOLLS (CONTRACTORS) LTD.

[1991] 1 Q.B. 1, [1990] 1 All E.R. 512
(C.A., Civ. Div., Purchas, Glidewell and Russell L.JJ.)

GLIDEWELL L.J.: — **[1]** This is an appeal against the decision of Mr. Rupert Jackson Q.C. sitting as an assistant recorder given on 31 January 1989 in the Kingston-upon-Thames County Court, entering judgment for the plaintiff for £3,500 damages with £1,400 interest and costs and dismissing the defendants' counterclaim.

[The plaintiff was a carpenter and the defendants were building contractors. The defendants had entered into a contract with the owner to refurbish 27 flats. The defendants engaged the plaintiff to carry out the carpentry work in the 27 flats and to repair the roof for £20,000. The defendant was required to make progress payments to the plaintiff. By 9 April 1986 the plaintiff had completed the work on the roof, had carried out the first repairs to all 27 flats and had substantially completed the second repairs to nine flats. By this date the defendants had made interim payments totalling £16,200. **GLIDEWELL L.J**. continued:]

[2]   By the end of March 1986 the plaintiff was in financial difficulty. The judge found that there were two reasons for this, namely: (i) that the agreed price of £20,000 was too low to enable the plaintiff to operate satisfactorily and at a profit. Mr. Cottrell, a surveyor employed by the defendants, said in evidence that a reasonable price for the works would have been £23,783 (ii) that the plaintiff failed to supervise his workmen adequately.

[3]   The defendants, as they made clear, were concerned lest the plaintiff did not complete the carpentry work on time. The main contract contained a penalty clause. The judge found that on 9 April 1986 the defendants promised to pay the plaintiff the further sum of £10,300, in addition to the £20,000, to be paid at the rate of £575 for each flat in which the carpentry work was completed.

[4]   The plaintiff and his men continued work on the flats until the end of May 1986. By that date the defendants, after their promise on 9 April 1986, had made only one further payment of £1,500. At the end of May the plaintiff ceased work on the flats. I will describe later the work which, according to the judge's findings, then remained to be done. Suffice it to say that the defendants engaged other carpenters to complete the work, but in the result incurred one week's time penalty in their contract with the building owners.

The Action

[5]   The plaintiff commenced this action by specially indorsed writ on 10 March 1987. He originally claimed the sum of £32,708.70. In a re-amended statement of claim served on 3 March 1988 his claim was reduced to £10,847.07. . . .

[6]   The defence then alleged that neither the balance of the original contract sum nor the £10,300 addition was payable until the work was completed, that the plaintiff did not complete the work before he left the site, and thus that no further sum was due to him. By their amended counterclaim the defendants claimed that the plaintiff was in breach of contract in ceasing work at the end of May 1986, as a result of which they had suffered damage to the extent of £18,121.46.

The Judge's Conclusions

[7]   The judge found that the defendants' promise to pay an additional £10,300, at the rate of £575 per completed flat, was part of an oral agreement made between the plaintiff and the defendants on 9 April 1986, by way of variation to the original contract.

[8]   The judge also found that before the plaintiff ceased work at the end of May 1986 the carpentry in 17 flats had been substantially (but not totally) completed. This means that between the making of the agreement on 9 April 1986 and the date when the plaintiff ceased work, eight further flats were substantially completed.

[9]   The judge calculated that this entitled the plaintiff to receive £4,600 (8 x £575) "less some small deduction for defective and incomplete items". He held that the plaintiff was also entitled to a reasonable proportion of the £2,200 which was outstanding from the original contract sum. (I believe this figure should be

£2,300, but this makes no practical difference.) Adding these two amounts, he decided that the plaintiff was entitled to further payments totalling £5,000 against which he had only received £1,500, and that the defendants were therefore in breach of contract, entitling the plaintiff to cease work.

The Issues

[10] Before us counsel for the defendants advances two arguments. His principal submission is that the defendants' admitted promise to pay an additional £10,300, at the rate of £575 per completed flat, is unenforceable since there was no consideration for it. . . .

[11] Counsel's secondary argument is that the additional payment was only payable as each flat was completed. On the judge's findings, eight further flats had been "substantially" completed. Substantial completion was something less than completion. Thus none of the eight flats had been completed, and no further payment was yet due from the defendants.

[The treatment of this argument is omitted. The Court of Appeal held that the plaintiff was not prevented from suing on the contract by the fact that he had not completely performed it. The issue raised by this argument will be considered in Chapter 4. **GLIDEWELL L.J.** continued:]

Was there consideration for the defendants' promise made on 9 April 1986 to pay an additional price at the rate of £575 per completed flat?

[12] The judge made the following findings of fact which are relevant on this issue: (i) The sub-contract price agreed was too low to enable the plaintiff to operate satisfactorily and at a profit. Mr. Cottrell, the defendants' surveyor, agreed that this was so. (ii) Mr. Roffey, the managing director of the defendants, was persuaded by Mr. Cottrell that the defendants should pay a bonus to the plaintiff. The figure agreed at the meeting on 9 April 1986 was £10,300.

[13] The judge quoted and accepted the evidence of Mr. Cottrell to the effect that a main contractor who agrees too low a price with a sub-contractor is acting contrary to his own interests. He will never get the job finished without paying more money.

[14] The judge therefore concluded:

> In my view where the original sub-contract price is too low, and the parties subsequently agree that the additional moneys shall be paid to the sub-contractor, this agreement is in the interests of both parties. This is what happened in the present case, and in my opinion the agreement of 9 April 1986 does not fail for lack of consideration.

[15] In his address to us counsel for the defendants outlined the benefits to the defendants which arose from their agreement to pay the additional £10,300 as (i) seeking to ensure that the plaintiff continued work and did not stop in breach of the sub-contract, (ii) avoiding the penalty for delay and (iii) avoiding the trouble and expense of engaging other people to complete the carpentry work.

[16] However, counsel submits that, though the defendants may have derived, or hoped to derive, practical benefits from their agreement to pay the "bonus", they derived no benefit in law, since the plaintiff was promising to do no more than he was already bound to do by his sub-contract, *i.e.*, continue with the carpentry work and complete it on time. Thus there was no consideration for the agreement.

[17] Counsel for the defendants relies on the principle of law which, traditionally, is based on the decision in *Stilk v. Myrick* (1809), 170 E.R. 1168. . . .

[18] There is, however, another legal concept of relatively recent development which is relevant, namely that of economic duress. Clearly, if a sub-contractor has agreed to undertake work at a fixed price, and before he has completed the work declines to continue with it unless the contractor agrees to pay an increased price, the sub-contractor may be held guilty of securing the contractor's promise by taking unfair advantage of the difficulties he will cause if he does not complete the work. In such a case an agreement to pay an increased price may well be voidable because it was entered into under duress. Thus this concept may provide another answer in law to the question of policy which has troubled the courts since before *Stilk v. Myrick* (1809), 170 E.R. 1168, and no doubt led at the date of that decision to a rigid adherence to the doctrine of consideration.

[19] This possible application of the concept of economic duress was referred to by Lord Scarman, delivering the judgment of the Judicial Committee of the Privy Council in *Pao On v. Lau Yiu*, [1980] A.C. 614 at 632 . . .

[20] Lord Scarman . . . referred to *Stilk v. Myrick* and its predecessor *Harris v. Watson* (1791), Peake 102, [1775-1802] All E.R. Rep. 493 and to *Williams v. Williams*, [[1957] 1 All E.R. 305, [1957] 1 W.L.R. 148, (C.A.)] before turning to the development of this branch of the law in the United States of America. He then said ([1980] A.C. 614 at 634-635):

> Their Lordships' knowledge of this developing branch of American law is necessarily limited. In their judgment it would be carrying audacity to the point of foolhardiness for them to attempt to extract from the American case law a principle to provide an answer to the question now under consideration. That question, their Lordships repeat, is whether, in a case where duress is not established, public policy may nevertheless invalidate the consideration if there has been a threat to repudiate a pre-existing contractual obligation or an unfair use of a dominating bargaining position. Their Lordships' conclusion is that where businessmen are negotiating at arm's length it is unnecessary for the achievement of justice, and unhelpful in the development of the law, to invoke such a rule of public policy. It would also create unacceptable anomaly. It is unnecessary because justice requires that men, who have negotiated at arm's length, be held to their bargains unless it can be shown that their consent was vitiated by fraud, mistake or duress. If a promise is induced by coercion of a man's will, the doctrine of duress suffices to do justice. The party coerced, if he chooses and acts in time, can avoid the contract. If there is no coercion, there can be no reason for avoiding the contract where there is shown to be a real consideration which is otherwise legal. Such a rule of public policy as is now being considered would be unhelpful because it would render the law uncertain. It would become a question of fact and degree to determine in each case whether there had been, short of duress, an unfair use of a strong bargaining position. It would create anomaly because, if public policy invalidates the consideration, the effect is to make the contract void. But unless the facts are such as to support a plea of non est factum, which is not suggested in this case, duress does no more than confer on the victim the opportunity, if taken in time, to avoid the contract. It would be strange if conduct less than duress could render a contract void, whereas duress does no more than render a contract voidable . . .

[21] . . . Lord Scarman's words seem to me to be of general application, equally applicable to a promise made by one of the original two parties to a contract.

[22] Accordingly, following the view of the majority in *Ward v. Byham*, [[1956] 2 All E.R. 318 (C.A.)] and of the whole court in *Williams v. Williams* and that of the Privy Council in *Pao On v. Lau Yiu* the present state of the law on this subject can be expressed in the following proposition: (i) if A has entered into a contract with B to do work for, or to supply goods or services to, B in return for payment by B and (ii) at some stage before A has completely performed his obligations under the contract B has reason to doubt whether A will, or will be able to, complete his side of the bargain and (iii) B thereupon promises A an additional payment in return for A's promise to perform his contractual obligations on time and (iv) as a result of giving his promise B obtains in practice a benefit, or obviates a disbenefit, and (v) B's promise is not given as a result of economic duress or fraud on the part of A, then (vi) the benefit to B is capable of being consideration for B's promise, so that the promise will be legally binding.

[23] As I have said, counsel for the defendants accepts that in the present case by promising to pay the extra £10,300 the defendants secured benefits. There is no finding, and no suggestion, that in this case the promise was given as a result of fraud or duress.

[24] If it be objected that the propositions above contravene the principle in *Stilk v. Myrick*, I answer that in my view they do not: they refine and limit the application of that principle, but they leave the principle unscathed, e.g., where B secures no benefit by his promise. It is not in my view surprising that a principle enunciated in relation to the rigours of seafaring life during the Napoleonic wars should be subjected during the succeeding 180 years to a process of refinement and limitation in its application in the present day.

[25] It is therefore my opinion that on his findings of fact in the present case, the judge was entitled to hold, as he did, that the defendants' promise to pay the extra £10,300 was supported by valuable consideration, and thus constituted an enforceable agreement.

[26] As a subsidiary argument, counsel for the defendants submits that on the facts of the present case the consideration, even if otherwise good, did not "move from the promisee". This submission is based on the principle illustrated in the decision in *Tweddle v. Atkinson* (1861), 1 B. & S. 393, [1861-73] All E.R. Rep. 369.

[27] My understanding of the meaning of the requirement that "consideration must move from the promisee" is that such consideration must be provided by the promisee, or arise out of his contractual relationship with the promisor. It is consideration provided by somebody else, not a party to the contract, which does not "move from the promisee". This was the situation in *Tweddle v. Atkinson*, but it is, of course, not the situation in the present case. Here the benefits to the defendants arose out of their agreement of 9 April 1986 with the plaintiff, the promisee. In this respect I would adopt the following passage from *Chitty on Contracts* (25th ed., 1983) para. 173, and refer to the authorities there cited:

> The requirement that consideration must move from the promisee is most generally satisfied where some detriment is suffered by him: e.g. where he parts with money or goods, or renders services, in exchange for the promise. But the requirement may

equally well be satisfied where the promisee confers a benefit on the promisor without *in fact* suffering any detriment. (Chitty's emphasis.)

[28] That is the situation in this case.

[29] I repeat, therefore, my opinion that the judge was, as a matter of law, entitled to hold that there was valid consideration to support the agreement under which the defendants promised to pay an additional £10,300 at the rate of £575 per flat. For these reasons I would dismiss this appeal.

RUSSELL L.J.: — . . . **[30]** For my part I wish to make it plain that I do not base my judgment on any reservation as to the correctness of the law long ago enunciated in *Stilk v. Myrick*. A gratuitous promise, pure and simple, remains unenforceable unless given under seal. But where, as in this case, a party undertakes to make a payment because by so doing it will gain an advantage arising out of the continuing relationship with the promisee the new bargain will not fail for want of consideration. As I read the judgment of the assistant recorder this was his true ratio on that part of the case wherein the absence of consideration was raised in argument. For the reasons that I have endeavoured to outline, I think that the assistant recorder came to a correct conclusion and I too would dismiss this appeal.

PURCHAS L.J.: — **[31]** In my judgment, therefore, the rule in *Stilk v. Myrick* remains valid as a matter of principle, namely that a contract not under seal must be supported by consideration. Thus, where the agreement on which reliance is placed provides that an extra payment is to be made for work to be done by the payee which he is already obliged to perform, then unless some other consideration is detected to support the agreement to pay the extra sum that agreement will not be enforceable. *Harris v. Watson* and *Stilk v. Myrick* involved circumstances of a very special nature, namely the extraordinary conditions existing at the turn of the eighteenth century under which seamen had to serve their contracts of employment on the high seas. There were strong public policy grounds at that time to protect the master and owners of a ship from being held to ransom by disaffected crews. Thus, the decision that the promise to pay extra wages even in the circumstances established in those cases was not supported by consideration is readily understandable. Of course, conditions today on the high seas have changed dramatically and it is at least questionable, counsel for the plaintiff submitted, whether these cases might not well have been decided differently if they were tried today. The modern cases tend to depend more on the defence of duress in a commercial context rather than lack of consideration for the second agreement. In the present case, the question of duress does not arise. The initiative in coming to the agreement of 9 April came from Mr. Cottrell and not from the plaintiff. It would not, therefore, lie in the defendants' mouth to assert a defence of duress. Nevertheless, the court is more ready in the presence of this defence being available in the commercial context to look for mutual advantages which would amount to sufficient consideration to support the second agreement under which the extra money is paid. . . .

[32] In the light of those authorities the question now must be addressed: was there evidence on which the judge was entitled to find that there was sufficient consideration to support the agreement of 9 April, as set out in the passage from his judgment already set out in the judgment of Glidewell L.J.? . . .

[33] The question must be posed: what consideration has moved from the plaintiff to support the promise to pay the extra £10,300 added to the lump sum provision? In the particular circumstances which I have outlined above, there was clearly a commercial advantage to both sides from a pragmatic point of view in reaching the agreement of 9 April. The defendants were on risk that as a result of the bargain they had struck the plaintiff would not or indeed possibly could not comply with his existing obligations without further finance. As a result of the agreement the defendants secured their position commercially. There was, however, no obligation added to the contractual duties imposed on the plaintiff under the original contact. Prima facie this would appear to be a classic *Stilk v. Myrick* case. It was, however, open to the plaintiff to be in deliberate breach of the contract in order to "cut his losses" commercially. In normal circumstances the suggestion that a contracting party can rely on his own breach to establish consideration is distinctly unattractive. In many cases it obviously would be and if there was any element of duress brought on the other contracting party under the modern development of this branch of the law the proposed breaker of the contract would not benefit. With some hesitation and comforted by the passage from the speech of Lord Hailsham L.C. [in *Woodhouse AC Israel Cocoa Ltd. S.A. v. Nigerian Produce Marketing Co. Ltd.*, [1972] A.C. 741 at 757-758] to which I have referred, I consider that the modern approach to the question of consideration would be that where there were benefits derived by each party to a contract of variation even though one party did not suffer a detriment this would not be fatal to the establishing of sufficient consideration to support the agreement. If both parties benefit from an agreement it is not necessary that each also suffers a detriment. In my judgment, on the facts as found by the judge, he was entitled to reach the conclusion that consideration existed and in those circumstances I would not disturb that finding. This is sufficient to determine the appeal. . . .

Appeal dismissed.

NOTES AND QUESTIONS

1. You will remember that one of the usual justifications for the rule that going-transaction adjustments are not enforceable was the statement of Pollock, *Principles of Contracts*, 12th ed., p. 143:

    > Neither the promise to do a thing nor the actual doing of it will be a good consideration if it is a thing which the party is already bound to do either by the general law or by a subsisting contract to the other party. It seems obvious that an express promise by A to B to do something which B can already call on him to do can in *contemplation of law* produce no fresh advantage to B or detriment to A. (Emphasis added.)

    Cheshire, Fifoot and Furmston, *Law of Contract*, 13th ed., p. 93 say, "The somewhat obvious rule, that there is no consideration if all that the plaintiff does is to perform, or to promise the performance of, an obligation already imposed upon him by a previous contract between him and the defendant" is illustrated by cases like *Stilk v. Myrick*.
    When the necessary consideration to support a promise is neither benefit, detriment nor the "price" requirement proposed by Pollock and accepted by the House of Lords but a thing "deemed" to be of no value, the capacity of the doctrine to catch people unawares is obvious. Similarly, the statement of Cheshire, Fifoot and Furmston that the rule is "obvious" is, as the cases just looked at illustrate, patently false.

2. The judgment of the English Court of Appeal in *Williams v. Roffey* is based on the argument that, if the promisee can show, *as a matter of fact*, that the promisor got a benefit, the promise to pay more is enforceable.
    While the Court of Appeal in *Williams v. Roffey* explicitly said that the authority of *Stilk v. Myrick* was not affected by the decision, what remains of it?

The going-transaction adjustment rule could only work if the courts refused to examine the circumstances of the promise to pay more; just as the majority of the House of Lords in *Foakes v. Beer* (the immediately following case) ignore Lord Blackburn's statement that payment by a debtor of less than the full amount owed was often a real benefit to the creditor. What happened in *Williams v. Roffey* was that, as happens elsewhere with the doctrine of consideration, a court finally decided that the doctrine simply cannot be applied when to do so would be plainly unjust. The court then makes an exception, purporting to leave the doctrine formally untouched and unchallenged. If enough cases of the *Gilbert Steel* type made it to court so that the judges (who after all want to sleep well at night) were constantly having to deal with the injustices that the rule creates, the judgment in *Williams v. Roffey* would soon demonstrate that the doctrine had received a mortal blow.

3.   If you were counsel in a Canadian case in which you represented a party like Gilbert Steel, what facts would you now seek to put before the court, and what arguments would you make?

4.   The issues of modification of ongoing contracts and "contractual hold-up", *i.e.*, threats of non-performance, are the subject of a considerable body of sophisticated jurisprudence in the United States, including law and economics analyses. See, *e.g.*, Oren Bar-Gill & Omri Ben-Shahar, "The Law of Duress and the Economics of Credible Threats" (2004), 33 J. Legal Stud. 391; Debora L. Threedy, "A Fish Story: *Alaska Packers' Association v. Domenico*, [2000] Utah L. Rev. 185.

The next case involves a doctrinal problem similar to what was considered in the last few cases. Once again, the problem has only limited practical importance, as it is often ignored and promises that are theoretically unenforceable are usually honoured. This case sets out all the issues and is the leading common law case on this aspect of the law.

FOAKES v. BEER

(1884), 9 App. Cas. 605
(H.L., Earl of Selborne L.C., Lords Blackburn, Fitzgerald and Watson)

[Mrs. Beer got a judgment for £990 19s 0d against Dr. Foakes. The parties entered into an agreement under which Dr. Foakes paid £500 on signing and the balance in instalments over about five years. Mrs. Beer promised not to claim any interest provided that the judgment was paid in instalments as promised. However, after Dr. Foakes had paid in accordance with the agreement, Mrs. Beer sued for the interest. The jury found that the principal had been paid as agreed and ruled in favour of the defendant. The Court of Appeal reversed and gave judgment for the interest. The defendant appealed.]

W.H. Holl, Q.C. for the appellant: Apart from the doctrine of *Cumber v. Wane* (1718), 1 Str. 426, there is no reason in sense or law why the agreement should not be valid, and the creditor prevented from enforcing his judgment if the agreement be performed. It may often be much more advantageous to the creditor to obtain immediate payment of part of his debt than to wait to enforce payment, or perhaps by pressing his debtor to force him into bankruptcy with the result of only a small dividend. Moreover if a composition is accepted, friends who would not otherwise do so may be willing to come forward to assist the debtor. And if the creditor thinks that the acceptance of part is for his benefit who is to say it is not? The doctrine of *Cumber v. Wane* has been continually assailed, as in *Couldery v. Bartrum*

(1881), 19 Ch. D. 394, 399 by Jessel M.R. In the note to *Cumber v. Wane* (1 *Smith's Leading Cases* 4th ed. p. 253, 8th ed. p. 367) which was written by J.W. Smith and never disapproved by any of the editors, including Willes and Keating JJ., it is said

> that its doctrine is founded upon vicious reasoning and false views of the office of a Court of law, which should rather strive to give effect to the engagements which persons have thought proper to enter into, than cast about for subtle reasons to defeat them upon the ground of being unreasonable. Carried to its full extent the doctrine of *Cumber v. Wane* embraces the exploded notion that in order to render valid a contract not under seal, the adequacy as well as the existence of the consideration must be established. Accordingly in modern times it has been, as appears by the preceding part of the note, subjected to modification in several instances.

Cumber v. Wane was decided on a ground now admitted to be erroneous, viz. that the satisfaction must be found by the Court to be reasonable. The Court cannot inquire into the adequacy of the consideration. *Reynolds v. Pinhowe* (1595), Cro. Eliz. 429, which was not cited in *Cumber v. Wane*, decided that the saving of trouble was a sufficient consideration; "for it is a benefit unto him to have his debt without suit or charge" . . . *Pinnel's Case* (1602), 5 Co. Rep. 1, 17a, was decided on a point of pleading: the dictum that payment of a smaller sum was no satisfaction of a larger, was extra judicial, and overlooked all considerations of mercantile convenience, such as mentioned in *Reynolds v. Pinhowe*; and it is also noticeable that it was a case of a bond debt sought to be set aside by a parol agreement. It is every day practice for tradesmen to take less in satisfaction of a larger sum, and give discount, where there is neither custom nor right to take credit . . . It has often been held that a sheet of paper or a stick of sealing wax is a sufficient consideration. The result of the cases is that if *Cumber v. Wane* be right, payment of a less sum than the debt due, by a bill, promissory note or cheque is a good discharge; but payment of such less sum by sovereigns or Bank of England notes is not. Here the agreement is not to take less than the debt, but to give time for payment of the whole without interest. Mankind have never acted on the doctrine of *Cumber v. Wane*, but the contrary; nay few are aware of it. By overruling it the House will only declare the universal practice to the good law as well as good sense.

EARL OF SELBORNE L.C.: — [1] Whatever may be the ultimate decision of this appeal the House is much indebted to Mr. Holl for his exceedingly able argument . . . The question, therefore, is nakedly raised by this appeal, whether your Lordships are now prepared, not only to overrule, as contrary to law, the doctrine stated by Sir Edward Coke to have been laid down by all the judges of the Common Pleas in *Pinnel's Case* in 1602, and repeated in his note to Littleton, sect. 344, but to treat a prospective agreement, not under seal, for satisfaction of a debt, by a series of payments on account to a total amount less than the whole debt, as binding in law, provided those payments are regularly made; the case not being one of a composition with a common debtor, agreed to, inter se, by several creditors. I prefer so to state the question instead of treating it (as it was put at the Bar) as depending on the authority of the case of *Cumber v. Wane*, decided in 1718. It may well be that distinctions, which in later cases have been held sufficient to exclude the application of that doctrine, existed and were improperly disregarded in *Cumber v. Wane*: and yet that the doctrine itself may be law, rightly recognised in *Cumber v. Wane*, and not really contradicted by any later authorities. And this appears to me to be the true state of the case. The doctrine itself, as laid down by Sir Edward Coke, may have been criticised, as questionable in principle, by some persons whose opinions are entitled to respect, but it has never been judicially overruled; on the contrary I think it has always, since the sixteenth century, been accepted as law. If so, I cannot think that your Lordships would do right, if you were now to reverse as erroneous, a judgment of the Court of Appeal, proceeding upon a doctrine which has been accepted as part of the law of England for 280 years.

[2]   The doctrine, as stated in *Pinnel's Case*, is "that payment of a lesser sum on the day" (it would of course be the same after the day), "in satisfaction of a greater, cannot be any satisfaction for the whole, because it appears to the Judges, that by no possibility a lesser sum can be a satisfaction to the plaintiff for a greater sum." As stated in Coke *Littleton*, 212(b), it is "where the condition is for payment of £20, the obligor or feoffer cannot at the time appointed pay a lesser sum in satisfaction of the whole, because it is apparent that a lesser sum of money cannot be a satisfaction of a greater;" adding (what is beyond controversy), that an acquittance under seal, in full satisfaction of the whole, would (under like circumstances) be valid and binding.

[3]   The distinction between the effect of a deed under seal, and that of an agreement by parol, or by writing not under seal, may seem arbitrary, but it is established in our law; nor is it really unreasonable or practically inconvenient that the law should require particular solemnities to give to a gratuitous contract the force of a binding obligation. If the question be (as, in the actual state of the law, I think it is), whether consideration is, or is not, given in a case of this kind, by the debtor who pays down part of the debt presently due from him, for a promise by the creditor to relinquish, after certain further payments on account, the residue of the debt, I cannot say that I think consideration is given, in the sense in which I have always understood that word as used in our law. It might be (and indeed I think it would be) an improvement in our law, if a release or acquittance of the whole debt, on payment of any sum which the creditor might be content to receive by way of accord and satisfaction (though less than the whole) were held to be, generally, binding though not under seal; nor should I be unwilling to see equal force given to a prospective agreement, like the present, in writing though not under seal; but I think it impossible, without refinements which practically alter the sense of the word, to treat such a release or acquittance as supported by any new consideration proceeding from the debtor. All the authorities subsequent to *Cumber v. Wane* which were relied upon by the appellant at your Lordships' Bar have proceeded upon the distinction, that, by giving negotiable paper or otherwise, there had been some new consideration for a new agreement, distinct from mere money payments in or towards discharge of the original liability. I think it unnecessary to go through those cases, or to examine the particular grounds on which each of them was decided. There are no such facts in the case now before your Lordships. What is called "any benefit, or even any legal possibility of benefit," in Mr. Smith's notes to *Cumber v. Wane*, is not (as I conceive) that sort of benefit which a creditor may derive from getting payment of part of the money due to him from a debtor who might otherwise keep him at arm's length, or possibly become insolvent, but is some independent benefit, actual or contingent, of a kind which might in law be a good and valuable consideration for any other sort of agreement not under seal.

[4]   My conclusion is, that the order appealed from should be affirmed, and the appeal dismissed, with costs, and I so move your Lordships.

LORD BLACKBURN [after making a thorough review of the cases, concluded]: —
[5] What principally weighs with me in thinking that Lord Coke made a mistake of fact is my conviction that all men of business, whether merchants or tradesmen, do every day recognise and act on the ground that prompt payment of a part of their demand may be more beneficial to them than it would be to insist on their rights and enforce payment of the whole. Even where the debtor is perfectly solvent, and sure to pay at last, this often is so. Where the credit of the debtor is doubtful it must be more so. I had persuaded myself that there was no such long-continued action on this dictum as to render it improper in this House to reconsider the question. I had written my reasons for so thinking; but as they were not satisfactory to the other noble and learned Lords who heard the case, I do not now repeat them nor persist in them.

[6] I assent to the judgment proposed, though it is not that which I had originally thought proper.

[**LORDS FITZGERALD** and **WATSON** gave judgment to the same effect as the **EARL OF SELBORNE**.]

NOTES AND QUESTIONS

1. In 1885, the year after *Foakes v. Beer* was decided, the Ontario legislature clearly rejected the approach of the House of Lords and passed what is now the *Mercantile Law Amendment Act*, R.S.O. 1990, c. M.10, s. 16:

   Part performance of an obligation either before or after a breach thereof when expressly accepted by the creditor or rendered in pursuance of an agreement for that purpose, though without any new consideration, shall be held to extinguish the obligation.

   Similar legislation has been enacted in British Columbia, Alberta, Saskatchewan and Manitoba.

2. If the debtor has paid part of the debt and that has been accepted by the creditor as sufficient, s. 16 of the *Mercantile Law Amendment Act* prevents the creditor going back on that. A creditor is not, of course, bound to accept less just because a debtor offers less or pays less than the full amount of the debt. A cheque that is expressed to be "in full payment" but that is for an amount less than the debt need not be accepted as being in full payment by the creditor, who is free to cross out the phrase "in full payment", cash the cheque and sue for any balance owing: *Champlain Ready Mixed Concrete v. Beaupré*, [1971] 3 O.R. 568, 21 D.L.R. (3d) 164 (C.A.).

   Section 16 does not explicitly deal with the problem of executory retraction that arises if the creditor purports to revoke the promise to accept less before the debtor has performed. If the right of the creditor to revoke the offer to accept less should be restricted, should any restriction apply if a debtor has not paid by the time that the debtor should have paid? If, for example, a creditor has agreed to accept payment of half the debt if a debtor pays by 1 November, what happens on 2 November if the debtor has not paid half the debt? The courts are likely to attach considerable importance to the question whether the debtor made a good faith effort to pay in accordance with the agreement.

   The Ontario Law Reform Commission in its *Report on Amendment of the Law of Contract* (1987) recommended (pp. 12, 13) that s. 16 be retained and that it be extended to prevent revocation of an offer to accept less before full payment of the amount stated to be sufficient has been paid. The Commission further recommended that if the debtor does not pay as the parties have agreed that it should (and the breach is not trivial or technical), the full amount of the debt should revive and the creditor should not be bound to accept what he had been prepared (and would have been forced) to accept had payment been made in a timely fashion. The argument in favour of this position is that the promise to take less should always have been regarded by the debtor as conditional on strict fulfilment of the promise to pay the new (lower) amount.

3.   At least in theory, the decision in *Foakes v. Beer* continues to apply where, as in England and Nova Scotia, there is no equivalent to s. 16. Even there, courts strain to avoid the rule.

In *Bank of Nova Scotia v. MacLellan* (1977), 78 D.L.R. (3d) 1, the Nova Scotia Supreme Court, Appellate Division, held that the bank could not recover on a promissory note jointly executed by the defendant and her husband in favour of the bank. She and her husband divorced after the note was executed, and he had disappeared. When the bank pressed her for payment, she made an agreement with an official of the bank that she would pay one-quarter of the note "in settlement" of the debt. She paid that sum, and the bank sued for the full debt, relying on *Foakes v. Beer*. The bank was held to be bound by the promise made on its behalf and to be unable to repudiate the agreement. In holding that the defendant had given consideration and hence could hold the bank to its promise, MacKeigan C.J.N.S. said: "The respondent [defendant] can be said to have at least faintly promised to help find her ex-husband. This promise, though slight and of little real value, is enough to meet the legal test of consideration."

4.   The English Court of Appeal in *Williams v. Roffey* did not cite *Foakes v. Beer*. Would *Foakes* still be decided as it was in the light of the Court of Appeal decision?

Contracts with a Third Party

An important variation on the preceding cases occurs when A promises to pay B a sum of money if B promises that he will perform his contract with C. It has occasionally been held that B can give no consideration for A's promise since he is already bound to perform the contract he has with C. These cases assume that B has in some sense "used up" his promising power by making one promise to do the thing. The better view is, however, represented by cases like *Scotson v. Pegg* (1861), 6 H. & N. 295, 158 E.R. 121 (Exch.). That case rejected this argument, and regarded the contract between A and B as one with consideration. By making the promise, B has assumed liability to A and may be liable in damages to A (as well as to C) should he breach his contract to C, and hence his contract with A. As stated by Wilde B. in *Scotson v. Pegg*:

> I accede to the proposition that if a person contracts with another to do a certain thing, he cannot make the performance of it a consideration for a new promise to the same individual. But there is no authority for the proposition that where there has been a promise to one person to do a certain thing, it is not possible to make a valid promise to another to do the same thing.

An example of the application of this rule is the following: a jockey has a contract with the owner of a horse to ride in a race for $1,000; implicit in the contract is a term that the jockey will use his best efforts to win, though there might also be a $250 bonus from the owner if the jockey wins. If a gambler offers the jockey another $500 if he wins, this promise from the gambler will be enforceable under the rule of *Scotson v. Pegg* if the jockey wins. Notice that the promise of the gambler is enforceable even though in this particular circumstance, since this a unilateral contract, there is no liability for not winning.

Although generally there is less possibility of economic duress in these situations than when one of two parties to a contract seeks modification, there are still some cases where there might be concerns about economic duress or public policy with a promise of this type. What about a promise made by a mother to a fireman that, if he will enter a burning building to save her child, the mother will pay him

$1,000? The fireman is already contractually obliged to the municipality to use his best efforts to save anyone endangered in a fire. Should the law encourage the making of such contracts? If there is concern about the enforcement of such promises, is there any reason to assume that they can be sensibly controlled by the doctrine of consideration?

RELIANCE AS A BASIS FOR THE ENFORCEMENT OF PROMISES

It is apparent from a number of the cases and problems studied that the doctrine of consideration is not a satisfactory tool for determining what promises should be enforced and what promises should not be. The doctrine of consideration generally has no impact on the ordinary commercial exchange, for in those situations the requirements of the doctrine are most obviously satisfied. The doctrine of consideration has a significant impact on a number of special situations, some of which were examined in the preceding sections.

The first (and by far the more destructive) effect of the doctrine of consideration is that it can make promises unenforceable that should be enforced. The cases of modification of existing contractual relations are in this category. In some of those cases, there is no economic or justice-related reason not to enforce the promise. In other cases, there may be good reasons for not enforcing the modified promises, but those reasons have to do with unconscionability or public policy, not with consideration.

A second effect of the doctrine of consideration is that the courts may, in some cases, be prepared to stretch the doctrine to make a non-commercial promise enforceable if it seems fair to do so. The courts have analyzed arrangements that are essentially donative promises as fitting into the exchange model in order to enforce a promise (*Hamer v. Sidway*, *Thomas v. Thomas*). They have "found" consideration to support promises, and have refused to find it when they see no need to enforce.

The courts have often done these things without giving a clear indication of why they decided to enforce a promise in one case or refused to enforce one in another. As revealed in the cases that follow on estoppel, the courts will sometimes avoid the effect of the strict application of the doctrine of consideration through use of such doctrinal tools as estoppel. The result is the creation of a significant element of "unreckonability" in the decisions. Finally, and this is perhaps its nastiest feature, the doctrine of consideration will only catch those who have not had the forethought, money or opportunity to consult a lawyer. *deliberateness & reliance*

Setting aside the doctrine of consideration, a number of factors are important in deciding which promises should be enforced. There are sound reasons for generally not enforcing gift promises. Evidence of deliberateness in the making of the contract is important. The fact that the transaction arises in a commercial context is important. What is perhaps the most important is whether the context in which the promise is made is likely to encourage people to rely on it or not. It is the fact of reliance that creates a strong pressure to enforce. This pressure is often hard to resist.

The cases that follow in this section explore reliance as a basis for enforcement of promises. It is impossible to separate fully reliance as a basis for enforcement from those cases where the courts are prepared to "find" consideration to protect reliance. The focus in the following cases is on the protection of reliance. To a significant extent, the cases here are those where the courts will enforce promises in order to protect reliance even though there is technically no consideration. In some cases the courts declare that consideration is not needed because there is some other doctrinal basis for enforcement, often relying on the concept known as estoppel. In some of the cases it is clear that the courts are protecting reliance, but they do not bother to make clear the doctrinal basis for enforcement. In some of the cases the courts could have found consideration, had the courts bothered to look. In other cases, the courts find consideration, but seem primarily motivated by protection of reliance.

A major purpose in studying these cases is to try to understand what "moved" the court to enforce the promise in any particular case so that you can (1) develop a sense of what factors will move a court to enforce a promise; and (2) offer a court a "peg" on which you as counsel and it as the adjudicator can "hang" an argument to justify enforcement.

The idea that counsel and courts use "pegs" to hang arguments on may sound a little odd, but it is the heart of legal argument. Clients do not walk in with a sign announcing their problems. A client does not say: "I have a problem of the doctrine of consideration." Rather, a client will say, "I had a deal with a buyer that it would pay more for the fabricated steel that I delivered after the price of the raw steel that I had to buy went up. Now they won't pay my invoices." It is the lawyer's job to put that problem into a legal category. If you say — to yourself, not to the client — "This is a problem of consideration", that classification will affect the facts that you will try to put to the court, the arguments that you will make, the cases and texts that you will regard as authorities and your attitude to the case.

If you see that, while you could frame the claim as one raising an issue of consideration, you could also frame it as one of reliance or even of some other issues, not only do you have more arguments to make to the court, you will be prepared to look at a client's problems with a different attitude. There will of course be situations where you do not have this freedom, but in most cases that go to litigation, the difference will be only in the degrees of freedom that counsel have. Most cases offer counsel some choice. You will not only have a choice when you start your analysis, you will have further choices throughout the case. As the following cases illustrate, the remedy obtained, *i.e.*, whether you may claim expectation or reliance damages, may depend on where or how you start your analysis.

The importance of the lawyer's imagination and creativity should become apparent as you read these materials, and is something that makes the law more interesting and challenging. It is unfortunate that the reported cases often obscure the creative role of the lawyer; the argument looks as if it followed from some established premise, not as if it was chosen from a number of possibilities by the lawyer who first thought about it.

The protection of reasonable reliance is a central theme of contract law, as illustrated in a number of doctrinal topics raised in this course. The present discussion focuses on a number of questions, including the following:

1. In what circumstances is reliance a sufficient reason for giving a remedy?

2. What are the respective roles to be played by the fact of reliance and by any promise made by one of the parties?

3. What remedy should be given when reliance is the basis for any relief?

4. To what extent can reliance be seen as a substitute for consideration so that the notion of an exchange or bargain as the principal basis for the enforcement of promises could be replaced by the need for the protection of reliance?

Reliance in the Commercial Context

The next cases raise explicitly the issue of reliance as a means of avoiding some of the undesirable features of the doctrine of consideration. In reading the cases, consider carefully what remedy will be sufficient to protect the party's reliance. There is no reason to assume that only a remedy in damages (or the "expectation" measure of damages) will do so. The remedy that the court sees as appropriate to protect reliance may have an important bearing on the court's willingness to give a remedy of any kind. A simplified analysis is that the less serious the remedy that the plaintiff needs to have its reliance protected (a remedy in damages to the full expectation measure being the most serious), the more willing the court will be to enforce the promise to protect that reliance. A corollary to this proposition is that the more extensive the plaintiff's acts of reliance, the greater the chance of its reliance being protected, either by an award of damages or even by some form of specific performance. *measure of reliance*

The following case is usually regarded as a leading precedent in the development of the legal rules protecting reliance. What is the nature of the reliance that is regarded as justifying the decision?

CENTRAL LONDON PROPERTY TRUST LTD. v. HIGH TREES HOUSE LTD.

[1947] 1 K.B. 130, 116 L.J. Rep. 77
(K.B.D., Denning J.)

Action tried by **DENNING J.** By a lease under seal made on September 24, 1937, the plaintiffs, Central London Property Trust Ltd., granted to the defendants, High Trees House Ltd., a subsidiary of the plaintiff company, a tenancy of a block of flats for the term of ninety-nine years from September 29, 1937, at a ground rent of £2,500 a year. The block of flats was a new one and had not been fully occupied at the beginning of the war owing to the absence of people from London. With war conditions prevailing, it was apparent to those responsible that the rent reserved under the lease could not be paid out of the profits of the flats and, accordingly, discussions took place between the directors of the two companies concerned, which were closely associated, and an arrangement was made between them which was put into writing. On January 3, 1940, the plaintiffs wrote to the defendants in these terms, "We confirm the arrangement made between us by which the ground rent should be reduced as from the commencement of the lease to £1,250 per annum," and on April 2, 1940, a confirmatory resolution to the same effect was passed by the plaintiff company. On March 20, 1941, a receiver was appointed by the debenture holders of the plaintiffs and on his death on February 28, 1944, his place was taken by his partner. The defendants paid the reduced rent from 1941 down to the beginning of 1945 by which time all the flats in the block were fully let, and continued to pay it thereafter. In September 1945, the then receiver of the plaintiff company looked into the matter of the lease and ascertained that the rent actually reserved by it was £2,500. On September 21, 1945, he wrote to the defendants saying that rent must be paid at the full rate and claiming that arrears amounting to £7,916 were due. Subsequently, he instituted the present friendly proceedings to test the legal position in regard to the rate at which rent was payable. In the action the plaintiffs sought to recover £625, being the amount represented by the difference between rent at the rate of £2,500 and £1,250 per annum

for the quarters ending September 29 and December 25, 1945. By their defence
the defendants pleaded (1) that the letter of January 3, 1940, constituted an agreement that the rent reserved should be £1,250 only, and that such agreement related
to the whole term of the lease; (2) they pleaded in the alternative that the plaintiff
company were estopped from alleging that the rent exceeded £1,250 per annum;
and (3) as a further alternative, that by failing to demand rent in excess of £1,250
before their letter of September 21, 1945 (received by the defendants on September 24), they had waived their rights in respect of any rent, in excess of that at the
rate of £1,250, which had accrued up to September 24, 1945 . . .

DENNING J. [stated the facts and continued:] — **[1]** If I were to consider this matter without regard to recent developments in the law, there is no doubt that had the
plaintiffs claimed it, they would have been entitled to recover ground rent at the
rate of £2,500 a year from the beginning of the term, since the lease under which it
was payable was a lease under seal which, according to the old common law,
could not be varied by an agreement by parol [the word "parol" refers to a writing
that is not under seal] (whether in writing or not), but only by deed. Equity, however, stepped in, and said that if there has been a variation of a deed by a simple
contract (which in the case of a lease required to be in writing would have to be
evidenced by writing), the courts may give effect to it . . . That equitable doctrine,
however, could hardly apply in the present case because the variation here might
be said to have been made without consideration. With regard to estoppel, the representation made in relation to reducing the rent was not a representation of an
existing fact. It was a representation, in effect, as to the future, namely, that payment of the rent would not be enforced at the full rate but only at the reduced rate.
Such a representation would not give rise to an estoppel, because, as was said in
Jorden v. Money (1854), 5 H.L.C. 185, a representation as to the future must be
embodied as a contract or be nothing.

[2]   But what is the position in view of developments in the law in recent years?
The law has not been standing still since *Jorden v. Money*. There has been a series
of decisions over the last fifty years which, although they are said to be cases of
estoppel, are not really such. They are cases in which a promise was made which
was intended to create legal relations and which to the knowledge of the person
making the promise, was going to be acted on by the person to whom it was made,
and which was in fact so acted on. In such cases the courts have said that the
promise must be honoured . . . As I have said they are not cases of estoppel in the
strict sense. They are really promises — promises intended to be binding, intended
to be acted on, and in fact acted on. *Jorden v. Money* can be distinguished, because there the promisor made it clear that she did not intend to be legally bound,
whereas in the cases to which I refer the proper inference was that the promisor
did intend to be bound. In each case the court held the promise to be binding on
the party making it, even though under the old common law it might be difficult to
find any consideration for it. The courts have not gone so far as to give a cause of
action in damages for the breach of such a promise, but they have refused to allow
the party making it to act inconsistently with it. It is in that sense, and that sense
only, that such a promise gives rise to an estoppel. The decisions are a natural result of the fusion of law and equity: for the [case] of *Hughes v. Metropolitan Railway* (1877), 2 App. Cas. 439 (H.L.) . . . [affords] a sufficient basis for saying that
a party would not be allowed in equity to go back on such a promise. In my opinion, the time has now come for the validity of such a promise to be recognized.

The logical consequence, no doubt, is that a promise to accept a smaller sum in discharge of a larger sum, if acted upon, is binding notwithstanding the absence of consideration: and if the fusion of law and equity leads to this result, so much the better. That aspect was not considered in *Foakes v. Beer* (1884), 9 App. Cas. 605 (H.L.). At this time of day, however, when law and equity have been joined together for over seventy years, principles must be reconsidered in the light of their combined effect. It is to be noticed that in the Sixth Interim Report of the Law Revision Committee, pars. 35, 40, it is recommended that such a promise as that to which I have referred, should be enforceable in law even though no consideration for it has been given by the promisee. It seems to me that, to the extent I have mentioned, that result has now been achieved by the decisions of the courts.

[3]　I am satisfied that a promise such as that to which I have referred is binding and the only question remaining for my consideration is the scope of the promise in the present case. I am satisfied on all the evidence that the promise here was that the ground rent should be reduced to £1,250 a year as a temporary expedient while the block of flats was not fully or substantially fully let, owing to the conditions prevailing. That means that the reduction in the rent applied throughout the years down to the end of 1944, but early in 1945 it is plain that the flats were fully let, and indeed the rents received from them (many of them not being affected by the Rent Restrictions Acts) were increased beyond the figure at which it was originally contemplated that they would be let. At all events the rent from them must have been very considerable. I find that the conditions prevailing at the time when the reduction in rent was made had completely passed away by the early months of 1945. I am satisfied that the promise was understood by all parties only to apply under the conditions prevailing at the time when it was made, namely, when the flats were only partially let, and that it did not extend any further than that. When the flats became fully let, early in 1945, the reduction ceased to apply.

[4]　In those circumstances, under the law as I hold it, it seems to me that rent is payable at the full rate for the quarters ending September 29 and December 15, 1945.　　　　*No estoppel*

[5]　If the case had been one of estoppel, it might be said that in any event the estoppel would cease when the conditions to which the representation applied came to an end, or it also might be said that it would only come to an end on notice. In either case it is only a way of ascertaining what is the scope of the representation. I prefer to apply the principle that a promise intended to be binding, intended to be acted on and in fact acted on, is binding so far as its terms properly apply. Here it was binding as covering the period down to the early part of 1945, and as from that time full rent is payable.

[6]　I therefore give judgment for the plaintiff company for the amount claimed.

QUESTIONS AND NOTES

1.　What was the nature of the defendant's reliance in *Central London Property*? How does it differ from the reliance of the plaintiff in *Gilbert Steel*?

2.　Do you think that Lord Denning was really relying on merger of the courts of equity and common law to justify ignoring the 1884 decision of the House of Lords in *Foakes v. Beer*? Or was this just an excuse to ignore a decision that would otherwise be a binding precedent?

3. The doctrine of estoppel has frequently been invoked where one party grants an extension of time for performance. The courts have repeatedly recognized the enforceability of extensions of time given by one party to permit the other to comply with the terms of the contract. If under a contract of sale, for example, delivery is to be made by a specified date and the buyer tells the seller that a delay is acceptable to him, the buyer cannot reimpose the time limit without giving the seller a reasonable time to comply: *Charles Rickards Ltd. v. Oppenheim*, [1950] 1 K.B. 616. *A fortiori* the buyer cannot use the seller's failure to comply with the original deadline as a breach of contract. Solicitors spend quite some time writing letters requesting extensions, granting extensions and re-imposing deadlines for performance. As you read the cases, consider what you should say in each type of letter.

4. The next case, while clearly not a commercial case, has often been regarded as a decision relevant to commercial cases. The case represents, depending on your point of view, a gloss on or headlong flight from *High Trees*.

COMBE v. COMBE

[1951] 2 K.B. 215, [1951] 1 All E.R. 767
(C.A., Asquith, Birkett and Denning L.JJ.)

DENNING L.J.: — **[1]** In this case a wife who has divorced her husband claims maintenance from him — not in the Divorce Court, but in the King's Bench — on an agreement which is said to be embodied in letters. The parties were married in 1915. They separated in 1939. On February 1, 1943, on the wife's petition, a decree nisi of divorce was pronounced. Shortly afterwards letters passed between the solicitors with regard to maintenance. [It was agreed that the husband would pay £100 a year maintenance to his former wife.]

[2]   He never paid anything. The wife pressed him for payment, but she did not follow it up by an application to the divorce court. It is to be observed that she herself has an income of her own of between £700 and £800 a year, whereas her husband has only £650 a year. Eventually, after nearly seven years had passed since the decree absolute, she brought this action in the King's Bench Division . . . claiming £675 being arrears for six years and three quarters at £100 a year. [The trial judge] held that the first three quarterly instalments of £25 were barred by the *Limitation Act*, 1939, but he gave judgment for £600 in respect of the instalments which accrued within the six years before the action was brought. He held . . . that there was no consideration for the husband's promise to pay his wife £100, but, nevertheless, he held that the promise was enforceable on the principle stated in [*High Trees*, above] . . . because it was an unequivocal acceptance of liability, intended to be binding, intended to be acted on, and, in fact, acted on.

[3]   Much as I am inclined to favour the principle of the *High Trees* case it is important that it should not be stretched too far lest it should be endangered. It does not create new causes of action where none existed before. It only prevents a party from insisting on his strict legal rights when it would be unjust to allow him to do so, having regard to the dealings which have taken place between the parties. That is the way it was put in the case in the House of Lords which first stated the principle — *Hughes v. Metropolitan Railway* [(1877), 2 App. Cas. 439] . . . It is also implicit in all the modern cases in which the principle has been developed. Sometimes it is a plaintiff who is not allowed to insist on his strict legal rights. Thus, a creditor is not allowed to enforce a debt which he has deliberately agreed to waive if the debtor has carried on business or in some other way changed his position in reliance on the waiver . . . [*High Trees*] . . . A landlord who has told his tenant that he can live in his cottage rent-free for the rest of his life is not allowed to go back on it if the tenant stays in the house on that footing: *Foster v. Robinson*, [1951] 1 K.B. 149. Sometimes it is a defendant who is not allowed to insist on his strict legal rights. His conduct may be such as to debar him from relying on some condition, denying some allegation, or taking some other point in answer to the claim. Thus, a government department, who had accepted a disease as due to war service, were not allowed afterwards to say it was not, when the soldier, in reliance on the assurance, had abstained from getting further evidence about it: *Robertson v. Minister of Pensions*, [1949] 1 K.B. 227, [1948] 2 All E.R. 767. A buyer who had waived the contract date for delivery was not allowed afterwards to set up the stipulated time as an answer to the seller: *Charles Rickards, Ltd. v. Oppenheim*, [1950] 1 K.B. 616. A tenant who had encroached on an adjoining building, asserting that it was comprised in the lease, was not allowed afterwards to say that it was not included in the lease: *J.F. Perrot & Co. Ltd. v. Cohen*, [1950] 1 K.B. 705. A tenant who had lived in a house rent-free by permission of his landlord, thereby asserting that his original tenancy had ended, was not afterwards allowed to say that his original tenancy continued: *Foster v. Robinson*. In none of these cases was the defendant sued on the promise, assurance, or assertion as a cause of action in itself. He was sued for some other cause, for example, a pension or a breach of contract, or possession, and the promise, assurance, or assertion only played a supplementary role, though, no doubt, an important one. That is, I think, its true function. It may be part of a cause of action, but not a cause of action in itself. The principle, as I understand it, is that where one party has, by his words or conduct, made to the other a promise or assurance which was intended to affect the legal relations between them and to be acted on accordingly, then, once the other party has taken him at his word and acted on it, the one who gave the promise or assurance cannot afterwards be allowed to revert to the previous legal relations as if no such promise or assurance had been made by him, but he must accept their legal relations subject to the qualification which he himself has so introduced, even though it is not supported in point of law by any consideration, but only by his word.

[4] Seeing that the principle never stands alone as giving a cause of action in itself, it can never do away with the necessity of consideration when that is an essential part of the cause of action. The doctrine of consideration is too firmly fixed to be overthrown by a side-wind. Its ill effects have been largely mitigated of late, but it still remains a cardinal necessity of the formation of a contract, although not of its modification or discharge. I fear that it was my failure to make this clear in [*High Trees*] Ltd., which misled [the trial judge] in the present case. He held that the wife could sue on the husband's promise as a separate and independent cause of action by itself, although, as he held, there was no consideration for it. That is not correct. The wife can only enforce the promise if there was consideration for it. That is, therefore, the real question in the case: Was there sufficient consideration to support the promise?

[5] If it were suggested that, in return for the husband's promise, the wife expressly or impliedly promised to forbear from applying to the court for maintenance — that is, a promise in return for a promise — there would clearly be no consideration because the wife's promise would not be binding on her and, therefore, would be worth nothing. Notwithstanding her promise, she could always ap-

ply to the divorce court for maintenance — perhaps, only with leave — but nevertheless she could apply. No agreement by her could take away that right . . . There was, however, clearly no promise by the wife, express or implied, to forbear from applying to the court. All that happened was that she did, in fact, forbear — that is, she did an act, in return for a promise. Is that sufficient consideration? Unilateral promises of this kind have long been enforced so long as the act or forbearance is done on the faith of the promise and at the request of the promisor, express or implied. The act done is then in itself sufficient consideration for the promise, even though it arises ex post facto . . . If the findings of [the trial judge] are accepted, they are sufficient to bring this principle into play. His finding that the husband's promise was intended to be binding, intended to be acted on, and was, in fact, acted on — although expressed to be a finding on the principle of the *High Trees House* case — is equivalent to a finding that there was consideration within this long-settled rule, because it comes to the same thing expressed in different words . . . My difficulty, however, is to accept the findings of [the trial judge] that the promise was "intended to be acted on." I cannot find any evidence of any intention by the husband that the wife should forbear from applying to the court for maintenance, or, in other words, any request by the husband, express or implied, that the wife should so forbear. He left her to apply, if she wished to do so. She did not do so, and I am not surprised, because it is very unlikely that the divorce court would have made any order in her favour, since she had a bigger income than her husband. Her forbearance was not intended by him, nor was it done at his request. It was, therefore, no consideration.

[6]   It may be that the wife has suffered some detriment because, after forbearing to apply to the court for seven years, she might not now get leave to apply . . . The court, however, is, nowadays much more ready to give leave than it used to be . . . and I should have thought that, if the wife fell on hard times, she would still get leave. Assuming, however, that she has suffered some detriment by her forbearance, nevertheless, as the forbearance was not at the husband's request, it is no consideration.

[7]   The doctrine of consideration is sometimes said to work injustice, but I see none in this case . . . I do not think it would be right for this wife, who is better off than her husband, to take no action for six or seven years and then demand from him the whole £600. The truth is that in these maintenance cases the real remedy of the wife is not by action in the King's Bench Division, but by application in the Divorce Court. I have always understood that no agreement for maintenance, which is made in the course of divorce proceedings prior to decree absolute, is valid unless it is sanctioned by the court . . . The reason why such agreements are invalid, unless approved, is because they are so apt to be collusive. Some wives are tempted to stipulate for extortionate maintenance as the price of giving their husbands their freedom. It is to remove this temptation that the sanction of the court is required. It would be a great pity if this salutary requirement could be evaded by taking action in the King's Bench Division. The Divorce Court can order the husband to pay whatever maintenance is just. Moreover, if justice so requires, it can make the order retrospective to decree absolute. That is the proper remedy of the wife here, and I do not think she has a right to any other. For these reasons I think the appeal should be allowed.

[ASQUITH and BIRKETT L.JJ. agreed in allowing the appeal. BIRKETT L.J. in his judgment said (p. 224, K.B.), acknowledging that the description came from coun-

shield ≠ sword

sel, that the doctrine of promissory estoppel was "to be used as a shield and not as a sword". Accordingly he too dismissed the wife's cause of action.]

NOTES AND QUESTIONS

1.   *High Trees* and *Combe v. Combe* are regarded as leading decisions on the doctrine of promissory or equitable estoppel, and are said to establish the proposition, quoted by the Ontario Court of Appeal in *Gilbert Steel*, that "estoppel is a shield and not a sword." Together these two English decisions have created a considerable amount of confusion.

2.   Leaving aside the significance of *Combe* in further refining the doctrine of estoppel, the actual outcome is quite understandable if one appreciates the factual context. At that time in England, it was only possible for a person to obtain a divorce if he or she could prove that his or her spouse was "guilty" of a matrimonial offence, *e.g.*, adultery. It is likely that Mr. Combe wanted a divorce, but he could not obtain one based on his own adultery. He and his wife probably entered an agreement in which he promised to pay her £100 a year, provided that she obtained the divorce, based on his adultery. If such an agreement was not a *bona fide* settlement of a spousal support claim, but rather in effect an attempt to bribe Mrs. Combe into "giving" Mr. Combe a divorce, it would be regarded by the courts as "collusive" and unenforceable. Since her income was higher than his, it seems unlikely that it was a genuine settlement of a claim for support since she would not have been awarded support by the Divorce Court in the absence of need. In that situation, the agreement might well have been characterized as "collusive".

     Mr. Combe, however, was understandably reluctant to argue in court that he and his wife had colluded to get the divorce since it might lead to the questioning of the validity of his divorce — at the date of the case there was an official, the King's Proctor, who had standing not only to oppose divorce petitions but to investigate collusive divorces and even to get them set aside — and the issue of collusion was not placed before the court by the parties. The decision of Lord Denning alludes to the issue of collusion; while he does not directly decide whether there was collusion in this case, these concerns may explain the judicial hostility to the enforcement of Mr. Combe's promise.

3.   It should be appreciated that in the context of English matrimonial law at that time, a settlement of a spousal support claim was not binding and did not preclude later judicial review. Outside the special circumstances of a possibly collusive matrimonial settlement, the promise to forego a court action — a compromise of an action — is clearly good consideration. This issue was explored in *Stott v. Merit Investment Corp.* (above).

     In Canada today, divorce law has evolved substantially and settlements of matrimonial support, property and child-related claims are very common and result in written "separation agreements". These agreements are generally negotiated with the assistance of lawyers and can usually be enforced as contracts. Divorce courts continue to exercise a supervisory jurisdiction, and may override agreements perceived to be unfair, though their jurisdiction to do so is limited, and courts appreciate that those who have made these agreements are likely to have relied upon them to plan their affairs. See *Miglin v. Miglin*, [2003] S.C.J. No. 21, [2003] 1 S.C.R. 303, 224 D.L.R. (4th) 193.

4.   The doctrine of estoppel is intended to protect the reliance of one person on the promise made by another. If that promise is part of an exchange, then it is enforceable as an ordinary contract, what we might call for want of a better term, a "Grade 'A' Contract". If it is not part of an exchange, the promisee can always try promissory estoppel and might succeed. Enforcing promises in either of these situations should not catch the promisor by surprise, for both the doctrine of consideration and promissory estoppel are concerned that the promise be made in circumstances where reliance on it would be reasonable and expected.

Surprise will occur when a promise that is relied on is *not* enforced, even though enforcement would not catch the promisor by surprise. Gilbert Steel was surprised; University Construction should not have been surprised if the promise to pay the higher price had been enforced.

cannot increase enforceability

The doctrine of promissory estoppel only limits the capacity of the doctrine of consideration to make unenforceable those promises that should be enforced, *i.e.,* it can be used to enforce promises where there is no valid reason to justify a refusal to enforce. The doctrine of promissory estoppel will not, any more than would the doctrine of consideration, make enforceable promises that are in some way objectionable, for example, because of duress. The confusion created by the doctrine of promissory estoppel relates to the scope of its capacity to increase enforceability. Estoppel will never make more promises *unenforceable*.

5. As the judgment of Denning J. in *High Trees* makes clear, what triggers the estoppel is the reliance of one person on what the other said that he or she would do. Denning J. said:

> I prefer to apply the principle that a promise intended to be binding, intended to be acted on and in fact acted on, is binding so far as its terms properly apply.

This language of *High Trees* led the trial judge in *Combe* to believe that it was enough to cover the facts in *Combe v. Combe*. Indeed, this language might be wide enough to offer an almost complete substitute for the doctrine of consideration. In *Combe v. Combe* Denning (now L.J. by then sitting in the English Court of Appeal) senses this consequence and backs off from such a conclusion. In doing so, he does two things in *Combe* that cause problems:

(1) he adopts an approach that is difficult to apply in other contexts; and

(2) he qualifies his original language in one of those rare cases where there are good reasons *not to enforce* the promise sued on, *i.e.,* where it would not have been necessary to have relied on what he said in *High Trees*.

6. As we examine the remaining cases in this section, *Combe v. Combe* raises some important questions:

(a) Is the famous "sword/shield" metaphor appropriate to distinguish the cases? In practical or economic terms, is the distinction between agreeing to take less and promising to pay more maintainable?

(b) What concept of contract law in an exchange economy must one have to be able to see a distinction between the two kinds of cases?

(c) What kind of evidence would you need to be convinced that the distinction reflects the way people, particularly merchants, think about contracts or promises? Does it reflect different forms that reliance might take?

The last point is especially important. *Combe* is regarded as an authority in commercial cases such as *Gilbert Steel*. It is *Combe v. Combe* that Wilson J.A. relies on in *Gilbert Steel* to justify her refusal to invoke estoppel to enforce the promise to pay more (¶ 13). This use of a case like *Combe v. Combe* is a good example of the traditional view that all contracts can be analyzed in the same way: they all present the same issues and require the same response from the courts; there is a unitary concept of contract liability, and in particular, a unitary concept of consideration. Consideration is seen an all-purpose tool.

There is, however, something odd about a rule that regards a dispute between a man and a woman who were once married to each other as having any relevance, let alone decisive authority, in a case between a steel supplier and a builder.

In spite of this fact, the law laid down in *Combe v. Combe* was approved by the House of Lords. As stated by the Privy Council in *Ajayi v. R.T. Briscoe (Nigeria) Ltd.,* [1964] 1 W.L.R. 1325, [1964] 3 All E.R. 556 (p. 559):

... when one party to a contract in the absence of fresh consideration agrees not to enforce his rights an equity will be raised in favour of the other party. This equity is, however, subject to the qualifications (1) that the other party has altered his position, (2) that the promisor can resile from his promise on giving reasonable notice . . . giving the promisee a reasonable opportunity of resuming his position, (3) the promise only becomes final and irrevocable if the promisee cannot resume his position.

In *Woodhouse A.C. Israel Cocoa Ltd. S.A. v. Nigerian Produce Marketing Co. Ltd.*, [1972] A.C. 741, [1972] 2 All E.R. 271 (H.L.), Lord Hailsham said (p. 758 A.C., p. 282 All E.R.):

I desire to add that the time may soon come when the whole sequence of cases based on promissory estoppel since the war, beginning with [*High Trees*] may need to be reviewed and reduced to a coherent body of doctrine by the courts. I do not mean to say that they are to be regarded with suspicion. But as is common with an expanding doctrine they do raise problems at coherent exposition which have never been systematically explored. However this may be, we are not in a position to carry out this exploration here and in the present proceedings.

7. To understand the problems caused by the treatment of a case about an agreement between people who were once married as one indistinguishable from a commercial case, you should note the general rules discussed earlier regarding spousal support and family arrangements.

At least in part, Lord Denning justified his decision in *Combe v. Combe* not to enforce the contract because of its setting in the English family law. It is too late now to argue that *Combe v. Combe* should be ignored in commercial cases, but it may be worthwhile to point out to a court that its applicability in such a setting is not inevitable. What is important to notice is that in *Combe* Denning L.J. realizes, almost with horror, the significance of what he had said in *High Trees* and attempts to limit that decision without throwing out his baby with the bath-water. (Do you see now the extent of the risk to the doctrine of consideration created by the decision in *Williams v. Roffey*?) The next two cases illustrate how well he succeeded in his efforts.

D. & C. BUILDERS LTD. v. REES

[1966] 2 Q.B. 617, [1965] 3 All E.R. 837
(C.A., Lord Denning M.R., Danckwerts and Winn L.JJ.)

LORD DENNING M.R.: — **[1]** D. & C. Builders Ltd. ("the plaintiffs") are a little company. "D" stands for Mr. Donaldson, a decorator, "C" for Mr. Casey, a plumber. They are jobbing builders. The defendant, Mr. Rees, has a shop where he sells builders' materials.

[2] In the spring of 1964 the defendant employed the plaintiffs to do work at his premises, 218, Brick Lane. The plaintiffs did the work and rendered accounts in May and June, which came to £746 13s. 1d. altogether. The defendant paid £250 on account. In addition the plaintiffs made an allowance of £14 off the bill. So in July 1964 there was owing to the plaintiffs the sum of £482 13s 1d. At this stage there was no dispute as to the work done. But the defendant did not pay.

[3] On Aug. 31, 1964, the plaintiffs wrote asking the defendant to pay the remainder of the bill. He did not reply. On Oct. 19, 1964, they wrote again, pointing out that the "outstanding account of £480 is well overdue". Still the defendant did not reply. He did not write or telephone for more than three weeks. Then on Friday, Nov. 13, 1964, the defendant was ill with influenza. His wife telephoned the plaintiffs. She spoke to Mr. Casey. She began to make complaints about the work: and then said: "My husband will offer you £300 in settlement. That is all you'll get. It is to be in satisfaction." Mr. Casey said he would have to discuss it with Mr. Donaldson. The two of them talked it over. Their company was in desperate financial straits. If they did not have the £300, they would be in a state of bankruptcy. So they decided to accept the £300 and see what they could do about the rest afterwards. Thereupon Mr. Donaldson telephoned to the defendant's wife. He said to her: "£300 will not even clear our commitments on the job. We will accept £300 and give you a year to find the balance." She said: "No, we will never have enough money to pay the balance. £300 is better than nothing." He said: "We have no choice but to accept." She said: "Would you like the money by cash or by cheque. If it is cash, you can have it on Monday. If by cheque, you can have it tomorrow (Saturday)." On Saturday, Nov. 14, 1964, Mr. Casey went to collect the money. He took with him a receipt prepared on the company's paper with the simple words: "Received the sum of £300 from Mr. Rees." She gave him a cheque for £300 and asked for a receipt. She insisted that the words "in completion of the account" be added. Mr. Casey did as she asked. He added the words to the receipt. So she had the clean receipt: "Received the sum of £300 from Mr. Rees in completion of the account. Paid, M. Casey." Mr. Casey gave in evidence his reason for giving it: "If I did not have the £300 the company would have gone bankrupt. The only reason we took it was to save the company. She knew the position we were in."

[4]   The plaintiffs were so worried about their position that they went to their solicitors. Within a few days, on Nov. 23, 1964, the solicitors wrote complaining that the defendant had "extricated a receipt of some sort or other" from them. They said that they were treating the £300 as a payment on account. On Nov. 28, 1964, the defendant replied alleging bad workmanship. He also set up the receipt which Mr. Casey gave to his wife, adding: "I assure you she had no gun on her." The plaintiffs brought this action for the balance. The defendant set up a defence of bad workmanship and also that there was a binding settlement. The question of settlement was tried as a preliminary issue. The judge made these findings:

> I concluded that by the middle of August the sum due to the plaintiffs was ascertained and not then in dispute. I also concluded that there was no consideration to support the agreement of Nov. 13 and 14. It was a case of agreeing to take a lesser sum, when a larger sum was already due to the plaintiffs. It was not a case of agreeing to take a cheque for a smaller amount instead of receiving cash for a larger amount. The payment by cheque was an incidental arrangement.

[5]   The judge decided, therefore, the preliminary issue in favour of the plaintiffs. The defendant appeals to this court. He says that there was here an accord and satisfaction — an *accord* when the plaintiffs agreed, however reluctantly, to accept £300 in settlement of the account — and *satisfaction* when they accepted the cheque for £300 and it was duly honoured. . . .

[6]   This case is of some consequence: for it is a daily occurrence that a merchant or tradesman, who is owed a sum of money, is asked to take less. The debtor says he is in difficulties. He offers a lesser sum in settlement, cash down. He says he cannot pay more. The creditor is considerate. He accepts the proffered sum and forgives him the rest of the debt. The question arises: is the settlement binding on the creditor? The answer is that, in point of law, the creditor is not bound by the settlement. He can the next day sue the debtor for the balance, and get judgment.

The law as so stated in 1602 by Lord Coke in *Pinnel's Case* [5 Co. Rep. 177a, 77 E.R. 237] — and accepted in 1884 by the House of Lords in *Foakes v. Beer* [above].

conditional vs. actual payment

[7] Now, suppose that the debtor, instead of paying the lesser sum in cash, pays it by cheque. He makes out a cheque for the amount. The creditor accepts the cheque and cashes it. Is the position any different? I think not. No sensible distinction can be taken between payment of a lesser sum by cash and payment of it by cheque. The cheque, when given, is conditional payment. When honoured, it is actual payment. It is then just the same as cash. If a creditor is not bound when he receives payment by cash, he should not be bound when he receives payment by cheque. This view is supported by the leading case of *Cumber v. Wane* (1721), 1 Stra. 426 [93 E.R. 613], which has suffered many vicissitudes but was, I think, rightly decided in point of law . . .

[8] In point of law payment of a lesser sum, whether by cash or by cheque, is no discharge of a greater sum.

[9] This doctrine of the common law has come under heavy fire. It was ridiculed by Sir George Jessel M.R. in *Couldery v. Bartrum* (1881), 19 Ch.D. 394, 399. . . . It was condemned by the Law Revision Committee in their Sixth Interim Report (Cmnd 5449), para. 20 and para. 22. But a remedy has been found. The harshness of the common law has been relieved. Equity has stretched out a merciful hand to help the debtor . . .

[10] In applying this principle, however, we must note the qualification. The creditor is barred from his legal rights only when it would be inequitable for him to insist on them. Where there has been a true accord, under which the creditor voluntarily agrees to accept a lesser sum in satisfaction, and the debtor acts on that accord by paying the lesser sum and the creditor accepts it, then it is *inequitable* for the creditor afterwards to insist on the balance. But he is not bound unless there has been truly an accord between them. In the present case, on the facts as found by the judge, it seems to me that there was no *true accord*. The debtor's wife held the creditor to ransom. The creditor was in need of money to meet his own commitments, and she knew it. When the creditor asked for payment of the £480 due to him, she said to him, in effect: "We cannot pay you the £480. But we will pay you £300 if you will accept it in settlement. If you do not accept it on those terms, you will get nothing. £300 is better than nothing." She had no right to say any such thing. She could properly have said: "We cannot pay you more than £300. Please accept it on account." But she had no right to insist on his taking it in settlement. When she said: "We will pay you nothing unless you accept £300 in settlement," she was putting undue pressure on the creditor. She was making a threat to break the contract (by paying nothing) and she was doing it so as to compel the creditor to do what he was unwilling to do (to accept £300 in settlement): and she succeeded. He complied with her demand . . . In these circumstances there was no true accord so as to found a defence of accord and satisfaction. There is also no equity in the defendant to warrant any departure from the due course of law. No person can insist on a settlement procured by intimidation.

intimid-ation

[11] In my opinion there is no reason in law or equity why the creditor should not enforce the full amount of the debt due to him. I would, therefore, dismiss this appeal.

DANCKWERTS L.J.: — **[12]** I agree with the judgment of Lord Denning M.R. *Foakes v. Beer*, applying the decision in *Pinnel's Case*, settled definitely the rule of law that payment of a lesser sum than the amount of a debt due cannot be a satisfaction of the debt, unless there is some benefit to the creditor added so that there is an accord and satisfaction . . .

[13] In my view the county judge was right in applying the rule in *Foakes v. Beer*, and I would dismiss the appeal.

WINN L.J.: — **[14]** . . . The question to be decided may be stated thus. Did the defendant's agreement to give his own cheque for £300 in full settlement of his existing debt to the plaintiffs of £482 13s. 1d. and the plaintiffs' agreement to accept it in full payment of that debt, followed by delivery and due payment of such a cheque, constitute a valid accord and satisfaction discharging the debt in law? . . .

[15] Apart altogether from any decided cases bearing on the matter, there might be a good deal to be said, as a matter of policy, in favour of holding any creditor bound by his promise to discharge a debtor of his paying some amount less than the debt due: some judges no doubt so thought when they held readily that acceptance by the creditor of something of a different nature from that to which he was entitled was a satisfaction of the liability . . . A like approach might at some time in the past have been adopted by the courts to all serious assurances of agreement, but as English law developed, it does not now permit in general of such treatment of mere promises. In the more specific field of discharge of monetary debt there has been some conflict of judicial opinion. . . .

[16] In my judgment it is an essential element of a valid accord and satisfaction that the agreement which constitutes the accord should itself be binding in law, and I do not think that any such agreement can be so binding unless it is either made under seal or supported by consideration. Satisfaction, viz., performance, of an agreement of accord does not provide retroactive validity to the accord, but depends for its effect on the legal validity of the accord as a binding contract at the time when it is made: this I think is apparent when it is remembered that, albeit rarely, existing obligations of debt may be replaced effectively by a contractually binding substitution of a new obligation . . .

[17] I would dismiss this appeal.

NOTES AND QUESTIONS

1. *D. & C. Builders* raises the question of what is "normal commercial pressure", and what constitutes "economic duress" or "undue pressure". In *Pau On v. Lau Yiu Long*, [1980] A.C. 614, [1979] 3 All E.R. 65 (P.C.), the Privy Council considered the question of what amount of pressure would be too much. The dispute in that case centred on the fact that the plaintiff, on discovering that he had, by mistake, signed an agreement which contained a clause that he objected to, refused to perform the original agreement until the clause was removed. The defendant, who was just in the process of taking a corporation public and could not risk litigation without jeopardizing the chances of a successful public offering, agreed to change the contract by deleting the clause. When the plaintiff sued to enforce the modified contract, the defendant raised the defence that the modification of the contract was executed under duress. This defence was disposed of by a finding by the judges in the lower courts that the defendant's acceptance of the modification was a calculated risk on his part that the particular clause would not cost him any money, and that in the circumstances it was better to agree than to risk the consequences of disagreement. (The court also held that

there was consideration for the amending promise, so that the result was that the amended agreement was enforceable.)

In *Pao On*, Lord Scarman said (pp. 78-79 All E.R.):   *Duress*

> Duress, whatever form it takes, is a coercion of the will so as to vitiate consent . . . In a contractual situation commercial pressure is not enough. There must be present some factor which could in law be regarded as a coercion of his will so as to vitiate his consent . . . In determining whether there was a coercion of will such that there was no true consent, it is material to enquire whether the person alleged to have been coerced did or did not protest; whether, at the time he was allegedly coerced into making the contract, he did or did not have an alternative course open to him such as an adequate legal remedy; whether he was independently advised; and whether after entering the contract he took steps to avoid it . . . there is nothing contrary to principle in recognizing economic duress as a factor which may render a contract voidable, provided always that the basis of such recognition is that it must amount to a coercion of will, which vitiates consent. It must be shown that the payment made or the contract entered into was not a voluntary act.

Could you argue that there was nothing more than "normal commercial pressure" present in *D. & C. Builders*?

2. What does Denning L.J. mean when he said that Mrs. Rees "had no right" to demand that Mr. Casey accept her payment as a settlement?

3. M.H. Ogilvie, in "Economic Duress in Contract: Departure, Detour or Dead-End?" (2000), 34 *Can. Bus. L.J.* 194, argues that cases like *Pao On* and *Stott v. Merit Investments*, *supra*, illustrate that "parties who voluntarily negotiate agreements that they believe to be economically advantageous cannot subsequently rely on economic duress to avoid these agreements". She points out that inequality of bargaining power is a common feature of many contractual relations: "Superior bargaining power is as prevalent as death and taxes." Accordingly she argues that a key element in a finding of economic duress is that "the conduct was analogous to extortion or blackmail: the victim had no choice but to submit . . . The victim had no other option. Where economic duress was not found, a choice of alternatives was available and a commercial decision was made; the presumption is that economic duress will rarely occur in commercial dealings."

    An example of physical duress leading to the setting aside of a contract is provided by the case of *Barton v. Armstrong*, [1976] A.C. 104, [1975] 2 All E.R. 465 (P.C.). In that case the Privy Council held that, it having been proved that the defendant had made credible threats against the plaintiff's life in order to force him to make an agreement advantageous to the defendant, the agreement was to be set aside.

4. Suppose that the defendant's wife in *D. & C. Builders*, in addition to her qualities as a hard bargainer, had had the forethought to give a peppercorn to Mr. Casey when he gave her the receipt; what would have happened then? Would Lord Denning have been able to carry the other members of the bench with him? Could he have given any relief in the terms of his own judgment? Does Lord Denning give any clear guidance on when he will relieve the debtor and when he will not?

5. Since *Foakes v. Beer* has been legislatively overruled in many provinces of Canada (see, for example in Ontario, the *Mercantile Law Amendment Act*, above), what would have happened had *D. & C. Builders* come up in Ontario?

    Assume that you are a County Court judge in England, which has not enacted an equivalent to Ontario's *Mercantile Law Amendment Act*, s. 16. A case exactly the same as *Foakes v. Beer* has just been argued before you. Would you regard yourself as bound by that 1885 House of Lords decision after *D. & C. Builders*? Would the decision of the English Court of Appeal in *Williams v. Roffey* lead you to question the continued applicability of *Foakes v. Beer*?

TUDALE EXPLORATIONS LTD. v. BRUCE

(1979), 20 O.R. (2d) 593, 88 D.L.R. (3d) 584
(Divisional Court, Grange, Southey, Griffiths JJ.)

GRANGE J.: — [1] This is an appeal from the order of the Mining and Lands Commissioner made on March 5, 1976, whereby he ordered that certain mining claims in Northwestern Ontario were vested in the respondent on this appeal or in its representatives. In so doing he denied to the appellant on this appeal rights which it claimed under an option agreement upon the grounds that the option had expired. The issue is whether the option had indeed expired or had been extended by the conduct of the parties and the operation of law.

[2]   The respondent in this appeal, Tudale Explorations Limited (Tudale), was the owner of the claims in question and by agreement dated May 28, 1969, granted to the appellant, then called Keevil Mining Group Limited, and now called Teck Mining Group Limited (Teck), the right and option to explore and develop the claims for a period of three years. Under the agreement the shares were held by an escrow agent and Teck could, at its option, require the claims to be transferred into the name of a company to be incorporated in a certain manner, the shares of which would be issued in certain proportions to the parties. The option was required to be exercised within three years and upon the failure of Teck to exercise it the shares would revert to Tudale. Under s. 11 of the agreement, it could be modified only by instrument in writing signed by the parties. The time for exercise of the option was by further written agreements extended to May 28, 1975, and then to June 30, 1975. Certain dealings took place in late June and early July between John Leslie May, land officer of Teck, and Stephen J. Lesavage, president of Tudale, aimed, at least so far as Teck was concerned, at a further extension. It is the nature of and the legal result of those dealings which give rise to the proceedings in appeal.

[3]   On June 25th, May and Lesavage had a telephone conversation concerning the agreement and there is a conflict between them with regard to it. According to May, the call was placed because he sought a further extension. He informed Lesavage that Teck wanted to proceed by a joint venture rather than a corporate approach, and would be submitting a proposal to that end; in the meantime he requested a 60-day extension. Lesavage declined that request but agreed to a 30-day extension.

[4]   Lesavage, on the other hand, testified to a rambling conversation in which both a 30- and a 60-day extension were mentioned but stated that neither extension was granted. In his reasons, the Commissioner stated: "I find as a fact that Lesavage, the president of Tudale, gave May his personal assurances that an extension of at least thirty days would be forthcoming and I accept May's version of the telephone conversation." On June 25, 1975, May wrote to Lesavage enclosing copies of an amendment extending the time. The amendment actually was for 60 days and May concluded his letter as follows: "I still feel we will need 60 days to properly finalize any new arrangement we might agree upon and would encourage you to approve of the extension on that basis." In his evidence which appears to have been accepted, May, in the words of the Commissioner, "explained the last paragraph as a request for a full sixty days rather than the thirty days agreed upon in the conversation."

[5]   A meeting of the directors of Tudale was held on June 27th, and thereafter Lesavage wrote to May and the full text follows:

> This will acknowledge receipt of your letter dated June 25, 1975. It is the opinion of the Directors of Tudale that, inasmuch as our original agreement is to be restructured, nothing can be served by extending it a further two months. However, as I have indicated to you in our telephone conversation, we will allow you sufficient time to submit your proposal for a joint venture.

[6]   May did not receive the letter until July 2nd. He immediately telephoned Lesavage complaining of the failure to confirm the extension. Lesavage said he would again seek the direction of his board but in the next day or two telephoned to say the directors had decided not to extend and the agreement was terminated.

[7]   On July 8, 1975, Teck purported to exercise the option by forwarding to the escrow agent a notice thereof together with a notarial copy of the letters patent of a company known as 305318 Ontario Limited (which had been incorporated as of June 30, 1975) and instructing him to transfer the claim to it. The escrow agent received contrary instructions from Tudale on July 11, 1975, and the claims remain with the agent, who has taken no part in these proceedings and has undertaken to be bound by the determination of the matter by the Court.

[8]   The proceeding itself was instituted by Tudale applying to the Commissioner's office for a vesting order. An appointment was issued for a hearing and the hearing took place in Thunder Bay on December 3, 1975. The Commissioner, after setting forth the facts in detail, considered the legal position of the parties. He discussed at length the doctrines of waiver and promissory estoppel but reached the conclusion that the conversation between May and Lesavage on June 25th was "an agreement extending the date of exercising the option a further thirty days" and was void under either para. 11 of the agreement or under s. 78(2) of the *Mining Act* R.S.O. 1970, c. 274, which requires contracts with respect to mining claims to be in writing signed by the person to be charged.

[9]   The Commissioner rejected waiver firstly because he found the conversation of June 25th to amount to a variation in the contract and not just a forbearance of the strict terms of the agreement. He also suggested it might fail for lack of consideration . . .

[10]   It is my view that the doctrine to be applied, whether it be called waiver or promissory estoppel or variation of the contract or simply binding promises, stems from the words of Lord Cairns in *Hughes v. Metropolitan R. Co.* (1877), 2 App. Cas. 439 (H.L.). [**GRANGE J.** here set out the passage from that case, above, and continued:] That principle was accepted by the Supreme Court of Canada in *Conwest Exploration Co. Ltd. v. Letain*, [1964] S.C.R. 20 at p. 28, 41 D.L.R. (2d) 198 at p. 206, and in numerous other Canadian cases. In [*High Trees*, above] Denning J. traced the principle first to justify an oral variation of a written contract, including one required to be in writing, to a representation without consideration and to a representation not just of an existing fact but to one as to the future. The essential features are an unambiguous representation which was intended to be acted upon and indeed was acted upon. The present rule is now expressed by Snell in his work *Snell's Principles of Equity*, 27th ed. (1973), p. 563, as follows:

> Where by his words or conduct one party to a transaction makes to the other an unambiguous promise or assurance which is intended to affect the legal relations between them (whether contractual or otherwise), and the other party acts upon it,

altering his position to his detriment, the party making the promise or assurance will
not be permitted to act inconsistently with it.

[11] It will be seen that the rule as so stated depends in no way upon consideration or formality and it matters not at all whether the effect of the promise is to
create a variation of contract nor whether the original contract was within or without the *Statute of Frauds*. . . .

[12] The rule as stated makes no mention of the shield/sword distinction, but
there have been cases, notably *Gilbert Steel Ltd. v. University Construction Ltd.*
[above] where the distinction appears to be preserved although on the facts no
reliance to his detriment was shown so the doctrine would not have applied in any
event.

[13] The sword/shield maxim has been heavily criticized: see "Courts, Consideration and Common Sense," by Professor B.J. Reiter, 27 *U. of Tor. L.J.* 439 (1977),
at p. 480 *et seq.*, and Waddams, *The Law of Contracts* (1977), pp. 130-1, and I
must confess to difficulty in seeing the logic of the distinction and it does not appear to be universally applied, but in this case, in my opinion it cannot matter because the promise is indeed set up as a shield and not as a sword. Not only is Teck
the respondent in the proceedings, but its claim to the property is based upon the
contract. The promise of extension is set up only as a defence to Tudale's assertion
that the rights under that contract had expired.

[14] The *Conwest* case, *supra*, is interesting, not only because the facts are
analogous, but also because the resolution there of the sword/shield problem is
helpful. In that case Letain optioned to Conwest certain mining claims, but it was a
condition precedent to the exercise of the option that a company be incorporated
by a certain date to receive the optioned shares. Letain first agreed to have his
name in the new company and later withdrew his consent. For that reason and others, the letters patent while bearing a date prior to the due date were actually issued later. Letain maintained that Conwest had lost all its rights. Conwest sued on
the option and was successful; Letain sued for the return of the claims and failed.
Judson J. for himself and Taschereau C.J.C. held that the condition of incorporation had been satisfied and also that Letain having treated the contracts as subsisting after the expiry of the time was not estopped. Martland and Ritchie JJ.
dissented upon the ground that the contract had not been performed. Martland J.
specifically rejected the application of equitable estoppel. As he put it (at p. 31
S.C.R., p. 202 D.L.R.):

> The basic question is as to whether, in the circumstances of the particular case, it is
> being used as a defence to the strict enforcement of contractual rights, or as a means
> of proving the existence of a contract made without consideration.

[15] Judson J. did not concern himself with the problem — perhaps he did not
consider it was a problem — and Cartwright J., while agreeing with Martland J.
that Conwest might not be able to enforce an agreement without consideration,
went on to say, at pp. 29-30, S.C.R., pp. 200-1 D.L.R.:

> In my view, however, Letain is the plaintiff in substance as well as in form. He is not
> simply resisting an attempt to enforce the option; he is seeking to compel the con-
> veyance to himself not only of the eight claims which he caused to be transferred to
> Conwest but also of a number of other claims which were never his. The foundation
> of his asserted right to a conveyance of these claims is the failure by Conwest to per-
> form strictly the term in the agreement of July 26, 1955, as to causing a company to

be incorporated on or before October 1, 1958. Assuming that this condition had not been varied by the acts of the parties and that it was not complied with until October 20, 1958, it is my opinion that by the dealings between the parties recited in the reasons of my brother Judson, Letain led Conwest to suppose that he would not exercise his right to insist on performance of the condition by the date mentioned; in my view it would be inequitable having regard to those dealings to allow Letain to take advantage of the delay which occurred. While, in my opinion, the other grounds upon which the judgment of my brother Judson is based are sufficient to entitle the appellant to succeed without the necessity of relying on the defence of equitable estoppel, that defence appears to me to be available in the circumstances of this case.

Accordingly, he upheld Conwest's position and rejected that of Letain.

[16] The parallel between the position of Conwest and of Teck in the case at bar is striking and on the authority of the Conwest case it would be difficult to strike down Teck's claim certainly on the ground that the promissory estoppel was being advanced as a sword. . . . *used as sword not shield*

[17] Here upon the finding of the Commissioner, Tudale by its president (whose authority was not seriously questioned) agreed to extend the time for exercising the option and then repudiated the agreement upon the ground the time had expired. Teck clearly acted upon that representation to its detriment. Upon the authorities I have cited, it makes no difference how the matter is viewed; Tudale cannot deny the extension or at the very least must give Teck a reasonable time to regain its position. It does not matter that the promise was oral, that it lacked consideration or that it related to a future event. All that matters was that it was intended to be and was acted upon to the other party's detriment. Nor can it, at least in the circumstances of this case, be said to be unavailable to Teck because of its being used as a sword and not a shield . . .

[18] For all these reasons, I would allow the appeal, dismiss Tudale's application and make an order vesting the claims in 305318 Ontario Limited. Teck is entitled to its costs, both in this Court and before the Commissioner.

NOTES

1. *Tudale Explorations* deals with an important type of contract in the Canadian mining industry, the contract between the junior exploration company, which owns the claim, and the senior mining company, which has the resources to explore and develop the claim. If, after exploration by the senior company, the claim seems worth developing fully, the two companies will jointly undertake to build a mine, usually on the basis of terms set out in the original agreement. The senior mining company is likely to rely on the initial option agreement to make significant expenditures in exploring the property, and will gain significant information about the likely viability of a mining project, information that will be shared with the junior company.

    In this case, it was clear that Teck wanted to proceed to develop a mine. It only wanted to change the legal form of the entity that would operate the mine, from a new company that each of the partners would have shares in to a joint venture. This change — from a jointly owned corporation and to a joint venture — would have had some practical implications, for example, in terms of the tax treatment of any profits in the hands of the partners, but would not have changed the general structure of the parties' relation because, from a functional perspective, the two entities are very similar, and Teck was clearly prepared to go ahead with a corporate structure, as revealed by its purported exercise of the option on July 8.

    In *Tudale*, if the court had not enforced the option agreement, the junior company could have sought out another partner and, using the information discovered by Teck, probably could have got a better deal with a new partner, since by that point more was known about the viability of the project. Does this help to explain the outcome?

2. Notice the remedy that the Divisional Court gives. It does not have to make a damage award; it has merely to hold that the time for exercising the option to buy had not expired when Teck purported to exercise it. When that step is taken, the original contract becomes enforceable. The resulting contract is one for which there is ample consideration. Does this help a court to avoid the problems of the sword/shield distinction?

3. The Ontario Court of Appeal in *Owen Sound Public Library Board v. Mial Developments Ltd.* (1979), 26 O.R. (2d) 459, 102 D.L.R. (3d) 658 (C.A.) was sufficiently concerned about the protection of reliance that it invoked estoppel to enforce a promise made "without consideration" to extend the time for payment. Why was the reliance of *Gilbert Steel* not protected by the same court? The latter case was not even mentioned in *Owen Sound*, even though Wilson J.A. sat on both appeals.

4. As noted by the court in *Tudale*, some commentators have argued that *Gilbert Steel* was incorrectly decided. It may also be argued that *Tudale* is inconsistent with *Gilbert Steel*, though in terms of *stare decisis*, the Divisional Court, which decided *Tudale*, is "lower" than the Ontario Court of Appeal, which decided *Gilbert Steel*.

    It is also possible to distinguish *Gilbert Steel* from other cases where estoppel was invoked. According to this view, a judge will consider both the protection of reliance, and what role the court should play in the active protection of reliance. *Gilbert Steel* was a case where the court was being asked to enforce a promise to pay more money for something that was already the subject of a contract. To enforce the promise, the court believed that it would have had to overrule almost 200 years of precedents on consideration. The traditional presentation of these cases obscures the fact that the important practical question is whether the court *wants* to find what it needs to justify enforcement.

    Gilbert Steel can be criticized on the ground that the Court of Appeal was unmoved in the face of the plaintiff's reliance, though the Court of Appeal considered that there had been no reliance. Arguably there was at least as much reliance as in *High Trees*. In *High Trees*, the promisee actually paid less, after being told by the promisor that it would accept this. In *High Trees* the court would not become actively involved to reverse the effect of the modified promise, and let the loss lie where it fell. Cases like *Tudale* are ones in which the promisee was clearly prepared to perform as originally contracted, but the promisor was prepared to allow a modification in the *manner* or *time* of performance. In *Tudale* the court was prepared actively to protect reliance.

    Does *Williams v. Roffey* make it easier to deal with these problems?

WALTONS STORES (INTERSTATE) LTD. v. MAHER

(1988), 164 C.L.R. 387, 88 A.J.L.R. 110
(H.C.A., Mason C.J. Wilson, Brennan, Deane and Gaudron JJ.)

[Waltons Stores Ltd. (the appellant-defendant) negotiated for some months with the Mahers (the respondents-plaintiffs) for a lease of land owned by the Mahers. It was envisaged that the Mahers would erect a building on the land, in accordance with specifications provided by Waltons. This would entail demolition of an existing building. On 7 November 1983, the Mahers' solicitors informed the appellant's solicitors of the need to "conclude the agreement within the next day or two" to enable completion of the building by the time of occupation envisaged by the proposed agreement. The solicitors for the parties were negotiating terms for the proposed lease. The solicitor for the Mahers sent a proposed document, and the solicitor for Waltons indicated that some amendments were wanted. The solicitor for Waltons said that he had verbal instructions on certain issues, but would need specific directions before the lease could be executed. On 7 November 1983 the solicitor for Waltons sent an amended draft lease back to the solicitor for the Mahers with a covering letter stating:

> You should note that we have not yet obtained our client's specific instructions to each amendment requested, but we believe that approval will be forthcoming. We shall let you know tomorrow if any amendments are not agreed to.

The letter also requested a schedule of finishes to be annexed to the executed documents prior to exchange. The Mahers were not notified of any objections. Four days later the documents, executed by the respondents and with a schedule of finishes annexed, were returned to the appellant's solicitors for execution and exchange. The documents were never executed by the appellant and were returned to the respondents' solicitors some months later with a letter stating the appellant's intention not to proceed. By this stage the demolition work had been finished and the new building was 40 per cent complete.

After the appellant refused to proceed with the transaction, the respondents commenced proceedings in the Supreme Court of New South Wales seeking a declaration that a binding agreement existed and specific performance of the lease, or, alternatively, damages. Kearney J. gave judgment in favour of the respondents (the Mahers — the owners) and awarded damages in lieu of specific performance, with the amount of damages referred to a master for determination. An appeal to the New South Wales Court of Appeal was dismissed. Waltons, the proposed tenant, appealed to the High Court of Australia.]

MASON C.J. and **WILSON J.**: — [1] The issue in this appeal is whether, in the light of the facts, the appellant is estopped from denying the existence of a binding contract that it would take a lease of the respondents' premises at Nowra and, if so, whether the respondents can support the order made by the primary judge (Kearney J.), affirmed by the New South Wales Court of Appeal, that the appellant pay to the respondent damages in lieu of specific performance of an agreement for a lease.

[2]   Kearney J. found that exchange was a prerequisite to the creation of a concluded contract between the parties. The respondents did not appeal against this finding so that its correctness is not an issue in this court. . . . The primary judge found that the appellant was estopped from denying that a concluded contract by way of exchange did exist between the parties. . . .

. . .

[14] . . . The facts justify the weaker inference drawn by the primary judge that the respondents assumed that the amendments were acceptable to the appellant so that the exchange of contracts was only a matter of formality. This assumption was a reasonable assumption because the terms of Dawson Waldron's letter of 7 November coupled with the failure to communicate any refusal by the appellant to agree to the amendments justified the inference that the appellant agreed to the amendments with the result that exchange would follow as a matter of course.

[15]   Kearney J. and the Court of Appeal considered that the appellant was under a duty to inform the respondents that their assumption that contracts had been exchanged or that there was a binding contract was incorrect. Kearney J. thought that the appellant, acting as a reasonable person would honestly and responsibly have done in the circumstances, should have told the respondents that it did not intend to exchange at all or until it made a final decision on its retailing strategy, when it

discovered on 10 December that the demolition was proceeding further. The Court of Appeal was of the same opinion.

[16] The estoppel set up by the respondents and found by the primary judge was a common law estoppel in the form of a representation by the appellant constituted by its silence in circumstances where it should have spoken. Likewise, the Court of Appeal based the estoppel on common law principles. . . .

[17] Our conclusion that the respondents assumed that exchange of contracts would take place as a matter of course, not that exchange had in fact taken place, undermines the factual foundation for the common law estoppel by representation found by Kearney J. and the common law estoppel based on omission to correct a mistake favoured by the Court of Appeal. There is, as Mason and Deane JJ. pointed out in *Legione v. Hateley* (1983), 152 C.L.R. 406 at 432, a long line of authority to support the proposition that, to make out a case of common law estoppel by representation, the representation must be as to an existing fact, a promise or representation as to future conduct being insufficient: *Jorden v. Money* (1854), 5 H.L.C. 185, 10 E.R. 868. . . . It was pointed out in *Legione* (at 432) that, although in *Thompson v. Palmer* [(1933) 49 C.L.R. 507], Dixon J. did not distinguish between an assumption founded upon a representation of existing fact and an assumption founded upon a representation as to future conduct, at the time the doctrine of consideration was thought to be a significant obstacle to the acceptance of an assumption founded upon a representation (or promise) as to future conduct as a basis for common law estoppel by representation. That this was so appears most clearly from the judgment of Isaacs J. in *Ferrier v. Stewart* [(1912), 15 C.L.R. 32] at 44. There, his Honour observed that estoppel refers "to an existing fact, and not to a promise de futuro, which must rest, if at all, on contract". However, he went on to say: "But a person's conduct has reference to an existing fact, if a given state of things is taken as the assumed basis on which another is induced to act".

[18] Because estoppel by representation is often treated as a separate category, it might be possible to confine the distinction between a representation as to existing fact and one as to future conduct to that category. The adoption of such a course would leave an estoppel based on an omission to correct a mistaken assumption free from that troublesome distinction. However, the result would be to fragment the unity of the common law conception of estoppel and to confine the troublesome distinction at the price of introducing another which is equally artificial. And the result would be even more difficult to justify in a case where, as here, the mistaken assumption as to future conduct arises as a direct consequence of a representation.

[19] If there is any basis at all for holding that common law estoppel arises where there is a mistaken assumption as to future events, that basis must lie in reversing *Jorden v. Money* and in accepting the powerful dissent of Lord St. Leonards in that case. The repeated acceptance of *Jorden v. Money* over the years by courts of the highest authority makes this a formidable exercise. We put it to one side as the respondents did not present any argument to us along these lines.

[20] This brings us to the doctrine of promissory estoppel on which the respondents relied in this Court to sustain the judgment in their favour. Promissory estoppel certainly extends to representations (or promises) as to future conduct . . . So far the doctrine has been mainly confined to precluding departure from a representation by a person in a pre-existing contractual relationship that he will not enforce his contractual rights, whether they be pre-existing or rights to be acquired as a result of the representation . . . But Denning J. in *Central London Property Trust, Ltd. v. High Trees House, Ltd.*, [1947] K.B. 130, at pp. 134-135, treated it as a wide-ranging doctrine operating outside the pre-existing contractual relationship . . . In principle there is certainly no reason why the doctrine should not apply so as to preclude departure by a person from a representation that he will not enforce a non-contractual right . . .

[21] There has been for many years a reluctance to allow promissory estoppel to become the vehicle for the positive enforcement of a representation by a party that he would do something in the future. Promissory estoppel, it has been said, is a defensive equity (*Hughes v. Metropolitan Railway Co.* (1877), 2 App. Cas. 439, at p. 448; *Combe v. Combe*, [1951] 2 K.B. 215, at pp. 219-220) and the traditional notion has been that estoppel could only be relied upon defensively as a shield and not as a sword . . . *High Trees* itself was an instance of the defensive use of promissory estoppel. But this does not mean that a plaintiff cannot rely on an estoppel. Even according to traditional orthodoxy, a plaintiff may rely on an estoppel if he has an independent cause of action, where in the words of Denning L.J. in *Combe v. Combe*, at p. 220, the estoppel "may be part of a cause of action, but not a cause of action in itself".

[22] But the respondents ask us to drive promissory estoppel one step further by enforcing directly in the absence of a pre-existing relationship of any kind a non-contractual promise on which the representee has relied to his detriment. For the purposes of discussion, we shall assume that there was such a promise in the present case. The principal objection to the enforcement of such a promise is that it would outflank the principles of the law of contract. Holmes J. expressed his objection to the operation of promissory estoppel in this situation when he said, "It would cut up the doctrine of consideration by the roots, if a promisee could make a gratuitous promise binding by subsequently acting in reliance on it": *Commonwealth v. Scituate Savings Bank* (1884), 137 Mass. 301, at p. 302. Likewise, Sir Owen Dixon considered that estoppel cut across the principles of the law of contract, notably offer and acceptance and consideration: "Concerning Judicial Method" (1956), 29 *Australian Law Journal* 468, at p. 475. And Denning L.J. in *Combe v. Combe*, after noting that "The doctrine of consideration is too firmly fixed to be overthrown by a side-wind", said (at p. 220) that such a promise could only be enforced if it was supported by sufficient consideration . . .

[23] There is force in these objections and it may not be a sufficient answer to repeat the words of Lord Denning M.R. in *Crabb v. Arun District Council*, [1976] Ch. 179, at p. 187, "Equity comes in, true to form, to mitigate the rigours of strict law". True it is that in the orthodox case of promissory estoppel, where the promisor promises that he will not exercise or enforce an existing right, the elements of reliance and detriment attract equitable intervention on the basis that it is unconscionable for the promisor to depart from his promise, if to do so will result in detriment to the promisee. And it can be argued (see, for example, Greig and Davis, *The Law of Contract*, p. 184) that there is no justification for applying the doctrine of promissory estoppel in this situation, yet denying it in the case of a non-contractual promise in the absence of a pre-existing relationship. The promise, if enforced, works a change in the relationship of the parties, by altering an existing legal relationship in the first situation and by creating a new legal relationship

in the second. The point has been made that it would be more logical to say that when the parties have agreed to pursue a course of action, an alteration of the relationship by non-contractual promise will not be countenanced, whereas the creation of a new relationship by a simple promise will be recognized: see D. Jackson, "Estoppel as a Sword" (1965), 81 *Law Quarterly Review* 223, at p. 242.

[24]   The direct enforcement of promises made without consideration by means of promissory estoppel has proceeded apace in the United States. The *Restatement on Contracts 2d* §90 states:

> (1) A promise which the promisor should reasonably expect to induce action or forbearance on the part of the promisee or a third person and which does induce such action or forbearance is binding if injustice can be avoided only by enforcement of the promise. The remedy granted for breach may be limited as justice requires.

This general proposition developed from the treatment in particular situations of promissory estoppel as the equivalent of consideration. Thus in *Allegheny College v. National Chautauqua County Bank* (1927), 246 N.Y. 369, Cardozo C.J. said (at p. 374):

> Certain . . . it is that we have adopted the doctrine of promissory estoppel as the equivalent of consideration in connection with our law of charitable subscriptions.

See Farnsworth, *Contracts* (1982) 2.19; Gilmore, *The Death of Contract* (1974), p. 129.

[25]   However, we need to view the development of the doctrine in the United States with some caution. There promissory estoppel developed partly in response to the limiting effects of the adoption of the bargain theory of consideration which has not been expressly adopted in Australia or England. It may be doubted whether our conception of consideration is substantially broader than the bargain theory . . . though we may be willing to imply consideration in situations where the bargain theory as implemented in the United States would deny the existence of consideration: see Atiyah, *Consideration in Contracts: A Fundamental Restatement* (1971), pp. 6-7, 27, fn. 35; Treitel, "Consideration: A Critical Analysis of Professor Atiyah's Fundamental Restatement" (1976), 50 *Australian Law Journal* 439, at pp. 440 *et seq*. It is perhaps sufficient to say that in the United States, as in Australia, there is an obvious interrelationship between the doctrines of consideration and promissory estoppel, promissory estoppel tending to occupy ground left vacant due to the constraints affecting consideration.

[26]   The proposition stated in §90(1) of the Restatement seems on its face to reflect a closer connection with the general law of contract than our doctrine of promissory estoppel, with its origins in the equitable concept of unconscionable conduct, might be thought to allow. This is because in the United States promissory estoppel has become an equivalent or substitute for consideration in contract formation, detriment being an element common to both doctrines. Nonetheless the proposition, by making the enforcement of the promise conditional on (a) a reasonable expectation on the part of the promisor that his promise will induce action or forbearance by the promisee and (b) the impossibility of avoiding injustice by other means, makes it clear that the promise is enforced in circumstances where departure from it is unconscionable. Note that the emphasis is on the promisor's reasonable expectation that his promise will induce action or forbearance, not on

the fact that he created or encouraged an expectation in the promisee of performance of the promise.

[27] Some recent English decisions are relevant to this general discussion. *Amalgamated Property Co. v. Texas Bank*, [1982] Q.B. 84 in the Court of Appeal and *Pacol Ltd. v. Trade Lines Ltd.*, [1982] 1 Lloyd's Rep. 456, are instances of common law or conventional estoppel. However, the comment of Goff J. in *Texas Bank* at first instance (at p. 107) is significant. His Honour observed:

> Such cases are very different from, for example, a mere promise by a party to make a gift or to increase his obligations under an existing contract; such promise will not generally give rise to an estoppel, even if acted on by the promisee, for the promisee may reasonably be expected to appreciate that, to render it binding, it must be incorporated in a binding contract or contractual variation, and that he cannot therefore safely rely upon it as a legally binding promise without first taking the necessary contractual steps.

The point is that, generally speaking, a plaintiff cannot enforce a voluntary promise because the promisee may reasonably be expected to appreciate that, to render it binding, it must form part of a binding contract.

[28] *Crabb* was an instance of promissory estoppel. It lends assistance to the view that promissory estoppel may in some circumstances extend to the enforcement of a right not previously in existence where the defendant has encouraged in the plaintiff the belief that it will be granted and has acquiesced in action taken by the plaintiff in that belief. There the defendants, knowing of the plaintiff's intention to sell his land in separate portions, encouraged the plaintiff to believe that he would be granted a right of access over their land and, by erecting gates and failing to disabuse him of his belief, encouraged the plaintiff to act to his detriment in selling part of the land without reservation of a right of way. This raised an equity in favour of the plaintiff which was satisfied by granting him a right of access and a right of way over the defendants' land. The Court of Appeal deduced from the circumstances an equity in the plaintiff to have these rights without having to pay for them. As Oliver J. pointed out in *Taylors Fashions Ltd. v. Liverpool Victoria Trustees Co. Ltd.*, [1982] Q.B. 133, at p. 153, the Court of Appeal treated promissory estoppel and proprietary estoppel or estoppel by acquiescence as mere facets of the same general principle, a point also made by Lord Denning M.R. in *Texas Bank*, at p. 122, and seemingly accepted by the Privy Council in *Attorney-General of Hong Kong v. Humphreys Estate Ltd.*, [1987] 1 A.C. 114, at pp. 123-124. In *Taylors Fashions* Oliver J. also remarked (at p. 153) that what gave rise to the need for the court to intervene was the defendants' unconscionable attempt to go back on the assumptions which were the foundation of their dealings. Indeed, Scarman L.J. in *Crabb* saw the question in terms of whether an equity had arisen from the conduct and relationship of the parties (at pp. 193-194), concluding that the court should determine what was "the minimum equity to do justice to the plaintiff" (at p. 198). See also *Pascoe v. Turner*, [1979] 1 W.L.R. 431, at p. 438; [1979] 2 All E.R. 945, at p. 951.

[29] The decision in *Crabb* is consistent with the principle of proprietary estoppel applied in *Ramsden v. Dyson* (1866), L.R. 1 H.L. 129. Under that principle a person whose conduct creates or lends force to an assumption by another that he will obtain an interest in the first person's land and on the basis of that expectation the other person alters his position or acts to his detriment, may bring into existence an equity in favour of that other person, the nature and extent of the equity depending

on the circumstances. And it should be noted that in *Crabb*, as in *Ramsden v. Dyson*, although equity acted by way of recognizing a proprietary interest in the plaintiff, that proprietary interest came into existence as the only appropriate means by which the defendants could be effectively estopped from exercising their existing legal rights.

[30]   One may therefore discern in the cases a common thread which links them together, namely, the principle that equity will come to the relief of a plaintiff who has acted to his detriment on the basis of a basic assumption in relation to which the other party to the transaction has "played such a part in the adoption of the assumption that it would be unfair or unjust if he were left free to ignore it": per Dixon J. in *Grundt* [*Grundt v. Great Boulder Pty. Gold Mines Ltd.* (1937), 59 C.L.R. 641], at p. 675; see also *Thompson* [*Thompson v. Palmer* (1933), 49 C.L.R. 507], at p. 547. Equity comes to the relief of such a plaintiff on the footing that it would be unconscionable conduct on the part of the other party to ignore the assumption.

[31]   Before we turn to the very recent decision of the Privy Council in *Humphreys Estate*, which was not a case of proprietary estoppel, but one, like the present, arising in the course of negotiations antecedent to the making of a contract, we should say something of equity's attitude to the enforcement of voluntary promises. So far equity has set its face against the enforcement of such promises and future representations as such. The support for the exercise of a general equitable jurisdiction to make good expectations created or encouraged by a defendant given by Lord Cottenham L.C. in *Hammersley v. De Biel* (1845), 12 Cl. & Fin. 45; 8 E.R. 1312, affirmed by the House of Lords in that case, was undermined by the insistence in *Jorden v. Money* on a representation of existing fact and destroyed by *Maddison v. Alderson* . . .

[32]   Because equitable estoppel has its basis in unconscionable conduct, rather than the making good of representations, the objection, grounded in *Maddison v. Alderson*, that promissory estoppel outflanks the doctrine of part performance loses much of its sting. Equitable estoppel is not a doctrine associated with part performance whose principal purpose is to overcome non-compliance with the formal requirements for the making of contracts. Equitable estoppel, though it may lead to the plaintiff acquiring an estate or interest in land, depends on considerations of a different kind from those on which part performance depends. Holding the representor to his representation is merely one way of doing justice between the parties.

[33]   In *Humphreys Estate* the defendants representing the Hong Kong government negotiated with a group of companies ("HKL"), which included the respondent Humphreys Estate, for an exchange whereby the government would acquire 83 flats, being part of property belonging to HKL, and in exchange HKL would take from the government a Crown lease of property known as Queen's Gardens and be granted the right to develop that property and certain adjoining property held by HKL. The negotiations did not result in a contract, though the exchange of properties was agreed in principle but subject to contract. The government took possession of HKL's property and expended a substantial sum on it. HKL took possession of Queen's Gardens and demolished existing buildings and paid to the government $103,865,608, the agreed difference between the value of the two properties. HKL withdrew from the negotiations and sued to recover the amount paid and possession of the first property. The defendants claimed that HKL was

estopped from withdrawing from the agreement in principle. The Privy Council rejected this claim on the ground that the government failed to show (a) that HKL created or encouraged a belief or expectation on the part of the government that HKL would not withdraw from the agreement in principle and (b) that the government relied on that belief or expectation (at p. 124). Their Lordships observed (at pp. 127-128):

> It is possible but unlikely that in circumstances at present unforeseeable a party to negotiations set out in a document expressed to be "subject to contract" would be able to satisfy the court that the parties had subsequently agreed to convert the document into a contract or that some form of estoppel had arisen to prevent both parties from refusing to proceed with the transactions envisaged by the document.

[34] The foregoing review of the doctrine of promissory estoppel indicates that the doctrine extends to the enforcement of voluntary promises on the footing that a departure from the basic assumptions underlying the transaction between the parties must be unconscionable. As failure to fulfil a promise does not of itself amount to unconscionable conduct, mere reliance on an executory promise to do something, resulting in the promisee changing his position or suffering detriment, does not bring promissory estoppel into play. Something more would be required. *Humphreys Estate* suggests that this may be found, if at all, in the creation or encouragement by the party estopped in the other party of an assumption that a contract will come into existence or a promise will be performed and that the other party relied on that assumption to his detriment to the knowledge of the first party. *Humphreys Estate* referred in terms to an assumption that the plaintiff would not exercise an existing legal right or liberty, the right or liberty to withdraw from the negotiations, but as a matter of substance such an assumption is indistinguishable from an assumption that a binding contract would eventuate. On the other hand the United States experience, distilled in the *Restatement* (2d § 90), suggests that the principle is to be expressed in terms of a reasonable expectation on the part of the promisor that his promise will induce action or forbearance by the promisee, the promise inducing such action or forbearance in circumstances where injustice arising from unconscionable conduct can only be avoided by holding the promisor to his promise.

[35] The application of these principles to the facts of the present case is not without difficulty. The parties were negotiating through their solicitors for an agreement for lease to be concluded by way of customary exchange. *Humphreys Estate* illustrates the difficulty of establishing an estoppel preventing parties from refusing to proceed with a transaction expressed to be "subject to contract". And there is the problem identified in *Texas Bank* (at p. 107) that a voluntary promise will not generally give rise to an estoppel because the promisee may reasonably be expected to appreciate that he cannot safely rely upon it. This problem is magnified in the present case where the parties were represented by their solicitors.

[36] All this may be conceded. But the crucial question remains: was the appellant entitled to stand by in silence when it must have known that the respondents were proceeding on the assumption that they had an agreement and that completion of the exchange was a formality? The mere exercise of its legal right not to exchange contracts could not be said to amount to unconscionable conduct on the part of the appellant. But there were two other factors present in the situation which require to be taken into consideration. The first was the element of urgency that pervaded the negotiation of the terms of the proposed lease. As we have

noted, the appellant was bound to give up possession of its existing commercial premises in Nowra in January 1984; the new building was to be available for fitting out by 15 January and completed by 5 February 1984. The respondents' solicitor had said to the appellant's solicitor on 7 November that it would be impossible for Maher to complete the building within the agreed time unless the agreement were concluded "within the next day or two". The outstanding details were agreed within a day or two thereafter, and the work of preparing the site commenced almost immediately.

[37]   The second factor of importance is that the respondents executed the counterpart deed and it was forwarded to the appellant's solicitor on 11 November. The assumption on which the respondents acted thereafter was that completion of the necessary exchange was a formality. The next their solicitor heard from the appellant was a letter from its solicitors dated 19 January, informing him that the appellant did not intend to proceed with the matter. It had known, at least since 10 December, that costly work was proceeding on the site.

[38]   It seems to us, in the light of these considerations, that the appellant was under an obligation to communicate with the respondents within a reasonable time after receiving the executed counterpart deed and certainly when it learnt on 10 December that demolition was proceeding. It had to choose whether to complete the contract or to warn the respondents that it had not yet decided upon the course it would take. It was not entitled simply to retain the counterpart deed executed by the respondents and do nothing . . . The appellant's inaction, in all the circumstances, constituted clear encouragement or inducement to the respondents to continue to act on the basis of the assumption which they had made. It was unconscionable for it, knowing that the respondents were exposing themselves to detriment by acting on the basis of a false assumption, to adopt a course of inaction which encouraged them in the course they had adopted. To express the point in the language of promissory estoppel the appellant is estopped in all the circumstances from retreating from its implied promise to complete the contract.

. . .

[40]   We therefore think that the Court of Appeal was correct in its conclusion. We would dismiss the appeal.

BRENNAN J.: —

. . .

[23]   Parties who are negotiating a contract may proceed in the expectation that the terms will be agreed and a contract made but, so long as both parties recognize that either party is at liberty to withdraw from the negotiations at any time before the contract is made, it cannot be unconscionable for one party to do so. Of course, the freedom to withdraw may be fettered or extinguished by agreement but, in the absence of agreement, either party ordinarily retains his freedom to withdraw. It is only if a party induces the other party to believe that he, the former party, is already bound and his freedom to withdraw has gone that it could be unconscionable for him subsequently to assert that he is legally free to withdraw.

[24]   It is essential to the existence of an equity created by estoppel that the party who induces the adoption of the assumption or expectation knows or intends that the party who adopts it will act or abstain from acting in reliance on the assumption or expectation: see per Lord Denning M.R. in *Crabb v. Arun District Council*,

at p. 188. When the adoption of an assumption or expectation is induced by the making of a promise, the knowledge or intention that the assumption or expectation will be acted upon may be easily inferred. But if a party encourages another to adhere to an assumption or expectation already formed or acquiesces in the making of an assumption or the entertainment of an expectation when he ought to object to the assumption or expectation — steps which are tantamount to inducing the other to adopt the assumption or expectation — the inference of knowledge or intention that the assumption or expectation will be acted on may be more difficult to draw.

[25] The unconscionable conduct which it is the object of equity to prevent is the failure of a party, who has induced the adoption of the assumption or expectation and who knew or intended that it would be relied on, to fulfil the assumption or expectation or otherwise to avoid the detriment which that failure would occasion. The object of the equity is not to compel the party bound to fulfil the assumption or expectation; it is to avoid the detriment which, if the assumption or expectation goes unfulfilled, will be suffered by the party who has been induced to act or to abstain from acting thereon.   *protect the promisee*

[26] If this object is kept steadily in mind, the concern that a general application of the principle of equitable estoppel would make non-contractual promises enforceable as contractual promises can be allayed. A non-contractual promise can give rise to an equitable estoppel only when the promisor induces the promisee to assume or expect that the promise is intended to affect their legal relations and he knows or intends that the promisee will act or abstain from acting in reliance on the promise, and when the promisee does so act or abstain from acting and the promisee would suffer detriment by his action or inaction if the promisor were not to fulfil the promise. When these elements are present, equitable estoppel almost wears the appearance of contract, for the action or inaction of the promisee looks like consideration for the promise on which, as the promisor knew or intended, the promisee would act or abstain from acting . . .

[**DEANE** and **GAUDRON JJ.** gave judgments to the same effect.]

QUESTION

How long and pointed can a shield become before it becomes a sword?

The next two cases explore other ways of protecting reliance. Their significance lies less in the specific doctrinal methods used than in the demonstration of the willingness of the courts to protect reliance when they believe that it was reasonable.

BAXTER v. JONES

(1903), 6 O.L.R. 360
(C.A., Moss C.J.O., Osler, McLennan and Garrow JJ.A.)

[The defendant, an insurance broker, had arranged insurance for the plaintiffs in January 1900, with coverage shared among several insurers. In January 1901 the plaintiffs arranged with the defendant to increase their insurance coverage on one policy by $500. Under the terms of their other existing policies, each of the insurers had to be informed of the increase in the amount of coverage on any other policy (a so-called "co-insurance notification clause"). Some time after the increase in coverage was arranged, the defendant told the plaintiffs that he would give the necessary notices to the other insurers, but he failed to do so. As a result, when a fire occurred, the other policies were not fully enforceable and the plaintiffs had inadequate insurance coverage. The plaintiffs sued the agent for the loss they had suffered. The action was brought in negligence. The trial judge found that the defendant had promised to give the other insurers notice and that it failed to do so. He gave judgment for the plaintiffs. The defendant appealed.]

OSLER J.A.: — [1] . . . If the defendant's employment and promise was entire to do both acts, viz., to procure the new insurance and to give the notices, then, even if it was, as it has been held in the Court below, a gratuitous promise, yet having proceeded upon his employment the defendant would be liable for negligently performing it in such a manner as to cause loss or injury to the plaintiffs. He knew the importance of giving the notices, and the effect of the omission to do so, upon the plaintiffs' other policies. To stop when he had only obtained the insurance was simply to go so far with the business as to cause a direct injury to the plaintiffs if he failed to follow it up by notice to the other insurers, and cannot be regarded otherwise than as actionable negligence. . . .

[2]   I think the learned Judge rightly regarded the transaction as one of mandate, so that if the defendant had not entered upon the execution of the business entrusted to him he would have incurred no liability, *Coggs v. Bernard* (1703), 2 Ld. Raym. 909, 1 *Smith's Leading Cases* 11th ed. p. 173, but "it is well established that one who enters upon the performance of a mandate or gratuitous undertaking on behalf of another, is responsible not only for what he does, but for what he leaves unfulfilled, and cannot rely on the want of consideration as an excuse for the omission of any step that is requisite for the protection of any interest intrusted to his care."

MACLENNAN J.A.: — [3] . . . But because he was procuring the insurance at the request of the plaintiffs, to that extent he was acting for them, which makes it necessary to consider how far, if at all, he was bound to give the notices, although all that he did was as between him and the plaintiffs purely voluntary. In *Coggs v. Bernard*, the defendant promised to hoist some hogsheads of brandy from one cellar and deposit them in another. In doing so a cask was staved, and the contents were lost. There the negligence was in doing the very act which was to be done, and the defendant was held to be liable though he was not to have any reward for what he undertook to do. That was a case of bailment, inasmuch as the defendant had taken the goods into his possession. But the judgment was not rested wholly upon that circumstance. At p. 181, Lord Holt in his elaborate judgment, refers to the case of a carpenter having undertaken to build a house, but who had not done it, and it was adjudged the action would not lie (i.e. the promise having been voluntary), and he adds: "But then the question was put to the Court — what if he had built the house unskilfully — and it is agreed in that case an action would have lain". . . . In *Skelton v. The London & North-Western R.W. Co.* (1867), L.R. 2 C.P. 631 at p. 636, Willes J., said the result of the decision in *Coggs v. Bernard* was that "if a person undertakes to perform a voluntary act, he is liable if he performs it improperly, but not if he neglects to perform it." Two insurance cases are cited in the notes to *Coggs v. Bernard*, p. 183, viz., *Wilkinson v. Coverdale*, 1 Esp. 75, and *Wallace v. Telfair* (1786), 2 T.R. 188 (n) in which these principles were applied to voluntary engagements to procure insurance.

QUESTIONS AND NOTES

1. What interest of the plaintiffs is protected by this judgment — expectation, restitution or reliance?

2. Is this a torts case or a contracts case? Since the action was brought in negligence, it seems to be a torts case. We shall explore later in these materials the tendency in recent years to collapse the divisions between contracts and torts. For the moment it is important to notice that the decision of counsel to frame the case in negligence enabled the court to find a way to avoid the argument of the defendant that his undertaking was gratuitous and therefore unenforceable for lack of consideration.

3. *Coggs v. Bernard* (1703), 2 Ld. Raym. 909, cited in *Baxter v. Jones*, is a famous bailment case. Bailment is a property law concept under which one person, the bailee, has lawful possession of the property of another, the bailor; a bailment relation may, for example, arise when a car is leased, or a person borrows a car from a friend. Under the law of bailment, even if a bailment is gratuitous, the bailee is liable for damage to the property of the bailor (owner). Thus, if A gratuitously promises to take care of B's chattel and A takes possession of it, A will generally be liable under the law of bailment for damage or loss of the chattel. However, if A promises to do anything beyond caring for the chattel (for example to repair it), he will only be bound by this promise if B provided some consideration.

4. There are other examples from the law of negligence of liability for gratuitous undertakings. For example, a doctor or lawyer will be liable for negligence in the performance of professional services, even if he or she is not being paid. It has also been recognized that a banker may be liable for economic losses that result from providing inaccurate information about the credit worthiness of a client to a third party, even if this information is provided gratuitously; see *Hedley Byrne & Co. Ltd. v. Heller & Partners Ltd.*, [1964] A.C. 465, [1963] 2 All E.R. 575 (H.L.).

    These are all situations in which the courts protect reasonable reliance, even in the absence of consideration.

5. *Baxter v. Jones* illustrates the common origin of tortious and contractual liability and the importance of both the relation between the parties and the undertaking of the defendant.

The next case illustrates that in some situations acts of reliance by a promisee may be regarded as satisfying the requirement for consideration, rendering the promise binding.

SLOAN v. UNION OIL OF CANADA CO. OF CANADA LTD.

[1955] 4 D.L.R. 664, 16 W.W.R. 225
(B.C.S.C., Wilson J.)

[The plaintiff had worked for many years for the defendant. In order to try to encourage employee loyalty during the Second World War, the defendant announced a policy of offering termination allowances; if the defendant terminated an employee (for any reason other than employee misconduct or retirement), the employee would receive a generous termination allowance, a sum larger than the statutory minimums. In August 1945, the defendant sold its assets to British-American Oil Co. Ltd. (B.A. Oil). A sale of assets involves a buyer, in this case B.A. Oil, acquiring all of the assets (*e.g.*, gas stations, oil refineries, etc.) of the vendor, Union Oil. But the vendor continues to exist as a legal entity, with its own contractual rights and obligations. The purchaser in this case, as is common in a sale of assets, wanted the employees of the original employer to work for it, but there was no legal assignment of the employment contracts.

By selling its assets, Union Oil in law terminated its employment contract with the plaintiff; although the plaintiff was able in effect to keep working at his old job, he was working for B.A. Oil. B.A. Oil did not offer the same fringe benefits as the defendant and, in particular, did not offer a termination allowance. The plaintiff was strongly discouraged by B.A. Oil from suing the defendant for his termination allowance while he worked for the new employer. When in 1950 he left his job with B.A. Oil, he brought an action against the defendant for payment of the termination allowance which he was entitled to when his employment with that company ceased on the sale of its assets to B.A. Oil.]

WILSON J.: — **[1]** . . . I must decide whether or not there was a contract by the defendant to pay the plaintiff a termination allowance if he was discharged without cause. . . .

[2]   The defendant had, in a series of communications from 1941 to 1945, told the plaintiff he would be paid such an allowance. I have no doubt that such statements constitute an offer by the defendant; a promise that it would, if he continued in its employment until such time, short of retirement age, as it should without cause, dismiss him from its service, pay him certain stated sums. The offer is clear. It is equally clear that there was no verbal or written acceptance of the offer; no consideration by way of a promise that he would so continue to serve. Therefore, if a consideration moved from the plaintiff to the defendant, that consideration was not a promise but a performance, the doing of an act. For undoubtedly he did fulfil the terms of the defendant's offer, he did serve them until dismissed, and it is this, and this only, that must be relied on as consideration.

[3]   Now he was, of course, already bound to serve them during his period of employment and the consideration for that service was his salary. But he was not bound to continue to serve them until he was dismissed. He could, at any time, have quit his employment. By staying until he was discharged he did something that was not required by his contract of employment and he says that his knowledge of the provision for a termination allowance was one of the factors which induced him to continue his employment.

[**WILSON J.** referred to *High Trees* and *Combe v. Combe* and continued:]

[4]   The decisive point in [*Combe v. Combe*] seems to me to have been not the rejection of the wife's forbearance as consideration but the finding that there was no offer by the husband to pay the money for the act of forbearance . . .

[5]   I think . . . that a majority of the Court would have enforced the promise to pay £100 per year if it had been coupled with a condition that the wife abstain from taking proceedings to collect alimony and if the wife had so abstained . . . The interesting thing here is that Denning L.J., if I read him correctly, would have enforced the husband's promise on a basis entirely unrelated to his judgment in the *High Trees House* case, and on what he calls a long-settled rule that a finding that there was a promise intended to be binding, intended to be acted upon and in fact acted upon is equivalent to a finding that there was consideration . . .

[6]   It appears to me that *Combe v. Combe* brings latter-day English law regarding consideration into a very near relationship with American law on the same subject. I propose to quote at some length from American authorities which seem to have anticipated the reasoning in *Combe v. Combe*, and have the added advantage of applying that reasoning to the relation of master and servant. I first cite this general statement from *Corbin on Contracts* vol. 1, p. 221:

> There are cases in which an employer has promised a "bonus", some form of benefit in addition to agreed wages or salary, on condition that the employee or employees remain in service for a stated period. In such cases the offered promise is almost always so made as to make it unnecessary for the employee to give any notice of his assent.

> It is sufficient that he continues in the employment as requested. It is certain that after so continuing in performance, the employer cannot withdraw or repudiate his promise without liability either in damages or for a proportionate part of the bonus promised. A unilateral contract exists.

[7]   . . . It seems to me there are here the essentials of a contract, offer and acceptance, promise and consideration. In the part of [the contract] where provision is made for termination allowance, certain paid holidays are listed and certain rights to vacations with pay are granted. Could it be argued that an employee who had taken the vacation granted would have no right of action against the company for wages for the period covered by the vacation? Surely not. The concession by an employer to an employee of the right to holiday pay or a termination allowance is as much a part of the consideration for his services as is his right to wages. It is part of the contract of employment . . .

NOTES

1.   The capacity of the doctrine of consideration to catch parties by surprise still exists. In *Watson v. Moore Corp.*, [1996] B.C.J. No. 525, [1996] 7 W.W.R. 564, 21 B.C.L.R. (3d) 157 (C.A.), the plaintiff had been employed by the defendant since 1968. Thirteen years after she started work, she was asked by her employer to sign a written contract of employment that limited the notice period in the event of dismissal. She signed other contracts afterwards. She was dismissed and given payment in lieu of notice in accordance with the terms of the last contract she had signed. The trial judge held that she was bound by the terms of this contract. The Court of Appeal held that there was no consideration for the last contract: the employer had not shown that, when she had been asked to sign the last contract, it had forborne from dismissing her — it simply had not dismissed her. Gibbs J.A. dissented on the ground that it had been accepted for a long time that giving continuing employment was sufficient consideration for an employment contract.

   What kind of human relations policy does the majority of the Court of Appeal imagine Canadian corporations should adopt?

   In *Techform Products Ltd. v. Wolda*, [2001] O.J. No. 3822, 56 O.R. (3d) 1, 206 D.L.R. (4th) 171 (C.A.), leave to appeal to S.C.C. refused, [2001] S.C.C.A. No. 603, the question was whether an employee who had created a valuable invention was the owner as the inventor. The plaintiff claimed that it owned the patent to the invention as the defendant had developed it while under contract to it. This question turned on the enforceability of an agreement made after the defendant had left the plaintiff's employment and had been retained by it as an independent consultant. The enforceability of the agreement, called the "Employee Technology Agreement" ("ETA"), depended on whether the plaintiff had given consideration for the defendant's promise to assign to the plaintiff any patent arising from any invention. Rosenberg J.A., giving the judgment of the Ontario Court of Appeal, held that whether there was consideration depended on whether the employer refrained from terminating the employment relation in consideration of the employee's acceptance of the terms of the new agreement. On the facts, Rosenberg J.A. held that there was consideration. He referred to the judgment of the British Columbia Court of Appeal in *Watson v. Moore Corp.* While

Rosenberg J.A. was able to say that the application of the principle of that case was consistent with the result he had reached, he indicated that on the facts of *Watson v. Moore Corp.*, he would have had a different outcome. Rosenberg J.A. held that an employer gives consideration for an amended employment contract provided that it offers "at least an implicit promise of reasonable forbearance [from dismissal] for some period of time" after the new agreement is made. The Court also dismissed an argument of duress in the circumstances, noting that the defendant had "ample opportunity to obtain independent legal advice" and, moreover, continued in the relation for years after signing the ETA. For a critical commentary on this decision, see M.H. Ogilvie, "Forbearance and Economic Duress: Three Strikes and You're Still Out at the Ontario Court of Appeal" (2004), 29 Queen's L.J. 809.

2. An interesting case involving the protection of reliance, though hardly in the mainstream of commercial relations, is *Budai v. Ontario Lottery Corp.* (1982), 142 D.L.R. (3d) 271 (Ont. Div. Ct.). A computer operated by an agent of the defendant generated a printout that informed the plaintiff that he had won $835.40 in a lottery, after which the plaintiff spent $480 that night on a binge in Buffalo with his friends. The next day he was informed that the lottery corporation's computer had made an error and that his actual prize was worth only $5. At trial in Small Claims Court, the plaintiff was awarded $835.40. The lottery corporation appealed to the Divisional Court and the judgment was varied to $480. What would the court have done if the plaintiff had been more cautious and less convivial and had agreed to buy a stereo set for $800? Could you justify an award of the full amount of $835.40? What policies do you think should be adopted by the law in dealing with this kind of statement by a lottery corporation?

McCUNN ESTATE v. CANADIAN IMPERIAL BANK OF COMMERCE

[2001] O.J. No. 486, 53 O.R. (3d) 304
(C.A., Catzman, Borins and Feldman JJ.A.)

BORINS J.A.: —

. . .

[2] The issue in this appeal is whether the estate of Mary Theresa McCunn can take advantage of the mistake of the appellant, the Canadian Imperial Bank of Commerce ("CIBC" or "the bank"), in debiting monthly insurance premiums to Mrs. McCunn's credit line after the insurance policy provided by the other appellant, the Mutual Life Assurance Company for Canada ("Mutual Life"), had come to an end. Chadwick J. [at trial (1999), 45 O.R. (3d) 112] held that the mistaken debiting of premiums extended the term of the insurance policy beyond its termination date. For the reasons that follow, it is my view that the decision of the applications judge is incorrect. I would, therefore, allow the appeal, set aside the judgment of Chadwick J. and direct that the application be dismissed.

Facts

[3]   The material facts are not in dispute. On January 22, 1990, Mrs. McCunn applied for and obtained a personal credit line from the CIBC. A few days later, her husband, Dr. McCunn also obtained a personal credit line from the bank. At that time, through Mutual Life, the bank provided, at its own expense, an insurance policy on the life of customers who had obtained credit lines. The purpose of the insurance was to reduce or liquidate any outstanding indebtedness under the credit

line upon a customer's death. As of January, 1990, Dr. and Mrs. McCunn were each insured under a Mutual Life group policy.

[4] The bank changed its policy of providing insurance without cost to its credit line customers in July, 1990, when it decided to pass along to them the responsibility for obtaining, at their own expense, insurance coverage. Customers were notified in writing of this decision and provided with an information package that explained, *inter alia*, that customers who were at that time insured were automatically enrolled in the new insurance plan "subject to the age 70 limit", unless they elected to opt out of the new plan. Customers also received a specimen insurance certificate which contained the following term: "Coverage will continue . . . until the date on which the Insured Person reaches age 70." Dr. and Mrs. McCunn each became automatically insured under the new plan on August 1, 1990. As before, the insurance was provided by Mutual Life. It was common ground that the coverage provided by the insurance policy terminated on Mrs. McCunn's 70th birthday.

[5] On May 21, 1993, Dr. and Mrs. McCunn decided to consolidate their credit lines into a single credit line. It was necessary that each sign a document effecting this change, with the result that the existing insurance coverage of their separate credit lines merged and coverage continued of their consolidated credit line. On June 2, 1993, the bank wrote to Mutual Life giving the insurer the particulars of this change and confirming that insurance coverage would continue on the new consolidated credit line.

[6] From August 1, 1990, when Mrs. McCunn became responsible for paying the cost of her insurance, monthly premiums were debited to her credit line. After the credit lines were consolidated on May 21, 1993, monthly premiums were debited to the joint credit line. Premiums were structured based on the average daily balance of the credit line and the customer's age. Mrs. McCunn reached her 70th birthday on December 7, 1996. Although the coverage on her life terminated on that day under the terms of the certificate of insurance, the bank continued to debit monthly premiums to the credit line for a further sixteen months until her death on March 25, 1998. Monthly statements sent to Mrs. McCunn reflected the debiting of the premiums.

[7] After Mrs. McCunn's death, a representative of her estate sought payment under the policy of an amount appropriate to reduce or liquidate any outstanding indebtedness under the credit line at the date of her death. The request was rejected by the bank, which pointed out that coverage had been terminated on Mrs. McCunn's 70th birthday. In a letter to the estate's solicitor, the bank wrote: "It would appear that insurance premiums did continue after Mrs. McCunn reached the age of 70, said premiums amounting to $1,067.38 have been reversed."

[8] It was the evidence of the bank's representative, Wayne Godin, that the premiums were debited to the credit line after Mrs. McCunn's 70th birthday as "a result of administrative oversight". . .

[**BORINS J.A.** outlined the reasons of Chadwick J., who said (p. 116 O.R.):

> In this particular case the deceased did not alter her conduct. *There is no evidence she was even aware the policy was still in effect although the premiums remained the same.* It would be speculation to try and determine whether the deceased would have gone to the marketplace to seek other insurance if she was aware her coverage had terminated at age 70. [Emphasis added by the Court of Appeal.]

He held, however, on the basis of the conduct of the bank, that the insurance contract had been extended to the date of Mrs. McCunn's death. The conduct of the bank which Chadwick J. found to be significant was the debiting of the premiums subsequent to Mrs. McCunn's 70th birthday, its awareness of her birth date and the fact it sent her monthly statements which reflected the debiting of the premiums.]

Analysis

[18]   Applying basic principles of contract law, it is my view the applications judge was incorrect in his conclusion that a new contract of insurance had resulted from the bank's debiting of monthly insurance premiums to Mrs. McCunn's credit line subsequent to the termination of the insurance policy by reason of her age. For the parties to have created a new contract of insurance it was necessary that the bank, with the requisite knowledge and intent, make an offer to provide insurance, and that Mrs. McCunn, with the requisite knowledge and intent, accept the offer. As I will explain, it cannot be said that either the bank made such an offer, or that there was an acceptance by Mrs. McCunn.

. . .

[20]   To extend the insurance contract beyond its termination date, it was necessary that there be an express agreement to do so between the bank and Mrs. McCunn. Either the insurer or the insured would have had to make an offer containing the material terms described above, and the other party would have had to accept it. On the reasons of the applications judge, the bank was deemed to have made an offer by erroneously continuing to debit monthly premiums after the termination of the original policy. I use the word "erroneously" because it is implicit in the conclusion reached by the applications judge that it was because the bank had failed to program its computer to take into account Mrs. McCunn's 70th birthday that the debiting of premiums continued. It was for this reason that he "deemed" that the bank intended to extend the contract.

[21]   The applications judge did not reject the bank's position that the debiting of the premiums was an administrative oversight as explained by Mr. Godin. An oversight is an inadvertent omission or error. This is precisely what occurred when the bank failed to program its computer properly. An act which is the result of an administrative oversight is not an intended act. As the bank was in error in debiting the premiums, it cannot be said that it intended to extend the contract. To act erroneously is inconsistent with acting knowingly. It follows that by inadvertently debiting the monthly premiums to Mrs. McCunn's credit line subsequent to the termination date of the contract, the bank cannot be seen to have knowingly intended to make an offer to extend the contract or, properly speaking, to enter into a new contract. Moreover, even if this could be said to amount to such an offer, there was no evidence that it was accepted by Mrs. McCunn. The applications judge made no such finding. Indeed, in considering the estate's estoppel argument he observed that there was no evidence that Mrs. McCunn "was ever aware that the policy was still in effect although the premiums remained the same".

[22]   In my view, *Saint John Tug Boat*, [[1964] S.C.R. 614, 46 D.L.R. (2d) 1], does not assist Mrs. McCunn's estate. It was an entirely different case where there was evidence that the plaintiff had offered the defendant the use of its tug boats. The issue was whether, in the absence of a written or verbal acceptance of the of-

fer, the defendant in some other manner had accepted it. It was found that by its conduct the defendant had accepted the offer. The case is not authority for any general legal principle. It was entirely fact driven and illustrates that a party may accept an offer by its conduct.

[23] What this case comes down to is a mistake by the bank which, as the applications judge found, was not relied on by Mrs. McCunn. Based on the clear language of the insurance contract, the insurer's duty to pay was discharged on her 70th birthday, a fact which was apparent on the face of the documents she signed. She must be taken to have known, or to have had reason to know, that by its terms the insurance coverage had come to an end when she reached age 70. Yet, in the face of these circumstances, the estate has attempted to take advantage of the bank's mistake to demand payment of the insurance. Where a party knows of another's mistake, or should reasonably know of it, she cannot expect that the law will permit her to take advantage of it, particularly in circumstances, as in this case, where she neither relied on it to her detriment, nor acted in the reasonable expectation that coverage had not come to an end. . . .

[24] This case is analogous to the situation in which a bank has mistakenly deposited a sum of money into a customer's account. Had the bank mistakenly deposited $1,000,000, or any other sum, into her account, Mrs. McCunn would not have been entitled to keep it and would be required to make restitution to the bank. . . .

. . .

Conclusion

[26] In summary, the application judge's finding that the bank's automated computer system had mistakenly continued to debit monthly premiums to Mrs. McCunn's credit line after the insurance coverage had terminated on her 70th birthday cannot be elevated to a knowing intention on the part of the bank to extend the coverage to some unspecified date in the future, particularly in light of his additional findings that Mrs. McCunn had neither relied to her detriment on the debiting of the premiums, nor formed any reasonable expectation that her life would be insured subsequent to her 70th birthday. In my view, there was no evidence that was capable of supporting a finding that the CIBC and Mrs. McCunn had entered into a contract extending the insurance contract that had terminated on her 70th birthday, or that they had agreed upon a new insurance contract. In reaching the conclusion that the CIBC had extended the insurance contract, the applications judge wrote an insurance contract. He erred in doing so.

[27] I would allow the appeal, set aside the judgment of Chadwick J. and order that the application be dismissed with costs in this court and below.

FELDMAN J.A. (dissenting): —

. . .

[33] The bank continued to deduct the joint life insurance premium from the McCunn account for 16 months after Mrs. McCunn reached the age of 70 and until her death. After deducting its administration fee, which was a percentage of the total aggregate premium, the bank forwarded the premiums to Mutual Life.

[34] The bank continued to deduct the joint premium notwithstanding that through the McCunns' branch, the bank was aware of Mrs. McCunn's birthdate and age. She was a "private banking" customer. When Mrs. McCunn was ap-

proaching her 70th birthday on December 7, 1996, the Bank recommended to her that she convert her R.R.S.P. funds into a Registered Retirement Income Fund (R.R.I.F). The bank also confirmed internally in its records and notified the branch by a report in early 1997, generated the month after the customer reaches age 70, that Mrs. McCunn had turned 70.

[35]   After Mrs. McCunn's death, when the estate sought to collect the life insurance, the bank took steps to reverse the charges to the account for Mrs. McCunn's portion of the premium for the 16 months after she had reached the age of 70, on the basis that the insurance coverage had terminated when she reached that age. On this application the bank took the position that its continued deduction of premiums after that time was an "administrative error" on its part.

[36]   How this error occurred was never explained by the bank in the evidence. In particular, there was no evidence as to whether this was an isolated incident limited to Mrs. McCunn, or whether the bank's computer also deducted premiums from other persons over the age of 70. The bank's deponent on the application, Mr. Godin, refused on cross examination to provide any documentation to substantiate that premiums were not deducted from other customers over age 70.

[37]   The issue articulated by the application judge [at p. 115 O.R.] was "whether C.I.B.C. and Mutual Life as a result of their conduct have extended a contract past the age of 70 to the point where Mary McCunn was covered at the time of her death."

[38]   Three legal avenues were argued by the respondent on the application. The application judge rejected both the arguments of reasonable expectation and of estoppel. However, he held that the contract of insurance had been extended beyond the date when Mrs. McCunn reached age 70 by the virtue of the following factors: (a) the bank continued to send statements and to debit Mrs. McCunn's account for premiums as if the insurance contract was still in place; (b) the bank advised Mrs. McCunn what steps she could take with her R.R.S.P's when she turned 70, evidencing that the bank clearly knew her birthdate and her age, and was in contact with her with respect to banking issues arising as a result of her age . . .

[39]   The application judge concluded [at p. 120 O.R.] that the bank's conduct was "more than acquiescent, and consistent with an active extension of the insurance. The bank's conduct was more than an administrative error." As a result, he found that the insurance contract remained in place at the date of Mrs. McCunn's death when she was 71 years old. . . .

[40]   The appellants' submission on the appeal is that the application judge erred in law by finding a contract where there was no consensus *ad idem*, on the basis that there was no evidence that Mrs. McCunn was aware that the insurance policy was still in effect after her 70th birthday. The appellants also argue that their conduct could not amount to waiver or estoppel . . .

[**FELDMAN J.A.** dealt with an argument that the trial judge had dealt with issues not pleaded. She held that he had not done so. She continued:]

2.   Consensus ad idem

[44]   In my view the application judge made no error in his analysis that by its conduct the bank (on behalf of Mutual Life) extended Mrs. McCunn's life insurance contract beyond the age of 70 and that Mrs. McCunn accepted that extension.

[45]   The appellant contends that there was no evidence of agreement because there was no evidence that Mrs. McCunn either knew about the extension or agreed with it, and in particular, no evidence that she relied on it to her detriment because there was no evidence that she could have obtained alternate insurance coverage had she attempted to do so.

[46]   The application judge referred to the case of *St. John Tug Boat v. Irving Refinery*, [1964] S.C.R. 614, 46 D.L.R. (2d) 1. In that case, the plaintiff tug boat company had offered to have on stand-by two tug boats for the use of the defendant to escort oil tankers into the harbour to its refinery. The advantage to the defendant of having boats on stand-by was that if it had to find a tug boat each time its tankers arrived, it would have had to incur significant demurrage charges while the tankers waited to unload their cargo. The defendant had initially accepted the offer first for one month, and then agreed to two two-week extensions thereafter. The defendant continued to use the services of the plaintiff's tugs for several months, but without a further formal extension of the terms of the stand-by facility. The defendant then refused to pay for the stand-by service.

[47]   The Supreme Court [of] Canada held that by continuing to make the stand-by services available after the extension period, and by sending invoices which showed that the same rates were being charged, the plaintiff made a new offer to the defendant to render the same services at the same rate. This offer was accepted by the defendant by its conduct of using the services from time to time.

[48]   The application judge noted that in this case, the roles of the parties were reversed, but with the bank as the offeror, the case on behalf of Mrs. McCunn was stronger. I agree with that analysis.

[49]   The system set up by the bank for premium payments and therefore for administration of the life insurance contract was fully within the control of the bank. The system put in place by the bank required no action by Mrs. McCunn because premiums were automatically debited from her account and her monthly statement referenced the deduction each month as "PLC life insurance charged". She could have complained upon receipt of her monthly statements, which provided on their face for a 30-day limit for doing so, but she did not do so. Her silence, if anything, is further evidence of her acceptance of the bank's actions in continuing to collect premiums after she turned 70.

[50]   In an offer and acceptance situation creating an agreement, there is no need for detrimental reliance. That may be necessary for promissory estoppel, but that is not the basis of the finding of liability in this case. In this case, the offer is the bank's deduction of premiums and sending of statements, while acceptance is demonstrated by Mrs. McCunn's lack of objection to the continuation of her life insurance policy regime by continuing to allow the deduction of premiums from her account. Furthermore, the element of consideration necessary for the formation of a [contract] is satisfied here. There is consideration flowing from Mrs. McCunn to the bank by the payment of the premiums from the line of credit account together with any interest charges incurred as a result. This is not a situation where a

party is clearly acting in error by taking or giving money because there is no consideration flowing from that act. Here the continued taking and application of premiums by the bank and the insurance company must be in consideration of the extension of the insurance contract.

[51] The bank asserted that the deduction of premiums did not indicate any intention to extend the contract because it was done merely as a result of administrative oversight. The application judge rejected that submission. He observed [at p. 119 O.R.] that the bank's conduct was "the direct result of automation in banking" because automatic processes may be set up without "the periodic monitoring of a thinking human being". He concluded: "On the face of its conduct, the bank must be deemed to have intended the consequences of these actions, and thus to have extended the contract."

[52] . . . Chadwick J. . . . concluded [at p. 120 O.R.] that "clearly the bank's conduct was more than acquiescent and consistent with an active extension of the insurance. The bank's conduct was more than an administrative error."

[53] This conclusion of the application judge is supported both by the evidence and by the law. Although the bank's deponent stated baldly that the bank's actions were a result of administrative oversight, there was no evidence as to how this oversight occurred within the automated structure set up to deduct the premiums from Mrs. McCunn's account. There was no evidence, for example, that her age had been programmed into the computer, but that there was an error in the computer's operation. The reasonable inference from the evidence was that the computer was programmed to continue deducting premiums from Mrs. McCunn's line of credit account without regard to her age. The fact that the bank was aware of her birthdate and of her age adds weight to this conclusion.

[54] Therefore, Chadwick J.'s conclusion that such an automatic process had been set in motion by the bank and could be considered as a continuing offer to Mrs. McCunn, was in accordance with the evidence on the application put forward by the appellants. There is no basis to overturn that finding on appeal and to treat the bank's action as an error or mistake.

[55] Chadwick J. also relied on basic principles of contract law referred to by the Supreme Court of Canada in the *St. John* case, including the following quote from *Smith v. Hughes* (1871), [1861-73] All E.R. Rep. 632, L.R. 6 Q.B. 597, at p. 637 All E.R., p. 607 Q.B.:

> If, whatever a man's real intention may be, he so conducts himself that a reasonable man would believe that he was assenting to the terms proposed by the other party, and that other party upon that belief enters into the contract with him, the man thus conducting himself would be equally bound as if he had intended to agree to the other party's terms.

[56] Thus, Chadwick J. effectively rejected the evidence of the bank that its actions were a result of administrative oversight, and also held that the actions of the bank, whatever its subjective intention, amounted to conduct which objectively demonstrated an intention that the life insurance contract would continue in force on payment of premiums without a limit on Mrs. McCunn's age . . .

[57] I agree with Chadwick J.'s findings on the evidence. . . .

. . .

[60] I would dismiss the appeal with costs.

. . .

[The Supreme Court of Canada granted leave to appeal on 4 October 2001, but the case was settled without the appeal being heard.]

QUESTIONS

1. What effect would the different approaches of Borins and Feldman JJ.A. have on how carefully banks conduct their business? Since it is inevitable that errors will occur, on whom should the risk of those errors fall?

2. Since Mrs. McCunn is dead, she cannot testify whether she relied on the bank's action or was even aware of it. Is it likely that she could have said anything useful about the extent of her reliance? Blackburn J. in *Smith v. Hughes* (the important passage is quoted by Feldman J.A. at ¶ 55 and the case is reproduced in Chapter 3) justifies the imposition of liability on the fact that there has been reliance on what was done. If no one, *as a matter of fact*, relies on those acts or statements that might reasonably have led someone to believe that an offer was being made or an undertaking given, what basis is there for imposing liability just because someone might have relied?

3. The bank led no evidence to explain how this error arose or how many people might have been similarly affected by it. Would it matter if there were many other people affected and the bank had made no effort to identify, notify and reimburse them? Would it matter if the bank had charged Mrs. McCunn higher premiums after her 70th birthday?

PROBLEMS

1. Judith had worked for the Granite Construction Co. Ltd. for many years. She had started at the bottom, and after 30 years had become its chief engineer. The company had never had a formal pension plan, but it had always been known that the company would pay a pension to its employees on their retirement. Judith worked until she reached the age of 65, when she decided to retire. At the farewell party given for her on her last day at work, as well as receiving a gold watch from the company, Judith was told by Anne, the president and owner of the company, that she would be paid a pension equal to 60 per cent of her final year's salary for the rest of her life. The company paid the pension for four years until the company was sold to a large conglomerate. The new owners have refused to pay the pension and deny any liability to do so. Is Judith entitled to the pension?

2. Walter had had a life insurance policy with Styx Life Insurance Co. He paid the premiums for 10 years and then stopped. In accordance with the terms of the policy, the company advised Walter that the cash surrender value of the policy was being used to provide insurance until 1 December 2006. The letter went on to say, "This means that you are fully covered until that date for the full amount of the policy, $50,000." Walter did not reply to this letter. Walter died on 1 November 2006. His executor submitted the necessary papers to the company and claimed the face value of the policy. The company rechecked its records and found that there had been an error in the original calculation and that the policy should have lapsed on 1 October 2006. Walter's executor sues the company. What result?

Note: The American Approach to Reliance

It is interesting to consider the historical development in the United States of the discussion about the appropriate remedy when reliance is used as the basis for enforcement. When it was proposed in the 1930's during the drafting of the original American *Restatement on Contracts* that a remedy be given for reliance, the Reporter (or chief author), Williston, thought that a promise enforceable on the ground of reliance should be treated like any other promise.

Controversy centred on the following problem that was much debated by the drafters of the *Restatement*: Uncle promises to give his nephew, Johnny, $1,000. In reliance on the promise, Johnny buys a car for $500. How much should Johnny get if Uncle refuses to perform his promise? (One can ask how useful it is to use examples like this in drafting documents such as a *Restatement*.) This view was reflected in §90 of the *Restatement* (1932):

> A promise which the promisor should reasonably expect to induce action or forbear-
> ance of a definite and substantial character on the part of the promisee and which
> does induce such action of forbearance is binding if injustice can be avoided only by
> enforcement of the promise.

Many people objected that this result did not have to follow from the proposition that reliance should be protected. If Johnny was entitled to any protection, it should be only to the extent that he was out of pocket by his reliance. To meet these criticisms, §90 of *Second Restatement on Contracts* (1969) was changed to read:

> A promise which the promisor should reasonably expect to induce action or forbear-
> ance on the part of the promisee or a third person and which does induce such action
> or forbearance is binding if injustice can be avoided only by enforcement of the
> promise. The remedy granted for breach may be limited as justice requires.

Do you agree that the change should have been made? Is the measure of recovery assumed by the amended §90 ($500) still more than the extent of Johnny's reli-
ance, since Johnny has the car, and can sell it for cash? The next cases raise the question of whether the Anglo-Canadian courts have gone as far as the Americans in protecting reliance.

Reliance in the Non-commercial Context   *gift-like promises*

Although there are suggestions that a single theory of enforceability, the doctrine of consideration, can be applicable to all contracts, there are serious difficulties in making that theory work outside the commercial exchange.

Earlier in this chapter, there was a discussion of the use of the doctrine of con-
sideration to determine the enforceability of promises that were gifts in substance, illustrated in cases like *Thomas v. Thomas*. In some of these gift promise cases, the results seem somewhat arbitrary. The doctrine of consideration may not provide a good device for predicting what the courts will do. The next few cases return to the problems posed by gift promises, including an examination of the issue of whether reliance should be a basis for determining whether a promise should be enforceable.

Most of the cases in this section are similar to the earlier ones on gift-like promises. In the typical case a person promised to make a donation, but died be-
fore completing the gift. The promise is not contained in a deed under seal, nor is the gift made by will. The problems arise precisely because these two standard ways of making gift promises (*i.e.*, when the gift is not completed by delivery) have not been used, and the law of contracts is left as the last refuge of the disappointed donee.

In large part the existence of these readily available substitutes predisposes the courts to be hostile to the enforcement of gift promises. The courts are tempted to ask: "Why didn't the donor complete the gift by will if he really wanted to make it?" It is not only the common law that is hostile to gifts; equity is also hostile. A donee is termed a "volunteer", a person who has given no consideration for the promise made to him, and it is a well-accepted maxim that "equity will not assist a volunteer". There are significant problems in deciding whether to enforce a promise to make a gift, and the general hostility of both the common law and equity is a factor to be considered. In many cases this attitude is amply justified, and there is little scope for offering disappointed donees a contractual way to get what the donor never gave them.

There are two questions to keep in mind as you read the materials that follow: Should the donee get a remedy? If so, what remedy? Remember the problem of the *Restatement* concerning the uncle, Johnny and the car; that was a case of an incomplete gift.

SKIDMORE v. BRADFORD
(1869), L.R. 8 Eq. 134, 21 L.T.R. 291
(Chancery, Stuart V.-C.)

[The testator, Jacob Bradford, had arranged to buy a warehouse from Charles Johnson for £5,000, intending to make a gift of it to his nephew, Edward Bradford. When Jacob came to pay the deposit on the purchase price, he asked Johnson to amend the agreement by writing in his nephew's name, Edward Bradford, as purchaser. At this time Jacob said, "I've bought the warehouse for my nephew." Johnson changed the name on the agreement, and Jacob paid Johnson £1,000 as a deposit. Johnson made out the receipt in Edward Bradford's name. Edward subsequently signed the agreement to purchase. Jacob paid a further £500 on the purchase price, but died before paying any more. Johnson required Edward to pay the balance of the purchase price of the warehouse. The court was asked to determine whether Jacob's estate was liable to Edward for the balance of the purchase price which he had paid (£3,500).]

SIR JOHN STUART V.-C.: — [1] . . . If Edward Bradford were a mere volunteer there is no principle on which he would be entitled to come to this Court to have the testator's intended act of bounty completed, and the balance of the purchase-money paid out of the assets. But if on the faith of the testator's representation he has involved himself in any liability, or has incurred any obligation, he cannot be regarded as a volunteer, and if so, the testator's assets are liable to make good the representation on the faith of which the nephew has entered into this contract.

[2] . . . In this case it is beyond all doubt that the real contracting party was Jacob Bradford, the testator, and that in making the purchase his intention was to confer a benefit upon his nephew. The vendor knew all the circumstances of the purchase. It is beyond all doubt that when the contract was prepared the testator desired the contract to be altered so as to have the name of the nephew inserted in the contract, and in consequence of that alteration the nephew came under a legal obligation to pay the purchase-money. The case, therefore, is one in which the purchaser became liable to be sued, and incurred that liability on the faith of the representations of the testator that he would give him the warehouse which was the subject matter of the contract and would provide the purchase-money . . .

[3] I am therefore of opinion that the assets of the testator are liable to make good the obligation which has been incurred by Edward Bradford, and he is entitled to have the balance of the purchase-money paid out of the testator's estate.

1. What is the extent of the nephew's reliance in *Skidmore*? Is this case the same as that of Uncle and Johnny in the *Restatement* discussion and, if so, which of the alternative versions of the *Restatement* does the judgment adopt? Is the nephew any worse off for having relied on the uncle's promise, or is he actually better off, since the warehouse can be sold?

2. Mary and Eleanor were good friends. Mary inherited a large lake-front lot from her father. She invited Eleanor to share the lot and said that she would give her one-quarter of the lot. Both women then walked the lot and marked out the part that was to be Eleanor's. Eleanor said that the place was so beautiful that she planned to build a house there, which she did. The friendship has now ended and Eleanor, who never had any deed to the property, would like a conveyance to protect the investment she has made in the house. Can she get one?

3. As illustrated in the problem in the *Restatement* of Johnny and the car, it is much harder to measure the reliance interest that should be protected outside the commercial exchange. The "net" reliance interest can be considered the amount by which the donee is out-of-pocket by reason of his or her reliance, or perhaps it is only the net costs to the donee, if any. The courts, however, sometimes award the "gross reliance" and that is much harder to justify. The following case provides an illustration of some further problems.

DALHOUSIE COLLEGE v. BOUTILIER

[1934] S.C.R. 642, [1934] 3 D.L.R. 593
(S.C.C., Duff C.J.C., Rinfret, Cannon, Crocket and Hughes JJ.)

[In 1920, Arthur Boutilier agreed to give $5,000 to Dalhousie College. His promise was made in writing in the following form:

> For the purpose of enabling Dalhousie College to maintain and improve the efficiency of its teaching, to construct new buildings and otherwise to keep pace with the growing need of its constituency and in consideration of the subscription of others, I promise to pay to the Treasurer of Dalhousie College the sum of Five Thousand Dollars, payment as follows. . . .

In response to a request that he make the payment, Boutilier had written to the President of Dalhousie in April 1926:

> In reply I desire to advise you that I have kept my promise to you in mind. As you are probably aware, since making my promise I suffered some rather severe reverses, but I expect before too long to be able to redeem my pledge.

By the time that Boutilier died in 1928, he had not written a letter describing how payment would be made, and no payment had been made. The College brought an action against the estate for the amount of the promised gift.]

CROCKET J.: — [1] . . .The claim was contested in the Probate Court by the Estate on two grounds, *viz.*: that in the absence of any letter from the deceased as to terms of payment, the claimant could not recover; and that the claim was barred by the *Statute of Limitations*. Dr. A. Stanley MacKenzie, who had retired from the Presidency of the University after 20 years' service shortly before the trial, and others gave evidence before the Registrar of Probate. Basing himself apparently upon Dr. MacKenzie's statement that in consideration of the moneys subscribed in the campaign referred to, large sums of money were expended by the College on the objects mentioned in the subscription card between the years 1920 and 1931, the Registrar decided that there was a good consideration for the deceased's subscription . . . and that no supplementary letter was necessary to complete the agreement. He further held that the deceased's letter of April 12, 1926, constituted a sufficient acknowledgment to take the case out of the *Statute of Limitations*.

[An appeal to the County Court was dismissed, but the Supreme Court of Nova Scotia allowed a further appeal. The College appealed to the Supreme Court of Canada.]

[2]   There is, of course, no doubt that the deceased's subscription can be sustained as a binding promise only upon one basis, *viz.*: as a contract, supported by a good and sufficient consideration. The whole controversy between the parties is as to whether such a consideration is to be found, either in the subscription paper itself or in the circumstances as disclosed by the evidence. . . .

[3]   The doctrine of mutual promises was also put forward on the argument as a ground upon which the deceased's promise might be held to be binding. It was suggested that the statement in the subscription of the purpose for which it was made, *viz.*: "of enabling Dalhousie College to maintain and improve the efficiency of its teaching, to construct new buildings and otherwise to keep pace with the growing need of its constituency," constituted an implied request on the part of the deceased to apply the promised subscription to this object and that the acceptance by the College of his promise created a contract between them, the consideration for the promise of the deceased to pay the money being the promise of the College to apply it to the purpose stated.

[4]   I cannot think that any such construction can fairly be placed upon the subscription paper and its acceptance by the College . . .

[5]   Chisholm C.J., in the case at bar, said that . . . he felt impelled to follow the decisions in the English cases. I am of opinion that he was fully justified in so doing, rather than apply the principle contended for by the appellant in reliance upon the decision in *Sargent v. Nicholson* (1915), 25 D.L.R. 638, 9 W.W.R. 883 (Man. C.A.) based, as the latter case is, upon the decisions of United States courts, which are not only in conflict with the English cases, but with decisions of the Court of Appeals of the State of New York, as I have, I think, shewn, and which have been subjected to very strong criticism by American legal authors, notably by Prof. Williston, as the learned Chief Justice of Nova Scotia has shewn in his exhaustive and, to my mind, very convincing judgment.

[6]   To hold otherwise would be to hold that a naked, voluntary promise may be converted into a binding legal contract by the subsequent action of the promisee alone without the consent, express or implied, of the promisor. There is no evidence here which in any way involves the deceased in carrying out of the work for which the promised subscription was made other than the signing of the subscription paper itself.

[7]   I may add that, had I come to the opposite conclusion upon the legal question involved, I should have felt impelled, as Chisholm C.J. did, to seriously question the accuracy of the statement relied upon by the appellant that "this work was done and the increased expenditures were made on the strength of the subscriptions promised," if that statement was meant to refer to all the increased expenditures listed in the comparative statements produced by Dr. MacKenzie . . . The statement produced of expenditures on buildings, grounds and equipment since 1920 shows a grand total for the more than ten years of but $1,491,687 — over

$700,000 less than the aggregate of the 1920 campaign subscriptions — and this grand total includes over $400,000 for Shirriff Hall, which it is well known was the object of a special donation contributed by a wealthy lady, now deceased, as a memorial to her father. In the light of this it becomes quite as difficult to believe that the College Corporation, in doing "this work" and making "the increased expenditures" did so in reliance upon the deceased's subscription . . . This evidence would assuredly seem to shut out all possibility of establishing a claim against the deceased's estate on any such ground as estoppel. The appeal, I think, should be dismissed with costs.

NOTES AND QUESTIONS

1.   One problem in *Dalhousie v. Boutilier* is that the issue arises after the donor's death. One might sympathize with the College if Boutilier had died with a net estate of $1,000,000. Why shouldn't Mr. Boutilier keep the promise made to it? On a person's death the assets of his or her estate are collected by the executors (now called the estate trustees) (or the administrator if no executors have been appointed in the will). The debts of the deceased are then paid, and the balance is distributed in accordance with the will, or if there is an intestacy (*i.e.*, no valid will) pursuant to a statutory scheme that favours close relatives, particularly the deceased's spouse, and makes no provision for gifts to charities.

From the point of view of the surviving spouse, anything that goes to charity before her — it is still and was in 1934 the fact that the majority of surviving spouses are women — represents a serious threat to her future well-being. The man who thought to purchase salvation for his soul by making a large death-bed gift to the church, for example, was seeking his salvation at the cost of her survival and the law has, at least since medieval times, treated such gifts to charity with hostility.

For some time Canadian provinces have had legislation that allowed dependants of the deceased to take even though the property was given away by the will. This power is vested in the court by legislation like the *Succession Law Reform Act*, R.S.O. 1990, c. S.26, and the *Testators' Family Maintenance Act*, R.S.N.S. 1989, c. 465. If a gift was made by will to a charity and if the deceased's dependants were not adequately taken care of, the gift could be postponed to the claims of the dependants.

But notice what happens if the "gift" to the charity is enforceable as a contract. As an enforceable promise, it is a debt of the estate and is paid before the claims of the dependants can even be considered. Enforcing gift promises as contracts is fraught with danger for the family of the deceased and, to the extent that society has to meet the cost in welfare, is potentially costly to society.

As if these dangers were not enough, there is another problem. If a person dies insolvent, that is, if his or her estate is not large enough to meet in full all the claims of the creditors, there is nothing for the family. The claims of the creditors are treated like any other case on insolvency: secured creditors (like those with a mortgage secured against a piece of land) take their security, while the unsecured creditors then take a *pro rata* share of what is left. A creditor will usually have a claim that is in substance restitutionary; it will principally be a claim to recover a benefit conferred on the deceased in the form of money lent or goods or services provided.

At best, the claim of the prospective donee, whether it be that of the nephew Johnny or Dalhousie, can be no more than a reliance claim, and, as in the case of Dalhousie, will often have no reliance component at all. To allow a donee to claim as a creditor not only threatens the family, but is potentially unfair to the deceased's other creditors.

There is legislation that allows a creditor to challenge any "non-arm's length" transfer if the transfer was an attempt to defeat creditors. See, *e.g.*, the *Fraudulent Conveyances Act*, R.S.O. 1990, c. F.29. An executed gift to a charity (or to a spouse for that matter) may therefore have to be repaid to the estate for the benefit of creditors if it was made shortly before the debtor's death and the deceased was insolvent. Even if a donee has a claim under a sealed instrument, the donee would be a "volunteer", *i.e.*, a person who has paid nothing for the property he or she is claiming, and the transaction could be set aside for the benefit of creditors.

2. The question of the enforceability of promises to charities involves more far-reaching issues than the application of the doctrine of consideration. These issues are not resolved by deciding if there was or was not satisfaction of the technical requirements of the doctrine of consideration. The presence of a seal would make the promise binding against the estate. But no one maintains that a person cannot make a valid promise to make a gift. It is only that it is necessary to be cautious in jumping to the conclusion that a gift promise is exactly the same as one made in the context of a commercial exchange. *gift promise ≠ commercial exchange*

3. Notice what the drafter of the Dalhousie pledge said and how the deceased's undertaking was presented as part of a bargain. How would you re-draft the document? Would you sign a United Way pledge card that had a seal, testimonium and attestation clause?

4. In *Re Ross*, [1932] S.C.R. 57, [1931] 4 D.L.R. 689 the Supreme Court of Canada, on appeal from the Quebec Court of Appeal, enforced a promise to give over $100,000 to McGill University. When the action was brought the donor was insolvent and the effect of the judgment was to allow the University to claim as a creditor. Newcombe J., in giving judgment for the University, suggested in *obiter* that the result reached under the Quebec *Civil Code*, which would allow enforcement of a subscription to the University, was preferable to that which the common law would have reached. Do you agree?

    In *Ross* the Court in any event found consideration since there was an initial promise by the University to name a building after the donor's family in exchange for the substantial pledge. As a matter of fact, the building was not named after the donor. Could the donor's estate bring an action against the University for breach of its undertaking? *Hmm ---*

5. The *Public Subscriptions Act*, R.S.N.S. 1989, c. 378, is an attempt to deal with the problems of charitable subscriptions and provides:

    > 2. Where any subscription list is opened and any subscription is made in aid of the erection of any road, bridge, place of worship or school-house, in aid of any other undertaking of public utility or which is designated in the subscription list as, or appears therefrom to be, a public undertaking, and such undertaking is commenced, every person who has engaged by written subscription to contribute money, labour or other aid towards the undertaking, shall be held liable to perform such engagement, notwithstanding any apparent want of consideration in the agreement for the same.

    > 3(1) The following persons may require every person who has subscribed to perform his engagement:

    > (a) where a public grant is made in aid of such undertaking, the commissioner or other person appointed to expend such grant;

    > (b) where no public grant is made, the person to whom the performance or superintendence of such undertaking has been entrusted; and

    > (c) the person who has engaged in, and is then carrying on, such undertaking.

    > (2) If any subscriber, after a written notice of at least one month, refuses or neglects to perform his engagement, he may be sued by such commissioner or other person in this Section mentioned, or by the person to whom the subscription is payable.

    > (3) Nothing in this Section shall be construed to bind or make liable the executors or administrators of, or the estate of, any subscriber, unless it ex-

pressly appears from the instrument subscribed by him that he intended that his estate should be liable by binding his executors or administrators.

4. All moneys or other aid so subscribed and recovered shall be applied and expended for the purpose for which the same have been so subscribed, and for no other purpose whatever.

Would this legislation have made the promise of Mr. Boutilier enforceable? There is no comparable legislation in Ontario. Do you understand now why the legislature might not have wanted to make promises to make such gifts enforceable?

6.   In *Brantford General Hospital Foundation v. Marquis Estate* (2003), 67 O.R. (3d) 432 (S.C.J.) a hospital foundation was unsuccessful in suing the estate of a wealthy woman to enforce a pledge for the construction of a new wing of the hospital, even though its coronary care unit was to be named after her and her late husband. A wealthy doctor bequeathed the hospital almost $3 million in his will. His widow later signed a pledge form to contribute another $1 million over five years. At the time she made the pledge, the hospital asked her permission to name its coronary care unit after the couple, to which she agreed. She honoured the first year's commitment, but died with $800,000 outstanding on the pledge. The hospital foundation sued her estate to enforce the pledge, first claiming that naming the unit after the couple was consideration. Justice Milanetti rejected this argument (at p. 437):

> ... the idea that the unit was to be named [after the couple] came from the hospital. ...This court finds that this was very clearly irrelevant to her in her decision to make the commitment. Further, it is clear that there was no mention whatsoever of the naming promise in the pledge document itself. Given that this is a document that the foundation seeks to use as evidence of the contractual pledge, it should have reflected such an important aspect of the bargain, and this is particularly so given that a professional fundraising firm had been engaged and likely prepared the documentation.

The Court also rejected an argument based on estoppel, finding that there was no reliance on the promise, and concluding that estoppel could not be used to enforce a donative promise (at pp. 439-440):

> ... the doctrine of estoppel can only succeed if there is a pre-existing legal relationship between the parties ... the court reiterates that no such legal or contractual relationship existed between the hospital foundation and [the deceased]. ... Whether categorized as a sword or a shield, the doctrine of estoppel is not sustainable in this case. Based upon the foregoing, this action is hereby dismissed.

Justice Milanetti commented on the difference between Canadian and American law in this area (at p. 439):

> What is clear to this court is that we have an incredibly generous individual, who out of devotion to this institution, makes a large gift to it. There is no doubt in this court's mind that Mrs. Marquis, indeed, intended to provide the foundation with this $1 million gift at the time of the pledge ... but, unfortunately, this court is unable to enforce her intentions in the absence of an enforceable binding contract. While the court would like to abide by the apparent wishes of the deceased, based on the Canadian law as currently framed, it feels it cannot enforce this agreement. It is abundantly clear that the American courts have taken a considerably different approach to subscriptions of this nature but the Canadian courts have chosen to follow the English lead in this regard and require that consideration, however slight, be proven. With that to guide me, it would appear that based on the evidentiary situation, the plaintiffs' case must fail.

Which do think is preferable, the Canadian approach or the American approach? If you represented the hospital when the pledge was being negotiated, what steps, if any, would you take to make the subscription enforceable?

INTENTION TO CREATE LEGAL RELATIONS

It is often stated that there must be an "intention to create legal relations" before an enforceable contract can exist. Such a rule is said to be as fundamental as the rule regarding the requirement of consideration. It is only sensible that there should be concern that the enforcement of a promise not catch the promisor by surprise. And in so far as the rule requiring "contractual intention" achieves this goal, it is perfectly justifiable.

In an ordinary commercial situation of parties making a contract — exchanging promises — there is a strong presumption that they intend to create a legally enforceable relation. That is, it is implicitly understood that if one party defaults, the other will be able to seek redress through the court system. The courts will regard parties as having this intention even though they frequently will not have actually considered what their position would be if there were to be a breach. Parties to a contract often do not actively contemplate what their legal position will be if there is a breach, as they are only considering performance. However, in most contractual situations, if they did consider the question, they would reasonably expect that in the event of breach or contractual dispute they would have recourse to the legal system.

There are, however, some situations in which courts may hold that a promise is not enforceable because there was "a lack of intent to create a legally enforceable relation". Problems with this issue most commonly arise:

(1) in regard to promises made between family members or in a social setting;

(2) when contracts are made in a commercial context and there is some indication that they are not intended to be legally binding; and

(3) when promises are made by a government.

It is very common for family members to make promises to one another. The courts will generally presume that members of a family did not reasonably expect to have recourse to the courts if their promises to one another were not honoured. This, however, is only a presumption, which may be rebutted. *family contract prot*

One of the leading cases in this area, *Balfour v. Balfour*, [1919] 2 K.B. 571 (C.A.), arose out of an action by a woman on a promise by her husband to support her while he was overseas. By the time that the woman commenced her action to enforce the man's earlier promise, the parties were in the middle of divorce proceedings and the woman had an order for alimony to provide her with future financial support. The contract action by the woman on the earlier promise was an attempt to get two years' arrears: the divorce court would be unlikely to have awarded her arrears of support in proceedings for alimony.

The English Court of Appeal rejected her claim. In the course of his judgment, Atkin L.J. talked about the promises between husband and wife as generally being outside the realm of the law:

> The consideration that really obtains for [these promises] is that natural love and affection which counts for so little in these cold Courts. The terms may be repudiated, varied or renewed as performance proceeds or as disagreements develop, and the principles of the common law as to exoneration and discharge and accord and satis-

faction are such as find no place in the domestic code . . . In respect of these promises each house is a domain into which the King's writ does not seek to run, and to which his officers do not seek to be admitted.

It can be argued that decisions like *Balfour*, which held that promises by one spouse to another were presumed to be unenforceable, typically worked to the disadvantage of women. In some situations a deserted wife like Mrs. Balfour might have had a statutory right to seek alimony, at least on a prospective basis, and would not have had to rely on a promise for support. However, alimony was not always available, as even a single act of adultery on a wife's part might preclude her from seeking alimony, despite the fact that her husband had already committed adultery or deserted her. So a woman's inability to rely on an agreement could work to her detriment.

The judicial attitude, expressed in the statement that the "King's writ does not seek to run" in a man's house, may also have reflected or contributed to a tolerance towards spousal abuse by the police and courts. In recent years, the legal system has become more responsive to the problem of domestic violence.

Despite the discriminatory history of the rules about family contracts, it makes some sense to presume that when members of an intact family unit make promises to one another, for example, about planned future expenditures, these will not be legally enforceable. Indeed, there are very few cases where spouses in an intact family unit have tried to seek redress in the courts.

Although spouses may be presumed not to have intended to create a legally enforceable relation in situations where there is an informal exchange of promises, when they sign formal documents, like a mortgage, this presumption may be rebutted.

Canadian law now recognizes, and even encourages, spouses to enter into written marriage contracts, and for unmarried partners, cohabitation agreements. These are legally enforceable contracts, usually negotiated and drafted with legal advice. While in popular myth these agreements could deal with such domestic matters as who will be responsible for household chores, in reality, the focus of these contracts is on the rights and responsibilities that the parties will have on termination of the relation — whether by death or separation. In particular, marriage contracts and cohabitation agreements establish respective property rights that will exist on termination of the relation, and are intended to avoid litigation that might arise in the context of termination of such personal relations. Clauses of a domestic contract that deal with any children who might be born to the parties are subject to judicial scrutiny to ensure that the interests of children are not prejudiced.

While marriage contracts and cohabitation agreements are increasingly common, most couples are still reluctant to enter into them. Indeed, most family lawyers have stories about individuals who planned to marry but broke off the engagement when they were unable to agree on the terms of a marriage contract. See Lorne Wolfson, *The New Family Law* (Toronto: Random House, 1987), pp. 47-50. As an aside, you might consider whether the law of contracts is operating as it should if the parties, having faced the need to specify the terms to govern their relation, decide not to proceed.

If spouses separate without having had a domestic contract, they are faced with a range of legal issues that must be resolved. While these can be resolved by a judge, it is most common for parties to negotiate a separation agreement to settle all potential causes of action between them. Family lawyers devote a considerable portion of their practice to the negotiation of separation agreements. These agreements are often negotiated against the backdrop of pending litigation, with the threat of an expensive and embittering trial if settlement is not reached. In the end, few separated spouses have a full court hearing. More common is the resolution of disputes through negotiation or mediation, with the terms set out in a separation agreement — a document that may be enforced as a contract.

The presumption against the legal enforceability of promises between members of intact families applies not only between spouses, but also between parents and children. As the next case illustrates, when there is significant reliance there is a strong pressure to enforce a promise in this situation as well.

JONES v. PADAVATTON

[1969] 2 All E.R. 616, [1969] 1 W.L.R. 328
(C.A., Danckwerts, Salmon and Fenton Atkinson L.JJ.)

[The plaintiff was the mother of the defendant. The parties came from Trinidad. The daughter lived in Washington, D.C. with her son, Tommy. She had a job at the Indian Embassy. The mother was very anxious for her daughter to get called to the English bar. She told her daughter that she would support her while she studied for the bar at the rate of $200 per month. The mother's solicitor in Trinidad, acting as the mother's agent, paid the daughter's fees to study for the bar at Lincoln's Inn and wrote the daughter a letter informing her of this and stating that the mother would give her $200 per month to support herself and her son while she pursued her legal studies. In 1962 the daughter went to England to study for the bar. In 1964 the arrangement was changed. The mother bought a house in England; rather than paying the daughter the allowance of $200 per month, the mother allowed the daughter to live in the house, and to receive the rental income from the portion of the house which was rented out. By 1967 the daughter had not made good progress in her studies; in five years she had passed exams that were normally completed in three years. In that year the mother came to England and tried to recover possession of the house that the daughter was living in. She eventually commenced proceedings to recover possession. The trial judge dismissed the mother's claim for possession, and, on the daughter's counter-claim, awarded her the value of repairs to the house made by her. The mother appealed.]

DANCKWERTS L.J.: — [1] . . . Before us a great deal of time was spent on discussions as to what were the terms of the arrangements between the parties, and it seemed to me that the further the discussions went, the more obscure and uncertain the terms alleged became. The acceptable duration of the daughter's studies was not finally settled, I think. There was a lack of evidence on the matter, and the members of the court were induced to supply suggestions based on their personal knowledge. At any rate, two questions emerged for argument: (i) Were the arrangements (such as they were) intended to produce legally binding agreements, or were they simply family arrangements depending for their fulfilment on good faith and trust, and not legally enforceable by legal proceedings? (ii) Were the arrangements made so obscure and uncertain that, though intended to be legally binding, a court could not enforce them?

[2] Counsel for the daughter argued strenuously for the view that the parties intended to create legally binding contracts . . . Counsel for the mother argued for the contrary view that there were no binding obligations, and that if there were they were too uncertain for the court to enforce. His stand-by was *Balfour v. Bal-*

four . . . Of course, there is no difficulty, if they so intend, in members of families entering into legally binding contracts in regard to family affairs. A competent equity draftsman would, if properly instructed, have no difficulty in drafting such a contract. But there is possibly in family affairs a presumption against such an intention (which, of course, can be rebutted). I would refer to Atkin L.J.'s magnificent exposition in regard to such arrangements in *Balfour v. Balfour.*

[3]   There is no doubt that this case is a most difficult one, but I have reached a conclusion that the present case is one of those family arrangements which depend on the good faith of the promises which are made and are not intended to be rigid, binding agreements. *Balfour v. Balfour* was a case of husband and wife, but there is no doubt that the same principles apply to dealings between other relations, such as father and son and daughter and mother. This, indeed, seems to me a compelling case. The mother and the daughter seem to have been on very good terms before 1967. The mother was arranging for a career for the daughter which she hoped would lead to success. This involved a visit to England in conditions which could not be wholly foreseen. What was required was an arrangement which was to be financed by the mother and was such as would be adaptable to circumstances, as it in fact was. The operation about the house was, in my view, not a completely fresh arrangement, but an adaptation of the mother's financial assistance to the daughter due to the situation which was found to exist in England. It was not a stiff contractual operation any more than the original arrangement.

[4]   In the result, of course, on this view, the daughter cannot resist the mother's rights as the owner of the house to the possession of which the mother is entitled. What the position is as regards the counterclaim is another matter. It may be, at least in honesty, that the daughter should be re-imbursed for the expenditure which she had incurred. In my opinion, therefore, the appeal should be allowed.

SALMON L.J.: *minority* — [5] I agree with the conclusion at which Danckwerts L.J., has arrived, but I have reached it by a different route. The first point to be decided is whether or not there was ever a legally binding agreement between the mother and the daughter in relation to the daughter's reading for the Bar in England. The daughter alleges that there was such an agreement, and the mother denies it. She says that there was nothing but a loose family arrangement which had no legal effect. The onus is clearly on the daughter. There is no dispute that the parties entered into some sort of arrangement. It really depends on: (a) whether the parties intended it to be legally binding; and (b) if so, whether it was sufficiently certain to be enforceable.

[handwritten margin note: Was there a binding contract?]

[6]   Did the parties intend the arrangement to be legally binding? This question has to be solved by applying what is sometimes (although perhaps unfortunately) called an objective test. The court has to consider what the parties said and wrote in the light of all the surrounding circumstances, and then decide whether the true inference is that the ordinary man and woman, speaking or writing thus in such circumstances, would have intended to create a legally binding agreement.

[7]   Counsel for the mother has said, quite rightly, that as a rule when arrangements are made between close relations, for example, between husband and wife, parent and child or uncle and nephew in relation to an allowance, there is a presumption against an intention of creating any legal relationship.

This is not a presumption of law, but of fact. It derives from experience of life and human nature which shows that in such circumstances men and women usually do not intend to create legal rights and obligations, but intend to rely solely on family ties of mutual trust and affection. This has all been explained by Atkin L.J., in his celebrated judgment in *Balfour v. Balfour*. There may, however, be circumstances in which this presumption, like all other presumptions of fact, can be rebutted. . . .

[SALMON L.J. reviewed the facts found by the trial judge. The trial judge had found that the mother's promise of support induced the daughter, then 34, to leave the excellent job that she had and to embark on a course that would, the mother hoped, lead to the daughter coming to work and live in Trinidad. He noted that the mother's solicitor confirmed the arrangements for the payment of support. SALMON L.J. continued:]

[8] In the very special circumstances of this case, I consider that the true inference must be that neither the mother nor the daughter could have intended that the daughter should have no legal right to receive, and the mother no legal obligation to pay, the allowance of $200 a month.

[9] The point was made by counsel for the mother that the parties cannot have had a contractual intention since it would be unthinkable for the daughter to be able to sue the mother if the mother fell on hard times. I am afraid that I am not impressed by this point. The evidence which the learned county court judge accepted showed that the mother was a woman of some substance, and prior to the agreement had assured the daughter that there would be no difficulty in finding the money. The fact that, if contrary to everyone's expectation the mother had lost her money, the daughter would have been unlikely to sue her throws no light on whether the parties had an intention to contract. The fact that a contracting party is in some circumstances unlikely to extract his pound of flesh does not mean that he has no right to it. Even today sometimes people forbear from mercy to enforce their undoubted legal rights.

[10] The next point made by counsel for the mother was that the arrangements between the mother and the daughter in 1962 were too uncertain to constitute a binding contract. . . . For two years from November 1962 until December 1964 the mother regularly paid her daughter £42, the equivalent of $ (West Indian) 200, a month, and the daughter accepted this sum without demur. Then it is said on the mother's behalf that the daughter's obligations are not sufficiently stated. I think that they are plain, to leave Washington, with all that entailed, come to London and genuinely study for the Bar there. If the daughter threw up her studies for the Bar, maybe the mother could not have recovered damages, but she would have been relieved of any obligation to continue the allowance.

[11] Then again it is said that the duration of the agreement was not specified. No doubt, but I see no difficulty in implying the usual term that it was to last for a reasonable time. The parties cannot have contemplated that the daughter should go on studying for the Bar and draw the allowance until she was seventy, nor on the other hand that the mother could have discontinued the allowance if the daughter did not pass her examinations within, say, 18 months. The promise was to pay the allowance until the daughter's studies were completed, and to my mind there was a clear implication that they were to be completed within a reasonable time. Studies are completed either by the student being called to the Bar or giving up the unequal struggle against the examiners. It may not be easy to decide, especially when there is such a paucity of evidence, what is a reasonable time. The daughter, however, was a well-educated intelligent woman capable of earning the equivalent of over £2,000 a year in Washington. It is true that she had a young son to look after, and may well (as the learned judge thought) have been hampered to some extent by the worry of this litigation. But, making all allowance for these factors and any other distraction, I cannot think that a reasonable time could possibly exceed five years from November 1962, the date when she began her studies.

[12]   It follows, therefore, that on no view can she now in November 1968 be entitled to anything further under the contract which the learned county court judge, rightly I think, held that she made with the mother in 1962. She has some of Part 1 of the Bar examination still to pass, and necessarily the final has not yet even been attempted. . . .

[**FENTON ATKINSON L.J.** wrote a judgment concurring with **DANCKWERTS L.J.** that the contract was unenforceable as there was no intent to enter a legally binding contract.]

QUESTIONS

1.   Suppose that one year after the daughter had come to England, the mother refused to pay any more. What would have happened:

    (a)   under the approach of Danckwerts L.J.?

    (b)   under the approach of Salmon L.J.?

    Which result is preferable?
        Most academic commentators consider the approach of Salmon L.J. preferable, with its protection of the daughter's reasonable reliance: see, *e.g.*, S.M. Waddams, *The Law of Contracts*, 5th ed. (Aurora, Ont.: Canada Law Book, 2005), ¶151.

2.   The trial judge in *Jones v. Padavatton* considered that the case was "entirely different from the ordinary case of a mother promising her daughter an allowance whilst the daughter read for the Bar, or a father promising his son an allowance at university if the son passed the necessary examinations to gain admission". The trial judge assumed that such promises are clearly unenforceable. Do you agree?

3.   *Jones v. Padavatton* illustrates that a rule like that in *Balfour v. Balfour* cannot be applied to all cases of agreements between family members. The rule should be seen as expressing the proper concern that any decision to enforce a promise between those who are in a close relation should be clearly justifiable in the sense that it meet some test of deliberateness on the part of the promisor, and that its enforcement not catch the promisor by surprise. Would evidence that there was reasonable and expected reliance on the promise meet this concern?

———————————

Although in most commercial situations there is no doubt of the parties' intention to create a legally enforceable relation, there are important commercial situations in which there is an express statement indicating that an agreement, or a part of an agreement, is not intended to be enforceable.

In *Rose & Frank Co. v. J.R. Crompton & Bros. Ltd.*, [1925] A.C. 445, [1924] All E.R. Rep. 245 (H.L.), a contract for the sale of goods provided that the agreement was intended to be "binding in honour only". The seller failed to deliver and the buyer sued for breach. The court held that the buyer could not recover damages on this contract. If the seller delivered and the buyer accepted the goods, there would, however, be an obligation to pay for the goods, at least on a *quantum meruit* basis, which presumptively would be the contract rate.

It is important to be clear about the effect of a clause like that in *Rose & Frank Co. v. J.R. Crompton*. In drafting an agreement with such a provision, the parties expressly addressed their minds to the way in which, or the extent to which, they wanted their agreement enforced. The only question before the court was whether or not their agreement should be enforced. That issue is whether one party should be able to say: "Though we have agreed to do certain things for you, you agree that if we do not do them, you will not sue us for breach." Although such an agreement has the potential for abuse, there are often commercial pressures to perform.

For a long time courts expressed hostility to contractual provisions which referred disputes to arbitration. The attitude at times bordered on the petulant: "Why don't you want us to decide your disputes for you?" When courts (and governments) came under severe pressure some years ago to deal with the huge backlog of cases waiting to be heard, they realized that arbitration, by getting the dispute out of the judicial system and into a forum (paid for by the parties), offered a good solution. Courts will now enforce arbitration clauses in almost all cases, sometimes even when the issue is whether or not the contract containing such a clause is valid.

A "letter of comfort" is a form of undertaking that is deliberately designed not to create enforceable obligations, but is intended to provide some "comfort" that something will be done. Such letters, for example, may be given by a parent corporation to a lender to one of the parent's subsidiary corporations.

When a loan is made to a subsidiary corporation, the lender can demand that the parent corporation guarantee the debts of the subsidiary, and if the parent corporation does so, it will be liable to the lender on the subsidiary's default. The lender may, however, be content to have something less than a full guarantee. The lender may be satisfied with a "letter of comfort" because the risk is thought to be good or because it can charge a higher rate of interest on the loan. Such a letter will typically set out the undertaking of the parent to run the subsidiary so that the lender's position is not jeopardized, or to run the subsidiary with due regard for the lender's rights. The lender in this situation will have willingly accepted "comfort" from the parent corporation rather than the protection of a guarantee. A person who receives a "comfort letter" may hope and expect that the obligation will be honoured, but the difference between a letter of comfort and a guarantee is that the letter of comfort generally does not give the lender any effective right to sue the maker for the loss the lender has suffered from the borrower's insolvency. There may, of course, be commercial consequences in terms of future borrowing by the parent corporation or other subsidiaries if the loan is not repaid.

Commercial lenders are, like the Canadian banks, large corporations with ample access to competent lawyers. These lenders know exactly what to do to obtain a binding guarantee from the parent corporation of a corporate borrower. A parent corporation would usually prefer not to give a guarantee and the negotiations between the parties are likely to centre on the degree of protection with which the lender will be satisfied. The next case illustrates how the parties may bargain over a comfort letter.

TORONTO-DOMINION BANK v. LEIGH INSTRUMENTS LTD. (TRUSTEE OF)

[1999] O.J. No. 3290, 45 O.R. (3d) 417, 178 D.L.R. (4th) 634
(C.A., Doherty, Austin and Sharpe JJ.A.)

BY THE COURT: — **[1]** This is an appeal from the judgment of Winkler J. dismissing all of the appellant's claims. Those claims were based on five letters of comfort provided to the appellant (the Bank) by the Plessey Company plc (Plessey) in connection with a series of loans made at the time of and following Plessey's takeover of Leigh Instruments Limited (Leigh). The respondent, General Electric Company plc (GEC) was in effective control of Plessey when the fifth letter of comfort was provided (December 19, 1989) and the claims against it arise out of that letter.

[2]   The court dismissed the appeal at the conclusion of oral argument with reasons to follow. These are the reasons.

[3]   Justice Winkler's reasons are reported at (1999), 40 B.L.R. (2d) 1. His detailed and careful review of the evidence and analysis of the issues have proved most helpful on the hearing of this appeal. The factual background necessary to an understanding of these reasons can be found in the reasons of Winkler J.

[4]   The trial took over a year. The wide-ranging attack launched by the Bank at trial has been replaced on appeal by a focused challenge to the trial judge's finding that the appellant had failed to establish negligent misrepresentation by Plessey in respect of any of the five letters of comfort or by GEC in respect of the fifth letter of comfort.

The Main Appeal

[5]   Mr. Finlay, with his usual consummate skill, advanced five grounds of appeal on behalf of the Bank. Four require him to convince us that the trial judge erred in his interpretation of the meaning of para. 3 of the letters of comfort provided by Plessey. Paragraph 3 reads:

> It is our policy that our wholly owned subsidiaries, including Leigh Instruments Limited, be managed in such a way as to be always in a position to meet their financial obligations including repayment of all amounts due under the above facility.

[6]   "The above facility" refers to the line of credit made available by the Bank to Leigh. That amount varied and reached $45 million when the fifth comfort letter was provided by Plessey in December 1989.

[7]   Throughout his submissions, Mr. Finlay stressed the differences between the contract claim advanced by the Bank and the tort claim in so far as they related to para. 3 of the comfort letters. He did not take issue with the trial judge's analysis of the contract claim, but submitted that the trial judge erroneously applied the same analysis when interpreting para. 3 for the purposes of the negligent misrepresentation claim.

[8]   No doubt there are important differences between the two claims; however, the task of determining the meaning to be given to the words in para. 3 was common to both. Before considering the legal effect of those words, the trial judge had to determine what they meant. The same words in the same document cannot have one meaning in the context of a contract claim and a different meaning in the context of a tort claim. Once the meaning of the words is fixed, the legal effect of those words must be considered. It is at this stage of the interpretative process that distinctions between contract and tort claims can become important.

[9] The process of determining the meaning to be given to words in a document is governed by the same principles regardless of whether the process is engaged in the context of a contract claim or a tort claim. Those principles are identified by the trial judge at pp. 105-11 and were recently reviewed by the Supreme Court of Canada in *Eli Lilly and Co. v. Novopharm Ltd.*, [1998] 2 S.C.R. 129 at 166-67, 161 D.L.R. (4th) 1. Essentially, the process is captured in the following question:

> Bearing in mind the relevant background, the purpose of the document, and considering the entirety of the document, what would the parties to the document reasonably have understood the contested words to mean?

[10] The Bank contends, and the respondents agree, that para. 3 contained a representation by Plessey to the Bank as to its policy with respect to the business affairs of Leigh. It is also common ground that the representation was a continuing one. The dispute centres on what the policy was represented to be. The Bank reads para. 3 as a representation by Plessey that it would manage Leigh's affairs in such a way that Leigh would always be in a position to meet its obligations to the Bank. The Bank contends that it was entitled to rely on this representation as to Plessey's policy unless and until given notice of a change in that policy.

[11] The respondents, emphasizing the words "be managed" in para. 3, submit that the paragraph was not a representation that Plessey would manage the affairs of Leigh, but rather a representation that it was Plessey's policy that its subsidiaries, including Leigh, should manage their own affairs in such a way as to be able to meet their financial obligations. The respondents rely not only on the language of para. 3, but on basic corporate law principles which they submit fixed the responsibility of management with the properly appointed officers of Leigh even though ultimate control of the company rested with the sole shareholder, Plessey.

[12] Winkler J. accepted the respondents' interpretation of para. 3. In reaching that conclusion, he emphasized the language of para. 3 considered in the context of the entire letter (pp. 111-16). He further held that his conclusion as to the meaning of the words in para. 3 was fortified by a consideration of the relevant background facts (pp. 116-18).

[13] Winkler J. construed para. 3 in the course of his consideration of the contract claim and applied that construction to both the contract claim and the tort claim. For the reasons set out above, we think this was a proper approach.

[14] There is some uncertainty as to the standard of review to be applied when addressing the appellant's submission that the trial judge misconstrued para. 3 of the comfort letters. We will assume that no deference is due to the trial judge's conclusion and that a correctness standard of review should be applied.

[15] After giving careful consideration to Mr. Finlay's submissions, we come to the same conclusion as the trial judge. We agree with the trial judge's observation, at p. 118, that the appellant's interpretation is inconsistent with the words "be managed" and would require that additional words be inserted in para. 3. The parties chose not to insert any such language. The phrase "be managed" does not suggest that Plessey itself would manage the affairs of Leigh.

[16] Whatever doubt might exist if only the words of para. 3 are considered is dispelled by a consideration of the relevant factual background. The Bank and Plessey were sophisticated commercial entities. Both were familiar with letters of comfort. The Bank knew full well that the letter of comfort was not security in the traditional sense and that its commercial value depended very much on the relationship which existed between the lender and the provider of the letter of comfort. The Bank was very anxious to establish an ongoing relationship with Plessey, a very large multinational corporation. It was well known that Plessey would not provide any guarantee on loans made to Leigh by the Bank. The letter was crafted to avoid any suggestion that Plessey had any legal responsibility for the loans. The interpretation of parag. 3 now advanced by the Bank would effectively put Plessey in the position of a guarantor subject to Plessey's ability, on notice to the Bank, to change its "policy". The interpretation urged by the Bank would give it almost exactly the security which it knew full well was not available to it when it chose to proceed with the loan in the hopes of doing more business with Plessey and its many subsidiaries.

[17] It was argued before Winkler J. and here that the respondents' interpretation of para. 3 meant that it amounted to no more than a "motherhood" statement having no real commercial purpose or value to the Bank. The trial judge, at pp. 116-18, considered and rejected this argument. He observed that other paragraphs in the letters contained valuable representations and undertakings by Plessey and that the third paragraph gave the Bank a basis, *albeit* not a legal one, upon which to request that Plessey stand behind the commercial activities of Leigh and honour Leigh's debts. That request, while not based on any legal obligation, had substance and value in the commercial world revealed by the extensive evidence heard by the trial judge.

[18] The trial judge, drawing on the language used by the English Court of Appeal in *Kleinwort Benson Ltd. v. Malaysia Mining*, [1989] 1 All E.R. 785, referred to para. 3 of the letter as imposing a "moral obligation" on Plessey or as constituting a "gentleman's agreement" between the Bank and Plessey. We prefer the description of the commercial value of comfort letters in general and this one in particular provided in the factum of the respondent GEC. Counsel wrote:

> In this marketplace, both parties have experience in situations where a parent, for reasons it deems appropriate, refuses to give a legally binding assurance and a bank, for reasons it similarly considers appropriate, agrees to accept something less, perhaps believing that when, and if, "push comes to shove", the parent would pay for any or all of the "non-legal" commercial considerations of reputation, fear of adverse publicity, higher future borrowing costs and a myriad other reasons and possibilities depending on the circumstances.

[19] The interpretation given to para. 3 by the trial judge did not render the letters of comfort valueless and it cannot be said that his interpretation yields a commercial absurdity. The Bank's primary submission must be rejected. The trial judge correctly construed para. 3 of the letters of comfort.

[20] The second ground of appeal assumes that the Bank's interpretation of para. 3 of the comfort letters is correct and goes on to contend that as Plessey had no such policy, para. 3 contained a misrepresentation. Obviously, the accuracy of the representation in para. 3 must be considered in the light of the meaning given to that paragraph by Winkler J. and affirmed by this court. The trial judge considered whether Plessey had a policy as he had found it described in para. 3. After an extensive review of the evidence (pp. 124-36), he concluded that Plessey had such a policy and that it remained in operation throughout the relevant time. This finding is clearly one of fact to which deference is due. There was ample evidence to support the finding.

[21] The Bank's third submission relates only to the fifth letter of comfort. The trial judge found that the fifth letter, like the first four, did not contain a material misrepresentation. He further held, at p. 146, that in the circumstances existing when the fifth letter was provided, the Bank could not reasonably have relied on any representation in the letter. In coming to that conclusion, the trial judge placed considerable emphasis on the concluding language of the fifth letter. In that letter Plessey indicated that the letter "does not constitute a legally binding commitment". That language did not appear in the earlier letters.

[22] As we are satisfied that the fifth letter contained no misrepresentation, it is not necessary to address the reliance argument. We will do so for the sake of completeness. The trial judge was entitled on all of the evidence to come to the conclusion that he did. His finding was reached not only on the basis of the closing language in the letter, but on all of the circumstances existing as of December 1989 when the fifth letter was provided. By that date, Plessey had been the subject of a hostile takeover and was controlled by commercial entities, one of which was the respondent, GEC, which had no ongoing working relationship with the Bank and no apparent need to look to the Bank for financing in the future. The commercial considerations which may have prompted Plessey to respond favourably to the Bank's request that Plessey honour these debts were not operative after Plessey itself was acquired by GEC and another corporate entity.

[23] The fourth submission made by the Bank is directed at GEC. The Bank seeks to hold GEC jointly liable with Plessey, the author of the letter, for negligent misrepresentation. This ground of appeal must fail as we are satisfied that the fifth letter did not contain any misrepresentation, and in any event any representation in that letter could not reasonably be relied on by the Bank.

[24] The Bank's fifth submission is somewhat different. For the purpose of this submission, the Bank accepts the interpretation of para. 3 given by the trial judge and adopted by this court. Counsel submits that even on that interpretation, the representation became untrue or at least misleading by January or February 1990 when Plessey realized that Leigh's continued fiscal viability was uncertain. Counsel submits that the continuing nature of the representation in para. 3 of the letters required Plessey to put the Bank on notice when it became clear to Plessey that Leigh might not be able to manage itself so as to meet its obligations to the Bank. If this submission is accepted, the Bank is entitled to recover the advances made to Leigh after Plessey knew that Leigh's prospects were not good.

[25] We cannot accept this submission. There is nothing inconsistent with the continued existence of a policy that Leigh should manage its affairs so as to be able to meet its financial obligations and the existence of circumstances which imperiled Leigh's ability to conduct its affairs in accordance with that policy. The policy may remain extant even if circumstances make compliance difficult or doubtful.

[26] The trial judge conducted an extensive review of the evidence surrounding Leigh's slide into insolvency in late 1989 and early 1990. He reviewed the extensive efforts made by Plessey and its owners to salvage Leigh's business. He

concluded, at p. 142, that the policy referred to in para. 3 of the letters remained in place throughout the material period of time right up until immediately before the bankruptcy of Leigh. We see no basis for interfering with that finding.

[27] There is a second reason why this submission must fail. It is premised on the representations made in the fifth letter of comfort. As indicated above, we agree with the trial judge's conclusion that the Bank could not reasonably rely on any representation in that letter. Consequently, even if we accepted the Bank's argument that the representations in para. 3 became misleading some time in January or February 1990, the Bank could still not establish the requisite reliance on the representations.

[28] We affirm the order of Winkler J. dismissing the Bank's action.

[The Court of Appeal also dismissed the bank's appeal against the order of the trial judge that the bank pay the defendant's solicitor and client costs. This amount would have been very large as the trial took over a year.]

NOTES AND QUESTIONS

1. Letters of comfort are used in many circumstances. The law firm that represents a corporation will be asked to give a "letter of comfort" to the corporation's auditor when the auditor is preparing the corporation's annual financial statements disclosing the existence of and making an assessment of the chances of liability or success in litigation against or by the corporation. The terms of this letter, the addressee and what must be disclosed are governed by a Joint Policy Statement of the Canadian Institute of Chartered Accountants and the Canadian Bar Association. The information from the law firm may be referred to in a note to the financial statements.

    In one situation a corporation had sued for over $100,000,000 from a customer under a "take or pay" contract for the supply of oil for electricity generation. The amount of this claim had been shown as an account receivable in the corporation's balance sheet for the previous year. The corporation's action for this amount was dismissed (and judgment given against the corporation for $20,000,000 on a counterclaim). The corporation was contemplating a large initial public offering of its shares and it was important that its balance sheet present as favourable a picture as possible. The auditor was able to leave the amount of the $100,000,000 claim as a receivable and not show the amount of the judgment on the counterclaim as a liability on the strength of a comfort letter from the law firm. In a note to the financial statement the auditors said, "We have been advised by management and counsel that an appeal from the trial judgment . . . *will be successful*." [Emphasis added.]

    What do you think that the law firm must have said for the auditor to be able to make this statement? If you were counsel to the auditing firm, what would you require the law firm to say? Should the corporation or a shareholder have an action against the law firm if this statement turned out to be an inaccurate forecast of what the Court of Appeal might do?

2. There are commercial situations in which parties choose to "opt out" of having legal regulation of their relation.

    It is not uncommon for parties to agree that any dispute arising out of their contractual relation will be resolved by an arbitrator rather than a judge. The arbitration process is relatively informal and expeditious in comparison with the judicial process. Commonly, the parties will have legal representation in the arbitration process, though this is not essential. The arbitrator, however, will generally apply the same legal principles as apply in court, and the decision of the arbitrator may be subject to some form of review or appeal by the courts. Further, unless reversed on appeal, the decision of an arbitrator can generally be registered with the courts and is as fully enforceable as a judgment of the courts.

3. There are some sophisticated commercial relations in which the parties agree that any disputes that arise will be resolved by arbitration, that the arbitrator will apply a special body of law relevant to that particular trade and that the decision is not legally enforceable. An example of this arises in the American cotton industry. The merchants and mills in this industry are relatively small in number and all belong to one of two trade associations. Agreements in the cotton industry all specify that disputes will be resolved by arbitrators, knowledgeable about the industry, acting under the auspices of one of the trade associations. The agreements further specify that the arbitrators will *not* apply the general commercial law, as embodied in the *Uniform Commercial Code*, but rather will use the body of association rules and customs of the trade, as reflected in previous arbitral decisions. This body of "private law" provides, among other things, for a narrower rule of damages for breach of contract, excluding consequential losses. While there are not infrequently factual disputes about shipments of cotton, the legal rules that govern these disputes are relatively clear and constant. The agreements also specify that the decisions of the arbitrators cannot be appealed to the courts and cannot be enforced in the courts. In practice, parties always honour the decisions of the arbitrator. A failure to honour the decision would result in a loss of reputation which would make it impossible for a party to carry on business among the relatively small group who trade in this area. The value of this type of "private legal system" for those in the cotton industry is that it is less expensive, more certain and better understood by the parties.

    See L. Bernstein, "Private Commercial Law in the Cotton Industry: Creating Cooperation through Rules, Norms and Institutions" (2001), 99 *Mich. L. Rev.* 1724.

Governments enter into legally enforceable commercial contracts of all kinds. Sometimes they are moved to "cancel" the contract for political reasons. The newly elected Liberal government decided in 1993 that it did not want helicopters that the previous Conservative government had contracted to buy. Such a cancellation would normally be subject to the government's obligation to provide full compensation for the manufacturers' loss of profits and wasted expenditures. Subject to *Canadian Charter of Rights and Freedoms* concerns (which are narrow in the field of economic interests, and probably non-existent in regard to purely commercial contractual matters), legislatures in Canada have the right to enact legislation to cancel contracts and to refuse to pay compensation. Governments are, however, very hesitant to do so, not only for political reasons, but because it will make people very reluctant to make contracts with any government in the future, or will cause them to do so only at a price that takes the risk into account.

In the United States, the courts have held that the government will be liable for damages for its breach of a contract that is the result of the enactment of legislation that prevents performance of its contractual obligations in the absence of an explicit provision in the legislation that limits the government's liability. In *Mobil Oil Exploration and Producing Southeast, Inc. v. United States*, 120 S.Ct. 2423 (2000), the government was liable for reliance-based damages to an oil company when the enactment of environmental legislation required the cancellation of an oil exploration agreement that the company has signed with the government.

In some situations the government announces that it will provide a subsidy or other benefit programs to individuals. Courts have traditionally been reluctant to treat these programs as binding unilateral contracts which the promisee could enforce by doing the specified acts and the courts have accordingly permitted governments some latitude in changing their policies and terminating programs. See, *e.g., Lethbridge Collieries Ltd. v. R.*, [1951] S.C.R. 138, [1950] 4 D.L.R. 785.

Lawyers have, however, been able to persuade courts that, in some cases, they should recognize that individuals may substantially rely on government policies, and that this reliance may be best protected through a contractual analysis. For example, in *Dale v. Manitoba* (1997), 147 D.L.R. (4th) 605, [1997] 8 W.W.R. 447 (Man. C.A.), it was held that a government's affirmative action program to support university studies for adults from disadvantaged backgrounds could not be discontinued for those who had commenced studying under it. While the government was entitled to discontinue the program for the future, those who had relied on the program to begin studies were held by the Manitoba Court of Appeal to be entitled to support until they completed their degrees.

The trial judge, Schulman J., noted that the students had each signed an application form describing the program, and concluded ((1995), 128 D.L.R. (4th) 512, at p. 517):

> In these circumstances, it is clear to me that the Government committed itself contractually to the students to pay to them the same level and character of funding during the second, third and fourth year of the program as committed in the first, provided they remained eligible for funding.

The judge also said (pp. 519-20):

> I find that the Government made much more than a statement of policy or mere directive for payment to the students. Not only did the Government demonstrate an intention to contract, but it executed an agreement in which it committed itself to pay. While the Government may not have realized that it was making a commitment directly to the students, I find that, objectively speaking, it demonstrated an intent to contract with them . . . The government knew that the students constituted a class of persons who would reasonably be expected to rely on the information communicated to them regarding the financial aspects of the program. The Government owed a higher duty of disclosure of all material facts to the students than it would have owed in a normal commercial dealing with the general public. The situation cried out for the students being told, prior to being admitted into the program, that there was no guarantee as to the level and character of funding for second, third and fourth years, if such was the case.

The Manitoba courts concluded that the promise of the government was not "gratuitously made" as the students gave consideration by in that they "altered their lifestyles", and gave an indirect benefit to the government by taking steps to acquire an education, improving their prospects of moving off the welfare rolls and eventually paying income tax.

In *Somerville Belkin Industries Ltd. v. Manitoba*, [1988] 3 W.W.R. 523, 51 Man. R. (2d) 232 (C.A.), the Government of Manitoba made a commitment in a letter sent to Somerville to pay $819,000 to Somerville to meet what were regarded as unusual costs relating to the purchase and modernization of the operations of a plant. It was clear that without this assistance, Somerville was not prepared to operate the plant. Somerville then proceeded to invest substantial money in the plant. Although approval of the payment had been obtained from the necessary members of the Cabinet, an order-in-council authorizing the payment was never received because a new government took office and refused to honour the commitment. Somerville brought an action to enforce payment and was successful at trial ([1987] 5 W.W.R. 553). The plaintiff claimed that the government was liable on the basis of a contract made by the responsible Minister. The trial judge held that the government would be held to the same standard for the acts of its agents as any other contracting party. In the circumstances, the awarding of the grant was within the authority of the Minister and the government was bound to pay in accordance with its promise. The government of Manitoba appealed, but the appeal was dismissed. On the facts, the Court found that a firm commitment had been made to Somerville. The Minister had the authority to, and intended to, bind the Crown in contract and did so by his letter of commitment. The question considered by the Court was this: absent an order-in-council, was the written commitment, which the Minister gave and which Somerville acted upon, binding on the government? The Court held that the non-completion of a "mere formality" could not enable a new government to renege on a valid and enforceable commitment, especially when the commitment had been relied upon. The Court also noted that, from a public policy perspective, the "ever-increasing role of government" in assisting businesses required that commitments of this nature be reliable.

There may also be situations in which institutions or individuals who have relied on promises of politicians may be able to use administrative law remedies to force governments to act on those promises; see *Mount Sinai Hospital Center v. Quebec (Minister of Health and Social Services)*, [2001] S.C.J. No. 43, [2001] 2 S.C.R. 281, 200 D.L.R. (4th) 193.

What limits, if any, do you think should be placed on governments that want to change policies and programs in times of shrinking resources? For example, could individuals who had children in the expectation of a certain level of support for family allowance, day care, school and social services make a contractual argument to prevent withdrawal of these supports? In these days of government cutbacks it is to be expected that there will be claims made to enforce government promises as contracts.

The promises that politicians make during election campaigns, no matter how explicit, even if blatantly dishonoured, do not give rise to a legal cause of action. In *Canadian Taxpayers Federation v. Ontario (Minister of Finance)*, [2004] O.J. No. 5239, 73 O.R. (3d) 621 (S.C.J.), during the 2003 election campaign, Dalton McGuinty, then leader of the Liberal Party in Ontario, made a highly publicized signing of a "Taxpayer Protection Promise", promising not to raise taxes unless the increase was approved in a referendum by the people of Ontario. After he was elected Premier, he decided not to honour that promise, claiming that the province's finances were in much worse shape than he anticipated when the promise was made (a claim that was challenged by his critics). The Canadian Taxpayers Federation, which had publicized the original promise and endorsed his campaign, brought an action against McGuinty, various members of the Cabinet and the government, claiming breach of contract and negligent misrepresentation. In a motion to strike out the claim, Rouleau J. dismissed the action as being without legal basis, concluding:

[53] In the course of election campaigns, politicians and their parties present their election platform to the electorate. In so doing they commonly make promises and pledge that they will or will not do various things if and when they are elected.

[54] It is hoped that, if elected, the politicians and their parties will keep their promises and will follow through with the pledges given. This said, however, few people would consider that all of the promises made and pledges given constitute legally-binding agreements between the candidate and the elector or electors to whom these promises or pledges were made.

[55] While the September 11, 2003 promise made by Mr. McGuinty was reduced to writing there is, in law, little difference between a promise made orally and one made in writing. The principal difference is that the promise made in writing will,

obviously, be easier to prove. There were doubtless many other promises and pledges made by various candidates and parties in the course of the 2003 election campaign. Some would have been made one-on-one during door-to-door campaigning; others would have been made to crowds or in the presence of media. Some were contained in campaign literature and others were in commercials. It is not unreasonable to expect that some of the promises led people to vote for the candidate or party making the pledge or promise and that individuals and groups would have expressed support for the candidate or party because of the promises or pledges made.

. . .

[58]   Pledges and promises are made in order to garner support in an election campaign but also to inform voters of a party's plans and intentions. If every individual or organization that expresses support for a politician or party or votes in favour of a politician or party by reason of a pledge or promise made is then free to bring an action in contract against the politician or party to compel the execution of that promise or pledge, our system of government would be rendered dysfunctional. The courts would be called upon to rule on which pledges and promises constitute contracts. The voter or group would then seek to use the court to enforce the promise or pledge. This would hinder if not paralyse the parliamentary system.

. . .

[62]   While it is no doubt desirable and important to the proper functioning of a democracy that candidates and parties do their best to follow through with the promises and pledges made, it is not the role of the courts, in circumstances such as in the present case, to intervene to enforce such promises and pledges. Rather, the remedy is for the electorate to consider and weigh the record of each candidate and party at the time of voting and in the intervening period to trust that the power entrusted to ministers will be "exercised from time to time as occasion may require in the public interest" (*Canada v. Dominion of Canada Postage Stamp Vending Co.*, [1930] S.C.R 500, [1930] 4 D.L.R. 241, at p. 506 S.C.R.).

Do you agree with Rouleau J.?

THIRD-PARTY BENEFICIARIES AND PRIVITY OF CONTRACT

The Background

Until this point, the focus of inquiry in this chapter has been on what types of promises are enforceable. We now turn to a related but distinct question — who can enforce or receive the benefit of a promise?

An important common law rule of enforceability is that only a "party" to the contract can enforce it; someone who is a "stranger" to the contract will have no rights or obligations under it. This is commonly referred to as the doctrine of "privity". The doctrine of privity was developed by judges as an aspect of the classical bargain model of contracts. Some judges and commentators regard privity as a distinct doctrine, while others treat it as an aspect of consideration — a third party who has given no consideration has no right to enforce a contract. As you read the following materials you should reflect on whether privity should be viewed as a distinct doctrinal issue, or part of consideration.

Most issues related to consideration have limited practical significance, and arise rarely in practice. Moreover, most consideration problems can be easily avoided with legal advice. Any promise may be made enforceable by use of a seal or nominal consideration. Third-party beneficiary issues, however, are more complex and have considerable practical significance. In many cases, courts refuse to give effect to certain types of agreements because of "lack of privity of contract". Some situations have been dealt with by legislation, but many court decisions in this area seem unjust. The 1992 decision of the Supreme Court of Canada in *London Drugs Ltd. v. Kuehne & Nagel International Ltd.*, [1992] 3 S.C.R. 299, [1993] 1 W.W.R. 1 demonstrates, however, that the courts are moving in a more sensible direction. It also remains true that competent legal advice can always avoid the problems of privity.

A common form of third-party contracts is that A and B make a contract, under which B promises to pay C, in exchange for A promising to do something for B. The contracting parties are A and B: C is a third party, and since the contract is for C's benefit, he or she is a third-party beneficiary and not "privy" to the contract. While A may enforce the obligation, there are a variety of situations in which A may be unwilling or unable to do so. The problem arises in those cases in which C seeks to sue B for breach of the promise made for his or her benefit. B's defence to C's action will make the two arguments that have been outlined: (i) C gave no consideration for the promise made by B to A (though for C's benefit); and (ii) C is not a party to the contract.

The law of third party beneficiary contracts was established — it is almost possible to say that it was created — by the Court of Queen's Bench in *Tweddle v. Atkinson* (1861), 1 B. & S. 393, 121 E.R. 762, and the rule about privity of contract became one of the maxims of the common law. In *Dunlop Pneumatic Tyre Co. Ltd. v. Selfridge & Co. Ltd.*, [1915] A.C. 847 (H.L.), Lord Haldane stated:

> My lords, in the law of England certain principles are fundamental. One is that only a person who is a party to a contract can sue upon it. Our law knows nothing of a *jus quaesitum tertio*[2] arising by way of contract.

This is a widely accepted statement of the common law rule and has caused many third-party problems. The problems created by the rule about privity can arise in a number of situations, both commercial and non-commercial, such as:

1. A is a person who takes out life insurance with an insurer, B, naming C as beneficiary.

2. A is an employee who pays into a pension plan run by B; B promises to pay a pension to A on his retirement, and on A's death to C, A's spouse.

3. A is a carrier, and agrees to carry B's goods if B will promise that it (B) will not sue A or anybody else who might be responsible for the goods during the course of transit; the goods are damaged by C, an employee of A.

In the first two of these examples C, at common law, cannot sue B for the promised benefit, and in the third example, B could not be prevented from suing C, regardless of the promise that he had made to A. As these examples suggest, problems with third-party beneficiaries contracts are common.

A particularly unpleasant example of the third-party beneficiary rule defeating the reasonable expectations of an individual occurred in *Vandepitte v. Preferred Accident Insurance Corporation of New York*, [1933] A.C. 70, [1932] All E.R. Rep. 527 (P.C.). This action was brought by a person injured in an automobile

---

2   The Latin phrase *jus quaesitum tertio* means the right of a third party to claim against the promisor. The phrase *jus tertii* is sometimes used as a synonym and literally means the "right of a third party".

accident by the negligence of the daughter of a person who had taken out insurance with the defendant insurer. The insurer had promised in the policy to indemnify the insured and "any person . . . operating the automobile . . . with the
permission of the insured". The *Insurance Act*, S.B.C. 1925, c. 20, s. 24, gave an
injured party a direct right of action against an insurer liable on a policy of insurance. The action of the accident victim failed; the daughter had no direct contractual relation with the insurer and there was no evidence that the father had
intended to insure for the benefit of his daughter. The insurer was therefore not
"liable" on the policy of insurance under the Act, and the injured person had no
right to sue the insurance company The most apt observation that one can make on
this case is to note that in 1932 (between the date of the decision in the Supreme
Court of Canada upholding the right of the insurer to repudiate liability and the
judgment of the Privy Council reaching the same conclusion), the legislature of
British Columbia amended the *Insurance Act* to provide that a person in the position of the daughter (an "insured not named in the policy") would be "deemed to
be a party to the contract and to have given consideration therefor". Thus, by the
time the Privy Council handed down its decision in *Vandepitte*, the result was of
little interest except to the particular litigants involved.

The doctrine of privity, based on the proposition of Lord Haldane in *Dunlop v.
Selfridge & Co.*, was applied in its most uncompromising form in the House of
Lords in *Scruttons Ltd. v. Midland Silicones Ltd.*, [1962] A.C. 446, [1962] 1 All
E.R. 1. The facts corresponded to those of the third example above. A drum of
pump fluid was shipped from the United States to England pursuant to a contract
found in the bill of lading, that contract having been made between the owner of
the goods and the carrier. The bill of lading defined the carrier to include "the
ship, her owner, operator . . . and also any . . . person to the extent bound by this
bill of lading, whether acting as carrier or bailee". The bill of lading limited the
liability of the "carrier" for any damage to $500. The carrier employed stevedores
to unload the ship, and the contract between the carrier and stevedores provided
that the stevedores would be responsible for any negligence on their part, but
should have "such protection as is afforded by the bill of lading". The drum was
damaged by the stevedores as it was being unloaded from the ship and the owner
of the drum (or more probably the owner's insurer under its right of subrogation)
sued the stevedores in negligence. Counsel for the stevedores argued that they
could take advantage of the provisions in the bill of lading that had been inserted
for their benefit. The lower courts refused to give the stevedores the protection of
the bill of lading, citing the doctrine of privity. The stevedores appealed to the
House of Lords, which rejected their claim to the benefit of the contract. In the
House of Lords, Viscount Simonds, in responding to the arguments of the appellant stevedores, said (at 476-78 A.C.):

> Learned counsel for the respondent met it, as they had successfully done in the
> courts below, by asserting a principle which is, I suppose, as well established as any
> in our law, a "fundamental" principle, as Lord Haldane called it in *Dunlop Pneu-
> matic Tyre Co. Ltd. v. Selfridge & Co. Ltd.* . . . an "elementary" principle, as it has
> been called times without number, that only a person who is a party to a contract can
> sue upon it. "Our law," said Lord Haldane, "knows nothing of a *jus quaesitum tertio*
> arising by way of contract." Learned counsel for the respondents claimed that this
> was the orthodox view and asked your Lordships to reject any proposition that im-
> pinged upon it. To that invitation I readily respond. For to me heterodoxy, or, as
> some might say, heresy, is not the more attractive because it is dignified by the name
> of reform. Nor will I easily be led by an undiscerning zeal for some abstract kind of

justice to ignore our first duty, which is to administer justice according to law, the law which is established for us by Act of Parliament or the binding authority of precedent.

The law is developed by the application of old principles to new circumstances. Therein lies its genius. Its reform by the abrogation of those principles is the task not of the courts of law but of Parliament. Therefore I reject the argument for the appellants under his head and invite your Lordships to say that certain statements which appear to support it in recent cases . . . be rejected. If the principle of *jus quaesitum tertio* is to be introduced into our law, it must be done by Parliament after a due consideration of its merits and demerits. I should not be prepared to give it my support without a greater knowledge than I at present possess of its operation in other systems of law.

The question that comes to mind after reading this speech is why Viscount Simonds felt so strongly about the third-party beneficiary rule. The stevedores were, after all, trying to have the respondent held to a promise that it had made, which promise (as part of a common form bill of lading used for the international carriage of goods) was fair, and merely allocated to the owner (the respondents) the risks of loss. It is not as if there was an issue of the fundamental unfairness of the agreement or of whether the parties should be able to make contracts of this type. They clearly can make such contracts, provided only that they use the correct form of words.

In fact, the original bill of lading was drafted in the expectation that the owner would get "all risks" insurance, which it undoubtedly did. The insurer for the owner then paid the owner for the loss and bought a subrogated claim in the name of its insured. Subrogation is a doctrine of equity that permits an insurer who has fully paid its insured's claim to sue in the name of the insured and recover from the tortfeasor. As a result of subrogation, the loss has been shifted from the insurer of the owner, which was paid to take this risk, to the stevedores, who reasonably believed that they were covered, and probably did not have insurance coverage.

Giving the stevedores the protection of the bill of lading is generally the most economically efficient arrangement in this situation. If the stevedores are liable, they will be encouraged to get their own insurance coverage to protect themselves from liability for any goods which they may happen to damage. This is likely to be relatively expensive insurance since the insurer will be uncertain of the maximum potential risk; the stevedores' act of negligence might result in the loss of relatively inexpensive cargo, like a container filled with cement, or it might result in the loss of a valuable product, like a container filled with computers. It will ordinarily be less expensive for the owner to obtain insurance for the goods being shipped, knowing the exact value of the goods and risk. In fact, the owner of the goods is very likely to have its own "all risks" insurance for the goods, since the bill of lading protects the carrier, and in any event the goods might be lost on the voyage without negligence of any party who could be held liable, for example, due to an act of God or a tortfeasor (like a pirate). The effect of *Scruttons* was to encourage expensive double insurance coverage for the goods, a cost which would be reflected in the rates that the stevedores charge, and ultimately in the costs of the goods sold to consumers.

The judgment of Viscount Simonds in *Scruttons Ltd. v. Midland Silicones Ltd.* on the role of the courts in the common law can be contrasted with his views in *Shaw v. Director of Public Prosecutions*, [1962] A.C. 220 (H.L.), where the House of Lords upheld a conviction for the judicially created crime of "conspiracy to corrupt public morals". Shaw had published a booklet containing the names and addresses of prostitutes, and in some cases pictures and a description of the type of services available. Prostitution *per se* was not a crime at that time in England, but Shaw was nevertheless found guilty of a common law crime, with Viscount Simonds commenting that a court has (p. 268):

> a residual power, where no statute has yet intervened to supersede the common law, to superintend those offences which are prejudicial to the public welfare.

Is it not odd that the House of Lords would assert a power to make a new criminal offence, yet deny that it has a power to remove a rule (i) that has no discernible purpose, (ii) that was, so to speak, brought forth fully formed only in 1861 and (iii) that frustrates a perfectly reasonable and common allocation of the risk of loss?

The Supreme Court of Canada followed *Scruttons Ltd. v. Midland Silicones Ltd.* in *Canadian General Electric Co. Ltd. v. Pickford & Black Ltd.*, [1971] S.C.R. 41. Ritchie J. simply said, "The law in this regard is, in my opinion, correctly stated in the reason for judgment of the majority of the House of Lords in [*Scruttons*] where the relevant cases are fully discussed" (at 43-44 S.C.R.).

The strong language of Viscount Simonds in *Scruttons* and the equally emphatic statement by Lord Haldane in *Dunlop v. Selfridge* may suggest that the third-party rule is particularly well established and represents how the law always deals with third parties. Such a conclusion would be incorrect. In spite of everything said in these and other cases, an examination of the law in more detail reveals that in many cases the courts get around the rule. The problem was that it was difficult to predict when the courts would strictly apply the rule and when they would evade it.

Historically, there were three principal legal institutions that lawyers and courts used to give a third party a benefit under a contract: agency, assignment and trust. Each of these legal institutions is important in its own right, and can be the subject of broad study. Our main concern here is to mention how they can be utilized to avoid the problems of privity.

1. Agency

An agent, A, can be employed by a principal, P, to make contracts on P's behalf with a third person, T. The contract is made as a result of negotiations between A and T, for the purpose of making a contract between T and P. While the negotiations are conducted between A and T, the contract, once formed, usually binds only P and T. There is no reason, however, that A may not also be a contracting party with T. So flexible is the agency device that a contract can be made between P and T even though T was not aware of P's existence when he dealt with A (who T might have thought was dealing on its own account, though the law protects T from being unpleasantly surprised when P appears.) A contract can also be made between P and T even though A had, at the time he made the contract, no authority to act for P, if P subsequently ratifies the contract and approves what A purported to do on his behalf.

2.   Assignment

If D, a debtor, owes $10,000 to C, a creditor, C, as assignor, can assign the debt to A, the assignee. Subject to certain restrictions, A can sue D for the amount of the debt. Purchases at an operator-owned gas station using an oil-company credit card involve such a transaction. The debt that the customer, D, owes to the gas station, C, is assigned to the oil company, A. The payment for the assignment by the assignee, A, is the oil company's agreement to sell the gas station gas against credit-card purchases. An assignment will be valid even if the debtor does not know about it. However, a debtor cannot be prejudiced by an assignment and in an action by the assignee may assert any defence or claim that it would have had if the action to enforce the debt were brought by the assignor, the original creditor.

3.   Trust

Under a trust, one party, called the trustee, agrees to hold an asset of some kind — land, securities or a debt — in trust for another, called the beneficiary or a *cestui que trust*. Thus, A and C may agree that A will hold B's promise to do something for C on trust for C. Such a situation could arise when a parent, A, agrees to hold a bank account on trust for her son, C. The bank would be B. The trust is a well-established equitable device for giving one person an interest in property held by another. A right to a benefit under a contract is a property right, a chose in action, that can be held on trust. If A is a trustee for C, then it is well established that C can bring an action against B and, if necessary, A will be compelled to allow the action to be brought in A's name. What is important is that A's unwillingness to sue B will not prejudice C's right to claim the benefit of the trust.

The existence of these three legal devices allowed parties to structure their legal affairs so that C can claim the benefit to which he was entitled under the arrangement with A and B. In determining whether a relation of agency, trust or assignment exists, the courts consider the words of the document and the intent of the parties.

In *Scruttons Ltd. v. Midland Silicones Ltd.*, Lord Reid accepted that, in principle, a stevedore could have the protection of a bill of lading between the owner and the carrier, provided that the bill of lading was properly drafted ([1962] A.C. 446, p. 474):

> I can see a possibility of success of the agency argument if (first) the bill of lading makes it clear that the stevedore is intended to be protected by the provisions in it which limit liability, (secondly) the bill of lading makes it clear that the carrier, in addition to contracting for these provisions on his own behalf, is also contracting as agent for the stevedore that these provisions should apply to the stevedore, (thirdly) the carrier has authority from the stevedore to do that, or perhaps later ratification by the stevedore would suffice, and (fourthly) that any difficulties about consideration moving from the stevedore were overcome. . . .

The acceptance of this principle led lawyers to try to draft agreements that would meet the criteria of Lord Reid and give the stevedores the protection of the bill of lading. Carriers began to use a more carefully drafted clause known as a "Himalaya clause". (The name comes from *Adler v. Dickson*, [1955] 1 Q.B. 158, [1954] 3 All E.R. 397, in which the ship *Himalaya* was involved.)

In *New Zealand Shipping Co. Ltd. v. A.M. Satterthwaite & Co. Ltd.*, [1975] A.C. 154, [1974] 1 All E.R. 1015, a majority of the Privy Council accepted that

prot

the following "*Himalaya* clause" in a bill of lading was effective to protect the stevedores (p. 1018 All E.R.):

> . . . It is hereby expressly agreed that no servant or agent of the Carrier (including every independent contractor from time to time employed by the Carrier) shall in any circumstances whatsoever be under any liability whatsoever to the Shipper, Consignee or Owner of the goods or to any holder of this Bill of Lading for any loss or damage or delay of whatsoever kind arising or resulting directly or indirectly from any act neglect or default on his part while acting in the course of or in connection with his employment and, without prejudice to the generality of the foregoing provisions in this Clause, every exemption, limitation, condition and liberty herein contained and every right, exemption from liability, defence and immunity of whatsoever nature applicable to the Carrier or to which the Carrier is entitled hereunder shall also be available and shall extend to protect every such servant or agent of the Carrier acting as aforesaid and for the purpose of all the foregoing provisions of this Clause the Carrier is or shall be deemed to be acting as agent or trustee on behalf of and for the benefit of all persons who are or might be his servants or agents from time to time (including independent contractors as aforesaid) and all such persons shall to this extent be or be deemed to be parties to the contract in or evidenced by this Bill of Lading . . .

Lord Wilberforce stated (p. 1019 All E.R.):

> If the choice, and the antithesis, is between a gratuitous promise, and a promise for consideration, as it must be, in the absence of a *tertium quid*, there can be little doubt which, in commercial reality, this is. The whole contract is of a commercial character, involving service on one side, rates of payment on the other, and qualifying stipulations as to both. The relations of all parties to each other are commercial relations entered into for business reasons of ultimate profit. To describe one set of promises, in this context, as gratuitous, or *nudum pactum*, seems paradoxical and is *prima facie* implausible. It is only the precise analysis of this complex of relations into the classical offer and acceptance, with identifiable consideration, that seems to present difficulty, but this same difficulty exists in many situations of daily life, e.g., sales at auction; supermarket purchases; boarding an omnibus; purchasing a train ticket; tenders for the supply of goods; offers of reward; acceptance by post; warranties of authority by agents; manufacturers' guarantees; gratuitous bailments; bankers' commercial credits. These are all examples which show that English law, having committed itself to a rather technical and schematic doctrine of contract, in application takes a practical approach, often at the cost of forcing the facts to fit uneasily into the marked slots of offer, acceptance and consideration.

> . . . The carrier assumes an obligation to transport the goods and to discharge at the port of arrival. The goods are to be carried and discharged, so the transaction is inherently contractual. It is contemplated that a part of this contract, *viz.* discharge, may be performed by independent contractors — *viz.*, the stevedore. By . . . the bill of lading the shipper agrees to exempt from liability the carrier, his servants and independent contractors in respect of the performance of this contract of carriage. Thus, if the carriage, including the discharge, is wholly carried out by the carrier, he is exempt. If part is carried out by him, and part by his servants, he and they are exempt. If part is carried out by him and part by an independent contractor, he and the independent contractor are exempt. The exemption is designed to cover the whole carriage from loading to discharge, by whomsoever it is performed: the performance attracts the exemption or immunity in favour of whoever the performer turns out to be. There is possibly more than one way of analysing this business transaction into the necessary components; that which their Lordships would accept is to say that the bill of lading brought into existence a bargain initially unilateral but capable of becoming mutual, between the shippers and the stevedore, made through the carrier as agent. This became a full contract when the stevedore performed services by discharging the goods. The performance of these services for the benefit of the shipper

prot

was the consideration for the agreement by the shipper that the stevedore should have the benefit of the exemptions and limitations contained in the bill of lading. The conception of a "unilateral" contract of this kind was recognised in *Great Northern Railway Co. v. Witham*, [above] and is well established. . . . the transaction [is] one of an offer open to acceptance by action such as was found in *Carlill v. Carbolic Smoke Ball Co.*, [[1893] 1 Q.B. 256]. But whether one describes the shipper's promise to exempt as an offer to be accepted by performance or as a promise in exchange for an act seems in the present context to be a matter of semantics. The words of Bowen L.J. in *Carlill v. Carbolic Smoke Ball*, ". . . why should not an offer be made to all the world which is to ripen into a contract with anybody who comes forward and performs the conditions?" seem to bridge both conceptions: he certainly seems to draw no distinction between an offer which matures into a contract when accepted and a promise which matures into a contract after performance and, though in some special contexts (such as in connection with the right to withdraw) some further refinement may be needed, either analysis may be equally valid.

On the issue of whether the stevedores provided consideration to the owner, Lord Wilberforce concluded (p. 1020 All E.R.):

In their Lordships' opinion, consideration may quite well be provided by the stevedore, as suggested, even though (or if) it was already under an obligation to discharge to the carrier. . . . An agreement to do an act which the promisor is under an existing obligation to a third party to do, may quite well amount to valid consideration and does so in the present case: the promisee obtains the benefit of a direct obligation which he can enforce. This proposition is illustrated and supported by *Scotson v. Pegg* [(1861), 158 E.R. 121] which their Lordships consider to be good law.

One can also see the Privy Council starting to be influenced by American jurisprudence and to recognize concerns about economic efficiency (p. 1021 All E.R.):

A clause very similar to the present was given effect by a United States District Court in *Carle and Montanari Inc. v. American Export Isbrantsen Lines Inc.*, [1968] 1 Lloyd's Rep. 260. The carrier in that case contracted, in an exemption clause, as agent for, *inter alios*, all stevedores and other independent contractors, and although it is no doubt true that the law in the United States is more liberal than ours as regards third-party contracts, their Lordships see no reason why the law of the Commonwealth should be more restrictive and technical as regards agency contracts. Commercial consideration should have the same force on both sides of the Pacific.

In the opinion of their Lordships, to give the stevedore the benefit of the exemptions and limitations contained in the bill of lading is to give effect to the clear intentions of a commercial document, and can be given within existing principles. They see no reason to strain the law or the facts in order to defeat these intentions. It should not be overlooked that the effect of denying validity to the clause would be to encourage actions against servants, agents and independent contractors in order to get round exemptions (which are almost invariable and often compulsory) accepted by shippers against carriers, the existence, and presumed efficacy, of which is reflected in the rates of freight. They see no attraction in this consequence.

In *ITO-International Terminal Operators Ltd. v. Miida Electronics Inc. and Mitsui O.S.K. Lines Ltd.*, [1986] 1 S.C.R. 752, 28 D.L.R. (4th) 641, the Supreme Court of Canada adopted the reasoning of the House of Lords in *New Zealand Shipping* and gave effect to a Himalaya cause. One must ask whether there is any social or economic utility to having lawyers continuously redraft ever more complex clauses and then re-litigate them in order to obtain judicial acknowledgement that they have finally succeeded in preparing a contract that reflects their obvious commercial intent.

While *New Zealand Shipping* and *ITO* were sensitive to the commercial realities of a stevedoring situation, the Supreme Court of Canada decision in *Greenwood Shopping Plaza Ltd.* (discussed below) was insensitive to commercial and social reality, and illustrates the damage that courts inflicted using the doctrine of privity.

———————————

While Canadian law dealing with bills of lading — at least those that are properly drafted — has now largely eliminated the problems caused by the third-party beneficiary rule, there remain pockets of the law where the rule can cause serious problems.   *welders no privity*

prof X   In *Greenwood Shopping Plaza Ltd. v. Beattie*, [1980] 2 S.C.R. 228, 111 D.L.R. (3d) 257, a landlord (actually, the landlord's insurer acting under its rights of subrogation) sued two welders personally for damages for negligence causing the loss by fire of a shopping centre. The welders had been employed by a Canadian Tire store, a tenant in the centre. The terms of the lease protected the tenant from being sued by the landlord or the landlord's insurer. The question before the Supreme Court was whether the tenant's employees would be similarly protected. Justice McIntyre, giving the judgment of the Supreme Court, held that the welders were not protected: their employer had not explicitly contracted on their behalf with the landlord to protect them from liability, and the Supreme Court concluded that there was no trust in their favour. As McIntyre J. remarked, they could not avoid the problems created by "the rigid mould imposed by the concept of privity". The effect of the judgment was to expose two labourers to liability and potential personal bankruptcy and, because the employees were tortfeasors, their employer had no legal obligation to provide them with an indemnity. The loss is placed on people who did not (and who likely would never have thought to) have insurance and who could not have bought it, had they tried, and this is done to vindicate a technical rule of the common law. The rule operates, like the doctrine of consideration itself, to catch only those who have not had or who have not had the opportunity to get competent legal advice.

In *New Zealand Shipping* the issue was, at base, which of two insurers would bear the risk of loss. As mentioned, it is almost always cheaper for the owner of property to insure than for equivalent protection to be taken out by someone else on a third-party basis. The insurer in *Greenwood v. Beattie* was not seeking to make labourers bankrupt — that result was "collateral damage". An employer may be under pressure to indemnify its employees. Any employer subject to a collective agreement would, if it did not protect its employees in a similar situation, promptly be faced with a demand that the collective agreement be modified to provide such protection: Canadian Tire employees have no union. This pressure gives any potential plaintiff significant power in extracting a settlement from the employer that may largely frustrate its attempts to allocate the risk to the party who under, for example, a lease, is contractually obliged to insure the property.

Later cases raise the possibility that the Supreme Court will not decide another *Greenwood* the same way.

———————————

The next decision is an extremely important decision of the Supreme Court of Canada, not only in terms of what was decided about the law of privity, but also in its general approach to the role of the courts and the evolution of contract law. As you read the decision, consider whether the Court is, in spite of what it says, reversing it own decision in *Greenwood v. Beattie*, rendered 12 years earlier.

LONDON DRUGS LTD. v. KUEHNE & NAGEL INTERNATIONAL LTD.

[1992] S.C.J. No. 84, 3 S.C.R. 299, 97 D.L.R. (4th) 261
(S.C.C., La Forest, L'Heureux-Dubé, Sopinka, McLachlin,
Cory and Iacobucci JJ.)

IACOBUCCI J. (**L'HEUREUX-DUBÉ**, **SOPINKA** and **CORY JJ.** concurring): — **[1]** This appeal and cross-appeal raise two principal issues: (1) the duty of care owed by employees to their employer's customers, and (2) the extent to which employees can claim the benefit of their employer's contractual limitation of liability clause.

I. *Facts*

[2]　The facts are not complicated. On August 31, 1981, London Drugs Limited (hereinafter "appellant"), delivered a transformer weighing some 7,500 pounds to Kuehne and Nagel International Ltd. (hereinafter "Kuehne & Nagel") for storage pursuant to the terms and conditions of a standard form contract of storage. The transformer had been purchased from its manufacturer, Federal Pioneer Limited, and was to be installed in the new warehouse facility being built by the appellant. The contract of storage included the following limitation of liability clause:

> LIABILITY - Sec. 11(a) The responsibility of a warehouseman in the absence of written provisions is the reasonable care and diligence required by the law.
>
> (b) The warehouseman's liability on any one package is limited to $40 unless the holder has declared in writing a valuation in excess of $40 and paid the additional charge specified to cover warehouse liability.

[3]　With full knowledge and understanding of this clause, the appellant chose not to obtain additional insurance from Kuehne & Nagel and instead arranged for its own all-risk coverage. At the time of entering into the contract, the appellant knew, or can be assumed to have known, that Kuehne & Nagel's employees would be responsible for moving and upkeeping the transformer.

[4]　On September 22, 1981, Dennis Gerrard Brassart and Hank Vanwinkel (hereinafter "respondents"), both employees of Kuehne & Nagel, received orders to load the transformer onto a truck which would deliver it to the appellant's new warehouse. The respondents attempted to move the transformer by lifting it with two forklift vehicles when safe practice required it to be lifted from above using brackets which were attached to the transformer and which were clearly marked for that purpose. While being lifted, the transformer toppled over and fell causing damages in the amount of $33,955.41.

[5]　Alleging breach of contract and negligence, the appellant brought an action for damages against Kuehne & Nagel, Federal Pioneer Limited, and the respondents. In a judgment rendered on April 14, 1986, Trainor J. of the Supreme Court of British Columbia held that the respondents were personally liable for the full amount of damages, limiting Kuehne & Nagel's liability to $40 and dismissing the claim against Federal Pioneer Limited. On March 30, 1990, the majority of the

Court of Appeal allowed the respondents' appeal and reduced their liability to $40. The appellant was granted leave to appeal to this Court on December 7, 1990. The respondents have cross appealed in order to argue that they should be completely free of liability. A written intervention was made by the General Truck Drivers & Helpers Local Union No. 31, the union authorized to negotiate the collective agreement with Kuehne & Nagel which, at all material times, governed the respondents' employment relationship. . . .

III. *Issues*

[6]   The cross-appeal raises the following question:

(1) Did the respondents, acting in the course of their employment and performing the very essence of their employer's contractual obligations with the appellant, owe a duty of care to the appellant?

If so, it is not disputed before this Court that the respondents were negligent in their handling of the appellant's transformer. . . . The next question which is raised by the appeal would thus become one of the appropriate liability for this breach, namely:

(2) Can the respondents obtain the benefit of the limitation of liability clause contained in the contract of storage between their employer and the appellant so as to limit their liability to $40?

[7]   For reasons that follow, I am of the opinion that both questions should be answered in the affirmative. By so concluding, both the cross-appeal and the appeal should therefore be dismissed.

IV. *Analysis*

A.   *Duty of Care*

[**IACOBUCCI J.** held that the employees owed a duty of care to the customer of their employer under ordinary tort principles. He concluded by saying, "There may well be cases where, having regards to the particular circumstances involved, an employee will not owe a duty of care to his or her employer's customer." The cross-appeal was accordingly dismissed. **IACOBUCCI J.** continued:]

B.   *Limitation of Liability Clause*

[8]   Accepting the finding of the trial judge that the respondents breached their duty of care thereby causing damages fixed at $33,955.41 to the appellant, I must now consider whether they are allowed to benefit from the limitation of liability clause found in the contract of storage between their employer, Kuehne & Nagel, and the appellant. The majority of the Court of Appeal reached a conclusion favourable to the respondents on this issue by using two different approaches (1) by implying a term in the contract extending the protection of s. 11(b) of the contract of storage to the respondents and by applying the exception to the doctrine of privity set out in *The Eurymedon* [*New Zealand Shipping Co. Ltd. v. A.M. Satterthwaite & Co. Ltd. (The "Eurymedon")*, [1975] A.C. 154, [1974] 1 All E.R. 1015] and *ITO-International Terminal Operators* [*ITO-International Operators Ltd. v. Miida Electronics Inc.*, [1986] 1 S.C.R. 752, 28 D.L.R. (4th) 641], (Lambert J.A.'s contract analysis); and (2) by taking into account the "contractual matrix" between Kuehne & Nagel and the appellant, including the limitation of liability clause, so as to qualify the respondents' duty of care and their ensuing liability to $40. . . .

. . .

[9]   In my view, the respondents were third party beneficiaries to the limitation of liability clause found in the contract of storage between their employer and the appellant and, in view of the circumstances involved, may benefit directly from this clause notwithstanding that they are not a signing party to the contract. I recognize that such a conclusion collides with privity of contract in its strictest sense; however, for reasons that follow, I believe that this Court is presented with an appropriate factual opportunity in which to reconsider the scope of this doctrine and decide whether its application in cases such as the one at bar should be limited or modified. It is my opinion that commercial reality and common sense require that it should. . . .

[10]   I will now turn to the heart of the present appeal, namely, privity of contract and third party beneficiaries. In dealing with this issue, I would like briefly to review what is understood by the doctrine of privity of contract, the decisions that support it, the reasons behind the doctrine, criticisms of the doctrine, and its treatment in other jurisdictions. I shall then go on to discuss previous decisions of this Court on the matter before turning to the doctrine in the circumstances of this appeal.

(3)   *The Doctrine of Privity of Contract and Third Party Beneficiaries*

A.   *Introduction*

[11]   The doctrine of privity of contract has been stated by many different authorities sometimes with varying effect. Broadly speaking, it stands for the proposition that a contract cannot, as a general rule, confer rights or impose obligations arising under it on any person except the parties to it. . . . It is now widely recognized that this doctrine has two very distinct components or aspects. On the one hand, it precludes parties to a contract from imposing liabilities or obligations on third parties. On the other, it prevents third parties from obtaining rights or benefits under a contract; it refuses to recognize a *jus quaesitum tertio* or a *jus tertii*. This latter aspect has not only applied to deny complete strangers from enforcing contractual provisions but has also applied in cases where the contract attempts, either expressly or impliedly, to confer benefits on a third party. In other words, it has equally applied in cases involving third party beneficiaries. This appeal is concerned only with the second aspect of privity, and particularly with its application to third party beneficiaries. Nothing in these reasons should be taken as affecting in any way the law as it relates to the imposition of obligations on third parties.

[12]   The decisions most often cited in Canadian courts in support of the doctrine of privity are: *Tweddle v. Atkinson* (1861), 1 B. & S. 393, 121 E.R. 762; *Dunlop Pneumatic Tyre Co. v. Selfridge & Co.*, [1915] A.C. 847 (H.L.); *Scruttons Ltd. v. Midland Silicones Ltd.*, [1962] A.C. 446 (H.L.); *Canadian General Electric* [*Canadian General Electric Co. v. Pickford & Black Ltd.*, [1971] S.C.R. 41, 14 D.L.R. (3d) 372]; and *Greenwood Shopping Plaza* [*Greenwood Shopping Plaza Ltd. v. Beattie*, [1980] 2 S.C.R. 228, 111 D.L.R. (3d) 257]. As confirmed by these and other decisions, privity of contract is an established principle of contract law. It is not, however, an ancient principle. As noted by this Court in *Greenwood Shopping Plaza*, the doctrine "has not always been applied with the rigour which has developed during modern times". Indeed, many have noted earlier decisions in the English

common law which have allowed third party beneficiaries to enforce contracts made for their benefit. . . . It is generally recognized that the law in this respect was not "settled" until the mid-nineteenth century. It is also accepted that there are certain exceptions to the doctrine of privity such as trust and agency. . . .

[13] Closely related to the doctrine of privity, but conceptually distinct, is the rule that consideration for a promise must move from the person entitled to sue or rely on that promise. Both rules have been used in the past, sometimes in an inter-changeable manner, in order to deny third parties the right to enforce contractual provisions made for their benefit. There is some debate in academic circles, sup-ported by *obiter dicta*, as to whether or not privity and consideration are really distinct concepts. For our purposes, however, I find it unnecessary to consider this question. I proceed on the basis that the major obstacle to the respondents' claim, as stated by the appellant, is that they are not a party to the contract from which they seek to obtain a benefit.

[14] The reasons behind the doctrine of privity have received very little judicial attention. Professor Treitel offers perhaps the most often cited (and debated) justi-fications for this doctrine in his treatise *The Law of Contract*, at p. 458. Maintain-ing a certain distance, he claims that the denial of third party rights under a contract may be justified for four reasons: (1) a contract is a very personal affair, affecting only the parties to it; (2) it would be unjust to allow a person to sue on a contract on which he or she could not be sued; (3) if third parties could enforce contracts made for their benefit, the rights of contracting parties to rescind or vary such contracts would be unduly hampered; and (4) the third party is often merely a donee and a "system of law which does not give a gratuitous promisee a right to enforce the promise is not likely to give this right to a gratuitous beneficiary who is not even a promisee".

[15] Professor Atiyah in *The Rise and Fall of Freedom of Contract* (1979), offers an economic explanation for the doctrine (at p. 414):

> There is a sense in which the new doctrine of privity was an important development in the law at a time of increasing complexity in multilateral commercial relation-ships. The appearance of middlemen in all sorts of commercial situations served to separate the parties at either end of the transaction, and it was generally accepted that no privity existed between them. Economically, this may have served a useful purpose, in that it encouraged the development of a more market-based concept of enterprise liability. But on some occasions the results were not only economically dubious but socially disastrous.

[16] Other possible justifications include preventing the promisor from being subject to double recovery and avoiding a floodgate of litigation brought about by third party beneficiaries.

B.   *Criticisms of the Doctrine*

[17] Few would argue that complete strangers to a contract should have the right to enforce its provisions. When it comes to third party beneficiaries, however, the doctrine of privity of contract has received much criticism in this century by law reformers, commentators, and judges. To date, three major law reform bodies in the Commonwealth have examined the doctrine; each has recommended its aboli-tion. . . .

[18] In Canada, the Ontario Law Reform Commission in its 1987 *Report on Amendment of the Law of Contract* recommended, persuasively in my view, the enactment of a general legislative provision to the effect that "contracts for the benefit of third parties should not be unenforceable for lack of consideration or want of privity" (at p. 71). The Commission, in the chapter of its Report entitled "Third Party Beneficiaries and Privity of Contract", offered the following general reasons for its recommendation: (1) the present state of the law is very complex and uncertain; (2) the traditional justifications for the doctrine of privity (only those in privity should be allowed to sue; consideration gives the right to sue; and preventing double recovery) are largely unfounded; (3) the doctrine impairs the enforcement of sensible commercial and personal arrangements made on a daily basis; (4) exceptions to the doctrine have developed with no rational basis except to avoid the application of the doctrine; (5) it is difficult, if not impossible, to reconcile the exceptions with the doctrine; (6) the exceptions are of limited use in many situations; (7) the possibility remains that meritorious claims will be defeated by the application of the doctrine; (8) the doctrine has been subject to legislative inroads as well as academic and judicial criticism; (9) many jurisdictions around the world (United States, New Zealand, Western Australia, Queensland and Quebec) have recognized third party rights by abolishing or modifying the doctrine of privity. . . .

[19] The Commission opted for a reform based on the enactment of a general provision abolishing the doctrine, rather than detailed legislation. This approach was considered to be more flexible; permitting courts to fashion principles on a case by case basis in order to enforce third party rights where justice required such a result. Moreover, it would avoid the many difficulties facing the drafter of specific legislation. It is apparent throughout the Report that the reform was also directed towards third parties seeking to enforce limitation of liability clauses made for their benefit.

[20] While noting that legislative reform along the lines mentioned above would be most welcome in this area of the law, many commentators have noted that uniform reform is unlikely in Canada owing to our present constitutional framework. . . . Despite the difficulty in the way of uniform legislative reform, Professor Reif [Linda C. Reif, "A Comment on *ITO Ltd. v. Miida Electronics Inc.* — The Supreme Court of Canada, Privity of Contract and the Himalaya Clause" (1988), 26 *Alta. L. Rev.* 372] is of the opinion that "the legislatures are still the most appropriate sites for any substantial amendment to the principle" since courts are limited in their response to "sporadic and factually limited opportunities" (p. 382). While this may be true, it does not mean that this Court should refuse to assist in the evolution of the common law when faced with appropriate circumstances.

[21] Most of the specific criticisms of the doctrine of privity and its application to third party beneficiaries have come from commentators. Some have questioned the application of the doctrine in general terms, that is, in its application to cases where a third party is attempting to enforce a contractual provision either by suit or by a defence to a suit, while others have dealt exclusively with the question of third party beneficiaries and limitation of liability (or exemption or exclusion) clauses. . . .

[22] These comments and others reveal many concerns about the doctrine of privity as it relates to third party beneficiaries. For our purposes, I think it sufficient to make the following observations. Many have noted that an application of the doctrine so as to prevent a third party from relying on a limitation of liability clause which was intended to benefit him or her frustrates sound commercial practice and justice. It does not respect allocations and assumptions of risk made by the parties to the contract and it ignores the practical realities of insurance coverage. In essence, it permits one party to make a unilateral modification to the contract by circumventing its provisions and the express or implied intention of the parties. In addition, it is inconsistent with the reasonable expectations of all the parties to the transaction, including the third party beneficiary who is made to support the entire burden of liability. The doctrine has also been criticized for creating uncertainty in the law. While most commentators welcome, at least in principle, the various judicial exceptions to privity of contract, concerns about the predictability of their use have been raised. Moreover, it is said, in cases where the recognized exceptions do not appear to apply, the underlying concerns of commercial reality and justice still militate for the recognition of a third party beneficiary right.

[23] There have been numerous calls from the judiciary for a reconsideration of the doctrine of privity and its refusal to allow third party beneficiaries to enforce provisions made for their benefit. . . .

[24] In the United States, third party rights are now recognized in every State, to a varying degree, by common law, uniform statutory legislation and/or specific state legislation. See, for example, §§ 302 - 315 of the *Restatement of Contract (Second)*. Ever since the cornerstone decision of the New York Court of Appeal in *Lawrence v. Fox*, 20 N.Y. 268 (1859), there has emerged what Professor Corbin refers to as a "trend" in the law, both judge-made and statutory, recognizing that third party beneficiaries are entitled, as a general rule, to enforce contractual provisions made for their benefit. The decision of the Massachussetts State Supreme Court in *Choate, Hall & Stewart v. SCA Services, Inc.*, 392 N.E.2d 1045 (1979), demonstrates that this trend has apparently now swept the entire country.

D.   *Previous Decisions of this Court*

[25] As mentioned above, the appellant in its argument places considerable if not exclusive reliance on the decisions of this Court in *Canadian General Electric*, *supra*, *Greenwood Shopping Plaza*, *supra*, and *ITO-International Terminal Operators*, *supra*. From these decisions it is submitted that a tortfeasor's liability cannot be excluded, limited or modified by the terms of a contract to which he or she is not a party, absent facts that can support a finding of trust or agency.

[26] . . . [W]hile *Canadian General Electric* confirms the doctrine of privity to the extent that a stranger cannot obtain a benefit from a contract to which he or she is not a party, it says nothing about the aspect of the doctrine which refuses to recognize a third party beneficiary right.

[27] Much of the same can be said about *Greenwood Shopping Plaza*, *supra*. In that case, employees of a company which was leasing premises in a shopping centre, while acting in the course of their employment, negligently caused a fire which destroyed part of the shopping centre. The lease between the owner of the centre and the company included in paragraphs 14 and 15 the provisions which dealt with the insurance of the demised premises. Although neither party to the contract took any steps towards the performance of the insurance undertakings, both were partially insured. Following the fire, an action was brought against the company and its employees on behalf of the owner of the shopping centre for the recovery of its

uninsured loss and on behalf of its fire insurers by way of subrogation for moneys paid. The company, even though it was vicariously liable for the negligence of its employees, was held to be protected from liability through the provisions of the lease. The sole question before this Court, as stated by McIntyre J., was the following (at pp. 235-36):

> ... whether the respondents, held to have been guilty of negligence which caused the loss, but not parties to the lease and the insuring agreement in paras. 14 and 15, may claim the benefit of those provisions and thereby receive the same protection as that afforded to the company, their employer, who was otherwise equally liable with them for their negligence.
>
> McIntyre J. answered the question in the negative by resorting to the doctrine of privity of contract. He noted that while certain exceptions to this doctrine had developed, such as agency and trust, on the limited evidence before this Court none was available to permit the employees to claim the benefit from the provisions of the lease.

[28] I should like to make four observations concerning this decision. First, the contract involved in *Greenwood Shopping Plaza* was a lease of premises rather than a contract for services such as a contract of storage. The contract was between a lessor (the owner of the shopping centre) and the lessee (the company) and the intervention of the lessee's employees was not at all necessary for the execution of this agreement. It was irrelevant to any aspect of this agreement, especially to paragraphs 14 and 15, whether the lessee had any employees and whether they would be present on the leased premises. Second, the provisions of the contract which the employees were seeking to obtain a benefit from in *Greenwood Shopping Plaza* were not general limitation of liability clauses. Rather they were stipulations containing mutual undertakings by the lessor and the lessee with respect to insurance of the premises and the granting of subrogation rights. Third, it was inferentially observed that there was little, if any, evidence to support a finding that the parties to the contract intended to confer a benefit on the employees by the provisions of the lease relied on. This appears from the comments made by McIntyre J. in the context of his analysis of both the agency exception (at pp. 238-39) and the trust exception (at p. 240) and, more clearly, in the following closing observations (at pp. 240-41):

> *It must also be observed that the clear and precise words of paras. 14 and 15 limit the application of the insurance provisions to the parties to the lease, the appellant and the company.* Courts must, in cases of this sort, be wary against drawing inferences upon vague and scanty evidence, where the result would be to contradict the clear words of a written agreement and where rectification is not sought or may not be had.

[29] Finally, and closely related to the preceding comment, there is the fact that . . . the parties seeking to obtain benefits from the contract in *Greenwood Shopping Plaza* were viewed as complete strangers and not third party beneficiaries. This appears clearly from the wording of the provisions in question as noted by McIntyre J. in the underlined passage reproduced above.

[30] In sum, the decision of this Court in *Greenwood Shopping Plaza*, while containing certain general statements relating to privity of contract, involved a contract and provisions which are different from the contract and provision in the case at bar. More importantly, however, is the fact that that case was not decided with reference to third party beneficiaries and with the aspect of privity denying a *jus tertii*, but rather with reference to complete strangers to a contract. Accordingly, Greenwood Shopping Plaza . . . is of limited use in a determination of whether third party beneficiary rights should be recognized in certain limited circumstances.

. . .

(4)   *The Doctrine of Privity and the Present Appeal*

[31] None of the traditional exceptions to privity is applicable in the case at bar. . . .

(a)   *Should the Doctrine of Privity be Relaxed?*

[32] Without doubt, major reforms to the rule denying third parties the right to enforce contractual provisions made for their benefit must come from the legislature. Although I have strong reservations about the rigid retention of a doctrine that has undergone systematic and substantial attack, privity of contract is an established principle in the law of contracts and should not be discarded lightly. Simply to abolish the doctrine of privity or to ignore it, without more, would represent a major change to the common law involving complex and uncertain ramifications. This Court has in the past indicated an unwillingness to sanction judge-made changes of this magnitude. . . .

[33] This Court has also recognized, however, that in appropriate circumstances courts have not only the power but the duty to make incremental changes to the common law to see that it reflects the emerging needs and values of our society. . . . It is my view that the present appeal is an appropriate situation for making such an incremental change to the doctrine of privity of contract in order to allow the respondents to benefit from the limitation of liability clause.

[34] As we have seen earlier, the doctrine of privity has come under serious attack for its refusal to recognize the right of a third party beneficiary to enforce contractual provisions made for his or her benefit. Law reformers, commentators and judges have pointed out the gaps that sometimes exist between contract theory on the one hand, and commercial reality and justice on the other. We have also seen that many jurisdictions around the world, including Quebec and the United States, have chosen from an early point . . . to recognize third party beneficiary rights in certain circumstances. As noted by the appellant, the common law recognizes certain exceptions to the doctrine, such as agency and trust, which enable courts, in appropriate circumstances, to arrive at results which conform with the true intentions of the contracting parties and commercial reality. However, as many have observed, the availability of these exceptions does not always correspond with their need. Accordingly, this Court should not be precluded from developing the common law so as to recognize a further exception to privity of contract merely on the ground that some exceptions already exist.

[35] While these comments may not, in themselves, justify doing away with the doctrine of privity, they nonetheless give a certain context to the principles that this Court is now dealing with. This context clearly supports in my view some type of reform or relaxation to the law relating to third party beneficiaries. Again, I reiterate that any substantial amendment to the doctrine of privity is a matter properly left with the legislature. But this does not mean that courts should shut their eyes to criticisms when faced with an opportunity, as in the case at bar, to make a very specific incremental change to the common law. . . .

[36] There are few principled reasons for upholding the doctrine of privity in the circumstances of this case. Maintaining the alleged status quo by itself is an unhelpful consideration since I am considering whether or not a relaxation, or change, to the law should be made. Similarly, most of the traditional reasons or justifications behind the doctrine are of little application in cases such as this one, when a third party beneficiary is relying on a contractual provision as a defence in an action brought by one of the contracting parties. There are no concerns about double recovery or floodgates of litigation brought by third party beneficiaries. The fact that a contract is a very personal affair, affecting only the parties to it, is simply a restatement of the doctrine of privity rather than a reason for its maintenance. Nor is there any concern about "reciprocity", that is, there is no concern that it would be unjust to allow a party to sue on a contract when he or she cannot be sued on it.

[37] Moreover, recognizing a right for a third party beneficiary to rely on a limitation of liability clause should have relatively little impact on the rights of contracting parties to rescind or vary their contracts, in comparison with the recognition of a third party right to sue on a contract. In the end, the most that can be said against the extension of exceptions to the doctrine of privity in this case is that the respondent employees are mere donees and have provided no consideration for the contractual limitation of liability.

[38] The doctrine of privity fails to appreciate the special considerations which arise from the relationships of employer-employee and employer-customer. There is clearly an identity of interest between the employer and his or her employees as far as the performance of the employer's contractual obligations is concerned. When a person contracts with an employer for certain services, there can be little doubt in most cases that employees will have the prime responsibilities related to the performance of the obligations which arise under the contract. This was the case in the present appeal, clearly to the knowledge of the appellant. While such a similarity or closeness might not be present when an employer performs his or her obligations through someone who is not an employee, it is virtually always present when employees are involved. Of course, I am in no way suggesting that employees are a party to their employer's contracts in the traditional sense so that they can bring an action on the contract or be sued for breach of contract. However, when an employer and a customer enter into a contract for services and include a clause limiting the liability of the employer for damages arising from what will normally be conduct contemplated by the contracting parties to be performed by the employer's employees, and in fact so performed, there is simply no valid reason for denying the benefit of the clause to employees who perform the contractual obligations. The nature and scope of the limitation of liability clause in such a case coincides essentially with the nature and scope of the contractual obligations performed by the third party beneficiaries (employees).

[39] Upholding a strict application of the doctrine of privity in the circumstances of this case would also have the effect of allowing the appellant to circumvent or escape the limitation of liability clause to which it had expressly consented. . . .

[40] In a similar fashion, it would be absurd in the circumstances of this case to let appellant go around the limitation of liability clause by suing the respondent employees in tort. The appellant consented to limit the "warehouseman'"s liability

to \$40 for anything that would happen during the performance of the contract. When the loss occurred, the respondents were acting in the course of their employment and performing the very services, albeit negligently, for which the appellant had contracted with Kuehne & Nagel. The appellant cannot obtain more than \$40 from Kuehne & Nagel, whether the action is based in contract or in tort, because of the limitation of liability clause. However, resorting to exactly the same actions, it is trying to obtain the full amount from the individuals ("warehousemen") who were directly responsible for the storing of its goods in accordance with the contract. As stated earlier, there is an identity of interest between the respondents and Kuehne & Nagel as far as performance of the latter's contractual obligations is concerned. When these facts are taken into account, and it is recalled that the appellant knew the role to be played by employees pursuant to the contract, it is clear to me that this Court is witnessing an attempt in effect to "circumvent or escape a contractual exclusion or limitation of liability for the act or omission that would constitute the tort". In my view, we should not sanction such an endeavour in the name of privity of contract.

[41] Finally, there are sound policy reasons why the doctrine of privity should be relaxed in the circumstances of this case. A clause such as one in a contract of storage limiting the liability of a "warehouseman" to \$40 in the absence of a declaration by the owner of the goods of their value and the payment of an additional insurance fee makes perfect commercial sense. It enables the contracting parties to allocate the risk of damage to the goods and to procure insurance accordingly. If the owner declares the value of the goods, which he or she alone knows, and pays the additional premium, the bargain will have placed the entire risk on the shoulders of the "warehouseman". On the other hand, if the owner refuses the offer of additional coverage, the bargain will have placed only a limited risk on the "warehouseman" and the owner will be left with the burden of procuring private insurance if he or she decides to diminish its own risk. In either scenario, the parties to the contract agree to a certain allocation and then proceed, based on this agreement, to make additional insurance arrangements if required. It stretches commercial credulity to suggest that a customer, acting prudently, will not obtain insurance because he or she is looking to the employees for recovery when generally little or nothing is known about the financial capacity and professional skills of the employees involved. That does not make sense in the modern world.

[42] In addition, employees such as the respondents do not reasonably expect to be subject to unlimited liability for damages that occur in the performance of the contract when said contract specifically limits the liability of the "warehouseman" to a fixed amount. According to modern commercial practice, an employer such as Kuehne & Nagel performs its contractual obligations with a party such as the appellant through its employees. As far as the contractual obligations are concerned, there is an identity of interest between the employer and the employees. It simply does not make commercial sense to hold that the term "warehouseman" was not intended to cover the respondent employees and as a result to deny them the benefit of the limitation of liability clause for a loss which occurred during the performance of the very services contracted for. Holding the employees liable in these circumstances could lead to serious injustice especially when one considers that the financial position of the affected employees could vary considerably such that, for example, more well off employees would be sued and left to look for contribution from their less well off colleagues. Such a result also creates uncertainty and

requires excessive expenditures on insurance in that it defeats the allocations of risk specifically made by the contracting parties and the reasonable expectations of everyone involved, including the employees. When parties enter into commercial agreements and decide that one of them and its employees will benefit from limited liability, or when these parties choose language such as "warehouseman" which implies that employees will also benefit from a protection, the doctrine of privity should not stand in the way of commercial reality and justice.

[43] For all the above reasons, I conclude that it is entirely appropriate in the circumstances of this case to call for a relaxation of the doctrine of privity.

(b) How Should the Doctrine of Privity be Relaxed?

[44] Regardless of the desirability of making a particular change to the law, I have already noted that complex changes with uncertain ramifications should be left to the legislature. Our power and duty as a court to adapt and develop the common law must only be exercised generally in a incremental fashion. This is particularly important when, as here, changes to substantive law are concerned, as opposed to changes to procedural law. . . .

[45] In my opinion, a threshold requirement for employees to obtain the benefit of their employer's contractual limitation of liability clause is the express or implied stipulation by the contracting parties that the benefit of the clause will also be shared by said employees. Without such a stipulation, it is my view that the employees are in a no better situation than this Court held those employees involved in *Greenwood Shopping Plaza, supra,* to be in, and should not therefore be able to rely on the clause as a means of defence. This Court found that the employees were strangers to the contract, as I discussed above. As for the other requirements proposed by the respondents, I agree with their substance although I would express them in a different manner.

[46] In the end, the narrow question before this Court is: in what circumstances should employees be entitled to benefit from a limitation of liability clause found in a contract between their employer and the plaintiff (customer)? Keeping in mind the comments made earlier and the circumstances of this appeal, I am of the view that employees may obtain such a benefit if the following requirements are satisfied:

(1) The limitation of liability clause must, either expressly or impliedly, extend its benefit to the employees (or employee) seeking to rely on it; and

(2) the employees (or employee) seeking the benefit of the limitation of liability clause must have been acting in the course of their employment and must have been performing the very services provided for in the contract between their employer and the plaintiff (customer) when the loss occurred.

[47] Although these requirements, if satisfied, permit a departure from the strict application of the doctrine of privity of contract, they represent an incremental change to the common law. I say "incremental change" for a number of reasons.

[48] First and foremost, this new exception to privity is dependent on the intention of the contracting parties. An employer and his or her customer may choose the appropriate language when drafting their contacts so as to extend, expressly or impliedly, the benefit of any limitation of liability to employees. It is their intention as stipulated in the contract which will determine whether the first require-

ment is met. In this connection, I agree with the view that the intention to extend the benefit of a limitation of liability clause to employees may be express or implied in all the circumstances. . . .

[49] Second, taken as a whole, this new exception involves very similar benchmarks to the recognized agency exception, applied . . .by this Court in *ITO-International Terminal Operators, supra.* As discussed in the latter decision, the four requirements for the agency exception were inspired from the following passage of Lord Reid's judgment in *Midland Silicones, supra* (at p. 474):

> I can see a possibility of success of the agency argument if (first) the bill of lading makes it clear that the stevedore is intended to be protected by the provisions in it which limit liability, (secondly) the bill of lading makes it clear that the carrier, in addition to contracting for these provisions on his own behalf, is also contracting as agent for the stevedore that these provisions should apply to the stevedore, (thirdly) the carrier has authority from the stevedore to do that, or perhaps later ratification by the stevedore would suffice, and (fourthly) that any difficulties about consideration moving from the stevedore were overcome.

[50] The first requirement of both exceptions is virtually identical. The second and third requirements of the agency exception are supplied by the identity of interest between an employer and his or her employees as far as the performance of contractual obligations are concerned; this is implicit in the recognition of this new exception. As for the fourth requirement of agency, while this new exception makes no specific mention of consideration moving from the employees to the customer, the second requirement of the new exception embraces the same elements which were adopted by courts to recognize consideration moving from stevedores in cases involving "Himalaya clauses".

[51] Third, it must be remembered that I am proposing a very specific and limited exception to privity in the case at bar; viz. permitting employees who qualify as third party beneficiaries to use their employer's limitation of liability clauses as "shields" in actions brought against them, when the damage they have caused was done in the course of their employment and while they were carrying out the very services for which the plaintiff (customer) had contracted with their employer. In sum, I am recognizing a limited *jus tertii*.

[52] In closing on this point, I wish to add the obvious comment that nothing in the above reasons should be taken as affecting in any way recognized exceptions to privity of contract such as trust and agency. In other words, even if the above requirements are not satisfied, an employee may still establish the existence of a trust or agency so as to obtain a benefit which the contracting parties intended him or her to have, notwithstanding lack of privity.

(c)   Application of the New Exception

[53] The only question in the case at bar is whether the respondents are third party beneficiaries with respect to the limitation of liability clause so as to come within the first requirement of the test I set forth above. Based on uncontested findings of fact, the respondents were acting in the course of their employment when they caused the transformer to topple over. Moreover, at that time they were performing the very services provided for in the contract between Kuehne & Nagel and the appellant, namely, the storage and upkeep of the transformer.

[54] For convenience, I reproduce again the limitation of liability clause:

LIABILITY - Sec. 11(a) The responsibility of a warehouseman in the absence of written provisions is the reasonable care and diligence required by the law.

(b) The warehouseman's liability on any one package is limited to $40 unless the holder has declared in writing a valuation in excess of $40 and paid the additional charge specified to cover warehouse liability.

Does the language chosen indicate that the benefit of the clause is specifically restricted to Kuehne & Nagel? I think not. On the contrary, when all of the relevant circumstances are considered, it is my view that the parties must be taken as having intended that the benefit of this clause would also extend to Kuehne & Nagel's employees.

[55] It is clear that the parties did not choose express language in order to extend the benefit of the clause to employees. For example, there is no mention of words such as "servants" or "employees" in s. 11(b) of the contract. As such, it cannot be said that the respondents are express third party beneficiaries with respect to the limitation of liability clause. However, this does not preclude a finding that they are implied third party beneficiaries. In view of the identity of interest between an employer and his or her employees with respect to the performance of the former's contractual obligations and the policy considerations discussed above, it is surely open to a court, in appropriate circumstances, to conclude that a limitation of liability clause in a commercial contract between an employer and his or her customer impliedly extends its benefit to employees.

[56] In the case at bar, the parties have not chosen language which inevitably leads to the conclusion that the respondents were not to benefit from s. 11(b) of the contract of storage. The term "warehouseman" as used in s. 11(b) is not defined in the contract and the definition provided in the *Warehouse Receipt Act*, s. 1, is of no use in determining whether it includes employees for the purpose of the contractual limitation of liability. While it is true that s. 10(e) of the contract uses the term "warehouse employee", this by itself does not preclude an interpretation of "warehouseman" in s. 11(b) of the same contract as implicitly including employees for the purposes of the limitation of liability clause. Such a conclusion does not offend the words chosen by the parties.

[57] When all the circumstances of this case are taken into account, including the nature of the relationship between employees and their employer, the identity of interest with respect to contractual obligations, the fact that the appellant knew that employees would be involved in performing the contractual obligations, and the absence of a clear indication in the contract to the contrary, the term "warehouseman" in s. 11(b) of the contract must be interpreted as meaning "warehousemen". As such, the respondents are not complete strangers to the limitation of liability clause. Rather, they are unexpressed or implicit third party beneficiaries with respect to this clause. Accordingly, the first requirement of this new exception to the doctrine of privity is also met.

C.   Conclusion

[58] The respondents owed a duty of care to the appellant in their handling of its transformer. According to the uncontested findings of the trial judge, they breached this duty causing damages in the amount of $33,955.41. While neither trust nor agency is applicable, the respondents are entitled to benefit directly from the limitation of liability clause in the contract between their employer and the

appellant. This is so because they are third party beneficiaries with respect to that clause and because they were acting in the course of their employment and performing the very services contracted for by the appellant when the damages occurred. I acknowledge that this, in effect, relaxes the doctrine of privity and creates a limited *jus tertii*. However, when viewed in its proper context, it merely represents an incremental change to the law, necessary to see that the common law develops in a manner that is consistent with modern notions of commercial reality and justice.

V. *Disposition*

[59] For the foregoing reasons, I would dismiss the appeal and cross-appeal, both with costs.

[**McLACHLIN J.** wrote a separately concurring judgment in which she suggested two preferable bases for the result: (i) the customer must impliedly have accepted the risk that its property would be handled by the employees of the defendant; and (ii) the limitation of liability in the contract can limit the employees' duty of care.

LA FOREST J., in a partially dissenting judgment, would have held that the employees were not liable in tort, because the tort was related to the performance of a contractual obligation, and the plaintiff could not reasonably rely on the employees as individuals, but rather was relying on the employer.]

NOTE AND QUESTIONS

1.   Notice the use by Iacobucci J. of the sword/shield distinction. If that distinction does not work effectively with promissory estoppel, is it any more likely to work well with third-party beneficiary contracts? The sword/shield distinction has obvious attractions for a judge trying to modify a "fundamental" common law rule to avoid a plainly unsatisfactory result; it looks to be no more than an "incremental" change.

2.   Did the Supreme Court overrule *Greenwood* in *London Drugs*? How would you advise a client about the likely outcome of litigation in a situation like *Greenwood*? *London Drugs* indicates that privity continues to be an important legal doctrine.

       Would you recommend to your clients, for example, that a standard employment contract or a standard limitation of liability clause intended to protect employees be redrafted in the light of the decision? What would you recommend, for example, that the clause in the lease in *Greenwood* be amended to say?

       It is possible, as Iacobucci J. said in *London Drugs*, to say that the parties to the lease in *Greenwood* did not intend to protect the tenant's employees, while the employer in *London Drugs* did intend to protect its employees. The concept of "intention" in such an analysis is artificial — it is almost certain that the landlord and the tenant or the customer and the storer never thought about the position that the tenant's or storer's employees might be in if they were to be sued by the landlord or customer for their negligence. Does an "intention analysis" allow a court to do whatever it wants?

The following decision of a provincial court of appeal takes what may be the next logical step after *London Drugs*. As you read it, consider what, if anything, is left of the 1980 Supreme Court of Canada decision in *Greenwood Shopping Plaza*.

LAING PROPERTY CORP. V. ALL SEASONS DISPLAY INC.

[2000] B.C.J. No. 1655, 190 D.L.R. (4th) 1, 79 B.C.L.R. (3d) 199
(Application for leave to appeal dismissed, 19 April 2001, [2001] S.C.C.A. No. 523)
(C.A., Rowles, Finch and Huddart, JJ.A.)

The judgment of the Court was delivered by **FINCH J.A.**: —

I

[1]   These three appeals are brought from the judgment of the Supreme Court of British Columbia pronounced on 4 February 1998 (reported at (1998), 53 B.C.L.R. (3d) 142, 39 B.L.R. (2d) 153, 3 C.C.L.I. (3d) 241). All appeals raise issues as to the correct interpretation of lease covenants requiring the tenants in a shopping mall to insure in the joint names of the tenant and the landlord against loss by fire, and to waive recourse and rights of subrogation against the landlord.

[2]   Three actions have been commenced in the Supreme Court. In two separate actions the tenants sued various defendants alleged to be responsible for a fire that occurred in the shopping mall on 26 December 1993. The landlord was not named as a defendant in either action. However, the defendants brought third party proceedings against the landlord and its employees claiming contribution or indemnity for their negligence. Those third parties pleaded the lease covenants as to insurance and waiver of rights in their defence.

[3]   In the third action, the landlord sued the same defendants as those sued by the tenants. The defendants again brought third party proceedings against the landlord and its employees. Again the third parties pleaded the same lease covenants in their defence.

[4]   The first appeal raises the question whether the learned trial judge erred in holding that the lease covenants were complete answers for the landlord against the defendants' third party claims.

[5]   The second appeal raises the question whether the learned trial judge erred in holding that the lease provisions did *not* protect the landlord's employees from liability for contribution or indemnity to the defendants in the tenants' two actions on the basis that the employees were not privy to the lease agreements.

[6]   The third appeal is brought by the City of Surrey, which was sued as a defendant in both of the tenants' actions. The City brought third party proceedings against the landlord, alleging breaches of various City by-laws as causes contributing to the fire and consequent losses. The learned trial judge struck out the City's third party notice on the basis that the landlord did not owe any duty to the City arising from any by-law and that the City could not therefore be in any better position than that of the other defendants. The City appeals this aspect of the decision.

[7]   The judgment in the court below arose from applications to strike out the third party notices, brought pursuant to Rules 18A, 19(24) and 57. On those applications the parties based their positions primarily on the pleadings. However, the lease agreements were placed in evidence, and the trial judge was also referred to the by-laws on which the City of Surrey relied. All appeals raise questions of law only, and none of the facts are in dispute.

II

[**FINCH J.A.**'s statement of the facts has been summarized. On Boxing Day 1993 a fire occurred in the Guildford Shopping Centre Mall, located in Surrey, B.C. The mall was owned by Laing Property Corporation ("Laing" or "the landlord"). The fire is alleged to have started in "Santa's Castle", a Christmas display. The fire caused substantial property damage and some of the tenants suffered losses due to the interruption of their businesses. "Santa's Castle" was created in a common area of the mall, not subject to any lease. The defendants in both the landlord's and the tenants' law suits are those alleged to be responsible for the cause and spread of the fire. The defendant All Seasons Display Inc. ("All Seasons") manufactured and designed Santa's Castle.

In the third party proceedings, Laing is alleged to be vicariously liable for the negligence of three of its employees, Michael Mylett, the mall manager, Jeri Lynne Cox, the mall's marketing director, and Frank Frost, the mall's maintenance supervisor. All are alleged to have been in breach of duties they owed to the tenants for failure to take various steps to ensure the safety of the display.

Laing leased retail premises in the mall to a large number of tenants, all of whom entered into written lease agreements. Three different forms of lease were used, but each form of lease, using slightly different wording, required the tenant to obtain property insurance in the joint names of the landlord and the tenant, and stipulated that the insurance policies so obtained would waive recourse and any subrogation rights against the landlord.

The wording of one of the lease forms is set out to illustrate the nature of all of the insurance and waiver covenants:

15. INSURANCE

The Tenant covenants and agrees to effect and maintain throughout the term of this lease in the joint names of the Landlord and Tenant the following Insurances in forms, amounts and with Insurance carriers satisfactory to the Landlord:

. . .

(c) *Fire and extended coverage risks including sprinkler leakage, sewer backup and burst water pipes, Insurance on Tenant's fixtures, fittings, equipment, leasehold improvements and stock in trade in an amount not less than the full replacement value thereof.*

. . .

All such policies shall waive recourse and any other rights of subrogation against the Landlord.

. . .

41. LANDLORD NOT RESPONSIBLE FOR ANY LOSS, DAMAGE ETC.

The Landlord shall not be responsible for any loss, damage or expenses caused to any tenant's fixtures, fittings, goods, stock, machinery, facilities or any other chattels or personal property of the Tenant occasioned by any loss or peril whatsoever, save and except any such loss occasioned solely by the negligence of the Landlord, its servants, agents or employees. [Emphasis added by **FINCH J.A.**]

FINCH J.A. rejected the first ground of appeal and dismissed the claim against the landlord, holding that it was protected by the terms of the leases. He continued:]

IV

THE SECOND APPEAL

Did the learned summary trial judge err in holding that the insurance covenants did not protect Laing's employees from liability because they were not privy to the lease agreements?

A.   *Introduction*

[82] Laing's three employees named as third parties are Michael Mylett, the mall manager, Jeri Lynne Cox, the mall's marketing director, and Frank Frost, the mall's maintenance supervisor. The learned summary trial judge held that although their employer (Laing) was protected from liability by the terms of the leases, the employees were not likewise protected because they were not privy to those contracts. He concluded that the case was indistinguishable from, and governed by, *Greenwood Shopping Plaza Ltd. v. Neil J. Buchanan Ltd.*, [1980] 2 S.C.R. 228, 111 D.L.R. (3d) 257. He held that the facts did not fall within the principled exception to the doctrine of privity as laid down in *London Drugs Ltd. v. Kuehne & Nagel International Ltd.*, [1992] 3 S.C.R. 299, 97 D.L.R. (4th) 261. The employees appealed this decision.

[83] The two-part test for extending a contractual benefit so as to include a contracting party's employees is described by Mr. Justice Iacobucci in *London Drugs*, *supra*, at p. 448 [S.C.R.]:

> . . . I am of the view that employees may obtain such a benefit if the following requirements are satisfied:
>
> (1) The limitation of liability clause must, either expressly or impliedly, extend its benefit to the employees (or employee) seeking to rely on it; and
>
> (2) the employees (or employee) seeking the benefit of the limitation of liability clause *must have been acting in the course of their employment and must have been performing the very services provided for* in the contract between their employer and the plaintiff (customer) when the loss occurred. [Mr. Justice Iacobucci's emphasis]

[84] The learned summary trial judge summarized his conclusion as to whether these requirements had been met at para. 70:

> [70] I have determined that the three employees involved here are alleged to have been acting in the course of their employment and it may be that they are alleged to have been performing the very services provided for in the lease agreements when, through their negligence, they caused the fire. If so, the second of the two requirements set out in *London Drugs* would, on the pleadings, be satisfied. But even if that be the case, it is my view, that the first or threshold requirement cannot be met. It cannot be said that the benefit of the insuring clauses was expressly or impliedly extended to these employees.

[85] The judge makes a clear finding that the employees' allegedly negligent conduct was performed in the course and scope of their employment (see also in this regard paras. 44 and 46 of the reasons). There is what might be called a tentative finding that the employees are alleged to have been performing "the very services" provided for in the leases, and there is a clear finding that the leases do not, either expressly or impliedly, evidence a mutual intention on behalf of the contracting parties to extend the benefits of the insuring clauses to the employees.

[86] That the employees are alleged to have been negligent while acting in the course and scope of their employment is, in my view, not open to doubt. [**FINCH J.A.** referred to the trial judge's reasoning on this point and agreed with him.]

[88] The issues on the employees' appeal, therefore, are whether the parties intended, expressly or impliedly, that the employees have the benefit of the insurance clauses along with their employer, and whether the employees were performing "the very services" provided for in the lease agreements.

B. Facts

[89] All three standard form leases, as well as the London Drugs Lease Modification Agreement, contain the following provision:

a)   The Tenant shall pay to the Landlord as additional rent . . . contribution towards
      the cost of carrying out sales promotions in connection with the Shopping Centre.
      Such contributions shall be used for sales promotions. . . . The cost of sales
      promotions may at the discretion of the Landlord include payment for the ser-
      vices of a full or part time director of promotion.

[90] All three leases also oblige the tenants to pay as additional rent a proportionate share of the operating expenses attributable to the maintenance, operation, supervision and administration of the shopping centre. In addition, the landlord covenants to maintain the common areas of the mall in "good tenantable condition".

[91] All forms of lease therefore contemplate that the tenants will pay Laing for the services described in the leases, and that Laing will spend the moneys received on this account to provide those services. The learned summary trial judge expressed his views of these lease provisions as follows (para. 64):

The leases here contain express obligations borne by the owner to manage and maintain the shopping centre, including in particular the common areas where the Christmas display was located, for the benefit of the tenants. Further, the leases provide for the tenants paying additional rent annually to contribute in proportionate shares to the operating expenses incurred by the owner in that regard, including the employing of personnel to fulfil its obligations. Unlike the lease in *Greenwood Shopping Plaza Ltd.*, these leases may then be said to be more than agreements for the letting of space which for their execution did not require the involvement of the employees alleged to have been negligent. They can, perhaps in a limited sense, be said to be contracts for services to be provided by the owner to the tenants for which the tenants are required to pay. The tenants can be taken to have been aware they were services to be provided by the owner's employees and there would then be a known employer-employee identity of interest that did not exist in *Greenwood Shopping Plaza Ltd.* such that the first distinction Iacobucci J. observed is, in this case, missing.

[92] With respect to whether the parties intended the protection of the leases to benefit the employees, the learned summary trial judge said:

[67] It appears to me that, if it was the intention of the parties to the leases in this case that the owner's employees have the benefit of the insurance covenants, it would mean they intended that the tenants would be obligated to obtain the several forms of liability and property insurances stipulated not just in the owner's name but in the name of all of its employees (presumably while acting in the course of their employment) as well. To imply such an intention would, to my mind, stretch the elasticity of implication beyond any reasonable bounds. In the absence of any expressed intention in the wording of the covenants regarding employees, I do not con-

sider it can be said that the parties shared any intention that the employees would derive any personal benefit from the tenants' obligation to obtain the insurances.

C.   *The Parties' Positions*

[93] Counsel for the employees says that an intention to extend the protection of the insuring covenants in the leases to the employees should be implied. The tenants would have known that the landlord's obligation to provide services under the leases would be fulfilled by the landlord's employees. There was therefore, as the judge found at para. 64, an identity of interest between the employee and employer. Moreover, the employees were powerless to protect themselves against liability. Counsel argues that it would be unjust and unfair for employees found negligent in the course of their employment to be held liable to an extent greater than that of their employer: *Edgeworth Construction Ltd. v. N.D. Lea and Associates*, [1993] 3 S.C.R. 206, 107 D.L.R. (4th) 169; and *Fraser River Pile & Dredge Ltd. v. Can-Dive Services Ltd.* (1999), 176 D.L.R. (4th) 257 (S.C.C.). Counsel submits that there should therefore be an implied intention that the employees benefit from the protection of the lease covenants.

[94] Counsel for the employees says that in light of the trial judge's finding that the employees were acting in the course and scope of their employment at the time of their alleged negligence, the second part of the *London Drugs* test is met by showing that the alleged acts of negligence occurred while the employees were performing Laing's service obligations under the leases.

[95] Counsel points to the particulars of the alleged negligence (quoted above). He relies on the judge's conclusions at paras. 45 and 46 that every act of negligence alleged related to the employees' responsibilities as mall manager, marketing director and maintenance supervisor. He says these duties clearly fall under Laing's service obligations under the leases to manage, maintain, supervise and promote the mall. He says the second part of the *London Drugs* test has therefore been met.

[96] Counsel for the defendants support the learned summary trial judge's application of the test in *London Drugs* in allowing the third party proceedings against the employees to stand. He says the employees were not performing a contract of service, nor were they "performing the very services" provided for in the contract between the employer and the plaintiff when the loss occurred. He points out that the leases are silent concerning the Christmas display and any specific activities relating to the alleged cause of the fire. Counsel suggests the only services contemplated by the leases were to maintain the common areas in "good tenantable condition" and to keep the outside areas well lighted until 11:00 p.m. For this reason, the defendants say there is no basis for implying an intention on behalf of the parties to benefit the employees with the protection of the leases.

[97] Counsel argues, as the judge found, that this case is indistinguishable from *Greenwood Shopping Plaza*.

D.   *Discussion*

[98] The first question to be answered is whether an intention to protect the employees can be implied in the leases. The rationale for implying an intention to extend to someone who is not privy to a contract the benefit of a clause providing one party with protection against liability was fully explored in *London Drugs*, *supra*. The parties' intention is critical. Iacobucci J. said at 449:

> First and foremost, this new exception to privity is dependent on the intention of the contracting parties. An employer and his or her customer may choose the appropriate language when drafting their contracts so as to extend, expressly or impliedly, the benefit of any limitation of liability to employees. It is their intention as stipulated in the contract which will determine whether the first requirement is met. In this connection, I agree with the view that the intention to extend the benefit of a limitation of liability clause to employees may be express or *implied* in all the circumstances: see *e.g., Mayfair Fabrics v. Henley*, 244 A.2d 344 (N.J. 1968); *Employers Casualty Co. v. Wainwright*, 473 P.2d 181 (Colo. Ct. App. 1970) (*cert.* denied).

[99] There appear to be a number of factors which assist in the determination of whether an intention to benefit a third party should be implied. The first is whether there is an identity of interest between the employee and employer as to the performance of the employer's contractual obligations. Where the employer, under the contract, is to provide services to the other party and the employees have the primary responsibility for performing those contractual obligations, the employees' interests are identical to those of the employer.

[100] A second factor is whether, in the circumstances of the contract's performance, a contracting party could be taken to know that the services to be provided under the contract would be performed by the employees of the other contracting party. In the case of a corporate contractor the provision of any services must be carried out by either employees or agents. A question to be asked is whether the contracting parties would normally expect that the service obligation of the contractor would be performed by its employees. Where there is an identity of interest between the employer and the employee and where the other party is aware of that identity of interest and would in the normal course of events expect the services to be performed by the employees, an intention to extend the benefit of any contractual protection to the employees will be implied. If it were not, the plaintiff would generally be able to circumvent the employer's contractual protection by suing the employees in tort. Such a result, in the language of *London Drugs*, "would be absurd" (at p. 444).

[101] The defendants argue that the leases were not contracts for services and that the employees were not performing the very services provided for in the leases. They say that Laing was not obliged to manage, maintain and promote the mall, but that those were merely tasks to be undertaken at Laing's discretion.

[102] However, when one looks at the particulars of negligence set out at para. 44 of the trial judge's reasons, it is clear that the defendants assert fault on the part of all three employees in the performance or non-performance of duties that could only have arisen as part of the obligations under the leases. In the absence of the leases, and but for their employment by Laing, none of the three employees could have owed any duty to the tenants in respect of any of the allegations made against them.

[103] Therefore, it would seem to be inconsistent for the defendants to contend that the leases were not contracts for services, or that the employees were not performing the very services called for under the lease, while at the same time alleging negligence against the employees in the performance of duties which could only arise under the leases.

[104] Whether the learned summary trial judge was correct therefore when he said that "[t]he leases here contain *express* obligations borne by the owner to manage and maintain the shopping centre" is not critical [para. 64, emphasis added]. The fact is that the tenants paid for, and the owner provided, services under the leases, and the tenants knew that those services would be performed by employees of the landlord.

[105] In these circumstances, there was, in my view, an implied mutual intention on behalf of the tenants and the landlord that the landlord's employees would have the benefit of any contractual protection afforded by the leases. It would make no commercial sense to infer otherwise, as the insuring clauses clearly show how the parties intended the risk of loss should be borne. If the employees could be sued for their negligence in performing services provided for under the contract, the tenant (or their insurers) would be able to avoid the clear meaning of the leases. Employees, who would then bear the risk, would have had no opportunity to protect themselves either by contract with the tenants or by insuring themselves against those risks which the contracting parties had already agreed would be borne by the tenants.

[106] We were referred in argument, and in the parties' written submissions, to a number of cases where the principles enunciated in *London Drugs* have been discussed and applied, including: *Edgeworth Construction Ltd. v. N.D. Lea and Associates, supra*; *Froese v. Montreal Trust Co. of Canada* (1996), 137 D.L.R. (4th) 725, 20 B.C.L.R. (3d) 193 (C.A.); *Madison Developments Ltd. v. Plan Electric Co. Ltd.* [(1997), 36 O.R. (3d) 80, 152 D.L.R. (4th) 653]; and *Tony & Jim's Holdings Ltd. v. Silva* [(1999), 43 O.R. (3d) 633, 170 D.L.R. (4th) 193], all of which I have read and considered.

[107] In my respectful view, this is another case where it can properly be implied that the parties intended the protection of the insuring clauses to extend to the landlord's employees. I am of the view that the learned summary trial judge erred in reaching the contrary conclusion.

[108] The remaining issue on the *London Drugs* test is whether the employees can be said to have been performing "the very services provided for in the contract between their employer and the plaintiff . . . when the loss occurred". I have already referred to the particulars of negligence alleged against the employees and the provisions of the lease requiring the tenants to pay for services to be provided by the landlord. As I have said, I do not see how the employees can be said to have been negligent as alleged while acting in the course and scope of their employment, and at the same time be said to be performing services that were not the very services which the employer had contracted to provide.

[109] As I understand the reasoning in *London Drugs*, I do not think it matters that the negligent conduct alleged does not comprise *all* of the services for which the landlord contracted, nor that the services provided were discretionary on the part of the landlord. For example, where a contract required one party to "inspect and maintain", and the only negligence complained of was in failing to maintain, it could not be said that maintenance services were not the very services called for by the contract. Similarly, where, as here, the contract confers a discretion on the landlord to provide some or all of a variety of services for which the tenants pay, and the landlord chooses to provide some of those services and not others, it could not be said that the services so provided at the landlord's discretion were not the very services called for under the lease.

[110] I am therefore of the view that the employees have met both parts of the *London Drugs* test, having shown an implied contractual intention that the insuring clauses should benefit them as well as their employer, and having shown that the negligent conduct alleged against them was performed in the course and scope of their employment and in the discharge of the very services the landlord was required to provide under the leases.

[111] I come then to the learned summary trial judge's conclusion that this case is not "distinguishable from *Greenwood Shopping Plaza* in any determinative way" (at para. 71). The points of similarity identified by the judge were:

    (1) the form of the agreement (a lease rather than a contract for services);

    (2) the nature of the clauses limiting liability (not a general limitation of liability clause);

    (3) the absence of evidence to support a finding of intention to benefit the employees; and

    (4) the employees in both cases were said to be viewed properly as complete strangers to the lease agreements rather than as third party beneficiaries.

[112] The learned summary trial judge accepted that in this case the lease might be viewed as a contract for services. For the reasons expressed above, I believe this issue must be decided squarely in favour of the employees.

[113] As to the form of the agreement, I see nothing in *London Drugs* to suggest that relaxing the doctrine of privity should turn on whether the contract in question is a lease, a contract of storage, or any other particular form of agreement. *Greenwood* was distinguished in *London Drugs* on the basis that no service obligations were contained in the *Greenwood* lease, not simply because the contract in question was a lease.

[114] Mr. Justice Iacobucci also referred with approval to *Mayfair Fabrics v. Henley*, *supra* and *Employers Casualty Co. v. Wainwright*, 473 P.2d 181 (1970). In both cases the benefits of exclusionary clauses were extended to employees of a party to a contract, and both cases involved exclusion clauses contained in commercial leases.

[115] As to whether there is sufficient evidence to support the finding of an intention to benefit the employees, it is of course correct to say that there is no direct evidence of such an intention. The intention, however, is to be found in the identity of interest between employer and employee, the tenants' knowledge of that identity of interest, and the performance by the employees of services which were provided for by the contract. In my view, there is evidence from which an intention to benefit the employees can and should be implied.

[116] Finally, the question of whether the employees in *Greenwood* could be considered third party beneficiaries to the contract was never addressed in that case. The analysis in *Greenwood* was based on the then accepted view of the doctrine of privity of contract, and whether the case, on its facts, could be said to fall into either the agency or trust exceptions to that doctrine. In the discussion of the trust exception, Mr. Justice McIntyre indirectly mentioned a third party right when he quoted at 239 from *Dunlop Pneumatic Tyre Co. Ltd. v. Selfridge & Co.*, [1915] A.C. 847 (H.L.): "Our law knows nothing of a *jus quaesitum tertio* arising by way of contract". But beyond that, there was no consideration of third party rights arising outside of the exceptions.

[117] So I think it must be taken as clear that no arguments were advanced in *Greenwood* based on the principles adopted in *London Drugs*. Therefore, the *Greenwood* case can properly be distinguished from the case at bar. But even if that were not so I would not follow it. To do so would produce a result that is directly contrary to the law as enunciated in *London Drugs*. I am also in agreement with the comments of Mr. Justice Carthy in *Madison Developments*, *supra*, where, speaking for the majority, he said at p. 91:

> As I read these lengthy excerpts from *London Drugs Ltd.*, the Supreme Court has not just distinguished the facts in *Greenwood*; it has applied new reasoning to create an incremental change in the law of privity, and has set forth a test for the application of that change which is not restricted to cases involving limited liability. In my view, it is now unnecessary to compare the facts of this case to those in *Greenwood*. It is rather a matter of applying the general principles enunciated in *London Drugs Ltd.* to a case involving an obligation to obtain fire insurance, as opposed to one imposing a limitation of liability.

[118] I am therefore of the view that the learned summary trial judge erred in holding that the three employees of Laing were not absolved from liability by the terms of the lease. I would allow their appeal and direct that the third party proceedings against them be struck out.

. . .

[140] I would allow the second appeal, being of the view that according to the principles enunciated in *London Drugs*, Laing's employees are entitled to the protection of the lease covenants.

. . .

NOTES AND QUESTIONS

1. The Supreme Court of Canada dismissed leave to appeal in *Laing Property* on April 19, 2001. Is *Greenwood* still "good law" after *Laing Property*?

2. Until the decision in *Laing Property*, it was possible for a court to get more or less satisfactory results simply by finding that every case was a "special case". This development was consistent with the history of the common law in this area as it did little more than neutralize cases that were obviously unsatisfactory. *Laing Property* suggests that *London Drugs* has, in spite of the very cautious language that Iacobucci J. uses and his unsatisfactory attempt to distinguish *Greenwood*, set the law off on a new course.

3. In *Tony and Jim's Holdings Ltd. v. Silva*, [1999] O.J. No. 705, 43 O.R. (3d) 633, 170 D.L.R. (4th) 193 (C.A.) there was a comprehensive waiver of subrogation rights under the landlord's insurance policy in favour of all those "with respect to which insurance is provided by" the policy. The insurer attempted to make the principal of a corporate tenant personally liable for a fire loss on which it had paid. The Court of Appeal held that, though the principal was not a party to the insuring agreement, his negligence could only be regarded as that of the corporation. This result was said to be consistent with the parties' intention in taking out the insurance in the first place.
   In giving the judgment of the Court, Charron J.A. said (pp. 643-44 O.R.):

   > [29] . . . While the language used in this clause is certainly not the clearest, it would seem to me that, in a case such as this one where fire coverage is extended to leased premises for fire caused by the negligence of anyone, the scope of this waiver can reasonably be interpreted to extend to the tenant who, in the words of the clause, has an "interest with respect to which insurance is provided" by the policy. Indeed, the insurer does not assert the right to make a

subrogated claim against the tenant. It is my view that the words used are also wide enough to include those individuals through which the corporate tenant, of necessity, must act.

[30] . . . [I]t is clear that the parties intended, by the terms of the lease, to allocate the risk of damage between them and then to procure insurance accordingly. The tenant paid the premiums, and the landlord procured the insurance. The [landlord's representative] confirmed in his examination for discovery that "we had to protect ourselves, and the tenants." Given that [the principal of the tenant] signed the lease which included the insurance provision on behalf of the corporation, it makes no commercial sense to expect in these circumstances that [he] would understand that he was obligated to procure separate insurance to cover the acts of those individuals through which the corporation would act. In my view, such an interpretation would clearly defeat the parties' allocation of risk and their reasonable expectations.

Another decision of the Supreme Court, *Fraser River Pile & Dredge Ltd. v. Can-Dive Services Ltd.*, [1999] S.C.J. No. 48, [1999] 3 S.C.R. 108, 176 D.L.R. (4th) 257, suggests that the Court will "relax" the doctrine of privity in order to produce results which "correspond" with "commercial reality". In that case, another one where an insurer tried to argue that it was not bound by a waiver of subrogation rights against a third party, Iacobucci J., again giving the judgment of the Supreme Court, held that the important factor was the parties' intention. He held that that intention was that the third party be protected. This development avoids the need to manipulate agency and trust doctrines to achieve the desired result, though it has limitations as it may not be clear exactly what the phrase "commercial reality" means.

As with the cases like *Gilbert Steel* and promissory estoppel, the important question is not whether contract principles or doctrine will support what the court wants to do, but whether the court wants to use the materials to hand to reach one result rather than another. The importance of decisions like *Laing Property*, *Tony and Jim's Holdings Ltd. v. Silva*, *Fraser River* and the other cases mentioned by Finch J.A., is that the courts seem to have rejected the attitude of indifference to the actual results and dominance of doctrine which characterized *Greenwood* and *Gilbert Steel.*

The result of the recent developments of promissory estoppel and of the third-party beneficiary rule is that courts seem more willing than they once were to reach results that acknowledge concerns, *e.g.*, for the protection of reliance and of the parties' reasonable expectations, that are at the heart of the law of contracts. To this extent, it may be that rules which, like the third-party beneficiary rule, ignore those concerns and apply traditional doctrine almost for its own sake, are on their way out.

4. While *London Drugs* affords important protections to "third party beneficiaries", the concept of privity remains a fundamental part of the law of contract, generally allowing those in a chain of transactions to seek relief only from parties with whom they have had contractual dealings. One illustration of its significance is the treatment in *Laing Property* of All Seasons Display Inc. Like the employees of the landlord, the display company had a contractual link with the landlord, but it clearly could not rely on the landlord's contract with the tenant to shield it from liability. It made "commercial sense" for the display company to get its own liability insurance; unlike employees, who would very likely have been caught by surprise if they had liability for actions taken in the course of their employment, there was no expectation that this independent contractor would have the protection of the lease. The display company was clearly expected to obtain its own liability insurance coverage.

5. An important way in which plaintiffs may, in some cases, circumvent the problem of lack of privity is by bringing a tort action (as occurred in *London Drugs*). For example, since *Donoghue v. Stevenson*, [1932] A.C. 562 a consumer can bring an action against a manufacturer for physical injury that is suffered by use of a product, even though the consumer's contract is with the retailer. As will be discussed in Chapter 5, a very important limitation on the use of tort actions is that they are generally limited

to situations where there is physical damage or injury, and cannot be used to recover for "purely economic losses". As will also be considered in Chapters 3 and 5, in some cases in which a person has relied on a statement made by a party with whom it has not had direct contractual dealings, it may be possible to impose liability based on the tort of negligent misrepresentation or by use of unilateral contract analysis. Consistent with *London Drugs*, the courts have recently weakened the rigid effects of privity and taken a broader view of situations in which negligent misrepresentation and unilateral contract can mitigate the rigours of privity doctrine. Nevertheless, privity of contract remains a fundamental doctrine that often limits those seeking compensation for losses to seeking relief from those with whom they have direct contractual links. This can create difficulties, for example, if a party in the "contractual chain" goes bankrupt. The limitations on liability resulting from the doctrine of privity and the extent to which plaintiffs can circumvent privity, are major themes in later chapters of this book.

Note on Legislative Reform of the Privity Rule

It might appear that a simple solution to the problems posed by the third-party beneficiary rule would be legislative abolition. One could envisage a statute that simply said that promises for the benefit of a third person would henceforth be enforceable. This simple solution would, however, be inadequate as it does not, for example, deal with the questions of the rights of the parties to the original contract to modify the contract without obtaining the consent of the third party. That there are difficulties in such a solution is clear, for even when the devices of agency or assignment are used to get around the rule, there are significant limits on the rights of the third party.

For example, if the assignee of a debt should sue, he can only do so "subject to the equities", that is, subject to the defences that the debtor could have raised if sued by the assignor. (This rule does not apply in the special case of a holder in due course of a negotiable instrument.) Similarly, a principal whose agent did not disclose the existence of an agency relation when she dealt with the third party can only sue the third party subject to any right of set-off that the third party may have against the agent.

An interesting example of legislative handling of the third-party issue is provided by contracts of life insurance. A common example of such a contract is one where the insurer agrees to pay the face value of the policy to a beneficiary (often the insured's spouse) designated by the insured. The insured will usually pay the premiums and be the contracting party. At common law, the beneficiary was a third party to the contract between the insurer and the insured and, therefore, had no enforceable claim for the amount of the policy. The representative of the estate could, for example, compromise a claim on the life insurance policy and direct payment to the estate. This result was intolerable, and so legislation was enacted to provide that the beneficiary can sue the insurer (*Insurance Act*, R.S.O. 1990, c. I.8, s. 195):

> 195. A beneficiary may enforce for the beneficiary's own benefit ... the payment of insurance money made payable to him, her or it in the contract or by a declaration and in accordance with the provisions thereof, but the insurer may set up any defence that it could have set up against the insured or the insured's personal representative.

The difficulty is that the insured may want to retain the freedom to deal with the policy. The insured may want to cancel it, to borrow money on the security of the policy or to change the beneficiary. The right of a beneficiary to sue must, therefore, be made subject to the right of the insured during his or her lifetime or in a will to change the arrangement with the insurer. The *Insurance Act* therefore provides:

> 197. Where a beneficiary,
>
> (a)   is not designated irrevocably . . .
>
> the insured may assign, exercise rights under or in respect of, surrender or otherwise deal with the contract as provided therein or in this Part or as may be agreed upon with the insurer.

The example of life insurance illustrates an important fact about the third-party rule: in many of the specific situations where the rule caused the greatest difficulties it was reversed by statute. It is unnecessary to give a complete listing of the legislative provisions. It is sufficient to note:

(1)   The driver of a car can sue the owner's insurer: *Insurance Act*, R.S.O. 1990, c. I.8, s. 244, reversing *Vandepitte v. Preferred Accident.*

(2)   An employee can claim the benefits of a collective agreement made between his employer and the union: *Labour Relations Act, 1995*, S.O. 1995, c. 1, Sched. A, s. 56, reversing *Young v. Canadian Northern Railway Co.*, [1931] A.C. 83, [1931] 1 D.L.R. 645 (P.C.).

(3)   A mortgagee can sue the transferee of the original mortgagor if the transferee promises the transferor to pay the mortgage: *Mortgages Act*, R.S.O. 1990, c. M.40, s. 20.

(4)   A consignee of goods can sue the shipper or carrier: *Mercantile Law Amendment Act*, R.S.O. 1990, c. M.10, s. 7; *Bills of Lading Act*, R.S.C. 1985, c. B-5, s. 2.

The legislative provisions of the other provinces parallel those of Ontario.

Given the large-scale legislative reversal of the third-party beneficiary rule, is the position of Iacobucci J. in *London Drugs* that legislative change, not judicial development, is the correct way to deal with the problems of the common law appropriate? Why is this legislative pattern not accepted as an authority (or authorities) on the law of third-party beneficiary contracts?

The Ontario Law Reform Commission in its *Report on Amendment of the Law of Contract* (1987) discussed in some detail the various proposals that have been suggested for the reform of the third-party beneficiary rule and the difficulties that must be overcome, and finally recommended that:

> There should be enacted a legislative provision to the effect that contracts for the benefit of third parties should not be unenforceable for lack of consideration or want of privity.

While this proposal has the merit of simplicity, it may be so brief as to create other problems. It does not deal with the kind of problems that, for example, the *Insurance Act* has had to consider, though it might avoid the harshness of the rule when applied to circumstances like *Greenwood v. Beattie*. The Supreme Court cited this *Report* in its judgment in *London Drugs*.

In England, legislation was enacted to abolish the third-party beneficiary rule. The Lord Chancellor, Lord Irving of Lairg, speaking on behalf of the government on second reading of the legislation in the House of Lords, said, "The one question

. . . about the Bill is not why it has been introduced, but why it has not been introduced before".

CONTRACTS (RIGHTS OF THIRD PARTIES) ACT, 1999

(U.K. 1999, Chapter c.31)

BE IT ENACTED by the Queen's most Excellent Majesty, by and with the advice and consent of the Lords Spiritual and Temporal, and Commons, in this present Parliament assembled, and by the authority of the same, as follows: —

Right of third party to enforce contractual term.

1(1) Subject to the provisions of this Act, a person who is not a party to a contract (a "third party") may in his own right enforce a term of the contract if-
(a)   the contract expressly provides that he may, or
(b)   subject to subsection (2), the term purports to confer a benefit on him.

(2) Subsection (1)(b) does not apply if on a proper construction of the contract it appears that the parties did not intend the term to be enforceable by the third party.

(3) The third party must be expressly identified in the contract by name, as a member of a class or as answering a particular description but need not be in existence when the contract is entered into.

(4) This section does not confer a right on a third party to enforce a term of a contract otherwise than subject to and in accordance with any other relevant terms of the contract.

(5) For the purpose of exercising his right to enforce a term of the contract, there shall be available to the third party any remedy that would have been available to him in an action for breach of contract if he had been a party to the contract (and the rules relating to damages, injunctions, specific performance and other relief shall apply accordingly).

(6) Where a term of a contract excludes or limits liability in relation to any matter references in this Act to the third party enforcing the term shall be construed as references to his availing himself of the exclusion or limitation.

(7) In this Act, in relation to a term of a contract which is enforceable by a third party-
"the promisor" means the party to the contract against whom the term is enforceable by the third party, and
"the promisee" means the party to the contract by whom the term is enforceable against the promisor.

Variation and rescission of contract.

2(1) Subject to the provisions of this section, where a third party has a right under section 1 to enforce a term of the contract, the parties to the contract may not, by agreement, rescind the contract, or vary it in such a way as to extinguish or alter his entitlement under that right, without his consent if-
(a)   the third party has communicated his assent to the term to the promisor,
(b)   the promisor is aware that the third party has relied on the term, or

    (c) the promisor can reasonably be expected to have foreseen that the third
        party would rely on the term and the third party has in fact relied on it.

            . . .

The Act goes on at considerable length to deal with the problems that a simple
abolition of the third party beneficiary rule entails. The number of points that Parliament considered it necessary to deal with illustrates that the simplicity of the
Ontario solution would be an illusion.

The following extract is a useful summary of the issues raised in this chapter, as
well as providing an introduction to some of the issues in the next chapter.

LLEWELLYN, "WHAT PRICE CONTRACT? AN ESSAY IN PERSPECTIVE"

(1931), 40 *Yale L.J.* 704 at 741-44

Consideration

[1] . . . In purpose consideration surely approximates closely the rough description
. . . of [the *Civil Code* concept of] *causa*: any sufficient justification for court-
enforcement. In broad effects, that purpose is accomplished. In detail, however,
the machinery is embarrassed by a number of rules not too well designed to meet
the purpose, yet sufficiently crystallized to make continuous trouble in such cases
as involve them.

[2]   Neither causes nor processes of the development of the consideration concept are at all clear in detail. We do not know how the Germanic system of awarding what one may speak of as the advantage of proof to the apparently sounder
side came to degenerate into the debt-defendant's power as of right to swear himself out of judgment. We do not know whether the fear of stout swearers or the
growth of commercial transactions was the more vital factor in developing assumpsit; we know little if anything of the details of the latter pressure on the courts
from, say, 1570 to 1620. We do not know in any clarity the process by which the
case-misfeasance-tort root and the *quid-pro-quo* root out of debt were built together. What is clear, is the emergence of a current definition in terms of benefit to
the promisor or detriment to the promisee as the agreed equivalent and inducing
cause of the promise; a definition which purports both to show what is adequate
and what is necessary to a successful action in assumpsit or its heirs. The current
formulation has the merit of covering most cases, even if it does not cover all. Indeed it is obvious that as soon as the arbitrary but utterly necessary logical jump is
made, of making mutual promises serve to support each other, the great bulk of
business promises are comfortably cared for.

[3]   Four troublesome classes of cases remain. There are business promises such
as "firm offers," understood to be good for a fixed time, but revoked before. They
are frequent; they are and should be relied on. As to them our consideration doctrine is badly out of joint. Closely related in orthodox doctrine, less so in practice,
is the second class: promises which call for acceptance by extended action (such as

laying twenty miles of track), revoked while the work is in process. A third and hugely important class is that of either additional or modifying business promises made after an original deal has been agreed upon. Law and logic go astray whenever such dealings are regarded as truly comparable to new agreements. They are not. No business man regards them so. They are going-transaction adjustments, as different from agreement-formation as are corporate organization and corporate management; and the line of legal dealing with them which runs over waiver and estoppel is based on sound intuition. The fourth main trouble-making class has only a doctrinal connection with business; it lies chiefly in the field of family affairs; it includes the promise made and relied on, but which did not bargain for reliance, and in the case of promises to provide it laps over into the third-party beneficiary problem. As to all of these classes but the first, a distinct but very uneven tendency is observable in the courts to strain by one dodge or another toward enforcement. That tendency is healthy. It may be expected to increase. It has already had some effects on orthodox doctrine. (e.g., *Restatement of Contracts* (Am. L. Inst. 1927) §§ 45, 90 & 135) and may be expected to have more. Meanwhile the first class mentioned goes largely untouched.

[4]   When one attempts to estimate the net value of the consideration requirement the first step is to repeat that it does fit most normal cases in life, that it gives trouble only on the fringes. As a test of what promises *not* to enforce, it must be regarded as somewhat formalistic. The existence of bargain equivalency does indeed commonly evidence positively that the promise was deliberate — considered — meant. Such equivalency gives also fair ground for believing that *some* promise was in fact made; and thereby much reduces the danger from possible perjury, and even from misunderstanding. The giving of a bargain equivalent, be it by promise or by action, is furthermore an excellent objective indication not only of the creation of expectation in the promisee, but of the reasonableness of there being expectation, and of its being related to the promise. (And the size of the equivalent may help to "interpret" the expectation.) Yet it will be observed that the handing over of a signed promise in writing (which is *not* enough for enforcement) would go far in most circumstances to assure the same values; no lawyer, *e.g.*, can fail to be struck by the closeness with which exemptions from the requirement of writing under the *Statute of Frauds* are related to the presence of unambiguous consideration which is *substantially equivalent in fact* to the promise claimed. Nor is it apparent why in many cases deliberateness, due assurance that the promise was made and relied on, and properly so, might not all be evidenced by circumstances apart from either writing or consideration. The problem is acute only within the family. Outside a writing might well be made a condition to "reasonableness" of any reliance; though very possibly, as with the *Statute of Frauds* on sales an exception might be needed for petty transactions. All in all, then, as a test for non-enforcement, our consideration requirements must be regarded as not yet wholly just to our needs.

[5]   As a positive test, a test for what promises *to* enforce, the same must be said. For here the requirement of the positive law runs in terms not of *factual* equivalency, but of *formal* equivalency under the bargain as stated. A consideration which in fact is largely, even wholly formal, may be enough; release of injury-claim for a dollar. This is well enough when the promise is one whose enforcement is in itself socially desirable: a charitable subscription, a promise to provide for a child on marriage, an option to buy land. And it is enforcement in such cases

which has given foothold for the draftsmen in cases of a — socially — different character. But when the courts in such cases recognize in general language the adequacy of thoroughly formal consideration, they obscure the problem discussed above, as to government by contract; the same problem so clearly seen by the courts in usury and mortgage cases, and by the legislature in regulation of employment: that of discrepancy in bargaining power and semi-duress in fact. Though obscured, that problem recurs. It is therefore not surprising that the last quarter century has seen — in business cases — the incursion into the doctrine of consideration of a further doctrine of so-called "mutuality" whereby particular promises are matched off against each other, and some equivalency in fact (*e.g.*, to buy if the other party has agreed to sell) frequently insisted on, even when formally adequate consideration is present. It is to be expected that this tendency will continue: and it is not unlikely that it will develop as in the past, peculiarly to relieve the weaker bargainer. The lop-sidedness of bargain-result is thus taken as the mark of lop-sidedness of bargain-making. But the motivation being apparently not wholly conscious, the result has been (as so often during case-law growth) confusion in doctrine and uncertainty in outcome; and — natural enough in a business economy — a relief of smaller business men which finds little counterpart in the case of the laborer.

Llewellyn wrote this article in 1931. Much of his analysis foresaw the legal developments of the past half-century, with the development of such doctrines as estoppel, unconscionability and economic duress.

CHAPTER THREE

THE FORMATION OF CONTRACTS

The rules governing the formation of contracts figure prominently at the start of the traditional approach to the study of the law of contracts. One reason for this is that the rules appear to reflect both the underlying values of the common law of contract and the desire of many lawyers, judges, academics and law students for certainty and predictability. Another reason is that the rules appear to be an important aspect of the intensely practical process of bargaining. But here, as with many other aspects of the law of contracts, the apparent simplicity and certainty of the rules mask many problems. The assumption that the rules respond to the practical problems of bargaining is largely false.

The approach in these materials is to provide a summary of the traditional black-letter rules of the common law, with some illustrations of the problems that arise. The second part of the chapter will explore some of the difficulties that typically arise in practice, their nature and what a solicitor may do about them. Many of these problems arise in situations where the traditional rules are either inapplicable or unable to respond satisfactorily to them.

This chapter includes a consideration of how the traditional legal rules governing contract formation have been applied to meet problems that arise with new means of communication, first with the introduction of the telegraph in the mid-nineteenth century, then, in the following century, with the use of telephones, fax machines, and most recently the Internet and e-commerce. The traditional rules have continued to hold intellectual appeal, though they have been adapted to apply to the new means of communication.

THE RULES OF OFFER AND ACCEPTANCE

The Mirror Image Rule of Offer and Acceptance

At common law the basic rules of contract formation developed in the nineteenth century as part of the bargain model of contracts. This model relies on the "mirror image" approach to contract formation. The recognized model for making a contract is for one party, called the "offeror", to state all the terms on which he is prepared to do business and to present these terms to the other as the "offer". (The personal pronouns "he" and "she" will often be used for convenience in this chapter, but always bear in mind that it is dangerous to forget that most problems of modern commercial contract involve corporations and that the pronoun "it" is more appropriate.) The other party, called the "offeree", can accept or reject the offered terms. If the offeree accepts all the terms, a contract is made. If the terms are rejected, the offer is "dead" and no contract can arise from a second purported acceptance. Once an offer is rejected, the offeror has the right to act as if there will be no contract with the offeree and may, for example, make a deal with someone else.

exchange of offers ⇒ contract

If the offeree does not accept all of the terms proposed, the offer has been rejected. If the offeree does not reject the terms outright but makes some changes in them, then the terms that she proposes become a new offer (and she becomes the offeror) and the other party (who becomes the offeree) is free to reject or accept that offer. Such a process permits the parties to bargain over the terms of a contract: the process is an exchange of offers that either party may, when his or her turn comes, accept and thus turn the offer into a contract. The process can go on for as long as the parties have the inclination. Its conclusion is either a clear breakdown of negotiations (as when an offer is rejected outright and no counter-offer is made), a clear agreement (as when one party says, "I accept all the terms you propose") in response to an offer or, somewhat less clearly, when the process just peters out and the parties turn to other things. The ultimate acceptance must mirror the final offer. The acceptance must in substance be: "I accept your offer," with "no ifs, ans or buts."

The courts have also recognized a type of "pre-offer" statement, called an "invitation to offer" or an "invitation to treat". (In the construction industry or for large projects, there may be three stages: an RFI, *i.e.*, a request for information on possible bidders to see if they are qualified; an RFP, *i.e.*, a request for proposals, inviting qualified parties to indicate their interest; a tender call, *i.e.*, an invitation to tenderers, perhaps those who have expressed an interest, to make an offer; and the final acceptance of the offer with the selection of the winning bid.) The invitation to treat expresses an interest in entering into negotiations, suggesting terms for an offer that might be accepted. Once a court concludes that a statement is only an invitation to treat, it cannot be "accepted"; only an offer confers on the offeree the power to make a contract.

In practice, it can be difficult to distinguish between an invitation to treat and an offer since the parties rarely make a clear statement indicating the legal significance of their communications. One party may make what might in some circumstances be an offer but which is not clearly so. If the other party purported to "accept" such an "offer", how can the courts tell if that "acceptance" created a contract? There are two sides to the dispute. The recipient of the "offer" would argue that she reasonably understood the statement to be an offer and that she was therefore entitled to accept. The "offeror" will argue that he never intended to do more than invite the other side to make an offer to him, which he in turn could choose to accept or not; his initial statement was one that preceded the stage of the negotiations where the offer is made. The issue of classifying a statement as an invitation to offer, an offer or an acceptance is generally undertaken retrospectively and in the context of litigation.

There are a great many cases on this issue and it is clear that no rule of law can resolve it. The inquiry that the court must make is, in a sense, factual: "What did the offeree reasonably understand by what the offeror said?" What is more important than the form of the inquiry is the attitude that the court brings to this factual determination.

Courts, for example, generally hold that a newspaper advertisement or the publication of a price list constitutes only an "invitation to treat", not an offer. If an advertisement were held to be an offer, the advertiser who "offers" to sell a single used car could find himself bound by two or more "acceptances". There are, however, circumstances in which an advertiser may be held to have made an offer. In *Lefkowitz v. Great Minneapolis Surplus Store*, 86 N.W.2d 689 (Minn. S.C. 1957) the defendant store published a newspaper advertisement announcing a sale at its store, stating: "3 brand new coats for sale, worth $100, $1 only: First come, first served." This statement was held to be an offer capable of acceptance by the plaintiff, who was among the first three people in the store to claim one of the coats. What is important in cases like *Lefkowitz* are such things as the reasonable understanding of the offeree and the risk that the offeror will be caught by unfair surprise.

The general approach of the courts to the interpretation of communications made in the process of contract formation was articulated in the classic English case of *Smith v. Hughes* (1871), L.R. 6 Q.B. 597. (The case is reproduced below.) Blackburn J. said (p. 607):

> If, whatever a man's real intention may be, he so conducts himself that a reasonable man would believe that he was assenting to the terms proposed by the other party, and the other party upon that belief enters into the contract with him, the man thus conducting himself would be equally bound as if he had intended to agree to the other party's terms.

The approach of Blackburn J. in *Smith v. Hughes* reflects an important theme for the law of contracts. The common law takes an "objective" approach to the analysis of contract formation and the interpretation of contracts. An "objective" agreement exists if one party reasonably believes that the other is assenting to the terms proposed by the first. The adoption of an objective approach facilitates the process of contract formation. A person can rely on the reasonable meaning of communications received without having to inquire into the other party's actual state of mind. If a "subjective" approach were adopted, the courts would have to engage in a difficult inquiry into what was actually in the mind of the contracting parties.

Though the courts now have clearly adopted an objective approach to the analysis of contract, they occasionally use language that suggests that what is subjectively in the minds of the parties is important. It is sometimes said that there has to be a *consensus ad idem* (in Latin, literally "agreement to the same thing") or that the parties "minds have to be at one". Statements like this are misleading. No legal system can require that there be an actual "meeting of the minds", for that would provide too much of an incentive to those who would like to contract with their "fingers crossed". The requirement that a subjective agreement exist would permit one party to stay with a contract only so long as it suited its convenience; when it did not, the party could claim that it had never really agreed to the other's terms. The law, at least with commercial contracts, must take an objective approach in the sense of the approach taken by the court in *Smith v. Hughes*.

A curious set of cases arising in the context of the rules of offer and acceptance deals with the display of goods in a self-service store. One so-called leading case, *Pharmaceutical Society of Great Britain v. Boots Cash Chemists (Southern) Ltd.*, [1952] 2 Q.B. 795, [1952] 2 All E.R. 456, affirmed [1953] 1 Q.B. 401, [1953] 1 All E.R. 482 (C.A.) arose out of a prosecution of a "self-serve pharmacy" for selling certain drugs in violation of a statute. The statute required that the "sale" of specified drugs was to be "effected by, or under the supervision of, a registered pharmacist". The drugs in question were displayed on a shelf in the store. The evidence was that a registered pharmacist was on duty near the cash register at the front of the store, but not near the display. The case turned on when (and therefore where) a contract for "sale" was made in a self-service store. The English Court of Appeal held that the sale was only made when the customer brought the goods to the cash register with the displayed sale price on the shelf being a mere "invitation to treat." The court analyzed the transaction on the basis that the customer made an offer at the cash register, implicitly offering to purchase the goods at the price on the sticker. The offer was accepted by the store when the check-out clerk entered the sale in the cash register, with a pharmacist nearby to supervise the sale. The result of this analysis was that the charge of "selling" drugs without the "supervision" of a pharmacist was dismissed. The prosecution probably arose out of the opposition of traditional "chemists" (pharmacists) in England to the "new" methods (in 1950) of marketing adopted by Boots, the British drug-store chain. The acquittal represented judicial sanction of the new, more efficient style of retail selling.

The *Boots* decision has been taken as authority for the proposition that the display of goods on a shelf in a self-serve store or in a store window (with price tag visible) is not an offer, but only an invitation to offer (or treat), *i.e.*, the stage in contract-making immediately preceding the offer. There is, however, no reason that this conclusion should necessarily be accepted as a statement of the law applicable to all situations. It has been said that this conclusion is required to accommodate the undoubted right of the customer in a self-serve store to pick up the goods and return them to the shelf. The right of a customer to pick up goods displayed in a store, to inspect them and to return them does not require the display to be treated as an invitation to treat. The display could just as easily be an offer with a right to inspect and return the goods prior to a cashier accepting payment. After all, many stores give the customer a right to return goods for any or no reason after the contract (on any analysis) has clearly been made, and even after the goods have been taken home.

The *Boots* case has led to some very odd decisions. The courts have held that the display of a switch-blade knife in a store window is not an "offering for sale" of the knife under a statute making it an offence to "offer" such a knife for sale, but a mere "invitation to treat": *Fisher v. Bell*, [1961] 1 Q.B. 394, [1960] 3 All E.R. 731. A woman was acquitted of the offence of theft in *R. v. Dawood*, [1976] 1 W.W.R. 262, 32 C.R.N.S. 382 (Alta. C.A.) when she switched price tags on some clothes, so that the price on the goods she took to the cash register was much lower than it should have been. When she took the goods to the cashier, the Court of Appeal held she was merely "offering" to purchase the goods at the lower price, which the cashier accepted by taking the money proffered. The contract was voidable due to fraud, but no theft occurred.

Why should it be assumed that the word "offer" must have the same meaning whenever it is used in the law? Is it likely that the accused in these two cases could claim to be unfairly surprised by being convicted for "offering" goods for sale or by being charged with theft? What language should the drafter of the legislation now use to stop the conduct obviously aimed at? These decisions demonstrate the power of the rules of offer and acceptance: they are what many people consider to be the "real" law of contract.

The Acceptance

As has just been explained, the courts have developed a bargain model of contract formation, generally requiring an offer and an acceptance of all the terms proposed for there to be a binding contract. This type of judicial approach resulted in a nineteenth-century decision that in a situation in which parties mail one another identi-

prof

cal "cross offers" there is no binding contract unless one party sends some form of acknowledgment or acceptance: *Tinn v. Hoffman & Co.* (1873), 29 L.T. 271 (Ex. Ch.). The rationale for this decision is that a bilateral contract is formed by *an exchange* of promises, and requires one party to indicate agreement to the terms proposed by the other.

The effect of an offer is that it confers on the offeree the power to accept it and thereby to create a binding contract. One issue that arises has to do with the time for a valid acceptance. If a time is specified within which the acceptance must be made, that will normally govern the offeree; an acceptance outside the time will be too late. If no time is specified, the rule is that an acceptance must be made within a "reasonable" time. What constitutes a "reasonable" time will depend on the circumstances, including the method of communication used and the subject matter of the contract. A reasonable time will usually be one or two business days. An acceptance that is too late is of no effect: the offer will have lapsed and the power to accept will be gone.

Issues arise in regard to acceptance of "firm offers." In *Dickinson v. Dodds* (1876), 2 Ch. D. 463 (C.A.) the defendant made an offer in writing to the plaintiff to sell a house for £800, stipulating that the offer was to be held open for 48 hours. Before the time was up, the agent for the plaintiff approached the defendant with a written acceptance, but as he approached, the defendant said: "You are too late. I have sold the property." The court stated the common law rule that in the absence of consideration, the promise to keep the offer open is not enforceable. Hence at common law an offer said to be "firm" or "irrevocable" for a fixed period is nevertheless revocable. As will be discussed later in this chapter, despite the rule of *Dickinson v. Dodds* there are ways that parties can ensure that an offer is irrevocable, and there are cases in which the courts stretch the rule to protect the reliance of an offeree on the (express or reasonably inferred) promise of the offeror to keep the offer open for the time promised.

Another set of problems concerns what the offeree must do to accept the offer. The offer can set out what the offeree must do to make a valid acceptance. The offeror is said to be "the master of the acceptance". An offeror can, for example, specify how and when an acceptance must be made. The offeror can require that an acceptance be in writing or that it be made by a specified time. *no duty to respond*

A person who receives an offer has, in general, no obligation to reply. A person generally cannot force another to respond or to be in a binding contractual relation by saying: "If I don't hear from you, we have a binding contract on my terms," as there is generally no duty to respond: *Felthouse v. Bindley* (1862), 11 C.B. (N.S.) *prof* 869, 142 E.R. 1037 (Ex. Ch.). Silence may, however, be sufficient if the parties are already in a commercial relationship and it would be reasonable to expect a rejection or response to the offer. *Saint John Tug Boat Co. v. Irving Refining Ltd.,* [1964] S.C.J. No. 38, [1964] S.C.R. 614, 46 D.L.R. (2d) 1 is a case where in the *silence* context of a prior commercial arrangement, acceptance was inferred from silence, despite the failure to communicate an acceptance. The defendant required tugs to guide incoming tankers to its refinery in Saint John harbour. After some communications between the parties, the plaintiff company sent a letter offering to have a tug available for use by the defendant on a "stand-by" basis. In exchange for a daily stand-by fee, the defendant would have priority for use of a tug when requested; the daily fee would be deducted from the normal rate for the use of the tug on any date that it was used, but the daily stand-by fee was payable whether or not the tug was used. There was no written acceptance of this offer, but an officer of the defendant orally agreed to have the tug available on a stand-by basis for six weeks, and acknowledged that it was liable for the daily stand-by fee as well the normal rate when the tug was used. Although no formal extension of the arrangement was agreed to, the defendant continued to make use of the tug for a further seven months. During the seven months the defendant did not pay any of the invoices, but it gave no indication to the plaintiff of any changes in the arrangements for the tug's use. The defendant never communicated its intent to extend (or terminate) the arrangement after the first six weeks, nor did it indicate that it did not expect to pay the daily stand-by fee and intended only to be treated like any other user, charged only for actual use, but without priority or assurance that the tug would be available. After seven months, the plaintiff launched an action and the defendant argued that after the six weeks, it was only liable for use of the tug at the normal rate, and was not liable for the daily stand-by fee. The Supreme Court of Canada upheld the decision of the trial judge that the daily rate was payable for the full period, with Ritchie J. writing, at 621-22 S.C.R.:

> The test of whether conduct, unaccompanied by any verbal or written undertaking, can constitute an acceptance of an offer so as to bind the acceptor to the fulfilment of the contract is made the subject of comment in *Anson on Contracts*, 21st ed., p. 28, where it is said:
>
>> The test of such a contract is an objective and not a subjective one; the intention to be attributed to a man is always that which his conduct bears when reasonably construed, and not that which was present in his own mind. ...
>
> ...
>
> It must be appreciated that mere failure to disown responsibility to pay compensation for services rendered is not of itself always enough to bind the person who has had the benefit of those services. The circumstances must be such as to give rise to an inference that the alleged acceptor has consented to the work being done on the terms upon which it was offered before a binding contract will be implied.

The common law rule that a person is generally not required to reject an offer is reinforced by some statutory provisions. The Ontario *Consumer Protection Act, 2002*, S.O. 2002, c. 30, Sched. A, s. 13(1), provides that a supplier shall not demand payment or even suggest that a "consumer" (*i.e.*, an "individual acting for personal, family or household purposes") must pay for "any unsolicited goods or services despite their use, receipt, misuse, loss, damage or theft". These provisions govern things like the sending of books by book clubs. The books have to be ordered at the beginning of the relation and thereafter the purchaser is liable for the books that arrive automatically as part of the plan.

It was a common practice in Canada for companies to enter into agreements with consumers (which the consumer would probably never have read) with a "negative option" clause. Such a clause stipulates that once a contract for regular receipt of some type of good or service is signed, the company may increase the price or change the service or good provided upon giving the consumer notice, and unless the consumer objects and writes to terminate the agreement or reject the added service, the consumer will be considered to have agreed to the change. This type of practice has been a concern to many people. A particularly egregious example was the practice of cable companies who added channels and services (and charged for them) *unless* the customer gave them notice that the new services were not wanted. Legislation in a number of provinces, including Alberta and British

Columbia, now regulates or prohibits negative option practices. In Ontario, the *Consumer Protection Act, 2002*, specifies:

> 13(3) A request for goods or services shall not be inferred solely on the basis of payment, inaction or the passing of time.

> 13(4) If a consumer is receiving goods or services on an ongoing or periodic basis and there is a material change in such goods or services, the goods or services shall be deemed to be unsolicited from the time of the material change forward unless the supplier is able to establish that the consumer consented to the material change.

These provisions effectively prohibit negative option billing for consumer contracts governed by this legislation. What these legislative provisions indicate is that commercial practices that are perceived as abuses, particularly those that, as with the "negative option" adopted by cable companies, are given great publicity in the press, will eventually be controlled by legislation because the rules of offer and acceptance cannot by themselves do the job.

Contracts Made by Mail

The legal model of contract formation was based on parties meeting in person to exchange an offer and acceptance (or acting through agents). Contracts made by mail presented special problems because there is necessarily a delay in any communication from one party to the other. The ordinary rule at common law is that an offer is accepted when the offeror receives notice of the acceptance. This rule is sometimes illustrated by the far-fetched (and imaginary) example of an offer being made orally in the presence of the offeree and the offeree's oral words of acceptance being drowned out by a passing train so that the offeror does not hear the words, "I accept," said by the offeree. Before the noise subsides and the offeree repeats the offer or the offeror asks the offeree what she said, one of the parties states that he or she has changed his or her mind about the deal. There is said to be no contract in such a case if the offeror does not hear what the offeree initially said.

In one late eighteenth-century case, the courts appeared to suggest that a binding contract might only be made if the parties were dealing with one another in a face-to-face situation: in *Cooke v. Oxley* (1790), 3 T.R. 653, 100 E.R. 785, it was held that an offeree could not accept an offer some hours after it had been made if the offeror had changed his mind about the offer at the time that it was received, even if there was no communication of a revocation. The court appeared to require that the parties' "minds meet" in some real sense (or at least that such a meeting not be precluded by the lapse of time) for a contract to exist. The offeree had to show that the offeror was still prepared to do business on the terms of the offer when the offer was accepted (J.M. Perillo, "The Origins of the Objective Theory of Contract Formation and Interpretation" (2000), 69 *Fordham L. Rev.* 427-77). Such conceptual problems would obviously cause serious difficulties in contracts made by mail, for there was bound to be a period of time between the making of the offer and its acceptance.

In one of the early cases to develop the "postal rule" to govern the formation of contracts made by mail, the court said that the offeror "must be considered in law as making, during every instant of time the letter was travelling" and repeating "the same identical offer" leading to a conceptual "meeting of the minds" up to the moment when the acceptance was placed in the mail: *Adams v. Lindsell* (1818), 1 B. & A. 681, 106 E.R. 250 (K.B.). Thus, a binding contract was formed by mailing an acceptance, even if the offeror no longer wished to do business at the time the acceptance was mailed.

With the use of the mail another problem arose. What would happen if the offeree accepted, but notice of acceptance was delayed or lost in the mail? The rule adopted is that, in the absence of a stipulation to the contrary made by the offeror, the contract is made when the offeree puts the notice of acceptance into the mail. The "postal acceptance rule", allocating the risk of loss to the offeror, was established in *Household Fire & Carriage Accident Insurance Co. Ltd. v. Grant* (1879), 4 Ex. D. 216 (C.A.). Of course, if the letter of acceptance is not received and the offeree wants to claim the benefit of the postal acceptance rule, it must provide reasonable proof of having mailed the acceptance to the correct address.

The issue of loss or delay of an acceptance in the mail requires the risk of a known and easily anticipated loss to be allocated in some way. Since the offeror controls the process of contract-making — the offeror makes the first communication — it makes sense for him to bear or control the risks. If the offeror does not wish to take the risk of loss or delay of the acceptance, he has only to include in the offer a term that the risk of loss or delay of the acceptance is on the offeree. He can do this either by providing that there is no binding contract unless he has received the acceptance by a stipulated date, or by requiring acceptance to be sent by a faster and more reliable method of communication, like a courier, fax or telephone.

The postal acceptance rule was historically justified on the basis that by using the mail for the offer, the offeror made the post office his agent, so that putting an acceptance in the mail constituted communication with the offeror through his agent. This analysis is highly artificial since the post office is no one's agent. A later and far preferable analysis was that the offeror, by selecting the use of mails without specifically stating that no contract was made until an acceptance was received, was choosing to run the risk of loss or delay in the mail.

Although it is rarely mentioned by the courts, it is interesting to observe that the postal acceptance rule is an economically efficient doctrine that facilitates contract formation. In the usual course of events, a binding contract can be made by mail by the sending of two letters, an offer and an acceptance. Once the acceptance is received, both parties know there is a binding contract. If the courts had not developed the postal acceptance rule, but required actual receipt of the acceptance for there to be a binding contract, both parties would only know that they had a binding contract if three letters were sent — the offer, the acceptance and an acknowledgment of receipt by the offeror informing the offeree of receipt and indicating that a binding contract had been formed.

However, the postal acceptance rule may require an offeror who wants to be certain of his position to make an inquiry if no news is received from an offeree, or to stipulate in the offer that he receive actual notice of the acceptance.

The following case illustrates how the courts may determine whether to apply the postal acceptance rules.

X **SCHILLER v. FISHER**

[1981] S.C.J. No. 51, [1981] 1 S.C.R. 593, 124 D.L.R. (3d) 577
(S.C.C., Laskin C.J.C., Martland, Ritchie, McIntyre and Chouinard JJ.)

MCINTYRE J.: — **[1]** This appeal raises the question of whether an enforceable contract for the sale and purchase of certain land arose out of correspondence which passed between the plaintiff Kingsmont Properties Limited (Kingsmont), the purchaser, and the defendant Nu-Towne Developments Incorporated (Nu-Towne), the vendor. Other parties were joined in these proceedings at their outset, but have all been either dismissed from the action or have agreed to the settlement of their claims. The sole remaining parties between whom the one issue arises are Kingsmont and Nu-Towne.

[2] The facts were agreed upon by the parties and were stated in the reasons for judgment of the trial Judge. They may be readily summarized. Negotiations between Kingsmont as purchaser and Nu-Towne as vendor, for the purchase and sale of 23 building lots had been in progress for a considerable time. During the negotiations the plaintiff Kingsmont gave the defendants a cheque, dated November 10, 1975, for $20,000. This sum was intended as a deposit on any agreement of purchase and sale which might be reached. On August 20, 1976, the solicitors for Nu-Towne, the proposed vendor, wrote to the solicitors for the purchaser, Kingsmont, in these terms:

> I am advised by my client that private negotiations have taken place between the parties involved and that an amended agreement was arrived at.

> Accordingly, I have re-drafted the proposed Agreement in accordance with my client's instructions and I submit the proposed agreement herein in duplicate for execution by the Purchaser. Will you kindly have each page initialled including Schedule "A" as substantial changes have been made since negotiations first commenced.

> The last day for execution is August 27, 1976. I look forward to receiving one fully executed copy in due course.

[3] The agreement forwarded with the above letter was executed by Nu-Towne as vendor on August 20, 1976. The letter and the form of agreement therefore amounted to an offer by Nu-Towne to sell to Kingsmont. The form of agreement provided in cl. 12 that the offer was to be accepted on or before August 27, 1976; otherwise it was to be void. By cl. 2 it provided that the deposit of $20,000 referred to above would be held, pending completion of the agreement, and be returned to Kingsmont with interest if the agreement was not completed for any reason other than the default of Kingsmont.

[4] With a letter dated August 27, 1976, the solicitor for Kingsmont returned two copies of the form of agreement, which had been received as above, executed by Kingsmont on that day. The letter said:

> We return two copies of the Agreement of Purchase and Sale executed by the purchaser. You will note the changes which have been made in clauses 4 changing the date of closing to September 30, 1976, 4(b) and 12. We would suggest that you arrange for initialling of these new changes and return one copy of the Agreement to us as soon as possible.

[5] Several changes had been made in the form of agreement and these changes had been initialled by the two signing officers of Kingsmont. No change was made regarding the terms on which the deposit was held, but the date of acceptance in cl. 12 was altered. The revised cl. 12 read:

> This Offer is to be accepted on or before the 1st. day of September, 1976, otherwise it is to be void but when accepted within that period shall constitute a binding contract of purchase and sale. It is agreed that there is no representation, warranty, collateral agreement or condition affecting this agreement or the real property or supported hereby other than as expressed herein in writing.

[6]   While the document which passed between the parties, as described above, was in form an agreement for the sale and purchase of land, it was referred to as an offer which would require an acceptance in Cls. 12 and 19. It was on this basis that the matter was argued and dealt with at trial and in the Court of Appeal and argued in this Court. I approach the case in like manner. The return of the form of agreement containing the changes referred to above constituted a counter-offer, since no actual acceptance of the agreement in its earlier form was given, but an offer to contract on the varied terms was made.

[7]   On September 1, 1976, the signing officers of Nu-Towne considered and initialled the various changes indicating their approval. One copy of the executed agreement was sent back to the plaintiff Kingsmont by a letter dated September 2, 1976. It was sent by registered post, mailed in Chatham on September 3, 1976. It was received in the Toronto Post Office on September 4, 1976, and by the solicitor for Kingsmont on September 7, 1976. By letter dated September 8, 1976, Kingsmont demanded the return of the deposit, the counter-offer not having been accepted within the time-limit. When the deposit was not returned action was commenced.

[8]   At trial the action was dismissed. The trial Judge considered and the parties before him agreed, that before a binding agreement of purchase and sale could be created, acceptance of the offer must be made and such acceptance must be communicated to the offeror. He noted that counsel had agreed that the conduct of the parties in this case had established that the appropriate mode of communication of any such acceptance was by mail and if one were to apply the postal acceptance rule expressed in *Adams et al. v. Lindsell et al.* (1818), 1 B. & Ald. 681, 106 E.R. 250, acceptance would be complete at the date of posting of the letter containing the initialled agreement, i.e., September 3, 1976. It may be remembered here that upon that basis the acceptance would be too late and ineffective. He was of the view, however, that the offer was accepted by the initialling of the changes by the officers of Nu-Towne on September 1, 1976. The plaintiff, Kingsmont, by its letter of August 27, 1976, had prescribed that method of acceptance and, in addition, had prescribed a method of communication, i.e., by mail, and a time for communication of acceptance by the use of the concluding words: "We would suggest that you arrange for initialling of these new changes and return one copy of the Agreement to us as soon as possible." Since the date for acceptance had been precisely stated, he considered that the concluding words of the letter could refer only to the time of communication of acceptance. Nu-Towne had clearly returned the document as soon as possible, and accordingly it had accepted the counter-offer and communicated acceptance in the manner and within the time stipulated. He, therefore, dismissed the plaintiff's action.

[9]   An appeal was allowed in the Ontario Court of Appeal, (Howland C.J.O., Weatherston and Morden JJ.A.) [25 O.R. (2d) 56, 100 D.L.R. (3d) 186]. Morden J.A., with whom Howland C.J.O. agreed, considered that the words "to be ac-

cepted" in para. 12 of the form of agreement included the act of communicating acceptance, and he did not consider it reasonable to construe the last sentence in the letter of August 27, 1976 [at p. 188] ". . . as in any way, contractually or by estoppel, qualifying the language and effect of paragraph 12". Weatherston J.A., dissenting, construed the letter of August 27, 1976, to mean that the terms of the agreement must be assented to on or before September 1st, but communication of acceptance must be made within a reasonable time.

[10] It is apparent at once that there is no real issue in law on the facts of this case. The trial Judge and the three appellate Judges all agreed that as a general rule acceptance of an offer, or in this case a counter-offer, would not be complete until communication of the acceptance was made. The trial Judge and Weatherston J.A., in his dissent in the Court of Appeal, were of the view, on the construction they placed upon the letter of August 27, 1976, that the offer had been accepted and communication of that fact had been made in accordance with the prescribed method and in the time limited for such purpose. The majority of the Court of Appeal construed the letter differently, considering that the concluding words of the letter of August 27, 1976, did not have the effect of permitting communication of acceptance of the counter-offer after September 1, 1976. The case has turned solely on a question of construction.

[11] The question before this Court then is: What is the effect, if any, of the letter of August 27, 1976, upon the provisions of cl. 12 of the form of agreement? In my view, the law was correctly stated in the judgments in the other Courts. Generally, the fact of acceptance of an offer must be communicated to the offeror before acceptance is complete and a binding contract is created. There are exceptions to this rule but none which apply here. In the facts of this case if the officers of Nu-Towne on receipt of the letter of August 27, 1976, had done nothing, or if after initialling the changes they had done nothing further, no binding contract would have been created. Silence or inaction in these circumstances on the part of Nu-Towne after receipt of the letter of August 27, 1976, could not be construed as a full acceptance. Some act of communication was required to complete acceptance and the nature and sufficiency of the act must be determined by reference to the letter of August 27, 1976, and cl. 12 of the form of agreement, for it is open to the parties to such a transaction to specify the mode and time of such communication and to vary the method of communication should they choose. I cannot agree in the circumstances of this case with the construction placed upon the letter by the majority of the Court of Appeal. Out of the negotiations between the parties a detailed and carefully prepared memorandum in the form of an agreement had emerged. It is evident from what followed the receipt by Kingsmont of the letter of August 20, 1976, with its enclosure, that the parties had agreed upon most of the matters in question. Kingsmont, on receiving the August 20th letter, was in accord with the essentials of the arrangement and made only a few minor changes before returning the form of agreement, duly executed, with the request that the changes be approved by initialling. It is evident that Kingsmont assumed that the changes would be accepted, which they were, and that agreement would therefore have been reached between the parties. The closing words of the letter, requesting that an initialled copy be returned as soon as possible, confirm this view and indicate that the prompt return of the initialled document, which was effected, would be accepted in satisfaction of any formal provision for acceptance contained in art. 12 of the form of agreement.

[12] I would allow the appeal and restore the judgment at trial with costs to the appellant.

NOTE AND QUESTION

1. Notice that, ordinarily, signing a document is a manifestation of agreement to its terms on which the other party may rely. Initialling changes to the document conveys the same message.

2. What do you think motivated the Supreme Court to take such a flexible interpretation of the rules of contract formation in *Schiller v. Fisher*?

Contracts Made by Fax

Many commercial contracts are made by an exchange of faxes. The risk that faxed documents may fade, that they may be illegible, that there may be difficulty in proving signing and the possibility of misdirection make lawyers cautious in relying on "fax formed" contracts when large sums of money may be at stake. A cautious lawyer may agree to have an offer and the acceptance recorded on documents sent by fax, with the condition that properly signed originals follow by ordinary mail. The Ontario Court of Appeal has, however, accepted the validity of use of facsimile transmission (fax) for forming a contract.

prof ✗

In *Rolling v. Willann Investments* (1989), 70 O.R. (2d) 578, 63 D.L.R. (4th) 760, the Ontario Court of Appeal dealt with an agreement which specified that notice of the exercise of an option had to be delivered by the prospective purchaser to the owner by a specific date. At the time that the agreement was made, the fax machine had not been invented, but by the date set for exercise, it was in widespread use, and both parties were using fax machines. The Court of Appeal held that a fax transmission was a valid method of delivery of an option to purchase land. Robins J.A. wrote (p. 763 D.L.R.):

> Willann next contends that the facsimile transmission of the offer could not constitute "delivery" under the terms of the option agreement. Given that the agreement was entered into in 1974, the parties could not have intended or contemplated that delivery would be made in this manner and, it is argued, this form of delivery is not in compliance with the contract. In Willann's submission, delivery to it could be effected only be personal service or by mail.

fax binding

> While it is true that the parties to the option agreement could not have anticipated delivery of a facsimile of the offer by means of a telephone transmission at the time the agreement was executed, they did not limit or restrict or, indeed, specify the way in which delivery was to be made for the purposes of their agreement. The purport of the agreement is that Willann is to be placed in receipt of a copy of the offer and is to exercise his option within a specified time following receipt. The manner in which delivery is to be made in order to place Willann in receipt of the document is of no real importance. What is important is whether and when Willann was in fact put in receipt of the offer or, put another way, whether and when the document was in fact delivered to him.

> Where technological advances have been made which facilitate communications and expedite the transmission of documents we see no reason why they should not be utilized. Indeed, they should be encouraged and approved. Nothing is to be gained in the circumstances of this case in requiring an attendance at Willann's offices to deliver the documents, and Willann suffered no prejudice by reason of the procedure followed. In our opinion, the transmission of a facsimile of the offer for the purpose of effecting delivery is not in violation of the option agreement. It follows that Willann properly received delivery of the offer.

While fax communication is commonly used for contract formation, there are still unresolved issues related to this form of telecommunication. If an acceptance is sent by fax, but not received, is a contract formed? Does the postal acceptance rule apply? Does it matter whether the failure to receive the fax was due to the mistake of the sender (offeree), the phone company, the two fax machines involved or the recipient (offeror), by, for example, failing to have paper in the receiving machine? Does it matter whether the offeror specified that the acceptance should be sent by fax?

Where Is a Contract Made?

For a range of procedural purposes, in particular to determine whether the courts of a particular province have jurisdiction over a contractual dispute, it is necessary to determine *where* a contract is made. This inquiry is necessitated by the rules of court of certain jurisdictions (See, *e.g.*, Alberta *Rules of Court*, Alta. Reg. 390/68, rule 30(f)(i); Ontario *Rules of Civil Procedure*, R.R.O. 1990, Reg. 194, rule 17.02), under which the court has jurisdiction over an absent defendant in respect of a "contract made in the jurisdiction". If the rule is that the contract is made when the offeror receives notice of the acceptance, the contract will be made where the offeror is. Conversely, if the postal acceptance rule is applied, the contract will be made where the acceptance is put in the mail.

The following case, *Eastern Power Ltd. v. Azienda Comunale Energia and Ambiente*, deals with the issue of "where" a contract was formed, in the context of a pre-trial jurisdictional motion. The plaintiff brought an action in Ontario and served the defendant with notice of the proceedings in Italy. Such service *ex juris*, *i.e.*, service on a party not physically present in the province, is permitted under rule 17.02(f)(i) of the Ontario *Rules of Civil Procedure* where the claim is "in respect of a contract . . . made in Ontario". Unless the contract could be held to be one "made in Ontario", the Ontario court would not have jurisdiction to hear the dispute. Further, the court was also dealing with question of the whether the courts of Ontario should regard themselves as "forum *conveniens*" (an appropriate or convenient forum for the trial), for which the question of "where" the contract is "made" is also an important factor.

EASTERN POWER LTD. v. AZIENDA COMMUNALE ENERGIA AND AMBIENTE

[1999] O.J. No. 3275, 178 D.L.R. (4th) 409
(Ont. C.A., Abella, Laskin and MacPherson JJ.A.)

MacPherson J.A.:—

Introduction

[1]   This is an appeal from the judgment of Juriansz J. ... in which he set aside service in Italy of a statement of claim by an Ontario company and stayed the company's action in Ontario on forum *non conveniens* grounds. In addition to the standard forum *non conveniens* factors that need to be addressed, the appeal poses the interesting question of where a contract is formed when the acceptance of an offer is communicated by facsimile transmission. Is the contract formed, in accordance with the general rule of contract law, in the place where the acceptance is received? Or should the postal exception to the general rule, which says that a contract is formed when and where an acceptance is placed in the mail, apply to acceptances communicated by facsimile transmission?

Factual Background

[2]   The appellant, Eastern Power Limited ("EP"), is a corporation organized under the laws of Ontario with its principal place of business in Toronto. Its business is the generation of power from non-conventional sources of energy such as landfill gas.

[3]   Azienda Communale Energia and Ambiente ("ACEA") is a corporation under the laws of Italy with its principal place of business in Rome. ACEA provides power to the City of Rome. ACEA generates some of its own power; however, it also purchases power from other sources.

[4]   In September 1994 representatives of ACEA came to Toronto to learn about EP's operations and to explore the possibility of developing power from non-conventional sources in Rome. In order to facilitate these discussions, a confidentiality agreement was prepared and signed. ACEA agreed to maintain as confidential any information specific to the proposed joint venture or related to proprietary processes and systems developed by EP. ACEA also agreed that it would not utilize such information and proceed independently or apart from EP.

[5]   In December 1994 EP met with ACEA in Italy. The parties drafted a Co-Operation Agreement. ACEA signed the agreement on December 9 and faxed it to EP in Ontario. EP signed the agreement in Ontario and faxed it to ACEA in Rome on December 21. It was an express term of the agreement that the two companies would co-operate and use their best efforts to enter into a project agreement. This agreement, relating to the implementation of the alternative energy project, would be based on proposals to be developed by EP and submitted to ACEA for approval. The project was described as "an electricity generating plant fuelled by landfill gas, sewage sludge and fossil fuel(s) located near Rome, Italy."

[6]   On January 29, 1996 ACEA signed a Letter of Intent relating to the project. The Letter of Intent was faxed by ACEA to EP in Ontario. On February 14 EP accepted and signed the Letter of Intent in Ontario and faxed it back to ACEA in Rome. The Letter of Intent indicated that the parties wanted to proceed with the project and set out how EP would structure itself in order to be permitted to carry out its work in Italy. The Letter of Intent contained these two provisions:

> The terms of reference between the parties of the new company are governed according to the Joint Venture Agreement which will be later signed by the parties. The intended contents of the present letter are subject to conditions such as:
>
> a) The acquisition of a favourable written opinion from the Ministry of Industry regarding the award of CIP 6 subsidy to the plant to be built, and also in relation to the Italian Law N. 481 dated 14.11.95 and every subsequent change and integrations which could occur in the meanwhile;

[7]   The parties worked to conclude a Joint Venture Agreement. Many drafts were prepared. However, none was ever signed. During these further negotiations EP was concerned that ACEA was not diligently pursuing the important CIP 6 subsidy. On January 24, 1997 the Ministry of Industry amended the subsidy program in a way that made it inapplicable to the proposed joint venture.

[8] On February 14, 1997, ACEA wrote to EP and effectively terminated their relationship. The letter, signed by ACEA's General Manager, Mario Diaco, cited three reasons: an inability to agree on some terms of the Joint Venture Agreement, the apparent inapplicability of the government subsidy to the project, and the legal requirement that ACEA award large contracts, like the proposed Rome generating plant, by way of public tender.

[9] On March 19, 1997 EP forwarded an invoice to ACEA for $478,547 for development and legal costs relating to the project. The time frame for this invoice was stated to be October 1994 - March 1997.

[10] On September 11, 1997 ACEA filed a summons with the Rome Civil Court. The summons essentially seeks a declaration that ACEA has no liability whatsoever to EP. EP was served with a copy of this claim about a week later. There is nothing in the record to indicate whether the court in Rome has disposed of the matter.

[11] On December 4, 1997 EP commenced its action against ACEA in Ontario. EP sought damages of $750,000 for development costs incurred and $160,000,000 for loss of profits as a result of the alleged negligence and breach of contract by ACEA with respect to the Co-operation Agreement.

[12] On January 19, 1998 ACEA was served with the statement of claim. ACEA did not serve a statement of defence and on March 25 was noted in default. EP then brought a motion for default judgment. This motion was adjourned to permit ACEA to bring its motion to set aside service of EP's statement of claim and to stay the action.

[13] Juriansz J. heard ACEA's motion on October 27, 1998. On November 26, 1998 he released his judgment. He set aside the service in Italy of EP's statement of claim and he stayed EP's action in Ontario on forum *non conveniens* grounds. By endorsement released on February 9, 1999, he awarded ACEA its costs of the motion fixed at $44,000.

[14] EP appeals from both components of Juriansz J.'s order of November 26, 1998 and from his costs award of February 9, 1999.

Issues

[15] The issues on this appeal are:

Was the motions judge correct to stay EP's action in Ontario on the basis of forum *non conveniens*?

Was the motions judge correct to set aside service in Italy of EP's statement of claim?

Was the motions judge correct to award ACEA costs of the motion fixed at $44,000?

[16] In the view I take of the appeal, the disposition of the first issue makes it unnecessary to consider the second issue. Accordingly, in these reasons I will address only the forum *non conveniens* and costs issues.

. . .

(a) Location where the contract was signed

[21] The contract which forms the basis of EP's action in contract and tort against ACEA is the Co-operation Agreement: see Statement of Claim, paragraphs 5, 26, 30 and 31. The motions judge found that the Co-operation Agreement was made in Italy because "acceptance was communicated to Italy." Since EP's acceptance was communicated by facsimile transmission, this raises the interesting question of the legal relationship between a faxed acceptance of an offer and the place where a contract is formed.

[22] The general rule of contract law is that a contract is made in the location where the offeror receives notification of the offeree's acceptance: see Fridman, *The Law of Contract in Canada*, 3rd ed., (1994), at p. 65; and *Re Viscount Supply Co.*, [1963] 1 O.R. 640 (S.C.). However, there is an exception to this general rule. It is the postal acceptance rule. As expressed by Ritchie J. in *Imperial Life Assurance Co. of Canada v. Colmenares*, [1967] S.C.R. 443 at 447:

> It has long been recognized that when contracts are to be concluded by post the place of mailing the acceptance is to be treated as the place where the contract was made. ...

[23] EP contends that the rule with respect to facsimile transmissions should follow the postal acceptance exception. With respect, I disagree. EP has cited no authority in support of its position. There is, however, case authority for the proposition that acceptance by facsimile transmission should follow the general rule, which would mean that a contract is formed when and where acceptance is received by the offeror.

[24] In *Brinkibon Ltd. v. Stahag Stahl G.m.b.H.*, [1983] 2 A.C. 34 (H.L.), a contract was concluded when the buyer in London transmitted its acceptance to the seller in Vienna. The mode of acceptance was a message sent by telex, a form of instantaneous communication like the telephone. The law lords were unanimous in concluding that the contract was formed in Vienna where the acceptance was received by the offeror. Lord Brandon of Oakbrook analyzed the issue in this fashion, at p. 48:

> Mr. Thompson's second and alternative case that the contract was concluded by the buyers transmitting to the sellers their telex of May 4, 1979, seems to me to be the correct analysis of the transaction. On this analysis, however, the buyers are up against the difficulty that it was decided by the Court of Appeal in *Entores Ltd. v. Miles Far East Corporation* [1955] 2 Q.B. 327 that, when an offer is accepted by telex, the contract thereby made is to be regarded as having been so made at the place where such telex was received (in this case Vienna) and not in the place from which such telex was sent (in this case London).

> Mr. Thompson invited your Lordships to hold that the *Entores* case was wrongly decided and should therefore be overruled. In this connection he said that it was well-established law that, when acceptance of an offer was notified to an offeror by post or telegram, the concluding of the contract took place when and where the letter of acceptance was posted or the telegram of acceptance was dispatched. He then argued that the same rule should apply to cases where the acceptance of an offer was communicated by telex, with the consequence that the contract so made should be regarded as having been made at the place from which the telex was sent and not the place where it was received.

> My Lords, I am not persuaded that the *Entores* case [1955] 2 Q.B. 327, was wrongly decided and should therefore be overruled. On the contrary, I think that it

was rightly decided and should be approved. The general principle of law applicable to the formation of a contract by offer and acceptance is that the acceptance of the offer by the offeree must be notified to the offeror before a contract can be regarded as concluded, *Carlill v. Carbolic Smoke Ball Co.*, [1893] 1 Q.B. 256, 262, per Lindley L.J. The cases on acceptance by letter and telegram constitute an exception to the general principle of the law of contract stated above. The reason for the exception is commercial expediency: see, for example, *Imperial Land Co. of Marseilles. In re (Harris' Case)* (1872) L.R. 7 Ch. App. 587, 692 per Mellish L.J. That reason of commercial expediency applies to cases where there is bound to be a substantial interval between the time when the acceptance is sent and the time when it is received. In such cases the exception to the general rule is more convenient, and makes on the whole for greater fairness, than the general rule itself would do. In my opinion, however, that reason of commercial expediency does not have any application when the means of communication employed between the offeror and the offeree is instantaneous in nature, as is the case when either the telephone or telex is used. In such cases the general principle relating to the formation of contracts remains applicable, with the result that the contract is made where and when the telex of acceptance is received by the offeror.

[25] In my view, this analysis is equally applicable to facsimile transmissions, another form of instantaneous communication. Indeed, there is at least one Canadian authority that has reached this conclusion. In *Joan Balcom Sales Inc. v. Poirier* (1991), 49 C.P.C. (2d) 180 (N.S. Co. Ct.), an acceptance of a real estate listing offer was communicated by two vendors in Ottawa to a real estate company in Berwick, Nova Scotia. The mode of communication was a facsimile transmission. The vendors' position was that the contract was formed in Ottawa; they argued that the "mailbox doctrine" should be applied to communication by facsimile transmission.

[26] Haliburton Co. Ct. J. did not accept the vendors' argument. He reviewed the English academic writing about the postal acceptance exception to the general rule of contract formation. He then concluded, at p. 187:

> The writers then discuss the practical need of special rules to be applied to contracts entered into by post in the age when post was the primary method of commercial communication. The considerations which made it highly practical, if not imperative, in the interests of commerce, for the offeree to have knowledge in a timely fashion that he had a firm contract do not apply to facsimile transmissions. The communication is instantaneous. The offeree could easily have confirmed within minutes that they had a binding contract.
>
> I, therefore, find that the contract was executed at Berwick.

[27] I agree with this analysis, and with the analysis of the law lords in *Brinkibon*. I would hold that in contract law an acceptance by facsimile transmission should follow the general rule of contract formation, not the postal acceptance exception.

[28] I do not say that this rule should be an absolute one; like Lord Wilberforce in his separate speech in *Brinkibon*, "I think it a sound rule, but not necessarily a universal rule" (p. 42). Lord Wilberforce discussed some of the factors that might suggest caution about applying the general rule to telex communications in all cases, including the many variants in such communications and whether the message was sent and received by the principals to the contemplated contract. However, he concluded, at p. 42:

The present case is ... the simple case of instantaneous communication between principals, and, in accordance with the general rule, involves that the contract (if any) was made when and where the acceptance was received.

[29] In my view, the present appeal is also "the simple case." The acceptance was faxed by the principals of EP in Ontario to the principals of ACEA in Italy. There is nothing to suggest that the communication between these principals was not instantaneous. Hence, applying the general rule, the contract was formed in Italy. ...

...

Disposition

[56] I would dismiss the appeal with costs.

[An application for leave to appeal to the Supreme Court was dismissed, [1999] S.C.C.A. No. 542.]

NOTES

1. When parties are negotiating a cross-border contract, whether an inter-provincial or international one, two issues usually have to be resolved. The first is the question of the law to govern the contract. The clause dealing with this issue, called a "choice of law clause", will typically say something like, "This agreement shall be governed and construed by the laws of the province of Ontario and the federal laws of Canada applicable therein." What this clause does is to indicate to the court before which any dispute may come that the parties intend their relation to be dealt with against the background of Ontario law. (It is not necessary, though it is common, to make the reference to the laws of Canada since those laws are part of the law of Ontario.)

2. A separate question will be whether the parties want to manage the litigation risks they face by choosing the place any dispute can be brought. A Canadian corporation may, for example, be very concerned if it were to be subject to being sued in those states in the United States where jury awards are unpredictable. Litigation risks can be managed by (i) avoiding courts and juries altogether by choosing arbitration; or (ii) by choosing a jurisdiction whose courts are respected. (There is some competition among courts in this respect. The courts of Delaware, New York and England, among foreign courts, are, for example, highly respected and will more often be chosen than courts of other jurisdictions.) A clause adopting the latter alternative may say something like, "The parties agree that the courts of the province of British Columbia shall have [exclusive/non-exclusive] jurisdiction over any dispute arising under this agreement." The Supreme Court has held that such a clause must be respected. See, *e.g.*, *Z.I. Pompey Industrie v. Ecu-Line N.V. (The "Canmar Fortune")*, [2003] S.C.J. No. 23, [2003] 1 S.C.R. 450, 224 D.L.R. (4th) 577, and *GreCon Dimter Inc. v. JR Normand Inc.*, [2005] S.C.J. No. 46, [2005] 2 S.C.R. 401.

3. The question of the law to govern an agreement and that of the jurisdiction before which any dispute may be brought are separate questions. The parties may agree to include both clauses (and choose the same jurisdiction), or they may choose one law but submit any disputes to another court or leave both clauses out. These choices may be made because one party has the stronger bargaining position and is able to insist that its choice, particularly of where to sue, will prevail, or because the parties have good reasons to leave those questions for later. (The first situation is very common in international lending transactions or in software licences — notice where Microsoft requires a purchaser of its products to sue. See, *e.g.*, *Rudder v. Microsoft*, below.)

4. The scope of a choice of law clause is never entirely clear because each jurisdiction will have laws that its courts believe should be applied whatever the parties may say. It is not, for example, possible to avoid the application of the *Securities Act* or the *Consumer Protection Act* by a choice of law clause which, for example, chooses some more accommodating jurisdiction. The issues raised by international contracts or even interprovincial contracts are complex and are a large part of any course on what is called "Conflict of Laws" or "Private International Law".

5. The analysis of the Court of Appeal in *Eastern Power v. Azienda* would have been affected had the parties had a choice of law clause or a choice of jurisdiction clause because the court might have had (i) to hear evidence of Italian law; or (ii) to consider whether it could even take jurisdiction in the face of a choice of the courts of Italy.

6. The case also illustrates the use of various pre-contractual documents, such as the "letter of intent". As will be more fully discussed later, terms of a letter of intent generally do not give rise to legal obligations, but in some circumstances some (or all) of the terms are enforceable. The issue of the legal significance of any of these terms would have to be resolved by a trial; ordinarily, signing a document is a manifestation of agreement to its forms on which the other party may rely. Initialling changes to the document conveys the same message.

Inquiries into the details of the process of offer and acceptance, illustrated by a case like *Eastern Power*, are rare and principally arise in the situation illustrated by that case: *viz.*, the application of a very technical rule limiting the court's jurisdiction to hear a dispute over a contract involving a foreign party.

It is unclear why the result of the kind of technical analysis related to contract formation should have any relevance to either the suitability of the particular court to hear the case or the fairness of a decision that an absent defendant should be required to answer the plaintiff's allegations in that court.

Should the outcome in *Eastern Power* have been different if the Ontario plaintiff had made and initialled a tiny amendment and the Italian defendant had faxed back its "acceptance" of that change?

The use of the place where the contract is made in the rules of court is based on a belief that a contract made in a jurisdiction should be subject to the courts of that jurisdiction. This belief is justifiable if the parties had been, for example, both carrying on business there, and one had subsequently left. The fact that the potential defendant has left the jurisdiction puts significant problems in the path of the potential plaintiff and perhaps these should be alleviated when the defendant is being sued on a contract that arose from a business relation created in the jurisdiction. When the connection to the jurisdiction is based only on the fact that the offeror was present there when the contract was "formed", the rules may have a less rational purpose. An unfortunate aspect of this situation is that if the rules governing contract formation are used in inappropriate ways, the original purpose for these rules may be forgotten.

The courts have begun to move away from an exclusive focus on the technical analysis of the process of contract formation to decide jurisdictional issues, at least if all of the parties are within Canada. The Supreme Court of Canada in *De Savoye v. Morguard Investments Ltd.*, [1990] 3 S.C.R. 1077, 76 D.L.R. (4th) 256, set some limits to the use of English common law ideas in the Canadian context by suggesting that whether the courts of one province may properly assert jurisdiction (power) over a contract dispute involving a person not present in the province may be limited by the *Constitution Act, 1867* and should not depend solely on artificial rules related to contract formation.

One of the curious features of the rules of offer and acceptance is that they are frequently used to resolve problems that have nothing to do with the process of bargaining. The questionable use of the rules of contract formation does not arise only in regard to jurisdictional issues; as discussed above, a similar issue arose in the context of the criminal liability of "offerors". There the issue was the purpose of the legislation (why would it be considered unlawful to display a switch-blade knife?) and the possibility of the defendant's being caught by unfair surprise.

This (mis)use of the rules of contract formation in other contexts may reflect the fact that the rules are regarded as "fundamental", as an integral and crucial part of the law of contracts. In reality, however, problems with the rules of offer and acceptance arise relatively rarely in practice. They are most frequently used by solicitors who want to control the process of bargaining so as to ensure that some advantage is obtained for their clients. For this purpose they must be known, but they will seldom cause problems that lead to litigation.

E-Commerce and Contracts Made Through the Use of Computers

Lawyers, scholars and judges are starting to deal with a range of interrelated issues related to the formation and enforcement of contracts formed through the issue of computers, including by an exchange of e-mails or by surfing websites. Many issues may need to be addressed when contracts are made over the Internet. Among them are questions about whether consumer protection (or, in Quebec, language) legislation applies to sellers whose only connection to a province is a province's resident's computer. Other issues deal with more technical problems. What counts as evidence of the terms of the contract? How may electronic documents be authenticated? What is the relation between an electronic document and one in a more traditional form?

Legislation has been enacted in a number of jurisdictions on the basis of an international convention developed under the sponsorship of the United Nations. Most Canadian legislation is based on that document. Ontario's *Electronic Commerce Act, 2000*, S.O. 2000, c. 17 (in force 16 October 2000) is an example of Canadian legislation on the topic. (The legislation in Quebec is, to the dismay of Quebec lawyers, wholly idiosyncratic.)

The Ontario legislation recognizes the validity of documents formed by electronic communication and the validity of electronic signatures. Such legislation has a limited, facilitative scope and does not attempt to regulate such matters as how an electronic contract is formed, which courts have jurisdiction over a contract formed on the Internet or what legal rules are to govern a contract formed through the use of computers. The reluctance of legislators to regulate contractual relations in cyberspace reflects the difficulties in enacting statutes governing a very rapidly developing field that often involves parties in many jurisdictions.

One of the questions to be faced in regard to contracts formed by e-mail is what rule will govern formation. Will the courts apply general rule, *i.e.*, the rule, applied in *Eastern Power*, that a contract is only formed when (and where) the offeror receives the acceptance, or the postal acceptance rule, *i.e.*, the rule that the contract is formed when (and where) the acceptance is sent to its destination? The decision in *Eastern Power* would suggest that the courts are not willing to extend the postal acceptance rule to other "instantaneous" forms of communication like e-mail. The weight of commentary is therefore that a contract is formed by e-mail when and where the acceptance is received. There is, however, an argument that it would be fairer to consumers to apply the postal acceptance rule; see P. Fasciano, "Internet Electronic Mail: A Last Bastion for the Mailbox Rule" (1997), 25 *Hofstra L. Rev.* 971-1003.

The development of e-commerce makes it increasingly hard to protect consumers from cases of outright fraud and cheating or even from simple bad service and shoddy goods. While the application of the postal acceptance rule might give some consumers additional leverage, the problem is that most of those who cheat are beyond the reach of provincial or Canadian control.

Businesses that operate websites usually have legal advice and are aware of contract formation issues. They attempt to control the process of contract formation through a combination of posted terms and appropriately placed icons. Websites commonly include terms that purport to regulate the selection of a forum for resolution of any dispute and the legal regime that is to govern the dispute. While there has not been a great deal of Canadian litigation about contracts formed on websites, it is apparent that common law courts will begin their analysis using familiar concepts. In some respects, a website is ideally suited to allowing the application of the mirror image rule of contract formation.

 RUDDER v. MICROSOFT CORP.

[1999] O.J. No. 3778, 40 C.P.C. (4th) 394, 2 C.P.R. (4th) 474
(Ont. S.C.J., Winkler J.)

[The plaintiffs wanted to bring a class action in the Ontario courts on behalf of all Canadian subscribers to the MSN network, which was operated by Microsoft. The plaintiffs claimed that Microsoft had breached its contract with them as subscribers to the Microsoft Network, and had breached its fiduciary duties to them and misappropriated their funds. The proposed class included all Canadian residents subscribing to the network from September 1, 1995, about 89,000 people. Most of the network's business activities, including billing and customer service, were carried out in the state of Washington. To become a subscriber, potential members "executed" an agreement online. All terms of the agreement were displayed on the computer screen and were also available on a computer diskette. One term was that the agreement was governed by the laws of Washington, which was to be the exclusive jurisdiction and venue for disputes arising out of network membership. The plaintiffs claimed that such terms were obscured because one could read the agreement only one computer screen at a time. The representative plaintiff, Rudder, said that he scanned through the terms, paying attention only when he came to the cost of the subscription, at which point he clicked his computer mouse on the "I Agree" button on the agreement. There were two opportunities during registration to withhold agreement, and a notice that subscribers were bound by the entire agreement whether they read it or not. The terms were all in the same type size, although some phrases were in capital letters.

The defendant brought a motion to stay the proposed class proceeding on the basis that any action had to be brought in Washington.

After dealing generally with the attitude that the court should take to a "forum selection clause" and concluding that it should be approached sympathetically, the court considered the way in which the defendant brought the clause in question to the attention of its customers.]

WINKLER J.: —

...

[10] The plaintiffs contend, first, that regardless of the deference to be shown to forum selection clauses, no effect should be given to the particular clause at issue in this case because it does not represent the true agreement of the parties. It is the plaintiffs' submission that the form in which the Member Agreement is provided to potential members of MSN is such that it obscures the forum selection clause. Therefore, the plaintiffs argue, the clause should be treated as if it were the fine print in a contract which must be brought specifically to the attention of the party accepting the terms. Since there was no specific notice given, in the plaintiffs' view, the forum selection clause should be severed from the Agreement which they otherwise seek to enforce.

[11] The argument advanced by the plaintiffs relies heavily on the alleged deficiencies in the technological aspects of electronic formats for presenting the terms of agreements. In other words, the plaintiffs contend that because only a portion of the Agreement was presented on the screen at one time, the terms of the Agreement which were not on the screen are essentially "fine print".

[12] I disagree. The Member Agreement is provided to potential members of MSN in a computer readable form through either individual computer disks or via the Internet at the MSN Web site. In this case, the plaintiff Rudder, whose affidavit was filed on the motion, received a computer disk as part of a promotion by MSN. The disk contained the operating software for MSN and included a multi-media sign-up procedure for persons who wished to obtain the MSN service. As part of the sign-up routine, potential members of MSN were required to acknowledge their acceptance of the terms of the Member Agreement by clicking on an "I Agree" button presented on the computer screen at the same time as the terms of the Member Agreement were displayed.

[**WINKLER J.** referred to the fact that the plaintiff admitted that the agreement was readily viewable by scrolling down his screen. The plaintiff also admitted that he had looked at the agreement to see what the cost of the service was, but that he had not looked carefully through it all.]

[14] I have viewed the Member Agreement as it was presented to Rudder during the sign-up procedure. All of the terms of the Agreement are displayed in the same format. Although, there are certain terms of the Agreement displayed entirely in upper-case letters, there are no physical differences which make a particular term of the agreement more difficult to read than any other term. In other words, there is no fine print as that term would be defined in a written document. The terms are set out in plain language, absent words that are commonly referred to as "legalese". Admittedly, the entire Agreement cannot be displayed at once on the computer screen, but this is not materially different from a multi-page written document which requires a party to turn the pages. Furthermore, the structure of the sign-up procedure is such that the potential member is presented with the terms of membership twice during the process and must signify acceptance each time. Each time the potential member is provided with the option of disagreeing which terminates the process. The second time the terms are displayed occurs during the online portion of the process and at that time, the potential member is advised via a clear notice on the computer screen of the following:

> . . . The membership agreement includes terms that govern how information about you and your membership may be used. To become a MSN Premier member, you must select "I Agree" to acknowledge your consent to the terms of the membership agreement. If you click "I Agree" without reading the membership agreement, you are still agreeing to be bound by all of the terms of the membership agreement, without limitation. . . .

[The court watched as the plaintiff was taken through an actual sign-up process and seemed to have difficulty accepting that the plaintiff still did not agree that the terms of the contract were obvious.]

[16] It is plain and obvious that there is no factual foundation for the plaintiffs' assertion that any term of the Membership Agreement was analogous to "fine print" in a written contract. What is equally clear is that the plaintiffs seek to avoid the consequences of specific terms of their agreement while at the same time seeking to have others enforced. Neither the form of this contract nor its manner of presentation to potential members are so aberrant as to lead to such an anomalous result. To give effect to the plaintiffs' argument would, rather than advancing the goal of "commercial certainty" . . . move this type of electronic transaction into the realm of commercial absurdity. It would lead to chaos in the marketplace, render ineffectual electronic commerce and undermine the integrity of any agreement entered into through this medium.

preserve e-commerce

[17] On the present facts, the Membership Agreement must be afforded the sanctity that must be given to any agreement in writing. The position of selectivity advanced by the plaintiffs runs contrary to this stated approach, both in principle and on the evidence, and must be rejected. Moreover, given that both of the representative plaintiffs are graduates of law schools and have a professed familiarity with Internet services, their position is particularly indefensible. *haha!*

[**WINKLER J.** refused to exercise his discretion to override the forum selection clause and dismissed the action.]

NOTES

1. The Global Business Dialogue on Electronic Commerce (GBDe), an association of the world's largest businesses firms, has developed a set of rules governing jurisdictional and choice of law issues for disputes regarding contracts formed over the internet or by e-mail. The GBDe concluded that the growth of e-commerce depends upon the adoption of both freedom of contract and rule-of-origin approaches to the problem of choice of forum for dispute resolution. See <http://www.gbd.org>.

    The GBDe rules provide that if the parties "agree", then a freedom of contract approach is to be used. The GBDe suggests that in the absence of any agreement, the "rule-of-origin" approach should be adopted, that is, the courts and laws of the seller of the goods or services would govern a dispute. The association argues that the adoption of any other alternative rule would increase legal uncertainty, force companies to familiarize themselves with multiple legal systems worldwide, and hence impede the growth of e-commerce. Operating in multiple jurisdictions would require companies to develop country-specific websites and to adjust their policies to reflect the local laws. While some large firms do modify some of their sites for specific countries, smaller and medium-sized companies cannot afford to develop worldwide compliance programs. Further, even large sellers prefer to be governed by familiar legal rules.

    The adoption of these rules may well be appropriate for business-to-business transactions (often called "B2B") where parties are usually sophisticated and large transactions are typical. Individual contracts can be negotiated by the parties. However, as the *Rudder* case illustrates, these rules may be inappropriate for business-to-consumer (often called "B2C") contracts, where the relatively small nature of the transactions makes the negotiation of specific legal terms inefficient for both buyer and seller.

For consumers, the freedom-of-contract rule usually means that they are bound by the legal regime that the seller chooses, usually one that is favourable to it, often its own. Further, in the absence of an explicit statement, the alternative rule-of-origin approach also means that the legal regime of the seller applies. Since few consumers would go to the trouble and expense of launching a law suit in the seller's jurisdiction, most consumers face the prospect of having no effective protection for online transactions. This lack of effective recourse may be one of the factors making Canadian consumers wary of e-commerce transactions.

If a corporation were to open a store, appoint a franchisee or a dealer or otherwise carry on business — a term that has been the focus of a great deal of litigation under legislation requiring corporations that "carry on business" in a province to be licensed — it is accepted that they would have to comply with all the rules of the province (or of Canada) for the protection of consumers or borrowers. (A significant part of the services that a Canadian law firm provides to its international clients consists of advice on how to comply with local law.)

The point of view of the GBDe suggests that, with e-commerce, provincial or Canadian concerns should be subordinated to those of the seller or supplier. Since it is possible for a seller to refuse to do business with a potential customer from a particular place — Internet gambling sites have to be careful that they do not *appear* to be doing business in Canada or the United States — it could be argued that, if an Internet seller chooses to do business with a person from Canada, the protection that that person would have under his or her law should be applicable.

2.   Legislation has now been enacted in a number of Canadian jurisdictions, including Nova Scotia, Alberta, Manitoba and British Columbia, to offer some protection to consumers who enter into contracts over the Internet. The Ontario *Consumer Protection Act, 2002*, S.O. 2002, c. 30, Sched. A., applies to those who sell goods or services to consumers in Ontario, wherever the seller is located. Section 39 requires that a seller in an Internet agreement shall "deliver … a copy" of the agreement to the consumer, though this delivery may be by e-mail, and specifies certain matters related to price and delivery that must be disclosed.

Sections 7(2) and 8 of the Ontario Act (which apply to all consumer contracts, whether formed on the Internet or otherwise) provide that a consumer contract cannot require a consumer to arbitrate or waive the right to participate in a class action against a commercial seller. These provisions reverse *Kanitz v. Rogers Cable Inc.*, [2002] O.J. No. 665 (S.C.J.), where it was held that a consumer was bound by the provision of an Internet-formed contract that provided that disputes with a cable company could only be resolved by individual arbitration of disputes. Given the small sums likely to be involved in a dispute with a cable company, the waiver of the right to participate in a class action denied consumers any practical way to seek legal relief for the company's breach of the service agreement.

3.   We will return later in this book to the problem that arose in *Rudder* when consumers sign or assent to contracts without reading or understanding the terms, although, as that case illustrates, courts tend to hold that an individual is bound by the terms of a contract that he or she has signed (or electronically adopted), even if the individual has chosen not to read it, though there are cases in which a consumer who hurriedly signs a contract without reading it may not be bound by all the terms; see *Tilden-Rent-A-Car Co. v Clendenning* (1978), 18 O.R. (2d) 601 (C.A.), in Chapter 6.

It is becoming increasingly common for websites and electronic commerce transactions to have provisions for dispute resolution through "e-tribunals", with the parties agreeing that any dispute will be resolved through a filing of electronic documents with an arbitrator in cyberspace. It seems likely that in certain areas of practice these private dispute-resolution bodies may be more important than courts. These bodies are

prot

developing their own legal rules, with competition between tribunals to have the most efficient procedures and substantive rules for dispute resolution. *choosing jurisdiction*

X 4. A similar problem to that in *Rudder v. Microsoft* can arise with the purchase of computer programs on floppy disk or CD-ROM discs. There the contract will typically be made — at least as the manufacturer intends — when the "shrink wrap" around the product is opened, and the consumer loads the disc onto the computer and first sees the licence agreement. Many of these software licence agreements — that is what the purchase of computer software gives the buyer — will contain a clause requiring the buyer to bring any complaints of product quality or performance before a court in the jurisdiction that is convenient for the manufacturer.

prot

X 5. There is another issue that arises in the retail sale of software, both online and in the "shrink-wrap" contract imposed on the buyer. The manufacturers and sellers of software are protected by the law of copyright. Under the terms of a retail contract, the retail buyer gets a licence to use the software for the purposes defined by the manufacturer, and the buyer may be liable for damages if he or she breaches the terms of the licence. The contract made when the program is downloaded or installed will typically impose on the buyer a prohibition on the unauthorized copying and distribution of the software. While the buyer may be surprised by the limited right given by the manufacturer — if he or she even bothers to read the terms of the licence — and the contract may not, at least before the package is opened, give the buyer any explicit indication of the extent of the licence, the protection of the manufacturer's intellectual property rights does not depend solely on the contract, but is also based on property rights.

It is only after the buyer has bought the product that the shrink-wrap seal can be broken and the buyer can learn any of the terms that the producer wishes to impose. The problem for the producer is that when a traditional offer and acceptance analysis is applied to this transaction, the court is likely to conclude that the contract is fully formed when the buyer pays for the software, and before the buyer has had the opportunity to learn any of the terms proposed by the producer. By the time the buyer opens the box and has any notice of the terms, the contract has been made and the explicit terms come "too late". This traditional type of analysis was applied by the courts to protect buyers in some decisions made early in the era of commercial software production; see, e.g., *North American Systemshops Ltd. v. King* (1989), 68 Alta. L.R. (2d) 145, 45 B.L.R. 242 (Q.B.).

Some more recent American decisions, however, have held that the producer of the software should be able to impose terms that can only be seen by the buyer after the sale, for example, those found inside the box or when the program is opened on a computer, provided that (1) something on the box that is visible at the time of purchase warns the buyer that there are terms inside the box; and (2) the buyer is advised of the right to return the product for a full refund after seeing the additional terms: *ProCD Inc. v. Zeidenberg*, 86 F.3d 1447 (7th Cir. 1996).

The solution to this problem is not so much a contractual one as a property one — no buyer of anything subject to copyright is likely to be successful in an argument that his or her ignorance of the law led him or her reasonably to believe that the licence was not limited. The important question will be whether the actual limitations imposed by the manufacturer will catch the buyer by unfair surprise. In any event, there is a problem of the doctrine of privity (Chapter 2) if the manufacturer should seek to claim a contractual right against a retail buyer who may have no contractual relation with the manufacturer.

There might be a practical problem with the suggestion that the buyer may return an opened software package, *viz.*, that the seller (or manufacturer) will be very reluctant to give a refund on an opened package of software. If the assumption that a contract is a bargain in which the two parties have agreed on a set of terms is accepted, it has to follow that, if either is to be bound by them, he or she must have had a chance to know them. If the consequence of this fact is that the buyer must have a right to reject and return the goods on discovering the terms the seller wants to impose on the transaction, then the way in which the terms of the contract are brought to the atten-

visible contract

tion of the buyer must be changed. If the return of the goods is not an acceptable solution for the seller, then the goods must be packaged so that all the terms are visible before the contract is made by opening the package.

The much greater legal control that is possible with the use of downloaded software (as opposed to software on a physical medium) may be one reason that form of delivery appears to be increasingly popular with software manufacturers.

For a discussion of the ways that technological change challenges traditional legal concepts based on the bargain theory of contract, see Arthur Cockfield, "Towards a Law and Technology Theory" (2004), 30 *Man. L.J.* 383, at 388-91.

6. At least in theory, the formation of a contract is premised on a model of two parties consenting to enter into a binding contractual relation. An interesting conceptual problem arises when contracts are made on a website, as in *Rudder v. Microsoft*. A person using a computer is in effect contracting with a machine. In some cases, a binding contract may be made by two machines, programmed to enter into a contract. (Such a situation may occur with Electronic Data Interchange (EDI) transactions. Such transactions are made in the context of a standard contract between the parties. Within the framework established by this contract, the parties, often a supplier and customer, will make purchases for the supply of goods. The arrangement will be established in accordance with well-recognized standards for the authentication of all orders and acknowledgments.) Such an arrangement may not fit well with a model of contracting based on consent. Nevertheless, the Ontario *Electronic Commerce Act, 2000*, S.O. 2000, c. 17, s. 20 is clear that two machines can form a legally binding contract for their owners. For a discussion of some of the conceptual and practical problems that arise when contracts are made on the Internet, see M. Radin, "Humans, Computers and Binding Commitment" (2000), 75 *Ind. L.J.* 1125 and Juliet M. Moringiello, "Signal, Assent and Internet Contracting" (2005), 57 *Rutgers L. Rev.* 1307.

Revocation of the Offer

The basic rule is that an offer can be revoked at any time before acceptance. The rule is, however, subject to some qualifications.

The first is that notice of the revocation must reach the offeree before acceptance occurs. If the parties are in a situation where the postal acceptance rule applies, then, to be effective, a revocation must reach the offeree before the acceptance has been put in the mail: *Henthorn v. Fraser*, [1892] 2 Ch. 27. If the mail rule does not apply, then revocation is possible before the acceptance reaches the offeror: *Byrne & Co. v. Van Tienhoven & Co.* (1880), 5 C.P.D. 344.

Firm Offers and Unilateral Contracts

There is nothing to prevent an offeror from stating that an offer is a "firm offer" that will remain open (or irrevocable) for a stated period. If the offer is accepted while it remains open, a contract will be made. This is a the traditional analysis of *Great Northern Railway Co. v. Witham* (Chapter 2, *supra*): Witham's offer to GNR to supply goods at stipulated prices for a whole year could be revoked or withdrawn by him at any time since GNR had not paid for Witham's promise to stand ready to supply for a year. GNR was equally free not to order any goods from Witham. Witham was, however, bound to supply the goods that the railway actually ordered before the offer was revoked, for with respect to a purchase order that was given, the standing offer had been accepted.

At common law, however, the offeror who has made a firm or irrevocable offer has, in spite of what she may have explicitly promised, a right to revoke this offer at any time before acceptance, as the promise to keep it open was made without consideration: *Dickinson v. Dodds* (1876), 2 Ch. D. 463, 45 L.J. Ch. 777 (C.A.). This common law rule has relatively little significance in practice — except when it catches someone by surprise.

The vast majority of businesses keep their promises and leave firm offers open for acceptance: good business practice requires nothing less. In situations where the stakes are high and the pressure to maintain a good business reputation is not present, the parties may arrange to ensure that any promise to keep an offer open is enforceable. This goal can be achieved by an "option contract", a contract in which the promise to keep an offer open is bought by payment. This payment may be nominal but is more likely to be substantial. Alternatively, the promise to leave the offer open for a fixed period may be executed under seal. In the standard land transaction in common law Canada (at least if the forms of real estate boards and agents are used), the offer and the promise to leave it open for a time is under seal.

[handwritten margin note: open offer]

There are, however, situations in which the parties did not have legal advice and the courts struggle to modify the harshness of the common law rule, especially to protect reliance by an offeree. In making promises to make a "firm offer" unenforceable, the doctrine of consideration is doing precisely what, unfortunately, it so often does: it is making unenforceable promises that should be enforced because, apart from the doctrine, there is no good reason not to enforce a promise freely made. The decision to enforce or not to enforce in any particular case should be justified, not by the presence or absence of consideration, but by the context of the deal, and the expectations and reliance of the parties. *[handwritten: enforceability]*

Enforcing a promise to keep an offer open is, of course, not always justified. An offeror may want to keep the freedom to revoke its offer at any time and, provided it does not catch the offeree by surprise, there is no reason not to give effect to its desire. It is common for businesses that make statements of prices in published lists to say something like: "Prices subject to change without notice", thus making it clear that there is no promise to deal on the basis of the quoted price. Other businesses, stores selling by catalogue, for example, will frequently state that a quoted price will be the maximum charged for, perhaps, a year or six months. It is inconceivable that a store would refuse, at least for the sale of the size typical of a consumer purchase order, to honour the price.

In many situations involving firm offers, problems do not arise in practice. Where such offers are common, they can be made enforceable if the promise to make the offer "firm" is under seal — as in the standard real estate deal — or is simply honoured because it is good business to do so. Sometimes, however, the problem of firm offers may arise in a manner that catches a party by surprise. The cases that follow illustrate that the problems of offers and the right of the offeror to revoke an offer are not always obvious.

What is important about the law regarding firm offers is the potential injustice of the common law rule and the courts' constant efforts to find ways around it. These efforts occur in a special class of cases where the problems are particularly intense. In the normal case of a firm offer, the time between the making of the offer and either acceptance or expiry of the time for acceptance is fairly short. In the problem cases, this time is far longer and one party will be seriously at risk in the sense that he or she may have relied on the offer.

Some of the difficult issues concerning revocation of offers related to "unilateral contracts"; this type of contract was discussed in Chapter 2 in *GNR v. Witham*. Before turning to the revocation issues related to unilateral contracts, it is necessary to understand the common law analysis of the process of formation of this type of contract. The classical precedent on the formation of "unilateral contracts" was decided late in the nineteenth century, although the case is still frequently cited, and the unusual facts are remembered by generations of law students.

CARLILL v. CARBOLIC SMOKE BALL CO.

[1893] 1 Q.B. 256 (C.A.)
(Lindley M.R., Bowen L.J., Smith L.J.)

[The defendants, who were the vendors of a medical preparation called "The Carbolic Smoke Ball", placed an advertisement in the *Pall Mall Gazette* of 13 November, 1891 stating:

> £100 reward will be paid by the Carbolic Smoke Ball Company to any person who contracts the increasing epidemic influenza, colds, or any disease caused by taking cold, after having used the ball three times daily for two weeks according to the printed directions supplied with each ball. £1000 is deposited with the Alliance Bank, Regent Street, shewing our sincerity in the matter.

> During the last epidemic of influenza many thousand carbolic smoke balls were sold as preventives against this disease, and in no ascertained case was the disease contracted by those using the carbolic smoke ball.

> One carbolic smoke ball will last a family several months, making it the cheapest remedy in the world at the price, 10s, post free. The ball can be refilled at a cost of 5s. Address, Carbolic Smoke Ball Company, 27, Princes Street, Hanover Square, London.

The plaintiff, a lady, on the faith of this advertisement, bought one of the balls at a chemist's, and used it as directed, three times a day, from November 20, 1891, to January 17, 1892, when she was attacked by influenza. Hawkins J. held that she was entitled to recover the £100. The defendants appealed.]

BOWEN, L.J.: — [1] ... The first observation which arises is that the document itself is not a contract at all, it is only an offer made to the public.

[2] . The defendants contend next, that it is an offer the terms of which are too vague to be treated as a definite offer, inasmuch as there is no limit of time fixed for the catching of the influenza, and it cannot be supposed that the advertisers seriously meant to promise to pay money to every person who catches the influenza at any time after the inhaling of the smoke ball. It was urged also, that if you look at this document you will find much vagueness as to the persons with whom the contract was intended to be made — that, in the first place, its terms are wide enough to include persons who may have used the smoke ball before the advertisement was issued; at all events, that it is an offer to the world in general, and, also, that it is unreasonable to suppose it to be a definite offer, because nobody in their senses would contract themselves out of the opportunity of checking the experiment which was going to be made at their own expense. It is also contended that the advertisement is rather in the nature of a puff or a proclamation than a promise or offer intended to mature into a contract when accepted. But the main point seems to be that the vagueness of the document shews that no contract whatever was intended. It seems to me that in order to arrive at a right conclusion we must read this advertisement in its plain meaning, as the public would understand it. It was intended to be issued to the public and to be read by the public. How would an ordinary person reading this document construe it?

[3] It was intended unquestionably to have some effect, and I think the effect which it was intended to have, was to make people use the smoke ball, because the suggestions and allegations which it contains are directed immediately to the use of the smoke ball as distinct from the purchase of it. It did not follow that the smoke ball was to be purchased from the defendants directly, or even from agents of theirs directly. The intention was that the circulation of the smoke ball should be promoted, and that the use of it should be increased. The advertisement begins by saying that a reward will be paid by the Carbolic Smoke Ball Company to any person who contracts the increasing epidemic after using the ball. It has been said that the words do not apply only to persons who contract the epidemic after the publication of the advertisement, but include persons who had previously contracted the influenza. I cannot so read the advertisement. It is written in colloquial and popular language, and I think that it is equivalent to this: "£100 will be paid to any person who shall contract the increasing epidemic after having used the carbolic smoke ball three times daily for two weeks." And it seems to me that the way in which the public would read it would be this, that if anybody, after the advertisement was published, used three times daily for two weeks the carbolic smoke ball, and then caught cold, he would be entitled to the reward. Then again it was said: "How long is this protection to endure? Is it to go on for ever, or for what limit of time?" I think that there are two constructions of this document, each of which is good sense, and each of which seems to me to satisfy the exigencies of the present action. It may mean that the protection is warranted to last during the epidemic, and it was during the epidemic that the plaintiff contracted the disease. I think, more probably, it means that the smoke ball will be a protection while it is in use. That seems to me the way in which an ordinary person would understand an advertisement about medicine, and about a specific against influenza. ... I think, on the construction of this advertisement, the protection was to enure during the time that the carbolic smoke ball was being used. ...

[4] Was it intended that the £100 should, if the conditions were fulfilled, be paid? The advertisement says that £1000 is lodged at the bank for the purpose. Therefore, it cannot be said that the statement that £100 would be paid was intended to be a mere puff. I think it was intended to be understood by the public as an offer which was to be acted upon.

[5] But it was said there was no check on the part of the persons who issued the advertisement, and that it would be an insensate thing to promise £100 to a person who used the smoke ball unless you could check or superintend his manner of using it. The answer to that argument seems to me to be that if a person chooses to make extravagant promises of this kind he probably does so because it pays him to make them, and, if he has made them, the extravagance of the promises is no reason in law why he should not be bound by them.

[6] It was also said that the contract is made with all the world — that is, with everybody; and that you cannot contract with everybody. It is not a contract made with all the world. There is the fallacy of the argument. It is an offer made to all the world; and why should not an offer be made to all the world which is to ripen into a contract with anybody who comes forward and performs the condition? It is an offer to become liable to any one who, before it is retracted, performs the condition, and, although the offer is made to the world, the contract is made with that limited portion of the public who come forward and perform the condition on the faith of the advertisement. It is not like cases in which you offer to negotiate, or you issue advertisements that you have got a stock of books to sell, or houses to let, in which case there is no offer to be bound by any contract. Such advertisements are offers to negotiate — offers to receive offers — offers to chaffer, as, I think, some learned judge in one of the cases has said. If this is an offer to be bound, then it is a contract the moment the person fulfils the condition. ...

[7] Then it was said that there was no notification of the acceptance of the contract. One cannot doubt that, as an ordinary rule of law, an acceptance of an offer made ought to be notified to the person who makes the offer, in order that the two minds may come together. Unless this is done the two minds may be apart, and there is not that consensus which is necessary according to the English law ... to make a contract. But there is this clear gloss to be made upon that doctrine, that as notification of acceptance is required for the benefit of the person who makes the offer, the person who makes the offer may dispense with notice to himself if he thinks it desirable to do so, and I suppose there can be no doubt that where a person in an offer made by him to another person, expressly or impliedly intimates a particular mode of acceptance as sufficient to make the bargain binding, it is only necessary for the other person to whom such offer is made to follow the indicated method of acceptance; and if the person making the offer, expressly or impliedly intimates in his offer that it will be sufficient to act on the proposal without communicating acceptance of it to himself, performance of the condition is a sufficient acceptance without notification. ...

[8] Now, if that is the law, how are we to find out whether the person who makes the offer does intimate that notification of acceptance will not be necessary in order to constitute a binding bargain? In many cases you look to the offer itself. In many cases you extract from the character of the transaction that notification is not required, and in the advertisement cases it seems to me to follow as an inference to be drawn from the transaction itself that a person is not to notify his acceptance of the offer before he performs the condition, but that if he performs the condition notification is dispensed with. It seems to me that from the point of view of common sense no other idea could be entertained. If I advertise to the world that my dog is lost, and that anybody who brings the dog to a particular place will be paid some money, are all the police or other persons whose business it is to find lost dogs to be expected to sit down and write me a note saying that they have accepted my proposal? Why, of course, they at once look after the dog, and as soon as they find the dog they have performed the condition. The essence of the transaction is that the dog should be found, and it is not necessary under such circumstances, as it seems to me, that in order to make the contract binding there should be any notification of acceptance. It follows from the nature of the thing that the performance of the condition is sufficient acceptance without the notification of it, and a person who makes an offer in an advertisement of that kind makes an offer which must be read by the light of that common sense reflection. He does, therefore, in his offer impliedly indicate that he does not require notification of the acceptance of the offer.

[9] A further argument for the defendants was that this was a *nudum pactum* - that there was no consideration for the promise — that taking the influenza was only a condition, and that the using the smoke ball was only a condition, and that there was no consideration at all; in fact, that there was no request, express or implied, to use the smoke ball. ... The short answer, to abstain from academical... discussion, is, it seems to me, that there is here a request to use involved in the

offer. Then as to the alleged want of consideration. The definition of "consideration" given in *Selwyn's Nisi Prius*, 8th ed. p. 47 … is this: "Any act of the plaintiff from which the defendant derives a benefit or advantage, or any labour, detriment, or inconvenience sustained by the plaintiff, provided such act is performed or such inconvenience suffered by the plaintiff, with the consent, either express or implied, of the defendant." Can it be said here that if the person who reads this advertisement applies thrice daily, for such time as may seem to him tolerable, the carbolic smoke ball to his nostrils for a whole fortnight, he is doing nothing at all — that it is a mere act which is not to count towards consideration to support a promise (for the law does not require us to measure the adequacy of the consideration). Inconvenience sustained by one party at the request of the other is enough to create a consideration. I think, therefore, that it is consideration enough that the plaintiff took the trouble of using the smoke ball. But I think also that the defendants received a benefit from this user, for the use of the smoke ball was contemplated by the defendants as being indirectly a benefit to them, because the use of the smoke balls would promote their sale. …

LINDLEY M.R.: — [This judgment preceded that of Bowen L.J. in the case report and included a rebuttal to the argument of the defendant's counsel that there was no contract because there had been no communication of the acceptance.]

[10] But then it is said, "Supposing that the performance of the conditions is an acceptance of the offer, that acceptance ought to have been notified." Unquestionably, as a general proposition, when an offer is made, it is necessary in order to make a binding contract, not only that it should be accepted, but that the acceptance should be notified. But is that so in cases of this kind? I apprehend that they are an exception to that rule, or, if not an exception, they are open to the observation that the notification of the acceptance need not precede the performance. This offer is a continuing offer. It was never revoked, and if notice of acceptance is required — which I doubt very much, for I rather think the true view is that which was expressed and explained by Lord Blackburn in the case of *Brogden v. Metropolitan Ry.* Co. 2 App. Cas. 666, 691 — if notice of acceptance is required, the person who makes the offer gets the notice of acceptance contemporaneously with his notice of the performance of the condition. If he gets notice of the acceptance before his offer is revoked, that in principle is all you want. I, however, think that the true view, in a case of this kind, is that the person who makes the over shews by his language and from the nature of the transaction that he does not expect and does not require notice of the acceptance apart from notice of the performance.

Smith L.J. wrote a concurring opinion.

Appeal dismissed.

The difficult issues that arise in regard to revocation in the case of a unilateral contract can be illustrated by the famous "walk to York" hypothetical, mentioned by Brett J. in *GNR v. Witham*. A promises to pay B £100 if B will walk to York. This transaction is traditionally analyzed in the following way: A makes an offer to B to pay B £100 if B walks to York. The only way that B can accept this offer is by completing his walk to York. If A were to revoke her offer when B was one kilometre short of his goal, this would be an effective revocation and, in strict common law theory, B would have no remedy even though he had performed 99 per cent of

what A had specified that he do. This is usually explained on the basis that B has
no right to be paid anything unless and until he walks to York; if B only walks half
way (or 99 per cent of the way) and he then quits, then B is not entitled to be paid
anything.   *unilateral contract defn*

Since there is only one promise, that of A, these kinds of contracts are often
called "unilateral" contracts, as distinguished from the more common "bilateral
contract" which is formed by an exchange of promises. With a unilateral contract,
one party makes an offer, either to the other party or to "the world". The offer is
accepted not by communication of an acceptance, but by performance. The contract is considered "unilateral", because until the offeree fully performs, the offeror
has no duty to perform. However, the term "unilateral" is not satisfactory since
these contracts are in the form of exchange transactions and, once there is full performance by the offeree, the offeror is also bound to perform — usually by making
the payment promised.

There is an obvious exchange: A's promise for B's action. B's action is then
both acceptance of the offer and consideration for A's promise, and that is, of
course, precisely why the problems arise.

With a unilateral offer of the "walk-to-York" type, there is considerable pressure to restrict the right of A to revoke her offer when B has completed a significant part of his journey.

A unilateral offer can be made "to the world", as in a newspaper advertisement
reading, "$100,000 reward for anyone with information leading to the arrest and
conviction of the Scarborough rapist." This offer is accepted by an offeree providing the needed information to the police: see *Smirnis v. Toronto Sun Publishing
Corp.* (1997), 37 O.R. (3d) 440 (Gen. Div.). If the person offering the reward
wishes to revoke it, notice of any revocation must be given before the person
comes forward with the information and must be done in a reasonable way, presumably with the same prominence as the original offer: *Shuey v. United States*, 92
U.S. 73 (1875).

The following cases are examples of such "unilateral" offers and of the courts'
efforts to restrict the right of the offeror to revoke. The devices used by the courts
to restrict the effect of the traditional rules are interesting. The result is that while
the courts have declined to abrogate the rule that offers can be revoked at any
time, it will be bypassed or ignored when its application would violate some concern that is more important than doctrinal purity.

It should be recognized that parties to a transaction rarely make use of terms
like "unilateral" or "bilateral contract". Even terms like "offer" and "acceptance",
unless lawyers are involved, are generally used by parties to a commercial transaction in a non-technical sense. Rather, these legal concepts are generally applied by
the courts in a retrospective fashion. It is understandable that if the application of
these traditional concepts seems unjust, courts will modify the application of the
traditional rules. As you read the cases, consider what other factors induce each
court to do what it does.

The Supreme Court of Canada in the first case states the classical rule that "an
offer in the unilateral sense can be revoked up to the last moment before *complete
performance*", but then determines that it does not need to apply such a harsh rule
in this particular case.

DAWSON v. HELICOPTER EXPLORATION CO. LTD.

[1955] S.C.R. 868, [1955] 5 D.L.R. 404
(S.C.C., Kerwin C.J.C., Rand, Estey, Cartwright and Fauteux JJ.)

[The plaintiff (appellant) had staked mineral deposit claims in northern British Columbia. These claims had lapsed. In 1951 the plaintiff wanted to interest a mining company in these claims. After hearing that the plaintiff wanted to get the claims developed, Springer wrote to the plaintiff on behalf of the defendant (respondent). Springer offered the plaintiff a 10 per cent interest in the claims in return for the plaintiff's help in finding them. The plaintiff was called up by the U.S. Army (he was an American and the Korean War was on) but expressed to Springer his continued willingness to co-operate in the development of the claims on the terms proposed by Springer. Springer repeated his offer in a subsequent letter of 5 March 1951, writing: "If you take us in to the showings and we think that they warrant staking, we will stake all claims and give you a 10 per cent non-assessable interest." The plaintiff replied on 12 April 1951: "If you will inform me [when you want to go] . . . I will immediately take steps for a temporary release in order to be on hand." Springer wrote on 7 June 1951 to say that they would not be going in that year. Later that summer, however, an exploration party sent by the defendant located the claims and made arrangements to develop them. The plaintiff commenced an action for his share. The trial judge and the British Columbia Court of Appeal dismissed the action. The plaintiff appealed.]

RAND J.: — [1] . . . The substantial contention of the respondent is that any offer contained in the correspondence and in particular the letter of March 5th called for an acceptance not by promise but by the performance of an act, the location of the claims by Dawson for the respondent. It is based upon the well-known conception which in its simplest form is illustrated by the case of a reward offered for some act to be done. To put it in other words, no intention was conveyed by Springer when he said "I hereby agree" that Dawson, if agreeable, should have replied "I hereby accept", or words to that effect: the offer called for and awaited only the act to be done and would remain revocable at any time until every element of that act had been completed.

[2] The error in this reasoning is that such an offer contemplates acts to be performed by the person only to whom it is made and in respect of which the offeror remains passive, and that is not so here. What Dawson was to do was to proceed to the area with Springer or persons acting for him by means of the respondent's helicopter and to locate the showings. It was necessarily implied by Springer that he would participate in his own proposal. This involved his promise that he would do so, and that the answer to the proposal would be either a refusal or a promise on the part of Dawson to a like participation. The offer was unconditional but contemplated a performance subject to the condition that a pilot could be obtained by the respondent.

[3] Dawson's answer of April 12th was, as I construe it, similarly an unqualified promissory acceptance, subject as to performance to his being able to obtain the necessary leave. It was the clear implication that Springer, controlling the means of making the trip, should fix the time and should notify Dawson accordingly. As the earlier letters show, Dawson was anxious to conclude some arrangement and if he could not make it with Springer he would seek it in other quarters.

[4]   Although in the circumstances, because the terms proposed involve such complementary action on the part of both parties as to put the implication beyond doubt, the precept is not required, this interpretation of the correspondence follows the tendency of Courts to treat offers as calling for bilateral rather than unilateral action when the language can be fairly so construed, in order that the transaction shall have such "business efficacy as both parties must have intended that at all events it should have": Bowen L.J. in *The "Moorcock"* (1889), 14 P.D. 64 at p. 68. In theory and as conceded by Mr. Guild, an offer in the unilateral sense can be revoked up to the last moment before complete performance. At such a consequence many Courts have balked; and it is in part that fact that has led to a promissory construction where that can be reasonably given. What is effectuated is the real intention of both parties to close a business bargain on the strength of which they may, thereafter, plan their courses.

[5]   This question is considered in *Williston on Contract* vol. 1, pp. 76-77, in which the author observes:

> Doubtless wherever possible, as matter of interpretation, a court would and should interpret an offer as contemplating a bilateral rather than a unilateral contract, since in a bilateral contract both parties are protected from a period prior to the beginning of performance on either side — that is from the making of the mutual promises.

> At the opening of the present century the courts were still looking for a clear promise on each side in bilateral contracts. A bargain which lacked such a promise by one of the parties was held to lack mutuality and, therefore, to be unenforceable. Courts are now more ready to recognize fair implications as effective: "A promise may be lacking, and yet the whole writing may be 'instinct with an obligation', imperfectly expressed" which the courts will regard as supplying the necessary reciprocal promise.

[6]   The expression "instinct with an obligation" . . . is employed by Cardozo J. in *Wood v. Lady Duff-Gordon* (1917), 222 N.Y. 88 at pp. 90-1, in the following passage:

> It is true that he does not promise in so many words that he will use reasonable efforts to place the defendant's indorsements and market her designs. We think, however, that such a promise is fairly to be implied. *The law has outgrown its primitive stage of formalism when the precise word was the sovereign talisman, and every slip was fatal* . . . A promise may be lacking, and yet the whole writing may be "instinct with an obligation" imperfectly expressed.

These observations apply obviously and equally to both offer and acceptance.

[7]   . . . Dawson was bound to remain ready during a reasonable time prior to that mentioned for the trip to endeavour, upon notice from Stringer, to obtain leave of absence. But in promising Dawson that the company would co-operate, Springer impliedly agreed that the company would not, by its own act, prevent the complementary performance by Dawson. In doing what it did, the company not only violated its engagement, but brought to an end the subject-matter of the contract. By that act it dispensed with any further duty of readiness on the part of Dawson whether or not he was aware of what had taken place. Even assuming the technical continuance of the obligations and the necessity of an affirmative step in order to treat an anticipatory breach as a repudiation, the action was not brought until long after the time for performance had passed. Being thus excused, Dawson's obtaining leave, apart from any pertinency to damages, became irrelevant to the cause of action arising from the final breach.

[8] I would, therefore, allow the appeal and remit the cause to the Supreme Court of British Columbia for the assessment of damages. The appellant will have his costs throughout.

[**KERWIN C.J.C.** dissented.]

NOTES AND QUESTIONS

1. Did the plaintiff in *Dawson* rely on the defendant in any way? Did the defendant gain any advantage at the expense of the plaintiff? Although not clear from the facts, it is possible that Helicopter Exploration derived some advantage in locating the claims from its discussions with Dawson. Should this affect the result? What interest of the plaintiff (in the sense of the expectation, restitution or reliance interest) did the Court ultimately protect? *revocability of unilateral offers*

2. Notice that in *Dawson v. Helicopter Exploration*, the Supreme Court reiterates the "traditional" common law rule of revocability of unilateral offers, but uses an approach based on the interpretation of the parties' arrangement to circumvent the rule.

3. Strong evidence that common law rules are unsatisfactory is found in the fact that the draft Canadian *Uniform Sale of Goods Act* makes some provision for the enforcement of firm offers, at least in the commercial context:

    Option Contract

    4.4(1) An offer by a merchant to buy or sell goods which expressly provides that it will be held open is not revocable for lack of consideration during the time stated or, if no time is stated, for a reasonable time not to exceed three months.

    4.4(2) Any such assurance of irrevocability in a form supplied by the offeree is not binding unless the assurance is separately signed by the offeror.

The next case is one of Lord Denning's characteristic judgments: he is determined to reach the result that he thinks is correct but he does not face the fact that the traditional common law rules make the achievement of that result difficult.

ERRINGTON v. ERRINGTON

[1952] 1 K.B. 290, [1952] 1 All E.R. 149
(C.A., Somervell, Denning and Hodson L.JJ.)

DENNING L.J.: — **[1]** The facts are reasonably clear. In 1936 the father bought the house for his son and daughter-in-law to live in. The father put down £250 in cash and borrowed £500 from a building society on the security of the house, repayable with interest by instalments of 15s. a week. He took the house in his own name and made himself responsible for the instalments. The father told the daughter-in-law that the £250 was a present for them, but he left them to pay the building society instalments of 15s a week themselves. He handed the building society book to the daughter-in-law and said to her: "Don't part with this book. The house will be your property when the mortgage is paid." He said that when he retired he would transfer it into their names. She has, in fact, paid the building society instalments regularly from that day to this with the result that much of the mortgage has been repaid, but there is a good deal yet to be paid. The rates [taxes] on the house came to

10s. a week. The couple found that they could not pay those as well as the building society instalments so the father said he would pay them and he did so.

[2]   It is to be noted that the couple never bound themselves to pay the instalments to the building society, and I see no reason why any such obligation should be implied. It is clear law that the court is not to imply a term unless it is necessary, and I do not see that it is necessary here. Ample content is given to the whole arrangement by holding that the father promised that the house should belong to the couple as soon as they had paid off the mortgage. The parties did not discuss what was to happen if the couple failed to pay the instalments to the building society, but I should have thought it clear that, if they did fail to pay the instalments, the father would not be bound to transfer the house to them. The father's promise was a unilateral contract — a promise of the house in return for their act of paying the instalments. It could not be revoked by him once the couple entered on performance of the act, but it would cease to bind him if they left it incomplete and unperformed, which they have not done. If that was the position during the father's lifetime, so it must be after his death. If the daughter-in-law continues to pay all the building society instalments, the couple will be entitled to have the property transferred to them as soon as the mortgage is paid off, but if she does not do so, then the building society will claim the instalments from the father's estate and the estate will have to pay them. I cannot think that in those circumstances the estate would be bound to transfer the house to them, any more than the father himself would have been. . . .

[3]   Applying the foregoing principles to the present case, it seems to me that, although the couple had exclusive possession of the house, there was clearly no relationship of landlord and tenant. They were not tenants at will, but licensees. They had a mere personal privilege to remain there, with no right to assign or sublet. They were, however, not bare licensees. They were licensees with a contractual right to remain. As such they have no right at law to remain, but only in equity, and equitable rights now prevail . . .

[4]   In the present case it is clear that the father expressly promised the couple that the property should belong to them as soon as the mortgage was paid, and impliedly promised that, so long as they paid the instalments to the building society, they should be allowed to remain in possession. They were not purchasers because they never bound themselves to pay the instalments, but nevertheless they were in a position analogous to purchasers. They have acted on the promise and neither the father nor his widow, his successor in title, can eject them in disregard of it. The result is that, in my opinion, the appeal should be dismissed and no order for possession should be made.

NOTES AND QUESTIONS

1.   Lord Denning was obviously determined to protect the young couple. It is not clear how he did it — at least if we are to be able to see in the case a solution to similar problems. One way of rationalizing what he did from the perspective of the law of contracts is to say that he prevented revocation while the son and daughter-in-law were "walking to York"; he moved forward in time the point at which the parties would be held to have entered into a binding contract. Under the traditional rules, there would be no binding contract until the offerees had walked the final steps to York or, on the facts of *Errington*, had paid the final instalment of the mortgage, when the couple would be entitled to call for a conveyance. What Lord Denning does is to prevent revocation for the time necessary to allow the couple to complete the "walk to York".

Under the doctrine of consideration, the "implied promise" of the father to allow the couple to remain in possession should not be enforceable by the couple, since they gave no consideration for it. Without referring to the concept, Lord Denning seems to be using an approach analogous to estoppel to protect the couple's reliance. Some of the language Lord Denning uses is similar to that he used in *Central London Property* (*supra*, Chapter 2).

2. Like all cases in which a problem is caused by the doctrine of consideration, the difficulty could have been easily avoided if the parties had seen a lawyer. In the context of *Errington*, one solution would have been for the father to have provided by his will that the couple could stay in the house so long as they kept up the mortgage payments. It is important to notice that this case is not a commercial case: it is, like the cases in Chapter 2, a case of an uncompleted gift. Uncompleted gift

3. The cases in Chapter 2 illustrated that courts have strong incentives to enforce promises or to give some relief to prevent the unjust enrichment of the defendant or to protect reliance. Was Lord Denning responding to these pressures in *Errington*? If so, what were the interests (in the sense of the expectation, restitution or reliance interests) that he could have seen and protected? What interest did he protect?

4. Why did the Supreme Court of Canada in its 1955 decision in *Dawson v. Helicopter Exploration* not follow the bolder approach of Lord Denning in *Errington*? More recent English cases seem sympathetic to Lord Denning's analysis; see Lord Goff in *Daulia Ltd. v. Four Millbank Nominees Ltd.*, [1978] Ch. 231, [1978] 2 All E.R. 557 (C.A.).

5. In *Ayerswood Development Corp. v. Hydro One Networks Inc.*, [2004] O.J. No. 4926 (S.C.J.), without citing *Errington* or *Dawson*, or discussing the common law rules, the court proceeded on the basis that an offer in a unilateral contract cannot be revoked once performance has commenced. Ontario Hydro had established a number of incentive programs to encourage energy efficiency, including one directed at the construction of new commercial buildings (the "NBC program"). Ontario Hydro knew that builders would rely upon the existence of the program to design their buildings in compliance with the energy requirements, and that this would involve additional expense for the builder. The design stage would have to be complete before a builder could even file the application for the program. In the program guide, Ontario Hydro stated: "These Basic incentives will only be available to projects applying on or before March 31, 1993." The plaintiff (Richmill) intended to construct a 17-storey apartment building. It had previously constructed a similar building nearby and intended to use a similar design for the new building. However, it was attracted by Ontario Hydro's NBC Program and decided to re-design the new building to fit those specifications and to thereby take advantage of the incentive payments. Richmill retained design engineers to do the design and complete the application form for the NBC program. That work was complete and Richmill was ready to start construction in early March 2003. The total incentive payment that Richmill would have been entitled to under the NBC program was approximately $340,000. Just prior to Richmill submitting its formal application, Ontario Hydro announced, without notice, that the program had been put on hold. Richmill went ahead and submitted its completed application on March 30, 1993, but Ontario Hydro refused to process it. Ontario Hydro took the position that it was free to cancel or modify these programs at will. Richmill went ahead and built the building with the energy efficient design and sued Hydro for the $340,000. In holding for the plaintiff, Molloy J. wrote:

> [7] In my opinion, Ontario Hydro's publication of the Program Guide and the Application Form/Agreement constituted an offer that was open to any customer who complied with its terms. Essentially, Ontario Hydro promised that if a customer submitted a qualifying design by March 31, 1993, incentive payments of a specific amount would be paid. Therefore, any customer who met those conditions was entitled to the payment. This is a unilateral contract, enforceable in nature. It is an offer to the world that anyone who complies

with the conditions set out in the offer will be paid a specific sum: *Carlill v. Carbolic Smoke Ball Company*, [1893] 1 Q.B. 256....

...

[17] Finally, Ontario Hydro argues that if there was an offer, it was revoked before being accepted by Richmill. In a unilateral contract, the person making the offer is not entitled to withdraw it once a party is in the process of performance. At the very least, the offeror is not entitled to put performance of a qualifying condition beyond the ability of the other party to satisfy: *Baughman v. Rampart Resources Ltd.* (1995), 124 D.L.R. 252 (B.C.C.A.) at paras 25-31. Here, Richmill had entered into the design stage for this building in October 1992 in reliance on the representation that the incentive payment was available if application was made by March 31, 1993. At this point, Richmill had not done everything it needed to do to complete the requirements for its eligibility for the payment, but it had commenced performance. It was too late at that point for Ontario Hydro to simply end all its obligations, particularly without any reasonable notice. Richmill did all it could do in terms of submitting the application on time. ...

This decision was affirmed by the Ontario Court of Appeal, [2005] O.J. No. 5059, 49 C.L.R. (3d) 181, without discussion of this issue, but a simple statement that the appeal court was "in essential agreement with the reasons of the trial judge".

6.   In a situation like *Errington*, where the performance is only partially complete at the time of the litigation, it might not be appropriate to use the *Dawson* analysis, which held both parties bound to a bilateral contract. Why?

7.   While there may be good reasons for restricting the power to revoke in cases like the ones we have just examined, there are other circumstances in which it may be fair to provide that there is a binding obligation to pay only if there has been complete performance. A more important example of a unilateral contract that courts have been reluctant to enforce without full performance is the usual form of listing agreement made between a real estate agent and a vendor of land.

      The standard listing agreement of the Toronto Real Estate Board (the agreement between the vendor of the land and the agent or broker, which will be signed before the agreement of purchase and sale is executed) provides:

> In consider of your listing the Property, I agree to pay the Listing Broker a commission of___% of the sale price of the Property ... for any valid offer to purchase ... the Property ... obtained during the Listing Period ....

      This clause appears to require payment of the commission if the agent produces an offer that is presented to the vendor and, what is most important, makes that commission payable *whether the transaction closes or not*. However, the expectation of most vendors is that the agent will be paid when (and only if) the deal has closed and the vendor has been paid.

      The literal effect of the agreements prepared by the real estate agents through the Real Estate Board (and other standard listing agreements in Canada follow the same pattern) is to "shorten the distance that they have to walk". However, this provision is very likely to catch the vendor by surprise. The general understanding of vendors is that the real estate agent has to bring an offer that the vendor will accept and that actually leads to a final sale of the property. The courts are not sympathetic to such an attempt by the agent and have held that, unless the agent expressly brings the effect of this clause to the attention of the vendor, the agent cannot sue for the commission unless the transaction closes, or unless its failure to close is the fault of the vendor.

      In *H.W. Liebig & Co. Ltd. v. Leading Investments Ltd.*, [1986] 1 S.C.R. 70, 25 D.L.R. (4th) 161, an action was brought by a real estate agent for an agreed commission after the agent brought an offer to the vendor that the vendor accepted, even though the deal did not close. In dismissing the agent's claim, La Forest J., giving the majority judgment, said (p. 87 S.C.R., pp. 182-83 D.L.R.):

It is not what these [real estate] boards may have intended a court might read into the clause that is determinative. It is what a court, from an objective standpoint, thinks both parties in the circumstances would have agreed to by the words used. And when one looks at the words in the light of the common understanding of people about this kind of contract, it becomes evident that this is not the meaning to be attached to them. Certainly they are very far from bringing home that meaning to the vendor.

Leading Investments is an interesting and important judgment. The judgment makes an important contribution in explaining the attitude of the court to interpretation. It is interesting from the point of view of the courts' treatment of standard form contracts like those of real estate boards. The Supreme Court has acknowledged that the standard forms used by real estate boards or individual agents are not "custom" contracts, *i.e.*, contracts drafted after careful negotiation between the parties, but rather contracts drafted for thousands of deals, working for the most part fairly, and reflecting by their terms what most people would expect such deals to involve. The parties have faith that the "undickered terms" are not unreasonable. They are likely to have expressly considered only the particular clauses, like those dealing with price, or, in the case of the listing agreement, the commission payable to the agent, that are special for their deal. When a standard deal is treated as if it were a "custom" deal, odd things may be expected to happen. We shall return to this point in Chapter 5.

Tendering in the Construction Industry and for Government Contracts

For the most part, the contracts examined to this point were made by a process of one-to-one bargaining, with each party trying to get the most favourable terms and the best price through negotiation. The classical model of contract formation characterizes this as a process of offer and acceptance. In certain situations, a party will try to get the best terms possible by having a competition between potential contracting parties. The principal forms such arrangements take are auctions and sealed tenders. This competitive process of contract formation is commercially (and socially) different from the process of contract formation based on one-to-one negotiation. (It is even becoming common for corporations to offer themselves for purchase by a process like an auction or tender. One interesting difference is that the draft contract prepared for the sale will be drafted by the seller, not as is common in the sale of a business, by the buyer: the terms of the sale are as much a part of the transaction and the price as the business and financial state of the corporation.)

The common law has developed a complex analysis of competitive contract formation. The courts began with the traditional offer and acceptance tools, gradually recognizing the specific problems that arise in this type of situation and modifying the analysis.

Sale of goods by public auction has long and widely been used by sellers to get the best price possible from potential buyers. In an auction with bidders present and making competing, increasingly high oral bids, the auctioneer's call for bids is considered an invitation to treat, a bid constitutes an offer, with the auctioneer then seeking other higher offers, and the auctioneer's "knocking down" the hammer and saying "sold" at the end of the process is the acceptance. As a consequence of this analysis, a bidder has the right to withdraw a bid before the auctioneer accepts his or her bid. The bidder who exercises this right may, of course, find it hard to get the auctioneer to accept any other bids. See *Payne v. Cave* (1789), 3 Term Rep. 148, 100 E.R. 502 and the Ontario *Sale of Goods Act*, R.S.O. 1990, c. S.1, s. 56(b), which provides that in cases of a sale of goods by auction, "a sale is complete when the auctioneer announces its completion by the fall of a hammer or in any other customary manner, and until such announcement is made any bidder may retract his, her or its bid." It is now common, particularly in the construction industry and in government procurement contracts, for the owner or buyer to solicit sealed written bids or tenders. The typical arrangement requires all bids to be submitted by a specified time, at which point they are all opened. In most cases the contract will be awarded to the lowest bidder. (It is almost invariable that all the terms of the contract other than price will have been specified by the owner or buyer in the "tender documents.") Public tendering is especially common when a government agency is involved, in part to ensure that there is no favouritism towards supporters of the governing party or Minister, and to ensure that the government gets the best terms possible. Public tendering is also used by private parties. Much of the recent litigation in Canada that deals with public tendering has arisen in the construction industry, though some has involved other types of procurement situations.

In the construction industry, the public bidding process is governed by "tender documents", which are prepared by the owner who wants competitive tenders (or bids) for a project. The tender documents give detailed specifications for the work to be done, and establish the terms for the bidding process, typically requiring the "general (or prime) contractors" to submit sealed tenders by a certain time, at which point they are opened in public. The tender documents invariably state that the sealed bids are "irrevocable" after the time for submission has passed, and require a "bid deposit" (usually a certified cheque) or a "bid bond" (a promise made by a commercial surety company, *i.e.*, an insurer, paid by the contractor to do so) that will be forfeited if the general contractor who is awarded the contract refuses to enter into the main contract.

In *Ron Engineering & Construction (Eastern) Ltd. v. Ontario*, [1981] 1 S.C.R. 111, 119 D.L.R. (3d) 267, the Supreme Court of Canada introduced a uniquely Canadian analysis of the tendering process (one that differs from the approach in England and the United States) which makes the tender (or bid) irrevocable once submitted. The Court did this by using a "two contract" analysis. The Court held that the owner, by issuing the tender documents and requesting irrevocable tenders, created a unilateral contract, what the Court called "Contract A". The tender documents constitute an offer to any prospective bidders that the owner will consider any bid and award the construction contract to the lowest bidder (or on such other competitive terms as the documents specify) in exchange for the bidder making an "irrevocable" bid. The general contractor's submission of a sealed tender to the owner is the "act" of acceptance that creates a unilateral contract ("Contract A") on the terms of the tender documents (which include irrevocability). The successful bidder and the owner will then enter into the construction contract, referred to as "Contract B". If the tender is not accepted within the specified period of time, the tenderer can recover any deposit or tender bond that accompanied the tender. If, after Contract A is formed (*i.e.* the bids are submitted), a tenderer claims that it has made a mistake in its bid, the court will only give relief if there was an "error on the face of the tender". As will be discussed in Chapter 5, giving relief on the basis that a contracting party made a mistake usually requires that the mistake be significant.

General contractors do not usually do all of the work on a big project themselves, but will use subcontractors to do specialized work, such as electrical, mechanical or plumbing work. Prior to the deadline for submission of sealed tenders by general contractors, subcontractors submit their own tenders — often over the phone — for work they want to do to one or more general contractors, who will incorporate the lowest subcontractor's tender into their own tender.

The process of submission of tenders by the subcontractors is usually governed by industry practice. Unlike the relation between the general contractor and the owner, which is governed by tender documents, the relation between subcontractors and general contractors may not be governed by formal tendering rules, but in a number of cases the courts have implied terms to govern this relation. In the construction industry there are industry-wide rules provided by the rules of the various bid depositories and by the Canadian Construction Documents Committee. These rules recognize certain practices designed to enhance the fairness and efficiency of the tendering process.

The following case explores the relation between general contractor and subcontractor in the context of the tendering process.

NORTHERN CONSTRUCTION CO. LTD. v. GLOGE HEATING AND PLUMBING LTD.

[1986] A.J. No. 10, 27 D.L.R. (4th) 264, [1986] 2 W.W.R. 649
(Alta. C.A., Lieberman, Harradence and Irving JJ.A.)

IRVING J.A.: — **[1]** The respondent Northern was a general contractor, and the appellant Gloge was a mechanical subcontractor. In August 1980 the government of Canada (the owner) invited tenders from contractors for the work proposed to be done at the Edmonton International Airport. The tender deadline was stipulated to be September 19, 1980; about September 3, 1980 Northern invited tenders from various subtrades, including the appellant Gloge.

[2] As the trial judge noted, the practice in the industry would cause an interested prospective subcontractor to obtain copies of the plans, specifications and tender documents from the owner so that it might prepare its tender. The subcontractor would know from such documents that general contractors tendering would be bound by their tenders for up to sixty days while the owner considered the various tenders. The subcontractors would also know that a general contractor was required to disclose in its tender the identity of the subcontractors it proposed to use.

[3] Tenders were to close on September 19, 1980; apparently the practice of many subcontractors, including Gloge, was to telephone their tenders to the general contractors minutes before the close of tenders, in order to deny any time for "bid-shopping" by general contractors. Following this practice, Gloge communicated its tender by telephone to Northern perhaps twenty minutes before tenders closed. Northern would then complete its own tender for submission to the owner in the few minutes remaining before tendering closed.

[4] Gloge's tender was the lowest of the mechanical subcontract tenders received by Northern, and was used by Northern in the computation of its own tender. Additionally, Northern nominated Gloge as its mechanical subcontractor in its tender to the owner. . . .

[5] By September 23 Gloge had realized that its tender seriously understated the cost of the work. This error resulted from incorrect extensions, etc., and resulted in a shortfall of approximately $180,000 below what the tender should have been.

Therefore on that date Gloge contacted several general contractors to whom it had tendered and learned that Northern was the lowest bidder. Upon enquiry to Northern, Gloge then learned that Northern's tender to the owner had relied on Gloge's mechanical tender. Gloge then explained that its tender was erroneous, and details were provided. After discussion, Gloge undertook to provide Northern with written details of the tender, including details of the error, so that Northern might assist Gloge, by urging the owner to permit substitution of Gloge by another mechanical tender, and presumably to permit Northern to adjust its own tender by the amount of the increase in the mechanical tender.

[6]   The owner agreed to the substitution, but refused to permit Northern to change the amount of its tender.

[7]   The owner duly accepted Northern's tender and awarded it the work. Gloge refused to perform the mechanical subcontract, so that Northern was required to make alternative arrangements by employing a subsidiary at an increase of $341,299 in the mechanical subcontract price. . . .

[8]   The real issue raised before us is Gloge's first submission — Was Gloge free to withdraw its bid, and did it do so? In our view, the decisions in *Ron Engineering & Construction v. Ontario*, [1981] 1 S.C.R. 111, and *The City of Calgary v. Northern Construction Company Division of Morrison-Knudsen Company Inc., et al.*, [1986] 2 W.W.R. 426 (Alta. C.A.), provide the answer.

[9]   Applying the analysis of Estey J. in *Ron Engineering*, Northern made an offer to Gloge to submit a tender for the mechanical subcontract; Gloge accepted the offer by submitting its tender on September 19, 1980, and contract A (as described by Estey J.) was made.

[10]   As Estey J. stated in *Ron Engineering*:

> The tender submitted by the respondent brought contract A into life. This is sometimes described in law as a unilateral contract, that is to say a contract which results from an act made in response to an offer, as for example in the simplest terms, "I will pay you a dollar if you will cut my lawn". No obligation to cut the lawn exists in law and the obligation to pay the dollar comes into being upon the performance of the invited act. Here the call for tenders created no obligation in the respondent or in anyone else in or out of the construction world. When a member of the construction industry responds to the call for tenders, as the respondent has done here, that response takes the form of the submission of a tender, or a bid as it is sometimes called. The significance of the bid in law is that it at once becomes irrevocable if filed in conformity with the terms and conditions under which the call for tenders was made and if such terms so provide. There is no disagreement between the parties here about the form and procedure in which the tender was submitted by the respondent and that it complied with the terms and conditions of the call for tenders. Consequently, contract A came into being. The principal term of contract A is the irrevocability of the bid, and the corollary term is the obligation in both parties to enter into a contract (contract B) upon the acceptance of the tender.

[11]   Was Gloge's tender revocable after close of tender? Gloge knew that Northern would select a mechanical tender and rely on it, and Gloge also knew that the tenders of the general contractors to the owner would be irrevocable for the time set out in the contract documents. Perhaps these facts of themselves might justify holding the Gloge tender to be irrevocable. But, in addition, the trial judge accepted certain expert evidence given at the trial by two witnesses who had been in the construction industry for many years. That evidence demonstrated that it was normal and standard practice for general contractors to accept last minute tele-

phone tenders from subcontractors, and that it was understood and accepted by those in the industry that while such tenders could be withdrawn prior to close of tendering, if not so withdrawn, that such tenders must remain irrevocable for the same term that the general contractors' tenders to the owner are irrevocable.

[12] This industry practice is eminent common sense. Without such accepted practice the tendering system would become unenforceable and meaningless. Estey J. observed in *Ron Engineering*:

> I share the view expressed by the Court of Appeal that the integrity of the bidding system must be protected where under the law of contracts it is possible so to do.

[13] Applying the industry practice to this case, Gloge could not withdraw its tender to Northern after tenders had closed, and its tender was irrevocable for the same period as Northern's. Accordingly Gloge was obligated to perform the work when Northern awarded it the subcontract, and is liable for failing to do so.

[14] We observe that Gloge's conduct after its tender error was discovered is consistent with the industry practice already described. Gloge did not take the position with Northern that it had the right to withdraw its bid. Instead, it sought Northern's assistance in an attempt to persuade the owner to consent to the substitution of a higher mechanical tender to replace Gloge's.

[15] In the result, the judgment at trial is affirmed. The appeal is dismissed with costs to be calculated on the same basis as ordered by the trial judge.

NOTES

1. The decision in *Northern Construction Co. v. Gloge Heating & Plumbing Ltd.* relies on the decision of the Supreme Court of Canada in *Ron Engineering*, which is considered in Chapter 5.

    While the courts have not abrogated the general common law rule that a "firm" offer is revocable, the decisions illustrate that a court can find a way to make an offer irrevocable if it really wants to do so. The judgment in *Northern Construction* makes practical sense and protects the general contractor's reliance on the industry practice. This reliance is both expected and, in the context of the industry, reasonable. The concerns of Estey and Irving JJ. are valid. The question that remains is why the common law insists on a rule, *viz.*, the rule that firm offers are revocable, when the courts are prepared to avoid it when it is necessary to do so. There is something about the common law rules of offer and acceptance and the doctrine of consideration that makes them peculiarly resistant to change.

2. The business of tendering for large-scale construction contracts is important and, as the concerns of Gloge, referred to by Irving J.A., indicate, possibilities for abuse exist. A written set of rules to deal with some of the most obvious problems has been developed by bodies that represent all parties in the construction industry with a continuing interest in the process. These bodies include the Canadian Construction Documents Committee and the Bid Depositories that exist in most large centres in Canada. (The Bid Depositories are operated by the construction industry and have rules governing any tendering that makes use of their services; the CCDC represents all those involved in construction — general contractors, subcontractors or trade contractors, architects, engineers and owners.) The rules of the Ontario Bid Depository are discussed in the next case, *Naylor Group Inc. v. Ellis-Don Construction Ltd.* Consensual rules like those of bid depositories illustrate that careful planning can provide methods to readily deal with the kind of problem the Alberta Court of Appeal faced, but those rules did not deal with the specific problem in *Northern Construction*, so the court was required to develop its own rules.

3.   *Northern Construction* dealt with the *obligations* of subcontractors in the construction
     bidding process. The next case deals with the *rights* that subcontractors have in this
     process, and considers the Ontario Bid Depository Rules.

NAYLOR GROUP INC. v. ELLIS-DON CONSTRUCTION LTD.

[2001] S.C.J. No. 56, [2001] 2 S.C.R. 943, 204 D.L.R. (4th) 513
(McLachlin, C.J.C., Iacobucci, Major, Bastarache, Binnie, Arbour and LeBel JJ.)

The judgment of the Court was delivered by

[1]   BINNIE J.: — This appeal raises the issue of a prime contractor's legal obligations (if any) to a prospective subcontractor whose bid it has incorporated in its
own successful tender for a construction project under the rules of a structured bid
depository. The appellant's Project Manager testified that a bid depository "is just
a fancy name for somebody collecting prices". This, as will be seen, is something
of an understatement.

[2]   The appellant, one of the largest construction firms in Ontario, acknowledges that it generally subcontracts with the trades "carried" in its own bid for a
job, but says it has no legal obligation to do so. In this case, the respondent subcontractor was deemed unacceptable because its employees belonged to the wrong
trade union. The respondent subcontractor replies that the appellant not only knew
from the outset that the respondent's workers belonged to an in-house union ("The
Employees Association of Naylor Group Incorporated"), but with full knowledge
of that fact invited it to bid for the electrical work on a multi-million dollar project
for renovations and additions to the Oakville-Trafalgar Memorial Hospital ("the
owner" or "OTMH"). Worse, the appellant used the respondent's low bid to get
the job, then "shopped" its bid elsewhere to get the work done at a very favourable
price. All of this, says the respondent, undermined the integrity of the Bid Depository process and breached the terms of the tender contract.

[3]   The Ontario Court of Appeal rejected the appellant's arguments. It held that
the terms of the contract governing this particular tender required the appellant to
enter into the electrical subcontract with the respondent in the absence of reasonable cause not to do so. I think that on the facts of this particular tender arrangement, this conclusion is correct. The issue, then, is whether reasonable cause existed. The appellant had invited the respondent to participate with the assurance
that there would be no objection at a later date to its union affiliation, and affirmed
this position repeatedly thereafter. The appellant's eventual reversal of that position was unreasonable. It is in accordance with the tendering contract that it bear
the commercial consequences. The appeal must therefore be dismissed.

[4]   The respondent subcontractor cross-appeals the award of damages. It says it
was entitled to its loss of profit on the lost contract (which the trial judge assessed
at $730,286) and that this figure was inappropriately reduced by the Ontario Court
of Appeal to $182,500 because of alleged "contingencies" which were not estab-
lished in the evidence. I think the respondent is partly correct in this respect. Accepting the dollar figures generated by the courts below, but deleting one of the
contingencies allowed by the Ontario Court of Appeal, I would allow the cross-
appeal and give judgment for the respondent in the sum of $365,143.

I.   *Facts*

[5]   In 1991, the OTMH called for tenders for the construction of an addition and renovation of its hospital through the Toronto Bid Depository.

1.   THE BID DEPOSITORY SYSTEM

[6]   A bid depository is, in effect, a structured bidding process. The model used here was devised in the late 1950s by the construction industry with the participation of the Ontario government. It is designed to achieve fairness on building construction projects where the owner requires a lump sum tender based on plans and specifications, and where a multitude of prime contractors, trade contractors and suppliers are expected to get involved in the tendering process. At the relevant time, it worked as follows.

[7]   The Bid Depository's staff was notified of a new project by an owner who wished to make use of their services. A date was fixed by which the pre-qualified subcontractors were to submit on a standard form document (for ease of comparison) a breakdown of their prices. Identical project documentation was made available to all interested bidders in each of the subtrades. Their tenders were sealed and delivered to the Bid Depository office by a specified date and time and deposited in a designated locked box. On the due date, the subtrade bid documents were made available to interested prime contractors who selected the subcontractors (not necessarily the lowest bidder) they wanted to carry as part of their own bid to the owner. Prime contractor bids were required to be filed on a standard form on a fixed date (here, two days after the opening of the subtrade bids). The system offered conformity and comparability. The prime contractor bids were open for the owner's acceptance for a fixed period (here 90 days) and the subcontractor bids were open for acceptance by the prime contractor for a fixed period after the award of the prime contract (here 7 days). Each prime contractor was required to undertake "to place a Sub-Contract with one of the trade contractors who used the Bid Depository" (Rule 13(c) of the Ontario Bid Depository Standard Rules and Procedures, also known as the rules of the Toronto Bid Depository). These were not informal arrangements for the convenience of prime contractors (i.e., "just a fancy name for somebody collecting prices"). Each participant in the tendering process bound itself by contract to certain obligations and acquired thereby certain rights. The content of those rights and obligations is the subject matter of this litigation.

[8]   Thomas Hitchman, President of the respondent, explained it thus:

> . . . the purpose of the Bid Depository is that the sub-trade contractors submit their price through the Bid Depository and then the general contractor has a time frame, in this case two days, to assemble his bid and in so doing he can use the numbers that come out of the various sub-trades that bid through the Bid Depository two days earlier.

> Q.   I gather in the process there are more than just electrical sub-contractors tendering, is that correct?

> A.   Yes.

[9]   The process is considered fair to all participants because all parties bid on identical information, and their bids are disclosed to the relevant parties at the same time. In particular, it assures subtrades that their bids will not be "shopped" by a prime contractor to competing subcontractors to lever a price advantage. "Bid shopping" was defined by the trial judge as "the practice of soliciting a bid from a contractor, with whom one has no intention of dealing, and then disclosing or using that in an attempt to drive prices down amongst contractors with whom one does intend to deal" ((1996), 30 C.L.R. (2d) 195 (Ont. Gen. Div.), at p. 200). The Court of Appeal thought it sufficient if the "shopping" was to get a bid "for the same value or less" ((1999), 43 O.R. (3d) 325, at p. 330, footnote 3).

2.   THE BIDDING HISTORY IN THIS CASE

[10]   The owner notified the Toronto Bid Depository of the project and a timetable was established whereby the bids of interested trade subcontractors were required to be made by December 10, 1991. A preliminary procedure was established by the owner and its architect to "pre-qualify" acceptable subcontractors by reference to such factors as their competence, track record on other projects, and financial viability. It being in the interest of prime contractors to have as many qualified firms as possible competing for the subcontracts, the appellant approached the respondent in early November 1991 to bid on the job. The respondent volunteered the important information that its workers were not affiliated with the International Brotherhood of Electrical Workers ("IBEW"). It was told there would be no objection on that account. . . .

. . .

[12]   The fact is that the appellant had been in a continuing if sporadic argument over bargaining rights with the IBEW for the previous 30 years. The dispute, in which the IBEW claimed to have been the *exclusive* bargaining agent for electrical workers on the appellant's jobs since 1962, came to a head in an 18-day hearing before the Ontario Labour Relations Board ("OLRB") in 1990. The issues before the OLRB were whether the IBEW had validly obtained bargaining rights in 1962 and, if so, whether those rights had been subsequently abandoned. The OLRB ruling was still under reserve in January 1991. The appellant was undoubtedly convinced of the correctness of its position before the OLRB, but it was aware, whereas the respondent was not, of the details of the IBEW grievance and whether or not an adverse ruling would cause it serious difficulty on the OTMH job.

[13]   The respondent tendered a price of $5,539,000. Approximately six weeks of work and 118 pages of calculations went into preparation of the bid. The next lowest bid for the electrical work was Comstock, an IBEW subcontractor, whose bid was $411,000 higher than the respondent's bid. Comstock also bid for the mechanical work.

[14]   The appellant carried the respondent's low bid for the electrical work and Comstock's bid for the mechanical work in its own tender for the prime contract. It was low bidder at $38,135,900 for the OTMH project. The trial judge found as a fact that if the appellant had carried Comstock's bid for the electrical work instead of the respondent's bid, it would not have been low bidder overall and might on that account have lost the prime contract.

[15]   By January 1992 it was common knowledge in the industry that the appellant had submitted the lowest bid. Acting on the appellant's assurances that its "in-house" union affiliation presented no problem, the respondent "assigned personnel to study drawings, set crew sizes and plan the phasing of the electrical work". At

no time did it receive any formal communication from the appellant that it would get the subcontract.

[16] Nor had the appellant received confirmation of the prime contract from the owner. The hospital is partly funded by the Ontario government, and there ensued an unexpected delay in obtaining a commitment of government funds. In February 1992, the owner, OTMH, asked the appellant to extend the date for acceptance of its tender for 60 days (i.e., until May 1992). The appellant, in turn, asked for similar extensions from the subcontractors it had carried in its tender, including the respondent. The respondent prudently requested from the appellant a letter confirming its intent to give it the subcontract for the electrical work, if its prime bid was accepted. The appellant declined, it said, "because it was Ellis-Dons practice not to enter into letters of intent prior to the award of the prime contract."

[17] The OLRB decision was released on February 28, 1992. . . . The IBEW grievance was upheld. The OLRB decision confirmed the appellant's collective bargaining commitment to use only electrical subcontractors whose employees were affiliated with the IBEW. . . . The appellant acknowledged in pre-trial discovery that the OLRB decision had been received by its in-house Director of Legal and Labour Operations, Mr. Paul Richer, on that date or soon thereafter although apparently it was not communicated to their manager on the OTMH project, Mr. Bruno Antidormi, until about March 10, 1992.

[18] In the meantime, the owner had incorporated various changes to its project into Bid Revision No. 1 (also known as Post Tender Addendum No. 1). Despite the OLRB ruling, the appellant asked the subtrades, *including the respondent*, to submit prices for the contract changes by March 12. The respondent quoted $132,192 (bringing its total bid to $5,671,192). This quote, too, was carried by the appellant in its tender to the owner on March 17, 1992, i.e., three weeks after the OLRB decision and seven days after the appellant's *project* management had been made fully aware of the contents of the decision, and had given themselves sufficient time to digest its impact.

[19] When word reached the respondent from some of its suppliers that the appellant was seeking bids from competing electrical subcontractors, one of its managers, Mr. Colin Harkness, called the appellant's Project Manager to confront him with this information. . . .

[20] The respondent concluded, quite understandably in the trial judge's view, that the appellant was now "shopping its bid" to rival firms.

[21] On May 4, 1992, the President of the respondent wrote a letter to the owner, OTMH, complaining of the appellant's apparent double game. He obtained no satisfaction. On May 6, 1992, the owner awarded the prime contract, incorporating Bid Revision No. 1 (Post Tender Addendum No. 1), to the appellant, who at that time still had no other electrical subcontractor prepared to do the project at the respondent's price. In fact, the prime contract contained Article 10.2 under which the appellant ostensibly undertook to hire the respondent:

> 10.2 The Contractor agrees to employ those Subcontractors proposed by him in writing and accepted by the Owner at the signing of the Contract.

[22] On May 5, 1992, the appellant offered to subcontract the electrical work to the respondent at the bid price if the respondent would align itself with the IBEW. The respondent, which already had a union, understandably saw this offer as a

ploy by the appellant to download its union problems onto the respondent and its workforce. It declined.

[23] On May 13, 1992, the appellant wrote to the respondent to say that because of the OLRB decision of February 28, 1992, "we regrettably will be unable to enter into a Subcontract Agreement with your firm for the electrical work".

[24] In July 1992, the appellant provided Guild Electric (an IBEW subcontractor) with a letter of intent to award the electrical subcontract for $5,671,192, precisely the same amount as had been bid by the respondent. Guild Electric had been pre-qualified for the OTMH project, but had decided not to submit a bid. It was therefore an ineligible subcontractor under Rule 13(c) of the Bid Depository, which was treated by the appellant as of no further relevance. The final subcontract was subsequently signed with Guild with a minor price difference which was conceded to be insignificant.

[25] The respondent sued for breach of contract and unjust enrichment. Its contractual claim was dismissed but it was awarded damages for unjust enrichment at trial in the amount of $14,560, an amount corresponding to the costs of preparing its bid. The respondent appealed and was awarded damages for breach of contract in the amount of $182,500 plus pre-judgment interest and costs. The appellant appeals from that decision on the issue of liability alone. The respondent cross-appeals on the issue of quantum of damages.

[**BINNIE J.**'s summary of the judgments in the Ontario courts is omitted.]

III. *Analysis*

[33] The prospect of a major construction job generally initiates a cascade of invitations to bid from the owner to prime contractors to the subcontractors to the suppliers and other participants. The invitations generate a corresponding flow of tenders upwards along the same food chain. The Bid Depository system promotes itself as designed to protect the reasonable expectations of all participants. It does this by establishing clear rules, fixed deadlines, simultaneous disclosure of bids, and an orderly contracting procedure. Those submitting bids incur the obligation to keep them open for acceptance for a fixed period of time. This of course ties up their resources and, depending on the circumstances, may incur some financial risk. In exchange, the tendering parties are assured that they will be fairly dealt with according to the rules established under the particular tendering procedure.

[34] For the last 20 years, the legal effect of tendering arrangements has been approached in accordance with the Contract A/Contract B analysis adopted in *Ron Engineering, supra*, per Estey J., at p. 119:

> There is no question when one reviews the terms and conditions under which the tender was made that a contract arose upon the submission of a tender between the contractor and the owner whereby the tenderer could not withdraw the tender for a period of sixty days after the date of the opening of the tenders. Later in these reasons this initial contract is referred to as contract A to distinguish it from the construction contract itself which would arise on the acceptance of a tender, and which I refer to as contract B.

[35] Subsequently, in *M.J.B. Enterprises Ltd. v. Defence Construction (1951) Ltd.*, [1999] 1 S.C.R. 619, the Court allowed the appeal of an unsuccessful bidder against the award of a prime contract to an unqualified bidder, contrary to an implied term in Contract A. The Court took the opportunity on that occasion to affirm that Contract A does not automatically spring into existence upon the making of a tender, and if it does, its terms must be ascertained as with any other contract, and not be derived from some abstract legal paradigm. Iacobucci J. reinforced this point at para. 17:

> . . . it is always possible that Contract A does not arise upon the submission of a tender, or that Contract A arises but the irrevocability of the tender is not one of its terms, all of this depending upon the terms and conditions of the tender call.

See also: *Martel Building Ltd. v. Canada*, [2000] 2 S.C.R. 860, 193 D.L.R. (4th) 1, at para. 80.

[36] Both *Ron Engineering*, *supra*, and *M.J.B. Enterprises* dealt with owners and prime contractors. The present appeal raises an issue at a lower level of the cascade. Nevertheless, as those decisions made clear, the Contract A/Contract B approach rests on ordinary principles of contract formation, and there is no reason in principle why the same approach should not apply at this lower level. The existence and content of Contract A will depend on the facts of the particular case. Accordingly, the prime contract having been awarded in this case to the appellant, the issue is whether the respondent had any contractual rights under its Contract A with the appellant either to the making of Contract B (the electrical subcontract) or to damages for the appellant's refusal to do so.

[37] This appeal thus raises five issues:

1. Was a Contract A formed between the appellant and respondent with respect to this project and, if so, what were its terms?

2. Was the contract frustrated by reason of the OLRB decision of February 28, 1992?

3. If not, did the appellant breach the terms of Contract A?

4. If so, what are the damages?

5. In the alternative, is the respondent entitled to recover on the basis of unjust enrichment?

. . .

1. WAS THERE A CONTRACT A AND, IF SO, WHAT WERE THE TERMS?

[39] The respondent contended at trial that the appellant, upon winning the prime contract, became automatically obligated to it under the terms of Contract A to enter into the electrical subcontract, i.e., Contract B. . . .

[40] It is possible that under a different set of bidding rules this *could* be the outcome, but there is nothing in the call for tender or related documents in this case to give rise to such a result. On the contrary, as pointed out by Weiler J.A. in the Ontario Court of Appeal, the tender documents clearly contemplate the possible substitution of a subcontractor that is different from the firm carried in the tender for the prime contract. Article 10.3 of the General Conditions that govern the tender provides that the owner may, on reasonable grounds, object to a subcontractor and, if so, the prime contractor is required to employ another subcontractor. Article 10.5 states that the prime contractor shall not be required to employ as a subcontractor a person or firm to whom he may reasonably object. These terms are incorporated into Contract A and are plainly inconsistent with the respondent's theory of a "deemed Contract B". In accordance with the usual principles of contract formation, communication of acceptance was required to make Contract B.

[41] The tender documents are equally clear, however, that the prime contractor is not free under Contract A of contractual obligation to the subtrades it has carried in its own bid. The Bid Depository does not operate simply for the prime contractor's convenience.

[42] The Ontario Bid Depository Standard Rules and Procedures assures participants that it "provides for the sanctity of the bid during the tendering process", and specifically assures a subcontractor that he [or she] is "[a]ble to bid Prime Contractors knowing his bid will not be 'shopped'". The mechanism by which this is achieved is by instructing prime contractors in Article 16.1 of the Instructions to Bidders:

> 16.1   Bidders shall submit with Bid Documents . . . names of the Subcontractors bidder proposes to perform work under the Contract, and to include in the Agreement he would sign with the Owner.

The attached printed form that is required of prime contractors to submit to the owner includes as Article 3 the term:

> 3.   In the Stipulated Price the following Subcontractors are carried and they *will* perform the work indicated. [Emphasis added.]

[43] The appellant was therefore required to and did include as Article 3 of its tender for the prime contract:

> In the Stipulated Price the following Subcontractors are carried and they *will* perform the work indicated: . . . Electrical . . . Naylor Group Incorporated. [Emphasis added.]

[44] Further, as noted above, the final contract between the owner and the appellant, which was in a standard form stipulated pursuant to the Bid Depository rules, provided as Article 10.2 of the General Conditions of the Stipulated Price Contract:

> 10.2   The Contractor agrees to employ those Subcontractors proposed by him in writing and accepted by the Owner at the signing of the Contract.

[45] Outside the framework of a bid depository or comparable scheme, such provisions might operate solely between the owner and the prime contractor, and be of no assistance to a stranger to their contract, such as an aspiring subcontractor. However, in this case, there was a structured Bid Depository, and these standard printed-form documents between the prime contractor and the owner constituted part of the Bid Depository regime as implemented, and formed the contractual basis on which the subcontractors tendered. Indeed, it was on this basis that the Bid Depository *could* assure them that their bids would not be "shopped". The assurance of a subcontract to the carried subcontractor, subject to *reasonable* objection, was for subcontractors the most important term of Contract A.

. . .

[47] I therefore reject the dismissive expression of the appellant's Project Manager that the Bid Depository was "just a fancy name for somebody collecting prices". It was contrary to the rules of the Bid Depository that a subcontractor's bid, once disclosed, would become merely a bargaining lever against other electrical subcontractors to obtain the same or a lower price.

[48] The appellant complains that it did not "shop" the respondent's bid, as the trial judge defined it, because at the time it solicited the bid *it did* intend to subcontract the work to the respondent if it turned out to be the low bidder, and it subsequently used the respondent's price as "a budget" to get the work done, not as a lever to obtain a still lower price from other subcontractors. This, while plausible, misses the point. The question at this stage is not whether the appellant engaged in bid shopping as defined by the trial judge but whether the rules of the Bid Depository created an effective contractual barrier to the practice, which was a leading selling point to the industry. In my view, the documentation referred to above, read in light of the rules of the Toronto Bid Depository, were intended to and did bring into existence, upon tender, a Contract A which required the successful prime contractor to subcontract to the firms carried in the absence of a reasonable objection.

[49] The appellant also complains that in effect the court here would be "implying" a term into Contract A without meeting the stringent requirements laid down in *Canadian Pacific Hotels Ltd. v. Bank of Montreal*, [1987] 1 S.C.R. 711, and *Martel Building, supra*. In my view, however, the obligation to contract, subject to reasonable objection, arises directly out of the rules of the Bid Depository and related (and required) standard form documentation, and does not resort to an "implied" term.

[50] Finally, the appellant warns that this conclusion "imposes highly dysfunctional constraints on the ability of prime contractors and owners to deal with unusual problems that may arise in the course of the tendering/bidding process". It seems to me the rules of the Bid Depository are *intended* to impose constraints. The prime contractor is protected by Article 10 of the General Conditions to the Stipulated Price Contract that would eliminate a subcontractor if the owner had "reasonable cause" to object (Art. 10.3) or if the prime contractor itself "may reasonably object" (Art. 10.5). The prime contractor's protection lies in the contractual right to object. The subcontractor's protection lies in the concept of "reasonableness". An *un*reasonable objection does not suffice. If other participants in the Bid Depository system agree with the appellant that such a constraint is "dysfunctional", the rules can always be amended.

[51] I therefore agree with Weiler J.A. that the various terms and conditions governing the Toronto Bid Depository, when read together, compel the conclusion that, when the appellant chose to carry the respondent's bid in its tender to the owner, it committed itself to subcontract the electrical work to the respondent in the absence of a reasonable objection. What is "reasonable" depends on the facts of the case.

2. WAS CONTRACT A FRUSTRATED BY REASON OF THE OLRB DECISION OF FEBRUARY 28, 1992?

[BINNIE J. discussed the argument that the OLRB decision had discharged the appellant. He concluded:]

[58] In my view, the OLRB decision no more qualified as a "supervening event" than would a court decision upholding the validity of the first of two inconsistent contracts for the sale of a house. The judicial decision, far from frustrating and

putting to an end the second contract, simply lays the basis for a claim in damages by the second purchaser. The OLRB merely affirmed a pre-existing obligation voluntarily entered into by the appellant that was too late disclosed to the respondent.

[59] There is another reason why the doctrine of frustration is inapplicable. Contract A left open the possibility that for some good reason the appellant might "reasonably object" to the awarding of the subcontract to the respondent. The owner and the appellant had satisfied themselves about the respondent's qualifications on the basis of information known to them at the time of carrying its bid in the tender for the prime contract. However, there might obviously have arisen subsequent events (e.g., loss of key personnel) or belatedly disclosed information (e.g., financial insolvency) that would render an objection reasonable. The parties to Contract A specifically provided their own test to deal with supervening circumstances by means of a flexible exit option based on reasonableness. As a matter of construction, there is no need here to consider court-imposed remedies based on the allegation of a radical change to the significance of the contractual obligation.

[60] The legal issue raised on these facts is not the doctrine of frustration but whether, in light of its conduct under the rules of the Bid Depository, it was "reasonable" of the appellant to object to the respondent's union affiliation.

3.   DID THE APPELLANT BREACH THE TERMS OF CONTRACT A?

[61] The appellant has throughout taken the position that its *only* objection to the respondent is the fact that it is not an IBEW subcontractor. In my view, its conduct throughout the OTMH project disentitled it from characterizing such an objection as "reasonable".

[62] This is not to understate the importance of the OLRB's affirmation of IBEW bargaining rights. . . . The IBEW, having established the correctness of its position at much effort and expense, could be expected to insist on the fruits of victory. The respondent says that the appellant simply acted duplicitously and crassly. Depending on who got the electrical subcontract, it knew it was going to be sued by either the IBEW or the respondent. It apparently viewed a suit by the respondent as the softer option. This observation may have a measure of truth, but the more important fact is that the OLRB ruling is backed up by a statutory enforcement scheme that the appellant is obliged to recognize as paramount. . . .

[63] The appellant's argument, with respect, sets up a straw man. The severity of the Act's provisions simply exposes the folly of the appellant's assurances and conduct at a time when the OLRB decision was looming. . . . The appellant chose to carry the respondent instead of its IBEW affiliated rival, Comstock, and thereby assured itself as low bidder of winning the prime contract. It was held by the OLRB to have previously promised the work to IBEW electricians. By reason of that earlier obligation, it was unable to fulfil its subsequent obligation under Contract A. It couldn't keep both sets of promises. It is perfectly fair that it compensate the respondent for its non-performance of Contract A.

[64] The appellant's dilemma is not without its sympathetic aspects. The OLRB decision was pending for about a year. In the meantime the appellant, as a practical operator, had either to bid carrying IBEW subcontractors (perhaps unnecessarily)

and risk losing major projects, or bid carrying non-IBEW subcontractors (perhaps wrongly) and risk the subsequent wrath of the IBEW and, perhaps, the OLRB. The problem, in the end, is that it purported to solve its dilemma at the respondent's expense.

[65] The appellant, with full knowledge of the IBEW situation, had gone out of its way to assure the respondent that its in-house union affiliation was no cause for concern and would be no basis for objection. It carried the respondent's bid in its tender for the prime contract in December 1991, with full knowledge both of the IBEW proceedings before the OLRB and the respondent's non-IBEW union affiliation. It affirmed its agreement to use the respondent when it put forward the respondent's addendum price in its submission to the owner on March 17, 1992, more than two weeks after its Director of Legal and Labour Operations had received full notice of the OLRB ruling and began to seek advice on its impact. It formally affirmed the respondent's expected role in the actual contract between the owner and the appellant dated May 6, 1992 because otherwise it would have been obliged to admit it was signing a multi-million dollar contract including major electrical work without anyone in sight who was prepared and IBEW-equipped to perform it at the respondent's price. The appellant was not prepared to give the electrical work to Comstock, which was already on the job as mechanical contractor, whose bid price had been $411,000 higher than the respondent.

[66] The evidence on these matters was clear and uncontradicted. The potential IBEW problem was flagged by the respondent itself at the initial contact in early November 1991. The "no problem" assurance was given after consultation within the appellant organization by Mr. Paul Quinless, who as the senior estimator had responsibility for bidding on the OTMH project. . . .

. . .

[68] On March 17, 1992 — well after the appellant acknowledges receiving and considering the OLRB decision — it affirmed its selection of the respondent by approving and submitting Naylor's price in its response to Bid Revision No. 1. . . .

[69] Even more remarkably, the appellant signed the prime contract dated May 6, 1992 — about two months after the appellant was fully aware of the OLRB decision — undertaking to the owner once again to use the respondent to do the electrical work. . . .

[70] I agree with the appellant that the OLRB ruling of February 28, 1992 put an end to the lawful ability to use the services of the respondent. In my view, however, the fact it lost its OLRB gamble is not sufficient to absolve it of the financial consequences to the respondent. Its belated objection to the respondent, in light of this history, was unreasonable.

[71] The respondent takes a darker view of the appellant's conduct. It contends that non-disclosure of the IBEW problem and the other matters referred to above were far from innocent. It insists that if the appellant had carried the lowest IBEW subcontractor (Comstock) for the electrical work, it would not have been low bidder on the OTMH project. The respondent says its bid was "used" to obtain the prime contract and "used" again to secure a substitute electrical subcontract at the same price from Guild Electric, all of which it says was contrary to the rules of the Toronto Bid Depository. . . .

[72] While both the trial judge and Weiler J.A. in the Ontario Court of Appeal found the appellant's conduct in this respect distasteful, I think it is sufficient to dispose of the case on the narrow contractual ground that the appellant could only extricate itself from Contract A by demonstrating that, in all the circumstances, its objection was "reasonable", and this it has failed to do.

4. WHAT ARE THE RESPONDENT'S DAMAGES FOR BREACH OF CONTRACT A?

[73] The well accepted principle is that the respondent should be put in as good a position, financially speaking, as it would have been in had the appellant performed its obligations under the tender contract. The normal measure of damages in the case of a wrongful refusal to contract in the building context is the contract price less the cost to the respondent of executing or completing the work, i.e., the loss of profit. . . .

[In the result, **BINNIE J.** assessed the plaintiff's damages at $365,143. In arriving at this figure, he varied the judgment of the Court of Appeal, which had discounted the plaintiff's award by 50 per cent to account for contingencies which might have adversely affected the profit that Naylor might have made.]

NOTES

1. Given the fact that many players in the construction industry have to maintain a reputation for reliability and co-operativeness, the extent of the litigation is surprising. Naylor and Eastern are both very big players in the Ontario construction scene and might be expected to have to work together in the future. The action of Gloge Heating & Plumbing Ltd. must have been prompted by desperation.

2. In *M.J.B. Enterprises Ltd. v. Defence Construction (1951) Co. Ltd.*, [1999] 1 S.C.R. 619, 170 D.L.R. (4th) 577, the defendant solicited bids for a construction project. The defendant owner (the Government of Canada) awarded the contract to the lowest tenderer of the four tenders received. It was held that this tender did not comply with the tender specifications. The question was whether the government had breached the terms of the contract with the other bidders in accepting a non-compliant bid.

    The defendant relied on a "privilege clause" in the tender documents. The clause in the tender documents was a standard one which provided: "The lowest or any tender shall not necessarily be accepted." The purpose of this clause is to reserve to the owner some discretion in the awarding of tenders. (A bid that is too low, *i.e.*, insufficient to permit the contractor to complete the work, is one that a prudent owner would not want to accept because the project is likely to run into problems that will almost certainly cost the owner more in the long run.)

    The plaintiff had submitted the second-lowest tender and brought an action for breach of contract, claiming that the winning tender should have been disqualified and that its tender should have been accepted as the lowest valid bid. The claim failed in the Alberta courts. In the Supreme Court of Canada, Iacobucci J., giving the judgment of the Court, held that the privilege clause did not permit acceptance of a noncompliant tender and that the owner, though it had acted in good faith, had breached the contract made when the plaintiff submitted a bid in response to the tender documents. Iacobucci J. considered and rejected an argument that the tender documents contained an express provision limiting the defendant's freedom. He then considered an argument that an appropriate undertaking should be implied in the tender documents. He concluded by saying:

    > [40] Therefore, according to the Instructions to Tenderers and the Tender Form, a contractor submitting a tender must submit a valid tender and, in submitting its tender, is not at liberty to negotiate over the terms of the tender documents. Given this, it is reasonable to infer that the respondent would *only* consider valid tenders. For the respondent to accept a non-compliant bid would be contrary to the express indication in the Instructions to Tenderers

that any negotiation of an amendment would have to take place according to the provisions of paragraph 12(b). It is also contrary to the entire tenor of the Tender Form, which was the only form required to be submitted in addition to the bid security, and which does not allow for any modification of the plans and specifications in the tender documents.

[41] The rationale for the tendering process, as can be seen from these documents, is to replace negotiation with competition. This competition entails certain risks for the appellant. The appellant must expend effort and incur expense in preparing its tender in accordance with strict specifications and may nonetheless not be awarded Contract B. It must submit its bid security which, although it is returned if the tender is not accepted, is a significant amount of money to raise and have tied up for the period of time between the submission of the tender and the decision regarding Contract B. . . . It appears obvious to me that exposing oneself to such risks makes little sense if the respondent is allowed, in effect, to circumscribe this process and accept a non-compliant bid. Therefore I find it reasonable, on the basis of the presumed intentions of the parties, to find an implied term that only a compliant bid would be accepted.

In considering the effect of the privilege clause, Iacobucci J. said:

[45] I do not find that the privilege clause overrode the obligation to accept only compliant bids, because on the contrary, there is a compatibility between the privilege clause and this obligation. . .

[46] Therefore even where, as in this case, almost nothing separates the tenderers except the different prices they submit, the rejection of the lowest bid would not imply that a tender could be accepted on the basis of some undisclosed criterion. The discretion to accept not necessarily the lowest bid, retained by the owner through the privilege clause, is a discretion to take a more nuanced view of "cost" than the prices quoted in the tenders. . . .

Iacobucci J. then considered the words of the privilege clause in the context of the tender documents. He said:

[48] Therefore, I conclude that the privilege clause is compatible with the obligation to accept only a compliant bid. As should be clear from this discussion, however, the privilege clause is incompatible with an obligation to accept only the *lowest* compliant bid. With respect to this latter proposition, the privilege clause must prevail.

After dealing with an argument of the plaintiff on the cases and evidence, he said:

[52] Applying the foregoing analysis to the case at bar, I find that the respondent was under no contractual obligation to award the contract to the appellant, who the parties agree was the lowest compliant bid. However, this does not mean that Contract A was not breached.

[53] [The non-compliant bidder] was only the lowest bidder because it failed to accept, and incorporate into its bid [certain risks]. As the Court of Appeal outlined, this risk was assigned to the contractor. Therefore [that] bid was based upon different specifications. Indeed, it is conceded that [that] . . . bid was non-compliant. Therefore, in awarding the contract to [that bidder], the respondent breached its obligation to the appellant and the other tenderers that it would accept only a compliant tender.

[54] The respondent's argument of good faith in considering the Sorochan bid to be compliant is no defence to a claim for breach of contract: it amounts to an argument that, because it thought it had interpreted the contract properly, it cannot be in breach. Acting in good faith or thinking that one has interpreted the contract correctly are not valid defences to an action for breach of contract.

Iacobucci J. held that, on a balance of probabilities, the plaintiff would have been awarded the contract, if the non-compliant bid had not been accepted. He held that the appellant was entitled to damages in the amount of the profits it would have realized had it been awarded the construction contract.

3.   Tendering contracts often include "privilege" clauses that are intended to give the buyer or owner some flexibility, though the courts tend to interpret them narrowly to ensure that the tendering process is fair.

In *Chinook Aggregates Ltd. v. Abbotsford (Municipal District)*, [1989] B.C.J. No. 2045, [1990] 1 W.W.R. 624, 35 C.L.R. 241 (C.A.), a municipality invited bids on a gravel crushing contract, including a statement in the instructions that "the lowest or any tender will not necessarily be accepted" (a privilege clause). Without any announcement to the parties who were bidding, the municipality applied a policy of preferring local contractors whose bids were within 10 per cent of the lowest bid in awarding the contract, and awarded the contract to a local firm. The out-of-town firm that had the lowest bid was successful in its action against the municipality for loss of profits on this job. The British Columbia Court of Appeal unanimously held that the party calling for tenders was under a duty to "treat all bidders fairly and not to give any of them an unfair advantage over the others". Legg J.A., speaking for the Court, concluded that the owner had breached this implied contractual obligation by adopting its preference policy; the privilege clause did not give the owner the right to attach an undisclosed condition to its offer.

In *Martel Building Ltd. v. Canada*, [2000] 2 S.C.R. 860, 193 D.L.R. (4th) 1, the Supreme Court considered a claim by a prospective landlord that had been bidding to offer the government of Canada office space in Ottawa. The plaintiff submitted the lowest dollar bid, but the Department of Public Works "adjusted" the bid to take account of "fit-up costs" and other expenses to meet the tenant's expectations. The tender documents included a privilege clause and specified that the lessee would complete a "financial analysis" of the project including fit-up costs. The process of adjusting each bid for fit-up costs was conducted by employees of the government using a method of calculation that took account of such factors as building layout and design. The Supreme Court, in a judgment by Iacobucci and Major JJ., rejected the claim of the lowest bidder, holding that the government was entitled to adjust the bids. They said:

> [88] In the circumstances of this case, we believe that implying a term to be fair and consistent in the assessment of the tender bids is justified based on the presumed intentions of the parties. Such implication is necessary to give business efficacy to the tendering process. . . . this Court agreed to imply a term in *M.J.B. Enterprises* that only compliant bids would be accepted since it believed that it would make little sense to expose oneself to the risks associated with the tendering process if the tender calling authority was "allowed, in effect, to circumscribe this process and accept a non-compliant bid" . . . Similarly, in light of the costs and effort associated with preparing and submitting a bid, we find it difficult to believe that the respondent [lowest bidder] in this case, or any of the other three tenderers, would have submitted a bid unless it was understood by those involved that all bidders would be treated fairly and equally. This implication has a certain degree of obviousness to it to the extent that the parties, if questioned, would clearly agree that this obligation had been assumed. Implying an obligation to treat all bidders fairly and equally is consistent with the goal of protecting and promoting the integrity of the bidding process, and benefits all participants involved. Without this implied term, tenderers, whose fate could be predetermined by some undisclosed standards, would either incur significant expenses in preparing futile bids or ultimately avoid participating in the tender process.

> [89] A privilege clause reserving the right not to accept the lowest or any bids does not exclude the obligation to treat all bidders fairly. Nevertheless, the tender documents must be examined closely to determine the full extent of the

obligation of fair and equal treatment. In order to respect the parties' intentions and reasonable expectations, such a duty must be defined with due consideration to the express contractual terms of the tender. A tendering authority has "the right to include stipulations and restrictions and to reserve privileges to itself in the tender documents".

. . .

[94] Admittedly, $812,736 was added to the Martel bid for fit-up costs. However, as the Department pointed out . . . fit-up costs were also added to the other three bidders. . . . These figures were derived from the Unit Price Tables submitted by each tenderer as part of their bid, using a general scenario to fit-up a 900 square metre area. This resulted in an average cost per square metre of fitted-up space. A certain percentage was then added uniformly to the four rates to account for increased costs that the Department had experienced in the past when using this computation.

[95] We cannot find any breach of Contract A related to the addition of fit-up costs. The Department was expressly entitled to add fit-up costs which it deemed necessary. Furthermore, fit-up costs were added to *all* bids, using the same standard or method of calculation. In this regard, the Department complied with its implied contractual obligation to treat all bidders fairly and equally. A duty to treat all bidders fairly in this context means treating all bids consistently, applying assumptions evenly. There is no evidence of any colourable attempt to use fit-ups to achieve a desired result. In light of the trial judge's finding that "it was fit-up costs . . . that made the plaintiff's bid the second lowest rather than the lowest bid", . . . the respondent's claim is considerably weakened.

The adoption of the Contract A / Contract B model of contracting has the advantage of giving some protection to those who respond to bid calls. These advantages come, however, at a price (and sometimes a very high price) because the irrevocability of a tender exposes a contractor to the risk that it will be held to a mistaken bid. The extent of the risks that now face contractors will be seen when we turn in Chapter 5 to the problems raised when one party claims to be excused from a contract on the basis of a mistake.

4. Since *M.J.B. Enterprises* some owners have been using broadly worded "discretion clauses" that purport to give owners the discretion to accept non-compliant bids. For example in *Kinetic Construction Ltd. v. Comox-Strathcona (Regional District)*, [2004] B.C.J. No. 2247, 245 D.L.R. (4th) 262 (C.A.), the owner included a clause providing:

> Tenders which contain qualifying conditions or otherwise fail to conform to the instructions to Tenderers may be disqualified or rejected. The Owner may, however, in its sole discretion, reject or retain for its consideration Tenderers which are nonconforming because they do not contain the content or form required by the Instructions to Tenderers or for failure to comply with the process for submission set out in these Instructions to Tenderers.

In that case, the British Columbia Court of Appeal upheld a decision that held that this clause permitted the owner to accept a non-compliant bid in preference to a compliant bid, with Southin J.A. concluding (at para. 5): "There was no breach [of Contract A] because [the discretion clause] ... construed in light of the whole of the invitation permitted the owner to do what the owner did."

5. It is possible for an owner or buyer to seek non-binding proposals from a number of potential partners and to be clear that it is *not* entering into a tendering process, but rather wishes to identify a possible partner to negotiate with. In *Buttcon Ltd. v. To-*

ronto Electric Commissioners, [2003] O.J. No 2796, 65 O.R. (3d) 601 (S.C.J.), Toronto Hydro decided on a two-step proposal process involving a "Request for Expressions of Interest" ("RFEI") and a "Request for Development Proposal" ("RFP") as its
approach to the construction of new facilities for its service centre operations. The
RFEI invited the construction community to propose project teams, from which four
or five would be invited to submit a more detailed proposal. The RFEI indicated that
Toronto Hydro anticipated that after a selection was made from the RFPs, a final
agreement would be negotiated with one team. The RFEI and RFP both contained
"Cautions" stating among other things that Toronto Hydro:

(a) Reserves the right to reject any or all proposals.

(b) Reserves the right to waive any irregularities in any proposal, to negotiate
for the modification of any single proposal, to request clarification and
additional information on any proposal, and to re-advertise for proposals
if desired.

(c) Reserves the right to accept the proposal which, in the sole opinion of
Toronto Hydro, is deemed the most advantageous to Toronto Hydro.

(d) Takes no responsibility for the accuracy of the information supplied
during this proposal call process by any official, employee or agent of
Toronto Hydro [unless provided in writing]. ...

The plaintiff, Buttcon Limited ("Buttcon"), was one of five proponents selected from
the RFEI to engage in the RFP stage of the process. Buttcon and three others responded to the RFP. From this group, Toronto Hydro eventually signed a construction
contract with Internorth Company Limited. Buttcon sued Toronto Hydro for an alleged breach of contract and for damages for unfairness in the tender process.

  MacFarland J. dismissed the action, concluding that the RFP was not a tender call
that created a "tender contract" (a "Contract A" in the terminology of *Ron Engineering*) that would oblige Toronto Hydro to enter into a construction contract ("Contract
B") upon receipt of the lowest tender. Here, the RFP was a non-binding invitation to
several parties to put forward proposals that could be the basis of negotiations for possible entry into a contract. The judge noted that while "established timelines and deposit requirements are common to both requests and formal tender situations, it was
clear from its language "to all proponents that [the RFP] was anything but a tender
call", (para. 43) and that subsequent discussions and negotiations would be required
concerning the contract. There was no intention by the issuance of the RFP to create
contractual relations, and Contract A did not arise on the facts of this case. Accordingly, there was no breach of contract. Toronto Hydro's only obligation was to run a
"fair process" and to ensure that no one participant was favoured over another; each
proponent was entitled to have its proposal considered in an "equitable and fair manner". One of the issues raised by Buttcon was that its proposal was based on the use of
electric heating for the building, which was more expensive than the gas-fired heating
included in the proposal that was accepted. Buttcon claimed that it was led to believe
by a Hydro employee that electrical heating was preferred for this project. McFarlane
J. concluded:

> [69] The RFP provides that only the terms of the written document and the
> written questions and answers provided to all will govern the process. Parties
> are not to rely on any statements made by any Hydro employees. The language
> is clear.

> [70] ... If a phone call to Mr. Clark [a Hydro employee] took place, I do not
> accept that he indicated that only an electrically sourced heating system would
> be acceptable. He had enough experience in this area to know better than to
> give such an answer. If he did, the language of the written document is to pre-
> vail in any event and further on Buttcon's evidence — it was too late for them
> to change their proposal anyway.

...

[72] Had the RFP provided that the heat source must be electrical — and in my view it did not — and Hydro in those circumstances selected Internorth, then I think Buttcon may have had a legitimate complaint. Those are not, however, the circumstances.

This decision illustrates that with careful drafting and use of a "request for proposals", the owner or buyer may have significant freedom to select the party that it wants to negotiate with, though of course none of the parties submitting a proposal is bound by it, unless it is incorporated into a later contract. Further, even in this situation there is an obligation on the owner or buyer to have "a fair process".

LIMITS OF THE TRADITIONAL RULES

Introduction

The common law rules governing contract formation are based on a simple model of contracting that often does not reflect what those making contracts actually do and, as a result, the application of these rules often runs into problems.

One kind of problem arises out of the unsatisfactory nature of some of the rules. An unsatisfactory rule that we have already considered is the rule that a firm offer can be revoked unless it is contained in an option contract or under seal.

In an important sense some of the rules of contract formation are obstacles around which a court or counsel must seek to find a way so that the result of a dispute can be socially or commercially desirable. These rules often operate very like the rules of consideration: a party with good legal advice can always achieve the desired result; parties without such advice may find their expectations disappointed. In these materials, the emphasis is on those situations where things have gone wrong. This creates the impression that parties must have the rules of contract formation constantly in mind. In a carefully planned transaction, the parties' lawyers will have the rules in mind and may well use them to control the negotiating process so that liability is accepted only when it is appropriate to do so.

Where the parties do not have legal advice, the process of making the deal in terms that accurately reflect their intentions may misfire and a number of things may go wrong. Faced with the problems that can then arise, a court will seldom apply the rules without an eye to the effects on the parties. The concepts of invitation to treat, offer and acceptance are analytical tools that are retrospectively applied to a situation. There is usually enough flexibility for the courts to characterize a communication as an offer, acceptance or an invitation to treat, or to do something else to achieve the desired result. It is important to know when the court will be moved to find that an offer exists; the skill of counsel lies in the ability to encourage the court to protect a client's expectations. Counsel must of course also be prepared to offer the court the doctrinal analysis to provide a justification for the socially or economically desired result.

It is not cynical to recognize that legal analysis is flexible and that factual context is important. The realization that neither facts nor rules operate automatically to permit deduction from agreed premises provides the explanation of almost every case we have looked at. It is equally true that courts are *not* free to choose any result that seems appropriate. The legal system will provide no guidance to anyone if there are not at least agreed standards for decisions and for debate about how disputes should be resolved.

Another kind of problem with the traditional rules represents a more serious challenge to the classical model of contract formation. In many situations, the whole process of bargaining envisaged by the traditional common law rules does not reflect what is occurring. There are cases in which it is inappropriate to look for the clearly accepted offer as the only basis for liability in a contractual situation. Finally, there are cases where the parties clearly have some kind of contractual relation, but it is hard to say exactly what it is. This situation can arise because the parties have made no effort or an inadequate effort to work out for themselves the terms of the relation they have created; it is not easy to determine what the proper response of the law should be in such a situation. These types of concerns, where it is difficult or not appropriate to strictly apply the traditional rules of contract formation, are the focus of the materials in the rest of the chapter.

These problems can be divided into two categories of cases. In the first class are cases where the terms of the agreement are simply not clear. It may not be clear, for example, that the parties have stopped bargaining. If it is clear that they thought that they had a bargain, there may be uncertainty about the terms on which the bargain should be enforced. The second class consists of cases where the parties exchanged documents and conducted "negotiations" that could be said to resemble bargaining in the classic model. However, on examination it turns out that whatever else was going on, it was not really "bargaining" in the classical sense. Unread documents were exchanged that did not respond to each other, but the parties acted on the basis that they had a contract; the parties achieved what one judge described as the "legal equivalent to the irresistible force colliding with the immovable object". The result is known as the "battle of the forms", and can produce complex problems.

It is useful to start by considering a couple of leading precedents that set out traditional rules and put the problems in perspective. These cases make it clear that even though the parties have, in form at least, reached an agreement, the determination of what that agreement might be is not easy. The first of these cases is considered one of the leading cases on the problem of mistakes in the process of contract formation.

RAFFLES v. WICHELHAUS

(1864), 2 H. & C. 906, 159 E.R. 375 (Exch.)
(Pollock, C.B., Martin and Pigott B.B.)

Declaration. For that it was agreed between the plaintiff and the defendants, to wit, at Liverpool, that the plaintiff should sell to the defendants, and the defendants buy of the plaintiff, certain goods, to wit, 125 bales of Surat cotton, guaranteed middling fair merchant's Dhollorah, to arrive ex "Peerless" from Bombay; and that the cotton should be taken from the quay, and that the defendants would pay the plaintiff for the same at a certain rate, to wit, at the rate of 17¼ pence per pound, within a certain time then agreed upon after the arrival of the said goods in England.

Averments: that the said goods did arrive by the said ship from Bombay in England, to wit, at Liverpool, and the plaintiff was then and there ready, and willing and offered to deliver the said goods to the defendants, &c. *Breach*: that the defendants refused to accept the said goods or pay the plaintiff for them.

Plea. That the said ship mentioned in the said agreement was meant and intended by the defendants to be the ship called the "Peerless," which sailed from Bombay, to wit, in October; and that the plaintiff was not ready and willing and did not offer to deliver to the defendants any bales of cotton which arrived by the last mentioned ship, but instead thereof was only ready and willing and offered to deliver to the defendants 125 bales of Surat cotton which arrived by another and different ship, which was also called the "Peerless," and which sailed from Bombay, to wit, in December. *Demurrer, and joinder therein.* [Broken into paragraphs by the editors]

[1]   Milward [counsel for the plaintiff], in support of the demurrer. The contract was for the sale of a number of bales of cotton of a particular description, which the plaintiff was ready to deliver. It is immaterial by what ship the cotton was to arrive, so that it was a ship called the "Peerless." The words "to arrive ex 'Peerless'" only mean that if the vessel is lost on the voyage, the contract is to be at an end.

[2]   **POLLOCK C.B.**: It would be a question for the jury whether both parties meant the same ship called the "Peerless."

[3]   Milward: That would be so if the contract was for the sale of a ship called the "Peerless"; but it is for the sale of cotton on board a ship of that name.

[4]   **POLLOCK C.B.**: The defendant only bought that cotton which was to arrive by a particular ship. It may as well be said, that if there is a contract for the purchase of certain goods in warehouse A, that is satisfied by the delivery of goods of the same description in warehouse B.

[5]   Milward: In that case there would be goods in both warehouses; here it does not appear that the plaintiff had any goods on board the other "Peerless."

[6]   **MARTIN B.**: It is imposing on the defendant a contract different from that which he entered into.

[7]   **POLLOCK C.B.**: It is like a contract for the purchase of wine coming from a particular estate in France or Spain, where there are two estates of that name.

[8]   Milward: The defendant has no right to contradict by parol evidence a written contract good upon the face of it. He does not impute misrepresentation or fraud, but only says that he fancied the ship was a different one. Intention is of no avail, unless stated at the time of the contract.

[9]   **POLLOCK C.B.**: One vessel sailed in October and the other in December.

[10]   Milward: The time of sailing is no part of the contract.

[11]   Mellish ... in support of the plea [for the defendant]: There is nothing on the face of the contract to shew that any particular ship called the "Peerless" was meant; but the moment it appears that two ships called the "Peerless" were about to sail from Bombay there is a latent ambiguity, and parol evidence may be given for the purpose of shewing that the defendant meant one "Peerless," and the plaintiff another. That being so, there was no *consensus ad idem,* and therefore no binding contract.

[Counsel were then stopped by the court.]

[12] *Per Curiam.* There must be judgment for the defendants.

NOTES AND QUESTIONS

1. *Raffles v. Wichelhaus* is a mysterious case. It has been the subject of considerable
    academic interest in the twentieth century. Grant Gilmore, in *The Death of Contract*
    (Columbus: Ohio State University Press, 1974), wrote what quickly became a classic
    work regarding the teaching of law during the nineteenth century in the United States,
    particularly at Harvard, and the development of contractual theory. Gilmore used the
    decision in *Raffles v. Wichelhaus* to illustrate some of his arguments. Gilmore's work
    has since been heavily criticized, both for his general discussion of the origins of the
    teaching of law at Harvard (see, *e.g.*, Bruce A. Kimball, "The Langdell Problem: His-
    toricizing the Century of Historiography, 1906–2000s" (2004), 22 L.H.R. No. 2,
    <http://www.historycooperative.org/journals/lhr/22.2/kimball.html>) and, with par-
    ticular regard to his analysis of *Raffles v. Wichelhaus*, by A.W.B. Simpson, in *Leading
    Cases in the Common Law* (Oxford: Clarendon Press, 1996). Simpson says (p. 162)
    that "absolutely everything Gilmore said about the case is wrong." Simpson suggests
    (pp. 152-54) that the litigation arose because the buyers had made a bad bargain —
    the market price of cotton on the arrival of either ship in Liverpool was less than the
    price the buyers had agreed to pay — and, what may be as important, because of the
    personal characteristics of the parties. Raffles was known as a quarrelsome man and
    the buyers, Wichelhaus and Busch, were foreigners and outside the relatively small
    circle of Liverpool cotton dealers. Raffles' mistake lay in not offering the cotton to the
    buyers when the first ship *Peerless* arrived (had he had any to tender), thus leaving it
    open to the buyers to allege that there was uncertainty over the ships. Simpson also
    points out that arbitration was the principal method by which the close-knit commu-
    nity of brokers dealt with the kind of problem that arose in the case and suggests that,
    had the dispute been dealt with in that way, it would have been unlikely that the buy-
    ers would have prevailed.

2. In *Raffles v. Wichelhaus* the plaintiff (seller) sued the defendant (buyer) for breach of
    a contract to purchase cotton. Milward's argument on behalf of the plaintiff was in
    support of the demurrer to the defendant's plea. The buyer by his plea says that there
    is no contract since the parties meant different ships: the seller "demurs" to this plea.
    As a result, the case was decided on the basis of the parties' written pleadings and
    without the court's hearing any evidence. A demurrer was a preliminary plea by a de-
    fendant who argued that the plaintiff's pleadings, even if true, would not support a
    judgment in its favour: it is as if the defendant said "So what?" to the plaintiff's claim.
    The modern equivalent of that pleading tactic is a defendant's motion to have the
    plaintiff's action dismissed because the pleadings do not disclose a cause of action
    against the defendant. The closest tactic that would now be adopted in facts like those
    in *Raffles v. Wichelhaus* would be a motion for summary judgment brought by the
    plaintiff, though on such a motion there could be discoveries and affidavit evidence
    submitted to the court.

    The effect of the demurrer was that the seller was taken to have accepted the
    buyer's claim that the parties *meant* different ships. Milward's tactic in arguing on
    demurrer may have been a serious error if, as a result, and as the comments from the
    Bench may suggest, he was not permitted to argue that as a matter of fact the name of
    the ship and the differing understandings of the parties were irrelevant.

3. *Raffles v. Wichelhaus* is a mid-nineteenth-century decision. From their questions the
    judges appear to be focusing on the subjective views of the parties and on their under-
    standings of the words used in the contract. Even if on an objective analysis of con-
    tract formation, neither could hold the other to his version of the contract so that there
    was no (objective) "meeting of the minds" and no contract, we have to deal with the
    uncontradicted statement of Milward that the name of the ship was completely irrele-
    vant to the issue before the court. The existence of even objective differences in the
    understandings of the parties should not make the underlying contract unenforceable if
    those differences do not affect the obligations of either party under the contract.

4. *Raffles v. Wichelhaus* is sometimes referred to as a "leading case" on the law of mistake (see, for example, Cheshire, Fifoot and Furmston, *Law of Contract*, 13th ed. (London: Butterworths, 1996) p. 256). Is there not something odd about a case that has a one-line judgment becoming a leading case? If it is to be so regarded, what proposition does it stand for? See G. Gilmore, *The Death of Contracts*, pp. 35-44.

5. In a case of mistake, the parties may be said to have made a mistake about the terms of the contract. The category of mistake is large and many of the cases are very hard to analyze satisfactorily (though *Raffles v. Wichelhaus* is not one of those). Cases of mistake will be examined in detail in Chapter 5.

    While there may in fact have been some mistake about the terms of the contract, the decision in *Raffles v. Wichelhaus* may be better understood as a situation where there is a misunderstanding or disagreement about the terms of the contract, and there is no reason to hold either party to the interpretation of the other. In other words, each party bore the risk that the term that he used was ambiguous, and in the absence of any reason to hold either party to the meaning attached to the term by the other party, there is no agreement that the law can enforce. There is no basis for the application of the reasoning in *Smith v. Hughes* (*infra*), since neither party gave the other party reasonable grounds to think that there was an agreement on the other's terms. In such a situation any result will catch one of the parties by surprise.

6. A says to B "I will sell you my cow for $100." B, knowing that A meant to say horse, and that the word "cow" was a slip of the tongue, says "I accept."

    (a) Is there a contract for the sale of the horse?

    (b) Is there a contract for the sale of the cow?

    (c) Is there a contract to sell either animal?

    Does the decision in *Raffles v. Wichelhaus* help you to answer any of these questions?

As discussed earlier, the modern approach to contract analysis is an objective or "reasonable person" approach. This approach is illustrated by the following case, still cited as a leading precedent.

SMITH v. HUGHES

(1871), L.R. 6 Q.B. 597
(Q.B., Cockburn C.J., Blackburn and Hannen JJ.)

APPEAL from the County Court of Surrey holden at Epsom.

The plaintiff sought to recover £34 15s. 8d., being the price of sixteen quarters of oats sold by the plaintiff to the defendant at 34s. per quarter, and the loss on the resale by the plaintiff of twenty-nine quarters of oats agreed to be purchased by the defendant, and which he refused to receive; and the storage of the quarters of oats for five weeks.

The plaintiff is a farmer. The defendant is an owner and trainer of racehorses.

The plaintiff's evidence was as follows: "In July last I had a quantity of new winter oats for sale. I was anxious to get rid of them, because oats were then dear, the supply of English oats being very short. On Saturday, the 31st of July, I took a sample of these oats to Hughes, who manages for the defendant, and asked him if he was a buyer of oats. He replied he was always a buyer of good oats. I said I had some good oats for sale; he asked me how many? I told him from forty to fifty quarters; he said he would have them all if they were good. I shewed him my sample, and asked 35s. a quarter; he took the sample, and said he would give me an answer next day. On the following Monday he wrote to me to say he would take the oats at 34s. a quarter, and I then sent in sixteen quarters. Soon afterwards I met the defendant, and he said, 'Why, those were new oats you sent me.' I replied, 'Well, I knew they were, and had none others.' He said, 'I thought I was buying old oats. New oats are useless to me; you must take them back again.' I refused to take them back." On cross-examination, the plaintiff said: "I was not aware that the defendant never bought new oats. I do not know that trainers never use new oats; a trainer has since this transaction offered me money for new oats. I never told defendant that they were old oats. Nothing was said about it: the word 'old' was not mentioned by either of us."

Hughes, the defendant's manager, stated: "The plaintiff asked me if I was a buyer of oats. I said I was always a buyer of good old oats. He said, 'I have some good old oats for sale,' and gave me a sample, and asked me 35s. a quarter. I said I would let him know. I wrote to say I would give him 34s. When I found they were new oats, I refused to have them, and they were immediately returned to the plaintiff on his refusal to fetch them back. I never buy new oats if I can get old. Trainers, as a rule, use old oats." On cross-examination, the witness hesitated and contradicted himself somewhat as to whether the word "old" was used at the time of making the contract.

Evidence was also given for the defendant, that at the time of the contract 34s. a quarter was a very high price for new oats, and such as a prudent man of business would not have given; but that oats were then very scarce.

In summing up, the judge told the jury that the first question for their consideration was, whether the word "old" had been used by the plaintiff or defendant in making the contract, and that the inclination of his opinion was that the word "old" had not been so used; but that was a question entirely for their consideration. If they were of opinion that the word "old" had been so used, they would return a verdict for the defendant. If, however, they thought that the word "old" had not been used, the second question would be, whether they were of opinion, on the state of the evidence, that the plaintiff believed the defendant to believe, or to be under the impression, that he was contracting for the purchase of old oats. If so, there would be a verdict for the defendant. But if the jury were of opinion that nothing was said as to the oats being old or new, and if they were of opinion that the plaintiff did not believe that the defendant believed or was under the impression that he was contracting for old oats, then they would find for the plaintiff.

The jury found a verdict for the defendant.

The question for the opinion of the Court was, whether the direction to the jury as above is or is not correct.

May 2. Pollock Q.C. (McKellar with him), for the plaintiff. The judge was wrong to leave the second question to the jury. If the plaintiff believed the defendant to believe that he was buying old oats, the plaintiff was under no legal obligation to undeceive him. The defendant had the sample; he could judge for himself what he was buying, and if he had any doubt as to the subject-matter of the contract he might have demanded a warranty. In *Benjamin on the Sale of Personal Property*, p. 315, it is stated: "The mistaken belief as to facts may be created by active means or by fraudulent concealment, or knowingly false representation; or passively, by mere silence, when it is a duty to speak. But it is only where a party is under some pledge or obligation to reveal facts to another that mere silence will be considered as a means of deception." So in *Story on Contracts*, s. 519, it is laid down: "A distinction should be observed between the concealment of extrinsic circumstances affecting the value of the subject-matter of sale, or operating as an inducement to a contract, such as the state of the market; and the concealment of intrinsic circumstances appertaining to its nature, character, and condition, such as natural defects and injuries. In respect of intrinsic circumstances, the rule is that mere silence as to anything which the other party might by proper diligence have discovered, and which is open to his examination, is not fraudulent unless a special trust or confidence exist between the parties, or be implied from the circumstance of the case . . . In respect to extrinsic circumstances, the rule is that neither party is ordinarily bound to notify them to the other, and mere concealment will not nullify the contract. But the party concealing a fault must be careful to do no act and say no word indicative of his assent to any mistaken proposition by the other; and must play an entirely negative part, for if he do anything positive he will render himself liable." If, therefore, the plaintiff believed that the defendant was under the impression that he was buying old oats, and did nothing by word or act to produce this impression on the mind of the defendant, but merely allowed him to remain under that impression, the plaintiff's conduct is not such as would avoid the contract. According to Paley [Paley's *Moral and Political Philosophy*, Book III, ch. 5], a promise is to be interpreted "in the sense in which the promiser apprehended at the time that the promisee received it." The judge's direction ought to have been, that if the plaintiff believed the defendant to believe that the plaintiff had contracted to sell to the defendant old oats, then they should find their verdict for the defendant. The question as to the difference between concealment and mere silence is discussed by Cicero [Cicero *de Officiis*, Lib. II, capp. xii, xiii.]. He puts the case of a merchant at Rhodes selling corn in a time of scarcity, and asks the question whether the seller is bound to inform the buyer of what he is aware but the buyer is not, *viz.*, that there are other ships laden with corn on their way to Rhodes. The conclusion arrived at appears to be that he is not acting dishonestly in not giving the information.

Arthur Wilson, for the defendant. The judge's direction, in substance, amounts to this: If the defendant contracted to buy old oats, he is not bound to accept new oats. And in that sense the direction is correct. If the plaintiff was selling new oats, and the defendant was buying old oats, the parties were not ad idem, and there was no contract; and that is what the jury have found. That the sale was by sample is immaterial; the sample only affects the quality, provided the subject-matter is the thing contracted for. . . . In *Chitty on Contracts*, 5th ed. p. 593, the law on the subject is thus stated: "It has been held that, where one party to a contract stands by and allows the other to enter into the contract under a delusion of the existence of which he was aware, and which he might have removed, the contract is void". . . .

COCKBURN C.J. [summarized the evidence and continued]: —

[1]   The learned judge of the county court left two questions to the jury: first, whether the word "old" had been used with reference to the oats in the conversation between the plaintiff and the defendant's manager; secondly, whether the plaintiff had believed that the defendant believed, or was under the impression, that he was contracting for old oats; in either of which cases he directed the jury to find for the defendant.

[2]   It is to be regretted that the jury were not required to give specific answers to the questions so left to them. For, it is quite possible that their verdict may have

been given for the defendant on the first ground; in which case there could, I think, be no doubt as to the propriety of the judge's direction; whereas now, as it is possible that the verdict of the jury — or at all events of some of them — may have proceeded on the second ground, we are called upon to consider and decide whether the ruling of the learned judge with reference to the second question was right.

[3]   For this purpose we must assume that nothing was said on the subject of the defendant's manager desiring to buy *old* oats, nor of the oats having been said to be old; while, on the other hand, we must assume that the defendant's manager believed the oats to be old oats, and that the plaintiff was conscious of the existence of such belief, but did nothing, directly or indirectly, to bring it about, simply offering his oats and exhibiting his sample, remaining perfectly passive as to what was passing in the mind of the other party. The question is whether, under such circumstances, the passive acquiescence of the seller in the self-deception of the buyer will entitle the latter to avoid the contract. I am of opinion that it will not.

[COCKBURN C.J. discussed the law of sales, the obligations of the seller and the risks that the buyer should run. He continued:]

[4]   In the case before us it must be taken that, as the defendant, on a portion of the oats being delivered, was able by inspection to ascertain that they were new oats, his manager might, by due inspection of the sample, have arrived at the same result. The case is, therefore, one of the sale and purchase of a specific article after inspection by the buyer. Under these circumstances the rule *caveat emptor* clearly applies; more especially as this cannot be put as a case of latent defect, but simply as one in which the seller did not make known to the buyer a circumstance affecting the quality of the thing sold. The oats in question were in no sense defective, on the contrary they were good oats, and all that can be said is that they had not acquired the quality which greater age would have given them. There is not, so far as I am aware, any authority for the position that a vendor who submits the subject-matter of sale to the inspection of the vendee, is bound to state circumstances which may tend to detract from the estimate which the buyer may injudiciously have formed of its value. Even the civil law, and the foreign law, founded upon it, which require that the seller shall answer for latent defects, have never gone the length of saying that, so long as the thing sold answers to the description under which it is sold, the seller is bound to disabuse the buyer as to any exaggerated estimate of its value.

[5]   It only remains to deal with an argument which was pressed upon us, that the defendant in the present case intended to buy old oats, and the plaintiff to sell new, so the two minds were not ad idem; and that consequently there was no contract. This argument proceeds on the fallacy of confounding what was merely a motive operating on the buyer to induce him to buy with one of the essential conditions of the contract. Both parties were agreed as to the sale and purchase of this particular parcel of oats. The defendant believed the oats to be old, and was thus induced to agree to buy them, but he omitted to make their age a condition of the contract. All that can be said is, that the two minds were not ad idem as to the age of the oats; they certainly were ad idem as to the sale and purchase of them. Suppose a person to buy a horse without a warranty, believing him to be sound, and the horse turns out unsound, could it be contended that it would be open to him to say that, as he had intended to buy a sound horse, and the seller to sell an unsound one, the con-

tract was void, because the seller must have known from the price the buyer was willing to give, or from his general habits as a buyer of horses, that he thought the horse was sound? The cases are exactly parallel.

[6]   The result is that, in my opinion, the learned judge of the county court was wrong in leaving the second question to the jury, and that, consequently, the case must go down to a new trial.

[**BLACKBURN J.** agreed with **COCKBURN C.J.** on the law of sale. He continued:]

[7]   But I have more difficulty about the second point raised in the case. I apprehend that if one of the parties intends to make a contract on one set of terms, and the other intends to make a contract on another set of terms, or, as it is sometimes expressed, if the parties are not *ad idem*, there is no contract, unless the circumstances are such as to preclude one of the parties from denying that he has agreed to the terms of the other. . . . If, whatever a man's real intention may be, he so conducts himself that a reasonable man would believe that he was assenting to the terms proposed by the other party, and that other party upon that belief enters into the contract with him, the man thus conducting himself would be equally bound as if he had intended to agree to the other party's terms.

[8]   The jury were directed that, if they believed the word "old" was used, they should find for the defendant — and this was right; for if that was the case, it is obvious that neither did the defendant intend to enter into a contract on the plaintiff's terms, that is, to buy this parcel of oats without any stipulation as to their quality; nor could the plaintiff have been led to believe he was intending to do so.

[9]   But the second direction raises the difficulty. I think that, if from that direction the jury would understand that they were first to consider whether they were satisfied that the defendant intended to buy this parcel of oats on the terms that it was part of his contract with the plaintiff that they were old oats, so as to have the warranty of the plaintiff to that effect, they were properly told that, if that was so, the defendant could not be bound to a contract without any such warranty unless the plaintiff was misled. But I doubt whether the direction would bring to the minds of the jury the distinction between agreeing to take the oats under the belief that they were old, and agreeing to take the oats under the belief that the plaintiff contracted that they were old.

[10]   The difference is the same as that between buying a horse believed to be sound, and buying one believed to be warranted sound; but I doubt if it was made obvious to the jury, and I doubt this the more because I do not see much evidence to justify a finding for the defendant on this latter ground if the word "old" was not used. There may have been more evidence than is stated in the case; and the demeanour of the witnesses may have strengthened the impression produced by the evidence there was; but it does not seem a very satisfactory verdict if it proceeded on this latter ground. I agree, therefore, in the result that there should be a new trial.

[**HANNEN J.** agreed in the result.]

Although judges and lawyers still sometimes use Latin expressions like "*consensus ad idem*" (*i.e.*, "agreement on the same thing"), or say that there has to be "meeting of the minds", which suggests that there has to be some subjective agreement before there can be a contract, the modern approach is to focus on the objective meaning of the parties' words and actions.

Whatever view one takes of contracts — the objective theory of Blackburn J. in *Smith v. Hughes*, or the apparently more subjective theory of Pollock C.B. in *Raffles v. Wichelhaus* — there are risks to be run by someone. Does the allocation of risk in *Raffles* make commercial sense? How would a prudent merchant protect himself from the risks allocated by the decision in that case?

HOBBS v. ESQUIMALT AND NANAIMO RAILWAY CO.

(1899), 29 S.C.R. 450
(S.C.C., Taschereau, Gwynne, Sedgewick, Girouard and King JJ.)

The action was brought by the appellant to enforce specific performance of an agreement by the railway company to sell to him certain land in British Columbia. The agreement is contained in the following document delivered to appellant in pursuance of his request for an allotment.

ESQUIMALT & NANAIMO RAILWAY CO. - LAND DEPARTMENT

VICTORIA, B.C., NOV. 28th, 1889.

> Received of Frank Vicker Hobbs, the sum of one hundred and twenty dollars ($120.00), being a first payment on account of his purchase from the E. & N. Ry. Company of one hundred and sixty (160) acres of land in Bright District, at the Price of three dollars ($3.00) an acre . . . the balance of purchase money to be paid in three equal instalments of seventy-five (75) cents an acre, at the expiration of one, two and three years from date, with interest at the rate of 6 per cent per annum.

(Sgd.) JOHN TRUTCH,

Land Commissioner.

The question in dispute between the parties is whether or not the railway company, in executing the conveyance to carry out this agreement, is entitled to reserve the minerals in the land therein described.

The company claims that Mr. Trutch had no authority to convey the minerals, and that in its forms of conveyance the word "land" is always used to mean surface rights only. The trial Judge held that the claim as to want of authority was well founded, but that the company had ratified the agreement. As he was of opinion, however, that the ratification was made under a mistake as to the legal effect of the agreement he refused to decree specific performance but declared in his judgment that the plaintiff was entitled at his option to a conveyance as offered by defendants or to repayment of the purchase money with interest and compensation for improvements. The plaintiff appealed and the decree was varied by a direction that the plaintiff was entitled to a conveyance reserving the minerals without option of repayment. The plaintiff then appealed to this court.

KING J.: — [1] . . . It is found by [the trial judge] that Mr. Trutch acted beyond the scope of his authority in agreeing to a sale of the land without reservation of the minerals, but that the contract so made was [ratified] by the company. He, however, was of opinion that, in so ratifying it, the company were under a mistake as to its legal effect, and upon this ground he declined to compel performance but left the plaintiff to his common law remedy for breach of contract.

[2] A first question is as to whether there was, by reason of the alleged mistake, a contract at all. . . .

[3] Here the parties were *ad idem* as to the terms of the contract. It was expressed in perfectly unambiguous language in the offer of the plaintiff and in the acceptance of defendants, and the alleged difference is in a wholly esoteric meaning which one of them gives to the plain words. . . .

[4] The alleged mistake is given in the evidence of Mr. Dunsmuir, the vice-president of the company. Speaking of the contract entered into by Mr. Trutch, he says: "It only sold the surface. That is, we term it land in our office. We do not say surface right, we say land, land minus the minerals."

[5] It is evident then that we may put Mr. Trutch aside, and treat the case on this point as if the company, upon an application by plaintiff for purchase of the 160 acres of land, had entered into an agreement to sell the land in the identical words used by Mr. Trutch. In effect they say: "We agreed to sell the land, but this means land reserving the minerals."

[6] It may well be that in the administration of their varied business a loose but convenient form of speech may have been used in the office, but it is not stated that it was supposed to be a correct one, and it appears incredible that a company, a large part of whose business is that of a land company, could reasonably suppose that in dealings with third persons for the sale of land, the word "land" means land with reservations of minerals. Mr. Trutch does not say that he misconceived the meaning of the word. His impression was that he had verbally notified the plaintiff that the minerals were to be reserved, and if he had done so the plaintiff would be precluded from obtaining the specific performance he seeks; but it has been found that notice was not given. The form of the company conveyances expressly reserving the minerals show that they were aware how to effect such object. The alleged mistake was therefore an unreasonable and careless one, and in view of the fact that the plaintiff went into possession under the contract, I do not think that it can be said to be unconscionable or highly unreasonable to enforce the specific performance of the contract.

TASCHEREAU J. (dissenting): — **[7]** I would dismiss this appeal. The reasons given in the courts below against the appellant's right to specific performance are, in my opinion, unanswerable. There has been no contract between this company and Hobbs. The company thought they were selling the land without the minerals; Hobbs thought he was buying the land with the minerals. So that the company did not sell what Hobbs thought he was buying, and Hobbs did not buy what the company thought they were selling. Therefore there was no contract between them. Hobbs would not have bought if he had known that the company were selling only surface rights, and the company would not have sold if they had thought that Hobbs intended to buy the land with the minerals. The ratification by the company stands upon no better ground. It was nothing but the ratification of a sale without the minerals. . . . The rule that any one dealing with another has the right to believe that this other one means what he says, or says what he means, is one that cannot be gainsaid. But it has no application here. Assuming that the agent sold the land with the minerals, he did what he had not the power to do. However, he did not do it. I would dismiss the appeal with costs.

[An appeal to the Privy Council was dismissed upon settlement: 31 S.C.R. xxviii.]

The Formation of Contracts

QUESTIONS AND NOTES

1.   Do King J. and Taschereau J. have the same view of the purpose of the law of contracts or, perhaps more pointedly, of the proper judicial response to problems of the
law of contracts? Do they agree on the role of a court that is asked to enforce a contract?

2.   The majority judgment of King J. is the logical extension of the decision in *Smith v.
Hughes*. The question is not whether there has been a subjective "meeting of the
minds" of the parties — though King J., says that the parties were *ad idem* — but
whether Hobbs can hold the railway to his understanding of the words used. This objective "reasonable person" approach taken by the majority is now the accepted
method of interpretation. It presents a fruitful method of dealing with many problems,
and we shall return to the decision as authority for a wide range of propositions. It is
not, however, free from problems. Consider the following questions:

(a)   To the extent that the law does not require that the promisor has understood the
promise being made before he or she may be made liable on the basis of *Smith v.
Hughes* or *Hobbs v. E & N Railway*, what legal or moral justification is there for
the imposition of liability?

(b)   If there is liability for a promise that was not understood by the promisor, how far
does it go? Are full expectation damages justifiable?

(c)   Would your answers to any of these questions be different in the following contexts:

(i)   the purchase of stock on a stock exchange through a broker,

(ii) the purchase of supplies for a manufacturer (General Motors, Toyota or a
potter making things for a crafts store),

(iii) an agreement by an employer to hire a person as

a.   a secretary,

b.   a plant manager, supervising 100 other workers, or

c.   a commission salesperson?

(d)   How far can the approach of *Smith v. Hughes* be pushed? Are there relations that
should not be created by such an approach?

(e)   Under Canadian legislation governing families, a person can become obliged to
support another simply by cohabiting together for a certain period of time, without ever marrying. Does this situation give legislative support to the approach of
Smith v. Hughes?

3.   Notice the intermediate position reached by the trial judge in *Hobbs v. E & N Railway*.
He would not allow either party to have the contract on their terms; instead, he would
have given Hobbs the option of a deal on the railway's terms or his money back. The
Court of Appeal gave Hobbs no option: a deal on the railway's terms and at the price
that one might assume that Hobbs reasonably thought was the price for land with the
minerals. This latter assumption is crucial to Hobbs' argument. If Hobbs should have
known that the price was too low for the purchase of land with mineral rights, he has
no basis for arguing that the railway should be held to the reasonable or objective
meaning of the word "land".

4.   Notice that the plaintiff, even though successful in the Supreme Court of Canada,
agreed to accept a settlement rather than defend that judgment in the Privy Council.
The power of the railway (the Esquimalt & Nanaimo was part of the Canadian Pacific
Railway — at the time Canada's largest corporation) to take every case to the Privy
Council in London must have operated as a strong inducement to Hobbs to settle. Sev-
eral large Canadian corporations, especially some in British Columbia, had a policy of

taking every case that they lost in a provincial court of appeal or in the Supreme Court of Canada to the Privy Council. This practice stopped only when Canadian appeals to the Privy Council were abolished in 1949.

5.   There are special rules that corporate bodies have to follow to bind themselves into contracts, though only one will be touched on here. The Supreme Court of Canada discussed the authority of Mr. Trutch, the Land Commissioner, to make the contract with Hobbs. The normal rule is that a principal is not bound by a contract made on its behalf by an agent who does not have actual authority from the principal to make the deal. Here, the court accepted that, while Mr. Trutch did not have the actual authority from the corporation to make the contract when he did, the corporation later ratified what he did and hence was bound.

   If this argument of ratification failed, Hobbs could also have argued that he relied on Mr. Trutch's appearance of authority. The law of agency provides that a principal, in this case the corporation, is bound by the acts of its agent who is acting within his or her ostensible or apparent authority. The "holding out" must be that of the corporation, not what the agent may say his or her authority is. A corporation may be similarly bound if an officer or other senior official, makes a contract that a person dealing with the corporation might reasonably believe to be within the scope of that person's authority because of his or her position in the corporation. These rules are an important way to protect the reasonable reliance of the person who deals with a corporation. The *Canada Business Corporations Act*, R.S.C. 1985, c. C-44, provides:

> 18(1) No corporation and no guarantor of an obligation of a corporation may assert against a person dealing with the corporation or against a person who acquired rights from the corporation that . . . (d) a person held out by a corporation as a director, an officer or an agent of the corporation has not been duly appointed or has no authority to exercise the powers and perform the duties that are customary in the business of the corporation or usual for a director, officer or agent; . . .

> (2) Subsection (1) does not apply in respect of a person who has, or ought to have, knowledge of a situation described in that subsection by virtue of their relationship to the corporation.

The judgment in the next case is a good example of a court dealing with the problem of what the process of bargaining was about and what the deal between the parties was.

STAIMAN STEEL LTD. v. COMMERCIAL & HOME BUILDERS LTD.

(1976), 13 O.R. (2d) 315, 71 D.L.R. (3d) 17
(H.C.J., Southey J.)

[The defendant (Commercial) had arranged for an auction of its construction equipment and its inventory of used steel in its fenced yard. The auctioneer, Caldarone (as agent for the defendant), separated the items into 383 numbered lots, which were tagged and listed in a catalogue made available to everyone attending the auction. There was also a pile of new prefabricated steel in the yard, piled separately from the rest of the steel and not tagged. This new steel was more valuable than the old steel and had been sold by the defendant a few weeks before the auction, but had not yet been delivered to the buyer.]

SOUTHEY J.: — [1] When the auctioneer started to offer the lots of used steel, one or two of the buyers suggested that the items of used steel be sold in bulk, instead of by individual lot. This procedure would save time and would eliminate any disputes as to the precise contents of each lot. Having satisfied himself that the buyers generally preferred to have such bulk sale, the auctioneer called a short break to enable the buyers to walk around the yard and inspect the lots which would be put up together.

[2] Before the bidding commenced, there was specific agreement that a number of items in the yard would not be included in the bulk sale, because they were not structural steel. Most of the items thus excluded were mechanical items. The auctioneer excluded them by referring to their lot numbers. . . .

[3] At one point, according to some of the witnesses, the auctioneer described the bulk lot in general terms as being all the steel in the yard except mechanical items. When this general description was given, Bernard Staiman, president of the plaintiff, picked up a piece of scrap steel from the ground and asked "Even this?". The auctioneer replied "Yes".

[4] The plaintiff was the successful bidder for the bulk lot at a unit price of $32 per ton.

[5] The action relates to a pile of steel beams, doors and other members, which were the component members of a prefabricated steel building with craneway. This steel had been sold by Commercial several weeks before the auction sale, but was still piled in the yard of Commercial on the day of the sale. The plaintiff contended that this pile of steel was included in the bulk lot, whereas the defendants asserted that it was never their intention to include this steel in the sale, because it did not belong to Commercial.

[6] The difference between the parties became apparent soon after the bulk lot was knocked down to the plaintiff and the auction sale was disrupted for a substantial time by a heated dispute between Staiman and the auctioneer as to the contents of the bulk lot. Staiman asserted that the steel he had purchased included the steel for the prefabricated building (hereinafter called the "building steel"). Commercial and the auctioneer both took the position that the steel purchased by the plaintiff in bulk did not include the building steel. . . .

[7] It is apparent from the evidence that Staiman behaved in a hot-tempered, quarrelsome and difficult manner throughout the incident in question. He refused to make the deposits on his purchases in the amounts and at the times required by the conditions of sale and he created a disturbance at the sale which threatened to disrupt it beyond repair. I find that Staiman became involved emotionally in the dispute that occurred and that I cannot accept as accurate his recollection of the matters in dispute.

[8] I was not impressed by Staiman's reliance on the question he put to the auctioneer as to whether the bulk lot included a piece of scrap steel and the answer received thereto as being of critical significance. I think the question may well have been intended to trap the auctioneer and set the stage for the dispute that occurred, but it is unnecessary for me to decide that point. If Staiman had any question that he genuinely wanted answered as to whether the building steel was included in the bulk lot, he should have made specific inquiries, as did [two other men] who were present at the auction and also gave evidence at trial.

[9] [On the question] as to whether the building steel was part of the bulk lot, I have concluded that it was never the intention of [the defendant] or [the auctioneer] to offer the building steel for sale at the auction. That steel had already been

sold. Furthermore, in my view, the defendants at no time manifested an intention to offer the building steel for sale. When the auctioneer agreed to sell the remaining inventory of steel in bulk, he was agreeing, in my view, to include in one bulk lot the items that had previously been offered for sale in separate lots. Even if he said that the bulk lot included all the steel in the yard except mechanical items, as some witnesses said he did, I think it should have been apparent to Staiman and the others at the sale that the auctioneer was offering only the steel belonging to [the defendant] that had been included in the auction sale. It should have been obvious that the auctioneer was not including the building steel in the bulk lot because that steel was separately piled from the rest; was not tagged; and was not listed in the catalogue. It was new steel painted grey, that had obviously been fabricated for a particular purpose. Whereas the other steel in the yard was all used.

[10] For the foregoing reasons, I find that the bulk lot for which the plaintiff was the successful bidder did not include the building steel. If, as appears to have been the case, the plaintiff thought the bulk lot he was purchasing included the building steel and the defendants thought that the bulk lot they were selling did not include the building steel, then the case was one of mutual mistake [and there may be no contract at all]. It is only in a case where the circumstances are so ambiguous that a reasonable bystander could not infer a common intention that the court will hold that no contract was created . . .

[11] Counsel for Commercial relied on *Raffles v. Wichelhaus et al.* (1864), 2 H. & C. 906, 159 E.R. 375, involving two ships named "Peerless" which sailed from Bombay, one in October and one in December, and *Scriven Brothers & Co. v. Hindley & Co.*, [1913] 3 K.B. 564, where the purchaser at an auction bid an extravagant price for the bales of tow in the mistaken belief that they were bales of hemp. In both cases the Courts held that there was no contract, apparently because there was no *consensus ad idem*.

[12] Counsel for the plaintiff, on the other hand, relied on the basic rule of contract law that it is not a party's actual intention that determines contractual relationships, but rather the intention manifested by the words and actions of the parties. Mr. Catzman referred to the following passage in the judgment of Middleton J.A., in *Lindsey v. Heron & Co.* (1921), 50 O.L.R. 1 at p. 8, 64 D.L.R. 92 at pp. 98-9:

> The apparent mutual assent of the parties essential to the formation of a contract, must be gathered from the language employed by them, and the law imputes to a person an intention corresponding to the reasonable meaning of his words and acts. It judges of his intention by his outward expressions and excludes all questions in regard to his unexpressed intention. If his words or acts, judged by a reasonable standard, manifest an intention to agree in regard to the matter in question, that agreement is established, and it is immaterial what may be the real but unexpressed state of his mind on the subject." [*Corpus Juris*, vol. 13, p. 265]

> "If, whatever a man's real intention may be, he so conducts himself that a reasonable man would believe that he was assenting to the terms proposed by the other party, and that other party upon that belief enters into the contract with him, the man thus conducting himself would be equally bound as if he had intended to agree to the other party's terms:" Blackburn J., in *Smith v. Hughes*, L.R. 6 Q.B. at p. 607.

. . .

[13] If, as appears to have been the case, the plaintiff thought the bulk lot he was purchasing included the building steel and the defendants thought that the bulk lot they were selling did not include the building steel, then the case was one of mutual mistake, as that expression is used in Cheshire and Fifoot's *Law of Contract*, 8th ed. (1972), p. 221. In such a case, the Court must decide what reasonable third parties would infer to be the contract from the words and conduct of the parties who entered into it. It is only in a case where the circumstances are so ambiguous that a reasonable bystander could not infer a common intention that the Court will hold that no contract was created. As pointed out in Cheshire and Fifoot at p. 212:

> If the evidence is so conflicting that there is nothing sufficiently solid from which to infer a contract in any final form without indulging in mere speculation, the court must of necessity declare that no contract whatsoever has been created.

[14]   In this case, in my judgment, a reasonable man would infer the existence of a contract to buy and sell the bulk lot without the building steel and therefore I have held that there was a contract to that effect binding on both parties, notwithstanding such mutual mistake.

[15]   The case is quite unlike *Raffles v. Wichelhaus* [*supra*] because, in [that case], it was impossible for the court to impute any definite [agreement] to the parties.

[16]   In *Raffles v. Wichelhaus* the court had no more reason to find that both parties had manifested an intention to deal in cotton shipped on the "Peerless" sailing in October than to deal with cotton shipped in the "Peerless" sailing in December.
. . .

[The court concluded that there was a binding contract to sell only the old steel in the yard; the new steel was not covered by this contract.]

Indefiniteness and the Process of Contract Negotiation

The traditional common law model of the process of contract formation is premised on the assumption that there is relatively little bargaining between the parties. The model envisages a fairly straightforward exchange of letters, faxes, e-mails or oral communications, which results in both of the parties having clearly agreed to a set of terms, or having clearly failed to reach an agreement. While this model of offer and acceptance accurately portrays some negotiations, in many situations it would be an odd and impractical process. The process would entail the exchange of offers between the parties, each of which represented all the terms that party would accept in the deal. Until one offer was accepted, each offer would lead to a counter-offer, and with each of these the parties would, so to speak, be back at the beginning. On the acceptance of one offer, the deal would be complete.

    In reality, the process of contract-making is as varied as the kinds of deals that may be made. Sometimes the process does reproduce what we would expect to see if offers of the traditional type were exchanged. Perhaps the paradigm example is the purchase of a house on the resale market. If a real estate agent is used, almost invariably a standard form prepared by the local real estate board is used. The prospective purchaser will initially complete the form and include all the terms that she wants. Do the drapes stay with the house? What about the appliances? Will the vendor take back a mortgage? Will the vendor permit the house to be inspected before a concluded contract is made? The vendor's willingness to agree to these terms may be known in advance through the listing or from conversations between the parties or their agents. The purchaser will sign the offer (which is under seal and which will be irrevocable for a short time — perhaps a few hours, probably not more than a day). The preliminaries to the offer, the time taken to visit an "open house", to discuss the proposed purchase with the agent, or a possible mort-gagee or to investigate schools, etc., will be time invested by the prospective pur-chaser and by the agent, even though there is no certainty that a deal will ever be made. As discussed earlier, the agent knows that she may have to put in a great deal of work without any certainty that any remuneration will be earned from it; almost invariably, the listing agreement is interpreted to provide that only if the house is sold will a commission be payable.

In this model of contracting it is easy to see how the rules of offer and accep-tance may be applied. The purchaser makes an offer that attempts to state all the terms that the purchaser wants in the deal. If the vendor does not like the deal, he may reject it outright or bargain over one or more of the items. If, for example, the price is too low, the vendor may "sign back" the document, crossing out and ini-tialling the price originally inserted and replacing it with an amended price, leav-ing the rest of the terms unchanged. If something else is unsatisfactory, the vendor may alter some other term. If the vendor wants to take the dishwasher, he may sign it back with that item removed from the list of appliances that stay. The vendor's "sign back" is itself a valid offer, containing all the terms on which the vendor is prepared to deal and which the purchasers may now accept. This process can go on as long as either party considers it useful. As we shall see, this process does not always work and there can be problems that are very difficult to solve. We shall look at some of these problems in this chapter and at some others in Chapter 4.

The deal is made when the formal offer of the purchaser or vendor is accepted by the other; typically this is clear when each party has signed the agreement and initialled all the changes proposed by the other. The deal does not "close" when the offer is accepted. The offer will contain a closing date that will normally be far enough in the future to permit the vendor's title to be searched and financing to be arranged by the purchaser. This "two-stage" process of dealing is an important aspect of sale transactions that involve large amounts of money. The contract is made at one point in time, with performance, often called "closing" or "comple-tion", at some later date. The time between formation and performance is used to give the purchaser an opportunity to make sure that the vendor owns what he pur-ports to be selling, and that it has all of the qualities that it was represented to have. In a real estate deal, the delay to closing gives the purchaser's lawyer a chance to "search title" to ascertain that the vendor has good title to the land, and will also allow for a home inspection. The delay also allows time for the parties to prepare to perform (in a house sale, to get ready to move).

Sale transactions of these types are not the only kinds of transactions that will concern us. Joint ventures, distribution and agency agreements, and long-term supply and requirements contracts may take a long time to negotiate. Such agree-ments will typically not be completed in two distinct stages; there will be one agreement that is both the contract and the creation of the relation. The problems that arise here are more likely to be due to the impatience of the parties who may begin the commercial relationship before a final agreement has been reached — at least according to the traditional contract formation rules. It is not uncommon for the terms of a relation to be found in many unsigned and different drafts of a pro-posed contract. When problems arise — "Can the vendor raise its prices just like that?" — the different unsigned drafts of the agreement may give little help in resolving the dispute. As we shall see, problems of this type exist in large and important classes of contracts.

In the asset or share purchase of a business there are two principal features that dramatically change the process of bargaining and the applicability of the rules of offer and acceptance. The first is that agreement may have an added stage. The first stage is not a binding contract like the real estate deal for the purchase and sale of a home, but an "agreement in principle" between the parties. This "agreement in principle" may be reached by the business people involved who leave the details "to be worked out by the lawyers". The agreement "in principle" may be contained in an exchange of letters, a complete but still draft agreement, or nothing more formal than an oral understanding and a handshake. As we shall see, the problem with an "agreement in principle" is that it is not a technical term, and it may or may not be regarded as a binding legal contract by the courts.

A second feature of complex negotiations is that they may be protracted and agreement may be reached in stages. It is expected by the parties that there will eventually be a document that states all the terms that the parties are prepared to accept, but agreement may be reached on a number of important items before agreement is reached on all. What is important is that the parties may not consider themselves free — or, at least, completely free — to go back and reopen the matters on which agreement has already been reached. The "incremental" nature of bargaining is a fact of commercial dealing. A breakdown of negotiations is unlikely to lead to litigation, though as we shall see, litigation is not unknown. The sanctions that encourage people (both the parties and their legal advisers) to accept as obligations what was agreed at an earlier negotiating session arise from the fact that negotiation is often an expensive process. People who ignore the transaction costs that the other party will incur if matters thought to be disposed of are re-opened may find themselves unpopular as prospective parties: they become too difficult and too expensive to deal with.

Parties do, of course, break off negotiations before the final agreement is executed and lawyers may work hard to make sure that their clients have this freedom, or have this weapon to use against the other party. A downturn in prices of land or in business prospects will have an immediate and obvious effect on the willingness of the purchaser to complete a deal that might have been based on optimism that is now seen to have been misplaced.

Three things are important to notice about this method of contracting. First, it is wrong to believe that the parties accept no obligations until there is a final executed deal. Obligations may arise simply from the fact that bargaining has taken place and that significant transaction costs have been incurred by both parties. Second, lawyers (when they are involved) have to be very careful to control the process so that, for example, their clients are not exposed to the risk of being held to a deal too soon. This risk is illustrated by the fact that "agreements in principle" sometimes lead to litigation. The third thing to appreciate is that the parties may not wait until the process of bargaining is complete before they begin to work together. Once agreement is reached on some key aspects of the deal, the parties may regard their relation as established, and the terms that still have to be negotiated may be left to be worked out later. Serious problems will arise if disagreements occur or the relation collapses before these details have been worked out.

Another potential source of confusion is the deliberate use of vague terms or the deliberate avoidance of a term dealing with an important point. The existence of such a situation may reflect the problems of the negotiations rather than carelessness. If the parties cannot agree, for example, on what to do if the relation breaks down, they may leave that issue unresolved. They may hope that the problem will not arise but, if it does, they may be content to let someone else sort out the mess. If the lawyers for the parties were to insist that every point be clearly resolved, there might be no deal, yet both clients might very much want a deal, even as their lawyers point out the dangers. It is no part of a lawyer's job to get in his or her client's way, once the client has been fully informed of the risks a transaction creates. Mysterious phrases like "reasonable best efforts" may appear in agreements because one party wants the other to use its "best efforts" to achieve some result while the other is only prepared to make "reasonable efforts". The phrase "reasonable best" accommodates both, though at the risk that disagreements may be harder to resolve than if there had been a clear agreement.

One way of expressing the problem of indefiniteness is to ask the question: "Have the parties done enough in making their agreement sufficiently precise that a court could reasonably be expected to enforce it?" The standard that is applied in answering this question discloses much about attitudes to the purpose of the law of contracts, and to the judicial responsibility for its development. Any classification of cases into a category of "indefiniteness" is necessarily arbitrary. In one sense, *Raffles v. Wichelhaus* raised the problem of indefiniteness: had the parties realized that they were at cross-purposes, they could have avoided the problems that later arose either by making it certain that they were agreed on what they were buying or selling or by making it clear that there was no deal.

Similarly, the problems of indefiniteness, like the problem in *Staiman Steel*, merge into problems of interpretation. If the parties have worked together for 10 years, it is no longer possible to say that the process of offer and acceptance "misfired"; the parties must have had a contract and the only question is its terms. Many of these problems will be the focus of concern in Chapter 5, when we turn to the problem of interpretation. In this chapter, we will examine a number of cases in which indefiniteness is relevant to the question of whether or not there is a binding contract, while the issues in Chapter 5 focus on interpretation of vague but valid contracts.

The line between some of the cases that deal with formation concerns and those dealing with interpretation issues is sometimes not easy to draw, and some cases considered now as formation problems could be studied as cases raising interpretation issues (and vice-versa).

A factor that bears on the way in which negotiations for large transactions are conducted today is the presence of lawyers at a very early stage in the process. This development is due, at least in part, to the very important role that tax planning plays in most corporate and commercial transactions — almost no significant transaction takes place now that does not depend on tax advice that one or both of the parties will have received — and to the need to comply with the large number of statutory rules. Legal advice may be needed at the outset of negotiations to ensure that the requirements imposed by tax, corporate, securities, competition and environmental legislation are properly addressed. Experienced lawyers also often provide advice about a range of legal, financial and tactical issues related to the negotiation process.

Agreements to Agree

It is often said that the court will not "make an agreement" for the parties. One important aspect of the rule is its use to justify the statement that the courts will not enforce "agreements to agree". An agreement to agree is an agreement that leaves all or, perhaps, only one point to be settled by the parties. A buyer and seller may, for example, agree to sell goods "at a price to be agreed". Another example is the statement in a commercial lease that the tenant shall be entitled to renew the lease for an additional term "at a rent to be agreed". Both of these contracts would be likely to come within the scope of the rule that courts will not make agreements for the parties, with the effect that there is no enforceable contract of sale or enforceable right in the tenant to renew the lease.

A refusal to enforce such an "agreement to agree" reflects a concern that it is not for the courts to make an agreement for the parties — they have not done what they should do to justify their bringing their dispute before the courts — or that, for breach of the promise to agree to a price or a rent, damages may be too uncertain.

The courts have drawn a distinction between agreements that omit some important term altogether, and those where the parties provide that they shall subsequently agree on some term. In the former case the courts may impose a reasonable term, while in the latter they will usually say that there has been no agreement. The difference in approach may seem arbitrary, but the courts tend to believe that if there is an "agreement to agree", the parties are not making a firm present commitment, and each is reserving the right to put forward a position that the other party may view as unreasonable. A judge will be reluctant to tell parties what they should agree to. However, if the parties say that they have an agreement, but are silent about an important term, or agree that it will be resolved by a "reasonable" term, there is more of a tendency to believe that the parties have made a present commitment and are willing to allow a judge to resolve any disagreements in a commercially "reasonable" fashion (*i.e.*, as the judge considers reasonable or fair).

The Ontario *Sale of Goods Act*, R.S.O. 1990, c. S.1, for example, provides:

> 9(1) The price in a contract of sale may be fixed by the contract or may be left to be fixed in a manner thereby agreed or may be determined by the course of dealing between the parties.

> (2) Where the price is not determined in accordance with the foregoing provisions, the buyer shall pay a reasonable price, and what constitutes a reasonable price is a question of fact dependent on the circumstances of each particular case.

However, it has been held that where a contract provides that the price of goods was to be "agreed upon from time to time between", the parties did not come under either subsection of s. 9 of the *Sale of Goods Act* and that a contract containing such a clause was void as an important term — the price — had been left unresolved and could not be supplied by the court: *May & Butcher v. The King* (1929, H.L.) (reported as a note to *Foley v. Classique Coaches, Ltd.*, [1934] 2 K.B. 1, at p. 17). Lord Buckmaster stated (p. 20):

> It has long been a well recognized principle of contract law that an agreement between two parties to enter into an agreement in which some critical matter is left undetermined is no contract at all.

The attitude of the House of Lords in *May & Butcher v. The King* may be contrasted with that of the same court in *Hillas & Co. Ltd. v. Arcos Ltd.*, [1932] All E.R. Rep. 494, 38 Com. Cas. 23 (H.L.). The background to *Hillas* is interesting and important and is mentioned in the judgment of Scrutton L.J. in the next case. In the early 1930's there was considerable hostility towards the Soviet Union in the United Kingdom. The Soviet Union was, however, a major supplier of lumber to the United Kingdom. Arcos Ltd. was an English corporation that was owned by the Russian state trading interests. The Russians, through Arcos Ltd., made their first sale to a major U.K. lumber importer, Hillas, with a contract to deliver 22,000 standards of lumber. At the time of the original deal in 1930, most English buyers were boycotting the Russians. As part of that deal, the Russians gave Hillas an option for the following year to be the exclusive importer of about 10 times the original amount on the same terms and at the same prices. By the next year, the boycott was over and the Russians had no need to give any importer a sweet deal, particularly as the price for Russian lumber had increased. Hillas took the position that Arcos was bound by the option contained in the earlier agreement; Arcos argued that it was not sufficiently definite. The agreement did not say what sizes of lumber would be sold or what the proportions of the various sizes would be in the total amount delivered in either year. The parties had made the deal work in the first year, but now the issue was whether an agreement could be imposed on Arcos when important terms were not stated. The House of Lords upheld the agreement.

The English courts had not finished with the Russians yet. The enforcement of the agreement in *Hillas v. Arcos* caused Arcos to breach an agreement with another English importer to whom it had promised lumber. Arcos had promised that importer that no other importer had a deal for better prices than it was offered. That importer sued and recovered damages: *Jewson & Son Ltd. v. Arcos Ltd.* (1933), 39 Com. Cas. 59. It is likely that before entering the second contract Arcos sought legal advice about whether it was not bound to sell to Hillas in the second year of that contract. If you imagine what advice you would have given in similar circumstances, you can understand how uncertain the law is. What advice would you give a client in the position of Arcos? What could a solicitor acting for Arcos have done to improve its position? Do you think that the English judges in the cases involving Arcos were influenced by a dislike for Russian Bolsheviks? Was it significant that in *May & Butcher v. The King* the judges upheld the argument of the British government that it had not made a binding contract?

Some of this English jurisprudence is usefully summarized in the following case.

FOLEY v. CLASSIQUE COACHES, LTD.

[1934] 2 K.B. 1, [1934] All E.R. Rep. 88
(C.A., Scrutton, Greer and Maugham L.JJ.)

[The plaintiff was a dealer in petrol [gasoline], and the defendants were operators of tour buses. In 1930 the parties made a contract by which the plaintiff sold land adjoining his premises to the defendant. In a separate document that was stated to be "supplemental" to the land contract, the defendants agreed to buy petrol from the plaintiff, on terms that included:

1.   The vendor shall sell to the company and the company shall purchase from the vendor all petrol which shall be required by the company for the running of their said business at a price to be agreed by the parties in writing and from time to time.

. . .

3.   This agreement shall remain in force during the life of the vendor and his present wife if she survives him.

. . .

6.   The company shall not purchase any petrol from any other person . . . so long as the vendor is able to supply them with sufficient petrol to satisfy their daily requirements. . . .

7.   The vendor shall supply the said petrol of a standard and quality at present supplied by the vendor or of such other standard and quality as the company may reasonably approve.

8.   If any dispute or difference shall arise . . . [it] shall be submitted to arbitration. . . .

The land was conveyed to the defendants. In 1933 the solicitor for the defendants purported to bring the agreement to an end. His letter said:

It appears that although you have supplied petrol to my clients as and when they have required it no agreement in writing as to price has ever been made . . . Having considered this alleged agreement . . . I have advised my clients that this document is of no force or effect, and therefore . . . my clients will be purchasing their petrol supplies elsewhere.

The trial judge, Lord Chief Justice Hewart, granted an injunction restraining the defendants from breach of clause 6, and awarded an amount of damages to be ascertained. The defendants appealed.]

SCRUTTON L.J.: — [1] In this appeal I think that the Lord Chief Justice's decision was right, and I am glad to come to that conclusion, because I do not regard the appellants' contention as an honest one. . . .

[2]   In the third year some one acting for the appellants thought he could get better petrol elsewhere, and on September 29, 1933, their solicitor, thinking he saw a way out of the agreement, wrote on behalf of the appellants the letter of September 29, 1933, repudiating the agreement. Possibly the solicitor had heard something about the decision of the House of Lords in *May & Butcher v. The King* [reported as a note following *Foley* at [1934] 2 K.B. 17] but probably had not heard of *Braithwaite v. Foreign Hardwood Co.*, [1905] 2 K.B. 543, in which the Court of Appeal decided that the wrongful repudiation of a contract by one party relieves the other party from the performance of any conditions precedent. If the solicitor had known of that decision he would not have written the letter in the terms he did. Thereafter the respondent brought his action claiming damages for breach of the agreement, a declaration that the agreement is binding, and an injunction to restrain the appellants from purchasing petrol from any other person. The Lord Chief Justice decided that the respondent was entitled to judgment, as there was a binding agreement by which the appellants got the land on condition that they should buy their petrol from the respondent. I observe that the appellants' solicitor in his letter made no suggestion that the land would be returned, and I suppose the appellants would have been extremely annoyed if they had been asked to return it when they repudiated the condition.

[3]   A good deal of the case turns upon the effect of two decisions of the House of Lords which are not easy to fit in with each other. The first of these cases is

May & Butcher v. The King (supra) . . . In the second case, *Hillas & Co. Ltd. v. Arcos Ltd. (supra)* the Court of Appeal, which included Greer L.J. and myself, both having a very large experience in these timber cases, came to the conclusion that as the House of Lords in *May & Butcher v. The King* considered that where a detail had to be agreed upon there was no agreement until that detail was agreed, we were bound to follow the decision in *May & Butcher v. The King* and hold that there was no effective agreement in respect of the option, because the terms had not been agreed. It was, however, held by the House of Lords in *Hillas & Co. v. Arcos* that we were wrong in so deciding and that we had misunderstood the decision in *May & Butcher v. The King.* The House took this line: it is quite true that there seems to be considerable vagueness about the agreement but the parties contrived to get through it on the contract for 22,000 standards, and so the House thought there was an agreement as to the option which the parties would be able to get through also despite the absence of details. It is true that in the first year the parties got through quite satisfactorily; that was because during that year the great bulk of English buyers were boycotting the Russian sellers. In the second year the position was different. The English buyers had changed their view and were buying large quantities of Russian timber, so that different conditions were then prevailing. In *Hillas & Co. v. Arcos* the House of Lords said that they had not laid down universal principles of construction in *May & Butcher v. The King,* and that each case must be decided on the construction of the particular document, while in *Hillas & Co. v. Arcos* they found that the parties believed they had a contract. In the present case the parties obviously believed they had a contract and they acted for three years as if they had; they had an arbitration clause which relates to the subject-matter of the agreement as to the supply of petrol, and it seems to me that this arbitration clause applies to any failure to agree as to the price. By analogy to the case of a tied house there is to be implied in this contract a term that the petrol shall be supplied at a reasonable price and shall be of reasonable quality. For these reasons I think the Lord Chief Justice was right in holding that there was an effective and enforceable contract, although as to the future no definite price had been agreed with regard to the petrol. . . .

[4]   The appeal therefore fails, and no alteration is required in the form of the injunction that has been granted.

NOTES AND QUESTIONS

1.   When considering how to treat an agreement, the courts consider more than the words of the agreement. In *Hillas v. Arcos*, the parties had made the agreement work for one year; the House of Lords may have asked itself: "Why couldn't it work for another — why should working out the mix of sizes be any more difficult?" Further, the buyer gave the seller a real advantage in the first year, when the buyer broke the boycott; it would be unfair to allow the seller to back out of the agreement in the second year.

In *Foley v. Classique Coaches, Ltd.*, not only had the agreement worked for three years, but it was partly performed by the plaintiff, who probably would not have made the deal to sell the land if the defendant had not promised a long-term contract to buy petrol. If the court in that case had held that the part of the deal that dealt with the sale of petrol could not be enforced because it was too indefinite, how could the deal ever be unwound? Would it have been fair to leave the defendant with the land and the plaintiff with benefits that he regarded as inadequate for the land he had given up?

The pressure to enforce will be a function of the extent to which one party has relied on the agreement, the degree to which the parties are committed to each other, and the problems of disentangling their relation. It is not possible to make a rational decision if these issues are ignored and the words of the agreement alone considered.

2.   If you were drafting an agreement for a deal like that in *Foley v. Classique Coaches, Ltd.*, now, how would you deal with the problem that the parties faced?

3.   A significant part of the problem of indefiniteness centres on the attitude of the judge deciding the case. Notice, for example, that in *Foley v. Classique Coaches, Ltd.*, Scrutton L.J., in discussing what he had said in *Hillas & Co. v. Arcos*, observed that he and Greer L.J. "both [had] a very large experience in these timber cases". The inference that can be drawn from this remark is that a judge with such a background might more readily understand whether or not a contract was sufficiently definite to be enforced.

       (a)   What do you think one would need to know before one could have confidence in the conclusion that a certain contract is or is not enforceable?

       (b)   What does this say about the problems counsel might have in giving a judge who lacks the kind of experience that Scrutton L.J. had sufficient information to make the proper decision?

       (c)   Do you think that a judge should make use of personal experience in this way? Is there a danger that the judge who does so is undercutting the effectiveness of the judicial process? Is there any satisfactory alternative to a judge's making use of personal experience in this way?

4.   As we shall see with letters of intent — pre-contractual letters that set out the major terms of a proposed agreement, but reserve the right not to enter into a contractual re-lation — there are situations where the parties deliberately plan not to have a relation that gives rise to legally enforceable rights and obligations. The parties may have cho-sen to use vague language as a means of keeping the courts out of their relation. It would be wrong to assume that enforcement of an "agreement to agree" is always preferable to leaving the parties alone. At the very least, the court should require evi-dence that they expected a legal relation, as opposed to something different. The ap-proach of *Hobbs v. E & N Railway* — taking a reasonable interpretation of their deal-ings — offers a method for a "default" assumption.

5.   The parties may even permit an arbitrator (but not the court) to set almost all the terms of the contract: *Calvan Consolidated Oil & Gas Ltd. v. Manning*, [1959] 1 S.C.R. 253, 17 D.L.R. (2d) 1. Such agreements, unlike those in *May & Butcher v. The King*, are enforceable because the terms can be made certain by a process provided for by the parties. The courts will not perform the job of an arbitrator. What reason might there be for the attitude of the court?
       The process of arbitration is characterized as "private adjudication". The parties se-lect an arbitrator, often a retired judge, a lawyer or a person with expertise in the sub-ject matter of the dispute, to hear the case. The parties present evidence and argu-ments before the arbitrator — the same characteristics as adjudication, though arbitra-tion is relatively expeditious, informal and inexpensive compared to litigation in the courts. The rules of evidence and procedure are generally less formal in an arbitration proceeding than in a court, and the arbitrator will usually be familiar with the com-mercial context of the dispute.
       Judges will be reluctant to impose their views about what parties should agree to. However, if the parties agree that they will abide by an arbitrator's decision about their disagreement, the courts will respect their selection of a method for rendering the contract sufficiently certain to be enforceable. While arbitration may be preferable to litigation, arbitration of a complex commercial dispute may also be expensive.
       Contractual arrangements that depend on the use of arbitrators are fairly common. There are at least two types of arbitration: "grievance" and "interest", both of which appear in contracts. Grievance arbitration involves an arbitrator resolving a retrospec-tive dispute, for example about whether there are grounds for dismissing a unionized employee. "Interest arbitration" requires an arbitrator to shape a future relation, or some aspect of a future relation. It is beyond the scope of this book to explore the problems of "interest" arbitration, but there are important problems in devising a

process and in making it work when an arbitrator is, for example, asked to fix the wages to be paid to employees in institutions where strikes are prohibited.

Parties often use interest arbitration in contracts where the agreement has to be flexible so that the parties can respond to changing circumstances. For example, some contracts have so many parties that it would be impracticable to have the parties agree to every change. Such contracts are often made for tax reasons and may involve hundreds of parties. These kinds of relations are not organized through corporations, because that form of organization is excluded by the tax rules that the parties want to take advantage of. Some contractual form for the relation is therefore necessary. A limited partnership, really a form of a contract between the partners, can operate like a corporation with power in the general partner to act as a manager, subject to the limited partners' "democratic" right to remove the general partner or to change the arrangement. A limited partnership confers on the limited partners a form of limited liability, the partners' liability being limited by the value of their investment.

6. Like arbitration, mediation is a form of "alternative dispute resolution" ("ADR") that parties may specify in a contract is to be used in the event of a dispute about the contract, instead of taking the matter to court. In mediation, the parties meet with a neutral third party who attempts to help the parties negotiate a settlement. Mediators, who may be lawyers, retired judges or other individuals with dispute resolution skills, help the parties to resolve their differences, suggesting various possible bases for an agreement, and facilitating the search for compromise. Unlike with arbitration (or adjudication by a judge), mediation may not result in the resolution of a dispute, and in some respects an agreement to mediate is similar to an agreement to negotiate a resolution of a disagreement, in that there is no certainty that the parties will reach a mediated agreement. There are, however, English cases which have held that if a commercial agreement includes a provision to mediate a dispute before the matter is referred to the courts, a judge may issue a stay or adjournment of the case until a good faith effort at mediation is tried. In *Cable & Wireless plc v. I.B.M.*, [2002] EWHC 2059 (Q.B.) Colman J. explained:

> For the courts now to decline to enforce contractual references to ADR on the grounds of intrinsic uncertainty would be to fly in the face of public policy…mediation as a tool for dispute resolution is not designed to achieve solutions which reflect the precise legal rights and obligations of the parties, but rather solutions which are mutually commercially acceptable at the time of the mediation.

In *Dunnett v. Railtrack*, [2002] 1 W.L.R. 2434 (Eng. C.A.), Brooke L.J. observed:

> Skilled mediators are now able to achieve results satisfactory to both parties in many cases which are quite beyond the power of lawyers and courts to achieve. This court has knowledge of cases where intense feelings have arisen. … But when the parties are brought together on neutral soil with a skilled mediator to help them resolve their differences, it may very well be that the mediator is able to achieve a result by which the parties shake hands at the end and feel that they have gone away having settled the dispute on terms with which they are happy to live.

If mediation is tried and failed, the parties will still have the right to resort to the courts (or an arbitrator if provided for in their contract). For a further discussion, see Kah Cheong Lye, "Agreements to Mediate: The Impact of *Cable & Wireless plc v. I.B.M*" (2004), 16 *Sing. Ac. L.J.* 530.

7. The line between relational contracts with procedures for decision-making and more formal business relations like the partnerships or corporations is sometimes not easy to draw in functional terms. A partnership is in essence a contractual arrangement between people who are in business together for profit. A large number of partners may be parties to the partnership agreement, and that agreement will almost always provide some method by which decisions for dealing with problems as they arise may be

made. Law firms are partnerships — often "limited liability partnerships" ("LLP's")
— and in large firms almost all decisions are made by executive or management com-
mittees. See, *e.g.*, *Mantini v. Smith Lyons LLP*, [2003] O.J. No. 1831, 64 O.R. (3d)
505 (C.A.). Corporations have shareholders who elect a board of directors to run the
corporation. Legislation like the *Canada Business Corporations Act*, R.S.C. 1985, c.
C-44, governs the election of directors and corporate decision-making.

   While the legal framework of the corporation differs dramatically from that of a
contract, the two institutions may in some situations be functionally interchangeable.
It may be a choice of form only whether vertical integration in an industry is achieved
by means of related corporations or long-term supply or requirements contracts.

   As we shall briefly explore in Chapter 6, some of the rules that protect the inevitable reliance of the shareholders of a corporation on the integrity of its board of directors are reflected in similar rules of contract law.

8.   Issues concerning agreements to agree illustrate once again the problems that arise
     from the focus of the law on the "discrete" transaction. The use of arbitration is one
     possible response to the pressures of relational contracts — contracts that provide a
     framework for co-operation. It is nearly inevitable that these kinds of contracts will
     have to respond to changes that occur during the term of the relation. The contract in
     Foley v. Classique Coaches, Ltd., for example, provided for expected (but unknown)
     changes in the agreement, and for arbitration in the event of differences.

9.   Like many legal aphorisms, the rule that courts will not enforce an agreement to agree
     has a particular meaning. Whenever the courts interpret a contract or fill in the blanks
     in an agreement, they are, in an important sense, "making the agreement" for the par-
     ties. As we shall see in Chapter 6, courts assert an even wider power to "make agree-
     ments" when they control the power given to the parties by the law of contract. Like
     so many legal "rules", the rule that courts will not make a contract is sometimes too
     uncritically accepted, and may be applied without discussion to justify a decision that
     a court has made.

COURTNEY AND FAIRBAIRN LTD. v. TOLAINI BROTHERS (HOTELS) LTD.

[1975] 1 W.L.R. 297, [1975] 1 All E.R. 716
(C.A., Lord Denning M.R., Lord Diplock and Lawton L.J.)

[The defendant wanted to build a hotel. It approached the plaintiff, a builder, who
agreed to introduce to the defendant a person who could supply the financing. In
return for this service, the defendant agreed in an exchange of letters to have the
plaintiff build the hotel, on the basis that they "negotiate fair and reasonable contract sums", based upon the "net cost of work and general overheads with a margin
for profit of 5%". The plaintiff fulfilled its part of the bargain and the defendant
obtained the financing it needed, but the parties could not agree on a price for the
construction. In the end the defendant had another contractor build the hotel, and
the plaintiff sought a declaration that there was a breach of contract and damages.
The defendant brought a preliminary motion to dismiss the action on the ground
that there was no enforceable contract between the parties.]

LORD DENNING M.R.: — [1] . . . But then this point was raised. Even if there was
not a contract actually to build, was not there a contract to negotiate? In this case
Mr. Tolaini did instruct his quantity surveyor to negotiate, but the negotiations
broke down. It may be suggested that the quantity surveyor was to blame for the
failure of the negotiations. But does that give rise to a cause of action? There is
very little guidance in the book about a contract to negotiate. It was touched on by
Lord Wright in *Hillas & Co. Ltd. v. Arcos Ltd.* (1932), 38 Com. Cas. 23, where he

said: "There is then no bargain except to negotiate, and negotiations may be fruit-
less and end without any contract ensuing." Then he went on: ". . . yet even then,
in strict theory, there is a contract (if there is good consideration) to negotiate,
though in the event of repudiation by one party the damages may be nominal,
unless a jury think that the opportunity to negotiate was of some appreciable value
to the injured party".

[2]   That tentative opinion by Lord Wright does not seem to me to be well
founded. If the law does not recognise a contract to enter into a contract (when
there is a fundamental term yet to be agreed) it seems to me it cannot recognise a
contract to negotiate. The reason is because it is too uncertain to have any binding
force. No court could estimate the damages because no one can tell whether the
negotiations would be successful or would fall through; or if successful, what the
result would be. It seems to me that a contract to negotiate, like a contract to enter
into a contract, is not a contract known to the law. . . . I think we must apply the
general principle that when there is a fundamental matter left undecided and to be
the subject of negotiation, there is no contract. So I would hold that there was not
any enforceable agreement in the letters between the plaintiff and the defendants. I
would allow the appeal accordingly.

LORD DIPLOCK: — **[3]** I agree and would only add my agreement that the dictum — for it is no more — of Lord Wright in *Hillas & Co. Ltd. v. Arcos Ltd.* to
which Lord Denning M.R. has referred, though an attractive theory, should in my
view be regarded as bad law.

NOTES AND QUESTIONS

1.   The type of service provided in *Courtney*, introducing a lender and a borrower, may
      be commercially provided by professionals who charge a "finder's fee" to the lender.
      The plaintiff in *Courtney* was suing for its loss of profits on the construction contract.
      Would it have made a difference if the plaintiff tried to recover for the value of the
      services it provided the defendant?

2.   A response to the proposition that an agreement to agree is unenforceable might be
      to argue that such an agreement could be given some force by holding that the par-
      ties have an obligation to negotiate in good faith. If, after so negotiating, no agree-
      ment is reached, neither would have a claim against the other. If, on the other hand,
      one party does not negotiate in good faith, the other could claim for breach of con-
      tract. In some cases it might be hard to say what the damages should be this case,
      but difficulty in quantifying damages is not generally a justification for a refusal to
      award any damages, though the court may be conservative in the amount that it
      awards. There is nothing that, in principle, would make it impossible or wrong to
      award damages for breach of an obligation to do something in good faith. For ex-
      ample, in a number of cases damages have been awarded for breach of an obligation
      to seek planning permission in good faith. Damages will reflect the chance that a
      good-faith effort would have been unsuccessful and be discounted accordingly. Ex-
      actly this method was used in *Multi-Malls Inc. v. Tex-Mall Properties Inc.* (1980),
      108 D.L.R. (3d) 399, 28 O.R. (2d) 6 (H.C.J.), affirmed 37 O.R. (2d) 133*n*, 128
      D.L.R. (3d) 192*n* (C.A.). If the courts have no problem in awarding damages for
      breach of an obligation to perform in good faith in one area, why should they have
      any more of a problem in another?

3.   Provisions in commercial leases that the tenant may renew the lease at a rent "to be
      agreed" will generally make the agreement to renew unenforceable. Although the
      problematic nature of this type of clause is well known to lawyers and commercial
      realtors, parties continue to use it, in part because they believe that (i) they will agree
      on a rent when the time for renewal arrives; or (ii) something will happen to make the

deal work. When it does not work, if the tenant has no right to renew, the lessor will be relieved, while the tenant will be disappointed. The tenant may well not have made the original deal if it was to have no right to renew. A tenant may be willing to make the investment to move and renovate premises if there is a chance that it may be recovered over 10 or 15 years, but be unwilling to make the same investment if it may be worthless in five years. The efforts that the courts will sometimes make to hold leases to be enforceable reflect judicial appreciation of this point. We shall see that the inability to re-make the deal when some later aspect turns out to disappoint one of the parties is a constant problem.

EMPRESS TOWERS LTD. v. BANK OF NOVA SCOTIA

[1990] B.C.J. No. 2054, 73 D.L.R. (4th) 400, [1991] 1 W.W.R. 537
(B.C.C.A., Taggart, Lambert and Wallace JJ.A.)

LAMBERT J.A.: — [1] The landlord, Empress Towers Ltd., brought a petition under . . . the *Commercial Tenancy Act* . . . against the tenant, the Bank of Nova Scotia, seeking to obtain a writ of possession . . .

[2]   The first lease between the parties was made in 1972. It expired in 1984. A new lease was made. It contained this clause:

> 23. RENEWAL: The Landlord hereby grants to the Tenant rights of renewal of this Lease for two successive periods of five (5) years each, such rights to be exercisable by three (3) months' written notice from the Tenant, subject to all the terms and conditions herein contained excepting any right of renewal beyond the second five (5) year period *and excepting the rental for any renewal period, which shall be the market rental prevailing at the commencement of that renewal term as mutually agreed between the Landlord and the Tenant.* If the Landlord and the Tenant do not agree upon the renewal rental within two (2) months following the exercise of a renewal option, then this agreement may be terminated at the option of either party. (Emphasis added)

[3]   The 1984 lease was due to expire on August 31, 1989. On May 25, 1989, the bank exercised its option to renew the lease for a further term of five years from September 1, 1989. On June 23, 1989 the bank proposed a rental rate of $5,400 a month, up from $3,097.92 under the lease that was about to expire. No written reply was received from Empress Towers. There may have been a telephone response. On July 26, 1989 the bank wrote again to Empress Towers. It said that its proposal of $5,400 a month was a rate which independent appraisers had advised the bank was appropriate. It said it was willing to negotiate. Also on July 26, the solicitor for Empress Towers wrote to the bank saying that his client was still reviewing the offer. On August 23, the bank asked whether Empress Towers was making progress in its deliberations and it said that it remained ready to discuss the matter at Empress Towers' convenience. On August 31, on the day when the first five-year term was due to expire, Empress Towers made its response. It said it would allow the bank to remain on a month-to-month basis if $15,000 was paid before September 15, 1989, and a rent of $5,400 a month was paid thereafter. The tenancy that Empress Towers wished to create in that way was to be terminable on 90 days' written notice. (There was evidence that an employee of Empress Towers had been robbed of $30,000 in a branch of the bank and that Empress Towers' insurance had paid only $15,000, leaving a loss to Empress Towers of $15,000.)

[4]   The petition was filed on October 3, 1989, and it was heard on October 30, 1989. The trial judge's reasons were not recorded. The parties are agreed that he said something like this:

> My view is that the landlord has not succeeded in clearing the first hurdle. I am not satisfied that the landlord has done anything with respect to negotiating in good faith. The landlord is now using his own default to justify terminating the lease. Accordingly the application fails and the petition is dismissed with costs in favour of the respondent.

[5]   This appeal has been brought by Empress Towers from that decision.

[6]   The principal question in the appeal is whether the renewal clause was void either for uncertainty or, what is fundamentally the same, as an agreement to agree. The obverse of that question is: If the renewal clause is not void, what does it mean?

[7]   What was said by this Court about interim agreements in *Griffin v. Martens* (1988), 27 B.C.L.R. (2d) 152 at p. 153, 10 A.C.W.S. (3d) 196 (C.A.) is equally true about leases:

> It is not the function of the courts to set interim agreements aside for uncertainty because they contain a clause that is not precisely expressed. If such a clause has an ascertainable meaning, then the courts should strive to find it. . . . As long as an agreement is not being constructed by the court, to the surprise of the parties, or at least one of them, the courts should try to retain and give effect to the agreement that the parties have created for themselves.

[8]   On the other hand, it is well established that if all that the parties say is that they will enter into a lease at a rental to be agreed, no enforceable lease obligation is created. . . . There may, however, be an obligation to negotiate.

[9]   The law is generally to the same effect in England. It is discussed by Mr. Justice Megarry in *Brown v. Gould*, [1972] 1 Ch. 53, where three categories of options are analyzed. The first category is where the rent is simply "to be agreed". Usually such a clause cannot be enforced. The second category is where the rent is to be established by a stated formula but no machinery is provided for applying the formula to produce the rental rate. Often the courts will supply the machinery. The third category is where the formula is set out but is defective and the machinery is provided for applying the formula to produce the rental rate. In those cases the machinery may be used to cure the defect in the formula. What is evident from a consideration of all three categories is that the courts will try, wherever possible, to give the proper legal effect to any clause that the parties understood and intended was to have legal effect.

[10]   In this case, if the parties had intended simply to say that if the tenant wished to renew it could only do so at a rent set by or acceptable to the landlord, then they could have said so. Instead, they said that if the tenant wished to renew it could do so at the market rental prevailing at the commencement of the renewal term. If nothing more had been said then the market rental could have been determined on the basis of valuations and, if necessary, a court could have made the determination. It would have been an objective matter. But the clause goes on to say that not only must the renewal rental be the prevailing market rental but also it must be the prevailing market rental as mutually agreed between the landlord and the tenant. It could be argued that the additional provision for mutual agreement meant only that the first step was to try to agree, but if that step failed then other steps should be adopted to set the market rental. However, the final sentence of cl. 23, which contemplates a failure to agree giving rise to a right of termination, precludes the acceptance of that argument. In my opinion, the effect of the requirement for mutual agreement must be that the landlord cannot be compelled to enter into a renewal tenancy at a rent which it has not accepted as the market rental. But, in my opinion, that is not the only effect of the requirement of mutual agreement. It also carries with it, first, an implied term that the landlord will negotiate in good faith with the tenant with the objective of reaching an agreement on the market rental rate and, second, that agreement on a market rental will not be unreasonably withheld. . . . Those terms are to be implied under the officious bystander and business efficacy principles in order to permit the renewal clause, which was clearly intended to have legal effect, from being struck down as uncertain. The key to implying the terms that I have set out is that the parties agreed that there should be a right of renewal at the prevailing market rental. (I do not have to decide in this case whether a bare right of renewal at a rental to be agreed carries with it an obligation to negotiate in good faith or not to withhold agreement unreasonably).

[11] The conclusion that I have reached is . . . that the requirements are to negotiate in good faith and not to withhold agreement unreasonably. Those requirements carry the same degree of diligence as "best efforts". One would suppose, certainly, that the landlord could not rent to anyone else at a rental rate that the Bank of Nova Scotia would be willing to pay.

[12] The chambers judge decided, on the basis of the affidavit evidence, that the landlord had not negotiated in good faith. It was suggested in argument on the appeal that the chambers judge's finding in that respect was wrong. But there is no basis for interfering with that finding. It was also suggested that the chambers judge erred in not admitting parol evidence, but I am satisfied that there was no sufficient foundation for the admission of parol evidence on the facts of this case.

[13] Section 21 of the *Commercial Tenancy Act* requires that if a writ of possession is not granted then the petition must be dismissed. That was what the chambers judge did. Other proceedings will be required if the parties are unable to resolve their differences.

[14] I would dismiss the appeal.

[WALLACE J.A., dissenting, stated the facts and the course of the negotiations between the parties and continued:] [15] The appellant made several submissions — only one of which I find it necessary to consider — namely, that the renewal clause was void and unenforceable and hence the appellant was not obliged to negotiate a new rental rate.

[16] In considering this submission, it is important to note that the original lease, to which the litigants were parties, provided that the renewal rental should be determined by negotiations or final and binding arbitration.

[17] When the 12-year lease expired, the parties negotiated a new five-year lease. From its form, it is apparent that the parties decided to reject the arbitration formula as a means of resolving any disagreement over the rental rate and to substitute the following provision:

> If the Landlord and the Tenant do not agree upon the renewal rental within two (2) months following the exercise of a renewal option, then this agreement may be terminated at the option of either party.

[18] Accordingly, it is clear that the parties expressly made the further renewal of the lease dependent upon the parties agreeing as to what was an acceptable rental. If the landlord or tenant, for whatever reason, did not agree upon the renewal rental either of them was entitled to terminate the lease.

[19] This court had occasion to consider a very similar provision in *Young v. Van Beneen*, [1953] 3 D.L.R. 702, 8 W.W.R. (N.S.) 702 (B.C.C.A.). . . . Mr. Justice Smith found (p. 703) "the so-called option . . . entirely illusory, being void for uncertainty". . . . Mr. Justice Bird (with whom Mr. Justice O'Halloran concurred) made the following observation (p. 704): "If a material term of a contract is left to future agreement, the contract is not enforceable until that term has been agreed to". . .

[20] In the instant case, to adopt the words of Vaughan Williams L.J., the landlord and the tenant were each to have a discretion, the one as to the rental he would pay, the other the rental he would accept. Until they agreed on that issue, the lease was not to be renewed for a further term and could be terminated by either party.

[21] Since the lease agreement expressly left the essential terms of renewal rent to be determined by the parties mutually at a future time it is unenforceable for uncertainty . . .

[22] It cannot be suggested that, failing agreement, the parties intended the lease rental to be the same as that which prevailed before expiration of the lease term. The parties made this clear when they provided that, in the event of failure to agree on a renewal rent, the lease would be terminated by either party. There is no reason why the court should not enforce their intention as expressed in the renewal cl. 23.

[23] It is a basic principle of the common law of contract that the parties are free to determine for themselves what primary obligations they will accept. Here, by deleting the arbitration provision for determining the market rental and substituting therefor a "market value . . . as mutually agreed between the landlord and tenant", they defined the nature of the obligation they would accept. There is no justification for the court qualifying or interfering with that exercise of their contractual prerogative to do so.

[24] The respondent submits that there should be implied, as a condition of the renewal provision, that each of the parties exercise "good faith" during the two month period provided for "mutually agreeing" on the market rental and that, since the landlord failed to negotiate at all during the two month period, it is open to the court to determine such rental.

[25] I have always had difficulty in determining what constitutes "good faith" in contract negotiations. If one of the parties "stubbornly" or "unreasonably" refuses to accept an offer or make a counter-offer, the other party usually categorizes the first person's conduct as "refusing to bargain in good faith". It usually reflects one party's view of the conduct of the other party where that person remains adamant and refuses to move from a bargaining position he or she has adopted. In the viewpoint of some negotiators, one is expected to commence negotiations by presenting an extreme position and then, in a series of meetings, gradually withdraw to a more reasonable position. Some characterize the procedure as "negotiating in good faith".

[26] In my view, where there is neither fraud nor deceit and one is simply exercising his or her contractual right to maintain a certain bargaining position, the question of "good faith" does not enter into the issue. The presence or absence of "good faith" in such circumstances is simply a subjective judgment by one party of the other's negotiating tactics. It does not afford a sound basis upon which to construe contractual obligations and privileges.

[27] As for implying a condition into cl. 23 that each of the parties "exercise good faith" in reaching a mutual agreement of the renewal rent, I would reject such a suggestion: firstly, because of the vague and indefinite nature of the phrase itself and, secondly, because it is not for the court to make the contract for the parties (*Trollope & Colls Ltd. v. North West Metropolitan Regional Hospital Board*, [1973] 2 All E.R. 260 (H.L.) at p. 268: "The court's function is to interpret and apply the contract the parties have made for themselves".). . . .

[28] In the instant case, the parties were well aware of various contractual provisions which would remove any uncertainty respecting the method of fixing of a renewal rental. They left the rental to be fixed by the future consensus of the parties. They anticipated such consensus might not be attained and provided what the rights of the respective parties would be in such an event. There is nothing before us to indicate such an agreement lacks "business efficacy". I would reject the submission that this contract be reformed by the court implying a term of "good faith".

[29] It is my view that the petitioner has demonstrated a *prima facie* case that the tenant is wrongfully in possession of the premises. I would allow the appeal with costs here and below. . . .

[Leave to appeal to S.C.C. refused (1991), 79 D.L.R. (4th) vii.]

NOTES AND QUESTIONS

1. Do you prefer the majority or the dissent in *Empress Towers*? What type of relief did the court grant? Is it significant that the court only dealt with an interim issue and did not impose an agreement on the parties? What is the effect of the majority judgment?

2. There are a number of factors in *Empress Towers v. Bank of Nova Scotia* that persuaded the majority of the Court of Appeal to give the plaintiff relief. The parties were in an existing commercial relationship and the bank did not claim that it had an enforceable lease, but rather that the lessor had not acted in good faith. The fact that the parties seemed to have agreed on the monthly rental and that a major issue was the lump sum payment that appeared to be related to the landlord's desire to resolve a collateral matter (the $15,000 from the robbery) may have been taken by the Court to be an indication of bad faith. Further, the way in which the issue was presented did not force the Court to do more than dismiss the application for the writ of possession. The bank was not guaranteed a lease; the obligation on the lessor to negotiate in good faith does not prevent the lessor from insisting on terms that might be reasonable but unacceptable to the bank.

     The Court in *Empress Towers* did not have to articulate what the "duty to bargain in good faith" might mean. One likely aspect of an obligation to negotiate in good faith in the context of *Empress Towers* would be to regard the lessor as in breach of this obligation if it gave a lease to a third party on terms that were either as favourable as or more favourable than those it offered to the bank. Such an obligation is often the subject of an express stipulation in a right of first refusal in a lease extension clause.

     A few years after deciding *Empress Towers* the British Columbia Court of Appeal in *Mannpar Enterprises v. Canada*, [1999] B.C.J. No. 850, 173 D.L.R. (4th) 243 (C.A.) did not impose an obligation to negotiate the renewal of a quarry lease when there was only a clause allowing for a five-year extension at a rate "subject to renegotiation". The Court in *Mannpar Enterprises* distinguished *Empress Towers* on the basis that in the earlier case there was reference to the "market rate" in the renegotiation clause, providing a "benchmark" for determining whether the parties were negotiating in good faith.

3. It is hard to believe that the parties to the agreement in *May & Butcher v. The King* or to a commercial lease would care — at least if they were asked at the beginning of the relation — if the court held:

    (a) that the price or rent payable on the renewable was to be treated as if there were no mention of price or rent so that the court could impose a reasonable price or rent; or

    (b) that the court had the power, in default of agreement, to impose a reasonable price or rent.

4. The *Sale of Goods Act* clearly assumes that the court can determine a reasonable price. It is important to remember that the *Sale of Goods Act* primarily envisages one-shot transactions, not long-term supply contracts. The agreement between a landlord and its tenant creates a relational contract, one that should last for an extended period. Neither party to the relation would want to be locked into a fixed rent when market conditions may make the price or rent too high or too low. In addition, there is likely to be a readily available "market" rent that would satisfy both parties. If the parties agree that the rent may be fixed by arbitration, the problems of uncertainty or indefiniteness are avoided and the agreement in enforceable.

5. In an effort to avoid the problems of "agreements to agree", rents on lease renewals are often tied to changes in an index of price levels like the Consumer Price Index. For contracts for the sale of goods, an escalator clause is within the provisions of s. 9(1) of the Ontario *Sale of Goods Act*, as a price "to be fixed", and it may work well in situations where there is likely to be a close correlation between the market price for the thing being bought and changes in price levels generally. However, an automatic escalator clause may not be appropriate for specific prices when changes in price are not closely correlated to prices generally.

The next case explores the issue of "agreements to agree" and is a modern example of the English courts' attitude to the problem.

WALFORD v. MILES

[1992] 2 A.C. 128, [1992] 1 All E.R. 453
(H.L., Lords Keith, Ackner, Goff, Jauncey and Browne-Wilkinson)

[The statement of facts is taken from the headnote. The respondents owned a company, together with premises that were let to the company where the company carried on a photographic processing business. In 1986 the respondents decided to sell the business and the premises, and received an offer of £1.9 million from a third party. In the meantime the appellants entered into negotiations with the respondents, and on 12 March 1987 the respondents agreed "in principle" to sell the business and the premises to them for £2 million and warranted that the trading profits in the 12 months following completion would be not less than £300,000; this written agreement was stated to be "subject to contract" [the English term meaning that there was to be no binding contract to sell until solicitors had drafted it and the parties had executed it]. On 17 March it was further agreed in a telephone conversation between the parties that if the appellants provided a comfort

letter from their bank by a specified date confirming that the bank had offered
them loan facilities to enable them to make the purchase for £2 million, the respondents "would terminate negotiations with any third party or consideration or
any alternative with a view to concluding agreements" with the appellants, and that
even if the respondents received a satisfactory proposal from any third party before the close of business on 20 March 1987, they "would not deal with that third
party and nor would [they] give further consideration to any alternative". [This
was known as the "lock out" agreement.] The appellants duly provided the comfort
letter from their bank in the time specified and on 25 March the respondents confirmed that, subject to contract, they agreed to the sale of the property and the
shares in the company at a total price of £2 million.

On 30 March the respondents withdrew from the negotiations with the appellants and decided to sell to the third party because they were concerned that their
staff would not get on with the appellants and that a loss of staff would put the
warranted £300,000 profit in jeopardy. The appellants brought an action against
the respondents for breach of the "lock-out" agreement of 17 March, collateral to
the negotiations which were proceeding to purchase the business and the premises
subject to contract, under which the appellants had been given an exclusive opportunity to try to come to terms with the respondents. The appellants alleged that it
was a term of the collateral agreement necessarily to be implied to give business
efficacy to it that, so long as the respondents continued to desire to sell the business and the premises, the respondents would continue to negotiate in good faith
with the appellants. It was contended that the consideration for the collateral contract was the appellants' agreement to continue negotiations and the provision of
the comfort letter from their bank.

The trial judge upheld the claim in principle, awarding £700 for special damages arising out of the expenses of the negotiations, with further damages on account of the repudiation to be assessed. The English Court of Appeal held that the
collateral agreement alleged was no more than an agreement to negotiate and was
therefore unenforceable, though allowing the claim for £700 for special damages
based on the misrepresentation of the respondent-vendor in continuing to deal with
third parties. This amount consisted of the expenses incurred in the negotiations
and in the preparation of contract documents. The appellants appealed to the
House of Lords, though the respondents accepted their liability for £700 for special damages and this issue was not argued in the House of Lords.

The appellants pleaded that there was an oral agreement that the respondents
would not deal with any third party, *i.e.*, a "lock-out" agreement, and that there
was also an agreement that the respondents would negotiate with the appellants in
good faith. The appellants further alleged that, by reason of the wrongful repudiation by the respondents of the oral agreement, the appellants lost the opportunity
of completing the sale and purchase of the shares and property, and that the true
market value of the shares and the property was £3 million. The appellants claimed
that they lost the difference between the price which they had agreed to pay of £2
million and the true market value.

LORD ACKNER, having stated the facts, described what had happened at trial and
before the Court of Appeal. He continued:]

*The validity of the agreement alleged in para. 5 of the statement of claim as
amended*

[1] The justification for the implied term in para. 5 of the amended statement of claim was that, in order to give the collateral agreement "business efficacy", Mr. Miles was obliged to "continue to negotiate in good faith". It was submitted to the Court of Appeal and initially to your Lordships that this collateral agreement could not be made to work, unless there was a positive duty imposed upon Mr. Miles to negotiate. It was of course conceded that the agreement made no specific provision for the period it was to last. It was however contended, albeit not pleaded, that the obligation to negotiate would endure for a reasonable time, and that such time was the time which was reasonably necessary to reach a binding agreement. It was however accepted that such period of time would not end when negotiations had ceased, because all such negotiations were conducted expressly under the umbrella of "subject to contract". The agreement alleged would thus be valueless if the alleged obligation to negotiate ended when negotiations as to the terms of the "subject to contract" agreement had ended, since at that stage the respondents would have been entitled at their whim to refuse to sign any contract.

[2] Apart from the absence of any term as to the duration of the collateral agreement, it contained no provision for the respondents to determine the negotiations, albeit that such a provision was essential. It was contended by Mr. Naughton that a term was to be implied giving the respondents a right to determine the negotiations, but only if they had "a proper reason". However, in order to determine whether a given reason was a proper one, he accepted that the test was not an objective one: would a hypothetical reasonable person consider the reason a reasonable one? The test was a subjective one: did the respondents honestly believe in the reason which they gave for the termination of the negotiations? Thus they could be quite irrational, so long as they behaved honestly.

[3] Mr. Naughton accepted that as the law now stands and has stood for approaching 20 years an agreement to negotiate is not recognised as an enforceable contract. This was first decided in terms in *Courtney v. Fairbairn Ltd. v. Tolaini Bros (Hotels) Ltd.* . . .

[4] In the Court of Appeal and before your Lordships Mr. Naughton submitted that . . . *Courtney & Fairbairn Ltd.* . . . [was] distinguishable from the present case, because that which was referred to negotiation with a view to agreement in [that case] . . . was an existing difference between the parties. In the present case, so it was contended, by the end of the telephone conversation on 17 March there was no existing difference. Every point that had been raised for discussion had been agreed. However this submission overlooked that what had been "agreed" on the telephone on 17 March was "subject to contract". Therefore the parties were still in negotiation even in relation to those matters. Further, there were many other matters which had still to be considered and agreed.

[5] Before your Lordships it was sought to argue that the decision in the *Courtney & Fairbairn Ltd.* case was wrong. Although the cases in the United States did not speak with one voice, your Lordships' attention was drawn to the decision of the United States Court of Appeals, Third Circuit in *Channel Home Centers Division of Grace Retail Corp v. Grossman* (1986), 795 F.2d 291, as being "the clearest example" of the American cases in the appellants' favour. That case raised the issue whether an agreement to negotiate in good faith, if supported by consideration, is an enforceable contract. I do not find the decision of any assistance. While accepting that an agreement to agree is not an enforceable contract, the United States Court of Appeals appears to have proceeded on the basis that an agreement to negotiate in good faith is synonymous with an agreement to use best endeavours and, as the latter is enforceable, so is the former. This appears to me, with respect, to be an unsustainable proposition. The reason why an agreement to negotiate, like an agreement to agree, is unenforceable is simply because it lacks the necessary certainty. The same does not apply to an agreement to use best endeavours. This uncertainty is demonstrated in the instant case by the provision which it is said has to be implied in the agreement for the determination of the negotiations. How can a court be expected to decide whether, subjectively, a proper reason existed for the termination of negotiations? The answer suggested depends upon whether the negotiations have been determined "in good faith". However, the concept of a duty to carry on negotiations in good faith is inherently repugnant to the adversarial position of the parties when involved in negotiations. Each party to the negotiations is entitled to pursue his (or her) own interest, so long as he avoids making misrepresentations. To advance that interest he must be entitled, if he thinks it appropriate, to threaten to withdraw from further negotiations or to withdraw in fact in the hope that the opposite party may seek to reopen the negotiations by offering him improved terms. Mr. Naughton of course, accepts that the agreement upon which he relies does not contain a duty to complete the negotiations. But that still leaves the vital question: how is a vendor ever to know that he is entitled to withdraw from further negotiations? How is the court to police such an "agreement"? A duty to negotiate in good faith is as unworkable in practice as it is inherently inconsistent with the position of a negotiating party. It is here that the uncertainty lies. In my judgment, while negotiations are in existence either party is entitled to withdraw from these negotiations, at any time and for any reason. There can be thus no obligation to continue to negotiate until there is a "proper reason" to withdraw. Accordingly, a bare agreement to negotiate has no legal content.

[**LORD ACKNER** also discussed the enforceability of the "lock-out" agreement. He concluded that while an agreement not to negotiate with others for a definite period may be enforceable, no obligation to negotiate with a party could be enforced.]

NOTES AND QUESTIONS

1.　Lord Ackner says (¶ 5) that a "duty to negotiate in good faith is as unworkable in practice as it is inherently inconsistent with the position of a negotiating party". Consider what this statement seems to entail. Bargaining can only be conducted if some agreed standards for communication are accepted. It is, for example, widely accepted that good-faith negotiations require that each party, or each party's lawyer, "black line" or "mark up" each copy of the draft agreement as it is exchanged to identify the changes made. It is customary for lawyers to exchange electronic versions of documents by e-mail to make black-lining easier. A lawyer who failed to do this likely would not be reported to the Law Society for unethical conduct, but he or she would be regarded as seriously hampering the process of negotiation. It is a small change in the law to expand the notion that bargaining in good faith requires the exchange of black-lined documents to other acts.

2.　What Lord Ackner says in *Walford* about the concept of the "duty to negotiate in good faith" being "unworkable" may not be totally consistent with what Denning L.J. says in *Brewer Street Investments Ltd. v. Barclays Woollen Co.*, [1954] 1 Q.B. 428, [1953] 2 All E.R. 1330 (C.A.), *infra*, and with much of what underlies the judgment of the Supreme Court of Canada in *Lac Minerals Ltd. v. International Corona Resources Ltd.*, [1989] 2 S.C.R. 574, 61 D.L.R. (4th) 14, *infra*.

3.   The contract in *Walford v. Miles* was a discrete transaction. In negotiations over relational contracts, the observance of standards of good faith in negotiations may well be an important factor in the overall deal. No one wants to deal on a long-term basis with a person who is hard and expensive to get along with.

4.   If the House of Lords had been faced with the issue in *Empress Towers*, what would it have done?

5.   In *EdperBrascan Corp. v. 117373 Canada Ltd.*, [2000] O.J. No. 4012, 50 O.R. (3d) 425, 9 B.L.R. (3d) 234 (S.C.J.), affirmed [2002] O.J. No. 759, 22 B.L.R. (3d) 42 (C.A.), EdperBrascan owned a controlling 38 per cent of Labatts. Labatts was heavily involved in financing various corporations with Edper. Edper agreed to sell its interest in Labatts to the public and as part of the deal a method was devised to get Labatts out of the Edper corporations, by liquidating its investments. Edper and Labatts entered into a letter agreement, *i.e.*, an agreement drafted as a letter, which, *inter alia*, provided:

> 4. In the event that not all of the Investments have been sold by March 31, 1998, Brascan will on March 31, 1998 purchase the remaining Investments at their Book Values: either for cash or, at Brascan's option, for listed common shares or convertible debentures of equivalent value of Brascan Limited, Great Lakes Power Limited, Noranda Inc., or London Insurance Group. To determine equivalent value, the shares chosen by Brascan shall be valued at (a) 95% of their average trading prices on the Toronto Stock Exchange over the 30 days immediately preceding March 31, 1998, or, (b) should Labatt determine that (a) does not represent equivalent value, at a price mutually agreed. Any shares or debentures transferred to Labatt will be market traded and will be either freely resaleable or, at Labatt's request, a prospectus will be promptly prepared and issued at Brascan's cost by the entity whose shares are being transferred to Labatt to permit the public distribution of such shares.

Edper, the plaintiff, tried to get Labatts to accept shares in a corporation other than one of the four listed in clause 4 in exchange for its investments. Labatts rejected the attempt on the basis that the shares being offered to it were not tradeable. The plaintiff sought a declaration that it had complied with the terms of the agreement; the defendant (Labatts) sought summary judgment dismissing the claim and an order compelling Edper to pay cash. The judge had to deal with the interpretation of the agreement and with the effect to be given to a clause providing that Labatts was to get shares of "equivalent value". Edper argued that the subjective intentions of the parties and evidence of their pre-contract negotiations supported its position. This argument was rejected on the basis that such evidence was excluded by the parol evidence rule.

Lane J. said:

> [47] It was urged upon me that I should follow *Empress Towers*, where there was . . .a finding by the majority that there was an obligation to negotiate in good faith to reach agreement on what was the prevailing market rental in order to enable an option to renew to have efficacy. But, as that court itself said [at ¶10], the key to that finding was the presence of the objective standard of the prevailing market. There was thus some standard against which to measure good faith. The *Empress Towers* court was careful to note that it was not deciding a case of a bare right to renew at a rate to be agreed. In our case, there is no such objective standard set up by the parties since equivalent value is a defined term. Further, the case before me is not a case where the matter to be negotiated was outside the contract, but rather is at the heart of the existing contract.

> [48] A problematic aspect of *Empress Towers* is the passage [at ¶11], in which the majority supports the decision by referring to the analogous case of an implied obligation to "use best efforts" where a contract is subject to the obtain-

ing of financing or a similar provision. That analogy was expressly rejected by
Lord Ackner in *Walford v. Miles*, [1992] 2 A.C. 128 (H.L.). . . .

[49] In the light of these cases, perhaps *Empress Towers* should be regarded as
confined to its very narrow set of facts, and not as authority for a general
proposition that the duty to bargain in good faith exists whenever a negotiation takes place within an existing contract. To some extent this seems to have
happened. In *Mannpar Enterprises Ltd. v. Canada* (1999), 173 D.L.R. (4th)
243 at p. 264, . . . the British Columbia Court of Appeal dealt with a case
where the lessors refused to negotiate a renewal of a licence to remove aggregates from an Indian reserve. There was no reference in the licence to any objective standard for the renewal rate. The court noted the importance in *Empress Towers* of the existence of the ". . . benchmark that could have been capable of objective assessment, namely 'market rental'." At para. 52, the court
reverted to the point, observing that without ". . . a benchmark or a standard
by which to measure such a duty, the negotiation concept is unworkable.". . .
More fundamentally, *Empress Towers*, even confined to its facts, seems out of
step with the high authority in the House of Lords, the Ontario Court of Appeal and elsewhere that a duty to bargain in good faith is not a workable concept from the point of view of enforcement through the courts. . . .

[50] There are certainly obligations upon contracting parties to act in good
faith in some circumstances. Examples include the exercise of a discretion,
Greenberg v. Meffert (1985), 50 O.R. (2d) 755, 18 D.L.R. (4th) 548 (C.A.),
and the duty to use best efforts, *Dynamic Transport Ltd. v. O.K. Detailing
Ltd.*, [1978] 2 S.C.R. 1072, 85 D.L.R. (3d) 19. But these sorts of cases differ
from our own because in them the parties did not expressly agree to a future
negotiation. Nor is the obligation universal: in *Wallace v. United Grain
Growers Ltd.*, [1997] 3 S.C.R. 701 at p. 735 *ff.*, 742, 152 D.L.R. (4th) 1,
Iacobucci J., for the majority of the Supreme Court, rejected the imposition of
a requirement of "good faith" reasons for the discharge of an employee,
whether in contract or in tort, describing the proposed tort as a "radical shift in
the law". However, because of the peculiarly vulnerable position of the employee at the time of discharge, there was an obligation of good faith and fair
dealing in the manner of dismissal, breach of which could be compensated for
by an extension of the period of notice.

[51] The common law rule is that contracts to negotiate are inherently uncertain and therefore incapable of creating binding and enforceable obligations. . .

6.   Do you agree with the assessment of Lane J. that *Empress Towers* is inconsistent with
     Walford?
     Suppose that in a classical bargaining session of the type where seller starts high
     and buyer starts low, the buyer decided part-way through the process to go back down
     again. Would that be bargaining in good faith? What is understood in that kind of bar-
     gaining process?

Letters of Intent

Negotiations are likely to begin with a discussion of the broad outlines of a proposed deal: what price will be paid for what assets or shares? As the negotiations
progress, the broad outlines will take shape and the details will be filled in, often
with the help of lawyers. Once the price has been determined, the method of payment will have to be settled and if that involves payment over time, there will be
questions of interest rates, payment schedules, security interests, etc., to be settled.
Ultimately the terms of the final contract that is signed may be many pages long,

and an untrained reader might find it very difficult to identify the salient parts of the deal.

In many situations, parties would be very reluctant to begin negotiations by putting all the details of the agreement in an offer; not only would it be a poor method of communicating the terms to the other side, it might be a great waste of time. Such a method of setting out all the proposed terms will sometimes be adopted when a party with a well-defined role in a particular business has a standard form of agreement that it either insists should be used or offers as a basis for negotiation. The familiarity of the other party (or its lawyer) with a standard form may make the problems of comprehension manageable. Banks, for example, in part because of their power and in part because their transactions are often highly standardized, are generally able to put their standard forms of agreement forward as the basis for the agreements that they may make with their borrowers.

In many business situations, however, there will not be a "standard form" and it is common for those negotiating a deal to have a "letter of intent" or "agreement in principle" after they have reached an initial agreement on the most important aspects of the deal. This document, often drafted by business persons, not lawyers, sets out the fundamental terms that have been agreed to. It is a basis for further negotiations or for indicating the general nature of the deal, and indicates that the parties are committed at least to the point of being prepared to acknowledge that the terms are the "principles" of the deal.

The problem is that there is not a fixed legal meaning to the term "letter of intent" or "agreement in principle", though with appropriate legal advice the parties can make clear whether or not they intend the document to constitute a binding legal contract. The fact that parties intend to sign a later, fuller and more formal document does not necessarily mean that the letter of intent is not itself a binding contract. As explained by Robins J.A. in *Bawitko Investments Ltd. v. Kernels Popcorn Ltd.* (1991), 79 D.L.R. (4th) 97 (Ont. C.A.) at 103-05:

> As a matter of normal business practice, parties planning to make a formal written document the expression of their agreement, necessarily discuss and negotiate the proposed terms of the agreement before they enter into it. They frequently agree upon all of the terms to be incorporated into the intended written document before it is prepared. Their agreement may be expressed orally or by way of memorandum, by exchange of correspondence, or other informal writings. The parties may "contract to make a contract", that is to say, they may bind themselves to execute at a future date a formal written agreement containing specific terms and conditions. When they agree on all of the essential provisions to be incorporated in a formal document with the intention that their agreement shall thereupon become binding, they will have fulfilled all the requisites for the formation of a contract. The fact that a formal written document to the same effect is to be thereafter prepared and signed does not alter the binding validity of the original contract.
>
> However, when the original contract is incomplete because essential provisions intended to govern the contractual relationship have not been settled or agreed upon; or the contract is too general or uncertain to be valid in itself and is dependent on the making of a formal contract; or the understanding or intention of the parties, even if there is no uncertainty as to the terms of their agreement, is that their legal obligations are to be deferred until a formal contract has been approved and executed, the original or preliminary agreement cannot constitute an enforceable contract. In other words, in such circumstances the "contract to make a contract" is not a contract at all. The execution of the contemplated formal document is not intended only as a solemn record or memorial of an already complete and binding contract but is essential to the formation of the contract itself. . . .

. . .

> If no agreement in respect to essential terms has been reached or the terms have
> not been agreed to with reasonable certainty, it can only be concluded that such
> terms were to be agreed upon at a later date and until that time there would be no
> completed agreement.

For many clients the ideal position from their point of view is to have the other
side irrevocably bound to the deal while they are free to accept it or not as they see
fit! Such an ideal position can, of course, usually only be obtained by paying for
an option and, outside that limited device, either both parties are bound or neither
is.

In some cases, the letter of intent, particularly one drafted by the buyer's solicitor, will make clear that the parties have proceeded some distance towards an
agreement, but that they have not yet reached the stage of a completed deal. Such a
letter will be more than a handshake, in that many of the details of the deal may
have been settled, but the parties may want to make sure (i) that further negotiations occur before a final deal is reached; (ii) that the conditions under which the
negotiations will take place are specified; and (iii) that there is a defined method
for bringing the negotiations to an end. When the parties are bargaining with lawyers at their sides, the letter of intent may make the existence — or more precisely
the non-existence — of an agreement very clear.

A letter of intent drafted by the Buyer's solicitor (and to be sent on the Buyer's
letterhead) may say something like the following:

> The purpose of this letter (the "Letter") is to set forth certain non-binding under-
> standings and certain binding agreements between [the "Buyer"] and [the "Seller"]
> with respect to the possible acquisition of the shares of [the Corporation], on the
> terms set forth below.

PART ONE — NON-BINDING PROVISIONS

> The following numbered paragraphs of this Letter (collectively, the "Non-binding
> Provisions") reflect our mutual understanding of the matters described in them, but
> each party acknowledges that neither the Non-binding Provisions nor any prior or
> subsequent conduct, dealings or action between the parties is intended to create or
> constitute and does not create or constitute any legally binding obligation or agree-
> ment between Buyer and Seller, and neither Buyer nor Seller shall have any recourse
> or liability to the other party based upon, arising from or relating to the Non-binding
> Provisions.
>
> 1. *Transaction.* Buyer would acquire from Seller the shares of [the Corporation]
>   (the "Acquired Shares"). The parties intend that the closing of the proposed
>   transaction would occur before [date] (the "Closing").
>
> 2. *Purchase Price.* [Based on the information known to Buyer on the date hereof],
>   the total consideration for the Acquired Shares would be $_____ (the
>   "Purchase Price"), of which: . . .

Note that in the non-binding provisions the drafter of the letter has not used either
the imperative voice, "Buyer *shall* acquire from Seller . . ." or the future tense,
"Buyer *will* acquire from Seller . . .", but the conditional, "would". The letter
would also deal in the non-binding section with a number of issues that will have
to be settled, *e.g.*, the basis for any purchase price adjustment, any employment
agreement for the principals of the seller and a possible non-competition clause.

The letter of intent will continue with the binding provisions:

PART TWO — BINDING PROVISIONS

In consideration of the significant costs to be borne by Buyer and Seller in pursuing this proposed transaction, and further in consideration of their mutual considerations as to the matters described herein, upon execution by Seller of this Letter or counterparts thereof, the following lettered paragraphs of this Letter (collectively, the "Binding Provisions") will constitute the legally binding and enforceable agreement of Buyer and Seller.

A. *Non-binding Provisions Not Enforceable.* Neither the Non-binding Provisions nor any prior or subsequent conduct, action or dealing between the parties is intended to create or constitute and does not create or constitute any legally binding obligation or agreement between Buyer and Seller, and neither Buyer nor Seller shall have any recourse or liability to the other party based upon, arising from, or relating to the Non-binding Provisions.

B. *Definitive Agreement.* Buyer and its counsel shall be responsible for preparing the initial draft of the Definitive Agreement.

C. *Access.* Seller shall cause [the President of the Corporation] to provide to Buyer complete access to [the Corporation's] facilities, books and records and shall cause the directors, employees, accountants, and other agents and representatives (individually a "Representative" and collectively, the "Representatives") of [the Corporation] to cooperate fully with Buyer and Buyer's Representatives in connection with Buyer's due diligence investigation of [the Corporation] and [the Corporation]'s assets, contracts, liabilities, operations, records and other aspects of its business. Buyer shall be under no obligation to continue with its due diligence investigation or negotiations regarding the consummation of the Definitive Agreement if, at any time, the results of its due diligence investigation are not satisfactory to Buyer for any reason in its sole discretion.

D. *Exclusive Dealing.* From the date hereof until •, Seller shall not [and shall cause [the Corporation] not to], directly or indirectly, through any Representative or otherwise solicit or entertain offers from, provide information to, negotiate with or in any manner encourage, discuss, accept or consider any proposal of any other person relating to the acquisition of the Acquired Shares, [the Corporation's] assets or business, in whole or in part, whether through direct or indirect purchase, amalgamation, consolidation or other business combination (other than sales of assets in the ordinary course). . . .

The binding provisions may include a confidentiality clause (if a confidentiality agreement has not already been signed), a break-up fee (a fee to be paid by the target company to the prospective buyer if the target company is sold to another, intended to compensate for its direct costs and lost opportunity costs), and the clause providing for termination of the negotiations.

Another form of letter of intent focuses on different concerns:

It is the intent of this letter that it set out with sufficient particularity the details of the transaction contemplated by the parties so that the parties may know the general terms of the formal, comprehensive asset purchase agreement (the "Agreement") to be executed by them. This letter is not a binding agreement except to the extent that it establishes:

(i) an obligation on each party to negotiate in good faith with a view to concluding the agreement that will set out their legal rights; and

(ii) mutual obligations of confidentiality between the parties.

Notice that even though this paragraph states that there is no binding contract between the parties, it makes it clear that the parties have a relation that imposes obligations on each of them. As we shall see when we look briefly at the consequences of beginning to negotiate, the relation then created may be not only important but perilous to ignore.

CANADA SQUARE CORP. LTD. v. VERSAFOOD SERVICES LTD.

(1981), 34 O.R. (2d) 250, 130 D.L.R. (3d) 205
(C.A., Brooke, Wilson and Morden JJ.A.)

[The issue was whether an enforceable agreement to lease space for a roof-top restaurant had been made by the parties. The president of the defendant (the prospective lessee) sent a letter to the president of the plaintiff (the developer and prospective lessor), to "confirm our verbal understandings" indicating that the letter "constitutes the general principles of our agreement". At that time, the project was still in the working drawings stage, but it was commercially necessary to make arrangements for a roof-top restaurant at that stage in the building process. (The decision to build a roof-top restaurant must be made at the building design stage; such a restaurant cannot easily be added later.) The letter set out which party was to have responsibility for major aspects of the restaurant design and operation, a formula for rental based on a percentage of gross sales, and the length of the lease, 30 years from the date of substantial completion of the restaurant. The letter specified that in addition to the roof-top restaurant, the defendant would operate coffee wagons and a food stand in the lobby. As requested by the defendant, upon receipt the president of the plaintiff also signed bottom of the letter and sent a copy back to the defendant stating that "This agreement is hereby accepted."

Both parties spent considerable sums to comply with the agreement, and the defendant put up a sign at the site stating that it would be operating the restaurant. Some 18 months after the letter was signed by both parties, the defendant ran into difficulty in arranging financing, and tried to argue that the letter did not constitute a binding agreement, since it was contemplated by both parties that a formal lease would be executed. Though the duration of the lease and a rental formula were set out, some significant terms, such as exactly when the lease was to commence, and when rental payments were due, were not specified. Furthermore, the letter did not specify the exact area to be leased, and referred to a food stand in the lobby "up to a gross amount of 600 square feet" to be operated by the defendant, with the exact location of this facility to be determined by the agreement of the parties.

The Court of Appeal held that a reasonable interpretation of the letter was that it provided for rental of the entire top floor, and that the uncertainty about the stand in the lobby was not fatal to the enforceability of the arrangement.]

MORDEN J.A.: — [1] . . . Alternatively, should it be the case that term lacks sufficient certainty I am prepared to rely upon the direct approach to the issue which is set forth in 1 *Williston on Contracts*, 3rd ed. (1957), at pp. 156-57, as part of his treatment of indefinite subsidiary promises: "It is evident that the question must be one of degree: Is the indefinite promise so essential to the bargain that inability to enforce that promise strictly according to its terms would make it unfair to enforce the remainder of the agreement? If the contract cannot be performed without settlement of the undetermined point, each party will be bound to agree to a reasonable determination of the unsettled point in order that the main promise may be enforced." This principle was applied by the Supreme Court of California in *City of Los Angeles v. Superior Court*, 333 P.2d 745 (1959). In that case one of the terms of an agreement, which was attacked in a taxpayers' suit, provided that the city

> will convey to the ball club 185 acres, more or less, of land presently owned by it in Chavez Ravine and will use its best efforts to acquire at a reasonable cost and convey additional land to make a total of about 300 acres, *reserving, among other things, an oil drilling site not to exceed five acres, the location of the site to be mutually agreed upon by the parties*. (Emphasis added.)

[2]   This is a quotation from p. 749 of the judgment and is a paraphrase of the contract. There were other provisions of a similar nature to which I need not refer at this point. The contract was claimed to be void because it contained promises to agree in the future. Gibson C.J. for the Court referred to the part of *Williston on Contracts* which I have quoted and then said on pp. 750-51:

> *The contract leaves to the future agreement of the parties the location and size, within five acres, of the site to be used for oil drilling*, the nature of the recreational facilities to be constructed and maintained over 20 years on the 40-acre parcel, and the rental to be paid to the city in the event the ball club exercises its right to use Wrigley Field prior to completion of the stadium. *The reservation of an oil drilling site* and the establishment and maintenance of the recreational facilities on the 40-acre parcel *are, of course, important features of the contract, but, in our opinion, the uncertainty with respect to the exact location and size of the drilling site* and the details with respect to the recreational facilities *are matters which should not be treated as rendering the contract void*. There is no indication that the city and the ball club are unable to come to an agreement as to them, and, if the parties cannot do so, the court may determine the matters within the test of reasonableness referred to above, in accordance with the general purposes of the contract. Similarly, the court could fix a reasonable rental for Wrigley Field, if this should ever become necessary. (Emphasis added.)

[3]   I emphasize those parts of the reasons which are particularly applicable to the present case.

[4]   This decision was relied upon in a later California judgment which was concerned with issues respecting the validity of an agreement to lease. I refer to *Wong v. DiGrazin*, 386 P.2d 817 (1963), at p. 827: "A minor possible ground of disagreement in an otherwise complete agreement will not render the agreement uncertain." "Where the matters left for future agreement are unessential, each party will be forced to accept a reasonable determination of the unsettled point."

[The Court held the agreement to be enforceable, observing that "it was very difficult to interpret what the parties had been doing" after the letter was signed by both as "negotiating the terms of an agreement to lease, as opposed to carrying out the project envisaged by the letter". The determination of damages was referred to a Master.]

NOTES

1.   While a lawyer might have foreseen the decision in *Versafood Services* in light of decisions like *Foley*, the decision in the *Versafood Services* case caused some surprise in the Toronto real estate industry as the parties had not signed a formal lease, and at the time there was some criticism of the decision as having taken the defendant by surprise. It is hard for anyone outside the industry involved to know what the expectations of the parties might have been when the letter was sent. If the parties had adequate legal advice when the letter was sent, they presumably could have made clear whether or not this was a binding agreement. In any event, the group of corporations

that make such deals in Toronto, Ontario or even in all of Canada, is fairly small and knowledge of the decision spread quickly among those in the industry, resulting in clearer statements by those involved in this particular industry when signing letters of intent.

2.   The risks created by a decision like that in *Versafood Services* are significantly affected by whether or not counsel realizes that evidence of the business background might be very important. If the judge has knowledge of the business, this may influence the decision, though this knowledge may be imperfect and the use of contextual information not put in evidence by the parties may impair the process of adjudication. Counsel may wish to call witnesses who have knowledge about industry practice and expectations, assuming that the court is willing to receive it and to listen to it.

L.C.D.H. AUDIO VISUAL LTD. v. I.S.T.S. VERBATIM LTD.

[1988] O.J. No. 633, B.L.R. 128
(Ont H.C.J., Southey J.)

[The City of Ottawa invited a number of firms to "pre-qualify" as prospective tenderers for a contract to supply audio-visual and simultaneous translation services to the Congress Centre that was being built. There were negotiations between the City and the firms that sought to be pre-qualified. The City was disappointed that only one bidder, the defendant, was pre-qualified (*i.e.*, had appropriate prior experience with all services), and even the defendant mainly had experience with translation and only limited experience with audio-visual services. The City encouraged the various interested firms to "caucus" and to form groups in which one party with strength in one area would bid for all the services, but subcontract with others with experience in other areas. Discussions occurred with the various companies interested in providing the services, and an arrangement was made that the defendant alone would bid on a contract to provide all the services to the City. Under this arrangement, the plaintiff gave up its chance to bid on the work from the City. The City was closely involved with this agreement, for its interests were affected by the arrangement between the parties. At the City's insistence, the parties signed an agreement that the responsible city employees would recommend that the defendant get the main contract, on condition that:

> I.S.T.S. will negotiate towards entering into a sub-contract . . . with one of the other two companies which were approved for pre-qualification . . .

Lengthy negotiations followed, and the defendant prepared a formal bid for the City. Early in that process, Dodwell Film Services Ltd., the only competitor of the plaintiff for the subcontract with the defendant for provision of audio-visual services, dropped out, and the plaintiff was led to believe that it would get the audio-visual work. Representatives of the plaintiff met several times with the defendant's employees to provide advice about the audio-visual services that would be required, assisting the defendant in preparing its bid to the City. Shortly after the defendant signed the main contract with the City for a five-year term, representatives of the defendant met representatives of the plaintiff in May 1983 and told them that they could only have a one-year subcontract. The plaintiff's representatives were "shocked" that discussions between the plaintiff and defendant had broken down, and the defendant entered into a contract with its own newly created subsidiary to provide audio-visual services. The plaintiff brought an action for damages, alleging that there had been a completed contract.

The court held that, after receiving the contract with the City, the defendant did not negotiate with the plaintiff "in good faith", but concluded that nevertheless the defendant had no liability to the plaintiff.]

SOUTHEY J.: — **[1]** The city representatives took great care to have the parties confirm in writing the agreement reached . . . at the meeting attended by the city and all three potential bidders for the main contract. What was confirmed was an agreement by I.S.T.S. to "negotiate towards entering into a subcontract" with the plaintiff or [the other pre-qualified party]. The general rule is that the law does not recognize a contract to enter into a contract, [or] a contract to negotiate. . . .

[2]　But even if the agreement made at the caucus was more than an agreement to negotiate, the most it could have been was an agreement by I.S.T.S. to subcontract to the plaintiff the video and visual portion of any contract I.S.T.S. might make for the provision of audio-visual and simultaneous translation services at the Centre. Such an agreement would still be a contract to enter into a contract, and would be one in which an essential provision had not yet been determined, namely, the percentage of gross revenues to be paid by the plaintiff for the concession. That term would have been a fundamental part of any subcontract. An agreement that lacks an essential or fundamental item is not a binding contract. . . .

[3]　The authorities on which Mr. Brennan [for the plaintiff] relied in submitting that there was a complete contract are all distinguishable, in my view, because the case at bar is one in which an essential term of the subcontract, namely, the percentage of gross profit to be repaid by the subcontractor, had not been agreed upon. There was no evidence of an understanding that it was to be the same percentage as would be paid by the main contractor, or that it was to be a reasonable percentage determinable by the court from the surrounding circumstances. It was necessary that there be a further meeting of the minds on this essential term. Until that occurred, in my opinion, there could have been no binding contract.

[4]　The plaintiff eventually was agreeable to the suggestion made by I.S.T.S. at the . . . meeting in May, 1983, for the percentages of gross revenue to be paid by the plaintiff in the subcontract under negotiation, but those percentages were part of a proposal by I.S.T.S. in which the duration of the subcontract was reduced from 5 years to one year. The reduced term was not acceptable to the plaintiff, with the result that the proposal of I.S.T.S. containing the percentages was never accepted by the plaintiff. The court must not construct an agreement for the parties. I do not know whether I.S.T.S. would have agreed to the percentages in question as part of a subcontract having a duration of more than one year. The participants in the 1981 discussions apparently contemplated a 5 year term for both the main contract and the subcontract, but that did not settle the term for the 1983 negotiations. To have a complete and binding agreement in 1983, it was necessary for the plaintiff and I.S.T.S. to agree on the duration of the said contract in the context of agreement on the other essential provisions of the subcontract. This did not occur. For the foregoing reasons, I find there was no binding subcontract between the plaintiff and I.S.T.S. for the provision of video and visual services at the Centre or requiring I.S.T.S. to enter into such subcontract with the plaintiff.

[5]　Robert and Harald Thiel [of I.S.T.S.] had enjoyed friendly relations with Kirk Lidbetter and other representatives of the plaintiff from March, 1981, until the spring of 1983. The Thiels gave assurances to representatives of the plaintiff during that period that the plaintiff would receive the subcontract. The conduct of the Thiels in abruptly informing the representatives of the plaintiff in August 1983 that they would not get the subcontract because I.S.T.S. had decided to do the video and visual work itself was, no doubt, a shock and a bitter disappointment to Kirk Lidbetter and the other representatives of the plaintiff. But the shock and disappointment was of the type that frequently occurs in the business world when an employer or customer, actual or prospective, decides to do business elsewhere after having raised a reasonable expectation in an employee or job applicant or supplier that he will be favoured with work or a purchase, but when no legally binding commitment has been made. The conduct of the Thiels showed no consideration for the feelings of their erstwhile friends, but they were under no legal obligation to do otherwise, in my opinion.

[6]   There is no question that the representatives of the plaintiff provided valuable assistance to the architects and engineers designing the Centre. Mr. Di Marino attended 5 or 6 meetings, and Mr. Lidbetter also attended some meetings, but cannot remember the number. No records were kept as to the time spent, and it never occurred to the plaintiff's representatives to make an arrangement for payment for their services in the event the plaintiff was not awarded the subcontract. I am not satisfied that the work done by the plaintiff in connection with the design was anything more than what would have been done by Messrs. Di Marino and Lidbetter for any potential customer from whom they hoped to obtain a valuable contract. It fell far short of constituting the plaintiff a joint venturer, in my judgment, and did not give rise to any promissory estoppel.

[7]   The action is dismissed with costs.

NOTES AND QUESTIONS

1.   Southey J. in *L.C.D.H. Audio v. I.S.T.S.* referred to *Courtney & Fairbairn v. Tolaini*, but made no reference to *Canada Square v. Versafood Services*. Do you think that *Canada Square* is relevant to this situation?

2.   Recall again the cases in Chapter 1 in which the courts awarded damages for the loss of a chance of a benefit. In one group of cases the breach consisted of a failure of the parties to seek in "good faith" to obtain permission to develop land. See, for example, *Multi-Malls Inc. v. Tex-Mall Properties Inc.* (1980), 28 O.R. (2d) 6, 108 D.L.R. (3d) 399 (H.C.J.), affirmed (1981), 128 D.L.R. (3d) 192 (C.A.). Are there justifiable differences between the cases of that type and those that we are now considering? Are there, perhaps, more obvious standards by which to judge the extent to which one "good faith" obligation is discharged when it is a matter of seeking planning permission rather than assessing the reasonableness of negotiating positions?

3.   Notice the issue before the court in *L.C.D.H.* and *Courtney v. Tolaini*. The court was asked whether or not there was a contract between the parties. Recall the problem with similar issues in Chapter 2 in the discussion of reliance as a basis for enforcement. We saw that it was possible to give a remedy to protect reliance even though it might have been hard to say that there was a contract. (See, for example, *Tudale Explorations Ltd. v. Bruce* (1979), 20 O.R. (2d) 593, 88 D.L.R. (3d) 584 (Div. Ct.), *supra*, Chapter 2.) If the case is not one where there is merely the claim for protection of the reliance interest, but the special case of the restitution interest, the claim of the plaintiff is even stronger.

     As we saw, *Foley v. Classique Coaches* would have been, at least partly, a restitution-based claim (though the court would have been unlikely then to have said so, even though it perceived the unfairness of the defendant's position).

     Courtney & Fairbairn v. Tolaini and *L.C.D.H.* might have been better argued (at least in the alternative) as restitutionary claims. Counsel for each plaintiff may have done their clients no favour by seeking, in effect, to enforce a contract seeking expectation-based damages when a restitutionary or reliance-based claim might have got the plaintiff some compensation for the benefit that it would never have gratuitously provided to the defendant.

4. A question that is important (but which would take us beyond the scope of these materials) is: "What are the characteristics of a relation or the bargaining process that would make it appropriate to hold the parties to an obligation to bargain in good faith and for example, to share information?" The question raises the issue of the context of bargaining and the parties' shared background and expectations. There is, for example, probably no basis for such an obligation to disclose unrequested information in the purchase and sale of a house on the resale market, but such an obligation may be at least indirectly imposed in sales of undeveloped land that cannot be developed without planning permission (as we shall see in Chapters 4 and 5).

5. In some cases the parties have concluded what might have been regarded as a final agreement, but have then treated it as if there were matters still to be negotiated. In some cases, the courts conclude that there was a binding contract, and the later attempt by one party to add or vary terms does not affect the validity of the prior contract unless the other party accepts these modifications. In other cases the courts conclude that while the parties might have been taken to have concluded an agreement on the fundamental terms, the fact that they kept negotiating indicates that there was not the intent to have a binding contract. It is essentially a question of interpretation of factual situations when a court determines whether further discussion — to use a neutral word — between the parties will have the effect of reopening the negotiations so that what might have been a final deal will not to be so treated. Once again, if lawyers are involved, the process may be controlled, but individuals have a tendency to do things without getting advice beforehand and then the best laid plans may go astray. The old cases of *Bristol, Cardiff, and Swansea Aërated Bread Co. v. Maggs* (1890), 44 Ch. D. 616 and *Bellamy v. Debenham* (1890), 45 Ch. D. 481, may be compared as illustrations of this problem.

6. One of the largest monetary awards in history, almost US $11 billion, turned on the question of whether a handshake could create a valid multi-billion dollar contract.

    In *Pennzoil v. Texaco* the crucial issue turned on whether a binding contract had been made to sell the shares of Getty Oil Co. to Pennzoil.

    Pennzoil made the offer for $112.50 per share, which the Board of Directors of Getty Oil voted to accept. The president of Getty came out of the Getty board meeting and shook hands with the president of Pennzoil, saying: "Congratulations . . . you've got a deal". A joint press release was issued setting out the terms and announcing "an agreement in principle". It was contemplated that there would be a detailed "transaction agreement" prepared by lawyers and signed by the parties. Two days later, however, the directors of Getty Oil voted to accept an offer from Texaco for $128 a share, and no agreement between Getty and Pennzoil was ever signed. Texaco believed that since no agreement had been signed, there was no binding contract, and agreed to indemnify Getty for any liability it might have to Pennzoil for breach of contract.

    Pennzoil sued Texaco for the tort of inducing a breach of contract, alleging that their contract with Getty Oil Co. had been breached. The central issue was whether there had been a binding contract between Pennzoil and Getty. The case was tried by a Texas civil jury, which found for Pennzoil after a three-month trial and awarded $11 billion to Pennzoil. Some commentators questioned how much the Texas jury was influenced by sympathy towards the Texas oil men who ran Pennzoil, over the business people who operated Texaco out of White Plains, New York. The case went through various appeals, and was ultimately settled out of court for $3 billion. In one of the Texas Court of Appeal judgments, the court considered whether the oral agreement could have legal effect [729 S.W.2d 768 (1987), pp. 788-89]:

    > . . . [I]f parties do not intend to be bound to an agreement until it is reduced to writing and signed by both parties, then there is no contract until that event occurs. . . . If there is no understanding that a signed writing is necessary before the parties will be bound, and the parties have agreed upon all substantial

terms, then an informal agreement can be binding, even though the parties contemplate evidencing their agreement in a formal document later. . . .

If the parties do intend to contract orally, the mere intention to commit the agreement to writing does not prevent contract formation before execution of that writing, and even a failure to reduce their promises to writing is immaterial to whether they are bound.

However, if either party communicates the intent not to be bound before a final formal document is executed, then no oral expression of agreement to specific terms will constitute a binding contract. . . . The emphasis in deciding when a binding contract exists is on intent rather than on form.

It is the parties' expressed intent that controls which rule of contract formation applies. To determine intent, a court must examine the words and deeds of the parties, because these constitute the objective signs of such intent. . . . Only the outward expressions of intent are considered — secret or subjective intent is immaterial to the question of whether the parties were bound.

Several factors have been articulated to help determine whether the parties intended to be bound only by a formal, signed writing: (1) whether a party expressly reserved the right to be bound only when a written agreement was signed; (2) whether there was any partial performance by one party that the party disclaiming the contract accepted; (3) whether all essential terms of the alleged contract had been agreed upon; and (4) whether the complexity or magnitude of the transaction was such that a formal, executed writing would normally be expected.

While the press release issued when the presidents of Getty and Pennzoil shook hands stated that the "agreement in principle" was "subject to execution of a definitive merger agreement", the Court declined to overturn the jury verdict that the oral agreement was binding.

PROBLEM

Your client wants to purchase a company, 5678 Ontario Ltd., through a share purchase agreement. The negotiations have been conducted with the owners of the company. On day 17 of the negotiations, the parties agree that the president of the company will be given a three-year employment contract on certain terms. The next day your client tells you that she has had second thoughts about the arrangement made to employ the president. She is worried that his character and his ability may be inappropriate for her organization. She instructs you to begin the day's negotiations by announcing this change. As her lawyer, how would you make this announcement? Would you feel obliged to give reasons for the change? (Your client has given you no instructions on this matter.) If you decided not to offer reasons, how would you respond to a request for them?

Do the answers that you come up with say anything about the issues raised in this chapter?

PROTECTION OF EXPECTATIONS ARISING FROM NEGOTIATIONS

The cases examined to this point in this chapter have dealt with the problem of determining whether or not there was an enforceable contract: have the parties have done enough so that the court could reasonably be asked to enforce the agreement? The traditional model of contract formation is based on the mirror image rule of offer and full acceptance, with complete certainty as to terms. Either there is a contract, on clear terms, with full expectancy damages, or there is no contract and no liability.

Canadian courts are struggling with the concept of "good faith" in a range of situations in the negotiation and performance of contracts. The following Supreme Court of Canada decision appears to suggest that Canadian courts have not recognized a "duty to bargain in good faith", but as we shall see later in these materials the courts will, in some cases, protect expectations and reliance, as well as preventing unjust enrichment that may arise as a result of pre-contractual negotiations.

MARTEL BUILDING LTD. v. CANADA

[2000] S.C.J. No. 60, [2000] 2 S.C.R. 860, 193 D.L.R. (4th) 1
(S.C.C., McLachlin C.J.C., Gonthier, Iacobucci, Major, Bastarache,
Binnie and Arbour JJ.)

[The respondent (Martel) leased most of a building it owned in Ottawa to an agency of the government of Canada. Prior to the end of the lease, the respondent's Chief Executive Officer (CEO) met a subordinate of the Chief of Leasing of the Department of Public Works to discuss a renewal of the lease. The Department instructed its Chief of Leasing to obtain a proposed rental rate from the respondent even though it intended to commence a tender process for space. The Chief of Leasing did not contact the respondent when directed to report on the status of negotiations and led his supervisors to believe that a proposed lease rate was forthcoming, but nobody informed the respondent of this expectation. The respondent's CEO twice contacted the Department and eventually had a meeting whose purpose, the CEO believed, was to commence negotiations. The CEO presented proposed rental rates that fell outside a range suggested by an appraisal commissioned by the Department. The CEO heard rumours that a tendering process was to begin and telephoned the Chief of Leasing. The parties met on the same day that an expression of interest was advertised to solicit interest in the tender. The CEO said he left the meeting with an understanding that the Chief of Leasing would recommend a lease renewal if he offered a rate of $220 per square metre. Two days after the meeting, the CEO advised the Chief of Leasing that he could offer that rate; however, the Department decided that remaining terms would have to be settled that day. The respondent could not respond that quickly. Its offer was rejected and tender documents were issued.

The respondent participated in the tendering competition, and submitted the lowest bid, but after adjustments the agency accepted another tender. The respondent sued the government. For reasons discussed above, the Supreme Court held that under the terms of the tender document, the Department had to conduct a "fair" tendering process but could adjust the bids to determine which bid to accept.

The Federal Court of Appeal, [1998] 4 F.C. 300, 163 D.L.R. (4th) 504, held that the government breached a tort duty of care in its conduct of the negotiations, depriving the respondent of the opportunity to negotiate a renewal of the lease. The Supreme Court of Canada held that there is no tort for liability for negligence in commercial negotiations.]

IACOBUCCI and MAJOR JJ.: —

. . .

[62] First, the very object of negotiation works against recovery. The primary goal of any economically rational actor engaged in commercial negotiation is to achieve the most advantageous financial bargain . . . in the context of bilateral negotiation, such gains are realized at the expense of the other negotiating party. . . .

. . .

[65] In essence, Martel claims that the appellant was negligent in not providing it with adequate information concerning the appellant's bargaining position or its readiness to conclude a renewal. The appellant's conduct in negotiating with Martel might be construed as "hard bargaining". The Department's agents displayed casual contempt towards Martel and its personnel as illustrated by broken appointments and general disregard of the minimal courtesy Martel could have reasonably expected. However indifferent the agents of the Department appear from the record, that by itself does not create a cause of action. Doubtless, the appellant's ability to assume such a position in relation to Martel was due to its dominant position in the Ottawa leasing market. The foregoing all point to the advantages enjoyed by the Crown, but do not point to liability.

[66] In many if not most commercial negotiations, an advantageous bargaining position is derived from the industrious generation of information not possessed by the opposite party as opposed to its market position as here. Helpful information is often a by-product of one party expending resources on due diligence, research or other information gathering activities. It is apparent that successful negotiating is the product of that kind of industry.

[67] It would defeat the essence of negotiation and hobble the marketplace to extend a duty of care to the conduct of negotiations, and to label a party's failure to disclose its bottom line, its motives or its final position as negligent. Such a conclusion would of necessity force the disclosure of privately acquired information and the dissipation of any competitive advantage derived from it, all of which is incompatible with the activity of negotiating and bargaining.

[68] . . . [T]o impose a duty in the circumstances of this appeal could interject tort law as after-the-fact insurance against failures to act with due diligence or to hedge the risk of failed negotiations through the pursuit of alternative strategies or opportunities. . . .

[69] Notwithstanding Martel's hope that the negotiations would produce a favourable outcome, it could at any point have concluded that the Department was not serious or interested in concluding a renewal of the Martel Building lease, but simply delaying for an undisclosed reason and seeking other potential landlords. While Martel may have suffered from its innocence and optimism, at least some of the responsibility for the delays in communication evident in this appeal can be attributed to it. The retention of self-vigilance is a necessary ingredient of commerce.

[70] . . . [T]o extend the tort of negligence into the conduct of commercial negotiations would introduce the courts to a significant regulatory function, scrutinizing the minutiae of pre-contractual conduct. It is undesirable to place further scrutiny upon commercial parties when other causes of action already provide remedies for many forms of conduct. Notably, the doctrines of undue influence, economic duress and unconscionability provide redress against bargains obtained as a result of improper negotiation. As well, negligent misrepresentation, fraud and the tort of deceit cover many aspects of negotiation which do not culminate in an agreement.

[71] A concluding but not conclusive fifth consideration is the extent to which needless litigation should be discouraged. To extend negligence into the conduct of negotiations could encourage a multiplicity of lawsuits. Given the number of negotiations that do not culminate in agreement, the potential for increased litigation in place of allowing market forces to operate seems obvious.

[72] For these reasons we are of the opinion that, in the circumstances of this case, any *prima facie* duty is significantly outweighed by the deleterious effects that would be occasioned through an extension of a duty of care into the conduct of negotiations. We conclude then that, as a general proposition, no duty of care arises in conducting negotiations. While there may well be a set of circumstances in which a duty of care may be found, it has not yet arisen.

[73] As a final note, we recognize that Martel's claim resembles the assertion of a duty to bargain in good faith. The breach of such a duty was alleged in the Federal Court, but not before this Court. As noted by the courts below, a duty to bargain in good faith has not been recognized to date in Canadian law. These reasons are restricted to whether or not the tort of negligence should be extended to include negotiation. Whether or not negotiations are to be governed by a duty of good faith is a question for another time.

. . .

NOTES AND QUESTIONS

1. The analysis of the Supreme Court is based on an argument that the government committed a tort. The tort claim was based on the argument that the government owed the plaintiff a duty of care. The Supreme Court asked (¶48):

    > Was there a sufficiently close relationship between Martel and the Department so that, in the reasonable contemplation of the Department, carelessness on its part might cause damage to a party such as Martel with whom it negotiated?

    This question was answered in the affirmative. The Court then asked (¶54):

    > Are there any policy considerations that serve to negative or limit (a) the scope of the *prima facie* duty of care (b) the class of persons to whom it is owed or (c) the damages to which a breach of it may give rise?

    The summary answer given to this question was:

    > [55] Notwithstanding our finding of proximity above, there are compelling policy reasons to conclude that one commercial party should not have to be mindful of another commercial party's legitimate interests in an arm's length negotiation.

    The "policy reasons" are outlined in the extract above. What is curious about the Supreme Court's reasoning is that it focuses on the law of torts and on the question of whether the defendant owed the plaintiff a tort duty to disclose information in the course of negotiations that did not result in the formation of a contract. As we shall see later in these materials, despite this seemingly broad statement, there are situations in which the courts do expect one commercial party to be mindful of another party's party's legitimate interests, even in an arm's-length negotiation.

2. Although it is certainly correct to say that parties negotiating do not, in general, have a positive duty to disclose information in the course of negotiating, and may, for example, "bluff" about their true intentions, there are clearly obligations that may arise in the course of negotiations. As we shall see later in this chapter, as well as later in these materials, there are situations in which a failure to engage in "decent conduct" in precontractual negotiations may result in legal liability. This could be characterized as a "duty to bargain in good faith", though the courts have generally chosen not to use this term. Perhaps one reason that the courts have tended to avoid articulating a general "duty to bargain in good faith" is that this term has a specific meaning in the context of negotiations governed by labour legislation (*i.e.*, collective bargaining with a

union), where the taking of an unreasonable position may have legal consequences. It is, however, important for students (and lawyers) to appreciate that the courts do impose obligations of "commercial decency" in regard to pre-contractual conduct.

An obligation to act in "good faith" may be seen as no more than an obligation to behave decently, which does not require one to be a whit less hard-nosed a bargainer or to disclose anything that one wants to keep confidential. It does not require one to subordinate one's interests to those of the other; it just means: behave decently and honourably, do not mislead and do not be unscrupulous. These standards of conduct are generally accepted by lawyers and their clients as part of the context within which bargaining takes place.

Decent behaviour is *as a matter of course,* scrupulously observed by solicitors acting in negotiations when they "black-line" a draft to bring to the attention of the other side the changes that have been made in the draft. Not only does the practice of black-lining reduce the costs of negotiation (because points settled on and not changed do not have to be checked for surreptitious changes), it is the open acknowledgment of the requirement of decent behaviour. The lawyer who does not black-line his or her drafts will quickly get a reputation as someone who is untrustworthy and expensive to deal with. In the long run, such a lawyer will only harm his or her career by ignoring the generally acknowledged requirement to behave decently.

The obligation to black-line will be acknowledged the moment one party receives a draft from the other and makes changes to it — there are computer programs to automate the process of black-lining. The recognition of the obligation does not depend on the existence of the contract or anything other than the fact that the parties are negotiating.

3. In *Big Quill Resources Inc. v. Potash Corp. of Saskatchewan Inc.*, [2000] S.J. No. 462, [2000] 10 W.W.R. 465, 195 Sask. R. 144 (Q. B.) varied, [2001] S.J. No. 128 [2001] 7 W.W.R. 221, 203 Sask. R. 298 (C.A.) the plaintiff bought feed-stock from the defendant under a contract which defined the price as an average of the defendant's costs. In the initial agreement, costs were defined as including only provincial *sales* taxes. When the agreement was amended, the word "sales" was surreptitiously removed on the instructions of the president of the defendant without notice to anyone else working for the defendant or to the plaintiff. (It is not clear from the facts whether counsel for the defendant simply did not bring the change to the attention of the plaintiff's counsel or was instructed not to do so: the latter is more probable.) The plaintiff paid the price calculated under the new formula for a time until it realized that the formula had been changed. The plaintiff claimed that the contract should be rectified, *i.e.*, that the secret amendment made by the defendant should be removed, and that it was entitled to recover what it had overpaid. The plaintiff's claim for rectification succeeded on the basis of "unilateral mistake". As a result, the plaintiff was entitled to recover the charges that it had had to pay under the amended agreement and to which the defendant was not entitled. The Court of Appeal, in a very short judgment, dismissed the appeal on the principal issue.

Big Quill can be seen as a simple case of a mistake made by the plaintiff that was induced by the defendant. (Similar cases and the legal remedy of rectification will be examined in Chapter 5.) The case can, however, also be regarded as a case in which the court recognized a duty on the part of the defendant to behave decently in the negotiations, *i.e.*, to bring the change proposed to the notice of the plaintiff so that it could at least be bargained over. Although the parties were bargaining over an amendment to an existing contract, it is hard to imagine that the result would have been different if the change had been made in the course of the negotiations for the first contract, *i.e.*, before the parties were in a contractual relation. (There was some evidence that it was the plaintiff who had surreptitiously inserted the word "sales" in the course of the earlier negotiations and, while the defendant argued that the "engineer was hoist with his own petard" (or that the "biter was bit"), the fact was that the defendant had not complained when it realized what had been done earlier. Had it complained, it might have been entitled to relief.)

It may, of course, be an important question whether one party has to bring to the other's attention all the significant terms of the document that the other is asked to sign. In *978011 Ontario Ltd. v. Cornell Engineering Co.* (2001), 198 D.L.R. (4th) 615, 12 B.L.R. (3d) 240 (Ont. C.A.), the plaintiff — actually his personal corporation — sued for breach of an employment contract. The question before the court was whether a special term of the contract of employment was enforceable by the plaintiff. The plaintiff had taken a standard form provided by his professional association of engineers and amended it to suit his situation. The amended standard form agreement was shown to the president of the defendant but the change made by the plaintiff was not drawn to the other's attention. The plaintiff made no effort to conceal the changes and he invited the president to read the contract over. (There was no evidence that the president was familiar with the standard contract.) In any event, the president signed the contract without reading it. The Ontario Court of Appeal held that a party has an obligation to read carefully what he is being asked to sign, and that it was not a breach of any obligation on the other party not to bring the special features of the agreement to the other's attention. Again, the Court of Appeal said that there was no obligation of "good faith" on parties who are negotiating.

Big Quill and *Cornell Engineering* are not necessarily inconsistent, and what was said in the latter case about the absence of a general obligation of good faith in negotiations was unnecessary to the decision. One difference between the two cases lies in the fact that in *Big Quill*, the defendant's president intended to mislead the plaintiff and (perhaps because he resented what the plaintiff had done to him before) was happy to sneak in the change to the draft. Another is to draw a distinction between the situation where the parties are exchanging drafts and one where, as it were, a first draft is shown to the other for the first time. In this latter case, the other can scarcely complain if it is caught by surprise if it signs the contract without reading it.

The practice of solicitors of black-lining documents will undoubtedly continue unaffected by the general comments about the absence of a duty to negotiate in good faith. The question that remains is why Canadian courts persist in denying an obligation that every solicitor acknowledges underlies his or her conduct of negotiations. If solicitors (and clients) acknowledge the obligation, what reasons can there be for the courts to deny that it exists? The legal profession undoubtedly recognizes certain obligations of "good faith" or "decency" in negotiations; indeed, so do the courts, though judges have been reluctant to use the term "good faith" to describe these duties or expectations for the negotiation of contracts.

4. There are similar issues of "good faith" or commercial decency that arise in regard to the performance of contracts. Case law widely recognizes an obligation to behave decently in the performance of contracts. Although there is also some judicial reluctance to explicitly use the term "good faith" in regard to issues of performance, courts seem somewhat more willing to explicitly recognize an obligation of good faith to act when performing a contract. In *Le Mesurier v. Andrus* (1986), 54 O.R. (2d) 1, 25 D.L.R. (4th) 424 (C.A.), where the defendant-purchaser relied on a very technical interpretation of a clause in the standard agreement of purchase and sale of land, Grange J.A., giving the judgment of the Court of Appeal, said (p. 7 O.R.):

> I think the purchaser's reliance upon this clause can be described as "capricious or arbitrary" where the vendors had removed the curb and replaced it within the lot line so that it did not encroach on the adjacent lot, and I cannot find her action to be "reasonable and in good faith" . . . Vendors and purchasers owe a duty to each other honestly to perform a contract honestly made. As Middleton J. put it in *Hurley v. Roy* (1921), 50 O.L.R. 281 at p. 285, 64 D.L.R. 375 at p. 377 "The policy of the Court ought to be in favour of the enforcement of honest bargains . . ."

> The approach may be merely an example of the development of an independent doctrine of good faith in contract law at least in the performance of contracts, one explicitly set forth in the American Uniform Commercial Code

and in the American Restatement and exhibited, although perhaps in disguised form, in many English and Canadian cases . . .

In *Gateway Realty Ltd. v. Arton Holdings Ltd.* (1991), 106 N.S.R. (2d) 180, 288 A.P.R. 180 (S.C.), the question was the extent to which the terms of a lease could be relied on deliberately to frustrate the efforts of a landlord to operate a shopping centre profitably. Kelly J. said (pp. 191-92):

> The law requires that parties to a contract exercise their rights under that agreement honestly, fairly and in good faith. This standard is breached when a party acts in a bad faith manner in the performance of its rights and obligations under the contract. "Good faith" conduct is the guide to the manner in which the parties should pursue their mutual contractual objectives. Such conduct is breached when a party acts in "bad faith" — conduct that is contrary to community standards of honesty, reasonableness or fairness. The insistence on a good faith requirement in discretionary conduct in contractual formation, performance, and enforcement is only the fulfilment of the obligation of the courts to do justice in the resolution of disputes between contending parties.

The decision of the trial judge was upheld by the Nova Scotia Court of Appeal, (1992), 112 N.S.R. (2d) 180, 307 A.P.R. 180. That Court did not expressly deal with the issue of good faith that formed an important aspect of the judgment of the trial judge. The Court of Appeal was content to agree with him that the lease had been breached and that the landlord was entitled to rescind the lease, re-take possession and re-let the premises. The conclusion that the lease had been breached is, however, consistent with the view of the trial judge that the breach consisted of a failure to act in good faith.

In *GATX Corp. v. Hawker Siddeley Canada Inc.* (1996), 27 B.L.R. (2d) 251 (Ont. Ct. (Gen. Div.) [Commercial List]), a case involving a "cute" attempt to avoid restrictions in a shareholders' agreement, Blair J., in enforcing the agreement, said (p. 276, ¶72): "This is an illustration of the application of the good faith doctrine of contractual performance, which in my view is part of the law of Ontario."

5. The Supreme Court in *Martel* acknowledged that there may be other tort actions that may arise in pre-contractual situations, such as negligent misrepresentation and fraud. These actions will be explored in Chapter 5.

The recognition of an obligation to behave decently, does not, as *Martel* and cases like *L.C.D.H. Audio Visual* indicate, mean that the expectations of those engaged in the negotiations will be met by the imposition of a deal. One important issue is whether, even if the courts are not prepared to find that there is an enforceable contract, there is some basis for an intermediate position. In the past half-century courts have begun to recognize some basis for finding an intermediate position — a position where there may be some protection for one party, but not necessarily the protection that would be afforded by an enforceable agreement.

There are, for example, cases in which there may be significant, reasonable reliance by one party on one part of an agreement, acting in the expectation that a full agreement will be concluded. If no deal is made, in some cases it may be appropriate to provide some compensation for losses without imposing full contractual (*i.e.*, expectancy) liability.

An important aspect of the beginning of negotiations is that one party, to interest the other in the proposed deal, may disclose to the other information that is confidential and very valuable. This disclosure would never have been made had the parties not had the intention — or at least the hope — of being able to reach an agreement on the terms of the deal. If the deal is made, the parties would both make use of the information that was disclosed. If no deal is made, is there an obligation not to disclose the information and, if so, what are the terms of this obligation?

Restitution and Reliance

In *Courtney and Fairbairn Ltd. v. Tolaini Brothers (Hotels) Ltd. (supra)*, Lord Denning stated that the courts would not enforce an agreement to agree, and that there was therefore no enforceable promise by the defendant to pay for the information about sources of financing that it had received. The English Court of Appeal was not asked in that case to consider whether the plaintiff's restitution interest could be protected by something other than the enforcement of the contract. The following cases illustrate that in some cases courts may find a way to protect what looks like what Fuller and Perdue called the reliance or restitution interests (though the judges in these cases do not use these terms in the same way as Fuller and Perdue).

The next case was decided by Lord Denning in 1954, though he did not mention it in *Courtney*, which he decided in 1975.

BREWER STREET INVESTMENTS LTD. v. BARCLAYS WOOLLEN CO.

[1954] 1 Q.B. 428, [1953] 2 All E.R. 1330
(C.A., Somervell, Denning and Romer L.JJ.)

[The parties were negotiating a lease. The prospective tenant wanted certain work done on the premises. After the rent had been agreed to for an initial 21-year term, the prospective tenant wrote to the owner requesting certain alterations to be made to meet its specific needs, and agreeing to pay for any work done. When the defendant-tenant wrote, it was clear that there was no binding lease, since the negotiations were "subject to contract" (an English legal term meaning that there is no binding contract until the solicitors negotiate a formal contract and it is signed by the parties). The landlord began work on the premises and incurred expenses. The lease was never executed, as the parties could not agree whether the tenant should have an option to purchase the premises at the end of the lease. The landlord sued to recover the costs incurred in doing the work, even though the work was stopped when negotiations broke down, and the defendant never took possession.]

DENNING L.J.: — [1] This case raises questions of considerable interest. The landlords seek to recover from the prospective tenants the moneys which they have had to pay to their own contractors for the work done on the alterations before the negotiations for the lease broke down. The question is whether they can do so.

[2] It is not easy to state the legal basis of the landlords' claim. The difficulty arises because, although the prospective tenants agreed to pay the cost of the alterations, nevertheless those alterations were never completed. The work was abandoned before it was finished. Once the negotiations for a lease broke down, both sides realized that the work must be stopped. It was a very sensible thing to do, but it means that the landlords cannot sue for the price as on a completed contract. Nor can they sue the prospective tenants for damages for breach of contract, because the prospective tenants have not been guilty of a breach.

[3] . . . They clearly cannot recover on a quantum meruit as ordinarily understood. The way they put their claim on this item and the others in the statement of claim is money paid on request. The prospective tenants, however, made no request in fact to the landlords to pay the money. Their request, if any, was to pay on completion of the work, and it was not completed. In these circumstances, the

proper way to formulate the claim is on a request implied in law, or, as I would prefer to put it in these days, on a claim in restitution.

[4]   It is clear on the facts that the parties proceeded on a fundamental assumption — that the lease would be granted — which has turned out to be wrong. The work done has been wasted. The question is: on whom is the loss to fall? The parties themselves did not envisage the situation which has emerged and did not provide for it; and we do not know what they would have provided if they had envisaged it. Only the law can resolve their rights and liabilities in the new situation, either by means of implying terms or, more simply, by asking on whom should the risk fall. . . .

[5]   [The question to ask is:] what was the reason for the negotiations breaking down? If it was the landlords' fault, as, for instance, if they refused to go on with the lease for no reason at all, or because they demanded a higher rent than that which had been already agreed, then they should not be allowed to recover any part of the cost of the alterations. Even if the landlords derived no benefit from the work, they should not be allowed to recover the cost from the prospective tenants, seeing that it was by their fault that the prospective tenants were deprived of it.

[6]   On the other hand, if it was the prospective tenants' fault that the negotiations broke down, as for instance, if they sought a lower rent than that which had been agreed upon, then the prospective tenants ought to pay the cost of the alterations up to the time they were stopped. After all, they did promise to pay for the work, and they should not be able to get out of their promise by their own fault, even though the alterations were not completed. It is a very old principle laid down by Sir Edward Coke that a man shall not be allowed to take advantage of a condition brought about by himself.

[7]   I do not think, however, that in the present case it can be said that either party was really at fault. Neither party sought to alter the rent or any other point which had been agreed upon. They fell out on a point which had not been agreed at all. From the very beginning the prospective tenants wanted an option to purchase, whereas the landlords were only ready to give them the first refusal. Each of them in the course of the negotiations sought on this point to get more favourable terms — the prospective tenants to get a firm option to purchase, the landlords to give a first refusal of little value — but their moves in the negotiations can hardly be considered a default by one or other.

[8]   What, then, is the position when the negotiations go off without the default of either? On whom should the risk fall? In my opinion the prospective tenants ought to pay all the costs thrown away. The work was done to meet their special requirements and was prima facie for their benefit and not for the benefit of the landlords. If and in so far as the work is shown to have been of benefit to the landlords, credit should be given in such sum as may be just. Subject to such credit, the prospective tenants ought to pay the cost of the work, because they in the first place agreed to take responsibility for it; and when the matter goes off without the default of either side, they should pay the costs thrown away. There is no finding here that the work was of any benefit to the landlords, and in the circumstances the prospective tenants should, I think, pay the amount claimed.

[9]   [Counsel for the defendant] argued that . . . it was not right . . . to ask whose fault it was, or on whom should the risk fall, because each side had an absolute right to withdraw from the negotiations: and could not be said to be at fault in do-

ing so. He . . . argued that, even if the landlord, for instance, demanded a higher rent and thus caused the negotiations to fall through, he could still recover the cost of the alterations. I do not think that that is right. Estate agents are employed on the footing that they get a large commission if a sale is completed, but nothing if it is not. They take the risk of the deal falling through. The cases on the subject are, therefore, illustrations of the same test; on whom in all the circumstances should the risk fall?

[10] In the present case I think that the risk should fall on the prospective tenants and that they should pay the costs of the alterations . . . the appeal should be dismissed.

QUESTIONS, NOTES AND PROBLEMS

1. What is the basis for the imposition of liability on the defendants? While Lord Denning refers to this as a claim "in restitution", he is clearly not using the term in the same way as Fuller and Perdue because the defendant obtained no benefit from the expenses incurred by the plaintiff; it is not a case of the "double difference".

2. Lord Denning says that the negotiations collapsed without the "fault" of either party. What do you think that he means by "fault" in this context? The idea that someone can be at fault assumes that there is a standard by which their conduct may be measured: fault is, after all, a failure to reach some applicable standard. Draft a statement of the standard that you think Denning L.J. is applying.

    If the word "fault" is used in this case as a possible basis for liability, why could there not be a similar finding of "fault" in respect of an obligation to bargain in good faith and an award of damages for such "fault"? The discussion about "fault" for negotiations breaking down, and the difficulty in determining it, may point to an important concern that has led the courts to say that ordinarily breach of an agreement to agree does not create liability.

3. Is it significant that the losses in *Brewer Street Investments* were easy to calculate?

4. Lord Denning clearly wanted to protect the plaintiff in *Brewer Street Investments* and counsel had the skill to offer him a way to do this. It is unclear whether counsel in *Courtney v. Tolaini* considered the possibility of an argument along the lines of *Brewer Street Investments* and rejected it as giving the client less than he wanted, or whether counsel did not see the relation between the two types of claims. Since Lord Denning also decided *Courtney v. Tolaini,* one might expect that if counsel for the plaintiff had put the case on some other basis than a claim for full expectancy damages, the plaintiff would have received something for the information that, on the facts of the case, he had no intention of providing gratuitously.

BREWER v. CHRYSLER CANADA LTD.

[1977] A.J. No. 420, [1977] 3 W.W.R. 69
(Alta. S.C., H.J. MacDonald J.)

[The plaintiff had several years' experience in the car-selling business, working as an employee for various dealers. The plaintiff had been approached in August 1975 by representatives of the defendant to see if he would be interested in establishing his own new dealership, selling the defendant's cars. The plaintiff agreed to make an application for the dealership. He was told that $55,000 capital would be needed, which he was able to raise. He began to make other preparations for opening his business. In October 1975, his employer, a dealer for a competitor of the defendant, required him either to abandon the plans for his own dealership or to resign. While he was told that his dealership application could only be formally accepted "by head office", the local representatives of the defendant told him that they highly recommended him and he was led to believe that the approval would "follow as a matter of course".

With the knowledge of the defendant's representatives, the plaintiff resigned his position. He continued to work on setting up the new dealership, and had the support of the defendant's representatives, who, for example, provided him with a car and took his order for 200 new cars for the proposed dealership. There was a delay in obtaining premises for the dealership, and the plaintiff had to use some of his capital to live and pay expenses for the business. When the defendant learned that he no longer had the full amount of required capital, it refused to give him the dealership. No contract had been executed by the parties when the negotiations were broken off. However, the defendant was able to secure another person to take over the dealership, using the staff whom the plaintiff had recruited, as well as receiving the benefit of some of the other preparatory work that the plaintiff had done. The plaintiff sued for breach of contract and in the alternative for *quantum meruit* relief.]

H.J. MacDonald J.: — **[1]** At this time [of deciding to resign from his employment] the plaintiff received a letter from the defendant stating:

> This letter will confirm that Chrysler Canada Ltd. is prepared to enter into an Agreement with yourself whereby you will merchandise Chrysler and Dodge automotive products, under the terms of the said Agreement, in the City of Calgary, upon the satisfactory resolution of the following items:
>
> 1. That approval is granted to your application as an investor in a dealership company under our Dealer Enterprise Investment Plan.
>
> 2. That a minimum of $55,000.00 will be invested by you in such a dealership company. . . .
>
> The commencement date of this proposed dealership is dependent upon the availability of the premises now occupied by Tower Dodge Ltd., 511 Centre Street, Calgary.
>
> We anticipate a response within the next few weeks on your application and will keep you informed of its progress so that we can work together in completing all other necessary details in establishing the dealership operation. . . .

[2] I find it was made plain to the plaintiff that he could not be appointed as dealer except by head office but he was given to understand that this would follow as a matter of course and that he "was in business". . . .

[3] In November and December 1975 the plaintiff devoted much of his time in visiting other dealerships in Calgary and becoming acquainted with aspects of their operation. This was, I find, suggested to him as a worthwhile activity. He also spent much of his time finding personnel who would be required as department heads or foremen when the new dealership got into business. He ended up by recruiting nine of the ten senior personnel that later became employees of the dealership [when opened by the person who took it over]. . . .

[4] It is obvious that the defendant considered the establishment of a new dealership to its advantage but also it went to a considerable length, after full knowledge of the situation of the plaintiff, to encourage him to carry on with the expectation that he would be accepted. During the months of November, December and January, to use a colloquialism, the plaintiff was "kept on a string". The defendant knew or should have known that the plaintiff had no income and that he would have to live on the capital resources he had at the end of October. The defendant knew the plaintiff was laying out not only his time but also money, which would be to the ultimate advantage of the dealership and therefore indirectly to the advantage of the defendant.

[5]   It is very clear that the expectation or a promise of a dealership was held out to the plaintiff and that after 10th November 1975 he was "in business", though it was recognized there was then no contract binding the defendant to give him a dealership. It was contemplated that the plaintiff would go to trouble and expense and in the normal course of events he would be eventually recompensed. There were assurances held out to the plaintiff as to his eventual position, upon which it was intended he would act and in effect upon which he did act.

[6]   I have considered the words of Denning L.J. in *Central London Property Trust v. High Trees House Ltd.*, [1947] K.B. 130, [1956] 1 All E.R. 256 at 258 where he says:

> But what is the position in view of developments in the law in recent years? The law has not been standing still since *Jorden v. Money*. There has been a series of decisions over the last fifty years which, although they are said to be cases of estoppel, are not really such. They are cases in which a promise was made which was intended to create legal relations and which to the knowledge of the person making the promise, was going to be acted on by the person to whom it was made, and which was in fact so acted on. In such cases the courts have said that the promise must be honoured.

[7]   Although the defendant as promisor did not intend to be bound by a contract, yet it must be inferred, in my opinion, that it did not expect to reap the benefits of the efforts and outlays of the plaintiff without some reasonable compensation. Under the circumstances it would seem to me an award by way of either unjust enrichment or *quantum meruit* would only be equitable.

[8]   As stated by Greer L.J. in *Craven-Ellis v. Canons Ltd.*, [1936] 2 K.B. 403, [1936] 2 All E.R. 1066:

> In my judgment, the obligation to pay reasonable remuneration for the work done when there is no binding contract between the parties is imposed by a rule of law, and not by an inference of fact arising from the acceptance of the services or goods.

[9]   In the text by Goff and Jones, *The Law of Restitution*, p. 270, it is stated:

> It is essential to a *quantum meruit* claim that the services should have been rendered in circumstances which disclose an intention that they should be paid for.

[10]   In the case at bar the services were rendered in the expectation of both parties that the plaintiff would be compensated by being granted a dealership. This did not come about but that fact does not "wipe out" the circumstances that the plaintiff was to be compensated. If it was not to be done by awarding him a contract, it must surely be done otherwise, namely, by an award for his services.

[The judge awarded the plaintiff the amount of the expenditures he had made and the salary he had lost, about $11,000.]

NOTES AND QUESTIONS

1.   Lord Denning denies that the basis for recovery in *Brewer Street Investments* is *quantum meruit* but says that it is "restitution" (using the term "restitution" in a procedural sense, *i.e.*, as a cause of action, rather than as Fuller and Perdue use the term). A claim in *quantum meruit*, *i.e.*, for as much as he deserves, before the procedural reforms of the nineteenth century, was one of the "common counts". These were standard plead-

ing formulae that permitted a party to recover, for example, "money had and received", "goods sold and delivered" and *"quantum meruit"*, *i.e.*, compensation for services rendered. *Deglman v. Guaranty Trust Co.* (*supra*, Chapter 2) was a case in
which the Supreme Court was concerned about the unjust enrichment of the aunt and
gave the nephew a *quantum meruit* claim based, not on what he might have had if the
aunt's contract had been enforced, but on "the fair value of the services rendered to
her".

2. H.J. MacDonald J. in *Brewer v. Chrysler* did not find a contract, either express or to
    be inferred from the parties' course of conduct, but he nevertheless imposed an obliga-
    tion to pay on the basis of a "quasi-contractual" or restitutionary claim. The court in-
    dicated that it was trying to prevent unjust enrichment, but it actually provided com-
    pensation on the basis of the plaintiff's loss. In Fuller and Perdue terms, the focus of
    judicial concern in *Brewer v. Chrysler* seemed to be protection of the restitution inter-
    est, though damages were assessed on a reliance basis. Why did the court, without dis-
    cussion of its rationale, use a reliance-based measure of damages?

3. It is hard to see how the defendant in *Brewer Street Investments* could have been un-
    justly enriched. However, two things are important:

    (a) both courts, the English Court of Appeal and the Alberta Supreme Court, were
         determined to support the claims of the plaintiffs who they felt deserved protec-
         tion; and

    (b) any difficulties in supporting the claims were swept away in broad statements that
         offered some plausible basis for relief, even if neither decision fits with tradi-
         tional legal approaches.

    It is the job of counsel involved in litigation to give the court some basis upon
    which a remedy can be based, some peg on which the court can hang its decision, and
    to convince the court that its sense of fairness not only should be expressed, but has
    adequate doctrinal support. Litigation counsel's task begins when the relation has dis-
    integrated.

4. Similarly, a solicitor involved in advising a party who is negotiating a contract cannot
    think exclusively in terms of "pegs" and legal doctrine. A solicitor who is advising a
    client about its possible rights and obligations under a contract, or in the context of
    negotiations that appear to be breaking down, has to think more broadly. While legal
    doctrine and traditional analysis will affect how negotiations are handled, a solicitor
    advising a client must recognize that a court's sense of fairness and the facts (the cli-
    ent's good faith and reasonableness) are likely to influence how a court will analyze a
    dispute that may be brought before it. An exclusive focus on the possible doctrinal
    "pegs" at any stage is almost certain to lead to advice that is incomplete or misleading.

5. H.J. MacDonald J. in *Brewer v. Chrysler* relies on the *High Trees* decision; he does
    not mention *Combe v. Combe*. Where has the distinction between "swords" and
    "shields" gone? Denning L.J. makes no effort to consider *Combe v. Combe* in *Brewer
    Street Investments*.

6. The general rule is that where a person expends resources in negotiating, or preparing
    a bid or a work proposal that is not accepted, there is no right to recover. This is a
    speculative expenditure. There may, however, be exceptional circumstances in which
    recovery is possible even if no contract is formed. As stated by Gautreau J., in *Magi-
    cal Waters Fountains v. Sarnia* (1990), 73 D.L.R. (4th) 734 (Ont. Gen. Div.) (p. 742):

    > If a person expends time and money to prepare a quotation or proposal, in
    > speculation that he will be awarded a contract and the contract fails to materi-
    > alize, he may get no relief even though the work is done at the request of the
    > other and it benefits the other. But, if the person's work goes beyond the work
    > normally involved in the preparation of a quotation or proposal, with a mutual
    > understanding that the work is not being done gratuitously then recovery

should be available, and this will be so even though the coming into existence of the contract is frustrated by something or somebody else.

(This quotation was accepted as correctly stating the law, though the judgment was reversed on the facts (1992), 91 D.L.R. (4th) 760 (Ont. Div. Ct.).)

For example, in *William Lacey (Hounslow) Ltd. v. Davis*, [1957] 2 All E.R. 712, [1957] 1 W.L.R. 932 (Q.B.D.), a firm of builders was held to be entitled to recover from the defendant the cost of preparing plans and estimates for rebuilding property owned by the defendant. The trial judge held that the builders were led to believe that they would obtain the contract for the actual work to be done. The work done in preparing the plans and estimates went far beyond that normally done by a builder who submits a tender, since it involved providing a detailed statement of costs of the work required to repair war damage, for which the defendant was to receive compensation from the government, as well as an ordinary contractual estimate of the work to be done. When the defendant sold the property without giving the work to the plaintiffs, he was liable to the plaintiffs for the costs of doing this extra work.

7. It is clear that, in appropriate cases, Canadian courts will provide relief for breach of an obligation to do something in "good faith". We have already seen some of the cases that have awarded damages for breach of the obligation to act in good faith in negotiations, and we consider other situations. The traditional statements that there is *no* obligation to act in good faith in negotiations may not accurately reflect what the courts do, though clearly there are limits to any legal obligations that arise to act in good faith in negotiations.

PROBLEM

Farmer makes an application for insurance on a form provided by Insurer that states that Farmer will pay all premiums, and that the policy, if issued, will run from the date of the application. One month later, Insurer notifies Farmer that his application has been rejected. That day Farmer suffers a loss that would have been covered by the policy if one had been issued. Farmer can show that if he had been notified earlier, he would have been able to obtain insurance elsewhere. What would you advise Farmer to do? What arguments would you make on Farmer's behalf in any action he might bring against Insurer?

Duty of Confidentiality

Duties of confidentiality arise in many different contexts. The employee who uses or discloses confidential information about his or her employer's business may be sued for damages. Brokers and others involved in the stock market may be prosecuted for using confidential information for their (or their clients') advantage, or may be sued for breach of the statutory restrictions on "insider trading," even if their clients or employers suffer no direct loss. The person who enters into negotiations with another and acquires information about the business and financial affairs of the other may acquire very valuable information. The use — or more accurately the misuse — of that information may entail very serious consequences.

The duties that the law imposes are part of a set of related obligations that protect those who have of necessity to depend on the integrity of others. Some of these duties are statutory, but many are based on well-established doctrines of the common law. Statutory duties include the fiduciary obligations of directors of a corporation and the conflict of interest rules of public officials — from Cabinet ministers to municipal councillors to civil servants. Lawyers have important duties arising under professional ethics codes not to disclose confidential information provided by a client, and prohibiting the use of such information for their own profit.

While a range of obligations of confidentiality may arise in different contexts, the focus of consideration here is on the obligations that may arise when a contractual relation is being negotiated. Additional duties may arise once a contract is formed. The next case is an important decision of the Supreme Court of Canada dealing with the obligations that arise when negotiations between two parties begin, and establishes that there are situations in which the Court will impose obligations of good faith on parties who are negotiating, even if an agreement is not concluded.

LAC MINERALS LTD. v. INTERNATIONAL CORONA RESOURCES LTD.

[1989] S.C.J. No. 83, [1989] 2 S.C.R. 574
(S.C.C., McIntyre, La Forest, Lamer, Wilson and Sopinka JJ.)

[The plaintiff, International Corona Resources Ltd. ("Corona") was a junior mining company, *i.e.*, a relatively new, small company with limited capital. It owned property in Northern Ontario that it believed had large deposits of gold. The development of mining property requires large amounts of capital; usually junior companies seek senior mining companies as partners to help to develop mines on properties that seem promising. Some of the results of exploration are publicized by junior mining companies so that prospective investors may be attracted to promising properties.

The results of some of the work done on the Corona property were noticed by an employee of the defendant, Lac Minerals Ltd. ("Lac"), a senior mining company, which approached Corona with a view to a joint development of the property. Corona offered Lac officials a site visit on 6 May 1981, at which the Lac employees were shown the drill cores and other information that Corona had on the property. From this information, it was clear that neighbouring property owned by a Mrs. Williams (the "Williams property") might also be very valuable and worth acquiring for development. In June 1981 Corona and Lac met to discuss a possible joint venture.

During the time that Lac and Corona were discussing the possible joint venture, Corona was trying first to find Mrs. Williams and then to buy the Williams property. In July 1981 Corona made an offer to Mrs. Williams for her property. Unknown to Corona, Lac was also making an offer to Mrs. Williams, basing its decision to acquire the Williams property on information received from Corona which had not been made public. Mrs. Williams eventually accepted the offer from Lac. When Corona found out what Lac had done, it immediately brought an action claiming that Lac had improperly taken advantage of the information that it had obtained from Corona. Corona later developed the David Bell Mine with Teck Corporation ("Teck") on its property, while Lac developed its mine, the Page Williams Mine, on the Williams property. Both mines were immensely valuable, with the potential to produce billions of dollars worth of gold.

The trial judge, R.E. Holland J., found that Lac and Corona had no contract, but that Lac owed Corona a duty of confidence and a fiduciary duty. The judge made a number of findings of fact which established that Lac knew, on the basis of industry practice, that the information it received from Corona was confidential and that it used that information in negotiating with Mrs. Williams.

At the time of the disclosure of the information, there was no explicit discussion about restrictions on the use of the confidential information by Lac. However, in determining the expectations of the mining industry, the trial judge placed great importance on the admissions made by the president of the defendant Lac during his examination for discovery:

> . . . If one geologist goes to another geologist and says, are you interested in making some sort of a deal and between the two of them, they agree that they should consider seriously the possibility of making a deal, I think for a short period of time that while they are exploring that, that any transference of data would be — I would hope the geologists would be competent enough to identify the difference between published, unpublished, confidential and so on but in the case that they weren't, there was just some exchange of conversation or physical data, then I would say that while both of them were seriously and honestly engaged in preparing a deal, that Lac and the other party would both have a duty towards each other not to hurt each other as the result of any information that was exchanged.

The trial judge awarded the Page Williams mine (at the time worth over $700 million) to Corona, though Lac was entitled to be paid about $200 million for its costs for development of the property. The Court of Appeal dismissed Lac's appeal. Lac appealed to the Supreme Court of Canada.

The principal judgment in that court was given by **LA FOREST J.**:]

[1]   Three issues must be addressed:

1.   What was the nature of the duty of confidence that was breached by Lac?

2.   Does the existence of the duty of confidence, alone or in conjunction with the other facts as found below, give rise to any fiduciary obligation or relation? If so, what is the nature of that obligation or relation?

3.   Is a constructive trust an available remedy for a breach of confidence as well as for breach of a fiduciary duty, and if so, should this Court interfere with the lower courts' imposition of that remedy?

[**LA FOREST J.** discussed the issues and the law relating to each of them. He continued:]

Conclusion on Fiduciary Obligations

[2]   Taking these factors together, I am of the view that the courts below did not err in finding that a fiduciary obligation existed and that it was breached. Lac urged this Court not to accept this finding, warning that imposing a fiduciary relationship in a case such as this would give rise to the greatest uncertainty in commercial law, and result in the determination of the rules of commercial conduct on the basis of *ad hoc* moral judgments rather than on the basis of established principles of commercial law.

[3]   I cannot accept either of these submissions. Certainty in commercial law is, no doubt, an important value, but it is not the only value. As Mr. Justice Grange has noted ("Good Faith in Commercial Transactions" (1985), *L.S.U.C. Special Lectures* 69), at p. 70:

> There are many limitations on the freedom of contract both in the common law and by statute. Every one of them carries within itself the seeds of debate as to its meaning or at least its applicability to a particular set of facts.

[4]   In any event, it is difficult to see how giving legal recognition to the parties' expectations will throw commercial law into turmoil.

[5]   Commercial relationships will more rarely involve fiduciary obligations. That is not because they are immune from them, but because in most cases, they would not be appropriately imposed. I agree with this comment of Mason J. in *Hospital Products Ltd. v. United States Surgical Corp.*, [(1984), 55 A.L.R. 417] at p. 455:

> There has been an understandable reluctance to subject commercial transactions to the equitable doctrine of constructive trust and constructive notice. But it is altogether too simplistic, if not superficial, to suggest that commercial transactions stand outside the fiduciary regime as though in some way commercial transactions do not lend themselves to the creation of a relationship in which one person comes under an obligation to act in the interests of another. The fact that in the great majority of commercial transactions the parties stand at arms' length does not enable us to make a generalization that is universally true in relation to every commercial transaction. In truth, every such transaction must be examined on its merits with a view to ascertaining whether it manifests the characteristics of a fiduciary relationship.

[6]   A fiduciary relationship is not precluded by the fact that the parties were involved in pre-contractual negotiations. That was made clear in the *United Dominions Corporation Ltd.* case, [*United Dominions Corporation Ltd. v. Brian Property Ltd.* (1985), A.L.J.R. 676] where the majority held, at p. 680, that:

> A fiduciary relationship can arise and fiduciary duties can exist between parties who have not reached, and who may never reach, agreement upon the consensual terms which are to govern the arrangement between them.

[7]   The fact that the relationship between the parties in that case was more advanced than in the case at bar does not affect the value of the conclusion. . . . It is a question to be determined on the facts whether the parties have reached a stage in their relationship where their expectations should be protected. In this case the facts support the existence of a fiduciary obligation not to act to the detriment of Corona's interest by acquiring the Williams property by using confidential information acquired during the negotiation process. The argument on morality is similarly misplaced. It is simply not the case that business and accepted morality are mutually exclusive domains. Indeed, the Court of Appeal, after holding that to find a fiduciary relationship here made no broad addition to the law, a view I take to be correct, noted that the practice established by the evidence to support the obligation was consistent with "business morality and with encouraging and enabling joint development of the natural resources of the country". This is not new. Texts from as early as 1903 refer to the obligation of "good faith by partners in their dealings with each other extend[ing] to negotiations culminating in the partnership, although in advance of its actual creation" (C.H. Lindley, *A Treatise on the American Law Relating to Mines and Mineral Lands* (1983), 2nd ed.). In my view, no distinction should be drawn here between negotiations culminating in a partnership or a joint venture.

[**LA FOREST J.** went on to hold that the court had considerable flexibility in the remedy that it could fashion. He continued:]

[8]   In view of this remedial flexibility, detailed consideration must be given to the reasons a remedy measured by Lac's gain at Corona's expense is more appropriate than a remedy compensating the plaintiff for the loss suffered. In this case, the Court of Appeal found that if compensatory damages were to be awarded, those damages in fact equalled the value of the property. This was premised on the finding that but for Lac's breach, Corona would have acquired the property. Neither at this point nor any other did either of the courts below find Corona would only acquire one half or less of the Williams property. While I agree that, if they could in fact be adequately assessed, compensation and restitution in this case would be equivalent measures, even if they would not, a restitutionary measure would be appropriate.

[9] The essence of the imposition of fiduciary obligations is its utility in the promotion and preservation of desired social behaviour and institutions. Likewise with the protection of confidences. In the modern world the exchange of confidential information is both necessary and expected. Evidence of an accepted business morality in the mining industry was given by the defendant, and the Court of Appeal found that the practice was not only reasonable, but that it would foster the exploration and development of our natural resources. The institution of bargaining in good faith is one that is worthy of legal protection in those circumstances where that protection accords with the expectations of the parties. The approach taken by my colleague, Sopinka J., would, in my view, have the effect not of encouraging bargaining in good faith, but of encouraging the contrary. If by breaching an obligation of confidence one party is able to acquire an asset entirely for itself, at a risk of only having to compensate the other for what the other would have received if a formal relationship between them were concluded, the former would be given a strong incentive to breach the obligation and acquire the asset. In the present case, it is true that had negotiations been concluded, Lac could also have acquired an interest in the Corona land, but that is only an expectation and not a certainty. Had Corona acquired the Williams property, as they would have but for Lac's breach, it seems probable that negotiations with Lac would have resulted in a concluded agreement. However, if Lac, during the negotiations, breached a duty of confidence owed to Corona, it seems certain that Corona would have broken off negotiations and Lac would be left with nothing. In such circumstances, many business people, weighing the risks, would breach the obligation and acquire the asset. This does nothing for the preservation of the institution of good faith bargaining or relationships of trust and confidence. The imposition of a remedy which restores an asset to the party who would have acquired it but for a breach of fiduciary duties or duties of confidence acts as a deterrent to the breach of duty and strengthens the social fabric those duties are imposed to protect. The elements of a claim in unjust enrichment having been made out, I have found no reason why the imposition of a restitutionary remedy should not be granted.

[**LA FOREST J.** held that the appropriate remedy was the imposition of a constructive trust so that, in effect, Lac held the Williams property for the benefit of Corona and had to transfer the mine to it.]

[**SOPINKA** and **MCINTYRE JJ.** (dissenting in part) held that Lac did not owe Corona a fiduciary obligation but was liable for breaching an obligation of confidence. He held that in the circumstances an appropriate remedy would be damages, not an order compelling Lac to hand the Page Williams mine to Corona.]

[**LAMER J.** agreed with **SOPINKA** and **MCINTYRE JJ.** that Lac did not owe Corona a fiduciary duty, but he agreed with **LA FOREST J.** that the appropriate remedy was a constructive trust.]

[**WILSON J.** agreed with **LA FOREST J.** that Lac owed Corona a fiduciary obligation.]

NOTES

1. "Non-User" agreements, agreements dealing specifically with the right of one party to use confidential information supplied by the other, are now much more common in the mining industry. They clarify and reinforce the effect of *Lac Minerals*. A prospective participant in a joint venture might now be asked to sign the following undertaking before being allowed to make a site visit:

    > In consideration of your agreeing to allow us to make a site visit to your . . . property and to inspect maps, plans, sections, drill cores and other information and samples, we hereby undertake that we will not for the period of one year from the date hereof:
    >
    > A. disclose any information that we receive from you to any person (other than our affiliates and associated corporations) without your express consent;
    >
    > B. use the information for any purpose other than for the preparation of a bona fide offer to you to participate with you in further exploration of the property; or
    >
    > C. use the information for any purpose that might adversely affect the interests of you or your shareholders.
    >
    > If we take away from the site any notes, copies of maps, plans or samples for the purpose of preparing a bona fide offer to participate in further exploration or development we further undertake not to make any copies of any material obtained from you (other than such as may be necessary to prepare the offer) and to return or to destroy any such notes, copies or samples (including all copies made by us) if our offer is either not made within a reasonable time or is rejected by you.
    >
    > Without restricting the generality of the foregoing, we acknowledge that the information that you will provide to us is confidential, that it is given for the limited purposes stated above and we acknowledge that we will hold in trust for you any benefits that we may obtain by use of the information that you have provided to us.
    >
    > We undertake to ensure that if any information dealt with by this agreement is disclosed to our affiliates or associated corporations, it will be subject to the same restrictions as apply to the information disclosed to us.

2. "Non-User" agreements have been in use for some time in the investment business when a potential investor is shown confidential information to enable him, her or it to make an investment decision such as an asset or share purchase. The "due diligence" performed by the purchaser (which the two-stage process of deal-making is designed to permit) will necessarily give the prospective purchaser a great deal of information that is confidential and of great value to competitors or other potential investors. An agreement that might be used in such a situation is the following:

    1. Target is furnishing the Evaluation Material to Purchaser solely for the purpose of assisting Purchaser in considering a proposed offer by Purchaser. Purchaser shall not use the Evaluation Material for any purpose other than evaluating the making of the Offer or in a manner which is in any way detrimental to the interests of Target or its shareholders.

    2. Purchaser acknowledges that the Evaluation Material is the property of Target which is confidential and material to the interests, business and affairs of Target and that disclosure thereof would be detrimental to the interests, business and affairs of Target and its shareholders. Accordingly, Purchaser agrees that it will maintain the confidentiality of the Evaluation Material and that the Purchaser will not disclose the Evaluation Material to any person except as expressly pro-

vided herein. Except as provided in paragraph 3, Purchaser shall not disclose the Evaluation Material to any person for any reason whatsoever other than those Representatives of Purchaser (who shall not exceed ten in number) who actually need to have knowledge of the Evaluation Material for the purpose of considering the Offer and whose names appear on the list attached hereto as Schedule A (the "Designated Representatives"). Each Designated Representative shall be informed by Purchaser of the confidential nature of the Evaluation Material and shall agree in writing and be required by Purchaser to treat the Evaluation Material as confidential and not to disclose the Evaluation Material to any person other than another Designated Representative.

3. Except with the express written consent of the Chairman, the Vice-President, Finance or the Vice-President and General Counsel or such other person as the Chairman of Target may expressly designate in writing, Purchaser shall not, and shall require that its Representatives do not:

    (a) make or cause to be made any copies of the Evaluation Material; or

    (b) disclose any of the Evaluation Material to any person other than a Designated Representative for any reason whatsoever unless:

        (i) in the reasonable opinion of Purchaser's counsel, disclosure is required to be made under the securities laws of any province of Canada or under the *Securities Act* of 1933 or the *Securities Exchange Act* of 1934 of the United States; or

        (ii) disclosure is required to be made by Purchaser pursuant to due legal process;

    provided that, prior to any such disclosure being made, Purchaser shall immediately notify and consult with Target concerning the information which it is proposed be disclosed.

4. In the event that the Offer has not been made by Purchaser or any of its Affiliates within 60 days from the date hereof all Evaluation Material and any and all copies thereof shall immediately be returned to Target by Purchaser.

5. Purchaser acknowledges that it is aware (and that its Representatives who have knowledge of the matters which arc the subject of this Agreement have been, or upon acquiring such knowledge will be, advised) of the restrictions imposed by the *Securities Act* (Ontario) and by other applicable securities legislation on a person processing material non-public information about a public company such as Target. In this regard, Purchaser agrees that it will not make an Offer or purchase or sell securities of Target with the knowledge of a material fact or material change in the affairs of Target that Purchaser knew or ought reasonably to have known had not been generally disclosed and that, if requested by Target, Purchaser shall cause its Representatives who have knowledge or who may hereafter acquire knowledge of the matters which are the subject of this agreement to give a written undertaking to the same effect to Purchaser or to Target.

6. This agreement shall terminate or be inoperative as to particular portions of the information forming part of the Evaluation Material if such information:

    (a) becomes generally available to the public (other than as a result of disclosure by or through Purchaser or any of its Affiliates or any of its Representatives);

    (b) is available to Purchaser on a non-confidential basis prior to its being provided to Purchaser by Target;

    (c) becomes available to Purchaser on a non-confidential basis from any source, provided that such source is not bound by a confidentiality or similar agreement with Target, or another insider of or person in a special relationship with Target, in respect of such information; or

(d) is required by law to be made available to Purchaser on a non-confidential basis and is generally disclosed.

7. Purchaser acknowledges and agrees that Target and its shareholders would be irreparably damaged if any provision of this agreement is not performed by Purchaser or its Affiliates or Representatives or Designated Representatives in accordance with its terms. Accordingly, Target shall be entitled to an injunction or injunctions to prevent breaches of any of the provisions of this agreement and may specifically enforce such provisions by an action instituted in court having jurisdiction. These specific remedies are in addition to any other remedy to which Target may be entitled at law or in equity.

3. In *Visagie v. TVX Gold Inc.*, [2000] O.J. No. 1992, 49 O.R. (3d) 198, 187 D.L.R. (4th) 193 (C.A.), the Ontario Court of Appeal considered a case where some junior partners entered into a joint venture agreement with a senior mining company to explore the possibility of jointly acquiring certain mines in Greece. Under the terms of the agreement, if the mine were acquired, the junior partners could have a 12 per cent interest based on their work, and could acquire another 12 per cent by putting up some capital. As part of the negotiations, confidentiality agreements were signed, and the senior company received information of value about the mines from the junior partners. One of the junior partners was a company that went into receivership and was unable to continue operations, so the senior company terminated the agreement. The senior company later acquired the mines on its own.

    The Ontario Court of Appeal concluded that there was a breach of the confidentiality agreement, but no breach of any fiduciary duty. Charron J.A. observed (pp. 208 and 210 O.R.) that "fiduciary obligations are seldom present in a commercial context when between parties acting at arm's length. . . . [In this case there is] not the kind of vulnerability that will serve to elevate the relationship between the parties to one that is fiduciary in nature." Since there was a breach of the confidentiality agreement, but no breach of a fiduciary duty, the Court only required the senior company to transfer to the other partners the minority interest that they would have had under the original agreement, upon paying the agreed capital amount, but the Court did not require the senior company to transfer all of its interest in the mines to the other partners. The remedy given was more limited than that in *Lac Minerals*. Why?

4. The problem that solicitors must now face is the effect of non-user agreements. If a junior mining company does not get a senior company to sign one before the latter makes a site visit, will the court draw an inference adverse to the former?

5. Confidentiality agreements are in common use when an inventor must disclose confidential intellectual property information, e.g., the details of a software program, to a potential licensee, manufacturer, joint venture partner, investor or purchaser. What issues should be considered by, for instance, the solicitor acting for a major corporation (Kodak, Sony, 3M, IBM) that is asked to sign a confidentiality agreement as a condition of receiving information about a product that it might want to exploit with the inventor? How might these issues be resolved in negotiations?

THE BATTLE OF THE FORMS

Seller, as a prudent manufacturer, has decided that it needs standard forms for its business. The Vice-President, Marketing calls the corporation's lawyer, and a form is drafted giving Seller certain advantages over Buyer when the form is used. A large supply of these forms is printed and the employee who handles orders for Seller is instructed to send a form with each order. The form is an invoice which contains a clause: "Goods cannot be returned for credit after delivery." Buyer, an equally prudent merchant, has its own stack of appropriately drafted forms which its employees use. Buyer's form, a purchase order, contains the following clause: "Goods subject to inspection. Buyer may reject goods as not being in accordance with specifications within seven days of delivery."

The typical transaction is that Buyer's employee phones Seller's employee — the two employees may be on a "first name" basis — and orders the goods. A purchase order is mailed the same day. When the goods are shipped, about three weeks later, a packing note is sent with them and an invoice is mailed about two days later. Neither party has read the printed clauses in the document sent by the other, though they may check each set of documents to ensure the accuracy of the "filled in terms" — the description of the goods, the price and delivery date. The parties carry on business this way for several years until one order is defective. The Buyer refuses to pay and tries to return the goods after five days.

What went on here between the seller and buyer is described as the "battle of the forms". It is clear that the parties had been doing business for years on the assumption that they had a valid contract each time that goods were shipped. No one in either corporation bothered to read all the documents and consider the significance of the fact that the forms did not coincide. Had anyone done so, one side or the other might have refused to do business except on the basis of its own form, or they might have tried to negotiate a consistent set of terms. It would not be fair to say that because of the failure of the parties to reach an agreement on all the terms of their relation, there were no contracts at all between them. If there is no contract, the only remedy of the seller would arise if the buyer retained the goods and refused to pay for them, in which case there would be an action "goods sold and delivered", based on the value of the goods and intended to prevent the buyer's unjust enrichment. If there is no contract at all, this might also be unfair to the buyer as it might mean that there are very limited remedies for defective goods.

One approach to analyzing this situation is to use the traditional rules of offer and acceptance to determine the terms for the particular transaction before the court. This approach provides an answer to the problem facing the court, but it would catch one of the parties by surprise — at least to the extent that either thought about the terms of their relation at all. The next cases raise the question of the extent to which the application of the traditional rules provides a satisfactory solution and, what is more difficult, what the alternatives are.

BUTLER MACHINE TOOL CO. LTD. v. EX-CELL-O CORP. (ENGLAND) LTD.

[1979] 1 All E.R. 965, [1979] 1 W.L.R. 401
(C.A., Lord Denning M.R., Lawton and Bridge L.JJ.)

LORD DENNING M.R.: — [1] This case is a "battle of forms". The suppliers of a machine, Butler Machine Tool Co. Ltd. ("the sellers"), on 23rd May 1969 quoted a price for a machine tool of £75,535. Delivery was to be given in ten months. On the back of the quotation there were terms and conditions. One of them was a price variation clause. It provided for an increase in the price if there was an increase in the costs and so forth. The machine tool was not delivered until November 1970. By that time costs had increased so much that the sellers claimed an additional sum of £2,892 as due to them under the price variation clause.

[2]   The buyers, Ex-Cell-O Corp., rejected the excess charge. They relied on their own terms and conditions. They said: "We did not accept the sellers' quotation as it was. We gave an order for the self-same machine at the self-same price, but on the back of our order we had our own terms and conditions. Our terms and conditions did not contain any price variation clause."

[3]   The judge held that the price variation clause in the sellers' form continued through the whole dealing and so the sellers were entitled to rely on it. He was clearly influenced by a passage in the 24th edition of Anson's *Law of Contract* [(1975), pp. 37-38] . . . The judge said that the sellers did all that was necessary and reasonable to bring the price variation clause to the notice of the buyers. He thought that the buyers would not "browse over the conditions" of the sellers, and then, by printed words in their (the buyers') document, trap the sellers into a fixed price contract.

[4]   I am afraid that I cannot agree with the suggestion that the buyers "trapped" the sellers in any way. Neither party called any oral evidence before the judge. The case was decided on the documents alone. I propose therefore to go through them.

[5]   On 23rd May 1969 the sellers offered to deliver one "Butler" double column plano-miller for the total price of £75,535, "DELIVERY: 10 months (Subject to confirmation at time of ordering) Other terms and conditions are on the reverse of this quotation". On the back there were 16 conditions in small print starting with this general condition:

> All orders are accepted only upon and subject to the terms set out in our quotation and the following conditions. These terms and conditions shall prevail over any terms and conditions in the Buyer's order.

[6]   Clause 3 was the price variation clause. It said:

> . . . Prices are based on present day costs of manufacture and design and having regard to the delivery quoted and uncertainty as to the cost of labour, materials etc. during the period of manufacture, we regret that we have no alternative but to make it a condition of acceptance of order that goods will be charged at prices ruling upon date of delivery.

[7]   The buyers, Ex-Cell-O, replied on 27th May 1969 giving an order in these words: "Please supply on terms and conditions as below and overleaf." Below there was a list of the goods ordered, but there were differences from the quotation of the sellers in these respects: (i) there was an additional item for the cost of installation, £3,100; (ii) there was a different delivery date: instead of 10 months, it was 10 to 11 months. Overleaf there were different terms as to the cost of carriage, in that it was to be paid to the delivery address of the buyers; whereas the sellers' terms were ex warehouse. There were different terms as to the right to cancel for late delivery. The buyers in their conditions reserved the right to cancel if delivery was not made by the agreed date, whereas the sellers in their conditions said that cancellation of order due to late delivery would not be accepted.

[8]   On the foot of the buyers' order there was a tear-off slip:

> ACKNOWLEDGEMENT: Please sign and return to EX-CELL-O CORP. (England) LTD.

> We accept your order on the Terms and Conditions stated thereon and undertake to deliver by . . . Date . . . Signed. . . .

In that slip the delivery date and signature were left blank ready to be filled in by the sellers.

[9]   On 5th June 1969 the sellers wrote this letter to the buyers:

> We have pleasure in acknowledging receipt of your official order dated 27th May covering the supply of one "Butler" Double Column Plano-Miller. . . . This is being entered in accordance with our revised quotation of 23rd May for delivery in 10/11 months, i.e., March/April, 1970. We return herewith, duly completed, your acknowledgment of order form.

They enclosed the acknowledgment form duly filled in with the delivery date, March/April 1970, and signed by the Butler Machine Tool Co. Ltd.

[10]   No doubt a contract was then concluded. But on what terms? The sellers rely on their general conditions and on their last letter which said "in accordance with our revised quotation of 23rd May" (which had on the back the price variation clause). The buyers rely on the acknowledgment signed by the sellers which accepted the buyers' order "on the terms and conditions stated thereon" (which did not include a price variation clause).

[11]   If those documents are analyzed in our traditional method, the result would seem to me to be this: the quotation of 23rd May 1969 was an offer by the sellers to the buyers containing the terms and conditions on the back. The order of 27th May 1969 purported to be an acceptance of that offer in that it was for the same machine at the same price, but it contained such additions as to cost of installation, date of delivery and so forth, that it was in law a rejection of the offer and constituted a counter-offer. The letter of the sellers of 5th June 1969 was an acceptance of that counter-offer, as is shown by the acknowledgment which the sellers signed and returned to the buyers. The reference to the quotation of 23rd May 1969 referred only to the price and identity of the machine.

[12]   To go on with the facts of the case. The important thing is that the sellers did not keep the contractual date of delivery which was March/April 1970. The machine was ready about September 1970 but by that time the buyers' production schedule had to be rearranged as they could not accept delivery until November 1970. Meanwhile the sellers had invoked the price increase clause. They sought to charge the buyers an increase due to the rise in costs between 27th May 1969 (when the order was given) and 1st April 1970 (when the machine ought to have been delivered). It came to £2,892. The buyers rejected the claim. The judge held that the sellers were entitled to the sum of £2,892 under the price variation clause. He did not apply the traditional method of analysis by way of offer and counter-offer. He said that in the quotation of 23rd May 1969 "one finds the price variation clause appearing under a most emphatic heading stating that it is a term or condition that is to prevail". So he held that it did prevail.

[13]   I have much sympathy with the judge's approach to this case. In many of these cases our traditional analysis of offer, counter-offer, rejection, acceptance and so forth is out-of-date. This was observed by Lord Wilberforce in *New Zealand Shipping Co. Ltd. v. A.M. Satterthwaite*, [1975] A.C. 154 at 167, [1974] 1 All E.R. 1015 at 1019-1020. The better way is to look at all the documents passing between the parties and glean from them, or from the conduct of the parties, whether they have reached agreement on all material points, even though there may be differences between the forms and conditions printed on the back of them.

As Lord Cairns L.C. said in *Brogden v. Metropolitan Railway Co* (1877), 2 App. Cas. 666 at 672:

> . . . there may be a consensus between the parties far short of a complete mode of expressing it, and that consensus may be discovered from letters or from other documents of an imperfect and incomplete description.

[14] Applying this guide, it will be found that in most cases when there is a "battle of forms" there is a contract as soon as the last of the forms is sent and received without objection being taken to it. . . . The difficulty is to decide which form, or which part of which form, is a term or condition of the contract. In some cases the battle is won by the man who fires the last shot. He is the man who puts forward the latest term and conditions: and, if they are not objected to by the other party, he may be taken to have agreed to them. Such was *British Road Services Ltd. v. Arthur v. Crutchley & Co. Ltd.*, [1968] 1 All E.R. 811 at 816-817, [1968] 1 Lloyd's Rep. 271 at 281-282, per Lord Pearson; and the illustration given by Professor Guest in Anson's *Law of Contract* 24th Edn. (1975), pp. 37-38, where he says that "the terms of the contract consist of the terms of the offer subject to the modifications contained in the acceptance". That may however go too far. In some cases, however, the battle is won by the man who gets the blow in first. If he offers to sell at a named price on the terms and conditions stated on the back and the buyer orders the goods purporting to accept the offer on an order form with his own different terms and conditions on the back, then, if the difference is so material that it would affect the price, the buyer ought not to be allowed to take advantage of the difference unless he draws it specifically to the attention of the seller. There are yet other cases where the battle depends on the shots fired on both sides. There is a concluded contract but the forms vary. The terms and conditions of both parties are to be construed together. If they can be reconciled so as to give a harmonious result, all well and good. If differences are irreconcilable, so that they are mutually contradictory, then the conflicting terms may have to be scrapped and replaced by a reasonable implication.

[15] In the present case the judge thought that the sellers in their original quotation got their blow in first; especially by the provision that "These terms and conditions shall prevail over any terms and conditions in the Buyer's order". It was so emphatic that the price variation clause continued through all the subsequent dealings and that the buyer must be taken to have agreed to it. I can understand that point of view. But I think that the documents have to be considered as a whole. And, as a matter of construction, I think the acknowledgment of 5th June 1969 is the decisive document. It makes it clear that the contract was on the buyers' terms and not on the sellers' terms: and the buyers' terms did not include a price variation clause.

[16] I would therefore allow the appeal and enter judgment for the buyers.

LAWTON L.J.: — [17] The modern commercial practice of making quotations and placing orders with conditions attached, usually in small print, is indeed likely, as in this case, to produce a battle of forms. The problem is how should that battle be conducted? The view taken by the judge was that the battle should extend over a wide area and the court should do its best to look into the minds of the parties and make certain assumptions. In my judgment, the battle has to be conducted in accordance with set rules. It is a battle more on classical 18th century lines when convention decided who had the right to open fire first rather than in accordance with the modern concept of attrition.

[18] The rules relating to a battle of this kind have been known for the past 130-odd years . . . those rules are still in force.

[19] When those rules are applied to this case, in my judgment, the answer is obvious. The sellers started by making an offer. That was in their quotation. . . .

[20] As I understand *Hyde v. Wrench* [(1840), 3 Beav. 334, 49 E.R. 132] and the cases which have followed, the consequence of placing the order in that way, if I may adopt Megaw J.'s words *Trollope & Colls Ltd. v. Atomic Power Constructions Ltd.*, [1962] 3 All E.R. 1035 at 1038, [1963] 1 W.L.R. 333 at 337, was "to kill the quotation". It follows that the court has to look at what happened after the buyers made their counter-offer. By letter dated 4th June 1969 the sellers' acknowledged receipt of the counter-offer, and they went on in this way: "Details of this order have been passed to our Halifax works for attention and a formal acknowledgement of order will follow in due course." That is clearly a reference to the printed tear-off slip which was at the bottom of the buyers' counter-offer. By letter dated 5th June 1969 the sales office manager at the sellers' Halifax factory completed that tear-off slip and sent it back to the buyers.

[21] It is true, as counsel for the sellers has reminded us, that the return of that printed slip was accompanied by a letter which had this sentence in it: "This is being entered in accordance with our revised quotation of 23rd May for delivery in 10/11 months." I agree with Lord Denning M.R. that, in a business sense, that refers to the quotation as to the price and the identity of the machine, and it does not bring into the contract the small print conditions on the back of the quotation. Those small print conditions had disappeared from the story. That was when the contract was made. At that date it was a fixed price contract without a price escalation clause.

[22] As I pointed out in the course of argument to counsel for the sellers, if the letter of 5th June which accompanied the form acknowledging the terms which the buyers had specified had amounted to a counter-offer, then in my judgment the parties never were *ad idem*. It cannot be said that the buyers accepted the counter-offer by reason of the fact that ultimately they took physical delivery of the machine. By the time they took physical delivery of the machine, they had made it clear by correspondence that they were not accepting that there was any price escalation clause in any contract which they had made with the plaintiffs.

[23] I agree with Lord Denning M.R. that this appeal should be allowed.

[**BRIDGE L.J.** wrote a concurring opinion, taking a similar approach to **LAWTON L.J.**]

QUESTION

1. Whose analytical approach is preferable, that of Lord Denning M.R. or that of Lawton L.J.?

TYWOOD INDUSTRIES LTD. v. ST. ANNE-NACKAWIC PULP & PAPER CO. LTD.

(1979), 25 O.R. (2d) 89, 100 D.L.R. (3d) 374
(H.C.J., Grange J.)

GRANGE J.: — **[1]** The plaintiff's action is for the price of goods sold. The defendant has moved to stay the action under s. 7 of the *Arbitrations Act*, R.S.O. 1970, c. 25, upon the ground that the agreement of sale contained a clause for submission to arbitration.

[2]   The plaintiff, which is an Ontario manufacturing company was invited by the defendant, a New Brunswick company, to tender for the sale of storage tanks. Eventually agreement was reached, at least as to the specifications and price, and three storage tanks were delivered from Ontario to New Brunswick and put into operation. The defendant alleged deficiencies in operation and stopped payment on the cheque for the third tank. The action followed. . . .

[3]   Much of the argument before me was concerned with whether in light of the nature of the dispute, I should impose a stay upon the action. It was recognized that there was a discretion and the problem was how that discretion should be exercised. There is, however, a preliminary question to be answered, *viz.*, whether there has indeed been an agreement for arbitration. . . . It may be also that if there is doubt on the matter that doubt will be a factor militating against the stay. To determine the question the dealings between the parties must be examined carefully.

[4]   The defendant's invitation to tender was dated September 19, 1977. The document on its face was entitled "A Request for Quotation" and set forth the goods required. On the reverse side were set forth the "Terms and Conditions". There were 13 of these, none of which dealt with arbitration. On September 26, 1977, the plaintiff replied with a quotation in a letter form, but the reverse side of the letter contained a list of 12 "Terms and Conditions of Sale", none of which made reference to arbitration. Condition 12 read as follows:

> 12. No modification of the above Conditions of Sale shall be effected by our receipt or acknowledgment of a purchase order containing additional or different conditions.

[5]   There followed some telephone and telex communications between the parties and a revised proposal was submitted by the plaintiff under date of November 7, 1977, with the same 12 "Terms and Conditions of Sale" on the reverse side. Then came two purchase orders from the defendant dated January 6, 1978 and July 3, 1978, each of which contained on the reverse "Terms and Conditions" of which the nineteenth and last read as follows:

> 19. This Contract shall be governed by and construed according to the laws of the Province of New Brunswick. Any controversy arising out of or relating to this Order, or the breach thereof, shall be settled by arbitration in Fredericton in accordance with the Arbitration Act of the Province of New Brunswick.

[6]   The plaintiff's copy was not produced but it is alleged to have printed thereon: "This order is accepted by the vendor subject to the terms and conditions on the face and reverse side of this order." It is also alleged to have printed thereon the instructions (to the vendor): "Mail acceptance copy of this order promptly giving definite shipment date." It appears to be common ground that neither purchase order was signed by the plaintiff nor returned to the defendant. The goods were then delivered.

[7]   This is what Professor Waddams in his work *The Law of Contracts* (1977), describes as "the battle of the forms" (p. 44), each party seeking to impose its terms upon the other and seeking to avoid being bound by that other. He suggests that the proper test is that laid down by Lord Pearce in *Kendall v. Lillico* [*Henry Kendall & Sons v. William Lillico & Sons Ltd.*], [1969] 2 A.C. 31 at p. 113, as follows:

The court's task is to decide what each party to an alleged contract would reasonably conclude from the utterances, writings or conduct of the other.

[8] Waddams also notes (pp. 50-1):

There are several signs of flexibility in the present structure of the law. One is the interconnection of notice requirements with the reasonableness of the terms sought to be incorporated. Another is the examination of the course of previous dealings in determining whether terms are incorporated. A third, and more general, trend that may prove to be the most significant of all is the development of doctrines of unconscionability.

[9] While the parties may have agreed to arbitration I am certainly not satisfied that this is so. I have the greatest doubt that the plaintiff put its mind to the question at all. Certainly it tried (perhaps not consciously) to impose its non-arbitrable condition upon the defendant when it quoted its price originally. It at no time acknowledged the supremacy of the defendant's terms. On the other hand, the defendant (again perhaps not consciously) did try to impose the arbitration term in the purchase orders, but it drew no particular attention to that term. Nor did it complain when the plaintiff failed to return the vendor's copy of the purchase orders with an acknowledgment of the terms sought to be imposed. This was a commercial transaction and terms might well have been expected, but the conduct of both parties seems to me to indicate that neither party considered any terms other than those found on the face of the documents (i.e., the specifications and the price) important. What was important to both was the consummation of the business deal that had been arranged between them. . . .

[10] The policy of the Courts seems still to be against clauses which would replace the Court's determination of issues with that of an arbitrator. . . .

[11] A . . . recent example of the reluctance to stay is found in the judgment of Lerner J., in *Jussem et al. v. Nissan Automobile Co. (Canada) Ltd. et al.*, [1973] 1 O.R. 697 . . . the Court found questions of law or mixed fact and law to be involved in the litigation and largely for that reason declined the stay. While the issues here may be mainly factual, i.e., the condition of the tanks, whether the condition found is in accord with the specifications is at least a question of mixed fact and law.

[12] More important, however, to the decision in the case at bar, is my doubt that the arbitration clause is a part of the contract, a problem which, in my view, might itself require a trial to resolve. It is stated in . . . *London Sack & Bag Co., Ltd. v. Dixon & Lugton, Ltd.*, [1943] 2 All E.R. 763 at p. 765: "Any doubt about the written submission being quite clearly established is . . . a sufficient reason for the judge's exercising his discretion against a stay."

[13] I do not find the arbitration clause clearly established in the case at bar. I would, therefore, not grant the stay and the motion must be dismissed.

QUESTIONS AND NOTES

1. *Tywood Industries* was decided in 1979. Since then, arbitration has become a more important a form of alternative dispute resolution. Would you now expect a court to approach the resolution of the "battle of the forms" as Grange J. did? Notice what Grange J. said in ¶ 10 about the "policy of the courts".

   If a court today would not do what Grange J. did because it weighed the effectiveness or desirability of an arbitration clause differently, what has changed to justify the different result? Has the law changed? Would a court need or consider evidence of the change? Would this change suggest a more general solution to the problem of the "battle of the forms"?

2. Notice that neither the English Court of Appeal nor Grange J. considered the context of the transaction. S.M. Waddams, *The Law of Contracts*, 5th ed. (Toronto: Carswell, 2005), pp. 50-62 suggests that the pattern of the parties' dealings or the practice in the industry may be the source of a solution. Such patterns may provide a solution, but presumably only if it can be proved that one party knew the expectations of the other. The context of the transaction in the broader sense of what is generally expected by traders or merchants similarly situated to the parties may suggest whether, for example, price adjustment clauses of the type used by the seller in *Butler Machine Tool Co. Ltd. v. Ex-Cell-O Corp.*, are common or unexpected in the sale of machine tools. This evidence would go far to provide a satisfactory solution to what has, under the rules of offer and acceptance, no easy solution.

3. In the United States, § 2-207 of the *Uniform Commercial Code* (UCC) attempts to deal with the battle of the forms, and is a partial model for the proposed Canadian *Uniform Sale of Goods Act* provision. The proposed Canadian Act states:

> 4.2(1) A contract of sale may be made in any manner sufficient to show agreement, including conduct by the parties which recognizes the existence of such a contract.
>
> (2) An agreement sufficient to constitute a contract of sale may be found even though the moment of its making is undetermined.
>
> (3) A reply to an offer purporting to be an acceptance but containing additional or different terms which do not materially alter the terms of the offer constitutes an acceptance and in such a case the terms of the contract are the terms of the offer with the modifications contained in the acceptance.
>
> (4) Subsection 3 does not apply if the offeror seasonably notifies the offeree of his objection to the additional or different terms.
>
> (5) For the purpose of subsection 3, additional or different terms relating to the price, payment, quality and quantity of the goods, place and time of delivery, extent of one party's liability to the other or the settlement of disputes are terms which materially alter the terms of the offer.

> *Official Comment*
>
> 1. Subsections (1) and (2) provide that no special formalities (such as writing) are required for a contract of sale. The provisions also indicate that a contract may be found by regarding the conduct of the parties, and that a court need not engage in the exercise of finding the precise moment when a contract is made.
>
> 2. Subsections (3) to (5) . . . deal with cases where an acceptance does not precisely mirror the terms of the offer. At common law this would prevent there being any contract. . . .

While Canada does not have the *Uniform Commercial Code*, a significant class of contracts is governed by legislation that is loosely modelled on Article 2. All the provinces of Canada and the federal government have made the *United Nations Convention on Contracts for the International Sale of Goods* (the "*Vienna Sales Convention*"), part of the law of Canada. This legislation applies to all international contracts for the sale of goods unless the parties have expressly excluded the operation of the *Convention*. The *Convention* provides:

Article 19

(1) A reply to an offer which purports to be an acceptance but contains additions, limitations or other modifications is a rejection of the offer and constitutes a counter-offer.

(2) However, a reply to an offer which purports to be an acceptance but contains additional or different terms which do not materially alter the terms of the offer constitutes an acceptance, unless the offeror, without undue delay, objects orally to the discrepancy or dispatches a notice to that effect. If he does not so object, the terms of the contract are the terms of the offer with the modifications contained in the acceptance.

(3) Additional or different terms relating, among other things, to the price, payment, quality and quantity of the goods, place and time of delivery, extent of one party's liability to the other or the settlement of disputes are considered to alter the terms of the offer materially.

The effect of Article 19 can result in outcomes that are different from those under the UCC § 2-207 and s. 4 of the *Uniform Sale of Goods Act*. The most significant difference between Article 19 of the *Convention* and s. 4.2 of the Act (and § 2-207 of the UCC) is the absence in the *Convention* of anything equivalent to s.-s. 4.2(1) of the Act. This omission denies the parties and the court the opportunity to impose on the parties the terms that they have actually agreed on and those terms which, from the parties' relation or shared background, they can reasonably be expected to have accepted as part of their deal.

For a comparison of the American statutory approach and the Anglo-Canadian common law approach, see Shanker, "'Battle of the Forms': A Comparison and Critique of Canadian, American and Historical Common Law Perspectives" (1979), 4 *Can. Bus. L.J.* 263. For a fuller comparative discussion, see A.T. von Mehren, "The Battle of the Forms: A Comparative View" (1990), 38 *Am. J. Comp. L.* 265.

4. There is a large body of American scholarship that deals with the complexities of the battle of the forms, and proposes a range of solutions. Some of this scholarship puts the problems into a wider context.

MACNEIL, THE NEW SOCIAL CONTRACT

(New Haven: Yale University Press, 1980)
(pp. 72-77; footnotes omitted)

Discreteness and Presentation in Contractual Relations

[1]   Because specificity and measurement are essential to the working of the modern economy, in modern law principles and rules implementing discreteness and presentation are always found. Many a problem occurs in performance, many an outfit skirts too close to the edge of nonperformance and falls off, and a few evildoers in every crowd cheat or welsh. Discrete and presentiated law such as neoclassical contract law will always remain necessary both to help set standards and to deal with disputes when standards are allegedly not met.

Neoclassical and Relational Contract Law

[2]   Neoclassical contract law is founded in theory and organization on the discrete transaction, but with many a relational concession. It can often deal ade-

quately with the more discrete issues in contractual relations. But when discrete
and relational principles conflict, neoclassical law lacks any overriding relational
foundation, and thus lacks a resource often needed in relational law. Two ways of
dealing with relational problems, one neoclassical, the other more relational, illustrate this point.

[3]   The neoclassical example is UCC § 2-207 [similar to s. 4.2(3) of the proposed Canadian Act, *supra*], the famous "Battle-of-the-Forms" section, and itself a
repeated battleground for legal scholars. It was aimed at doing away with the ri-
gidities of the mirror-image rule of the common law. This rule required an
acceptance to be precisely the same as the offer at the peril of being treated as no
more than a new offer. This older rule is admirably fitted to the discrete transaction, where consent is either on or off. Thus, in a discrete transaction no room exists for "we accept, but do not accept."

[4]   But businessmen regularly do exactly that. Consider a businessman receiving a buyer's printed purchase order for 100 widgets at $700, delivery on or before
July 30. He replies by sending his printed sales order, for 100 widgets at $700,
delivery on or before July 30. Irrespective of its printed words, the sales order will
normally be understood in much of the American business world as reflecting a
sliding scale of consent: 99 percent consent to selling 100 widgets at $700, 90
percent to delivery within a week or so of July 30, 70 percent to delivery by July
30, a sliding scale of 85 percent down to 5 percent insistence on compliance with
various printed terms on the sales order and willingness to go along with various
of buyer's printed terms. Buyer's consent will be understood as reflecting a similar, although partially conflicting, pattern.

[5]   Section 2-207 deals with this messy phenomenon by providing in part: "A
definite . . . expression of acceptance . . . operates as an acceptance even though it
states terms . . . different from those offered . . ." It thereby makes "we accept, but
do not accept" a contract. This is a start, but only a start, on a good relational principle. Some definition of the relation created is needed, since the conflicts preclude total dependence on mutual consent. . . .

[6]   . . . 2-207(1) illustrates the error of modifying the wisdom of the law of discrete transactions, without at the same time building relational foundations. To
build such foundations here requires an answer to this question: How can people
regularly do business on the basis of "we accept, but do not accept"? They can do
so only because they trust each other. Trust may arise from prior dealings with the
same party or with similar parties, from the mores of the general or particular
business community, from a recognition of the accommodating effects even of a
very positive law of contracts, from a great many potential sources. But trust must
exist or businessmen would be little inclined to take the risks of the "we accept,
but do not accept" game. These relational elements could form a proper conceptual base for legal rules governing the Battle-of-the-Forms. . . .

Macneil refers to an English study: Beale and Dugdale, "Contracts Between Businessmen: Planning and the Use of Contractual Remedies" (1975), 2 *British Journal of Law and Society* 45. Beale and Dugdale observe (pp. 47-48 and 50-51):

[B]esides there being a common acceptance of certain norms within the trade, there was a considerable degree of trust among firms. This was particularly so among smaller firms who obtained most of their orders locally and who frequently placed great trust in the fairness of one or two very large firms. No doubt belief in mutual fairness was reinforced by the considerable degree of personal contact between officers, usually in the business context but sometimes on social occasions. The firm's general reputation was also at stake. Not only did salesmen stress the need to have a good product and to stand behind it, buyers also emphasized the need to maintain a reputation for the firm as fair and efficient, and both said that any attempt to shelter behind contractual provisions or even frequent citation of contractual terms would destroy the firm's reputation very quickly. But even more important than the general reputation of the firm was the desire to do business again with the other party, or with other firms in the same group of companies. Each side had to be prepared to make concessions and to do so in a spirit of co-operation.

There was considerable awareness of the fact that in many cases an exchange of conditions would not necessarily lead to an enforceable contract, and some that the last set of conditions might prevail . . . But most firms seemed unconcerned about the failure to make a contract. They usually tried to ensure that they referred to their conditions in any written communications, which would prevent the letter "accepting" the other party's terms, but no more, and some were not even concerned with that . . .

[W]e were told of and saw signs of a gradual change in attitude towards tightening up procedures and creating legally enforceable agreements . . . This may be entirely explicable by the recent inflation and economic troubles which make it desirable to have clear agreement on such matters as price increases and delays, but we were told by several representatives that it was the result of a new professionalism among young managers, many of whom have studied contract law.

The notion of trust referred to by Beale and Dugdale should not be seen as a modern phenomenon. It is as old as the existence of exchange transactions. Fernand Braudel, in *The Wheels of Commerce*, vol. 2 of *Civilization & Capitalism 15th-18th Century* (New York: Harper and Row, 1979; English translation by Sian Reynolds, 1982), refers to the standards of conduct expected of merchants (pp. 150-51):

Whatever the form of agreement or cooperation between merchants, it required loyalty, personal confidence, scrupulousness and respect for instructions. There was quite a strict code of behaviour among merchants. Hebenstreit and Son, an Amsterdam firm, had agreed [to] a fifty-fifty contract with Dugard Fils of Rouen. On 6 January 1766, they wrote a stiff letter to the French firm, because it had sold "very cheaply," "without any necessity and even against our express instructions," the [goods] they had dispatched to Rouen. The conclusion is plain: "We insist that you replace our half-share yourself at the same price you have sold it for so inopportunely." At least they are proposing an amicable settlement, "so that we do not have to appeal to a third party," evidence that in an affair like this, merchant solidarity, even in Rouen, would have operated in favour of an Amsterdam supplier.

Braudel attributes the importance in commercial dealings of minority groups such as Jews and Armenians to the high degree of trust that existed among them. He also details many examples where merchant trust was, in practice, far more important and powerful than the law. He cites the involvement of foreign merchants in the Spanish trade from America at a time when that trade was supposedly by Spanish decree confined to Spanish merchants. A foreign merchant had to trust a Spanish merchant, as it was clear that the Spanish courts not only would have upheld the claim of the Spanish merchant in any dispute, but also would have severely punished the foreigner.

The problem that Macneil discusses may be seen as part of a much larger problem. This problem is the failure of the law to "connect" with the activities of the people that it is seeking to control. This failure does not occur only in contracts. In "Law's Precarious Hold on Life" (1969), 3 *Georgia L. Rev.* 530, Fuller discusses the failure in the conventional areas of property and torts as well as in contracts (where he uses the battle of the forms to illustrate his argument), and in establishing the idea of law among people who have no notion of law as either something "made" or as involving the separation of power and property.

There is a body of legal scholarship in the United States that has combined empirical and doctrinal analysis, and reached similar conclusions to the English study of Beale and Dugale about the importance of trust, though somewhat different conclusions about whether those engaged in these types of transactions actually read the documents they sign. Professor J.E. Murray, in "The Chaos of the 'Battle of the Forms': Solutions" (1986), 39 *Vand. L. Rev.* 1307, reports on having spoken to over 5,000 purchasing agents, and never finding one who had actually read the seller's form; indeed most could not even explain the significance of the terms on their own forms, much less on the other party's.

Daniel Keating, in "Exploring the Battle of the Forms in Action" (2000), 98 *Mich. L. Rev.* 267, found that while the "battle of the forms" situation does lead to litigation, as a result of the long-standing nature of the relation that is typical of these situations there is considerable pressure to settle the disputes that arise. One in-house counsel for a major department store retailer gave a succinct reason why after-the-fact form disputes typically do not amount to much: "We're more interested in being in the retail business . . . [than] in the litigation business . . ." Another lawyer for a paper products manufacturer commented: "[A] couple of golf games can get a lot solved." Keating observed that in repeated transactions of limited value, it is often not efficient for parties to worry about inconsistencies in their forms. As transactions become larger in size and less standardized, legal departments are more likely to be involved at the time of contract formation and have a "fully dickered contract."

Butler Machine Tool and *Tywood Industries* both involved relatively large contracts between parties to a discrete transaction.

CHAPTER FOUR

EXCUSES FOR NON-PERFORMANCE

INTRODUCTION

It is sometimes said that contractual obligations, unlike tort obligations, are "strict" or "absolute". This is true in the sense that it is not usually a defence for a party being sued for breach of contract to establish that it did its best to perform. In a broader sense, however, it is not accurate to say that contractual obligations are "absolute" and such a statement would give a misleading picture of the law. This chapter and the latter part of Chapter 5 examine a range of situations in which contractual obligations will be excused.

It is hard to think of any legal obligations that are "absolute" in the sense that breach of the obligation will in every case lead to punishment or a judgment for specific performance or damages: the standard bank guarantee comes close, but even it can, in some limited situations, be successfully challenged on the ground that, in the circumstances, the guarantor should be excused from performance. Important moral obligations, such as the obligations not to kill, steal or tell a lie, are all subject to exceptions or excuses. A person who kills in self-defence commits no crime. A starving person who steals may, morally at least, be blameless and we all know when the obligation not to tell a lie must be subordinated to concerns for kindness, prudence or necessity.

Contractual obligations are also subject to the same limits. In this chapter we shall examine part of the "law of excuses". The first part examines the law of excuses as a deliberate planning device in the parties' arrangement or relation. The second part focuses on those cases where one party asks the court to recognize that it had in the circumstances an excuse for its non-performance, even though there is no express provision for this in the contract. Chapter 5 will examine the law of excuses as part of the law of mistake and frustration, *i.e.*, cases where the excuse arises because the deal either arose or was to be performed in circumstances that differed significantly from those that the parties had expected.

There is no "bright line" test to distinguish the two areas and the same cases and the same tests will often be referred to in both areas.

The law of excuses expresses a simple idea: performance by one or both parties may be excused because an event has occurred, which, in the context of the particular contract, provides an excuse, or, even when there is no express reference to the event, it is so serious that a court will decide that an excuse for not performing exists. Excuses come, therefore, from two sources: the agreement of the parties; or the background to the deal and the standards established by the courts.

The inclusion in a contract of a term that, unless some specified event occurs or if some specified event occurs, one party is discharged from its obligation to perform, reflects the intensely practical view that it is best not to spend money if there is a risk that the expenditure will not be as valuable as hoped, or, more generally, that good money should not be thrown after bad. The fact that, if the risk arises from the possibility that the other might breach its obligations, a party may have a claim against the other in damages, is often small comfort for the disappointment for all the reasons that, as the cases in Chapter 1 made plain, damages are an expensive and often inadequate remedy.

When the parties have provided that one party will be excused from performance in specified circumstances, it is usual to refer to the clause providing for that excuse as a "condition" or an "express condition". When there is no express condition, but the court holds nevertheless that one party is excused, the court may say that it is doing so because of an "implied condition". Apart from the fact that the word "condition" is common to both phrases and that they both deal with excuses, they have little in common. An express condition is a deliberate planning device negotiated between the parties; an implied condition simply represents a court's view that, in all the circumstances, one party should be excused from performance.

The following clause, taken from a standard or share purchase agreement (a business acquisition agreement), illustrates how an express condition might operate.

ARTICLE 6 — Conditions

6(1) *Conditions to the Obligations of the Purchaser.* Notwithstanding anything herein contained, the obligation of the Buyer to complete the transactions provided for herein will be subject to the fulfilment of the following conditions at or prior to the Closing Time, and the Seller and the Shareholder jointly and severally covenant to use their best efforts to ensure that such conditions are fulfilled.

. . .

(2) *Material Adverse Changes.* During the Interim Period there will have been no change in the Condition of the Business, howsoever arising, except changes which have occurred in the ordinary course of the Business and which, individually or in the aggregate, have not affected and may not affect the Condition of the Business in any material adverse respect. . . .

Such a clause has an obvious purpose in excusing the buyer if there is some materially adverse change in the business being bought. Note that the change does not have to have been brought about by the fault of the seller or to have any specified source: the buyer will be excused because the event occurred.

EXPRESS CONDITIONS

The term "condition" can be defined as: "An explicit contractual provision which provides either: (1) that a party to the contract is not obliged to perform one or more of its duties thereunder unless some state of events occurs or fails to occur; or (2) that, if some state of events occurs or fails to occur, the obligation of a party to perform one or more of its duties thereunder is suspended or terminated." (Fuller and Eisenberg, *Basic Contract Law*, 4th ed. (St. Paul: West Publishing Co., 1981), at 956).

Sometimes the first part of this definition is divided into two separate situations and these are referred to as "conditions precedent" and "conditions subsequent". There are judicial statements that suggest differences in the analysis depending on the classification of a condition as precedent or subsequent. It has, for example, been said that with a condition precedent, if the condition precedent is not satisfied, the contract never comes into existence. With a condition subsequent, on the other hand, the contract came into existence, but obligations under it come to an end if the condition is not satisfied.

The idea that a condition precedent suspends the operation of any contractual obligations is often no more than a vivid way of describing the condition's effect. Like many vivid aphorisms — the "shield/sword" distinction in promissory estoppel, for example — it can mislead if it is taken literally. The making of a contract, whether or not it is wholly enforceable, can, like the obligation arising from the starting of negotiations in *Lac Minerals* (*supra*, Chapter 3), impose duties that will be recognized and enforced by the courts.

The use of conditions permits contract planning of two kinds. The first kind, illustrated by the condition quoted above, permits the buyer to walk away from the deal while the seller remains bound. This lopsided effect has occasionally led courts to restrict the buyer's right to enforce a contract by waiving compliance with the condition. The second use of conditions in contract planning permits a party to walk away from a deal that has not worked out as had been hoped and to avoid throwing good money after bad. If the event which provides the excuse is a breach, one party might have a claim in damages, but that will always be perceived by those in contractual relations as far less valuable than being able to get out of the deal or having an excuse for doing no more under the contract.

A condition of the type quoted is also of value to the seller. First, the seller may, by accepting the condition, get at least the chance that someone will undertake to buy its business (provided, of course, that no materially adverse change occurs and many other conditions are satisfied). If the seller did not accept the condition, it might be asked to promise that no materially adverse change would occur. There are many reasons why a seller would be unwilling to give such an undertaking. Both parties would much prefer to abort the transaction rather than face the risks of litigation.

The two-stage bargaining process that was described in Chapter 3 is a situation where conditions are likely to be used. A commitment from the parties in the form of an executed asset or share purchase agreement provides a basis for seeking such things as the necessary consents to carry on the business, prevents the seller from making a deal with another buyer, and may deal with the problems arising from the fact that extensive disclosure of the details of the seller's business may be involved in obtaining the consents (or in satisfying other conditions).

Another common form of two-stage transaction is the standard sale of a house on the resale market. The parties make a deal on the price and other terms when the agreement of purchase and sale is signed by the purchaser and the vendor. That agreement states when closing is to occur and the other details of the deal. The time that must elapse between the making of the agreement and date of closing specified by the parties permits the purchaser to examine the vendor's title to ascertain that the vendor has clear title. A standard clause in Canadian real estate agreements is a condition that provides that the inability of the vendor to provide good title to the property operates to excuse the purchaser from going ahead and closing the deal rather than as the basis for a claim for damages. Other common clauses may, for example, make it a condition of the deal that the purchaser "obtain satisfactory financing" or have the right to refuse to go ahead if an inspection by a certified home inspector reveals any structural defects.

An express condition can only be included in an agreement with the consent of both parties, and a party may refuse to allow the other to have an excuse for non-performance. Bargaining for inclusion of conditions is much like bargaining for an option: both give one party the right to hold the other to the deal without being similarly bound itself.

The asymmetrical obligations resulting from a condition can create possibilities for abuse and for the kind of concern that was reflected in the judicial attitudes toward letters of intent in Chapter 3; that is, a reluctance to hold one side bound to the contract unless the other is similarly bound. There is nothing objectionable about a condition requiring that all necessary governmental consents to the continued operation of the business be obtained before the purchaser pays the purchase price, for the consents are either given or not given (though, as we shall see, there may be a dispute over which party is to seek the consents).

On the other hand, giving the purchaser of a house the right to terminate the deal unless she "obtains satisfactory financing" raises the problem of the standard by which to judge the financing she is offered. What if she is offered a standard institutional mortgage at market rates? Can she avoid the deal by claiming that "satisfactory" to her meant a mortgage half a point below market rates or for a larger proportion of the purchase price than is customary? The following case raises these issues.

DYNAMIC TRANSPORT LTD. v. O.K. DETAILING LTD.

[1978] S.C.J. No. 52, [1978] 2 S.C.R. 1072, 85 D.L.R. (3d) 19
(S.C.C., Laskin C.J.C., Martland, Ritchie, Pigeon and Dickson JJ.)

[The plaintiff, appellant, purchaser had agreed to purchase land described as "4 acres, more or less" from the defendant, respondent, vendor. The land was part of a 5.42-acre parcel occupied by the defendant. The defendant ultimately refused to complete the transaction (the land having risen substantially in value) and the plaintiff sued for specific performance of the agreement. The trial judge gave judgment for the plaintiff. The defendant's appeal was allowed by the Alberta Court of Appeal. The plaintiff appealed to the Supreme Court of Canada. There were two issues raised on the appeal: the validity of the description of the land under the *Statute of Frauds* and the effect of a requirement that planning permission be obtained before the land could be subdivided. The Supreme Court, in a judgment by Dickson J., held that the description, when taken in conjunction with all the facts, was sufficiently precise to meet the requirements of the *Statute of Frauds*. **DICKSON J.** then turned to the second issue and continued:]

[1]   Both parties were aware that subdivision approval, pursuant to *The Planning Act* [R.S.A. 1970, c. 276], was required, but the agreement is silent as to whether vendor or purchaser would obtain this approval. The statutory prerequisite became an implied term of the agreement. The obtaining of subdivision approval was, in effect, a condition precedent to the performance of the obligations to sell and to buy . . . The parties created a binding agreement. It is true that the performance of some of the provisions of that agreement was not due unless and until the condition was fulfilled, but that in no way negates or dilutes the force of the obligations imposed by those provisions, in particular, the obligation of the vendor to sell and the obligation of the purchaser to buy. These obligations were merely in suspense pending the occurrence of the event constituting the condition precedent.

[2]   The existence of a condition precedent does not preclude the possibility of some provisions of a contract being operative before the condition is fulfilled, as

for example, a provision obligating one party to take steps to bring about the event constituting the condition precedent. . . .

[3] In appropriate circumstances the courts will find an implied promise by one party to take steps to bring about the event constituting the condition present: see Cheshire and Fifoot's *Law of Contract*, 9th ed. (1976), at pp. 137-8:

> Where there is a contract but the obligations of one or both parties are subject to conditions a number of subsidiary problems arise. So there may be a question of whether one of the parties has undertaken to bring the condition about . . . There is a clear distinction between a promise, for breach of which an action lies and a condition, upon which an obligation is dependent. But the same event may be both promised and conditional, when it may be called a promissory condition. A common form of contract is one where land is sold "subject to planning permission." In such a contract one could hardly imply a promise to obtain planning permission, since this would be without the control of the parties but the courts have frequently implied a promise by the purchaser to use his best endeavours to obtain planning permission.

[4] There are many cases in which provisions of a contract were subject to the condition precedent of an approval or a licence being obtained, and one party was by inference in the circumstances held to have undertaken to apply for the approval or licence. . . This type of case is merely a specific instance of the general principle that "the court will readily imply a promise on the part of each party to do all that is necessary to secure performance of the contract": 9 *Hals.* (4th ed.), p. 234, para. 350: see also *Chitty on Contracts*, "General Principles" (23rd ed.), p. 316, para. 698, where it is said: "The court will also imply that each party is under an obligation to do all that is necessary on his part to secure performance of the contract."

[5] Section 19(1) of *The Planning Act* of Alberta provides:

> 19.(1) A person who proposes to carry out a division of land shall apply for approval of the proposed subdivision in the manner prescribed by The Subdivision and Transfer Regulations.

"Subdivision" is defined in s. 2(s) as follows:

> (s)   "subdivision" means a division of a parcel by means of a plan of subdivision, plan of survey, agreement or any instrument, including a caveat, transferring or creating an estate or interest in part of the parcel.

[6] In a purchase and sale situation, the "person who proposes to carry out a subdivision of land" is the intending vendor. It is he who must divide his parcel of land, which has hitherto been one unit, for the purpose of sale. If a purchaser carried out the actual work in connection with the application, he could only do so in the vendor's name and as his agent. The vendor is under a duty to act in good faith and to take all reasonable steps to complete the sale. I cannot accept the proposition that failure to fix responsibility for obtaining planning approval renders a contract unenforceable. The common intention to transfer a parcel of land in the knowledge that a subdivision is required in order to effect such transfer must be taken to include agreement that the vendor will make a proper application for subdivision and use his best efforts to obtain such subdivision. This is the only way in which business efficacy can be given to their agreement. In the circumstances of this case, the only reasonable inference to be drawn is that an implied obligation rested on the vendor to apply for subdivision. In making a similar finding on the facts in *Hogg v. Wilken* [(1974), 5 O.R. (2d) 759], Lerner J. said at p. 761:

In this contract the only inference to be drawn is that it was the vendors' obligation to make the application. An application for such consent would have to be carried out in good faith to its logical conclusion by presentation of same to the committee, the necessary appearance before the committee and furnishing any answers or material that would be reasonably within the power of the vendors to supply if requested by that committee.

[7]   In *Hogg v. Wilken* a mandatory order was made in these terms.

[8]   The procedure for application is set forth in detail in *The Planning Act* and the *Regulations* promulgated thereunder. There is no problem in determining the mechanics of what is to be done. The planning approval point was not raised as a possible defence in the statement of defence nor, it would seem, at trial. After delivering oral judgment the trial judge, in discussion with counsel, spoke of this matter as a "practical problem which I am sure you will be able to resolve without difficulty".

[**DICKSON J**. referred to several cases where it had been stated that a person could be compelled to do that which he had undertaken to do. He continued:]

[9]   In the case at bar, the trial judge said:

The plaintiff is entitled to an order for specific performance, and that order will go. In the alternative, the plaintiff is entitled to damages in the sum of $200,000, which I find is the present value of the land.

The judge overlooked the fact of the purchase price of $53,000. Therefore, the correct figure would be $147,000.

[10]   In my opinion, the appellant is entitled to a declaration that the contract between the parties mentioned above is a binding contract in accordance with its terms, including the implied term that the respondent will seek subdivision approval. The appellant is further entitled to an order that the respondent make and pursue a *bona fide* application as may be necessary to obtain registration of the approved plan of subdivision, including registration of the approved plan with the Registrar of the North Alberta Land Registration District if approval is obtained. Such application shall be at the expense of the respondent and shall be made within sixty days following delivery of this judgment, or such extended period as may be ordered by a judge of the Trial Division of the Supreme Court of Alberta in Chambers. In the event that the respondent does not make such application within the time stated, or does not pursue such application with due diligence, the appellant shall be entitled to damages for loss of its bargain in an amount of $147,000. Upon the application for subdivision being successfully made and completed, including registration of the approved plan, the remaining provisions of the agreement, concerning the actual sale and purchase of the land, shall be specifically performed and carried into effect. The date of closing, date of adjustments, and any other matters incidental to closing the transaction shall be as ordered by a judge of the Trial Division of the Supreme Court of Alberta in Chambers. In the event that the respondent makes and pursues a *bona fide* application as aforesaid, and such application is rejected, then the appellant's claim for specific performance of the provisions concerning sale and purchase stands dismissed, as does the claim for damages in the alternative, and the caveat filed by the appellant shall be discharged. Until that time, the caveat may be maintained.

[11] I would allow the appeal, set aside the judgment of the Appellate Division and substitute therefor an order as aforementioned.

NOTES AND QUESTIONS

1. Every contract is incomplete in the sense that the words used may have to be interpreted in the context in which their meaning or force has to be considered. Contracts are incomplete in another sense when some kind of machinery or some extended course of action has to be imposed on (or expected of) one party or the other to make the arrangement work. Whether a contract will be completed in either of these senses can often be a difficult problem to decide.

    Dickson J. in *Dynamic Transport* imposed an obligation to make "good faith" efforts to perform to give effect to what he assumed the parties must have intended by the deal that they made. He said (¶ 6): "The vendor is under a duty to act in good faith and to take all reasonable steps to complete the sale." Dickson J. went on (¶ 6) to show precisely where the obligation came from:

    > I cannot accept the proposition that failure to fix responsibility for obtaining planning approval renders a contract unenforceable. The common intention to transfer a parcel of land in the knowledge that a subdivision is required in order to effect such transfer must be taken to include agreement that the vendor will make a proper application for subdivision and use his best efforts to obtain such subdivision. This is the only way in which business efficacy can be given to their agreement.

    What is important in every case is the attitude of the court to the job of making the parties' arrangement work. Dickson J. sees the court's role as facilitating the parties' task of making the agreement work: the parties can rely on the court adding obligations to the agreement or on drawing inferences from it to "fill in the blanks".

2. It has become routine to impose obligations of good faith performance on developers who enter into agreements conditional on planning permission being obtained. Similarly, if a transaction is conditional on a lessor's or a mortgagee's consent, a failure to seek the consent in good faith may well expose a party to substantial damages: *Metropolitan Trust Co. of Canada v. Pressure Concrete Services Ltd.* (1976), 9 O.R. (2d) 375, 60 D.L.R. (3d) 431 (C.A.), affirming [1973] 3 O.R. 629, 37 D.L.R. (3d) 649. The scope of contractual obligations to perform in good faith is further explored in Chapter 6. What is important now is to note that such obligations may be imposed and the effect of the imposition of an obligation to perform in good faith.

3. It is not uncommon for conditions to be included in agreements to purchase real estate that make performance of the agreement conditional upon the purchaser being "satisfied" about some matter related to the purchase, such as "arranging satisfactory financing" or having a "satisfactory home inspection". This type of clause gives a purchaser significant discretion, but despite its widespread use, there is no judicial consensus about how this type of clause is to be interpreted.

    In *869125 Ontario Inc. v. Angeli* (1997), 27 O.T.C. 296, 10 R.P.R. (3d) 18 (Gen. Div.) an agreement for the sale of vacant land for development purposes gave the purchaser almost one year from the date of signing the agreement to "satisfy itself as to the development status, the development potential, the economic feasibility and the soil conditions of the subject property. . . . If the purchaser cannot satisfy itself as to [this] Feasibility Condition, within the time limit, the Purchaser shall have the right in its sole and unlimited discretion to elect to cancel this Agreement" and have its deposit returned. Boyko J. held (p. 28 R.P.R.) that adding the word 'unlimited' to the phrase 'sole discretion' gives the purchaser "great latitude", but does not relieve the purchaser from having to provide the vendor with "some explanation, backed by some evidence, capable of establishing that the discretion was exercised honestly, in good faith and reasonably in the circumstances". Boyko J. thus took what has been charac-

terized as an "objective and good faith approach" to the judicial supervision of the
purchaser's exercise of discretion.

In *Marshall v. Bernard Place Corp.* [2002] O.J. No. 463, 58 O.R. (3d) 97 (C.A.)
the purchaser agreed to buy a renovated house in Toronto for $1,510,000 with a
$150,000 deposit. The agreement was conditional upon the purchaser's obtaining a
home inspection report "satisfactory to him in his sole and absolute discretion". The
inspection report identified some minor deficiencies that could be remedied by the expenditure of about $2,200. The purchaser had wanted to acquire a "carefree house"
and decided not to proceed with the transaction. The vendor claimed that there was no
"reasonable" basis for not proceeding, since the deficiencies were very minor compared to the value of the house. At trial, Keenan J. held that the purchaser was entitled
to rely on this condition and ordered the deposit returned. In considering whether this
type of clause is "subjective" or "objective", he wrote (36 R.P.R. (3d) 153, at pp. 159-
63):

. . .

. . . In the present case, the use of the words "a report satisfactory to him in his
sole and absolute discretion" would clearly express an intention to create an
option. It would then be subject only to the provision that it be exercised honestly. I would not go so far as to call the condition clause an option because
there remains a requirement of reasonableness, honesty and good faith. However, the very broadly worded discretion imputes a very broad subjective element and comes very close to an option.

. . .

. . . [T]he condition clause which was agreed by the parties contains clear
words that gave to the Marshalls the right to engage a building inspector of
their own choice and at their own expense and to receive a report satisfactory to them in their sole and absolute discretion. The parties also agreed
that the condition is included in the Agreement for the sole benefit of the
Purchaser and may be waived at the Purchaser's sole option. The wording
clearly excludes any participation by the Vendor in the property inspection
or the decision whether the report is satisfactory or should be satisfactory to
the Purchaser. It is not open to the Vendor to say that the Purchaser ought
to have been satisfied.

The Ontario Court of Appeal upheld the trial decision, ruling that the vendor had
the right to rely on the condition to excuse performance and to have the deposit returned. However, Cronk J.A., giving the judgment of the Court, took a different view
of the standard for the exercise of a "discretion clause", rejecting a subjective approach. She said:

[19] ... the contract controls the standard to be applied to a sole discretion
clause. The determination of whether a discretionary condition imposes a subjective or objective standard depends upon "the intention of the parties as disclosed by their contract".

[20] The requirement of honesty and good faith applies whether the exercise
of discretion is measured by an objective or subjective standard. ... No contractual discretion is absolute, in the sense of authorizing the capricious or arbitrary exercise of the discretion. ... even a broadly stated contractual discretion is not "unbridled" and is subject to established limits.

[21] In my view, absent express contractual language to the contrary, an inspection report which identifies deficiencies in the construction or integrity of
a house provides an objective basis on which to assess the potential exercise
of discretion under a discretionary property inspection condition. The intention of the parties, as reflected in the language of the condition, then deter-

mines the scope for subjective assessment of the materiality of the identified deficiencies. The language of a contract may afford considerable latitude to a party seeking to rely on a discretionary property inspection condition where an inspection report provides objective evidence on which to base a decision that the deficiencies identified in the report are sufficiently unacceptable as to warrant a decision not to complete the transaction.

Cronk J.A. concluded that the vendor had to exercise the discretion granted by this clause with "good faith, honesty and reasonableness," and held that this standard was met in this case. She said:

[26] … it is also my view that the subject-matter of this Agreement attracts elements of an objective standard of reasonableness. The Agreement relates to the acquisition of a residential property. The integrity of the property and its condition are matters which are capable of objective measurement. As indicated above, this suggests that, in the first instance, objective factors must ground the exercise of discretion under the condition. If such objective factors exist, the language of the condition will then establish what latitude is given to the party seeking to rely on the condition in determining whether the risks associated with the identified deficiencies in the property are acceptable in the circumstances. This determination must be reasonably based, and the discretion must be exercised honestly and in good faith. In the circumstances of this case, therefore, the contract between the parties dictates that a standard of reasonableness containing, first, objective, and second, subjective, elements governs the exercise of discretion under the property inspection condition. It remains, then, to consider whether the respondents met this standard in relying on the inspection condition, acting honestly and in good faith.

[27] The inspection report identified physical deficiencies which could be remedied at minimal cost; however, the true risks associated with some of the deficiencies could not be determined at the time of the inspection. In addition, the report gave rise to the prospect of coping with the deficiencies, and effecting necessary repairs, when a tenant was in possession of the premises. These were legitimate uncertainties and inconveniences which the respondents were entitled to take into account.

There is clearly a growing judicial acceptance that the power granted by a discretionary condition must be exercised reasonably and in good faith, that is, honestly and consistently with the purpose for which it was conferred. The decisions also illustrate that it can be difficult for lawyers to predict exactly what the courts will accept as a "good faith" and "reasonable" exercise of discretion.

The attitude of the courts to the kind of power conferred on the buyer by the language of the clause used in *Marshall v. Bernard Place*, is further illustrated by the courts' attitude to the power of a lender under a demand loan — a very common financing arrangement in which the lender may demand payment at any time. The courts have held that the lender, in spite of the clear words in the credit agreement must give notice before taking steps (usually the appointment of a receiver to manage or realize on the borrower's assets) when the demand for immediate payment of the loan is not met. This limit on the banks' power was imposed by the Supreme Court in *Ronald Elwyn Lister Ltd. v. Dunlop Canada Ltd.*, [1982] S.C.J. No. 38, [1982] 1 S.C.R. 726, 135 D.L.R. (3d) 1, and *Houle v. National Bank of Canada*, [1990] S.C.J. No. 120, [1990] 3 S.C.R. 122, 74 D.L.R. (4th) 577. Another example is *Kavcar Investments Ltd. v. Aetna Financial Services Ltd.*, [1989] O.J. No. 1723, 70 O.R. (2d) 225, 62 D.L.R. (4th) 277 (C.A.).

In spite of what the courts say, many parties, particularly those in a relatively stronger bargaining position, really want their "sole and absolute discretion" to be precisely that and wholly subject to their subjective reasons.

Waiver of Conditions

A condition is usually made a term of a contract at the insistence of or for the benefit of one party. In some situations the party who wanted the condition included in the contract or who is to benefit from the term, wants to "waive" the condition and require performance even if the condition is not satisfied. The question of whether this is permissible is surprisingly complex.

The issue of waiver may, for example, arise when there is a contract for the sale of vacant land which the purchaser plans to develop. The purchaser knows that planning permission will have to be obtained. To protect itself, the purchaser will make the grant of planning permission a condition of the purchaser's obligation to pay for the land. The Supreme Court of Canada in *Dynamic Transport v. O.K. Detailing* imposed the obligation to seek planning permission on the vendor under an "implied condition" of the contract. It is more common for an agreement for the sale of land that requires planning permission to specify that the purchaser will have the obligation to seek that approval. Even with the order of specific performance, the purchaser in *Dynamic Transport* might have preferred to be the one to seek permission.

A person who buys land for development must usually incur the costs of seeking permission to develop the land. The process involved in obtaining development permission may be very expensive and drawn out, particularly if the application is opposed by ratepayer or other groups. Concerns for the environment may make the process even longer and more expensive, as the amount of information needed by all levels of government has increased. The vendor, especially if he or she is a farmer or the owner of a large lot, will not want to incur, and indeed may not be able to afford, the expenses of seeking permission without a buyer for the land. In any event, permission may be dependent on the plans of a specific purchaser, so that it may simply be a waste of time for the owner to seek permission to develop the land. The purchaser who is prepared to incur the costs of seeking permission will not want to incur those costs without an assurance that, if permission is given, it will be able to buy the land. Similarly, the purchaser will not want to pay the full development value of the land until it is sure that permission will be given, and the vendor will want to obtain a higher value than the land has as "raw land" and appropriate for himself or herself some of the development value of the land. The risks and chances of gain that each party faces will be allocated by the use of express conditions.

The chances of breach of a contract for the sale of land are directly proportional to the relative change in the value of the land over the time between the original agreement and closing, and the extent of the change will be a function of the length of that period and the rate of change. The longer the period for satisfaction of the condition, the greater the chance that price shifts will make the deal less attractive to one of the parties. The more difficult it is to obtain permission, the higher the costs facing the purchaser.

Changes in the value of the land may, for example, make the deal very much more favourable to the purchaser so that it might believe that the deal is a good deal even if planning permission has not actually been given. If the development proposal seems close to the point where permission will be given, the purchaser may be prepared to take whatever risk there is that permission will not be obtained and may want to go ahead with the deal. A purchaser who believes that a deal will be worthwhile even if permission has not yet been obtained may try to "waive" the condition, rather than using the fact that the condition has not been satisfied to end the deal. If, however, the value of the land has risen significantly, the vendor may be very happy to have the deal die, as the land, perhaps with permission very nearly obtained, can now be sold for a much higher price.

Unfortunately, the law regarding waiver of conditions is not as simple as it might be. The next few cases explore this issue.

TURNEY v. ZHILKA

[1959] S.C.J. No. 37, [1959] S.C.R. 578, 18 D.L.R. (2d) 447
(S.C.C., Taschereau, Locke, Cartwright, Martland and Judson JJ.)

[Zhilka agreed to purchase property from the Turneys. The agreement contained a condition that stated: "Providing the property can be annexed to the Village of Streetsville and a plan is approved by the Village Council for subdivision." Neither party agreed to fulfil this condition and neither party expressly reserved a power of waiver. The purchaser Zhilka made some enquiries of the Village Council, but made little progress and received little encouragement, and the prospects of annexation were, on the evidence, remote. Later, Zhilka purported to waive this condition on the ground that it was solely for his benefit and was severable, and he sued for specific performance without reference to the condition.]

JUDSON J.: — **[1]** The learned trial judge found that the condition was one introduced for the sole benefit of the purchaser and that he could waive it.

[2] I have doubts whether this inference may be drawn from the evidence adduced in this case, but, in any event, the defence falls to be decided on broader grounds. The cases on which the judgment is founded are *Hawksley v. Outram*, [[1892] 3 Ch. 359], and *Morrell v. Studd*, [[1913] 2 Ch. 648]. In the first case a purchaser of a business stipulated in the contract of sale that he should have the right to carry on under the old name and that the vendors would not compete within a certain area. A dispute arose whether one of the vendors, who had signed the contract of sale under a power of attorney from another, had acted within his power. The purchaser then said that he would waive these rights and successfully sued for specific performance. In the second case, the contract provided that the purchaser should pay a certain sum on completion and the balance within two years. He also promised to secure the balance to the vendor's satisfaction. The purchaser raised difficulties about the performance of this promise, and the vendor said that he would waive it and take the purchaser's unsecured promise. It was held that he was entitled to do so. All that waiver means in these circumstances is that one party to a contract may forgo a promised advantage or may dispense with part of the promised performance of the other party which is simply and solely for the benefit of the first party and is severable from the rest of the contract.

[3] But here there is no right to be waived. The obligations under the contract, on both sides, depend upon a future uncertain event, the happening of which depends entirely on the will of a third party, the Village Council. This is a true condition precedent, an external condition upon which the existence of the obligation depends. Until the event occurs there is no right to performance on either side. The parties have not promised that it will occur. In the absence of such a promise there can be no breach of contract until the event does occur. The purchaser now seeks to make the vendor liable on his promise to convey in spite of the non-performance of the condition and this to suit his own convenience only. This is not a case of renunciation or relinquishment of a right but rather an attempt by one party, without the consent of the other, to write a new contract. Waiver has often been referred to as a troublesome and uncertain term in the law but it does at least presuppose the existence of a right to be relinquished.

[The action was dismissed with costs.]

BEAUCHAMP v. BEAUCHAMP

[1973] 2 O.R. 43, 32 D.L.R. (3d) 693
(C.A., Gale C.J.O., Jessup and Arnup JJ.A.)

GALE C.J.O.: — **[1]** On April 13, 1971, the appellants signed an offer to purchase certain lands in the Township of Gloucester for the sum of $15,500 in cash. I emphasize that the purchasers were to pay cash and nothing else, in the form of a deposit of $500, and the balance on closing. The closing was to take place on July 1st. The agreement also had the following condition included in it:

> This sale is conditional for a period of 15 days from date of acceptance of same upon the Purchaser of his Agent being able to obtain a first mortgage in the amount of Ten Thousand Dollars ($10,000.00) bearing interest at the current rate otherwise, this offer shall be null and void and all deposit monies shall be returned to the Purchaser without interest or any other charge. This offer is also conditional for a period of 15 days from date of acceptance of same upon the Purchaser or his Agent being able to secure a second mortgage in the amount of $2,500.00 for a period of five (5) years, bearing interest at the current rate, otherwise, this offer shall be null and void and all deposit monies returned to the Purchaser without interest or any other charge.

[2] The appellants were able to arrange for a first mortgage of $12,000 and, on April 28, 1971, as found by the trial Judge, they caused a notice in the following form to be delivered to the respondents:

> This is to notify you that the condition specified on the agreement of purchase and sale between Mr. Vianney Beauchamp and Carmen Beauchamp herein called the Vendors and Mr. Ronald Beauchamp and Pauline Beauchamp herein called the Purchasers has been met. The transaction will therefore close as per the agreement.

[3] The Judge . . . dismissed the appellant's action for specific performance, holding that the respondents were excused from completing the sale on the ground that the condition which I have quoted was a condition precedent which had not been strictly complied with by the appellants' arranging of a first mortgage of $10,000 and a second mortgage of $2,500.

[4] We point out, as did the trial judge, that the condition was solely for the protection of the appellants, and all the respondents were interested in was receiving the sum of $15,500 in cash. The notice to which I have referred brought home to the respondents the fact that payment of the $15,500 in cash would be made and that the appellants had met the condition referred to in the offer, or, alternatively, were waiving it.

[5] In those circumstances, we are of the view that the learned trial Judge erred in declining to order specific performance. Counsel for the respondents relied upon the cases of *Turney et al. v. Zhilka* [*supra*] and *Aldercrest Developments Ltd. v. Hunter et al.*, [1970] 2 O.R. 562, 11 D.L.R. (3d) 439, for the proposition that a true condition precedent cannot be waived, even though it is in favour of one party only and the fulfilment of the condition is completely within the control of that one party. We do not think that those cases are appropriate to the circumstances here; they are distinguishable, as the condition herein is not such as is dealt with in those cases.

[6] The appeal will therefore be allowed and judgment given for specific performance, with costs to the appellants throughout.

[An appeal to the Supreme Court of Canada was dismissed without reasons or requiring the respondent to argue; per Laskin C.J.C., Martland, Judson, Spence, and Dickson JJ. See [1974] S.C.R. v, 40 D.L.R. (3d) 160.]

QUESTION

Why was the condition in *Beauchamp* not "such as was dealt with" in *Turney v. Zhilka*?

BARNETT v. HARRISON

[1975] S.C.J. No. 88, [1976] 2 S.C.R. 531, 57 D.L.R. (3d) 225
(S.C.C., Laskin C.J.C., Judson, Martland, Ritchie, Pigeon, Beetz,
Dickson, Spence and de Grandpré JJ.)

[An agreement for the purchase by Barnett of lands owned by Harrison contained the following clause:

> If this offer is accepted by the vendors, the contract of purchase and sale will be subject to the condition that the necessary approvals of the Ontario Municipal Board and the Town of Stoney Creek to the site plan and proposed changes in zoning, and any approval of the Committee of Adjustment or Planning Board required are given. The applications for and all matters and appearances relating to such approval shall be prepared by and at the expense of the purchaser but may be brought in the names of the vendors. The vendors agree and undertake to give all help and co-operation required by the purchaser and to execute all necessary documents and make all attendances necessary (without costs to the purchaser) to assist in and facilitate the obtaining of the approvals and registrations required by the purchaser. It is agreed between the parties that the Application and hearing before the Ontario Municipal Board shall be completed on or before the 30th day of September, 1968 (without the decision necessarily having been made). Provided however, if any adjournment results from opposition beyond the control of the purchaser, then the said date for completion of the application and hearing shall be extended to the 31st day of January, 1969 at the latest. Provided further, that the purchaser shall within two months after all Municipal approvals have been granted, cause an appointment to be obtained for a hearing before the Ontario Municipal Board. In the event that these conditions are not complied with, then notwithstanding anything herein contained, the agreement of purchase and sale shall be null and void and the deposit monies returned to the purchaser.

Barnett made assiduous efforts to obtain the requisite approvals, but the Town planning authorities were processing his application in a lethargic way. On September 30, Barnett "in a last minute attempt to save the agreement" gave notice to Harrison that he waived the condition. Harrison replied that as the conditions had not been fulfilled, the agreement was "null and void". Barnett sued for specific performance.]

DICKSON J.: — [1] . . . This case raises once again the question whether a contracting party may waive a condition of the contract on the ground it is intended only for his benefit, and then bring an action for specific performance.

[2] . . . There can be no doubt on the evidence that the purchaser seriously planned and assiduously sought approval of a major housing development. The approval, a future uncertain event, was entirely dependent upon the will of third parties, the Town of Stoney Creek, the Planning Board, the Minister and the Ontario Municipal Board. The factual infrastructure of this case may differ in detail from *Turney v. Zhilka* [*supra*] . . . I do not think, however, it can be very seriously questioned that the general principle laid down in *Turney v. Zhilka* applies.

[3] The Court was invited by counsel for the appellant to reappraise the rule in *Turney v. Zhilka* if that case was found to be controlling. Counsel cited a number of American and English authorities which support the broad proposition that a party to a contract can waive a condition that is for his benefit. Despite the support elsewhere for such a general proposition, I am of the view the rule expressed in *Turney v. Zhilka* should not be disturbed for several reasons. First, the distinction made in *Turney v. Zhilka* between (i) the manifest right of A to waive default by B in the performance of a severable condition intended for the benefit of A and (ii) the attempt by A to waive his own default or the default of C, upon whom depends the performance which gives rise to the obligation, i.e., the true condition precedent, seems to me, with respect, to be valid. Second, when parties, as here, aided by legal advisors, make a contract subject to explicit conditions precedent and provide therein specifically that in the event of non-compliance with one or more of the conditions, the contract shall be void, the Court runs roughshod over the agreement by introducing an implied provision conceding to the purchaser the right to waive compliance. In the instant case the conditions for water and sewer requirements were expressed to be subject to waiver at the option of the purchaser but the conditions respecting site plan and zoning were not; if all of these various conditions were to be placed on the same footing, the Court would be simply rewriting the agreement. Third, if the purchaser is to be put in the position of being able to rely on the conditions precedent or to waive them, depending on which course is to his greater benefit, the result may be that the purchaser has been given an option to purchase, for which he has paid nothing; if the property increases in value, the purchaser waives compliance and demands specific performance but if the property declines in value, the purchaser does not waive compliance and the agreement becomes null and void in accordance with its terms. It is right to say that this opportunity to select against the vendors will not arise in every case. The zoning changes or other contingency, the subject-matter of the condition precedent, may be approved by the third party or otherwise satisfied within the purchase. He will not be permitted purposely to fail to perform his obligations in order to avoid the contract. But even when, as here, no question of bad faith arises, approvals may not be forthcoming within the prescribed time, and the vendors, whose lands have been tied up for 20 months, can be in the position where they do not know until the final day whether or not the purchaser will waive compliance and whether or not the sale will be completed. If what has been termed an agreement of purchase and sale is to be in reality an option, the purchaser will take the benefit of the appreciation in land value during the intervening months but if the agreement takes effect in accordance with its terms the vendors will have that benefit. I can see no injustice to the purchaser if the contract terms prevail and possible injustice to vendors if they do not. Fourth, application of the rule in *Turney v. Zhilka* may avoid determination of two questions which can give rise to difficulty (i) whether the condition precedent is for the benefit of the purchaser alone or for the joint benefit and (ii) whether the conditions precedent are severable from the balance of the agreement. I am inclined to the view in the present case that they are not. Finally, the rule in *Turney v. Zhilka* has been in effect since 1959, and has been applied many times. In the interests of certainty and predictability in the law, the rule should endure unless compelling reason for change be shown. If in any case the parties agree that the rule shall not apply, that can be readily written into the agreement . . .

[4]   [The case of *Beauchamp v. Beauchamp* was cited by counsel for the appellant. There,] the vendors refused to close on the ground the condition precedent had not been strictly complied with but the position was untenable. The patent purpose of the condition was to afford the purchasers an opportunity of raising the moneys with which to complete the purchase; in this they were successful and so advised the vendors timeously. It was of no importance whatever that the funds required by the purchasers came from a first mortgage for $12,000 rather than a first mortgage for $10,000 and a second mortgage of $2,500. That case should, I think, be regarded as one in which the condition precedent was satisfied and not as one in which it was waived. I would dismiss the appeal with costs.

[**JUDSON, MARTLAND, RITCHIE, PIGEON, BEETZ** and **DE GRANDPRÉ JJ.** concurred with **DICKSON J.**]

LASKIN C.J.C. (Dissenting): — [5] I pass now to a consideration of *Turney v. Zhilka* and to the principle on which it was based . . . Judson J. speaking for this Court read [the condition in that case] as depending (to use his words) entirely on the will of a third party. That is not the present case, it being quite clear under the contract (even apart from the evidence of the vendors) that it was the purchaser who was to prepare and seek approval of a site plan, and of necessary rezoning, in order to carry out his apartment project which was the known and particularized use to which the land was to be put. Since the obligation to proceed with a site plan and to seek rezoning was expressly put on the purchaser, and since, on the evidence, the condition was exacted by him solely for his benefit, there is a marked difference between the present case and *Turney v. Zhilka*.

[6]   The issue raised by [that case] . . . appears to me to require a proper understanding of the phrase "true condition precedent" which was used by Judson J. . . .

[7]   A condition which is characterized as a condition precedent may be one in which both parties have an interest and yet it may be subject to waiver at the suit of one only of the parties. That is because their interest in it may not be the same. The condition may be for the protection of one party only in the sense that it is solely for his benefit, but it may be important to the other party in the sense that he is entitled to know the consequence of its performance or waiver by the date fixed for its performance so that he may, if he is the vendor, either collect his money or be free to look for another purchaser. It would, in my view, be a mistake to move from the fact that both parties have an interest in the performance or non-performance of a condition of the contract to the conclusion that the condition cannot therefore be waived at the suit of the one party for whose sole benefit the condition was introduced into the contract. Some of the submissions made here, especially on the re-argument of the appeal, failed to draw this distinction which, to me, is a vital one.

[8] Another distinction that appears to me to be vital is one that is clear upon a comparison of the relevant conditions in *Turney v. Zhilka* and in the present case. The fact that the conduct or action of a third party is involved in the proper per- formance of a condition does not on that ground alone make it a "true condition precedent" which cannot be waived. Thus, to take a homely example, the fact that a purchaser may make it a condition of completion that he be able to obtain mort- gage financing within a fixed period does not, in my opinion, preclude him from waiving the condition and paying in cash, provided, of course, he makes his elec- tion to waive the condition within the period fixed by the contract. . . . In principle, there is no difference between the foregoing situation and one where the duty of one of the parties to the contract arises only upon the act of a third party, as for example, the obligation to pay money upon the certificate of an architect or engi- neer. Of course, the obligor is not likely to make the payment unless the certificate is provided, but the fact that he could insist on its production does not mean that he could not waive this condition of his duty to pay. . . .

[9] What has sometimes complicated the application of this principle are cases which involved not the performance of a concluded contract but rather the ques- tion whether there was a concluded contract. . . . Thus, where a transaction was subject to "the preparation by my solicitor and completion of a formal contract," it could not be said that the vendor could waive this provision and create a contract by his unilateral act. . . .

[10] I take *Turney v. Zhilka* to have involved, as a matter of construction, a con- dition which was applicable to the duty of both parties. As Judson J. put it . . . "the obligations under the contract, *on both sides* depend upon a future uncertain event, the happening of which depends entirely on the will of a third party, the Village council." (The emphasis is mine.) It is on this basis only that it can be said, as Judson J. did, that there was here a "true condition precedent," that is one external to the obligations of both parties and one where the contract did not give the car- riage of the matter to either one of the parties so as to provide a basis for contend- ing that it was for his benefit alone and could be waived by him. This construction of a condition involving some action of a third party is not a necessary one. . . . Nevertheless, there can be no doubt that, in particular situations of which *Turney v. Zhilka* is illustrative, a provision for rezoning or redevelopment consent may be construed as one for the mutual advantage or benefit of both of the parties to a contract of sale of land and hence not open to unilateral waiver. . . .

[11] I cannot but think that if the condition in the present case [is not an instance] of [a condition] which can be waived by the one party to whose duty of perform- ance they go, there can hardly be any case in which waiver can be lawfully ef- fected short of an express provision therefor in the contract of sale. No doubt this is a salutary procedure, but the law of contract has long ago ceased to depend on exact expression of every consequence of a contractual provision.

[12] An examination of the case law in England, in Australia, in New Zealand and the United States discloses no differentiation in applicable principle between those provisions where action of a third party is involved and those where only the action of the opposite party is involved so far as concerns the right of waiver of a provision which is found to be for the benefit of one party only. Of course, a party cannot base a claim for performance by the opposite party of a conditional obliga- tion on his own failure to perform, unless it can be said that the failure relates to a mere promise rather than to the condition; but, even as to a condition to which a party is obliged in favour of the opposite party, the latter may elect to enforce the contract rather than rescind upon breach of the condition.

[13] The present case, in a sense, shows the opposite side of the coin because if the provision in question is solely for the benefit of a party who decides to renounce that benefit, there is then no impediment to calling for the opposite party's performance provided the provision waived is not tied in with other terms from which it cannot be now extricated by way of unilateral relinquishment. What the earlier observation shows, however, is that failure to perform a condition does not necessarily mean that there is no contract to enforce since the innocent party may elect to keep it alive. . . .

[14] Having had the benefit of seeing the reasons prepared by my brother Dickson before completing my own, I would underline two of the points of difference between us. I do not view waiver as involving a rewriting of an agreement any more than I regard estoppel of a party from insisting upon a term of an agreement as a rewriting thereof. A party that is entitled to a range of benefits under an agreement does not rewrite it against the opposite party by forgoing some of those benefits. Second, I find nothing offensive or prejudicial in the fact that a vendor may not know until completion date whether there will be a waiver so as to give the purchaser a choice to opt out or to insist on performance by the vendor. This is not an uncommon situation in contracts and depends simply on their terms.

[15] In the result, while recognizing the basis upon which *Turney v. Zhilka* proceeded, I do not find that it precludes a contrary conclusion in the present case. . . .

[**SPENCE J.** agreed with **LASKIN C.J.C.**]

QUESTIONS AND NOTES

1. What is the effect of the judgment in *Barnett v. Harrison*? What do each of the parties end up with? Are questions of this sort relevant?

2. In *Kitsilano Enterprises Ltd. v. G. & A. Developments Ltd.* (1990), 48 B.C.L.R. (2d) 70, [1990] 6 W.W.R. 38 (S.C.) Macdonell J. said (p. 84 B.C.L.R.):

   Having analyzed the various lines of authority, it is my view that they can be neatly rationalized by looking first to the conditions to see whether they are true conditions precedent which require nothing to be done to fulfil them. If this is the case, then the agreement cannot be turned into a binding agreement until the conditions are removed and remains an offer until then. If, on the other hand, it can be said that a condition is a promissory condition which requires one of the parties to do something to bring about the fulfilment of the condition in proper circumstances, such an agreement can result in a binding agreement.

   Is there any reason to assume that a distinction, developed in the context of deciding if there is an agreement that can be enforced, can be equally well or as easily applied in another context where the issues are quite different?

3. It is possible to argue that Judson J. made a serious error in *Turney v. Zhilka*. The distinction drawn there between a "true condition precedent" and a "waivable right" seems hard to justify. The two cases referred to by Judson J. are both cases where the right waived was a contractual claim. It makes sense to permit a person to waive a right that he or she is owed under contract. Judson J. appears to believe that only rights under promises can be waived. This conclusion does not follow. The question is

not whether the satisfaction of the condition depends on a person not a party to the contract, but what risks the condition allocated. In other words, if one asks what the purpose of the condition in *Barnett v. Harrison* was, it was fairly obviously to protect the purchaser. If the vendor got the agreed purchase price of the land, why should he care whether permission had or had not been obtained?

It is, of course, possible that a vendor might care whether the condition is satisfied, and the facts of *Turney v. Zhilka* might perhaps provide such an example because the vendors retained land close to the land that was the subject of the contract. The vendors might then have a stake in development permission that transcended the particular deal involved in the case. (It has to be admitted that this explanation for the result in *Turney v. Zhilka* may, on the facts, be farfetched.) If, however, it is assumed that the condition was not solely for the benefit of the purchaser, then waiver should not be allowed. That decision has nothing to do with what a purchaser should be able to do, absent evidence that the condition was for the benefit of *both* parties, but everything to do with the nature of the deal and the allocation of the risks the parties made. As the treatment of *Turney v. Zhilka* in *Beauchamp v. Beauchamp* demonstrates, the courts will tend not to follow a decision that they find leads to unpalatable results.

4. Dickson J. suggests in *Barnett v. Harrison* that to allow the plaintiff to waive any condition that is not clearly stated to be waivable would make the agreement of purchase and sale no more than an "option contract". This seems hard to accept. It is clearly established that the party who has the obligation to have any condition satisfied must seek in good faith to do so. In any case, the vendor has accepted (and been paid to accept) the risk that the purchaser may have a right to get out of the deal if the condition is not satisfied.

The decisions of the Supreme Court in *Turney v. Zhilka* and *Barnett v. Harrison* created serious confusion, particularly in real estate transactions. Of course, if parties have had good legal advice and have expressly included the right to waive any condition, then the decisions would cause no problems but, as always, bad cases are bad precisely because they catch those who do not have good legal advice. Many cases that have been decided since *Barnett v. Harrison* illustrate the dubious quality of the claim that the decision in that case provided a means for achieving certainty and predictability. Courts have sometimes simply chosen not to follow *Turney v. Zhilka* (as in *Beauchamp v. Beauchamp*) or they have decided that the key lies in being able to decide when a condition is or is not a "true condition precedent" or some other kind of condition precedent. (Whenever courts use the epithet "true" to refer to something which, like a condition, cannot be true or false, it is usually a sign that the decision is based on grounds that the court does not want to or cannot disclose.)

5. In the end, *Barnett v. Harrison* is of limited significance. It can fairly be treated as a case that "on its true interpretation" involved a condition that was precedent to certain duties of each of the parties (in the same way as Laskin C.J.C. regarded *Turney v. Zhilka* as such a case in his dissent in *Barnett v. Harrison*). The *Beauchamp v. Beauchamp* line of cases leaves it open to a willing court to put much into the "interpretive process" so as to find that the condition is precedent to the duty of one party only, a potential escape for it alone. Thus "interpreted," the issues presented by *Barnett v. Harrison* do not arise and "waiver" is permissible.

More open recognition of the importance of the "interpretive process" would enhance certainty and predictability as well as justice in judicial decision-making in this area of law. It should be no more inherently difficult for judges to recognize the need to protect reasonable expectations here than it was for them to do so (with candour and consistency) when they imposed duties of good-faith dealing on parties who seek to rely on the failure of conditions to escape from their obligations.

6. Judson J. in *Turney v. Zhilka*, above, ¶ 3, said that a true condition precedent is "an external condition upon which the existence of the obligation depends". Based on this view, it has sometimes been said that until a condition precedent is satisfied, the agreement is "null and void" or inoperative. This conclusion may be applicable as regards what we may call the substance of the obligation, *i.e.*, the obligation to pay the

purchase price in exchange for the land. As *Dynamic Transport Ltd. v. O.K. Detailing Ltd.* illustrates, an agreement, even before the condition has been waived or satisfied, may impose significant obligations on one party. Broad statements that a contract is "valid" or "null and void" (notice the hallowed legal pleonasm) seldom assist the analysis and often do more harm than good because some judge might believe them.

7. It is now almost universal for transactions where there are conditions for the agreement to state something like:

> The conditions contained in section *.* hereof are inserted for the exclusive benefit of the Purchaser and may be waived in whole or in part by the Purchaser at any time.

No seller is likely to reject a request by a buyer that the agreement contain language to this effect.

8. The following section of the *Law and Equity Act*, R.S.B.C. 1996, c. 253, was first enacted in 1979:

> 54. If the performance of a contract is suspended until the fulfillment of a condition precedent, a party to the contract may waive the fulfillment of the condition precedent, even if the fulfillment of the condition precedent is dependent on the will or actions of a person who is not a party to the contract if
>
> (a) the condition precedent benefits only that party to the contract,
>
> (b) the contract is capable of being performed without fulfillment of the condition precedent, and
>
> (c) where a time is stipulated for fulfillment of the condition precedent, the waiver is made before the time stipulated, and where a time is not stipulated for fulfillment of the condition precedent, the waiver is made within a reasonable time.

This provision was enacted after the British Columbia Law Reform Commission recommended this change. Was "waiver of conditions precedent" an appropriate issue for Law Reform Commission study? Was reform in these terms necessary? Was it desirable?

Would (or should) application of the statute change the result in *Barnett v. Harrison*?

Conditions Subsequent

The conditions examined in the preceding section are considered "conditions precedent": their legal effect is to provide an excuse to the party seeking protection from some risk. They operate to prevent a contract from becoming effective. Conditions subsequent, conditions that provide an excuse for one party's refusal to continue to perform a contract, are also very common. Conditions precedent will operate both in discrete transactions of the *Turney v. Zhilka* or *Barnett v. Harrison* type, and in contracts that establish a framework for future co-operation, a relational contract. Conditions subsequent have little or no role in discrete transactions: once the contract is performed, once the price has been paid for the land, the purchaser can have no remedy other than a claim for damages. In long-term contracts — leases, loans, distribution agreements, agency relations — the parties may well plan that one or other of them may have an excuse for stopping performance. Even if the parties do not include express conditions subsequent in the agreement, the courts are much more likely to draw an inference that an event has occurred that operates to discharge one of the parties in the circumstances, that is, to imply a condition.

There are a number of standard clauses that operate as conditions subsequent. In many agreements there will be a list of "events of default". For example, in standard bank credit agreements, the agreements that govern almost all lending by Canadian chartered banks to their corporate customers, there will be a long list of these default events, typically in a clause like the following:

> **12.01 Events of Default.** Upon the occurrence of any one or more of the following events:
>
> (a) the non-payment of any amount due hereunder within five Banking Days after notice of non-payment has been given to the Borrower by the Bank;
>
> (b) the commencement of proceedings for the dissolution, liquidation or winding-up of the Borrower or for the suspension of the operations of the Borrower unless such proceedings are being contested in good faith by the Borrower by proper legal proceedings;
>
> (c) if the Borrower ceases or threatens to cease to carry on its business, or is adjudged or declared bankrupt or insolvent or makes an assignment for the general benefit of creditors, petitions or applies to any tribunal for the appointment of a receiver or trustee for it or for any part of its property, or. . . .
>
> the right of the Borrower to obtain any further credit hereunder and all of the obligations of the Bank hereunder to extend such further credit shall automatically terminate and the Bank may, by notice to the Borrower, declare all indebtedness of the Borrower to the Bank pursuant to this agreement . . . to be immediately due and payable whereupon all such indebtedness shall immediately become and be due and payable. . . .

Not only does the occurrence of an event of default discharge the bank from any further obligation to advance money to the borrower under the agreement, but it also gives the bank the right to demand immediate payment. The planning aspects of this kind of clause are obvious.

A similar kind of clause is often found in long-term supply or sale contracts. The clause that follows is taken from a contract for the long-term supply of fuel to foreign utilities for electricity generation.

> **8.01 Party Not Liable for Non-Performance**: A party hereto (in this Article a "Defaulting Party") shall not be liable to the other party hereto for the Defaulting Party's failure to fulfil its obligations under any section of this agreement (other than Article 5 which imposes on the Purchaser the obligation to pay for the goods) if such failure is caused by the occurrence of an Event of Force Majeure. . . .

and an "Event of Force Majeure" is defined in the contract to mean:

> an event which is beyond the reasonable control of a party hereto including an act of God, action or failure to act of any government or governmental board, commission, department, bureau or authority, confiscation, war, blockade, insurrection, riot, terrorist act, sabotage, flood, fire, explosion, epidemic, landslide, lightning, earthquake, storm, accident, strike, lockout, work slowdown, work stoppage, power failure or shortage and any failure (other than a failure caused by the negligence or deliberate act or inaction of a party hereto) of supplies, equipment, labour or transportation.

The occurrence of an event of "force majeure" operates to provide one party (probably the seller in the agreement from which the preceding extract has been taken) with an excuse for its failure to deliver the goods under the contract.

If you were acting for the buyer and were revising this agreement and, in particular, the force majeure clause, would you remove any of the listed catastrophes? Would you draft something entirely different and, if so, what would you say?

IMPLIED CONDITIONS

One practical problem that occasionally causes difficulties with the legal rules applicable to it is the question of the order in which the parties are to perform. It is, for example, almost the invariable practice of an employer to pay an employee his or her wages *after* the latter has worked for a time. The technical response to an employee who sued for his or her wages *before* doing any work would be the argument that the employee's performance is a condition of the employer's obligation to pay anything. There are practical reasons for employers to do what they do, though the parties to an employment contract could of course provide otherwise.

It is similarly common for a meal in a restaurant to be paid for after the meal has been eaten. An action by a restaurant for the price of the meal based on the argument that ordering the meal from the menu was acceptance of the restaurant's offer would, like the employee's claim, be met by the argument that providing the meal was a condition of the customer's obligation to pay. Again, there will be many situations — at fast-food restaurants, for example — where it is payment first, meal later.

The general rule of the common law is that performance of the parties' contractual obligations must be simultaneous. As the examples that have just been given illustrate, that rule will be departed from in many common situations. The *Sale of Goods Act*, R.S.O. 1990, c. S.1, for example, states:

> 27. Unless otherwise agreed, delivery of the goods and payment of the price are concurrent conditions, that is to say, the seller shall be ready and willing to give possession of the goods to the buyer in exchange for the price and the buyer shall be ready and willing to pay the price in exchange for possession of the goods.

The closing of a formal transaction like a contract for the purchase and sale of land, a negotiated bank loan or a business acquisition will involve the (almost) simultaneous handing over of cheques and documents, the transfer in the first case and the credit agreement and general security agreement in the second.

Where parties do not entirely trust each other or where they are dealing at a distance, carefully planned steps will be taken to make sure that performance is simultaneous. A seller, for example, will not ship goods until the buyer has provided security for payment in the form of a letter of credit. (A letter of credit, also known as an "lc" or, in this case, a "documentary lc", is an undertaking by a bank to pay the amount specified in the letter in return for the documents giving title to the goods. The attraction of an lc from the seller's point of view is that it is equivalent to cash. A "standby lc" is a general form of security under which a bank promises to pay if its customer does not. A bank will have taken security from its customer to cover the risk that it is taking.) The buyer will be protected by requiring the bank to be satisfied that the proper documents have been received.

If one party's performance is a condition of the other's, the obligations are said to be dependent. The obligation of a party to show that it is "ready, willing and able" to perform will then be a condition of the other's performance and an action for breach of the other's obligation will require the first party to meet the condition. The requirements of tender in a contract for the purchase and sale of land recognize that the parties' obligations are dependent. A party "makes tender" by producing evidence that it is ready, willing and able to perform.

Some obligations are independent. It is, for example, well established that a tenant's obligation to pay rent is independent of, for example, the landlord's obligation to repair. This means that a tenant may not withhold rent because the landlord has not repaired the premises.

The purpose of an express condition is that it permits the more careful planning of an exchange relation than would be possible without it. The essence of this planning is that the agreement provides one party (or, possibly, both parties) with an excuse for non-performance. This kind of planning is an explicit allocation of the risks necessarily created by the fact that the parties have made any kind of arrangement for the future, and both parties may benefit from this type of planning.

It is not, however, uncommon for parties to agree that one party will do something, without explicitly providing that one will be excused from further obligations if the other fails to perform. The failure to specify the consequences of non-performance may be a result of lack of adequate legal advice, or because the difficulty of predicting the consequences of breach at the time of formation of the contract makes it very complex for the parties to agree in advance about the consequences of breach. In this situation, if there is a breach by one party, the other party may want to argue that it is excused from performance by the breach. This argument will be put on the basis that the term of the contract should be interpreted to be a condition, or treated as an "implied condition".

When the court says that it is "implying" things into the contract, it may mean that it is drawing an inference from what the parties have said and from the background to the deal. Alternatively, it may mean that the court thinks that certain things *should* have been provided by the parties, or that something *should* happen in the events that have occurred. When the court implies a condition in the contract, it is saying that, in the circumstances, one party should be excused from further performance (or any performance). This way of thinking about the role of courts and their function in dealing with contracts problems suggests that the court is giving effect to the agreement that the parties have made, or to their intention. It is, however, likely that the court is as much motivated by what it thinks is a fair solution to a problem that, *ex hypothesi*, the parties did *not* resolve, as it is by its concern for what they intended. The courts' decisions here are understandably similar to what they do when they consider the nature and extent of the remedies available for breach of contract.

In *Trollope & Colls Ltd. v. North West Metropolitan Regional Hospital Board*, [1973] 2 All E.R. 260, [1973] 1 W.L.R. 601 (H.L.), Lord Pearson said (p. 268 E.R.):

> An unexpressed term can be implied, if and only if the court finds that the parties must have intended that term to form part of their contract: It is not enough for the court to find that such a term would have been adopted by the parties as reasonable men if it had been suggested to them: it must have been a term that went without saying, a term *necessary* to give business efficacy to the contract, a term which, although tacit, formed part of the contract which the parties made for themselves.

A contract will typically be made up of a number of components. When an agreement has been drafted by solicitors, the various components may be identified and explicit provision made for what is to happen if some events do not occur or if one of the parties does not do what it undertook to do. The drafter may have used conditions to excuse one party's performance in some situation. Sometimes it is not possible to give one's client an excuse and then the client's only remedy may be an action for damages. If something has been sold and paid for, the buyer's only remedy may be to sue the seller for breach of contract. Such a remedy was the only thing that the buyer in *Canlin Ltd. v. Thiokol Fibres Can. Ltd.* (*supra*, Chapter 1) could do: it was too late to argue that it had an excuse for not paying the price.

When solicitors have not been involved or if the particular difficulty that has arisen is dealt with by the agreement, the court will be faced with determining whether the event provides one party with an excuse or, if the other has breached the contract, with a remedy in damages. It is broadly true that the more serious the effect of the event on the expectations of the parties (or the party facing a loss because of the event), the more likely it is that the court will regard the event as an excuse. The conclusion that one party is to have an excuse may be expressed by saying that the occurrence (or non-occurrence) of the event is a condition. If the event is not so serious, the party may be compelled to perform, but, if the event was due to the other's breach of contract, may have an action for damages. Such an action is often, as in *Canlin Ltd. v. Thiokol Fibres Can. Ltd.*, one for breach of warranty, *i.e.*, a promise that the goods sold will meet some standard of quality. Warranties are another type of contract term. The special features of warranties and the other kinds of contractual terms that are used will be examined in Chapter 5.

The next case illustrates how a court can approach the problem of deciding whether or not an event, whether caused by external circumstances or by one of the parties, provides an excuse. As you read the case, consider the source of the criteria that the court uses to justify the result that it reaches.

HONGKONG FIR SHIPPING CO. v. KAWASAKI KISEN KAISHA LTD.

[1962] 2 Q.B. 26, [1962] 1 All E.R. 474
(C.A., Sellers, Upjohn and Diplock L.JJ.)

[The plaintiffs bought a ship and chartered it to the defendants. Under the terms of the contract of charterparty, the owners promised that the vessel was "in every way fitted for ordinary cargo service", and that they would "maintain her in a thoroughly efficient state in hull and machinery during service". The charterers promised to pay hire, but under the contract were excused from payment for the time when the ship was in port for repairs. The ship sailed from Liverpool to Newport News, Virginia in February 1957, where coal was picked up to take to Osaka. There were many problems on the voyage: the engine repeatedly broke down and the ship had an incompetent and insufficient crew. The ship reached Osaka on 25 May. It was not ready for sea again until 15 September. Between Liverpool and Osaka it was at sea for eight and one-half weeks, and off hire for five weeks. The ship needed 15 more weeks to get it ready for sea once it reached Osaka. In Osaka the incompetent crew were replaced with a competent crew, and the ship was properly repaired.

On 5 and 6 June and 27 July the charterers wrote repudiating the charter and claiming damages for breach of contract; on 8 and 12 August the owners wrote intimating that they would treat the contract as cancelled by the charterers' wrongful repudiation and claim damages. On 11 September the charterers wrote again repudiating the charter and the owners formally accepted that repudiation on 13

September. Between the time the contract was made and the time of repudiation, there had been a very steep fall in the rate for sea freight, and the defendants could charter another ship for less than half the rate they were paying the plaintiff.

On 8 November 1957, the owners issued a writ against the charterers claiming damages for wrongful repudiation of the charterparty. The charterers alleged breaches by the plaintiffs in that, *inter alia*, the vessel was unseaworthy by reason of her machinery, that the owners had failed to exercise due diligence to make her seaworthy and fitted for the voyage, and that the description in the charterparty of the vessel's steaming capacity was inaccurate; alternatively, they alleged that the charterparty was frustrated by reason of the breakdown and repairs and delays consequent thereon; the charterers also counterclaimed for damages.

The trial judge, Salmon J., held that the shipowners were entitled to damages for breach of contract. The charterer appealed. Only the judgment of Diplock L.J. is reproduced. The other judges agreed in the result.]

DIPLOCK L.J.: — [1] The contract, the familiar Baltime 1939 charter, and the facts on which this case turns have been already stated in the judgment of Sellers L.J. who has also referred to many of the relevant cases. With his analysis of the cases, as with the clear and careful judgment of Salmon J., I am in agreement, and I desire to add only some general observations upon the legal questions which this case involves.

[2]   Every synallagmatic contract contains in it the seeds of the problem: in what event will a party be relieved of his undertaking to do that which he has agreed to do but has not yet done? The contract may itself expressly define some of these events, as in the cancellation clause in a charterparty; but, human prescience being limited, it seldom does so exhaustively and often fails to do so at all. In some classes of contracts, such as sale of goods, marine insurance, contracts of af-freightment evidenced by bills of lading and those between parties to bills of exchange, Parliament has defined by statute some of the events not provided for expressly in individual contracts of that class; but where an event occurs the occurrence of which neither the parties nor Parliament have expressly stated will discharge one of the parties from further performance of his undertakings, it is for the court to determine whether the event has this effect or not.

[3]   The test whether an event has this effect or not has been stated in a number of metaphors all of which I think amount to the same thing: does the occurrence of the event deprive the party who has further undertakings still to perform of substantially the whole benefit which it was the intention of the parties as expressed in the contract that he should obtain as the consideration for performing those undertakings?

[4]   This test is applicable whether or not the event occurs as a result of the default of one of the parties to the contract, but the consequences of the event are different in the two cases. Where the event occurs as a result of the default of one party, the party in default cannot rely upon it as relieving himself of the performance of any further undertakings on his part, and the innocent party, although entitled to, need not treat the event as relieving him of the further performance of his own undertakings. This is only a specific application of the fundamental legal and moral rule that a man should not be allowed to take advantage of his own wrong. Where the event occurs as a result of the default of neither party, each is relieved

of the further performance of his own undertakings, and their rights in respect of undertakings previously performed are now regulated by the *Law Reform (Frustrated Contracts) Act, 1943*.

[5]   This branch of the common law has reached its present stage by the normal process of historical growth, and the fallacy in Mr. Ashton Roskill's contention that a different test is applicable when the event occurs as a result of the default of one party from that applicable in cases of frustration where the event occurs as a result of the default of neither party lies, in my view, from a failure to view the cases in their historical context. The problem: in what event will a party to a contract be relieved of his undertaking to do that which he has agreed to do but has not yet done? has exercised the English courts for centuries, probably ever since assumpsit emerged as a form of action distinct from covenant and debt and long before even the earliest cases which we have been invited to examine. . . .

[6]   In the earlier cases before the *Common Law Procedure Act, 1852*, the problem tends to be obscured to modern readers by the rules of pleading peculiar to the relevant forms of action, covenant, debt and assumpsit, and the nomenclature adopted in the judgments, which were mainly on demurrer, reflects this. It was early recognised that contractual undertakings were of two different kinds: those collateral to the main purpose of the parties as expressed in the contract and those which were mutually dependent so that the non-performance by one party of an undertaking of this class was an event which excused the other party from the performance of his corresponding undertaking. In the nomenclature of the eighteenth and early nineteenth centuries undertakings of the latter class were called "conditions precedent" and a plaintiff under the rules of pleading had to aver specially in his declaration his performance or readiness and willingness to perform all those contractual undertakings on his part which constituted conditions precedent to the defendant's undertaking for non-performance of which the action was brought. In the earliest cases such as *Pordage v. Cole* [(1669), 1 Wms. Saund. 319], and *Thorpe v. Thorpe* [(1701), 12 Mod. 455], the question whether an undertaking was a condition precedent appears to have turned upon the verbal niceties of the particular phrases used in the written contract and it was not until 1773 that Lord Mansfield, in the case which is a legal landmark, *Boone v. Eyre*, swept away these arid technicalities. "The distinction", he said, "is very clear, *where mutual covenants go to the whole of the consideration on both sides, they are mutual conditions, the one precedent to the other.* But where they go only to a part, where a breach may be paid for in damages, there the defendant has a remedy on his covenant, and shall not plead it as a condition precedent". . . .

[7]   The fact that the emphasis in the earlier cases was upon the breach by one party to the contract of his contractual undertakings, for this was the commonest circumstance in which the question arose, tended to obscure the fact that it was really the event resulting from the breach which relieved the other party of further performance of his obligations; but the principle was applied early in the nineteenth century and without analysis to cases where the event relied upon was one brought about by a party to a contract before the time for performance of his undertakings arose but which would make it impossible to perform those obligations when the time to do so did arrive . . . It was not, however, until *Jackson v. Union Marine Insurance Co. Ltd.* [(1874), L.R. 10 C.P. 125] that it was recognised that it was the happening of the event and not the fact that the event was the result of a

breach by one party of his contractual obligations that relieved the other party from further performance of his obligations.

[8] "There are the cases," said Bramwell B. [p. 147], "which hold that, where the shipowner has not merely broken his contract, but has so broken it that the condition precedent is not performed, the charterer is discharged . . . Why? Not merely because the contract is broken. If it is not a condition precedent, what matters it whether it is unperformed with or without excuse? Not arriving with due diligence, or at a day named, is the subject of a cross-action only. But not arriving in time for the voyage contemplated, but at such a time that it is frustrated, is not only a breach of contract, but discharges the charterer. And so it should, though he has such an excuse that no action lies."

[9] Once it is appreciated that it is the event and not the fact that the event is a result of a breach of contract which relieves the party not in default of further performance of his obligations, two consequences follow. (1) The test whether the event relied upon has this consequence is the same whether the event is the result of the other party's breach of contract or not . . . (2) The question whether an event which is the result of the other party's breach of contract has this consequence cannot be answered by treating all contractual undertakings as falling into one of two separate categories: "conditions" the breach of which gives rise to an event which relieves the party not in default of further performance of his obligations, and "warranties" the breach of which does not give rise to such an event. . . .

[10] No doubt there are many simple contractual undertakings, sometimes express but more often because of their very simplicity ("It goes without saying") to be implied, of which it can be predicated that every breach of such an undertaking must give rise to an event which will deprive the party not in default of substantially the whole benefit which it was intended that he should obtain from the contract. And such a stipulation, unless the parties have agreed that breach of it shall not entitle the non-defaulting party to treat the contract as repudiated, is a "condition." So too there may be other simple contractual undertakings of which it can be predicated that *no* breach can give rise to an event which will deprive the party not in default of substantially the whole benefit which it was intended that he should obtain from the contract; and such a stipulation, unless the parties have agreed that breach of it shall entitle the non-defaulting party to treat the contract as repudiated, is a "warranty."

[11] There are, however, many contractual undertakings of a more complex character which cannot be categorised as being "conditions" or "warranties," if the late nineteenth-century meaning adopted in the *Sale of Goods Act, 1893*, and used by Bowen L.J. in *Bentsen v. Taylor, Sons & Co.*, [[1893] 2 Q.B. 274], be given to those terms. Of such undertakings all that can be predicated is that some breaches will and others will not give rise to an event which will deprive the party not in default of substantially the whole benefit which it was intended that he should obtain from the contract; and the legal consequences of a breach of such an undertaking, unless provided for expressly in the contract, depend upon the nature of the event to which the breach gives rise and do not follow automatically from a prior classification of the undertaking as a "condition" or a "warranty." For instance, to take Bramwell B.'s example in *Jackson v. Union Marine Insurance Co. Ltd.* itself, breach of an undertaking by a shipowner to sail with all possible dispatch to a named port does not necessarily relieve the charterer of further performance of his obligation under the charterparty, but if the breach is so prolonged that the contemplated voyage is frustrated it does have this effect. . . .

[12] As my brethren have already pointed out, the shipowners' undertaking to tender a seaworthy ship has, as a result of numerous decisions as to what can amount to "unseaworthiness," become one of the most complex of contractual undertakings. It embraces obligations with respect to every part of the hull and machinery, stores and equipment and the crew itself. It can be broken by the presence of trivial defects easily and rapidly remediable as well as by defects which must inevitably result in a total loss of the vessel. . . .

[13] What the judge had to do in the present case, as in any other case where one party to a contract relies upon a breach by the other party as giving him a right to elect to rescind the contract, and the contract itself makes no express provision as to this, was to look at the events which had occurred as a result of the breach at the time at which the charterers purported to rescind the charterparty and to decide whether the occurrence of those events deprived the charterers of substantially the whole benefit which it was the intention of the parties as expressed in the charterparty that the charterers should obtain from the further performance of their own contractual undertakings.

[14] One turns therefore to the contract, the Baltime 1939 charter, of which Sellers L.J. has already cited the relevant terms. Clause 13, the "due diligence" clause, which exempts the shipowners from responsibility for delay or loss or damage to goods on board due to unseaworthiness, unless such delay or loss or damage has been caused by want of due diligence of the owners in making the vessel seaworthy and fitted for the voyage, is in itself sufficient to show that the mere occurrence of the events that the vessel was in some respect unseaworthy when tendered or that such unseaworthiness had caused some delay in performance of the charterparty would not deprive the charterer of the whole benefit which it was the intention of the parties he should obtain from the performance of his obligations under the contract, for he undertakes to continue to perform his obligations notwithstanding the occurrence of such events if they fall short of frustration of the contract and even deprives himself of any remedy in damages unless such events are the consequence of want of due diligence on the part of the shipowner.

[15] The question which the judge had to ask himself was, as he rightly decided, whether or not at the date when the charterers purported to rescind the contract, namely, June 6, 1957, or when the shipowners purported to accept such rescission, namely, August 8, 1957, the delay which had already occurred as a result of the incompetence of the engine-room staff, and the delay which was likely to occur in repairing the engines of the vessel and the conduct of the shipowners by that date in taking steps to remedy these two matters, were, when taken together, such as to deprive the charterers of substantially the whole benefit which it was the intention of the parties they should obtain from further use of the vessel under the charterparty.

[16] In my view, in his judgment . . . the judge took into account and gave due weight to all the relevant considerations and arrived at the right answer for the right reasons.

NOTES AND QUESTIONS

1. Although it was not mentioned by Diplock L.J., Salmon J., the trial judge, remarked that in light of the "catastrophic fall in the freight market between February [when the contract was made] and June [when the charter was repudiated] of 1957 [due to the resolution of the Suez crisis] . . . it would only be natural . . . for the charterers to wish to escape from the charterparty if they lawfully may".

2. Some commentators refer to the type of term that was involved in *Hongkong Fir* as an "innominate" or "intermediate" term, that is, a term between a condition and a warranty (*e.g.*, John McCamus, *The Law of Contracts* (Toronto: Irwin Law, 2005) at 627). The legal significance of such a term is not specified in the contract (hence it is "innominate", unnamed), and its legal effect can only be determined in the context of a specific breach, rather than on an abstract basis when the contract is formed. While it is useful to understand that there are terms that may be neither conditions nor warranties, in the sense that their legal effect cannot be conclusively determined when the contract is made, Lord Diplock did not use the "innominate" or "intermediate" vocabulary. What is important is that you appreciate that there are many situations in which lawyers and courts must determine whether there has been a "Hongkong Fir event", *i.e.*, an event that provides a party with an excuse for its non-performance.

3. In *Jacob & Youngs v. Kent*, 129 N.E. 889 (N.Y.C.A. 1921), a case similar to (and referred to in) *Peevyhouse v. Garland Coal* and *Ruxley v. Forsyth*, *supra*, Chapter 1, a builder sued the owner for the balance owed on a contract for the construction of a house. The owner had not yet paid the full price for the construction of the house. The owner claimed to be excused from full payment (about five per cent of the total cost remained unpaid) on the ground that the builder had not complied with an obligation to install a particular brand of water pipe in the house as the construction specifications required. It was proved that the pipe that was installed was as good as that which should have been installed. On the *Peevyhouse* reasoning, the owner should get no damages for the breach since he had suffered no economic loss from the breach. The question was then whether the fact that the owner had not paid should make his position better.

    The New York Court of Appeal, like the Oklahoma court, was divided. The majority, in a judgment by Cardozo J., held that the breach did not offer an excuse. In one of his typical passages, Cardozo J. said:

    > Some promises are so plainly independent that they can never by fair construction be conditions of one another. . . . Others are so plainly dependent that they must always be conditions. Others, though dependent and thus conditions when there is departure in point of substance, will be viewed as independent and collateral when the departure is insignificant. . . . Considerations partly of justice and partly of presumable intention are to tell us whether this or that promise shall be placed in one class or in another. The simple and the uniform will call for different remedies from the multifarious and the intricate. The margin of departure within the range of normal expectation upon a sale of common chattels will vary from the margin to be expected upon a contract for the construction of a mansion or a "skyscraper." There will be harshness sometimes and oppression in the implication of a condition when the thing upon which labor has been expended is incapable of surrender because united to the land, and equity and reason in the implication of a like condition when the subject-matter, if defective, is in shape to be returned. From the conclusion that promises may not be treated as dependent to the extent of their uttermost minutiae without a sacrifice of justice, the progress is a short one to the conclusion that they may not be so treated without a perversion of intention. Intention not otherwise revealed may be presumed to hold in contemplation the reasonable and probable. If something else is in view, it must not be left to implication. There will be no assumption of a purpose to visit venial faults with oppressive retribution.

Those who think more of symmetry and logic in the development of legal rules than of practical adaptation to the attainment of a just result will be troubled by a classification where the lines of division are so wavering and blurred. Something, doubtless, may be said on the score of consistency and certainty in favor of a stricter standard. The courts have balanced such considerations against those of equity and fairness, and found the latter to be the weightier.

McLaughlin J. wrote a judgment for the dissent:

The defendant had a right to contract for what he wanted. He had a right before making payment to get what the contract called for. It is no answer to this suggestion to say that the pipe put in was just as good as that made by the Reading Manufacturing Company, or that the difference in value between such pipe and the pipe made by the Reading Manufacturing Company would be either "nominal or nothing." Defendant contracted for pipe made by the Reading Manufacturing Company. What his reason was for requiring this kind of pipe is of no importance. He wanted that and was entitled to it. It may have been a mere whim on his part, but even so, he had a right to this kind of pipe, regardless of whether some other kind, according to the opinion of the contractor or experts, would have been "just as good, better, or done just as well." He agreed to pay only upon condition that the pipes installed were made by that company and he ought not to be compelled to pay unless that condition be performed.

(a) What does McLaughlin J. mean by the word "right" in the extract from his judgment?

(b) Would McLaughlin J. have reached the same decision if the whole cost of replacing the wrong pipe (say, 50 per cent of the total price) happened to be the amount of the price of construction that had remained unpaid?

The following decision provides an illustration of a case in which a court decides that a breach of a term is sufficiently significant to discharge the innocent party from further performance, as well offering a discussion of the concepts of "repudiation" and "rescission," and of "substantial breach"

968703 ONTARIO LTD. v. VERNON

[1999] O.J. No. 580, 58 O.R. (3d) 215, 22 B.L.R. (3d) 161
(Ont. C.A., Carthy, Weiler and Cronk JJ.A.)

[In June 1995, the defendant Vernon hired the plaintiff Headline Industries, an auctioneering firm, to sell assets at an auction that took place on August 23 and 24. Under the written agreement, all proceeds were to be deposited into a joint bank account. In breach of the contract, Headline did not deposit over $100,000 into the joint account and, at the end of August, Vernon refused to permit Headline to sell the remaining assets in accordance with the written agreement, which provided for a division of the proceeds in specified amounts. Headline then sued for damages for loss of profit on the sale of the remaining assets, and Vernon counterclaimed against Headline for breach of contract and breach of fiduciary duty.

After finding that Ernest Wilson, the principal shareholder of Headline, had breached his fiduciary duty by attempting, albeit unsuccessfully, to secretly sell assets to three companies that he controlled, with a view to making a profit for himself, and by further attempting to make a secret profit on the sale of scrap metal, MacKinnon J. dismissed Headline's claim and awarded Vernon $5,000 on its counterclaim. MacKinnon J. also found that contrary to three interlocutory orders, Headline had delayed paying the funds into a joint account until just before trial and failed to reasonably account until 26 months after the auction. The Divisional Court reversed the trial judgment, and Vernon appealed to the Court of Appeal. The Court of Appeal held that the decision of the Divisional Court should be reversed, and restored the decision of the trial judge.]

WEILER J.A.: — **[12]** There is some ambiguity in the trial judge's reasons on the issue of whether the Vernon companies were excused from further performance of the contract because of Headline's failure to pay a large sum of the money from the auction into the joint bank account. Under the heading, Failure to Act in Good Faith, the trial judge stated:

> This is not a case of anticipatory breach going to the root of the contract, but rather a dispute over the application and division of proceeds of the auction, failure to comply with contractual obligation for payment into the trust account, and one involving the plaintiff's flouting of court orders. These breaches entitle the Vernon companies to damages but do not in the circumstances entitle Spencer Vernon and his companies to repudiate the entire contract.

[13] It was at this point in his reasons that the trial judge awarded damages to the Vernon companies of $5,000. Under the next heading, "Contractual Accounting Analysis", the trial judge stated:

> Having breached the agreement by failing to pay all funds into the joint account, the plaintiff is not entitled, in my view, to the value of any assets remaining.

[14] Before dealing with the merits of the parties' arguments, clarification of the trial judge's reasons respecting his decision will be of assistance. The trial judge's statement that the Vernon companies were not entitled to repudiate the entire contract is problematic. The term rescission, is sometimes used to indicate total abrogation of the contract with all its obligations. A repudiation means that the contract is ended in the sense that the innocent party is released from the duty of future performance. The contract is not totally abrogated because the innocent party can, however, sue for damages for the other party's breach of its obligations before the termination. See Waddams, *The Law of Contracts*, 3rd ed. (Toronto: Canada Law Book, 1993), at pp. 427-28. Having regard to the reasons as a whole, I am of the opinion that the trial judge meant to say that the Vernon companies were not entitled to rescind the entire contract. This conclusion is supported by the trial judge's later holding that Headline's breach of contract by failing to pay the money into the joint bank account excused the Vernon companies from further performance of their obligations under the contract. Headline's breach, however, did not deprive it of the commissions it had already been paid from the auction sale.

[15] Was the trial judge correct in law to excuse Vernon from further performance of the contract and did the Divisional Court err in reversing this conclusion? Only a substantial, not a minor, breach of contract will excuse the innocent party from continued performance of a contract: *Robson v. Thorne, Ernst & Whinney* (1999), 127 O.A.C. 215 (C.A.); *Bayer Aktiengesellschaft v. Apotex Inc.* (1998), 113 O.A.C. 1 (C.A.).

[16] There are several factors that provide guidance in determining whether or not a breach is a substantial breach justifying future non-performance of the innocent party's obligations. They are: (a) the ratio of the party's obligation not performed to the obligation as a whole; (b) the seriousness of the breach to the innocent party;

(c) the likelihood of repetition of the breach; (d) the seriousness of the consequences of the breach; and (e) the relationship of the part of the obligation performed to the whole obligation. See Waddams, *supra*, at pp. 401-02.

[17] Without getting into an exact ratio, Headline's failure to deposit in excess of
$100,000 into the joint bank account was significant in relation to the entire obli-
gation under the contract. The seriousness of the breach in this instance, however,
cannot be addressed strictly in monetary terms. Headline did not cure its breach
within a few days. Instead, refusing to comply with court orders, and refusing to
account until over two years had passed, it repeated or continued the breach of
contract. This failure was in itself sufficient to justify Vernon's refusal to perform
the rest of the contract. Headline's failure to deposit the money into the joint bank
account justified Vernon's refusal to go ahead and put more assets into cash that
might disappear.

[18] During this time, Vernon discovered that Wilson had caused Headline to
breach its fiduciary duty as agent. In conducting the auction, Wilson had caused
Headline to sell some of the Vernon companies' goods to Wilson's companies
below their appraised value. Wilson's breach of trust meant that the Vernon companies could not trust Headline to sell the remaining goods, including scrap metal,
following the auction. That Vernon could not trust Wilson was confirmed by Wilson's attempt to have Stephen Lehmann of Francoz Metals pay Headline alone for
every fourth load of scrap metal in order to remove it. Vernon is entitled to rely on
this after-discovered breach of fiduciary duty as a further basis to excuse it from
future performance under the contract. ...

[19] In my opinion, the Divisional Court therefore erred in not holding that
Vernon and his companies were excused from further performance under the contract.

The following decision deals with a very common problem: what happens if one
party is late in performing some of its obligations under the contract.

SAIL LABRADOR LTD. v. "CHALLENGE ONE" (THE)

[1999] 1 S.C.R. 265, 169 D.L.R. (4th) 1
(S.C.C., Lamer C.J.C. and Gonthier, Cory, Iacobucci, Major,
Bastarache and Binnie JJ.)

[The appellant entered into a five-year agreement with the respondent to charter a
vessel. Under clause 30 of the charterparty, the appellant had an option to purchase the vessel at the end of the five-year period subject to "full performance of
all its obligations in th[e] Charter Party including but not limited to payments being made promptly and in accordance with the schedule" in the agreement. The
accepted practice between the parties was for the appellant to submit seven post-
dated, uncertified cheques to the respondent at the beginning of each operating
season. While there were no problems with the cheques for the first four years, the
cheque for the first payment in the fifth year was returned by reason of insufficient
funds. The trial judge found that the bank's refusal to honour the appellant's
cheque was due to an error by a bank employee. The respondent wrote to the ap-

pellant informing it that the option to purchase was void and of no further effect because of the appellant's failure to make the payment as required. In this same letter, the respondent gave the appellant instructions on how it could remedy its late payment. The appellant promptly made the payment with interest in accordance with the respondent's instructions. All subsequent payments were made on time. At the end of the five-year lease the appellant gave the respondent notice of its intention to exercise the option to purchase and tendered payment. The respondent refused to execute a bill of sale. The Federal Court, Trial Division, granted the appellant's action for a declaration that it was entitled to exercise the option. The Federal Court of Appeal allowed the respondent's appeal. The Supreme Court of Canada upheld the trial decision, ruling that in the circumstances the one late payment did not constitute a breach sufficient to allow the respondent to rely on Clause 30.]

BASTARACHE J.: — [31] Both Treitel [*The Law of Contract*, 9th ed. (London: Sweet & Maxwell, 1995)] and Waddams [*The Law of Contracts*, 3rd ed. (Toronto: Canada Law Book, 1993)] recognize that, as a general rule, parties to a contract must perform their obligations specifically as dictated by the contract. However, if the performance is deficient, for example in quality, quantity or timeliness, it is accepted that the defect in performance must attain a certain minimum degree of seriousness to entitle the non-offending party to rescind the contract. The failure in performance must substantially deprive the other party of what was bargained for. This concept is referred to as substantial non-performance or as a requirement that a breach go to the "root" of the contract. In English legal literature, the expression "substantial failure" is used. If this minimum standard is not met, rescission will not be available to the non-offending party. This party will be forced to settle for a remedy in damages. Thus, courts are concerned with the consequences of the deficient performance and the nature of the prejudice caused to the non-offending party when determining whether rescission is available (Treitel, at pp. 685-86; Waddams, at pp. 394-96). The case of *Hongkong Fir Shipping Co. v. Kawasaki Kisen Kaisha Ltd.*, [1962] 2 Q.B. 26 (C.A.), stands for the proposition that courts will apply this type of substantial non-performance test to determine if rescission is available in cases involving charter party contracts like the one in question.

. . .

[52] In [*United Scientific Holdings Ltd. v. Burnley Borough Council*, [1978] A.C. 904] Lord Diplock reiterated the historic approach of equity to the issue of the timeliness of performance as follows, at p. 927:

> . . . the rules of equity . . . did not regard stipulations in contracts as to the time by which various steps should be taken by the parties as being of the essence of the contract *unless the express words of the contract, the nature of its subject matter or the surrounding circumstances made it inequitable not to treat the failure of one party to comply exactly with the stipulation as relieving the other party from the duty to perform his obligations under the contract.* [Emphasis added.]

. . .

[54] This Court must therefore begin from the presumption that time is not of the essence in the contract in the present case. However, keeping in mind that parties to commercial contracts are free to make time of the essence in relation to the performance of any contractual obligations. . . . I must assess whether these parties have expressly made time the essence of this contract through the incorporation of

a "time of the essence" clause. If they have not, this Court may still conclude that time is of the essence if the nature of the property involved or the circumstance of this case call for such an interpretation.

Is Clause 30 a "Time of the Essence" Clause?

[55] This Court must look to the actual language used by these parties in clause 30, the option clause, to determine whether it was their intention to expressly make time of the essence. The respondent submits that since this is a commercial contract entered into by equal parties, the wording of clause 30 must be strictly construed. The respondent further submits that the words "promptly and in accordance with the schedule" make time of the essence in relation to the lease payments. Accordingly, the argument goes, the appellant's single late payment, even though it was caused by a bank error and quickly remedied with interest, allows the respondent to put an end to the option.

[56] Before discussing the strict interpretation urged by the respondent, I would point out that commercial parties should be familiar enough with the applicable law to know that they must use very precise words if their intention is to make time the essence of a contract. This is self-evident given that the reason for the inclusion of a clause of this nature in the first place is to provide certainty about the consequences of breach which the substantial non-performance doctrine cannot provide. Furthermore, because of the real possibility of an unjust enrichment, courts must be certain that it was the parties' intention to allow any breach of the timing of performance, no matter how minor or non-prejudicial, to justify rescission of the entire contract.

[57] In my opinion, the words used in clause 30 are simply not precise enough to satisfy this Court that these parties intended to make timely lease payments the essence of this contract. The word "promptly" adds nothing to the words "in accordance with the schedule". Read together, these words call for regular payment. Nothing exceptional about the obligations of the parties can be inferred. This conclusion is bolstered by the respondent's admission in oral argument that contracts used in this industry often include the actual words "time is of the essence" when the parties intend to, in fact, make time of the essence.

[**BINNIE J**. concurred in the result.]

NOTE

It is common for commercial contracts, such as those involving an agreement to sell land, to have a clause stipulating that "time is of the essence".

In *Union Eagle Ltd. v. Golden Achievement Ltd.*, [1997] A.C. 514 (Hong Kong P.C.) the Privy Council on an appeal from a case from Hong Kong dealt with a case where the purchaser was just 10 minutes late in tendering funds, and held that since there was a "time is of the essence" clause, the vendor was discharged from the obligation to sell. Union Eagle agreed to purchase a condominium unit in Hong Kong for HK$4.2 million. The sale was to be closed on or before 5:00 p.m. on Sept. 30, 1991, at the offices of the vendor's solicitors, and the contract had a standard "time is of the essence" clause. On the closing date, but before the 5:00 p.m. deadline, the purchaser's solicitor called the vendor's solicitor to say that his clerk was in transit with the closing documents and funds. Traffic was unusually congested on that day (even by Hong Kong standards) and the clerk arrived at approximately 5:10 p.m. The vendor's solicitor immediately noted that the purchaser was in default by being too late, and terminated the contract by invoking the "time of the essence" clause. The vendor kept the deposit, as it was entitled to do under the purchase agreement. The vendor would not have suffered any prejudice by closing at 5:10 p.m. as opposed to 5:00 p.m. There was no back-to-back purchase, no bank deposit deadline and no registration deadline. The delay was purely accidental. However, at that time the Hong Kong condominium market was in the grip of some of the most spectacular hyper-inflation that it had ever seen, and the vendor knew that between the date that the contract was signed and the closing date, prices had already skyrocketed and would likely continue to do so if this sale could somehow be avoided. The unit was later resold for HK $15 million!

In *1473587 Ontario Inc. v. Jackson*, [2005] O.J. No. 710, 74 O.R. (3d) 539 (S.C.J.), an agreement for the sale of land provided that the deposit was to be paid within five days of signing, and included a "time of the essence clause". By inadvertence, the purchaser was five days late in getting the deposit to the vendor, by which time the vendor had received another, higher offer. As in *Union Eagle*, the delay was innocent and the vendor had done nothing to induce the purchaser to miss the payment deadline. Although the time delay was longer than in *Union Eagle*, Rutherford J. in *1473587 Ontario Inc. v. Jackson* cited and relied upon *Union Eagle*, concluding that the vendor had the right to terminate the contract with the purchaser because the purchaser was late. *Sail Labrador* was distinguished as there was no time is of the essence clause. Rutherford J. rejected the purchaser's argument that the vendor was not acting in good faith, and concluded that the vendor was not acting "unfairly" by exercising its strict legal rights. The trial decision was affirmed by the Court of Appeal in a brief written decision at [2005] O.J. No. 3145, 75 O.R. (3d) 484 (C.A.).

Were the vendors in *Union Eagle* and *1473587 Ontario Inc.* acting in good faith? Should it matter? Are these cases distinguishable from decisions considered earlier in this chapter dealing with conditions precedent, like *Marshall v. Bernard Place Corp.*, [2002] O.J. No. 463, 58 O.R. (3d) 97 (C.A.), which imposed an obligation on a purchaser to exercise a discretionary home inspection clause with "honesty and good faith"?

THE RIGHT OF THE PARTY WHO HAS NOT PERFORMED TO SUE

The cases in this section present some difficult problems for the lawyer called upon to give advice to a client in circumstances where the other party has indicated that it is unlikely to perform.

If there has been a breach of condition or, under the test of the *Hongkong Fir* case, a party has an excuse for non-performance arising from the other's breach, the right of the party not in breach to sue for damages should not be affected by that party's own failure to perform subsequent to the breach. The fact that the plaintiff has not performed will, of course, affect the amount of the claim for damages, but it should not preclude the innocent party from having any recovery. This simple proposition was established in the following case:

CORT v. THE AMBERGATE RAILWAY CO.

(1851), 17 Q.B. 127, 117 E.R. 1229
(Q.B., Campbell C.J., Patteson, Coleridge and Erle JJ.)

[The parties had made a contract under which the plaintiff would manufacture and sell to the defendant railway chairs (iron pieces with a notch for the rail by which the rail is fixed to the tie) for the building of the defendant's railway. The total amount of the chairs under the contract was about 4,000 tons. The defendant accepted and paid for about 1,800 tons (costing £12,000). Subsequently the defendants became insolvent and gave notice to the plaintiff that they would not take any more chairs. The plaintiff sued for damages for breach of the contract to take the full 4,000 tons, and in its pleadings claimed that it was "ready and willing" to perform. The defendant argued that the plaintiff had not proved that he was ready and willing to deliver the remaining chairs.]

LORD CAMPBELL C.J.: — **[1]** Next we have to consider whether the plaintiffs were entitled to a verdict on the issue whether they were ready and willing to execute and perform the said contract according to the said conditions and stipulations, in manner and form, &c.; and on the issue whether the defendants did refuse to accept or receive the residue of the chairs, or prevent or discharge the plaintiffs from supplying the said residue, and from the further execution and performance of the said contract. It is not denied that, if the defendants would have regularly accepted and paid for the chairs, the plaintiffs would have gone on regularly making and delivering them according to the contract; the objection is that, although the plaintiffs were desirous that the contract should be fully performed, yet, after receiving the notice that the company did not wish to have any more chairs, and would not accept any more, they ceased to make any more, insomuch that the residue which the company are alleged to have refused to accept never were made. The defendants contend that, as the plaintiffs did not make and tender the residue of the chairs, they cannot be said to have been ready and willing to perform the contract; that the defendants cannot be charged with a breach of it; that, after the notice from the defendants, which in truth amounted to a declaration that they had broken and thenceforward renounced the contract, the plaintiffs, if they wished to have any redress, were bound to buy the requisite quantity of the peculiar sort of iron suited for these railway chairs, to make the whole of them according to the pattern, with the name of the company upon them, and to bring them to the appointed places of delivery and tender them to the defendants, who, from insolvency, had abandoned the completion of the line for which the chairs were intended, desiring that no more chairs might be made, and declaring, in effect, that no more should be accepted or paid for. We are of opinion, however, that the jury were fully justified upon the evidence in finding that the plaintiffs were ready and willing to perform the contract, although they never made and tendered the residue of the chairs. In common sense the meaning of such an averment of readiness and willingness must be that the noncompletion of the contract was not the fault of the plaintiffs, and that they were disposed and able to complete it if it had not been renounced by the defendants. What more can reasonably be required by the parties for whom the goods are to be manufactured? If, having accepted a part, they are unable to pay for the residue, and have resolved not to accept them, no benefit can accrue to them from a useless waste of materials and labour, which might possibly enhance the amount of damages to be awarded against them . . .

[2] Upon the whole, we think we are justified, on principle and without trenching on any former decision, in holding that, when there is an executory contract for the manufacturing and supply of goods from time to time, to be paid for after delivery, if the purchaser, having accepted and paid for a portion of the goods contracted for, gives notice to the vendor not to manufacture any more as he has no occasion for them and will not accept or pay for them, the vendor having been desirous and able to complete the contract, he may, without manufacturing and tendering the rest of the goods, maintain an action against the purchaser for breach of contract; and that he is entitled to a verdict on pleas traversing allegations that he was ready and willing to perform the contract, that the defendant refused to accept the residue of the goods, and that he prevented and discharged the plaintiff from manufacturing and delivering them.

[3] We are likewise of opinion that, in this case, the damages are not excessive, as the jury were justified in taking into their calculation all the chairs which remained to be delivered, and which the defendants refused to accept. They were all included in the declaration and in the issues joined: the time mentioned in the proposal for the delivery of some of them had arrived before the notice was given; but the time of delivery was not of the essence of the contract; and the obligation was still incumbent upon the defendants to accept the whole of the residue.

[4]   The rule must therefore be discharged.

The next development in the law was to allow the plaintiff to sue before the time for performance had arrived. To support such an action, the plaintiff had to show that the defendant had clearly indicated his unwillingness to perform: the defendant had to have repudiated the contract. Since the repudiation must have occurred *before* the time for performance, the plaintiff's cause of action was based on the defendant's "anticipatory repudiation" (or "anticipatory breach").

HOCHSTER v. DE LA TOUR

(1853), 2 El. & Bl. 678, 118 E.R. 922
(Campbell C.J., Coleridge, Erle and Compton JJ.)

[On 12 April 1852 the defendant agreed to employ the plaintiff as a courier (or valet) to accompany him on a trip through Europe. The engagement was to begin on 1 June 1852. On 11 May 1852 the defendant told the plaintiff that he had changed his mind and would not need his services. The plaintiff commenced this action on 22 May. It was argued on behalf of the defendant that the action had been brought too soon, that there could be no breach before 1 June.]

LORD CAMPBELL C.J. now delivered the judgment of the Court:

[1]   On this motion in arrest of judgment, the question arises, Whether, if there be an agreement between A and B, whereby B engages to employ A on and from a future day for a given period of time, to travel with him into a foreign country as a courier, and to start with him in that capacity on that day, A being to receive a monthly salary during the continuance of such service, B may, before the day, refuse to perform the agreement and break and renounce it, so as to entitle A before the day to commence an action against B to recover damages for breach of the agreement; A having been ready and willing to perform it, till it was broken and renounced by B. The defendant's counsel very powerfully contended that, if the plaintiff was not contented to dissolve the contract, and to abandon all remedy upon it, he was bound to remain ready and willing to perform it till the day when the actual employment as courier in the service of the defendant was to begin; and that there could be no breach of the agreement, before that day, to give a right of action. But it cannot be laid down as a universal rule that, where by agreement an act is to be done on a future day, no action can be brought for a breach of the agreement till the day for doing the act has arrived. If a man promises to marry a woman on a future day, and before that day marries another woman, he is instantly liable to an action for breach of promise of marriage . . . If a man contracts to execute a lease on and from a future day for a certain term, and, before that day, executes a lease to another for the same term, he may be immediately sued for breaking the contract . . . So, if a man contracts to sell and deliver specific goods on a future day, and before the day he sells and delivers them to another, he is immediately liable to an action at the suit of the person with whom he first contracted to sell and deliver them . . . One reason alleged in support of such an action is, that the defendant has, before the day, rendered it impossible for him to perform the contract at the day: but this does not necessarily follow; for, prior to the day fixed for doing the act, the first wife may have died, a surrender of the lease executed might be obtained, and the defendant might have repurchased the goods so as to be in a situation to sell and deliver them to the plaintiff. Another reason may be, that, where there is a contract to do an act on a future day, there is a relation constituted between the parties in the meantime by the contract, and that they impliedly promise that in the meantime neither will do any thing to the prejudice of the other inconsistent with that relation. As an example, a man and woman engaged to marry are affianced to one another during the period between the time of the engagement and the celebration of the marriage. In this very case, of traveller and courier, from the day of the hiring till the day when the employment was to begin, they were engaged to each other; and it seems to be a breach of an implied contract if either of them renounces the engagement . . . The declaration in the present case, in alleging a breach, states a great deal more than a passing intention on the part of the defendant which he may repent of, and could only be proved by evidence that he had utterly renounced the contract, or done some act which rendered it impossible for him to perform it. If the plaintiff has no remedy for breach of the contract unless he treats the contract as in force, and acts upon it down to the 1st June 1852, it follows that, till then, he must enter into no employment which will interfere with his promise "to start with the defendant on such travels on the day and year," and that he must then be properly equipped in all respects as a courier for a three months' tour on the continent of Europe. But it is surely much more rational, and more for the benefit of both parties, that, after the renunciation of the agreement by the defendant, the plaintiff should be at liberty to consider himself absolved from any future performance of it, retaining his right to sue for any damage he has suffered from the breach of it. Thus, instead of remaining idle and laying out money in preparations which must be useless, he is at liberty to seek service under another employer, which would go in mitigation of the damages to which he would otherwise be entitled for a breach of the contract . . . The man who wrongfully renounces a contract into which he has deliberately entered cannot justly complain if he is immediately sued for a compensation in damages by the man whom he has injured: and it seems reasonable to allow an option to the injured party, either to sue immediately, or to wait till the time when the act was to be done, still holding it as prospectively binding for the exercise of this option, which may be advantageous to the innocent party, and cannot be prejudicial to the wrongdoer. An argument against the action before the 1st of June is urged from the difficulty of calculating the damages: but this argument is equally strong against an action before the 1st of September, when the three months would expire. In either case, the jury in assessing the damages would be justified in looking to all that had happened, or was likely to happen, to increase or mitigate the loss of the plaintiff down to the day of trial. We do not find any decision contrary to the view we are taking of this case. . . . If it should be held that, upon a contract to do an act on a future day, a renunciation of the contract by one party dispenses with a condition to be performed in the meantime by the other, there seems no reason for requiring that other to wait till the day arrives before seeking his remedy by action: and the only ground on which the condition can be dispensed with seems to be, that the renunciation may be treated as a breach of the contract.

[2] Upon the whole, we think that the declaration in this case is sufficient. It gives us great satisfaction to reflect that, the question being on the record, our opinion may be reviewed in a Court of Error. In the meantime we must give judgment for the plaintiff.

The rule in *Hochster v. De la Tour* was elaborated in the following case, in what is regarded as the classic statement of the law.

FROST v. KNIGHT

(1872), L.R. 7 Exch. 111
(Exchequer Chamber, Cockburn C.J., Byles, Keating and Lush JJ.)

[The plaintiff sought damages for breach of promise of marriage. The parties had agreed to marry after the defendant's father died. The defendant, before his father's death, said that he would not marry the plaintiff. The plaintiff immediately sued for damages. In giving judgment for the plaintiff, **COCKBURN C.J.** said: —]

[1] The law with reference to a contract to be performed at a future time, where the party bound to performance announces prior to the time his intention not to perform it, as established in . . . *Hochster v. De la Tour* . . . may be thus stated. The promisee, if he pleases, may treat the notice of intention as inoperative, and await the time when the contract is to be executed, and then hold the other party responsible for all the consequences of non-performance; but in that case he keeps the contract alive for the benefit of the other party as well as his own; he remains subject to all his own obligations and liabilities under it, and enables the other party not only to complete the contract, if so advised, notwithstanding his previous repudiation of it, but also to take advantage of any supervening circumstance which would justify him in declining to complete it.

[2] On the other hand, the promisee may, if he thinks proper, treat the repudiation of the other party as a wrongful [act] putting an end to the contract, and may at once bring his action as on a breach of it; and in such action he will be entitled to such damages as would have arisen from the non-performance of the contract at the appointed time, subject, however, to abatement in respect of any circumstances which may have afforded him the means of mitigating his loss. . . .

[3] The contract having been thus broken by the promisor, and treated as broken by the promisee, performance at the appointed time becomes excluded, and the breach by reason of the future non-performance becomes virtually involved in the action as one of the consequences of the repudiation of the contract; and the eventual non-performance may therefore, by anticipation, be treated as a cause of action, and damages be assessed and recovered in respect of it, though the time for performance may yet be remote.

[4] It is obvious that such a course must lead to the convenience of both parties; and though we should be unwilling to found our opinion on grounds of convenience alone, yet the latter tend strongly to support the view that such an action ought to be admitted and upheld. By acting on such a notice of the intention of the promisor, and taking timely measures, the promisee may in many cases avert, or at all events materially lessen, the injurious effects which would otherwise flow from the non-fulfilment of the contract; and in assessing the damages for breach of performance, a jury will of course take into account whatever the plaintiff has done, or has had the means of doing, and, as a prudent man, ought in reason to have done, whereby his loss has been, or would have been, diminished.

[5]   It appears to us that the foregoing considerations apply to the case of a contract the performance of which is made to depend on a contingency, as much as to one in which the performance is to take place at a future time; and we are, therefore, of opinion that the principle of the decision of *Hochster v. De la Tour* is equally applicable to such a case as the present.

[COCKBURN C.J. further said that allowing the plaintiff to sue immediately would reduce the damages suffered by the plaintiff since she would become less marriageable as she got older.]

DOMICILE DEVELOPMENTS INC. v. MacTAVISH

[1999] O.J. No. 1998, 45 O.R. (3d) 302, 175 D.L.R. (4th) 334
(Ont. C.A., Brooke, Laskin and Rosenberg JJ.A.)

LASKIN J.A.: — [1] The appellant Duncan MacTavish appeals from the judgment of Binks J. awarding the respondent Domicile Developments Inc. $97,975.88 for damages for breach of an agreement of purchase and sale. The appeal raises the question of the obligation of a vendor under an agreement making time of the essence, when the purchaser is in default but the vendor also is not ready to complete the transaction on the closing date.

The Facts

[2]   On February 1, 1995, MacTavish and Domicile signed an agreement of purchase and sale by which MacTavish agreed to buy a semi-detached house in Ottawa to be built by Domicile. The purchase price was $450,000. The agreement called for a $5,000 deposit on execution of the agreement and a further $15,000 deposit on notice that a building permit had been obtained. MacTavish was to obtain vacant possession on the closing date, September 15, 1995. If the house was substantially completed on September 15, 1995, MacTavish was obliged to complete the transaction. The agreement provided that the house was deemed to be substantially completed when a municipal occupancy permit was issued. Typically, and importantly in this case, the agreement stated that "time shall in all respects be of the essence hereof".

[3]   MacTavish paid the $5,000 deposit when he signed the agreement. However, two and one-half months later, on April 13, 1995, he repudiated the agreement. His lawyer wrote Domicile that "our client has no intention of proceeding with the purchase of the property" and asked for the return of the $5,000 deposit. Domicile chose not to accept MacTavish's anticipatory repudiation. Instead its lawyer wrote that the deposit would not be returned and that "Domicile remains ready, willing and able to perform its side of the bargain."

[4]   On July 7, 1995, Domicile obtained a building permit for the house. On July 19, 1995, Domicile's lawyer wrote MacTavish's lawyer reiterating that Domicile did not accept MacTavish's anticipatory repudiation of the agreement, that Domicile considered the agreement in force and that it would "pursue the remedies

available to it under these circumstances." The letter also notified MacTavish of the building permit and asked for the further $15,000 deposit required by the agreement. MacTavish did not pay this deposit.

[5] On August 15, 1995, Domicile's lawyer wrote another letter to MacTavish's lawyer, again saying that Domicile did not accept the repudiation and that it considered the agreement to still be in effect. On the same day Domicile issued a statement of claim, seeking specific performance of the agreement or alternatively, damages. The trial judge found that "Domicile did not accept MacTavish's repudiation, but elected to keep the contract alive and proceed with the construction which commenced on July 15, 1995, after approvals were obtained from the city."

[6] However, on the closing date, September 15, 1995, Domicile had not substantially completed the house. Therefore neither party tendered on the closing date. MacTavish did not intend to close and Domicile had not finished the house. Indeed the house was not substantially completed until May 1996. At no point did Domicile give MacTavish notice of a new closing date.

[7] Meanwhile housing prices in Ottawa declined in late 1995 and early 1996. On February 21, 1996, Domicile agreed to sell the house to one of its shareholders for $365,000 — $85,000 less than the price MacTavish had agreed to pay. A municipal occupancy permit for the house was issued in early May. Thus, as the trial judge found: "the house was not completed and ready for occupancy until May 3, 1996." Domicile closed the transaction with its shareholder that day.

[8] At trial Domicile sought damages. The trial judge awarded Domicile damages of $97,975.88, representing the difference in the sale price less the $5,000 deposit ($80,000) and Domicile's cost of carrying the house between September 15, 1995 and May 3, 1996 ($17,975.88). MacTavish appeals against the finding of liability and raises several grounds of appeal against the award of damages. I will deal only with liability because in my view the trial judge erred in finding Mac-Tavish liable.

Discussion

[9] In April 1995, MacTavish stated that he did not intend to close the transaction. His conduct amounted to an anticipatory repudiation of the agreement. On being notified of MacTavish's anticipatory repudiation, Domicile, the innocent party, had a choice: it could "accept" or reject the repudiation. Had Domicile "accepted" the repudiation it would have been discharged from closing the transaction and could have sued for damages for breach of contract. (See the discussion in Waddams, *The Law of Contracts*, at pp. 419-32.) Domicile, however, rejected the repudiation and therefore the agreement remained in effect. Because of the view I take of this case, I need not consider the difficult and important question whether in April 1995 Domicile should have taken reasonable steps to reduce its losses, instead of ignoring the repudiation and waiting for the closing date. (See *Asamera Oil Corp. v. Sea Oil & General Corp.*, [1979] 1 S.C.R. 633, 89 D.L.R. (3d) 1.)

[10] Because Domicile's rejection of MacTavish's anticipatory repudiation kept the agreement alive, time remained of the essence. A time is of the essence provision means that on the closing date an innocent party may treat the contract as ended and sue the defaulting party for damages or it may keep the contract alive and sue for specific performance or damages [footnote omitted]. In order to take advantage of a time of the essence provision the innocent party must itself be "ready, desirous, prompt and eager" to carry out the agreement [footnote omitted]. Domicile could not satisfy this requirement on the closing date. Because it had not yet substantially completed construction of the house it could not carry out the agreement. Equally MacTavish could not rely on the time of the essence provision to end the agreement. A time of the essence provision can be raised as a defence only by a party who is ready, willing and able to close on the agreed date and MacTavish was not ready, willing and able to close on September 15, 1995 [footnote omitted].

[11] Therefore, on the closing date neither Domicile nor MacTavish was entitled to enforce or end the agreement. A similar situation arose in *King v. Urban & Country Transport Ltd.* (1974), 1 O.R. (2d) 449, 40 D.L.R. (3d) 641, a decision of this court relied on by Binks J. In *King v. Urban,* the purchaser was not in a position to close on the closing date; but the vendor was also in default and not entitled to rely on the time of the essence provision in the contract. Arnup J.A. resolved the stalemate by applying two propositions (at pp. 454-56):

1. When time is of the essence and neither party is ready to close on the agreed date the agreement remains in effect.

2. Either party may reinstate time of the essence by setting a new date for closing and providing reasonable notice to the other party.

[12] An important corollary of Arnup J.A.'s second proposition is that a party who is not ready to close on the agreed date and who subsequently terminates the transaction without having set a new closing date and without having reinstated time of the essence will itself breach or repudiate the agreement [footnote omitted].

[13] The corollary applies to the facts of this case. Domicile did not give Mac-Tavish reasonable notice of a new closing date. Instead it unilaterally ended the agreement by selling to a third party and seeking damages from MacTavish. Because it did not reinstate time of the essence by setting a new closing date, Domicile was not entitled to end its agreement with MacTavish. Therefore, in failing to give MacTavish an opportunity to close the transaction after September 15, Domicile itself breached the agreement. Because of Domicile's breach, MacTavish could no longer be held liable. The trial judge came to the opposite conclusion because he did not consider the effect of Domicile's inability to close on September 15. As a consequence, he did not consider Domicile's obligation to set a new closing date on reasonable notice to reinstate time of the essence. . . .

[14] Having decided to keep the agreement alive and then having been unable to carry out its part of the bargain on closing, Domicile could not continue to hold MacTavish liable without also giving MacTavish a further and reasonable opportunity to perform.

[15] Requiring that time of the essence be reinstated by giving notice of a new closing date is sensible and produces a just result. This requirement also ensures that the cost of carrying the property will be properly allocated between the vendor and the purchaser. To be effective the new closing date must be reasonable. And, although a provision making time of the essence may be implied from the surround-

ing circumstances or from the conduct of the parties, to avoid any dispute the notice should state that time is of the essence for this new date [footnote omitted].

[16] I would allow the appeal and set aside the judgment of Binks J. In its place I would issue a judgment dismissing Domicile's action with costs and ordering it to return to MacTavish his $5,000 deposit together with accrued interest. MacTavish is also entitled to his costs of the appeal.

NOTES, QUESTIONS AND PROBLEMS

1. The action of "breach of promise" of marriage, the cause of action in *Frost v. Knight*, is now regarded as an anachronism and it has been statutorily abolished in some jurisdictions. In the nineteenth century, upper- and middle-class women had no "career" options, and the failure of a man to keep his promise to marry could cause enormous economic loss to the woman, particularly if, in reliance on the engagement, she had foregone other opportunities of marriage. *Frost v. Knight* is a case with as much at stake for the plaintiff as any commercial or property case now. It is, unlike cases like *Combe v. Combe (supra*, Chapter 2), an entirely appropriate authority for a case like *Domicile Developments* and it illustrates one of the general principles of contract law.

2. In *White & Carter (Councils) Ltd. v. McGregor (supra*, Chapter 1), Lord Reid held that the plaintiff, faced with the defender's repudiation, could ignore it if it chose to do so. *Frost v. Knight* is cited as the source of that option. The party who ignores the other's anticipatory repudiation faces one risk that arises directly from *Frost v. Knight*: by treating the repudiation as inoperative (to use the word Cockburn C.J. uses), the promisee keeps the "contract alive" (or "affirms the contract"). The effect of this rule is that the promisor may change his mind and perform when the time for performance arrives and the promisee is bound to accept that performance or be in breach itself. Similarly, the promisee has no excuse for its non-performance, and may be in breach or otherwise disentitled to sue if it does not perform its obligations under the contract.

3. The biological metaphor used by Cockburn C.J. in *Frost v. Knight* causes some problems. One of the problems that must be faced after the Supreme Court of Canada decision in *Asamera Oil Corp. Ltd. v. Sea Oil & General Corp. (supra*, Chapter 1), is the effect of any repudiation on the promisee's "duty to mitigate". It may be inconsistent with *Asamera* and the principle of avoidable harms if, regardless of whether the contract is "alive" or "dead", the repudiation had no effect on the promisee's right to damages. In other words, it may be necessary to take a more sophisticated approach than simply asking whether or not the contract "exists". The promisee may be regarded as having had an opportunity to avoid the harmful consequences of the breach, and when damages come to be assessed, this fact should be considered.

4. If a case like *Hochster* were to arise today and the prospective employer makes clear that the job is cancelled, when is the plaintiff obliged to seek alternative employment in an effort to avoid the harmful consequences of the defendant's breach? In *Domicile Developments*, at ¶ 9, Laskin J.A. referred to this as a "difficult and important" question that he did not have to resolve. *Frost v. Knight* and *White & Carter Councils* might suggest that the employee could at least wait until 1 June, *i.e.*, when his employment was to have started, but if it is clear that the defendant will not perform, *Asamera* strongly suggests that the plaintiff's right to collect damages will be reduced if reasonable steps are not taken to find alternative employment as soon as it is clear that the defendant will not perform.

5. As the law now is, and even if the full effect of *Asamera* is assimilated, there are still difficulties in dealing with the practical problems facing a lawyer who has to give advice to a client.

    (a) Suppose that Sarah has a binding contract to sell Bob 200 cartons of paper, and the following conversation takes place:

> SARAH: I know that I promised that I would have 100 cartons of paper ready for you at the end of the month, but I'm afraid that it looks as if I can't make it.
>
> BOB: This is really serious for me. I have several orders to fill and I need the paper for them. I'll have to go and find some other supplier, and I expect you to pay the difference.

Can Bob sue Sarah for breach of contract at this point?

(b) Suppose that Bob replies to Sarah as follows:

> BOB: I really need that paper. I have a lot riding on what I can produce in the next few weeks. Please do what you can to meet my order.
>
> SARAH: Okay, I'll do what I can, but I'm not optimistic.

A week later Bob believes that there is almost no chance that Sarah can perform her contract with him. Can Bob safely go out to obtain an alternative supply? What steps can he take to make it safe for him to do so?

(c) Suppose Sarah indicates that she will not be able to deliver the paper and Bob is silent. What is the reasonable inference of silence in the face of anticipatory repudiation?

6. An equally plausible problem might be the following: A vendor agrees to sell a vacant lot on the standard local Real Estate Board form. The sale is conditional on the land being re-zoned to permit the construction of a small condominium. There is no financing condition. The obligation to obtain the re-zoning is assumed by the purchaser and the vendor agrees to co-operate in the application. Closing is set to take place six months after the acceptance of the offer. Consider the following two situations:

(a) Two months before the date fixed for closing, the purchaser tells the vendor that she thinks it unlikely that she will be able to complete because, given the rapid rise in interest rates, she is having more difficulty than she expected in obtaining financing at rates that she can afford.

(b) Three months before closing the vendor has grounds for believing that the purchaser is not making any efforts to pursue the re-zoning because the value of the land has fallen.

Outline the general form of the advice that you would give your client, the vendor. Draft letters that might be sent to the purchaser. Draft the replies that the purchaser's solicitor might send to the vendor.

7. Problems arise in instalment contracts. If the seller fails to deliver one instalment on time, does that excuse the buyer from accepting any more deliveries? Similarly, if the buyer fails to pay one instalment on time, does that excuse the seller from its obligation to deliver? These are not easy questions to resolve. The *Sale of Goods Act*, R.S.O. 1990, c. S.1, s. 30(2), provides that whether either party has an excuse depends in each case on the terms of the contract and the circumstances of the case. Could legislation say anything else?

8. In *Maredelanto Compania Naviera S.A. v. Bergbau-Handel GmbH (The "Mihalis Angelos")*, [1971] 1 Q.B. 183, [1970] 3 All E.R. 125 (C.A.), the court considered the question of how to deal with a situation where, subsequent to the repudiation, events occur which would have excused the repudiating party from performing. Lord Denning said:

> You must take into account all the contingencies which might have reduced or extinguished the loss. . . . It follows that if the defendant has under the contract an option which would reduce or extinguish the loss, it will be assumed that he will exercise it. . . . In short the plaintiff must be compensated for such

loss as he would have suffered if there had been no renunciation: but not if he would have lost nothing.

9.   By contract dated 1 July Mary promised to sell goods to Tom. She promised to deliver on 1 October. On 1 September Tom tells Mary that he will not accept delivery of the goods. Mary does nothing. Mary sues for breach of contract on 15 September.

   (a)   Suppose that on 20 September Mary sells the goods to another buyer at 10 per cent less than the price she agreed to sell to Tom?

   (b)   On 30 September, the goods that Mary would have delivered to Tom are destroyed by fire so that she cannot perform her contract with Tom before 2 January. Assume that the goods tendered on 2 January could be refused by Tom. Is Tom liable to Mary?

10.   The *Uniform Commercial Code* contains the following provisions:

   § 2-609. Right to Adequate Assurance of Performance

      (1) A contract for sale imposes an obligation on each party that the other's expectation of receiving due performance will not be impaired. When reasonable grounds for insecurity arise with respect to the performance of either party the other may in writing demand adequate assurance of due performance and until he receives such assurance may if commercially reasonable suspend any performance for which he has not already received the agreed return.

      (2) Between merchants the reasonableness of grounds for insecurity and the adequacy of any assurance offered shall be determined according to commercial standards.

   § 2-610. Anticipatory Repudiation

   When either party repudiates the contract with respect to a performance not yet due the loss of which will substantially impair the value of the contract to the other, the aggrieved party may

   (a)   for a commercially reasonable time await performance by the repudiating party; or

   (b)   resort to any remedy for breach (Section 2-703 or Section 2-711), even though he has notified the repudiating party that he would await the latter's performance and has urged retraction; and

   (c)   in either case suspend his own performance or proceed in accordance with the provisions of this Article on the seller's right to identify goods to the contract notwithstanding breach or to salvage unfinished goods (Section 2-704).

The UCC in § 2-611 deals with the situation where the promisee seeks to retract its repudiation.

   The United Nations Convention on Contracts for the International Sale of Goods (Schedule E of the International Sale of Goods Act, R.S.O. 1990, c. I.10) provides:

   Article 71

      (1) A party may suspend the performance of his obligations if, after the conclusion of the contract, it becomes apparent that the other party will not perform a substantial part of his obligations as a result of:

      (a)   a serious deficiency in his ability to perform or in his creditworthiness; or

      (b)   his conduct in preparing to perform or in performing the contract.

      (2) If the seller has already dispatched the goods before the grounds described in the preceding paragraph become evident, he may prevent the hand-

ing over of the goods to the buyer even though the buyer holds a document which entitles him to obtain them. The present paragraph relates only to the rights in the goods as between the buyer and the seller.

(3) A party suspending performance, whether before or after dispatch of the goods, must immediately give notice of the suspension to the other party and must continue with performance if the other party provides adequate assurance of his performance.

Article 72

(1) If prior to the date for performance of the contract it is clear that one of the parties will commit a fundamental breach of contract, the other party may declare the contract avoided.

(2) If time allows, the party intending to declare the contract avoided must give reasonable notice to the other party in order to permit him to provide adequate assurance of his performance.

(3) The requirements of the preceding paragraph do not apply if the other party has declared that he will not perform his obligations.

How well do these statutory provisions deal with the problems of anticipatory breach?

11. In some situations the party who elects to treat the contract as discharged due to a fundamental breach by the other party will seek restitutionary relief for services provided: see N. Rafferty, "Contracts Discharged Through Breach: Restitution for Services Rendered by the Innocent Party" (1999), 37 *Alta. L. Rev.* 51-72.

THE RIGHT OF A PARTY IN BREACH TO CLAIM RESTITUTION

The mere existence of an excuse for further obligations to perform does not deal with all the problems that have to be resolved. For example, there is the question of whether a party who is excused from performance by reason of the other's breach may still be compelled to pay for the benefits received under the contract prior to the breach.

There are two common situations where one party has a right to recover even though he admits that he is in breach and that, as a result, the other party is discharged from further obligations and may also have a right to damages. The first occurs when a plaintiff has made an advance payment of the price and seeks to recover it. The second occurs when a plaintiff has partly performed and has supplied work or materials to the defendant, but has not completed the required performance. In both of these situations, the plaintiff cannot sue for the contractual performance of the defendant since the plaintiff has not done what he promised to do. The following cases explore some of the difficulties in the plaintiff's claim that he should be paid to prevent the unjust enrichment of the defendant.

Recovery of Money

HOWE v. SMITH

(1884), 27 Ch. D. 89
(C.A., Cotton, Bowen and Fry L.JJ.)

FRY L.J.: — **[1]** On the 24th of March, 1881, the Defendant and Plaintiff entered into an agreement in writing, by which the Defendant agreed to sell and the purchaser agreed to buy certain real estate for £12,500, of which £500 was in the contract stated to have been paid on the signing of the agreement as a deposit and in part payment of the purchase-money. The contract provided for the payment of the balance on the 24th of April, 1881, and it further provided by the 8th condition that if the purchaser should fail to comply with the agreement the vendor should be at liberty to resell the premises, and the deficiency on such second sale thereof, with all expenses attending the same, should be made good by the defaulter and be recoverable as liquidated damages.

[2]   The Plaintiff, the purchaser, did not pay the balance of his purchase-money on the day stipulated, and he has been guilty of such delay and neglect in completing that, according to our judgment already expressed, he has lost all right to the specific performance of the contract in equity.

[3]   The question then arises which has been argued before us, although not before Mr. Justice Kay, whether or not the Plaintiff is entitled to recover the £500 paid on the signing of the contract.

[4]   The £500 was paid, in the words of the contract, as "a deposit and in part payment of the purchase-money." What is the meaning of this expression? The authorities seem to leave the matter in some doubt. . . .

[5]   [The] authorities appear to afford no certain light to answer the inquiry whether, in the absence of express stipulation, money paid as a deposit on the signing of a contract can be recovered by the payer if he has made such default in performance of his part as to have lost all right to performance by the other party to the contract or damages for his own non-performance.

[6]   Money paid as a deposit must, I conceive, be paid on some terms implied or expressed. In this case no terms are expressed, and we must therefore inquire what terms are to be implied. The terms most naturally to be implied appear to me in the case of money paid on the signing of a contract to be that in the event of the contract being performed it shall be brought into account, but if the contract is not performed by the payer it shall remain the property of the payee. It is not merely a part payment, but is then also an earnest to bind the bargain so entered into, and creates by the fear of its forfeiture a motive in the payer to perform the rest of the contract.

[7]   The practice of giving something to signify the conclusion of the contract, sometimes a sum of money, sometimes a ring or other object, to be repaid or redelivered on the completion of the contract, appears to be one of great antiquity and very general prevalence. It may not be unimportant to observe as evidence of this antiquity that our own word "earnest" has been supposed to flow from a Phoenician source through . . . the Greeks, the *arra* or *arrha* of the Latins, and the *arrhes* of the French. It was familiar to the law of Rome. . . .

[8]   Taking these early authorities into consideration, I think we may conclude that the deposit in the present case is the earnest or *arrha* of our earlier writers; that the expression used in the present contract that the money is paid "as a deposit and in part payment of the purchase-money," relates to the two alternatives, and declares that in the event of the purchaser making default the money is to be forfeited, and that in the event of the purchase being completed the sum is to be taken in part payment.

[9] Such being my view of the nature of the deposit, it appears to me to be clear that the purchaser has lost all right to recover it if he has lost both his right to specific performance in equity and his right to sue for damages for its non-performance at law. That the purchaser has by his delay lost all right to specific performance we have already decided. It remains to inquire whether he has also lost all right to sue for damages for its non-performance.

[10] . . . But in my opinion there has been such default as justifies the vendor in treating the contract as rescinded; it affords the vendor an alternative remedy, so that he may either affirm the contract and sell under this clause or rescind the contract and sell under his absolute title. If he act under the clause, he must bring the deposit into account in his claim for the deficiency: if he sells as owner, he may retain the deposit, but loses his claim for the deficiency under the clause in question.

[11] For these reasons I conclude that the appeal must be dismissed, with costs.

[**COTTON** and **BOWEN L.JJ.** agreed with **FRY L.J.**]

NOTES AND QUESTIONS

1.   What if after the buyer defaulted, the seller was able to sell the land to another buyer for £13,500? Was the seller obliged to return the deposit?

2.   Suppose after the buyer defaulted, the seller was only able to sell the land for £11,000. Does the use of the term "deposit" serve as a limitation of liability? In *Lozcal Holdings v. Brassos Development Ltd.* (1980), 111 D.L.R. (3d) 598, 12 Alta. L.R. (2d) 227, the Alberta Court of Appeal held that the mere use of the term "deposit" does not limit the amount of damages unless it is clearly indicated that the forfeiture limits the liability.

   In some circumstances, the amount of forfeiture resulting from a deposit may be regarded as so large relative to any conceivable loss, that it may be viewed as "extravagant" or "unconscionable", and a court will refuse to enforce it. See *Stockloser v. Johnson*, [1954] 1 All E.R. 630, [1954] 1 Q.B. 476 (C.A.). These cases and related issues are considered in Chapter 6.

DIES v. BRITISH AND INTERNATIONAL MINING AND FINANCE CORP. LTD.

[1939] 1 K.B. 724
(K.B.D., Stable J.)

STABLE J.: — **[1]** The facts, so far as they are material, are not in dispute, and no evidence was called by either side except as to the meaning of certain French words and as to the amount of damages, if any, recoverable by the defendant corporation against the plaintiffs. The facts may shortly be summarized as follows: Mr. Quintana, the plaintiff, being minded to buy a large quantity of Mauser rifles and the appropriate ammunition, entered into a contract with the defendant corporation, the terms of which are set out in the two letters dated November 14, 1936. For the purposes of the present action the second letter may be ignored. Subsequently this contract was either varied or a new contract was substituted in its place, it matters not which, but in the result the terms of the contract which it is accepted was ultimately made between the parties are to be found in the three letters.

[2]   The contract was a contract governed by the law of England. The language employed by the contracting parties was French. The translations of the contractual letters into the English language have been agreed, with the exception of certain words the meanings of which are in dispute and which were the subject-matter of evidence called before me. In substance, the contract provided for the sale by the defendant corporation to Mr. Quintana of a number of Mauser rifles and a quantity of ammunition at the price of £270,000. The goods were stated in the contract to be destined for Turkey. Delivery was to be made by December 15, 1936, which date was extended by mutual agreement, and it appears for the mutual convenience of both of the contracting parties, to January 15, 1937.

[3]   As regards the price £100,000 was paid on or about November 14, 1936, and the plaintiff, Mr. Quintana, was to provide for the balance of the purchase price by means of an irrevocable credit to be opened in favour of the defendant corporation with a bank in Prague. ... Mr. Quintana paid to the corporation the sum of £100,000 and no more, and it is this sum or part of this sum that the plaintiffs claim to be entitled to recover in this action.

[4]   Notwithstanding the fact that he had made this substantial payment, for reasons which have not been disclosed to me Mr. Quintana was unable to take delivery of any of the rifles or ammunition sold to him. It is admitted in the statement of claim that the contract was broken by Mr. Quintana in that he never paid the additional £100,000 or opened the additional credit of £35,000, and was never ready or willing to take delivery. A certain amount of reticence has been observed as to the causes or circumstances which occasioned this breach, but the breach itself is admitted. By a letter dated February 4, 1937, the defendant corporation, as they were lawfully entitled to do in view of the breach or breaches of contract by Mr. Quintana going to the root of the contract, elected to treat the contract as being at an end in the sense that it ceased to impose any obligation of further performance on either party. As from the letter of February 4, 1937, the right of the defendant corporation was to sue Mr. Quintana, the other contracting party, for the damages they had sustained by reason of his breach of contract, and their obligation to deliver the goods was at an end.

[5]   . . . The matter has to be decided, in my judgment, not on any express or implied term contained in the contract, but on the principle of law applicable where the contract itself is silent, except in so far as the intention of the parties can be ascertained from the designation used to indicate the nature of the sum that was paid. On this basis the plaintiff's contention can, I think, be fairly summarized as follows: Where there is a contract for the sale of goods, and a part payment for the goods is made, but no goods are delivered or tendered by reason of the default of the buyer, the seller's only remedy is to recover damages for the default, while the buyer, notwithstanding that it is by reason of his default that the contract has not been performed, is entitled to recover the purchase price that he has paid, subject possibly to the right of the seller to set off against that claim the damages to which he can establish his title. . . .

[6]   In the present case, neither by the use of the word "deposit" or otherwise, is there anything to indicate that the payment of £100,000 was intended or was believed by either party to be in the nature of a guarantee or earnest for the due performance of the contract. It was part payment of the price of the goods sold and was so described.

[7] . . . [T]he general rule is that the law confers on the purchaser the right to recover his money, and that to enable the seller to keep it he must be able to point to some language in the contract from which the inference to be drawn is that the parties intended and agreed that he should.

[8] The argument on behalf of the defendant corporation was supported by the submission that the action for money had and received would not lie, since on the present facts the only possible basis was a total failure of consideration, which basis was ruled out by the fact that it was the purchaser who had made default. . . .

[9] I was, however, quite satisfied that in the present case the foundation of the right, if right there be, is not a total failure of consideration. There was no failure of consideration, total or partial. It was not the consideration that failed but the party to the contract.

[10] This objection, in my judgment, really goes to a question of form and not of substance, for if under the present circumstances there is a right in the buyer to recover a payment he has made in part, it is wholly immaterial in point of form whether the basis of right depends on a total failure of consideration, or something else. In my judgment, the real foundation of the right which I hold exists in the present case is not a total failure of consideration but the right of the purchaser, derived from the terms of the contract and the principle of law applicable, to recover back his money . . .

[11] In the result I find that the plaintiffs have a right of action for the recovery of the £100,000.

[12] The defendants, on the other hand, are, or may be, entitled to damages. . . .

[13] In my judgment, the true measure of damages is the loss of profit that the sellers would have made on the deal. This is measured by the difference between the price at which they could have bought and the contract price. There must also be brought into account such incidental expenses as delivery charges and the cost of sending the goods to the port to be selected by the buyers, an obligation which fell on the sellers. . . .

[14] The precise form which the order must take will have to be considered. There must be an inquiry to ascertain the damage, and, when this figure has been arrived at, if it is less than the sum of £100,000, the defendant corporation will have to pay the balance to the plaintiffs. If the damages are more than £100,000 the claim will be extinguished to the extent of £100,000 by the money which the defendant corporation have in their hands, and judgment will be entered for the defendant corporation for the balance. Mr. Pritt suggested that the £100,000 should carry interest, but I do not think that this is a case in which interest ought to be allowed. It is true that the defendant corporation has had the £100,000. Equally, it is hoped that Mr. Quintana has had the use of the money which he will have to pay to the defendant corporation in damages.

Recovery for the Supply of Goods or Services

The courts have had considerable difficulty in dealing with claims for recovery of the price for the supply of goods or services in partially completed contracts.

Part of the problem arises from one of the rules of the common law that was laid down at the end of the eighteenth century, known as the "entire contract" rule. The rule is usually associated with the case of *Cutter v. Powell* (1795), 6 T.R. 320, 101 E.R. 573 (K.B.). Lord Kenyon refused to allow any claim by the widow of a ship's officer for part of the pay he was alleged to have earned on a voyage from Jamaica to Liverpool. The officer had been promised £31 10s 0d for the voyage. He died after completing about two-thirds of the voyage. The obligation of the defendant to pay was said to arise only on the completion of the voyage. The entire contract rule was applied in the following nineteenth-century case.

BLAKE v. SHAW

(1853), 10 U.C.Q.B. 180
(Robinson C.J., Draper and Burns JJ.)

Assumpsit on the common counts. Pleas, Non-assumpsit, payment, and set-off.

At the trial, before Sullivan J. at Niagara, it was proved on behalf of the plaintiff that the defendant was a merchant in St. Catharines, in large business; that the plaintiff was in his service as a clerk, from the 13th of November, 1848, till the 20th of September, 1850, and that his service was worth from £75 to £100 a year, besides his board; that in September 1850, the plaintiff went to California, and that by his instructions a relative of his afterwards went to the defendant to demand payment of his wages; that the defendant said he would not pay until he saw the plaintiff himself, who would be more in want of his wages when he returned than at that time. This witness swore that she had herself lent the plaintiff £35 when he went away.

On the defence it was sworn, by Shaw, the defendant, that he had agreed with the plaintiff about the 15th of November, 1848, to pay him £60 a year; that in September 1850, he left the defendant's service without notice or permission, and sent his sister-in-law to the defendant with an order. The defendant swore that he had paid the plaintiff more than his wages for the first year, and that he told his sister-in-law if he wished to settle he must come himself, for that he did not believe he owed him anything. He swore that the plaintiff agreed with him to serve by the year. The defendant admitted that he offered to give £25 and costs to settle this suit, but not because it was a balance due.

A fellow clerk of the plaintiff swore that he knew nothing of the plaintiff's intention to leave; he went with the permission of the defendant to a fair in the neighbourhood, and never returned; the witness recommended him to come back, but the plaintiff said he had got tired of working at £60 a year. This clerk swore that if he were to leave in the same manner, he should expect to lose his wages.

The learned judge ruled that although it appeared by the evidence that there might be a balance of £45 due to the plaintiff on account of his current year's wages, yet that he was not entitled to sue for it, being hired for a year, and having left without permission before the year had ended.

The jury gave a verdict for the plaintiff for £25.

ROBINSON C.J. delivered the judgment of the court: — **[1]** We have no doubt that upon the evidence the verdict given in this cause was against the law, which is clear that where a clerk or other person hired for a year, departs without consent before the year is up, he forfeits his wages, and cannot recover for the part of the year that he has served. And in this case the footing on which the parties were is plain. It was not merely a constructive hiring for a year, but an actual contract of that kind; and courts of justice have expressed themselves strongly on the importance to society of enforcing such engagements, by making parties bear the legal consequences of breaking them. The only room for a doubt whether we may not properly decline to grant a new trial is, that there was certainly no misdirection. The jury were not misled; and it may be said, and perhaps thought, that the verdict is consistent with justice, and ought not therefore to be disturbed. But . . . "If that argument were to prevail, it would encourage juries to commit a breach of duty, by finding verdicts contrary to law, and would enable them to set aside the contracts of mankind."

[2]   The jury, we think it probable, awarded the plaintiff £25 in this case, because it was sworn that the defendant, while this action was pending offered that sum, if the action were dropped, at the same time contending that he was under no obligation to pay anything. The very object of such offer is to stop a law suit, and when the party to whom it is made rejects it, and will persevere in his action; he should derive no advantage from having refused it; but as he has thought proper to insist on his supposed legal right, in the hope of compelling the defendant to pay more, he should be left to abide by the proper legal result of that action.

[3]   We are of opinion that there ought to be a new trial without costs.

NOTES AND QUESTIONS

1.   The entire contract rule was developed by common law judges in the eighteenth and nineteenth centuries. In general, which economic class do you think benefitted from the rule? Do you think it is a fair rule?

2.   In theory, an employee could negotiate a contract to be paid by the day or the hour, rather than the year, or the voyage, but in an era before unions and employment legislation, the economics of the labour market generally allowed employers to determine the terms of employment contracts for unskilled workers.

3.   Notice that in *Blake v. Shaw* the trial judge rejected a claim based on the value of the services provided, *i.e.*, a claim in *quantum meruit*. This is because there was no "unjust" enrichment in this situation. There was a deprivation to the plaintiff and an enrichment of the defendant, but it arose as a result of the term of the contract and hence was not considered "unjust".

The next case is an example of the application of the "entire contract rule" to a building contract. The court recognizes some exceptions to this rule for building contracts.

SUMPTER v. HEDGES

[1898] 1 Q.B. 673
(C.A., A.L. Smith, Collins and Chitty L.JJ.)

Appeal from the judgment of Bruce J. at the trial before him without a jury.

The action was for work done and materials provided. The plaintiff, a builder, had contracted with the defendant to build upon the defendant's land two houses and stables for the sum of £565. The plaintiff did part of the work, amounting in value to about £333, and had received payment of part of the price. He then informed the defendant that he had no money, and could not go on with the work. The learned judge found that he had abandoned the contract. The defendant thereupon finished the buildings on his own account, using for that purpose certain building materials which the plaintiff had left on the ground. The judge gave judgment for the plaintiff for the value of the materials so used, but allowed him nothing in respect of the work which he had done upon the buildings.

A.L. SMITH L.J.: — [1] In this case the plaintiff, a builder, entered into a contract to build two houses and stables on the defendant's land for a lump sum. When the buildings were still in an unfinished state the plaintiff informed the defendant that he had no money, and was not going on with the work any more. The learned judge has found as a fact that he abandoned the contract. Under such circumstances, what is a building owner to do? He cannot keep the buildings on his land in an unfinished state for ever. The law is that, where there is a contract to do work for a lump sum, until the work is completed the price of it cannot be recovered. Therefore the plaintiff could not recover on the original contract. It is suggested however that the plaintiff was entitled to recover for the work he did on a quantum meruit. But, in order that that may be so, there must be evidence of a fresh contract to pay for the work already done. With regard to that, the case of *Munro v. Butt* [(1858), 8 E. & B. 738] appears to be exactly in point. That case decides that, unless the building owner does something from which a new contract can be inferred to pay for the work already done, the plaintiff in such a case as this cannot recover on a quantum meruit. In the case of *Lysaght v. Pearson* (reported in the *Times*, 3 March 1879), to which we have been referred, the case of *Munro v. Butt* does not appear to have been referred to. There the plaintiff had contracted to erect on the defendant's land two corrugated iron roofs. When he had completed one of them, he does not seem to have said that he abandoned the contract, but merely that he would not go on unless the defendant paid him for what he had already done. The defendant thereupon proceeded to erect for himself the second roof. The Court of Appeal held that there was in that case something from which a new contract might be inferred to pay for the work done by the plaintiff. That is not this case. In the case of *Whitaker v. Dunn* (1887), 3 T.L.R. 602 there was a contract to erect a laundry on defendant's land, and the laundry erected was not in accordance with the contract, but the official referee held that the plaintiff could recover on a quantum meruit. The case came before a Divisional Court, consisting of Lord Coleridge C.J. and myself, and we said that the decision in *Munro v. Butt* applied, and there being no circumstances to justify an inference of a fresh contract the plaintiff must fail. My brother Collins thinks that that case went to the Court of Appeal, and that he argued it there, and the Court affirmed the decision of the Queen's Bench Division. I think the appeal must be dismissed.

CHITTY L.J.: — [2] I am of the same opinion. The plaintiff had contracted to erect certain buildings for a lump sum. When the work was only partly done, the plaintiff said that he could not go on with it, and the judge has found that he abandoned the contract. The position therefore was that the defendant found his land with unfinished buildings upon it, and he thereupon completed the work. That is no evidence from which the inference can be drawn that he entered into a fresh contract to pay for the work done by the plaintiff. If we held that the plaintiff could recover, we should in my opinion be overruling *Cutter v. Powell* (1795), 6 T.R. 320, and a long series of cases in which it has been decided that there must in such a case be some evidence of a new contract to enable the plaintiff to recover on a quantum meruit. There was nothing new in the decision in *Pattinson v. Luckley* (1875), L.R. 10 Ex. 330, but Bramwell B. there pointed out with his usual clearness that in the case of a building erected upon land the mere fact that the defendant remains in possession of his land is no evidence upon which an inference of a new contract can be founded. He says: "In the case of goods sold and delivered, it is easy to shew a contract from the retention of the goods; but that is not so where work is done on real property." I think the learned judge was quite right in holding that in this case there was no evidence from which a fresh contract to pay for the work done could be inferred.

[**COLLINS L.J.** wrote a concurring judgment.]

QUESTIONS AND NOTES

1. Are you satisfied with how *Lysaght v. Pearson* is distinguished from *Sumpter v. Hedges*?

2. What do you think would be evidence of a fresh contract to pay for the work already done? Could such evidence be inferred? If so, what kinds of things would lead the court to draw such an inference?

3. Some contracts, especially modern building contracts, are contractually apportionable or severable. That is, the contracts are written to provide that the builder is entitled to stipulated payments after each stage of construction, regardless of whether the entire project is completed.

4. For building contracts there is an important exception to the entire contract rule. The contractor who has "substantially" performed can sue for the contract price, less any amount that the promisee can claim as damages for the breach. This rule was part of the issue in *Jacob and Youngs v. Kent, supra*. This rule goes further than the prevention of unjust enrichment since it allows the contractor to sue for the price as the starting point of its claim. In *Dakin & Co. Ltd. v. Lee*, [1916] 1 K.B. 566 (C.A.), Lord Cozens-Hardy M.R. had to deal with a claim by a builder for work done repairing a house. In one part of the house, the concrete foundation was only two feet deep, while the specifications called for four-foot depth; the columns used to support one bay window were four inches of solid iron, while the specifications called for five inches of hollow iron; and the finishing work around one window was not done in the manner contractually specified. Lord Cozens-Hardy M.R. stated (pp. 578-80):

> In these circumstances it has been argued before us that, in a contract of this kind to do work for a lump sum, the defect in some of the items in the specification, or the failure to do every item contained in the specification, puts an end to the whole contract, and prevents the builders from making any claim upon it; and therefore, where there is no ground for presuming any fresh contract, he cannot obtain any payment. The matter has been treated in the argument as though the omission to do every item perfectly was an abandonment of the contract. That seems to me, with great respect, to be absolutely and entirely wrong. An illustration of the abandonment of a contract which was given from one of the authorities was that of a builder who, when he had half finished his work, said to the employer "I cannot finish it, because I have no money," and left the job undone at that stage. That is an abandonment of the contract, and prevents the builder, therefore, from making any claim, unless there be some other circumstances leading to a different conclusion. But to say that a builder cannot recover from a building owner merely because some item of the work has been done negligently or inefficiently or improperly is a proposition which I should not listen to unless compelled by a decision of the House of Lords. Take a contract for a lump sum to decorate a house; the con-

tract provides that there shall be three coats of oil paint, but in one of the rooms only two coats of paint are put on. Can anybody seriously say that under these circumstances the building owner could go and occupy the house and take the benefit of all the decorations which had been done in the other rooms without paying a penny for all the work done by the builder, just because only two coats of paint had been put on in one room where there ought to have been three? . . .

It seems to me that the result is that the builders are entitled to recover the contract price, less so much as it is found ought to be allowed in respect of the items which the official referee has found to be defective. There is no finding by the referee as to what the precise figures should be, and unless they are agreed, the matter must go back to him to decide what ought to be allowed in respect of the concrete not being 4 feet and the wrong joining of the rolled steel joists, and what, if anything, ought to be allowed in respect of the concrete not having been properly mixed.

The appeal substantially fails and must be dismissed; but the case must go back, if necessary, to the official referee to find what allowance ought to be made from the sum to be paid the builders in respect of those items.

5.   Why do you think that common law judges seemed to create more exceptions to the entire contract rule for builders than for workers?

6.   Legislatures have mitigated some of the rigours of the entire contract rule, especially as it might apply to employment contracts. See for example, the *Apportionment Act*, R.S.O. 1990, c. A.23:

> 1. In this Act,
>
> "annuities" includes salaries and pensions;
>
> . . .
>
> 3. All rents, annuities, dividends, and other periodical payments in the nature of income, whether reserved or made payable under an instrument in writing or otherwise, shall, like interest on money lent, be considered as accruing from day to day, and are apportionable in respect of time accordingly.

This legislation is based on the original English legislation of 1870. What is the effect of this statute on a case like *Blake v. Shaw*?

PART TWO

CHAPTER FIVE

CONTRACTUAL UNDERTAKINGS: THEIR DETERMINATION, RANGE, AND REMEDIES FOR BREACH

INTRODUCTION

The first four chapters of this book dealt with some of the fundamental concepts of contract law. The rules that govern the formation of contracts, and the requirements for having a legally enforceable contract, as well as the consequences of breach of a contract, were examined; some of the contract concepts that lawyers and judges use, such as "consideration" and "condition", were introduced. This chapter deals with a range of related problems that arise in connection with the interpretation and performance of contracts. These problems not only are dealt with by the barristers and the courts, but much more frequently are encountered by solicitors in their negotiation and drafting of contracts, and in their informal resolution of disputes connected with the performance of contracts.

The best way to understand the real-life problems faced by solicitors who work in what can broadly be called the "contracts field" would be to study not the decisions of the courts, but actual deals made by the parties, the background of the negotiations, the expectations and understandings of the parties, the general nature of the commercial arrangement the contract was intended to reflect, the standard agreements that each solicitor or firm uses as templates for each common transaction, the way in which performance is actually carried out, and the flexibility or tolerance of (non-)performance by parties trying (generally) to work things out in a relation of mutual co-operation. Unfortunately, direct access to this type of information is not readily available, and what material is available tends not to be easily comprehensible to students starting their legal studies. Developing an understanding of the commercial and legal context of different types of contractual situations is the focus of study in a number of upper-year courses. Indeed, a considerable amount of time and effort in the early years of the practice of law is devoted to gaining a better understanding of these issues.

In a first-year contracts course, the primary focus tends to be on court decisions, which are the most accessible materials for study, though for students starting the study of law it can be difficult to understand the legal and commercial context of many of the cases that deal with contractual undertakings. As mentioned earlier, it is important to appreciate that a judicial decision about a contractual case is in a sense, pathological: it represents the "living" contractual relation only as accurately as a judgment in a divorce action represents — or helps one to understand — a living marriage. There is also a real danger that one will be led to believe that one "dead" contract laid out, so to speak, on the mortuary slab is much the same as any other dead contract. The belief that the traditional rules apply to *all* contracts is thus strengthened. Exactly this effect could be observed in many of the cases on consideration and third-party beneficiary contracts: too often judicial analysis is driven by abstract principles taken from precedents, without an assessment being made of the effect of judicial action.

An important aspect of this casebook is an investigation of the extent to which the traditional rules do not apply, or do not apply satisfactorily, to many contractual situations. As has already been seen, those traditional rules do not account adequately for the fundamental difference between discrete contracts and relational ones, or for the patterns of modern business practices and organizations. Another example of this discrepancy is the failure of the traditional rules to deal adequately with the large corporation as a contracting party (as could be seen in some of the cases dealing with third-party beneficiary contracts).

One of the most frequently performed judicial functions regarding contracts is the interpretation of what the parties meant by the words that they used. One of the most valuable functions performed by solicitors is their ability to draft contracts with a view to the ways that the courts are likely to approach the job of interpretation. The language of lawyers is sometimes, perhaps often, unfamiliar and hard for the layperson to understand. Much more often than not (but unfortunately not always), that language is precise and makes a substantial contribution to the reduction of the risks of misinterpretation by the courts. Perhaps more importantly, use of precise language increases the likelihood that both parties, who usually intend (at least at the beginning) to perform, will understand the obligations being undertaken and will perform as agreed. Contracts function much more frequently as rules for the parties as they work within the framework of the agreement than as sources for judicially imposed resolutions of disputes. A well-drafted contract helps parties avoid disputes, not only by avoiding misunderstandings at the contract's inception but during its lifetime, as the employees of the parties manage their relations within the framework of the contract.

Within this context, there are proper places for technical language as well as for "plain language" drafting, and some of the issues raised by the form of language used in contracts will be considered in this chapter. There is also an important point of efficiency to be remembered. Most agreements drafted by lawyers have a structure and language that is familiar to other lawyers. Adherence to the expected order of the clauses and even to the expected words makes the job of drafting and understanding them easier and, of course, cheaper. Standard language, like standard sizes and measuring units, cuts down on the transaction costs of most deals.

It is important to understand how courts will approach the problem of interpretation: what the parties meant by the agreement they made (if they had any common idea of the meaning of the agreement); the problem of the relevance of the murky background of negotiations; and the possibly inconsistent expectations out of which the contract arose.

The extracts and notes at the start of this chapter introduce some of the fundamental issues of the law of contract. An important point to remember is that a wide range of relations may be brought within the realm of "contract". At one extreme is the paradigm of the classical or traditional law of contract: the one-shot deal of two parties who come together for a single transaction and who conduct themselves during the negotiation and performance of that deal as if they had never had any previous dealings and never expected to have any in the future. As has been argued, this view of how contracts are made is often inaccurate, though not entirely wrong. At the other end of the spectrum are complex long-term economic relations that involve multiple parties.

The following extract suggests that the range of contractual relations is very broad: so broad, in fact, that some startling consequences can be seen as necessarily linked to such a view.

MACNEIL, THE NEW SOCIAL CONTRACT

(New Haven: Yale University Press, 1980) (pp. 4-10, 70)

[1]   By contract I mean no more and no less than the relations among parties to the process of projecting exchange into the future. This projection emanates from combining in a society the other three contract roots. A sense of choice and an awareness of future regularly cause people to do things and to make plans for the future. When these actions and plans relate to exchange, it is projected forward in time. That is, some of the elements of exchange, instead of occurring immediately, will occur in the future. This, or rather the relations between people when this occurs, is what I mean by contract.

[2]   Let me compare this with a more traditional definition, that in *Restatement (Second)*: "A contract is a promise or a set of promises for the breach of which the law gives a remedy, or the performance of which the law in some way recognizes as a duty." Now, this is a definition not of contract-in-fact, but of contract-in-law. Under it, any relation, no matter how full of exchange, not potentially giving rise to *legal* remedies or *legal* recognition of duties is not a contract. In our law-ridden society — and I agree with Pashukanis that any society ridden with exchange will be ridden with law — this limitation of the contract concept is in some ways less serious than it might seem. Most of our exchange relations do in fact give rise to legal rights. But in Britain, for example, collective bargaining is in theory outside legal enforceability. And there exist in our society exchange relations, of which marriage is but an extreme example, where much occurs to which the law does not, in any practical sense, extend its remedies or recognize legal duties.

[3]   More important than possible omission of particular relations from the domain of a law-oriented definition of contracts is the bias it gives our thinking. While law may be an integral part of virtually all contractual relations, one not to be ignored, law is not what contracts are all about. Contracts are about getting things done in the real world — building things, selling things, co-operating in enterprise, achieving power and prestige, sharing and competing in a family structure. Thus, even if a law-oriented definition encompasses every contract included in an exchange-oriented definition, it will inevitably be perceived as narrower because it immediately tells us to think about law. If we wish to understand contract, and indeed if we wish to understand contract law, we must think about exchange and such things first, and law second.

[4]   But an even more serious hindrance to understanding is the limitation of contract to "a promise or a set of promises." Promise is an illusive concept, but the Restatement tries to put us on the right track by defining it as the "manifestation of intention to act or refrain from acting in a specified way, so made as to justify a promisee in understanding that a commitment has been made." Unfortunately this seems merely a Gertrude Steinian "a promise is a promise is a promise."

[5]   Those of us who try to define promise may be under eternal sentence to do so in Steinian terms, but hope is as eternal as the sentence, so let me try something else. Since many of the important applications of promise in contracts have to do with exchange, I shall limit this discussion of promise to its role as an exchange-projector.

[6]   The idea of promise is an affirmation of the power of the human will to affect the future. It affirms that an individual can affect the future now. But a promise is made *to* someone. Thus, the first two elements of promise in its contractual context are the wills of *two* or more individuals with beliefs in the power of one to affect the future — subject to the linkage of the social matrix essential to exchange.

[7]   A third element of promise is the doing of something now to limit the choices otherwise available to the promisor in the future. This is part of the notion of commitment encompassed in the *Restatement* definition. For example, a person entering an agreement to sell a house no longer may choose to sell it elsewhere without suffering the consequences of breaching his promise. These may be as intangible as a loss of reputation or as concrete as a judgment awarding damages.

[8]   Two other closely linked elements of promise as an exchange-projector must now be added: communication and measured reciprocity. Communication is required by the division between "you" and "me" postulated by the existence of separate wills. Finally, the separation of selfish "you" from selfish "me," together with the existence of commitment, and communication, all go to guarantee that promise-based exchange-projection will indeed encompass *measured* reciprocity, the fifth element.

[9]   We have thus five elements of promise in exchange, always to be viewed in their particular society. These are: (1) the will of the promisor and (2) the will of the promisee; (3) present action to limit future choice; (4) communication; and (5) measured reciprocity. These may be more conveniently summarized in this definition of promise as an exchange-projector: "Present communication of a commitment to engage in a reciprocal measured exchange." This extraordinarily powerful mechanism for projecting exchange into the future is the essence of discrete contract.

[10]   But we are seeking to understand contract as the relations among parties to the processes of future exchange. Only if promise as defined is the *sole* way exchange can be and is projected do we stop with it. And, of course, it is not. Indeed, in many circumstances promise is neither the most effective nor the most important exchange-projector in contractual relations.

[11]   Nonpromissory exchange-projectors — those lacking one or more of the elements of promise — come in a great many forms. In all societies, custom, status, habit, and other internalizations project exchange into the future. In some primitive societies these may be the primary projectors, with promise relating to exchange playing only a very minor role, if that. Moreover, we err if we fail to recognize that such nonpromissory mechanisms continue to play vital parts in the most modern and developed of societies. Even kinship, a form of status which plays major roles in so many societies, is by no means absent as an exchange-projector in ours, although it may now be overshadowed by class or other structures with partially related roles.

[12] More dynamic nonpromissory exchange-projectors than these are positions of command, vital not only in many simple societies but even more so in immensely complex societies. The internal hierarchies of corporations are a modern example. Complicating this pattern in complex structures is the existence of bureaucracies which, while in theory merely tools of higher commanders, in fact develop self-interests inevitably both affecting and effecting exchange-projection.

[13] Finally, the very existence of ongoing contractual relations creates expectations that future exchange will occur, and in partially predictable patterns, simply through the dynamics of the existing relations whether or not hierarchical. For example, the existence of an ongoing market for a product creates, without hierarchical command, expectations that production for that market may be worthwhile. Such markets remain among our most important relational exchange-projectors, even though the relational web they create may be highly impersonal.

[14] Thus we find a great range of nonpromissory exchange-projectors. Key ones include custom, status, habit and other internalizations, command in hierarchical structures, and expectations created by the dynamics of any status quo, including markets.

[15] These nonpromissory types may be and often are accompanied by promises. But more important to understanding contract is the other side of the coin: promissory projectors are *always* accompanied by nonpromissory projectors. This emanates from the interplay of the always present social matrix with the nature of promises themselves. Promises are inherently fragmentary. The human mind can focus on only a limited number of things at the same time, and, for reasons of efficiency in fact focuses on even fewer than it can. Thus, promises can never encompass more than a fragment of the total situation. At least as fundamental, the amount of information available about the future is always only partial, and promises, however sweeping, can be understood only against this background. All this is part of what Herbert Simon calls bounded rationality. Moreover, promises are further narrowed by the need to fit them into symbolic forms required for communication. The latter narrowing is aggravated by the effort required to transform promises into communication symbols; effort is a cost, and therefore not everything that *can* be transformed into promises will be. For all these reasons, promises are inescapably but fragments of any contractual relation or even transaction, no matter how discrete.

[16] A second factor in the inevitably limited role of promises is overt or tacit recognition that the promise made is never exactly the same as the promise received. Every promise is always *two* promises, the sender's and the receiver's. The resulting nonmutuality ranges from subtle to gross differences in understanding. These differences can be resolved only by bringing into the picture something other than the promises themselves. This something, whatever else it may be, is a nonpromissory projection of exchange into the future.

[17] Partly because of the foregoing factors, both individuals and societies always view promises as less than absolute. Much promise breaking is tolerated, expected, and, indeed, desired. This is true not only respecting the parties, as demonstrated, for example, by Professor Macaulay's studies of the behavior of manufacturers,

but also respecting the rest of society, including the legal system. Were it not, we would find legal contract remedies to be real guns, ready for hire at low cost, rather than expensive cap pistols.

[18]   Once promises are viewed as less than absolute, other exchange-projectors inevitably must come into play. Thus throughout the realm of contract, albeit in greatly varying degrees, we find promise always accompanied by significant non-promissory projectors of exchange. This fact gives rise to troublesome questions concerning the relations between the promissory and nonpromissory aspects of any given contractual relations.

[19]   In 1961 . . . Harold Havighurst said that in certain primitive societies "con-tract . . . is only a ripple upon the great sea of custom." In contrast, the systematics of a neoclassical contract law, such as that of *Restatement (Second)*, treats custom and other nonpromissory exchange-projectors as "only a ripple upon the great sea of promise." In modern society, neither of these conditions obtains; there are two deep ocean currents, the promissory and the nonpromissory; the ripple — no, the waves, even storms — come wherever these cross. . . .

[20]   As contractual relations expand, those relations take on more and more the characteristics of minisocieties and ministates . . . In the case of huge bundles of contractual relations, such as a major national or multinational corporation, they take on the characteristics of large societies and large states. But whether large or small, the whole range of social and political norms becomes pertinent *within* the contractual relations. In ongoing contractual relations we find such broad norms as distributive justice, liberty, human dignity, social equality and inequality, and pro-cedural justice, to mention some of the more vital.

[21]   At this point, just as contractual relations exceed the capacities of the neo-classical contract law system, so too the issues exceed the capacities of neoclassi-cal contract law scholars. They must become something else — anthropologists, sociologists, economists, political theorists, and philosophers — to do reasonable justice to the issues raised by contractual relations. Exchange and planning, the basic areas of expertise of the contracts scholar, have now become just two of the many factors in a complete social organism.

One other general point can be raised here. It is important to think carefully about the role of the law and, in particular, about the role of lawyers in developing the law. There are a number of competing views of the proper role of the law and law-yers. The following excerpt presents an extreme view of what that role should be. If you find that you cannot accept that view, what alternative do you support? On what basis do you defend your view?

RENNER, THE INSTITUTIONS OF PRIVATE LAW AND THEIR SOCIAL FUNCTION

(1906) (London: Routledge & Kegan Paul, 1949, translated by
Agnes Schwartzchild, p. 48)

[Karl Renner was born in 1870 and died in 1950. He was an Austrian politician and scholar. Renner, a Marxist, held interesting views of the function of the law of contract. This extract concerns his ideas about the lawyer's function.]

[1] Of greater interest to us is another part of legal theory which I will call the analysis of positive law; distinguishing it as a separate branch from general legal theory, for it has its own functions and methodology. It is not the object of positive legal analysis to investigate the origin of the common will, its essence, its growth or decay. Its object is to analyse the legal norms contained in the sum total of positive legal provisions, arranging them in accordance with their inherent nature, and to reduce them to a system. For the chaotic multitude of norms can neither be understood nor expounded, neither taught nor applied, without previous co-ordination. We have to classify the norms according to their constituent elements, which we will call "legal characteristics." Positive legal analysis distinguishes rules of private law and rules of public law, and divides the former, in accordance with the particular relations of individual wills with which they are concerned, into rules of the law of property, of obligations, of family relationships, and of succession. Such analysis treats a loan, for example, invariably as a relationship between the wills of two persons, creditor and debtor, concerning the giving and returning of an object; it pays no regard to whether the creditor exploits the debtor — as is usually the case — or whether the debtor exploits the creditor — which may also happen — or to whether the loan concerns a debt of honour or a commercial credit. Positive legal analysis has no other task than to ascertain all the legal norms relevant to the facts and to apply them to the case in hand. This exhausts the function of positive legal analysis. The question how loan transactions collectively react upon the economic system, upon particular classes or upon society as a whole, in short the social effect of the norm, transcends its legal structure. However interesting these social repercussions may be to the lawyer as a side-line, they are the province of the economist and sociologist. They lie outside the province of systematic legal analysis, just as the economic use of the tobacco leaf lies outside the province of botany.

NOTE

Materials based on Renner's view of the proper focus of the lawyer would look very different from these materials. While Renner's view is extreme, there are attitudes to law (or philosophies of law) that share some of his views.

Each law student, lawyer and judge must develop and articulate his or her own view of the proper focus of legal inquiry, the permissible role of lawyers as advocates and as critics of the law's values, and the result of these considerations on the judicial function. These are important questions.

To return to the issues raised by Macneil, his perception of the breadth of contractual relations and issues must be kept in mind in trying to understand the rules of the law of contracts. As has been repeatedly seen in the cases in the first four chapters of this book, the courts frequently take a narrow view of the scope of the relations created by contract. Yet the pressures to view relations of exchange more broadly are sometimes so strong that the courts cannot resist them, and the result is that a broad range of relations is sometimes given some kind of protection. Examples of this pressure can be seen in the protection given to reliance. Paradoxically, the very fact that protected relations are expanded creates problems of controlling or limiting, rather than extending, the range of relations given protection. Courts now face serious problems in setting limits to the range of undertakings that will be seen as justifying reliance or creating expectations. The problem becomes one of respecting the limits to the responsibilities that they might otherwise be seen as having undertaken. These limits may be set by the parties or inherent in their relation.

An example of such a problem is provided by *Dale v. Manitoba* (1997), 147 D.L.R. (4th) 605, [1997] 8 W.W.R. 447 (Man. C.A.) (*supra*, Chapter 2), a case that deals with the question of the intent to form a legally binding contractual relation. By establishing a program to support individual disadvantaged students attending university, the government of Manitoba was held to have contractually committed itself to fund their continued attendance at university. The court used a contractual analysis to require the provincial government to continue funding for those students who began their studies in reliance on the government's commitment. It was irrelevant that the province had responded to a reduction in federal support for the program. Such a decision illustrates an extension of contractual analysis to a relation far from the traditional two-party, one-time, commercial exchange. The case may also illustrate a situation in which, while the students' expectations may have been protected, the government may have been caught by surprise in being held to be contractually bound.

Part of the problem of understanding the law of contracts arises from the fact that its pervasiveness makes analysis difficult. If every relation arising from the agreement of two parties to a future course of action or to a future pattern of cooperation is a contract, can there be principles that are equally applicable to the relations within a family as they are to relations between two large corporations, or to relations between citizens and the government? One response to this pervasiveness has been to subdivide the law into narrower categories: the law of insurance, labour relations, sale of goods, etc.

The consequence of this multiplication of categories of contract has been serious: the law of contracts has been Balkanized. The law of insurance has often developed in ways that seem to ignore what has happened in what can be called the "general part" of the law of contracts. Similarly, areas like labour law have developed in ways that differ from "general" contract law, and the guidance labour law could offer the law generally is not taken. (We saw an example of this potential guidance in the extract from Brown, "Contract Remedies in a Planned Economy: Labour Arbitration Leads the Way", reproduced in Chapter 1.) It is the unwillingness of the courts to make use of the labour law model that simultaneously exacerbates the problem of giving fair compensation for wrongful dismissal and leaves the category of "labour law" as a separate area of the law. The "general part" of the law of contracts is what is dealt with in textbooks that purport to cover the "law of contracts"; the other parts are dealt with in the specialized texts: the law of insurance, the law of labour arbitration, etc.

The process of Balkanization has in some ways been exacerbated by the proliferation of specialized reporting series and electronic case report databases. If real estate cases are reported in real property reports, then each "real estate" case will tend only to cite other "real estate" cases. If you do a search on an electronic database of all the cases that have facts similar to your own, it is not easy to stand back from the resulting list of names and the plethora of facts to find a general principle.

There seems also to be an increasing tendency for the courts of one province to refer only to the judgments of the courts of that province. Perhaps this tendency is caused by the proliferation of provincial series of reports and the possibility of searching online for the decisions of, for example, the judgments of the courts of Saskatchewan. The huge increase in the availability of decisions through the large number of reports and online means that it is possible to find relevant precedents in the decisions of one province. The consequences are serious for it soon becomes impossible to talk of a "Canadian common law": we shall be reduced to talking of a "British Columbia common law" or an "Ontario common law".

Little can be done here to counteract this development other than to make you aware of it. It is important to be aware of the twin dangers of inappropriate principles that are applied too broadly (the doctrine of consideration, for example), and of the failure to see that cases with quite different facts are often, at base, about the same problem. There is, for example, a close parallel between promissory estoppel and the cases giving a remedy when negotiations had not led to a contract, but where one party suffered a loss that the court believed should be shifted to the other.

This chapter introduces a range of problems related to the interpretation of contracts that will be further developed in the next chapter. This chapter will deal with the problems of agreements, the terms of which are more or less free from judicial control by the common law or legislation. "Free" in this context means that the parties are able by agreement to arrange their affairs as they see fit, and the problems that the courts face arise because of a lack of clear agreement on the issue. In the next chapter the focus will be explicitly on the forms and extent of the control exercised by the law over the parties' arrangements in situations where the agreement is considered in some way unfair.

The first section of this chapter deals with the problem of interpretation — the problem of "discovering" the meaning of the terms used by the parties — and what can be regarded as the source of the terms of the agreement. The second section deals with the problems that arise when one party does not get all that it expected from the agreement. The usual classification of the problems in this area puts them into a heading called "Misrepresentations and Warranties". Here the problems of breach of contract and issues of damages will surface again. It will be important to determine what it is that can be regarded as representing, containing or being the source of the expectations that the court is asked to protect.

The final part of the chapter deals with the endemic problem of mistakes. The law of mistake is a broad and confusing category — everything that goes wrong with contracts can in one sense be viewed as a type of mistake. The traditional division of the law of "mistake" is narrower and is focussed on: (1) mistakes or misunderstandings made at the time the contract was made; and (2) mistaken assumptions about the future as a result of a change in circumstances arising after the contract was made. The first category is traditionally put under the heading of "Mistake". When the "mistake" relates to events that occur after the contract was made or performance has begun, the problems are put in a legal category called "Frustration" or "Impossibility of Performance".

When a party to a contract argues that the contract was made "by mistake", he or she usually wants to be relieved from performance and to recover anything that might have been paid to the other before the mistake was discovered. The courts may say that a contract made in some sense by mistake has been "vitiated" by the mistake. If there has been a substantial change in circumstances, the parties may be discharged from further performance, an effect that may be caused either by an explicit term of the contract, or by the court's conclusion that what happened has resulted in a change that renders performance "fundamentally different" from what the contract contemplated, a situation referred to as "frustration". What the law can do about the problems that arise when the parties realize that they have made a mistake, either in their understanding at the beginning of the deal or in their assumptions about the factual background against which performance would be carried out, will be examined.

The relation of mistake and frustration to the previous sections on contractual interpretation, misrepresentation and warranties lies in the fact that all of these issues can be regarded as concerned with the allocation of the risks of loss or disappointment that can arise in any effort to project arrangements into the future. The entire chapter is, in a sense, concerned with the problems of disappointed expectations. In the earlier sections of the chapter it is possible to argue (though, of course, not always successfully) that one side assumed the risk of loss or disappointment. In the later sections the party who is seeking to avoid the disappointment is reduced to arguing that even though no one expressly assumed the risk of loss or disappointment, it is the other side that should bear it. In this sense the law of mistake — those rules of law that focus explicitly on the mistake as the only basis for relief — is the argument of last resort: it is usually tried only when all else has failed or is likely to fail.

INTERPRETATION

Problems of interpretation are probably the most commonly litigated issue in contracts. There are thousands of cases that could be used to illustrate judicial approaches to the problems of interpretation. Some special rules related to contracts where one party has a stronger bargaining position will be postponed to the next chapter. What is most important in this chapter is to understand the approach of the courts to the problem rather than the detailed rules of interpretation. The cases in this section discuss some of the relevant values that the courts must consider.

The word "contract" refers to a set of related promises. Many contracts are very simple documents (or even oral communications) in which one party transfers title of a good to the other, who pays the price. Others are long and complex documents in which the parties undertake to perform services over a long time or give extensive undertakings about the nature of the thing being bought. The final price paid by one party will be a function not only of the value of the thing being sold or the service being provided but of the extent to which there are collateral undertakings regarding quality and the allocation of the risks inherent in the transaction or relation. The amount that the buyer of a car or a large appliance will pay will depend not just on the price of the item, but on the price of, for example, the extended warranty that the buyer wants. The function of such a warranty is to transfer to the seller the risks (and worries) associated with the ownership of the good. This kind of separate pricing is obvious in, for example, the contract for the rental of a car. The renter will be asked to accept or reject particular clauses (usually having to do with insurance on the car), each of which may have a price attached to it. In other words, the price that a buyer will pay or that a seller will demand will frequently depend on the terms of the transaction as much as on the value of the goods. It is important to remember that the terms of a negotiated contract are often separately priced. The interrelation between price and terms is made clear in the following case extract.

FEDERAL COMMERCE & NAVIGATION CO. v. TRADAX EXPORT SA (THE "MARATHA ENVOY")

[1978] A.C. 1, [1977] 2 All E.R. 849
(H.L., Viscount Dilhorne, Lords Diplock, Simon, Edmund-Davies and Fraser)

[An issue arose as to the interpretation of a standard charterparty. The narrow question was which party was to bear the costs of delay arising from congestion at the port of discharge. In the course of a judgment disposing of this issue, **LORD DIPLOCK** said (at 851-52)]: —

[1]   My Lords, the freight market for chartered vessels still remains a classic example of a free market. It is world-wide in coverage, highly competitive and sensitive to fluctuations in supply and demand. It is a market in which the individual charterers and shipowners are matched in bargaining power and are at liberty to enter into charterparties in whatever contractual terms they please.

[2]   In practice the contracts negotiated in this market by the parties or their brokers are based on one or other of a number of printed forms of charterparties appropriate to the various kinds of use to which vessels are put. These forms incorporate numerous standard clauses to which additions, often in the form of other well-known standard clauses, and deletions are agreed in the course of the bargaining process in which agreement is also reached on such basic terms as rates of freight, demurrage and despatch money.

[3]   So far as the profitability of the transaction to each party is concerned, there is an inter-relationship between rates of freight, demurrage and despatch money and clauses of the charterparty which deal with the allocation between the charterer and shipowner of those risks of delay in the prosecution of the adventure contemplated by the charterparty which, being beyond the control of either party, have been conveniently called "misfortune risks" as distinguished from "fault risks." Among the most prevalent of misfortune risks is congestion at a loading or discharging port causing the vessel to wait idly until a berth falls vacant at which her cargo can be loaded or discharged. If it is to wait at the shipowner's expense he will endeavour to secure that this risk is covered in the freight rate that he charges. If it is to wait at the expense of the charterer and be paid for as demurrage or by reduction in despatch money he will expect this to be reflected in a lower freight rate charged.

[4]   No market such as a freight, insurance, or commodity market, in which dealings involve the parties entering into legal relations of some complexity with one another, can operate efficiently without the use of standard forms of contract and standard clauses to be used in them. Apart from enabling negotiations to be conducted quickly, standard clauses serve two purposes. First, they enable those making use of the market to compare one offer with another to see which is the better; and this . . . involves considering not only the figures for freight, demurrage, and despatch money, but those clauses of the charterparty that deal with the allocation of misfortune risks between charterer and shipowner, particularly those risks which may result in delay. The second purpose served by standard clauses is that they become the subject of exegesis by the courts so that the way in which they will apply to the adventure contemplated by the charterparty will be understood in the same sense by both the parties when they are negotiating its terms and carrying them out.

[5]   It is no part of the function of a court of justice to dictate to charterers and shipowners the terms of the contracts into which they ought to enter on the freight market; but it is an important function of a court, and particularly of your Lordships' House, to provide them with legal certainty at the negotiation stage as to what it is that they are agreeing to. And if there is that certainty, then when occasion arises for a court to enforce the contract or to award damages for its breach, the fact that the members of the court themselves may think that one of the parties was unwise in agreeing to assume a particular misfortune risk or unlucky in its proving more expensive to him than he expected, has nothing to do with the merits of the case or with enabling justice to be done. The only merits of the case are that parties who have bargained on equal terms in a free market should stick to their agreements. Justice is done by seeing that they do so or [by] compensating the party who has kept his promise for any loss he has sustained by the failure of the other party to keep his. [**LORD DIPLOCK** went on to castigate the members of the Court of Appeal for ignoring these factors in their judgments.]

The next case dramatically illustrates how the different views of the members of the Supreme Court of Canada on their proper role in the interpretation of a contract can influence the result.

SCOTT v. WAWANESA MUTUAL INSURANCE CO.

[1989] S.C.J. No. 55, [1989] 1 S.C.R. 1445, 59 D.L.R. (4th) 660
(S.C.C., Dickson C.J.C., La Forest, L'Heureux-Dubé, McIntyre, Lamer, Wilson
and Sopinka JJ.)

The judgment of **L'HEUREUX-DUBÉ, MCINTYRE, LAMER** and **WILSON JJ.** was delivered by **L'HEUREUX-DUBÉ J.**: —

[1]   The Appellants were the holders of a valid and in force insurance policy with the respondent insurance company. On March 29, 1983, Charles Scott, the fifteen-year-old son of appellant Cecil Scott, deliberately set fire to the insured premises. The appellants, who were not in any way implicated in the setting of the fire, filed a Proof of Loss with the respondent company. Their insurance claim was denied.

[2]   The clause of the insurance policy which is at issue in this case reads as follows:

LOSSES EXCLUDED

This policy does not insure:

. . .

(d)   loss or damage caused by a criminal or wilful act or omission of the Insured or of any person whose property is insured hereunder;

The policy defines the "Insured" in the following manner:

The unqualified word "Insured" includes

(1)   The Named Insured

(2)   if residents of his household, his spouse, the relatives of either, and any other person under the age of 21 in the care of an Insured; . . .

[3]   The issue in this case is whether Charles Scott, the son of appellant Cecil Scott, is included within this definition of the "Insured", such that the loss incurred is excluded from compensation by the above cited exception clause. . . .

[4]   In my view, the terms of the insurance policy are perfectly clear and unambiguous. The policy does not cover the type of risk which occasioned this loss. Such risk was specifically excluded. The wording of the exclusion clause for the purposes of the present case is unambiguous, as is the definition of "Insured". I am in complete agreement with the statement of Macdonald J.A., writing for the Court of Appeal [(1986), 6 B.C.L.R. (2d) 56], at p. 62, that:

> In the case at bar the policy does not insure "loss or damage caused by a criminal or wilful act or omission of the Insured or of any person whose property is insured hereunder". Clearly Charles Scott falls within the definition of "Insured" which I quoted earlier. He was a resident of the household and a relative of a named insured. And he was an "other person under the age of 21 in the care of an Insured".

> It is unnecessary to decide whether the indemnification obligation is joint or several. The exclusionary clause is unambiguous. Assuming the position more favourable to the respondents [appellants in the S.C.C.], that it is several, the exclusionary clause bars recovery where the loss is caused by a wilful act of the insured. This clause is therefore fatal to the respondent's [here appellant's] claim. . . .

[5]   In this particular case, the plain meaning of the clause at issue is given additional support by another term of the policy itself:

PERILS INSURED AGAINST

> The Insurance provided by Section I of this Policy is against direct loss or damage caused by the following perils, as defined and limited:

. . .

> 13. VANDALISM OR MALICIOUS ACTS: There is no liability for loss or damage

. . .

> (c)   caused by the Insured's spouse or any member of the same household.

. . .

[6]   Were I convinced that a different interpretation would advance the true intent of the parties, I would gladly subscribe to it. However, when the wording of a contract is unambiguous, as in my view it is in this case, courts should not give it a meaning different from that which is expressed by its clear terms, unless the contract is unreasonable or has an effect contrary to the intention of the parties. In the present case, the policy of insurance excludes liability of the insurer for damage caused by the criminal or wilful acts of the insured. The definition of "insured" clearly includes the minor children living in the home. It may well be that insurance companies do not wish to pay for the delinquency of teenagers within the home. I do not see how they could word their policy to exclude such a risk other than by the precise terms used in this policy.

[7]   Given the facts of the case, the exclusion clause, and the definition of insured contained in the policy, the damages suffered by the appellants in this case are clearly excluded. I cannot think of any words which could more clearly exclude coverage in these circumstances than those used in the policy.

[8]   In the result, I would dismiss the appeal with costs.

[The judgment of **DICKSON C.J.C.**, **LA FOREST** and **SOPINKA JJ.** was delivered by **LA FOREST J.** (dissenting)]: —

The Issue

[9] There can be no gainsaying the insurer's proposition that the Scotts' son was an insured. His property was covered by the policy. That, however, is not the issue. The issue is whether the exclusion from coverage caused by the wrongful act or omission of an insured applies only to the insured responsible for the act or omission or whether it applies not only to that insured but also to an innocent insured. The answer to this question cannot be determined by a simple logical exercise like that outlined by the Court of Appeal. It requires interpretation, a task, as will be seen, not so much dictated by adamantine logic as by reference to divergent public policies underlying the clause. That issue, as we shall see, is related to the issue whether the insurer's indemnification obligation is joint or several. That, too, is a matter of interpretation. As Corbin puts it: "The question whether two or more promisors have promised a single undivided performance, or have each promised a limited and separate performance, is wholly a problem of interpretation"; see *Corbin on Contracts* (1951), vol. 4, § 926, at p. 704.

[10] Strong conflicting lines of authority clearly attest to the fact that the interpretation of the exclusionary clause is far from clear and unambiguous. The Ontario Court of Appeal and Newfoundland trial courts have held that the exclusion applies only to the wrongdoer . . . The British Columbia courts, on the other hand, have now taken the view that the wrongdoing of one insured also excludes recovery of the others . . . A similar division of opinion exists in the United States where the cases are legion, though by far the predominant view nowadays is that only the wrongdoer is excluded. . . .

The Two Approaches

[11] The decisions of the trial judge and the Court of Appeal, then, are representative of two divergent streams of jurisprudence dealing with the problem posed when an innocent insured seeks to recover for a loss occasioned by the wrongful act of a co-insured. The most common scenario in the case reports, and one that decidedly does not serve as an encomium to matrimonial bliss, sees husband or wife burn down the matrimonial home. One of these decisions, the leading case of *Hedtcke v. Sentry Insurance Co.*, 326 N.W.2d 727 (Wis. 1982), provides the most comprehensive and probing summary of the two judicial responses to the problem.

[12] As noted by Abrahamson J. in *Hedtcke*, the approach at one time was to make recovery depend upon whether the interests of the co-insured were joint or several. Where interests were held to be joint, the misconduct of one insured was considered the misconduct of the other, and neither could recover under the policy. As noted, a minority of state courts still follow that approach. This line of authority is premised on several considerations of public policy. Chief among them is the principle that a wrongdoer must not be allowed to profit, be it directly or indirectly, from his act. Abrahamson J. also cited the desire to deter crime and to avoid fraud against insurers. I agree with James A. Rendall's comment that the latter considerations are "not very persuasive"; see an *Annotation* to Wood J.'s judgment in the present case (1984), 8 C.C.L.I. 216.

[13] The modern approach, followed in *Hedtcke*, focuses, first and foremost, on the contract of insurance. The result is made to depend upon whether "the insureds have promised the same performance, or a separate performance as to each, that is, whether each insured has promised that all insured parties will use 'reasonable means' to preserve the property, or whether each has promised that he or she will protect the property" (see *Hedtcke*, at p. 739). This depends on the language of the policy.

[14] This approach, however, takes as its starting point the "fundamental principle of individual responsibility for wrongdoing" (*Hedtcke*, at p. 740). Consequently in the interpretation of the insurance contract the courts have held that, absent unambiguous provisions to the contrary, a reasonable person, unversed in the niceties of insurance law, would expect that his individual interest in the policy was covered by a policy which named him without qualification as one of the persons insured. Thus the reasonable person, though he or she might not choose to express it in these terms, would view the obligations of the insurer as several as to each of the parties involved.

[15] The modern approach does not lose sight of the fundamental rule that a wrongdoer should not profit by his act. It attempts, however, to avoid the harshness that must necessarily follow when the sins of the guilty are visited on the innocent. That harshness is well expressed by Abrahamson J. in the following passage in *Hedtcke*, at p. 740:

> Contrary to our basic notions of fair play and justice, the [rule denying coverage] punishes the innocent victim. An absolute bar to recovery by an innocent insured is particularly harsh in a case in which the arson appears to be retribution against the innocent insured. Having lost the property, the innocent insured is victimized once again by the denial of the proceeds forthcoming under the fire insurance policy.

[16] Accordingly, the focus is on tailoring "the recovery permitted the innocent insured to guard against the possibility that the arsonist might receive financial benefit as a result of the arson" (*Hedtcke*, at p. 740). The modern approach, as noted earlier, is today accepted in the vast majority of decisions on the point.

The Modern Approach

[17] I am firmly of the view that the modern approach's primary focus on the meaning of the insurance contract is to be preferred to the old approach which is principally undergirded by public policy considerations extraneous to the contract. The modern approach seems to me to be entirely consonant with this Court's approach to the interpretation of insurance contracts. The guidelines for the interpretation of insurance contracts set out by this Court in *Consolidated-Bathurst Export Ltd. v. Mutual Boiler and Machinery Insurance Co.*, [1980] 1 S.C.R. 888, provide an appropriate starting point for this analysis. In that case, Estey J. had this to say at p. 901:

> Even apart from the doctrine of *contra proferentem* as it may be applied in the construction of contracts, *the normal rules of construction lead a court to search for an interpretation which, from the whole of the contract, would appear to promote or advance the true intent of the parties at the time of entry into the contract.* Consequently, literal meaning should not be applied where to do so would bring about an unrealistic result or a result which would not be contemplated in the commercial atmosphere in which the insurance was contracted. Where words may bear two constructions, the more reasonable one, that which produces a fair result, must certainly

be taken as the interpretation which would promote the intention of the parties. Similarly, an interpretation which defeats the intentions of the parties and their objective in entering into the commercial transaction in the first place should be discarded in favour of an interpretation of the policy which promotes a sensible commercial result.

(Emphasis added.)

[18] Though Estey J. was speaking in the context of a commercial contract of insurance, the same reasoning would apply here. In other words, in construing an insurance policy, the courts must be guided by the reasonable expectation and purpose of an ordinary person in entering such contract, and the language employed in the policy is to be given its ordinary meaning, such as the average policy holder of ordinary intelligence, as well as the insurer, would attach to it. . . .

[19] Bearing the above principles in mind, I shall now attempt to assess whether the indemnification obligation in the policy here is joint or several. In my view, the latter is the case. As I see it, reasonable persons, unversed in the niceties of insurance law, would, in purchasing fire insurance, expect that a policy naming them as an insured without qualification would insure them to the extent of their interest. Moreover, reasonable persons would expect that they would lose the right to recover for their own wilful destruction. But the same persons would find it an anomalous result if informed that they stood to lose all if their spouse burned down their house. The following responses would be forthcoming: "I had nothing to do with that act of arson so why am I being punished for it? My 50 per cent interest in the house belongs to me. I could have taken out my own insurance policy on my interest; in that case if my spouse burnt down the house I was protected. Why should my getting paid depend on whether there is one policy or two? If it had been made clear to me, why would I have ever agreed to take out a joint policy? I only stood to lose."

[20] If this logic is sound, it has definite application to the facts of this case. The Scotts did not take out fire insurance to insure their son's possessions: they insured to protect their house. It is both unrealistic and unreasonable to assume that the named insured would view the indemnification obligation of the insurer as joint because their son's possessions were included. These were only marginal to the transaction.

[21] It is true, as the respondent insurer contends, that the appellants by the terms of the policy had exclusive control over who was to be co-insured. As it puts it in its factum:

> They had the right, without seeking the Respondent's permission or paying an additional premium, to admit others into their insurance, thereby providing them with a right against the Respondent for indemnity against third party liability, personal property damage and additional living expense claims. It is not unreasonable to require that, having opted to exercise this right to create co-insureds, they must take the burden of their co-insured's acts.

[22] While this, I suppose, may be technically correct, it does not take into account the realities of the situation. The clause is a standard one in a homeowner's policy. It is scarcely believable that an ordinary insured would ever consider the possibility to which the respondent alludes. Besides, the respondent misses a vital point. If it were made clear to an insured in the position of the appellants that the insurer would admit whom the insured asked, but on the implied condition that the

indemnification obligation assumed was joint and not several, no one would choose to exercise the option. It would be absurd to do so in the case under appeal; it would amount to saying: "I will insure my son's possessions. The 'X' dollars I will recover for them if the house burns down by accident more than makes up for the fact that if he burns my house down I will recover nothing at all."

[23] A more realistic interpretation of the indemnification obligation is that where the definition of "Insured" is defined so as to extend to others than the named insured, that definition should not be construed so as to restrict or limit the coverage enjoyed by the named insured. If the policy in this case is interpreted in this manner, it would reflect the result contemplated in the commercial atmosphere in which the insurance was contracted. This issue was discussed in *Morgan v. Greater New York Taxpayers Mutual Ins. Ass'n.* [112 N.E.2d 273 (N.Y.C.A. 1953)], dealing with the cognate situation involving an owner's public liability policy which contained an exclusion clause similar to the one in question here. The following observations of Conway J., at p. 275, are apposite:

> But that argument, based upon the "Definitions" section, cannot withstand analysis. Defendant, we think, seeks to turn to its own advantage a provision of the policy intended to benefit, not to prejudice, the named assured. The "Definitions" section, by assigning a broad meaning to the term "Assured", extends coverage to various persons in addition to the named assured. That section which might be termed an "additional assured" provision serves as an inducement to purchase insurance to one contemplating taking out a liability policy, by affording coverage, without added premium, to others in addition to the applicant. To hold that such a provision, purporting as it does to broaden coverage by extending it to additional assureds, works a reduction in the coverage which would be afforded to the named assured in the absence of such provision is not in harmony with the true, beneficial purpose of the provision . . .

[24] Clearly, an insurer might choose to contract on the basis that it considered its indemnification obligation joint with regard to both the named insured and other insured. But in offering to contract on such terms, it would be incumbent on an insurer to manifest this intention in the very clearest of language. This is because a person entering such a contract would be agreeing to assume vicarious liability for the criminal conduct of another. This, it is fair to say, is fundamentally at odds with the expectation of the reasonable person when buying fire insurance. He or she insures on the assumption that his or her undivided interest is protected. That is the whole point of taking out insurance. . . .

[25] To summarize on this point, while it is true that the exemption clause as worded can be made to bear the interpretation urged by the respondent, the language is far from clear; in a word, it is ambiguous. In the face of this ambiguity, the Ontario Court of Appeal in *Rankin v. North Waterloo Farmers Mutual Insurance Co.* [(1979), 25 O.R. (2d) 102, 100 D.L.R. (3d) 564], applied the *contra proferentem* doctrine and construed the language in a manner favourable to the insured. In my opinion, they were correct to do so. Policies of insurance are prepared by the insurers and in doing so they not unnaturally are minded to protect their own interests. To avoid the consequent injustices that may ensue to an insured, courts have long insisted that any ambiguity be resolved in favour of the insured. And where, as is the case here, the ambiguity bears on a clause that stands significantly to defeat the objective of the purchaser in buying insurance, the case for application of the doctrine is compelling. A clause intended to achieve the purpose argued

for by the insurer would, in my view, have to be drawn so as to bring it clearly to the attention of the insured . . .

NOTES AND QUESTIONS

1. The quotation from the judgment of Estey J. in *Consolidated-Bathurst Export Ltd. v. Mutual Boiler and Machinery Insurance Co.*, *supra*, ¶ 17, emphasizes the "true intent of the parties", while La Forest J. in his comments on this quotation says: "the courts must be guided by the reasonable expectation and purpose of an ordinary person in entering such contract". There is an important issue hidden in this shift. Leaving aside the problem of what a *true* intent might be, any concept of "intent" (or intention) is elusive. Parties enter into exchange relations because they have *differing* goals, expectations and even hopes. A seller agrees to sell goods to a buyer because it wants the buyer's money more than it wants its own goods; a buyer buys because it wants the seller's goods more than its money. To this extent, buyers and sellers intend to achieve different things though, because of this, they may jointly intend an exchange. It would be hard to imagine what evidence either might lead on what its intentions were. A focus on the parties' expectations is a focus on what is real and on which the parties can lead readily imaginable evidence. A focus on expectations permits a consideration of the extent to which one interpretation rather than another might defeat those expectations.

2. The differing approaches of L'Heureux-Dubé J., La Forest J. and Lord Diplock vividly illustrate the issues of interpretation. The problem facing the Supreme Court of Canada in *Scott* was caused by the fact that the Mr. and Mrs. Scott had never thought about the consequences of their son's committing arson, though if they had, La Forest J.'s interpretation of their expectations is almost certainly correct. Lord Diplock had a far easier task in *Federal Commerce*. The parties to the contract he had to deal with were both intimately familiar with its terms and the background expectations of the industry. They were also "institutional litigants"; they had a stake in more than the particular litigation. Such a litigant would like to win the case (though the costs of taking it to the House of Lords might well exceed any possible recovery), but the important point for such litigants is to have the meaning of the clause settled for the future when both parties would have the chance to bargain over the allocation of the risk in future contracts.

3. Before the judgment of the Supreme Court in *Scott v. Wawanesa*, the insurer could not, in light of the cases and what it *as a matter of fact* knew about the law, reasonably have expected that, in the circumstances, the interpretation of the contract which it argued for was probable, let alone inevitable. While the insureds had no clear expectation regarding what might happen were their son to burn down their home, they almost certainly did not expect that, if that happened, they would have no insurance. A focus on the parties' expectations makes these facts relevant.

   The result of the judgment of the Supreme Court of Canada is that insurers now know the position that they can take in similar circumstances. Insured individuals, however, are rarely likely to consider in detail the risks they run. (Again, you might consider how this lopsidedness in the information available to each party might be overcome.) The judgment of the Ontario Court of Appeal in *Rankin v. North Waterloo Farmers Mutual Insurance Co.* (1979), 25 O.R. (2d) 102, 100 D.L.R. (3d) 564, and that of the dissent in *Scott v. Wawanesa* would, at least, have made insurers consider the need to re-draft their policies and, perhaps, to make their insureds aware of the risks that they would be exposed to.

4. *Scott* is a case in which one party is an institutional litigant that drafted the contract; that party will have other chances to "get it right", *i.e.*, to draft the contract so that future insureds will understand that they have to bear the risk of another person's wrongdoing. The approach to interpretation of the minority encourages a kind of "dialogue" between the court and solicitors who draft their clients' contracts: the approach

of the majority makes such a dialogue quite unnecessary for the insurer now has no need to worry about informing its insureds of the risks that they run.

It is possible to see in many agreements, for example, bank guarantees, traces of the decisions that interpreted earlier versions of the agreement. Like a designer building a better machine as earlier versions were shown to fail or to be inadequate to their task, a solicitor will read judicial decisions to see how his or her client's agreements can be perfected.

5. The three judgments illustrate the importance of judges' attitudes. Each judgment illustrates the central fact that each judge had a choice to make in his or her judgment — it is the tragedy of L'Heureux-Dubé J.'s judgment that she denies that she had and was making a choice. The practical problem facing any lawyer at any stage of a contract, at its drafting, on its breakdown or in litigation, is to foresee what a judge is likely to *want* to do with the contract. It is the existence of this choice that makes the jurisprudential and philosophical issues touched on by Llewellyn, Corbin, Macneil and Renner in various extracts in this book so important.

    The important question is whether the judge offers a justification for what he or she does that would permit counsel to debate usefully the correct attitude to be taken to the problems raised by the cases.

6. The case of *Toronto-Dominion Bank v. Leigh Instruments Ltd. (Trustee of) [No. 3]* (1999), 45 O.R. (3d) 417, 178 D.L.R. (4th) 634 (C.A.), excerpted in Chapter 2, in the discussion of the topic of "Intention to Create Legal Relations", illustrates that the nature of the parties' relation in that case was as much an issue of interpretation as was the meaning of the words that they used. The court concluded that the parent corporation had not given a guarantee for the debt of its subsidiary to the bank, but only a letter of comfort, and that there was no intention to create a legally enforceable guarantee. It is assumed by solicitors that a letter of comfort is not a guarantee, and that a lender who wants a guarantee will not be content with a letter of comfort and will, moreover, know exactly what obligations the guarantor must undertake to satisfy it. Standard bank guarantees are very explicit documents and they clearly and explicitly spell out the extensive obligations of the guarantor.

7. As discussed in Chapter 2, leaving aside the question of arson, the son in *Scott* would have been a third-party beneficiary of his parent's policy and, as such, would have had no enforceable claim against the insurer — *Vandepitte v. Preferred Accident* was not overruled by *London Drugs* — had it chosen to dispute any claim made by him. Given this fact, does one have to accept the argument that the son was, in fact, an "insured" under the policy? The assumption in *Scott v. Wawanesa* that the son was an insured was used by Esson J.A. in the British Columbia Court of Appeal in *Fraser River Pile & Dredge Ltd. v. Can-Dive Services Ltd.* (1997), 39 B.C.L.R. (3d) 187, [1998] 3 W.W.R. 177 (¶45) (affirmed [1999] 3 S.C.R. 108, 176 D.L.R. (4th) 257), to bolster his argument that *Vandepitte* was now a "dead letter" and did not have to be followed. In fact, the same insurance company in *Fenrich v. Wawanesa Mutual Insurance Co.* [2005] A.J. No. 788, 256 D.L.R. (4th) 395 (C.A.) successfully argued that it owed no contractual obligations to the insureds' son, who wanted to challenge the amount that he had received from the insurance company under the policy in respect of a loss to property owned by him.

The Parol Evidence Rule

Beyond the relatively narrow range of situations that are required to be in writing because of the *Statute of Frauds*, an oral contract is as valid and enforceable as any written one. It is, however, a very common practice to have a written, signed document, particularly for any significant transaction. Given the complexity and number of terms in most contracts, it is unlikely that parties could accurately remember all of the terms without a written document. In the large organizations that typically make such contracts, a written record is also important to give guidance to those in the organization who must conduct themselves in accordance with the contract.

Despite the pervasive use of written contracts, one of the most difficult problems of interpretation is to determine exactly where the agreement between the parties is to be found. At first sight, this may seem to be an easy issue to resolve: the agreement is found in the written document that the parties will usually have signed. It is possible that such a simple answer can sometimes be given, but as a practical matter, this simple response will be possible only in a minority of contracts. The reason for this statement and for the existence of the problem referred to is the fact that the parties rarely make it absolutely clear (or even intend, let alone conduct themselves to make it always apparent) that the written contract is to be the *only* source of the terms of their agreement. In other words, the agreement will often be "infected", obscured or perhaps illuminated by the often murky background facts out of which it arose, and the actions of the parties before, during and even after the negotiation of the contract.

An agreement arises out of a process of negotiation that will very often determine the expectations of one or both parties as to the details of the deal. The problem for the courts is to determine whether this background is part of the final terms of the deal, or is just something that has been replaced by the (more) formal written contract that represents the final expression of the agreement. Courts have had great difficulty in making these kinds of decisions.

An analogous problem arose in Chapter 3. The traditional legal approach to contract formation regards the parties' relation as arising suddenly and perfectly formed on the acceptance of the offer, while up to that point the parties are no more than total strangers. This approach, however, cannot be sustained when there is a need to protect the reliance or even the expectations resulting from the negotiations. Courts, as in *Brewer Street Investments v. Barclays Woollen* and *Brewer v. Chrysler*, find ways to hold that legally protected relations existed before the final moment of the creation of the contract.

A large part of the difficulty the courts face arises from the legal rules that give priority to a written agreement. These rules often cannot be applied in practice. At the same time, the context of the modern contract, the negotiation and administration of the contract by employees of corporations, not the corporation itself, is frequently ignored, and the rules are projected onto facts that differ significantly from those the traditional rules "expect".

A rule that causes great difficulty is known as the "parol evidence rule". The word "parol" historically derives from the old "Law French" word for "spoken", but now refers to any source of the terms of the contract that is not part of the written contract, and includes both oral statements and written documents. (There are cases in which the rule is called the "parole" evidence rule. This spelling is incorrect. The word "parole" refers to the promise, originally made by a prisoner of war on his release not to fight again, or, in its modern use, to the "promise" of the released prisoner, released on "parole", to be of good conduct.)

In practice, the principal difficulties of the parol evidence rule arise with oral evidence that is alleged to qualify or affect a written agreement. The rule is sometimes stated in the following form: "The fundamental rule is that if the language of the written contract is clear and unambiguous, then no extrinsic parol evidence may be admitted to alter, vary, or interpret in any way the words used in the writing." (G.H.L. Fridman, *The Law of Contract in Canada*, 4th ed. (Toronto: Carswell, 1999), p. 480.)

The importance of this articulation of the parol evidence rule is that it makes *inadmissible* the evidence that would "alter, vary or interpret" the written contract. As the rule is conventionally stated, it has a superficial appearance to a rule of evidence. Rules about the inadmissibility of evidence are part of the laws of evidence and are justified on the ground either that the proposed evidence is irrelevant, or that some other value, for example, the risk of severe prejudice to a party, outweighs the relevance of the evidence. If evidence is "inadmissible" it should not even be considered by the trier of fact. In a jury trial, the issue of the admissibility of evidence is generally considered in the absence of the jury, so that the jury will not even hear inadmissible evidence. In civil cases, issues of the admissibility of evidence are generally decided on the ground that the evidence is admissible if relevant to an issue in the litigation, and inadmissible if it is not.

The parol evidence rule is not, as the cases below make clear, an evidentiary rule of the ordinary kind that actually makes the evidence inadmissible. Contracts cases are almost always tried by a judge sitting without a jury, and the parol evidence rule is almost never applied so that evidence submitted by a party is actually excluded: the evidence will be heard and the dispute will be over its legal effect. (In any case, questions of the interpretation of a contract are not questions for a jury.) If the judge considers that the evidence is caught by the parol evidence rule, the judge may say that the evidence is "inadmissible", but what is really being said is that the parol evidence was considered by the court, but was ultimately not accepted as determinative.

The parol evidence rule is sometimes stated in ways that are potentially seriously misleading. For example, in *Eli Lilly & Co. v. Novopharm Ltd.; Eli Lilly & Co. v. Apotex Inc.*, [1998] 2 S.C.R. 129, 161 D.L.R. (4th) 1, ¶55, Iacobucci J. said that because of the parol evidence rule it is "unnecessary to consider any extrinsic evidence at all when the document is clear and unambiguous on its face".

In support of this strict articulation of the parol evidence rule, Iacobucci J. quoted from the judgment of Lord Atkinson in *Lampson v. City of Quebec* (1920), 54 D.L.R. 344 (P.C.), who said (p. 350):

> . . . the intention by which the deed is to be construed is that of the parties as revealed by the language they have chosen to use in the deed itself . . . [I]f the meaning of the deed, reading its words in their ordinary sense, be plain and unambiguous it is not permissible for the parties to it . . . to come into a Court of Justice and say: "Our intention was wholly different from that which the language of our deed expresses."

Lord Atkinson, by using the phrase "*our* intention" appears to say that an agreement may be interpreted in a way that ignores what *both* parties intended. If this is what he meant, he has entered an Alice-in-Wonderland world where contracts are not regarded as agreements of parties that have a rational purpose and context, but rather are documents whose significance is determined by whatever the courts say they mean, regardless of the intention, expectations or understandings of the parties.

In *Eli Lilly* Iacobucci J. goes on to say (¶56):

> [a]dmittedly, it would be absurd to adopt an interpretation which is clearly inconsistent with the commercial interests of the parties, if the goal is to ascertain their true contractual intent. However, to interpret a plainly worded document in accordance with the true contractual intent of the parties is not difficult, if it is presumed that the parties intended the legal consequences of their words.

These sentences indicate that the Supreme Court of Canada would probably not do what Lord Atkinson's statement suggests that he would.

The definition section of an agreement may give common expressions used in the document a quite surprising meaning that is very different from the ordinary usuage of the terms, and no one would could argue that the defined terms should have any other meaning than the one given to them by the parties. Each party is equally free to allege that they had such a provision in a separate document or as part of a shared oral or even tacit understanding of the meanings of the terms used in the agreement. If parties use a word in a wholly idiosyncratic and eccentric way in their agreement, that is their business and a court has no basis for giving the agreement any effect other than that which the parties intended, even though one of them may later decide that it would prefer to give the word its ordinary meaning or to escape the agreement altogether: after all, the parties have to be disagreeing about something to have resorted to litigation.

In *Smith v. Wilson* (1832), 3 B. & Ad. 728, 110 E.R. 266 (K.B.), the court stated that written "instruments [are] to be expounded according to the custom" of the merchants or parties who make them. The court held that, in a dispute over a written lease that included a term for the sale of rabbits, oral evidence was admissible to prove that "the word thousand meant more than its ordinary sense." The court accepted that "the ordinary meaning of the word 'thousand,' as applied to rabbits, in the place where the agreement was made, was one hundred dozen." Accordingly, the court held that the written agreement for the sale of "10,000 rabbits" was actually enforceable as a contract for the sale of 12,000 rabbits. One would usually expect the figure "1,000" to be "clear and unambiguous on its face", yet the case is evidence that a court can be satisfied that it did not have that meaning to the parties.

It has to be accepted that no word (or anything else) can be interpreted by the court without allowing the parties to show that it meant something special to them, and statements that "unambiguous terms" are to be given their natural meaning cannot be taken to mean what those statements might unambiguously seem to suggest. Lord Hoffmann in *Investors Compensation Scheme Ltd. v. West Bromwich Building Society*, [1998] 1 All E.R. 98, p. 114, [1998] 1 W.L.R. 896, pp. 912-13, said that the background to a contract (apart from evidence of the negotiations and of the parties' subjective intent) "includes absolutely anything which would have affected the way in which the language of the document would have been understood by a reasonable man".

Three questions have to be considered when any contract comes for enforcement before a court: (1) Have the parties made a contract? (2) Did the parties assent to a particular writing as the complete and accurate expression of their agreement? and (3) Is the contract affected by any mistake, fraud or illegality? The first of these questions was the focus of Chapter 3; the second and third are the focus of this chapter.

Each of these questions can only be determined by the court's hearing evidence: evidence of what the parties expected, of the course of negotiations and of the place of the agreement in the parties' relation. Such evidence was, for example, heard by the trial judge in *Toronto-Dominion Bank v. Leigh Instruments Ltd. (Trustee of) [No. 3]* (1999), 45 O.R. (3d) 417, 178 D.L.R. (4th) 634, *supra*, Chapter 2, when the background to the letter of comfort given by the debtor's parent was examined.

In other words, it is difficult to regard relevant evidence as *inadmissible* for the purpose of determining these three questions: no agreement, even though it is written and comes complete with seals and recitals of all kinds, can possibly prove that all these issues have been determined in favour of the validity of the agreement and that the writing is the final expression of the parties' agreement simply by existing — particularly if one party proposes to lead evidence to the contrary! There has to be *some* evidence to prove these points, though the court may draw inferences from some proved facts to establish others.

The most appropriate understanding of the parol evidence rule is the simple and nearly obvious proposition that once the court determines that a written document is the final and complete expression of the parties' agreement, then, and only then, can it be said that evidence of what the parties may have said during the negotiations or in other writings must be irrelevant. Even then, this extrinsic evidence is only irrelevant as regards past understandings or events. The parties are *always* free to make a new agreement, and to replace an earlier writing by another later writing or by an oral understanding. Evidence that they have or have not replaced the earlier writing must also be admissible.

This understanding of the parol evidence rule may acknowledge a presumption in favour of the written document, but it allows the parties to adduce evidence to show the document does not embody all the terms of their agreement, or to help understand the meaning that the parties may have given to words used in the document. Nevertheless, the courts sometimes apply the parol evidence rule in the same way as the quotation from Fridman, *supra*, would suggest that they should. An example of a court taking a strict approach to the parol evidence rule is supplied by the following case.

BAUER v. BANK OF MONTREAL

[1980] S.C.J. No. 46, [1980] 2 S.C.R. 102, 110 D.L.R. (3d) 424
(S.C.C., Ritchie, Dickson, Estey, McIntyre and Chouinard JJ.)

MCINTYRE J.: — [1] This appeal raises the question of the effect upon the liability of a guarantor to the creditor when the creditor, by reason of its dealing with security for the debt, has rendered it impossible to deliver the security to the guarantor upon the guarantor paying the debt.

[**MCINTYRE J.** set out the facts: Bauer, the defendant, appellant, was, in March 1971, the principal officer and major shareholder of a company known as Grey Electronics Supply Limited. This company was a customer of the respondent bank. The bank lent money to the company, taking as security an assignment of the company's book accounts (accounts receivable) and a guarantee from the defendant. This guarantee was on the bank's standard form. The defendant sold his business but the bank would not release him from his guarantee. The company subsequently failed and the defendant was sued on the guarantee. At that time it was discovered that the bank had, through it own fault, failed to properly register its security interest in the company's book debts. As a result, the bank lost its security in the book debts and became an ordinary unsecured creditor of the company. Thus, the amount demanded of the defendant was far larger than it would otherwise have been. **MCINTYRE J.** continued:]

[2]   At trial before Galligan J. the bank's action was dismissed [(1977), 15 O.R. (2d) 746, 76 D.L.R. (3d) 636]. The trial judge held that a creditor was under an obligation to "safeguard securities given to him in the same condition as when the guarantee was given and if registration is necessary to make the security valid and effective, then the creditor must properly register the securities." He went on to hold that where a creditor fails to preserve the security, and it therefore became unavailable for delivery to the guarantor upon payment of the debt, the guarantor would be relieved wholly or partially from his liability depending on the extent of the injury suffered. He held as well that since the bank had not met the onus of showing to what extent the guarantor was prejudiced by the loss of the accounts, the guarantor was entitled to be fully discharged. On appeal by the bank, the Court of Appeal [(1978), 19 O.R. (2d) 425, 85 D.L.R. (3d) 752], per Arnup J.A., agreed with the trial judge upon his disposition of the case as it was presented to him, but allowed the appeal on a new point not raised or argued at trial.

[3]   As has been stated earlier, the guarantee was on the bank's standard form which is used regularly for this purpose. It provided for a continuing guarantee by the guarantor of all indebtedness of the company to the bank from time to time owing up to $50,000 and provided as well:

> It is further agreed that said bank, without exonerating in whole or in part the under-signed, or any of them (if more than one), may grant time, renewals, extensions, in-dulgences, releases and discharges to, may take securities from and give the same and any or all existing securities up to, may abstain from taking securities from, or from perfecting securities of . . . the customer.

[4]   The inclusion of this provision in the guarantee raised the only point considered of significance in the Court of Appeal, and Arnup J.A. for the court dealt with it in these words:

> In the circumstances of this case, the words "perfecting securities" in the guarantee included registration of the assignment of book debts in the right place. The guarantee contains in express terms an agreement by the signatory with the bank that the bank may abstain from perfecting securities without exonerating in whole or in part the guarantor. In our view, this language precisely covers the situation that arose, and accordingly it was not open to the defendant to assert, by way of defence, the alleged negligent dealing with the securities by the bank.

[5]   The duty of a creditor holding security for the performance of the obligations of a debtor or a surety is clearly established. The creditor, in the absence of agreement to the contrary with the debtor or the surety, must protect and preserve the security and be in a position, unless excused by other agreement, to return to reassign the security to the debtor or surety on repayment of the debt. . . .

[6]   In this court, the appellant argued several points. In summary, his argument embraced four principal propositions. He contended in the first place that the clause in the guarantee relied upon by the Court of Appeal was an exemption or exclusion clause, and as such it should be construed *contra proferentem*, that is, against the bank whose standard printed form embodied the guarantee. He then contended that the bank could not rely on the clause because it was unusual, onerous, and unreasonable. Further, it was said that the execution of the guarantee was procured by a misrepresentation of its nature and effect by the bank and it should be set aside. Finally, it was argued that it had been specifically agreed in a collateral agreement that the assigned accounts would be preserved for reassignment to the guarantor upon payment of the debt. . . .

[**MCINTYRE J.** rejected the appellant's arguments on the first two propositions.]

[7]   The third argument involves the assertion that the execution of the guarantee was procured by misrepresentation of its full nature and effect by the bank or, alternatively, that there was a failure to explain its nature and effect. The misrepresentation alleged is that the bank manager told the guarantor that upon his paying the amount secured under the guarantee, the book debts would be reassigned to him. This representation was false for the reason that it contradicted the bank's own document. It was contended that the guarantee would not have been executed in its absence. Various authorities were cited for the proposition that a contract induced by misrepresentation or by an oral representation, inconsistent with the form of the written contract, would not stand and could not bind the party to whom the representation had been made. . . .

[8]   No quarrel can be made with the general proposition advanced on this point by the appellant. To succeed, however, this argument must rest upon a finding of some misrepresentation by the bank, innocent or not, or on some oral representation inconsistent with the written document which caused a misimpression in the guarantor's mind, or upon some omission on the part of the bank manager to explain the contents of the document which induced the guarantor to enter into the guarantee upon a misunderstanding as to its nature. For reasons which will appear later in that part of this judgment dealing with the collateral contract argument, I am of the view that there is no evidence which would support any such finding against the bank. The cases referred to above support the general proposition advanced but rest upon a factual basis providing support for the argument. In each case there is a clear finding of a specific misrepresentation which led to the formation of the contract in question, a circumstance not to be found here. This argument must fail as well.

[9]   Finally, it was the contention of the guarantor that the bank could not rely on the above-quoted provision in the facts of this case because it was an express condition of the giving of the guarantee that the accounts be preserved for the benefit of the guarantor and reassigned to him on payment of the company's indebtedness. The bank was, therefore, in breach of its undertaking in this regard and was not entitled to take advantage of the provision. The argument had not been raised at trial presumably because no reliance had been placed upon the relieving provision above-quoted.

[10]   I have examined the evidence with care and find it difficult to discover any very clear support for the existence of any such collateral or qualifying agreement. However, Galligan J. considered there was such an agreement, for he said:

> Not only is it the law that a surety upon payment of the debt is entitled to the benefit of the security held by the creditor . . . in this case I am satisfied that it was understood between the plaintiff's branch manager and the defendant that if the defendant paid the indebtedness of Grey Electronic to the plaintiff, the plaintiff would deliver to him the book debts of Grey Electronic, the assignment of which was held by it.

[11]   To make such a finding, he would necessarily have had to rely on evidence. The only evidence I can find in the record of such an arrangement is a statement by the bank manager that the bank would have reassigned the accounts on payment by the guarantor as normal practice, and the assertion by the guarantor that he had been told by the bank manager that if he made good on his guarantee the accounts would be reassigned to him. He said as well that he would not have given his guarantee otherwise. There was then some evidence for the finding of the trial judge, and its sufficiency is not for this court to judge. However, it seems clear to me that this evidence would go towards imposing a limit on the bank's rights with respect to the security given by the debtor. This would clearly contradict the terms of the guarantee which, as has been pointed out, gave the bank the right to abstain from registration and perfection of security. On this basis, it would be inadmissible under the parol evidence rule and any collateral agreement founded upon it could not stand. I can see no distinction between the case at bar and that of *Hawrish v. Bank of Montreal*, [1969] S.C.R. 515, 520, 2 D.L.R. (3d) 600, 605-6, where in almost identical circumstances, Judson J., speaking for this court, said:

> Bearing in mind these remarks to the effect that there must be a clear intention to create a binding agreement, I am not convinced that the evidence in this case indicates clearly the existence of such intention. Indeed, I am disposed to agree with what the Court of Appeal said on this point. However, this is not in issue in this appeal. My opinion is that the appellant's argument fails on the ground that the collateral agreement allowing for the discharge of the appellant cannot stand as it clearly contradicts the terms of the guarantee bond which state that it is a continuing guarantee.

[12] . . . Any such collateral oral agreement as contended for by the appellant therefore may not stand in the face of the written guarantee. It follows that an additional argument raised by the guarantor relating to a claim that the collateral contract had been fundamentally breached will not require to be dealt with. I would dismiss the appeal. In all circumstances of this case, I would not award costs to the respondent in any of the courts.

QUESTIONS AND NOTES

1. Does McIntyre J. say that he does not believe that there was such a promise as the guarantor claimed, or that evidence of such a promise, assuming that there was credible evidence of it, would be inadmissible? Would the same result have been reached if, at the trial, clear and credible evidence had been led in support of the statements alleged by the defendant to have been made by the bank?

    If the Supreme Court accepts that the statement was made by the bank manager but chooses to give it no legal effect, the Court would be saying: "We accept the guarantor's evidence that the bank made the representation on which he relied, but even so, the fact that the representation is not noted or referred to on the bank's standard form of guarantee means that we will ignore it." Such a decision is hard to defend. It requires a finding that the parties, particularly the guarantor, understood that, in signing the guarantee, the guarantor was content to ignore what has been found to be the basis on which he signed the guarantee. It is not impossible for the parties to make such an agreement; many documents are drafted that state that the parties admit they are not relying on anything that may have been said during the course of the negotiations and, in the ordinary course, such a clause may well be effective.

    At the very least, when there is a finding that the employee of the creditor made the representation on which the guarantor has, as a matter of fact, relied, fairness would require some evidence that the guarantor understood that, in spite of what was said, the representation was not to be relied on. This argument explains why trial courts are frequently moved to find ways to avoid the application of the strict form of the parol evidence rule articulated by the Supreme Court in *Bauer*.

2. The bank in both *Hawrish v. Bank of Montreal*, [1969] S.C.R. 515, 2 D.L.R. (3d) 600 and *Bauer* was able to enforce the guarantee even though the bank's employees had

done things that might have given a court with a different motivation a basis for giving relief to the guarantor. From the point of view of a well-run bank, the cases illustrate clear risks that the bank would prefer to avoid.

Draft a letter to be sent from the bank's head office to all managers and loan officers explaining how they should conduct themselves in negotiations with customers over guarantees. Remember that managers and loan officers are frequently transferred from one branch to another, so that a relation between a manager and a customer may be temporary.

Bank employees may have incentives (built into their jobs by the loan and collection policies of the bank) to encourage customers to take out loans (banks do advertise, after all; where do their profits come from?) and then to collect on the loans. These two pressures may explain the conduct of the bank in these cases. Should the courts put the risk of the bank's failure to control its employees onto its customers?

3. As a matter of practice, the biggest threat to the careful planning of solicitors for their clients is the careless use of words by the parties and their employees. The best-devised scheme for allocating losses may be completely undermined by assurances given by an employee. This problem will be examined in the next chapter.

4. What values are at stake in a case like *Bauer*? Is it relevant that the contract is a standard bank guarantee? What do you think is more important, the protection of the expectations created by the document or the relation of mutual trust built up by the bank and the customer over the years? Do you think that the bank, as an institution, had any reasonable expectations of the enforceability of the guarantee? What is the "bank" for the purposes of determining its expectations? Whom would you call as a witness to testify to the bank's expectations?

5. As you read the cases involving the parol evidence rule, you may notice that it is invariably banks and other large commercial entities that seek to invoke a broad formulation of this rule to the disadvantage of economically weaker individuals. Should this affect how the courts apply the rule?

The following decision gives a response to the problems of the parol evidence rule that differs from *Bauer*.

GALLEN v. ALLSTATE GRAIN CO.

[1984] B.C.J. No. 1621, 9 D.L.R. (4th) 496, 53 B.C.L.R. 38
(C.A., Seaton, Lambert and Anderson JJ.A.)

[The plaintiffs were farmers. The defendant was a grain dealer. The defendant agreed to sell buckwheat seed to the plaintiffs and to buy the crop when it was harvested. The defendant's manager, Nunweiler, orally assured the plaintiffs that there would be no problem with weeds. The buckwheat would "grow up and cover the field like an umbrella" and any weeds would be smothered. The plaintiffs signed a written contract that included a clause that stated:

> 23. Allstate gives no warranty as to the productiveness or any other matter pertaining to the seed sold to the producer and will not in any way be responsible for the crop.

The plaintiffs planted the seed. The crop was a total failure — it was choked by weeds. The plaintiffs sued for the profit they would have made had they planted their usual crop. The trial judge, Paris J., gave judgment for the plaintiffs. The defendant appealed.]

LAMBERT J.A.: — [1] The parol evidence rule is not only a rule about the admissibility of evidence. It reaches into questions of substantive law. But it is a rule of evidence, as well as a body of principles of substantive law, and if the evidence of the oral representation in this case was improperly admitted, the appeal should be allowed.

[2]   The rule of evidence may be stated in this way: Subject to certain exceptions, when the parties to an agreement have apparently set down all its terms in a document, extrinsic evidence is not admissible to add to, subtract from, vary or contradict those terms.

[3]   So the rule does not extend to cases where the document may not embody all the terms of the agreement. And even in cases where the document seems to embody all the terms of the agreement, there is a myriad of exceptions to the rule. I will set out some of them. Evidence of an oral statement is relevant and may be admitted, even where its effect may be to add to, subtract from, vary or contradict the document:

(a) to show that the contract was invalid because of fraud, misrepresentation, mistake, incapacity, lack of consideration, or lack of contracting intention;

(b) to dispel ambiguities, to establish a term implied by custom, or to demonstrate the factual matrix of the agreement;

(c) in support of a claim for rectification;

(d) to establish a condition precedent to the agreement;

(e) to establish a collateral agreement;

(f) in support of an allegation that the document itself was not intended by the parties to constitute the whole agreement;

(g) in support of a claim for an equitable remedy, such as specific performance or rescission, on any ground that supports such a claim in equity, including misrepresentation of any kind, innocent, negligent, or fraudulent; and

(h) in support of a claim in tort that the oral statement was in breach of a duty of care.

[4]   I do not consider that I am setting out an exhaustive list. I am only showing that appropriate allegations in the pleadings will require that the evidence be admitted.

[5]   So, if it is said that an oral representation that was made before the contract document was signed contains a warranty giving rise to a claim for damages, evidence can be given of the representation, even if the representation adds to, subtracts from, varies, or contradicts the document, if the pleadings are appropriate, and if the party on whose behalf the evidence is tendered asserts that from the factual matrix it can be shown that the document does not contain the whole agreement. The oral representation may be part of a single agreement, other parts of which appear in the document. (The one-contract theory.) Alternatively, the document may record a complete agreement but there may be a separate collateral agreement with different terms, one of which is the oral representation. (The two-contract theory.)

[6] On the basis of the pleadings in this case, I do not doubt that the evidence was properly admitted on the question of whether the document constituted a record of the whole agreement.

[7] I should add that I can see very little residual practicality in the parol evidence rule, as a rule of evidence, in cases tried by a judge alone . . .

Can the Oral Representation Add to, Subtract from, Vary or Contradict the Signed Document?

[8] Once the oral evidence has been properly admitted under the application of the parol evidence rule, the body of principles of substantive law that are also customarily treated as being encompassed by the rule must be considered.

[9] [Earlier in these reasons] I concluded that evidence of the oral representation was admissible in this case either on the basis that the document did not contain the whole agreement (the "one-contract" theory), or on the basis that the document contained one complete agreement, but that the oral representation formed the basic term of another complete agreement (the "two-contract" theory).

[10] But I wish to emphasize that these theories are legal analysis only. They are not real life. So the substantive law ought to be the same, whichever theory is adopted. It makes no sense to say that if the warranty is cast as part of a single contract ("I am selling you a rust-proof car"), the consequence in law is different than if the warranty is cast as part of a separate collateral contract ("If you buy this car from me, I will guarantee that it is rust-proof").

[11] The crucial parol evidence principle of substantive law, for the purposes of this case, is the principle that forms one of the reasons for decision in *Hawrish v. Bank of Montreal* . . . *Bauer v. Bank of Montreal* . . . *Carman Construction Ltd. v. CPR Co.*, [1982] 1 S.C.R. 958. . . [briefly discussed below] all decisions of the Supreme Court of Canada. . . . That principle was stated in this way by Mr. Justice Martland, for the Supreme Court of Canada, in the *Carman Construction* case, at p. 969: "a collateral agreement cannot be established where it is inconsistent with or contradicts the written agreement."

[12] I propose to make eight comments about that principle.

[A] The first is that the principle has its root in the parol evidence rule as a rule of evidence, and in the "two-contract" or "collateral contract" exception to that rule of evidence. There is no objection to the introduction of evidence to establish an oral agreement separate from the written agreement and made at the same time: see *Heilbut, Symons & Co. v. Buckleton*, [1913] A.C. 30. But it is unreasonable to contemplate that, at the same time, and between the same parties, two contracts will be made dealing with the same subject-matter, one of which contradicts the other. So, since the written one was clearly and demonstrably made, reason requires one to conclude that the oral one, contradicting it, was never made. . . .

[B] The second is that the principle can not be an absolute one.

. . .

[C] The fourth point is that *Bauer v. Bank of Montreal* explicitly recognizes a particular exception to the principle. . . . So, if the contract is induced by an oral misrepresentation that is inconsistent with the written contract, the written contract cannot stand.

· · ·

Conclusion

[13] Once it has been decided that the oral representation was a warranty, then, in my opinion,

    (a) evidence accepted on the basis that there would be a subsequent ruling on admissibility, becomes admissible;

    (b) the oral warranty and the document must be interpreted together, and, if possible, harmoniously, to attach the correct contractual effect to each;

    (c) if no contradiction becomes apparent in following that process, then the principle in *Hawrish*, *Bauer*, and *Carman* has no application; and

    (d) if there is a contradiction, then the principle in *Hawrish, Bauer*, and *Carman* is that there is a strong presumption in favour of the written document, but the rule is not absolute, and if on the evidence it is clear that the oral warranty was intended to prevail, it will prevail.

[14] Since, in my opinion, there is no contradiction in this case between the specific oral warranty and the signed standard form Buckwheat Marketing Agreement, 1980, I have concluded that the warranty has contractual effect and that the defendant, Allstate Grain Co. Ltd., is liable to the plaintiffs for breach of that warranty.

[15] But if it were correct, in this case, to conclude that the oral representation and the Buckwheat Marketing Agreement, 1980 contradicted each other, then, on the basis of the facts found by the trial judge and his conclusion that the oral representation was intended to affect the contractual relationship of the parties, as a warranty, I would have concluded that, in spite of the strong presumption in favour of the document, the oral warranty should prevail.

[16] I would dismiss the appeal.

[**ANDERSON J.A.** agreed with the reasons of **LAMBERT J.A.** but also concluded that the words of clause 23 were not so clear and unequivocal as to exclude the assurances given in respect of weed control. **SEATON J.A.** dissented. He said: "I am of the view that the parol evidence, if admitted, falls short of showing the requisite contractual intention, cannot create a contractual term that is capable of standing with the written term, and cannot create a term that overwhelms the written term."

Leave to appeal to the Supreme Court was dismissed (1984), 56 N.R. 233.]

NOTES AND QUESTIONS

1.   As stated by Lambert J.A., the parol evidence rule can be avoided by appropriately drafted pleadings and a sympathetic judge. If the party seeking to have the parol evidence admitted pleads that the document is ambiguous, that there is a "collateral" (separate) agreement, or that the document was executed by mistake, the evidence to establish these propositions will always be considered by a judge.

2.   As a practical matter, the parol evidence rule can never operate to exclude any evidence, so long as counsel make the necessary *pro forma* allegations in the pleadings.

Nevertheless, the rule still causes problems and, as with all similar rules, some judges give the rule a strict, literal effect, as illustrated by *Bauer*.

3. Sometimes the drafter of a contract, in an effort to convince the court that the writing really is the final expression of the parties' agreement, adds an "entire agreement clause" (the written document sets out "the entire agreement") or an "integration clause" (the written document integrates all previous statements and undertakings). It should not surprise you that such a clause will not always be effective to exclude evidence that the court considers relevant.

In *Shelanu Inc. v. Print Three Franchising Corp.*,[2003] O.J. No. 1919, 64 O.R. (3d) 533 (C.A.), the Ontario Court of Appeal considered a written franchise agreement that was varied by a later oral agreement; the written contract had an "entire agreement clause". Weiler J.A. wrote:

> [46] Paragraph 27 of the agreement reads as follows:
>
>> This agreement constitutes the entire Agreement between the parties with respect to all of the matters herein and its execution has not been induced by, nor do any of the parties hereto rely upon or regard as material, any representation or right not incorporated herein. Any representations, inducements, promises, and agreements, oral or otherwise not contained herein shall have no force or effect in the construction of the rights and obligations of the parties created by this Agreement.
>
> [47] Paragraph 27 deals "with . . . all of the matters herein" and states that any oral or other representations have no force or effect in the "construction of the rights and obligations of the parties created by this Agreement". The rights and obligations of the parties to the oral agreement, namely, BCD, Shelanu and Print Three are, as I have said, not "matters herein" and were not "created" by the franchise agreement between Shelanu and Print Three or, for that matter, BCD and Print Three.
>
> [48] Further, the ordinary meaning of the language used in para. 27 is that the written agreement represented the entire agreement between the parties at the time it was signed. J. Beatson, in *Anson's Law of Contract*, 27th ed. (Oxford: Oxford University Press, 1998) at pp. 494-95 states:
>
>> A simple contract, . . . whether in writing or not, may be varied by a subsequent agreement either written or oral. This in no way conflicts with the rule that extrinsic evidence is not admissible to vary or add to the contents of the written document, for that principle merely refers to the ascertainment of the original intention of the parties.
>
> [49] Indeed, an exception to the parol evidence rule is the existence of any subsequent oral agreement to rescind or modify a written contract. ...
>
> [50] Clauses such as the entire agreement clause in issue here are normally used to try to exclude representations made prior to the signing of the written agreement. See P.M. Perell, "A Riddle Inside an Enigma: The Entire Agreement Clause" (1998) Advocates' Q. 287. Nothing in para. 27 suggests that an oral agreement to surrender the franchise several years later would be of no effect. It cannot be said the entire agreement clause was clearly intended to cover any and all future contractual relations between Shelanu and Print Three. ... The fact that Print Three and Shelanu entered into and acted upon an oral agreement respecting the surrender of the franchise at 200 Bloor Street West indicates this was not the case. Indeed, J.M. Perillo, ed., *Corbin on Contracts* (St. Paul, MN: Western Publishing Co., 1993) states at para. 1295 that an express provision in a written contract forbidding oral variation of the terms of a contract or its discharge is generally unsuccessful with respect to subsequent agreements. The reason he gives is that:

> Two contractors cannot by mutual agreement limit their power to control their legal relations by future mutual agreement. Nor can they in this manner prescribe new rules of evidence and procedure in the proof of facts and events.
>
> [51] Paragraph 27 has no application either.
>
> [52] The wording of the exclusion paragraphs does not conflict with the subsequent … oral agreement … and does not prevent effect being given to this oral agreement.

On the other hand, in appropriate cases the courts may give effect to such clauses, as occurred in *MacMillan v. Kaiser Equipment Ltd.*, [2004] B.C.J. No. 969, 33 B.C.L.R. (4th) 44 (C.A.), where the British Columbia Court of Appeal upheld a trial decision that gave effect to an "entire agreement clause". After discussing cases in which the Court had refused to give effect to entire agreement clauses, such as *Zippy Print Enterprises Ltd. v. Pawliuk*, [2004] B.C.J. No. 2778, 100 B.C.L.R. (2d) 55 (C.A.) and *Turner v. Visscher Holdings Inc.* [1996] B.C.J. No. 998, 23 B.C.L.R. (3d) 304 (C.A.), Oppal J.A. concluded:

> [45] In this case it is apparent that Mr. MacMillan failed to establish that the alleged collateral agreement for or promises of shares survived the entire agreement clause in the written agreement. It is important to note that the 1995 Employment Agreement was negotiated between knowledgeable, sophisticated businesspersons. Mr. MacMillan was represented by independent counsel who presumably gave him legal advice relating to his rights and obligations. Clearly, from a policy perspective, an agreement that is negotiated between sophisticated businesspersons ought to be enforced in accordance with the terms they select in all but the most exceptional circumstances. There is no suggestion that the parties to the agreement in this case were unequal in any sense. Moreover, there is no evidence of mistake or fraud.
>
> [46] In my view both *Turner* … and *Zippy Print* … are distinguishable on their facts. In *Turner*, the parties acted on a collateral agreement, and by doing so, gave every indication that the written agreement containing the entire agreement clause did not actually constitute the entire agreement. Similarly, in *Zippy Print,* it was clear that the oral representations were made in order to induce the defendants to enter into the written contract and that the defendants relied on those representations.

4. Appellate courts are never anxious to expand the grounds upon which parties may appeal. One important limit on appeals is the rule that the findings of fact of the trial judge will not ordinarily be reconsidered. The judges of a court of appeal, however, are not unaware of the risk that a trial judge may have made a serious mistake in the facts that he or she considered. The parol evidence rule is one way for courts of appeal to control findings of fact without actually saying that they are doing so.

   It might be a mistake to think that the issue in *Bauer* was really about the parol evidence rule. It may well be that the Supreme Court simply did not accept the trial judge's findings and wanted to reverse his decision without opening the floodgates of appeals against findings of fact by trial judges.

5. The judgment in *Bauer* may, for example, be contrasted with the decision of the Ontario Court of Appeal in *Bank of Nova Scotia v. Zackheim* (1983), 42 O.R. (2d) 592, 3 D.L.R (4th) 760. The plaintiff bank sued the defendant guarantor on a guarantee. The defendant successfully argued before the Master that he had a good defence to the plaintiff's claim for summary judgment. The trial judge, Griffiths J., had reversed the Master and the defendant appealed. The question was whether a triable issue had been raised by the defendant. Zuber J.A., giving the judgment of the Court of Appeal, allowed the appeal and held that there should be a trial. Zuber J.A. said (p. 761 D.L.R.):

The defendant entered into a guarantee agreeing with the plaintiff bank whereby he guaranteed the liability of a limited company. Paragraph 14 of the guarantee reads in part:

> 14. This guarantee embodies all the agreements between the parties hereto relative to the guarantee, assignment and postponement and none of the parties shall be bound by any representation or promise made by any person relative thereto which is not embodied herein; and it is specifically agreed that the Bank shall not be bound by any representations or promises made by the Customer to the Guarantor.

The principal defence of the defendant was that he had been induced to enter into this guarantee by the innocent misrepresentation of the bank manager as to its effect. . . .

Mr. Justice Griffiths was of the view that the parol evidence rule excluded evidence of oral innocent misrepresentations that contradict the terms of a written guarantee and therefore there was no triable issue raised by the defendant. Mr. Justice Griffiths premised this view on his interpretation of a decision of the Supreme Court of Canada: *Bauer v. Bank of Montreal.* . . .

In our respectful view, the learned judge was in error. [Zuber J.A. here quoted ¶¶ 7 and 8 of the judgment of McIntyre J. in *Bauer, supra.*]

It appears to us that the defence of innocent misrepresentation has not been precluded or diminished. In the *Bauer* case, which was a case which proceeded to trial, there was simply no evidence of misrepresentation. This defence, of course, requires an evidentiary basis and in this case the defendant seeks an opportunity to adduce such evidence. . . .

We, of course, do not pass upon the merits of this case. It will be for the trial judge to determine whether the defendant is able to establish his defence. However, an arguable defence has been raised and the defendant is entitled to a trial.

6. In a number of provinces, including Alberta, British Columbia, Prince Edward Island and Ontario, legislation has been enacted to eliminate the effect of the parol evidence rule in cases where a consumer is dealing with a business. In Ontario, the *Consumer Protection Act, 2002*, S.O. 2002, c. 30, Sched. A provides:

> 18(10) In [a] trial [by a consumer seeking relief for having relied on any statement or representation of a business], oral evidence . . . is admissible despite the existence of a written agreement and despite the fact that the evidence pertains to a representation in respect of a term, condition or undertaking that is or is not provided for in the agreement.

A corporation can only make contracts through agents. There are difficult problems in deciding how the law should treat communications to and from employees and agents of large business enterprises.

The problem of communicating to large business organizations was already apparent in 1854 in *Hadley v. Baxendale, supra*, Chapter 1. As noted after that case, in the headnote to the law report, there is a statement that the servant of the plaintiff "told the clerk" employed by the defendant that the mill was stopped, but in the judgment Alderson B. says that "the special circumstances" of the mill being stopped were "never communicated" to the defendant. In *Hadley v. Baxendale* the defendant was a partnership, and the court may have considered that communication to an employee of the partnership was not communication to the partnership.

Similar problems arise in deciding what can be a communication *from* a firm, *i.e.*, a partnership or a corporation.

An agent may be an employee like the check-out person in a supermarket who is authorized by the corporation operating the store to sell, *i.e.*, transfer title in the goods to the customer in return for cash or a charge to a credit card. When the corporation bought the land on which the store was to be built, or bought the corporation that had previously operated the store, that contract was not made by a person who might operate a cash register. That contract would normally have been made by an officer, the president or a vice-president, who would have been authorized to enter into negotiations by a resolution of the boards of directors of the corporations involved, and the agreement would probably have been approved by the board of directors before being executed. The solicitors acting for each of the vendor and purchaser would have had to give an opinion to the other party that the transaction had been properly authorized by their respective clients.

This concern that the contract be properly authorized arises from the rule that a person (T) who makes a contract with an agent (A) will not be able to sue the principal (P) on a contract made between T and P if the person acting as P's agent (A) is not authorized by P to act as P's agent. In other words, T deals with A at its peril. It is up to T to make sure that A has authority to act for the corporation. The risks that T runs are, in practice, limited by the rule that T may rely on (i) P's representation that A has authority, (ii) the fact that A has the usual authority of a person in A's position, or (iii) the fact that A has been held out by P as having authority sufficient to conclude the contract with T. The agent is then said to have "ostensible" authority, even if there is a lack of actual authority, and the principal is bound by the "ostensible agent". A customer of a supermarket may, for example, reasonably rely on a cashier to have the authority to sell groceries, and on a vice-president to sell 100 used cash registers.

The rules of the law of agency have an important effect on the allocation of the risk of loss arising from the misbehaviour of employees. A customer who accepted the offer of a disgruntled cashier to buy the store's cash register for $10 would only have herself to blame if the store asked for it back. When a court holds that the terms of a bank guarantee have been varied by a bank manager, the court must have assumed (or found) that the bank manager had authority from the bank to do what was done.

Some cases involving business enterprises in which the courts apply the parol evidence rule might be more appropriately analyzed by a careful examination of the authority of the employee whose words are alleged to have modified the written agreement.

Carman Construction Ltd. v. Canadian Pacific Railway, [1982] 1 S.C.R. 958, 136 D.L.R. (3d) 193, dealt with the relation between the parol evidence rule and the issue of an employee's ability to change the terms of the contract between him and his employer. The plaintiff-contractor had submitted a tender to do some work for the defendant. The work involved the removal of rock and overburden for a new railway siding. The plaintiff received the invitation to tender on Tuesday, 6 September 1977 and the tenders were to be submitted by 10:00 a.m. Friday, 9 September 1977. The tender documents contained no estimate of the amount of rock to be removed. A technician employed by the defendant had done a survey of the proposed siding and, as a result of this survey, the amount of rock to be removed was estimated at about 7,000 cubic yards. On 7 September 1977, Fielding, the general manager of the plaintiff, visited the offices of the defendant in Sudbury.

He told someone — he did not know the person's name — in the defendant's engineering department that, without more information on what the job required, the plaintiff could not submit a bid. An employee of the railway, who was never identified, told Fielding that there were between 7,000 and 7,500 cubic yards to be removed. The plaintiff then submitted a bid on the basis that there were 7,500 yards of rock. The plaintiff's bid was accepted by the defendant. The formal contract between the parties contained the following clauses:

> 3.1 It is hereby declared and agreed by the Contractor that this Agreement has been entered into by him on his own knowledge respecting the nature and conformation of the ground upon which the work is to be done, the location, character, quality and quantities of material to be removed, the character of the equipment and facilities needed, the general and local conditions and all other matters which can in any way affect the work under this Agreement, and the Contractor does not rely upon any information given or statement made to him in relation to the work by the Company.

> . . .

> 4. *Familiarity with Site*

> Each tenderer must make himself personally acquainted with the location of the proposed work, and must inform himself by such means as he may prefer as to all conditions of the site and all other factors which may affect his tender and the performance of the work, and shall not claim at any time after tendering that there was any misunderstanding in regard to conditions at the site or of conditions imposed by the Agreement.

Fielding admitted that he had read the provisions of clause 3.1, which had been included in the draft contract sent with the tender package. It later was determined that there were about 11,000 cubic yards of rock to be removed. The plaintiff claimed to be entitled to an extra $32,000 under the contract to reflect the greater amount of rock to be excavated.

The trial judge dismissed the action on the ground that the parties' relation was governed by clause 3.1. The Ontario Court of Appeal dismissed the appeal: (1981), 33 O.R. (2d) 472, 124 D.L.R. (3d) 680. In the Court of Appeal, Wilson J.A. said (pp. 472-73 O.R., p. 680 D.L.R.):

> The majority of the Court sees no reason why in the circumstances of this case the defendant should be precluded from putting forward the non-reliance provisions of the tender documents. The plaintiff was aware of these provisions before it approached the defendant's employees seeking information as to the quantity of the rock to be removed. It knew that this precise matter was dealt with in clear and unambiguous terms in the contract on which it was tendering. Indeed, the provisions were clearly meant for the sole purpose of ensuring that, if prospective bidders got any information on this subject from the defendant's employees, they would be relying upon it at their own risk. Likewise the defendant knew that if its employees gave out any information or made an estimate in response to requests from prospective bidders, the risk of the information's being wrong was not on it but on the bidders who used it. This was the context in which they conducted their business. . . .

> . . . This is a case in which the plaintiff tendered knowing that in the very contract on which it was tendering it had agreed to assume the risk of using any information obtained by it from the defendant's employees. There is no basis for the exercise of the Court's equitable jurisdiction.

The plaintiff appealed to the Supreme Court of Canada, basing its argument on:

(a) a claim in contract for breach of a collateral warranty; and

(b)   a claim in tort for negligent misrepresentation.

In rejecting the contract-based claim, Martland J., giving the judgment of the Supreme Court, said ([1982] 1 S.C.R. 958 at 966, 136 D.L.R. (3d) 193 at 198):

> *Collateral Warranty*
>
> A collateral warranty is a contract collateral to the primary agreement. Its existence must be established, as in the case of any other contract, by proof of intention to contract. . . .
>
> In my opinion there is no evidence in the present case to establish an intention to warrant the accuracy of the statement made by the C.P.R. employee to Fielding, i.e., no promise to make it good. . .
>
> There is an additional ground for denying the existence of a collateral warranty. Such a warranty, if it existed, would contradict the express terms of the contract as contained in clause 3.1. This court held in Hawrish v. Bank of Montreal . . . that a collateral agreement cannot be established where it is inconsistent with or contradicts the written agreement.
>
> The Hawrish case was followed on this point by this court recently in the case of *Bauer v. Bank of Montreal* [*supra*].

Martland J. also rejected the claim based on negligent misrepresentation (pp. 972-73 S.C.R., p. 203 D.L.R.):

> I reach this conclusion in the light of the facts to which I have already referred in dealing with the issue of collateral warranty. Carman was made aware, when Fielding received the tender documents, and read and understood clause 3.1, that if it entered into an agreement with C.P.R. it was doing so on its own knowledge as to quantities of material to be removed and that it would not rely upon any information or statement made to it by C.P.R. in relation to the work. Fielding was aware of this when he sought information from a C.P.R. employee. He knew that if information was obtained, Carman would be relying on it at its own risk. . . .

QUESTIONS AND NOTES

1.   What does the fact that the C.P.R. employee who gave Fielding the information was unnamed and never identified suggest about the reasonableness of Fielding's reliance on what he was told by him?

2.   It would be comparatively easy to draft instructions to employees to deal with the problem of information raised in *Carman*, but would such instructions deal with the practical problem facing *both* the C.P.R. and Carman, *viz.*, how to get a tender in the very short time allowed by the C.P.R? It was in C.P.R.'s interest to get bids from as many as possible of the contractors from whom it invited tenders. It might have been significant that Carman was the only bidder prepared to bid under the conditions imposed by C.P.R. In addition, both C.P.R. and Carman must deal with each other again. Good relations between them over the long term require that the individuals who must deal face to face have trust and confidence in each other. It is apparent from the facts that Fielding and at least some of the employees in the C.P.R. engineering department knew each other.

3.   The organizational structure of a corporation as large as C.P.R. requires that its relations with the outside world be formalized to a considerable degree. It would make its operation very difficult if every employee could, by careless language or by ignoring his or her employer's instructions, alter the terms of the relations that C.P.R. has tried to create with the outside world. Carman was a much smaller corporation than C.P.R., but it too must have had problems of a similar kind. Recall how the courts' willingness to regard an employee as having more authority than his employer probably in-

tended him to have, frustrated the planned risk allocation in *Cornwall Gravel Co. Ltd. v. Purolator Courier Ltd.* (1978), 18 O.R. (2d) 551, 83 D.L.R. (3d) 267 (affirmed (1979), 28 O.R. (2d) 704, 115 D.L.R. (3d) 511 (C.A.), affirmed [1980] 2 S.C.R. 118, 120 D.L.R. (3d) 575), examined in Chapter 1.

The problems of controlling employees so that their actions do not jeopardize the allocation of risks that the employers have made is also an important theme in the next chapter. We shall there note some of the specific risks and methods for dealing with them.

4. One can, perhaps, reconcile the pressure on the parties to co-operate (at the corporate and individual levels) by using the concept of authority in the relations of the principal, its agent and the person who deals with the agent that was mentioned earlier. One could then argue that, whether or not Fielding [T, the Third Party] knew the terms of the contract, he would, in dealing with an unnamed employee [A, the Agent], do so at his own risk, because he should have realized that such a person could not, within the structure of C.P.R. [P, the Principal], have the authority to change the terms of the standard-form contract used for all construction tenders. If Fielding had wanted to bid and was unwilling to do so with the information he had, he should have gone further up the corporate organization to find out what he wanted to know. The person, for example, the division engineer, who had authorized the invitation to tender, would be able to balance the need for Carman to have information against the risk that would be created by giving the information. Fielding's reliance on such an official of C.P.R. would have been reasonable. If the court had focused on this issue, the interests of C.P.R. would have been protected because the responsibility for disclosing the information necessary to enable Carman to bid on the contract would have been placed on a person who would know if there was likely to be more than one bid and if Carman needed to be given assurance of the size of the contract. Similarly, Carman's interests would have been protected because there would have been no risk that this person was not authorized to change the terms of the contract.

An analysis that looks at the relation of the parties, not just at the terms of the contract, is likely to work better and to offer a better basis for understanding the pressures that the court should respond to. An analysis that treats the contract as the sole event in the parties' relation is almost certain to get the correct answer only by chance.

5. The trial judge in *Carman* made a finding that the employee who gave the information was authorized to do so. Martland J. said that "the trial judge felt satisfied that [he] was an employee of C.P.R. authorized to give out such information."

In light of the written contract, this employee was almost certainly not in fact authorized to do so. Given the fact that the employee was never identified or called as a witness and that there was no evidence that he had any actual authority from C.P.R. management, it is hard to know exactly what to make of the statement. Presumably it was a finding that the employee had the ostensible authority to give out this information, though any evidence to support that conclusion is entirely lacking. It was not further referred to by Martland J. and appears to have played no part in his analysis.

6. Later in this chapter we will look at the problems of negligent misrepresentation and of clauses which, like clause 3.1 in *Carman Construction*, allocate risks of loss. The underlying problem of authority will be one of the difficulties that any satisfactory solution must deal with.

Apart from the parol evidence rule, it has been held that evidence of the course of negotiations between the parties is generally not to be admitted, or considered, by a court when interpreting a contract. Issues of admissibility are those that relate to the relevance of evidence. Such issues are distinct from issues of the weight to be given to admitted evidence. In other words, evidence that is admitted may not be believed or, even if it is believed, may not convince the court that the proposition argued for has been established. The judgment in the next case talks about admissibility, but you have to consider whether the issue is the admissibility in the narrow sense, or the weight to be given to the evidence on the assumption that it cannot be excluded.

HI-TECH GROUP INC. v. SEARS CANADA INC.

[2001] O.J. No. 33, 52 O.R. (3d) 97, 11 B.L.R. (3d) 197
(C.A., Morden, Goudge and Feldman JJ.A.)

The judgment of the court was delivered by

MORDEN J.A.: — **[1]** This is an appeal by the plaintiff from a summary judgment granted by John A.B. Macdonald J. dismissing one of the plaintiff's claims in this action.

[2]   The grounds of the appeal are that the motions judge erred: (1) in interpreting the termination provision in an agreement between the plaintiff and the defendant; (2) in holding that extrinsic evidence relating to the agreement was inadmissible; and (3) in granting partial summary judgment, on part only of a larger claim, in the circumstances of this case.

[3]   The facts, insofar as they are relevant to the issues that must be addressed on this appeal, are as follows. The plaintiff is in the business of organizing and managing consumer clubs on behalf of retailers, such as the defendant, to offer benefits and costs savings to consumer members as well as increase retail sales for the retailer.

[4]   The plaintiff entered into an agreement with the defendant dated May 1, 1994 which established the "Mature Outlook Program" that was designed for the defendant's customers who were over 50 years of age. Customers purchased membership in the program for $9.99. Out of this membership fee, the plaintiff received $8.99 and the defendant kept $1. The plaintiff provided various benefits to members and administered the program. The defendant provided other benefits, notably discount coupons on purchases by members.

[5]   The term of the agreement is set forth in s. 4.1 as follows:

> The term of this Agreement will commence as of the date first above written [May 1, 1994] and will end at midnight on May 31, 1995 ("Initial Term") subject to termination as hereinafter provided. *Thereafter, it will automatically renew for successive terms of one year, subject to termination by either party upon 120 days prior written notice.* Upon any such termination, if the Program is to continue in operation under the management of SEARS or a third party, SEARS and MANAGER [the plaintiff] will agree on procedures for the orderly transfer of MANAGER's functions to SEARS or SEARS designee, and MANAGER will be compensated for its reasonable costs incurred therein.

(Emphasis added)

[6]   The program was established in May, 1994. The defendant delivered a notice of termination to the plaintiff on February 21, 1996, to be effective no later than June 30, 1996. The plaintiff's position was that under s. 4.1 of the agreement, the notice was ineffective to terminate the agreement before May 31, 1997. Put shortly, it submitted that the 120 days' notice was to precede the commencement of the renewal term beginning on May 31, 1996 and, if it did not, the agreement would renew automatically for a further year from that date.

[7]   The plaintiff commenced this action in November 1996. In its statement of claim, it claimed damages in the amount of $12,000,000 based on various alleged breaches of the agreement by the defendant. One of the breaches, the one in question in the motion and in this appeal, is the alleged breach of the termination provision described in the preceding paragraph.

[8]   The defendant, after delivering its statement of defence, brought a motion for "partial summary judgment" dismissing the claim against it relating to the termination of the agreement. This was a claim for damages for the period July 1, 1996 to May 31, 1997. The motions judge granted the relief sought. The formal judgment provided that "partial summary judgment be granted to the defendant, dismissing the plaintiff's claim for damages for breach or repudiation of the agreement dated May 1, 1994, on the basis that the defendant did not validly terminate the Agreement effective June 30, 1996".

[9]   Both the plaintiff and the defendant filed extrinsic evidence on the motion for summary judgment and, indeed, in the statement of claim, the plaintiff pleaded as material facts what it considered to be the general effect of part of this evidence. This related to its "significant start-up costs for the Program" and the expectation that the program would not become profitable until it had been established for some time. The plaintiff also alleged that it relied on the automatic renewal clause to reduce the risk it was assuming. It submitted that this clause would provide a reasonable opportunity for it to obtain a return on its initial investment in establishing the program under the agreement.

[10]   In its evidence filed on the motion, the plaintiff furnished details to support the allegation. It is the plaintiff's position that this evidence, which it submits relates to the genesis and one of the aims of the transaction, supports the interpretation that the agreement was to renew automatically for one-year periods subject to 120 days' notice of termination before a renewal date.

[11]   The defendant challenges this evidence and, in fact, relies on evidence that the plaintiff was prepared to accept the risk of the contract running not longer than its initial term.

[12]   Both parties filed and relied upon evidence of earlier drafts of the agreement and on the parties' conduct under the agreement, submitting that this evidence casts light on its meaning.

[MORDEN J.A. dealt with the proper test to be applied in a motion for summary judgment.]

[14]   The motions judge then reviewed the basic submissions of the parties and examined "the law which determines how to ascertain the meaning of a written agreement" [para. 7]. In doing so, he made several references to the reasons of Iacobucci J. for the Supreme Court of Canada in *Eli Lilly & Co. v. Novopharm Ltd.*, [1998] 2 S.C.R. 129, 161 D.L.R. (4th) 1, particularly, passages in paras. 52, 54, 55, 57, 58 and 59.

[15]   A major issue considered by the court in *Eli Lilly* was the admissibility of extrinsic evidence to aid in the interpretation of the agreement in question in that

case. Iacobucci J. concluded that the agreement did not contain any ambiguity that could not be resolved by reference to the text itself and "[n]o further interpretive aids are necessary" [para. 57]. He then said at para. 58:

> More specifically, there is no need to resort to any of the evidence tendered by either Apotex or Novopharm as to the subjective intentions of their principals at the time of drafting. Consequently, I find this evidence to be inadmissible by virtue of the parol evidence rule. . . .

[16] The motions judge in his reasons said [at paras. 9-12]:

> If it were open to the parties to lead evidence of "surrounding circumstances", that evidence could not properly include evidence of the subjective intention of either one party (per Iacobucci J. in *Lilly* para. 54) or of all parties to the agreement (per Iacobucci J. in *Lilly* at para. 59). The surrounding circumstances, if admissible in evidence, will encompass factors which assist the Court "to search for an interpretation which, from the whole of the contract would appear to promote or advance the true intent of the parties at the time of entry into the contract". See *Consolidated Bathurst Export Ltd. v. Mutual Boiler & Machinery Insce. Co.*, [1980] 1 S.C.R. 888 at p. 901, *Kentucky Fried Chicken v. Scotts Food Services Ltd.* (1998), 41 B.L.R. (2d) 42 (O.C.A.) at p. 51.

> However, I conclude that, as a question of law, it is not open to the respondent in the circumstances here to lead such evidence, based on the authority of *Eli Lilly v. Novopharm (supra)*.

> . . .

> Where, as here, the agreement is a negotiated commercial agreement, it should be interpreted objectively, rather than from the perspective of one or the other of the parties: see *Kentucky Fried Chicken* at p. 51 (supra).

> In my opinion, based on these legal principles, the applicant has established that there is no genuine issue of material fact which requires a trial to determine what the parties intended by their termination language in para. 4.1, interpreted in the light of all of the contractual language. The respondent has failed, in my opinion, to establish that its claim has a real chance of success, whether it is its claim that it has the right to lead evidence in aid of interpretation of the contract, or its claim of breach of para. 4.1 of the agreement.

[17] The motions judge then dealt with the interpretation of s. 4.1 in the agreement [at paras. 13-14]:

> In my opinion, the respondent's argument that termination rights may be exercised only on a May 31st renewal date, and only on 120 days written notice given prior to the renewal date is inconsistent with and incompatible with the usual and ordinary meaning of the language which the *contracting* parties used. That language is clear and unambiguous in its meaning, and it determines clearly the rights of the parties to terminate the agreement: either party may terminate the agreement by written notice delivered on the other party 120 days prior to the date of termination.

> In my opinion, the case is like *Lilly (supra)*. The language used in the agreement, in its relevant provision is so clear and unambiguous that the meaning the parties intended to give to the language may be determined simply by having reference to the agreement itself. In the result, no further interpretive aids are necessary (per Iacobucci J. in *Lilly* at para. [57]) and it is "unnecessary to consider any extrinsic evidence at all" (per Iacobucci J. in *Lilly* at para. [55]). Given the applicability of these conclusions of Iacobucci J., I conclude that evidence of "surrounding circumstances" is not admissible herein. In para. [55] of *Lilly*, after he had mentioned that there is some jurisdiction to read *contractual* language in the light of "surrounding

circumstances", Iacobucci J. held that "it is unnecessary to consider any extrinsic evidence at all when the document is clear and unambiguous on its face." Surrounding circumstances are before the Court only if established by extrinsic evidence; that is, evidence of matters extrinsic to the contractual document.

(Emphasis added.)

[18] According to *Eli Lilly*, the first step in the process of determining the admissibility of extrinsic evidence in this case is to determine whether the text of s. 4.1 of the agreement is clear and unambiguous. On this question I disagree, with respect, with the views of the motions judge. I think that the provision is ambiguous in the sense that it is reasonably susceptible of more than one meaning. One of them supports the plaintiff's position.

[19] For convenience, I repeat the most relevant part of s. 4.1:

> The term of this Agreement will commence as of the date first above written [May 1, 1994] and will end at midnight on May 31, 1995 ("Initial Term") subject to termination as hereinafter provided. Thereafter, *it will automatically renew for successive terms of one year, subject to termination by either party upon 120 days prior written notice.* . . .

(Emphasis added)

[20] The plaintiff's submission, which I think is reasonably open to it to make, is that the statement "it will automatically renew for successive terms of one year" is the dominant part of the sentence that is "subject to" the phrase providing for termination on 120 days' prior notice. The court should read the renewal term and the notice provision together and not in opposition to each other. This is done by reading the notice provision as qualifying the automatic renewal. In other words, there *will* be an automatic renewal unless appropriate notice is given. There is no ability under s. 4.1 to abridge the renewal term; there is only the right to prevent further renewal by giving appropriate notice.

[21] The plaintiff's submission continues along the following lines. To read s. 4.1 otherwise is to give no meaning to the provision for an initial term and for subsequent automatic one-year terms. If it had been intended that the parties could terminate the agreement at any time on 120 days' notice, there would be no point to the stipulation of an initial term and of successive renewal terms of one year. If the contract could be terminated at any time, the provision of the successive terms serves no purpose. Support is also found in the use of "prior" in the phrase "prior written notice". Prior to what? The plaintiff answers that the 120 days' notice must be read as being "prior" to the end of the annual term then in effect. If it is not, the word "prior" is mere surplusage.

[22] The defendant has not responded to the submission that the "subject to" clause relates to the automatic renewal feature in the preceding clause, but does respond to the submission relating to treating as redundant the provision of an initial term and successive renewal terms. The defendant submits that it bears upon merely a question of the "efficiency" of the language used and has no bearing on the meaning of the term. Against this response the plaintiff relies upon the principle of interpretation that effect must, if possible, be given to every word and every clause in an agreement: *Brown Brothers Ltd. v. Popham*, [1940] O.R. 102, [1939] 4 D.L.R. 662 (C.A.) at p. 670; and 13 *Halsbury's Laws of England*, 4th ed. reissue, at para. 174.

[23] What is said in *Eli Lilly* respecting the admissibility of extrinsic evidence has no application in this case if I am right that s. 4.1 is ambiguous. Indeed, because words always take their meaning from their context, evidence of the circumstances surrounding the making of a contract has been regarded as admissible in every case: *Prenn v. Simmonds*, [1971] 3 All E.R. 237, [1971] 1 W.L.R. 1381 (H.L.) at pp. 1383-84; *Reardon Smith Line Ltd. v. Hansen-Tangen*, [1976] 3 All E.R. 570, [1976] 1 W.L.R. 989 (H.L.) at pp. 995-96; *Hill v. Nova Scotia (Attorney General)*, [1997] 1 S.C.R. 69 at pp. 78-79, 157 N.S.R. (2d) 181; Waddams, *The Law of Contracts*, 4th ed. (Aurora: Canada Law Book, 1999), at p. 232.

[24] A frequently quoted and useful statement respecting surrounding circumstances is that of Lord Wilberforce in *Reardon Smith Line Ltd. v. Hansen-Tangen*, *supra*, at pp. 995-96. After indicating that particular evidence in that case "would exceed what is permissible" in construing the contract in question, he went on to say:

> But it does not follow that, renouncing this evidence, one must be confined within the four corners of the document. No contracts are made in a vacuum: there is always a setting in which they have to be placed. The nature of what is legitimate to have regard to is usually described as "the surrounding circumstances" but this phrase is imprecise: it can be illustrated but hardly defined. In a commercial contract it is certainly right that the court should know the commercial purpose of the contract and this in turn presupposes knowledge of the genesis of the transaction, the background, the context, the market in which the parties are operating.

[25] The contract in this case must be interpreted in the context of properly admissible evidence. This process cannot be fully carried out until findings of fact have been made on the evidence. From at least the first part of the 19th century it was the function of the jury to find the surrounding circumstances as part of the process of interpreting documents: 13 *Halsbury's*, *supra*, at para. 166.

[26] This court is clearly not in a position to make the proper findings because the evidence is open to differing interpretations and inferences, and differing views on what weight should be given to it. In short, it gives rise to a genuine issue for trial. It will be the responsibility of the trial judge, in the context of the issues arising at the trial and the submissions made on them, to determine the extent of the admissibility of the evidence and to make the proper findings on it.

[**MORDEN J.A.** concluded with several paragraphs on the question of the parties' burdens of proof in a motion for summary judgment and held that the trial judge had imposed the wrong burden on the plaintiff in the circumstances.]

Appeal allowed.

NOTES

1.   What role did the "extrinsic evidence" play in the question before the Court of Appeal in *Hi-Tech Group*? Given his approach in *Hi-Tech*, would Morden J.A. be likely to take the same view of the guarantor's arguments about the parol evidence rule in *Bauer v. Bank of Montreal* that McIntyre J. did in that case?

2.   The harm done by the incorrect and unhelpful statement of the parol evidence rule in *Eli Lilly* can be seen in the motions court and appeal judgments in *Hi-Tech Group*. Rather than considering dispassionately the evidence as it might have borne on the parties' understandings of s. 4.1, the motions judge felt constrained by Iacobucci J.'s language to focus on the words and not on the relation of the clause to the whole

structure of the parties' relation. How did the Ontario Court of Appeal deal with the statements in *Eli Lilly* that led the motions judge to conclude that the Court could not consider evidence of the "surrounding circumstances" to help interpret a contract?

3. In *White v. E.B.F. Manufacturing Ltd.*, [2005] N.S.J. No. 518, 12 B.L.R. (4th) 1 (C.A.), the Court had to interpret the provisions of a licensing agreement that dealt with how royalties were to be calculated, and when and by whom they were to be paid. The trial judge had considered extrinsic evidence to help interpret such words as the term "Company" (*i.e.*, whether the Court should consider the revenues of a company closely affiliated with one of the parties to the agreement in determining the revenues on which royalties were to be calculated). In affirming this approach, Saunders J.A. accepted the following as a statement of principle: (at paras. 42-43) :

> In *Investors Compensation Scheme Ltd. v. West Bromwich Building Society*, [1998] 1 W.L.R. 896 (H.L.), at page 913, Lord Hoffman summarises the principles of interpretation of a written contract. He says:

> > (1)   Interpretation is the ascertainment of the meaning which the document would convey to a reasonable person having all the background knowledge which would reasonably have been available to the parties in the situation in which they were at the time of the contract.

> > ...

> > (4)   The meaning which a document (or any other utterance) would convey to a reasonable man is not the same thing as the meaning of its words. The meaning of words is a matter of dictionaries and grammars; the meaning of the document is what the parties using those words against the relevant background would reasonably have been understood to mean. The background may not merely enable the reasonable man to choose between the possible meanings of words which are ambiguous but even (as occasionally happens in ordinary life) to conclude that the parties must, for whatever reason, have used the wrong words or syntax ...

> In *Kentucky Fried Chicken Canada v. Scott's Food Services Inc.*, [1998] O.J. No. 4368, 41 B.L.R. (2d) 42 (C.A.) at para. 27, the Court states:

> > Where, as here, the document to be construed is a negotiated commercial document, the court should avoid an interpretation that would result in a commercial absurdity. Rather, the document should be construed in accordance with sound commercial principles and good business sense. Care must be taken, however, to do this objectively rather than from the perspective of one contracting party or the other, since what might make good business sense to one party would not necessarily do so for the other.

4. It is sometimes argued that evidence of the course of the negotiations over the agreement is "inadmissible". This suggests that the process of negotiation can be neatly separated from the agreement itself. It is often hard to draw a neat line. The buyer (to the knowledge of the seller) may have negotiated the agreement under a mistake. The question, "Is the buyer liable to pay the price of the goods to the seller?" may be answered by saying that there is no contract, that there is no contract on the terms alleged by the seller (using an argument based on *Smith v. Hughes*), or that the agreement is not to be given the meaning asserted by the seller.

5. Suppose that in *Hobbs v. Esquimalt & Nanaimo Railway* (*supra*, Chapter 3) the facts were as follows:

(a)   Trutch said to Hobbs, "By 'land' we mean land without the mineral rights," or

(b)   the price paid by Hobbs was such that any reasonable purchaser would know that the land was being sold either without mineral rights or at a price substantially less than that for which land with mineral rights would normally be sold.

Should these facts be *inadmissible*?

6.   It is sometimes said that evidence of what the parties have done under the agreement, *i.e.*, after it has been made and performance started, is inadmissible to establish the meaning to be given to the agreement. Suppose that in *Hobbs v. Esquimalt & Nanaimo Railway* after the sale had been completed (assuming no litigation) Hobbs had gone into possession of the land, and over the course of the following year had regularly allowed teams of geologists employed by the railway to enter his land to prospect for minerals. Suppose it is proved that he said to an official of the railway: "If I had known that you guys were going to be tramping all over my land pursuing your mineral rights, I would never have bought it." Would this evidence be admissible in Hobbs' action to get the mineral rights?

7.   The role that the courts see for themselves in interpreting contracts says a great deal about the relation between agreements, freedom of contract, the judicial function and, ultimately, the nature of the law of contract.

8.   On the closing of a loan or asset or share transfer transaction, it is customary for the solicitor for each party to supply the other with an opinion stating that the agreement entered into by the solicitor's client is enforceable against it. Such opinions are referred to as "transaction opinions" or "enforceability opinions". They differ from the kind of opinion given in, say, a litigation matter, because they are understood by the lawyers who will sign them (on behalf of their firms) as being a guarantee that the lawyers' work has been properly done. The core of the opinion is a statement along the following lines:

> All necessary corporate action has been taken by or on behalf of the Borrower to authorize the execution and delivery of, and the Borrower has duly executed and delivered, the Credit Agreement and the Security Documents (collectively, the "Borrower's Documents"). Each of the Borrower's Documents is a legal, valid and binding obligation of the Borrower, enforceable by the Bank against the Borrower in accordance with its terms.

This example is taken from an opinion that would be given by the solicitor for the borrower to the creditor in a loan transaction.

Explain to a person who, perhaps as a junior officer of a bank, is unfamiliar with transaction opinions, what the phrase "enforceable in accordance with its terms" in an opinion might mean.

It is permissible to qualify the statement in an opinion by pointing out the situations where the agreement may not be enforceable strictly in accordance with its terms. The standard opinion is usually qualified by the following language:

> The foregoing opinion as to the enforceability of the Borrower's Documents is subject to or may be limited by the general laws relating to bankruptcy, insolvency, reorganization, arrangement, moratorium or other similar laws relating to or affecting the rights of creditors and to the fact that equitable remedies, such as specific performance and injunctive relief, are subject to the discretion of the court and may not be awarded where damages are considered an adequate remedy.

Would you like to consider adding any other qualification? Remember that many lawyers consider that signing an opinion exposes the law firm (and to the extent that its liability insurance may be unavailable or inadequate, the partners personally) to liability to the firm's client or the lender.

9.   In *R. v. Marshall*, [1999] 3 S.C.R. 456, 177 D.L.R. (4th) 513, the Supreme Court of Canada interpreted a series of a treaties entered into between the British government

and the Mi'kmaq Indian nation in the 1760's in order to determine whether they gave the accused Indian the right to fish for eel without a licence in 1993.

There was extrinsic evidence that the negotiation of these treaties was conducted orally, with the treaty then reduced to writing, which the Indians who signed the treaty could not read. There was also extrinsic evidence that the aboriginal leaders expected that they would have the right to hunt and fish, and exchange the "harvest of wildlife" with the British at "truckhouses" (or trading posts) for such manufactured "necessaries" as firearms and ammunition. The written treaty did not mention hunting or fishing, containing only the promise by the Mi'kmaq not to "Traffick, Barter or Exchange any Commodities in any manner but with such persons, or the Manager of such Truckhouses as shall be appointed or established by His majesty's Governor". The Nova Scotia Court of Appeal took a strict approach to the interpretation of the treaties, ruling that "extrinsic evidence cannot be used in the absence of ambiguity." That Court held that there was no express mention of the right to hunt or fish in the treaties, and upheld the conviction of the accused.

The majority of the Supreme Court of Canada recognized that a treaty is a type of agreement that can be treated in much the same way that a modern commercial contract can be treated and took a broader approach to the admissibility of extrinsic evidence and to the meaning of the treaty. The Court held that the treaty afforded a continuing right to aboriginal peoples to hunt and fish, though recognizing the authority of the federal government to regulate this right.

Binnie J. compared modern contract law to treaty law:

> [10] Firstly, even in a modern commercial context, extrinsic evidence is available to show that a written document does not include all of the terms of an agreement. Rules of interpretation in contract law are in general more strict than those applicable to treaties, yet Professor Waddams states in *The Law of Contracts* (3rd ed. 1993), at para. 316:
>
>> The parol evidence rule does not purport to exclude evidence designed to show whether or not the agreement has been "reduced to writing", or whether it was, or was not, the intention of the parties that it should be the exclusive record of their agreement. Proof of this question is a precondition to the operation of the rule, and all relevant evidence is admissible on it. This is the view taken by Corbin and other writers, and followed in the Second Restatement

> . . .

> [43] The law has long recognized that parties make assumptions when they enter into agreements about certain things that give their arrangements efficacy. Courts will imply a contractual term on the basis of presumed intentions of the parties where it is necessary to assure the efficacy of the contract, e.g., where it meets the "officious bystander test": *M.J.B. Enterprises Ltd. v. Defence Construction (1951) Ltd.*, [1999] 1 S.C.R. 619, [170 D.L.R. (4th) 577,] at para. 30 . . . Waddams *supra*, at para 490. . . . Here, if the ubiquitous officious bystander had said, "This talk about truckhouses is all very well, but if the Mi'kmaq are to make these promises, will they have the right to hunt and fish to catch something to trade at the truckhouses?", the answer would have to be, having regard to the honour of the Crown, "of course". If the law is prepared to supply the deficiencies of written contracts prepared by sophisticated parties and their legal advisors in order to produce a sensible result that accords with the intent of both parties, though unexpressed, the law cannot ask less of the honour and dignity of the Crown in its dealings with First Nations.

MISREPRESENTATIONS AND WARRANTIES

The Classification of Contractual Statements

A great deal of judicial and academic ink has been used to deal with the problems caused by the fact that, in the negotiating and making of a contract, the parties may make a variety of statements about the quality of the thing being sold, or adopt a variety of methods for controlling their liability and the allocation of the risks inherent in the transaction. The courts and the parties generally recognize that some things said about the quality of the goods are not particularly important while other things are very important. Similarly, the parties may choose, as the cases on conditions precedent in Chapter 4 illustrated, to make a certain set of circumstances a requirement for an enforceable contract. The response of the parties — at least of those who are acting with legal advice in the preparation or negotiation of the agreement — has been to identify and classify the various statements as, for example, ones giving the buyer a right only to damages, or others as providing an excuse for the buyer's performance, *i.e.*, as deal-breakers.

The courts have similarly developed a range of legal responses for dealing with the problems that arise if the expectations of the buyer — and for simplicity a sale will be taken as the example — are disappointed. The nature of the remedy that is available to the disappointed buyer depends on how the statement is classified. The approach of the courts to how statements are to be classified has evolved considerably over the past one hundred years or so, and is now quite complex.

The terms "puff", "misrepresentation" and "warranty" refer to statements or promises that might be made by the seller. A "puff", frequently referred to as a "mere puff", is the kind of legally meaningless statement that sellers sometimes make about the goods or services being sold. An example of a puff would be the statement of a salesperson in a clothing store to a woman who is trying on a new dress: "That looks gorgeous on you." A "representation" is a statement of fact — "These financial statements correctly state the financial situation of the corporation you are buying" — that may entail liability on the seller if it is incorrect, *i.e.*, if it is a "*mis*representation". Misrepresentations may be innocent, negligent or fraudulent, with different remedies for each.

A "warranty" is a contractual promise by the seller that the subject of the sale has certain qualities or characteristics. A warranty may be a term of the contract, but may also be "outside" the contract as a "collateral contract", *i.e.*, as a separate contract between buyer and seller to induce the making of the "main" contract.

The word "condition" as used in a case like *Hongkong Fir Shipping Co. v. Kawasaki Kisen Kaisha Ltd.*, *supra*, examined in Chapter 4, is sometimes brought into the classification as an even more serious term of the contract than a warranty, the breach of which gives the innocent party an excuse for non-performance as well as the right to damages. Express conditions can provide an excuse for non-performance, and are in a sense, the antithesis of warranties, for which only expectation damages can be awarded. While a prospective buyer may much prefer to get out of a deal before it has performed by paying the price, rather than paying the price and then suing for damages for breach, a condition is not always an important term of the contract or a more important term than a warranty.

When something is called an "innominate term", as in a case like *Hongkong Fir*, that classification reflects the fact that the term is not a condition — because the parties did not expressly make it one — but that it may be treated as if it were one in the sense that the occurrence (or non-occurrence) of the event covered by the term may provide one party with an excuse for its non-performance. Used in this way, the concept of an "innominate term" is a retrospective classification used to bring about a particular result that the court considers proper — *ex hypothesi* the parties will not have dealt with the event themselves because, if they had, it would be either a breach of warranty (giving rise only to a claim for damages) or an express condition, providing for the excuse that one party now claims to have.

It is tempting to think of the progress from "puff", "representations", "warranties", "conditions" as going from things that have no relevance to the contract to things that are very important. Such a classification process is often undertaken by courts and legal scholars. The difficulty is, of course, that the things that are written or said by the seller or simply understood by the buyer from the context of the deal will not always be easily classified into one of these terms: the classification is likely to be made because, as we shall see, the court *wants* to reach some particular result and will classify the statement to achieve that end, or because a lawyer argues for one classification rather than another because that argument forwards his or her client's case. The words are simply pegs on which a lawyer (or a judge) can hang an argument to justify the result that he or she wants to reach.

Where the buyer has fully performed its obligations when the seller's breach occurs (or becomes known to the buyer), there will be no practical significance in the distinctions between warranty and condition, as the buyer's remedy will be limited to damages measured by the compensation principle. In these situations there is a tendency to simply refer to the term that has been breached as a "warranty".

Solicitors drafting an asset or share purchase of a business will use words like "representation", "warranty" and "condition" in a precise and technical fashion, in senses that are widely accepted by lawyers but with consequences that are usually clearly spelled out. In this context, a representation, if false, may give rise to a claim for damages or it may provide the buyer with the opportunity to walk away from the deal. In this last situation the truthfulness of the representation (or the performance of a warranty) will have become a condition of the buyer's performance.

A special class of warranties comprises the pre-closing covenants (promises) of the seller to run its business in the period between the making of the agreement and the closing date (during which time the buyer will be completing its due diligence) in the manner specified by the buyer. The seller will, for example, usually promise not to incur any expenses out of the ordinary course of business. The seller will also often give post-closing covenants under which it might, for example, agree to buy back some of the corporation's bad debts or assist the buyer in getting any necessary permissions to complete the transaction.

In these cases the courts have no reason not to accept the consequences of the words that the parties have used. Parties must be free to determine if the occurrence of a particular event gives rise to an excuse for one party's non-performance or to a claim for damages. When the parties are not precise in stating the consequences of the event, the court will have to determine what should be done if a particular term is breached.

Examples of the actual use of the terms "representation", "warranty" and "covenant" are provided by the following examples in asset purchase agreements:

5.01   *Representations and Warranties by the Seller*

The Seller hereby represents and warrants to the Buyer as follows, and acknowledges that the Buyer is relying upon the accuracy of each of the representations and warranties in connection with the purchase of the Purchased Assets and the completion of the other transactions hereunder. . . .

The list that will follow such an opening will cover many pages and a wide range of topics, from a statement that the books have been kept in accordance with the usual accounting standards to a statement that there has been full disclosure of all material facts.

6.01   *Covenants by the Seller*

The Seller hereby covenants to the Purchaser that it will do or cause to be done the following: . . .

(4)   Evidence Concerning Satisfaction of Representations, Warranties and Covenants of the Seller

At the Closing Time, the Seller shall deliver to the Purchaser such certificates of the Seller and certificates or statutory declarations of senior officers of the Seller as the Purchaser may reasonably think necessary establishing that, as of the Closing Date,

(i)   the representations and warranties of the Seller contained in this agreement are true and accurate and not misleading in any respect. . . .

7.01   *Conditions for the Benefit of the Purchaser*

Notwithstanding anything herein contained, the obligations of the Purchaser to complete the purchase of the Purchased Assets and to carry out the other transactions provided for by this agreement will be subject to the fulfillment of each of the following conditions at or before the Closing Time, and the Seller hereby covenants to perform and comply with each of the conditions and to cause each condition to be performed and complied with and fulfilled to the extent that the condition relates to matters within the control of the Seller:

(1) Accuracy of Representations and Warranties

The representations and warranties of the Seller contained herein shall be true and correct in all material respects as at the Closing Time, with the same force and effect as if made at and as of the Closing Time, and the Purchaser shall have received a certificate from a senior officer of the Seller confirming that such representations and warranties are true and correct as at the Closing Time.

At first glance it may appear that the solicitor who drafted this agreement — it will, in fact, be a template on the solicitor's (or his or her firm's) word-processor, to be used by the solicitor for the buyer as the model from which the actual first draft of the agreement will be produced — is using a "belt-and-suspenders approach", *i.e.*, using every term that he or she can think of. That conclusion would not, however, be correct: the solicitor is using the words "representation" and "warranty" very precisely. The use of the word "covenant" is simply a conventional word to describe a special class of undertakings common in all business acquisition agreements.

The transformation of the representations and warranties into what are, in effect, conditions in paragraph 7.01(1), illustrates the desire of the buyer's solicitor to make sure that his or her client does not have to pay the price if there is any risk that the buyer will not be getting exactly what it expected.

Judges are sometimes quite casual about their use of terms "representation", "warranty" and even "condition", and it is important to appreciate the limitations, arbitrariness and confusion surrounding them. The classification process is often arbitrary, and in many cases not very helpful. What is important to understand is that there is a range of remedies that a buyer may seek if it is disappointed in the deal that it made with the seller. Sometimes being excused from performance (or further performance) is all that is necessary to protect the buyer. In other situations, the buyer needs a damage award if it is to be compensated for the loss it has suffered. As has been mentioned, the job of the buyer's counsel will be to offer the court a "peg" on which to hang an argument to justify the remedy sought by the client.

In other words, clients can plan their relations with others by using express conditions or by making the seller promise in a warranty that the goods being bought are of some specified quality. Not infrequently, however, the classification will be done by counsel and the court only after the deal has collapsed, and it will, moreover, be done to support or deny the buyer's claim to relief.

The interrelation of representations and warranties on the one hand and conditions on the other is illustrated by the arguments made in *Transamerica Life Canada Inc. v. ING Canada Inc.*, [2003] O.J. No. 4656, 68 O.R. (3d) 457, 234 D.L.R. (4th) 367 (C.A.). The plaintiff had bought all of the shares of a life insurance company from the defendant. After the transaction had closed, the plaintiff sued for damages for breach of representations and warranties about the company's financial statements. The defendant pleaded that the plaintiff knew all the facts before it closed the deal and should have brought the matter up prior to closing so that the purchase price could have been adjusted. In particular, the defendant pleaded that the buyer had breached an implied obligation of good faith owed to the seller, by not notifying the seller of its concerns prior to the closing. The motions judge had struck out these allegations in the seller's pleadings. The Court of Appeal held, reversing the trial judge, that the allegations should not be struck out; the defendant was entitled to argue that the buyer had breached an implied obligation of good faith. The Court of Appeal accepted that there was sufficient uncertainty about the legal existence of a duty of good faith to merit a trial on this issue.

The facts of *Transamerica Life* illustrate a common bone of contention between solicitors drafting an agreement. The question is whether the buyer can close the deal, knowing that there are misrepresentations or breaches of warranty, and then sue for damages, or bring the deficiencies or breaches up at the time they are discovered and have them dealt with in the context of the negotiations or used as an excuse for the buyer's non-performance. In practical terms, the question is whether the buyer may "ambush" the seller by raising the question of deficiencies only after the closing. In order to prevent an ambush, a seller may try to insert a "no-ambush" clause in the agreement.

Misrepresentations

Outside those situations where the agreement in question has been carefully drafted by solicitors, the law is much less tidy. In general, the remedy for breach of an *innocent misrepresentation* is limited to rescission of the contract. Rescission for an innocent misrepresentation is subject to an important qualification, namely, that the remedy must be promptly sought. The nineteenth-century rule was that rescission had to be sought before both parties had performed the contract. This rule was sometimes expressed by saying that the remedy had to be sought before the contract was executed. Relief for breach of warranty can, however, be sought even after performance, but is limited to expectation-based damages.

Another distinction between misrepresentations and warranties lies in the relation between the time at which the remedy is sought and the seriousness of the breach that is alleged. The law can be seen as expressing the common sense idea that the longer a buyer waits to assert a right to a remedy, the more serious the breach must be for relief to be given. Conversely, the sooner a buyer claims to be disappointed by the seller's performance and seeks relief, the easier it will be to argue that the seller assumed the risk that the buyer would not be disappointed. In general, if a buyer wants a remedy late in the deal or after the performance of both parties has been completed, the buyer will face greater difficulties in establishing that the statement was a warranty rather than a misrepresentation. Once the buyer's performance has occurred, it is pointless to worry about a condition or the occurrence of a "*Hongkong Fir* event" because the only remedy that will be of any use to the buyer is a claim for damages.

In addition to the timeliness of the disappointed party's assertion of a claim to relief, the relative ability of the parties to have prevented the loss is significant. It may be important that one party has greater or easier (often cheaper) access to the information that would eliminate or reduce the chance of disappointment. If the party who makes a false statement was in the best position to have discovered that the statement was false, this will have a significant bearing on the decision of a court to treat the statement as a warranty rather than a representation. Conversely, if a party makes a statement that is clearly a matter of opinion about an issue which both parties are equally well placed to assess, this supports the argument that it is a representation rather than a warranty.

In practice, as already mentioned, the distinction between a representation and a warranty is often "result-selective". That is, the judge determines an appropriate result, and classifies the term accordingly. The distinction is, moreover, sometimes regarded as a question of fact, so that it is appropriate for the trial judge to make this decision as part of his or her fact-finding function, and the decision is then less subject to review by an appellate court.

It can be difficult to distinguish a representation from a warranty. If the problem is dealt with as a question of fact, it is hard to see where or how that question differs from a conclusion of law. The "factual" inquiry assumes that the facts of the case — which can be sworn to by the parties or established by evidence — can support a distinction that may have no real-world existence. The "factual" element in this inquiry is as hard to deal with as the factual element about the likelihood of loss in the context of the rules of *Hadley v. Baxendale*. The policy-based judgment — the issue of what the courts want to do — ultimately provides the only sure and honest basis for any decision on the issues raised by remoteness of damages. So, too, a policy-based focus must be explicitly acknowledged if one is to make sense of the issue of the remedy given for disappointment due to a false statement made at the time of contract formation.

Some of the issues involved in the choice between misrepresentation and warranty can be seen in an example taken from one of the leading cases, *Redgrave v. Hurd* (1881), 20 Ch. D. 1. The plaintiff, a solicitor, advertised his practice, which was in Birmingham, for sale. The defendant expressed an interest in purchasing it. The vendor, who wanted to retire, insisted that the purchaser buy his house as well as the practice. The purchaser met the vendor and enquired whether the practice was profitable; to satisfy the purchaser, the vendor showed him a collection of papers that he said indicated a practice bringing in about £300 per year. The purchaser did not examine the papers closely, but was satisfied with the oral statement of the vendor. A careful examination of the papers by the purchaser would have revealed that the vendor's statement about the income of the practice was false. A written agreement was made that the purchaser would buy the vendor's house for £1,600, and the purchaser paid a deposit of £100. The vendor was unwilling to have any written contract about the sale of the practice, though it was understood that the £1,600 was for the sale of both the house and the practice. Before the purchaser had paid more than part of the price, but after he had taken possession of the house, the purchaser discovered that the practice was bringing in less than £200 a year. He refused to complete the deal. The vendor sued for specific performance of the agreement of purchase and sale of the house.

The court held that the vendor had misrepresented the income from the practice. This misrepresentation was held to be "innocent" and not fraudulent — as discussed later, establishing proof of fraud is difficult. The remedy for such an innocent misrepresentation is the right of the purchaser to have the agreement rescinded. "Rescission" as used in this sense is a decree of a court of equity setting aside an agreement. The effect of the decree is that the parties are put back in the position that they would have been in had the agreement never been made.

There are two principal limitations on the remedy of rescission. First, the promisee must be able to give back that which he got from the promisor: the promisee must be able to make *restitutio in integrum*, *i.e.*, restoration to the former state. The second limitation is that the promisee cannot get reliance (or expectation) damages; he can only get back what he paid the promisor — that is, the amount by which the promisor would be enriched if it were allowed to keep what the promisee paid. This limitation arises because rescission is an equitable remedy: the Court of Chancery could not give damages, but it could set an agreement aside. On the facts of *Redgrave v. Hurd*, the purchaser recovered the deposit, but he could not recover the costs of moving his family to Birmingham from another part of England.

Had the vendor been held to be guilty of fraud (that is, had he made a fraudulent misrepresentation), the purchaser's remedies would have been rescission as well as damages for deceit. The remedy of rescission is available for both innocent and fraudulent misrepresentation. Deceit is a common law tort giving a remedy in damages. Such damages would be the usual tort measure, *i.e.*, reliance damages. Neither of these remedies is promissory in the sense that damages for breach of contract can be so described. As with equitable remedies generally, the fact that rescission may not be available (the thing having been destroyed or damaged) does not have any effect on the right of the injured party to seek a common law remedy. Such a remedy in this situation would be damages for deceit.

The basis for the interference of equity in the case of fraudulent misrepresentation is that it would be against conscience for the promisor to insist on the promisee's performance when he has misrepresented the quality of what he is selling. The basis for the tort remedy of deceit is the deliberate (or reckless) misrepresentation of the facts by the promisor.

Fraud is, however, a serious allegation to make, since it involves an allegation of serious wrongdoing and may involve a criminal offence. Even in civil cases, the courts insist on clear evidence that the defendant intended to mislead the plaintiff. The usual requirement for fraud is that the false representation must have been made "knowingly, or without belief in its truth, or recklessly, careless whether it be true or false." This requirement was established in *Derry v. Peek* (1889), 13 App. Cas. 337 (H.L.), in the speech of Lord Herschell. Because the allegation of fraud may affect a person's reputation, a party who alleges fraud but is unable to establish it may be penalized in costs, even if otherwise successful in the case. On the other hand, if fraud is proven, the court may well consider that this is the type of reprehensible conduct that merits exemplary or punitive damages or an award of full or substantial indemnity costs (*i.e.*, what used to be called "solicitor and client" costs) in addition to whatever damages are awarded.

The result in *Derry v. Peek*, *viz.*, the imposition of a very high threshold for a finding of fraud, has been resisted on several fronts, as it appears to protect apparently blameworthy parties. Parliament quickly overturned the actual result by statute (see *Directors Liability Act, 1890*, 53 & 54 Vict. c. 64). This statute, in turn, influenced James Landis and others when they drafted the American *Securities Act of 1933*. Judges also resisted the result in *Derry v. Peek*. The most famous example of this is Lord Haldane's speech in *Nocton v. Lord Ashburton*, [1914] A.C. 932 (H.L.), where he held that the *Derry v. Peek* standard for a finding of fraud did not apply to relations that were historically protected by equity.

There is another possible limitation on the right of a promisee to get rescission for innocent misrepresentation. The traditional rule is that the remedy for innocent misrepresentation has to be sought before the contract had been executed or fully performed by both parties — that is, relief is available only while the contract remained executory. If the purchaser in *Redgrave v. Hurd* had completed the deal by paying the full price of the house, he would not have been entitled to rescission on the ground of innocent misrepresentation, and as the vendor was not guilty of fraud, the purchaser would have had no remedy in damages.

The courts have taken a number of different approaches to mitigate the rigour of the traditional rule that there is no remedy for an innocent misrepresentation after execution.

There are a large number of cases on the issue of whether a contract remains executory, and hence whether there is still a right to relief for an innocent misrepresentation. The cases are not easily reconciled with each other. In some cases the courts have been concerned with a technical test: has the deal been completed in the legal sense, for example, by the transfer of a cheque? In other cases the courts have been more concerned with completion in a broader sense: has everything been done under the agreement that the parties promised to do? In *Redican v. Nesbitt*, [1924] S.C.R. 135, [1924] 1 D.L.R. 536, the vendor's agent made certain representations about a leasehold property, in particular that it was electrically lighted. The purchaser was not able to inspect the property until two days after the purchase price was paid, the documents executed and the keys handed over. She then discovered that the house was not lighted by electricity. The trial judge held that there could be no relief for the innocent misrepresentation since the contract was "executed" upon delivery of the purchase price in exchange for the keys and the title documents.

In some more recent cases the courts are more inclined to give relief and they have taken a more flexible approach in deciding when the remedy for an innocent misrepresentation will no longer be available. In *Ennis v. Klassen* (1990), 70 D.L.R. (4th) 321, [1990] 4 W.W.R. 609 (Man. C.A.), the plaintiff bought a car described as a "BMW 733i" from the defendant. In fact, the car was a different, inferior model of BMW. The plaintiff paid the price, took delivery and registered the car in his name. Three days after taking delivery, the plaintiff learned of the misdescription and sought rescission. The action was dismissed at trial, but the Manitoba Court of Appeal granted rescission. The Court of Appeal recognized the principle that "rescission ceases to be available where the contract has been accepted" but limited the effect of this traditional doctrine by saying that in the case of a sale of goods "in most instances [this] will mean after the passage of a reasonable period of time for the purchaser to determine whether representations are true."

Another approach to avoiding the harshness of the traditional rule denying relief for an innocent misrepresentation after execution has been by a broadening of the remedy of warranty or, more precisely, by a greater willingness of the courts to find a warranty that in the past might have been treated as misrepresentation. Relief for misrepresentation has also come from another direction with the development of the tort of negligent misrepresentation causing pure economic loss.

The development of the law of mistake may now also give a remedy in situations where there may have been no relief a hundred years ago. Courts may sometimes find that a "mistake" has deprived the buyer of substantially the whole benefit the contract was to have provided. A mistake of this kind is sometimes referred to as an "error *in substantialibus*" — the Latin phrase is a clear indication of the fact that the court's conclusion is based on criteria that the court does not want to disclose or discuss (because no one knows exactly what the expression means) — and the instances of it arise principally in real estate transactions. See, e.g., *Holmes v. Walker*, *infra*. The effect of such a mistake is to provide the buyer with an excuse to avoid the contract even after the property has been transferred. The effect of the mistake is even more drastic than that of a *Hongkong Fir* event because the transaction will be unwound. These developments will be more fully explored later in this chapter. One consequence of their availability is that claims for rescission for innocent misrepresentation are comparatively rare now.

As you read the materials that follow, consider whether the courts classify the undertaking and then decide on the remedy, or decide on the remedy (or on the desirability of a remedy) and then classify the undertaking appropriately. Consider also how you would, had you had the chance to have advised either party when the contract was being negotiated, have avoided the problems that arose in each of the following cases.

The next four cases explore the development of the law governing innocent misrepresentation and breach of warranty.

HEILBUT, SYMONS & CO. v. BUCKLETON

[1913] A.C. 30
(H.L., Viscount Haldane L.C., Lords Atkinson and Moulton)

[The defendant was a stock underwriter or promoter who was selling shares in a new rubber company, at a time when there was a rubber boom. The plaintiff telephoned Johnston, a representative of the defendant, and the following conversation took place.

Buckleton: "I understand you are bringing out a rubber company."

Johnston: "We are."

Buckleton: "Is it all right?"

Johnston: "We are bringing it out."

Buckleton: "That is good enough for me."

The plaintiff explained in his evidence in chief that his reason for being willing to do this was that the position the defendants occupied in the rubber trade was of such high standing that "any company they should see fit to bring out was a sufficient warranty" to him "that it was all right in every respect". Afterwards, as the result of the conversation, a large number of shares were allotted to the plaintiff by the defendant pursuant to a written contract. No written statements were made about the company by the defendant, though the company issued its own written prospectus.

Later on it was discovered that there was a large deficiency in the rubber trees that were said in the company's prospectus to exist on the company's plantations, and the shares fell in value. There is no doubt that the plaintiff would have had an action against the company based on the false statements in the prospectus, but it was bankrupt. The plaintiff brought an action against the defendant for fraudulent misrepresentation, and alternatively for damages for breach of a warranty that the company was a "rubber company" — that is, a company whose main object was to produce rubber. The plaintiff had bought 6,000 shares, which ultimately were worthless, and the plaintiff sued the defendant.

The jury found:

(1)   that the company could not properly be described as a rubber company;

(2)   that the defendants did not make a fraudulent representation; but that

(3)   they did warrant that it was a rubber company.

No appeal was taken against the second finding. The appeal was limited to the other two findings.]

LORD MOULTON [after stating the facts continued]: — [1] The alleged warranty rested entirely upon the following evidence. The plaintiff got a friend to ring up on the telephone Mr. Johnston (a representative of the defendants, for whose acts they accept the full responsibility) to tell him that the plaintiff wished to speak to him. The plaintiff's evidence continues thus: "I went to the telephone and I said 'Is that you, Johnston?' He said, 'Yes.' I said, 'I understand that you are bringing out a rubber company,' and he said, 'We are.'"

[2]   The material part of the evidence ends here. . . .

[3]   The plaintiff then asked if he could have some shares.

[4]   There is no controversy between the parties as to certain points of fact and of law . . . [T]here [is no] controversy as to the legal nature of that which the plaintiff must establish. He must shew a warranty, *i.e.*, a contract collateral to the main contract to take the shares, whereby the defendants in consideration of the plaintiff taking the shares promised that the company itself was a rubber company. The question in issue is whether there was any evidence that such a contract was made between the parties.

[5]   It is evident, both on principle and on authority, that there may be a contract the consideration for which is the making of some other contract. "If you will make such and such a contract I will give you one hundred pounds," is in every sense of the word a complete legal contract. It is collateral to the main contract, but each has an independent existence, and they do not differ in respect of their

possessing to the full the character and status of a contract. But such collateral contracts must from their very nature be rare. The effect of a collateral contract such as that which I have instanced would be to increase the consideration of the main contract by £100, and the more natural and usual way of carrying this out would be by so modifying the main contract and not by executing a concurrent and collateral contract. Such collateral contracts, the sole effect of which is to vary or add to the terms of the principal contract, are therefore viewed with suspicion by the law. They must be proved strictly. Not only the terms of such contracts but the existence of an *animus contrahendi* on the part of all the parties to them must be clearly shewn. Any laxity on these points would enable parties to escape from the full performance of the obligations of contracts unquestionably entered into by them and more especially would have the effect of lessening the authority of written contracts by making it possible to vary them by suggesting the existence of verbal collateral agreements relating to the same subject-matter.

[6]   There is in the present case an entire absence of any evidence to support the existence of such a collateral contract. The statement of Mr. Johnston in answer to plaintiff's question was beyond controversy a mere statement of fact, for it was in reply to a question for information and nothing more. No doubt it was a representation as to fact, and indeed it was the actual representation upon which the main case of the plaintiff rested. It was this representation which he alleged to have been false and fraudulent and which he alleged induced him to enter into the contracts and take the shares. There is no suggestion throughout the whole of his evidence that he regarded it as anything but a representation. Neither the plaintiff nor the defendants were asked any question or gave any evidence tending to shew the existence of any *animus contrahendi* other than as regards the main contracts. The whole case for the existence of a collateral contract therefore rests on the mere fact that the statement was made as to the character of the company, and if this is to be treated as evidence sufficient to establish the existence of a collateral contract of the kind alleged the same result must follow with regard to any other statement relating to the subject-matter of a contract made by a contracting party prior to its execution. This would negative entirely the firmly established rule that an innocent representation gives no right to damages. It would amount to saying that the making of any representation prior to a contract relating to its subject-matter is sufficient to establish the existence of a collateral contract that the statement is true and therefore to give a right to damages if such should not be the case.

[7]   In the history of English law we find many attempts to make persons responsible in damages by reason of innocent misrepresentations, and at times it has seemed as though the attempts would succeed. On the Chancery side of the Court the decisions favouring this view usually took the form of extending the scope of the action for deceit. There was a tendency to recognize the existence of what was sometimes called "legal fraud," *i.e.*, that the making of an incorrect statement of fact without reasonable grounds, or of one which was inconsistent with information which the person had received or had the means of obtaining, entailed the same legal consequences as making it fraudulently. Such a doctrine would make a man liable for forgetfulness or mistake or even for honestly interpreting the facts known to him or drawing conclusions from them in a way which the Court did not think to be legally warranted. . . . The opinions pronounced in your Lordships' House in [*Derry v. Peek*] shew that both in substance and in form the decision was, and was intended to be, a reaffirmation of the old common-law doctrine that

actual fraud was essential to an action for deceit, and it finally settled the law that an innocent misrepresentation gives no right of action sounding in damages.

[8]   On the Common Law side of the Court the attempts to make a person liable for an innocent misrepresentation have usually taken the form of attempts to extend the doctrine of warranty beyond its just limits and to find that a warranty existed in cases where there was nothing more than an innocent misrepresentation. The present case is, in my opinion, an instance of this. But in respect of the question of the existence of a warranty the Courts have had the advantage of an admirable enunciation of the true principle of law which was made in very early days by Holt C.J. with respect to the contract of sale. He says: "An affirmation at the time of the sale is a warranty, provided it appear on evidence to be so intended." [*Medina v. Stoughton* (1700), 1 Salk. 210, 91 E.R. 188.] So far as decisions are concerned, this has, on the whole, been consistently followed in the Courts of Common Law. . . . A still more serious deviation from the correct principle is to be found in a passage in the judgment of the Court of Appeal in *De Lassalle v. Guildford*, [1901] 2 K.B. 215, which was cited to us in the argument in the present case. In discussing the question whether a representation amounts to a warranty or not the judgment says: "In determining whether it was so intended, a decisive test is whether the vendor assumes to assert a fact of which the buyer is ignorant, or merely states an opinion or judgment upon a matter of which the vendor has no special knowledge, and on which the buyer may be expected also to have an opinion and to exercise his judgment."

[9]   With all deference to the authority of the Court that decided that case, the proposition which it thus formulates cannot be supported. It is clear that the Court did not intend to depart from the law laid down by Holt C.J. and cited above, for in the same judgment that dictum is referred to and accepted as a correct statement of the law. It is, therefore, evident that the use of the phrase "decisive test" cannot be defended. Otherwise it would be the duty of a judge to direct a jury that if a vendor states a fact of which the buyer is ignorant, they must, as a matter of law, find the existence of a warranty, whether or not the totality of the evidence shews that the parties intended the affirmation to form part of the contract; and this would be inconsistent with the law as laid down by Holt C.J. It may well be that the features thus referred to in the judgment of the Court of Appeal in that case may be criteria of value in guiding a jury in coming to a decision whether or not a warranty was intended; but they cannot be said to furnish decisive tests, because it cannot be said as a matter of law that the presence or absence of those features is conclusive of the intention of the parties. The intention of the parties can only be deduced from the totality of the evidence, and no secondary principles of such a kind can be universally true.

[10]   It is, my Lords, of the greatest importance, in my opinion, that this House should maintain in its full integrity the principle that a person is not liable in damages for an innocent misrepresentation, no matter in what way or under what form the attack is made. In the present case the statement was made in answer to an inquiry for information. There is nothing which can by any possibility be taken as evidence of an intention on the part of either or both of the parties that there should be a contractual liability in respect of the accuracy of the statement. It is a representation as to a specific thing and nothing more. The judge, therefore, ought not to have left the question of warranty to the jury, and if, as a matter of prudence,

he did so in order to obtain their opinion in case of appeal, he ought then to have entered judgment for the defendants notwithstanding the verdict.

[**VISCOUNT HALDANE** and **LORD ATKINSON** gave judgments to the same effect.]

NOTES AND QUESTIONS

1. The plaintiff argued that in addition to the written contract to buy the shares, there was an oral contract based on an implicit promise by the vendor in the form: "We promise that, if you buy the shares, they are shares of a rubber company." It is in this sense that the warranty is regarded as a "collateral contract." It is this other contract that Lord Moulton refused to find on the facts.

   The parol evidence rule requires the court to conclude that there is a warranty only if the oral assertion constitutes a contract "collateral" to the main written contract. The consideration given for the collateral warranty would be the buyer's agreement to enter into the main contract of sale.

2. *Heilbut, Symons & Co. v. Buckleton* is still regarded as a leading case on the law of warranties and it is frequently cited, though the law has evolved significantly, as the cases set out below indicate. The narrow view of warranties that *Heilbut Symons* articulates is typical of decisions of the nineteenth and early twentieth century that restricted liability and favoured sellers.

3. Lord Moulton's judgment is one of the clearest statements of the principle of *caveat emptor*. Had the courts adopted the argument rejected by Lord Moulton, perhaps we would not have needed as much of the expensive machinery of the various provincial securities commissions as we now have. The extensive disclosure requirements under the *Securities Acts* and the various *Business Corporations Acts* have made people dealing in the purchase and sale of both shares and business assets accustomed to full disclosure.

4. One impression given by the conversation between Johnston and the plaintiff is that Johnston was being "cute". He carefully avoided answering the crucial question asked by the purchaser: "Is it all right?" Such conduct would clearly be a breach of the present statutory obligations of disclosure on investment dealers and stockbrokers.

5. On its actual facts, the decision in *Heilbut, Symons & Co. v. Buckleton* has been overtaken by other developments in the law. The law regarding the information that a potential investor must have is now found in the securities legislation of the provinces. Generally, new issues of shares must be accompanied by a prospectus. The contents of the prospectus and its accuracy and completeness will be reviewed by a securities commission. The issuer, promoter and underwriter (someone in the position of the defendant in *Heilbut*) are liable for any misrepresentations in the prospectus (including omissions that make what is included misleading).

   In addition, the purchaser has the right to get out of the deal for any or no reason if he moves to do so within some short period (often 48 hours) after receipt of a prospectus. The obligation to disclose in a prospectus is stated in, for example, the *Securities Act*, R.S.O. 1990, c. S.5:

   > 56(1) A prospectus shall provide full, true and plain disclosure of all material facts relating to the securities issued or proposed to be distributed and shall comply with the requirements of Ontario securities law.

   > 58(1) ... a prospectus filed under subsection 53 (1) or subsection 62 (1) shall contain a certificate in the following form, signed by the chief executive officer, the chief financial officer, and, on behalf of the board of directors, any two directors of the issuer, other than the foregoing, duly authorized to sign, and any person or company who is a promoter of the issuer:

The foregoing constitutes full, true and plain disclosure of all material facts relating to the securities offered by this prospectus as required by Part XV of the *Securities Act* and the regulations thereunder.

It is an indication of the seriousness with which these undertakings are regarded by securities commissions in Canada and by the Securities and Exchange Commission in the United States that directors and officers may not be indemnified by the corporation in respect of their liability under these provisions.

6. The standard language of asset and share purchase agreements frequently adopts an approach that is strongly based on the statutory provisions. The following clause is taken from such a standard contract:

    Full Disclosure

    None of the foregoing representations and statements of fact contains any untrue statement of material fact or omits to state any material fact necessary to make any such statement or representation not misleading to a prospective purchaser of the Business seeking full information as to the Business, its assets and liabilities.

7. One consequence of the enactment of securities legislation and the routine use of clauses like the "full disclosure" clause is that the traditional common law attitude to non-disclosure, as opposed to mis-disclosure — generally treating the former as less serious than the latter — becomes less defensible. The risks that now arise from unknown environmental hazards when purchasing or taking over (for example, after a default on a mortgage) land makes everyone much more conscious about disclosure.

    What, for example, would you do if:

    (a) your client, the seller of a business, has indicated that she is unwilling to sign a contract containing the "Full Disclosure" clause set out above, and you have been asked to negotiate its removal from the buyer's draft contract?

    (b) you are asked by your client, the buyer, for advice in a situation where the seller has indicated an unwillingness to sign an agreement with the standard "full disclosure" language?

8. Should the courts take any notice of the development of such statutory liability in deciding whether the law should "lean" in favour of or against giving some kind of protection? Does the next case show how such a change in attitude may be achieved?

DICK BENTLEY PRODUCTIONS LTD. v. HAROLD SMITH MOTORS LTD.

[1965] 2 All E.R. 65, [1965] 1 W.L.R. 623
(C.A., Lord Denning M.R., Danckwerts and Salmon L.JJ.)

[The plaintiff bought a car from the defendant, a car dealership. The representative of the defendant told the plaintiff before the purchase was completed that the car had been owned by a German Baron and had been driven only 20,000 miles since its engine had been replaced. The representative of the defendant had told the plaintiff that he was in a position to find out the history of the cars he sold. The purchase price was £1,850. The car was a considerable disappointment to the plaintiff, and had actually been driven 100,000 miles since the engine had been replaced. Eventually the plaintiff brought an action for breach of warranty. The trial judge found that there was a warranty which had been breached, and awarded damages based on the difference in value between a car whose engine had 20,000 miles on it and one that had gone 100,000 miles on it. The vendor appealed. After summarizing the facts, **LORD DENNING M.R.** continued:]

[1] The first point is whether this representation, namely that the car had done twenty thousand miles only since it had been fitted with a replacement engine and gearbox, was an innocent misrepresentation (which does not give rise to damages), or whether it was a warranty. It was said by Holt C.J. (*supra*), and repeated in *Heilbut, Symons v. Buckleton*: "An affirmation at the time of the sale is a warranty, provided it appear on evidence to be so intended." But that word "intended" has given rise to difficulties . . . [T]he question whether a warranty was intended depends on the conduct of the parties, on their words and behaviour, rather than on their thoughts. If an intelligent bystander would reasonably infer that a warranty was intended, that will suffice. What conduct, then, what words and behaviour lead to the inference of a warranty?

[2] Looking at the cases once more, as we have done so often, it seems to me that if a representation is made in the course of dealings for a contract for the very purpose of inducing the other party to act on it, and it actually induces him to act on it by entering into the contract, that is prima facie ground for inferring that the representation was intended as a warranty. It is not necessary to speak of it as being collateral. Suffice it that the representation was intended to be acted on and was in fact acted on. But the maker of the representation can rebut this inference if he can show that it really was an innocent misrepresentation, in that he was in fact innocent of fault in making it, and that it would not be reasonable in the circumstances for him to be bound by it. In *Oscar Chess* [*Ltd. v. Williams*, [1957] 1 All E.R. 325, [1957] 1 W.L.R. 370], the inference was rebutted. There a man had bought a second-hand car and received with it a log-book, which stated the year of the car, 1948. He afterwards resold the car. When he resold it he simply repeated what was in the log-book and passed it on to the buyer. He honestly believed on reasonable grounds that it was true. He was completely innocent of any fault. There was no warranty by him but only an innocent misrepresentation. Whereas in the present case it is very different. The inference is not rebutted. Here we have a dealer, Mr. Smith, who was in a position to know, or at least to find out, the history of the car. He could get it by writing to the makers. He did not do so. Indeed it was done later. When the history of this car was examined, his statement turned out to be quite wrong. He ought to have known better. There was no reasonable foundation for it.

[**LORD DENNING M.R.** summarized the history of the car, and continued:]

[3] The county court judge found that the representations were not dishonest. Mr. Smith was not guilty of fraud. But he made the statement as to twenty thousand miles without any foundation. And the judge was well justified in finding that there was a warranty. He said: "I have no hesitation that as a matter of law the statement was a warranty. Mr. Smith stated a fact that should be within his own knowledge. He had jumped to a conclusion and stated it as a fact. A fact that a buyer would act on." That is ample foundation for the inference of a warranty. So much for this point. I hold that the appeal fails and should be dismissed.

[**DANCKWERTS** and **SALMON L.JJ.** agreed.]

QUESTIONS AND NOTES

1. What changed between *Heilbut* (decided in 1913) and *Dick Bentley* (1965) to justify or explain the difference in judicial attitude?

2. If you had the chance to cross-examine Johnston, the defendant's salesman in *Heilbut*, what questions would you ask him in the light of Lord Denning's judgment in *Dick Bentley*?

3. In *Dick Bentley Productions,* Lord Denning noted the importance of relative knowledge as a factor in deciding whether a statement is a warranty. The relative knowledge of the parties is now accepted as a significant factor in determining whether a statement is a warranty. However, the absence of fault as a basis for rebutting a claim that a statement is a warranty has generally not been accepted. S.M. Waddams, *The Law of Contracts*, 5th ed. (Aurora, Ont.: Canada Law Book, 2005), ¶ 407 comments:

    > The question of fault is clearly quite unrelated to contractual intention and its introduction in this context was, no doubt, influenced by the then recent development of an action in tort for damages for negligent misrepresentations. Fault, however, does not seem a satisfactory test. In cases where the seller is enriched by a representation the buyer should have the right to restitution of the enrichment even if the seller was careful. On the other hand, other kinds of damages for breach of warranty, in particular damages based on the buyer's expectation or consequential damages . . . may not be justified, at least against a non-business seller, even if the latter can be said to be negligent.

    Professor Waddams offers no citations to support his position on the extent of damages for breach of warranty in these situations (set out in the last three sentences of this quotation). Do you agree with him?

The importance of what the court wants to do is illustrated by the following case.

FRASER-REID v. DROUMTSEKAS

[1980] S.C.J. No. 125, [1980] 1 S.C.R. 720, 103 D.L.R. (3d) 385
(S.C.C., Martland, Ritchie, Dickson, Estey and McIntyre JJ.)

DICKSON J. delivered the judgment of the Court: —

[1]   Although the common-law doctrine of *caveat emptor* has long since ceased to play any significant part in the sale of goods, it has lost little of its pristine force in the sale of land. In 1931, a breach was created in the doctrine that the buyer must beware, with recognition by an English Court of an implied warranty of fitness for habitation in the sale of an *uncompleted* house. The breach has since been opened a little wider in some of the States of the United States by extending the warranty to *completed* houses when the seller is the builder and the defect is latent. Otherwise, notwithstanding new methods of house merchandising and, in general, increased concern for consumer protection, *caveat emptor* remains a force to be reckoned with by the credulous or indolent purchaser of housing property. Lacking express warranties, he may be in difficulty because there is no implied warranty of fitness for human habitation upon the purchase of a house already completed at the time of sale. The rationale stems from the *laissez-faire* attitudes of the eighteenth and nineteenth centuries and the notion that a purchaser must fend for himself, seeking protection by express warranty or by independent examination of the premises. If he fails to do either, he is without remedy either at law or in equity, in

the absence of fraud or fundamental difference between that which was bargained for and that obtained.

I

[2] The facts are unremarkable. On October 1, 1969, the plaintiffs, Dr. and Mrs. Fraser-Reid, purchased a newly completed house in the City of Waterloo from Ken Droumtsekas Construction Limited, a builder-vendor. The following spring, serious basement flooding occurred. Thereafter, every heavy rain brought more water into the basement. The agreement of purchase and sale contained the following provision:

> This transaction of purchase and sale is to be completed on or before the 1st day of November, 1969, on which date vacant possession of the Real Property is to be given to the Purchaser, unless otherwise provided herein.

> *Providing that the Vendor has disclosed to the Purchaser all outstanding infractions* and orders requiring work to be done on the premises issued by any Municipal or Provincial or Federal Authority *in respect to the premises referred to herein.* (Italics added.)

[3] At the material time, s. 13B of the building by-law of the City of Waterloo provided:

> Unless otherwise permitted by the authority having jurisdiction, all exterior foundation walls shall be drained by drainage tile or pipe laid around the exterior of the foundation so that the top of the tile or pipe is below the bottom of the floor slab or crawl space floor.

[4] The agreement of purchase and sale contained an exclusion clause in these terms:

> It is agreed that there is no representation, warranty, collateral agreement or condition affecting this agreement or the real property or supported hereby other than as expressed herein in writing.

[The trial judge found (a) that there was no express warranty; (b) that, based on the distinction between completed and uncompleted houses, there was no implied warranty; (c) that the defendant was in breach of the building code in not installing weeping tile; and (d) that damages should be assessed at $4,412.78. The Ontario Court of Appeal dismissed the purchasers' appeal. **DICKSON J.** disposed of the argument that there could be an express warranty based on the builder's statement that he "built good houses and this is a good house". This statement was dismissed as "mere trade puffery". An argument was also raised at the Supreme Court that there was liability in negligence, but this was dismissed for being raised too late in the proceedings. **DICKSON J.** continued:]

V

[5] The case is accordingly narrowed to (i) implied warranty, and (ii) express warranty, in the provision of the sale agreement quoted earlier. As to implied warranty, the appellants argue that the house was not, in fact, completed at the time of purchase. This runs counter to the explicit finding of the judge at trial, who found the deficiencies in the construction of the house to be "evidence of faulty workmanship, not of incompleteness" and thus "the house which was purchased on October 1, 1969, was a completed house." The sale agreement does not mention any work to be completed other than sodding. I would not be prepared to alter the judge's finding. . . .

[6]   The appellants must rest their case for implied warranty upon the novel proposition stated in their factum:

> It is respectfully submitted that there is implied by law, in the sale of a new, unoccu-
> pied home, where the vendor is also the builder with special knowledge of the
> method of construction that the home: (1) was built in compliance with all applica-
> ble building by-laws, (2) was built in a good and workmanlike manner, (3) would be
> fit for human habitation.

[7]   To support this proposition, the appellants look to American authority.

[8]   American case law has tended to give recognition to the change in the housing market from the pre-war situation in which a prospective house owner bought
a lot, engaged an architect, and then hired a contractor to construct, to the post-war
position in which the great bulk of housing is mass-produced, according to sample
or "show-house," and sold by the builder-vendor. . . .

[9]   The American case law upon which the appellants must rely, however, is far
from consistent . . . There is, however, a distinct trend towards convergence of
traditional products-liability principles and those applying to new homes. The shift
countenanced in the American Courts has been to take the English principles applicable to a home under construction and to extend those principles to completed
houses, but only where the seller of the house is also the developer or builder and
the house is a new unoccupied house. . . . It has specifically not been extended to
the case of an unoccupied home sold by one owner to a new owner.

[10]   There has been some criticism of the resulting confusion of the American
Courts in handling these cases. In a useful review of the trend up to 1966 by Roberts, "The Case of the Unwary Home Buyer: The Housing Merchant Did It"
(1967), 52 *Cornell L. Rev.* 835, the author points up the simple fact that the Courts
have found it easier to abolish the rule of *caveat emptor* in new home sales than to
elaborate a new set of rules to guarantee some predictability in the ambit and content of the warranties applicable to the industry. In the result, Roberts argues that
the complexity of the warranty required necessitates legislative intervention, and
warns of the impact upon the structure of the housing industry, and the cost of
homes, of a wide-ranging warranty in such situations.

[11]   At the same time, it must be observed that the decided English and Canadian
cases in this area point up the irrationality and odd results derived from the rigid
"completed/incomplete" distinction. Take the case of the prospective home buyer
who views a model home in a subdivision development and decides to buy a house
yet to be built on a lot in that subdivision. In his case, the Courts will be willing to
imply a warranty as to fitness for habitation and workmanship. But the unfortunate
who buys the "show" home is without warranty even if both models reveal the
same structural defects. Or, take the case of the buyer who enters into a contract
for a home that is "99 per cent complete." The Courts will imply a warranty . . .
[but had] the contract been entered into the next day, when the work was completed, there is no warranty. One can easily multiply the incongruities.

[**DICKSON J.** made reference to the *Ontario New Home Warranties Plan Act*, R.S.O. 1980, c. 350 (HUDAC), but that scheme was not in effect when this house was built.]

[12] The only real question for debate in the present case is whether removal of the irrational distinction between completed and incomplete houses is better left to legislative intervention. One can argue that *caveat emptor* was a judicial creation and what the courts created, the courts can delimit. But the complexities of the problem, the difficulties of spelling out the ambit of a court-imposed warranty, the major cost impact upon the construction industry and, in due course, upon consumers through increased house prices, all counsel judicial restraint.

[13] I would be inclined to reject the proposition advanced on behalf of the appellants for an extended implied warranty. It appears to me at this time that if the sale of a completed house by a vendor-builder is to carry a non-contractual warranty, it should be of statutory origin, and spelled out in detail. Even if the Court were to recognize an implied warranty of the amplitude urged by the appellants, here the exclusion clause contained in the agreement they signed is of such breadth that they might well be unable to avail themselves of the warranty. In the circumstances, it is unnecessary to canvass this point.

VI

[14] Finally, it is submitted that the proviso in the agreement of sale which states that the vendor has disclosed to the purchaser all outstanding infractions in respect of the premises constitutes an express warranty, breach of which entitles the plaintiffs to succeed. Two questions must be answered: (i) do the words constitute an express warranty? and if so (ii) was the warranty "merged" in the conveyance and thereby extinguished?

[15] The words "providing that" ordinarily signify or denote a limitation upon something preceding, or a condition on the performance or non-performance of which the validity of the instrument may depend. That is not invariably so. It may also affirm that a proposition of fact is true and take effect as a warranty. The mere use of a technical word should not obscure its true nature. A warranty is a term in a contract which does not go to the root of the agreement between the parties but simply expresses some lesser obligation, the failure to perform which can give rise to an action for damages, but never to the right to rescind or repudiate the contract. . . . An affirmation at the time of sale is a warranty provided it appears on the evidence to have been so intended. . . . No special form of words is necessary. [*De Lassalle v. Guildford*] . . . "It must be a collateral undertaking forming part of the contract by agreement of the parties express or implied, and must be given during the course of the dealing which leads to the bargain, and should then enter into the bargain as part of it." The assertion by the vendor of a fact of which the buyer is ignorant is a criterion of value in determining whether a warranty was intended: *Heilbut, Symons v. Buckleton* [*supra*]. In the present agreement, I would read the proviso as an undertaking or promise on the part of the vendor to disclose to the purchaser, in respect of the premises, (a) all outstanding infractions, and (b) all orders requiring work to be done on the premises issued by any municipal, or provincial, or federal authority. The clause is an assurance of compliance with statutory duty. It is an affirmation of fact and not merely a matter of opinion. The word

"infractions" obviously refers to infractions of applicable building by-laws, rules, or regulations.

[16] The respondents submit that the words "issued by any municipal . . . authority" modify not only "orders requiring work to be done," but also "infractions," and that the plaintiffs must therefore show that the infraction was issued by a municipal authority. Such a construction would be a plain distortion of language. An infraction is a breach, or violation, or infringement of a law, or duty, or contract. It is not something "issued."

[17] The clause in question here is a proviso to the provision made as to the closing date. The closing is to occur on or before November 1, 1969, providing the Vendor has disclosed to the Purchaser all infractions, etc. This is a legal duty imposed by the agreement upon the Vendor, and which he failed to perform.

[18] In the result, because of the Vendor's silence, the closing proceeded and title passed to the Purchaser, but the Purchaser was deprived of his opportunity to refuse to close. Had he been aware of the infraction he could have insisted upon the Vendor complying with the by-law before the agreement was closed. He has, therefore, suffered damage and in the amount assessed by the trial Judge.

[19] It was also contended that the words in question constituted a representation, not a warranty, and that the misrepresentation was innocently made and, therefore, not actionable. The distinction between representation and warranty is often tenuous. It is said that a representation is that which precedes and induces the contract, whereas a warranty is embodied in, and is given contemporaneously with the contract. . . .

[20] The provision in the agreement in the case at bar is, in my opinion, neither a representation nor innocent. It was a promise as to a certain state of affairs and collateral to the main purpose of the contract, which was the transfer of the property in the land. It was knowingly breached by the builder. There was an infraction of the building by-law, affecting a vital part of the building, the foundation. The breach was one which could not possibly have been discovered by ordinary inspection for the foundation had been covered up, and the defect hidden, before the sale agreement was entered into. The infraction was not disclosed to the purchaser. The words in question, in my view, constituted a warranty.

[**DICKSON J.** turned to the question of merger, *i.e.*, the argument by the defendant that any rights that the plaintiff would have had under the warranty would have merged in the conveyance of the title to the house to the plaintiff. **DICKSON J.** rejected this argument on the ground that the parties could not have intended that the warranty would cease to exist upon the conveyance. He concluded:]

[21] I would accordingly allow the appeal, set aside the judgment of the trial court and the order of the Court of Appeal, and enter judgment in favour of the appellants in the amount of $4,412.78 with costs in all courts.

QUESTIONS AND NOTES

1. Do you agree that the job of removing an "irrational" common law distinction is one for the legislature and not for the courts in the context of the law discussed in *Fraser-Reid*?

2. It is apparent that Dickson J. was strongly moved to protect the purchasers. What are the reasons for this desire? Should a judge respond to such pressures or should the protection of home purchasers be left to the legislature if protection can only be provided by distorting the common law and the parties' agreement?

3. What is the role played by the express warranty in the judgment? Is this the role the defendant expected it to play?

    At the time the Supreme Court rendered its decision in *Fraser-Reid*, the clause in question was a standard clause in real estate transactions and most real estate solicitors assumed that it only required the owner to inform a purchaser about any outstanding work orders or infraction notices that the municipality had issued to the owner. The broader interpretation given to the clause by the Supreme Court was contrary to that taken by the trial judge and the judges of Ontario Court of Appeal, who had more familiarity with standard agreements of purchase and sale of a house, and caught most real estate solicitors by surprise. Why did the Supreme Court give the clause the interpretation that it did? What advice would you, as solicitor to the builder, now give to your client, who is anxious to minimize the risks of its being similarly caught next time?

4. In the decisions in this section there is an explicit judicial allocation of the risk of loss or disappointment. An issue that is also introduced here, and further developed in Chapter 6, is the power of the parties to allocate the risk of loss by their agreement. A significant problem raised by some of the cases is whether the allocation of risk that the court imposes as a "default" allocation — the allocation that is made by the law, failing or in the absence of any allocation by the parties — is likely to upset what might be the expected allocation given the background of the deal.

In the next case, *Murray v. Sperry Rand Corp.*, the judge uses terminology that confuses representations and warranties, though his ultimate ruling is that the statements were warranties.

In *Heilbut*, a warranty is defined as a "collateral contract". Note the arguments invoked to support the conclusion that there is a contract, complete with consideration. The method used is a good example of the technique of finding a peg to hang an argument on. What really is at stake in a case like *Murray v. Sperry Rand Corp.*?

MURRAY v. SPERRY RAND CORP.

(1979), 23 O.R. (2d) 456, 96 D.L.R. (3d) 113
(H.C., Reid J.)

[The plaintiff bought a forage harvester from the defendant dealer in the products of the co-defendant manufacturer, a U.S. corporation. The machine was distributed in Canada by the Canadian subsidiary of the manufacturer and was sold through the dealer. The plaintiff bought the machine in reliance on a brochure published by the defendant manufacturer that he had picked up from a salesman employed by the dealer. The brochure said:

> You'll fine-chop forage to 3/16 of an inch . . . season after season!
>
> You'll harvest over 45 tons per hour with ease . . . Under test conditions, the big New Holland harvesters have harvested well over 60 tons per hour.
>
> And Micro-Shear cutting action gives you a choice of crop fineness — from 3/16 of an inch to 2 1/4 inches.

In a visit to the plaintiff's farm by the dealer, his salesman and a representative of the Canadian distributor, the plaintiff received assurances that the harvester would perform as described in the brochure; that it was ideally suited to the plaintiff's type of farming, and that it would do a better job than his existing machine. The plaintiff bought the machine from the dealer. The machine was not a success and, though the defendant's representatives made repeated efforts to make it work as the brochure had said it would, it only cut 16 tons per hour, not even close to the 45 tons per hour that the brochure stated that the machine would cut. As a result the plaintiff was unable to expand his farming operations and left farming. The plaintiff sued the dealer (Church), the Canadian distributor and the American manufacturer. **REID J.** set out his findings of fact and continued: —]

[1]   On the evidence I make the following findings:

(1) Plaintiff was induced to purchase the harvester through oral representations made by the personnel of Church and Sperry Rand Canada and through the sales brochure prepared and published by Sperry Rand Corporation.

(2) The performance of the machine fell seriously short of that represented in the sales brochure.

[2]   In relation to liability, the real questions in this litigation are not questions of fact. There is no doubt about the failure of the machine. It was confirmed very clearly by the evidence of both defendants. Defendants' attempts, particularly those of Sperry Rand Corporation, to blame the failure of the machine upon plaintiff were unsuccessful. There is no question in my mind that the machine failed because of an inherent defect or because the machine was not suitable for plaintiff's farming conditions, or both. Defendant manufacturer denied that the machine suffered from an inherent defect. Yet it was not able to explain why in the hands of its own people the machine would not perform properly.

(3) I find also that the consequence of the machine's failure was damage suffered by plaintiff.

[3]   *The liability of Church.* Church was a signatory to the purchase-order contract. Plaintiff was induced to sign that contract by representations made by or on behalf of Church. . . .

[4]   I am satisfied that these representations were made with the single purpose of inducing plaintiff to buy the machine.

[5]   *The representations as collateral warranties.* It has long been the law that an affirmation made with the intention of inducing contractual relations is a warranty . . . the breach of which creates liability in damages. . . .

[6]   The representations made to plaintiff were, in my opinion, collateral warranties.

[7]   The failure of the machine was a clear breach of those warranties. On that ground Church is liable to plaintiff.

[**REID J.** here examined the provisions of the *Sale of Goods Act*, R.S.O. 1970, c. 421, and concluded that under the Act (s. 15 (1) and (2)) the vendor, Church, was liable to the plaintiff. He went on to hold that the disclaimer in the contract was ineffective to protect Church.]

[8] *The liability of the manufacturer.* Sperry Rand Corporation was not a party to the written contract between plaintiff and Church. It had manufactured the harvester. It had also published the sales brochure.

[9] I refer to it as a sales brochure notwithstanding evidence from an official of Sperry Rand Corporation that it was not intended to persuade people to buy the machines it describes. That view is, in my opinion, contradicted by the brochure itself. Its tone is strongly promotional. It goes far beyond any simple intention to furnish specifications. It was, in my opinion, a sales tool. It was intended to be one and was used in this case as one.

[10] The representations contained in it, so far as they related to this litigation, have already been set out. In the circumstances of this case those representations amounted to collateral warranties given by the manufacturer.

[11] It is, in my opinion, the law that a person may be liable for breach of a warranty notwithstanding that he has no contractual relationship with the person to whom the warranty is given. . . .

[12] Dissemination of a sale brochure through dealers is a well-known and normal method of distribution for manufacturers whose products are not sold directly to the public. Through the brochure, the manufacturer presents his case to the potential customer just as directly as he would if they were sitting down together to discuss the matter.

[13] Plaintiff's purchase from the dealer in this case seems clearly to be "some other act for the benefit of the manufacturer" contemplated by McNair J. [in *Shanklin Pier Ltd. v. Detel Products Ltd.* [1951] 2 K.B. 854]. . . .

[14] I cannot see any significant difference in the situation of the . . . manufacturer in *Shanklin* . . . and the harvester manufacturer in this case.

[15] *The liability of the distributor.* It could hardly be argued that Sperry Rand Canada Ltd. was not the agent of Sperry Rand Corporation. Its liability could rest on that ground. It seems to me, however, to be a fair inference from the evidence that this defendant is directly liable as a warrantor in the same way in which I have held the manufacturer liable.

[16] Again, the evidence is not overwhelming . . .

[17] [But w]hile I recognize difficulties with this evidence, I am satisfied that this has been established on the balance of probabilities.

[18] The defendant is therefore liable to plaintiff directly for breach of warranty.

[19] *Damages.* Again, the evidence on this gave me difficulty. At this remove from the events it is not surprising that witnesses have difficulty in recalling things with exactitude. Plaintiff's claim is that his plans to board cattle on a substantial scale were frustrated and that he lost profits on this and from the sale of crops. He sold the machine itself for $4,050, for a loss of $8,550. He claims also for loss of the value of crops and for extra expenses in 1968 and 1969. His claims and how he arrived at them were gone over at length and challenged thoroughly. . . . I have, however, come to the conclusion that plaintiff has in a general way made out his claim. That is, he has proved that he did suffer the kinds of damages he claimed. On the other hand, apart from the loss on the sale of the machine, which could be exactly calculated, the other calculations that he put forward could not be accepted entirely at face value. I allow the loss on the machine at $8,550.

[20] I allow the other losses claimed at the sum of $20,000.

[21] Plaintiff is entitled to the costs of the action against all defendants.

NOTES AND QUESTIONS

1. Does the plaintiff get expectation or reliance damages?

2. In *Shanklin Pier v. Detel Products*, [1951] 2 K.B. 854, cited in *Murray v. Sperry Rand*, the plaintiffs were the owners of a pier. They wished to paint the pier and consulted the defendant, a firm of paint manufacturers. The defendant told them that its paint was suitable for the purpose, and, acting on the faith of this statement, the plaintiffs caused to be inserted in their agreement with the contractors who were to paint the pier a term requiring the use of the defendant's paint. The paint proved unsuitable and the plaintiffs sued the defendant for breach of warranty. McNair J. held that the plaintiffs were entitled to damages. In his judgment he said (p. 856):

> I see no reason why there may not be an enforceable warranty between A and B supported by the consideration that B should cause C to enter into a contract with A or that B should do some other act for the benefit of A.

Under this analysis, a manufacturer's advertising creates a "collateral warranty" by means of a unilateral contract. The manufacturer in effect promises anyone who reads and relies on the advertisement: "We promise that anyone who buys our product from a retailer that it will have the qualities set out in this advertisement." The buyer's consideration is entering the contract with the retailer, which constitutes consideration under *Scotson v. Pegg*, discussed in Chapter 2.

REVIEW PROBLEM

You act for a small Canadian corporation that has developed a very successful software program. Unfortunately, your client cannot generate the sales that the quality of its product might well justify because, as a small corporation, it does not have the reputation or resources to offer purchasers assurance that warranty and upgrade protection will be available for long enough to make an investment in the software prudent. Your client has received an offer from a major U.S. software manufacturer to purchase the software and all the business assets. In the course of negotiating the deal, the purchaser wants a warranty with respect to your client's right to transfer the copyright in the software. Your client is fairly sure that there are no copyright problems, but litigation over software, particularly very successful software, is becoming common in the U.S. and the risks of being sued are not trivial.

Outline the arguments that you would make in the course of negotiations for a more restricted undertaking — using that word in its broadest sense — on the part of your client. What are the crucial terms of the clause that you would like to see in the contract? How would you try to persuade the purchaser to accept your arguments?

Note on Discrete and Relational Contracts in Commercial Situations

It is important to consider again a distinction that permeates the law: the distinction between discrete contracts — where the only relation between the parties is a single transaction, like the sale of a business — and a relational contract — where there is a long-term economic relation such as that between a franchisor and a franchisee.

Almost all of the contracts examined in this section of the book are discrete contracts.

Major commercial contracts that involve discrete transactions are, in general, characterized by a two-stage process of completion. An asset or share purchase of a business (the latter to be distinguished from the purchase of shares on a Stock Exchange or take-over bid) provides the buyer with the opportunity, as in the purchase of real estate, to check that it is getting what it expects out of the deal. The buyer will have the opportunity to do what is called a "due diligence" examination, that is, the inspection of the assets of the business being bought. The buyer will have the chance to make a physical examination of the business, its buildings, equipment, land, etc. The buyer will also be able to check the accounting records of the seller, its list of employees, its suppliers and its customers.

A clause giving the buyer the right to its due diligence might be one like the following:

Investigation

From the date hereof to and including the Closing Date, the Seller shall permit representatives of the Buyer to make such investigation of the Purchased Assets and the Business and of the financial and legal condition of the Business as they may require or deem advisable or necessary to familiarize themselves with the Purchased Assets and Business and the Seller will assist and cooperate in any such investigation.

The Seller shall make available all books, records and documents as may be required in connection with any such investigation.

The extent to which the buyer may be permitted to do any of these things may be bargained over. (It is likely that the buyer and seller are or have been in competition and the seller may be very reluctant to give a competitor — the transaction may not, after all, be completed — access to particularly sensitive information. How much the buyer gets to see may be a function of the extent of the confidentiality agreement that the buyer signs.) The incidence of the costs involved in something as expensive as an accounting or environmental audit, *i.e.*, the check to make sure that there are no environmental "land mines", may also be the subject of negotiation.

It is customary for the buyer's solicitor to prepare the first draft of an asset purchase agreement that will be negotiated by the parties. The terms that might be offered by the buyer would be those that it would like to have in the deal. A seller may be unwilling to do other than to state that, for example, "to the best of its knowledge" certain facts are true and that it will not *promise* that they are true. The implication of such a position is that the buyer will have either to rely on the statement of the seller or satisfy itself, by using "due diligence", that the fact is true. In either situation, the buyer may not get damages if the statement is untrue. The process of settling such terms will be a very important part of the negotiations and much will depend on each solicitor's awareness of the risks facing his or her client from each formulation of the terms.

It is worth noting two observations:

(a) given the sensitive nature of the business information that is being disclosed and the fact that the deal may not be executed, it is very important to have a confidentiality agreement between the seller and buyer preventing misuse of any information that may be disclosed by the seller to a prospective buyer in the context of negotiations or the due diligence examination; and

(b) the right of buyers and lenders to require environmental audits, and extensive representations and warranties on the environmental risks of land being bought or used as collateral, may do more to improve the quality of the environment than much direct government regulatory effort.

The ability of the buyer to investigate the seller's affairs may, but probably will not, induce the buyer not to require extensive representations and warranties by the seller.

What is important about this two-stage process of completing a discrete commercial transaction is the ability of the buyer, the party that is paying money, to make sure that it gets value for it. While discrete transactions are very common, there are, in fact, few litigated cases involving asset or share purchase agreements. The typical remedy that a prospective buyer has, if its due diligence has turned up undesirable facts, is to walk away from the transaction.

In contrast, relational contracts, *viz.*, employment and management contracts, franchises, agency and distribution agreements, will usually be made and structured in very different ways from discrete contracts. There will usually be little real opportunity for due diligence (though the extent of any disclosure will depend on the particular situation and on the parties' relative bargaining strength), and the parties will generally be less concerned about disclosure at the beginning and things like representations and warranties. Once a relation has commenced, there is considerable commercial pressure to resolve differences amicably. Litigation is most likely to arise after the performance has commenced, and will focus on whether future events or the performance by one party will justify one or other of them in bringing the relation to an end. For example, the franchisee will deny that the franchisor can terminate the franchise.

Several provinces have enacted legislation that gives a prospective franchisee a right to the kind of disclosure that an investor in an initial public offering of shares would get under the *Securities Acts* of the provinces. The original statute was that of Alberta (see *Franchises Act*, R.S.A. 2000, c. F-23) and it has now been followed by Ontario (see *Arthur Wishart Act (Franchise Disclosure), 2000*, S.O. 2000, c. 3, discussed in Chapter 6).

A commercial loan agreement is an example of an important type of relational contract. Actions on agreements to lend — where the lender has promised to lend money but then does not do so because it discovers concerns about the borrower before the loan is made — are very rare, but do arise. See e.g., *Abba Ventures Inc. v. Royal Trust Corp. of Canada* (1996), 25 B.L.R. (2d) 211, 176 N.B.R. (2d) 33 (Q.B.). (It is worth remembering the aphorism that if you borrow $10,000, you are at the lender's mercy, while if you borrow $100,000,000, the lender is at your mercy.) Actions for default on repayment of a loan are, of course, another matter and exactly what we would expect from a relational contract that has not worked out. Defaults on loans typically occur, not because the lender did not know the state of the borrower's affairs when the loan was made, but because the parties' plans, expectations or hopes were not, as things turned out, realized.

The right of one party to terminate a relational contract is, of course, determined by the agreement that was initially negotiated and drafted. As discussed in Chapter 4, in some cases a lender, like a bank, will have a wide power when an "event of default" occurs. The judicial method of controlling the contractual power to terminate a relational contract is generally found in the use of the concepts of unconscionability and good faith, which are considered in Chapter 6. The law governing wrongful dismissal is, of course, an example of the law's treatment of the problems arising on the termination of a relational contract. Since the focus in this chapter is largely on the terms of the deal and the allocation of risks by planning, it is not surprising that most of the cases involve discrete transactions.

Warranties and the Doctrine of Privity

A warranty is a legally enforceable promise given by one party to a contract to the other party. A range of issues and problems arise from the fact that a party to the contract can rely on the warranty to seek relief. As you read the cases in this section, consider why the rules about privity of contract developed in this context, and why there are sound reasons for continuing them.

Two aspects of the *Sale of Goods Act*, R.S.O. 1990, c. S.1 illustrate important issues related to the law of warranties. The Act, which largely codified the common law rules of the late nineteenth century that governed the sale of goods, imposes obligations on the seller of goods by implying terms in each contract of sale. The Act permits the parties, by an appropriately drafted contract, to "exclude" the implied terms of the Act and to put all the risks of, for example, poor quality, on the buyer. However, the ability of buyers to waive or forego the protection of the "implied terms" of the Act is now limited by legislation like the Ontario *Consumer Protection Act* and by judicial methods that we shall examine in the next chapter. A second point is that whatever protection is provided by the *Sale of Goods Act*, is available only to the *buyer*. No protection is available under the Act either to the buyer's spouse or children, who might well be injured if, for example, a car were defective, or to a person who bought the goods from the original buyer. The person who is not a buyer is not privy to the contract of sale and hence can claim no rights under the *Sale of Goods Act*.

The law regarding implied terms in the sale of goods is based on the provisions of the *Sale of Goods Act*. The following sections are relevant for our purposes. (We have numbered the sections in accordance with the Ontario Act. These provisions in other provincial Acts are identical, though their numbering varies.)

13. In a contract of sale, unless the circumstances of the contract are such as to show a different intention, there is

  (a)　an implied condition on the part of the seller that in the case of a sale he has a right to sell the goods, and that in the case of an agreement to sell the seller will have a right to sell the goods at the time when the property is to pass;

  (b)　an implied warranty that the buyer will have and enjoy quiet possession of the goods; and

  (c)　an implied warranty that the goods will be free from any charge or encumbrance in favour of any third party, not declared or known to the buyer before or at the time when the contract is made.

14. Where there is a contract for the sale of goods by description, there is an implied condition that the goods will correspond with the description, and, if the sale is by sample as well as by description, it is not sufficient that the bulk of the goods corresponds with the sample if the goods do not also correspond with the description.

15. Subject to this Act and any statute in that behalf, there is no implied warranty or condition as to the quality or fitness for any particular purpose of goods supplied under a contract of sale, except as follows:

1. Where the buyer, expressly or by implication, makes known to the seller the particular purpose for which the goods are required so as to show that the buyer relies on the seller's skill or judgment, and the goods are of a description that it is in the course of the seller's business to supply (whether he is the manufacturer or not), there is an implied condition that the goods will be reasonably fit for such purpose, but in the case of a contract for the sale of a specified article under its patent or other trade name there is no implied condition as to its fitness for any particular purpose.

2. Where goods are bought by description from a seller who deals in goods of that description (whether he is the manufacturer or not), there is an implied condition that the goods will be of merchantable quality, but if the buyer has examined the goods, there is no implied condition as regards defects that such examination ought to have revealed.

3. An implied warranty or condition as to quality or fitness for a particular purpose may be annexed by the usage of trade.

4. An express warranty or condition does not negative a warranty or condition implied by this Act unless inconsistent therewith.

The Act is premised on there being a significant distinction between "conditions" and "warranties", whether implied by section 13 or section 15, or by the express terms of the contract. Conditions are in theory more important than warranties. If a seller breaches a condition, the buyer has the right to reject the goods, whereas if there is a breach of warranty, there is still an obligation to accept and pay for the goods, subject to the right to claim damages.

Section 12(2) governs express conditions and warranties, while s-s. 12(3) stipulates that once goods have been "accepted", the buyer loses the right to reject the goods for a breach of condition.

12(2) Whether a stipulation in a contract of sale is a condition the breach of which may give rise to a right to treat the contract as a repudiated or a warranty the breach of which may give rise to a claim for damages but not to a right to reject the goods and treat the contract as repudiated depends in each case on the construction of the contract, and a stipulation may be a condition, though called a warranty in the contract.

(3) Where a contract of sale is not severable and the buyer has accepted the goods or part thereof, or where the contract is for specific goods the property in which has passed to the buyer, the breach of any condition to be fulfilled by the seller can only be treated as a breach of warranty and not as a ground for rejecting the goods and treating the contract as repudiated, unless there is a term of the contract, express or implied, to that effect.

The effect of s-s. 12(3) is to limit severely the right of the buyer to get out of the contract. The use of the word "condition" in s. 15, for example, in practice rarely gives any more right than a claim for damages for breach of warranty, since a defect in the goods is not likely to be discovered until after the goods are in use and "accepted" under s-s. 12(3). The buyer's acceptance of the goods will, in effect, transform a condition, *i.e.*, an excuse to refuse to perform, into a warranty, *i.e.*, a claim to damages.

The provisions of the *Sale of Goods Act* will not be explored in detail here, though its provisions are important for cases like *Murray v. Sperry Rand*. The general effect of these sections is to incorporate into every contract of sale certain terms regarding the quality, broadly defined, of the goods being sold. It does not, however, apply to other contracts, such as those for the sale of services, financial assets or real property.

The Ontario Law Reform Commission recommended extensive changes to the *Sale of Goods Act*. The Law Reform Commission was concerned that, in the case of consumer transactions at least, the seller should be unable to contract out of the basic warranty. This was one of the principal problems with the implied terms under the Act. It is clear in the Act that the seller can, if it wants to, contract out of any of the warranties provided in s. 15. Chapter 6 will examine some of the methods by which the courts and the legislature can control the exercise of this power.

The Ontario legislature in effect amended the *Sale of Goods Act* by enacting the following section of the *Consumer Protection Act, 2002* (S.O. 2002, c. 30, Sched. A):

9(1)   The supplier is deemed to warrant that the services supplied under a consumer agreement are of a reasonably acceptable quality.

(2) The implied conditions and warranties applying to the sale of goods by virtue of the *Sale of Goods Act* are deemed to apply with necessary modifications to goods that are leased or traded or otherwise supplied under a consumer agreement.

(3) Any term or acknowledgement, whether part of the consumer agreement or not, that purports to negate or vary any implied condition or warranty under the *Sale of Goods Act* or any deemed condition or warranty under this Act is void.

(4) If a term or acknowledgement referenced in subsection (3) is a term of the agreement, it is severable from the agreement and shall not be evidence of circumstances showing an intent that the deemed or implied warranty or condition does not apply.

Note that the Act applies not only to the sale of goods but to the provision of services. Services are very broadly defined to mean "anything other than goods, including any service, right, entitlement or benefit".

The provisions of the *Sale of Goods Act* only apply to contracts of sale. As far as the ultimate purchaser of goods is concerned, the contract of sale is made only with the retailer. The retailer may have bought goods from a wholesaler, who may have bought them from the manufacturer. The Act, therefore, gives no contractual remedy to the ultimate purchaser against the manufacturer, though if there has been advertising, a consumer might be able to establish a contractual claim against the manufacturer based on the advertising, as in *Murray v. Sperry Rand*.

This is known as the problem of "vertical privity" in the chain of commercial distribution of goods. In many cases the problem of vertical privity will mean that the ultimate purchaser has no remedy against the manufacturer (or wholesaler); a remedy against the retailer sometimes is of no practical value, since the retailer is sometimes less substantial than the manufacturer and not worth suing. There are strong policy reasons for imposing liability on the manufacturer. The Ontario Law Reform Commission said in its *Report on Consumer Warranties and Guarantees in the Sale of Goods* (1972):

It has often been remarked that in the modern marketing milieu it is the manufacturer who plays the dominant role. It is he who is responsible for putting the goods into the stream of commerce and, in most cases, of creating the consumer demand for them by continuous advertising. The retailer is little more than a way station. It is the manufacturer who endows the goods with their characteristics and it is he who determines the type of material and components that shall be used and who establishes the quality control mechanism. It is also he who determines what express guarantees shall be given to the consumer and who is responsible for the availability of spare parts and the adequacy of servicing facilities. Almost all the consumer's knowledge about the goods is derived from the labels or markings attached to the goods on the sales literature that accompanies them — and these too originate from the manufacturer.

In 1976 the Ontario government introduced a *Consumer Products Warranties Act*, which would have allowed a direct action against the manufacturer by the consumer. That Act was not passed.

The problem of "horizontal privity" arises when, for example, a member of the consumer's family is injured by defective goods. The purchase may have been made by the husband and the injury may have been suffered by his wife or child. The injured person has given no consideration to anyone and so cannot sue anyone in contract. Again, the Ontario Law Reform Commission recommended that the problems of horizontal privity be avoided by broadening the definition of "consumer". The 1990 proposal for a *Consumer and Business Practices Code* addressed the problem of horizontal privity by providing:

> 34. If a consumer acquires goods or services as a gift for an individual, the individual is entitled to every warranty that the consumer would be entitled to.
>
> . . .
>
> 36. An individual who is entitled to a warranty under this Part may sue a person for breach of a warranty under this Part.

Notice the style of drafting in the new code. It was intended to be understood by someone who knows nothing about the law. Do you think that it succeeds? Do you think that the provisions would be easy to interpret? These issues remain academic as the expanded definition of "consumer" was not enacted.

Both Saskatchewan (*Consumer Protection Act*, S.S. 1996, c. C-30.1) and New Brunswick (*Consumer Product Warranty and Liability Act*, S.N.B. 1978, c. C-18.1) have legislation that addresses some of the problems of privity. Compare the Ontario language with that of the New Brunswick Act, which provides:

> 23. Where the seller is in breach of a warranty provided by this Act, any person who is not a party to the contract but who suffers a consumer loss because of the breach may recover damages against the seller for the loss if it was reasonably foreseeable at the time of the contract as liable to result from the breach.

The Act defines a "consumer loss" as (a) a loss that a person does not suffer in a business capacity; or (b) a loss that a person suffers in a business capacity to the extent that it consists of liability that he or another person incurs for a loss that is not suffered in a business capacity.

Thus, in a few provinces, some of the problems caused for consumers by the rules regarding privity of contract and breach of warranty or condition have been addressed by the use of legislation.

Note that there are cases that followed *Jarvis v. Swan's Tours* (*supra*, Chapter 1), such as *Jackson v. Horizon Holidays Ltd.*, [1975] 3 All E.R. 92, [1975] 1 W.L.R. 1468 (C.A.); and *Kent v. Conquest Vacations*, [2005] O.J. No. 312 (Div. Ct.), where parents or spouses have recovered damages in respect of the loss of enjoyment suffered by family members while on a vacation. These cases are hard to fit within either the law of damages or the doctrine of privity, but reflect a desire to protect disappointed vacationers and hold travel companies to their advertising. The disappointed vacationer cases, however, may be regarded as anomalous and have largely suffered the indignity of being "confined to their special facts".

The two cases that follow deal with the issue of privity and third-party beneficiary contracts in ways that are entirely typical in the common law. Consider whether and to what extent the devices used by the courts are satisfactory ways of solving the problems caused by the rules about privity of contract.

McMORRAN v. DOMINION STORES LTD.

(1977), 14 O.R. (2d) 559, 74 D.L.R. (3d) 186
(H.C., Lerner J.)

LERNER J.: — [1] This action is for breach of warranty in the sale and negligence in the manufacture of a bottle of carbonated soda-water.

[2]   The defendants, Dominion Stores Limited, will be referred to as "Dominion" and Crush International Limited, as "Crush." The breach of warranty is alleged against Dominion as the vendor of a bottle of carbonated soda-water. Crush is alleged to be liable for negligence in the manufacture of this bottle of soda-water. In the third-party proceedings, Dominion, if found liable, claims indemnity from Crush.

[The facts as found by the judge were: The plaintiff purchased a bottle of soda-water from a Dominion store. As he was opening the bottle, it exploded, injuring him in the eye. There was no evidence of any carelessness by the plaintiff, or any damage to the bottle occurring after it was filled by Crush.]

[3]   *Liability of Dominion Stores Limited.* The plaintiff's claim against Dominion is in contract, basing his claim for damages on a breach of the implied warranties set out in the *Sale of Goods Act*, s. 15 . . . The plaintiff, by implication, made known to Dominion that he intended to remove the crown by hand from the bottle and use its contents. It was also the ordinary or usual use to which, by implication, the plaintiff as buyer would be expected to put the bottle of beverage. The defendant knew that the bottle of soda-water was purchased to use its contents which use would be impossible without removing the crown. Paragraph 1 of s. 15 spells out a warranty of fitness of the bottled beverage for its ordinary purposes and no special communication needed to be made to the seller for that purpose. The warning printed on the crown was not intended to warn the buyer to examine the crown to determine whether it would fly off prematurely in his hand, but was a warning not to accept the bottle for use if the seal was broken because that kind of defect in the seal might allow the pressure of the gas to escape prematurely and leave the liquid without "carbonization" or "flat" and unpalatable after it was opened. From the words of warning an arrow led down to the lower edge of the crown where the seal was located. I find as fact that the warning was not directed to the defect described *supra* and located well above the warning words. On the balance of probabilities, the defect in the crown was present when the plaintiff selected the bottle of beverage from the shelf at Dominion's store which therefore brings home liability to this defendant for breach of warranty. Liability in this type of case, it would seem to me, is long since beyond doubt where the necessary facts are present.

[4] *Liability of Crush International Limited.* I begin with the finding that the bottle of soda-water left Crush in a defective condition resulting in the plaintiff's injuries. Has the plaintiff satisfied the onus that the defect was caused by the manufacturer's negligence in the application of the crown to the thread on the bottle?

[5] Where the defect arises in the manufacturing process controlled by the defendant, the inference of negligence is practically irresistible . . . Either the manufacturer's system was at fault or, if the system was sound, then an individual employee must have been negligent . . .

[6] In the result, the defendant, Crush, is liable in negligence to the plaintiff for his damages. . . . [for injuries suffered and the loss of employment.]

[7] *Third-party proceedings.* The defendant, Dominion, claims indemnity from its co-defendant for breach of contract and relies on s. 15 of the *Sale of Goods Act*. . . .

[8] Dominion having been found liable to the plaintiff for breach of contract pursuant to s. 15 of the *Sale of Goods Act*, Crush has the same legal obligation to Dominion as the latter had to the plaintiff. The negligence of Crush in the manufacture of the bottle of soda-water precipitated the plaintiff's injuries and damages. . . .

[9] Dominion will therefore have judgment against Crush for the amounts that it pays the plaintiff for damages and costs in the main action. Dominion will also have the costs of the third-party proceedings against Crush.

SIGURDSON V. HILLCREST SERVICE LTD.

[1976] S.J. No. 389, 73 D.L.R. (3d) 132, [1977] 1 W.W.R. 740
(Sask. Q.B., Estey J.)

[The plaintiffs were Mr. and Mrs. Sigurdson and their sons. All the plaintiffs were injured in an accident caused by the installation on Mr. Sigurdson's car of a defective brake hose. There was expert evidence that the defects in the hose could not have been discovered except by cutting the hose in half. The plaintiffs sued the service station that had installed the hose. The service station joined the supplier of the hose as a third party.]

ESTEY J. [after stating the facts, continued]: — **[1]** I take the view that there were no circumstances in the present case which would suggest to an employee of the defendant that the brake hose was or might be defective when it was delivered to the defendant's place of business by the third party. Indeed there was, prior to installation of the brake hose, no test or examination which could be conducted by the defendant which would locate the foreign object short of destruction of the brake hose. Moreover, the operation of the vehicle from May 1st to June 16th suggests in itself that the actual installation of the brake hose was proper. There is therefore in my opinion no negligence on the part of the defendant in either the installation of the brake hose or in the failure to inspect such hose prior to installation. As I have held that there is no negligence on the part of the defendant, I dismiss the actions of the plaintiffs Mrs. Sigurdson and her son Christopher.

[2] The liability of the defendant towards the plaintiff Mr. Sigurdson involves other considerations. While I have already held that the defendant's employees were not guilty of negligence, the defendant, in so far as the plaintiff Mr. Sigurdson is concerned, is faced with the provision of the *Sale of Goods Act* [s. 16 of the Saskatchewan Act being the same as s. 15 of the Ontario Act] . . . I am of the view on the facts of the present case that there was by virtue of the [Act], an implied warranty or condition that the brake hose would be "reasonably fit" for the purpose for which it was intended. I find that the said brake hose was not "reasonably fit" in that it contained foreign bodies which eventually caused a rupture and brake failure which failure was the cause of the accident. . . .

[3] My view is that the defendant may successfully recover from its supplier the third party for a breach of warranty, *i.e.*, that the brake hose was defective or not reasonably fit for the purpose for which it was intended. . . .

QUESTIONS

1. What reasons might there be to explain why the plaintiffs, as well as the defendant retailer and the supplier, did not sue the manufacturer of the hose?

    Though not indicated in the report, it is very likely that the manufacturer was bankrupt or not worth pursuing for some other reason.

    Although the other members of the family of Mr. Sigurdson could not recover for their injuries in contract against the service station because of the horizontal privity problem, they would have had a strong tort-based claim in negligence against the manufacturer.

2. The implication of terms in the context of a sale of goods may be justified on the ground that to do so, by offering a kind of "default" allocation of risk, is consistent with commercial expectations. Where do you think the standards for the addition (or implication) of terms come or should come from? In other words, when are the courts justified in drawing an inference that the agreement should be expanded to impose obligations not specifically agreed to by the parties?

In *Winnipeg Condominium Corporation No. 36 v. Bird Construction Co. Ltd.*, [1995] 1 S.C.R. 85, 121 D.L.R. (4th) 193, the Supreme Court of Canada was willing to address some of the problems created by the doctrine of privity by extending tort liability. The defendant, respondent, a builder, had constructed a building for a developer, who was likely bankrupt and not worth suing. The appellant, plaintiff, became the owner in 1978 when the developer sold the units in the building. The directors of the plaintiff became concerned about exterior masonry work on the building in 1982 and they retained an architect and an engineering firm to make an assessment of the quality of the construction. A favourable report was provided. In 1989 a large slab of the exterior wall fell from the building, though fortunately no one was injured. The plaintiff sued the builder, the architect and the subcontractor who had done the work in negligence.

The question before the Supreme Court was whether a general contractor responsible for the construction of a building may be held liable in tort for negligence to a subsequent purchaser of the building, who was not in contractual privity with the contractor, for the cost of repairing defects in the building arising out of negligence in its construction.

La Forest J., giving the judgment of the Court, said (p. 103 S.C.R.) that his conclusion "that the type of economic loss claimed by the Condominium Corporation is recoverable in tort is . . . based in large part upon what seem to me to be compelling policy considerations". He said (p. 121 S.C.R.):

> I conclude that the law in Canada has now progressed to the point where it can be said that contractors (as well as subcontractors, architects and engineers) who take part in the design and construction of a building will owe a duty in tort to subsequent purchasers of the building if it can be shown that it was foreseeable that a failure to take reasonable care in constructing the building would create defects that pose a substantial danger to the health and safety of the occupants. Where negligence is established and such defects manifest themselves before any damage to persons or property occurs, they should, in my view, be liable for the reasonable cost of repairing the defects and putting the building back into a non-dangerous state.

La Forest J. then held that there were no compelling policy considerations that should limit the consequences of the duty he imposed on the defendants. He rejected an argument that the imposition of tort liability in the circumstances — which amounted to a transmissible warranty by the builder to the subsequent purchaser — could not be easily defined or limited. He also rejected an argument that *caveat emptor* applied to limit the defendants' liability. He said (pp. 122-23 S.C.R.):

> [t]hese concerns are both merely versions of the more general and traditional concern that allowing recovery for economic loss in tort will subject a defendant to what Cardozo C.J. in *Ultramares Corp. v. Touche*, 174 N.E. 441 (N.Y.C.A. 1931), at p. 444, called "liability in an indeterminate amount for an indeterminate time to an indeterminate class."

He continued (p. 123 S.C.R.):

> . . . In light of the fact that most buildings have a relatively long useful life, the concern is that a contractor will be subject potentially to an indeterminate amount of liability to an indeterminate number of successive owners over an indeterminate time period. The doctrines of privity of contract and *caveat emptor* provide courts with a useful mechanism for limiting liability in tort. But the problem . . . is that it is difficult to justify the employment of these doctrines in the tort context in any principled manner apart from their utility as mechanisms for limiting liability.

As regards the duty on the contractor, he said (pp. 123-25 S.C.R.):

> As I see it, the duty to construct a building according to reasonable standards and without dangerous defects arises independently of the contractual stipulations between the original owner and the contractor because it arises from a duty to create the building safely and not merely according to contractual standards of quality. It must be remembered that we are speaking here of a duty to construct the building according to reasonable standards of safety in such a manner that it does not contain *dangerous* defects. As this duty arises independently of any contract, there is no logical reason for allowing the contractor to rely upon a contract made with the original owner to shield him or her from liability to subsequent purchasers arising from a dangerously constructed building. . . .

> . . .

> The tort duty to construct a building safely is thus a circumscribed duty that is not parasitic upon any contractual duties between the contractor and the original owner. Seen in this way, no serious risk of indeterminate liability arises with respect to this tort duty. . . .

. . .

However, in my view, any danger of indeterminacy in damages is averted by the requirement that the defect for which the costs of repair are claimed must constitute a real and substantial danger to the inhabitants of the building, and the fact that the inhabitants of the building can only claim the reasonable cost of repairing the defect and mitigating the danger. The burden of proof will always fall on the plaintiff to demonstrate that there is a serious risk to safety, that the risk was caused by the contractor's negligence, and that the repairs are required to alleviate the risk.

He rejected the *"caveat emptor"* concern (p. 126 S.C.R.) on the basis that "a subsequent purchaser is not the best placed to bear the risk of the emergence of latent defects".

The judgment in *Bird Construction* illustrates that the law of torts can impose significant restrictions on the freedom of an owner of land and a builder to build as they please. La Forest J. mentions specifically that a builder cannot plead in answer to a claim by an injured party that it performed its contract to the standard required by the then owner of the land. It is not clear whether this standard will differ from that imposed by legislation; the legislative standard arguably formed the basis for the imposition of "additional" obligations in *Fraser-Reid*. What is important to notice is that there are now similar limits, coming from different directions, on parties' freedom of contract.

In a number of recent cases, including *Bird Construction*, the Supreme Court has made it very clear that concurrent duties in tort and contract can exist. This issue will be dealt with later in this chapter. What is important will be the extent to which contractual values, values connected to or arising out of a relation of exchange, can be preserved when this development is carried any distance.

While the existence of a contractual relation between parties does not preclude concurrent tort liability, contractual arrangements may affect tort liability. The following decision examines further issues related to the tort doctrine of "economic loss". This tort doctrine is based on some concerns that are similar to the concerns that lie at the base of the contract doctrine of privity.

BOW VALLEY HUSKY (BERMUDA) LTD. v. SAINT JOHN SHIPBUILDING LTD.

[1997] S.C.J. No. 111, [1997] 3 S.C.R. 1210, 153 D.L.R. (4th) 385
(S.C.C., La Forest, Gonthier, Cory, McLachlin, Iacobucci and Major JJ.)

[Husky Oil Operations Ltd. ("HOOL") and Bow Valley Industries Ltd. ("BVI") made arrangements to have an oil drilling rig constructed by Saint John Shipbuilding Limited ("SJSL"). In order to take advantage of government financing, HOOL and BVI incorporated an offshore company, Bow Valley Husky (Bermuda) Ltd. ("BVHB"). Before construction began, ownership of the rig and the construction contract with SJSL were transferred to BVHB. HOOL and BVI entered into contracts with BVHB for the hire of the rig to conduct drilling operations at sites chosen by HOOL and BVI. These contracts provided that HOOL and BVI would continue to pay day rates to BVHB in the event that the rig was out of service. A heat trace system was required in order to prevent the rig's pipes from freezing during the winter. BVHB chose the Raychem system, which used Thermaclad wrap to keep moisture from the insulation and heat trace wire. The specifications for the Raychem heat trace system required the installation of a ground fault circuit breaker system to cut off the power in the event of an electrical fault, to prevent arcing of the heat trace wire. A functioning system was not installed until after a fire broke out on the rig, causing damage to a tray of electrical and communications cables. As a result of the damage, the rig had to be towed to port for repairs and was out of service for several months. BVHB, HOOL and BVI commenced an action against SJSL alleging breach of contract and negligence, and an action against Raychem for negligence. BVHB claimed both for the cost of the repairs to the rig and for the revenue lost as a result of the rig being out of service for several months. HOOL and BVI sought to recover the day rates that they were contractually required to pay to BVHB during the period the rig was out of service, as well as expenses they incurred for supplies to the rig, including food, drilling mud and additional equipment.

The trial judge held that the defendant SJSL was liable in contract and tort for failing to provide certificates of approval for the Thermaclad, and in tort for breach of duty to warn of the inflammability of Thermaclad. He also held that the defendant Raychem was liable in tort for breach of its duty to warn. The trial judge went on to hold that the major fault lay with BVHB for its operation of the heat trace system without a functioning ground fault circuit breaker system. Moreover, it kept the heat trace system on, even when it might not have been required, despite incidents of arcing on the heat trace wires. He apportioned the fault 60 per cent to BVHB and 40 per cent to SJSL and Raychem. He did not award damages for breach of contract. The trial judge dismissed the plaintiffs' claim, however, on the ground that the case arose out of negligence at sea and was governed by Canadian maritime law, which precluded application of the Newfoundland *Contributory Negligence Act*, R.S.N. 1990, c. C-33 and made contributory negligence a bar to recovery.

The Court of Appeal held that because the loss suffered by HOOL and BVI was economic in nature, it was not recoverable. It agreed with the trial judge that maritime law applied, but held that provincial negligence legislation applied to maritime cases in some situations, including this case. Alternatively, if the Newfoundland *Contributory Negligence Act* did not apply, the court held that maritime law no longer made contributory negligence a bar to recovery. In the result, BVHB was held entitled to recover 40 per cent of its loss from SJSL and Raychem.

HOOL and BVI appealed from the judgment of the Newfoundland Court of Appeal; BVHB, SJSL and Raychem cross-appealed.

The principal judgment on the appeal was given by **McLACHLIN J.**, with whom **LA FOREST J.** concurred. **McLACHLIN** and **LA FOREST JJ.**, however, dissented on the cross-appeal; they would have dismissed the cross-appeal of SJSL and made it liable for its failure to warn the plaintiffs. (See Part V, Section B, of **McLACHLIN J.**'s judgment.) The majority, **GONTHIER, CORY, IACOBUCCI** and **MAJOR JJ.**, in a judgment by **IACOBUCCI J.**, held that the liability of SJSL for not warning the plaintiffs was excluded by the terms of the contract and that the cross-appeal by SJSL on that point should be allowed.]

McLACHLIN J. [after stating the facts and the judgments in the Newfoundland courts, continued:] —

IV.   Issues

[17]

(1) Are the defendants liable to the plaintiffs in tort?

(a) Did the circumstances impose on SJSL and Raychem a duty to warn BVHB of the risks associated with using Thermaclad?

(b) Was SJSL's duty to warn excluded by its contract with BVHB?

(c) Is Raychem entitled to rely on the "learned intermediary" defence?

(d) Is causation established?

(e) How should fault be allocated between SJSL and Raychem?

(f) Did SJSL and Raychem owe BVI and HOOL a duty to warn? (Recovery of contractual relational economic loss)

(g) Was BVHB contributorily negligent?

(h) Does BVHB's contributory negligence bar its claims?

(2) Is SJSL liable to BVHB in contract?

V.   Are the Defendants Liable to the Plaintiffs in Tort?

[**McLACHLIN J.** held that SJSL and Raychem were liable to BVHB in tort. She concluded her analysis of the facts and the cases by saying:]

[23] The evidence establishes that the plaintiff BVHB knew that Thermaclad would burn under some circumstances. The defendants SJSL and Raychem, however, had much more detailed knowledge of the specific inflammability characteristics of the Thermaclad. Raychem gained this knowledge through its own testing as manufacturer. SJSL gained it through its request to Raychem for information on Thermaclad's inflammability. BVHB did not have the degree of knowledge necessary to negate reliance on SJSL and Raychem. SJSL and Raychem did not demonstrate that BVHB accepted the risk of using Thermaclad. It follows that both SJSL and Raychem owed BVHB a duty to warn, subject to the special defences raised by SJSL and Raychem, to which I now turn.

B.   *Was SJSL's Duty to Warn Excluded by Its Contract With BVHB?*

[24] SJSL argues that any duty to warn BVHB which might otherwise arise from the circumstances is negatived by the contract between them. The trial judge rejected this submission, as did the Court of Appeal, on the ground that the contract provisions did not deal with or impact on SJSL's duty to warn. I agree.

[25] SJSL relies on clauses 702, 905 and 907 of its contract with BVHB. Clause 702, under Article VII (Inspection), stipulates that upon delivery SJSL's "sole obligation with respect to the Vessel shall be as specified in Article IX" (Warranties). Clause 905 excludes claims for defects except as provided in the warranty provision:

> 905.   The remedies provided in this Article are exclusive, and Builder shall have no liability whatever for any consequential loss, damage or expense arising from any defects.

Finally, clause 907 excludes liability for "owner directed supply":

> 907.   Builder's liability with respect to the Owner Directed Supply shall extend only to installation thereof in accordance with the certified equipment drawings and manuals furnished by the supplier in those instances where such equipment is actu-

ally installed by Builder. In all other instances, the sole risk and responsibility for Owner Directed Supply shall, as between Builder and Owner, be borne by Owner.

[26]   While BVHB's claim sounds in tort, the contract remains relevant to determining whether a tort duty arises, and if so, its scope. As this Court stated in *BG Checo International Ltd. v. British Columbia Hydro and Power Authority*, [1993] 1 S.C.R. 12, *per* La Forest and McLachlin JJ., parties are free to contract "to limit or waive the duties which the common law would impose on them for negligence" (pp. 26-27). However, "[i]n so far as the tort duty is not contradicted by the contract, it remains intact and may be sued upon" (p. 27).

[27]   To borrow the language of La Forest J. in *London Drugs Ltd. v. Kuehne & Nagel International Ltd.*, [1992] 3 S.C.R. 299, at p. 327, tort liability in a case such as this falls to be assessed in a contractual matrix. The parties' planned obligations must be given appropriate pre-eminence. Where those planned obligations negate tort liability, contract "trumps" tort: see J. Fleming, "Tort in a Contractual Matrix" (1993), 5 *Canterbury L. Rev.* 269, at p. 270, citing P. Cane, *Tort Law and Economic Interests* (1991), at p. 293. It follows that a tort claim cannot be used to escape an otherwise applicable contractual exclusion or limitation clause: *Central Trust Co. v. Rafuse*, [1986] 2 S.C.R. 147.

[28]   In order to determine the extent to which the parties' planned obligations affect their tort liabilities, it is necessary to ascertain the intention of the parties with respect to the particular issue from the contract documents as a whole: *BG Checo, supra*. In doing so, it must be kept in mind that generally limitation and exclusion clauses are strictly construed against the party seeking to invoke the clause: see e.g. *Hunter Engineering Co. v. Syncrude Canada Ltd.*, [1989] 1 S.C.R. 426, *per* Wilson J., at p. 497.

[29]   The provisions of the contract relied on by SJSL do not directly address responsibility for negligence or duty to warn. While the absence of a term expressly excluding tort liability is not determinative, the contract provisions, considered as a whole, relate to the finding of and responsibility for defects. They function, as the label of Article IX states, as a "warranty" of workmanship and materials. More specifically, clauses 702, 905 and 907, taken in combination, provide that in situations of "owner directed supply", SJSL bears the responsibility for installation while BVHB bears the responsibility for defects.

[30]   Warranties usually relate to the quality of goods and workmanship and do not relate to warnings about the risks associated with the use of products. In *University of Regina v. Pettick* (1991), 45 C.L.R. 1, a majority of the Saskatchewan Court of Appeal dismissed a contractor's argument that a one-year warranty it gave to the owner excluded any liability that it might have in tort. In concluding that a warranty does not necessarily exclude tort liability, Sherstobitoff J.A. stated (at pp. 52-53):

> There is nothing in a warranty by itself that suggests that further liability should be excluded. The warranty is a bargain that holds the contractor liable irrespective of negligence for a period of time. A tort claim requires proof of negligence. That it should continue beyond the warranty period does not interfere with the legitimate expectations of the parties as to their contractual relationship.

Without concluding decisively that warranty provisions could never negative a duty to warn, it may be noted that we have been referred to no case in which a warranty like that set out in Articles VII and IX was found to limit tort liability for duty to warn.

[31] This case is distinguishable from *Giffels Associates Ltd. v. Eastern Construction Co.*, [1978] 2 S.C.R. 1346, where a warranty coupled with a provision excluding liability for "all claims by the Owner" except those under the warranty (p. 1351) was held to exclude recovery for negligence in "the performance of the contract" (pp. 1354-55). First, the wording of clause 702 (obligations "with respect to the Vessel") is narrower than the wording of the contract in *Giffels* ("all claims by the Owner"). Second, the claim in *Giffels* was for damage due to faulty workmanship, which was specifically covered by the warranty clauses. The tort claim constituted an attempt to avoid express contractual exclusions, something that cannot be done: see *Central Trust, supra.* BVHB's claim against SJSL, by contrast, is not for negligence relating to the choice of, installation of, or defects in, the Thermaclad or other materials, but for failure to warn of the inflammability of Thermaclad. SJSL's duty to warn arose independently of the contract, through its greater knowledge of the inflammability characteristics of Thermaclad: see e.g. *Rivtow* [*Rivtow Marine Ltd. v. Washington Iron Works*, [1974] S.C.R. 1189], at pp. 1207 and 1214, and, more generally, *Queen v. Cognos Inc.*, [1993] 1 S.C.R. 87.

[32] SJSL places special emphasis on the fact that Thermaclad was "owner directed supply". Clause 907, it submits, excludes all liability for owner-directed supply, including liability for breach of duty to warn of the risks associated with the use of a product. I do not read clause 907 as extending to duty to warn. The starting point in construing clause 907 is that it functions to exclude or exempt from liability. As such, it must be narrowly construed. With this in mind, one turns to the wording and context of the clause 907 exemption. The first thing to note is that it falls under Article IX, entitled "Warranties". This suggests, as argued earlier, that the parties intended clause 907 to apply to defects in materials and workmanship. The words of clause 907 are consistent with this interpretation. The words "owner directed supply" connote goods supplied, not damages that might flow from the inappropriate use of a product. The purpose of owner-directed supply clauses in the context of construction contract warranties is to narrow the scope of the warranty for owner-directed materials or "supply". The builder is not responsible for defects in the materials chosen by the owner, only for defective installation. This is fair, since the owner has directed the use of the materials. In this sense, SJSL limited its liability "for the choice of Thermaclad": *per* Cameron J.A., at p. 114. Through its contract, it stated that it would not be liable for defects in the product supplied. Clause 907, however, does not address the quite different problem of whether, in all the circumstances, SJSL was under a duty to warn BVHB of the fire risks associated with the use of Thermaclad. That duty arose independently of the contract. It is grounded not in the contract but in SJSL's particular knowledge of the inflammability of Thermaclad.

[33] To put it another way, clause 907 addresses defects in products or their installation. If BVHB alleged that the Thermaclad supplied was defective, clause 907 would provide a complete defence. But BVHB does not allege that the Thermaclad supplied was defective. It makes the quite different claim that perfectly sound Thermaclad, properly installed, introduced a risk which SJSL was under a duty to warn it about. To that claim, clause 907 provides no defence.

[34] I conclude that the contractual matrix in which the duty to warn of the inflammability of Thermaclad arose does not negate or "contradict", to use the language of *BG Checo, supra,* that duty. It follows that BVHB was entitled to claim against SJSL based on the tort duty to warn.

. . .

F.   *Did SJSL and Raychem Owe BVI and HOOL a Duty to Warn? (Recovery of Contractual Relational Economic Loss)*

   (1)   *The Law*

[42] The plaintiffs HOOL and BVI had contracts with BVHB for the use of the rig owned by BVHB. They seek damages for economic loss incurred as a result of the shutdown of the drilling rig during the period it was being repaired. In other words, the plaintiffs HOOL and BVI seek to recover the economic loss they suffered as a result of damage to the property of a third party. This sort of loss is often called "contractual relational economic loss". The issue is whether the loss suffered by HOOL and BVI is recoverable.

[43] The issue arises because common law courts have traditionally regarded many types of contractual relational economic loss as irrecoverable. The reasons for this were summarized by this Court, *per* Major J., in *D'Amato v. Badger,* [1996] 2 S.C.R. 1071. First, economic interests have customarily been seen by the common law courts as less worthy of protection than either bodily security or property. Second, relational economic loss presents the spectre of "liability in an indeterminate amount for an indeterminate time to an indeterminate class": *Ultramares Corp. v. Touche,* 174 N.E. 441 (N.Y. 1931), at p. 444, *per* Cardozo C.J. Third, it may be more efficient to place the burden of economic loss on the victim, who may be better placed to anticipate and insure its risk. Fourth, confining economic claims to contract discourages a multiplicity of lawsuits.

[44] In England the situation is clear — no relational economic loss can ever be recovered: *Murphy v. Brentwood District Council,* [1991] 1 A.C. 398 (H.L.). Although *Murphy* concerned the liability of a public authority for approval of a negligently constructed building, not relational economic loss, the House of Lords stipulated that pure economic loss is recoverable only where there is actual physical damage to property of the plaintiff, thus excluding recovery for relational economic loss. In the civil law jurisdictions of Quebec and France, by contrast, the law does not distinguish between loss arising from damage of one's own property and loss arising from damage to the property of another. If civil law judges restrict recovery, it is not as a matter of law, but on the basis of the facts and causal connection. The law in the common law provinces of Canada falls somewhere between these two extremes. While treating recovery in tort of contractual relational economic loss as exceptional, it is accepted in Canadian jurisprudence that there may be cases where it may be recovered.

[45] The foregoing suggests the need for a rule to distinguish between cases where contractual relational economic loss can be recovered and cases where it cannot be recovered. Such a rule, as I wrote in *Canadian National Railway Co. v. Norsk Pacific Steamship Co.,* [1992] 1 S.C.R. 1021, should be morally and economically defensible and provide a logical basis upon which individuals can predicate their conduct and courts can decide future cases (p. 1147). Although this Court attempted to formulate such a rule in *Norsk*, a split decision prevented the emergence of a clear rule. Given the commercial importance of the issue, it is important that the rule be settled. It is therefore necessary for this Court to revisit the issue.

[46] The differences between the reasons of La Forest J. and myself in *Norsk* are of two orders: difference in result and difference in methodology. The difference in result, taken at its narrowest, is a difference in the definition of what constitutes a "joint venture" for the purposes of determining whether recovery for contractual relational economic loss should be allowed. We both agreed that if the plaintiff is in a joint venture with the person whose property is damaged, the plaintiff may claim consequential economic loss related to that property. We parted company because La Forest J. took a stricter view of what constituted a joint venture than I did.

[47] The difference in methodology is not, on close analysis, as great as might be supposed. Broadly put, La Forest J. started from a general exclusionary rule and proceeded to articulate exceptions to that rule where recovery would be permitted. I, by contrast, stressed the two-step test for when recovery would be available, based on the general principles of recovery in tort as set out in *Anns v. Merton London Borough Council*, [1978] A.C. 728 (H.L.), and *Kamloops (City of) v. Nielsen*, [1984] 2 S.C.R. 2: (1) whether the relationship between the plaintiff and defendant was sufficiently proximate to give rise to a *prima facie* duty of care; and (2) whether, if such a *prima facie* duty existed, it was negated for policy reasons and recovery should be denied.

[48] Despite this difference in approach, La Forest J. and I agreed on several important propositions: (1) relational economic loss is recoverable only in special circumstances where the appropriate conditions are met; (2) these circumstances can be defined by reference to categories, which will make the law generally predictable; (3) the categories are not closed. La Forest J. identified the categories of recovery of relational economic loss defined to date as: (1) cases where the claimant has a possessory or proprietary interest in the damaged property; (2) general average cases; and (3) cases where the relationship between the claimant and property owner constitutes a joint venture.

[49] The case at bar does not fall into any of the above three categories. The plaintiffs here had no possessory or proprietary interest in the rig and the case is not one of general averaging. While related contractually, the Court of Appeal correctly held that the plaintiff and the property owner cannot, on any view of the term, be viewed as joint venturers.

[50] However, that is not the end of the matter. The categories of recoverable contractual relational economic loss in tort are not closed. Where a case does not fall within a recognized category the court may go on to consider whether the situation is one where the right to recover contractual relational economic loss should nevertheless be recognized. This is in accordance with *Norsk*, *per* La Forest J., at p. 1134:

> Thus I do not say that the right to recovery in all cases of contractual relational economic loss depends exclusively on the terms of the contract. Rather, I note that such

is the tenor of the exclusionary rule and that *departures from that rule should be justified on defensible policy grounds.* [Emphasis added.]

More particularly, La Forest J. suggested that the general rule against recovery for policy-based reasons might be relaxed where the deterrent effect of potential liability to the property owner is low, or, despite a degree of indeterminate liability, where the claimant's opportunity to allocate the risk by contract is slight, either because of the type of transaction or an inequality of bargaining power. I agreed with La Forest J. that policy considerations relating to increased costs of processing claims and contractual allocation of the risk are important (p. 1164). I concluded that the test for recovery "should be flexible enough to meet the complexities of commercial reality and to permit the recognition of new situations in which liability ought, in justice, to lie as such situations arise" (p. 1166). It thus appears that new categories of recoverable contractual relational economic loss may be recognized where justified by policy considerations and required by justice. At the same time, courts should not assiduously seek new categories; what is required is a clear rule predicting when recovery is available.

[51] More recently, in *Hercules Managements Ltd. v. Ernst & Young*, [1997] 2 S.C.R. 165, this Court described the general approach that should be followed in determining when tort recovery for economic loss is appropriate. The plaintiffs in that case were shareholders in a company, Hercules Managements Ltd. The auditors for the company allegedly failed to disclose in their annual audits matters detrimental to the company. The company failed and the plaintiffs suffered financial loss. The plaintiff shareholders sued the auditors. The first issue was whether the plaintiffs' action against the auditors could be maintained in law. Although styled as an action for negligent misrepresentation, the plaintiffs' claim was treated as a case of relational economic loss owing to the fact that the services were performed pursuant to a contract with the company. The primary loser was the company, which had contracted with the auditors. The plaintiffs' loss was derivative of, or relational to, the company's loss. The defendant auditors asserted that their only duty was to the company with which they had contracted. They argued that no relational tort duty to third parties lay in the circumstances. To affirm such a duty, they maintained, would be contrary to the policy considerations that had led courts in the past to deny recovery for relational economic loss. The Court, *per* La Forest J., unanimously held that the shareholders had no cause of action against the auditors.

[52] La Forest J. set out the methodology that courts should follow in determining whether a tort action lies for relational economic loss. He held that the two-part methodology of *Anns, supra*, adopted by this Court in *Kamloops, supra*, should be followed: (1) whether a *prima facie* duty of care is owed; and (2) whether that duty, if it exists, is negated or limited by policy considerations. In applying the second step, La Forest J. wrote that while policy considerations will sometimes result in the *prima facie* duty being negated, in certain categories of cases such considerations may give way to other overriding policy considerations.

[53] La Forest J. held that the existence of a relationship of "neighbourhood" or "proximity" distinguishes those circumstances in which the defendant owes a *prima facie* duty of care to the plaintiff from those where no such duty exists. The term "proximity" is a label expressing the fact of a relationship of neighbourhood sufficient to attract a *prima facie* legal duty. Whether the duty arises depends on

the nature of the case and its facts. Policy concerns are best dealt with under the second branch of the test. Criteria that in other cases have been used to define the legal test for the duty of care can now be recognised as policy-based ways by which to curtail indeterminate or inappropriate recovery.

[54] Following this analysis, La Forest J. concluded that the first branch of the *Anns* test was satisfied and the defendant auditors owed a *prima facie* duty of care to the plaintiffs. First, the possibility that the plaintiffs would rely on the audited statements prepared for the company was reasonably foreseeable. Second, the relationship between the parties and nature of the statements themselves made the plaintiffs' reliance reasonable.

[55] Policy considerations under the second branch of the test, however, negatived a duty of care. La Forest J. began by noting that while policy concerns surrounding indeterminate liability will serve to negate a *prima facie* duty of care in many auditors' negligence cases, there may be particular situations where such concerns do not inhere. The specific factual matrix of a given case may bring it within a category which, for policy reasons, is identified as an exception to the exclusionary rule; considerations of proximity may militate in favour of finding a *prima facie* duty of care at the first stage, and the policy considerations which usually negate it may be absent. In such cases, liability would appropriately lie. The main policy consideration at stake in *Hercules* was the spectre of indeterminate liability. Not everyone who picks up a financial statement and relies on it can sue for financial loss incurred as a result of reliance on the statement. Only persons that the makers of the statement can reasonably be expected to have foreseen relying on the statements can sue, and then only for uses that the auditors could reasonably have foreseen. The question thus became whether the plaintiffs had used the statements for the purpose for which they had been prepared. The Court held they had not. The statements had been prepared for the purpose of permitting the shareholders to collectively oversee the management of the company, not for the purpose of assisting individual shareholders in investment decisions. The policy considerations surrounding indeterminate liability accordingly inhered, negating the *prima facie* duty of care.

[56] The same approach may be applied to the contractual relational economic loss at stake in the case at bar. The first step is to inquire whether the relationship of neighbourhood or proximity necessary to found a *prima facie* duty of care is present. If so, one moves to the second step of inquiring whether the policy concerns that usually preclude recovery of contractual relational economic loss, such as indeterminacy, are overridden.

(2) *Application of the Law*

[57] Before applying the law set out above to the facts of this case, a preliminary point arises: is the loss claimed by the plaintiffs contractual relational economic loss at all? The plaintiffs argue that the loss they claim against the defendants is really loss transferred from BVHB, the rig owner. The plaintiffs argue that they were in a "common venture" (as distinguished from a joint venture) with BVHB, which resulted in BVHB's losses being transferred to them. Therefore, they argue, they should be able to claim the losses as though they stand in the shoes of BVHB. BVHB could have claimed consequential losses for loss of use of the drilling rig; so then, on this theory, can HOOL and BVI.

[58] This argument suffers from a number of difficulties. First, insofar as courts have recognized transferred loss, it has been confined to physical damage: *Norsk*, *supra*. Applied to relational economic loss, it would need to meet the criteria for recovery of that category of loss, and hence would seem not to advance the plaintiffs' case. Second, the plaintiffs claim not only for loss of use of the drilling rig, but for losses related to unavoidable expenses they incurred for other supplies, including food, drilling mud and additional equipment. It is more difficult to see how these losses, based entirely on contracts between the plaintiffs and others, independent of BVHB, can be said to be transferred from BVHB. Third, there is nothing to show that the day rates paid by HOOL and BVI while the rig was idle are identical to what BVHB's consequential losses would have been. Finally, what does one do about the contributory negligence of BVHB? Given that BVHB is 60 per cent at fault, under the transferred loss theory would the plaintiffs be able to recover only 40 per cent of their claim? These difficulties suggest that the plaintiffs' loss is not the transferred loss of BVHB, the owner of the damaged rig. It is contractual relational economic loss, and should be treated as such.

[59] I return to the question of whether, on the approach articulated in *Hercules*, *supra*, the plaintiffs' claim for contractual relational economic loss is actionable. The Newfoundland Court of Appeal, without the benefit of *Hercules*, essentially followed the two-step process outlined in that case. It held that the defendants owed a *prima facie* duty of care to BVI and HOOL. The duty arose because BVI and HOOL's economic interests could foreseeably have been affected by a failure to warn BVHB of the danger of fire resulting from the use of products supplied by the defendants. The Court of Appeal went on to hold that there should be no recovery for other reasons. It held that it would be totally impractical to warn every person who could foreseeably suffer economic loss arising from the shutdown of the drilling rig. If there was a duty to warn BVI and HOOL, then there would also be a duty to warn other potential investors in the project, such as Mobil Oil Canada Ltd. and Petro Canada, as well as a host of other persons who stood to gain from the uninterrupted operation of the drilling rig, including employees and suppliers of the rig. In these circumstances, in the Court of Appeal's view, the only duty on the defendants was to warn the person in control and possession of the rig of the dangers of fire associated with the use of Thermaclad.

[60] As in *Hercules*, the decision as to whether a *prima facie* duty of care exists requires an investigation into whether the defendant and the plaintiff can be said to be in a relationship of proximity or neighbourhood. Proximity exists on a given set of facts if the defendant may be said to be under an obligation to be mindful of the plaintiff's legitimate interests in conducting his or her affairs: *Hercules*, at para. 28. On the facts of this case, I agree with the Court of Appeal that a *prima facie* duty of care arises. Indeed, the duty to warn raised against the defendants is the correlative of the duty to disclose financial facts raised against the auditors in *Hercules*.

[61] Where a duty to warn is alleged, the issue is not reliance (there being nothing to rely upon), but whether the defendants ought reasonably to have foreseen that the plaintiffs might suffer loss as a result of use of the product about which the warning should have been made. I have already found that the duty to warn extended to BVHB. The question is, however, whether it extended as far as HOOL and BVI. The facts establish that this was the case. The defendants knew of the existence of the plaintiffs and others like them and knew or ought to have known that they stood to lose money if the drilling rig was shut down.

[62] The next question is whether this *prima facie* duty of care is negatived by policy considerations. In my view, it is. The most serious problem is that seized on by the Court of Appeal — the problem of indeterminate liability. If the defendants owed a duty to warn the plaintiffs, it is difficult to see why they would not owe a similar duty to a host of other persons who would foreseeably lose money if the rig was shut down as a result of being damaged. Other investors in the project are the most obvious persons who would also be owed a duty, although the list could arguably be extended to additional classes of persons. What has been referred to as the ripple effect is present in this case. A number of investment companies which contracted with HOOL are making claims against it, as has BVI.

[63] No sound reason to permit the plaintiffs to recover while denying recovery to these other persons emerges. To hold otherwise would pose problems for defendants, who would face liability in an indeterminate amount for an indeterminate time to an indeterminate class. It also would pose problems for potential plaintiffs. Which of all the potential plaintiffs can expect and anticipate they will succeed? Why should one type of contractual relationship, that of HOOL, be treated as more worthy than another, e.g., that of the employees on the rig? In this state, what contractual and insurance arrangements should potential plaintiffs make against future loss?

[64] The plaintiffs propose a number of solutions to the problem of indeterminacy. None of them succeeds, in my respectful view. The first proposal is to confine liability to persons whose identity was known to the defendants. This is a reversion to the "known plaintiff" test, rejected by a majority of this Court in *Norsk, supra*. As commentators have pointed out, the fact that the defendant knew the identity of the plaintiff should not in logic or justice determine recovery. On such a test, the notorious would recover, the private would lose: *Norsk*. The problem of indeterminate liability cannot be avoided by arbitrary distinctions for which there is no legal or social justification: *Norsk*, at p. 1112. There must be something which, for policy reasons, permits the court to say this category of person can recover and that category cannot, something which justifies the line being drawn at one point rather than another.

[65] Second, and in a similar vein, the plaintiffs argue that determinacy can be achieved by restricting recovery to the users of the rig, a class which they say is analogous in time and extent to the owners and occupiers of the building in *Winnipeg Condominium Corporation No. 36 v. Bird Construction Co.*, [1995] 1 S.C.R. 85. This argument fails for the same reasons as the known plaintiff test. There is no logical reason for drawing the line at users rather than somewhere else.

[66] Third, the plaintiffs attempt to distinguish themselves from other potential claimants through the concept of reliance. The defendants correctly answer this argument by pointing out that any person who is contractually dependent on a product or a structure owned by another "relies" on the manufacturer or builder to supply a safe product.

[67] Finally, the plaintiffs argue that a finding of a duty to warn negates the spectre of indeterminate liability as the duty to warn does not extend to everyone in any way connected to the manufactured product. This argument begs the question. The duty to warn found to this point is only a *prima facie* duty to warn in accordance with the first requirement of *Anns*, *supra*, that there be sufficient proximity or neighbourhood to found a duty of care. It is not circumscribed and imports no limits on liability. Considerations of indeterminate liability arise in the second step of the *Anns* analysis. Hence the *prima facie* duty of care, by itself, cannot resolve the problem of indeterminate liability.

[68] The problem of indeterminate liability constitutes a policy consideration tending to negative a duty of care for contractual relational economic loss. However, the courts have recognized positive policy considerations tending to support the imposition of such a duty of care. One of these, discussed by La Forest J. in *Norsk*, is the need to provide additional deterrence against negligence. The potential liability to the owner of the damaged property usually satisfies the goal of encouraging persons to exercise due care not to damage the property. However, situations may arise where this is not the case. In such a case, the additional deterrent of liability to others might be justified. The facts in the case at bar do not support liability to the plaintiffs on this basis. BVHB, the owner of the drilling rig, suffered property damage in excess of five million dollars. This is a significant sum. It is not apparent that increasing the defendants' potential liability would have led to different behaviour and avoidance of the loss.

[69] Another situation which may support imposition of liability for contractual relational economic loss, recognized by La Forest J. in *Norsk*, is the case where the plaintiff's ability to allocate the risk to the property owner by contract is slight, either because of the type of the transaction or inequality of bargaining power. Again, this does not assist the plaintiffs in this case. BVI and HOOL not only had the ability to allocate their risks; they did just that. It cannot be said that BVI and HOOL suffered from inequality of bargaining power with BVHB, the very company they created. Moreover, the record shows they exercised that power. The risk of loss caused by down-time of the rig was specifically allocated under the Drilling Contracts between BVI, HOOL and BVHB. The contracts provided for day rate payments to BVHB and/or termination rights in the event of lost or diminished use of the rig. The parties also set out in the contracts their liability to each other and made provision for third party claims arising out of rig operations. Finally, the contracts contained provisions related to the purchase and maintenance of insurance.

[70] I conclude that the policy considerations relevant to the case at bar negative the *prima facie* duty of care to BVI and HOOL.

. . .

[**MCLACHLIN J.** concluded her analysis of the tort issues by saying:]

[103] The defendants SJSL and Raychem owed the plaintiff BVHB a duty to warn of the dangers of using Thermaclad on the rig. The contract did not exclude SJSL's tort liability to BVHB. SJSL and Raychem did not discharge their duty to warn and are equally responsible for failing to do so.

[104] The plaintiff BVHB was contributorily negligent, and responsible for 60 per cent of its loss. Its contributory negligence does not bar recovery of the balance of its losses.

. . .

[The judgment of **IACOBUCCI, GONTHIER, CORY** and **MAJOR JJ.** was delivered by]

[112] IACOBUCCI J.: — I have had the advantage of reading the lucid reasons of my colleague, Justice McLachlin. At the outset, I wish to commend my colleague for her treatment of the approaches taken by her and La Forest J. in *Canadian National Railway Co. v. Norsk Pacific Steamship Co.*, [1992] 1 S.C.R. 1021. In that respect, I simply wish to add one comment regarding the issue of contractual relational economic loss.

[113] I understand my colleague's discussion of this matter to mean that she has adopted the general exclusionary rule and categorical exceptions approach set forth by La Forest J. in *Norsk*. My colleague has found that the circumstances of the present case do not fall within any of the three exceptions identified in that case. She points out that both her reasons and those of La Forest J. in *Norsk* recognize that the categories of recoverable contractual relational economic loss are not closed and that whether or not a new category ought to be created is determined on a case-by-case basis. In that connection, I approve of her analysis of the facts of this case and applaud the approach she has taken to meld her reasoning in *Norsk* with that of La Forest J. in this very difficult area of the law.

[114] While I agree with most of her analysis in this case, I cannot, with respect, concur with her interpretation of clauses 702, 905 and 907 of the contract between SJSL and BVHB. I agree with my colleague when she points out that limitation and exclusion clauses are to be strictly construed against the party seeking to invoke the clause. I also agree that, where the planned contractual obligations of two parties negate tort liability, contract will "trump" tort. But, I disagree with her conclusion that the clauses in question do not negate SJSL's duty to warn.

[115] Clause 907 states in part that, "Builder's liability with respect to the Owner Directed Supply shall extend *only* to installation thereof . . ." (emphasis added). As I read this clause, the parties have chosen to specify the *only* ground of builder liability related to the use of Thermaclad, namely, negligence in the installation thereof. By expressly limiting liability to only these circumstances, the parties have, in my view, by necessary implication excluded all other grounds of builder liability, including the duty to warn.

[116] The fact that Thermaclad is "owner directed supply" reinforces my reading of the provisions in question. In the instant case, Thermaclad was chosen by the owner, BVHB, and the builder, SJSL, was obliged to use that product. Indeed, SJSL would have breached the contract if it had refused to use this material. It seems to me that where the owner specifies a particular product to be used, it is generally the owner and not the builder who, unless otherwise specified in the contract, should bear the losses that flow from the risk associated with that product's use.

[117] Additional reinforcement for my conclusion that the contract provisions create exclusive liability limited to installation is found in the concluding language of clause 907, which reads: "In *all* other instances, the *sole* risk and responsibility for Owner Directed Supply shall, as between Builder and Owner, be borne by Owner" (emphasis added). I also draw support from clause 905 which states in part that, the "remedies provided in this Article are *exclusive*" (emphasis added). In addition, clause 702 states that "the Builder's *sole* obligation with respect to the Vessel shall be as specified in Article IX" (emphasis added). That article contains both clauses 905 and 907.

[118] In concluding that the present contract does not exclude liability for negligence, my colleague puts much emphasis on the placement of the relevant provisions within the contract. Clauses 905 and 907, both found in the "warranty" section of the contract, are said to function as a "'warranty' of workmanship and materials" (para. 29). My colleague notes that warranties generally do not relate to the duty to warn about the risks associated with the use of the products they cover. However, in my opinion, the placement of clauses within a contract, while a factor to be considered, is not determinative. Rather, in my view, one should examine the contract as a whole with a view to searching for the intention of the parties by recognizing the natural meaning that flows from the language chosen.

[119] When examined in the context of cases which have held parties responsible for negligence without any express contractual reference to that head of liability, it is clear that the clauses in the instant contract are of a very different nature. For example, in *Falcon Lumber Ltd. v. Canada Wood Specialty Co.* (1978), 95 D.L.R. (3d) 503 (Ont. H.C.), the court found the defendant liable for negligence despite the following at paragraph 13 of the defendant's price list: "The Canada Wood Specialty Company Limited is not responsible for damages or theft that may occur whilst customer lumber and/or property is on The Canada Wood Specialty Co. Ltd. premises." Whereas clauses such as this provide for general *exclusion* from liability, the language of the clauses at issue in the case at bar expressly provides for the *assumption* of liability limited to a specific circumstance, namely, negligent installation of owner-directed supply. I do not accept that contract clauses which are so fundamentally different should necessarily be interpreted in the same manner.

[120] An alternative analysis set forth by this Court in *ITO-International Terminal Operators Ltd. v. Miida Electronics Inc.*, [1986] 1 S.C.R. 752, leads me to the same conclusion. In *Miida Electronics*, a marine carrier (Mitsui) agreed in a contract evidenced by a bill of lading to carry goods from Japan to Montreal where the respondent Miida, the other party to the contract and the owner of the goods, could take delivery. The goods arrived in Montreal and were picked up by the appellant, ITO, a cargo-handling company and terminal operator. ITO had agreed with Mitsui to store the goods until delivery was made to Miida. Before the goods could be delivered to Miida, thieves broke into the storage facility operated by ITO and a large number of Miida's goods were stolen. Miida alleged that the theft would not have occurred but for the negligence of ITO.

[121] One of the key issues in *Miida Electronics* was whether a "Himalaya" clause in Mitsui's bill of lading extended limitation of liability to those it employed in the performance of the contract of carriage. However, having decided that the Himalaya clause could be effective, the Court went on to consider whether the exemption clause in the bill of lading, which imposed limits on liability but did not expressly refer to negligence, could relieve ITO of liability for its own negligence. McIntyre J., writing for the majority, relied heavily upon *Lamport & Holt Lines Ltd. v. Coubro & Scrutton (M. & I.) Ltd. (The "Raphael")*, [1982] 2 Lloyd's Rep. 42 (C.A.), where May L.J. canvassed the jurisprudence in the area and stated (at pp. 49-50):

. . . if an exemption clause of the kind we are considering excludes liability for negligence expressly, then the Courts will give effect to the exemption. If it does not do so expressly, but its wording is clear and wide enough to do so by implication, then the question becomes whether the contracting parties so intended. If the only head of liability upon which the clause can bite in the circumstances of a given case is negligence, and the parties did or must be deemed to have applied their minds to this eventuality, then clearly it is not difficult for a Court to hold that this was what the parties intended — that this is its proper construction. Indeed, to hold otherwise would be contrary to common sense. On the other hand if there is a head of liability upon which the clause could bite in addition to negligence then, because it is more unlikely than not that a party will be ready to excuse his other contracting party from the consequences of the latter's negligence, the clause will generally be construed as not covering negligence. If the parties did or must be deemed to have applied their minds to the potential alternative head of liability at the time the contract was made then, in the absence of any express reference to negligence, the Courts can sensibly only conclude that the relevant clause was not intended to cover negligence and will refuse so to construe it.

The Ontario Court of Appeal recently relied upon this same line of reasoning in *Upper Lakes Shipping Ltd. v. St. Lawrence Cement Inc.* (1992), 89 D.L.R. (4th) 722.

[122] In *Miida Electronics*, *supra*, McIntyre J. found that, as the goods were in short-term storage awaiting delivery, the only liability that could be imposed on ITO would be based on negligence. Therefore, the exemption clause in the bill of lading, despite the absence of an express reference to negligence, was found to relieve ITO of liability for negligence. In my opinion, the contract provisions in the instant case warrant the same treatment. By the wording of clause 905, SJSL is relieved of any liability arising from defects. Clause 907 states that SJSL's liability shall extend only to installation of owner-directed supply and that in *all other instances*, BVHB bears the risk and responsibility for these products. Therefore, it seems to me that the natural meaning of these clauses indicates that the only head of liability upon which these clauses can bite is negligence in installation. As such, based upon the authority of *Miida Electronics*, SJSL ought to be relieved of any liability for failing to warn BVHB of the dangers associated with the use of Thermaclad.

[123] Accordingly, I must respectfully disagree with McLachlin J.'s conclusion that BVHB was entitled to claim against SJSL based on the tort duty to warn. I note that it is not open to Raychem to seek contribution from SJSL, as a contractor which has protected itself against liability cannot be said to have contributed to any actionable loss suffered by the plaintiff: *Giffels Associates Ltd. v. Eastern Construction Co.*, [1978] 2 S.C.R. 1346. Consequently, Raychem is liable for the entire 40 per cent quantum found by the trial judge.

[124] I would therefore dismiss the appeal brought by HOOL and BVI. Further, I would dismiss all of the cross-appeals save for that of SJSL with regard to the duty to warn, which I would allow with costs throughout. As to costs on the main appeal and all other cross-appeals, I would assess these in the same manner as McLachlin J.

PLAS-TEX CANADA LTD. v. DOW CHEMICAL OF CANADA LTD.

[2004] A.J. No. 1098, 245 D.L.R. (4th) 650, [2005] 7 W.W.R. 419
(Alta. C.A., Conrad, O'Leary and Picard JJ.A.)
[Leave to appeal denied, April 28, 2005]

[The plaintiffs were affiliated companies providing pipeline systems to carry natural gas. They shared common ownership and management and goals. The defendant Dow sold defective resin to two of the plaintiffs, which sold it to other related plaintiff companies. Dow did not have a contractual relationship with the other plaintiffs. One of the contracts contained clauses limiting Dow's liability by stating that the plaintiff buyer accepted all liability for loss or damage resulting from use of the resin. At the time of the sale Dow knew that that the resin was defective and that some plaintiffs would use the resin to manufacture pipe installed by other plaintiffs to carry natural gas. The pipe was dangerous and allowed natural gas to escape. The plaintiffs were forced to undertake major remedial operations and use of the pipe was eventually prohibited. The plaintiffs' reputation was damaged, which caused them to lose some of their customers and be petitioned into bankruptcy. The trial judge found Dow liable to all of the plaintiffs in contract and tort. The plaintiffs were awarded damages for the purchase price of the resin, cost of pipe repairs and lost profits. The Alberta Court of Appeal upheld the trial decision.

A significant portion of the Court of Appeal decision dealt with the issues related to the contract of sale. Before signing the contract with the plaintiff, Dow knew that defects in the product would cause the pipe manufactured from it to fail. Rather than disclosing this knowledge, Dow protected itself with limitation of liability clauses. Dow breached implied warranties under the *Sale of Goods Act*; for reasons discussed in Chapter 6, the Court refused to give effect to the exclusion clause, concluding that it was unconscionable.

The issue of interest here is the extent of liability in tort of Dow to the companies that did not have a privity of contract with Dow. The trial judge accepted that Dow knew of the corporate structure of the plaintiffs and of their working relationships. The court concluded that Dow had a duty to warn all the plaintiffs of the resin dangers and to take reasonable care not to distribute a dangerous product. There was a reasonable foreseeability of harm to each plaintiff and no policy reason to limit the duty of care. The portion of the Court of Appeal decision that deals with the doctrine of economic loss is set out here.]

PICARD J.A.: — **[111]** In a negligence action, the defendant must be found to be the cause-in-fact and the cause-in-law of the injury to the plaintiff. The former is measured by the "but-for" test which is often difficult to apply. The latter involves legal tests and requires the determination of the limits of the plaintiff's liability: it is often dealt with under the heading of "remoteness" of damage and usually requires an analysis of policy considerations similar to that done under duty of care. ...

(1) Cause-in-fact

[113] What injuries did the defective resin cause? The trial judge found that pipes manufactured with N5303, the resin produced by Dow, were brittle and cracked and that this was caused by the "intrinsically defective" resin. ... Indeed, this causal connection was acknowledged by Dow in its brief in that litigation. According to the expert evidence, accepted by the trial judge, the level of antioxidant in the resin was enormously below industry standards and pipe made from it was, therefore, subject to "thermo-oxidant degradation"... the respondents have proven that "but-for" the deficient resin, the pipes it fabricated and placed in the ground would not have cracked.

[114] What damages resulted from the injuries caused by the defective resin? Firstly, the gas co-ops refused to pay the respondents and by mid-1976 the respondents were owed $1.2 million. Secondly, refunds were demanded for all pipe held in inventory. Thirdly, the pipe was no longer saleable and there was no evidence that it had any salvage value. Lastly, there were unrecoverable repair costs, mounting operating expenses, and accelerated demands for payment from suppliers. ...

(2) Cause-in-law (remoteness)

[116] There is a legal test to measure the extent to which a negligent defendant ought to be held liable for the damages suffered by a plaintiff. The principle is that injured parties should be restored to the position that they would have been in had the wrong not been committed. Often the question asked is: what damages were reasonably foreseeable, or, to put it another way, what damages are not too remote? The application of this test is difficult where the loss is economic.

[117] The claim for lost profits for the year of the receivership, 1976, and the following five years is a claim for loss of profits and therefore is for economic loss. Since there was no physical damage recognized by law, it is a claim for "pure" economic loss. The trial judge found that the receivership of all of the respondents was foreseeable. However, the trial judge did not do the analysis required to determine whether relevant policy concerns should limit the extent of Dow's liability for the pure economic loss. That was an error of law because a policy analysis is now part of the legal test to determine foreseeability, or remoteness, of pure economic loss ...

[118] When the loss is economic loss, courts are concerned about maintaining control: in the words of Justice Cardozo, the fear is of "liability in an indeterminate amount for an indeterminate time to an indeterminate class": *Ultramares Corp. v. Touche* (1931), 255 N.Y. Supp. 170 (C.A.) at 179. The Supreme Court of Canada has been searching for a "principled mechanism" that would provide assistance to the courts in deciding when an award for economic loss would be appropriate but it has proven to be elusive: *Canadian National Railway Co. v. Norsk Pacific Steamship Co.*, [1992] 1 S.C.R 1021, at 1137 per McLachlin J. (as she then was). Some of the earlier requirements were: to prove there was an "independent tort"; to fit the claim into a category, such as negligent misrepresentation; or, to found the claim on the physical loss of a third party, sometimes called a contractual relational loss. However, as stated by McLachlin J., in *Norsk, supra*, there is no single universal formula and the categories are not closed. What is required is a case-by-case analysis, where the appropriate legal tests for duty and causation and a thorough policy review are done.

[119] In a new situation where the loss is pure economic loss, a policy analysis is especially critical. A policy analysis must be done to establish a duty of care (using the *Anns* tests), and also to determine the extent to which a defendant should have to compensate the plaintiff. This analysis is easier to describe than to carry out. That there is overlap is not surprising. For example, it is necessary in both to determine foreseeability of harm. But there is also a basis for distinction with a difference.

[120] In deciding whether there is a duty of care, the focus is on the relationship, proximity, and foreseeability of some harm and on relevant policy considerations. In determining scope of liability for damages for pure economic loss, the focus is on the nature of the negligent action and the foreseeability of the extent of the harm and relevant policy considerations.

[121] In this case, a duty was found to warn and not to manufacture a dangerous product. The duty was breached because the appropriate standard of care was not met. The negligent actions caused harm, including pure economic loss. Dow says it should not be liable for any economic loss because the respondents suffered no physical harm and, further, it is not a case of "contractual relational economic loss" that is, economic loss suffered as a result of damage to the property of a third party. It relies on *Bow Valley Husky, supra*.

[122] The lay person or the scientist might find it hard to believe that in this case the respondents' property has suffered no harm. After all, the defective resin was a critical component in the pipe and made the pipe defective also. However, finding property damage in this manner, described as "complex structure theory", was rejected by La Forest J. in *Winnipeg Condominium, supra*. He expressed concern that the theory would "circumvent and obscure underlying policy questions" and emphasized that "it is preferable for courts to weigh the policy issues openly": *Winnipeg Condominium, supra* at para. 15. Thus, Dow is correct, as far as the law is concerned (at least at this time) the respondents have suffered no physical damage.

[123] This is not a case of "contract relational economic loss" and can be distinguished from the *Bow Valley* case on its facts. In *Bow Valley*, the plaintiffs sued to recover money that they were required by contract to pay for the rental of an oil rig that was not useable because of the defendant's negligence. The plaintiffs suffered pure economic loss because of the damage to the rig that was owned by a third party. The parties similarly located in this case would be the gas co-ops who are not a party to this action.

[124] This is a case where the claims are for pure economic loss and cost of repairs resulting from failure to warn (at any time) and is a products liability case based on the manufacture of a product known by the manufacturer to be dangerous. Both the *Rivtow* and *Winnipeg Condominium* cases are applicable. Like *Rivtow*, it is a case where repairs had to be done and there were economic consequences beyond just the cost of repairs. Like *Winnipeg*, it is a case where a defect posed a real and substantial danger to the public and compensation for timely repair and pure economic loss was held to be recoverable and supported by policy considerations. The respondents here did have a property interest in the pipe as the plaintiffs in those cases had in the crane and building. However, the nature of the pure economic loss here differs from both as it involved not only the loss but also the total termination of profits of the respondents.

[125] In all of its recent decisions on pure economic loss, the Supreme Court of Canada has undertaken a policy analysis in order to determine whether a defendant ought to be held liable and to what extent, and has made it clear that lower courts must do the same. I must do the policy analysis not done by the trial judge using both a narrow and a broad focus. There is an overlap with the policy analysis done for duty of care, especially with that done for the second step of the *Anns* test.

[126] Looking at Dow's situation through the lens of policy, are there reasons that Dow should not be required to pay for any part or all of the economic loss of the respondents? Are there reasons that it ought to? What is the effect on law and on society of a decision one way or the other?

[127] This takes us back to some of the basic facts. Dow, a major petrochemical company, sold resin that it knew was defective and dangerous when used as it knew it would be. It never warned any of the respondents about the risk. The respondents were small companies with no relevant expertise who relied for that on Dow. While Dow did acknowledge the critical facts in litigation in which it claimed indemnity from its insurer, it required the respondents to prove them in the trial of this action. The respondents did not stop manufacturing pipe and installing it, when it became apparent that the pipe was cracking because the respondents did not know the cause. They carried on trying to satisfy customers and doing repairs under the warranties.

[128] They did question Dow about the quality of the resin in August 1975 and sent back some resin that they had received. Dow responded in writing, saying that they had tested some of the pipe and found it "indicated very uniform blending and consistent black levels ... Well done!" It is possible to interpret this as an intentional evasion of the question. In any case, Dow never did admit to the respondents that they had a problem with the resin. Later, the respondents asked for financial assistance but were refused. They carried on business until their financial position became untenable and they were forced into receivership by the Canadian Imperial Bank of Commerce. The respondents went from flourishing to moribund in two years. The expert evidence was that they missed out on an opportunity to participate in the booming oil and gas industry in Alberta.

[129] The contractual matrix does not assist Dow in limiting liability because it was found to have fundamentally breached its contractual obligations and its attempt to limit its liability [was] unconscionable.

[130] From a narrow, or case-specific perspective, are there policy reasons why Dow should not be liable for the cost of repairs and loss of profits suffered by the respondents? I find there are none.

[131] What are the relevant policy considerations from the broader perspective? Given that the tort was the negligent manufacture of a product as well as that its intended use was dangerous followed by a failure to warn of the known dangers, policy considerations support the tortfeasor paying the entire loss suffered by the injured parties. I agree with the statement by D.F. Edgell in *Product Liability in Canada*, (Toronto: Butterworths Canada, 2000) at 245, that there is a strong public interest in deterring manufacturers from marketing dangerous products. This case is not atypical in that there was a significant difference in knowledge and expertise between the parties. Indeed, here there was an intentional withholding of information. There are policy reasons to support liability so that consumers can reasonably expect that they can rely on manufacturers not to supply products that they know to be dangerous and to warn them if risks are discovered.

[132] As for compensation for the cost of repairs, it is now clear that the ruling in *Rivtow* precluding such an award is no longer good law. As La Forest J. said later in *Norsk*, *supra*, at para. 37, it is important to encourage the prevention of harm

and reduction of risk goals achieved by timely repairs: see also *Product Liability*, *supra*, at 238. LaForest J. went on to say in *Winnipeg Condominium*, *supra*, that barring recovery for the cost of repair of dangerous defects had a chilling effect on incentive and action to effect repairs.

[133] In summary, policy considerations support liability in this, a products liability case where the defect presented a known danger to the public and the consumer was reasonable in relying on the manufacturer's expertise. I find that the trial judge committed no error in deciding that Dow should be liable for economic loss, that is the loss of profits, of the respondents and also for the cost of repairs.

NOTES

1. Is the extension of tort liability in *Plas-tex* to allow for a recovery of profit for a tort consistent with *Bow Valley*?

2. The relation between contractual liability and the tort doctrine of "economic loss" is further explored later in this chapter, in particular in *Hercules Managements Ltd. v. Ernst & Young*, [1997] 2 S.C.R. 165, 146 D.L.R. (4th) 577, excerpted below.

3. In *Murphy v. Brentwood District Council*, [1991] 1 A.C. 398, [1990] 2 All E.R. 908 (H.L.), the plaintiff bought a house from a builder in 1970. The foundation of the house was badly designed. The defendant, the local authority, had approved the plans after having had them checked by a firm of consulting engineers. In 1981, the plaintiff noticed cracks in the house. The plaintiff could not afford to repair the house and sold it for £35,000 less than it would have been worth had it been properly designed and built. The plaintiff recovered judgment against the Council from the trial judge and the Court of Appeal. The defendant Council appealed to the House of Lords. The appeal was heard by seven judges and the House was invited to and had agreed to address the question whether it should reconsider and, if necessary, overrule *Anns v. Merton London Borough*, [1978] A.C. 728, [1977] 2 All E.R. 492. In the result, the House of Lords reversed the lower court rulings and held that the Council was not liable for these purely economic losses.

    In overruling *Anns*, the House of Lords cast some doubt on *Kamloops (City) v. Nielsen*, [1984] 2 S.C.R. 2, 10 D.L.R. (4th) 641, in which the Supreme Court of Canada had applied *Anns* to find that a municipality could be liable for negligence in carrying out its inspection of houses under construction. The Supreme Court has, however, consistently refused to follow *Murphy v. Brentwood* and has equally consistently stated its determination to apply *Kamloops (City) v. Nielsen*. The Supreme Court is thus continuing to take the broader approach to tort liability of *Anns*. *Anns* has been the seminal case for extending the scope of recovery in respect of pure economic losses, that is, for providing "ancillary" protection to interests arising out of relations close to contracts. As will become apparent in the cases and discussion below, the scope of liability that follows from the adoption of the *Anns* test is too extensive and the Supreme Court has had to find other methods for limiting it. These methods are illustrated in *Hercules Management Ltd. v. Ernst & Young*, *infra*.

    See also discussion in Russell Brown, "Still Crazy After All These Years: *Anns*, *Cooper v. Hobart* and Pure Economic Loss" (2003), 36 *U.B.C. L. Rev.* 159.

NEGLIGENT MISREPRESENTATION

One of the historical features of the law of contracts is the existence of various devices to keep contractual liability separate from other kinds of liability. As we have seen, the law of contracts is, in theory at least, to be sharply distinguished from other kinds of moral obligation. This separation is achieved principally by the doctrine of consideration, which, again in theory, is supposed to restrict enforcement to those relations that are part of bargains. As was clear in the cases dealing with third-party beneficiary contracts, the doctrine of consideration operates to limit the scope of duties to those who are parties to a contract.

Implicit in the judgment of Lord Moulton in *Heilbut, Symons & Co.* is the idea that it would be improper to expand the notion of warranty. Lord Moulton does not make it clear *why* it would be improper to do so. He says that a warranty must be proved strictly and that "any laxity on these points would enable parties to escape from the full performance of obligations of contracts unquestionably entered into by them." (Notice that this argument avoids the issue: the question is, what were the obligations of the parties? Was the plaintiff agreeing to buy shares promoted by the defendant or shares *of a rubber company*?) At a later point in his judgment Lord Moulton says: "On the Common Law side of the Court the attempts to make a person liable for innocent misrepresentation have usually taken the form of attempts to extend the doctrine of warranty beyond its just limits" (¶ 8).

These arguments assume that the bargain that the parties made is known, and that this agreement should be given its minimum scope. Both of these arguments overlook the question of what bargain the parties made and whether it would be appropriate to put the risk of disappointment on one side rather than the other. It is as if there was some notion of the "correct" kind of contractual obligation, to be identified by the court and enforced.

The result of the cases is considerable confusion in determining what a warranty is. How would we know whether a statement is a warranty? What do we do when we have one? We know there are situations in which the court will be moved to find some basis for relief, and that the court will often defend the giving of relief on the ground that a warranty exists. This kind of justification underlies the judgment of Lord Denning in *Dick Bentley*. The question is always what the courts want to do and why, not what kind of contracting the parties should engage in. The court will decide whether or not to give relief by considering such matters as the relative knowledge of the parties and which party might be the least-cost avoider of the risk of disappointment.

As happens sometimes in the law, a problem is simultaneously dealt with from two directions. Just as the law of warranty was being liberated from the limitations of *Heilbut* by decisions such as *Dick Bentley*, the law of torts was being expanded to perform a similar function — that of providing a remedy for the party who is induced to enter into a contract by the misrepresentation of the other party. To understand the significance of this development a brief historical review of the law is necessary.

For breach of warranty, only a remedy in damages was available; for an innocent misrepresentation there was no claim to damages, only a basis for claiming rescission. The latter remedy was limited as it had to be sought before performance and by the requirement that *restitutio in integrum* (*i.e.*, a complete return to the pre-contract situation) be possible. In addition to these contract remedies, there was a tort remedy for fraudulent misrepresentations. As we have mentioned, the remedy for fraud was also limited. The person who alleged fraud had to meet a heavy evidentiary burden and fraud, being also a criminal offence, was narrowly defined. A fraudulent misrepresentation has to be made "knowingly, or without belief in its truth, or recklessly, careless whether it be true or false": *Derry v. Peek* (1889), 13 App. Cas. 337 (H.L.).

Until the last few decades, there was no remedy after performance had occurred for non-fraudulent misrepresentation where there was no warranty. There were two reasons for this limitation on the right to damages. One rationale was an illogical response to the law regarding fraud. This response may have been based on the idea that, since the measure of damages for non-fraudulent misrepresentation would be the same as for fraud (*i.e.*, reliance losses), it would be wrong to give a remedy for non-fraudulent misrepresentation. A second concern was the general reluctance of the courts to award damages in tort for pure economic loss. This latter reason appeared in the judgment of the majority of the Court of Appeal in *Candler v. Crane, Christmas & Co.*, [1951] 2 K.B. 164. Such a remedy was seen as being potentially too dangerous and uncontrollable. La Forest J. in *Bird Construction* referred to the American case *Ultramares Corp. v. Touche*, 174 N.E. 441 (N.Y.C.A. 1931), at p. 444, where Cardozo C.J., made a response similar to *Candler*, stating that a tort remedy for economic losses would create "liability in an indeterminate amount for an indeterminate time to an indeterminate class".

Note that the duty of care stated in *Donoghue v. Stevenson*, [1932] A.C. 562, 101 L.J.P.C. 119, *viz.*, that one owes a duty of care to those whom one should reasonably consider might be harmed by one's actions, is broad enough to cover not only physical injury or damage to property but what can be called "pure economic loss" cases, *i.e.*, cases where the plaintiff suffered economic losses arising without any physical injury or damage. Cardozo's response was motivated by the fear that allowing recovery for pure economic loss would extend tort liability too far. This fear justified the prohibition of all such claims, not just those that might be, on whatever grounds could be imagined, beyond some proper limit.

The facts of *Candler* illustrate the problems of pure economic loss and one court's response to the problems that had to be resolved. A, an accountant, was instructed by B to provide financial statements for a corporation owned by B. A was told by B that the statements would be shown to C, a prospective investor in the corporation. A prepared the statements negligently, indicating that the company was profitable when it was not, and C, who relied on them to invest in the company, later lost his investment. A could be made liable to the corporation, if it had suffered a loss and could establish that it had employed him to prepare the statements. Perhaps A could be made liable to B on the same basis. The person who needs protection is C, but no protection was available: C and A were not in a contractual relation, and at best C would be a third-party beneficiary to the contract between A and the corporation. As long as A was not fraudulent, C would have no remedy in deceit and, of course, there would be no remedy through rescission, since there was no contract between A and C and, in any event, rescission would be pointless.

As will be seen, the law has changed radically since 1951 and *Candler v. Crane, Christmas* has now been overruled. It remains interesting as an example of the problems that the law made for itself. The third-party beneficiary rule limited the scope of contractual remedies, and the limited role of the law of torts in actions for damages for pure economic loss meant that many losses that one might have thought should be shifted to the person at fault were left to lie where they fell.

Notice also that *Candler v. Crane, Christmas* illustrates a kind of circular reasoning. A court that is moved to recognize the importance of reliance will only protect "reasonable" reliance. How does one know what reliance is reasonable? Reasonable reliance is the reliance that the court will protect! This argument appears circular if we ignore the fact that neither the court's view nor the views of those who might rely are projected into a void. The courts as much as individuals treat the fact of reliance as part of an existing, functioning system. There is no need to ask which came first; both exist and can only exist together. With warranties, innocent misrepresentations and negligent misrepresentations, the situation is the converse of the reliance argument. A court may refuse to find a warranty, for example, because there was not enough (or not enough justifiable) reliance, and make that decision because it does not think that the law should help this plaintiff in these circumstances: this plaintiff should bear the loss it has suffered. The fundamental problem of all rules in contracts remains: what do we *want* to do — *i.e.*, what *should* the law do, and why? These questions, though not often expressly stated, underlay much of the law of consideration: if the court wanted to enforce a promise it would find consideration if it had to. Conversely, if the court was not moved to protect the plaintiff, it would not easily be convinced that it should make the necessary findings of fact.

The tort of negligent misrepresentation has developed from the decision of the House of Lords in *Hedley Byrne & Co. Ltd. v. Heller & Partners Ltd.*, [1964] A.C. 465, [1963] 2 All E.R. 575. The basis for liability for negligent misrepresentation (or negligent misstatement) is the recognition of the applicability of the concept of the duty of care in *Donoghue v. Stevenson* to pure economic loss. The basis for liability was that the defendant negligently made a false statement that was reasonably relied upon by another person in a relation to the plaintiff of sufficient "proximity" to justify the imposition of the duty of care. This tort has in some respects "filled the gap" between the remedy for fraud and that for innocent misrepresentation. The result is that a plaintiff may claim damages for non-fraudulent, negligent misrepresentation. The measure of damages should be the tort measure, *i.e.*, to compensate the plaintiff for the loss (or harm) suffered by entering into the relation or in reliance on the defendant's statements. This measure is not (or may not be) the same as the compensation principle because it is backward looking: it seeks to put the plaintiff in the position that it would have been in if the contract had not been made or if the steps taken in reliance had not been taken. It is interesting to consider the extent to which, in terms of the size of the cheque that the unsuccessful defendant will write, two measures lead to different results.

The tort of negligent misrepresentation can give rise to a cause of action in situations where there is no contract between the parties. The next case illustrates how a court can also use negligent misrepresentation to impose liability where there is a contract between the parties but where a contractual analysis will not "work".

ESSO PETROLEUM CO. v. MARDON

[1976] Q.B. 801, [1976] 2 All E.R. 5
(C.A., Lord Denning M.R., Ormrod and Shaw L.JJ.)

[In 1961 Esso Petroleum wanted an outlet to sell gas in Southport. They found a vacant site which appeared very suitable. To determine if it would be a profitable site, they made an estimate of the annual consumption ("e.a.c."). That figure was 200,000 gallons a year. This figure was based on the assumption that the gas station would have access from a busy street. Before the station was built, the local planning authority forced Esso to build the pumps where they could not be seen from the main street and gave access to the site only from a side street. Esso did not, however, change the e.a.c. in the light of these changes. Esso then leased the gas station to the defendant.]

LORD DENNING M.R.: — **[1]** "This is," said the judge, "a tragic story of wasted endeavour and financial disaster." It is a long story starting as long ago as 1961, and finishing in 1967. Since then eight years have been spent in litigation. . . .

[2] I will give what took place [at the meeting between the defendant and two representatives of the plaintiff] in the words of the judge:

> Mr. Mardon was told that Esso estimated that the throughput of the . . . site, in its third year of operation, would amount to 200,000 gallons a year. I also find that Mr. Mardon then indicated that he thought 100,000 to 150,000 gallons would be a more realistic estimate, but he was convinced by the far greater expertise of, particularly, Mr. Leitch. Mr. Allen is a far younger man and, although on his appointment as manager for the area I am satisfied he made his own observations as to the potentiality of the Eastbank Street site, in the result he accepted Mr. Leitch's estimate. Mr. Mardon, having indicated that he thought that a lower figure would be a more realistic estimate, had his doubts quelled by the experience and the estimate furnished by Mr. Leitch; and it was for that reason, I am satisfied, because of what he was told about the estimated throughput in the third year, that he then proceeded to negotiate for and obtain the grant of a three-year tenancy at a rent of £2,500 a year for the first two years, rising to £3,000 yearly in the last year.

[3] . . . All the dealings were based on that estimate of a throughput of 200,000 gallons. It was on that estimate that Esso developed the site at a cost of £40,000: and that the tenant agreed to pay a rent of £2,500, rising to £3,000. . . .

[4] Having induced Mr. Mardon to accept . . . a tenancy was granted to Mr. Mardon. It was dated April 10, 1963, and was for three years at a rent of £2,500 for the first two years, and £3,000 for the third year. It required him to keep open all day every day of the week, including Sunday. It forbade him to assign or under-let.

[5] On the next day Mr. Mardon went into occupation of the service station and did everything that could be desired of him. He was an extremely good tenant and he tried every method to increase the sales and profitability of the service station. Esso freely acknowledge this.

[Mr. Mardon threatened to quit. The rent was reduced to £1,000 per year. But even so the station could not be made to pay. Eventually, Esso, not being paid, drained the tanks, and then sued for the petrol sold. This put Mr. Mardon out of business. He had lost all his capital.]

[6] . . . Such being the facts, I turn to consider the law. It is founded on the representation that the estimated throughput of the service station was 200,000 gallons. No claim can be brought under the Misrepresentation Act 1967, because that Act did not come into force until April 22, 1967: whereas this representation was made in April 1963. So the claim is put in two ways. First, that the representation was a collateral warranty. Second, that it was a negligent misrepresentation. I will take them in order.

[7] *Collateral warranty.* Ever since *Heilbut, Symons & Co. v. Buckleton* [*supra*], we have had to contend with the law as laid down by the House of Lords that an innocent misrepresentation gives no right to damages. In order to escape from that rule, the pleader used to allege — I often did it myself — that the misrepresentation was fraudulent, or alternatively a collateral warranty. At the trial we nearly always succeeded on collateral warranty. We had to reckon, of course, with the dictum of Lord Moulton . . . that "such collateral contracts must from their very nature be rare." But more often than not the court elevated the innocent misrepresentation into a collateral warranty: and thereby did justice. . . . A representation as to the profits that had been made in the past was invariably held to be a warranty. Besides that experience, there have been many cases since I have sat in this court where we have readily held a representation — which induces a person to enter into a contract — to be a warranty sounding in damages. I summarized them in *Dick Bentley v. Smith* [*supra*] . . . [Counsel for Esso] submitted that the forecast here of 200,000 gallons was an expression of opinion and not a statement of fact: and that it could not be interpreted as a warranty or promise.

[8]   Now I would quite agree with [him] that it was not a warranty — in this sense — that it did not *guarantee* that the throughput *would be* 200,000 gallons. But, nevertheless, it was a forecast made by a party — Esso — who had special knowledge and skill. It was the yardstick (the e.a.c.) by which they measured the worth of a filling station. They knew the facts. They knew the traffic in the town. They knew the throughput of comparable stations. They had much experience and expertise at their disposal. They were in a much better position than Mr. Mardon to make a forecast. It seems to me that if such a person makes a forecast, intending that the other should act upon it — and he does act upon it, it can well be interpreted as a warranty that the forecast is sound and reliable in the sense that they made it with reasonable care and skill. It is just as if Esso said to Mr. Mardon: "Our forecast of throughput is 200,000 gallons. You can rely upon it as being a sound forecast of what the service station should do. The rent is calculated on that footing." If the forecast turned out to be an unsound forecast such as no person of skill or experience should have made, there is a breach of warranty . . .

[9]   In the present case it seems to me that there was a warranty that the forecast was sound, that is, Esso made it with reasonable care and skill. That warranty was broken. Most negligently Esso made a "fatal error" in the forecast they stated to Mr. Mardon, and on which he took the tenancy. For this they are liable in damages. The judge, however, declined to find a warranty. So I must go further.

[10]   *Negligent misrepresentation.* Assuming that there was no warranty, the question arises whether Esso are liable for negligent misstatement under the doctrine of *Hedley Byrne v. Heller.* It has been suggested that *Hedley Byrne* cannot be used so as to impose liability for negligent pre-contractual statements: and that, in a pre-contract situation, the remedy . . . was only in warranty or nothing. Thus in *Hedley Byrne* itself Lord Reid said, "Where there is a contract there is no difficulty as regards the contracting parties: the question is whether there is a warranty". . . .

[11]   In arguing this point [counsel for Esso] took his stand in this way. He submitted that when the negotiations between two parties resulted in a contract between them, their rights and duties were governed by the law of contract and not by the law of tort. There was, therefore, no place in their relationship for *Hedley Byrne* which was solely on liability in tort. . . . But I venture to suggest that [the cases relied on by counsel for Esso] are in conflict with other decisions of high authority which were not cited in them. These decisions show that, in the case of a professional man, the duty to use reasonable care arises not only in contract, but is also imposed by the law apart from contract, and is therefore actionable in tort. It is comparable to the duty of reasonable care which is owed by a master to his servant, or vice versa. It can be put either in contract or in tort. . . .

[12] That seems to me right. A professional man may give advice under a contract for reward; or without a contract, in pursuance of a voluntary assumption of responsibility, gratuitously without reward. In either case he is under one and the same duty to use reasonable care. . . . In the one case it is by reason of a term implied by law. In the other, it is by reason of a duty imposed by law. For a breach of that duty he is liable in damages; and those damages should be, and are, the same, whether he is sued in contract or in tort.

[13] It follows that I cannot accept [counsel's] proposition. It seems to me that *Hedley Byrne*, properly understood, covers this particular proposition: if a man, who has or professes to have special knowledge or skill, makes a representation by virtue thereof to another — be it advice, information or opinion — with the intention of inducing him to enter into a contract with him, he is under a duty to use reasonable care to see that the representation is correct, and that the advice, information or opinion is reliable. If he negligently gives unsound advice or misleading information or expresses an erroneous opinion, and thereby induces the other side to enter into a contract with him, he is liable in damages. . . .

[14] Applying this principle, it is plain that Esso professed to have — and did in fact have — special knowledge or skill in estimating the throughput of a filling station. They made the representation — they forecast a throughput of 200,000 gallons — intending to induce Mr. Mardon to enter into a tenancy on the faith of it. They made it negligently. It was a "fatal error." And thereby induced Mr. Mardon to enter into a contract of tenancy that was disastrous to him. For this misrepresentation they are liable in damages.

[15] *The measure of damages.* Mr. Mardon is not to be compensated here for "loss of a bargain." He was given no bargain that the throughput would amount to 200,000 gallons a year. He is only to be compensated for having been induced to enter into a contract which turned out to be disastrous for him. Whether it be called breach of warranty or negligent misrepresentation, its effect was *not* to warrant the throughput, but only to induce him to enter the contract. So the damages in either case are to be measured by the loss he suffered . . . [H]e can say: "I would not have entered into this contract at all but for your representation. Owing to it, I have lost all the capital I put into it. I also incurred a large overdraft. I have spent four years of my life in wasted endeavour without reward; and it will take me some time to re-establish myself."

[16] For all such loss he is entitled to recover damages. It is to be measured in a similar way as the loss due to a personal injury. You should look into the future so as to forecast what would have been likely to happen if he had never entered into this contract: and contrast it with his position as it is now as a result of entering into it. The future is necessarily problematical and can only be a rough-and-ready estimate. But it must be done in assessing the loss.

[**LORD DENNING** did not regard the new agreement as changing the responsibility of Esso.]

[17] . . . If Mr. Mardon had not been induced to enter into the contract, it is fair to assume that he would have found an alternative business in which to invest his capital. (The judge said so.) It is also fair to assume (as he is a very good man of business) that he would have invested it sufficiently well so that he would not have lost the capital. Nor would he have incurred any overdraft or liabilities that were not covered by his assets. And it may be assumed that he would have made a reasonable return by way of earnings for his own work (in addition to return from his capital). But equally it must be remembered that after March 1967 (when he gave up the site at Southport) he should have been able (if fit) to take other employment or start another business and thus mitigate his loss: and gradually get restored to a position equal to that which he would have had if he had never gone into the Esso business. It would take him some time to do this. So the loss of earnings could only be for a limited number of years.

[18] On this footing, the loss which he has suffered would seem to be as follows (subject to further argument by the parties): Capital loss: cash put into the business and lost, £6,270; overdraft incurred in running the business, £7,774. Loss of earnings to be discussed. There will be interest to be added for a period to be discussed.

[19] Mr. Mardon also claimed damages for having to sell his house to pay off the overdraft. That seems to me too remote and should be compensated by interest on the overdraft. He also suffered in health by reason of all the worry over this disaster, and was off work. That should be compensated by loss of future earnings. . . .

[ORMROD and SHAW L.JJ. wrote judgments agreeing with LORD DENNING.]

QUESTIONS AND NOTES

1.   Lord Denning appears to pay deference to the decision of the trial judge that there was no warranty. Lord Denning had said in *Dick Bentley v. Harold Smith* that "if a representation is made in the course of dealings for a contract for the very purpose of inducing the other party to act on it, and it actually induces him to act on it by entering into the contract, that is prima facie ground for inferring that the representation was intended as a warranty." What was the reason that Esso made the representation to Mr. Mardon? What findings of fact would the trial judge have had to make to justify his decision? How much of a purely factual inquiry is involved in the conclusion that a statement inducing the making of a contract is a warranty? In the final result, did it matter that Lord Denning accepted that there was no warranty?

2.   Notice that Lord Denning admits (¶ 7) that counsel and courts adopted a result-selective process of choosing between (fraudulent) misrepresentations and (collateral) warranties.

3.   If Mr. Mardon gets compensation for (i) the capital he invested (or borrowed to put) in the business; (ii) interest on those amounts; and (iii) something for his own time, is an award based on these factors putting him in (a) the position he would have been in if the representation had not been made; or (b) the position he would have been in if the representation had been true? If not, what, precisely, is the difference between the two measures?

4.   Lord Denning refers to cases of professional negligence as examples of the congruence of contract and tort.
       The duty of a solicitor, for example, is said to involve obligations in both contract and tort. Thus, a lawyer might be sued for negligence even if advice is provided gratuitously, provided that it was "reasonably relied upon".
       A client's contract with a lawyer is often created by a conversation like this:

       Client: "Will you act for me in this house purchase?"

       Lawyer: "Yes."

       If the client suffers loss, the problem will be to establish that the lawyer did not reach the standard of performance that the client was entitled to expect. Since the contract says nothing about the standard, it is up to the law to "fill in the blanks" in the agreement. The standard to which the lawyer is generally held is that of the "average practitioner" exercising reasonable care in the performance of the obligations undertaken, though if the lawyer claims to be a specialist there may be a higher standard of care. This standard looks much like a tort standard, for it refers to the taking of reasonable professional care or to the assumption of reasonable skill in the discharge of the duty. The tort view of liability is, of course, reinforced by the common use of the term "malpractice". While the basis of liability generally is contractual, the standard of care is tort based. There is often only a semantic issue in categorizing the claim as based in contract or tort.

In some circumstances, however, the argument over whether a lawyer's professional liability is based in contract or in tort will have a direct bearing on the measure of damages or on the length of the limitation period. The tort limitation period, running from the date at which the breach reasonably became known to the plaintiff, is, in effect, longer than the contract limitation period, which runs from the date of breach of the contractual duty, the date on which the negligent act occurred. In the case of solicitors' negligence it is often impossible for the client to know that there has been a breach of duty until after the contract limitation period has run. Clients may not know, for example, that they have not received good title to property that they bought until the time comes to sell it and the new purchaser's lawyer points out the problem. This event may occur many years after the original lawyer's contractual obligation was breached. The Supreme Court of Canada held in *Central & Eastern Trust Co. v. Rafuse*, [1986] 2 S.C.R. 147, 31 D.L.R. (4th) 481, that the client of a negligent lawyer could sue in either contract or tort, and could have the benefit of the longer limitation period.

The tendency to regard the contract between a lawyer and his or her client as creating tort liabilities only is based on the very early development of the common law forms of action that led, ultimately, to the action of *assumpsit* and the modern law of contracts. A lawyer is liable because he or she *undertook* to do something for his or her client and did it badly. In a tort claim, it would not matter if this undertaking was given gratuitously or in return for payment — payment here being the commercial price of the service, not merely technical compliance with the doctrine of consideration. If the law ignores the fact of payment, there is a risk that the expectations of the client will be disappointed and un-remedied. This issue will be further explored shortly.

5.   Consider the position of a lawyer who agrees to act for the purchaser of a house. In such a situation, the lawyer will often "certify" to the client and to a mortgage lender that the client has a "good and marketable title" to the property: the lawyer's opinion (given in a letter to his or her client after the completion of the transaction) will state that the client has a "good and marketable title".

Sometimes the lawyer makes no such express statement and the lawyer may then argue that the liability to the client is limited. A court, however, will not care what exact words the lawyer actually uses; he or she will be held to the same standard of care, unless there is some explicit limitation of liability. The expectations of the client are generally that the lawyer will check to ensure that at least there are no surprises. The contract between the parties is one almost entirely created by the law, at least in the absence of express stipulations (and there are limitations on how far a court will allow a professional like a lawyer or doctor to go in contracting out of a professional standard of care.)

What are its terms so far as the issue of damages is concerned? There are two promises that the lawyer can make (or be held to have made) to the client: "I promise that you will not suffer loss through your reliance on my skill" or "I promise that you will get whatever benefits you would have received had you obtained the title to the property that you have bought."

Which promise do you think the client might have expected a lawyer to make? How do you think that this question should be answered?

If one takes a careful look at the relation between lawyer and client, it is possible to see that in some situations the conventional distinction between expectation and reliance damages may collapse. Suppose that a client comes to a lawyer and asks her to act on the client's purchase of land for investment. If the lawyer is careless and if, as a result, the client does not get a "good and marketable title", the client has lost not only the actual costs incurred in making the useless investment — its reliance losses — but also the opportunity to put its money into a profitable investment — its expectation losses. Both losses were incurred in reliance on the lawyer's promise to act properly; both losses can be shown to be reliance losses. If we use the economic term, "opportunity costs" — the costs of not making the next most profitable investment — to describe the client's lost profit, their nature as reliance losses becomes clear.

On this analysis, the question is not whether the law compensates the plaintiff for lost profit or for costs thrown away, or for the expectation interest or the reliance interest, but whether a court awards a higher or lower measure of damages. In other words, there is not always a satisfactory distinction between "expectation" damages or "reliance" damages; both terms suggest the same measure.

6. The effect of the decision in *Esso v. Mardon*, or perhaps, its capacity to make analysis difficult, is similar to that of Lord Denning's judgment in *High Trees* (*supra*, Chapter 2). Lord Denning has articulated a principle that is difficult to control. The next case explores some further implications of the tort of negligent misrepresentation. We shall then look more closely at methods of controlling the scope of the tort.

The following judgment of the Supreme Court of Canada in *V.K. Mason Construction Ltd. v. Bank of Nova Scotia* illustrates the problems of deciding what damages to award, and how an award that is nominally regarded as "reliance based" may in fact give an expectation-like award.

V.K. MASON CONSTRUCTION LTD. v. BANK OF NOVA SCOTIA

[1985] S.C.J. No. 12, [1985] 1 S.C.R. 271, 16 D.L.R. (4th) 598
(S.C.C., Dickson C.J.C., Estey, McIntyre, Chouinard, Lamer and Wilson JJ.)

WILSON J.: — **[1]** The court is confronted in this case with appeals in two lawsuits which have been consolidated. The first lawsuit involved an action on the alternative footing of contract and tort brought by V. K. Mason Construction Ltd. ("Mason"), against the Bank of Nova Scotia ("the Bank"). The second action involved a claim by Mason under the *Mechanics' Lien Act*, R.S.O. 1970, c. 267, as amended, against Courtot Investments Ltd. ("Courtot") and the Bank. The claim against Courtot was settled but the claim against the Bank is before us . . .

1. The Facts

[2] Both actions arose out of the financing and construction of an office and retail shopping complex in Toronto known as the "Courtot Centre". [It is on the north side of Bloor Street just west of Bay Street.] The owner and developer of the complex was Courtot, the general contractor in charge of construction was Mason and the Bank provided bridge financing for the construction, taking as part of its security a mortgage contained in a demand debenture on the property.

[3] Courtot was a valued client of the Bank but was inexperienced in the field of property development. It was also shortsighted in its planning for financial contingencies and failed to obtain adequate funding to cope with rising interest rates and costly architectural changes implemented subsequent to the project's getting underway. As a consequence the litigation between Mason and the Bank took place in the aftermath of the commercial failure of the Courtot Centre project and the inability of Courtot to raise sufficient financing to meet its indebtedness to its general contractor.

[4]   The story commences in March, 1972, when Mason submitted a tender for construction of the project containing the following stipulation:

> Our tender and any contract entered into following acceptance of our tender are conditional upon production to us prior to execution of any construction contract, satisfactory evidence of the ability of the Owner to meet the payments as they become due under such contract.

[5]   By July 17, 1972, Mason was prepared to sign a fixed price construction contract with Courtot provided it was satisfied of Courtot's ability to meet the payments. Mason had begun construction before a contract was signed but O'Leary J. expressly found at trial that it would not have signed the contract had it not been for assurances from the Bank. The reason for his conclusion on this point was that Mason's investment in the project up to the time of the signing of the contract was small enough that it would have been able, had it abandoned the project, to recover its investment from Courtot on a *quantum meruit* basis under the *Mechanics' Lien Act* or otherwise.

[6]   Courtot meanwhile had been trying to arrange financing for the project from the Bank. In October, 1971, the Bank rejected his application for bridge financing and in January, 1972, it turned down a further application for a loan of $865,500 to cover pre-construction costs. In February, 1972, however, the latter decision was reversed and by July 6, 1972, the branch manager, Mr. Hway, was prepared to recommend a loan of $9,000,000 to provide bridge financing. By August the Bank decided to loan Courtot $8,850,000 U.S., one of the bases for that decision being the fact that Courtot had been able to arrange a fixed price construction contract with Mason for $6,100,000. The Bank's commitment to Courtot, expressed in the form of a letter approving the loan in principle, was conveyed to Mason but this was not sufficient to convince Mason of Courtot's ability to meet the payments.

[7]   The events of August 30 through September 12 are crucial to the case and are covered in detail by O'Leary J. Mason through its solicitor sought assurances from the Bank that Courtot had sufficient financing. There was an exchange of telephone conversations and, although the oral evidence is unclear about the outcome of these conversations, the documentary evidence indicates that as of September 7, 1972, Mason was still not satisfied that Courtot was able to pay the contract price. O'Leary J. found that, if Mason had continued to be unsatisfied about Courtot's ability to pay, it would not have continued with the project. He further found that the Bank knew or ought to have known this and that it was apparent that further assurances would be necessary.

[8]   Mr. Hway, the branch manager, on September 8, 1972, drafted a letter to Mason giving those assurances. He did not send it immediately but discussed the wording of the letter with the Bank's solicitor on September 11 or 12. The solicitor did not recommend any changes and on September 12, 1972, the letter was delivered to Mason. It read as follows:

We wish to advise that we have accorded Courtot Investments Limited interim financing sufficient to cover the construction of the subject complex. We shall therefore provide funds for your progress billings as they occur against architect's certificates (Bregman & Hamann) of work completed subject to the usual search for liens by our solicitor.

[9]   Acting upon the strength of this assurance, Mason signed the construction contract with Courtot on September 14, 1972. Construction went ahead and Mason performed its part of the bargain, substantially completing construction in August, 1974. The completion of construction had originally been scheduled for December 31, 1973, but changes in the specifications by Courtot had both added to the cost of construction (which resulted in an agreed increase in the contract price) and delayed the completion date. O'Leary J. expressly exonerated Mason from any responsibility for the construction delays.

[10]   By April 19, 1974, it had become apparent both to Courtot and to the Bank that the amount of the Bank's loan to Courtot would not cover the cost of construction. The Bank did not, however, offer to extend Courtot more money or agree to Courtot's request for an extension of the due date of the loan. By July 31, 1974, Courtot had called down $8,413,000 U.S. of the $8,850,000 U.S. which the Bank had agreed to lend it. Rather than call for the rest of the money in order to provide at least part payment to Mason, Courtot tried to find excuses in order to delay paying Mason and then engaged in vexatious litigation against Mason for this purpose. The Bank at no point informed Mason that Courtot had insufficient funds to cover the cost of construction.

[11]   By August 30, 1974, Mason had substantially completed construction and had not been paid on architects' certificates dating back as far as July 10, 1974. Mason took out mechanics' liens on the property of $1,057,941.98 in work for which it had not been paid. In August, 1975, the Bank demanded payment from Courtot on its loans and exercised its power of sale of the Courtot Centre as mortgagee under the demand debenture. On February 9, 1976, the complex was sold for $11,000,000.

[12]   In December, 1977, Mason settled its mechanics' lien action against Courtot and Courtot acceded to the entry of judgment in favour of Mason in the amount of $1,427,487.17. The Bank asserted its priority as mortgagee over the proceeds of the sale and, after it had been paid, there were insufficient funds to pay Mason in full. In the mechanics' lien action, therefore, Mason asserted that by virtue of s. 4 of the *Interest Act*, R.S.C. 1970, c. I-18, the Bank was limited to interest at the rate of 5 per cent. The learned trial judge agreed with this submission and the result was that, by reducing the amount of the Bank's claim, Mason would be enabled to have its claim satisfied out of the proceeds of sale. Mason had also argued that the Bank was estopped from asserting its priority as mortgagee but, in light of his ruling on the *Interest Act* point, the learned judge did not find it necessary to make a ruling on this issue.

[13]   Returning to the contract and tort action, O'Leary J. found on the facts as stated above that there was a contract between Mason and the Bank and that the Bank had breached that contract. He awarded damages in the amount of $1,057,941.98. The trial judge also found that the Bank was liable to Mason on the alternative basis of negligent misrepresentation. Specifically, he found that the representation in the Bank's letter of September 8, 1972, was false in that the Bank

had not committed itself to provide sufficient funds to Courtot to complete the project but only a specified sum of money toward the financing of the project. Furthermore, O'Leary J. found that, even at the date the statement was made, the amount of the Bank's loan to Courtot was significantly less than the projected cost of the project, a fact known to the Bank. The learned trial judge awarded damages of $897,941.98 for negligent misrepresentation, this sum being calculated by removing Mason's projected profit of $160,000 from the value of the contract damages.

[14] The Bank's appeal in both actions was heard by Houlden, Goodman and Cory JJ.A. At the conclusion of argument Houlden J.A. gave an oral judgment for the court. With respect to the contract/tort action, he dismissed the Bank's appeal with respect to the breach of contract claim and did not find it necessary to comment on the negligent misrepresentation issue. With respect to the mechanics' lien case, he allowed the Bank's appeal, holding that s. 4 of the *Interest Act* was inapplicable in this case because the Bank's loan was a mortgage on real estate and therefore expressly excluded from the operation of the section. He further held that the Bank was not estopped from asserting its priority as mortgagee over Mason under the *Mechanics' Lien Act*.

2.   *The Issues*

[15] The issues in the two actions may be conveniently dealt with under four main headings, namely: (1) contract; (2) negligent misrepresentation; (3) s. 4 of the *Interest Act*; and (4) estoppel.

[16] It might, however, be useful at the outset to put the case in perspective. This is not a simple situation in which a bank makes a representation about the creditworthiness of one of its clients to a third party. This is a case in which the Bank made a representation to a third party for the specific purpose of inducing the third party to enter into a contract with one of the Bank's own clients, thereby enabling that client to enter into a substantial loan transaction with the Bank. I do not think it is realistic to portray the Bank manager, Mr. Hway, as an inexperienced person who had no motive or intention to mislead anyone. It is quite clear that Mr. Hway wished to check the letter with the Bank's solicitor precisely because he realized that the Bank was inducing Mason to enter into a contract and he wanted to avoid the prospect of the Bank's incurring a liability to Mason.

[17] Mr. Hway, like Courtot, no doubt thought that the transaction would be a profitable one. Had Courtot been able to arrange permanent mortgage financing or find a buyer for the building there would have been no problem about the shortfall in the Bank's bridge financing. Unfortunately for all concerned, the market for commercial properties in that part of Toronto was soft at the time Courtot was looking for commercial tenants for the centre. Also, Courtot was caught by having a floating interest loan at a time when interest rates were rising, thereby significantly increasing the amount of interest which it owed to the Bank. Furthermore, having taken out a loan in U.S. funds Courtot was hurt by currency fluctuations which resulted from the strength of the Canadian dollar as compared to the American dollar. Finally, Mr. Courtot was, as already mentioned, an inexperienced developer and he had not allowed himself sufficient flexibility by taking contingencies of this kind into account in arranging his financing. As a result the project, from Courtot's perspective at least, was a failure and the contest among the creditors was on.

(i)   *Contract*

[18] Mr. Sopinka, counsel for the Bank, put forward three main lines of argument against the existence of a contract in this case, namely: (1) absence of an intention on the part of the Bank and Mason to create legal relations between themselves; (2) absence of offer and acceptance; and (3) absence of consideration. He submitted, moreover, that even if there was a contract between Mason and the Bank there was no breach of it by the Bank.

[19] It seems to me that if there were a contract in existence between these two parties it must be characterized, in the terms of traditional contract analysis, as a unilateral contract. The Bank's letter to Mason would, on this analysis, be construed as an offer that, if Mason would sign a fixed price contract with Courtot, the Bank would supply Courtot with sufficient interim financing to complete the report. Mason was entitled to accept this offer either by communication or by performance, *i.e.*, by signing the contract with Courtot: see *Carlill v. Carbolic Smoke Ball Co.*, [1893] 1 Q.B. 256 (C.A.). The consideration which passed to the Bank would be that Mason had obligated itself to Courtot to enter into a fixed price contract, thereby giving the Bank the assurance that the project was sufficiently sound that it could lend money to Courtot.

[20] The problem with this analysis is that it requires a great deal to be implied into the course of conduct of the parties. By implying a contract into this course of conduct one is left unsure of the exact nature of the Bank's obligations. Was the Bank obliged to advance money to Courtot so that Mason would be paid even if Courtot did not demand the money? The trial judge held, in effect, that it was, but I find it difficult to say that sophisticated business people, taking into account the course of conduct leading up to the Bank's statement, would construe the September 8, 1972 letter as imposing that kind of obligation. It is, of course, always a matter of judgment whether the requisite certainty of intention exists as a foundation for implying a contract out of a combination of documents and a course of conduct. I tend to view this as a case which falls on the far side of the line in the sense that I do not believe that reasonable business people would have construed the Bank's letter as an absolute and unqualified guarantee, which is what the courts below have effectively held.

[21] Negligent misrepresentation is, in my view, the appropriate basis of liability in this case. The disadvantage in implying a contract in a commercial context like this is that much of the value of commercial contracts lies in their ability to produce certainty. Parties are enabled to regulate their relationship by means of words rather than by means of their understanding of what each others actions are intended to imply. I think this is one reason why the common law imposes an objective rather than a subjective test for the creation of an agreement. The objective test is important because it prevents parties from avoiding obligations which a reasonable person would assume they had undertaken, simply on the ground that there is no document embodying the precise nature of the obligation. On the other hand, if too broad a view is taken of what a reasonable person assumes will give rise to an agreement or obligation, the certainty which is one of the principle virtues of contract may be undermined. Obviously, there are circumstances in which a

Bank's conduct could give rise to contractual liability as a guarantor, but I do not believe that this case falls into that category. I conclude therefore that there was no contractual relationship between the Bank and Mason.

(ii)   *Negligent misrepresentation*

[22] It seems to me that a negligent misrepresentation analysis properly focuses attention on the gravamen of the cause of action in this case, namely, the fact that the Bank's representation to Mason was false. The parties are in agreement that the applicable law is to be found in the decision of the House of Lords in *Hedley Byrne & Co. Ltd. v. Heller & Partners Ltd.*, [1964] A.C. 465, [1963] 2 All E.R. 575 (H.L.). Mr. Sopinka sums up the requirements for liability as follows: (a) there must be an untrue statement; (b) it must have been made negligently; (c) there must be a special relationship giving rise to a duty of care; and (d) there must be reliance which is foreseeable. His submission to the court comprised a reconstruction of the facts to show that none of these prerequisites was present. His problem is that O'Leary J. made very clear findings of fact against the Bank on all four requirements.

[23] The main difficulty I have with Mr. Sopinka's approach to the facts is that he attempts to isolate them from their context when it is the context that gives them meaning. For example, with respect to the falsity of the September 8, 1972 letter, Mr. Sopinka attempts to show that, on the basis of Courtot's estimates of total project costs minus soft costs, the Bank was justified in representing that it was loaning Courtot sufficient money to complete the project. This seems to me to completely overlook the fact that what Mason was seeking was an assurance that Courtot would have sufficient funds at a time when Mason already knew the basic terms of the Bank's loan to Courtot. In other words, the September 8, 1972 letter would, as the Bank knew, be construed as an assurance of something over and above the terms of the loan, yet the Bank went ahead and gave that assurance relying solely on the terms of the loan and Courtot's cost estimates. Mr. Hway may have felt at the time that he was justified in assuring Mason that there would be sufficient funds without informing them that his assurance was based on the assumption that soft costs would not be incurred.

[24] The same general comment can be made with respect to Mr. Sopinka's submissions on negligence, particularly in relation to special relationship and reliance. The Bank had a special relationship with Mason because it was inducing Mason to sign a contract with Courtot in reliance on the Bank's assurance of adequate financing. The statement was negligent because it was made without revealing that the Bank was giving an assurance based solely on a loan arrangement which Mason had already said was insufficient assurance to it of the existence of adequate financing.

[25] Not only was the Bank's misrepresentation made negligently but it is clear from the finding of fact of O'Leary J. that Mason relied on it and that such reliance was foreseeable by the Bank. I believe therefore that all the requirements for negligent misrepresentation are met in this case.

[26] One of the interesting legal issues with respect to negligent misrepresentation is the issue of damages. Mason cross-appealed on this issue. The Bank concedes that in principle the proper aim of a damage award is to restore the plaintiff to the position in which he would have been if the negligent misrepresentation had

never been made: see *McGregor on Damages*, 14th ed. (1980), p. 996. The Bank argues that Mason would have lost money in any event even if the misrepresentation had not been made because it would have lost money in severing its relationship with Courtot. The problem with this submission is that the trial judge made an express finding to the contrary. What we have to assume, I believe, is that but for the misrepresentation Mason would have ceased work for Courtot, recovered its expenses for work already done and found another construction project to work on.

[27] The learned trial judge awarded damages for misrepresentation on the basis that they were equal to contract damages minus Mason's anticipated profit. Counsel for Mason submits that the trial judge was wrong in subtracting the anticipated profit because damages in contract and tort are the same. He also submitted that interest should have been awarded on the damages at 12 per cent from the completion of the project on October 7, 1974. While I tend to the view that there is a conceptual difference between damages in contract and in tort, I believe that in many instances the same quantum will be arrived at, albeit by somewhat different routes.

[28] I agree with the submission of counsel for Mason that the trial judge was wrong in subtracting profit. I believe that in principle one is entitled to assume that Mason would have found a profitable means of employing itself had it not been induced to work on the Courtot project by the Bank's misrepresentation. This, in my view, is a reasonably foreseeable head of damage: see *Patrick L. Roberts Ltd. v. Sollinger Industries Ltd. and Ontario Development Corp.* (1978), 84 D.L.R. (3d) 113, 19 O.R. (2d) 44 (C.A.). In equating Mason's lost profit with the profit estimated on the Courtot project we are simply saying that this is a reasonable estimate of what Mason would have been likely to have made if it had decided to abandon the Courtot project and find other work. That is to say, the lost profit on *this* contract represents the lost opportunity for profit on *any* contract.

[29] On the basis of the same reasoning it seems to me that Mason ought to be entitled to prejudgment interest as of the date of completion of the project. In other words, to put Mason in the position it would have been in absent the misrepresentation we must assume that it would have in hand at the time it completed the project that amount of outlay and anticipated profit which is lost in completing the project. It seems to me to be only reasonable to assume that it would have been able to put that money to profitable use. Interest is the court's way of compensating Mason for the loss of the opportunity to invest that money.

[30] I note that in connection with the issue of negligent misrepresentation the learned trial judge found that the Bank had a duty to warn Mason in April, 1974, that Courtot did not have enough money to complete the project. This, in my view, is a separate (although related) head of liability. However, because the original negligent misrepresentation encompasses a greater liability than the duty to warn, I do not consider it necessary to deal with this aspect of the case.

[The discussion of the *Interest Act* and the estoppel argument is omitted. Mason's appeal on these issues was dismissed.]

Conclusions

[31] (1) The Bank is not liable to Mason in contract but is liable in negligent misrepresentation.

[32] (2) Although damages for negligent misrepresentation would normally be assessed in terms of actual loss, including lost opportunity, rather than loss of anticipated profit, in this case the commercial context in which the parties operated dictates that Mason's loss should be calculated in the same way in tort as it would be in contract. Mason is accordingly entitled to damages in the sum of $1,138,151.63, being the entire balance outstanding under its contract with Courtot, plus interest on this amount at the rate of 9 per cent per annum from October 7, 1974, to March 21, 1980.

QUESTIONS AND NOTES

1.   The imposition on the Bank of liability for negligent misrepresentation is based on the breach by the Bank of a duty owed to Mason. What are the terms of that duty? In other words, what should the Bank have done to discharge its duty to Mason? If this duty could be limited or affected by the language of the letter that the bank wrote to Mason, is the letter the source of the duty? If the letter is the source, why couldn't it support a contract duty?

2.   What are the terms of the contract that Mason would have alleged that the Bank breached? Do the terms of this contract have to be different from the duty that the Bank should have met under its tort duty? What would have been the difference if the court had recognized a contract-based claim?

3.   *V.K. Mason* raises some challenging issues in its approach to the assessment of damages. Wilson J. accepts the "principle" that "the proper aim" of the damage award in a case like this is to restore the plaintiff to the position he would have been in "if the negligent misrepresentation had never been made". This sounds like a statement that there will be a reliance-based assessment of damages, but she includes the plaintiff's loss of profits in the award, which suggests an expectation-based approach.
     Does Wilson J. mean that in all cases of negligent misrepresentation the court may award the same amount of damages as may be awarded for breach of contract?
     It is significant that both *Mardon* and *V.K. Mason* involve situations where there has been reliance on the negligent misstatement *and* performance of the contractual obligations. In a situation where the plaintiff has in fact relied on the defendant's statement to perform a contract with the defendant, the plaintiff may have given up the opportunity to work with others, and a reliance-based damage assessment may include opportunity costs, resulting in the same award as an expectation-based approach. These cases illustrate the argument made by Fuller and Perdue that in some situations the distinction between expectation and reliance losses collapses, as the reliance measure of damages includes opportunity costs.
     Does the fact that a loss results from the breach of an obligation arising from an undertaking that was bought (*i.e.*, from a contract) ever justify a larger damage award than would be made if similar losses resulted from the breach of an obligation that is imposed but not paid for (*i.e.*, a negligent misstatement)?

4.   If the liability of a party to a contract for a misrepresentation can be based in either contract (breach of warranty) or tort (negligent misstatement), there is a need to determine the effect of a contractual allocation of the risk of loss. It should follow from general contract principles (freedom of contract and party autonomy, both issues to be more fully examined in Chapter 6) that the parties to a contract can plan the allocation of risk in any way they see fit. Will that allocation be threatened by the imposition on the parties of tort duties? The issue is complex, and forces us to be precise about the

basis of any liability imposed on anyone. In principle it is, however, usually possible to limit tort liability by the terms of a contract.

5. The liability of a bank for an assurance given by it was again raised in *Keith Plumbing & Heating Co. v. Newport City Club Ltd. (sub nom. Micron Construction Ltd. v. Hongkong Bank of Canada)* (2000), 184 D.L.R. (4th) 75, [2000] 6 W.W.R. 65 (B.C.C.A.). The plaintiff, Micron Construction Ltd., was a contractor retained by developers (Newport City Club Ltd.) at an early stage in the construction of a building. The plaintiff and other building traders involved were anxious about the financing for the building. Eventually the bank provided a letter in the following form:

    Confidential

    September 29, 1994

    TO WHOM IT MAY CONCERN

    Dear Sir/Madam

    RE: NEWPORT CITY CLUB LTD.

    This is to confirm that the captioned company has maintained an operating account with this Bank, to which loan facilities of low to medium eight figures have been authorized, on secured basis, to finance the acquisition and renovation of their premises at 1155 West Georgia Street, Vancouver.

    The said account is being operated as agreed.

    This bank reference is given at the request of the captioned and without any responsibility on the Bank and its signing officers.

    In reliance on the letter, the plaintiff did work for the developers for which it was not paid, as the developers were insolvent. The bank's letter falsely misrepresented that construction financing was in place, despite the bank's knowledge that security had not been provided.

    The plaintiff sued the bank for fraudulent misrepresentation and negligent misrepresentation. The British Columbia Court of Appeal, affirming the trial judge on this point, held that there was no fraud, though the actions of the bank's employees were close to being reckless. The Court concluded that no bank exercising reasonable care towards those it knew would rely upon the information would have drafted such a letter. In the claim for negligent misrepresentation, one question was the effect of the final sentence in the bank's letter, which stated that the letter was provided "without any responsibility". Esson J.A., giving the judgment of the majority of the Court, said:

    > [99] In my view, it was reasonable in these circumstances, even with knowledge of the disclaimer, for the plaintiff to rely on the Bank's assurances and it was reasonably foreseeable to the Bank that the plaintiff would rely. The fact that the plaintiff, to the knowledge of the Bank, had no alternative source of information available to it is critical to that conclusion. That circumstance distinguishes this case from the more typical situation in which the recipient of the information decides to rely upon it rather than going to the trouble or expense of obtaining it elsewhere. . . .

    A further basis for the Court's decision to make the bank liable was that, in a subsequent conversation between an employee of the bank and the plaintiff's banker, the bank repeated its assurances that there would be adequate funds to pay the plaintiff.

While politicians frequently make promises in elections, it is clear that for a variety of public policy reasons, these promises are not (and should not be) legally enforceable. In *Hogan v. Newfoundland (Attorney General)*, [2000] N.J. 54 (C.A.), the court made clear that purely political promises could not be the basis for a claim in contract or negligent misrepresentation, even if a person (or group) claimed reliance on the promise in casting his or her (or their) votes in an election. Cameron J.A. stated (para. 38): "Supremacy of Parliament is also at the foundation of the view that election promises do not amount to an offer to contract and do not create legally enforceable rights."

In *Friesen v. Hammell*, [1999] 5 W.W.R. 345, 57 B.C.L.R. (3d) 276 (C.A.), three voters sought a declaration under s. 150 of the *Election Act*, R.S.B.C. 1996, c. 106, that the elections of 39 members of the New Democratic Party (NDP) to the Legislative Assembly were invalid by virtue of breaches of s. 256(2) of the Act. That subsection provided:

> (2) An individual or organization must not, by abduction, duress or fraudulent means, do any of the following:
>
> (a) impede, prevent or otherwise interfere with an individual's right to vote;
>
> (b) compel, persuade or otherwise cause an individual to vote or refrain from voting;
>
> (c) compel, persuade or otherwise cause an individual to vote or refrain from voting for a particular candidate or for a candidate of a particular political party.

The NDP and the 39 members sought to have the application dismissed. The trial judge had refused to grant either the petitioners' or the respondents' applications.

The petitioners claimed that the respondents made knowingly false representations concerning the 1995-96 and 1996-97 provincial budgets and the government's ability to sustain a capital development program. They alleged that these misrepresentations induced the electorate to vote for NDP members. Both appeals focused on para. 256(2)(c) of the *Election Act*, and, in particular, on whether the fraud statements alleged to have been made constituted "fraudulent means" within the paragraph. The petitioners argued that the legislature intended to control not only fraudulent conduct aimed at the voting process itself, but also fraudulent conduct aimed at influencing the decisions of the voters.

The British Columbia Court of Appeal held that it had no jurisdiction to grant the relief claimed by the petitioners. The respondents' appeal was dismissed, but the petition against them was directed to proceed to trial. The Court of Appeal held that "fraudulent means" for the purpose of s. 256 included fraudulent misrepresentations of material facts, made knowingly or recklessly, that induced potential voters to vote a party or candidate other than the one for whom the voter would have voted but for the misrepresentation.

Do you think that this result is what the NDP had in mind when the legislature amended the *Election Act* and added s-s. 256(2)?

Ultimately this petition was dismissed after a full hearing, with Humphries J. concluding that there was no evidence that the statements made by the Premier and Finance Minister were known to be false or that they were made without regard to truth or falsity: [2002] B.C.J. No. 1618, 190 D.L.R. (4th) 210 (S.C.). While the evidence established that the politicians were "optimistic" (and wrong) in their forecasts, it did *not* establish that they inserted "grossly exaggerated numbers into this budget, ones which they knew could never materialize".

Once the courts permitted a plaintiff to sue in either contract or tort, the problem of the co-existence of the two remedies had to be faced. There are two general circumstances when co-existence has to be considered. The first is whether a representation that induced the making of the contract may be made the basis for a claim after the contract is made; this question was the issue in *Esso Petroleum v Mardon*. The second is whether a representation made during the contract is effective to displace a contractual allocation of risk.

The Supreme Court has struggled with these issues and, while the results of the cases are generally satisfactory, the basis for the decisions is not always clear. The earliest case in the Supreme Court where the issue was raised (though in a post-contractual setting) was *J. Nunes Diamonds Ltd. v. Dominion Electric Protection Co.*, [1972] S.C.R. 769, 26 D.L.R. (3d) 699. The defendant supplied a burglar alarm system to the plaintiff, appellant, a diamond merchant. The contract between the parties expressly allocated the risk of loss from burglary to the plaintiff, *i.e.*, from the defendant's liability insurer to the plaintiff's casualty insurer. The main benefit from the contract for the plaintiff was that, with the system, it was able to obtain insurance at a more reasonable — or at least a lower — premium than would have been the case had there been no burglar alarm. Indeed, without the alarm system, insurance of any kind might not have been available.

The defendant's alarm system was circumvented at the premises of another diamond merchant. The plaintiff's insurer sought assurances from the defendant that its system was not at fault. An assurance given by an unnamed employee of the defendant to the insurer was, for the purposes of the judgment, assumed to have been negligently given. When burglars stole diamonds from the plaintiff's premises, the insurer paid under the policy and then brought a subrogated claim against the defendant. The plaintiff's claim was dismissed.

Pigeon J. suggested that, for the tort of negligent misrepresentation to be actionable the tort has to be "independent" of the contract. A tort may be "independent" in at least two ways: (i) the representation may have been made to a party who was not a party to the contract; or (ii) the duty owed by the defendant may be unaffected by the contract. The first (and less common) situation may, as a matter of fact, have occurred in *J. Nunes Diamonds*, though the form of the action, *i.e.*, a claim by the insurer under its rights of subrogation, may have obscured this possibility. The person who relied on the representation was not the plaintiff but the plaintiff's insurer. If the insurer had had an opportunity to protect itself by, for example, requiring more of the diamonds to be stored in a bank vault, and if it had, in reliance on the defendant's assurance, not taken that opportunity, the insurer may have had a cause of action against the alarm company that would be entirely independent of the contract because the insurer was not a party to it. The insurer's (more or less automatic) response of suing in a subrogated action in the name of the insured may then have been a mistake.

The test of independence stated by Pigeon J. (pp. 777-78 S.C.R.) was that "where the relationship between the parties is governed by a contract, [it has to be] considered as an 'independent tort' unconnected with the performance of the contract. . . . Would these representations have been made if the parties had not been in the contractual relationship . . . ?" This might seem to be a difficult test to meet, but in other parts of the judgment, Pigeon J. indicated that the critical issue was the assessment of tort liability in light of the other contractual provisions. He noted that here the parties clearly expected that the plaintiff and its insurer would bear the risk of burglary. There was "no doubt", he said (p. 778 S.C.R.), that the parties did not intend that the contract of service would be "turned into the equivalent of a contract of insurance, by virtue of inaccurate or incomplete representations respecting the actual value of the protection service provided".

While the discussion of Pigeon J. about the requirement for an "independent tort" has not featured in later Supreme Court cases, the courts must often consider the relevance of contractual provisions when assessing the possibility of tort liability. In *J. Nunes Diamonds* Pigeon J. found that neither the nominal plaintiff nor the insurer actually relied on the defendant's assurance, as at the time there was no realistic alternative to the limited protection afforded by the defendant's system.

An example of a pre-contractual misrepresentation that survived the contract is provided by the next case.

QUEEN v. COGNOS INC.

[1993] S.C.J. No. 3, [1993] 1 S.C.R. 87, 99 D.L.R. (4th) 626
(S.C.C., La Forest, L'Heureux-Dubé, Gonthier, Sopinka and Iacobucci JJ.)

[The plaintiff was living with his wife and children in Calgary, where he had a relatively well-paid and secure managerial position. He responded to an advertisement for a position with the defendant (then called Quasar Systems Ltd.), which was located in Ottawa. At the interview the plaintiff was told that the defendant was hiring someone for a "major project", which was fully described and would utilize his skills. He was led to believe that the project would last at least two years. He was offered the position, and moved with his family from Calgary to take the position. The contract of employment that the plaintiff signed provided for one month's notice of termination. The plaintiff accepted employment without being told that the project on which he was to be employed had not been approved by the defendant corporation's board of directors.

After the plaintiff began work for the defendant he learned that the board of directors had decided not to proceed with the project. The defendant attempted to find other projects for the plaintiff to work on, but after a few months the plaintiff was dismissed as there was no work for someone with his skill set. He received only his contractual notice of termination. The trial judge held that there was a negligent misrepresentation, and assessed the damages at $67,000. This amount was necessary "to put the plaintiff in the same position as he would have been if the negligent misrepresentation had not been made". It consisted of $50,000 for loss of income, $200 for costs of obtaining a new employment, $11,800 for the loss on the purchase and sale of his home in the Ottawa area, and $5,000 in general damages for emotional stress. The Ontario Court of Appeal allowed the appeal (1990), 78 O.R. (2d) 176, observing that the plaintiff had no separate claim for compensation in tort under negligent misrepresentation: his rights were given under the contract and he had received his full contractual entitlement.

On appeal to the Supreme Court of Canada, counsel for the plaintiff put the case squarely on the ground of negligence, and not on contract. The Supreme Court allowed the appeal, and affirmed the trial judgment. The damage assessment was upheld without discussion. The principal judgment was given by Iacobucci J., with whom Sopinka J. agreed. La Forest, L'Heureux-Dubé and Gonthier JJ. agreed with the result reached by Iacobucci J., but on a much shorter ground, *viz.*, that the tort committed by the defendant was independent of the contract and the defendant's liability was not limited by an exclusion clause in the contract. McLachlin J. also agreed with Iacobucci J., but she would have held that the fact that the parties entered into a contract which contained a specific term governing termination did not preclude the appellant's action in tort for negligent misrepresentation: the pre-contractual representation was different in scope and effect from the contractual obligation.

In giving his judgment, **IACOBUCCI J.** said: —]

IV. *Analysis*

A. *Introduction*

[1] This appeal involves an action in tort to recover damages caused by alleged negligent misrepresentations made in the course of a hiring interview by an employer (the respondent), through its representative, to a prospective employee (the appellant) with respect to the employer and the nature and existence of the employment opportunity. Though a relatively recent feature of the common law, the tort of negligent misrepresentation relied on by the appellant and first recognized by the House of Lords in *Hedley Byrne* [*Hedley Byrne & Co. Ltd. v. Heller & Partners Ltd.*, [1964] A.C. 465, [1963] 2 All E.R. 575] is now an established principle of Canadian tort law. This Court has confirmed on many occasions, sometimes tacitly, that an action in tort may lie, in appropriate circumstances, for damages caused by a misrepresentation made in a negligent manner. . . .

[2] The required elements for a successful *Hedley Byrne* claim have been stated in many authorities, sometimes in varying forms. The decisions of this Court cited above suggest five general requirements: (1) there must be a duty of care based on a "special relationship" between the representor and the representee; (2) the representation in question must be untrue, inaccurate, or misleading; (3) the representor must have acted negligently in making said misrepresentation; (4) the representee must have relied, in a reasonable manner, on said negligent misrepresentation; and (5) the reliance must have been detrimental to the representee in the sense that damages resulted.

[After mentioning that the tort of negligent misrepresentation has been used in several pre-contract settings, including *Esso v. Mardon*, *supra*, Iacobucci J. went on to say:]

[3] This is not to say that the contract in such a case is irrelevant and that a court should dispose of the plaintiff's tort claim independently of the contractual arrangement. On the contrary, depending on the circumstances, the subsequent contract may play a very important role in determining whether or not, and to what extent, a claim for negligent misrepresentation shall succeed. Indeed, as evidenced by my conclusion in *BG Checo* [*BG Checo International Ltd. v. British Columbia Hydro and Power Authority*, [1993] 1 S.C.R. 12, 99 D.L.R. (4th) 577], such a contract can have the effect of negating the action in tort and of confining the plaintiff to whatever remedies are available under the law of contract. On the other hand, even if the tort claim is not barred altogether by the contract, the duty or liability of the defendant with respect to negligent misrepresentations may be limited or excluded by a term of the subsequent contract so as to diminish or extinguish the plaintiff's remedy in tort: see, for example, *Hedley Byrne* (although this case did not involve a contract) and *Carman Construction* (although this case involved mostly post-contractual representations) . . . Equally true, however, is that there are cases where the subsequent contract will have no effect whatsoever on the plaintiff's claim for damages in tort. As will be apparent from these reasons, it is my view that the employment agreement signed by the appellant in March of 1983 is governed by this last proposition.

[4] When considering the effect of the subsequent contract on the representee's tort action, everything revolves around the nature of the contractual obligations assumed by the parties and the nature of the alleged negligent misrepresentation. The first and foremost question should be whether there is a specific contractual duty created by an express term of the contract which is co-extensive with the common law duty of care which the representee alleges the representor has breached. Put another way, did the pre-contractual representation relied on by the plaintiff become an express term of the subsequent contract? If so, absent any overriding considerations arising from the context in which the transaction occurred, the plaintiff cannot bring a concurrent action in tort for negligent misrepresentation and is confined to whatever remedies are available under the law of contract. The authorities supporting this proposition, including the decision of this Court in *Central Trust Co. v. Rafuse*, [1986] 2 S.C.R. 147 [*sub nom. Central & Eastern Trust Co. v. Rafuse*, 31 D.L.R. (4th) 481, varied [1988] 1 S.C.R. 1206], are fully canvassed in my reasons in *BG Checo*. As alluded to in *BG Checo*, this principle is an exception to the general rule of concurrency espoused by this Court in *Central Trust v. Rafuse*. . . .

[5] There lies, in my view, the fundamental difference between the present appeal and *BG Checo*, *supra*. In the latter case, the alleged pre-contractual misrepresentation had been incorporated verbatim as an express term of the subsequent contract. As such, the common law duty of care relied on by the plaintiff in its tort action was co-extensive with a duty imposed on the defendant in contract by an express term of their agreement. Thus, it was my view that the plaintiff was barred from exercising a concurrent action in tort for the alleged breach of said duty, and this view was reinforced by the commercial context in which the transaction occurred. In the case at bar, however, there is no such concurrency. The employment agreement signed by the appellant in March of 1983 does not contain any express contractual obligation co-extensive with the duty of care the respondent is alleged to have breached. The provisions most relevant to this appeal (clauses 13 and 14) contain contractual duties clearly different from, not co-extensive with, the common law duty invoked by the appellant in his tort action.

[6] Having said this, it does not follow that the employment agreement is irrelevant to the disposition of this appeal. As I mentioned earlier, even if the tort claim is not barred altogether by the contract as in *BG Checo*, the duty or liability of the representor in tort may be limited or excluded by a term of the subsequent contract. In this respect, the respondent submits that the Court of Appeal was correct in finding that clauses 13 and 14 of the employment agreement represent a valid disclaimer for the misrepresentations allegedly made during the hiring interview, thereby negating any duty of care.

[**IACOBUCCI J.** then discussed the duty of care owed by the defendant to the plaintiff and concluded that one was owed and that it had been breached. He returned to analyze the impact of the contract of employment that the plaintiff executed on the tort duty of care. He held that, unlike the situation in *BG Checo*, the contract did not affect the tortious liability that the defendant had incurred. He set out the terms of the employment contract:]

Transfer

13. Quasar Systems reserves the right to reassign you to another position with the Company without reduction of your salary or benefits and upon one month's notice to you. Should such reassignment require your permanent relocation to another city, the Company will reimburse you for your expenses in accordance with the then current relocation policy.

Termination Notice — One Month

14. This Agreement may be terminated at any time and without cause by Quasar Systems Ltd. or by you. In the event of termination, Quasar Systems Ltd. will give you one month's notice of termination plus any additional notice that may be required by any applicable legislation. Similarly, you shall give Quasar Systems Ltd. one month's notice if you voluntarily terminate this Agreement. Quasar Systems Ltd. may pay you one month's salary in lieu of the aforesaid notice in which event this Agreement and your employment will be terminated on the date such payment in lieu of notice is made.

[IACOBUCCI J. continued:]

[7]   As for the respondent's liability, clauses 13 and 14 of the employment agreement are clearly not, on their face, general limitation or exclusion of liability clauses as these expressions are commonly used. The language adopted by the parties is unambiguous. By stretching the common definition of "limitation of liability clause", one could interpret clauses 13 and 14 as "limiting" the respondent's "liability" in the event of a transfer or termination to what is specifically provided therein. However, even if this interpretation were adopted, the respondent's liability for *pre-contractual negligent misrepresentations* is clearly beyond the scope of these provisions. It is trite law that, in determining whether or not a limitation (or exclusion) of liability clause protects a defendant in a particular situation, the first step is to interpret the clause to see if it applies to the tort or breach of contract complained of. If the clause is wide enough to cover, for example, the defendant's negligence, then it may operate to limit effectively the defendant's liability for the breach of a common law duty of care, subject to any overriding considerations. This is not, however, the situation facing this Court.

[8]   Clauses 13 and 14 of the employment agreement, even if characterized as "limitation of liability" clauses, cannot support an interpretation which would enable them to protect the respondent from the breach of a common law duty of care, let alone the breach of the particular duty invoked by the appellant in his action for negligent misrepresentation. These provisions are no more relevant to the outcome of this case than is clause 15 of the contract, permitting Cognos to terminate the appellant's employment for cause. Thus, contrary to the respondent's submission, the third proposition set out in *Central Trust v. Rafuse*, at p. 206, is of no assistance to this appeal, that is, the appellant is not attempting by his tort claim to "circumvent or escape a contractual exclusion or limitation of liability for the act or omission that would constitute the tort". Simply put, there is nothing in the employment agreement for the appellant to circumvent or to escape.

NOTES AND PROBLEMS

1.   The problem of the co-existence of contract and tort remedies has had prominence in Canada because of some of the statements of the Supreme Court suggesting that a plaintiff has an almost unrestricted option of suing in either contract or tort. In *BG Checo International Ltd. v. British Columbia Hydro and Power Authority*, [1993] 1

S.C.R. 12, 99 D.L.R. (4th) 577, La Forest J. and McLachlin J., in a joint judgment said (p. 26 S.C.R., p. 584 D.L.R.):

> In our view, the general rule emerging from this Court's decision in *Central Trust Co. v. Rafuse*, [1986] 2 S.C.R. 147, is that where a given wrong *prima facie* supports an action in contract and in tort, the party may sue in either or both, except where the contract indicates that the parties intended to limit or negative the right to sue in tort.

2.   The issue of the relation between contract and tort was raised in the Supreme Court decision in *Hamilton v. Open Window Bakery Ltd.*, [2004] S.C.J. No. 72, [2004] 1 S.C.R. 303, 235 D.L.R. (4th) 193. The plaintiff undertook to provide services to the defendant for 36 months. The defendant had a right to terminate the contract at the end of 18 months, on giving three months' notice. The defendant wrongfully terminated the contract after 15 months (and then terminated her again in the nineteenth month). The trial judge concluded that the early termination was not legally justified, and found that, as a matter of fact, had the contract not been terminated, the defendant would not have done so on the earliest possible date. He awarded damages based on the assumption that the plaintiff's services would have been provided for the full balance of the term of the contract, discounted by 25 per cent to reflect the possibility that the contract might have been terminated short of its full term. On appeal, the majority of the Ontario Court of Appeal held that, regardless of what the facts might have been if the contract had not been terminated, damages had to be based on the minimum obligation of the defendant, that is, three months' payments. Simmons J.A. justified this approach (at para. 56) as a reflection of the "reasonable expectations of the parties concerning minimum guaranteed benefits under the contract". Goudge J.A. dissented on the basis that the trial judge's approach was correct. On further appeal to the Supreme Court, Arbour J. upheld the Court of Appeal decision that damages for breach of contract should be based on the minimum contractual obligation on the defendant, *i.e.*, the "least burdensome" obligations of the defendant, and that it was wrong in law to consider what might have happened. She said (at para. 15):

> This tort-like analysis proposed by Hamilton is not an established part of Canadian law. There are compelling reasons for this. Contractual obligations are voluntarily assumed by parties and given effect to by the courts. The failure to perform certain promised positive contractual obligations in contract law is conceptually distinct from the breach of unpromised negative obligations to not harm another's interests in tort law.

Arbour J. did not refer to *Rafuse* or *BG Checo*. Is this statement consistent with that of McLachlin and La Forest JJ. in *BG Checo*, set out in note 1 above? Does the statement of Arbour J. obscure the relation between contract and tort liability?

3.   The issues raised by the co-existence of both contract and tort liability are difficult for the same reason that the representation/warranty cases are difficult: there is no easy test to determine how to characterize the two claims. In a certain sense, there is no distinction between the claims. There is a contract that is valid and enforceable, and there may also be a tort duty. Which should govern the relation in the circumstances that the court is faced with is very much a matter of the inferences to be drawn from things that cannot be directly tied to one or the other, or to a judicial choice of the more appropriate remedy. In this situation, the role of the lawyer in offering a court a peg on which to hang an argument is clear.

4.   Scarman L.J. in *Parsons (Livestock) Ltd. v. Uttley Ingham & Co. Ltd.*, [1978] 1 Q.B. 791, [1978] 1 All E.R. 525, [1977] 2 Lloyd's Rep. 522, said that "the law is not so absurd as to differentiate between contract and tort save in situations where the agreement, or the factual relationship, of the parties with each other requires it in the interests of justice." Is "justice" synonymous with or does it find expression in what the judges *want* to do?

5.   If you were now to draft an employment contract for an employer, would you advise drafting to avoid the consequences of *Queen v. Cognos*? How would you draft around them?

In *Hercules Managements Ltd. v. Ernst & Young*, [1997] 2 S.C.R. 165, 146 D.L.R. (4th) 577, the Supreme Court had to deal with a claim in negligence against a firm of accountants. Investors in two corporations lost money when the corporations went into receivership. They claimed damages against the accountants. The defendant accountants brought a motion for summary judgment in the Manitoba Court of Queen's Bench seeking to have the plaintiffs' claims dismissed. The grounds for the motion were (a) that there was no contract between the plaintiffs and the defendants; (b) that the defendants did not owe the individual plaintiffs any duty of care in tort; and (c) that the claims asserted by the plaintiffs could only properly be brought by the corporations themselves and not by the shareholders individually. The motions judge granted the motion with respect to four plaintiffs, including the appellants, and dismissed their actions on the basis that they raised no genuine issues for trial. By agreement, the claims of the remaining plaintiffs were adjourned *sine die*. An appeal to the Manitoba Court of Appeal was unanimously dismissed with costs.

La Forest J. gave the judgment of the Supreme Court. He reiterated the view of the Supreme Court that, following the decision in *Anns v. Merton London Borough Council*, [1978] A.C. 728 (H.L.), the accountants owed the defendants a *prima facie* duty of care. The question then was whether the scope of that duty should be limited by policy concerns. He said:

[32]   The general area of auditors' liability is a case in point. In modern commercial society, the fact that audit reports will be relied on by many different people (e.g., shareholders, creditors, potential takeover bidders, investors, etc.) for a wide variety of purposes will almost always be reasonably foreseeable to auditors themselves. Similarly, the very nature of audited financial statements — produced, as they are, by professionals whose reputations (and, thereby, whose livelihoods) are at stake — will very often mean that any of those people would act wholly reasonably in placing their reliance on such statements in conducting their affairs. . . . In light of these considerations, the reasonable foreseeability/reasonable reliance test for ascertaining a *prima facie* duty of care may well be satisfied in many (even if not all) negligent misstatement suits against auditors and, consequently, the problem of indeterminate liability will often arise.

La Forest J. referred to a number of articles in which the consequences of making auditors liable were discussed. He continued:

[36]   As I have thus far attempted to demonstrate, the possible repercussions of exposing auditors to indeterminate liability are significant. In applying the two-stage *Anns/Kamloops* test to negligent misrepresentation actions against auditors, therefore, policy considerations reflecting those repercussions should be taken into account. In the general run of auditors' cases, concerns over indeterminate liability will serve to negate a *prima facie* duty of care. But while such concerns may exist in most such cases, there may be particular situations where they do not. In other words, the specific factual matrix of a given case may render it an "exception" to the general class of cases in that while (as in most auditors' liability cases) considerations of proximity under the first branch of the *Anns/Kamloops* test might militate in favour of finding that a duty of care inheres, the typical concerns surrounding indeterminate liability do *not* arise. . . .

La Forest J. distinguished the general case of auditors preparing financial statements from the special case where the accountant knows the identity of the plaintiff (or a class of plaintiffs) and where the accountant's statements are used for the specific purpose or transaction for which they were made. In the latter case, policy considerations surrounding indeterminate liability will not be of any concern since the scope of liability can readily be circumscribed. He offered the same justification to explain *Hedley Byrne v. Heller*.

He said (at para. 39):

[T]he defendant bank provided a negligently prepared credit reference in respect of one of its customers to another bank which, to the knowledge of the defendants, passed on the information to the plaintiff for a stipulated purpose. The plaintiff relied on the credit reference for the specific purpose for which it was prepared. The House of Lords found that but for the presence of a disclaimer, the defendants would have been liable to the plaintiff in negligence. While indeterminate liability would have raised some concern to the Lords had the plaintiff not been known to the defendants or had the credit reference been used for a purpose or transaction other than that for which it was actually prepared, no such difficulties about indeterminacy arose on the particular facts of the case.

La Forest J. concluded by saying:

[41]   The foregoing analysis should render the following points clear. A *prima facie* duty of care will arise on the part of a defendant in a negligent misrepresentation action when it can be said (a) that the defendant ought reasonably to have foreseen that the plaintiff would rely on his representation and (b) that reliance by the plaintiff, in the circumstances, would be reasonable. Even though, in the context of auditors' liability cases, such a duty will often (even if not always) be found to exist, the problem of indeterminate liability will frequently result in the duty being negated by the kinds of policy considerations already discussed. Where, however, indeterminate liability can be shown not to be a concern on the facts of a particular case, a duty of care will be found to exist. . . .

He held that, while the accountants owed a *prima facie* duty of care to the plaintiffs, that duty was, in the circumstances, negated.

NOTES AND PROBLEMS

1.   Though nothing turned on the fact in *Hercules*, the facts state that the accountant who performed the audit had personal investments in the corporations he audited. Do you think that, in the light of Enron's collapse and the role of its auditor in that event, a court might now take a different view of the auditor's liability?

2.   The decision of the Supreme Court in *Hercules Managements* represents the response of the Court to the problems created by its adherence to the *Anns* basis for liability in tort causing pure economic loss. Consider how well the decision operates in the context of the process of adjudication. What kind of evidence does the court require in order to have sufficient information to make the policy decision that must now be faced? Is the burden of obtaining this information one that can fairly be put on the parties?

3.   *Hercules Managements Ltd. v. Ernst & Young* was seen as an important case in determining the liability of accountants for negligence in the preparation of financial statements. The Canadian Institute of Chartered Accountants was an intervener in the litigation. The decision clearly limits the liability of accountants, but there may still be cases in which accountants have liability to investors.

4. In *Kripps v. Touche Ross & Co.*, [1997] 6 W.W.R. 421, 33 B.C.L.R. (3d) 254 (C.A.) (leave to appeal refused (1997), 225 N.R. 236*n* (S.C.C.)), investors who purchased debentures issued by a mortgage company that went bankrupt sued the auditors for negligence in the financial statements published in the prospectus and on which the investors had relied. Finch J.A. described the regulatory background:

    > [6] The *Securities Act*, R.S.B.C. 1979, c. 380 (subsequently replaced by S.B.C. 1985, c. 83) prohibited the sale of debentures to the public unless, annually, a prospectus was filed with the Superintendent of Brokers and given to prospective purchasers. The Act required that the prospectus include financial statements and an auditor's report. Section 42 of the Act required that this auditor's report state that the financial statements presented the financial position of the company fairly according to GAAP [Generally Accepted Accounting Principles], and that otherwise the report be unqualified. The Act also required the company to obtain and file the written consent of its auditor to the use of its report, which consent had to state that the auditor had read the prospectus and that the information derived from the financial statements in the prospectus or within the auditor's knowledge was presented fairly and was not misleading.

    The plaintiffs claimed to recover damages for the losses that they incurred in reliance on the defendant's audit. The auditors had a contractual relationship with the company, but not with the investors. The plaintiffs argued that the auditors should have been aware that investors would rely on their certification that the company's financial statements were accurate. The British Columbia Court of Appeal held that the auditors were liable. Although the auditors followed the standards of their profession — Generally Accepted Accounting Principles — they allowed the company to understate its losses in a fashion that could mislead investors. The Court accepted the argument that the plaintiffs did not have to prove that the misrepresentation was a fundamental factor in their decision to invest. Finch J.A. wrote:

    > [103] It is sufficient . . . for the plaintiff in an action for negligent misrepresentation to prove that the misrepresentation was at least one factor which induced the plaintiff to act to his or her detriment. . . . where the misrepresentation in question is one which . . . would naturally tend to induce the plaintiff to act upon it, the plaintiff's reliance may be inferred. The inference of reliance is one which may be rebutted but the onus of doing so rests on the representor.

    The British Columbia Court of Appeal decided *Kripps* before the Supreme Court rendered its decision in *Hercules Managements*, but the Supreme Court of Canada denied leave to appeal after *Hercules Managements*. The distinction between the two cases would appear to be that in *Kripps* the auditor had to sign the statement filed with the prospectus that was sent to investors, and so the auditor was held to have had notice that investors would rely on the financial statements. It is, however, unfortunate that there is no authoritative judicial attempt to reconcile the two decisions reaching differing conclusions on an auditor's duty of care. See J. Blackier and M. Paskell-Mede, "Auditor Liability in Canada: The Past, Present and Future" (1999), 48 *U.N.B.L.J.* 65-94.

5. There is a very serious problem with the judgment of the Supreme Court in *Hercules Managements* as the proceedings, a motion to have the plaintiffs' pleadings struck out, denied both parties any opportunity to present any evidence: the case went off on the allegations in the pleadings and there was no trial. What basis is there for the Supreme Court to make an important policy statement on the liability of auditors when it has no facts, other than those alleged in the pleadings, on which to base its decision? Do you think that the plaintiffs were fairly treated by the Court? If the process of adjudication is characterized by the way in which the parties participate in it and if the central feature of that participation is the right of each party to present proofs and reasoned arguments, did the plaintiffs get a chance to have a meaningful participation in the deci-

sion? This argument does not mean that the result in *Hercules Managements* is necessarily wrong, only that a proper justification for the result does not exist.

6.   Amendments to Ontario *Securities Act* (see S.O. 2002, c. 22, s. 185), enacted Part XXIII.1 of the Act and impose liability on auditors to purchasers of securities in publicly traded companies for negligence that results in misrepresentations appearing in the audited financial statements, though in the absence of actual knowledge of the misrepresentation their liability is limited to the amount of their fees over the prior year. This is a limited statutory reversal of *Hercules Managements*. There continues to be writing advocating broader liability for auditors in Canada: see, *e.g.*, Leon Trakman and Jason Trainor, "The Rights and Responsibilities of Auditors to Third Parties" (2005), 31 *Queen's L.J.* 148.

Note on the Relation between Contract and Tort Liability

The extent to which changes in tort law will affect contractual relations, or relations "equivalent" to contract, is clear. The narrower the scope for recovery in tort for pure economic loss, the narrower the range of claims that are alternative to or independent of contract.

The reluctance of courts to continue the historical distinction between liability in contract and that in tort has led to statements in some academic writing which suggest that there are no real differences between contract and tort liability, and that there is now a generalized form of liability in "contorts". See, *e.g.*, the discussion in Charles Miller, "Contortions over contorts: a distinct damages requirement?" (1997), 28 *Tex. Tech L. Rev.* 1257-1280. This idea is seductive — it coincides with a belief that conceptualism is bad — but it seems misguided.

There are important issues that require separate treatment depending on whether or not there is a contract. One issue already mentioned is the problems that arise in assessing damages if the reasons for awarding a larger amount rather than a smaller amount — "big cheque" or "small cheque" damages — are not carefully articulated. An important factor in many assessments of damages, for example, is whether or not the plaintiff paid for the defendant's undertaking.

Another aspect of the relation between contract and tort is whether damages should be apportioned between the defendants. In tort it is possible, under, for example, the British Columbia *Negligence Act*, R.S.B.C. 1996, c. 333 or the Ontario *Negligence Act*, R.S.O. 1990, c. N.1, and equivalent legislation in other provinces, to apportion losses caused by negligence. Apportionment refers to the allocation of responsibility (and liability for damages) between two or more defendants, while contribution refers to the allocation of responsibility to the plaintiff as well as the defendant, so that the plaintiff, being held responsible for part of the loss, only recovers a proportion of the damages from the defendant. The basis of apportionment or contribution in tort is that both defendants (or the defendant and the plaintiff) have been guilty of fault, and both should bear the loss in the proportion of their fault. There are serious difficulties in applying the concept of apportionment of liability in contract cases, though courts sometimes do it.

There are, for example, a number of cases where lawyers have been sued for professional negligence and the lawyers have argued that if the client had used its own procedures for checking, say, the vendor's title to property or a survey of the property, the lawyer's mistake would have come to light and the client would not have suffered a loss. See, *e.g.*, *Coopers & Lybrand v. H.E. Kane Agencies Ltd.* (1985), 17 D.L.R. (4th) 695 (N.B.C.A.), and *Doiron v. Caisse Populaire D'Inkerman Ltée* (1985), 17 D.L.R. (4th) 660 (N.B.C.A.), where contribution was allowed. In the latter case, La Forest J.A. said (p. 680) that there should be no wa-ter-tight compartments between contract and tort and that it made sense in the modern world to consider all the circumstances, including "the public expectations about the types of contract involved as well as the particular expectations one must assume the party had". He acknowledged that the express provisions of the con-tract may influence the application of any contribution and that contribution could be justified under the rules of *Hadley v. Baxendale*. On this last point he said (p. 683):

> I think liability should be apportioned on the basis of what might reasonably have been in the contemplation of the parties had an eventuality such as the present oc-curred to them.

In the result he split the loss 50:50. Liability for losses on stock purchases was also divided equally between a stockbroker and a client based on contributory negli-gence in *Transpacific Sales Ltd. (Trustee for) v. Sprott Securities Ltd.*, [2003] O.J. No. 3900, 67 O.R. (3d) 368 (C.A.).

There are many cases in which it is not appropriate to use the concept of con-tributory negligence to apportion liability. For example, the Court denied a claim that the plaintiff client was contributorily negligent in *Chedore v. Bank of Mont-real* (1986), 34 D.L.R. (4th) 177 (N.B.C.A.), noting that the client was entitled to rely on the defendant's skill. There may well be relations where the parties agree to split the responsibility so that it would be reasonable for the court to conclude that the client was to some extent responsible for the loss. Absent clear evidence that there was such an allocation of risk — and the evidence might have to be something like a reduced fee — is there adequate justification for making the cli-ent responsible for any part of the loss?

Apportionment of liability between defendants has some of the same problems, but here the issue is complicated by the fact that the two contract breakers have probably not allocated any risk of loss between themselves, though both may have undertaken obligations to the other contracting party that have different risks. One party may have a clause limiting its liability; the other may not. It would be unsat-isfactory if this contractual limitation were to be eviscerated in a tort action brought by another contracting party that was itself in breach of its contract.

Where two parties, each having a contractual obligation to another person, both breach their obligations and together cause the plaintiff loss, apportionment may, if permitted under the legislation regarding joint torts and its applicability to con-tractual undertakings, be justifiable, but even then, differences in the terms of the two undertakings and in the amount paid for each may make the determination of each party's respective share of the loss very difficult. Apportionment and contri-bution are both based on comparative fault. There is considerable difficulty in ap-plying any fault-based concepts to claims based on breach of contract.

What all these different problems illustrate is that the enforcement of contrac-tual allocations of risk goes on in a number of different ways where the law of contracts runs up against or co-exists with the law of torts. What is common in these various areas (and in most of the cases) is a concern that one party is not able by a choice of the cause of action to change dramatically the incidence of risk. Even when the court permits the plaintiff to sue in either contract or tort, that choice will be likely to give effect to the expectations of the parties, whatever their source. Where the choice seems to threaten the contractual allocations of risk, the courts will generally deny it. This concern is apparent in the Supreme Court decision in *London Drugs v. Kuehne & Nagel* in Chapter 2.

PROBLEMS AND NOTES

1. Cases dealing with the law of warranties and negligent misrepresentation are of great interest to barristers. They are of comparatively little interest to solicitors. It is unlikely that any judicial decision dealing with the distinction between a warranty and an innocent misrepresentation would lead solicitors to re-draft the standard agreements that they use for most common commercial transactions.

    The problems of *Esso v. Mardon* or *Queen v. Cognos* could, of course, have been dealt with by more carefully drafted agreements. (Some employment agreements now explicitly exclude liability for any statements made in the course of the interview process and not embodied in the employment contract.) In some cases, however, the costs of detailed negotiation and careful drafting are out of all proportion to the risks that the parties run, not to mention the business problem faced by a company like Esso in saying that its expert's estimate may not be worth anything. Remember that these costs must be incurred in all agreements, for the solicitor can never know which agreements might lead to problems later.

    The problem in *V.K. Mason Construction Ltd. v. Bank of Nova Scotia* arose only because the bank manager did not use the bank's standard letter for dealing with the situation, though he did obtain the advice of the bank's lawyer before sending the letter. The bank's standard letter would have protected the bank. As mentioned in connection with the parol evidence rule (and as discussed further in the next chapter), the inability of parties to control their employees causes more problems than any standard language in any agreement.

    The fact that lawyers look at these cases in these two very different ways illustrates the very different role that cases play for barristers and solicitors.

    Review the judgments in this section and consider how you would re-draft the agreements that led to the disputes.

2. A client has come to you and has asked you to draft an agreement for her in the following circumstances.

    The client, Patricia, and a friend, Henry, are avid sailors. They want to build two small yachts in Henry's backyard. The yachts will be about seven metres long and will be made of wood and fibreglass. Both parties have experience in building boats, but neither has built anything as large as the boats that are now planned. Each boat will require a considerable investment in time and materials from both parties. The parties propose to share the cost of the materials equally, and each party expects to put in as much time as the other in the actual work. The result should be two identical yachts.

    Patricia would like to have an agreement that would help to avoid any disputes that might arise later between her and Henry.

    Outline the terms of an agreement that the parties might use to implement the arrangement that they propose. Draft as many of the terms as you have time to do. A careful outline is of more use than a few clauses, however well drafted they may be.

Note on the Personal Liability of Employees for Negligent Misrepresentation

An employee who enters into a contract as an agent of his or her employer incurs no contractual liability to the third party. Since the basis for liability for negligent misrepresentation is tortious, the individual employee who makes the misrepresentation might in some circumstances be personally liable as a tortfeasor. (His or her employer may also be vicariously liable for any tortious conduct of the employee that occurs within the scope of the employee's work.) The cases dealing with negligent misstatement tend to slide over this fact and assume that the corporate defendant was the only tortfeasor, rather than a corporate entity made vicariously liable for the torts of its employees acting in the course and scope of their employment. The fact that the employees were personally liable in tort to the plaintiffs, was, of course, the source of the problems in *Greenwood Shopping Plaza Ltd. v. Beattie*, [1980] 2 S.C.R. 228, 111 D.L.R. (3d) 257, *London Drugs Ltd. v. Kuehne & Nagel International Ltd.*, [1992] 3 S.C.R. 299, 97 D.L.R. (4th) 261, and the most recent case, *Laing Property Corp. v. All Seasons Display Inc.* (2000), 190 D.L.R. (4th) 1, 79 B.C.L.R. (3d) 199 (C.A.), leave to appeal to S.C.C. refused, 19 April 2001, [2001] S.C.C.A. No. 523 (all *supra*, Chapter 2).

Outside the context of *London Drugs*, *Laing Property* and similar cases where the employees are protected by the contract between the plaintiff and their employer, the issue of the personal liability of employees (and employees include the officers, but not the directors, of corporations) will, as a matter of practice, arise in two situations. The first is when the corporation is insolvent, and the plaintiff is very anxious to find a solvent defendant to sue. The second is when the plaintiff may have a particular grudge against the employee and is anxious to make him or her personally liable. The wrongfully dismissed employee may, for example, want to sue the person who, the argument will go, wrongfully induced the corporation to terminate the employee's contract of employment.

The courts have wrestled with these problems in a number of cases. Broadly speaking, the courts have held that employees acting within the scope of their employment will not be exposed to the risk of personal liability for negligent misrepresentations made in the course of their employment and for the benefit of the employer. Recall that in *Edgeworth Construction Ltd. v. N.D. Lea & Associates Ltd.*, [1993] 3 S.C.R. 206, *supra*, Chapter 2, the Supreme Court of Canada concluded, without any significant discussion, that individual engineers had no personal liability for negligent misrepresentations that may have occurred in the course of their employment, though their employer may have been liable.

This protection also recognizes, particularly in the case of actions based on inducing breach of contract, that an employee has to balance his or her duty to the employer and to the employee who may have been dismissed. Nevertheless, there remain many situations where an employee may be personally liable to the victim of his or her tortious behaviour. In *ADGA Systems International Ltd. v. Valcom Ltd.* (1999), 43 O.R. (3d) 101, 168 D.L.R. (4th) 351 (C.A.) (leave to appeal to S.C.C. dismissed, 6 April 2000), the plaintiff sued the defendant corporation, its sole director and two senior employees for wrongful interference with economic relations, *i.e.*, inducing another to breach its contract with the plaintiff. The defendant moved for summary judgment to dismiss the action against the individual defendants. The trial judge had rejected the motion to dismiss on the ground that there was a triable issue. The Ontario Court of Appeal, in a careful judgment, disentangled the issues of personal liability, "immunity" and the corporate veil and held that when a director or employee acts to induce a person to breach his or her contract with a third party, the director or employee is *prima facie* liable in tort. The Court noted that an exception might arise if the views of La Forest J. in *London Drugs*, *i.e.*, the view that individual employees acting in the course and scope of their employment did not individually owe a duty of care to the plaintiff, were generally accepted, though even that limitation on liability would not apply on the facts of the case.

In *ScotiaMcLeod Inc. v. Peoples Jewellers Ltd.* (1995), 26 O.R. (3d) 481, 129 D.L.R. (4th) 711 (C.A.), Finlayson J.A. described the protection as follows (p. 491 O.R.):

. . . officers or employees of limited companies are protected from personal liability
unless it can be shown that their actions are themselves tortious or exhibit a separate
identity or interest from that of the company so as to make the act or conduct complained of their own.

In *NBD Bank, Canada v. Dofasco Inc.* (1999), 46 O.R. (3d) 514, 181 D.L.R.
(4th) 37 (C.A.) (application for leave to appeal to S.C.C. dismissed (2000), 254
N.R. 400*n*), the plaintiff bank lent money to Algoma Steel just before it became
insolvent. It sued both Dofasco and the Chief Financial Officer (CFO) of Algoma
personally for fraud and misrepresentation. The judge held that there was no fraud.
The CFO, personally, and Dofasco were, however, held liable in misrepresentation. The Court of Appeal dismissed the appeal. While Dofasco had no duty to
make disclosures about the financial state of its subsidiary, once it offered the bank
assurances, it had a duty of care. The officer owed the bank a duty in his personal
capacity. There was a "special" relation and he should have foreseen that the bank
would rely on his representation. He was not protected by the fact that he was acting as an officer of Dofasco.

In *Lana International Ltd. v. Menasco Aerospace Ltd.* (2000), 50 O.R. (3d) 97,
190 D.L.R. (4th) 340 (C.A.), an action was started against the CEO of the defendant corporation for damages for negligence, improper purpose, malice, etc., arising out of the purchase by the plaintiff of aircraft landing gear from the defendant.
The gear was defective and had to be recalled. The trial judge had summarily dismissed the claim against the individual defendant, principally on technical evidentiary grounds. The appeal was allowed and the summary judgment set aside. The
Court of Appeal held that there was no blanket protection of employees and that, if
the claim were properly pleaded, employees (and directors) might be made personally liable as tortfeasors.

MISTAKE

The law of mistake is doctrinally, academically and practically challenging. A key
to an understanding of the law of mistake is the realization that it is a residual
category: it is invoked as a last-ditch effort by those whose claim for relief can find
no better "peg" on which their argument can be hung. There is no definite border
between the problems relating to interpretation, representations, warranties, negligent misrepresentation and even conditions or excuses, examined in the previous
sections, and the problems of "mistake" to be examined here. In all of the cases we
have looked at, the parties could be said to have made "mistakes" of one kind or
another: in not making the terms of the contract clear or clearer, in not dealing
with all the various risks of disappointment that should have been foreseen or in
trusting someone who turned out not to be as trustworthy as expected or hoped.
The difference between those cases and the ones that follow is that in the former
there was some basis (such as the words used by the parties or in the reliance of
one party on the skill or knowledge of the other) for the allocation of the risk of
disappointment to one side.

Because the law of mistake is a residual category, a wide range of problems can
be put under this heading, not just problems that might be similar to the issues of
misrepresentation and warranties. Problems of offer and acceptance, of good faith
in negotiations, and of unexpected catastrophes are all dealt with under the general
heading of "Mistake". It is a catch-all of arguments that have, so to speak, no other

home. The underlying issue in all of the cases is, however, the same as that in the cases on interpretation, warranties and representations: on which party should the courts place the risk of disappointment, and why?

The cases on mistake can be seen as falling into several categories. Two of these categories are composed of cases in which, if the mistaken party can maintain a claim, the allocation of risk to one side or the other is relatively simple. The easier cases are represented by two types of mistake: (i) where there has been a mistake in transcribing the agreement; and (ii) where a party has mistakenly made a payment that is not owing or due to the payee.

The difficult cases are those where it is very hard to find a basis for allocating the risk of the loss that has occurred. This group of cases typically involves disputes where one or both parties made a mistake about some underlying assumptions related to the contract. The mistake may have been made in the assumptions about the context of the deal, such as an assumption that government legislation would not affect the financial plans for the contract. A mistake may have been made in the nature of the thing being sold: the seller may have thought that he was selling a barren cow when in fact he sold a cow that was fertile and in calf. Another group consists of cases where there is some mistake or misunderstanding about the terms of a contract or in the formulation of the offer. This type of mistake in communication was considered in Chapter 3, in cases like *Raffles v. Wichelhaus* and *Hobbs v. Esquimalt & Nanaimo Railway Co.*

In dealing with cases of mistake, we again find that judges frequently fail to address explicitly the allocation of risk, and we are left to try to work out for ourselves the factors that moved or are likely to move the court to reach one result rather than another. The general pattern of the law presents the familiar picture of the courts reaching results that often are satisfactory on their facts, even though the reasons for the result are often not well articulated. We will also see a familiar pattern of historical development of the law, starting with rigid rules that gave little scope for relief, and moving towards a more flexible position with broader scope for relief. There are, however, some recent decisions that continue to take a narrow approach and that are difficult to justify. The rules are, as one might expect in these circumstances, quite manipulable.

Rectification: Correcting the Written Contract

One class of mistake occurs when the written agreement of the parties fails to record accurately the terms of the parties' agreement. Courts of equity have long been prepared to give the remedy of "rectification" in these situations — to "correct" the written document. The simplest example is the case in which the parties have agreed in negotiating the deal on the price of the land being sold as $110,000; when the agreement is typed up the price is, by mistake, entered as $100,000. The mistake is only discovered after the agreement has been signed. To obtain the remedy of rectification, there must be a finding by the court that the written agreement does not correctly record the true antecedent agreement made by the parties.

Oral evidence is admitted to rectify the written document. The courts have long accepted that parol evidence will be admitted in this situation, on the basis that, once the written agreement is rectified, it is that written document that is enforced. The courts have understandably taken this purposive interpretation of the parol evidence rule.

Of course, when the mistake is pointed out, the parties will often agree to correct the agreement. One may well ask why such a case would ever go to court: why wouldn't the purchaser simply agree to have the price changed? There are two reasons why the purchaser might try to resist the rectification of the agreement (apart from sheer bloody-mindedness). The first is that the purchaser now has some kind of bargaining lever that he may want to use to get a lower price; even if a court were to uphold the right of the vendor to rectification, the vendor would face the expense and inconvenience of litigation and to avoid this, the vendor might settle the dispute advantageously to the purchaser. The second and more defensible reason is that rectification requires that the court be convinced that the antecedent agreement really was for a price of $110,000. The parties may have differing memories or interpretations of the negotiations and the agreement; there may be some factual disagreement about what was the true antecedent agreement. Before a court will grant rectification, it must be satisfied that there truly was an error in the written document.

Rectification is not a broad remedy that is intended to deal with all "mistakes" in a written document: it is a narrow remedy to deal with a precise problem. Rectification is not a substitute for interpretation (though there are cases where it is so used, and authors who support this use). It is meant to deal with the problem of typographical or transcription mistakes and similar kinds of errors. Counsel sometimes try to use the concept more broadly than this limited purpose would suggest as a *pro forma* pleading device to get around the parol evidence rule, and this contributes to the notion that it is widely available.

When a party wants a court order to enforce an agreement, or needs an official record, rectification must be sought if the document does not reflect the true accord. It is essential in those situations that the written contract be the correct expression of the parties' agreement. Rectification is an equitable remedy and, before the merger of law and equity, would have been a necessary preliminary step to an action at common law or at equity to enforce the agreement.

The following judgment is the most recent decision of the Supreme Court on the issue:

PERFORMANCE INDUSTRIES LTD. v. SYLVAN LAKE GOLF & TENNIS CLUB LTD.

[2002] S.C.J. No. 20, [2002] 1 S.C.R. 678, 209 D.L.R. (4th) 318
(S.C.C., McLachlin C.J.C., L'Heureux-Dubé, Gonthier, Major,
Binnie, Arbour and LeBel JJ.)

[The plaintiff-respondent operated an 18-hole golf course. The defendant-appellant O'Connor entered into negotiations with Bell, the respondent's principal, for a joint venture which would allow the plaintiff to develop part of the lands. The trial judge found that Bell and O'Connor made an oral agreement that gave the plaintiff an option to purchase land on the eighteenth fairway for a specific residential development to be undertaken by Bell. During the negotiations, Bell discussed with O'Connor photographs and plans for a double row of houses clustered around a *cul-de-sac* along the length of the eighteenth fairway. When O'Connor's lawyer reduced the terms of the oral agreement to writing, the option clause accurately specified the 480-yard length of the proposed development, but instead of sufficient width to permit a double row of houses (110 yards), the clause as written allowed only enough land for a single row of houses (110 *feet*). Bell signed the contract without reading it.

When Bell sought to exercise the option some five years after the signing of the contract, O'Connor insisted on the written terms, despite knowing that these terms did not accurately reflect the prior oral option agreement. The respondent sued the appellants for rectification of the agreement or damages in lieu thereof, punitive damages and solicitor-client costs. The trial judge held that the respondent was entitled to rectification of the option clause and awarded damages on the basis of the loss of profit on a fully built residential development. Punitive damages were assessed at $200,000. The Alberta Court of Appeal set aside the punitive damages award, but otherwise affirmed the trial judgment.

The Supreme Court of Canada affirmed the decision of the Court of Appeal, dismissing both an appeal by the defendant, who argued that the action should be dismissed, and a cross-appeal by the plaintiff, who argued for a restoration of punitive damages.

BINNIE J. delivered the judgment of all the members of the Court except **LEBEL J.**: —]

III. *Analysis*

[29] When reasonably sophisticated business people reduce their oral agreements to written form, which are prepared and reviewed by lawyers, and changes made, and the documents are then executed, there is usually little scope for rectification. Nor does a falling out between business partners usually attract an award of punitive damages. This case is unusual because of the findings of fraud and deceit made against the appellant O'Connor by the trial judge. The appellants are therefore obliged to try to make their case, if at all, out of the mouth of Bell, with such help as they can find in the law books for their position.

[30] Counsel for the appellants (who was not counsel at trial) seeks to raise three issues, which he describes as follows: (1) the relationship between the plea of unilateral mistake and the remedy of rectification (particularly where the mistake is the product of the plaintiff's own negligence); (2) the kind of pleading and proof that a plaintiff who seeks rectification must offer, as well as the proper standard of proof to apply in rectification cases; and, (3) the proper method of quantifying damages ordered in lieu of rectification in cases where the subject matter of the rectified contract is an option for the sale of land. The respondent, as stated, cross appeals against the quashing of the award of punitive damages.

A. *Rectification of the Contract*

[31] Rectification is an equitable remedy whose purpose is to prevent a written document from being used as an engine of fraud or misconduct "equivalent to fraud". The traditional rule was to permit rectification only for mutual mistake, but rectification is now available for unilateral mistake (as here), provided certain demanding preconditions are met. Insofar as they are relevant to this appeal, these preconditions can be summarized as follows. Rectification is predicated on the existence of a prior oral contract whose terms are definite and ascertainable. The plaintiff must establish that the terms agreed to orally were not written down properly. The error may be fraudulent, or it may be innocent. What is essential is that at

the time of execution of the written document the defendant knew or ought to have known of the error and the plaintiff did not. Moreover, the attempt of the defendant to rely on the erroneous written document must amount to "fraud or the equivalent of fraud". The court's task in a rectification case is corrective, not speculative. It is to restore the parties to their original bargain, not to rectify a belatedly recognized error of judgment by one party or the other: *Hart v. Boutilier* (1916), 56 D.L.R. 620 (S.C.C.), at p. 630; *Ship M.F. Whalen v. Pointe Anne Quarries Ltd.* (1921), 63 S.C.R. 109, at pp. 126-27; *Downtown King West Development Corp. v. Massey Ferguson Industries Ltd.* (1996), 133 D.L.R. (4th) 550 (Ont. C.A.), at p. 558; G.H.L. Fridman, *The Law of Contract in Canada* (4th ed. 1999), at p. 867; S.M. Waddams, *The Law of Contracts* (4th ed. 1999), para. 336. In *Hart, supra*, at p. 630, Duff J. (as he then was) stressed that "[t]he power of rectification must be used with great caution". Apart from everything else, a relaxed approach to rectification as a substitute for due diligence at the time a document is signed would undermine the confidence of the commercial world in written contracts.

...

C.   *The Conditions Precedent to Rectification*

[35] As stated, high hurdles are placed in the way of a business person who relies on his or her own unilateral mistake to resile from the written terms of a document which he or she has signed and which, on its face, seems perfectly clear. The law is determined not to open the proverbial floodgates to dissatisfied contract makers who want to extricate themselves from a poor bargain.

[36] I referred earlier to the four conditions precedent, or "hurdles" that a plaintiff must overcome. To these the appellants wish to add a fifth. Rectification, they say, should not be available to a plaintiff who is negligent in reviewing the documentation of a commercial agreement. To the extent the appellants' argument is that in such circumstances the Court *may* exercise its discretion to refuse the equitable remedy to such a plaintiff, I agree with them. To the extent they say the want of due diligence (or negligence) on the plaintiff's part is an absolute bar, I think their proposition is inconsistent with principle and authority and should be rejected.

[37] The first of the traditional hurdles is that Sylvan (Bell) must show the existence and content of the inconsistent prior oral agreement. Rectification is "[t]he most venerable breach in the parol evidence rule" (Waddams, *supra*, at para. 336). The requirement of a prior oral agreement closes the "floodgate" to unhappy contract makers who simply failed to read the contractual documents, or who now have misgivings about the merits of what they have signed.

[38] The second hurdle is that not only must Sylvan (Bell) show that the written document does not correspond with the prior oral agreement, but that O'Connor either knew or ought to have known of the mistake in reducing the oral terms to writing. It is only where permitting O'Connor to take advantage of the error would amount to "fraud or the equivalent of fraud" that rectification is available. This requirement closes the "floodgate" to unhappy contract makers who simply made a mistake. Equity acts on the conscience of a defendant who seeks to take advantage of an error which he or she either knew or ought reasonably to have known about

at the time the document was signed. Mere unilateral mistake alone is not sufficient to support rectification but if permitting the non-mistaken party to take advantage of the document would be fraud or equivalent to fraud, rectification may
be available: *Hart, supra*, at p. 630; *Ship M.F. Whalen, supra*, at pp. 126-27.

[39] What amounts to "fraud or the equivalent of fraud" is, of course, a crucial
question. In *First City Capital Ltd. v. British Columbia Building Corp.* (1989), 43
B.L.R. 29 (B.C.S.C.), McLachlin C.J.S.C. (as she then was) observed that "in this
context 'fraud or the equivalent of fraud' refers not to the tort of deceit or strict
fraud in the legal sense, but rather to the broader category of equitable fraud or
constructive fraud. . . . Fraud in this wider sense refers to transactions falling short
of deceit but where the Court is of the opinion that it is unconscientious for a person to avail himself of the advantage obtained" (p. 37). Fraud in the "wider sense"
of a ground for equitable relief "is so infinite in its varieties that the Courts have
not attempted to define it", but "'all kinds of unfair dealing and unconscionable
conduct in matters of contract come within its ken'": *McMaster University v. Wilchar Construction Ltd.* (1971), 22 D.L.R. (3d) 9 (Ont. H.C.), at p. 19 . . . *Stepps
Investments Ltd. v. Security Capital Corp. Ltd.* (1976), 73 D.L.R. (3d) 351
(Ont. H.C.), *per* Grange J. (as he then was), at pp. 362-63; and Waddams, *supra*,
at para. 342.

[40] The third hurdle is that Sylvan (Bell) must show "the precise form" in which
the written instrument can be made to express the prior intention (*Hart, supra, per*
Duff J., at p. 630). This requirement closes the "floodgates" to those who would
invite the court to speculate about the parties' unexpressed intentions, or impose
what in hindsight seems to be a sensible arrangement that the parties might have
made but did not. The court's equitable jurisdiction is limited to putting into words
that — and only that — which the parties had already orally agreed to.

[41] The fourth hurdle is that all of the foregoing must be established by proof
which this Court has variously described as "beyond reasonable doubt" (*Ship M.F.
Whalen, supra*, at p. 127), or "evidence which leaves no 'fair and reasonable
doubt'" (*Hart, supra*, at p. 630), or "convincing proof" or "more than sufficient
evidence" (*Augdome Corp. v. Gray*, [1975] 2 S.C.R. 354, at pp. 371-72). The
modern approach, I think, is captured by the expression "convincing proof", i.e.,
proof that may fall well short of the criminal standard, but which goes beyond the
sort of proof that only reluctantly and with hesitation scrapes over the low end of
the civil "more probable than not" standard.

[42] Some critics argue that anything more demanding than the ordinary civil
standard of proof is unnecessary (e.g., Waddams, *supra*, at para. 343), but, again,
the objective is to promote the utility of written agreements by closing the "floodgate" against marginal cases that dilute what are rightly seen to be demanding preconditions to rectification.

[43] It was formerly held that it was not sufficient if the evidence merely comes
from the party seeking rectification. In *Ship M.F. Whalen, supra*, Duff J. (as he
then was) said, at p. 127, "[s]uch parol evidence must be adequately supported by
documentary evidence and by considerations arising from the conduct of the parties". Modern practice has moved away from insistence on documentary corroboration (Waddams, *supra*, at para. 337, Fridman, *supra*, at p. 879). In some situations, documentary corroboration is simply not available, but if the parol evidence

is corroborated by the conduct of the parties or other proof, rectification may, in the discretion of the Court, be available.

...

(1) *The Existence and Content of the Prior Oral Agreement*

[47] The Court should attempt to uphold the parties' bargain where the terms can be ascertained with a reasonable level of comfort, i.e., convincing proof. Here the trial judge predicated his award of compensatory damages on the finding that the optioned land could accommodate 58 single family houses located along the 480 yard length of the 18th fairway. There is no argument about the 480 yards. O'Connor himself plucked the 480 figure from the length of play listed on the Sylvan Lake Golf Club score card. O'Connor's number for the width of the development (110) may also be accepted. The issue is whether the number was intended to express yards or feet. The trial judge appears to have concluded that the dispute about the depth of the residential development (which is all that divided the parties) came down to a simple choice between Bell's version (Plan A) and O'Connor's version (Plan B). Both plans were predicated on the length of the 18th fairway, namely 480 yards. Plan B, which O'Connor had described in the document, contemplated a single row of houses on a development plan 110 *feet* deep. Bell's Plan A was based on two rows of housing separated by a road allowance, in a configuration similar to that shown in the aerial photo of the Bayview development discussed by Bell and O'Connor at their December 16-17 meeting. Plan A called for a depth of about 110 *yards*. If Plan B's 110-*foot* depth is tripled to 110 *yards*, the acreage under option would be roughly tripled from about 3.6 acres (Plan B) to about 10.8 acres (Plan A), which accommodates the 58 lots plus the standard municipal road allowance. The problem in *I.C.R.V. Holdings Ltd.*, *supra*, was that the parties never agreed on the boundary. Here the trial judge concluded that there *was* agreement even though the parties did not express themselves to each other in lawyerly language. This not infrequently happens: *Bloom v. Averbach*, [1927] S.C.R. 615, *per* Lamont J., at p. 621:

> It is suggested that had the letters been handed to a lawyer to prepare a formal contract therefrom, he would not have been able to determine what assets were to be included in the term "building, machinery and fixtures," or what were to be covered by "stock, etc." It may be that he would not, but that is not the test. *The test is, did the parties themselves clearly understand what was comprised in each. In other words were their minds ad idem as to these expressions?* [Emphasis added.]

[48] The trial judge thus found that the parties had made a verbal agreement with reference to a residential development along the 18th hole. It was more than an agreement to agree. He concluded that there was a definite project in a definite location to which O'Connor and Bell had given their definite assent.

[49] Although the parties did not discuss a metes and bounds description, they were working on a defined development proposal. O'Connor cannot complain if the numbers he inserted in clause 18 (110 x 480) are accepted and confirmed. The issue, then, is the error created by his apparently duplicitous substitution of feet for yards in one dimension. We know the 480 must be yards because it measures the 18th fairway. If the 110 is converted from feet to yards, symmetry is achieved, certainty is preserved and Bell's position is vindicated.

(2) *Fraud or Conduct Equivalent to Fraud*

[50] The notion of "*equivalent* to fraud" as distinguished from fraud itself, is often utilized where "the court is unwilling to go so far as to find actual knowledge on the side of the party seeking enforcement" (Waddams, *supra*, at para. 342). The trial judge had no such hesitation in this case. He characterized O'Connor's actions as "fraudulent, dishonest and deceitful" (para. 114).

...

[52] O'Connor thus fraudulently misrepresented the written document as accurately reflecting the terms of the prior oral contract. He knew that Bell would not sign an agreement without the option for sufficient land to create the "Bayview" layout development with two rows of housing as specified in the prior oral contract. O'Connor therefore knew when Bell signed the document that he had not detected the substitution of 110 feet for 110 yards. O'Connor knowingly snapped at Bell's mistake "to thwart or reduce any plan by Bell to develop an increased area of the golf course for residential development". Bell's loss would be O'Connor's gain, as O'Connor (Performance) would come into sole ownership of the optioned land as of December 31, 1994.

[53] Although on occasion the trial judge describes O'Connor's conduct as "equivalent to fraud", and elsewhere he describes it as actual fraud, his reasons taken as a whole can only be characterized as a finding of actual fraud.

(3) *Precise Terms of Rectification*

[54] It follows from the foregoing that "the precise form" in which the written document can be made to conform to the oral agreement would be simply to change the word "feet" in the phrase "one hundred and ten (110) *feet* in width" to "yards".

(4) *Existence of "Convincing Proof"*

[55] The trial judge made his key findings in respect of the prior oral agreement, Bell's unilateral mistake and O'Connor's knowledge of that mistake to a standard of "beyond any reasonable doubt".

[56] He also found that Bell's version of the verbal agreement was sufficiently corroborated on significant points by other witnesses (including his wife, his former partner, his lawyer and, subsequently, the development consultants), and documents (including his lawyer's notes and the plan of the Bayview Golf Course development discussed in mid-December 1989).

D. *Bell's Lack of Due Diligence*

[57] The appellants seek, in effect, to add a fifth hurdle (or condition precedent) to the availability of rectification. A plaintiff, they say, should be denied such a remedy unless the error in the written document could not have been discovered with due diligence.

[58] O'Connor says that Bell's failure to read clause 18 and note the mixture of yards and feet should be fatal to his claim because the Court ought not to assist businesspersons who are negligent in protecting their own interests. Alternatively, the effective cause of Bell's loss is not the fraudulent document but Bell's failure to detect the fraud when he had an opportunity to do so.

[59] I agree that Bell, an experienced businessman, ought to have examined the text of clause 18 before signing the document. The terms of clause 18 were clear on their face (even though many readers might have misread a description of land that mixed units of measurement as clause 18 did here). He had time to review the document with his lawyer. He did so. Changes were requested. He did not catch the substitution of 110 feet for 110 yards; indeed, he says he did not read clause 18 at all.

[60] The trial judge, at para. 76, accepted the evidence of Bell's lawyer who admitted that he had not directed his mind to the limitations of the size of the development parcel found in clause 18, nor had he made any note of bringing those to Bell's attention which would have been his normal practice.

> He could offer no explanation for why he had not done so other than the fact that his focus on receipt of the Agreement signed by Bell was to ensure the completion and registration of documentation to facilitate the closing of [the purchase] on or before December 31, 1989. This court accepts the evidence offered by Mr. Hancock and that of Bell that they at no time discussed the description of property contained in clause 18.

[61] It is undoubtedly true that courts ought to hold commercial entities to a reasonable level of due diligence in documenting their transactions. Otherwise, written agreements will lose their utility and commercial life will suffer. Rectification should not become a belated substitute for due diligence.

[62] On the other hand, most cases of unilateral mistake involve a degree of carelessness on the part of the plaintiff. A diligent reading of the written document would generally have disclosed the error that the plaintiff, after the fact, seeks to have corrected. The mistaken party will often have failed to read the document entirely, or may have read it too hastily or without parsing each word. As the American *Restatement of the Law, Second: Contracts, (2d)* (1981) points out in its commentary under § 157 ("Effect of Fault of Party Seeking Relief"), "since a party can often avoid a mistake by the exercise of such care, the availability of relief would be severely circumscribed if he were to be barred by his negligence". Comment B discusses "failure to read writing". "Generally, one who assents to a writing is presumed to know its contents and cannot escape being bound by its terms merely by contending that he did not read them; his assent is deemed to cover unknown as well as known terms". But this proposition is qualified by that Comment's further statement that the "exceptional rule" in s. 157 (which permits rectification or "reformation" of the contract) applies only where there has been an agreement that preceded the writing. "In such a case, a party's negligence in failing to read the writing does not preclude reformation if the writing does not correctly express the prior agreement".

[63] One reason why the defence of contributory negligence or want of due diligence is not persuasive in a rectification case is because the plaintiff seeks no more than enforcement of the prior oral agreement to which the defendant has already bound itself.

...

E. *Discretionary Relief*

[66] I conclude, therefore, that due diligence on the part of the plaintiff is not a condition precedent to rectification. However, it should be added at once that rectification is an equitable remedy and its award is in the discretion of the court. The conduct of the plaintiff is relevant to the exercise of that discretion. In a case where the court concludes that it would be unjust to impose on a defendant a liability that ought more properly to be attributed to the plaintiff's negligence, rectification may be denied. That was not the case here.

F. *Fraud*

[67] There is, on the facts of this case, a more fundamental reason why the appellants' complaint about Bell's lack of due diligence provides no defence. O'Connor did more than "snap" at a business partner's mistake. O'Connor undertook as part of the verbal agreement to have a document prepared that set out its terms. According to the trial judge, he not only breached that term, it became part of his fraudulent scheme to have the document wrongly state the terms of the option, to fraudulently misrepresent to Bell that it did accurately set out their verbal agreement, to allow Bell to sign it when O'Connor knew Bell was mistaken in doing so, then to delay any response to Bell's development proposals (and thus bring the error to Bell's attention) until it was almost too late for the development to proceed. O'Connor admitted providing his lawyer with the erroneous metes and bounds description in clause 18. It should not, I think, lie in his mouth to say that he should not be responsible for what followed because his fraud was so obvious that it ought to have been detected.

[68] "[F]raud 'unravels everything'": *Farah v. Barki*, [1955] S.C.R. 107, at p. 115 (Kellock J. quoting Farwell J. in *May v. Platt*, [1900] 1 Ch. 616, at p. 623).

[69] The appellants' concept of a due diligence defence in a fraud case was rejected over 125 years ago by Lord Chelmsford L.C. who said, "when once it is established that there has been any fraudulent misrepresentation or wilful concealment by which a person has been induced to enter into a contract, it is no answer to his claim to be relieved from it to tell him that he might have known the truth by proper inquiry. He has a right to retort upon his objector, "You, at least, who have stated what is untrue, or have concealed the truth, for the purpose of drawing me into a contract, cannot accuse me of want of caution because I relied implicitly upon your fairness and honesty": *Central R. Co. of Venezuela v. Kisch* (1867), L.R. 2 H.L. 99, at pp. 120-21.

[70] Lord Chelmsford's strictures were quoted and applied by Southin J. (as she then was) in *United Services Funds (Trustees) v. Richardson Greenshields of Canada Ltd.* (1988), 48 D.L.R. (4th) 98 (B.C.S.C.), where she observed that "[c]arelessness on the part of the victim has never been a defence to an action for fraud" (p. 109):

> Once the plaintiff knows of the fraud he must mitigate his loss but until he knows of it, in my view, no issue of reasonable care or anything resembling it arises at law.
>
> And in my opinion, a good thing, too. There may be greater damages to civilized society than endemic dishonesty. But I can think of nothing which will contribute to dishonesty more than a rule of law which requires us all to be on perpetual guard

against rogues lest we be faced with a defence of "Ha, ha, your own fault I fool you." Such a defence should not be countenanced from a rogue.

(p. 111)

...

G.   *Damages in Lieu of Rectification*

[72] The trial judge awarded $620,100 in compensatory damages representing the loss of profit on a fully built residential development on the 18th fairway. The appellants argue that damages should be limited to the difference between the market value of the land and the option price of $400,000. They say compensatory damages should not include the "reasonably expected profit" from a 58-lot housing development.

[73] The finding of fact is, however, that the parties specifically contemplated (even on O'Connor's evidence) that the optioned land would be put to the use of residential housing. Damages for breach of the contract, as rectified, therefore must include losses flowing from the special circumstances known to the parties at the time they made their contract . . .

...

H.   *Should the Award of Punitive Damages be Restored?*

[77] The respondent in its cross-appeal seeks restoration of the $200,000 award of punitive damages disallowed by the Alberta Court of Appeal. . . .

...

[79] Punitive damages are awarded against a defendant in exceptional cases for "malicious, oppressive and high-handed" misconduct that "offends the court's sense of decency". . . .

[80] The misconduct found against O'Connor was his contemptuous disregard for Bell's rights under the verbal agreement of December 1989, together with his subsequent use of the written document (which he knew misstated their verbal agreement) leading up to and including court proceedings filed January 4, 1995, to obtain possession of the golf course property and thereby to destroy the value of Bell's option to develop the agreed-upon residential project.

[81] Torts such as deceit or fraud already incorporate a type of misconduct that to some extent "offends the court's sense of decency" and which "represents a marked departure from ordinary standards of decent behaviour", yet not all fraud cases lead to an award of punitive damages.

...

[87] O'Connor's fraud was, of course, reprehensible. Indeed, fraud is generally reprehensible, but only in exceptional cases does it attract punitive damages. In this case, the trial judge . . . thought punishment above and beyond the payment of generous compensatory damages was required for two reasons, namely that O'Connor's actions (1) "demand an award which will stand as an example to others" and (2) "at the same time assure that O'Connor does not unduly profit from his conduct". These are both legitimate objectives for the award of punitive dam-

ages. . . . However, it must be kept in mind that an award of punitive damages is rational "if, but only if" compensatory damages do not adequately achieve the objectives of retribution, deterrence and denunciation.

[88] This was a commercial relationship between two businessmen. One tried to pull a fast one on the other. There was no abuse of a dominant position. O'Connor's misconduct was planned and deliberate and he persisted in it over a period of four and a half years, but in the end the courts did their work and Bell obtained full compensation plus costs on a solicitor-client basis, all of which undoubtedly had a punitive effect on O'Connor. In addition, O'Connor is stigmatized with a judicial finding (now upheld by two appellate courts) that he acted in a way that was "fraudulent, dishonest and deceitful". His conduct has been soundly denounced and he has been required personally to pay a large amount of money in compensation. The respondent is unable to identify any aggravating circumstances that would not be present in almost any case of business fraud except that O'Connor was found to have behaved abominably in the conduct of the litigation. However, as stated, the trial judge excluded this consideration from the award of punitive damages because he identified it as the basis for his award of solicitor-client costs. . . .

[**LeBel J.** wrote a short concurring judgment.]

NOTES AND QUESTIONS

1. In some cases courts take a broader view of rectification. In *Juliar v. Canada (Attorney General)*, [2000] O.J. No. 3706, 50 O.R. (3d) 728, 8 B.L.R. (3d) 167 (C.A.), members of a family entered into a transaction to restructure a business. The form of the restructuring chosen was the result of the mistaken belief of an accountant that it was tax-neutral, *i.e.*, that it would not expose the parties to tax liability. When the tax consequences were known, the parties sought to have the agreement rectified. The trial judge held that the agreement could be rectified because the intention of the parties had always been to achieve the restructuring without tax liability. The Minister appealed, principally on the ground that the facts did not support the evidence of the intention on which the trial judge had relied. The Court of Appeal found that the facts could support what the trial judge had done and that the appeal should be dismissed. In giving the judgment of the Court of Appeal, Austin J.A. quoted from the decision in *Re Slocock's Will Trusts*, [1979] 1 All E.R. 358 (Ch. D.), where the court was concerned with an application for rectification of a deed designed to reduce or avoid payment of tax on the death of a party, but which deed misdescribed the property involved due to a solicitor's error. Graham J. said (p. 363):

    > The true principles governing these matters I conceive to be as follows. (1) The court has a discretion to rectify where it is satisfied that the document does not carry out the intention of the parties. This is the basic principle. (2) Parties are entitled to enter into any transaction which is legal, and, in particular, are entitled to arrange their affairs to avoid payment of tax if they legitimately can. . . . (3) If a mistake is made in a document legitimately designed to avoid the payment of tax, there is no reason why it should not be corrected. The Crown is in no privileged position qua such a document. It would not be a correct exercise of the discretion in such circumstances to refuse rectification merely because the Crown would thereby be deprived of an accidental and unexpected windfall. (4) [Nothing] . . . compels the court to the conclusion that rectification of a document should be refused where the sole purpose of seeking it is to enable the parties to obtain a legitimate fiscal advantage which it was their common intention to obtain at the time of the execution of the document.

2. In *771225 Ontario Inc. v. Bramco Holdings Co.* (1995), 21 O.R. (3d) 739, 43 R.P.R. (2d) 70 (C.A.) (leave to appeal to S.C.C. refused (1995), 48 R.P.R. (2d) 320*n*), rectification of an agreement for the purchase and sale of land to reduce the land transfer tax payable was refused. A majority of the Court of Appeal gave two reasons: (i) the court should not usurp the discretion give by the legislation to the Minister to remit the tax; and (ii) it would be inappropriate for the court to rewrite history for the sole purpose of reducing the tax payable by a taxpayer.

3. Rectification in tax cases raises difficulties that have almost nothing to do with the law of contracts: the parties are not arguing about the need to give relief for a mistake. Only the government is concerned — and it is not even a party to the agreement being rectified. *Juliar* and *Re Slocock* represent one approach, *771225* another. While Austin J.A. referred to *771225* in *Juliar*, he distinguished it on the basis that in *Juliar* the parties had an intention to avoid tax, suggesting that the tax consequences in *771225* were somehow incidental. Such a distinction is hard to maintain because it depends on the slippery concept of "intention" and in tax matters the taxpayer might always be assumed to want to pay less tax. How does wanting to pay less tax differ from intending to pay less tax?

Mistaken Payments

A second class of relatively easy cases is made up of those situations where the plaintiff has made a mistaken (over)payment. Tom owes Mary $1,000. By mistake, he pays her $1,100. (Perhaps he forgot an earlier part payment.) As we saw in Chapter 2, this case is the paradigm of the restitutionary claim. Mary is unjustly enriched by the payment; she has no right to it, since it was never due. This type of case is considered part of the law of mistake, as the courts regard the payment as having been made by mistake. There are many cases on mistakes of this kind: the bank that mistakenly credits a customer with money that the customer has no right to; the insurer who pays a claim without appreciating that the policy has lapsed. In all these cases the law requires repayment unless the payee can show that repayment would in the circumstances defeat some significant reliance by the defendant. The payee cannot simply claim that the payer made a mistake, a mistake that the payee neither encouraged nor expected, and that it is just bad luck on those who make mistakes.

The relation between the parties may be based on contract: there is a contract between the bank and its customer, or between the insurer and the insured, but the right to repayment is not dependent on the existence of any contract. The right arises simply from the existence of unjust enrichment. There are some limitations on the right to recover in these situations if it can be shown that, in essence, it not unjust for this defendant in the particular circumstances to keep the enrichment.

One historically significant limitation on the right to recover mistaken payments was the traditional rule that there could only be relief if an overpayment was made due to a "mistake of fact" and not if it was due to a "mistake of law". This distinction, while of some antiquity, is no longer accepted, and relief can be obtained whether the mistake that led to the overpayment is one of fact or one of law. In any event, the distinction was never clear and could be manipulated by a court that wanted to give relief.

In *Hydro-Electric Commission of the Township of Nepean v. Ontario Hydro*, [1982] 1 S.C.R. 347, 132 D.L.R. (3d) 193, the majority of the Supreme Court, in a judgment by Estey J., upheld the old rule regarding the unavailability of relief for mistakes of law. Dickson J. (with whom Laskin C.J.C. agreed) dissented and would have abolished the distinction.

The distinction has now been removed from the law in Canada by the judgment of the Supreme Court in *Air Canada v. British Columbia*, [1989] 1 S.C.R. 1161, 59 D.L.R. (4th) 161. The main issue in that case was the right of the province to tax gasoline bought by airlines. Part of the tax was held to be constitutionally invalid and the question then arose whether the airlines could recover what they had paid under the invalid legislation. The province argued that the airlines had made a mistake of law and hence could not recover the previous payments — they should have refused to pay in the first place. The Court rejected this argument, and abolished the distinction between mistake of law and mistake of fact. In giving the judgment of the majority of the court, La Forest J. said (pp. 1198-1201 S.C.R., pp. 190-92 D.L.R.):

> Counsel for Canadian Pacific Airlines invited us to do away with the mistake of law rule. As she noted, the common law has largely permitted recovery of payments made under a mistake of fact. The same approach should, she contended, be followed in the case of a mistake of law. The distinction between the two, she stated, has resulted in confusion, ambiguity and injustice, and should no longer be recognized. She urged us to adopt the dissenting reasons of Dickson J., as he was, in [*Hydro-Electric Commission of the Township of Nepean v. Ontario Hydro, supra*].

> I do not intend to regurgitate what was said by Dickson J. in his judgment. Suffice it to say that it constitutes a thorough, scholarly and damning analysis of the mistake of law doctrine from its beginning and through the egregious error of Lord Ellenborough C.J. in the case of *Bilbie v. Lumley* (1802), 2 East. 469, 102 E.R. 448, to the present day: see Goff and Jones, *The Law of Restitution*, 3rd ed. (1986), at p. 117. What the judgment reveals is a rule built on inadequate foundations, lacking in clarity (the distinction between a mistake of fact and mistake of law can best be described as a fluttering, shadowy will-o'-the-wisp), and whose harshness has led to a luxuriant growth of exceptions (twelve perhaps, though the identity and scope of the exceptions I am told has led to considerable learned esoteric debate). Despite this, and despite almost universal criticism, the doctrine has spread from its original place in contract law into other areas, including public law (such as in *Nepean* itself), and it now even more ambitiously threatens to invade the domain of constitutional law. This explosion has, as Corbin has observed, probably occurred because of the temptation under the pressure of work for judges to seize upon the first plausible rule that becomes handy to dispose of a case that has no merit: *Corbin on Contracts* (1960), vol. 3, para. 617 at p. 756. The result is that while the rule undoubtedly serves some useful functions, these could be achieved by other means. As Dickson J. himself put it at p. 362:

>> The modern justification for the existence of the rule against recovery of moneys paid under a mistake of law has been the stability of contractual relations. The rule though is often used as a handy means of disposing of cases where, in fact, recovery of money *should* be barred, and would be, under a more searching analysis of the case. (Emphasis in original.)

> From his analysis, Dickson J. concluded that the judicial development of the law of restitution or unjust (or as Dickson J. noted, "unjustified") enrichment renders otiose the distinction between mistakes of fact and mistakes of law. He would abolish the distinction, and would allow recovery in any case of enrichment at the plaintiff's expense provided the enrichment was caused by the mistake and the payment was not made to compromise an honest claim, subject of course to any available defenses or equitable reasons for denying recovery, such as change of position or estoppel. Dickson J. considered the finality of transactions to be an important, but not an absolute value, and its weight in a particular context was best assessed within the context of the principles of the law of restitution. He preferred to do this rather than engrafting new exceptions to a rule that has over the years been variously described as "most unfortunate", "monstrous", "decrepit" and "unjust".

I am aware that Dickson J. was speaking in minority (for himself and Laskin C.J.C.), but it can scarcely be maintained that the three judges who formed the majority rejected this position. Indeed, they never really faced this issue at all. The case, we saw, was argued on the basis that it fell within one of the exceptions to the mistake of law rule, that the parties were not *in pari delicto*, and they dealt with it accordingly. After having read Dickson J.'s judgment, Estey J. was at pains to note that in the argument unjust enrichment had only been tangentially mentioned and that the distinction between mistake of fact and mistake of law was not raised; indeed, it was accepted. "Accordingly," he concluded, "my considerations have been confined to the operation of the doctrine of mistake of law as argued".

This can hardly constitute an expression of opinion — let alone a definitive one — by this court on the issues raised by Dickson J., and I therefore have no hesitation in following his lead in these matters. In my view the distinction between mistake of fact and mistake of law should play no part in the law of restitution. Both species of mistake, if one can be distinguished from the other, should, in an appropriate case, be considered as factors which can make an enrichment at the plaintiff's expense "unjust" or "unjustified". This does not imply, however, that recovery will follow in every case where a mistake has been shown to exist. If the defendant can show that the payment was made in settlement of an honest claim, or that he has changed his position as a result of the enrichment, then restitution will be denied.

As noted by La Forest J., an important limitation on the right to recover for a mistakenly made payment is that the right to recover will be lost if the recipient has, in reliance on the receipt of the money, changed its position. A "change of position" defence does not arise from simply spending the money but from the doing of some act (the discharge of indebtedness or possibly the making of a gift) that would make it unfair to require that the money be repaid.

Budai v. Ontario Lottery Corp. (1983), 142 D.L.R. (3d) 271, 24 C.C.L.T. 1 (Ont. Div. Ct.) (briefly considered in Chapter 2) raised a similar issue in terms of protection of reliance in the context of mistake. The defendant lottery corporation mistakenly told the plaintiff that he had won $430, when in fact he had only won $5. In reliance on the assurance, the plaintiff had a big party for his friends, spending the money that he expected to get. The plaintiff sued the lottery corporation after it refused to pay more than $5. The court protected the plaintiff's reliance and awarded him the $430. If Budai had actually been paid by the lottery corporation, and the corporation tried to recover the money paid by "mistake", Budai would have a strong case for resisting the claim for restitution. Budai's reliance on the lottery corporation mistake in spending the money mistakenly paid out on a big party, might be the kind of reliance that would be protected. There is nothing odd in this coincidence of result; it would only be odd if the results were not the same.

A common feature of the conceptually "easy cases" — those involving rectification and mistakenly made payments — is that it is hard to make the argument that the risk of disappointment should be on the party who is complaining of the mistake. In the rectification cases, given the requirement that there must be an antecedent agreement that has been incorrectly recorded in the written agreement, it cannot plausibly be argued that the party adversely affected by the mistake should bear the risk of typographical errors. Similarly, in the mistaken payment cases, the risk of loss arising from the payment cannot normally be said to be on the payor, at least not before the payee has changed its position. There is nothing inconsistent with the general approach to these mistakes to suggest that the risk could shift with the passing of time. Such a shift would be in accordance with the proposition that the person who moves promptly to seek relief is better off than the person who waits. Apart from the argument that the analysis of what risks each party should bear justifies the legal rules, it can also be argued that no expectations of the defendant are defeated by the giving of relief. No one can plausibly argue that they relied on getting an advantage from a typographical error or a windfall from a mistaken payment.

Mistaken Assumptions

In some cases of mistake, the decision about how to allocate the risk of loss is far more difficult than in cases of rectification or mistakenly made payments. Some of the difficulties in the law of mistake arise because some of the "leading decisions" in this area have articulated unsatisfactory legal "rules". From the point of view of trying to understand how rules work and then how to use them in advising clients, rules are unsatisfactory if they do not provide useful guidance or do not permit reasoned arguments to be made before a court. Rules are also unsatisfactory if they are framed in terms that appear to make each decision depend on a matter of arbitrary choice between categories, with that choice leading more or less automatically to a particular result. Such rules make it possible that the court will not even be aware that the issue before it is, for example, one of the allocation of risk.

A further problem is that, while all the cases in this book are in a sense pathological, the ones in this section are doubly so. They have only come to court because the mistake has been serious and unexpected and has arisen in a way that does not permit any kind of "structured" argument to deal with it. That is, the argument that counsel must make cannot be structured around familiar contractual concepts, like misrepresentation, warranty or reliance. The lack of "structure" in this area is reflected in the fact that while in some the cases it is clear that good work by a solicitor would have prevented the problem, in others no reasonable amount of planning could have avoided it.

The cases in this section are sometimes referred to as ones involving a "mistake in assumptions". This term was developed by George Palmer, in *Mistake and Unjust Enrichment* (Columbus, Ohio: S.U.P., 1962), and occurs when "an agreement is reached and is correctly recorded, but one or both parties makes a false assumption concerning some matter relevant to the decision to enter into the contract" (p. 6). The mistake relates to the underlying reason of one or both parties for entering into the transaction, as opposed to a mistake in expressing the transaction (rectification), or a misunderstanding relating to the transaction, such as arose in *Raffles v. Wichelhaus* ("mistake in formation"). The unjust enrichment (overpayment) cases are referred to by Palmer as involving a "mistake in performance". Although situations shade into one another and drawing bright lines between them is impossible, the concept of the mistake in assumptions is widely accepted.

The next case is one of the most famous American decisions in the law of contracts, and is studied by many American law students. It deals with the issue whether the argument of mistake can be used to reallocate the chance of gain.

SHERWOOD v. WALKER

33 N.W. 919 (1887)
(Mich. S.C., Campbell C.J., Morse, Champlin and Sherwood JJ.)

MORSE J.: — **[1]** Replevin for a cow . . . The defendants reside at Detroit, but are in business at Walkerville, Ontario, and have a farm at Greenfield, in Wayne county, upon which were some blooded cattle supposed to be barren as breeders. The Walkers are importers and breeders of polled Angus cattle. The plaintiff is a banker living at Plymouth, in Wayne county. He called upon the defendants at Walkerville for the purchase of some of their stock, but found none there that suited him. Meeting one of the defendants afterwards, he was informed that they had a few head upon their Greenfield farm. He was asked to go out and look at them, with the statement at the time that they were probably barren, and would not breed. May 5, 1886, plaintiff went out to Greenfield, and saw the cattle. A few days thereafter, he called upon one of the defendants with the view of purchasing a cow, known as "Rose 2nd of Aberlone." After considerable talk, it was agreed that defendants would telephone Sherwood at his home in Plymouth in reference to the price. The second morning after this talk he was called up by telephone, and the terms of the sale were finally agreed upon. He was to pay five and one-half cents per pound, live weight, fifty pounds shrinkage. He was asked how he intended to take the cow home, and replied that he might ship her from King's cattle-yard. He requested defendants to confirm the sale in writing, which they did by sending him the following letter: . . . "We confirm sale to you of the cow Rose 2nd of Aberlone . . . at five and a half cents per pound, less fifty pounds shrink. We enclose herewith order on Mr. Graham for the cow. . . ."

[2]　　On the twenty-first of the same month the plaintiff went to defendants' farm at Greenfield, and presented the order and letter to Graham, who informed him that the defendants had instructed him not to deliver the cow. Soon after, the plaintiff tendered to Hiram Walker, one of the defendants, $80, and demanded the cow. Walker refused to take the money or deliver the cow. The plaintiff then instituted this suit. After he had secured possession of the cow under the writ of replevin, the plaintiff caused her to be weighed by the constable who served the writ, at a place other than King's cattle-yard. She weighed 1,420 pounds. . . .

[3]　　The defendants then introduced evidence tending to show that at the time of the alleged sale it was believed by both the plaintiff and themselves that the cow was barren and would not breed; that she cost $850, and if not barren would be worth from $750 to $1,000 [Graham later thought that the cow was in calf, and as a consequence the defendants would not sell her]. The cow had a calf in the month of October following. . . .

[4]　　It appears from the record that both parties supposed this cow was barren and would not breed, and she was sold by the pound for an insignificant sum as compared with her real value if a breeder. She was evidently sold and purchased on the relation of her value for beef, unless the plaintiff had learned of her true condition, and concealed such knowledge from the defendants. . . .

[5]　　It seems to me, however, in the case made by this record, that the mistake or misapprehension of the parties went to the whole substance of the agreement. If the cow was a breeder, she was worth at least $750; if barren, she was worth not over $80. The parties would not have made the contract of sale except upon the understanding and belief that she was incapable of breeding, and of no use as a cow. It is true she is now the identical animal that they thought her to be when the contract was made; there is no mistake as to the identity of the creature. Yet the mistake was not of the mere quality of the animal, but went to the very nature of the thing. A barren cow is substantially a different creature than a breeding one. There is as much difference between them for all purposes of use as there is between an ox and a cow that is capable of breeding and giving milk . . . She was not in fact the animal, or the kind of animal, the defendants intended to sell or the plaintiff to buy. She was not a barren cow, and, if this fact had been known, there would have been no contract. The mistake affected the substance of the whole consideration, and it must be considered that there was no contract to sell or [for] sale of the cow as she actually was. The thing sold and bought had in fact no existence. She was sold as a beef creature would be sold; she is in fact a breeding cow, and a valuable one. The court should have instructed the jury that if they found the cow was sold, or contracted to be sold, upon the understanding of both parties that she was barren, and useless for the purpose of breeding, and that in fact she was not barren, but capable of breeding, then the defendants had a right to rescind, and to refuse to deliver, and the verdict should be in their favour.

[6]   The judgment of the court below must be reversed, and a new trial granted. . . .

[**CAMPBELL C.J.** and **CHAMPLIN J.** concurred.]

SHERWOOD J. (dissenting): — [7] . . . In this case neither party knew the actual quality and condition of this cow at the time of the sale. The defendants say, or rather said, to the plaintiff, "they had a few head left on their farm in Greenfield, and asked plaintiff to go and see them, stating to plaintiff that in all probability they were sterile and would not breed." Plaintiff did go as requested, and found there these cows, including the one purchased, with a bull. The cow had been exposed, but neither knew she was with calf nor whether she would breed. The defendants thought she would not, but the plaintiff says that he thought she could be made to breed, but believed she was not with calf. The defendants sold the cow for what they believed her to be, and the plaintiff bought her as he believed she was, after the statements made by the defendants. No conditions whatever were attached to the terms of sale by either party. It was in fact as absolute as it could well be made, and I know of no precedent as authority by which this court can alter the contract thus made by these parties in writing — interpolate in it a condition by which, if the defendants should be mistaken in their belief that the cow was barren, she could be returned to them and their contract should be annulled. It is not the duty of courts to destroy contracts when called upon to enforce them, after they have been legally made. There was no mistake of any material fact by either of the parties in the case as would license the vendors to rescind. There was no difference between the parties, nor misapprehension, as to the substance of the thing bargained for, which was a cow supposed to be barren by one party, and believed not to be by the other. As to the quality of the animal, subsequently developed, both parties were equally ignorant, and as to this each party took his chances. If this were not the law, there would be no safety in purchasing this kind of stock. . . .

QUESTIONS AND NOTES

1.   Do the judgments disagree on the facts or the law?

2.   If the facts had been reversed, that is, if the buyer had believed that he was buying a cow in calf and had paid the appropriate price and she turned out to be barren, the buyer could probably have sued for breach of a warranty or perhaps for negligent misrepresentation. The seller has no analogous right because there are no implied warranties running from the buyer to the seller. All the seller can use for his claim that the loss he will suffer should not be visited on him is the law of mistake.

3.   You are acting for a person in the position of the plaintiff. How do you conduct the negotiations with the other side to minimize the risk of the court's doing what it did in this case? There are two issues to keep in mind. How do you make it clear to the court that you wanted to buy the chance that "Rose" was in calf? How do you conduct the negotiations to avoid the risk that the other party will allege that you breached an obligation of disclosure?

4.   Was it significant that the buyer was a banker rather than a butcher? What might be the effects of the majority decision on the supply of cows available for breeding?

5.   Which judgment do you find preferable? Why?

   Most scholars who have written about the decision in *Sherwood v. Walker* prefer the dissent, and consider its risk-based analysis ("each party took his chances") to be the best approach to this type of case. See, e.g., J. Swan, "The Allocation of Risk in the Analysis of Mistake and Frustration", in Reiter and Swan, eds., *Studies in Contract Law* (Toronto: Butterworths, 1980), 181.

The decision that follows has been regarded as the leading precedent on the law of mistake, though after reading some of the cases decided later, it may be an open question whether the courts are still following it, or are only saying that they are still following it.

BELL v. LEVER BROTHERS LTD.

[1932] A.C. 161
(H.L., Viscount Hailsham, Lords Atkin, Blanesburgh, Thankerton and Warrington)

LORD ATKIN: — **[1]** My Lords, this case involves a question of much importance in the formation and dissolution of contracts.

[The appellants, Bell and Snelling, were hired by Lever on a five-year contract to manage the Niger Company Ltd., a subsidiary of Lever that was in financial difficulty when they took over. Bell was to be paid £8,000 a year, and Snelling was to be paid £6,000. The Niger Company prospered under their direction. After two and one-half years the Niger Company was amalgamated with another company and the services of Bell and Snelling were no longer required. Lever agreed to pay them £30,000 and £40,000 respectively, amounts which represented more than the balance owing under their five-year employment contracts. After making the payments Lever discovered that it could have dismissed both men without compensation, as they had breached their contracts of employment by trading in cocoa on their own accounts while they were working for the Niger Company. While these acts of "insider trading" would have given Lever Bros. the right to terminate them for cause without notice, they were not acts of fraud against Lever Bros. Lever sued to recover the amounts that it had paid. The jury held that there was no fraud on the part of the appellants; that had it known of the breaches, Lever would have dismissed them; and that Lever would not have promised to pay what it did had it known of the breaches. The trial judge gave judgment for Lever. This decision was upheld by a unanimous Court of Appeal. The appeal to the House of Lords concentrates on the position of Bell alone.]

[2] Two points present themselves for decision. Was the agreement [between Lever and Bell and Snelling] void by reason of a mutual mistake of [Lever] and Mr. Bell?

[3] Could the agreement . . . be avoided by reason of the failure of Mr. Bell to disclose his misconduct in regard to the cocoa dealings?

[4] My Lords, the rules of law dealing with the effect of mistake on contract appear to be established with reasonable clearness. If mistake operates at all it operates so as to negative or in some cases to nullify consent. The parties may be mistaken in the identity of the contracting parties, or in the existence of the subject-matter of the contract at the date of the contract, or in the quality of the subject-matter of the contract. These mistakes may be by one party, or by both, and the legal effect may depend upon the class of mistake above mentioned. Thus a mistaken belief by A that he is contracting with B, whereas in fact he is contracting with C, will negative consent where it is clear that the intention of A was to contract only with B. So the agreement of A and B to purchase a specific article is void if in fact the article had perished before the date of sale. In this case, though the parties in fact were agreed about the subject-matter, yet a consent to transfer or take delivery of something not existent is deemed useless, the consent is nullified. As codified in the Sale of Goods Act the contract is expressed to be void if the seller was in ignorance of the destruction of the specific chattel. I apprehend that if the seller with knowledge that a chattel was destroyed purported to sell it to a purchaser, the latter might sue for damages for non-delivery though the former could not sue for non-acceptance, but I know of no case where a seller has so committed himself. This is a case where mutual mistake certainly and unilateral mistake by the seller of goods will prevent a contract from arising. Corresponding to mistake as to the existence of the subject-matter is mistake as to title in cases where, unknown to the parties, the buyer is already the owner of that which the seller purports to sell to him. The parties intended to effectuate a transfer of ownership: such a transfer is impossible: the stipulation is *naturali ratione inutilis*. This is the case of *Cooper v. Phibbs* (1867), L.R. 2 H.L. 149, where A agreed to take a lease of a fishery from B, though contrary to the belief of both parties at the time A was tenant for life of the fishery and B appears to have had no title at all. To such a case Lord Westbury applied the principle that if parties contract under a mutual mistake and misapprehension as to their relative and respective rights the result is that the agreement is liable to be set aside as having proceeded upon a common mistake. Applied to the context the statement is only subject to the criticism that the agreement would appear to be void rather than voidable. Applied to mistake as to rights generally it would appear to be too wide. Even where the vendor has no title, though both parties think he has, the correct view would appear to be that there is a contract: but that the vendor has either committed a breach of a stipulation as to title, or is not able to perform his contract. The contract is unenforceable by him but is not void.

[5] Mistake as to quality of the thing contracted for raises more difficult questions. In such a case a mistake will not affect assent unless it is the mistake of both parties, and is as to the existence of some quality which makes the thing without the quality essentially different from the thing as it was believed to be. Of course it may appear that the parties contracted that the article should possess the quality which one or other or both mistakenly believed it to possess. But in such a case there is a contract and the inquiry is a different one, being whether the contract as to quality amounts to a condition or a warranty, a different branch of the law. The principles to be applied are to be found in two cases which, as far as my knowledge goes, have always been treated as authoritative expositions of the law. The first is *Kennedy v. Panama, etc. Mail Co.* [(1867), L.R. 2 Q.B. 580].

[6]   In that case the plaintiff had applied for shares in the defendant company on the faith of a prospectus which stated falsely but innocently that the company had a binding contract with the Government of New Zealand for the carriage of mails. On discovering the true facts the plaintiff brought an action for the recovery of the sums he had paid on calls. The defendants brought a cross action for further calls. Blackburn J., in delivering the judgment of the Court, said. . . .

> There is, however, a very important difference between cases where a contract may be rescinded on account of fraud, and those in which it may be rescinded on the ground that there is a difference in substance between the thing bargained for and that obtained. It is enough to show that there was a fraudulent representation as to any part of that which induced the party to enter into the contract which he seeks to rescind; but where there has been an innocent misrepresentation or misapprehension, it does not authorize a rescission unless it is such as to show that there is a complete difference in substance between what was supposed to be and what was taken, so as to constitute a failure of consideration.

[7]   The Court came to the conclusion in that case that, though there was a misapprehension as to that which was a material part of the motive inducing the applicant to ask for the shares, it did not prevent the shares from being in substance those he applied for.

[**LORD ATKIN** then discussed *Smith v. Hughes* (1871), L.R. 6 Q.B. 597, and continued:]

[8]   In these cases I am inclined to think that the true analysis is that there is a contract, but that the one party is not able to supply the very thing whether goods or services that the other party contracted to take; and therefore the contract is unenforceable by the one if executory, while if executed the other can recover back money paid on the ground of failure of the consideration.

[9]   We are now in a position to apply to the facts of this case the law as to mistake so far as it has been stated. It is essential on this part of the discussion to keep in mind the finding of the jury acquitting the defendants of fraudulent misrepresentation or concealment in procuring the agreements in question. Grave injustice may be done to the defendants and confusion introduced into the legal conclusion, unless it is quite clear that in considering mistake in this case no suggestion of fraud is admissible and cannot strictly be regarded by the judge who has to determine the legal issues raised. The agreement which is said to be void is the agreement . . . that Bell would retire from the Board of the Niger Company and its subsidiaries, and that in consideration of his doing so Levers would pay him as compensation for the termination of his agreements and consequent loss of office the sum of £30,000. . . . The agreement, which as part of the contract was terminated, had been broken so that it could be repudiated.

[10] Is an agreement to terminate a broken contract different in kind from an agreement to terminate an unbroken contract, assuming that the breach has given the one party the right to declare the contract at an end? . . . But, on the whole, I have come to the conclusion that it would be wrong to decide that an agreement to terminate a definite specified contract is void if it turns out that the agreement had already been broken and could have been terminated otherwise. The contract released is the identical contract in both cases, and the party paying for release gets exactly what he bargains for. It seems immaterial that he could have got the same result in another way, or that if he had known the true facts he would not have entered into the bargain. . . .

[11] This brings the discussion to the alternative mode of expressing the result of a mutual mistake. It is said that in such a case as the present there is to be implied a stipulation in the contract that a condition of its efficacy is that the facts should be as understood by both parties — namely, that the contract could not be terminated till the end of the current term. The question of the existence of conditions, express or implied, is obviously one that affects not the formation of contract, but the investigation of the terms of the contract when made. A condition derives its efficacy from the consent of the parties, express or implied. They have agreed, but on what terms. One term may be that unless the facts are or are not of a particular nature, or unless an event has or has not happened, the contract is not to take effect. With regard to future facts such a condition is obviously contractual. Till the event occurs the parties are bound. . . .

[12] Sir John Simon formulated for the assistance of your Lordships a proposition which should be recorded: "Whenever it is to be inferred from the terms of a contract or its surrounding circumstances that the consensus has been reached upon the basis of a particular contractual assumption, and that assumption is not true, the contract is avoided: *i.e.*, it is void *ab initio* if the assumption is of present fact and it ceases to bind if the assumption is of future fact."

[13] I think few would demur to this statement, but its value depends upon the meaning of "a contractual assumption," and also upon the true meaning to be attached to "basis," a metaphor which may mislead. When used expressly in contracts, for instance, in policies of insurance, which state that the truth of the statements in the proposal is to be the basis of the contract of insurance, the meaning is clear. The truth of the statements is made a condition of the contract, which failing, the contract is void unless the condition is waived. The proposition does not amount to more than this: that, if the contract expressly or impliedly contains a term that a particular assumption is a condition of the contract, the contract is avoided if the assumption is not true. But we have not advanced far on the inquiry how to ascertain whether the contract does contain such a condition. Various words are to be found to define the state of things which make a condition. "In the contemplation of both parties fundamental to the continued validity of the contract", "a foundation essential to its existence", "a fundamental reason for making it", are phrases found in the important judgment of Scrutton L.J. in the present case. The first two phrases appear to me to be unexceptionable. They cover the case of a contract to serve in a particular place, the existence of which is fundamental to the service, or to procure the services of a professional vocalist, whose continued health is essential to performance. But "a fundamental reason for making a contract" may, with respect, be misleading. The reason of one party only is presumably not intended, but in the cases I have suggested above, of the sale of a horse or of a picture, it might be said that the fundamental reason for making the contract was the belief of both parties that the horse was sound or the picture an old master, yet in neither case would the condition as I think exist. Nothing is more dangerous than to allow oneself liberty to construct for the parties contracts which they have not in terms made by importing implications which would appear to make the contract more businesslike or more just. The implications to be made are to be no more than are "necessary" for giving business efficacy to the transaction, and it appears to me that, both as to existing facts and future facts, a condition would not be implied unless the new state of facts makes the contract something different in kind from the contract in the original state of facts. . . .

[14] We therefore get a common standard for mutual mistake, and implied conditions whether as to existing or as to future facts. Does the state of the new facts destroy the identity of the subject-matter as it was in the original state of facts? To apply the principle to the infinite combinations of facts that arise in actual experience will continue to be difficult, but if this case results in establishing order into what has been a somewhat confused and difficult branch of the law it will have served a useful purpose. . . .

[15] The result is that in the present case servants unfaithful in some of their work retain large compensation which some will think they do not deserve. Nevertheless it is of greater importance that well-established principles of contract should be maintained than that a particular hardship should be redressed; and I see no way of giving relief to the plaintiffs in the present circumstances except by confiding to the Courts loose powers of introducing terms into contracts which would only serve to introduce doubt and confusion where certainty is essential.

[16] I think therefore that this appeal should be allowed. . . .

[LORDS BLANESBURGH and THANKERTON agreed in the result reached by LORD ATKIN.]

LORD WARRINGTON (dissenting): — [17] . . . The real question, therefore, is whether the erroneous assumption on the part of both parties to the agreements that the service contracts were undeterminable except by agreement was of such a fundamental character as to constitute an underlying assumption without which the parties would not have made the contract they in fact made, or whether it was only a common error as to a material element, but one not going to the root of the matter and not affecting the substance of the consideration.

[18] With the knowledge that I am differing from the majority of your Lordships, I am unable to arrive at any conclusion except that in this case the erroneous assumption was essential to the contract which without it would not have been made.

[19] It is true that the error was not one as to the terms of the service agreements, but it was one which, having regard to the matter on which the parties were negotiating — namely, the terms on which the service agreements were to be prematurely determined and the compensation to be paid therefor — was in my opinion as fundamental to the bargain as any error one can imagine.

[20] The compensation agreed to be paid was in each case the amount of the full salary for the two years and a half unexpired with the addition in Mr. Bell's case of £10,000 and in Mr. Snelling's of £5,000. It is difficult to believe that the jury

were otherwise than correct in their answer . . . namely, that had Levers known of the actings of the appellants in regard to the dealings in question they would not have made the agreements now impeached or either of them. . . .

[VISCOUNT HAILSHAM agreed with LORD WARRINGTON.]

NOTES AND QUESTIONS

1. Lord Warrington in his dissent points out that the compensation paid to Bell and Snelling included amounts in the nature of gratuitous payments. Bell got an additional £10,000 and Snelling £5,000. Do the arguments on the issue of mistake apply to the part of the compensation that is the gratuitous payment (a bonus for work well done) as well as to the pre-payment of salary? The statement of the jury verdict is not conclusive on this issue.

2. How should a court determine if something is "fundamentally different" or "different in substance" from something else? A man and a woman may be different, but what kind of judgment is implicit in the statement that they are "fundamentally different"? If you were asked if they were "fundamentally different", would you not want to know why the question was being asked and what depended on your answer?

    So too the answers given by Lord Atkin and Lord Warrington to the question of which type of mistake will give the court the basis for awarding must involve important value questions of the familiar type: "What do the courts want to do, and why do they want to do it?"

3. Recall that in *Raffles v. Wichelhaus* (*supra*, Chapter 3) the court concluded that there was no enforceable agreement because the parties had not agreed on the terms of the contract. The case was also referred to as one of the leading cases on the law of mistake. Notice the similar structure of reasoning by Lord Atkin. He sees the operation of mistake in the context of the rules of offer and acceptance: mistake either "negatives" or "nullifies" consent. If there is an operative mistake, *i.e.*, a mistake that is legally relevant, its effect is in the context of the rules of offer and acceptance, so that the process of "creating" a contract misfires and either nothing (legally) happens or whatever happens has no legal effect.

    This focus on issues of contract formation as a central feature of the traditional mistake analysis has created serious difficulties. Any decision to give or to deny relief on the basis of mistake is justified on the same grounds that justify the use of the rules of offer and acceptance. In other words, just as the traditional rules of offer and acceptance have been cut loose (or developed in isolation) from serious consideration of the kind of contracting that parties actually engage in and from the need for the law to respect the values that underlie the actual processes of exchange, so too the law of mistake, as analyzed by Lord Atkin, bears little relation to the values inherent in the law of contract and what the rules of contract exist for.

    So long as the focus is on the rules of contract formation — notice the first sentence of Lord Atkin's judgment — the court cannot deal with two important issues:

    (a) If you wanted to give relief to Lever, why should the completed gift, *i.e.*, the bonus, be treated in the same way as the pre-payment of the employees' salary? Do the breaches of duty diminish the value of their services *as they were perceived* by Lever when it made the gratuitous payments?

    (b) There is an important issue respecting the duty of disclosure an employee has to make when he or she is fired with compensation. Must the employee disclose all breaches that would justify dismissal without compensation, at the risk that, after he or she has left, the employer can dig around to see if the payment can be recovered? The House of Lords touches on this issue in dealing with the jury's finding that Bell and Snelling were not guilty of fraud. What might fraud mean in this context? Would a finding that there was fraud mean that the breaches were considered (by the trier of fact) to be so serious that they should have been disclosed or that the employee in some particularly objectionable way hid his or her offences?

4.   In *Courtright v. Canadian Pacific Ltd.* (1983), 45 O.R. (2d) 52, 5 D.L.R. (4th) 488, (H.C.J.), affirmed (1985), 50 O.R. (2d) 560, 18 D.L.R. (4th) 639 (C.A.), the plaintiff sued for damages for wrongful dismissal in a situation where he had just been hired and his employer refused to allow him to start work. The defence was that he had not disclosed in the course of his application or interview for employment as a solicitor that the police were investigating him for allegations of "influence peddling", and there was a possibility that he might be charged. While he had not been charged at the time of his application or job interview, by the time that the job was to start, he had been charged, though he was later acquitted. The Court of Appeal held that his failure to disclose the fact that he was under investigation at the time of his job interview was a breach of his obligation to deal with a prospective employer in good faith. The existence of such an obligation provides at least a defensible basis for allocating the risk of loss to the employee, and the duty that arises at the beginning of the relation may, presumably, arise at its termination.

The report of *Courtright* raises two wider issues. The judgment of the Court of Appeal refers to *Bell v. Lever Brothers* in the context of the duty of the employee to disclose facts which might affect his "acceptability" to his employer, yet the "catch-lines" in the Ontario Reports and Dominion Law Reports mention "Mistake" as one of the topics in the case, as if the mere citation of *Bell v. Lever Brothers* means that the case has to be one of mistake. There was no mistake made by anyone (except perhaps by Mr. Courtright in not mentioning his situation), and no argument on "mistake" was made. *Bell v. Lever Brothers* was referred to by Mr. Courtright as authority for the proposition that the employee owes his or her employer no duty of disclosure, at least on termination. The development of the law of warranties, as we have seen, and of obligations of good faith in negotiations, illustrates that problems of non-disclosure do not have to be dealt with as "mistakes", though in 1932 counsel for Lever may have had little choice but to do what he did.

A second aspect of *Courtright* that is worth noting is that there was ultimately no basis for any concern by the defendant about the plaintiff's integrity. He was the victim of an overly wide criminal investigation. However, the judgments emphasized that being employed as a lawyer constitutes a "confidential relation". The court referred to a contract *uberrimae fidei*, *i.e.*, of utmost good faith, for which there is a duty of "good faith" that requires disclosure of any material information before a contract is formed.

Does a law student going for an articling interview have a similar obligation?

5.   In many standard form contracts, asset and share purchase agreements, for example, the vendor may give an undertaking that there are no facts not disclosed, which, if disclosed, would be material to the purchaser. Such clause might be in the following form:

> There is no fact known to the Corporation or the Seller which materially and adversely affects the affairs, prospects, operations or condition of the Corporation, the Assets or the Business which has not been set forth in this Agreement.

(The capitalized terms would all have been defined in the agreement.) In such situations there is a clear allocation of some of the risks of mistake to the seller. What arguments would you, as solicitor for the seller, make against the inclusion of a clause of this type? How would you argue for a limit to its scope?

In *Solle v. Butcher*, [1950] 1 K.B. 671, [1949] 2 All E.R. 1107 (C.A.), the parties had been partners in a business that bought houses for renovation. The defendant bought a house, renovated it, and leased a flat in it to the plaintiff. The parties were concerned that the rent charged would not be caught by the *Rent Acts*. These acts, originally passed in 1920, prohibited any increase in rent during the term of a tenancy. Rents could be increased with permission of a government agency at the end of one tenancy and the beginning of another. The pre-war rent had been £140 per annum for the flat rented by the plaintiff. The plaintiff undertook to get legal advice on the applicability of the *Rent Acts*. After advice had been obtained that the flats were not subject to the pre-war rents, the parties agreed on a rent of £250 per annum without obtaining the agency's permission, and the plaintiff entered into a seven-year lease. Relations between the parties subsequently deteriorated. During the tenancy, the plaintiff brought an action claiming that the rent legislation applied, that the maximum rent was £140 and that the overpayment should be returned to him. The county court judge held that the *Rent Acts* applied and that the rent should have been £140, and gave judgment for the plaintiff. The defendant appealed to the Court of Appeal.

Lord Denning, then Denning L.J., held that, since the rent could not be increased during the term of the lease, the only way in which the defendant could be protected was by avoiding the lease on the ground of mistake. He held that *Bell v. Lever Brothers* limited the scope of mistake at common law, *i.e.*, when it is argued that the contract is void. He went on to hold that there was a wider jurisdiction in equity to hold contracts voidable for mistake. Accordingly, the lease was set aside "on terms." The terms protected the tenant while the landlord made an application to have the rent increased (but not above the agreed rent) and, after the rent had been lawfully increased, the tenant would have a lease for the original term. The plaintiff could stay in the house but he would have to pay the agreed rent.

Solle v. Butcher illustrates the "residual" nature of an argument based on "mistake". The operation of the legislation forced the landlord to leave a tenant in possession under a lease at a rent that was almost one-half of what the landlord would have been able to charge if he had made a proper application for rent review. In 1949, when *Solle* was decided, it was accepted that the remedy available for non-fraudulent misrepresentation was limited and that there was no action for negligent misrepresentation causing pure economic loss. (A year later, a majority of the Court of Appeal, over a vigorous dissent by Denning L.J., held in *Candler v. Crane, Christmas & Co.*, [1951] 2 K.B. 164, [1951] 1 All E.R. 426, that there was no action for negligent misreprentation that did not cause physical loss. This case was overruled by the House of Lords in *Hedley Byrne & Co. Ltd. v. Heller & Partners Ltd.*) Without that basis for liability, there was no basis for imposing liability on the plaintiff for the mistaken information that he gave the defendant. The only basis for relief for the landlord was to have the lease set aside so that an application could be made under the legislation to permit the higher rent to be charged. Once again, Lord Denning uses equity to provide a basis for relief. What limits are there on this use of equity that would permit a court to make a justifiable allocation of the risk of loss inherent in the fact that the parties made a mistake? In other words, did Lord Denning once again let the genie out of the bottle?

You can see the explicit allocation of the risk of loss through mistake being made in this case. What reasons are there to support this allocation? Which party has the least-cost access to facts? Which party induced reliance on what he said?

Is there any need to use a "mistake" analysis to deal with the allocation of the risk of loss in a case like this after *Hedley Byrne v. Heller*?

In the recent decision in *Great Peace Shipping Ltd. v. Tsavliris Salvage (International) Ltd.*, [2003] Q.B. 679, the English Court of Appeal strongly disapproved of the decision in *Solle v. Butcher* and held that the correct analysis of mistake was that established by Lord Atkin in *Bell v. Lever Brothers*. The mistake in *Great Peace* arose in the context of a contract for salvage. The defendants wanted to get help to a damaged ship in the south Indian Ocean. They were led to believe that the "Great Peace", owned by the plaintiff, was the closest ship and they made an agreement that the "Great Peace" would go to the damaged ship and that the defendants would pay a minimum of five days' hire. It turned out that the "Great Peace" was more than 10 times as far away as the defendants believed, so the defendants arranged for another ship to carry out the salvage and sought to escape their liability for the five days' hire (some £80,000) on the basis that they had made a mistake, from the consequences of which, under *Solle v. Butcher*, they could be relieved. The Court of Appeal made a very thorough analysis of *Bell v. Lever Brothers*, the cases that had preceded it and those that had followed it. The Court held that the application of the test set out by Lord Atkin, *i.e.*, whether the contract made was "fundamentally different" from that which the parties had intended, led to the conclusion that no relief should be given.

The problem with the judgment in *Great Peace* is that, by focusing on Lord Atkin's test, the measure of flexibility provided by *Solle v. Butcher* was removed. This argument does not suggest that the result in *Great Peace* was necessarily wrong; only that, by focusing on whether the parties' assent to the terms of the contract was negatived or nullified, we have no basis for an examination of which party should, in the circumstances, bear the risk of loss. It is certainly not obvious that the loss should be borne by the plaintiff and arguments, perhaps special to the shipping industry, might well be made to suggest that undertakings to pay for one ship to go to the rescue of another should, at least in general, be enforced, even if there has been a mistake made by the party seeking the other's help. The Court of Appeal did not consider *Solle v. Butcher* in the light of the modern law of negligent misrepresentation and the possibility that, leaving issues of mistake, whether equitable or not, entirely aside, the result in that case was the only justifiable one. The result in "Great Peace" has been severely criticized and it has been said that "it would be unfortunate indeed if Canadian courts were to embrace the reasoning in *The Great Peace*" (John McCamus, "Mistaken Assumptions in Equity: Sound Doctrine or Chimera?" (2004), 40 *Can. Bus. L.J.* 85).

The next case raises the problem of the limit to Lord Denning's reasoning in *Solle v. Butcher,* and the relation of that judgment to *Bell v. Lever Brothers*.

The case involved an insurance contract; it is a rule of the law of insurance that a misrepresentation in the application for insurance by an insured provides the insurer with an excuse not to pay on a claim. In general, this rule applies even though the misrepresentation is innocent and the insured has been paying premiums for years; it may make the policy unenforceable even though the misrepresentation may have no bearing (either at the date of the original policy or when the loss occurs) on the decision of the insurer to accept the risk and issue the policy. This rule developed because the insured usually knows much more about the subject matter of the contract than the insurance company.

As you read this case, consider whether this rule of insurance law is fair, especially in a situation like this one, in which the mistake in filling in the insurance application is made by a third party who was selected by the insurance company to help sell its insurance policies.

MAGEE v. PENNINE INSURANCE CO.

[1969] 2 All E.R. 891
(C.A., Lord Denning M.R., Winn and Fenton Atkinson L.JJ.)

[The plaintiff bought a car in 1961. He applied for insurance. The application for insurance was filled in by the car salesman, but the plaintiff signed it. The application stated that the car was for the plaintiff to drive. This was untrue. The plaintiff had never had a driver's licence, and the car was really for his son, then aged 18. In any event, the policy was issued by the defendant insurer and renewed several times. The original car was replaced by another. In 1965 an accident occurred and a claim was made under the collision coverage. The defendant's adjuster assessed the damage and, in a letter written to the plaintiff, offered to pay £385 (£410 less £25 deductible), which the plaintiff orally accepted. The defendant insurer then discovered that there had been a misrepresentation in the original application, and refused to pay.

An action was brought on both the insurance policy and the letter (which was regarded as an agreement of compromise). The representatives of the insurance company testified at the trial that they would not have insured the son. The trial judge dismissed the claim on the policy (based on the failure of the insured when the policy was issued to disclose that his son was driving the vehicle) but allowed the claim on the letter.]

LORD DENNING M.R. [after stating the facts, continued: —] **[1]** But then comes the next point. Accepting that the agreement to pay £385 was an agreement of compromise. Is it vitiated by mistake? The insurance company was clearly under a mistake. They thought that the policy was good and binding. They did not know, at the time of that letter, that there had been misrepresentations in the proposal form. If Mr. Magee knew of their mistake — if he knew that the policy was bad — he certainly could not take advantage of the agreement to pay £385. He would be "snapping at an offer which he knew was made under a mistake": and no man is allowed to get away with that. But I prefer to assume that Mr. Magee was innocent. I think we should take it that both parties were under a common mistake. Both parties thought that the policy was good and binding. The letter . . . was written on the assumption that the policy was good whereas it was in truth voidable.

[2] What is the effect in law of this common mistake? [Counsel for the plaintiff] said that the agreement to pay £385 was good, despite this common mistake. He relied much on *Bell v. Lever Bros.* and its similarity to the present case. He submitted that, inasmuch as the mistake there did not vitiate that contract, the mistake here should not vitiate this one. I do not propose today to go through the speeches in that case. They have given enough trouble to commentators already. I would say simply this: A common mistake, even on a most fundamental matter, does not make a contract void at law: but it makes it voidable in equity. I analyzed the cases in *Solle v. Butcher*, and I would repeat what I said there: "A contract is also liable in equity to be set aside if the parties were under a common misapprehension either as to facts or as to their relative and respective rights, provided that the misapprehension was fundamental and that the party seeking to set it aside was not himself at fault." Now applying that principle here, it is clear that, when the insurance company and Mr. Magee made this agreement to pay £385, they were both under a common mistake which was fundamental to the whole agreement. Both thought that Mr. Magee was entitled to claim under the policy of insurance, whereas he was not so entitled. That common mistake does not make the agreement to pay £385 a nullity, but it makes it liable to be set aside in equity.

[3]   This brings me to a question which has caused me much difficulty. Is this a case in which we ought to set the agreement aside in equity? I have hesitated on this point, but I cannot shut my eyes to the fact that Mr. Magee had no valid claim on the insurance policy: and, if he had no claim on the policy, it is not equitable that he should have a good claim on the agreement to pay £385, seeing that it was made under a fundamental mistake. It is not fair to hold the insurance company to an agreement which they would not have dreamt of making if they had not been under a mistake. I would, therefore, uphold the appeal and give judgment for the insurance company.

WINN L.J. (dissenting): — [4] This appeal has given me pleasure because it has been so well argued by both the counsel who have appeared in it; and, of course, the problem which it presents is not one the solution of which is going to impose frightful actual loss or consequences on the particular individuals or companies who are involved. It is a neat and teasing problem, the difficulty of which is slightly indicated, though by no means established, by the regrettable circumstance that I find myself respectfully having to dissent from the views of my Lord and of my brother Fenton Atkinson L.J. . . .

[5]   For my part, I think that here there was a misapprehension as to rights, but no misapprehension whatsoever as to the subject-matter of the contract, namely, the settlement of the rights of the assured with regard to the accident that happened. The insurance company was settling his rights, if he had any. He understood them to be settling his rights; but each of them, on the assumption that the county court judge's view of the facts was right, thought his rights against the insurers were very much more valuable than in fact they were, since in reality they were worthless: the insurers could have repudiated — or avoided, that being the more accurate phrase on the basis of the mis-statements which my Lord has narrated.

[6]   In my view the mistake must be a mistake as to the nature or at the very least the quality of the subject-matter and not as to the reason why either party desires to deal with the subject-matter as the contract provides that it should be dealt with. . . .

FENTON ATKINSON L.J.: — [7] . . . Applying the rule [laid down in *Bell v. Lever Brothers Ltd.* and stated in *Chitty on Contracts* (1968)] to the facts of this case, I think it is clear that, when the agreement relied upon by the plaintiff was made, it was made on the basis of a particular and essential contractual assumption, namely, that there was in existence a valid and enforceable policy of insurance, and that assumption was not true. In my view it is the right and equitable result of this case that the insurers should be entitled to avoid that agreement on the ground of mutual mistake in a fundamental and vital matter.

[8]   I agree that this appeal should succeed on that ground.

QUESTIONS AND NOTES

1.   Is the decision in *Magee v. Pennine* an application of the rule in *Bell v. Lever Brothers*? Do Lord Denning and Fenton Atkinson L.J. take the same approach to *Bell*?

2. Could an analysis of the allocation of the risks run by each party provide an answer to the problem of *Magee v. Pennine*? The effect of the decision is to preserve the right of the insurer to use the defence of misrepresentation at any time and regardless of any intervening agreement. Is there any type of "change of position" argument that Magee could have made?

3. Notice the parallel in the development of the law of mistake in *Bell v. Lever Brothers*, *Solle v. Butcher* and *Magee v. Pennine*, and the development of the law of consideration in *High Trees*, *Combe v. Combe* and *D & C Builders v. Rees*. In each set of cases there is an unsatisfactory common law rule articulated by the House of Lords. Then Lord Denning "invokes equity" and reaches a satisfactory result in one case, but with implications that turn out to be hard to control. He deals with the later problems by developing a limit on his earlier articulated doctrine that is difficult to apply. While some of his fellow judges in the final case in the series continue to apply the original decision of the House of Lords, Lord Denning does not deal with the underlying problems in a comprehensive fashion. Nevertheless, the approach of Lord Denning in *Solle v. Butcher* and *High Trees* is very influential. Can you see why?

4. The traditional rules about the law of mistake have been outlined in the preceding cases. A principal feature of that approach is that mistake is a very limited remedy. There are a number of "control devices": that the mistake must be "fundamental", that it must violate or disappoint some essential contractual assumption, and that it must not be the "fault" of the party seeking relief.

As we saw in Chapter 2, in *Stott v. Merit Investments*, there is a strong presumption in favour of upholding a compromise agreement, even if one party should later argue that the agreement was made by "mistake", and had a much stronger claim or defence than it thought at the time. Nevertheless, there are situations in which the courts will accept such an argument.

TORONTO-DOMINION BANK v. FORTIN (NO. 2)

(1979), 88 D.L.R. (3d) 232, [1978] 5 W.W.R. 302
(B.C.S.C., Andrews J.)

Application for repayment of money paid to a receiver-manager.

[On 21 June 1976, Harold Sigurdson was appointed receiver/manager of Chimo Structures Ltd., Chimo Industries Ltd. and Chimo Construction Ltd. (hereinafter referred to as the "Chimo Companies") by the Toronto-Dominion Bank. The receiver/manager invited offers for the Chimo Companies as a going concern. On 14 October 1976, Flynn, the applicant, through his solicitor, tendered an offer for the purchase of the property and assets of the Chimo Companies. Flynn's offer was, as required by the terms of the invitation, accompanied by a certified cheque for 5 per cent of the offered purchase price, in the amount of $24,658. After some further negotiations between the parties, Sigurdson accepted Flynn's offer on 3 November 1976. Court approval of this transaction was never obtained as Flynn refused to proceed with the transaction, claiming that the terms of the contract he signed were so unclear that the contract was not binding. Flynn's solicitor asked for the return of the deposit that he had paid. This request was refused, but the receiver/manager stated that he would accept $10,000 as a compromise in satisfaction of all claims against Flynn arising out of the agreement.

Flynn agreed to the terms of the compromise agreement on 18 November 1976. On 30 November 1976, when Sigurdson, the receiver/manager, sought to get court approval of another offer to purchase the Chimo Companies, the court ruled that the receiver had acted beyond the powers given him by the order of the court appointing him in offering the assets for sale and in entering into an agreement for sale without leave of the court. This ruling was upheld by the Court of Appeal on 11 February 1977.]

[**ANDREWS J.**, having stated the facts, continued: —] **[1]** As a result of that decision the applicant now contends that the receiver/manager had no legal right to enter into a contract with the applicant for the sale of the assets of the Chimo Companies. Thus, the applicant feels that the receiver/manager's position as an officer of the Court obliges him to return the $10,000 paid under the compromise agreement, as the said sum was paid under a mistake of law.

[2]   The basic rule respecting a compromise agreement is that it cannot be attacked by reason of a common mistake of law provided the claim compromised is a *bona fide* or "honest" claim, however mistaken the parties are as to its validity. Thus forbearance to sue is said to be good consideration regardless of whether the claim compromised is unfounded and could not be sustained.

[3]   One rationale for this rule is given in Cheshire & Fifoot's *Law of Contract*, 9th ed. (1976), p. 76, where the learned author states that the consideration for a compromise agreement is not found in the compromise of a legal right but rather in the surrender of the *claim* to such a right. The traditional reason cited in the case law is the policy desire to effect reasonable settlements. Such a desire would be frustrated if the compromise of a doubtful claim could be set aside on demonstration that the claim could not succeed.

[**ANDREWS J.** referred to several cases supporting the rule and holding that the validity or invalidity of the claim is not a relevant factor. He continued:]

[4]   The applicant in the case at bar says that the receiver's powers are derived from an order of the Court appointing him, and since that appointment did not contain the power to sell the assets he therefore could not have any power to compromise an agreement for sale. A similar position was advanced in the *Deeks* [*A.-G. B.C. v. Deeks Sand & Gravel Co. Ltd.*, [1956] S.C.R. 336, 2 D.L.R. (2d) 305] case where the Province of British Columbia sought to enforce a compromise relating to the renewal of certain leases. The compromise provided that there would be an adjustment both as regard to rental and royalties. It was later determined to be beyond the powers of the Province to impose a royalty on the leases in question; thus it was argued that the compromise must be invalid as the subject-matter of the attempted compromise was *ultra vires* the Province. The Supreme Court of Canada in rejecting that argument found the compromise valid as affecting the settlement of an honest disagreement over the construction of the leases. The *Deeks* case is distinguished from the case at bar in that, in the *Deeks* case, the parties specifically sought legal advice on that part of the compromise settlement later in dispute. In the *Deeks* case at p. 345 S.C.R., p. 313 D.L.R. the Court says:

> Although the respondent was at the time acting under the advice of solicitors and had been advised that it was entitled to receive renewals free from the claims being put forward by the Province, it saw fit to enter into the compromise which involved concessions on both sides.

[5]   Thus the parties had put their minds to the capacity of the Province to impose the royalties. This is different from the case at bar, where neither party had considered the capacity of the receiver to enter the contract of sale or the compromise. Had they sought legal advice on this point and decided, even if erroneously, that the receiver had the capacity to enter into the agreement of sale, they would be bound by the compromise agreement. This is a recurring theme running throughout the case law as to whether the parties at any time considered and received legal advice respecting the validity of the claim to be compromised. In *Rogers v. Ingham* (1876), 3 Ch. D. 351, the compromise was effected where all the facts were known and legal opinion was considered. Thus the Court would not exercise its equitable power of relief. On the other hand, in *Lawton v. Campion* (1854), 52 E.R. 35, 18 Beav. 87, the compromise did not consider whether there was any liability at all to pay and the Court set aside the compromise agreement.

[6]   At some point a mistake can be so fundamental that the compromise agreement cannot stand. Such a proposition is set out by S. M. Waddams in the *Law of Contracts* (1977), p. 85. Similarly, G. H. Treitel in the *Law of Contracts*, 4th ed. (1975), p. 60, comments that where the claim is clearly untenable the compromise of it should not be good consideration. This concept of a fundamental mistake was enunciated by the House of Lords in *Bell v. Lever Bros. Ltd. . . .* and cited with approval . . . in the judgment of Fenton Atkinson L.J., in *Magee v. Pennine Ins. Co. Ltd. . . .*

[7]   The *Magee* case is analogous to the case at bar. In the *Magee* case a compromise was effected on an insurance claim, with both parties operating under the assumption that the insurance company was bound by the policy. On the basis of misstatements in the application, which were not the fault of either party, the company challenged the compromise and at trial was found to have the right to repudiate the policy.

[**ANDREWS J.** referred to the judgments of Lord Denning M.R. in *Magee v. Pennine* (¶ 2) on the distinction between mistake at common law and mistake in equity. He continued:]

[8]   In the context of the case at bar the contract of sale is void *ab initio* and, it being the basis of the later compromise that compromise, following *Magee*, though not a nullity at law is liable to be set aside in equity. The case at bar is stronger for the applicant, as the contract of insurance in *Magee* was merely voidable for misrepresentation as opposed to being void from inception, as here. . . .

NOTE

In *Toronto-Dominion Bank v. Fortin (No. 2)* the court accepted the fact that in negotiating the settlement contract the plaintiff did not contemplate or "take the risk" that the receiver had no legal authority even to offer the business for sale. The receiver was in a much better position than the purchaser to know what his authority was. Allocating this risk to him, *i.e.*, in effect to the secured creditors that he represents, puts the loss on the person with greater or easier access to the information necessary to avoid the mistake.

HOLMES v. WALKER

[1997] O.J. No. 4404, 35 O.R. (3d) 699, 15 R.P.R. (3d) 78, affirmed [1998] O.J.
No. 4725, 41 O.R. (3d) 160*n*
(Gen. Div., Archie Campbell J.; C.A., McMurtry C.J.O., Abella and O'Connor JJ.A.)

ARCHIE CAMPBELL J.: —

The Application

[1]   Mrs. Holmes moves by stated case under Rule 22 of the Rules of Civil Procedure for a judgment rescinding her 1989 purchase, from Mr. Walker, of a cottage
property on Georgian Bay. She discovered from a 1993 survey that the cottage was
not built on the land she bought. Although one corner of the cottage grazes the
boundary of her land 95 per cent to 99 per cent of the cottage is built on the 66 foot
township road allowance that runs between her property and the shoreline.

[2]   The township will not sell Mrs. Holmes the land underneath her cottage but it
will let her keep and use the cottage in return for an occupation rent of $25.00 a year.

The Facts

[3]   The agreed facts in the special case under Rule 22 are set out in Appendix A
[omitted]. Some additional facts emerge from the documents that form part of the
special case.

[4]   The four-bedroom woodframe cottage in Saugeen Township was built by Mr.
Walker's father around 1936 and Mr. Walker came into possession in 1983. The lot
has about 50 feet of frontage on Lake Huron and a depth of 122 to 140 feet. It is
agreed that Mr. Walker always believed the cottage was on his property. It is agreed
that there was no reason for him to believe otherwise, that nothing ever came to his
attention to make him think otherwise, and that he acted in good faith at all times.

[5]   Mrs. Holmes bought the property in 1989 for $170,000. Had she known the
cottage was situated, even partly, on the road allowance, she would not have
bought the land.

The Purchaser's Failure to Obtain a Survey

[6]   The most significant fact, in my view, is that Mrs. Holmes failed to get a
survey before she bought the property.

[7]   The agreement of purchase and sale, completed on April 11, 1989, provided
that Mrs. Holmes had until June 7 to examine the title and that the transaction
would close on July 7. The deposit of $1,000 was to be returned if there was a
valid objection to title. Clause 10 of the agreement provided:

> Purchaser shall not call for the production of any title deed, abstract, survey or other
> evidence of title to the property except such as are in the possession or control of
> Vendor. Vendor agrees that, if requested by the Purchaser, he will deliver any sketch
> or survey of the property in his possession or within his control to Purchaser as soon
> as possible and prior to the last day for examining title.

[8]   Mrs. Holmes was represented by a lawyer whom she has sued in respect of
his work on the purchase. That lawsuit is in abeyance pending the outcome of this
motion. The lawyer is not a party to this motion and he has had no opportunity to
make submissions on any matter affecting his communications with Mrs. Holmes

about the absence of a survey. Those are matters for the other lawsuit if it is not settled.

[9] Mrs. Holmes' lawyer wrote the Township and asked whether the cottage and property complied with all building and zoning by-laws and regulations. The Township replied on June 22:

> Without a survey of the subject property we cannot comment on whether the building complies with zoning regulations. The lot is an existing lot and in my opinion does not comply with the current zoning requirements regarding lot area, frontage, and depth.

[10] Mrs. Holmes' lawyer on June 13 requisitioned from Mr. Walker's lawyer production of a survey showing that the cottage was situated wholly within the lot lines:

> REQUIRED: Survey indicating that the structures located on the property are situate entirely within the lot lines and that there are no encroachments, easements or adverse claims respecting the property. We reserve the right to submit such further and other requisitions as may be necessary with reference to zoning compliance, work orders, etc. until we have had a reasonable opportunity to forward the survey to the municipal authorities for their inspection.

[11] Mr. Walker's lawyer replied on June 20 that there was no survey available: "There is no survey available." There is no evidence in this case whether Mrs. Holmes' lawyer discussed with her the obvious need for a survey. The only fact relevant to this case is that Mrs. Holmes never got a survey before closing.

[12] On July 6, the day prior to closing, Mr. Walker at the request of Mrs. Holmes' lawyer, signed a preprinted statutory declaration stating in part:

> To the best of my knowledge and belief the buildings used in connection with the premises are situate wholly within the limits of the lands above described . . .

It is agreed that Mr. Walker signed this declaration in good faith, ignorant of the fact that the cottage was 95 per cent to 99 per cent on the road allowance.

[13] The deal closed as scheduled on July 7, 1989.

[14] On September 11 Mrs. Holmes' lawyer, together with his account for $650, sent her a standard reporting letter that said:

> We are of the opinion that you have a good and marketable title subject to . . . any discrepancies that an up-to-date survey might reveal if the survey of the property was not current . . .

The Aftermath

[15] In July of 1993, four years after she bought the land, Mrs. Holmes got a survey. As noted above, it showed that 95 per cent to 99 per cent of the cottage was built on the township shore road allowance, not on the land she bought. She commenced these proceedings against Mr. Walker in November of 1994.

[16] The cottage, because of its age and construction, cannot be moved. It may not be possible to build a new cottage of the same size on the property.

[17] The township will not sell to Mrs. Holmes the road allowance under the cottage. But it will give her an occupation licence for $25.00 a year. This is unacceptable to Mrs. Holmes because she says the occupation licence prohibits her from exercising normal rights of ownership, prevents her from rebuilding the cottage if it is destroyed, prevents her from repairing the cottage, and prevents her from renovating or making additions.

Non-Issues

[18] The actual conveyance is not part of the stated case. No submissions were made about vendor's undertaking that the warranties in the agreement of purchase and sale shall continue in full force and not merge on closing. There is no evidence or argument in respect of any possible claim for adverse possession and no evidence or argument based on s. 50 of the *Conveyancing and Law of Property Act*, R.S.O. 1990, c. C.34, s. 37.

The Basic Legal Position

[19] After closing, a purchaser of land can only set aside the transaction on the basis of:

1. some covenant, condition or warranty in the conveyance;

2. fraud;

3. mutual mistake that results in a total failure of consideration;

4. some deficiency in the land conveyed that amounts to error *in substantialibus*; or

5. a contractual condition or a warranty collateral to the contract that survives the closing.

. . .

The Plaintiff's Position

[20] Mrs. Holmes puts her case entirely on the basis that the location of the cottage on the road allowance, instead of her land, constitutes an error *in substantialibus*.

The Doctrine of Error in substantialibus

[21] Error *in substantialibus* translates badly into English. It does not mean substantial error. It means more. It means that the buyer and the seller made a mistake about some fundamental quality of the thing sold. It means an error in the very substance of what is sold, an error so fundamental that it goes to the real identity and character of the thing sold.

[22] The leading Ontario cases are *Hyrsky v. Smith*, [1969] 2 O.R. 360, 5 D.L.R. (3d) 385 (H.C.J.) (Lieff J.), *Di Cenzo Construction v. Glassco* [(1978), 21 O.R. (2d) 186, 90 D.L.R. (3d) 127 (C.A.)], and *Zeitel v. Ellscheid* (1991), 5 O.R. (3d) 449, 85 D.L.R. (4th) 654 (C.A.) (Carthy and Arbour JJ.A., Finlayson J.A. dissenting).

[23] To trigger the doctrine, the buyer must end up with something totally different from what he expected to buy and the vendor expected to sell: *Zeitel v. Ellscheid*, per Finlayson J.A. at p. 463, dissenting on other grounds.

. . .

Application of the Principles

[24] The mistake here was a fundamental mistake about the nature of the thing purchased. Mrs. Holmes thought she was buying, and Mr. Walker thought he was selling, a piece of land with a cottage. In fact Mr. Walker sold and Mrs. Holmes bought a piece of land without a cottage. The mistake involved ownership of the cottage, the very thing the purchaser wanted to buy.

[25] It was fundamental to the agreement and the conveyance that Mrs. Holmes was buying a cottage and not a vacant lot. The real estate listing shows a picture of the cottage and describes its structure and heating and electrical system and water system. The agreement of purchase and sale shows that they addressed their minds to the existence of the cottage ("present use seasonal residential") and to the furnishings in the cottage and to the fire insurability of the "principal building" and the payment of insurance pending closing. The vendor's statutory declaration just before closing said that to the best of his knowledge and belief the buildings were situate wholly within the limits of the lands.

[26] It was fundamental to the agreement that there was a cottage on the property. Mrs. Holmes was buying a cottage, not just a vacant lot. The thing contracted for was a cottage and the thing conveyed was a piece of vacant land.

[27] The proposed occupation licence, although significant to the impact of the error and the availability of rescission, has no effect on the nature of the error itself. Although relevant to the equities of the motion to rescind, the occupation licence is irrelevant to the question of error *in substantialibus.*

[28] To paraphrase Chief Justice Meredith [in *Freear v. Gilders* (1921), 50 O.L.R. 217 at p. 220, 64 D.L.R. 274 at p. 276 (C.A.)], there was a difference in substance between the nature of the thing bargained for, a summer cottage, and the thing obtained, a piece of vacant land grazed by the corner of a cottage built on township property.

[29] For these reasons I conclude that there was an error *in substantialibus.*

Rescission: Factors to Consider

[30] The next question is whether Mrs. Holmes has established a basis for rescission.

[31] Rescission is not an automatic remedy. The court must weigh the equities and determine in its discretion, as between two parties who acted in good faith, which one is most entitled to relief from the consequences of their mutual mistake.

[32] On the one hand, Mr. Walker did not own the thing he purported to sell — the cottage. If rescission is denied he retains a benefit from the sale of something he did not own.

[33] On the other hand, if rescission is granted, it relieves Mrs. Holmes from the foreseeable consequences of her failure to take the easy, obvious, and prudent step of getting a survey before closing.

[34] If rescission is granted it will be necessary, in order to compensate both Mr. Walker and Mrs. Holmes for their respective interests in the transaction, to unscramble the egg more than eight years after the closing. The cottage would be returned to Walker and the purchase price refunded to Mrs. Holmes after appropriate adjustments. Occupation rent would be calculated and adjustments made for taxes, maintenance, and any other matter that might come into play such as interest and, arguably, the effect of any rise or fall in the value of the property and any economic loss or gain to either party. Conveyances and statements of adjustment would be drafted, exchanged, negotiated, and finally executed and implemented. A further reference to the court might well be required. It would be difficult, after eight years, to restore the parties to the positions they would have enjoyed had they not closed the deal. The process of unscrambling the egg would be inexact, complex, lengthy, and expensive.

Rescission: Weighing the Factors

[35] In favour of rescission we have the fact that Mr. Walker would otherwise retain the benefit of selling something he did not own.

[36] Against rescission we have

— The fact that Mrs. Holmes is not, in the sense in which the expression is used in rescission, an innocent party. She caused the problem by failing to get a survey before closing when it was such an obvious, easy and prudent thing to do.

— The fact that Mrs. Holmes by failing to get a survey before closing assumed the very risk that she now seeks to shift to Mr. Walker. It would be unfair to visit Mr. Walker with the foreseeable consequences of the risk assumed by Mrs. Holmes.

— The delay from the date of closing in July 1989.

— The difficulty and expense and further delay of unscrambling the egg.

— The unfairness of suddenly visiting Mr. Walker, after governing himself for years on the premise that the sale was final, with the consequences of Mrs. Holmes' failure to get a survey before closing.

— The fact that Mrs. Holmes, although she will not end up with the full legal incidents of ownership if rescission is denied, will be able to keep, use, and enjoy the cottage by paying the township $25.00 a year for the licence of occupation.

— The strong public interest in the finality of property transactions, the principle that vendors should be entitled to treat a final sale as final without having the transaction reversed years later because the purchaser did not bother to get a survey on closing. Rescission should not be too lightly granted lest the bright line disappear between sales that are final and sales that are subject to reversal years later.

[37] The equities, on balance, weigh against rescission.

Conclusion

[38] The answer to the question in the special case under Rule 22 is that, although there was an error *in substantialibus*, Mrs. Holmes is not entitled to rescission.

[39] An order will go dismissing the action against Mr. Walker.

[In the Court of Appeal, **McMurtry C.J.O.** said: —]

It is incumbent upon the appellant to satisfy the court that Campbell J. made an error in principle in the exercise of his discretion. We are not so satisfied. It is clear from the reasons of Campbell J. that the key factor in deciding not to grant rescission was the appellant's failure to obtain a survey prior to closing. The subsequent events were all directly related to her failure to do so. For these reasons, the appeal is dismissed with costs fixed at $2,000.

QUESTIONS

1. How does the solution reached by Campbell J. to the problem of the mistake made by Mrs. Holmes square with the analysis of mistake in a case like *Bell v. Lever Brothers Ltd.*? What is the basis for the result?

2. Note that the trial judge concludes that the facts present an error *in substantialibus*. It is clear that the plaintiff made a serious mistake, but the basis for the decision, as the very short judgment in the Court of Appeal makes clear, is that the mistake was solely due to the plaintiff's failure to get a survey. The decision can be seen as one based on the allocation to the plaintiff of the risk of not getting a survey. The seriousness of the mistake had nothing to do with the decision. The only role that the question of seriousness, *i.e.*, the fact that the mistake was *really* serious, would have played is that it might have prevented the defendant from successfully moving to have the plaintiff's claim struck out. The case illustrates the fact that the seriousness of the mistake is not, by itself, a reason for doing anything (except, perhaps, expressing sympathy for the plaintiff's situation).

The next decision explicitly adopts an analysis of risk as the basis for decision.

AMALGAMATED INVESTMENT PROPERTY CO. v. JOHN WALKER & SONS LTD.

[1976] 3 All E.R. 509, [1977] 1 W.L.R. 164
(C.A., Buckley, Lawton and Pennycuick L.JJ.)

[The defendants wanted to sell a large warehouse. It was advertised as being "for sale for occupation or redevelopment". The plaintiff offered £1,710,000 for the property. This was accepted by the defendants. As is typical of major commercial land transactions, written enquiries were made before the contract was signed, and amongst other questions asked was this:

> Although the Purchaser will be making the usual searches and enquiries of the local and planning authorities, the Vendor is asked specifically to state whether he is aware of any order, designation or proposal of any local or other authority or body having compulsory powers involving any of the following . . .

Then there were a number of subparagraphs, the only relevant one being (iv), which reads: "The designation of the property as a building of special architectural or historic interest." A negative answer was given to that question by the vendors on 14 August.

The formal contract was signed on 25 September 1973. The contract incorporated the English Law Society's General Conditions of Sale (1973 Revision) which contained, amongst other provisions, a condition that nothing in the conditions should entitle the vendor to compel the purchaser to accept or the purchaser to compel the vendor to convey (with or without compensation) property which "differed substantially" from the property agreed to be sold and purchased, whether in quantity, quality, tenure or otherwise, if the purchaser or the vendor respectively would be prejudiced by reason of such difference.

On 26 September 1973, that is, the day after the formal contract was signed, the Department of the Environment wrote a letter to the defendants notifying them that the property, the subject matter of the contract, had been selected for inclusion in the statutory list of buildings of special architectural or historic interest compiled by the Secretary of State, and that that list was about to be given legal effect. The effect of "listing" the property as of historic interest was to make redevelopment that would alter the building's exterior virtually impossible, and to cause the value of the property to drop from £1,700,000 to £200,000. The purchasers refused to go ahead with the deal, and the vendors sued.

In holding for the vendor, **BUCKLEY L.J.** said: —]

[1]   It seems to me that the risk of property being listed as property of architectural or historical interest is a risk which inheres in all ownership of buildings. In many cases it may be an extremely remote risk. In many cases it may be a marginal risk. In some cases it may be a substantial risk. But it is a risk, I think, which attaches to all buildings and it is a risk that every owner and every purchaser of property must recognise that he is subject to. The purchasers in the present case bought knowing that they would have to obtain planning permission in order to develop the property. The effect of listing under the sections of the 1971 Act to which I have referred makes the obtaining of planning permission, it may be, more difficult, and it may also make it a longer and more complicated process. But still, in essence, the position is that the would-be developer has to obtain the appropriate planning permissions, one form of permission being the "listed building permission." The plaintiffs, when they entered into the contract, must obviously be taken to have known that they would need to get planning permission. They must also, in my judgment, be taken to have known that there was the risk, although they may not have regarded it as a substantial risk, that the building might at some time be listed, and that their chances of obtaining planning permission might possibly be adversely affected to some extent by that, or at any rate their chances of obtaining speedy planning permission. But, in my judgment, this is a risk of a kind which every purchaser should be regarded as knowing that he is subject to when he enters into his contract of purchase. It is a risk which I think the purchaser must carry, and any loss that may result from the maturing of that risk is a loss which must lie where it falls . . .

NOTES

1.   Although *Amalgamated Investment Property* could be regarded as a case of "frustration" rather than "mistake" (since the "mistake" related to developments subsequent to the formation of the contract), the court's explicit adoption of a "risk analysis" is a useful way of dealing with this type of problem. A similar analysis could have been applied had the designation been made earlier and only become known to the parties

after the contract had been made but before the transaction closed. Should the result have been the same in that situation?

2. There is no basis in this case for an argument that the advertisement was a warranty. The formal contract drawn up by the parties would have most likely expressly excluded any such undertaking by the vendor.

    In *Hayward v. Mellick* (1984), 45 O.R. (2d) 110, 5 D.L.R. (4th) 740 (C.A.) the vendor and his real estate agent orally told the buyer that there were 65 workable acres on a 95-acre farm. The agreement of purchase and sale excluded any "representation warranty, collateral agreement or condition", other than one written in the agreement of purchase and sale. After taking possession, the buyer discovered that there were only 51.7 workable acres, but the seller's error was an "honest" mistake. The Court of Appeal held, reversing the trial judge, that the statement as to the acreage was a negligent misrepresentation. It would have been the basis for a remedy had it not been for the exclusion clause in the contract.

    Another option for the disappointed purchaser is to sue his or her lawyer or real estate agent. See, for example, *Hauck v. Dixon* (1975), 10 O.R. (2d) 605, 64 D.L.R. (3d) 201 (H.C.J.).

Note on the Terminology of Mistake

Some authors divide mistakes into two or three different kinds. Cheshire, Fifoot and Furmston, *Law of Contract*, 14th ed. (London: Butterworths, 2001), pp. 252-53, adopt three classifications of mistake: common mistakes, mutual mistakes, and unilateral mistakes. They offer the following explanation of the three terms:

> In common mistake, both parties make the same mistake. Each knows the intention of the other and accepts it, but each is mistaken about some underlying and fundamental fact. The parties, for example, are unaware that the subject matter of their contract has already perished.
>
> In mutual mistake, the parties misunderstand each other and are at cross-purposes. A, for example, intends to offer his Ford Sierra car for sale, but B believes that the offer relates to the Ford Grenada also owned by A.
>
> In unilateral mistake, only one of the parties is mistaken. The other knows, or must be taken to know, of his [the first party's] mistake. Suppose, for instance, that A agrees to buy from B a specific picture which A believes to be a genuine Constable but which is in fact a copy. If B is ignorant of A's erroneous belief, the case is one of mutual mistake, but, if he knows of it, of unilateral mistake.

In accordance with the rules of *Bell v. Lever Brothers*, Cheshire, Fifoot and Furmston suggest that there is an agreement in the case of "common mistake", but, if the mistake is "fundamental", the agreement is "robbed of all efficacy" by reason of the mistake. If a party seeks relief in the circumstances of a mutual or unilateral mistake, the "very existence of the agreement is denied".

Others use the terms "common" and "mutual" interchangeably. See, for example, Lord Atkin's judgment in *Bell v. Lever Brothers* (¶ 4) and Thompson J. in *McMaster University v. Wilchar Construction Ltd.*, [1971] 3 O.R. 801 at 809, 22 D.L.R. (3d) 9 at 17 (H.C.J.); affirmed (1973), 12 O.R. (2d) 512, 69 D.L.R. (3d) 400, who said:

> In mutual or common mistake, the error or mistake in order to avoid the contract at law must have been based either upon a fundamental mistaken assumption as to the subject matter of the contract or upon a mistake relating to a fundamental term of the contract.

A major difficulty with the traditional analysis is that mistake can come in a wide variety of forms. Some of these are easy to resolve, others hard. Any application of the analysis of *Bell v. Lever Brothers* is difficult, for the test of "difference in kind" or "fundamental difference" is not easily controlled. When the verbiage is stripped away, the only important question in *Bell v. Lever Brothers* was whether Bell and Snelling had a duty to disclose what they had done. This is not an easy question to decide. It raises many important issues of the content of such a contract (the content imposed by judges rather than from the express agreement of the parties) and of the expectations of the parties. Significant research would probably be required to discover what both employers and employees thought on this issue. The fact that this question is so well hidden (even though a similar issue arises in *Magee v. Pennine*) illustrates the difficulty of the issues of mistake and the inadequacies of the assumption that the only kind of contracting model relevant is the discrete exchange. *Bell v. Lever Brothers* and even *Solle v. Butcher* and *Magee v. Pennine* are not discrete transactions or, to speak more precisely, the problems do not arise out of discrete transactions. The underlying contract in each had lasted for several years and might well have lasted for far longer. Notice that all of the examples given by Cheshire, Fifoot and Furmston are discrete contracts.

When one examines the situations where mistake is accepted as the basis for the relief, it is clear that the cases present complex patterns. It is suggested that the best analysis of a situation where there has been a mistake as to underlying assumptions is to ask which party should bear the risk of the loss or, which is really the same thing, which should get the advantage of the chance of gain. Factors that are likely to be important in this analysis include: the nature of the contract and the relation of the parties; the size, significance or nature of the mistake; communications between the parties and the terms and context of the contract; the relative fault, responsibility or knowledge (or ease of access to knowledge) of the parties; and the timeliness of any claim for relief.

Use of the terminology "common", "mutual" and "unilateral" mistake should be avoided, since those terms are not used consistently by the courts and, in any event, may not be helpful.

Mistakes in the Formation of Contracts

The next cases, which deal with issues related to the formation of contracts, are also commonly considered under the heading of "mistake".

These cases raise a range of issues related to the communications between the parties about the terms or nature of the contract. Some similar situations were explored in Chapter 3. Recall that ordinarily parties are held to the reasonable meaning of their communications but, where a mistake or misunderstanding occurs without the fault of either party, the courts have generally held that no contract is formed. *Raffles v. Wichelhaus* and *Staiman Steel* were cases where mistakes of one kind or another were made in the formation of the contact.

In *Raffles v. Wichelhaus* the parties agreed that there was to be a sale of cotton on board a ship named "Peerless" sailing from Bombay to Liverpool but, as it subsequently turned out, there were two ships with that name sailing from Bombay at different times. The court held that there was no enforceable contract. This decision can best be understood as putting the risk of the parties' confusion on both of them: neither could enforce the contract on his terms. It happened that the seller wanted to enforce the contract but, had the situation been reversed, the buyer would equally have been unable to enforce the contract on his terms. In *Raffles* there was no single "reasonable" interpretation of the contract, and the misunderstanding or mistake arose without the fault of either party.

In *Staiman Steel* the plaintiff was a buyer at an auction conducted on the premises of an insolvent corporation. The auctioneer invited bids on what was described as "all the steel in the yard". There was both old and new steel in the yard. The plaintiff knew that the auctioneer had not meant to sell the new steel but, relying on what had been said, bid for the steel and was the successful bidder. The plaintiff sued for damages based on the defendant's refusal, not only to sell him the new steel, but also the other steel "in the yard". The trial judge held that, given what the plaintiff actually knew, he could not insist on buying what was not for sale. On the other hand, despite the fact that the defendant was thoroughly annoyed at what the plaintiff had done and the attitude he had taken, the defendant was nevertheless bound to sell such steel as came within the description of what was for sale.

While Esquimalt & Nanaimo Railway in *Hobbs v. Esquimalt & Nanaimo Railway* made a mistake in believing that the word "land" would be interpreted to mean surface rights only, that mistake did not make the contract void or unenforceable and the risk of loss arising from that mistake was placed on it. In *Staiman Steel* and *Hobbs*, the parties were held to the "reasonable" interpretation of their agreement.

The important factors that move a court are exactly what one would expect to find: a concern for fairness and relative fault; for the protection of the parties' reasonable expectations, or, in the more difficult cases, a choice being made as to which party will have its expectations protected. In addition to cases like *Hobbs v. Esquimalt & Nanaimo Railway* and *Staiman Steel*, the following cases illustrate these principles:

(a) *Smith v. Hughes* (1871), L.R. 6 Q.B. 597, reproduced in Chapter 3, is still frequently quoted. Blackburn J. said (p. 607):

> If, whatever a man's real intention may be, he so conducts himself that a reasonable man would believe that he was assenting to the terms proposed by the other party, and the other party upon that belief enters into a contract with him, the man thus conducting himself would be bound as if he had intended to agree to the other party's terms.

(b) *McMaster University v. Wilchar Construction Ltd.* (*supra*). The plaintiff was trying to hold the defendant contractor to an agreement to construct a building for a fixed price, rejecting the defendant's claim that the agreement was subject to a price escalation clause. The defendant prepared and signed the agreement, and then sent it to the plaintiff for signing. The defendant accidentally omitted the page that had a price escalator clause. The pages were numbered, and the trial judge found that the plaintiff knew that the defendant had made a mistake in omitting from its bid the page with the price escalation clause. From the defendant's point of view, it had made a significant mistake, but it might have been hard to show that it was "fundamental". The court, however, held that the plaintiff could not enforce the agreement since it knew that the defendant had made a mistake. Thompson J. said: "Fraud, in a sense to which equity has attached its disapproval, extends to any transactions in which the Court is of the opinion that it is unconscientious for a person to avail himself of the legal advantage which he has obtained."

(c) *Stepps Investments Ltd. v. Security Capital Corp.* (1976), 14 O.R. (2d) 259,
73 D.L.R. (3d) 351 (H.C.J., Grange J.) The parties were involved in negotiating a complex share transaction, and various drafts of the contract were exchanged. Towards the very end of the negotiations, the plaintiff made a few
small but significant changes in the text of some of the clauses, without alert-
ing the defendant. The defendant signed the agreement. The plaintiff then
sought to enforce its terms. The court refused to enforce the agreement as
signed. Grange J. said: (p. 272):

> It is not unreasonable, in my view, in modern commercial relations, to re-
> quire the parties, where an important amendment is being made, to ensure
> that knowledge of such amendment comes to the other side. I do not mean
> that a party must overcome obtuseness in his opposite number but he must at
> least give him real opportunity to appreciate the change. And if the circum-
> stances are such that the amendment might readily be missed he should be
> particularly reluctant to assume such knowledge.

In the result, the court held that the plaintiff had an option: it could have the
agreement on the defendant's terms or no agreement (rectification or rescission). In the circumstances, neither party could force its terms on the other.
Stepps Investments can be seen as a case that enforces an obligation to bargain
in good faith.

In one sense these are relatively easy cases. They could possibly be put in the
category of "unilateral" mistake under the Cheshire, Fifoot and Furmston analysis.
But this would be to miss their importance. They are important because the courts
are engaging in an analysis that looks at the nature of the transaction and determining which party should bear the risk of what occurred. In *Stepps Investments*
Grange J. was aware of modern commercial practice and the standard of good
faith behaviour that would justify the allocation of risk in that case. In other words,
the courts face the same basic problem as in other areas of contract law: what do
we want to do, and on whom do we want to put the risk of loss? While a case like
Bell v. Lever Brothers could have taken this approach, there is no indication in that
case of what a principled solution or a defensible allocation of the risk of loss
would look like. There is no discussion of the standards of good faith that should
be imported into the usual contract of employment.

Many of the more recent cases display a creative and defensible treatment of
the law of mistake. There is no concern that the mistake be "fundamental". Rather,
the question is whether as between the parties, the risk of disappointment is justifiably allocated to one side. It is interesting that Grange J. in *Stepps Investments*
makes specific reference to modern commercial practice. If it were not for cases
like *Smith v. Hughes*, one might be tempted to see the importation of notions of
good faith as a strictly modern phenomenon. Such notions give a clear indication
of what kind of standards will justify an allocation of the risk of disappointment to
one side rather than the other.

The common practice of "black-lining" changes (underlining or putting a line in
the margin) in drafts of an agreement as each successive draft is prepared can be
seen as an assumption of an obligation to bargain in good faith. A court would not
have much difficulty in providing relief to a party who had been misled by the
other's deliberate failure to indicate a change from one draft to the next. If parties
and their lawyers could not rely on the practice of black-lining, the transaction
costs involved in negotiating a complex agreement would be greatly increased. An

analysis on the basis of mistake, as illustrated in these cases, reaches or justifies the same result as would be achieved if the courts explicitly accepted that there is an obligation to bargain in good faith. It does not matter whether this situation is analyzed from the perspective of mistake or failure to bargain in good faith — the same basic principles govern. From a practical point of view, a failure to black-line a document is a serious impediment to efficient bargaining and, as in *Stepps Investments*, by denying a party the right to enforce the terms covertly inserted in the agreement, the court is providing a strong incentive to openness and efficiency in negotiations.

In *AMJ Campbell Inc. v. Kord Products Inc.*, [2003] O.J. No. 329, 63 O.R. (3d) 375, 32 B.L.R. (3d) 90 (S.C.J.), the solicitors for the parties were negotiating over the valuation of the inventory being sold. The initial definition proposed by the solicitor for the buyer was that the agreed selling price was to be defined as "net of taxes, rebates and discounts". The buyer's solicitor further amended the clause to say, "net of taxes, freight rebates and discounts". This clause was, again at the request of the buyer's solicitor, amended to read, "net of taxes, freight, re-bates and discounts". The added comma after the word "freight" was duly black-lined. The seller's officer signed the agreement without carefully reading the changes. When the seller realized the significance of the change, it sought rectifi-cation. Epstein J. held that the changes had been properly brought to the seller's attention; that it knew of the change, through the knowledge of its solicitors (who may not have appreciated its significance); that the buyer had no reason to think that the seller did not know of the change; and that the conditions for rectification had not been met. She described the case as that of the "million dollar comma".

The following case is a decision of the Supreme Court of Canada on a common problem of mistake related to the formation of contracts. Consider how an analysis of the risks run by each side in the transaction would deal with the problem, and compare this with the actual analysis of the Court.

RON ENGINEERING & CONSTRUCTION (EASTERN) LTD. v. ONTARIO

[1981] 1 S.C.R. 111, 119 D.L.R. (3d) 267
(S.C.C., Martland, Dickson, Estey, McIntyre and Lamer JJ.)

[The respondent, plaintiff, contractor had submitted a tender for the construction of works for the owner, the Ontario Water Resources Commission, the appellant, defendant. The tendering process was governed by a document issued by the owner entitled "Information for Tenderers". The tender was submitted by the con-tractor at 3:00 p.m. on the day fixed for the submission of tenders and was accom-panied by the required deposit of $150,000. The deposit was required from all contractors who submitted a tender and was intended to ensure that each was fi-nancially stable and serious about the bidding process. The "Information for Ten-derers" included a statement under the heading "Tender Deposit", providing:

. . . the tenderer guarantees that if his tender is withdrawn before the Commission shall have considered the tenders or before or after he has been notified that his ten-der has been recommended to the Commission for acceptance or that if the Commis-sion does not for any reason receive within the period of seven days as stipulated and as required herein, the agreement executed by the tenderer . . . the Commission may retain the tender deposit for the use of the Commission and may accept any tender, advertise for new tenders, negotiate a contract and not accept any tender as the Commission may deem advisable.

The tender was by far the lowest of those submitted and the employee of the contractor who was present when the tenders were opened realized immediately that a mistake in the calculation of the price must have been made.

(Tendering in the construction industry is a frantic exercise. A general contractor like Ron Engineering has to get quotations from its subcontractors and these are coming in by phone and are being added into the final tender document up to the last minute. In fact, Ron Engineering's employee was already at the government building where the tenders had to be submitted and she entered the final amount on the tender documents when she was told over the phone what it should be. A witness at the trial described the process in this case as "normal — complete chaos".)

By 4:15 p.m. of the same day the contractor informed the owner by telex that a mistake had been made and that the tender price should have been about 27 per cent larger (about $750,000). While the tender of the plaintiff was just about $632,000 lower than the next lowest tender, it was very close to the amount that the owner's consulting engineers had estimated as a reasonable cost. The owner took the position, based on the provisions of the "Information for Tenderers", that the tender could not be revoked and that the contractor could be required to execute a contract for the works at the price of the tender. The contractor refused to execute the contract when it was submitted to it and the owner then took the position that the deposit was forfeited.

The contractor sued to recover its deposit on the ground that the owner could neither accept the tender once it was known to have been affected by a mistake, nor claim to keep the deposit because the formal construction contract was not executed by the contractor. The claim for the return of the deposit was dismissed by the trial judge. The Ontario Court of Appeal reversed this decision and the deposit was ordered refunded. The defendant owner appealed to the Supreme Court of Canada.]

The judgment of the court was given by **ESTEY J.**: —

[**ESTEY J.** regarded the normal procedure of tendering as involving two contracts. The first, which he referred to as "contract A", was a contract that would arise on the submission of the tender together with the tender deposit by the contractor. Assuming that the contractor's tender was accepted, the parties would then execute the construction contract, "contract B".]

[1]   . . . We are then left with the bare submission on behalf of the contractor that while the offer was not withdrawn it was not capable of acceptance and that by reason thereof the contractor is entitled to a return of the deposit.

[2]   I share the view expressed by the Court of Appeal that integrity of the bidding system must be protected where under the law of contracts it is possible so to do. I further share the view expressed by that Court that there may be circumstances where a tender may not be accepted as for example where in law it does not constitute a tender, and hence the bid deposit might not be forfeited. That is so in my view, however, simply because contract A cannot come into being. It puts it another way to say that the purported tender does not in law amount to an acceptance of the call for tenders and hence the unilateral contract does not come into existence. Therefore, with the greatest of respect, I diverge from that Court where it is stated in the judgment below: "However, when that mistake is proven by the production of reasonable evidence, the person to whom the tender is made is not in a position to accept the tender or to seek to forfeit the bid deposit." The test, in my respectful view, must be imposed at the time the tender is submitted and not at some later date after a demonstration by the tenderer of a calculation error. Contract A (being the contract arising forthwith upon the submission of the tender) comes into being forthwith and without further formality upon the submission of the tender. If the tenderer has committed an error in the calculation leading to the tender submitted with the tender deposit, and at least in those circumstances where at that moment the tender is capable of acceptance in law, the rights of the parties under contract A have thereupon crystallized. The tender deposit, designed to ensure the performance of the obligations of the tenderer under contract A, must therefore stand exposed to the risk of forfeiture upon the breach of those obligations by the tenderer. Where the conduct of the tenderer might indeed expose him to other claims in damages by the owner, the tender deposit might well be the lesser pain to be suffered by reason of the error in the preparation of the tender. This I will return to later.

[3]   Much argument was undertaken in this Court on the bearing of the law of mistake on the outcome of this appeal. In approaching the application of the principles of mistake it is imperative here to bear in mind that the only contract up to now in existence between the parties to this appeal is the contract arising on the submission of the tender whereunder the tender is irrevocable during the period of time stipulated in the contract. Contract B (the construction contract, the form of which is set out in the documents relating to the call for tenders) has not and did not come into existence. We are concerned therefore with the law of mistake, if at all, only in connection with contract A.

[4]   The tender submitted by the respondent brought contract A into life. This is sometimes described in law as a unilateral contract, that is to say a contract which results from an act made in response to an offer, as for example in the simplest terms, "I will pay you a dollar if you will cut my lawn." No obligation to cut the lawn exists in law and the obligation to pay the dollar comes into being upon the performance of the invited act. Here the call for tenders created no obligation in the respondent or in anyone else in or out of the construction world. When a member of the construction industry responds to the call for tenders, as the respondent has done here, that response takes the form of the submission of a tender, or a bid as it is sometimes called. The significance of the bid in law is that it at once becomes irrevocable if filed in conformity with the terms and conditions under which the call for tenders was made and if such terms so provide. There is no disagreement between the parties here about the form and procedure in which the tender was submitted by the respondent and that it complied with the terms and conditions of the call for tenders. Consequently, contract A came into being. The principal term of contract A is the irrevocability of the bid, and the corollary term is the obligation in both parties to enter into a contract (contract B) under the acceptance of the tender. Other terms include the qualified obligations of the owner to accept the lowest tender, and the degree of this obligation is controlled by the terms and conditions established in the call for tenders.

[5]   The role of the deposit under contract A is clear and simple. The deposit was required in order to ensure the performance by the contractor-tenderer of its obli-

gations under contract A. The deposit was recoverable by the contractor under certain conditions, none of which were met; and also was subject to forfeiture under another term of the contract, the provisions of which in my view have been met.

[6]   There is no question of a mistake on the part of either party up to the moment in time when contract A came into existence. The employee of the respondent intended to submit the very tender submitted, including the price therein stipulated. Indeed, the President, in instructing the respondent's employee, intended the tender to be as submitted. However, the contractor submits that as the tender was the product of a mistake in calculation, it cannot form the basis of a construction contract since it is not capable of acceptance and hence it cannot be subject to the terms and conditions of contract A so as to cause a forfeiture thereunder of the deposit. The fallacy in this argument is twofold. Firstly, there was no mistake in the sense that the contractor did not intend to submit the tender as in form and substance it was. Secondly, there is no principle in law under which the tender was rendered incapable of acceptance by the appellant. For a mutual contract such as contract B to arise, there must of course be a meeting of the minds, a shared *animus contrahendi*, but when the contract in question is the product of other contractual arrangements, different considerations apply. However, as already stated, we never reach that problem here as the rights of the parties fall to be decided according to the tender arrangements, contract A. At the point when the tender was submitted the owner had not been told about the mistake in calculation. Unlike the case of *McMaster University v. Wilchar Construction* [*supra*], there was nothing on the face of the tender to reveal an error. There was no inference to be drawn by the quantum of the tender . . . that there had indeed been a miscalculation. . . .

[7]   [In the *McMaster University* case] [t]he court was . . . not so much concerned with mistake as with the inability of the parties to comply on the facts with the fundamental rules pertaining to the formation of contracts. There could be no *consensus ad idem* and hence construction contract B could not come into being. More important to the issue now before us, the document submitted by the contractor was on its face incomplete and could not in law amount to a tender as required by the conditions established in the call for tenders. . . .

NOTES AND QUESTIONS

1.   Has Estey J. changed the common law rule that a promise to keep an offer open that is not "bought" with payment or executed under seal is unenforceable?

2.   In the late 1970's two cases progressed through the Ontario courts to the Supreme Court of Canada. One, *Ron Engineering*, we have just examined. The other (unreported) case, *Municipality of Metropolitan Toronto v. Poole Construction Ltd.*, went up through the courts at about the same time. In *Poole Construction*, the plaintiff sought to enforce a contract made by a tendering process like that in *Ron Engineering*. As in that case, the defendant contractor had made a serious mistake in its bid. The trial judge, Cromarty J., in a short oral judgment delivered on 16 May 1979, dismissed the action. This decision was upheld by the Court of Appeal in a judgment delivered on 21 February 1980. In *Poole Construction*, the plaintiff sought to recover from the defendant the difference between its bid and the next lowest bid. The Ontario courts had consistently denied relief to both the Commission in *Ron Engineering* and to Metro Toronto in *Poole Construction*. Only the judgments in *Ron Engineering* are reported: the editor of the D.L.R. (and O.R.) chose to report *Ron Engineering*, but not

Poole Construction, believing that they raised the same issues and the profession did not need two similar cases.

Both cases were appealed to the Supreme Court of Canada and while leave was given in *Ron Engineering* on 20 November 1979, the decision to give leave in *Poole Construction* was reserved on 22 April 1980. The appeal in *Ron Engineering* was heard on 13 November 1980, and judgment was delivered on 21 January 1981. The application for leave to appeal in the *Poole Construction* case had been outstanding since April of the previous year. *On the same day* that *Ron Engineering* was decided, the application by Metro Toronto for leave to appeal was dismissed.

3. What does Estey J. mean when he says, "The employee of the respondent intended to submit the very tender submitted, including the price therein stipulated"? How can one *not* intend to do that which one does (arguments of insanity, drunkenness, etc., aside) in the sense that Estey J. uses the word "intended"? Is it not true that in all the cases we have looked at in this section the parties intended to do that which they did? What scope is left under the rule stated by Estey J. for the operation of mistake?

4. The analysis of the tendering process by the Supreme Court in *Ron Engineering* was for a time generally accepted as the basis for dealing with problems in the tendering process. In *M.J.B. Enterprises Ltd. v. Defence Construction (1951) Ltd.*, [1999] 1 S.C.R. 619, 170 D.L.R. (4th) 577, Iacobucci J., after quoting from Estey J.'s judgment in *Ron Engineering*, and in dealing with the scope and terms of "Contract A", said:

> [17] . . . Therefore it is always possible that Contract A does not arise upon the submission of a tender, or that Contract A arises but the irrevocability of the tender is not one of its terms, all of this depending upon the terms and conditions of the tender call. To the extent that *Ron Engineering* suggests otherwise, I decline to follow it.

Iacobucci J. went on to say that he also did not wish to endorse Estey J.'s characterization of "Contract A" in *Ron Engineering* as a unilateral contract (¶ 18), because both parties had obligations under it.

5. The result in *Ron Engineering* is very hard to justify. There was no reliance or loss suffered by the owner on the bid, and there was ample proof that the contractor had made an honest error. The Court stated that the decision was intended to "protect the integrity" of the tendering system. All those involved in tendering (at least on the contracting side) were appalled by the decision and the idea that it protected the integrity of the system has to be understood as meaning only that it eliminated the need for courts to engage in sometimes difficult factual enquiries about the nature of the "mistake" that the contractor alone made. The decision of the Supreme Court resulted in a windfall gain to the owner and similar gains to hundreds of owners since then.

The decision also frustrated the efforts of the Ontario courts, particularly the Court of Appeal, which had been developing a workable and soundly based law of mistakes in the formulation of offers. See, *e.g.*, *Belle River Community Arena v. Kaufmann* (1978), 20 O.R. (2d) 447, 87 D.L.R. (3d) 761, as well as the Court of Appeal judgment in *Ron Engineering* (1979), 24 O.R. (2d) 332, 98 D.L.R. (3d) 548, itself. The most recent case before the Ontario Court of Appeal, *Toronto Transit Commission v. Gottardo Construction Ltd.*, [2005] O.J. No. 3689, 77 O.R. (3d) 269, 257 D.L.R. (4th) 539, had exactly the same result and effect as *Ron Engineering*: the contractor who made an innocent mistake was made to pay some $400,000 to the TTC. The trial judge had done all she could to give the contractor relief, but the Court of Appeal was having none of it. It reversed the trial judge, and awarded damages of $434,000. The Court of Appeal held that a contract was formed as soon as the Commission opened Gottardo's tender, and that Gottardo could not argue there was an error on the face of the tender because the supplementary document it sent showed a different amount. Rouleau J.A. wrote (at paras. 30-32):

> It is well established that rescission may only be granted in cases of unilateral mistake when the unmistaken party engaged in fraud or some other un-

conscionable conduct or where the unmistaken party contributed to the mistake. As set out in G.H.L. Friedman, *The Law of Contract in Canada*, 4th ed. (Toronto: Carswell, 1999), at 273-74:

> As long as the unmistaken party knows of the mistake, without having caused it, the party cannot resist a suit for rectification on the grounds of mistake. The same will apply if the other party had good reason to know of the mistake and to know what was intended. The converse of the proposition as to knowledge of the other party's mistake is that if the unmistaken party is ignorant of the other's mistake, the contract will be valid and neither rescission nor rectification will be possible.

In the case of tenders, the rights of the parties crystallize and Contract A is formed upon the opening of the tenders. Nothing on the face of the documents then in existence, including the form of tender, suggested that the tender amount was in error. At that point in time no one was aware of an error and the tender was compliant and capable of acceptance.

The trial judge's reasons make it clear that the mistake was unilateral and that there was no fraud. The trial judge, however, found that since the mistake was honestly made and inadvertent and because enforcement would cause Gottardo financial hardship, she would grant rescission. With respect, I do not agree. In my view, there are no unique circumstances in this case which distinguish it from *Ron Engineering* and which would operate so as to entitle the tenderer to have the contract rescinded. While it is conceded that some financial hardship will flow from enforcement of the contract, this is not sufficient to warrant rescission. The burden imposed on Gottardo by the enforcement of the contract freely entered into is not so grossly disproportionate so as to make enforcement of it by the courts unconscionable. In the circumstances, there are simply no grounds for equitable intervention.

6. Evidence that the rule stated by the Supreme Court in *Ron Engineering* is not, in fact, appropriate from the point of view of the construction industry may be seen from the standard rules of the Ontario Bid Depository (reproduced after *Northern Construction Co. Ltd. v. Gloge Heating and Plumbing Ltd.*, *supra*, Chapter 3) and the Canadian Construction Documents Committee ("CCDC"). The CCDC rules deal with the relations between owners and contractors. These rules did not apply in *Ron Engineering*, but if these rules had applied, they would have resolved the issue in favour of the contractor.

What is known as Document 23 of the CCDC provides:

3. *Bid Call*

. . .

(n) If a bidder informs the bid calling authority reasonably promptly after Bid closing and before the authority communicates acceptance of the Bid, that a serious and demonstrable mistake has been made in his Bid and requests to withdraw, he should normally be allowed to do so without penalty.

. . .

(p) The Owner reserves the right to reject any and all Bids for satisfactory reasons. However, he should not reject Bids for the purpose of appointing a Contractor who did not submit a Bid, or appointing a bidder selected in advance, or appointing a bidder who did not submit a Bid in accordance with the Bid procedures. Also, the Owner should not call Bids to obtain an estimate of the cost of the work.

5. *Contract Award*

. . .

(g) Prior to the award of the Contract it is customary for the Consultant to review with the Owner the list of proposed Subcontractors submitted by the successful bidder. Should the Consultant or Owner have had unsatisfactory experience on other projects with one or more of the proposed Subcontractors, the bidder may be asked to change such proposed Subcontractors. In the event that a change is required and the Contractor agrees, the bid price shall be adjusted by the difference in cost and mark-up occasioned by such required change.

(h) An Owner contemplating the changing of one or more of the proposed Subcontractors should respect reasons a bidder may have for not wishing to work with another particular Subcontractor.

Notice the assumptions underlying this code. The rules do not speak in legal terms. It is assumed that bidders are acting in good faith (though all those who submit bids are concerned that their prices not be "shopped") and that the rules should fairly reflect the different interests of owners (very often governmental bodies), contractors ("Prime Contractors") and subcontractors ("Trade Contractors"). It is reasonable to assume that the allocation of the risks of mistake provided for in the CCDC Documents — the Committee represents all those involved in the industry — is what would be most appropriate for the construction industry.

7.   Notice that Rules 3(p) and 5(g) give the Owner and the Contractor the explicit power to reject any subcontractor with whom they have had an "unsatisfactory experience". Contracts with the (Federal) Department of Public Works and Government Services sometimes contain a clause stating that: "The Department has the right to exclude the use of specified suppliers with whom it has had a poor working experience." These clauses are further evidence that few commercial contracts are discrete; no contracting party can afford to deal only in the context of the current deal. That deal, even after it is done, has a future. It is this fact that, in part at least, makes a case like *Gilbert Steel v. University Construction* so hard to understand.

8.   The importance of the parties' reputations would suggest that a subcontractor like Gloge Heating and Plumbing Ltd. must have been really pushed to the wall to fight a prime contractor like Northern Construction Co. in *Northern Construction Co. v. Gloge Heating & Plumbing Ltd.* The decision to fight must have been very expensive for Gloge.

9.   The decision in *Ron Engineering* was followed in *Calgary (City) v. Northern Construction Co. Division of Morrison-Knudsen Co. Inc.*, [1987] 2 S.C.R. 757, [1988] 2 W.W.R. 193, affirming (1985), [1986] 2 W.W.R. 426, 42 Alta. L.R. (2d) 1 (C.A.). The facts in *Northern Construction* are similar to those in *Ron Engineering*, a fairly typical example of the mistaken bid made in response to a call for tenders. The invitation for tenders issued by the City of Calgary provided that any tender submitted would be irrevocable for a fixed period. The bid documents required a 10 per cent deposit, and stipulated that if the tenderer for any reason failed to enter a contract with the City, the City was "entitled to retain the deposit . . . as liquidated damages, or require the Tenderer to pay the City the difference between the offer made in this Tender and any other Tender which the City accepts . . .".

The defendant, a contractor, submitted its tender, but made a mathematical error in its tender. The plaintiff, the City, agreed that the error was honestly made and that the error had been reported to it before the tender was accepted. The City accepted the next lowest tender and brought an action against the contractor for the difference in the two bids. The trial judge ((1982), 23 Alta. L.R. (2d) 338), had dismissed the action, on the ground that the City could not accept an offer known to have been made under mistake. The Alberta Court of Appeal reversed this decision ((1985), 42 Alta. L.R. 1, 67 A.R. 95), relying on *Ron Engineering*, commenting that it would not have required the forfeiture of the deposit in this case, since that would be "unconscionable". The contractor appealed. The Supreme Court of Canada, in very short judgments by McIntyre and Wilson JJ., dismissed the appeal on the basis that it was governed by the earlier decision in *Ron Engineering*.

10. *Northern Construction* and *Ron Engineering* are troubling. As Kerans J.A. noted in *Northern Construction* (p. 16 A.R.): "No loss to [the] City arises except the loss of the chance to take advantage of the mistakes of others. Nevertheless the preponderance of authority is that equity will not intervene to protect a party from a bad bargain unless it can be seen that one contracting party held unequal bargaining power."

11. *Ron Engineering* continues to produce unfair results in case after case in every province. Owners, *i.e.*, the party in the position of the province in that case, continue to extract money from contractors who have made a careless mistake in the chaos of the final few moments of bidding, even though the owner has suffered no loss. No notice is taken of the rules of the CCDC or of the bid depositories. The whole issue of procurement by public authorities is a burgeoning area of legal practice and perhaps, as governments address the issues arising in the area, the result in *Ron Engineering* will be reconsidered.

Leaving aside *Ron Engineering*, most of the cases on mistake contained in this book can be fairly analyzed on the basis of a rational allocation of the risks of loss. General economic theories suggest that the risk should be on the party with the cheapest access to the information to avoid the mistake on the ground that this would be an economically efficient solution.

Perhaps a solution might be to allocate where one can and then, where no obvious basis for allocation offers itself, do one of two things:

(a) let the loss lie where it has fallen, on the ground that the plaintiff has shown no good reason that it should be shifted; or

(b) split the loss between the parties.

Neither of these solutions is wholly satisfactory. Loss (or gain) splitting in *Sherwood v. Walker* is almost as bad from the purchaser's point of view as the decision of the majority. Letting the loss lie where it has fallen is, at least in actions between vendors and purchasers, an asymmetric allocation: purchasers have the vendor's implied conditions and warranties, vendors have nothing. On the other hand, the vendor will often have the lowest cost access to the facts necessary to avoid the mistake. As the cases studied illustrate, most situations of a mistake can be resolved by identifying which party could most easily have prevented the mistake, and having that party bear the loss.

Some of these issues will be further explored in the next section of this chapter, which deals with frustration.

REVIEW PROBLEM

A lawyer comes to you asking whether his client, the purchaser in a land contract, has grounds to appeal a judgment dismissing his claim to rescind a contract. Advise about possible grounds for appeal. The judgment was delivered by Palmer J.:

> This is an action for rescission of a contract of sale of a 100-acre parcel of land brought by the purchaser. The vendor has counterclaimed for damages. The agreement was entered into on 26 June 2002, and the sale was to be closed on 31 October 2002. In June 2002 the Ontario legislature passed two acts: *The Ontario Planning and Development Act, 2002*, and *The Parkway Belt Planning and Development Act,*

2002. By their respective terms each Act came into effect on 4 June 2002. By regulation made under the latter Act all development of (*inter alia*) the land in question was prohibited.

Neither party was aware of this legislation at the time the agreement was signed. The agreed price for the land was $500,000 and the purchaser paid a deposit of $50,000. I find as a fact that the price of $500,000 would only have been paid by the purchaser in the belief that the land could be developed. The development restrictions were discovered by the purchaser on 30 June 2002 during the course of the search for zoning regulations routinely carried out by purchasers after agreement and before closing. Immediately upon making the discovery the purchaser refused to complete the transaction and the defendant subsequently resold the land for $100,000, the agreed market value of land thus restricted in its development potential.

The argument of the purchaser is that the agreement is vitiated by the mistake made by the parties in agreeing to sell land when development — the purpose of the contract — was impossible. Counsel for the plaintiff submits that the law is that where "the very foundation of the agreement" is destroyed, the agreement can be set aside on the ground of mistake.

In my view, in the present instance, "the very foundation of the agreement" has not been destroyed. Though it was, as I have found, well known to the vendor that the purchaser intended to make commercial use of its property by some form of subdivision, the agreement is in no sense made conditional upon the ability of the purchaser to carry out its intention. The "very foundation of the agreement" was that the vendor would sell and the purchaser would buy the property therein described upon the terms set out. The only obligations assumed by the vendor were to provide a deed and to join in or consent to any subsequent applications respecting the zoning and to give partial discharges of the mortgage it was taking back under certain circumstances. The only obligation of the purchaser was to pay the cash balance agreed to, execute and give back a mortgage, and pay such mortgage in accordance with its terms. Nothing in legislation affects, in the slightest degree, the abilities of the parties to carry out their respective obligations.

As it was put by counsel for the vendor, a developer in purchasing land is always conscious of the risk that zoning or similar changes may make the carrying out of his intention impossible, or may delay it. He may attempt to guard against risk by the insertion of proper conditions in the contract and thereby persuade the vendor to assume some of the risk. In the present case he has not done so and, indeed, there is no evidence that he has attempted to do so. "The very foundation of the agreement" is not affected and there is no room for the application of the doctrine of mistake.

I regard the case as coming within the well-known case of *Bell v. Lever Brothers*, [1932] A.C. 161. Counsel for the purchaser has argued that recent cases have expanded the scope of the relief for mistake and that the law has changed since 1932. It is worth noting that *Bell v. Lever Brothers* was decided in the same year as *Donoghue v. Stevenson*, [1932] A.C. 562, and by courts with substantial overlapping membership, and no one has suggested that the latter case is out of date or subject to criticism.

I therefore conclude that the purchaser is not entitled to relief and that the vendor's action must succeed. I give judgment therefore for the vendor for $400,000 and costs. Since the vendor still has the deposit paid by the purchaser, that amount shall be taken into account.

FRUSTRATION

Another broad class of mistakes is made up of those that occur because the assumed background to the transaction changes *after* the parties have made their contract. For conceptual and historical reasons, the law in this area has developed separately from the doctrine of "mistake", though the issues are similar and the most promising methods of analysis are essentially the same.

The effect of a conclusion that a contract is "frustrated" is that both parties are excused from further performance. A test that is commonly applied to determine if there is a "frustrating event" that will discharge future obligations is that laid down in the *Hongkong Fir* case (*supra*, Chapter 4, (¶ 3)): "Does the occurrence of the event deprive the party who has further undertakings still to perform of substantially the whole benefit that it was the intention of the parties as expressed in the contract that he should obtain as the consideration for performing those undertakings?"

This test is similar to the approach to relief for mistake where relief can only be given where the mistake is "fundamental". As a single test, and as it is sometimes used, it is therefore subject to all the criticisms of the mistake test. The key to an understanding of the problem is the realization that the *Hongkong Fir* test must be applied in the specific contractual context that arises, in the sense that the event must be assessed against the benefits that the contract was to provide. It is necessary to ascertain the risks that the contract has allocated to each side to determine if the risk of the event that has occurred should be borne by one side rather than the other. This task will sometimes be easy, at other times difficult. Recall that this is exactly what was done in the *Hongkong Fir* case itself: Diplock L.J. held that the contract allocated the risk of the events that occurred to the charterer so that it was *not* to be excused in the circumstances.

It is not uncommon for parties to a contract to deal explicitly with a variety of possible changes in circumstances. The cases that end up in litigation are generally those where the parties did not allocate the risk of loss in the contract; careful drafting and imaginative foresight can avoid many potential problems. Nevertheless, in all contracts, because they are attempts to project present knowledge and expectations into the future, there will remain a risk of the some unforeseen event and there may arise situations where the courts need to deal with the resulting disappointment in ways that do not catch parties by surprise and that, so far as possible, are consistent with commercial expectations.

The first reported case on frustration — though that term was not used by the court — is *Paradine v. Jane* (1647), Aleyn. 26, 82 E.R. 897. The case appears to have been forgotten for about 150 years after it was decided until it was revived (or rediscovered) by a Serjeant Williams, who paraphrased it in a note to the case of *Walton v. Waterhouse* (1684), 2 Wms Saunders 420, 8 E.R. 1233. Williams' notes were published in 1802. *Paradine v. Jane* was regarded as the foundation of the idea that contractual liability was not only strict (no showing of fault was required to establish liability) but absolute (there were no excuses for non-performance). Since 1802, the development of the law has been one long sustained attempt, first, to deny that contractual liability is absolute, and, second, to sort out the resulting problems.

PARADINE v. JANE

(1647), Aleyn 26, 82 E.R. 897
(Common Pleas)

[The plaintiff leased land to the defendant for three years. The defendant was put out of possession for all but four months of the term by the royalist forces during the civil wars in England and did not pay the rent. The plaintiff brought an action in debt for the rent. The narrow question was whether the defendant could plead the occupation of his land by the royalists as an excuse for his non-payment of the rent.]

. . . It was resolved, that the matter of the plea was insufficient; for though the whole army had been alien enemies, yet he ought to pay his rent. And this difference was taken, that where the law creates a duty or charge, and the party is disabled to perform it without any default in him, and hath no remedy over, there the law will excuse him. As in the case of waste, if a house be destroyed by tempest, or by enemies, the lessee is excused . . . but when the party by his own contract creates a duty or charge upon himself, he is bound to make it good, if he may, notwithstanding any accident by inevitable necessity, because he might have provided against it by his contract. . . .

The first reported case to depart from the absolute rule of *Paradine v. Jane* was *Taylor v. Caldwell*. Notice how the court rationalizes the departure from the law as it might have been understood after *Paradine v. Jane*.

TAYLOR v. CALDWELL

(1863), 3 B. and S. 826, 122 E.R. 309
(Q.B., Cockburn C.J., Blackburn, Wightman and Crompton JJ.)

[An agreement was made between the parties that the plaintiff would have the use of the Surrey Gardens and Music Hall on four days during the summer of 1861, in order to stage a series of concerts. The defendant was the owner of the music hall. Less than one week before the first performance, the music hall was destroyed by fire. The plaintiff sued for damages for breach of contract.]

The judgment of the court was given by **BLACKBURN J.**: — [1] After the making of the agreement and before the first day on which a concert was to be given, the Hall was destroyed by fire. This destruction, we must take it on the evidence, was without the fault of either party, and was so complete that in consequence the concerts could not be given as intended. And the question we have to decide is whether, under these circumstances, the loss which the plaintiffs have sustained is to fall upon the defendants. The parties when framing their agreement evidently had not present to their minds the possibility of such a disaster, and have made no express stipulation with reference to it, so that the answer to the question must depend upon the general rules of law applicable to such a contract.

[2] There seems no doubt that where there is a positive contract to do a thing not in itself unlawful, the contractor must perform it or pay damages for not doing it, although in consequence of unforeseen accidents, the performance of his contract has become unexpectedly burdensome or even impossible. . . . But this rule is only applicable when the contract is positive and absolute, and not subject to any condi-

tion either express or implied: and there are authorities which, as we think, establish the principle that where, from the nature of the contract, it appears that the parties must from the beginning have known that it could not be fulfilled unless when the time for the fulfilment of the contract arrived some particular specified thing continued to exist, so that, when entering into the contract, they must have contemplated such continuing existence as the foundation of what was to be done; there, in the absence of any express or implied warranty that the thing shall exist, the contract is not to be construed as a positive contract, but as subject to an implied condition that the parties shall be excused in case, before breach, performance becomes impossible from the perishing of the thing without default of the contractor.

[3]   There seems little doubt that this implication tends to further the great object of making the legal construction such as to fulfil the intention of those who entered into the contract. For in the course of affairs men in making such contracts in general would, if it were brought to their minds, say that there should be such a condition. . . .

[After referring to a number of cases, **BLACKBURN J.** continued:]

[4]   It seems that in those cases the only ground on which the parties or their executors can be excused from the consequences of the breach of the contract is, that from the nature of the contract there is an implied condition of the continued existence of the life of the contractor [as in the case of a promise to marry] and, perhaps in the case of the painter [contracting to paint a picture] of his eyesight. . . .

[5]   In none of these cases [including *Hall v. Wright* (1859), 120 E.R. 695 and *Coggs v. Bernard* (1703), 92 E.R. 107] is the promise in words other than positive, nor is there any express stipulation that the destruction of the person or thing shall excuse the performance; but that excuse is by law implied, because from the nature of the contract it is apparent that the parties contracted on the basis of the continued existence of the particular person or chattel. In the present case, looking at the whole contract, we find that the parties contracted on the basis of the continued existence of the Music Hall at the time when the concerts were to be given; that being essential to their performance.

[6]   We think, therefore, that the Music Hall having ceased to exist, without fault of either party, both parties are excused, the plaintiffs from taking the gardens and paying the money, the defendants from performing their promise to give the use of the Hall and Gardens and other things.

[7]   Consequently the rule must be absolute to enter the verdict for the defendants.

NOTES AND QUESTIONS

1.   Blackburn J. made extensive references to the civil law, and it is from that source that he developed the notion of the implied term as the basis for relief. What limits are suggested on the power of the court to imply such terms that it thinks fit?

2.   It might appear that the decision does not allocate any loss between the parties, but this appearance would be false, for there is a loss to be allocated. The question is whether this loss is allocated in a commercially sensible way.

In 1863, when *Taylor v. Caldwell* was decided, there was no business interruption insurance, but it is now possible to get insurance for a broad range of events that might result in the interruption of business or cancellation of a concert. Should the availability of insurance protection be relevant to the outcome?

Can the allocation of the risk of loss be understood apart from the insurance protection that each party might have had? Was one party expecting the certainty of gain while the other had a much more speculative interest? Should this fact be relevant?

3. Is there any evidence that the parties had considered what might happen if the Music Hall should burn down? If not, what basis is there for the decision of the court?

4. Is the rule laid down in *Paradine v. Jane* good law after *Taylor v. Caldwell*?

The next case is one of the group of cases known as the "Coronation Cases". They arose because the coronation of Edward VII had to be postponed. The processions were supposed to take place on 26 and 27 June 1902. On 24 June the King came down with appendicitis. The King's operation was one of the first successful operations for appendicitis. The coronation eventually took place on 9 August 1902.

KRELL v. HENRY

[1903] 2 K.B. 740
(C.A., Vaughan Williams, Romer and Stirling L.JJ.)

[The plaintiff had a flat that looked out over the proposed route for the coronation procession of Edward VII. The flat was advertised as being available with "windows to view the Coronation Procession" for rent for the days (but not the nights) of 26 and 27 June, the planned days for the coronation. On 20 June 1902, the plaintiff had agreed to rent the rooms to the defendant for £75. The exchange of letters that formed the contract did not explicitly mention the coronation. The defendant paid £25 as a deposit. The balance was payable on 24 June 1902. On that day the king was taken ill and the processions were cancelled. The defendant refused to pay the balance of the £50, still owing. The plaintiff sued for £50. The trial judge (Darling J.) dismissed the action. The plaintiff appealed.]

VAUGHAN WILLIAMS L.J. read the following written judgment [broken into paragraphs by the editors]: — **[1]** The real question in this case is the extent of the application in English law of the principle of the Roman law which has been adopted and acted on in many English decisions, and notably in the case of *Taylor v. Caldwell*. . . .

[2] I do not think that the principle of the civil law as introduced into the English law [by that case and others] is limited to cases in which the event causing the impossibility of performance is the destruction or non-existence of some thing which is the subject-matter of the contract or of some condition or state of things expressly specified as a condition of it. I think that you first have to ascertain, not necessarily from the terms of the contract, but, if required, from necessary inferences, drawn from surrounding circumstances recognized by both contracting parties, what is the substance of the contract, and then to ask the question whether that substantial contract needs for its foundation the assumption of the existence of a particular state of things. If it does, this will limit the operation of the general words, and in such case, if the contract becomes impossible of performance by reason of the non-existence of the state of things assumed by both contracting parties as the foundation of the contract, there will be no breach of the contract thus limited.

[3]   Now what are the facts of the present case? . . . In my judgment the use of the rooms was let and taken for the purpose of seeing the Royal procession. It was not a demise of the rooms, or even an agreement to let and take the rooms. It is a licence to use rooms for a particular purpose and none other. And in my judgment the taking place of those processions on the days proclaimed along the proclaimed route . . . was regarded by both contracting parties as the foundation of the contract; and I think that it cannot reasonably be supposed to have been in the contemplation of the contracting parties, when the contract was made, that the coronation would not be held on the proclaimed days, or the processions not take place on those days along the proclaimed route; and I think that the words imposing on the defendant the obligation to accept and pay for the use of the rooms for the named days, although general and unconditional, were not used with reference to the possibility of the particular contingency which afterwards occurred.

[4]   It was suggested in the course of the argument that if the occurrence, on the proclaimed days, of the coronation and the procession in this case were the foundation of the contract, and if the general words are thereby limited or qualified, so that in the event of the non-occurrence of the coronation and procession along the proclaimed route they would discharge both parties from further performance of the contract, it would follow that if a cabman was engaged to take some one to Epsom on Derby Day at a suitably enhanced price for such a journey, say £10, both parties to the contract would be discharged in the contingency of the race at Epsom for some reason becoming impossible; but I do not think this follows, for I do not think that in the cab case the happening of the race would be the foundation of the contract. No doubt the purpose of the engager would be to go to see the Derby, and the price would be proportionately high; but the cab had no special qualifications for the purpose which led to the selection of the cab for this particular occasion. Any other cab would have done as well.

[5]   Moreover, I think that, under the cab contract, the hirer, even if the race went off, could have said, "Drive me to Epsom; I will pay you the agreed sum; you have nothing to do with the purpose for which I hired the cab," and that if the cabman refused he would have been guilty of a breach of contract, there being nothing to qualify his promise to drive the hirer to Epsom on a particular day. Whereas in the case of the coronation, there is not merely the purpose of the hirer to see the coronation procession, but it is the coronation procession and the relative position of the rooms which is the basis of the contract as much for the lessor as the hirer; and I think that if the King, before the coronation day and after the contract, had died, the hirer could not have insisted on having the rooms on the days named.

[6]   It could not in the cab case be reasonably said that seeing the Derby race was the foundation of the contract, as it was of the licence in this case. Whereas in the present case, where the rooms were offered and taken, by reason of their peculiar suitability from the position of the rooms for a view of the coronation procession, surely the view of the coronation procession was the foundation of the contract, which is a very different thing from the purpose of the man who engaged the cab — namely, to see the race — being held to be the foundation of the contract.

[7]   Each case must be judged by its own circumstances. In each case one must ask oneself, first, what, having regard to all the circumstances, was the foundation of the contract? Secondly, was the performance of the contract prevented? Thirdly, was the event which prevented the performance of the contract of such a character that it cannot reasonably be said to have been in the contemplation of the parties at the date of the contract? If all these questions are answered in the affirmative (as I think they should be in this case), I think both parties are discharged from further performance of the contract . . . I think this appeal ought to be dismissed.

[**ROMER** and **STIRLING L.JJ.** agreed with **VAUGHAN WILLIAMS L.J.**]

NOTES AND QUESTIONS

1.   *Krell v. Henry* may be contrasted with another coronation case, *Herne Bay Steamboat Co. v. Hutton*, [1903] 2 K.B. 683. In that case the defendant had agreed to charter a boat to watch the Review (or parade of ships) of the fleet at Spithead by the King. Like the other coronation ceremonies, the Review was cancelled due to the King's illness. The cancellation was held not to frustrate the contract to charter a boat to view the fleet. The contract specified that charter was to be "for the purpose of viewing the naval review and for a day's cruise around the fleet". The basis for the distinction between the two cases was that the fleet remained at Spithead in spite of the King's illness, and the court observed that it was "very well worth seeing the fleet without the Review".

2.   Do you think that Vaughan Williams L.J. adequately distinguished his example of the Epsom cab from the dispute before him? Note that underlying the cab example is the assumption that the customer could require the cab-driver to honour his undertaking. There was no question on the facts of *Krell v. Henry* of the "tenant" seeking to hold the owner of the rooms to the contract and, presumably, the owner would have been delighted to provide the rooms for the agreed price. Does this shift in focus matter?

3.   The decision in *Krell v. Henry* is regarded as doctrinally correct, establishing that frustration may apply even if performance of the contract is rendered without purpose but not impossible. As a decision allocating the risk of loss to one of the parties in this particular situation, the decision is harder to understand. What other facts would you want to know before you could accept the conclusion that the risk of loss was appropriately allocated? Which party bore the risk of fog or rain that might have totally obstructed or largely obscured the view but which would not have led to the cancellation of the parade? How would you know whether or not fog or rain during the processions went to the "foundation" of the contract? What factors are likely to determine the price paid to have rooms available to look at a coronation procession?

    Part of the problem with contracts to watch coronation processions is that there is no context within which the risks run by the parties might be understood. In a contract of sale, for example, it is possible to adopt, as a default rule, the point of view that unless the buyer gets a warranty or some other protection from the seller, the risk is on it. The last coronation before that of King Edward VII had been that of his mother, Queen Victoria, in 1837. There were probably few people alive in 1902 who would have remembered Queen Victoria's and fewer still (if any) who would have considered how the risk of her illness might have been allocated at that time. The absence of a context makes the court's task much more difficult because it has nothing outside the contract to fall back on to justify any allocation of the risk. It is worth noting that the actual result in *Krell v. Henry* is that the incidence of the risk is split: the plaintiff keeps what the defendant prepaid and the defendant does not have to pay the balance. Perhaps this result is as fair as could be imagined.

4.   If you buy an opera ticket and get appendicitis and are unable to attend, can you claim that the contract was frustrated?

5. The defendant in *Krell v. Henry* had prepaid £25 of the total price of £75. His claim for the return of this deposit was abandoned. There were coronation cases like *Chandler v. Webster*, [1904] 1 K.B. 493, in which the courts denied a party the right to get back what had been paid to the other. In *Krell v. Henry*, Vaughan Williams L.J. points out that the £50 over which the parties were arguing was not due until the end of the day on which the announcement of the king's illness was made. Should it have made any difference if the money had been due the day before?

   The issue of the appropriate remedy in the event of frustration is discussed later in this section.

6. It is sometimes hard to draw the line between problems of frustration and interpretation. Thus, in *Atlantic Paper Stock Ltd. v. St. Anne-Nackawic Pulp & Paper Co.*, [1975] 1 S.C.R. 580, 56 D.L.R. (3d) 409, a contract for the purchase and sale of raw materials for corrugated cardboard was alleged by the buyer to be frustrated by the lack of economic markets for the buyer's product. Dickson J. in the Supreme Court held that the cause of the lack of a market was the failure of the buyer to do a good market analysis and that there had not been a change of circumstances that would justify giving the buyer an excuse for non-performance. The buyer had simply priced itself out of the market and, the buyer's obligations not being excused, it was liable to the seller for breach of contract.

7. The problems of frustration are not just caused by physical disasters or royal appendicitis, but by legislation that may make a planned activity illegal. The issues are the same: which party should, in the events that have occurred, bear the risk of loss? Some years ago there was a furore over exploding pop bottles. The bottles that exploded were 1.5 litre glass bottles. In *Ahlstrom Canada Ltd. v. Browning Harvey Ltd.* (1986), 31 D.L.R. (4th) 316 (Nfld. C.A.), the plaintiff, a Pepsi bottler, had ordered 1.5 litre glass pop bottles (costing over $9,000) from the defendant manufacturer and paid for them. Before the bottles could be used, their use was prohibited under the *Hazardous Products Act*, R.S.C. 1970, c. H-3. The plaintiff returned the bottles to the defendant and sought to recover what it had paid the defendant. The trial judge had given judgment for the plaintiff on the ground that the defendant, as the manufacturer, could make better use of the glass than the plaintiff. The defendant appealed. The Court of Appeal held that there had been no breach of condition by the defendant, and that property (and the risk of loss in the circumstances) had passed to the plaintiff.

   Is the point when title passes under the *Sale of Goods Act* an appropriate point in the circumstances to transfer the risk of loss from the seller to the buyer? There was no discussion in *Ahlstrom Canada Ltd. v. Browning Harvey Ltd.* of either frustration or impossibility in either court. The decision of the trial judge put the whole loss on the seller; the appeal decision put the loss on the buyer. Would a splitting of the loss be preferable or even possible?

8. It is common in many commercial agreements to provide for the allocation of the risk of frustration or impossibility. A clause allocating these risks is usually referred to as a "force majeure" clause. A typical clause dealing with problems of "force majeure" is the following:

   ### Force Majeure

   8.01 *Party Not Liable for Non-Performance*: A party hereto (hereinafter in this Article called a "Defaulting Party") shall not be liable to the other party hereto for the Defaulting Party's failure to fulfil its obligations under any section of this agreement (other than Article 5 which imposes on the Purchaser the obligation to pay for the goods) if such failure is caused by the occurrence of an Event of Force Majeure. In the case of any such failure so caused (other than a failure by the Defaulting Party to fulfil its obligations under Article 5 [regarding payment of the price]), then except for the rights of the other party hereto under Article 9 to terminate the Agreement, the other party hereto shall have no claim for damages or specific performance or other right of action against the Defaulting Party.

8.02 *Obligations Arising Out of Event of Force Majeure*: A Defaulting Party shall

(a) forthwith give notice to the other party hereto of the occurrence of an Event of Force Majeure;

(b) unless such Event of Force Majeure is a strike, work slowdown or work stoppage, use its best efforts to eliminate such Event of Force Majeure;

(c) forthwith give notice to the other party when such Event of Force Majeure has been eliminated or has ceased to prevent the Defaulting Party from fulfilling such obligations; and

(d) proceed to fulfil such obligations as soon as reasonably possible after such Event of Force Majeure has been eliminated or has ceased to prevent the Defaulting Party from fulfilling such obligations.

The definition section of the Agreement defines an Event of Force Majeure as:

"Event of Force Majeure" means an event which is beyond the reasonable control of a party hereto including an act of God, action or failure to act of any government or governmental board, commission, department, bureau or authority, confiscation, war, blockade, insurrection, riot, sabotage, flood, fire, explosion, epidemic, landslide, lightning, earthquake, storm, accident, strike, lockout, work slowdown, work stoppage, power failure or shortage and any failure (other than a failure caused by the negligence or deliberate act or inaction of a party hereto) of supplies, equipment, labour or transportation;

Termination of Agreement

9.01 *Notice of Default*: If a party hereto (hereinafter in this Article called the "Defaulting Party") fails to fulfil any obligation of such party hereunder, the other party hereto (hereinafter in this Article called the "Non-defaulting Party") shall be entitled to give to the Defaulting Party a notice requiring the Defaulting Party to fulfil such obligation (hereinafter in this Article called the "Defaulted Obligation").

9.02 *Default Due to Event of Force Majeure*: If a Defaulting Party's failure to fulfil a Defaulted Obligation (other than an obligation under Article 5) is caused by the occurrence of an Event of Force Majeure and if, pursuant to section 9.01, the Non-defaulting Party gives to the Defaulting Party a notice requiring the Defaulting Party to fulfil such Defaulted Obligation, then unless the Defaulting Party fulfils such Defaulted Obligation within 6 months after receipt by the Defaulting Party of such notice, the Non-defaulting Party shall be entitled, by notice given to the Defaulting Party, to terminate all further obligations of the parties hereto under the preceding articles (other than Article 7) of this agreement.

9.03 *Default Not Due to Event of Force Majeure*: If the Defaulted Obligation which a Defaulting Party fails to fulfil is an obligation under Article 5 or if a Defaulting Party's failure to fulfil a Defaulted Obligation is not caused by the occurrence of an Event of Force Majeure and, in either case, if pursuant to section 9.01 the Non-defaulting Party gives to the Defaulting Party a notice requiring the Defaulting Party to fulfil such Defaulted Obligation, then unless the Defaulting Party fulfils such Defaulted Obligation within 30 days after receipt by the Defaulting Party of such notice, the Non-defaulting Party shall be entitled, by notice given to the Defaulting Party, to terminate all further obligations of the parties hereto under the preceding articles (other than Article 7) of this agreement.

9.04 *Time of Termination*: If at any time a party hereto is entitled to give, and does give, a notice terminating all further obligations of the parties hereto un-

der the preceding articles (other than Article 7) of this agreement, all such obligations shall terminate on the day on which such notice is received by the
party to which such notice is given.

9.05 *Consequences of Termination*: In the event of the termination of all further obligations of the parties hereto under the preceding articles (other than
Article 7) of this agreement,

(a) Vendor shall, if directed by the Purchaser so to do, transfer to the account
     of a specified Customer or Customers, all Goods (including Accepted
     Goods) title to which (as between Vendor and the Purchaser) is vested in
     the Purchaser at the time of such termination; or

(b) Vendor shall, if directed by the Purchaser so to do, deliver to the
     Purchaser, on board highway transport vehicles at Vendor's Facilities all
     Goods (including Accepted Goods) title to which (as between Vendor
     and the Purchaser) is vested in the Purchaser at the time of such
     termination; and

(c) each party hereto shall continue to be liable to pay, on the terms herein
     specified, any amount accrued or accruing and payable by such party to
     the other party hereto up to the time of such termination.

Accepted Goods delivered pursuant to this section shall conform to the specifications contained in this Agreement. The conformance to such specifications
of such Accepted Goods as determined by Vendor shall be final and conclusive for the purposes of this agreement and shall be binding as between Vendor and the Purchaser.

9.06 *Costs of Termination*: All costs and expenses incurred by Vendor in delivering Goods pursuant to section 9.05 shall be borne and paid by the Purchaser.

Another example of a *force majeure* clause is the following:

Force Majeure means an event: that (i) was unforeseen by the parties, (ii) was
not controllable by the parties, (iii) could not reasonably have been foreseen
by the parties, and (iv) against which the parties could not have taken precaution; and includes: acts of God, strikes, lock-outs, fires, riots, arson, intervention by civil or military authorities, governmental regulations and orders and
acts of war (declared and undeclared).

Notice the interrelation of notice, demands and excuses and the eventual right of the
parties to get out of the deal.

9. The *Atlantic Paper Stock* case illustrates one of the serious practical problems of the
    law of frustration. Long-term contracts for the supply of goods are common. The par-
    ties, often large and sophisticated companies, have planned for many of the obvious
    contingencies that might arise during performance of the contract.
        An interesting example of the problems of these contracts and the judicial response
    is provided by the American case of *Aluminum Co. of America (ALCOA) v. Essex
    Group Inc.*, 499 F.Supp. 53 (W.D. Penn. 1980). The plaintiff agreed to process molten
    aluminum for the defendant under a contract that contained a complicated escalator
    clause. The price to be paid by the buyer Essex was to vary in accordance with two
    factors. Twenty per cent of the original price was to vary with changes in the Whole-
    sale Price Index — Industrial Commodities (WPI-IC). This charge was referred to as
    the "production charge". A further 20 per cent of the price was to vary with changes in
    the hourly wage rates paid to Alcoa employees. A large component of the production
    charge for aluminum smelting is the cost of electricity.
        After the Organization of Petroleum Exporting Countries (OPEC) oil embargo of
    1973, the cost of electricity rose at a rate far in excess of the rate of increase in WPI
    (which contained factors other than energy costs). Had the contract run its course, Al-

coa would have lost about $60,000,000. Alcoa sought to have the terms of the contract modified on the basis of mistake or frustration.

The trial judge held that the parties' mistake was one of fact rather than one of simple prediction of future events in that both parties to the contract assumed that the index they adopted was adequate to fulfil its purpose. This mistaken assumption was "essentially a present actuarial error". He further held that to give relief to Alcoa, the mistake had to relate to a basic assumption underlying the contract, and had to have caused a "severe imbalance in the agreed exchange". These requirements were held to have been met in the case. The form of relief was not a discharge of the contract, releasing each from its obligations to the other, but judicially imposed revised escalator clause. The judge said (p. 80):

> For the duration of the contract the price for each pound of aluminum converted by Alcoa shall be the lesser of the current Price A or Price B indicated below.
>
> Price A shall be the contract ceiling price computed periodically as specified in the contract.
>
> Price B shall be the greater of the current Price B1 or Price B2. Price B1 shall be the price specified in the contract, computed according to the terms of the contract. Price B2 shall be that price which yields Alcoa a profit of one cent per pound of aluminum converted. . . .

The judge concluded by saying that the approach that he had taken represented a "new spirit of commercial law". He said that, without such an approach, people might not enter into long-term contractual relations. He saw the court's response as (i) helping to avoid the need for more complicated drafting; (ii) limiting the risk in long-term commercial relations; and (iii) reflective of the duties, responsibilities and problems facing management of large enterprises.

The remedy given by the court in *Alcoa* is known as "reformation" of the contract. It has not been a remedy that Anglo-Canadian courts have utilized to respond to frustrating events. Do you think that they should?

10. The *Alcoa* decision was sympathetic to the indirect problems created for a producer due to the dramatic 1973 rise in price of oil as a result of the actions of the OPEC cartel. However, courts were much less sympathetic to suppliers who had made long-term contracts to supply oil or other sources of energy and suffered dramatic losses. This was exactly the type of risk that a supplier undertakes in entering into a long-term contract.

In *Eastern Air Lines v. Gulf Oil*, 415 F.Supp. 429 (S.D. Fla. 1975), an oil company had a long-term fuel supply contract with an airline, with the price set by reference to the price for domestically produced American oil. In response to the OPEC crisis, the government began to control the price of American-produced oil, but not that of imported oil. The oil company in fact relied heavily on imported oil, and argued that the contract was frustrated, or rendered commercially impractical. The court refused to accept this argument.

11. In an effort to encourage the sale of its nuclear reactors in the 1970's, a manufacturer, Westinghouse, offered to the utilities that bought its reactors a guaranteed supply of uranium at a price of about $8 per pound. When the price of uranium reached $26 per pound, Westinghouse defaulted on its supply contracts. (It was alleged that the activities of the uranium cartel, of which Canada was a member, were responsible for the price increase. The price eventually reached $40 per pound.) Westinghouse settled some of the claims for about $900,000,000. Westinghouse was not excused from the obligation to supply the uranium by reason of the catastrophic price rise: *Re Westinghouse Electric Corp.*, 517 F.Supp. 440 (1981). Should Westinghouse have been excused from performance?

Another area in which problems frequently arise when the parties' expectations are seriously upset is agreements for the purchase and sale of land. One such example has already been considered in the case of *Amalgamated Investment* (*supra*). A more general form of the problem arises when the zoning changes after the contract has been made but before the deal closes. On whom is the risk of loss in these circumstances? Historically the development of the law in this area was affected by a rule that contracts for the sale (or lease) of land cannot, as a matter of law, be frustrated. This rule has now largely disappeared, and the modern law appears in the next case.

KBK NO. 138 VENTURES LTD. v. CANADA SAFEWAY LTD.

[2000] B.C.J. No. 938, 185 D.L.R. (4th) 650, 74 B.C.L.R. (3d) 331
(C.A., McEachern C.J.B.C., Cumming and Braidwood JJ.A.)

The judgment of the Court was delivered by

[1]   BRAIDWOOD J.A.: — The issue in this appeal is whether or not an agreement between the parties for the sale of land has been frustrated and is void so that the appellant must return the $150,000 deposit that it received pursuant to the contract of sale.

Facts

[2]   The facts are not in dispute. The appellant Canada Safeway Limited ("Safeway") owned certain property on Victoria Drive in East Vancouver. It decided to sell the property as "prime redevelopment opportunity" and issued an advertisement providing a description of the property and listing the price at $8.5 million. The property was described as being zoned C-2 with a maximum floor space ratio ("FSR") of 3.22 except where the property was used for dwelling purposes for which the maximum FSR was 2.5.

[3]   The respondent KBK No. 138 Ventures Ltd. ("KBK") was interested in purchasing the property and developing it as a mixed commercial and residential condominium project. An employee of KBK contacted the City of Vancouver ("the City") and learned that the maximum FSR for such a project would be 3.0, meaning that it was likely that the City would issue a development permit allowing an FSR of about 2.3 to 2.5. The development both parties expected was dependent on the floor area, which in turn was dependent on the maximum allowable FSR.

[4]   On 28 October 1996, KBK and Safeway entered into a contract for the sale of the property. The contract specified that the purchase price would be the greater of $8.8 million or $38 multiplied by the number of square feet of floor area (as determined by the maximum FSR permitted by the City on the closing date).

[5]   Pursuant to the contract, KBK paid Safeway $150,000 as a first instalment on the purchase price. This is the sum of money now in dispute.

[6]   On 29 November 1996, the Director of Planning for the City ("the Director") submitted an application on his own motion to the City to rezone the property from C-2 to CD-1 and to decrease the maximum FSR to 0.3.

[7] On 2 December 1996, the parties received letters advising them of the Director's application. Neither party had contemplated such an eventuality. If the application were accepted, floor space would be restricted to one-tenth of the maximum allowed under C-2 zoning. It would be impossible for KBK to pursue the project as contemplated and develop the property if the purchase price remained at $8.8 million.

[8] Both KBK and Safeway registered their objections to the Director's application. However, on 25 March 1997, after a public hearing and a second reading by Council, a bylaw was passed that formally rezoned the property from C-2 to CD-1. This zoning change had the result of restricting the FSR of any new buildings to a maximum of 0.3.

[9] On 13 March 1997, KBK advised Safeway that the contract had been frustrated and demanded that Safeway return the first instalment. Safeway refused to do so.

[10] Safeway ultimately entered into another agreement to sell the property to Westbank Holdings Ltd. The purchase price was now set at $5.4 million to reflect the development restrictions associated with the rezoning of the property.

[11] In her reasons for judgment, reported at (1999), 26 R.P.R. (3d) 88 (B.C.S.C.), the trial judge found that the contract between the parties had been frustrated. Pursuant to s. 5(2) of the *Frustrated Contract Act*, R.S.B.C. 1996, c. 166, she ordered that KBK is entitled to restitution of the first instalment that it made to Safeway, which amounted to $150,000.

Discussion

[12] The issue in this appeal is whether the trial judge erred in finding that the contract had been frustrated. In *National Carriers Ltd. v. Panalpina (Northern) Ltd.*, [1981] 1 All E.R. 161 (H.L.), Lord Simon of Glaisdale put forth the following definition of "frustration" at p. 175:

> Frustration of a contract takes place when there supervenes an event (without default of either party and for which the contract makes no sufficient provision) which *so significantly changes that nature (not merely the expense or onerousness) of the outstanding contractual rights* and/or obligations from what the parties could reasonably have contemplated at the time of its execution that *it would be unjust to hold them to the literal sense of its stipulations in the new circumstances*; in such case the law declares both parties to be discharged from further performance.

[Emphasis added.]

1. *The Test for Frustration*

[13] The leading case on the doctrine of frustration is *Davis Contractors Ltd. v. Fareham U.D.C.*, [1956] A.C. 696, [1956] 2 All E.R. 145 (H.L.), in which the House of Lords articulated the so-called "radical change in the obligation" test. Lord Radcliffe stated at p. 728-29 (A.C.):

> So perhaps it would be simpler to say at the outset that frustration occurs whenever the law recognizes that without default of either party *a contractual obligation has become incapable of being performed because the circumstances in which perform-*

ance is called for would render it a thing radically different from that which was undertaken by the contract. Non haec in foedera veni. It was not this that I promised to do.

There is, however, no uncertainty as to the materials upon which the court must proceed. "The data for decision are, on the one hand, the terms and construction of the contract, read in the light of the then existing circumstances, and on the other hand the events which have occurred" (*Denny, Mott & Dickson Ltd. v. James B. Fraser & Co. Ltd.*, [1944] A.C. 265 at 274-275 *per* Lord Wright). In the nature of things there is often no room for any elaborate inquiry. The court must act upon a general impression of what its rule requires. It is for that reason that special importance is necessarily attached to the occurrence of any unexpected event that, as it were, changes the face of things. But, even so, *it is not hardship or inconvenience or material loss itself which calls the principle of frustration into play. There must be as well such a change in the significance of the obligation that the thing undertaken would, if performed, be a different thing from that contracted for.*

[Emphasis added.]

In a concurring judgment, Lord Reid stated at pp. 720-21 that a finding of frustration depends "on the true construction of the terms which are in the contract read in light of the nature of the contract and of the relevant surrounding circumstances when the contract was made".

[14] The test for frustration was neatly summarized by Mr. Justice Sigurdson in *Folia v. Trelinski* (1997), 14 R.P.R. (3d) 5 (B.C.S.C.). He stated at paragraph 18:

In order to find that the contract at issue has been frustrated the following criteria would have to be satisfied. The event in question *must have occurred after the formation of the contract and cannot be self-induced.* The contract must, as a result, be *totally different* from what the parties had intended. This difference must take into account *the distinction between complete fruitlessness and mere inconvenience.* The disruption *must be permanent*, not temporary or transient. The *change must totally affect the nature, meaning, purpose, effect and consequences of the contract* so far as concerns either or both parties. Finally, the act or event that brought about such radical change *must not have been foreseeable.*

[Emphasis added.]

[15] There is no doubt that the *Davis Contractors* decision is the law in Canada. The Supreme Court of Canada applied this test as early as 1960: *Peter Kiewit Sons' Co. of Canada v. Eakins Construction Ltd.*, [1960] S.C.R. 361, 22 D.L.R. (2d) 465. What is important for the purpose of this appeal is that the "radical change in the obligation" test has also been applied to real estate contracts in Canada. I make this point because there is still a considerable amount of debate in England as to whether the doctrine of frustration can apply to land conveyances. However, the Ontario Court of Appeal has ruled in a long line of cases that the doctrine should apply to land: see *Capital Quality Homes Ltd. v. Colwyn Construction Ltd.* (1975), 9 O.R. (2d) 617 at 629, 61 D.L.R. (3d) 385 (C.A.); *Dinicola v. Huang & Danczkay Properties* (1996), 29 O.R. (3d) 161, 135 D.L.R. (4th) 525 (Gen. Div.); affirmed (1998), 40 O.R. (3d) 252, 163 D.L.R. (4th) 286 (C.A.). . . . Such case law is in harmony with the well-established idea in Canada that commercial conveyances of land are also contracts: *Highway Properties Ltd. v. Kelly, Douglas & Co.*, [1971] S.C.R. 562, 17 D.L.R. (3d) 710.

[16] In her reasons for judgment, the trial judge also referred to the English Court of Appeal decision of *Krell v. Henry*, [1903] 2 K.B. 740 (C.A.). I do not find there to be a necessary inconsistency in the "radical change in the obligation" test set out in the *Davis Contractors* case and the principles set out in the well-known case of *Krell.*

[17] The court in *Krell* laid down three conditions to be satisfied for the doctrine of frustration to apply. These are:

1. What, having regard to all the circumstances, was the foundation of the contract?

2. Was the performance of the contract prevented?

3. Was the event which prevented the performance of the contract of such a character that it cannot reasonably be said to have been in the contemplation of the parties at the date of the contract?

[18] The learned trial judge found that each of these conditions were satisfied and I agree with that result.

2. *The Victoria Wood Decision*

[19] Counsel for Safeway argued that the facts in this case are similar to *Victoria Wood Development Corp. v. Ondrey* (1978), 22 O.R. (2d) 1, 7 R.P.R. 60, 92 D.L.R. (3d) 22 (C.A.). The vendors in *Victoria Wood* were interested in selling 89 acres of land in Oakville, a suburb of Toronto. They knew that the land was zoned for industrial use. The buyer, Victoria Wood, entered into a contract with the vendors with the intention of subdividing and developing the lands for industrial or commercial use. The vendor was fully aware of this intention. After the contract had been completed, however, the Ontario Legislature enacted a statute which effectively restricted the land to agricultural uses. The Court found that the land in question was "rendered useless for development for industrial, commercial or residential use". The buyer then argued that the contract had been frustrated.

[20] The trial judge held that the contract had not been frustrated. He concluded that the "foundation of the contract" was that the vendor would sell the property, and the buyer would purchase the property. The supervening legislation did not affect these obligations in any way: 14 O.R. (2d) 723 at 727, 74 D.L.R. (3d) 528 (H.C.J.).

[21] The Ontario Court of Appeal affirmed this ruling. It also affirmed the decision in *Capital Quality Homes, supra,* that the doctrine of frustration could apply to land. Arnup J.A. stated the test in this way at p. 13 (O.R.):

> Has the contractual obligation become impossible to perform because its performance would be radically different from that undertaken by the contract? [*Davis Contractors*] Has there occurred an intervening event or change of circumstances so fundamental as to be regarded by the law both as striking at the root of the agreement, and as entirely beyond what was contemplated by the parties [*Cricklewood Property & Investment Trust Ltd. v. Leighton's Investment Trust Ltd.,* [1945] A.C. 221 (H.L.) at 228 *per* Viscount Simon, L.C.] . . . Viscount Simon, L.C., had defined frustration in these terms:
>
> > . . . the premature determination of an agreement between parties, lawfully entered into and in course of operation at the time of its premature determina-

tion, owing to the occurrence of an intervening event or change of circumstances so fundamental as to be regarded by the law both as striking at the root of the agreement, and as entirely beyond what was contemplated by the parties when they entered into the agreement.

Reverting to my questions: Is the effect of the legislation of such a nature that the law would consider the fundamental character of the agreement to have been so altered as to no longer reflect the original basis of the agreement? [*Capital Quality Homes*, supra at p. 626.]

The Court in *Victoria Wood* answered these questions in the negative. Arnup J.A. continued at pp. 13-14:

I do not think *mere knowledge of the vendor* that land was being bought for development, or even for a particular kind of development, is sufficient to bring into operation the doctrine of frustration when an entirely unexpected governmental enactment makes the purchaser's purpose incapable of realization, or so difficult that great hardship is occasioned to it in carrying out that purpose. As I have stated earlier, there was no "common venture" here. As [Viscount Simonds] said in *Davis Contractors Ltd.*, *supra*, at p. 715, "*it by no means follows that disappointed expectations lead to frustrated contracts*".

Professor Reiter observes that "it is sometimes a very complex matter to ascertain what is the 'foundation,' 'basis,' or 'purpose' of a contract, or what is the 'implicit undertaking' of the parties": [(1978), 56 *Can. Bar Rev.* 98 at 106]. In the present case, the ascertainment has to be based on *implications* from the contract (which is silent on the subject). *The parties themselves never met. The vendors called no evidence at all.* The purchaser called no evidence of any generally understood practice of vendors and developers as to allocation of the risk."

[Emphasis added.]

Therefore, the Court found that the contract had not been frustrated.

3. *The Case at Bar*

[22] It was argued before us that the purpose of the agreement in this case was not the development of the Victoria Drive property as prime commercial and residential property; rather, it was simply the sale and purchase of property. This Court should therefore follow the decision of *Victoria Wood* and find that the contract has not been frustrated. However, I think that the facts of the case at bar clearly distinguish it from the facts in *Victoria Wood*. In particular, the circumstances surrounding the contract demonstrate that Safeway had more than "mere knowledge" that KBK had the intention of redeveloping the property.

[23] I first turn to the advertisement placed by Safeway that introduced the property to KBK. It read in part:

FOR SALE

PRIME RE-DEVELOPMENT OPPORTUNITY

. . .

Zoning:

The subject property is zoned C-2, a commercial zoning district intended to provide a wide range of goods and services and commercial activities to serve large neighbourhoods.

Some, but not all, permitted uses include: general office; financial institution; retail store; grocery or drug store; restaurant — Class 1. Conditional approval uses include dwelling units in conjunction with any of the outright approved uses but limited generally to the upper floors of a building; and also liquor stores.

The maximum floor space ratio shall not exceed 3.22, except that the FSR for dwelling uses shall not exceed 2.50. . . .

[Emphasis added.]

[24] I next turn to the clauses in the contract itself. Clause 1 specifically referred to KBK's intentions in purchasing the property when it defined the term "development" as follows:

. . . the Buyer's intended development on the Lands, being a condominium development for mixed commercial and/or residential use.

I also point to Clause 6.2 of the contract, which the learned trial judge also noted. It read in part:

The Purchase Price shall also be adjusted on the Closing Date *by increasing the Purchase Price to an amount equal to the product of $38.00 times the number of square feet of floor area for the Lands approved in accordance with the FSR for the Lands.* . . . The Purchase Price will not be adjusted if the above calculation gives a result of less than the original Purchase Price, or if the FSR is not determined on the Closing Date due to a final development permit not having been approved and issued by the City of Vancouver.

[Emphasis added.]

The deal was therefore structured with an eye on KBK's ultimate goal of redeveloping the property as a condominium development for mixed commercial and/or residential use. It was on the basis of the FSR allowable for such a development that the purchase price of $8.5 million was calculated.

[25] Schedule 3 of the contract included a non-competition clause prohibiting KBK from using the property as a grocery store, drugstore or convenience store. The implication of this provision is that KBK was bound to develop the land into something other than a grocery store like Safeway. Such a non-competition clause was *not* included in the agreement of purchase and sale concluded between Safeway and Westbank at the reduced price of $5.4 million.

[26] The appellant Safeway argued that other clauses in the contract specifically allocated the risk of such a downzoning to KBK. However, I agree with the trial judge that the contract cannot be interpreted in this manner. She stated at paragraph 30:

Safeway submitted that clauses 4.2, 7.1 and 9.0, all operated to expressly allocate the risk of inability to develop the Property to the Plaintiff. Clause 4.2 stated that:

The transaction contemplated by this agreement is not conditional on the Buyer obtaining a development permit for the Development, and the transaction contemplated hereby shall be completed on the closing date whether or not a development permit is obtained by the Buyer.

Clause 7.2 stated [that] the Buyer acknowledges and agrees that the seller neither makes nor gives any representation, warranty or covenant with respect to:

(a)   zoning, inclusive of permitted uses, of the lands;

(b) the availability of the development permit or building permit in respect of the lands, for any development and construction by the buyer of any building or structure, which the buyer may desire at any time to develop and construct upon the lands. . . .

I do not find that the above clauses expressly allocate to [KBK] the risk of the Director's application to re-zone the Property. At best, these clauses are of general wording and serve as a disclaimer, by Safeway, as to anything it may have said during the course of negotiations with respect to the zoning or development of the Property.

[27] Finally, I turn to the question as to whether the change in zoning was foreseeable. The learned trial judge wrote at paragraph 39:

It is clear from the evidence that the parties did not actually contemplate the event which I have found to have frustrated the Contract. I am satisfied that any reasonable person in the position of the parties likely would not have contemplated such an event. It was most unusual for the Director to take such a step on his own accord. He appeared to have done so as a result of a new concept amongst planning authorities of "visioning" by communities. It was both the Plaintiff's and the Defendant's misfortune that the Property was located in one of the areas chosen to be a pilot project for input from the community as to its vision of the future for that community.

This finding of fact made in the course of the Rule 18A trial cannot be lightly interfered with by this Court: *Orangeville Raceway Ltd. v. Wood Gundy Inc.* (1995), 6 B.C.L.R. (3d) 391 (C.A.) at 400.

Summary and Disposition

[28] In all the circumstances, I agree with the conclusion of the trial judge. This is not a case like *Victoria Wood, supra*, since there is more than "mere knowledge of the vendor that land was being bought for development or even for a particular kind of development". Rather, there is an intervening event and change of circumstances so fundamental as to be regarded as striking at the root of the agreement and as entirely beyond what was contemplated by the parties when they entered into the agreement. The Director's application "radically altered" the contract between the parties within the meaning of the test set out in *Davis Contractors* and the above cases. The change in zoning and the consequent reduction in FSR from 3.22 to 0.3, which meant a change in the allowable buildable square footage from 231,800 square feet to 30,230 square feet, did not amount to a mere inconvenience but, rather, transformed the contract into something totally different than what the parties intended.

[29] Accordingly, I would dismiss this appeal.

QUESTIONS AND NOTES

1. Does the judgment in *KBK No. 138 Ventures* acknowledge the same concerns as the judgment in *Amalgamated Investment*? Can the cases be distinguished?

2. To what extent could the solution in this case be regarded as a simple question of the interpretation of the contract and the identification of the allocation of the risks made by the parties? What is it that triggers a concern for "frustration" as opposed to, say, the purchaser's unwillingness to pay the price after the extraordinary intervention by the city?

3. Contracts to rent rooms to view coronation processions are rare. (Queen Victoria ascended the throne and was crowned in 1837, and she died in 1901; most of those who would have watched her son's (cancelled) coronation would not even have been born when she was crowned.) Contracts to sell land are common. To what extent do these facts force the courts to adopt a different form of reasoning in the two classes of case? Is there any evidence of the expectations of those engaged in the business of buying and selling land for development?

4. If the decision whether or not a contract is frustrated is an allocation of the risk of loss arising from the happening of an unexpected event, it follows that a "self-induced" frustration cannot operate to put the risk of loss on the party not causing the loss. In other words, if the music hall in *Taylor v. Caldwell* had been burnt down by the fault of the owner, could he have claimed to be excused from his obligation to make it available to the other party?

   The simple proposition that frustration does not apply if it is self-induced sometimes runs into difficulties. Consider the following problem:

   > Owner has two ships registered in Vancouver under the *Canada Shipping Act*. The ships are chartered to Margaret and Maureen respectively. The Canadian government, acting under statutory authority, tells Owner that one of his ships is to be requisitioned, but that he can nominate the one to be taken. The nomination will frustrate the charter in each case. If the owner nominates the ship chartered to Margaret can she sue?

   Would it make any difference if the owner was operating one of the ships himself and nominated the other one?

Difficult problems similar to frustration arise when courts deal with domestic contracts between spouses who are separating or divorcing. In these separation agreements, usually negotiated with legal advice and the pending threat of litigation, separated spouses often settle all outstanding matters between them, such as dividing property, dealing with custody of and access to children and child support, and resolving issues of spousal support.

Sometimes separation agreements have contractual variation clauses, dealing with one or more issues in the agreement, such as an arbitration clause to alter access to children, or a price inflation clause for amounts of monthly support, but some agreements have no variation clause or provide only very narrow grounds for variation.

These agreements deal with the most significant issues in the spouses' lives, and are often the most important contracts that the parties will enter into in their lives. The courts do not want lightly to interfere with separation agreements, as they wish to promote finality and allow people to get on with their lives. But courts also recognize that the circumstances of individuals may change dramatically after the agreements are made.

There has been a great deal of litigation about when and how courts should allow variation in the absence of contractual provisions. In regard to child-related issues, including custody, access and child support, the courts have consistently held that they can vary any provision to promote "the best interests of the child".

Wilson J. in the Supreme Court of Canada in 1987 held that when dealing with the issue of spousal support under the *Divorce Act*, R.S.C. 1985, c. 3 (2nd Supp.), judges could override the spousal support provisions of a separation agreement, but only if there was a "radical change in circumstances, causally connected to the marriage": *Pelech v. Pelech*, [1987] 1 S.C.R. 801, 38 D.L.R. (4th) 641. This type of narrow judicial approach often worked to the disadvantage of women, who most frequently sought variation if they were unable to achieve or maintain the economic circumstances that they hoped for or expected. The "causal connection test" of *Pelech* was heavily criticized, especially by feminist scholars; see, e.g., C.J. Rogerson, "The Causal Connection Test in Spousal Support Law" (1989), 8 *Can. J. Fam. L.* 95.

In *Miglin v. Miglin*, [2003] S.C.J. No. 21, [2003] 1 S.C.R. 303, 34 R.F.L. (5th) 255, the Supreme Court of Canada revisited the question of what effect should be given to the spousal provisions of a separation agreement. The Court recognized that the courts should scrutinize the circumstances in which a domestic contract was negotiated and executed. The doctrine of unconscionability, considered in Chapter 6, has an important role in family law cases, and can be invoked to challenge any of the provisions of a separation agreement, including those that deal with property issues. A consideration of unconscionability and the circumstances of formation of a domestic contract is likely to occur if a spouse was vulnerable when the agreement was signed, for example, due to spousal abuse or a lack of independent legal advice. However, the Court acknowledged (at para. 82) that competent "professional assistance received by the parties will often overcome any systemic imbalances between the parties".

Beyond situations of unconscionability and cases where the circumstances of execution of the agreement should be used to invalidate an agreement, the Supreme Court recognized a continuing jurisdiction under the *Divorce Act* to vary spousal support provisions of a separation agreement "if parties ... find themselves down the road of their post-divorce life in circumstances not contemplated". Thus, even if an agreement provides that monthly amounts of spousal support will be payable only for a limited period of time, a judge could override those provisions of the agreement. This was the very issue in *Miglin*, where the agreement provided for monthly payments of spousal support to the former wife for five years, after which time it was expected that she would become self-supporting. In fact, in *Miglin*, the former wife, who had given up work to look after the children of the marriage, was still not employed five years after the agreement was executed. The Supreme Court reversed the trial judge and the Ontario Court of Appeal, and upheld the provisions of this agreement that limited support. Bastarache and Arbour JJ., writing for a majority of the Court, articulated when the Court should override the spousal support provisions of an agreement (at paras. 88-91):

> The parties' intentions, as reflected by the agreement, are the backdrop against which the court must consider whether the situation of the parties at the time of the application makes it no longer appropriate to accord the agreement conclusive weight. We note that it is unlikely that the court will be persuaded to disregard the agreement in its entirety but for a significant change in the parties' circumstances from what could reasonably be anticipated at the time of negotiation. Although the change need not be "radically unforeseen", and the applicant need not demonstrate a causal connection to the marriage, the applicant must nevertheless clearly show that, in light of the new circumstances, the terms of the agreement no longer reflect the parties' intentions at the time of execution and the objectives of the Act. Accordingly, it will be necessary to show that these new circumstances were not reasonably anticipated by the parties, and have led to a situation that cannot be condoned.

> We stress that a certain degree of change is foreseeable most of the time. The prospective nature of these agreements cannot be lost on the parties and they must be presumed to be aware that the future is, to a greater or lesser extent, uncertain. It will be unconvincing, for example, to tell a judge that an agreement never contem-

plated that the job market might change, or that parenting responsibilities under an agreement might be somewhat more onerous than imagined, or that a transition into the workforce might be challenging. Negotiating parties should know that each person's health cannot be guaranteed as a constant. An agreement must also contemplate, for example, that the relative values of assets in a property division will not necessarily remain the same. Housing prices may rise or fall. A business may take a downturn or become more profitable. Moreover, some changes may be caused or provoked by the parties themselves. A party may remarry or decide not to work. Where the parties have demonstrated their intention to release one another from all claims to spousal support, changes of this nature are unlikely to be considered sufficient to justify dispensing with that declared intention.... The test here is not strict foreseeability; a thorough review of case law leaves virtually no change entirely unforeseeable. The question, rather, is the extent to which the unimpeachably negotiated agreement can be said to have contemplated the situation before the court at the time of the application.

...

Although we recognize the unique nature of separation agreements and their differences from commercial contracts, they are contracts nonetheless. Parties must take responsibility for the contract they execute as well as for their own lives. It is only where the current circumstances represent a significant departure from the range of reasonable outcomes anticipated by the parties, in a manner that puts them at odds with the objectives of the Act, that the court may be persuaded to give the agreement little weight.

The decision produced a vigorous dissent by LeBel and Deschamps JJ., and academic critics have argued that the majority approach fails to take sufficient account of the familial and gendered context of separation agreements, and that "certainty, finality and autonomy are emphasized to the detriment of fairness" Carol Rogerson, *"Miglin v. Miglin*: They Are Agreements Nonetheless" (2003), 20 *Can J. Fam. L.* 197. The decision in *Miglin* clearly gives judges broader discretion to vary support provisions than under the earlier decisions like *Pelech.* Does the approach give judges a wider discretion to deal with changes in circumstances when dealing with spousal support under the *Divorce Act* than when they are dealing with commercial contracts and the doctrine of frustration? Is a difference in approach justified?

If you were representing a wealthy spouse who wished to settle a claim for spousal support (as well as other issues) after a long "traditional marriage", what kind of variation clause would you want? What if you were representing the wife in a 20-year marriage who stayed home to raise three children, and now hopes to go back to university to gain employment? Would you want the variation clause to deal with the possibility of the woman cohabiting with another man?

The next case illustrates a common problem and the need for the doctrine of frustration to be carefully applied; a simple decision that a contract is frustrated may not be responsive to the issues that have to be resolved.

H.R. & S. SAINSBURY LTD. v. STREET

[1972] 3 All E.R. 1126, [1972] 1 W.L.R. 834
(Q.B., MacKenna J.)

[The defendant was a farmer and the plaintiff was a grain dealer. The defendant had planted barley on his land. Before the harvest came in, the parties entered a contract with the intent that the defendant would sell his entire crop to the plaintiff. They estimated that the yield would be 1.5 tons per acre. Since the defendant had 182 arable acres, the parties estimated that he would have 275 tons for sale. On 1 July 1970, the parties signed the plaintiff's standard contract, under which the defendant agreed to sell "about 275 tons" of barley from his farm to the plaintiff at the price of £20 per ton. That year the harvest in England and the United States was poor and throughout July and August the price of barley was rising rapidly. As a result of the bad weather, the defendant's total crop only came to 140 tons.

The defendant did not sell his crop to the plaintiff. He sold 100 tons to another grain dealer for £27.5 per ton, keeping about 40 tons for himself. The plaintiff bought barley against the contract at £30 per ton, and sued the defendant for breach of contract.]

MACKENNA J. [after stating the facts, continued: —] [1] . . . I am prepared to assume, consistently with the plaintiffs' abandonment of their claim for damages for the tonnage not in fact produced, that it was an implied condition of the contract that if the defendant, through no fault of his, failed to produce the stipulated tonnage of his growing crop, he should not be required to pay damages. It seems a very reasonable condition, considering the risks of agriculture and the fact that the crop was at the contract date still growing. But a condition that he need not deliver any if, through some misfortune, he could not deliver the whole is a very different one, and in my opinion so unreasonable that I would not imply it unless compelled to do so by authority. The way in which the parties chose the more or less conventional figure of [1.5 tons] per acre as the estimated yield of the crop is, I think, an additional reason in this case against the implication. If they had intended that a failure to achieve this optimistic tonnage would mean the end of the contract for both of them, they would have gone about the business of estimating the yield in a much more cautious manner. Counsel for the defendant argued that it was reasonable that the defendant should be freed of all his obligations under the contract if without his fault he failed to produce the whole tonnage. 275 tons (5 per cent more or less) set an upper limit to the quantity which the plaintiffs could be compelled to take. It was reasonable, he said, that there should be a lower limit to the amount which the defendant could be compelled to deliver. In a year when the defendant's yield was high market prices would probably be low and it would be a benefit to the plaintiffs not to be required to take more than an agreed tonnage at the contract price fixed in advance. In a year when the yield was low, as in the present case, it would be a benefit to the defendant if he were free to disregard his contract and to sell his crop to some other buyer at the higher market price. The contract should, if possible, be construed as giving him this freedom. I am not persuaded by the argument. The upper limit of 275 tons might in the circumstances of a particular case be beneficial to both parties. But even if it could be beneficial only to the buyer that is no reason for implying a term that the same figure shall serve as a lower limit to the seller's obligation to deliver, so that his failure to reach that figure, if blameless, would release him from the contract.

[MACKENNA J. first considered *Howell v. Coupland* (1876), 1 Q.B.D. 258. In that case, the defendant, a farmer, had promised before the harvest to sell his crop of potatoes to the plaintiff. When the contract was made the estimated crop was 200 tons but only 80 tons were produced. The plaintiff sued for damages for breach of contract. The court held that the farmer was excused from any obligation to deliver more than the land had produced. The judge next referred to the *Sale of Goods Act*, which in s. 5(2) provides that "there may be a contract for the sale of goods, the acquisition of which by the seller depends upon a contingency which may or may not happen." Sections 6 and 7, dealing with the destruction of existing goods, were held to be inapplicable to a contract to sell growing crops. In any case, the act preserved the common law, so that if it did not apply, the common law would. A third reference was to *Barrow, Lane & Ballard Ltd. v. Phillip Phillips & Co. Ltd.*, [1929] 1 K.B. 574, where the amount of goods that the buyer had agreed to buy was (unknown to the parties) more than the amount of goods available to be sold. The buyer was held to be discharged in this event. MACKENNA J. continued:]

[2]   . . . The condition which excuses the defendant can be cast either in the form of a condition precedent to the existence of an obligation to deliver, or in the form of a condition subsequent to the existence of such an obligation determining the same, without affecting the substance of the matter. "He shall be under an obligation to deliver in the future if he produces. . ." would be in form a condition precedent. "He is under an obligation to deliver in the future but that obligation shall be discharged if he does not produce . . ." would be in form a condition subsequent. The difference is a matter of words, not of substance. . . . For this reason I should not wish to rest anything, in this case at least, on the distinction between the two kinds of condition.

[3]   . . . What is said in this passage about the presumed intention of the parties seems to me very relevant in determining what condition shall be implied. It should be a condition which will give effect to the presumed intention of reasonable men. In the case which [*Benjamin on Sale*, 7th ed. (1931), pp. 156-57] supposes, it would be unreasonable to compel the buyer to accept delivery of the odd volume. This difficulty could be met in one of two ways, either by implying a condition in cases of that kind that the contract shall be wholly discharged, or by implying a condition in such cases, or indeed in all cases when the seller is excused, that the buyer shall have an option of accepting part delivery. The United States *Sales Act* cited in *Williston on Sales* [rev. ed. (1948)] expressly allows the buyer, in case of deterioration or partial destruction of the subject-matter of a sale or contract to sell, to require such performance as remains possible.

[4]   So much for the authorities, which do not, I think, oblige me to decide this case in the defendant's favour. Therefore my judgment will be for the plaintiffs for £1,050.

NOTE AND QUESTIONS

1.   MacKenna J. refers to the U.S. *Sales Act* (actually the *Uniform Sales Act* of 1906) and to *Williston on Sales* (1948). The provisions of that Act have been replaced by the following provision of the *Uniform Commercial Code*:

   § 2-615. Except so far as a seller may have assumed a greater obligation and subject to the preceding section on substituted performance:

   (a) Delay in delivery or non-delivery in whole or in part by a seller who complies with paragraphs (b) and (c) is not a breach of his duty under a contract of sale if performance as agreed has been made impracticable by the occurrence of a contingency the non-occurrence of which was a basic assumption on which the contract was made or by compliance in good faith with any applicable foreign or domestic governmental regulation or order whether or not it later proves to be invalid.

(b)   Where the causes mentioned in paragraph (a) affect only a part of the seller's capacity to perform, he must allocate production and deliveries among his customers but may include regular customers not then under contract as well as his own requirements for further manufacture. He may so allocate in any manner which is fair and reasonable.

(c)   The seller must notify the buyer seasonably that there will be a delay or non-delivery and, when allocation is required under paragraph (b), of the estimated quota thus made available for the buyer.

The *Uniform Commercial Code* is an attempt to balance the claims of buyers and sellers.

2.   The result in *Sainsbury v. Street* and the cases cited there seems to give the seller the worst of both worlds. Since the seller has less than the contract amount to deliver, the buyer has no obligation to buy, but the seller is obliged to deliver all that he has grown and has no power to allocate the production among any of his regular customers or to retain any part of it for his own use.

3.   Consider carefully the economics of the relation created in *Sainsbury v. Street*. Suppose that the farmer and the agent of the buyer had thought about the allocation of the crop between them in the event that it was less than expected, where would they have found the typical provisions of any arrangement that they might have made? Why is there no evidence of the commercial background to what must be a common transaction? Which is more likely to be faithful to that background, the decision in the case or the *Uniform Commercial Code* rules?

4.   The parties in *Sainsbury* agreed that damages should be assessed at £1,050, being £7.5 multiplied by 140, the farmer's gain from breaching the contract. It is not clear from the report why this restitutionary measure was chosen, though it might have represented the seller's expectation interest as being the difference between the contract and market price at the date of breach.

The contracts we have so far examined have largely been executory, that is, neither side has paid the full price nor completely performed its part of the bargain. (In *KBK No. 138 Ventures Ltd. v. Canada Safeway Ltd.*, the purchaser had paid a deposit that the decision of the court gave back to it.) Where the relation is discrete and one side has fully performed, there are serious problems if a court decides that a contract has been frustrated.

As the next case discloses, saying that frustration results in a contract coming to "an end" can create awkward problems.

FIBROSA SPOLKA AKCYJNA v. FAIRBAIRN LAWSON COMBE BARBOUR LTD.

[1943] A.C. 32, [1942] 2 All E.R. 122
(H.L., Viscount Simon L.C., Lords Atkin, Russell, Macmillan, Wright, Roche and Porter)

[The appellants, a Polish company, agreed by a contract dated 12 July 1939 to purchase from the respondents certain machinery that was to be delivered to Poland. The appellants paid a deposit of £1,000. When war was declared between Great Britain and Germany, the appellant's agents asked for the return of the deposit on the ground that performance of the contract was now impossible. The respondents refused on the ground that they had done considerable work on the machinery. They also argued that, the contract being frustrated, the loss should lie where it fell. The trial judge dismissed the action, and his decision was upheld by the Court of Appeal.]

LORD WRIGHT: — **[1]** My Lords, the claim in the action was to recover a prepayment of £1,000 made on account of the price under a contract which had been frustrated. The claim was for money paid for a consideration which had failed. It is clear that any civilized system of law is bound to provide remedies for cases of what has been called unjust enrichment or unjust benefit, that is, to prevent a man from retaining the money of or some benefit derived from another which it is against conscience that he should keep. Such remedies in English law are generically different from remedies in contract or in tort, and are now recognized to fall within a third category of the common law which has been called quasi-contract or restitution. . . .

[2]   By 1760 actions for money had and received had increased in number and variety. Lord Mansfield C.J., in a familiar passage in *Moses v. Macferlan* [(1760), 97 E.R. 676, 2 Burr. 1005], sought to rationalize the action for money had and received, and illustrated it by some typical instances. "It lies," he said, "for money paid by mistake; or upon a consideration which happens to fail; or for money got through imposition (express, or implied;) or extortion; or oppression; or an undue advantage taken of the plaintiff's situation, contrary to laws made for the protection of persons under those circumstances. In one word, the gist of this kind of action is, that the defendant, upon the circumstances of the case, is obliged by the ties of natural justice and equity to refund the money." Lord Mansfield prefaced this pronouncement by observations which are to be noted. "If the defendant be under an obligation from the ties of natural justice, to refund; the law implies a debt and gives this action [*indebitatus assumpsit*] founded in the equity of the plaintiff's case, as it were, upon a contract ("*quasi ex contractu*" as the Roman law expresses it)." Lord Mansfield does not say that the law implies a promise. The law implies a debt or obligation which is a different thing. In fact, he denies that there is a contract; the obligation is as efficacious as if it were upon a contract. The obligation is a creation of the law, just as much as an obligation in tort. The obligation belongs to a third class, distinct from either contract or tort, though it resembles contract rather than tort. This statement of Lord Mansfield has been the basis of the modern law of quasi-contract, notwithstanding the criticisms which have been launched against it. Like all large generalizations, it has needed and received qualifications in practice . . . The standard of what is against conscience in this context has become more or less canalized or defined, but in substance the juristic concept remains as Lord Mansfield left it. . . .

[3]   Must, then, the court stay its hand in what would otherwise appear to be an ordinary case for the repayment of money paid in advance on account of the purchase price under a contract for the sale of goods merely because the contract has become impossible of performance and the consideration has failed for that reason? The defendant has the plaintiff's money. There was no intention to enrich him in the events which happened. No doubt, when money is paid under a contract it can only be claimed back as for failure of consideration where the contract is terminated as to the future. Characteristic instances are where it is dissolved by frustration or impossibility or by the contract becoming abortive for any reason not involving fault on the part of the plaintiff where the consideration, if entire, has entirely failed, or where, if it is severable, it has entirely failed as to the severable residue . . . The claim for repayment is not based on the contract which is dissolved on the frustration but on the fact that the defendant has received the money and has on the events which have supervened no right to keep it. The same event which automatically renders performance of the consideration for the payment impossible, not only terminates the contract as to the future, but terminates the right of the payee to retain the money which he has received only on the terms of the contract performance. . . .

[4]   It is clear that the failure of consideration need not be attributable to breach of contract or misconduct on the part of the defendant, as the cases I have cited and many others show. Impossibility of performance or frustration is only a particular type of circumstance in which a party who is disabled from performing his contract is entitled to say that the contract is terminated as to the future, and in which repayment of money paid on account of performance may be demanded.

[5]   These principles, however, only apply where the payment is not of such a character that by the express or implied terms of the contract it is irrecoverable even though the consideration fails. The contract may exclude the repayment. . . .

[6]   [I]n *Chandler v. Webster*, [1904] 1 K.B. 493 [one of the "Coronation cases", where part payment had been made by the plaintiff under the contract that he had made with the defendant to view the processions], Collins M.R. discussed the matter more elaborately, but he still ignored the principles and authorities on the action for money had and received to which I have referred, though the claim was to recover as on a total failure of consideration. He indeed discussed the case from that point of view. The hirer was claiming to recover what he had paid in advance and was resisting a counterclaim for the balance which was by the contract payable before the date when the procession became impossible. He ought, in my opinion, to have succeeded on both issues, but by the judgment of the Court of Appeal he failed on both. The reasoning of the Master of the Rolls may, I think, fairly be summarized to be that impossibility through the fault of neither party leaves the parties where they were but relieves them from further performance, and that it is only if the contract is wiped out altogether that money paid under it would have to be repaid as on a failure of consideration, but that the only effect of impossibility is to release the parties from further performance. The rule, he said, is arbitrary, but it is really impossible to work or adjust with any exactitude what the rights of the parties in the event should be. I hesitate to criticize the ruling of so great a lawyer as the Master of the Rolls, but I cannot concur in these propositions. I need scarcely repeat my reasons for doing so, which are apparent from what I have already said. The claim for money had and received is not, in my opinion, a claim for further performance of the contract. It is a claim outside the contract. If the parties are left where they are, one feature of the position is that the one who has received the prepayment is left in possession of a sum of money which belongs to the other. The frustration does not change the property in the money, nor is the contract wiped out altogether, but only the future performance. . . . No one who reads the reported cases can ignore how inveterate is this theory or explanation in English law. I do not see any objection to this mode of expression so long as it is understood that what is implied is what the court thinks the parties ought to have agreed on the basis of what is fair and reasonable, not what as individuals they would or might have agreed. "It is," said Lord Sumner, "irrespective of the individuals concerned, their temperaments and failings, their interest and circum-

stances." The court is thus taken to assume the role of the reasonable man, and decides what the reasonable man would regard as just on the facts of the case. The hypothetical "reasonable man" is personified by the court itself. It is the court which decides. The position is thus somewhat like the position in the cases in which the court imports a term in a contract on the basis of what is reasonable. As frustration is automatic, so equally the claim for money had and received here follows automatically.

[7] [*Chandler v. Webster* should be overruled.] In my judgment the appeal should be allowed.

[Only the judgment of **LORD WRIGHT** is reproduced here. The other judges all wrote judgments agreeing in allowing the appeal.]

NOTES

1. War is invariably regarded by the courts as a frustrating event if the hostilities prevent performance. Even though when the contract in *Fibrosa* was made in July 1939, the outbreak of war was not unexpected, this did not affect how the courts assessed the event.

2. While the judgment in *Fibrosa* articulates important equitable or restitutionary principles and is frequently cited when courts are dealing with restitutionary remedies (for example in *Deglman v. Guaranty Trust* in Chapter 2), the "equities" of the case do not all point in the same direction. Lord Wright completely ignores the claim of the respondent to some reimbursement for the work that it did on the machinery. The result of *Fibrosa* was to attach a somewhat artificial meaning to the word "unjust" in the phrase "unjust enrichment". It may be true that, on the reasoning of Lord Wright, there can be no *contractual* claim by the respondent to keep the deposit, but that argument does not dispose of the issues raised by the case.

3. As evidence of the validity of this criticism, the United Kingdom Parliament enacted legislation in 1943 to partially reverse the effect of the decision in *Fibrosa*. That legislation formed the basis for the legislation enacted in all common law provinces except Nova Scotia.

   The Ontario Act is reproduced in part here.

FRUSTRATED CONTRACTS ACT

R.S.O. 1990, c. F.34

1. In this Act,

"contract" includes a contract to which the Crown is a party;

"court" means the court or arbitrator by or before whom a matter falls to be determined;

"discharged" means relieved from further performance of the contract.

2(1) This Act applies to any contract that is governed by the law of Ontario and that has become impossible of performance or been otherwise frustrated and to the parties which for that reason have been discharged.

(2) This Act does not apply,

(a) to a charterparty or a contract for the carriage of goods by sea, except a time charterparty or a charterparty by way of demise;

(b) to a contract of insurance; or

(c) to a contract for the sale of specific goods where the goods, without the knowledge of the seller, have perished at the time the contract was made, or where the goods, without any fault on the part of the seller or buyer, perished before the risk passed to the buyer.

3(1) The sums paid or payable to a party in pursuance of a contract before the parties were discharged,

(a) in the case of sums paid, are recoverable from the party as money received for the use of the party by whom the sums were paid; and

(b) in the case of sums payable, cease to be payable.

(2) If, before the parties were discharged, the party to whom the sums were paid or payable incurred expenses in connection with the performance of the contract, the court, if it considers it just to do so having regard to all the circumstances, may allow the party to retain or to recover, as the case may be, the whole or any part of the sums paid or payable not exceeding the amount of the expenses, and, without restricting the generality of the foregoing, the court, in estimating the amount of the expenses, may include such sum as appears to be reasonable in respect of overhead expenses and in respect of any work or services performed personally by the party incurring the expenses.

(3) If, before the parties were discharged, any of them has, by reason of anything done by any other party in connection with the performance of the contract, obtained a valuable benefit other than a payment of money, the court, if it considers it just to do so having regard to all the circumstances, may allow the other party to recover from the party benefited the whole or any part of the value of the benefit.

QUESTION AND NOTE

1. To what extent would the adoption of the legislation change the result in any of the cases we have looked at?

2. While the Ontario Act is clearly an improvement over *Fibrosa Spolka*, it is unsatisfactory in a number of respects; see discussion, *e.g.*, in Ontario Law Reform Commission, *Report on Amendment of the Law of Contract* (1987), 14. As a result, the Uniform Law Commission wrote a second *Uniform Frustrated Contracts Act* in 1974 (the first was in 1948 and was based on the 1944 English statute). This *Uniform Act* was modelled on legislation in British Columbia, and has now been enacted in the Yukon, and in modified form in Saskatchewan.

   The provisions of the British Columbia *Frustrated Contract Act*, R.S.B.C. 1996, c. 166, and the second *Uniform Frustrated Contracts Act* differ from the statute adopted in Ontario and most other provinces in three significant ways. First, there is a right to restitutionary relief if a benefit has been conferred prior to the frustrating event, rather than making this relief discretionary. Second, there is a loss apportionment scheme to deal with cases where the expenditures of one party have not resulted in a gain to the other party, or alternatively where the gain has been destroyed by the frustrating event. This is achieved by defining "benefit", as used in s. 3(3) of the Ontario Act, to "mean something done in the fulfillment of contractual obligations, whether or not the person for whose benefit it was done received the benefit". Third, the second *Uniform Act* provides that recovery may be denied in any case where the course of prior dealing or trade custom indicates that the party which incurred the expenditures should "bear the risk" of that loss. This would, for example, apply in a case where the prior course of dealing reveals that the party incurring the expenditures would normally have obtained insurance that would cover the situation of frustration.

THIRD PARTIES AND MISTAKES

The "mistake" analysis of *Bell v. Lever Brothers* has also been applied to a number of cases requiring the courts to decide which of two innocent parties should bear the cost of a loss from contracts entered into a result of "mistaken" beliefs induced by the fraudulent acts of a third party.

The common feature of these cases is that one person, sometimes referred to as the "rogue", induces another person to contract with him. That other person has the mistaken belief, carefully induced by the rogue, that he is dealing with an honest person. There are two general kinds of situations that fall into this category. In the first situation, the rogue induces a person to "buy" a chattel that the rogue has obtained from another innocent party by means of fraud. The litigation arises when the original owner seeks to recover the goods from the innocent purchaser. In the second situation the rogue induces the other person to sign a document, the full impact of which the signer does not understand, and the rogue then uses the document to gain something from another innocent party. The problem arises when the party who has relied on the signed document tries to enforce his claim against the other innocent party.

In the first situation, the original owner of the chattel will have been induced to part with it by the rogue's statement that he is someone who can be trusted. The rogue may have produced stolen or counterfeit identification papers to induce the owner to accept a cheque that later bounces. By the time the initial owner discovers the fraud, the rogue has sold the goods to the innocent third party. A "mistake" argument can be based on what Lord Atkin said in *Bell v. Lever Brothers* to invalidate the first contract and have the goods returned to the original owner. Lord Atkin said that where a person, A, makes a contract with B thinking that he is C, there is no contract; A's consent is said to be "negatived". The difficulty with this analysis is that the innocent purchaser, the person who bought the chattel from the rogue, B, also has an argument to claim the protection of the law.

In some older cases, the courts relied on *Bell v. Lever Brothers* to develop a distinction based on whether the original owner made a mistake as to "identity" as opposed to "attributes". If the court concluded that the initial owner, A, contracted with the rogue B thinking that he was C, there would be no valid initial contract and the initial owner recovers. However, if the court concluded that A made a mistake about the attributes of B, for example believing that B was an honest person with sufficient resources to pay for the goods, there would be a valid contract and the innocent purchaser from the rogue gets to keep the goods. If the sale to the innocent party was made before the contract was set aside by A, *i.e.*, before the first contract was nullified by a court order, then the rogue could pass good title to the chattel to the innocent party. The right to have a contract that is induced by fraud avoided — that is, to have a voidable contract made void — was protected by the equitable remedy of rescission. But equity would not threaten the right of a *bona fide* third-party purchaser for value without notice of the fraud. Equity therefore provided significant protection to the innocent party in a situation where the original contract was only voidable, *i.e.*, where the owner had made a mistake as to the "attributes" of the rogue.

There are a large number of these cases, and they are impossible to reconcile. The law has to determine which of two innocent people will suffer for the fraud of another. A focus on the belief of only one of them is bound to be inadequate.

A number of cases after *Bell* analyzed this situation in a similar fashion to tort cases: on whom should the loss fall, given that the defrauded seller can more easily protect him or herself than can the innocent purchaser? These decisions rejected an analysis based on *Bell v. Lever Brothers* and adopted an analysis based on the proposition that the loss should fall on the person who could most easily and cheaply have protected him or herself. This person will usually be the original owner. After all, no one ever has to take anything other than cash before giving up possession of a chattel. Most notable among the cases adopting this analysis was *Lewis v. Averay*, [1972] 1 Q.B. 198, [1971] 3 All E.R. 907 (C.A.). Lord Denning M.R. dismissed the claim of the original owner and protected the innocent purchaser even though there was a mistake as to the "identity" of the rogue since he had produced false identification papers. This decision abolished the distinction between mistakes as to "identity" as opposed to "attributes" in the situation where the owner sells goods to a rogue who then sells to an innocent third party.

Lewis v. Averay was overruled by the House of Lords in *Shogun Finance Ltd. v. Hudson*, [2004] 1 A.C. 919, and the old rule, laid down in *Cundy v. Lindsay* (1878), 3 App. Cas. 459, that the risk is always on the innocent purchaser was reinstated. The decision was by a closely divided court and is unlikely to be followed by Canadian courts. In any case, the very different regimes for dealing with security interests in personal property in Canada and England make the incidence of the problems very different in the two countries.

The second class of cases has bothered common lawyers for a long time. In the Middle Ages, when the bulk of the population could not read, the signer of a document might have been led to believe that he was signing something different from what he was actually signing. The defence of the mistaken signer who was sued on the document was to plead that the document was not his deed. The signer would say, in Latin of course: *Haec scriptum non est factum meum* — "This writing is not my deed." The defence is now generally referred to as that of *non est factum*.

At common law, a defence based on *non est factum*, if established, made the deed void. This result would have the same effect on the rights of those who had relied on the document as if the contract for the sale of the chattel to the rogue were held to be void, *i.e.*, third parties could take no rights under the document. The law of *non est factum* has gone through a significant change. The most recent case in the Supreme Court of Canada on this issue is reproduced here, and the nature of the changes can be seen. As you read the case, consider how useful an analogy it offers for the sensible treatment of the cases in which a chattel is obtained by fraud.

In all of these cases the person who was guilty of fraud can, of course, be sued for damages for deceit or for rescission. The practical difficulty is that rogues have usually disappeared, are penniless, or are languishing in prison with no assets.

MARVCO COLOR RESEARCH LTD. v. HARRIS

[1982] S.C.J. No. 98, [1982] 2 S.C.R. 774, 141 D.L.R. (3d) 577
(S.C.C., Laskin C.J.C., Ritchie, Dickson, Estey and Lamer JJ.)

[The plaintiff sold its business to Johnston and Suwald. Suwald and Johnston gave the plaintiff a chattel mortgage to secure their obligation to it. Johnston, who was living with the defendants' daughter, wanted to purchase Suwald's interest. The defendants were prepared to give Johnston limited help in this transaction. The defendants agreed to sign a mortgage in favour of the Bank of Montreal for $15,000; the Bank then loaned Johnston $15,000, so that he could buy Suwald's interest. However, as a condition of selling his interest to Johnston, Suwald also required Johnston to have the plaintiff cancel his debt. The plaintiff was only willing to release Suwald if Johnston could find another creditworthy guarantor, like the defendants, but Johnston did not ask them if they were willing to undertake this larger obligation — $55,000. Rather, after having the defendants sign the $15,000 mortgage to the Bank of Montreal — an obligation they knowingly assumed — Johnston put documents in front of them that were a mortgage and guarantee for $55,000 in favour of the plaintiff. He told them that the documents were part of the mortgage transaction with the Bank for $15,000. The defendants did not read the documents but rather relied on Johnston, and signed the documents out of love for their daughter. Accordingly, they executed a guarantee in favour of the plaintiff for about $55,000, in addition to the mortgage to the Bank for $15,000 that they knowingly signed. Unfortunately, the defendants were victims of Johnston's deception. Johnston defaulted on all obligations, and was bankrupt and imprisoned.

The plaintiff brought an action on the personal covenant in the mortgage for $55,000. The defendants pleaded *non est factum*. The trial judge, Grange J., dismissed the action. This decision was upheld by the Ontario Court of Appeal in a short oral judgment. The plaintiff appealed.]

The judgment of the court was given by **ESTEY J.**: — **[1]** . . . The mortgage in favour of the Bank of Montreal has been paid off and the only issue arising on this appeal concerns the mortgage which is the subject of the action, and in that connection this issue was put by the appellant: "Is the defence of *non est factum* available to a party who, knowing that a document has legal effect, carelessly fails to read the document thereby permitting a third party to perpetrate a fraud on another innocent party?" This issue turns on the decision of this Court in *Prudential Trust Co. Ltd. v. Cugnet*, [1956] S.C.R. 914, 5 D.L.R. (2d) 1, a four-to-one decision. The majority, applying the decision of the English Court of Appeal in *Carlisle & Cumberland Banking Co. v. Bragg*, [1911] 1 K.B. 489, found that where a document was executed as a result of a misrepresentation as to its nature and character and not merely its contents the defendant was entitled to raise the plea of *non est factum* on basis that his mind at the time of the execution of the document did not follow his hand. In such a circumstance the document was void *ab initio*. So went the judgment of Nolan J. with whom Taschereau and Fauteux JJ., as they then were, concurred. Locke J. reached the same result, but added the following comment at p. 929 [S.C.R., p. 4 D.L.R.] on the effect of careless conduct on the ability of the defendant to raise the plea of *non est factum*:

> It is my opinion that the result of the authorities was correctly stated in the *Bragg's* case. To say that a person may be estopped by careless conduct such as that in the present case, when the instrument is not negotiable, is to assert the existence of some

duty on the part of the person owing to the public at large, or to other persons unknown to him who might suffer damage by acting upon the instrument on the footing that it is valid in the hands of the holder. I do not consider that the authorities
support the view that there is any such general duty, the breach of which imposes a
liability in negligence.

[2] Cartwright J., as he then was, dissented. His Lordship commenced with a
recitation of the general proprieties (932 S.C.R., 7 D.L.R.):

> . . . [G]enerally speaking, a person who executes a document without taking the
> trouble to read it is liable on it and cannot plead that he mistook its contents, at all
> events, as against a person who acting in good faith in the ordinary course of busi-
> ness has changed his position in reliance on such document.

and then moved to the exception arising under the principle of *non est factum*.
After making reference to *Carlisle v. Bragg, supra*, His Lordship said (934 S.C.R.,
9 D.L.R.):

> An anxious consideration of all the authorities referred to by counsel and in the
> Courts below has brought me to the conclusion that, in so far as *Carlisle v. Bragg*
> decides that the rule that negligence excludes a plea of *non est factum* is limited to
> the case of negotiable instruments and does not extend to a deed such as the one be-
> fore us, we should refuse to follow it.

[3] He concluded, therefore, that any person who fails to exercise reasonable
care in signing a document is precluded from relying on the plea of *non est factum*
as against a person who relies upon that document in good faith and for value.

[4] As the basis for the judgments of Justice Nolan, concurred in by two other
members of the court, and of Justice Locke was the judgment of the Court of Appeal of England in *Carlisle v. Bragg, supra*, it should be pointed out at once that
case has been overruled by the House of Lords in *Saunders v. Anglia Building
Society*, [1971] A.C. 1004, [1971] 2 All E.R. 322 (H.L.).

[5] The doctrine of *non est factum* sprang into prominence with the judgment in
Foster v. Mackinnon (1869), L.R. 4 C.P. 704.

[6] The decision of the Court of Appeal in *Carlisle v. Bragg* may be summarized as follows:

(1) *Foster v. Mackinnon* applies only to bills of exchange.

(2) Negligence on the part of the signor is therefore relevant only to bills of
exchange.

(3) Negligence is used in the tortious sense, and therefore, only when a duty
of care exists in the signor and his act is the proximate cause of the loss
by the third party, can it be a bar to a successful plea of *non est factum*.

(4) In all other cases negligence is irrelevant, and *non est factum* may be
pleaded where the document signed is of a different nature from that
which the signor intended to execute: *vide Chitty on Contracts* 18th ed.
(1930) at 803, and Anson *Law of Contracts* 14th ed. (1917) at 164.

Carlisle v. Bragg has attracted unfavourable comment in legal writings. . . .

[7] Although the decision in *Carlisle v. Bragg* was the subject of much criticism, it was adopted by the majority of this court in *Prudential Trust Co. Ltd. v.*

Cugnet, supra. As previously mentioned, Cartwright J. in his dissenting judgment recognized the flaws in the Court of Appeal's decision and refused to follow it, adopting instead the rule recognized prior to *Carlisle v. Bragg* that a person who was negligent in executing a written instrument, whether or not it was a bill of exchange, was estopped, as against an innocent transferee, from denying the validity of the document. He also recognized that negligence in the sense that the term was used in relation to the plea of *non est factum* connoted carelessness, rather than the attributes of the term in the law of tort. . . .

[8]   It was not until *Saunders v. Anglia Building Society, supra*, that the law was put back to the position which it was in after *Foster v. Mackinnon*. It is interesting to note that in doing so all the judges dealt with the meaning of the word negligence as employed by the court in *Foster v. Mackinnon* as meaning "carelessness" in the same way that Cartwright J. did in *Prudential, supra*. Thus the rule with reference to *non est factum* in the United Kingdom requires that the defendant be not guilty of carelessness in order to be entitled to raise the defence of *non est factum*. . . .

[9]   In my view, with all due respect to those who have expressed views to the contrary, the dissenting view of Cartwright J. (as he then was) in *Prudential, supra*, correctly enunciated the principles of the law of *non est factum*. In the result the defendants-respondents are barred by reason of their carelessness from pleading that their minds did not follow their hands when executing the mortgage so as to be able to plead that the mortgage is not binding upon them. The rationale of the rule is simple and clear. As between an innocent party (the appellant) and the respondents, the law must take into account the fact that the appellant was completely innocent of any negligence, carelessness or wrongdoing, whereas the respondents by their careless conduct have made it possible for the wrongdoers to inflict a loss. As between the appellant and the respondents, simple justice requires that the party, who by the application of reasonable care was in a position to avoid a loss to any of the parties, should bear any loss that results when the only alternative available to the courts would be to place the loss upon the innocent appellant. In the final analysis, therefore, the question raised cannot be put more aptly than in the words of Cartwright J. in *Prudential, supra*, at 929 S.C.R., 5 D.L.R.: ". . . which of two innocent parties is to suffer for the fraud of a third." The two parties are innocent in the sense that they were not guilty of wrongdoing as against any other person, but as between the two innocent parties there remains a distinction significant in the law, namely, that the respondents, by their carelessness, have exposed the innocent appellant to risk of loss, and even though no duty in law was owed by the respondents to the appellant to safeguard the appellant from such loss, nonetheless the law must take this discarded opportunity into account.

[10]   In my view, this is so for the compelling reason that in this case, and no doubt generally in similar cases, the respondents' carelessness is but another description of a state of mind into which the respondents have fallen because of their determination to assist themselves and/or a third party for whom the transaction has been entered into in the first place. Here the respondents apparently sought to attain some advantage indirectly for their daughter by assisting Johnston in his commercial venture. In the *Saunders* case, *supra*, the aunt set out to apply her property for the benefit of her nephew. In both cases the carelessness took the form of a failure to determine the nature of the document the respective defendants

were executing. Whether the carelessness stemmed from an enthusiasm for their immediate purpose or from a confidence in the intended beneficiary to save them harmless matters not. This may explain the origin of the careless state of mind but is not a factor limiting the operation of the principle of *non est factum* and its application. The defendants, in executing the security without the simple precaution of ascertaining its nature in fact and in law, have nonetheless taken an intended and deliberate step in signing the document and have caused it to be legally binding upon themselves. In the words of *Foster v. Mackinnon* this negligence, even though it may have sprung from good intentions, precludes the defendants in this circumstance from disowning the document, that is to say, from pleading that their minds did not follow their respective hands when signing the document and hence that no document in law was executed by them.

[11] This principle of law is based not only upon the principle of placing the loss on the person guilty of carelessness, but also upon a recognition of the need for certainty and security in commerce.

[12] I wish only to add that the application of the principle that carelessness will disentitle a party to the document of the right to disown the document in law must depend upon the circumstances of each case. This has been said throughout the judgments written on the principle of *non est factum* from the earliest times. The magnitude and extent of the carelessness, the circumstances which may have contributed to such carelessness, and all other circumstances must be taken into account in each case before a court may determine whether estoppel shall arise in the defendant so as to prevent the raising of this defence. The policy considerations inherent in the plea of *non est factum* were well stated by Lord Wilberforce in his judgment in *Saunders, supra*, at 1023-24:

> The law . . . has two conflicting objectives: relief to a signer whose consent is genuinely lacking . . . protection to innocent third parties who have acted upon an apparently regular and properly executed document. Because each of these factors may involve questions of degree or shading any rule of law must represent a compromise and must allow to the court some flexibility in application.

[13] The result in this case has depended upon the intervention by this court in the development of the principle of *non est factum* and its invocation in a way inconsistent with that applied many years ago in the *Prudential* case, *supra*. The respondents have pleaded their case in the courts below and in this court consistent with the result in the *Prudential* judgment. In these circumstances consideration can and should be given to the application of the general principle that costs follow the event. The appellant, of course, was required to persevere to the level of this court in order to bring about the review of the reasoning which led to the determination in the *Prudential* case. The respondents, on the other hand, acted reasonably in founding their position upon that decision notwithstanding the revision of the law of England consequent upon the judgments in *Saunders*. In all these circumstances, therefore, I would award to the appellant costs only before the court of first instance with no costs being awarded either party in the Court of Appeal or in this court.

QUESTIONS AND NOTES

1.   Did the Ontario Court of Appeal do what it should have done in the case?

2.   What message does the decision on the issue of costs give to subsequent litigants? Should this message be given by the Supreme Court of Canada?

3.   What should a provincial court of appeal do with a contracts decision or, indeed, with any decision of the Supreme Court, that it feels was wrongly decided and that it believes is likely to be reversed by the Supreme Court when it is reconsidered by it? Does the answer to this question depend on the likelihood that the Supreme Court will give leave to appeal? Does the answer depend on the likelihood that the particular parties before it have or have not adequate resources to meet the costs of an appeal? Does the refusal of the Supreme Court to give reasons for denying leave to appeal bear on these questions?

4.   In *Saunders v. Anglia Building Society*, [1971] A.C. 1004, [1971] 2 All E.R. 322 (H.L.), a 78-year-old woman whose glasses were broken relied on her nephew and his friend to explain documents to her that she signed. The House of Lords held that she could not rely on the defence of *non est factum* to defeat the claim of an innocent third party who had relied on the document that she signed. Lord Wilberforce noted that it is a "rare" case in which an adult who is literate will be able to rely on *non est factum* against a third party, if the person has chosen not to read the document he or she signed. Even for those who are "illiterate or blind", the law "ought only to give relief if satisfied that consent was truly lacking but will require of signers even in this class that they act responsibly and carefully according to their circumstances in putting their signatures to legal documents".

5.   Owner carelessly leaves his goods outside where they are stolen. The thief sells the goods to an innocent third party who has no notice of the theft. The law is that the owner can recover against the innocent third party. How is this situation to be distinguished from *Marvco*?

CHAPTER SIX

THE CONTROL OF CONTRACT POWER

INTRODUCTION

These materials have repeatedly stressed the importance of contractual relations to the economic and social structure of Canadian society, and the fact that the law of contracts reflects both fundamental societal values and concerns about economic efficiency.

In this chapter, the focus is more explicitly on the values implicit and explicitly found in the law of contracts, and the value choices to be made by lawyers and judges. Ultimately the law can only be understood by considering carefully its purposes and values. What makes the law interesting, and the roles of lawyers and judges difficult, is that there are often no easy answers to the conflicts in values that arise. The question is not one of choosing a single value, but of making a hard choice between two (and sometimes more) strongly competing values.

In considering the role of values in the law of contracts, four major concepts should be kept in mind: the first two of these relate to the values of the law of contract: freedom of contract and the protection of reasonable expectations. The second two are of special concern to lawyers and to the way that they understand the law of contracts, relational contracts and the role of lawyers.

Freedom of contract: Fuller ("Consideration and Form," *supra*, Chapter 2) pointed out that one of the purposes of the enforcement of promises is the realization of the principle of individual autonomy. Individual autonomy translates into claims that the right of parties to make contracts with each other is an aspect of individual liberty. How much weight should be given to freedom of contract when it is realized that the freedom of one party may be the negation of the freedom of the other? The issue of judicial intervention to prevent exploitation was raised when the doctrine of economic duress and its judicial antecedents were considered in *The Port Caledonia* and *D. & C. Builders* in Chapter 2. This chapter will further explore when and how the courts or legislatures should be concerned about contractual power being used to exploit the vulnerable in society.

Good faith and the protection of reasonable expectations: These two concepts are among the most powerful ideas for dealing with the problems of contracts. Their use as tools for the resolution of contract problems lies, almost paradoxically, in their ability to be simultaneously capable of providing broad and general standards of conduct and highly individualized solutions to particular issues. We shall explore their contribution to an analysis of the issues in this chapter, and the limits upon it.

Relational contracts: Almost from the beginning of our examination of the problems of contracts we have seen the importance of relational contracts. Because many of the traditional common law rules of contract law are premised on the discrete exchange transaction, relational contracts have caused special problems. Relational contracts pose special problems in providing satisfactory remedies for breach, in the applicability of the rules of consideration, and in determining the content of the arrangement that the parties have made. In this chapter we will explore how relational contracts present difficult problems in controlling the power that they confer on one party (and occasionally on both parties). This result follows from the fact that relational contracts often create an intense dependence of one side on the other. As Macneil points out (*supra*, Chapter 5), relational contracts possess some of the features of political organizations. They are structures for co-operation, and as such they may last for a long time and require from both parties a large, shared investment in the common enterprise. Protecting one party from exploitation by the other is far more challenging than the provision of measures to protect the consumer in the "ordinary" lop-sided deal between a merchant and a consumer.

Marriages and other long-term cohabiting relations are consensual relations with high degrees of interdependence that have some contractual aspects. Though the study of these familial issues is beyond the scope of this book, some of the themes of a Contracts course may find some resonance in the study of Family Law, with the law protecting reasonable expectations and vulnerabilities.

The role of lawyers: Throughout this book there has been an emphasis on the role of the lawyer in the planning of contractual relations. This chapter continues to explore the contribution that lawyers can make to the sensible solution of contract problems. It also examines the guidance that the law gives to the lawyer and the difficulties the lawyer faces in planning the affairs of clients. While much of the material in this chapter is comprised of judgments decided by the courts — suggesting an emphasis on the role of the barrister — in the notes and comments, this chapter again attempts to present a more balanced, realistic view of the operation of the law and of the work that lawyers actually do in negotiating and planning.

Freedom of Contract

The extracts reproduced here illustrate the nature of the claims made in the name of "freedom of contract". The first view expresses a nineteenth-century judicial articulation of freedom of contract in terms that are almost a caricature of the present doctrine.

> [I]f there is one thing which more than another public policy requires it is that men of full age and competent understanding shall have the utmost liberty of contracting, and that their contracts when entered into freely and voluntarily should be held sacred.

(Jessel M.R. in *Printing & Numerical Registering Co. v. Sampson* (1875), L.R. 19 Eq. 462 at 465.)

This view of Jessel M.R. is not even a fully accurate statement of the law when it was made. (The scope of the doctrine depended on the meaning to be given to the words "freely and voluntarily"; even in 1875 the courts had given those words a potentially "controllable" meaning. The courts had, for example, accepted such defences to the strict enforcement of contractual rights as duress, undue influence and frustration.) However, this view of contract was widely accepted as the correct place to begin thinking about contracts problems in the nineteenth century.

Another more modern view of the meaning of freedom of contract recognizes that contracting occurs in the context of an existing economic, social and legal framework which affects and constrains any contractual relation. This extract is taken from a review by Mensch of Atiyah's *The Rise and Fall of Freedom of Contract* (Oxford: The Clarendon Press, 1979). It is a small sample of a large literature on the historical and philosophical development of ideas of freedom of contract.

B. MENSCH, "FREEDOM OF CONTRACT AS IDEOLOGY"

(1981), 33 *Stan. L. Rev.* 753 (excerpt)

[1]   But the free will contradiction appears deeper than the problem of formal rules; ultimately, it impeaches the coherence of the free value-enhancing exchange mechanism. In theory, exchanges are a function of autonomous will, not legal force: While state control is required to secure *future* performance, a present exchange of goods or promises is a pure expression of voluntarism. In turn, this expression of voluntarism required intelligible legal rules to separate free bargains from those formed under fraud, duress, or undue influence. Dawson's brilliant essay ["Duress — An Essay in Perspective" (1947), 45 Mich. L. Rev. 253] convincingly demonstrated, however, that a natural separation simply does not exist. Instead, the legal boundary identifying freedom is a function of legal decision-making, and has varied over the course of history.

[2]   In particular, it has arbitrarily excluded economic pressure from the legal definition of duress. That exclusion concealed the fact that coercion, including legal coercion, lies at the heart of *every* bargain. Coercion is inherent in each party's legally protected threat to withhold what is owned. The right to withhold creates the right to force submission to one's own terms. Since ownership is a function of legal entitlement, every bargain (and, taken collectively, the "natural" market price) is a function of the legal order — including legal decisions about whether and to what extent bargained-for advantages should be protected as rights. It is therefore wrong to dissociate private bargaining from legal decision-making: The results of the former are a function of the latter. This conclusion dissolves the theoretical distinctions between public and private spheres, and between free and regulated markets. Since the inner sphere of free bargaining and the outer framework of fixed rules collapse into each other, the problem of state coercion in the ideal of free contract is not simply a messy inconvenience caused by temporal change; it is a problem deep in the core of the ideology itself. The assumption that the state was not implicated in the outcomes of free market bargaining was *never* true — a quite different point from saying . . . that it is *no longer* true.

[3]   Still, the image of the autonomous bargainer was a powerful one, profoundly believed in by those who added to its credibility by constructing around it the elaborate structure of contract law. There may be reasons in concrete experience that made this particular myth more credible in the early nineteenth century than it is today. Nevertheless, the problem of contradiction undercuts the conclusion that legal doctrine mirrored reality and progressively served its needs. The legal myth was too obviously only an ideological myth. If the free contract ideal seemed to

accurately reflect life under capitalism, that is surely in large part attributable to the power of the ideology, rather than to the accuracy of the reflected image.

It may be widely accepted that the use of exchanges and contractual arrangements is a good, or at least a defensible, method of providing for the satisfaction of basic human necessities and that economic and "efficiency" arguments are relevant to an analysis of contracts: it does not follow that contractual arrangements and efficiency arguments are appropriate to all situations or transactions. There are, for example, ethical and social policy concerns about exchange transactions involving drugs, babies, human organs for transplant or even sexual services. These types of transactions do occur, and different countries have different attitudes towards them. For example, in Canada, prostitution is not itself illegal, though many aspects of the "sex trade" are prohibited. Also, in Canada, a donor of an organ, such as a kidney, cannot be paid, but in some other countries the sale of kidneys and other organs is legal. While commercial surrogate motherhood contracts are illegal or at least unenforceable in Canada and in many jurisdictions, they are legal in some American states. A "contractual analysis" may be of very limited value for deciding whether to allow these types of relations.

Just because an economist can discuss the effects, advantages and disadvantages of markets for babies, human bodily organs or anything else, it does not mean that these kinds of relations are necessarily part of every study of the law of contracts. A discussion of the limits to contractual freedom on ethical and social policy grounds, economic issues, and moral and ethical questions that need to be considered are usefully collected in Michael Trebilcock, *The Limits of Freedom of Contract* (Cambridge & London: Harvard University Press, 1993).

The following extract is a feminist commentary that deals with freedom of contract and the limitations of an economic analysis of contractual relations.

WANDA A. WEIGERS, "ECONOMIC ANALYSIS OF LAW AND 'PRIVATE ORDERING': A FEMINIST CRITIQUE"

(1992), 42 *U.T.L.J.* 170

[Footnotes omitted.]

III   *The Paretian Framework of Exchange*

[1]   The primary goal or concern of welfare economics is allocative efficiency or the distribution of resources to their most highly "valued" uses. The concept of efficiency most relevant to individual exchanges in a market context is Pareto efficiency. A policy, decision, or transaction is Pareto optimal (and resources are allocated efficiently) if no one can be made any better off without making another worse off. A policy, decision, or transaction that generates losses for one or more parties may still constitute a potential Pareto improvement if those who benefit from the policy or decision can hypothetically compensate the losers and still be better off. Since a Pareto-optimal outcome can by hypothesis only make people better off, the standard of Pareto efficiency is presumed by many to be ethically and politically uncontroversial. In this part, I examine and challenge certain assumptions and conditions underlying the Paretian framework of exchange as it

applies to disempowered groups such as women. I argue that the legal economist's exclusive focus on efficiency and reliance on market exchange as an indicator of social welfare obscures and validates the conditions and effects of social inequality.

[2]   Neoclassical economics in both its positive and normative uses relies upon several basic assumptions about human behaviour: that individuals have autonomous and stable preferences, that they are motivated to maximize their self-interest or satisfaction, and that they act rationally in doing so, given their preferences. Pareto efficiency is closely linked to the use of markets primarily because a perfectly competitive market can be shown in economic theory to produce a Pareto-efficient allocation of resources. In a perfectly competitive market, all resources are being used where their value as registered in the market is greatest, no further mutually beneficial trades are possible, and goods are being produced at minimum average long-run cost. For economists, the model of the competitive market is "the benchmark against which the performance of all real-world institutions should be measured." Legal economists view legal rules as a means of inducing behaviour that would be consistent with the conditions or outcomes of a competitive market (for example, by reducing transaction costs) where real markets fail to conform to the competitive model because of conditions such as imperfect information or externalities.

[3]   According to Michael Trebilcock ["Economic Analysis of Law" in Richard F. Devlin, *Canadian Perspectives on Legal Theory* (Toronto: Edmond Montgomery, 1991], neoclassical economists generally "attach strong normative value to regimes of private exchange and private ordering" relative to collective decision-making because the former is believed to provide the most accurate revelation of preferences. Since individual utility functions are not directly observable, this "predilection for private ordering" is based upon the simple premise that parties who voluntarily trade do so because they perceive themselves as being better off. The normative criterion of Pareto efficiency is premised on the assumptions that social welfare is a product of the welfare of individuals and that the individual is the best judge of his or her well-being. The assumption that individual preferences as revealed through the process of exchange correspond to enhanced well-being thus grounds the more far-reaching normative claim that markets generally promote aggregate social welfare and that refusal to permit and respect an exchange results in a welfare loss. Some political economists also regard market ordering as most compatible with the value of individual autonomy "because it minimizes the extent to which individuals are subjected to externally imposed forms of coercion or socially ordained forms of status. Private ordering is the quintessential form of government with the consent of the governed.

[4]   James Boyd White ["Economics and Law: Two Cultures in Tension" (1986), 54 *Tenn. L. Rev.* 161, 171] argues that the economic approach to social welfare destroys the possibility of making meaningful ethical distinctions. In attaching normative significance only to the expression of preferences, normative economic theory abstracts from the cultural, historical, and socio-economic context of agents and reduces all issues of value, principle, and need to quantifiable units that can be registered on a single scale. On such premises, entry into a contract to sell oneself into slavery or to sell bodily organs, as expressions of preference, can be no more morally problematic than entry into a contract to buy invest-

ment bonds. Within the economic model, there is no way of understanding or evaluating the profoundly different meaning and importance of a person's choices in the context of his or her life. Thus any attempt to distinguish between feminist objections to commodification and the moral majoritarian position on abortion or between feminist objections to pornography and moral majoritarian objections to unmarried cohabitation can only be regarded as arbitrary discrimination between preferences. Economic theory provides no basis upon which to exclude or discount any preferences, even those that are parasitic on past or present structures of domination.

[5]   The "real story" of gender relations — of women's subordination to men — has often been described in terms of an exchange. Through marriage, women have exchanged sexual access to their bodies, their reproductive capacity, household services, and often their wage labour for physical and economic security from men. Viewing marriage as a "bargain," however, tends falsely to imply that women got what they "bargained for" rather than what they were forced to live with. The "guarantee of lifelong security" for married women has often meant a subsistence income or less and also physical violence if not death. The concept of "bargain" also implies that women were "free" and equal parties to such arrangements. But if many, if not most, women have married for economic security rather than for love, they have done so because they have had few alternative means of support. Moreover, women have not been equal participants in fashioning or determining the limited set of life options and alternatives available to them.

[6]   Historically, women's response to male dominance in Western societies has included active resistance, submission, and collaboration. If consent is defined only in terms of rational, deliberate choice, women could be said to have largely "consented" to their subordinate social roles. Whether these choices were voluntary or free, however, depends upon the conditions under which choice was exercised. The consent, submission, or accommodation by women to a system of male dominance has been secured through a number of means including physical force, socialization, a lack of education and economic alternatives, and economic incentives, as well as through the stigma and physical danger facing non-conforming women. Only by ignoring such factors could women's submission to a social structure that was systematically unfair and exploitative be described as a Pareto-superior if not Pareto-optimal move.

[7]   In practice, market methodology tends implicitly to assume that unless patently coerced or directly constrained, the choices made by parties to an exchange are equally voluntary and autonomous. In ignoring the "different degrees and kinds of freedom" under which choices are made, such a method is unable to address the social context of inequity that both directly and indirectly constrains and systematically structures choice. The legal economist's reliance on willingness to pay as a measure of the "value" attached to a "voluntary" exchange abstracts from the obvious constraints related to an unequal distribution of wealth. The assumption that workers "freely choose" their working conditions under capitalism also obscures the fact that workers have no claim to or control over the means or processes of production or the product of their labour that they must sell in order to subsist.

[8]   Market methodology will likewise tend to obscure the extent to which women's choices reflect a "structured inequality of life conditions." Thus, Richard

Posner's description of the traditional sexual division of labour as a voluntary and efficient exchange ignores entrenched barriers to the equal participation of women in the workplace, such as unequal pay, sex discrimination, and a sex-segregated labour market, as well as the refusal of men and male-dominated institutions to accommodate, support, and perform child care. Posner's analysis not only obscures the extent to which choice is structured by such factors, but simultaneously validates and reinforces market outcomes by presenting them as consensual or as the result of "free" choice. In his analysis, choice plays a legitimizing role in rendering market outcomes fair, acceptable, or deserved.

[9] Elizabeth Anderson ["Values, Risks and Market Norms" (1988), 17 *Phil. & Pub. Affairs* 59] argues that "revealed preference theory can make claims only about what people choose, not about how they view their choices". Any attempt to understand human action must deal with the perspectives of agents themselves and with complex contextual factors including real and perceived constraints, the role of responsibility to others, and the social relations in which choice occurs. Robin West ["Authority, Autonomy and Choices: The Role of Consent in the Moral and Political Visions of Franz Kafka and Richard Posner" (1985), 99 *Harv. L. Rev.* 384] contrasts Posnerian economics with the nightmarish world of Kafka and argues that isolating entry into a contract as the only relevant moment of "choice" ignores the complex psychological motivations or desires of subjects and the actual consequences of their "choices." A commitment to "private" ordering as presumptively welfare maximizing does not allow for the possibility of mistake, regret, or ambivalence. People may "consent" to transactions out of a desire or a need to obey authority rather than to increase their well-being or autonomy. According to West, Posner "defines the problem of victimization out of existence." Victims cannot exist because they are presumed to have enhanced their welfare or to have consented to risk. Anderson notes that circumstances such as isolation and social inequality can undermine an individual's ability to choose and result in self-blame, fatalism, conditioned subservience, a tendency to defer to the judgment of others, and a fear of making just demands.

[10] In another context, West has argued that the assumed correlation between consent and well-being or autonomy is empirically more false for women as a group than for men. According to West, women "consent to increase the pleasure or satisfy the desires of others" for reasons that include an attempt to control danger or suppress the pervasive fear of male violence. Other writers have noted that women have traditionally been expected to give the interests of others greater weight than their own interests or to further the interests of others at the expense of their own. I am not suggesting that men as individuals are incapable of altruism or have never been altruistic, nor that women's happiness is not intimately connected to the happiness of others. However, men have never been expected to adhere to a morality of self-sacrifice simply on account of their gender. For some women, by contrast, self-sacrifice or self-denial remans a "way of life" and a "consistent duty." Women who have internalized this role have been and are particularly vulnerable to exploitation.

[11] It has been argued that prospective birth mothers, for example, offer little resistance to exploitation by private surrogacy agencies. Most mothers claim to be motivated at least in part by "altruistic" feelings towards the adoptive parents. Surrogacy agencies allegedly manipulate such "altruistic" motivations to gain favourable terms for their clients. Agencies screen mothers for deference and submissiveness, stress the importance of acts of love and generosity, and intimidate them by challenging their sense of morality. According to Elizabeth Anderson, "the model of altruism which is held up to women in the industry" is one of self-sacrifice and self-effacement, involving the subordination of their interests to those of the adoptive parents. Some feminists have also questioned the degree to which such an agreement fosters personal autonomy if autonomy is defined in a more positive sense as enablement, competence, or self-development. Standard contractual provisions permit or require extensive monitoring of the birth mother's conduct during pregnancy, her subjection to all prescribed medical orders including medication and surgery, and the subordination of all other interests including her job, travel plans, and recreational activities for the sake of producing a child for the adoptive parents.

[12] Related concerns arise with respect to the binding impact of separation agreements. One strain of feminist thought is supportive of mediation as a more participatory alternative to an abstract, adversarial, and inflexible process of formal adjudication. However, others have argued that women as a group will likely be relatively disadvantaged by the trend towards divorce mediation and the binding impact of separation agreements, given the power imbalances that now exist between men and women as groups. Because of socialization, women may tend to be submissive or to undervalue our contribution and fail to insist upon a fair share. Because we are typically the primary child rearers, women may also feel compelled to sacrifice a fair return in order to secure an agreement granting them custody of and maintenance for their children. Some feminists have suggested that the closed and confidential nature of mediation amounts to a "re-privatization" of the family, leaving "women subject to the prevailing values of a patriarchal culture" but in a context where such values are no longer open to external scrutiny and challenge.

[13] Paying attention to the context of inequality inevitably complicates the general claim that voluntary exchange enhances individual welfare. Ascertaining whether these exchanges are voluntary involves a counter-factual inquiry into whether the exchange would increase the well-being of women in the absence of coercion. The definition of coercion (or what constitutes a fair context for choice) is a normative judgment of an explicitly political, ethical, and distributive nature. Admittedly, in the absence of widespread restructuring and redistribution of opportunities, women's entry into the types of agreements canvassed may well reflect a realistic assessment of their welfare *given* their constraints. To an indeterminate degree, however, these agreements may also reflect a failure to take women's own needs seriously that is a predictable outcome of entrenched patterns of socialization and a pervasive ideology of male supremacy. The assumption that exchange increases welfare also ignores the possibility that many women might simply prefer to foreclose certain options, particularly ones that may require the sacrifice of their own interests in order to ensure the economic welfare of dependents. Women may wish to avoid altogether feeling pressured to "rent out" their bodies as a way of earning money for their dependents or feeling compelled in circumstances of unequal bargaining power to discount their just economic claims upon divorce. In the contexts I have addressed, the possibility of exchange will not alleviate the underlying structural conditions that shape and perpetuate women's inequality. Indeed, women's entry into these contracts may well be perceived as an accep-

tance of their fairness or as a legitimate reason to do nothing to address the conditions in which choice is exercised. One concern with validating prostitution as an occupation, for example, is that women will then be viewed as having "freely" chosen it, rendering less visible the social conditions that make prostitution a palatable choice for many women. To the extent that prostitution is seen as a legitimate choice, women on welfare and unemployment insurance may also be encouraged or required to turn to it.

[14] Neoclassical economics ignores the question of the just organization and distribution of power and wealth in society. Economists readily acknowledge that the results of "voluntary" Pareto exchanges depend upon a predetermined distribution of endowments that are not necessarily just or equitable. However, the question of the just distribution of wealth or endowments is typically considered either irrelevant to questions of efficiency, reflecting the assumption that the Paretian framework of exchange is not dependent upon resolution of the complex ethical and distributive issues I have raised, or simply beyond the expertise of the economist. Numerous critics have questioned the appropriateness of a measure of "value" that is based on an unjust distribution of wealth or on a distribution that may not serve to maximize welfare. If issues of distribution are broached at all in economic analysis, they are typically discussed in terms of the "efficiency costs" of implementing distributive change. Such a framework of analysis tends to privilege the existing distribution of wealth and power by virtue of what it systematically omits and excludes from extensive study — namely, the benefits of a more egalitarian distribution, the real social costs of present inequalities, and the values (like the desire for community, creative work, and so forth) that are not monetizable and cannot be directly registered in a market. What many might describe as an ideological tilt is a basic conceptual feature of the discipline.

[15] According to Duncan Kennedy ["Distributive and Paternalistic Motives in Contract and Tort Law" (1982), 41 *Md. L. Rev.* 563], the apparent neutrality of the Pareto criterion of efficiency — its concern for making everyone better off and no one worse off — serves to mediate and defuse the conflict that is inherent in an unequal distribution of power. The attempt to attach normative significance to choice without regard to its social context can systematically obscure and impair our understanding of the conditions and pervasive effects of social inequality. The economist's exclusive focus on efficiency can "sub silentio" powerfully legitimize the status quo.

NOTE

One class of contracts — the domestic contract — merits special mention, as the courts do take at least some account of the social, emotional and relational aspects of these contracts. Even here, notions of freedom of contract are important.

A study of domestic contracts is beyond the scope of this book and requires separate study, especially to understand the need to protect those who may be subject to exploitation or domination — most frequently women, who are often socially, economically or psychologically disadvantaged in comparison to their partners. Recent developments in family law and changes in patterns of family living have made marriage contracts, cohabitation agreements and separation agreements very important. For both parties to the relation, the consequences of the deal that they make can be both serious and persistent: it is likely the most important contract they will ever sign. As a consequence of the tendency of lawyers and judges dealing with any kind of agreement to apply the general law of contracts to questions arising under them, there are important issues of how far general contracts rules should be applied in domestic contracts, particularly to enforce against a woman the terms of a contract that may operate in ways that she had not foreseen and which are not responsive to her needs. The range of choices that are available to deal with this problem are limited, in large part because of the influence of either the classical Western idea of the individual as free to make choices for herself or the (both older and newer) idea that cultural conditioning may significantly impair the individual's ability to make decisions that will be in her best interest in the long term.

Canadian courts have accepted that parents cannot make binding agreements about the care or support of their children, as there is always a continuing judicial jurisdiction to set aside provisions of a domestic contract that are not in the "best interests" of children. Further, courts have a somewhat broader range of supervisory powers when dealing with spousal support provisions of a domestic contract than for ordinary consumer or commercial contracts. In particular, there may be circumstances in which a court will intervene to override provisions of an agreement that make inadequate provisions for the support of a dependent spouse after separation. However, in *Hartshorne v. Hartshorne*, [2004] S.C.J. No. 20, [2004] 1 S.C.R. 550 and *Miglin v. Miglin*, [2003] S.C.J. No. 21, [2003] 1 S.C.R 303, 224 D.L.R. (4th) 193, the Supreme Court held that, if the parties have independent legal advice when entering a domestic contract, the judicial authority to override a waiver or limitation of spousal support is narrow. In *Miglin*, the majority judgement of Arbour and Bastarache JJ. endorsed the importance of freedom of contract in the domestic sphere, and cautioned against "unduly interfering with agreements freely entered into and on which the parties reasonably expected to rely" (para. 45). As discussed later in this chapter, any contract may be set aside if it is "unconscionable" (or very unfair), and there continues to be a significant amount of litigation about whether individual domestic contracts are unconscionable, especially if they are entered into by persons who are in an emotionally vulnerable condition. Further, *Hartshorne* and *Miglin* recognize the "unique environment" in which domestic contracts are negotiated and give courts a jurisdiction to override spousal support provisions that are considered unfair, even if they do not meet the common law test of "unconscionability". See discussion in Martha Bailey, "Marriage à la carte: A Comment on *Hartshorne v. Hartshorne*" (2004), 20 *Can. J. Fam. L.* 249-259; and Martha Shaffer, "Domestic Contracts, Part II: The Supreme Court's Decision in *Hartshorne v. Hartshorne*" (2004) 20 *Can. J. Fam. L.* 261-289.This chapter considers some aspects of the special nature of contracts involving spouses and other family members, especially in the context of the enforceability of loan guarantees.

In an important sense the notion of freedom of contract has had a broader and more subtle influence on the law than these extracts might suggest. Freedom of contract is an aspect of the ideology of contracts that forms a basis for many of the traditional rules of contract law, such as those governing formation expressed in the rules of offer and acceptance, and the rules about consideration. The model of contracting that underlies the traditional rules is based on the assumption that *all* contracts are discrete contracts — a relation created for one transaction that has neither history nor future, and that is lacking in a social or economic context. The parties are assumed to make their agreement on a clean slate and, at the end of the deal, to go their separate ways. They are also assumed to be autonomous, capable of protecting their interests, and able to choose when "freely and voluntarily" to enter into contracts.

In this chapter, where the focus is on judicial control over contract power, relatively few of the cases involve discrete transactions, like the sale of land. Most contracts have significant relational elements. Consumer contracts may tend towards the discrete end of the spectrum, but it would be a short-sighted merchant who ignored the possibility of repeat business. Much of modern advertising is designed to foster a sense of loyalty to brand names or to particular stores, banks, or insurance companies.

When pushed, the courts take account of the fact that relations of dependence exist and that they may have to be protected, as they are, for example, in *Lac Minerals Ltd. v. International Corona Resources Ltd.* (*supra*, Chapter 3), and in many of the cases in this chapter. The development of more useful rules requires that the model of contracts come closer to the reality of the economic and social relations that it reflects. This task is one that can only be accomplished over the long term and by those who have a clear idea of the role of alternative models of contracting in the development of the law. Keep these questions and issues in mind as you study the materials in this chapter.

1. What should be the role of consent and the intention of the parties in the modern world of contracting? What kind of consent should be shown to have existed in what kind of contract? Is the consent required in an individually negotiated deal the same as that required in a standardized transaction where, as with so many modern contracts, the terms are offered on a take-it-or-leave-it basis?

2. The classical model of contracts assumed a world of small, autonomous traders. How can one accommodate a world of huge corporations linked with others in a network of associated corporations with assets of billions of dollars?

3. What about a situation in which the use of a contractual relation as opposed, for example, to vertical or horizontal corporate integration in an industry is a matter of institutional design? What is the point of being concerned with any undesirable feature of the contractual relation if the relation can be transformed into something that is not a contractual relation — at least in the sense that the law on it would be found in the "Contracts" section of the *Canadian Abridgment* — but could instead be based on a corporation or a partnership? If the relation is not contractual, then devices to control it that are based on the law of contract will not work. The materials in this chapter briefly consider some of the issues that arise with the corporate form of business organization.

4. The classical view of contracts (and economics) assumed a world of more or less perfect competition. The economic analysis of the "evils" of monopoly powers and how they should be controlled is limited and controversial; many economists question whether monopolies are harmful to the economy, or argue that they can be controlled. How should the law of contract, which functions at the level of individual exchanges, deal with the situation where competition is significantly impaired by a structural (*i.e.*, long term) monopoly?

5. The theory of the corporation is that management functions as an agent of the shareholders and that all employees, from the president down, are agents of the corporation. How can we accommodate the reality, already observed by Macneil in *The New Social Contract* (1980) and by Galbraith, *The New Industrial State* (1967), that in many cases there is no true principal or owner? With ownership of the shares spread among many individuals, management may effectively control the corporation. The supposed agents may, in reality, be agents without principals. An agent without a principal operates without many of the constraints that one might assume would govern the agent. Such a

corporate manager functions more like a bureaucrat seeking to balance the claims of customers, employees, shareholders and even politicians, with the desire to protect his or her job, rather than as a participant in a process of economic exchange designed to maximize the financial return to the corporate principal. Or corporate managers may be seeking to enhance their own wealth and power, not only at the expense of employees and customers, but also at the expense of shareholders.

6. It is often suggested that the law of contract is "private law". In reality the distinction between "private law" and "public law" is often difficult to perceive and maintain. Almost every area of economic life is affected by government regulation: employment standards; consumer purchasing; landlord-tenant relations; hours of work; minimum wages; health and safety rules; standards of cleanliness and content in food; and extensive obligations of disclosure in many areas. The models of disclosure required under legislation like the *Securities Acts* of the various provinces provide the now expected pattern of disclosure in many commercial deals; this is a vivid example of the relation between "public" law standards and "private" law standards.

7. If it is decided to control the power of contract, who should exercise that power? Should it be the courts or some other governmental body — a licensing tribunal or an independent board or commission, for example? Each method of control has its special features that make it more or less appropriate to perform some particular task. Can a court, with its limited access to the social and economic context of a contract, and with the costs of supplying any necessary information to it borne directly by the parties, do an adequate job of controlling contractual power? Can the system of private litigation offer any realistic protection to consumers who have been treated unfairly in a large number of small deals?

8. As Mensch notes, an element of coercion lies at the heart of every bargain. This fact has usually been dealt with in one of three ways:

    (a) it is ignored: everyone is assumed to be competent to make such contracts as he or she sees fit to make;

    (b) certain classes of people are singled out for special protection. The principal identified classes now consist of "minors", *i.e.*, those under the age of majority, and consumers (Although there were at one time "protections" (or restrictions) on the capacity of married women to enter into enforceable contracts, these have been abolished by statute.); and

    (c) individual deals might be examined by the courts (or some other body) to see if they met some extra test of enforceability.

The primary focus of this chapter is on the third method, judicial scrutiny of individual contracts to determine their enforceability. It must, however, be appreciated that there is a great deal of statutory regulation of contract powers with legislation focused on specific types of transactions, such as employment relations, landlord-tenant relations, consumer sales and domestic contracts.

There are no easy answers to these questions (and there are many more that could be asked). These questions present for discussion some issues that are pervasive in the modern law of contract. The materials in this chapter address these questions, but the treatment given here is a mere introduction to complex and pervasive issues. It is important to address explicitly the underlying economic and social context within which the law of contract must function. Many of the almost unconscious responses that have been made to these issues — often taking the form of an almost wilful blindness to them — are bound up with ideas of "freedom of contract" and the role of individual autonomy. These unconscious or at least unarticulated responses form the basis for many of the decisions in this chapter.

The following section introduces the problems caused by the standard-form contract: the mass-produced arrangement that is so much a part of modern economic arrangements. One focus of inquiry will be the extent to which the notion that one of the functions of the law of contract is the protection of the parties' reasonable expectations is a helpful notion.

TECHNIQUES OF CONTROL

There are a number of techniques used by judges to control what they perceive as objectionable uses of contract power. The techniques include the methods that were considered earlier in these materials: broad (or narrow) interpretation of contractual provisions; the explicit control of unfairness through use of concepts like unconscionability and duress; and the limitation of the remedies for breach. The methods are sometimes expressly justified as devices to support control of contract power; sometimes the control is almost an incidental (though not necessarily an unconscious) consequence of the use of a particular interpretative approach.

The more open the court is about what it is doing, the more direction it gives to those who need guidance, and the more predictable its decisions will be. It does not, however, follow that any device used will be less effective in particular cases just because the courts do not clearly state the reasons for their interference. There are cases in which the court's stated reasons may not reflect the real justification for its interference.

Interference in a contractual arrangement is rarely costless. The courts impose costs not only on the parties, but also on others in similar situations. Too often the question of the costs of judicial interference are not directly acknowledged by the courts. It is important in each case to assess the costs as well as the benefits of judicial interference with contractual freedom. In some of the cases in these materials, you may conclude that the courts have not correctly balanced the costs and benefits of interference, and decide that they interfered when they should not have, or that they failed to intervene when they should have.

Interpretation

Some techniques used by courts in an attempt to protect reasonable expectations or control contractual power are fairly simple. For instance, a court can use the process of interpretation or construction of an agreement to expand obligations or to narrow the scope of exemptions. In *Fraser-Reid v. Droumtsekas* (*supra*, Chapter 5) the Supreme Court of Canada was faced with a situation in which a builder had built a new house that did not satisfy the requirements of the Building Code. As we saw, the Court was unwilling to create an implied warranty for new homes because of concerns about the effects that this might have on the housing market, and held that, absent an express warranty, the purchaser should get no relief. But this result was regarded by the Supreme Court as intolerable, for it would mean that the very person for whose protection the Building Code was enacted would get no protection from it. The Supreme Court, therefore, protected the purchasers' expectations by "finding" an express warranty that the Building Code would be complied with in the following words, which commonly appeared in standard form agreements for the purchase and sale of homes:

> Providing that the Vendor has disclosed to the Purchaser all outstanding infractions and orders requiring work to be done on the premises issued by any Municipal or Provincial or Federal Authority in respect of the premises referred to herein.

Before the Supreme Court interpreted the clause in this way, few solicitors, real estate agents, or builders thought that these words compromised the builder's basic common law, "no-warranty" position for newly constructed homes. Nevertheless, the Court was able to achieve the result it wanted by interpreting the words in this way. This decision imposed costs on the many builders who had this standard clause in their contracts; it may not be a coincidence that after the cause of action arose in *Fraser-Reid*, but before the case was decided by the Supreme Court, legislation was enacted to impose on all builders in the province the costs of failing to comply with the Building Code (the *Ontario Home Owners' Warranty Act*).

In *Wallis v. Pratt*, [1911] A.C. 394, the defendant sold seed to the plaintiff. The seed was described in the contract as "common English Sainfoin." The contract of sale contained a clause saying that "the seller gives no warranty express or implied as to growth, description or any other matter." The seed was accepted by the buyer but turned out to be the seed of a different plant. The buyer claimed damages for breach of contract. The House of Lords held that the exemption clause, because it used the word "warranty", did not apply to exclude the implied statutory "condition" of the *Sale of Goods Act*, *viz.*, that goods must correspond with their description. (See, e.g., Ontario *Sale of Goods Act*, s. 14). The buyer was able to recover for breach of the implied "condition" that the seeds would correspond to their description as "common English Sainfoin". (The distinction in the *Sale of Goods Act* between implied warranties and implied conditions was briefly examined in Chapter 5, *supra*.)

Similarly, judges have sometimes held that an exclusion of any "warranty or condition" does not avail a seller if there has been a "negligent misstatement"; see *Sodd Corp. v. Tessis* (1977), 17 O.R. (2d) 158 (C.A.). This technique of reading down the effect of a contractual clause allocating the risk of loss is obviously capable of rendering many exemption clauses ineffective.

A more general example of the same approach is the judicial hostility to attempts to obtain exemption from liability for negligence. In the absence of an explicit mention of negligence (or gross negligence), a judge is likely to find that exemption clauses do not exclude liability for negligence. Perhaps judges feel that since negligence requires fault, it is not proper that anyone should avoid liability when he or she has been guilty of fault.

Courts will sometimes refer to these approaches to interpretation as an application of interpretation *contra proferentem*, *i.e.*, an interpretation of the language of the contract against the interest of the party who drafted it. If, for example, there is any ambiguity in a clause, especially an exemption clause, it will be resolved against the party who drafted the clause and who is seeking to rely on it. This approach is justified on the basis that the party who drafted the contract could have avoided the ambiguity and, not having done so, should bear the risk of an unfavourable interpretation. In practice, however, the courts sometimes go quite far in finding ambiguity so that they can achieve a result that they want.

The approach of the minority in *Scott v. Wawanesa Insurance* (reproduced in Chapter 5, above) could be characterized as interpretation *contra proferentem*, *i.e.*, as putting on the insurer the risk that its desired interpretation of the clause in question will not be given effect because the insurer did not make clear to the insureds the risk that they ran by permitting their son to be an insured.

Inconsistency

Another technique that the courts sometimes use to achieve a desired result is to find that an exemption clause is inconsistent with other terms of the contract, and hence is ineffective.

In a number of cases the courts have held an exemption clause ineffective if, at the time the contract is made, an employee of the party seeking to rely on the clause has orally assured the other that he "does not have to worry" or that the clause is more limited in scope than it is intended to be. In *Mendelssohn v. Normand Ltd.*, [1970] 1 Q.B. 177, [1969] 2 All E.R. 1215 (C.A.), the plaintiff had parked his car, a Rolls Royce, in the defendant's garage. He wanted to lock his car but was told by the attendant that he could not do so. He told the attendant that there were valuables in the car. The attendant promised to lock up the car. The valuables disappeared. The contract contained two clauses: (i) that the defendant accepted no liability for loss and, (ii) that the terms could be varied only if the variance was in writing and signed by the defendant's manager. Lord Denning found no problem in holding the defendant liable:

> [The plaintiff] relies on the conversation which Mr. Mendelssohn had with the attendant. The man promised to lock up the car. In other words, he promised to see that the contents were safe. He did not do so. Instead he left the car unlocked. It was probably he who took the suitcase himself. What is the effect of such a promise? It was not within the *actual* authority of the attendant to give it but it was within his *ostensible* authority. He was there to receive cars on behalf of the garage company. He had apparent authority to make a statement relating to its custody. Such a statement is binding on the company. It takes priority over any printed condition. There are many cases in the books when a man has made, by word of mouth, a promise or a representation of fact, on which the other party acts by entering into the contract. In all such cases the man is not allowed to repudiate his representation by reference to a printed condition . . . nor is he allowed to go back on his promise by reliance on a written clause . . . The reason is because the oral promise or representation has a decisive influence on the transaction — it is the very thing which induces the other to contract — and it would be most unjust to allow the maker to go back on it. The printed condition is rejected because it is repugnant to the express oral promise or representation. As Devlin J. said in *Firestone Tyre and Rubber Co. Ltd. v. Vokins & Co. Ltd.*, [1951] 1 Lloyd's Rep. 32, 39: It is illusory to say: "We promise to do a thing, but we are not liable if we do not do it!" To avoid this illusion, the law gives the oral promise priority over the printed clause.

Again, it can easily be seen that this kind of approach gives the court a wide power to undo whatever the drafter of the contract may have intended.

The risk that the defendant faced in *Mendelssohn v. Normand* is a reflection of problems examined earlier in this book. The problem of the parol evidence rule, the problem of authority (*Carman Construction v. CPR, supra*, Chapter 5) and the problem of negligent misrepresentation in the context of contractual relations (*V.K. Mason Construction v. Bank of Nova Scotia* and *J. Nunes Diamonds Ltd. v.*

Dominion Electric Protection, supra, Chapter 5) are all implicated in Lord Denning's judgment. It is clear that the employee would not have had authority to make a contract on behalf of his employer under the general law of agency. An employee employed to park cars would not be held out by his employer as an agent with authority to amend the terms of a written standard form contract that expressly requires that any change be in writing and signed by the manager.

Notice that Lord Denning, through what may be no more than his vivid literary style, turns the corporate defendant into a person — a "man". Such a shift in "personality" obscures the very real problems of contracts made on behalf of corporations. Would Mr. Mendelssohn — he was, after all, driving a Rolls Royce and had used the garage "many times before" — have been surprised to be held to the consequences of dealing with a corporation?

A corporation is said to have the powers of a "natural person". The *Canada Business Corporations Act*, s. 15(1), states: "A corporation has the capacity and, subject to this Act, the rights, powers and privileges of a natural person." This type of legislative statement does not justify the assumption that a corporation *is* the same as a natural person. The difficulty with Lord Denning's approach — confounding a corporation and a human being — is that it fails to address the issues of the law of agency.

Finally and to anticipate an issue dealt with later, who are the real parties in the dispute between Mr. Mendelssohn and the garage and what effect should that have on any analysis of the problem? Would it matter if it was really Mr. Mendelssohn's insurer suing the insurer of the parking lot? The least-cost insurer will always be the owner's insurer.

A more general example of the same approach is judicial hostility to attempts to obtain exemption from liability for negligence. The original motive for such an attitude was the view of judges that, since negligence requires fault, it is not proper that anyone should avoid liability when he or she has been guilty of fault. While there are still echoes of this attitude, the widespread recognition (even by judges) of the ubiquity of insurance has led to the realization that, whatever the result, the person "at fault" will not, as a matter of fact, have to pay: his or her insurer will.

As you read the cases in this chapter, keep the following questions in mind:

1. What purpose does the clause in question serve?

2. Have the parties agreed to an allocation of risk that can be insured against?

3. To what extent is there an imbalance of bargaining power?

    There are two possible sources of imbalance:

    (a) an inequality of information (the buyer does not know very much about the thing or service he or she is buying), and

    (b) an inequality of power arising from a structural or temporary monopoly position enjoyed by one person (a phone company that has lines throughout a province enjoys a structural monopoly; the sole tow truck on a deserted highway on Christmas Eve has a temporary monopoly, as had the plaintiff in *The Port Caledonia, supra*, Chapter 2). So too, a builder might have a form of temporary monopoly as regards an owner once construction has commenced (see *Williams v. Roffey Bros., supra*, Chapter 2).

4. To what extent has this imbalance resulted in the ability of one side to impose terms on the other?

5. Should one distinguish between cases involving merchants only and those involving consumers buying from commercial sellers?

6. If the court, as in *Fraser-Reid v. Droumtsekas*, *Wallis v. Pratt* or *Mendelssohn v. Normand*, eviscerates an exemption clause or makes an attempted alloca- tion of risk ineffective, what response does the decision encourage? Has much good — giving that word whatever meaning you like — been done if the price for the protection of one unsuspecting person is the more effective taking by surprise of many others? Consider what effect the decision will have on future transactions. Who will pay the cost of implementing the decision in future transactions?

7. As you read each case in this chapter, put yourself in the position of the solici- tor for the defendant and consider what advice you would give your client, both before and after the decision. In particular, consider how you would re- draft the contract.

Standard Form Contracts

Issues of exploitation of contractual power often, though by no means always, in- volve standard form contracts. While some standard-form contracts are drafted by one party, invariably the economically more powerful party, others are a product of a process of negotiation between organizations that represent the different inter- ests affected by the contract. Contracts such as the international charter party re- ferred to in *Federal Commerce and Navigation Co. Ltd. v. Tradax Export SA* (*su- pra*, Chapter 5) are standard-form contracts, the terms of which are negotiated between organizations of shipowners and charterers.

Standard-form contracts with the terms set by one side are sometimes called "contracts of adhesion". These contracts are mass-produced and are often used on a "take-it-or-leave-it" basis. It is commonly assumed that these contracts are found only in consumer transactions and that their use is characterized by the unfair ex- ploitation of the weaker party. Indeed, the term "contract of adhesion" was first associated with contracts in which there was overwhelming power on the part of one side and relative weakness on the other: the consumer was forced to accept *all* the other's terms if he or she wanted what the other was offering. Small busi- nesses, particularly franchisees, are often, though by no means always, in much the same situation as consumers. The use of such contracts is widespread, and the reasons for their use are far more defensible than might at first appear. The fea- tures of such contracts will be explored in the materials that follow.

The following extract is from a famous article on such contracts.

KESSLER, "CONTRACTS OF ADHESION — SOME THOUGHTS ABOUT FREEDOM OF CONTRACT"

(1943), 43 *Colum. L. Rev.* 629

[1]   . . . The development of large scale enterprise with its mass production and mass distribution made a new type of contract inevitable — the standardized mass contract. A standardized contract, once its contents have been formulated by a

business firm, is used in every bargain dealing with the same product or service. The individuality of the parties which so frequently gave color to the old type contract has disappeared. The stereotyped contract of today reflects the impersonality of the market. It has reached its greatest perfection in the different types of contracts used on the various exchanges. Once the usefulness of these contracts was discovered and perfected in the transportation, insurance, and banking business, their use spread into all other fields of large scale enterprise, into international as well as national trade, and into labor relations. It is to be noted that uniformity of terms of contracts typically recurring in a business enterprise is an important factor in the exact calculation of risks. Risks which are difficult to calculate can be excluded altogether. Unforeseeable contingencies affecting performance, such as strikes, fire, and transportation difficulties can be taken care of. The standard clauses in insurance policies are the most striking illustrations of successful attempts on the part of business enterprises to select and control risks assumed under a contract. The insurance business probably deserves credit also for having first realized the full importance of the so-called juridical risk, the danger that a court or jury may be swayed by "irrational factors" to decide against a powerful defendant. Ingenious clauses have been the result. Once their practical utility was proven, they were made use of in other lines of business. It is highly probable that the desire to avoid juridical risks has been a motivating factor in the widespread use of warranty clauses in the machine industry limiting the common-law remedies of the buyer to breach of an implied warranty of quality and particularly excluding his right to claim damages. The same is true for arbitration clauses in international trade. Standardized contracts have thus become an important means of excluding or controlling the "irrational factor" in litigation. In this respect they are a true reflection of the spirit of our time with its hostility to irrational factors in the judicial process, and they belong in the same category as codifications and restatements.

[2]   In so far as the reduction of costs of production and distribution thus achieved is reflected in reduced prices, society as a whole ultimately benefits from the use of standard contracts. And there can be no doubt that this has been the case to a considerable extent. The use of standard contracts has, however, another aspect which has become increasingly important. Standard contracts are typically used by enterprises with strong bargaining power. The weaker party, in need of the goods or services, is frequently not in a position to shop around for better terms, either because the author of the standard contract has a monopoly (natural or artificial) or because all competitors use the same clauses. His contractual intention is but a subjection more or less voluntary to terms dictated by the stronger party, terms whose consequences are often understood only in a vague way, if at all. Thus, standardized contracts are frequently contracts of adhesion; they are *à prendre ou à laisser*. Not infrequently the weaker party to a prospective contract even agrees in advance not to retract his offer while the offeree reserves for himself the power to accept or refuse; or he submits to terms or change of terms which will be communicated to him later. To be sure, the latter type of clauses regularly provide for a power to disaffirm, but as a practical matter they are acquiesced in frequently, thus becoming part of the "living law." Lastly, standardized contracts have also been used to control and regulate the distribution of goods from producer all the way down to the ultimate consumer. They have become one of the many devices to build up and strengthen industrial empires.

[3] And yet the tremendous economic importance of contracts of adhesion is hardly reflected in the great texts on contracts or in the *Restatement*. As a matter of fact, the term "contract of adhesion" or a similar symbol has not even found general recognition in our legal vocabulary. This will not do any harm if we remain fully aware that the use of the word "contract" does not commit us to an indiscriminate extension of the ordinary contract rules to all contracts. But apparently the realization of the deep-going antinomies in the structure of our system of contracts is too painful an experience to be permitted to rise to the full level of our consciousness. Consequently, courts have made great efforts to protect the weaker contracting party and still keep "the elementary rules" of the law of contracts intact. As a result, our common law of standardized contracts is highly contradictory and confusing, and the potentialities inherent in the common-law system for coping with contracts of adhesion have not been fully developed. The law of insurance contracts furnishes excellent illustrations. Handicapped by the axiom that courts can only interpret but cannot make contracts for the parties, courts had to rely heavily on their prerogative of interpretation to protect a policy holder. To be sure, many courts have shown a remarkable skill in reaching "just" decisions by construing ambiguous clauses against their author even in cases where there was no ambiguity. Still, this roundabout method has its disadvantages as the story of the treatment of warranties in life insurance contracts strikingly demonstrates. Courts, when protecting an innocent policy holder against the harshness of the doctrine, did not state clearly that as a matter of public policy an insurance company cannot avoid liability merely because of the falsity of a statement which has been labelled "warranty." They felt that freedom of contract prevented them from saying so. Instead they disguised as "interpretation" their efforts to change warranties into representations. But this makeshift solution tempted insurance companies to try the usefulness of "warranties" again and again.

The following extract examines standard-form contracts from a different perspective.

HAVIGHURST, THE NATURE OF PRIVATE CONTRACT

(Evanston, Ill.: Northwestern University Press, 1961), at 115-118

[1] Whenever parties who know and trust each other enter into a transaction or relation, a few words to make plain the specificities are ordinarily all in the way of a contract that is needed. Quite apart from any catalogue of terms, each one, if he has had any experience in similar matters, will have a fairly clear idea of what he expects from the other party in a course of events that does not veer too far from the usual, and a fairly clear idea of what the other party expects from him. Each one is willing to accommodate himself within reasonable limits to a fixed idea of the other and to compromise in the unusual event that fixed ideas should conflict. Neither anticipates any difficulty. Law is far from their thoughts.

[2] This pleasant state of affairs, however, does not always exist. If the relation is to extend over a period and the parties are uncertain about what the future holds, if they have reason to expect the unexpected, they may not, even when they know and trust each other, be confident of their ability to meet all contingencies in a spirit of peace and friendship. It may seem desirable to try to anticipate what may happen and to make specific provision for everything that can be foreseen. The lawyer properly encourages this state of mind. In my first lecture I mentioned the contribution of the profession to the cause of peace. "Nip controversy before it even buds!" is good advice.

[3]   Yet, though an elaborate contract is drawn, it is not with a view to litigation. Unless either imagination or expression proves inadequate there will be no controversy, and even if differences should arise, the parties expect to be able to resolve them.

[4]   It is only when a party is dealing with someone he does not know and trust that he begins to think about the law and to feel that for legal reasons he needs a contract of many words. In a deal in which credit is extended no words, however voluminous, will take the place of an investigation, but the need of which I am now speaking has nothing to do with credit. The drawer of the contract is not concerned about the other party's performance nor with his own legal remedies. His worry is that the other party will prove to be an evil person, that the other party will trump up a lawsuit against him.

[5]   This is not an idle fear. Fraudulent lawsuits are common. Some persons will commit arson or even murder with a view to establishing an insurance claim. Others may be honest, but they are neurotic and easily moved without provocation to pursue an aggressive course of action.

[6]   A business that deals with many customers or suppliers or employees or holders of dealer franchises or tenants does not ordinarily find it feasible to conduct a thorough investigation in each case of character and emotional stability. Furthermore, if the dealing is expected to extend over a long period, character and emotional stability, unexceptionable at the time, may later suffer deterioration. It is far simpler to require adhesion to a contract that commits the business legally to a performance far less than it expects to render, to hedge promises about with conditions that it does not expect to insist upon, unless the other party proves to be evil or unstable. If carefully prepared, the contract, supplemented by verbal assurances, may yield the advantage of raising the expectations necessary to induce the desired performance and at the same time insulate against legal liability.

[7]   Such a course cannot always be characterized as sharp dealing. These are not harsh terms imposed in every instance by reason of superior bargaining power. The business may be quite competitive. But informed, intelligent and well-balanced people are not as a rule too much concerned about the extent of the legal pressures available in the event of dispute. In deciding with whom they will deal they are apt to take more account of the attractiveness of other terms and of the company's reputation for fair dealing. For the business enterprise, then, good judgment prompts elimination, as far as possible, of the legal hazard. If a few are constrained to deal elsewhere because the proposition is not attractive from a legal standpoint, they are probably the litigious-minded people and their loss is good riddance.

[8]   I have several wealthy neighbors who apparently are obsessed with worry about burglars. They have great iron fences surrounding their properties and fierce dogs. When the fierce dogs bark behind the iron fences, the evil person bent upon intrusion tends to be dissuaded. For the business enterprise, possessed of assets

and obsessed with worry about evil litigants, the contract of adhesion is a great iron fence. The business may not have fierce dogs, but it has lawyers — lawyers who keep the fences in repair and lawyers who make appropriate noises when prospective litigants approach. The evil person bent upon a lawsuit tends to be dissuaded.

[9]   However, as you readily see, there is here a problem. The iron fence that excludes the bad man also excludes the good. And a man who sincerely believes that his claim is just may sometimes be regarded by the enterpriser as evil. The contract of adhesion, though conceived in a worthy cause, has the effect of depriving every adherent of a day in court.

[10]   The question is: To what extent is this deprivation of public concern?

[11]   In many situations, in my opinion, it is not a matter of concern; and the reason is that there is no real need for legal enforcement. The non-legal pressures are ample to insure performance. Many firms in their dealing lean over backward to preserve good will and to keep the peace. They pursue a course epitomized in the slogan "The customer is always right." When a claim is denied, it is more certain that it had no substance than if, there having been no contract spelling out the terms, it had been dismissed in a court of law. . . .

[12]   But in . . . two situations where legal pressures attain maximum importance, the power of one party to deprive the other of a day in court *is* a matter of public concern. In these instances the need is for enforcement against the stronger party, and he is the one in a position to prepare the contract of adhesion — to build the iron fence. Here it has been necessary to impose limitations upon freedom of contract.

[13]   First among the principal situations in which legal enforcement is advantageous . . . is the one found in a class of dealing that lends itself easily to fly-by-night operation. The best example is the insurance business. Here, when contract is completely free, the contract of adhesion, filled with multifarious conditions and warranties, utterly destroys the day in court of the policyholder or his beneficiary; and, as I have said, the non-legal sanctions are entirely inadequate. . . .

[14]   The second situation . . . in which legal enforcement is essential is one in which the contracting parties are subject to unequal competitive pressures. It is typified by the contract by which the powerful enterpriser obtains the co-operation of the small man. In the labor field generally collective bargaining, fostered by limitations upon contract freedom of a kind I have yet to discuss, has redressed the imbalance. But there are other relations involving disparate competitive pressures in which organization of those in the weaker position has not been and perhaps cannot be achieved.

[15]   The most obvious example of such a relation is that between the large manufacturer of nationally advertised products and its sales agencies. In some businesses of this kind, dealers frequently are deprived of a needed day in court. Contracts of adhesion still commit the manufacturer to a performance far less than he expects to render, and in the event of controversy the dealer's only hope is for a drastic judicial distortion of the contract language. In the automobile business, however, an act of Congress and laws in a number of states have limited the power

of the manufacturer, no matter how the contract reads, to terminate the agency at will. It has provided for the automobile dealer a day in court.

NOTES

1. Consider the conditions that have to be met before the benefits of standard-form contracts outlined by Kessler may accrue to society. The extent to which lower costs for a seller, for example, will result in lower prices for buyers will be a function of the market in which the seller competes. Arguments that increased costs to a seller will be directly passed on to buyers in higher prices are commonly made to oppose government measures which are seen as being costly to business. However, in some situations, sellers rather than consumers may bear the extra costs.

2. While it is sometimes hard without a great deal of economic data to determine the effects of standardization of contractual relations, the standardization of contractual relations is a powerful method of preventing or, at least reducing, the risk that arises from an employer's inability to control its employees. Having standardized terms also substantially reduces the costs of contract formation.

   Standard-form contracts also permit, not just the mass-production of contracts, but the "mass-administration" of contracts. A mechanic servicing a car has to know whether the car is under a warranty or not, and it is very expensive to have disputes about this issue at the level of the service station and car owner. A department store has to have standardized methods for dealing with its customers' charge accounts. A corporation renting cars needs to know whether the renter has agreed to pay for extra insurance or not as well as many other things about the deal. If nothing else, a standardized contract is a good way to make sure that standard information on the other party is collected.

3. There is a large literature on standard form contracts and economic power: see, *e.g.*, Todd Rakoff, "Contracts of Adhesion: An Essay in Reconstruction" (1983), 96 *Harv. L. Rev.* 1174; and the 2006 Symposium Issue (vol. 104) of the *Michigan Law Review,* "Boilerplate: Foundation of Market Contracts".

4. You can easily conduct a simple experiment to test the extent to which contracts may be "custom designed". The next time you are faced with a standardized contract, try to negotiate special terms for yourself, and note:

   (a) how far up the corporate structure you have to go before,

      (i) you become exhausted by the effort, or

      (ii) someone will actually consider your request, and

   (b) what aspects, if any, of such a contract are, in fact, negotiable.

The Ticket Cases

Several cases have illustrated the problems that arise when one party asserts that certain written terms are "*the* terms of the bargain" while the other party asserts that they are not — the battle of the forms, *supra*, Chapter 3, and the problems of the parol evidence rule, *supra*, Chapter 5. The "battle of the forms" cases involve merchants who are expected to recognize that the writing on one of their forms will constitute the contract; indeed, each tries to assure that its form will govern. The problems become more acute if one party claims that the terms of the contract are those that it has "imposed" on the other party by posting them or by printing them on a ticket or invoice. Courts are concerned that the other party should have a reasonable chance to see these terms and to decide whether they are an acceptable basis for doing business.

Concerns of fairness and of the possible abuse of the power of the party who imposes the terms may lead the courts to protect the person on whom the terms are sought to be imposed. Protection may be given if the terms do not reflect the reasonable expectations that one might have for that type of transaction (checking a coat, parking a car, etc.). The courts' approach in such cases shows a determination to prevent injustice which might occur if internal legal logic of traditional contract formation rules were allowed to run unchecked, balanced against a concern for not being overly solicitous to those who are careless in protecting their commercial interests.

PARKER v. SOUTH EASTERN RAILWAY CO.

(1877), 2 C.P.D. 416
(C.A., Mellish, Bramwell and Baggallay L.JJ.)

[Action] against the South Eastern Railway Company for the value of a bag and its contents lost to the [plaintiff] . . . by the negligence of the company's servants.

The plaintiff had deposited a bag in a cloak-room at the defendants' railway station, had paid the clerk 2d. [two pence], and had received a paper ticket, on one side of which were written a number and a date, and were printed notices as to when the office would be opened and closed, and the words "See back." On the other side were printed several clauses relating to articles left by passengers, the last of which was, "The company will not be responsible for any package exceeding the value of £10." The plaintiff on the same day presented his ticket and demanded his bag, and the bag could not be found, and had not been since found. Parker claimed £24 10s as the value of his bag. The company pleaded that they had accepted the goods on the condition that they would not be responsible for the value if it exceeded £10; and on the trial they relied on the words printed on the back of the ticket, and also on the fact that a notice to the same effect was printed and hung up in the cloak-room. The plaintiff gave evidence and denied that he had seen the notice, or read what was printed on the ticket. The plaintiff admitted that he had often received such tickets, and knew there was printed matter on them, but said that he did not know what it was: . . . that he imagined the ticket to be a receipt for the money paid by him. . . .

The questions left in each case by the judge to the jury were: (1) Did the plaintiff read or was he aware of the special condition upon which the articles were deposited? (2) Was the plaintiff, under the circumstances, under any obligation, in the exercise of reasonable and proper caution, to read or make himself aware of the condition?

The jury in each case answered both questions in the negative, and the judge thereupon directed judgment to be entered for the plaintiff for the amount claimed, reserving leave to the defendants to move to enter judgment for them. . . .

MELLISH L.J.: — [1] . . . The question then is, whether the plaintiff was bound by the conditions contained in the ticket. In an ordinary case, where an action is brought on a written agreement which is signed by the defendant, the agreement is proved by proving his signature, and, in the absence of fraud, it is wholly immaterial that he has not read the agreement and does not know its contents. The parties may, however, reduce their agreement into writing, so that the writing constitutes the sole evidence of the agreement, without signing it; but in that case there must be evidence independently of the agreement itself to prove that the defendant has assented to it. In that case, also, if it is proved that the defendant has assented to the writing constituting the agreement between the parties, it is, in the absence of fraud, immaterial that the defendant had not read the agreement and did not know its contents. Now if in the course of making a contract one party delivers to another a paper containing writing, and the party receiving the paper knows that the paper contains conditions which the party delivering it intends to constitute the contract, I have no doubt that the party receiving the paper does, by receiving and keeping it, assent to the conditions contained in it, although he does not read them, and does not know what they are. . . .

[2]   Now, I am of opinion that we cannot lay down, as a matter of law, either that the plaintiff was bound or that he was not bound by the conditions printed on the ticket, from the mere fact that he knew there was writing on the ticket, but did not know that the writing contained conditions. I think there may be cases in which a paper containing writing is delivered by one party to another in the course of a business transaction, where it would be quite reasonable that the party receiving it should assume that the writing contained in it no condition, and should put it in his pocket unread. . . .

[3]   Now the question we have to consider is whether the railway company were entitled to assume that a person depositing luggage, and receiving a ticket in such a way that he could see that some writing was printed on it, would understand that the writing contained the conditions of contract, and this seems to me to depend upon whether people in general would in fact, and naturally, draw that inference. The railway company, as it seems to me, must be entitled to make some assumptions respecting the person who deposits luggage with them: I think they are entitled to assume that he can read, and that he understands the English language, and that he pays such attention to what he is about as may be reasonably expected from a person in such a transaction as that of depositing luggage in a cloak-room. The railway company must however, take mankind as they find them, and if what they do is sufficient to inform people in general that the ticket contains conditions, I think that a particular plaintiff ought not to be in a better position than other persons on account of his exceptional ignorance or stupidity or carelessness. But if what the railway company do is not sufficient to convey to the minds of people in general that the ticket contains conditions, then they have received goods on deposit without obtaining the consent of the persons depositing them to the conditions limiting their liability. I am of opinion, therefore, that the proper direction to leave to the jury in these cases is, that if the person receiving the ticket did not see or know that there was any writing on the ticket, he is not bound by the conditions; that if he knew there was writing, and knew or believed that the writing contained conditions, then he is bound by the conditions, that if he knew there was writing on the ticket, but did not know or believe that the writing contained conditions, nevertheless he would be bound, if the delivering of the ticket to him in such a manner that he could see there was writing upon it, was, in the opinion of the jury, reasonable notice that the writing contained conditions.

[4]   I have lastly to consider whether the direction of the learned judge was correct, namely, "Was the plaintiff, under the circumstances, under any obligation, in the exercise of reasonable and proper caution, to read or to make himself aware of the condition?" I think that this direction was not strictly accurate, and was calculated to mislead the jury. The plaintiff was certainly under no obligation to read

the ticket, but was entitled to leave it unread if he pleased, and the question does not appear to me to direct the attention of the jury to the real question, namely, whether the railway company did what was reasonably sufficient to give the plaintiff notice of the condition.

[5] On the whole, I am of opinion that there ought to be a new trial.

[**BAGGALLAY L.J.** delivered an opinion concurring with **MELLISH L.J.**]

BRAMWELL L.J.: — **[6]** It is clear that if the [plaintiff] . . . had read the conditions on the tickets and not objected, [he] would have been bound by them. No point was or could be made that the contract was complete before the ticket was given. If then reading the conditions [he] would have been bound, it follows that had [he] been told they were the conditions of the contract and invited to read them, and [he] had refused, saying [he was] content to take them whatever they might be, then also, [he] would be bound by them. So also would [he] be if [he was] so told, and made no answer, and did nothing; for in that case [he] would have tacitly said the same thing, viz., that [he was] content to take them, whatever they might be. If follows, further, that if [he] knew that what was on the tickets was the contract which the defendants were willing to enter into, [he], the plaintiff, would be bound, though not told they were the conditions; for it cannot make a difference that [he was] not told what by the hypothesis [he] knew already. We have it, then, that if the plaintiff knew that what was printed was the contract which the defendants were willing to enter into, the [plaintiff], not objecting, is bound by its terms, though [he] did not inform [himself] what they were. The plaintiff [has] sworn that [he] did not know that the printing was the contract, and we must act as though that was true and we believed it, at least as far as entering the verdict for the defendants is concerned. Does this make any difference? The plaintiff knew of the printed matter. [He admits he] knew it concerned [him] in some way, though [he] said [he] did not know what it was; yet [he does not pretend] that he knew or believed it was not the contract. [He does not pretend] he thought it had nothing to do with the business in hand; that he thought it was an advertisement or other matter unconnected with his deposit of a parcel at the defendants' cloak-room. [He admits] that, for anything [he] knew or believed, it might be, only [he] did not know or believe it was, the contract. [His] evidence is very much that [he] did not think, or, thinking, did not care about it. Now [he claims] to charge the company, and to have the benefit of [his] own indifference. Is this just? Is it reasonable? Is it the way in which any other business is allowed to be conducted? Is it even allowed to a man to "think," "judge," "guess," "chance" a matter, without informing himself when he can, and then when his "thought," "judgment," "guess," or "chance" turns out wrong or unsuccessful, claim to impose a burthen or duty on another which he could not have done had he informed himself as he might? Suppose the clerk or porter at the cloak-room had said to the [plaintiff], "Read that, it concerns you," and [he] had not read it, would [he] be at liberty to set up that though told to read [he] did not, because [he] thought something or other? But what is the difference between that case and the present? Why is there printing on the paper, except that it may be read? The putting of it into [his] hands was equivalent to saying, "Read that." Could the defendants practically do more than they did? Had they not a right to suppose either that the [plaintiff] knew the conditions, or that [he was] content to take on trust whatever is printed? Let us for the moment forget that the defendants are a *caput lupinum* — a railway company. Take any other case — any case of money being paid and a paper given by the receiver, or goods bought on credit and a paper given with them. . . . Has not the giver of the paper a right to suppose that the receiver is content to deal on the terms in the paper? What more can be done? Must he say, "Read that?" As I have said, he does so in effect when he puts it into the other's hands. The truth is, people are content to take these things on trust. They know that there is a form which is always used — they are satisfied it is not unreasonable, because people do not usually put unreasonable terms in their contracts. If they did, then dealing would soon be stopped. Besides, unreasonable practices would be known. The very fact of not looking at the paper shews that this confidence exists. It is asked: What if there was some unreasonable condition, as for instance to forfeit £1,000 if the goods were not removed in forty-eight hours? Would the depositor be bound? I might content myself by asking: Would he be, if he were told "our conditions are on this ticket," and he did not read them. In my judgment, he would not be bound in either case. I think there is an implied understanding that there is no condition unreasonable to the knowledge of the party tendering the document and not insisting on its being read — no condition not relevant to the matter in hand. I am of opinion, therefore, that the plaintiffs, having notice of the printing, were in the same situation as though the porter had said, "Read that, it concerns the matter in hand," that if the plaintiffs did not read it, they were as much bound as if they had read it and had not objected.

[7] The difficulty I feel as to what I have written is that it is too demonstrative. But, put in practical language, it is this: The defendants put into the hands of the plaintiff a paper with printed matter on it, which in all good sense and reason must be supposed to relate to the matter in hand. This printed matter the plaintiff sees, and must either read it, and object if he does not agree to it, or if he does read it and not object, or does not read it, he must be held to consent to its terms; therefore, on the facts, the judges should have directed verdicts for the defendants. . . .

QUESTIONS

1. What conflicting principles did the Court consider in *Parker*? Did either Mellish L.J. or Bramwell L.J. consider the conflicting principles? Given the assumptions about the nature of contract and the theory underlying issues of the "formation of contract", do you think that they were able to see the issues that they faced?

2. Have you ever *not* read a ticket that was handed to you? Was this an example of "exceptional ignorance or stupidity or carelessness"?

3. What do you think that Bramwell L.J. meant when he said, "It is clear that if the plaintiffs in these actions had read the conditions and not objected, they would have been bound by them"? What would the plaintiffs have been told if they had objected? In a world where assent must operate like an on/off switch, the law has to treat a "grumbling" assent as an (unqualified) assent. What options, as matters simply of what is practically possible, are there in dealing with a grumbling assent? What is the process of contract formation that Bramwell develops in terms of the "offer-acceptance" model?

4. Outline specifically the points under each of the judgments that should be covered in a proper charge to the jury. (Even if we do not use juries in such cases now, the trial judge would have to ask the same questions.) Consider specifically the following:

 (a) Would each side be likely to agree on the range of facts that the jury should consider?

 (b) Outline the points at which you think disagreement might occur.

(c) At what point does the inquiry into the facts risk the values that must be held by a system of adjudication or by the process of private ordering?

5. In *J. Spurling Ltd. v. Bradshaw*, [1956] 2 All E.R. 121, [1956] 1 W.L.R. 461 (C.A.), Denning L.J. dealt with an exemption clause in a contract between the plaintiff, a warehouse operator, and the defendant, the owner of eight casks of orange juice. The plaintiff had sued for its charges and the defendant had counterclaimed for negligence in the storage of the casks. Nearly all the juice had been lost before the casks had been picked up. In upholding a decision of the trial judge who had held that the exemption clause would protect the plaintiff, Lord Denning said:

> This brings me to the question whether this clause was part of the contract. Counsel for the defendant urged us to hold that the plaintiffs did not do what was reasonably sufficient to give notice of the conditions within *Parker v. South Eastern Ry. Co.* I agree that the more unreasonable a clause is, the greater the notice which must be given of it. Some clauses which I have seen would need to be printed in red ink on the face of the document with a red hand pointing to it before the notice could be held to be sufficient. The clause in this case, however, in my judgment, does not call for such exceptional treatment, especially when it is construed, as it should be, subject to the proviso that it only applies when the warehouseman is carrying out his contract and not when he is deviating from it or breaking it in a radical respect. So construed, the judge was, I think entitled to find that sufficient notice was given. It is to be noticed that the landing account on its face told the defendant that the goods would be insured if he gave instructions; otherwise they were not insured. The invoice, on its face, told him they were warehoused "at owner's risk." The printed conditions, when read subject to the proviso which I have mentioned, added little or nothing to those explicit statements taken together. Next it was said that the landing account and invoice were issued after the goods had been received and could not therefore be part of the contract of bailment: but the defendant admitted that he had received many landing accounts before. True, he had not troubled to read them. On receiving this account, he took no objection to it, left the goods there, and went on paying the warehouse rent for months afterwards. It seems to me that by the course of business and conduct of the parties, these conditions were part of the contract. In these circumstances, the plaintiffs were entitled to rely on this exempting condition . . .

> I think, therefore, that the counterclaim was properly dismissed, and this appeal also should be dismissed.

Is Lord Denning's decision a departure from either judgment in *Parker*? Does *Spurling* take account of important facts ignored in either judgment in *Parker*?

6. How far can the notion of "reasonable notice" serve as an instrument to control contract power? To what extent is this notion a reflection of the real issues that arise in such cases?

7. The analysis of the Court of Appeal in *Parker v. South Eastern Railway Co.* was applied by the English Court of Appeal in *Interfoto Picture Library Ltd. v. Stiletto Visual Programmes Ltd.*, [1989] 1 Q.B. 433, [1988] 1 All E.R. 348. The facts were that the plaintiff provided file photographs to the defendant. The written conditions that came when the photographs were delivered to the defendant provided that there would be a *per diem* charge if the photographs were kept longer than a few days, even if they were not used. The defendant forgot about the photographs and kept them for two weeks longer than it should have. As provided in the conditions, the defendant was billed for more than £3,700. It was accepted by the court that it was unlikely that the employee of the defendant had read the printed conditions on the delivery note that accompanied the photographs, though the defendant was taken to have known when the package was opened that there were contractual terms included in the package.

The question which the court addressed was whether the defendant was bound by the terms of the contract. The Court of Appeal held that, in view of the fact that the terms were neither common nor usual, the plaintiff should have done more to bring them to the defendant's attention. The court regarded the obligation of the plaintiff to bring the terms explicitly to the defendant's attention as directly related to the extent that the terms departed from what the defendant should have expected. Bingham L.J. said:

> The defendants are not to be relieved of [their] liability because they did not read the condition, although doubtless they did not, but in my judgment they are to be relieved because the plaintiffs did not do what was necessary to draw this unreasonable and extortionate clause fairly to their attention.

Bingham L.J. focuses on the expectations — though he does not use that word — and on the need to protect the reasonable expectations of the defendants, and requires a contracting party to bring an unusual clause to the attention of the other. Bingham L.J. rejected any general principle of good faith as a basis for protecting the defendant's expectations. He said:

> English law has, characteristically, committed itself to no such overriding principle [of good faith] but has developed piecemeal solutions in response to demonstrated problems of unfairness.

While it is possible that a general principle of good faith might provide a basis for protecting the expectations of the defendants on the facts of *Interfoto*, such a principle is not necessary to protect reasonable expectations. What is necessary is the willingness of the court to look at a party's expectations and at the factors that went to create those expectations in the first place. That inquiry will establish that the expectations were (or were not) reasonable, that the other party knew or should have known (or did not know) what they were and focus on the question whether the other party should have pointed out that those expectations were not going to be met under the terms of the transaction.

Cases like *Interfoto* could, as Bingham L.J. suggested, possibly be re-cast as cases involving some duty of good faith if the issue were seen more in terms of one party's duty to make the terms of the contract clear to the other: the idea of good faith as "fair dealing" would similarly encompass this duty. The importance of good faith in the law of contracts is hard to over-emphasize, but there is a need to be careful about what the duty requires and where it is needed. A focus on the need to protect one party's reasonable expectations does not need any finding that the other did not act in good faith: protection can be provided simply by considering whether one party had expectations which, in the context of the parties' relation, should be protected.

The significance of decisions like *Interfoto* is that they illustrate how easy it is to do what has to be done to forward the values that the law of contracts must reflect. There are many cases where one party, in the course of negotiations, did not draw an amendment it had inserted in the written agreement explicitly to the other's attention. The courts regularly denied enforcement of the clause if the other missed it. Long before "good faith" became a fashionable term, the Courts were able to prevent unfairness or to protect the expectations that one party had been led to believe the agreement created. In other words, the goals of discouraging bad conduct or bad faith and of enhancing the utility of contracts can often be achieved without an explicit focus on good faith. The plaintiff in *Interfoto* now knows what it has to do — *i.e.*, use the red ink and provide the "red hand" that Lord Denning M.R. suggested in *Spurling v. Bradshaw* might be needed in such circumstances — to make the terms that it wants enforceable — though it may be an important business decision for it whether enforceability is worth the cost in rejected deals.

The real threats to the important values of the law of contracts lie in ignoring expectations and the need to protect them. Cases in which courts focus on the process of offer and acceptance — the Court of Appeal in *Interfoto* could have held that the defendant was bound because it knew that there were conditions attached to the delivery of the photographs, whether it read them or not — or on the plain meaning of the words of the contract, regardless of whether doing so would catch one party by surprise, illustrate that the threats exist. The articulation of general duties of good faith and fair dealing would help to eliminate these threats, but those are principally standards of conduct that operate in conjunction with a concern to protect the parties' (or a party's) reasonable expectations and to prevent unfair surprise.

HEFFRON v. IMPERIAL PARKING CO. LTD.

(1973), 3 O.R. (2d) 722, 46 D.L.R. (3d) 642
(C.A., Evans, Brooke and Estey JJ.A.)

The judgment of the court was delivered by **ESTEY J.A.**: —

[1] This is an appeal from a judgment . . . wherein the plaintiff was awarded $1,251.92 as damages for the loss of an automobile left by the respondent with the appellants, the operators of a parking lot, together with costs.

[2] The respondent on October 10, 1970, parked his motor vehicle in the parking lot of the appellants in downtown Toronto paying the evening flat rate charge and receiving in return a ticket whereupon there was printed:

No. 49801

PARKING CONDITIONS

We are not responsible for
theft or damage of car or
contents, however caused.

IMPERIAL PARKING CO.

237 Victoria Street
364-4611
Corner Bond & Dundas Sts.

Open 8:00 a.m. - 12:00 p.m.

---

[3] At the request of the appellants' attendant the respondent left the keys in the automobile. The lot was marked with three signs on which the same message was set out as appeared on the ticket. The learned trial judge came to the conclusion "that the defendants took reasonable steps under the circumstances to draw the conditions of parking to the plaintiff's attention even though, as he admitted, he had not read the parking ticket but merely slipped it into his pocket." In addition to these signs there was a sign announcing the hours in which the parking lot was open and which were the same set out on the ticket described above. I can find no reason to disturb the learned trial judge's conclusion that the appellant had taken all reasonable measures to communicate to the respondent the parking conditions including the hours of operation.

[4] The respondent returned to the parking lot about one hour after it had closed and was unable to locate his car. Three days later it was discovered abandoned in a damaged condition. The evidence is that when the car was left with the appellants by the respondent it contained some personal property of the respondent including clothing, a tape player and an electric razor; there is no evidence to indicate that the tape player was affixed to or formed part of the car. These items of personal property were not in the car when it was recovered.

[5]   There was evidence indicating that the appellants operated a parking garage across the street from the parking lot in question and that it was a normal practice for the attendant when leaving the lot at midnight to take the keys of any cars remaining on the lot to the office of the parking garage across the street which was operated by the appellant. The keys to the respondent's car were not found in either the kiosk on the parking lot or in the office of the parking garage. . . .

[6]   The appellant relies upon the decision of this Court in *Samuel Smith & Sons Ltd. v. Silverman*, [1961] O.R. 648, 29 D.L.R. (2d) 98, in support of its submission that the exculpatory condition in the ticket together with the same message in the signs posted on the parking lot are sufficiently broad in their terms to exonerate the appellant even when the damage occurred through negligence of the appellant, its servants, or a third party. The appellant also submits that it is under no onus or obligation to advance any explanation for the non-delivery of the respondent's automobile and since the respondent was unable to show that its loss was occasioned by a fundamental breach of the contract by the appellant, the respondent's action should be dismissed. The appellant alternatively submits that the respondent in parking his automobile on the appellant's premises is a mere licensee and consequently, no bailment arose and therefore no duty in the appellants to explain the loss. . . .

[7]   The respective characteristics of the bailment and the licence relationships are guides to the application of the appropriate relationship to the case at hand. Bailment has been defined as "a delivery of personal chattels in trust, on a contract, express or implied, that the trust shall be duly executed, and the chattels redelivered in either their original or an altered form, as soon as the time or use for, or condition on which they were bailed, shall have elapsed or been performed": *Bacon's Abridgement*, adopted in *Re S. Davis & Co. Ltd.*, [1945] Ch. 402 at 405. A licence on the other hand is simply the grant of such authority to another to enter upon land for an agreed purpose as to justify that which otherwise would be a trespass and its only legal effect is that the licensor until the licence is revoked is precluded from bringing an action for trespass. . . .

[8]   While no single fact may be of controlling importance in the isolation and categorization of the relationship between the parties to this appeal, the combination of the following factors favour the relationship of bailor-bailee, rather than licensor-licensee:

(a) The owner of the car delivered the keys and therefore the control over the movement of his automobile to the attendant at the attendant's request;

(b) the parking ticket had a serial number which would indicate that the surrender of the specific ticket would be necessary in order to obtain delivery from the attendant of the automobile;

(c) the provision of the attendant raises a reasonable inference that he is supplied by the owner of the business for more than the mere function of receiving money upon the parking of the car;

(d) the parking lot closed, according to the conditions announced on the ticket and signs, at midnight and no conditions were imposed concerning the removal of cars prior thereto;

(e) the notice of a closing hour reasonably infers an active operation of the parking lot rather than a passive allotment of parking stations from which the car owner could at any time, day or night, unilaterally withdraw his parked vehicle, and

(f) the practice of the parking lot owner (although unknown to the owner of the car) was to place the keys left in automobiles at the end of the day in the office of the appellants' car-parking garage across the road.

[9]   In my view, the special circumstances of this case, which I have summarized above, indicate that there was no mutual intention of a mere parking of the car by the respondent owner on the appellants' lot without any action required by the appellants beyond the collection of the fee, The appellants did not hold out a single identified unit of parking space for the exclusive use of the respondent nor did the appellants represent to the respondent that there would be identified a small rectangular island of land somewhere in the appellants' parking lot on which either the respondent or the appellants would place the respondent's vehicle as an alternative to leaving it at the side of the street. The ticket system, the hours of operation, the operating habits of the appellants, including the disposition of car keys at the close of business, and the stipulation that the keys be left in the car so as to enable the appellants to place and move the car at their convenience anywhere within the appellants' parking facility, all indicate a relationship quite different from that of a licence passively granted by the appellant as licensor to the respondent . . . Here the respondent surrendered and the appellant accepted (indeed required) control of this valuable and highly mobile item of property. I therefore conclude that there was a delivery of possession by the respondent to the appellants of the automobile under a contract of bailment. . . .

[10]   The appellant has submitted that should it be found that it was a bailee the exculpatory terms of the contract relieve it from any liability including negligence of the appellant's servants. The respondent in turn has argued that by reason of the fundamental breach of the contract of bailment by the appellant the contract has been terminated including the exculpatory term and the appellant is therefore liable to the respondent for damages thereby occasioned.

[11]   Linked inextricably with the answer to the question of applicability of the exempting clause in any such transaction, is the determination of what onus, if any, lies upon the bailee once the bailor proves non-delivery. Lord Denning in *J. Spurling Ltd. v. Bradshaw*, [1956] 1 W.L.R. 461 at 466, stated:

> A bailor, by pleading and presenting his case properly, can always put on the bailee the burden of proof. In the case of non-delivery, for instance, all he need plead is the contract and a failure to deliver on demand. That puts on the bailee the burden of proving either loss without his fault (which, of course, would be a complete answer at common law) or, if it was due to his fault, it was a fault from which he is excused by the exempting clause. . . .

[12]   . . . The onus in the case of a licence relationship is of course quite different and the licensor is not ordinarily called upon to discharge any burden or onus other than to demonstrate that he has honoured the existence of the licence.

[13] We are left, therefore, with the unexplained disappearance of the respondent's automobile and the last question remaining to be answered is whether the exculpatory clause exonerates the appellants notwithstanding the appellants' complete failure to explain the cause of disappearance, or whether the clause ceased to operate upon the happening of the unexplained loss of the automobile by reason of a breach of a fundamental term of the contract.

[**ESTEY J.A.** here discussed the doctrine of "fundamental breach," a topic which will be introduced in the next section. He concluded that, on the basis of the doctrine, the appellant could not rely on the exemption clause.]

[14] On the facts now before this Court the question is whether the parties to this car-parking transaction contemplated that upon the delivery of the complete possession and control over the car, the operator of the parking lot would be free to maintain silence and escape any liability upon his failure to deliver the car to the respondent on surrender of the appropriate serial parking ticket? To answer the question in the affirmative one must find that the owner, on surrendering his car to the lot operator upon payment of the requested fee for this service, thereupon accepted the implied condition that the operator could, when closing or at the end of the day, leave the car and its keys unprotected and available to any thief or joy-rider who might happen upon the lot. Such an assumption would make meaningless the purpose of parking a car off the highway on a lot supervised by an attendant and equipped with a kiosk from which the lot and the properties placed thereon could be supervised. Furthermore, the issue of a serially numbered ticket upon delivery of possession of the car would either be a meaningless ritual or, worse still, a practice intended to induce a false sense of security. Such an interpretation is denied by the strongest inference by the appellant itself whose president in evidence partially excerpted above detailed the steps followed at the end of the day for safeguarding the keys of automobiles still on the parking lot. . . .

[15] In a recent decision of this court, *Bata v. City Parking Canada Ltd.* (1973), 2 O.R. (2d) 446, 43 D.L.R. (3d) 190, . . . [t]he ticket emphasized the charges were for "parking space only" and similar wording appeared on signs on the premises. The actual wording in all instances was "charges are for use of parking space only." For that reason the court found the relationship to be that of licence rather than bailment and, in my view, is clearly distinguishable from the facts now before us.

[16] But there is a further circumstance in this case which requires examination to completely dispose of this transaction and the rights and obligations of the parties therein. As stated earlier, both the signs on the lot and the ticket referred to the closing of the lot at 12:00 p.m., which the parties agreed in this instance means midnight. When the appellants asked the respondent to leave the keys in the car there arose the clearest implied duty in the appellants to take reasonable steps at the close of business to retain custody of the keys in a manner appropriate to the need of the respondent to recover his car and the necessity of protecting the keys and the car from loss. The appellants are unable to explain what became of the keys. They were never located in either the kiosk on the lot or in the appellants' parking garage across the road. Thus, the keys were either stolen during the day or after the lot closed. In either case the appellants must fail, in the first instance as bailee of the keys and the car for the reasons I have outlined earlier, and in the second instance for breach of duty to exercise reasonable care to safeguard the keys after the closing of the lot. This latter understanding and the duty arising therefrom are entirely unrelated to the exculpatory term set out in the parking ticket. It could not be otherwise as the law would then be unable to imply a duty to exercise reasonable care in the second stage of the custodial arrangement . . .

Appeal dismissed.

THORNTON v. SHOE LANE PARKING LTD.

[1971] 2 Q.B. 163, [1971] 1 All E.R. 686
(C.A., Lord Denning M.R., Megaw and Willmer L.JJ.)

[The plaintiff parked his car in a multi-storey parking garage operated by the defendant. At the entrance was a sign saying, "All cars parked at owner's risk." On entering the plaintiff was faced with a red light which turned to green when he took a ticket offered to him by an automatic machine. The ticket stated that it was "subject to the conditions of issue as displayed on the premises". The plaintiff saw no conditions when he entered the garage, but there were conditions posted in a few places in the garage. These posted conditions purported to exempt the garage from liability for any damage to the car, as well as "any injury to the customer ... howsoever that loss ... damage or injury is caused" that might occur on the defendant's premises. The plaintiff was severely injured in an accident in the defendant's elevator that was found to be 50 per cent the fault of the employees of the garage. The trial judge awarded damages, and the defendant appealed from that decision. After stating the facts, **LORD DENNING M.R.** continued: —]

[1]   . . . The important thing to notice is that the [defendants] seek by this condition to exempt themselves from liability, not only for damage to the car, but also for injury to the customer howsoever caused. The condition talks about insurance [stating that "the customer is deemed to be fully insured at all times against all risks".] It is well known that the customer is usually insured against damage to the car. But he is not insured against damage to himself. If the condition is incorporated into the contract of parking, it means that [the plaintiff] will be unable to recover any damages for his personal injuries which were caused by the negligence of the company. . . .

[2]   The offer was accepted when the plaintiff drove up to the entrance and, by the movement of his car, turned the light from red to green, and the ticket was thrust at him. The contract was then concluded, and it could not be altered by any words printed on the ticket itself. In particular, it could not be altered so as to exempt the company from liability for personal injury due to their negligence.

[3]   Assuming, however, that an automatic machine is a booking clerk in disguise, so that the old fashioned ticket cases still apply to it, we then have to go back to the three questions put by Mellish L.J. in *Parker v. South Eastern Ry Co.* subject to this qualification: Mellish L.J. used the word "conditions" in the plural, whereas it would be more apt to use the word "condition" in the singular, as indeed Mellish L.J. himself did at the end of his judgment. After all, the only condition that matters for this purpose is the exempting condition. It is no use telling the customer that the ticket is issued subject to some "conditions" or other, without more; for he may reasonably regard "conditions" in general as merely regulatory, and not as taking away his rights, unless the exempting condition is drawn specifically to his attention. (Alternatively, if the plural "conditions" is used, it would be better prefaced with the word "exempting," because the exempting conditions are

the only conditions that matter for this purpose.) Telescoping the three questions, they come to this: the customer is bound by the exempting condition if he knows that the ticket is issued subject to it; or, if the company did what was reasonably sufficient to give him notice of it.

[4]   Counsel for the defendants admitted here that the defendants did not do what was reasonably sufficient to give the plaintiff notice of the exempting condition. That admission was properly made. I do not pause to enquire whether the exempting condition is void for unreasonableness. All I say is that it is so wide and so destructive of rights that the court should not hold any man bound by it unless it is drawn to his attention in the most explicit way. It is an instance of what I had in mind in *J. Spurling Ltd. v. Bradshaw*. In order to give sufficient notice, it would need to be printed in red ink with a red hand pointing to it, or something equally startling.

[5]   However, although reasonable notice of it was not given, counsel for the defendants said that this case came within the second question propounded by Mellish L.J., namely that the plaintiff "knew or believed that the writing contained conditions." There was no finding to that effect. The burden was on the defendants to prove it, and they did not do so. Certainly there was no evidence that the plaintiff knew of this exempting condition. He is not, therefore, bound by it. . . .

[6]   I do not think the defendants can escape liability by reason of the exempting condition. I would, therefore, dismiss the appeal. [MEGAW and WILLMER L.JJ. agreed.]

NOTES AND QUESTIONS

1.   Is it possible and desirable to draft a clause that would exempt a party to a contract from liability for personal injuries (whether or not caused by negligence), by way of a posted notice, *i.e.*, by an *unsigned* contract? Consider specifically the following situations:

      (a)   spectators at a hockey game;

      (b)   occupants of a car in a parking lot;

      (c)   spectators at a rock concert; and

      (d)   participants in an aerobic exercise class.

      If you answer these questions affirmatively, draft such a clause. If you think that it is not possible to do so, justify your conclusion.

2.   Peter parks his car in the parking lot operated by Alice. There are signs in large letters on the lot saying "Charges are for use of parking space only" and "Cars parked at owner's risk. For conditions see back of ticket." Peter gets a ticket when he drives in but does not read it. On the back is the following clause: "In order to reduce the risk of theft to cars parked in this lot, it is closed from 2:00 a.m. to 8:00 a.m. No car can be removed during that time." Peter returns at 2:10 a.m. to find the lot locked up and a heavy gate across the entrance. Peter is forced to take a cab home at a cost of $50 and, as a further result, is unable to make an important early meeting the next day. Has he any remedy against Alice?

3.   To what extent was the decision that a "bailment" rather than a licence was involved in *Heffron* (a) a finding of "fact" or (b) a legal conclusion? Could the answer to this question help counsel or a court faced with a similar issue in a subsequent case? To the extent that the decision was based on a finding of fact, what are the facts that sug-

gest that the relation between the parties was a bailment rather than a licence? Which party, the parking lot or the car-owner's insurer, might want to broaden the courts' access to or consideration of the facts?

In *Heffron*, the Court of Appeal refers to its own decision rendered a few months earlier in *Bata v. City Parking Canada Ltd.* (1973), 2 O.R. (2d) 446, 43 D.L.R. (3d) 190 (C.A.). In *Bata*, the parking lot attendant told the car owner to leave his keys in the car, but the ticket and sign said "Charges for use of Parking Space Only". As noted in *Heffron*, the Court in *Bata* ruled that this was a licence relation and refused to impose liability on the parking lot operator for the loss of the car. Do you think that a valid distinction can be made based on the fact that an unread ticket has different words?

Was the result in *Heffron* a fair result? What is the significance of the availability and widespread use of automobile theft insurance to your answer to this question? What is the significance of the availability and use (or non-use) of liability insurance by the operators of parking lots?

4. We shall later look briefly at some of the issues raised by "plain language" drafting. The goals of the movement in favour of such drafting are fairly obvious: people should be aware of the risks that they face when they make a contract. Does the common language found on almost every parking lot (since *Bata* and *Heffron*), "Charges are for use of parking space only", usefully inform the average driver of the allocation of risks? In one sense, these words are in "plain language": none are words that are obviously technical lawyers' words. Are they "plain language" in the sense that that term connotes? What would a truly "plain language" sign at a parking garage or lot say?

5. How useful is the analysis of the issues, repeated in *Thornton v. Shoe Lane*, as one of offer and acceptance? Does such an analysis reflect the values that should be considered?

6. Would Lord Denning have treated a claim for the theft of the contents of Mr. Thornton's car in the same way as the claim for personal injuries? Should he do so? On what basis should one distinguish between the two claims? Does it make a difference that it is relatively easy to obtain theft insurance for a motor vehicle, but that insuring against injury that might occur on a parking lot (through disability insurance) is more expensive, and in some cases impossible to obtain or not universal in the sense that car insurance is?

    Can you suggest a better way of addressing the concerns raised in the cases in the "ticket cases"?

7. *Specht v. Netscape Communications Corp.*, 150 F.Supp. 2d 585 (S.D. N.Y. 2001), considered whether a person who downloaded free computer software from an Internet website was bound by the terms of an arbitration clause in the Licence Agreement that was posted on the site, when there was no requirement for the user to click an "I agree" icon before downloading. The court held that the notice provided was insufficient to form a binding "browse wrap" contract. Hellerstein J. said:

    > Promises become binding when there is a meeting of the minds and consideration is exchanged. So it was at King's Bench in common law England; so it was under the common law in the American colonies; so it was through more than two centuries of jurisprudence in this country; and so it is today. Assent may be registered by a signature, a handshake, or a click of a computer mouse transmitted across the invisible ether of the Internet. Formality is not a requisite; any sign, symbol or action, or even willful inaction, as long as it is unequivocally referable to the promise, may create a contract. . . .

    > Netscape argues that the mere act of downloading indicates assent. However, downloading is hardly an unambiguous indication of assent. The primary purpose of downloading is to obtain a product, not to assent to an agreement. In contrast, clicking on an icon stating "I assent" has no meaning or purpose

other than to indicate such assent. Netscape's failure to require users of SmartDownload to indicate assent to its license as a precondition to downloading and using its software is fatal to its argument that a contract has been formed.

Furthermore, unlike the user of Netscape Navigator or other click-wrap or shrink-wrap licensees, the individual obtaining SmartDownload is not made aware that he is entering into a contract. SmartDownload is available from Netscape's web site free of charge. Before downloading the software, the user need not view any license agreement terms or even any reference to a license agreement, and need not do anything to manifest assent to such a license agreement other than actually taking possession of the product. From the user's vantage point, SmartDownload could be analogized to a free neighborhood newspaper, readily obtained from a sidewalk box or supermarket counter without any exchange with a seller or vender. It is there for the taking. . . .

The only hint that a contract is being formed is one small box of text referring to the license agreement, text that appears below the screen used for downloading and that a user need not even see before obtaining the product:

> Please review and agree to the terms of the Netscape SmartDownload software license agreement before downloading and using the software.

Couched in the mild request, "Please review," this language reads as a mere invitation, not as a condition. The language does not indicate that a user must agree to the license terms before downloading and using the software. While clearer language appears in the License Agreement itself, the language of the invitation does not require the reading of those terms or provide adequate notice either that a contract is being created or that the terms of the License Agreement will bind the user.

The case law on software licensing has not eroded the importance of assent in contract formation. Mutual assent is the bedrock of any agreement to which the law will give force. Defendants' position, if accepted, would so expand the definition of assent as to render it meaningless. Because the user Plaintiffs did not assent to the License Agreement, they are not subject to the arbitration clause contained therein and cannot be compelled to arbitrate their claims against the Defendants.

How would you advise a website operator to design its site in order to ensure that a person who downloads free software is bound by terms it might like to impose, for example, concerning use and distribution of the software, liability and dispute resolution?

Signed Contracts

One of the major issues in the ticket cases was whether or not the party seeking to impose its terms had given the other party adequate notice of the terms. When a contract is signed, the normal rule is that the person signing is bound by all the terms of the signed contract whether he or she had read the contract or not. Signing is regarded as a manifestation of assent to the terms and is sometimes thought to dispose conclusively of the issue of notice. The case that is usually cited in support of this proposition is *L'Estrange v. Graucob, Ltd.*, [1934] 2 K.B. 394 (C.A.). There Scrutton L.J. referred to the judgment of Mellish L.J. in *Parker v. South Eastern Railway Co.*, *supra*, where it was said, "In an ordinary case, where an action is brought on a written agreement which is signed by the defendant, the agreement is proved by proving his signature, and, in the absence of fraud, it is wholly immaterial that he has not read the agreement and does not know the contents." Scrutton L.J. then said much the same thing in a sentence that has been frequently quoted (p. 403): "When a document containing contractual terms is signed, then, in the absence of fraud, or I will add, misrepresentation, the party signing is bound, as it is wholly immaterial whether he has read the document or not."

This was the rule of the nineteenth and early twentieth centuries, and as with other rigid rules of that era, it tended to favour the economically powerful. By the last half of the twentieth century, the courts began to develop more flexible but less certain approaches. The concerns that motivated courts to refuse to give effect to exemption clauses in some of the ticket cases apply to the signed contract.

In reading the cases that follow, consider how well the courts are doing the job of controlling contract power. Keep the following questions in mind:

(a) What purpose does the clause in question serve? Might the clause have been drafted differently and, thereby not have been subject to judicial control?

(b) Have the parties agreed to an allocation of risk against which insurance is available? (If you do not know if insurance is available, consider if the allocation of the risk appears sensible or if it is likely that the same deal could have been offered with alternative prices, the actual price depending on the chosen allocation of the risk. You should bear in mind that it is almost always cheaper for the owner of property to insure than it is for a third party, like a parking lot operator, to insure the property.)

(c) If a court finds or assumes that there was an "imbalance of bargaining power", consider what facts it relied on to support its conclusion. Does the breadth of the factual inquiry necessitated by the conclusion threaten the process of adjudication? What was the precise effect of any "imbalance" that the court found? Was the court's solution the only one possible, or was it the most satisfactory one to deal with the imbalance?

(d) Should one distinguish between cases involving merchants only and those involving consumers and, if so, why?

We have already seen some of the examples of the devices used by the courts to avoid or lessen the effect of a contractual allocation of risk when they felt it desirable to do so. Those devices included the use of strict construction, interpretation *contra proferentem*, and the evisceration of clauses purporting to exclude liability for negligence. We now turn to a more drastic and controversial example of the courts' treatment of contractual allocations of risk. This device is referred to as the "doctrine of fundamental breach".

The earliest cases where the doctrine of "fundamental breach" was applied were English cases (in many of which Lord Denning played a prominent role) and they all fitted into a common pattern. That pattern involved the purchase of durable goods by a consumer, or a person treated by the court as a consumer. The purchase would have been financed by the granting of credit to the consumer by a finance company. The legal form of the transaction common in England (and not unlike the Canadian form for similar transactions) would have been one in which the consumer "hired" (leased) the goods from the finance company, which, at the consumer's explicit direction (contained in the financing agreement signed by the consumer) would have bought them from the ostensible seller — the dealer that the consumer had seen whose salesperson he or she had talked to and with whom he or she thought a deal had been made.

The consumer would agree to pay the purchase price to the finance company in instalments. The transaction would have been structured as a lease so that the finance company would retain title to the goods until the purchase price was fully paid (through the rental payments). If the consumer defaulted in his or her payments, the goods could be seized. When, as of course happened in the litigated cases, the goods turned out to be unsatisfactory, the consumer would refuse to pay any more, adopting the reasonable position that he or she should not be compelled to pay for goods that were now of no use. This reasonable position was not (unfortunately, though perhaps not unexpectedly) supported by the law as found in the *Sale of Goods Act* and, the agreement being signed, *L'Estrange v. Graucob* was ritually invoked to justify, in Karl Llewellyn's immortal words, "the spitting of the victim for the barbecue". Llewellyn, *The Common Law Tradition* (Boston: Little, Brown, 1960), pp. 362-71.

The standard legal analysis was of the following form: Since the dealer had not sold the goods to the consumer, it did not, therefore, assume the duties of a seller. The finance company had bought the goods at the explicit direction of the consumer and would, therefore, not be caught by the implied terms of the *Sale of Goods Act*. In any event, since the transaction with the consumer would have been a lease and not a sale, the *Sale of Goods Act* would not have applied. Moreover, the contract between the consumer and the finance company would have been replete with enough exemption clauses to exclude the terms of the *Sale of Goods Act* several times over.

In most cases where a consumer buys goods that are defective, either the seller will replace them or the consumer will do nothing, make the required payments and chalk the loss up to experience. Where the consumer is, however, sued by the finance company, he or she has little to lose by defending and trusting the court to get him or her out of the mess. In the original cases of fundamental breach the action was brought by the finance company to collect the full amount of the loan outstanding. (The finance company would almost certainly have had an action against the dealer for any loss suffered on the loan to the consumer, but that right would not help the consumer, who, in fact, might be in the process of being sued precisely because the dealer was insolvent or had gone out of business.) In an effort to protect the consumer in these circumstances, the courts developed the doctrine of fundamental breach.

There were initially two approaches to the defence provided by the doctrine of "fundamental breach". One, the "rule of construction approach", made the result depend on whether the contract could be interpreted so as to give the consumer a defence in the circumstances that had occurred. It was implicit in this approach that the parties could, by better drafting, put the risk of loss in the circumstances on the consumer. The other, the "rule of law" approach, made the result, *i.e.*, the provision of an excuse to the consumer, depend on a rule that would operate independently of the parties' intention.

One of the first cases to articulate the "rule of law" approach to the doctrine of fundamental breach was *Karsales (Harrow) Ltd. v. Wallis*, [1956] 2 All E.R. 866, [1956] 1 W.L.R. 936 (C.A.). The defendant bought a used car, a Buick, on a "hire purchase" agreement (similar in effect to the common conditional sales contract frequently used in Canada). The defendant met the seller one evening, and signed the agreement without having test driven the car. The contract included an exemption clause which read:

> 3(g)   No condition or warranty that the vehicle is roadworthy or as to its age, condition or fitness for any purpose is given by the owner [seller] or implied herein.

When the defendant returned the next morning, planning to drive away with the car, he found it to be "in deplorable condition and incapable of self-propulsion". He refused to pay for the car and the seller sued for the price. The English Court of Appeal held that there was a "fundamental breach of contract" which disentitled the plaintiff seller from relying on the exemption clause. Lord Denning stated: (pp. 868-69 All E.R.):

> The law about exempting clauses . . . has been much developed in recent years, at any rate about printed exempting clauses, which so often pass unread. Notwithstanding earlier cases which might suggest the contrary, it is now settled that exempting clauses of this kind, no matter how widely they are expressed, only avail the party when he is carrying out his contract in its essential respects. He is not allowed to use them as a cover for misconduct or indifference or to enable him to turn a blind eye to his obligations. They do not avail him when he is guilty of a breach which goes to the root of the contract. It is necessary to look at the contract apart from the exempting clauses and see what are the terms, express or implied, which impose an obligation on the party. If he has been guilty of a breach of those obligations in a respect which goes to the very root of the contract, he cannot rely on the exempting clauses.

In the same case Parker L.J. said (p. 871):

> Accordingly . . . the plaintiff [seller] said (in effect) that it does not matter what is delivered so long as it bears the appellation of a "Buick" car as described in the agreement, and that the hirer [buyer] is bound to take it. In my judgment, however extensive the exception clause may be, it has no application if there has been a breach of a fundamental term.

> Applying that to the facts of this case, it seems to me that the vehicle delivered in effect is not properly described (as the agreement describes it) as a motor vehicle, "Buick," giving the chassis and engine number. By that I am not saying that every defect in a car which renders it for the moment unusable on the road amounts to a breach of a fundamental term; but where, as here, a vehicle is delivered incapable of self-propulsion except after a complete overhaul and in the condition referred to by [the trial judge] . . . it seems to me that it is abundantly clear that there was a breach of a fundamental term and that accordingly the exceptions in cl. 3(g) do not apply.

The original English cases articulating the rule of law approach to the doctrine of fundamental breach were all consumer cases, and the courts might well have held that the reasonable expectations of the consumer would be defeated if he or she were given no relief. (It should be noted that in Canada legislation now gives individual consumers special protections when a loan is made to finance the purchase of goods and the goods are defective, regardless of the exact form of the financing transaction.)

The courts did not, however, discuss this feature of the cases since orthodox theory made no distinction between the kinds of contracting parties: all transactions were the same. As a result, the doctrine was made applicable to exemption clauses in commercial cases. In *Canso Chemicals Ltd. v. Canadian Westinghouse Co.* (1974), 10 N.S.R. (2d) 306, 54 D.L.R. (3d) 517 (C.A.), the Nova Scotia Court of Appeal applied the doctrine to a contract between two large corporations. In *Harbutt's "Plasticine" Ltd. v. Wayne Tank & Pump Co.*, [1970] 1 Q.B. 447, [1970] 1 All E.R. 225 (C.A.), Lord Denning applied the doctrine of fundamental breach in a contractual dispute involving two large companies, and refused to give effect to an exemption clause, despite the absence of any evidence of unfairness in the process of contract formation or in the terms of the contract.

It may well have been (and may still be) justifiable for courts to refuse to give effect to exemption clauses in consumer cases where doing so would defeat the reasonable expectations of the consumer. Indeed, consumers are often unaware of the terms of the contracts they sign, or at least do not appreciate the significance of the terms of the contract.

The law regarding sales to consumers was changed by legislation in the period from 1960 to 1977. All Canadian provinces have various *Consumer Protection Acts* which, *inter alia*, prevent sellers from excluding the implied terms under the *Sale of Goods Act*. In England consumer law was changed by the *Unfair Contract Terms Act, 1977*. After 1977 the rule of law approach to the doctrine of fundamental breach served no useful function, and judges began to reconsider it. It was rejected in the following case.

PHOTO PRODUCTION LTD. v. SECURICOR TRANSPORT LTD

[1980] A.C. 827, [1980] 1 All E.R. 556
(H.L., Lords Wilberforce, Diplock, Salmon, Keith and Scarman)

LORD WILBERFORCE: — **[1]** My Lords, this appeal arises from the destruction by fire of a factory owned by the respondents ("Photo Productions") involving loss and damage agreed to amount to £615,000. The question is whether the appellants ("Securicor") are liable to the respondent for this sum.

[2]   Securicor are [*sic*] a company which provides security services. In 1968 they entered into a contract with Photo Productions by which it agreed to provide their "Night Patrol Service" . . . The contract incorporated printed standard conditions which, in some circumstances, might exclude or limit Securicor's liability. The questions in this appeal are (i) whether these conditions can be invoked at all in the events which happened and (ii) if so, whether either the exclusion provision, or a provision limiting liability, can be applied on the facts. The trial judge (MacKenna J.) decided these issues in favour of Securicor. The Court of Appeal [[1978] 3 All E.R. 146, [1978] 1 W.L.R. 856] decided issue (i) in Photo Productions' favour invoking the doctrine of fundamental breach. Waller L.J. in addition would have decided for Photo Productions on issue (ii).

[3]   What happened was that on a Sunday night the duty employee of Securicor was one Musgrove. It was not suggested that he was unsuitable for the job or that Securicor were negligent in employing him. He visited the factory at the correct time, but when inside he deliberately started a fire by throwing a match onto some cartons. The fire got out of control and a large part of the premises was burnt down. Though what he did was deliberate, it was not established that he intended to destroy the factory. The judge's finding was in these words:

> Whether Musgrove intended to light only a small fire (which was the very least he meant to do) or whether he intended to cause much more serious damage, and, in either case, what was the reason for his act, are mysteries I am unable to solve.

[4]   This, and it is important to bear in mind when considering the judgments in the Court of Appeal, falls short of a finding that Musgrove deliberately burnt or intended to burn Photo Productions' factory.

[5]   The condition on which Securicor relies reads, relevantly, as follows:

> Under no circumstances shall the Company [Securicor] be responsible for any inju-
> rious act or default by any employee of the Company unless such act or default
> could have been foreseen and avoided by the exercise of due diligence on the part of
> the Company as his employer; nor, in any event, shall the Company be held respon-
> sible for: (a) Any loss suffered by the customer through burglary, theft, fire or any
> other cause, except insofar as such loss is solely attributable to the negligence of the
> Company's employees acting within the course of their employment. . . .

[6]   There are further provisions limiting to stated amounts the liability of Securicor on which it relies in the alternative if held not to be totally exempt.

[7]   It is first necessary to decide on the correct approach to a case such as this
where it is sought to invoke an exception or limitation clause in the contract. The
approach of Lord Denning M.R. in the Court of Appeal was to consider first
whether the breach was "fundamental." If so, he said, the court itself deprives the
party of the benefit of an exemption or limitation clause. Shaw and Waller L.JJ.
substantially followed him in this argument.

[8]   Lord Denning M.R. in this was following the earlier decision of the Court of
Appeal, and in particular his own judgment in *Harbutt's "Plasticine" Ltd. v.
Wayne Tank & Pump Co.* [1970] 1 Q.B. 447, [1970] 1 All E.R. 225]. In that case
Lord Denning M.R. distinguished two cases: (a) the case where as the result of a
breach of contract the innocent party has, and exercises, the right to bring the contract to an end; and (b) the case where the breach automatically brings the contract
to an end, without the innocent party having to make an election whether to terminate the contract or to continue it. In the first case Lord Denning M.R., purportedly
applying this House's decision in *Suisse Atlantique Société d'Armement Maritime
SA v. N.V. Rotterdamsche Kolen Centrale* [[1967] 1 A.C. 361, [1966] 2 All E.R.
61 (H.L.)], but in effect two citations from two of their Lordships' speeches, extracted a rule of law that the "termination" of the contract brings it, and with it the
exclusion clause, to an end. The *Suisse Atlantique* case in his view

> affirms the long line of cases in this court that when one party has been guilty of a
> fundamental breach of the contract . . . and the other side accepts it, so that the con-
> tract comes to an end . . . then the guilty party cannot rely on an exception or limita-
> tion clause to escape from his liability for the breach. (*Harbutt's* case . . .)

He then applied the same principle to the second case.

[9]   My Lords, whatever the intrinsic merit of this doctrine, as to which I shall
have something to say later, it is clear to me that so far from following this
House's decision in the *Suisse Atlantique* case, it is directly opposed to it and that
the whole purpose and tenor of the *Suisse Atlantique* case was to repudiate it. The
lengthy, and perhaps I may say sometimes indigestible speeches of their Lordships, are correctly summarised in the headnote — holding No. 3 [[1967] 1 A.C.
361, at 362] — "That the question whether an exceptions clause was applicable
where there was a fundamental breach of contract was one of the true construction
of the contract." That there was any rule of law by which exception clauses are
eliminated, or deprived of effect, regardless of their terms, was clearly not the
view of Viscount Dilhorne, Lord Hodson or myself. The passages invoked for the
contrary view of a rule of law consist only of two short extracts from two of the
speeches — on any view a minority. But the case for the doctrine does not even go
so far as that. Lord Reid, in my respectful opinion, and I recognize that I might not

be the best judge in this matter, in his speech read as a whole, cannot be claimed as a supporter of a rule of law.

[10] My Lords, in the light of this, the passage from the *Suisse Atlantique* case cited by Lord Denning M.R. has to be considered. For convenience I restate it [p. 398]:

> If fundamental breach is established, the next question is what effect, if any, that has on the applicability of other terms of the contract. This question has often arisen with regard to clauses excluding liability, in whole or in part, of the party in breach. I do not think that there is generally much difficulty where the innocent party has elected to treat the breach as a repudiation, bring the contract to an end and sue for damages. Then the whole contract has ceased to exist including the exclusion clause, and I do not see how that clause can then be used to exclude an action for loss which will be suffered by the innocent party after it has ceased to exist, such as loss of the profit which would have accrued if the contract had run its full term.

[11] It is with the utmost reluctance that, not forgetting the "beams" that may exist elsewhere, I have to detect here a mote of ambiguity or perhaps even of inconsistency. What is referred to is "loss which will be suffered by the innocent party after [the contract] has ceased to exist" and I venture to think that all that is being said, rather elliptically, relates only to what is to happen in the future, and is not a proposition as to the immediate consequences caused by the breach; if it were, that would be inconsistent with the full and reasoned discussion which follows.

[12] It is only because of Lord Reid's great authority in the law that I have found it necessary to embark on what in the end may be superfluous analysis. For I am convinced that, with the possible exception of Lord Upjohn, whose critical passage, when read in full, is somewhat ambiguous, their Lordships, fairly read, can only be taken to have rejected those suggestions for a rule of law which had appeared in the Court of Appeal and to have firmly stated that the question is one of construction, not merely of course of the exclusion clause alone, but of the whole contract. . . .

[13] 1. The doctrine of "fundamental breach" in spite of its imperfections and doubtful parentage has served a useful purpose. There were a large number of problems, productive of injustice, in which it was worse than unsatisfactory to leave exception clauses to operate. Lord Reid referred to these in the *Suisse Atlantique* case, pointing out at the same time that the doctrine of fundamental breach was a dubious specific. But since then Parliament has taken a hand: it has passed the *Unfair Contract Terms Act 1977*. This act applies to consumer contracts and those based on standard terms and enables exception clauses to be applied with regard to what is just and reasonable. It is significant that Parliament refrained from legislating over the whole field of contract. After this act, in commercial matters generally, when the parties are not of unequal bargaining power, and when risks are normally borne by insurance, not only is the case for judicial intervention undemonstrated, but there is everything to be said, and this seems to have been Parliament's intention, for leaving the parties free to apportion the risks as they think fit and for respecting their decisions.

[14] At the stage of negotiation as to the consequences of a breach, there is everything to be said for allowing the parties to estimate their respective claims according to the contractual provisions they have themselves made, rather than for facing

them with a legal complex so uncertain as the doctrine of fundamental breach must be. What, for example, would have been the position of Photo Productions' factory if instead of being destroyed it had been damaged, slightly or moderately or severely? At what point does the doctrine (with what logical justification I have not understood) decide, ex post facto, that the breach was (factually) fundamental before going on to ask whether legally it is to be regarded as fundamental? How is the date of "termination" to be fixed? Is it the date of the incident causing the damage, or the date of the innocent party's election, or some other date? All these difficulties arise from the doctrine and are left unsolved by it.

[15] At the judicial stage there is still more to be said for leaving cases to be decided straightforwardly on what the parties have bargained for rather than on analysis, which becomes progressively more refined, of decisions in other cases leading to inevitable appeals. The learned judge was able to decide this case on normal principles of contractual law with minimal citation of authority. I am sure that most commercial judges have wished to be able to do the same. In my opinion they can and should.

[16] 2. *Harbutt's Plasticine Ltd. v. Wayne Tank & Pump Co.* must clearly be overruled. It would be enough to put that on its radical inconsistency with the *Suisse Atlantique* case. But even if the matter were res integra I would find the decision to be based on unsatisfactory reasoning as to the "termination" of the contract and the effect of "termination" on the plaintiffs' claim for damage. I have, indeed, been unable to understand how the doctrine can be reconciled with the well-accepted principle of law, stated by the highest modern authority, that when in the context of a breach of contract one speaks of "termination" what is meant is not more than that the innocent party or, in some cases, both parties are excused from further performance. Damages, in such cases, are then claimed under the contract, so what reason in principle can there be for disregarding what the contract itself says about damages, whether it "liquidates" them, or limits them, or excludes them? These difficulties arise in part from uncertain or inconsistent terminology. A vast number of expressions are used to describe situations where a breach has been committed by one party of such a character as to entitle the other party to refuse further performance: discharge, rescission, termination, the contract is at an end, or dead, or displaced; clauses cannot survive, or simply go. I have come to think that some of these difficulties can be avoided; in particular the use of "rescission," even if distinguished from rescission ab initio, as an equivalent for discharge, though justifiable in some contexts . . . may lead to confusion in others. To plead for complete uniformity may be to cry for the moon. But what can and ought to be avoided is to make use of these confusions in order to produce a concealed and unreasoned legal innovation: to pass, for example, from saying that a party, victim of a breach of contract, is entitled to refuse further performance, to saying that he may treat the contract as at an end, or as rescinded, and to draw from this the proposition, which is not analytical but one of policy, that all or (arbitrarily) some of the clauses of the contract lose, automatically, their force, regardless of intention.

[17] If this process is discontinued the way is free to use such words as "discharge" or "termination" consistently with principles as stated by modern authority which *Harbutt's* case disregards. . . .

[18] These passages I believe to state correctly the modern law of contract in the relevant respects; they demonstrate that the whole foundation of *Harbutt's* case is unsound. . . .

[19] In this situation the present case has to be decided. As a preliminary, the nature of the contract has to be understood. Securicor undertook to provide a service of periodical visits for a very modest charge which works out at 26p per visit. It did not agree to provide equipment. It would have no knowledge of the value of Photo Productions' factory; that, and the efficacy of their fire precautions, would be known to Photo Productions. In these circumstances nobody could consider it unreasonable that as between these two equal parties the risk assumed by Securicor should be a modest one, and that Photo Productions should carry the substantial risk of damage or destruction.

[20] The duty of Securicor was, as stated, to provide a service. There must be implied an obligation to use care in selecting their patrolmen, to take care of the keys and, I would think, to operate the service with due and proper regard to the safety and security of the premises. The breach of duty committed by Securicor lay in a failure to discharge this latter obligation. Alternatively it could be put on a vicarious responsibility for the wrongful act of Musgrove, viz starting a fire on the premises; Securicor would be responsible for this . . . This being the breach, does condition 1 apply? It is drafted in strong terms: "Under no circumstances, any injurious act or default by any employee." These words have to be approached with the aid of the cardinal rules of construction that they must be read *contra proferentem* and that in order to escape from the consequences of one's own wrongdoing, or that of one's servant, clear words are necessary. I think that these words are clear. Photo Productions in fact relied on them for an argument that since they exempted from negligence they must be taken as not exempting from the consequence of deliberate acts. But this is a perversion of the rule that if a clause can cover something other than negligence it will not be applied to negligence. Whether, in addition to negligence, it covers other, e.g., deliberate, acts, remains a matter of construction requiring, of course, clear words. I am of opinion that it does and, being free to construe and apply the clause, I must hold that liability is excluded. On this part of the case I agree with the judge and adopt his reasons for judgment. I would allow the appeal.

[**LORDS SALMON, KEITH OF KINKEL, SCARMAN** and **DIPLOCK** delivered judgments agreeing with **LORD WILBERFORCE.**]

NOTES AND QUESTIONS

1. In *Beaufort Realties (1964) Inc. v. Chomedey Aluminum Co. Ltd.*, [1980] 2 S.C.R. 718, 116 D.L.R. (3d) 193, the Supreme Court of Canada, in spite of the decision of the House of Lords in *Photo Production*, applied the doctrine of fundamental breach without much thought for its justification. Chomedey Aluminum Co. Ltd., was a subcontractor on a construction project. The general contractor was Belcourt Construction (Ottawa) Ltd. The work was being done for the owner, Beaufort Realties. Chomedey agreed in the contract with Belcourt that it would not assert a mechanic's lien against the property. A dispute arose between Belcourt and Chomedey over the quality of the work done by Chomedey, and Belcourt, alleging that the work had been done badly, refused to make a progress payment. Chomedey filed a mechanics' lien; the owner challenged Chomedey's right to do so. In the lien action the trial judge held that Belcourt's refusal to pay was a "fundamental breach" and that Chomedey would be allowed to assert its lien. This decision was reversed by the Divisional Court. The Court

of Appeal upheld the trial judge. The contractor and owner appealed to the Supreme Court. The appeal was dismissed.

The substance of the decision of the Supreme Court was the following paragraph from the judgment of Ritchie J. (who gave the judgment of the Court, p. 726 (S.C.R.)):

> Like Madam Justice Wilson [in the Court of Appeal], and having particular regard to the judgment of the House of Lords in the *Photo Production* case, . . . I am satisfied that, considering the fundamental breach by the contractor (Belcourt Construction (Ottawa) Limited), in the context of the contract as a whole the true construction to be placed on article 6 is that the waiver [of lien] therein contained ceased to bind the respondent upon it having communicated to the appellant its election to treat the contract as at an end.

As a result of the decision in *Beaufort Realties*, the "rule of construction" approach to doctrine of fundamental breach was accepted in Canada.

The Court of Appeal and the Supreme Court treated Belcourt's refusal to make the progress payment as a "fundamental breach", but there was no investigation of the significance of the general contractor's action in light of the parties' contractual obligations and, in particular, the standard of performance reached by the subcontractor.

2. One of the major problems of the doctrine of fundamental breach was that it was triggered only by the presence of an "exemption clause". (Such a clause is sometimes called an "exclusion clause" or an "exempting clause".) In order to give relief on the basis that it did in *Beaufort Realties*, the Supreme Court had to treat the clause waiving the subcontractor's right to a lien as an "exemption" clause. This conclusion was due, in part at least, to the fact that counsel for the contractor apparently accepted the ruling of the trial judge that it was an "exemption clause": it was almost as if the trial judge's decision were a finding of fact, not subject to review on appeal.

There are many cases discussing the correct way to define such a clause. A standard textbook definition is the following one taken from *Chitty on Contracts*, 25th ed. (London: Sweet & Maxwell, 1983), vol. 1, p. 466:

> Exemption clauses may be broadly divided into three categories. First, there are clauses which purport to limit or reduce what would otherwise be the defendant's duty, i.e., the substantive obligations to which he would otherwise be subject under the contract, for example, by excluding express or implied terms, by limiting liability to cases of wilful neglect or fault, or by binding a buyer of land or goods to accept the property sold subject to "faults," "defects" or "errors of description." Secondly, there are clauses which purport to relieve a party in default from the sanctions which would otherwise attach to his breach of contract, such as liability to be sued for breach or to be liable in damages, or which take away from the other party the right to rescind or repudiate the agreement. Thirdly, there are clauses which purport to qualify the duty of the party in default fully to indemnify the other party, for example, by limiting the amount of damages recoverable against him, or by providing a time-limit within which claims must be made.

There is no unanimity on how one identifies such a clause, and the Supreme Court has delivered inconsistent judgments. The waiver of lien in *Beaufort Realties* was held to be an exemption clause, but the clause in *Bauer v. Bank of Montreal* (*supra*, Chapter 5) was held not to be one. The clause in *Beaufort Realties* stated (p. 720 (S.C.R.)):

> The Subcontractor hereby waives, releases and renounces all privileges or rights of privilege, and all lien or rights of lien now existing or that may hereinafter exist for work done or materials furnished under this Contract, upon the premises and upon the land on which the same is situated, and upon any money or monies due or to become due from any person or persons to Contractor, and agrees to furnish a good and sufficient waiver of the privilege and

lien on said building, lands and monies from every person or corporation furnishing labour or material under the Subcontractor. . . .

The clause in *Bauer v. Bank of Montreal* ([1980] 2 S.C.R. 102, p. 105) stated:

It is further agreed that said bank, without exonerating in whole or in part the undersigned, or any of them (if more than one), may grant time, renewals, extensions, indulgences, releases and discharges to, may take securities from and give the same and any or all existing securities up to, may abstain from taking securities from, or from perfecting securities of, . . . the customer.

The definition from the 23rd edition of *Chitty on Contracts*, Vol. 1, p. 362, was quoted by McIntyre J. in *Bauer v. Bank of Montreal*, to justify his conclusion that the clause in the bank guarantee was not an "exemption" clause, and hence the doctrine of fundamental breach did not apply, and the individual was liable to the Bank. That definition was almost identical to that set out above, with the exception that the second sentence then stated ([1980] 2 S.C.R. 102, p. 108):

First, there are clauses which purport to exempt one party from a substantive obligation to which he would otherwise be subject under the contract, for example, by excluding express or implied terms, by limiting liability to cases of wilful neglect or default, or by binding a buyer of land or goods to accept the property sold subject to "faults", "defects" or "errors of description".

If an exemption clause is a clause that allocates to one side a risk that, were it not for the clause, would be on the other, what is the difference between the clauses in the two cases? Do both not allocate risks between the parties?

3.   In *B.G. Linton Construction Ltd. v. Canadian National Railway Co.*, [1975] 2 S.C.R. 678, 49 D.L.R. (3d) 548, a contractor wanted to amend a bid that was about to be submitted to the federal government. According to the tender documents, the amendment had to be in writing; a telegram would be an effective amendment, but a telex message would not. The contractor went to the offices of the respondent in Fort Nelson to send a telegram to reduce his bid. He informed the clerk of the importance of a telegram, as opposed to a telex, and of the deadline for the submission of bids. He was assured that the amending bid would be delivered in time and in the form required. It was delivered late. The contractor was able to show that, had the amendment been delivered on time, its bid would have been accepted. The respondent relied on a clause in its standard telegram form that exempted it from liability. The form was approved by the Railway Commissioners for Canada (at the time the appropriate body for granting such approval), and provided (p. 681 (S.C.R.)):

It is agreed between the sender of the message on the face of this form and this Company that said Company shall not be liable for damages arising from failure to transmit or deliver, or for any error in the transmission or delivery of any unrepeated telegram, whether happening from negligence of its servants or otherwise. . . .

A majority of the Supreme Court, in a judgment delivered by Ritchie J., held that the contractor could not sue in the face of the exemption clause. Laskin C.J.C. dissented, and would have held the respondent liable, saying (p. 684 S.C.R.):

The ultimate situation that arises here is a complete negation of any obligation which the transaction may have appeared to contemplate, but that is a result which . . . can hardly be reached where the parties have not been trifling and did have reciprocal obligations in view . . . There must be a residue of obligation that is not cancelled out by concurrent exemption, otherwise it is illusory to speak of a contract. . . .

Spence J., with whom Laskin C.J.C. agreed, also dissented. He did so on the ground that there had been a fundamental breach by the respondent.

Ritchie J. (p. 692 (S.C.R.)) referred to these arguments, and in particular to a statement by Laskin C.J.C., and commented:

> It seems to me a rather monstrous proposition, if it is seriously advanced, that Parliament in its legislation authorized total immunity from liability to be conferred upon a carrier which, under its cover, could decide when and if it would send a requested telegram.

Ritchie J. said that he could see no basis in the facts to support these statements. All that had happened was that a telegram had been delivered one hour late.

4. On what basis (or evidence), if we were to accept the analysis of Laskin C.J.C., could a court determine the minimum obligation that a party must be taken to have assumed by contract? Should it make any difference that the seller of a car promises to sell "a metal box on four wheels, more or less", or that he promises to sell a specified car, excluding all warranties that the car will work or last for any length of time, and charges the same price in both situations?

5. Should it make any difference to the analysis of the effect, or to the application of such devices as *contra proferentem* construction if the exemption clause has a statutory basis, as was the case in *B.G. Linton*?

6. Canadian courts did not find it easy to follow the decision of the Supreme Court in *Beaufort*. There were cases that cited *Beaufort* as authority for the adoption in Canada of the decision in *Photo Production*, and which then refused to reallocate the risk of loss allocated by the contract. There were also cases that applied the "construction" approach to fundamental breach set out in *Photo Production* doctrine.

    In *Canadian-Dominion Leasing Ltd. v. Welch* (1981), 33 O.R. (2d) 826, 125 D.L.R. (3d) 723 (C.A.), the Court of Appeal had to deal with the claim of the defendant that the plaintiff (who had financed the defendant's purchase) had fundamentally breached a contract to lease a photocopier (which never worked) in the face of an exemption clause which stated that the plaintiff was not liable for defects in the quality of what it had provided. The Court of Appeal said (p. 829 (O.R.)):

> In our view, having regard to all the circumstances of the case, including the dealings between the parties and their clear intent as expressed in the language they have used, the "no warranties" clause in the lease set out heretofore in this judgment was applicable notwithstanding the breach might be regarded as fundamental. The facts come squarely within the relevant contractual language.

The following decision of the Supreme Court of Canada deals with the general problems of "exemption clauses" and offers contrasting views of the proper role or scope of the doctrine of fundamental breach.

HUNTER ENGINEERING CO., INC. v. SYNCRUDE CANADA LTD.

[1989] S.C.J. No. 23, [1989] 1 S.C.R. 426, 57 D.L.R. (4th) 321
(S.C.C., Dickson C.J.C., McIntyre, Wilson, L'Heureux-Dubé and La Forest JJ.)

[The appellants, defendants, Hunter Engineering Co. Inc. and Allis-Chalmers Canada Ltd., had supplied large gears to the respondent, plaintiff, Syncrude Canada Ltd., for use on a conveyor belt on the plaintiff's Alberta tar sands project. The facts were complex and a number of issues were dealt with by the Supreme Court. The issue relevant here is the interpretation of the warranty given by the defendants to the plaintiff and the effect of clauses limiting the defendants' liability in the events that happened. Allis-Chalmers also claimed, in third party proceedings, against Hunter Engineering (U.S.), the designer of the gear boxes. The contracts between the two defendants and Syncrude were similar, with both providing Syncrude with a warranty in the following words:

> **8. Warranties — Guarantees**: Seller warrants that the goods shall be free from defects in design, material, workmanship, and title, and shall conform in all respects to the terms of this purchase order, and shall be of the best quality, if no quality is specified. If it appears within one year from the date of placing the equipment in service for the purpose for which it was purchased, that the equipment, or any part thereof, does not conform to these warranties and Buyer so notifies Seller within a reasonable time after its discovery, Seller shall thereupon promptly correct such nonconformity as its sole expense. . . . Except as otherwise provided in this purchase order, Seller's liability hereunder shall extend to all damages proximately caused by the breach of any of the foregoing warranties or guarantees, but such liability shall in no event include loss of profit or loss of use.

This warranty was subsequently amended by each of the defendants. The amendment in the Hunter Engineering contract was the addition of the following words:

> *Warranty*: Twenty four (24) months from date of shipment to twelve (12) months from date of start-up whichever occurs first.

The amendment in the Allis-Chalmers contract was:

> *Warranty*: 24 months from date of shipment or 12 months from date of start-up, whichever occurs first.

> . . .

> A. Paragraph 8 — "Warranties and Guarantees"

> The final sentence of paragraph 8 is hereby deleted. In its place shall be, "The provisions of this paragraph represent the only warranty of the Seller and no other warranty or conditions, statutory or otherwise shall be implied." The warranty period shall be twelve (12) months from the date of operation or 24 months from the date of shipment, whichever occurs first. . . .

The plaintiff made a claim against both defendants under the warranties. The claims were made more than 12 months after the date of start-up of the equipment. The issue before the Supreme Court of Canada was whether the claims were limited by the terms of the warranty. This issue was subdivided into two aspects:

(a) were the claims of the plaintiff barred by the terms of the warranty; and

(b) could the doctrine of fundamental breach apply to allow the plaintiff to claim, even if the defendants were protected by the terms of the express warranties?

The Court held that in the case of Hunter Engineering, the warranty did not exclude the statutory warranty under the *Sale of Goods Act* (the reference was to s. 15(1) of the Ontario Act) while the claim against Allis-Chalmers under the Act was barred by the terms of the warranty.

DICKSON C.J.C. (LA FOREST J. concurring) justified his conclusion that Hunter Engineering was liable under the *Sale of Goods Act* on the grounds that if one wishes to contract out of statutory protections, this must be done by clear and direct language, particularly where the parties are two large, commercially sophisticated companies.

DICKSON C.J.C. then dealt with the argument that the doctrine of fundamental breach applied to the breaches by the defendants.]

[1] . . . It will now be convenient to consider the liability to Syncrude of Allis-Chalmers and in turn of Hunter U.S. on the third party claim of Allis-Chalmers. The facts can be briefly stated. The purchase agreement contained in para. 8 a warranty modified . . . to exclude statutory warranties or conditions. Paragraph 14 of the agreement read:

> . . . Notwithstanding any other provision in this contract or any applicable statutory provisions neither the Seller nor the Buyer shall be liable to the other for special or consequential damages or damages for loss of use arising directly or indirectly from any breach of this contract, fundamental or otherwise or from any tortious acts or omissions of their respective employees or agents and in no event shall the liability of the Seller exceed the unit price of the defective product or of the product subject to late delivery.

[2] The price of the 14 conveyor systems and accessories purchased from Allis-Chalmers was $4,166,464. The agreed cost of the repairs was $400,000; including prejudgment interest, $535,000. In the face of the contractual provisions, Allis-Chalmers can only be found liable under the doctrine of fundamental breach.

[3] The Court of Appeal differed with the trial judge on the question of fundamental breach. At trial Gibbs J., at pp. 74-6, quoted with approval from the judgment of Stratton J.A., as he then was, in *Sperry Rand Canada Ltd. v. Thomas Equipment Ltd.* (1982), 135 D.L.R. (3d) 197 at pp. 205-6, 40 N.B.R. (2d) 271 (N.B.C.A.), and the judgment of Harradence J.A. in *Gafco Enterprises Ltd. v. Schofield*, [1983] 4 W.W.R. 135 at pp. 139-41, 25 Alta. L.R. (2d) 238, 23 B.L.R. 9 (Alta. C.A.).

[4] Applying the principle of these cases to the purchase order and the nature of the defect in the bull gears, Gibbs J. concluded that the case for fundamental breach had not been made out. He said at pp. 77-78:

> As to the nature of the defect, in my opinion it was not so fundamental that it went to the root of the contract. The contract between the parties was still a contract for gearboxes. Gearboxes were supplied. They were capable of performing their function and did perform it for in excess of a year which, given the agreed time limitations, was the "cost free to Syncrude" period contemplated by the parties. It was conceded that the gearboxes were not fit for the service. However, the unfitness, or defect, was repairable and was repaired at a cost significantly less than the original purchase price. No doubt the bull gear is an important component of the gearbox but no more important than the engine in an automobile and in the *Gafco Ent.* case the failure of the engine was not a sufficiently fundamental breach to lead the Court to set aside the contract of sale. On my appreciation of the evidence Syncrude got what it bargained for . . . It has not convinced me that there was fundamental breach.

[5] On appeal, Anderson J.A. reviewed a number of authorities . . . and held that Allis-Chalmers was in fundamental breach because Syncrude was deprived of substantially the whole benefit of the contract.

[6] In reaching that conclusion he said at p. 393:

> It follows that the cost of repair was not significantly less than the original purchase price but, on the contrary, the cost of repair constituted 86 per cent of the purchase price. Moreover, the expected life of a gearbox is 20 years. The expected life of a

bull gear is at least ten years. The bull gear failed within less than two years after Syncrude's operations commenced.

[7]   He rejected as without merit the argument of counsel for Allis-Chalmers that Syncrude's contract with Allis-Chalmers was not just a "contract for gearboxes" but was rather a contract for the purchase of a package of 14 conveyor systems for a price of over $4,000,000, and viewed in relation to the total purchase price actually paid by Syncrude, the cost of repair of one component, whether it is considered to be the bull gear or the gearbox, was indeed "significantly less than the original purchase price."

[8]   Hunter U.S., ultimately liable on account of the third-party claim against it, submits that the British Columbia Court of Appeal was wrong on this branch of the case because the effect of its decision is to re-establish the doctrine of fundamental breach as a rule of law invalidating a clause limiting liability. . . .

[9]   It was contended by Hunter U.S. that . . . the Court of Appeal approached the matter by asking whether the warranty in the contract excluded liability for fundamental breach. Upon finding it did not, the Court of Appeal then found as a fact, contrary to the finding of fact made by the trial judge, that the breach was fundamental, and awarded the buyer the full amount of its claim.

[10]   It was submitted that by doing this, the Court of Appeal erroneously adopted the approach . . . that to be effective a limitation of liability clause must expressly exclude liability for fundamental breach. It was submitted this approach involves returning to the notion of treating fundamental breach as something which, as a rule of law, will displace the terms of the contract; to paraphrase Lord Bridge's decision in *George Mitchell (Chesterhall) Ltd. v. Finney Lock Seeds Ltd.*, [1983] 2 All E.R. 737 (H.L.) at p. 741: it reintroduces by the back door a doctrine which the *Suisse Atlantique* case, and cases following, had evicted by the front.

[11]   Allis-Chalmers adopted in its entirety the argument of Hunter U.S. with respect to the fundamental breach issue. The argument in the factum of Allis-Chalmers was directed to the further question whether the Court of Appeal erred in failing to construe properly the warranty clause in ascertaining whether it applied to the instant breach.

[12]   Allis-Chalmers argued that the words of cl. 8 are clear and fairly susceptible of only one meaning, and the Court of Appeal erred in failing to give effect to them; instead of giving effect to the language of the contract, the Court of Appeal imported its own implied warranty and erroneously embarked on a consideration of whether cl. 8 was effective to eliminate the "essential undertaking of Allis-Chalmers to provide gearboxes capable of meeting the requirements of the extraction process". In proceeding in this fashion, the Court of Appeal in effect resurrected a term analogous to the implied statutory warranty of fitness for the purpose required, which the parties had expressly excluded. By importing this additional term into the contract the court rewrote the bargain which the parties had made for themselves.

[13]   Syncrude argues in response that the seller's fundamental obligation does not derive from, and is not dependent upon, the existence of express or implied warranties or conditions. It is inherent in the contract of sale.

[14] Syncrude relied upon the pronouncement of the doctrine of fundamental obligation of the seller enunciated by Weatherston J. in *Cain v. Bird Chevrolet-Oldsmobile Ltd.* (1976), 69 D.L.R. (3d) 484, 12 O.R. (2d) 532 (H.C.) affirmed 88 D.L.R. (3d) 607*n* (Ont. C.A.)). The court stated at pp. 486-7 D.L.R., pp. 534-5 O.R.:

> The first and most important thing in any case is to determine what are the terms of the contract, so as to decide what performance was required by the defaulting party. . . .

Where a machine has been delivered which has such a defect, or "such a congeries of defects" as to destroy the workable character of the machine, there is said to be a fundamental breach of contract by the seller. This is so because the purported performance of the contract is quite different than that which the contract contemplated. . . . There has been no failure of consideration, no failure to deliver the thing contracted for, but it is implicit in the transaction, as a fundamental term, that the thing contracted for is what it seems to be.

[15] The House of Lords' cases decided that liability for breach of a fundamental term may be excluded by a suitably worded exclusion clause. However, counsel contended that there is a rule of construction that exemption clauses must be very clearly worded if they are to be sufficient to exclude liability for fundamental breach. It was said that this approach to the construction of a contract was confirmed in this court in *Beaufort Realties (1964) Inc. v. Chomedey Aluminum Co. Ltd.* [*supra*]

[16] On the application of the principles to the present case, Syncrude asked the question whether Allis-Chalmers and Syncrude intended that Allis-Chalmers could supply gearboxes which were so fundamentally defective as to require complete replacement, or in this case, complete reconstruction, after 15 months' service, at Syncrude's sole cost. Syncrude would give a negative response to this question.

[17] I have had the advantage of reading the reasons for judgment prepared by my colleague, Justice Wilson, in this appeal and I agree with her disposition of the liability of Allis-Chalmers. In my view, the warranty clauses in the Allis-Chalmers contract effectively excluded liability for defective gearboxes after the warranty period expired. With respect, I disagree, however, with Wilson J.'s approach to the doctrine of fundamental breach. I am inclined to adopt the course charted by the House of Lords in *Photo Production Ltd. v. Securicor Transport Ltd.*, [*supra*], and to treat fundamental breach as a matter of contract construction. I do not favour, as suggested by Wilson J., requiring the court to assess the reasonableness of enforcing the contract terms after the court has already determined the meaning of the contract based on ordinary principles of contract interpretation. In my view, the courts should not disturb the bargain the parties have struck, and I am inclined to replace the doctrine of fundamental breach with a rule that holds the parties to the terms of their agreement, provided the agreement is not unconscionable.

[18] The doctrine of fundamental breach in the context of clauses excluding a party from contractual liability has been confusing at the best of times. Simply put, the doctrine has served to relieve parties from the effects of contractual terms, excluding liability for deficient performance where the effects of these terms have seemed particularly harsh. Lord Wilberforce acknowledged this in *Photo Production*, at p. 843:

1.   The doctrine of "fundamental breach" in spite of its imperfections and doubtful parentage has served a useful purpose. There was a large number of problems, productive of injustice, in which it was worse than unsatisfactory to leave exception clauses to operate.

[19]   In cases where extreme unfairness would result from the operation of an exclusion clause, a fundamental breach of contract was said to have occurred. The consequence of fundamental breach was that the party in breach was not entitled to rely on the contractual exclusion of liability but was required to pay damages for contract breach. In the doctrine's most common formulation, by Lord Denning in *Karsales (Harrow) Ltd. v. Wallis*, [1956] 1 W.L.R. 936 (C.A.), fundamental breach was said to be a rule of law that operated regardless of the intentions of the contracting parties. Thus, even if the parties excluded liability by clear and express language, they could still be liable for fundamental breach of contract. This rule of law was rapidly embraced by both English and Canadian courts.

[20]   A decade later in the *Suisse Atlantique* case, the House of Lords rejected the rule of law concept in favour of an approach based on the true construction of the contract. The Law Lords expressed the view that a court considering the concept of fundamental breach must determine whether the contract, properly interpreted, excluded liability for the fundamental breach. If the parties clearly intended an exclusion clause to apply in the event of fundamental breach, the party in breach would be exempted from liability. In *B.G. Linton Construction Ltd. v. C.N.R. Co.* [[1975] 2 S.C.R. 678, 49 D.L.R. (3d) 548], this court approved of the *Suisse Atlantique* formulation. The renunciation of the rule of law approach by the House of Lords and by this court, however, had little effect on the practice of lower courts in England or in Canada. Lord Denning quickly resuscitated the rule of law doctrine in *Harbutt's "Plasticine" Ltd. v. Wayne Tank & Pump Co. Ltd.*, [1970] 1 Q.B. 447 (C.A.).

[21]   Finally, in 1980, the House of Lords definitively rejected the rule of law approach to fundamental breach in *Photo Production, supra*. . . .

[22]   Lord Diplock [in *Photo Production*] alluded to the importance of negotiated risk allocation at p. 851:

> My Lords, the reports are full of cases in which what would appear to be very strained constructions have been placed on exclusion clauses, mainly in what to-day would be called consumer contracts and contracts of adhesion. . . . In commercial contracts negotiated between business-men capable of looking after their own interests and of deciding how risks inherent in the performance of various kinds of contract can be most economically borne (generally by insurance), it is, in my view, wrong to place a strained construction upon words in an exclusion clause which are clear and fairly susceptible of one meaning only even after due allowance has been made for the presumption in favour of the implied primary and secondary obligations.

[23]   In *Beaufort Realties (1964) Inc., supra*, Ritchie J., delivering the judgment of this court, stated, p. 196 D.L.R., p. 723 S.C.R.:

> Stated bluntly, the difference of opinion as to the true intent and meaning of their Lordships' judgment in the *Suisse Atlantique* case centered around the question of whether a rule of law exists to the effect that a fundamental breach going to the root of a contract eliminates once and for all the effect of all clauses exempting or excluding the party in breach from rights which it would otherwise have been entitled to exercise, or whether the true construction of the contract is the governing consid-

eration in determining whether or not an exclusionary clause remains unaffected and enforceable notwithstanding the fundamental breach. The former view was espoused by Lord Denning M.R. and is illustrated by his judgment which he delivered on behalf of the Court of Appeal in the *Photo Production* case, *supra*. . . .

and at p. 197 D.L.R., p. 725 S.C.R.:

It has been concurrently found by the learned trial judge and the Court of Appeal that art. 6 of this contract constituted an exclusionary or exception clause and Madam Justice Wilson adopted the same considerations as those which governed the House of Lords in the Photo case in holding that the question of whether such a clause was applicable where there was a fundamental breach was to be determined according to the true construction of the contract. I concur in this approach to the case.

[24] As Wilson J. notes in her reasons, Canadian courts have tended to pay lip service to contract construction but to apply the doctrine of fundamental breach as if it were a rule of law. While the motivation underlying the continuing use of fundamental breach as a rule of law may be laudatory, as a tool for relieving parties from the effects of unfair bargains, the doctrine of fundamental breach has spawned a host of difficulties; the most obvious is how to determine whether a particular breach is fundamental. From this very first step the doctrine of fundamental breach invites the parties to engage in games of characterization, each party emphasizing different aspects of the contract to show either that the breach that occurred went to the very root of the contract or that it did not. The difficulty of characterizing a breach as fundamental for the purposes of exclusion clauses is vividly illustrated by the differing views of the trial judge and the Court of Appeal in the present case.

[25] The many shortcomings of the doctrine as a means of circumventing the effects of unfair contracts are succinctly explained by Professor Waddams (*The Law of Contracts*, 2nd ed. (Toronto: C.L.B. Inc., 1984), at pp. 352-53):

The doctrine of fundamental breach has, however, many serious deficiencies as a technique of controlling unfair agreements. The doctrine requires the court to identify the offending provision as an "exemption clause", then to consider the agreement apart from the exemption clause, to ask itself whether there would have been a breach of that part of the agreement and then to consider whether that breach was "fundamental". These enquiries are artificial and irrelevant to the real questions at issue. An exemption clause is not always unfair and there are many unfair provisions that are not exemption clauses. It is quite unsatisfactory to look at the agreement apart from the exemption clause, because the exemption clause is itself part of the agreement, and if fair and reasonable a perfectly legitimate part. Nor is there any reason to associate unfairness with breach or with fundamental breach. . . .

[26] More serious is the danger that suppression of the true criterion leads, as elsewhere, to the striking down of agreements that are perfectly fair and reasonable.

[27] Professor Waddams makes two crucially important points. One is that not all exclusion clauses are unreasonable. This fact is ignored by the rule of law approach to fundamental breach. In the commercial context, clauses limiting or excluding liability are negotiated as part of the general contract. As they do with all other contractual terms, the parties bargain for the consequences of deficient performance. In the usual situation, exclusion clauses will be reflected in the contract price. Professor Waddams' second point is that exclusion clauses are not the only

contractual provisions which may lead to unfairness. There appears to be no sound reason for applying special rules in the case of clauses excluding liability than for other clauses producing harsh results.

[28] In light of the unnecessary complexities the doctrine of fundamental breach has created, the resulting uncertainty in the law, and the unrefined nature of the doctrine as a tool for averting unfairness, I am much inclined to lay the doctrine of fundamental breach to rest, and where necessary and appropriate, to deal explicitly with unconscionability. In my view, there is much to be gained by addressing directly the protection of the weak from over-reaching by the strong, rather than relying on the artificial legal doctrine of "fundamental breach". There is little value in cloaking the inquiry behind a construction that takes on its own idiosyncratic traits, sometimes at odds with concerns of fairness. This is precisely what has happened with the doctrine of fundamental breach. It is preferable to interpret the terms of the contract, in an attempt to determine exactly what the parties agreed. If on its true construction the contract excludes liability for the kind of breach that occurred, the party in breach will generally be saved from liability. Only where the contract is unconscionable, as might arise from situations of unequal bargaining power between the parties, should the courts interfere with agreements the parties have freely concluded. The courts do not blindly enforce harsh or unconscionable bargains and, as Professor Waddams has argued, the doctrine of "fundamental breach" may best be understood as but one manifestation of a general underlying principle which explains judicial intervention in a variety of contractual settings. Explicitly addressing concerns of unconscionability and inequality of bargaining power allows the courts to focus expressly on the real grounds for refusing to give force to a contractual term said to have been agreed to by the parties.

[29] I wish to add that, in my view, directly considering the issues of contract construction and unconscionability will often lead to the same result as would have been reached using the doctrine of fundamental breach, but with the advantage of clearly addressing the real issues at stake.

[30] In rejecting the doctrine of fundamental breach and adopting an approach that binds the parties to the bargains they make, subject to unconscionability, I do not wish to be taken as expressing an opinion on the substantial failure of contract performance, sometimes described as fundamental breach, that will relieve a party from future obligations under the contract. The concept of fundamental breach in the context of refusal to enforce exclusion clauses and of substantial failure of performance have often been confused, even though the two are quite distinct. In *Suisse Atlantique*, Lord Wilberforce noted the importance of distinguishing the two uses of the term fundamental breach, at p. 431:

> Next for consideration is the argument based on "fundamental breach" or, which is presumably the same thing, a breach going "to the root of the contract." These expressions are used in the cases to denote two quite different things, namely, (i) a performance totally different from that which the contract contemplates, (ii) a breach of contract more serious than one which would entitle the other party merely to damages and which (at least) would entitle him to refuse performance or further performance under the contract.

> Both of these situations have long been familiar in the English law of contract . . . What is certain is that to use the expression without distinguishing to which of these, or to what other, situations it refers is to invite confusion.

The importance of the difference between these meanings lies in this, that they relate to two separate questions which may arise in relation to any contract.

[31] I wish to be clear that my comments are restricted to the use of fundamental breach in the context of enforcing contractual exclusion clauses.

[32] Turning to the case at bar, I am of the view that Allis-Chalmers is not liable for the defective gearboxes. The warranty provision of the contract between Allis-Chalmers and Syncrude clearly limited the liability of Allis-Chalmers' to defects appearing within one year from the date of placing the equipment into service. The trial judge found that the defects in the gearboxes did not become apparent until after the warranty of Allis-Chalmers had expired. It is clear, therefore, that the warranty clause excluded liability for the defects that materialized, and subject to the existence of any unconscionability between the two parties there can be no liability on the part of Allis-Chalmers. I have no doubt that unconscionability is not an issue in this case. Both Allis-Chalmers and Syncrude are large and commercially sophisticated companies. Both parties knew or should have known what they were doing and what they had bargained for when they entered into the contract. There is no suggestion that Syncrude was pressured in any way to agree to terms to which it did not wish to assent. I am therefore of the view that the parties should be held to the terms of their bargain and that the warranty clause freed Allis-Chalmers from any liability for the defective gearboxes. . . .

[WILSON J. (with whom **L'HEUREUX-DUBÉ J.** agreed) said:]

[33] . . . Prior to 1980, in both the United Kingdom and in Canada, there were two competing views of the consequences of fundamental breach. One held that there was a rule of law that a fundamental breach brought a contract to an end, thereby preventing the contract breaker from relying on any clause exempting liability. This view was most closely identified with Lord Denning in the English Court of Appeal: see *Karsales (Harrow) Ltd. v. Wallis* . . . [and] *Harbutt's "Plasticine" Ltd. v. Wayne Tank & Pump Co.* . . . The other view was that exemption clauses should be construed by the same rules of contract interpretation whether a fundamental breach had occurred or not. Whether or not liability was excluded was to be decided simply on the construction of the contract: see *Suisse Atlantique*, *supra*; *Traders Finance Corp. v. Halverson* (1968), 2 D.L.R. (3d) 666 (B.C.C.A.); *R.G. McLean Ltd. v. Canadian Vickers Ltd.*, [[1971] 1 O.R. 207, 15 D.L.R. (3d) 15, at p. 20 (C.A.)].

[34] In England the issue was unequivocally resolved by the House of Lords in favour of the construction approach in the *Photo Production* case. . . .The construction approach to exclusionary clauses in the face of a fundamental breach affirmed in *Photo Production* was adopted by this court as the law in Canada in *Beaufort Realties (1964) Inc. v. Chomedey Aluminum Co. Ltd.* [*supra*]. The court did not, however, reject the concept of fundamental breach . . .

[35] Thus, the law in Canada on this point appears to be settled. Some uncertainty, however, does remain primarily with regard to the application of the construction approach. . . .

[36] Commentators seem to be in agreement, however, that the courts, while paying lip service to the construction approach, have continued to apply a modified "rule of law" doctrine in some cases. Professor Fridman in *Law of Contract in Canada*, 2nd ed. (1986), has suggested at p. 558 that:

> Under the guise of "construction", some courts appear to be utilizing something very much akin to the "rule of law" doctrine. What Canadian courts may be doing is to apply a concept of "fair and reasonable" construction in relation to the survival of the exclusion clause after a fundamental breach, and the application of such a clause where the breach in question involves not just a negligent performance of the contract, but the complete failure of the party obliged to fulfil the contract in any way whatsoever.

[37] Professor Ogilvie, in a review of Canadian cases decided shortly after *Photo Production*, including *Beaufort Realties* itself, argues that the rule of law approach "has been replaced by a substantive test of reasonableness which bestows on the courts at least as much judicial discretion to intervene in contractual relationships as fundamental breach ever did": see Ogilvie, "The Reception of *Photo Production Ltd. v. Securicor Transport Ltd.* in Canada: *Nec Tamen Consumebatur*" (1982), 27 *McGill L.J.* 424 at p. 441.

[38] Little is to be gained from a review of the recent cases which have inspired these comments. Suffice it to say that the law in this area seems to be in need of clarification. The uncertainty might be resolved in either of two ways. The first way would be to adopt *Photo Production* in its entirety. This would include discarding the concept of fundamental breach. The courts would give effect to exclusion clauses on their true construction regardless of the nature of the breach. Even the party who had committed a breach such that the foundation of the contract was undermined and the very thing bargained for not provided could rely on provisions in the contract limiting or excluding his or her liability. The only relevant question for the court would be: on a true and natural construction of the provisions of the contract did the parties, *at the time the contract was made*, succeed in excluding liability? This approach would have the merit of importing greater simplicity into the law and consequently greater certainty into commercial dealings, although the results of enforcing such exclusion clauses could be harsh if the parties had not adequately anticipated or considered the possibility of the contract's disintegration through fundamental breach.

[39] The other way would be to import some "reasonableness" requirement into the law so that courts could refuse to enforce exclusion clauses in strict accordance with their terms if to do so would be unfair and unreasonable. One far-reaching "reasonableness" requirement which I would reject (and which I believe was rejected in *Beaufort Realties* both by this court and the Ontario Court of Appeal) would be to require that the exclusion clause be *per se* a fair and reasonable contractual term in the contractual setting or bargain made by the parties. I would reject this approach because the courts, in my view, are quite unsuited to assess the fairness or reasonableness of contractual provisions as the parties negotiated them. Too many elements are involved in such an assessment, some of them quite subjective. It was partly for this reason that this court in *Beaufort Realties* and the House of Lords in *Photo Production* clearly stated that exclusion clauses, like all contractual provisions, should be given their natural and true construction. Great uncertainty and needless complications in the drafting of contracts will obviously result if courts give exclusion clauses strained and artificial interpretations in order, indirectly and obliquely, to avoid the impact of what seems to them ex post facto to have been an unfair and unreasonable clause.

[40] I would accordingly reject the concept that an exclusion clause in order to be enforceable must be *per se* a fair and reasonable provision at the time it was negotiated. The exclusion clause cannot be considered in isolation from the other provisions of the contract and the circumstances in which it was entered into. The purchaser may have been prepared to assume some risk if he could get the article at a modest price or if he was very anxious to get it. Conversely, if he was having to pay a high price for the article and had to be talked into the purchase, he may have been concerned to impose the broadest possible liability on his vendor. A contractual provision that seems unfair to a third party may have been the product of hard bargaining between the parties and, in my view, deserves to be enforced by the courts in accordance with its terms.

[41] It is, however, in my view an entirely different matter for the courts to determine *after a particular breach has occurred* whether an exclusion clause should be enforced or not. This, I believe, was the issue addressed by this court in *Beaufort Realties*. In *Beaufort* this court accepted the proposition enunciated in *Photo Production* that no rule of law invalidated or extinguished exclusion clauses in the event of fundamental breach but rather that they should be given their natural and true construction so that the parties' agreement would be given effect. Nevertheless the court, in approving the approach taken by the Ontario Court of Appeal in *Beaufort*, recognized at the same time the need for courts to determine whether in the context of the particular breach which had occurred it was fair and reasonable to enforce the clause in favour of the party who had committed that breach even if the exclusion clause was clear and unambiguous. The relevant question for the court in *Beaufort* was: is it fair and reasonable in the context of this fundamental breach that the exclusion clause continue to operate for the benefit of the party responsible for the fundamental breach? In other words, should a party be able to commit a fundamental breach secure in the knowledge that no liability can attend it? Or should there be room for the courts to say: this party is now trying to have his cake and eat it too. He is seeking to escape almost entirely the burdens of the transaction but enlist the support of the courts to enforce its benefits.

[42] It seems to me that the House of Lords was able to come to a decision in *Photo Production* untrammelled by the need to reconcile the competing values sought to be advanced in a system of contract law such as ours. We do not have in this country legislation comparable to the United Kingdom's *Unfair Contract Terms Act 1977*. I believe that in the absence of such legislation Canadian courts must continue to develop through the common law a balance between the obvious desirability of allowing the parties to make their own bargains and have them enforced through the courts and the obvious undesirability of having the courts used to enforce bargains in favour of parties who are totally repudiating such bargains themselves. I fully agree with the commentators that the balance which the courts reach will be made much clearer if we do not clothe our reasoning "in the guise of interpretation". Exclusion clauses do not automatically lose their validity in the event of a fundamental breach by virtue of some hard and fast rule of law. They should be given their natural and true construction so that the meaning and effect of the exclusion clause the parties agreed to at the time the contract was entered into is fully understood and appreciated. But, in my view, the court must still decide, having ascertained the parties' intention at the time the contract was made, whether or not to give effect to it in the context of subsequent events such as a fundamental breach committed by the party seeking its enforcement through the

courts. Whether the courts address this narrowly in terms of fairness as between
the parties (and I believe this has been a source of confusion, the parties being, in
the absence of inequality of bargaining power, the best judges of what is fair as
between themselves) or on the broader policy basis of the need for the courts
(apart from the interests of the parties) to balance conflicting values inherent in our
contract law (the approach which I prefer), I believe the result will be the same
since the question essentially is: in the circumstances that have happened should
the court lend its aid to A to hold B to this clause?

[43] In affirming the legitimate role of our courts at common law to decide
whether or not to enforce an exclusion clause in the event of a fundamental breach,
I am not unmindful of the fact that means are available to render exclusion clauses
unenforceable even in the absence of a finding of fundamental breach. While we
do not have legislation comparable to the United Kingdom's *Unfair Contract
Terms Act 1977*, we do have some legislative protection in this area. Six provinces
prevent sellers from excluding their obligations under Sale of Goods Acts where
consumer sales are concerned: see *Consumer Protection Act*, R.S.O. 1980, c. 87,
s. 34(1) . . .; *Consumer Product Warranty and Liability Act*, S.N.B. 1978, c. C-
18.1., ss. 24-26 (except in so far as an exclusion is fair and reasonable); the *Consumer Products Warranties Act*, R.S.S. 1978, c. C-30, ss. 8 and 11. In addition,
some provinces have legislation dealing with unfair business practices which affects the application of some exclusion clauses: see *Business Practices Act*, R.S.O.
1980, c. 55, s. 2(b)(vi); *Trade Practice Act*, R.S.B.C. 1979, c. 406, s. 4(e); *Unfair
Trade Practices Act*, R.S.A. 1980, c. U-3, s. 4(b). . . . Such legislation, in effect,
imposes limits on freedom of contract for policy reasons.

[44] There are, moreover, other avenues in our law through which the courts (as
opposed to the legislatures) can control the impact of exclusion clauses in appropriate circumstances. Fundamental breach has its origins in that aspect of the doctrine of unconscionability which deals with inequality of bargaining power: see
Waddams, "Unconscionability in Contracts" (1976), 39 *Mod. L. Rev.* 369. As Professor Ziegel notes in "Comment" (1979), 57 *Can. Bar Rev.* 105 at p. 113:

> The initial impulse that prompted the development of the doctrine of fundamental
> breach was very sound insofar as it was designed to prevent overreaching of a
> weaker party by a stronger party. The impulse became distorted when subsequent
> courts confused cause and effect and treated the doctrine, albeit covertly, as express-
> ing a conclusive rule of public policy regardless of the circumstances of the particu-
> lar case. *What is needed therefore is a return to a regime of natural construction
> coupled with an explicit test of unfairness tailored to meet the facts of particular
> cases.*

(Emphasis added.)

[45] The availability of a plea of unconscionability in circumstances where the
contractual term is *per se* unreasonable *and* the unreasonableness stems from inequality of bargaining power was confirmed in Canada over a century ago in *Waters v. Donnelly* (1884), 9 O.R. 391 (Ch.). It has been used on many subsequent
occasions: see *Morrison v. Coast Finance Ltd.* (1965), 55 D.L.R. (2d) 710, 54
W.W.R. 257 (B.C.C.A.); *Harry v. Kreutziger* (1978), 95 D.L.R. (3d) 231, 9
B.C.L.R. 166 (C.A.); *Taylor v. Armstrong* (1979), 99 D.L.R. (3d) 547, 24 O.R.
(2d) 614 (H.C.).

[46] While this is perhaps not the place for a detailed examination of the doctrine of unconscionability as it relates to exclusion clauses, I believe that the equitable principles on which the doctrine is based are broad enough to cover many of the factual situations which have perhaps deservedly attracted the application of the "fair and reasonable" approach in cases of fundamental breach. In particular, the circumstances surrounding the making of a consumer standard-form contract could permit the purchaser to argue that it would be unconscionable to enforce an exclusion clause. . .

[47] As I have noted, this is not the place for an exposition of the doctrine of unconscionability as it relates to inequality of bargaining power and I do not necessarily endorse the approaches taken in the cases to which I have just referred. I use them merely to illustrate the broader point that in situations involving contractual terms which result from inequality of bargaining power the judicial armoury has weapons apart from strained and artificial constructions of exclusion clauses. Where, however, there is no such inequality of bargaining power (as in the present case) the courts should, as a general rule, give effect to the bargain freely negotiated by the parties. The question is whether this is an absolute rule or whether *as a policy matter* the courts should have the power to refuse to enforce a clear and unambiguous exclusion clause freely negotiated by parties of equal bargaining power and, if so, in what circumstances? In the present state of the law in Canada the doctrine of fundamental breach provides one answer.

[48] To dispense with the doctrine of fundamental breach and rely solely on the principle of unconscionability, as has been suggested by some commentators, would, in my view, require an extension of the principle of unconscionability beyond its traditional bounds of inequality of bargaining power. The court, in effect, would be in the position of saying that terms freely negotiated by parties of equal bargaining power were unconscionable. Yet it was the inequality of bargaining power which traditionally was the source of the unconscionability. What was unconscionable was to permit the strong to take advantage of the weak in the making of the contract. Remove the inequality and we must ask, wherein lies the unconscionability? It seems to me that it must have its roots in subsequent events, given that the parties themselves are the best judges of what is fair at the time they make their bargain. The policy of the common law is, I believe, that having regard to the conduct (pursuant to the contract) of the party seeking the indulgence of the court to enforce the clause, the court refuses. This conduct is described for convenience as "fundamental breach". It marks off the boundaries of tolerable conduct. But the boundaries are admittedly uncertain. Will replacing it with a general concept of unconscionability reduce the uncertainty?

[49] When and in what circumstances will an exclusion clause in a contract freely negotiated by parties of equal bargaining power be unconscionable? If both fundamental breach and unconscionability are properly viewed as legal tools designed to relieve parties in light of subsequent events from the harsh consequences of an automatic enforcement of an exclusion clause in accordance with its terms, is there anything to choose between them as far as certainty in the law is concerned? Arguably, unconscionability is even less certain than fundamental breach. Indeed, it may be described as "the length of the Chancellor's foot". Lord Wilberforce may be right that parties of equal bargaining power should be left to live with their bargains regardless of subsequent events. I believe, however, that there is some virtue in a residual power residing in the court to withhold its assistance on policy grounds in appropriate circumstances.

[50]   Turning to the case at bar, it seems to me that, even if the breach of contract was a fundamental one, there would be nothing unfair or unreasonable (and even less so unconscionable, if this is a stricter test) in giving effect to the exclusion clause. The contract was made between two companies in the commercial market place who are of roughly equal bargaining power. Both are familiar and experienced with this type of contract . . .

[51]   There is no evidence to suggest that Allis-Chalmers who seeks to rely on the exclusion clause was guilty of any sharp or unfair dealing. It supplied what was bargained for (even although it had defects) and its contractual relationship with Syncrude, which included not only the gears but the entire conveyer system, continued on after the supply of the gears. It cannot be said, in Lord Diplock's words, that Syncrude was "deprived of substantially the whole benefit" of the contract. This is not a case in which the vendor or supplier was seeking to repudiate almost entirely the burdens of the transaction and invoking the assistance of the courts to enforce its benefits. There is no abuse of freedom of contract here.

[52]   In deciding to enforce the exclusion clause the trial judge relied in part on the fact that the exclusion clause limited but did not completely exclude the liability of Allis-Chalmers (p. 77). In relying on this fact the trial judge was supported by some dicta of Lord Wilberforce in the House of Lords in *Ailsa Craig Fishing Co..v. Malvern Fishing Co.*, [1983] 1 All E.R. 101 (H.L.) at pp. 102-3. It seems to me, however, that any categorical distinction between clauses limiting and clauses excluding liability is inherently unreliable in that, depending on the circumstances, "exclusions can be perfectly fair and limitations very unfair": Waddams, *The Law of Contracts*, 2nd ed. (1977), at p. 349. It is preferable, I believe, to determine whether or not the impugned clause should be enforced in all the circumstances of the case and avoid reliance on awkward and artificial labels. When this is done, it becomes clear that there is no reason in this case not to enforce the clause excluding the statutory warranty.

[MCINTYRE J. held that he did not have to deal with the issue of the vitality of the doctrine of fundamental breach.]

QUESTIONS

1.   Part of what concerned Wilson J. is a problem of timing. If an agreement is fair and reasonable when it is made, is that determination the limit of the court's inquiry? In other words, may an originally fair agreement later become unfair or unconscionable? Notice that on this point, Wilson J. and Dickson C.J.C. have quite different concerns.

     The "timing" issue that leads to the very different concerns of Dickson C.J.C. and Wilson J. is another consequence of the traditional focus of the law on discrete relations. That focus suggests that everything be dealt with in the original contract. If an event occurs that does not fit within that framework, the contract does not deal with it and the court is free to allocate the risk as it sees fit. The doctrine of fundamental breach gives the court a wide and potentially uncontrollable power to re-allocate risks. A focus on relational contracts would suggest that the answer to the question whether a contract was originally enforceable in every respect does not deal with the problem of the later application of or exercise of the powers conferred by the contract in circumstances that may not have been envisaged at the beginning.

The original "exemption clause" (*i.e.*, "fundamental breach") cases like *Karsales v. Wallis* were not relational contracts in the sense in which that term is used here. A person obliged to pay off a loan faces a long-term obligation, but that obligation does not arise in a relation that is a framework for future co-operation. In the same way, the contract between Syncrude and its suppliers was not a relational contract.

2. In *Fraser Jewellers (1982) Ltd. v. Dominion Electric Protection Ltd.* (1997), 34 O.R. (3d) 1, 148 D.L.R. (4th) 496, the Ontario Court of Appeal gave effect to an exemption clause that limited the liability of an electronic security company to the annual cost of its services in the event of any breach of contract "from negligence or otherwise". The exemption clause was in bold block letters and stated that the security company "is not an insurer and makes no guarantee or warranty". Due to the defendant's negligence there was a 10-minute delay in sending a message to the police during a robbery. Robins J.A. noted that this was a commercial relation and that the plaintiff had ample opportunity to read the contract before signing, although the owner claimed that he had not done so. Although the plaintiff chose not to insure its inventory due to cost of doing so, insurance was readily available for robbery and other thefts.

    Citing *Hunter Engineering,* Robins J.A. concluded (pp. 10-12 (O.R.), pp. 504-06 (D.L.R.)):

    > Relief [from a contractual limitation of liability] should be granted only if the clause, seen in the light of the entire agreement, can be said, on Dickson C.J.C.'s test, to be "unconscionable" or, on Wilson J's test to be "unfair or unreasonable". The difference in practice between these alternatives, as Professor Waddams has observed, "is unlikely to be large": Waddams, *The Law of Contracts*, 3rd ed. (1993), at p. 323. . . . This is an ordinary commercial contract between business people . . . [the security company] has no control over the value of its customer's inventory and can hardly be expected, in exchange for a relatively modest annual fee, to insure a jeweller against negligent acts on the part of its employees . . . .

    Do you agree with Robins J.A. about the limited significance of the difference between the approaches of Wilson J. and Dickson C.J.C.? Can you think of circumstances in which there might be a practical effect to the difference in approach?

3. In *Solway v. Davis Moving & Storage Inc.*, [2002] O.J. No. 4760, 62 O.R. (3d) 522, 222 D.L.R. (4th) 251 (C.A.), leave to appeal dismissed [2003] S.C.C.A. 57, the plaintiffs entered into a contract with the defendant to have their household goods removed from their house, stored briefly and delivered to their new home. The plaintiffs were particularly concerned about security since their household goods included rare and valuable artefacts and antiques, and were reassured by statements of the representative of the defendant that the trailer containing their goods would be locked and parked in their moving yard. The trailer was parked in the lot but had to be removed for one night while the lot was being snowploughed and was left, unattended, on a public street. While it was on the street, the trailer was stolen. The defendant admitted liability for the loss of the goods, but only to the extent of the terms of the bill of lading to $0.60 per pound, for a total of $7,089.60. The trial judge found that the plaintiffs were never advised that their goods would be left in an unattended trailer on a public street, that the defendant had given false assurances that the goods would be secured, which had induced the plaintiffs to agree to the limitation clause, and that it would be unreasonable in the circumstances to enforce the limitation clause. The plaintiffs' action for the value of the goods was allowed. In upholding the trial decision, Labrosse J.A. wrote (at paras. 19-21):

    > Despite Kennedy Moving's assurances to the contrary, the plaintiffs' goods were not, however, kept in secure conditions. The trailer containing their goods was left overnight on the street with no surveillance. As the trial judge noted, Kennedy Moving should have anticipated that a theft might occur if the trailer was left unattended overnight on a public street. The plaintiffs were

never advised that their goods would be stored in these conditions, and they certainly never agreed to such an arrangement.

In deciding not to enforce the limitation clause, the trial judge appears to have equated the words, "unconscionable" and "unreasonable" as these terms were discussed in *Hunter Engineering*. In our view, on the facts as found by the trial judge, to limit the loss of the plaintiffs to $7,089.60 would, in the words of Dickson C.J.C. be "unconscionable", or in the words of Wilson J. be "unfair or unreasonable". This is one of those cases where relief should be granted.

The conclusion of the trial judge is amply supported by the evidence. It also accords with principles of contract law. We see no basis to interfere.

In dissent, Carthy J.A. wrote (at paras. 27, 40 and 45):

The trial judge found that the homeowners were intelligent and sophisticated business people, that they knew of the limitation of liability provision in the contract, and that they arranged their own insurance (said now to be insufficient) to protect against loss during the move. … There is no need for an undefined discretion in the enforceability of exclusion clauses. Contracting parties, insurers, business persons and litigants are all better served by the certainty of standards. … The carrier has no means of knowing the value of the goods and, even if it did, the cost of insurance for the most valuable of goods in a cargo would impose prohibitive charges on the consignor of lesser valued goods. Thus statutes or regulations emerged maintaining the concept of absolute liability but limiting that liability to a declared value or, more often, to a value measured by weight. In this fashion the consignor can either insure the goods or bear the risk of their loss or damage, knowing the value of such goods. The carrier also bears some risk, which will act as an incentive to act prudently, while knowing that the extent of liability is tied to the weight of the goods being transported.

Notice the radically different starting positions of the majority and the dissenting judge. The majority see the transaction as having very few relevant facts, these being principally the assurance given by the defendant and its breach of that undertaking. Carthy J.A. in dissent, on the other hand, sees the transaction in a commercial context, the features of which are set in part by legislation and the actual insurance background to transactions of this type. A fuller consideration of the commercial background suggests, like the judgment of the same court in *Fraser Jewellers* (mentioned briefly above), that the answer to the question of which party should bear the risk of loss is to a large extent independent of the particular circumstances of the litigation before the court, but far more dependent on the legislative and insuring background to the transaction. A glimpse of the insuring background in this case is provided by *Solway v. Lloyd's Underwriters*, [2005] O.J. No. 1331, 75 O.R. (3d) 129 (S.C.J.) varied [2006] O.J. No. 2059 (C.A.), where the issue was which of the available insurers should bear the risk of loss (with a very significant difference in the amount of coverage available).

4.   Abolishing the doctrine of fundamental breach as it was articulated in the original class of cases, like *Karsales v. Wallis*, where it arose, says nothing about the issue that underlies either Wilson J.'s concern or a case like *Hongkong Fir* (*supra*, Chapter 4), *viz.*, the possible existence of an excuse for further performance on the occurrence of an event that seriously deprives one party of the benefits that the contract was to provide. The law of excuses is, however, crude: it permits a party to walk from the relation, but does not give the courts any power to revise or re-draft the contract to make it work better. This power is not, apart from some American cases like *Aluminum Co. of America v. Essex Group, Inc.*, 499 F.Supp. 53 (WD Pa. 1980) (*supra*, Chapter 5), exercised by courts operating in the common law. We draw an explicit comparison later in this chapter to the existence of a power given to Canadian courts by the *Canada Business Corporations Act* and most other provincial business corporation statutes to

give relief from "oppression". The legislative grant of power to give relief for oppression is a very wide jurisdiction that permits courts to make both retrospective and prospective changes to the parties' relation. The full scope of the power has not yet been tested. The existence of a wide power, even if conferred by statute, to re-make relations for the future as well as to undo past wrongs, illustrates the narrow range of alternatives that the courts are now prepared to exercise in the general law of contract. No one would argue that a court which would seek to re-make or re-draft the parties' relation has an easy task. The question is, however, if what we now do is preferable to the courts' having a wider power.

5. A curious feature of the law relating to "exemption clauses" is that the courts and commentators generally ignore the fact that there are many functional equivalents of exemption clauses. If an exemption clause is a clause that allocates to one party a risk which, were it not for the clause would be on the other party, then one obvious method (among many other methods) of achieving this is, for example, to provide that the parties' agreement is to be binding in "honour only" or that it shall not be legally enforceable. As noted in the discussion of the "intention to create legal relations" in Chapter 2, such an "honour" arrangement was made in *Rose & Frank Co. v. J.R. Crompton & Bros. Ltd.*, [1925] A.C. 445 (H.L.). If, as happened in that case, the seller has received cash for what it has actually delivered, it may be happy to deny the purchaser any legal remedy for future non-deliveries by providing that the contract should not be legally binding. How far should a seller be permitted to go with this argument?

6. In *Lattavo v. 770373 Ontario Ltd.*, [2004] O.J. No. 3334, 24 R.P.R. (4th) 114, (S.C.J.), the plaintiffs entered a contract to have a new house built for them by the defendant builder on a lot that they purchased from the builder, based on a design chosen by the plaintiffs from the builder's artistic rendering. During construction, it became apparent that the lot had a severe slope which affected the ability of the builder to complete the house according to the original design. As a result of the slope, the town required the design of the front entrance to be modified to make it conform to building regulations concerning the allowable degree of slope. The agreement included an exclusionary clause providing that the builder could "modify the plans and specifications pertaining to the Property including [...] architectural, structural [...] grading ..." without the purchaser's consent. The purchasers learned of the change prior to closing, but decided to close the deal and seek damages. Stewart J. refused to give effect to this clause, writing (at para. 37):

> In my view, the changes required by this grading problem are so major and fundamental as to render the exclusionary provisions of the Agreement ineffective. The placement of steps to the side of a majestic entrance design is not only unsatisfactory from a practical standpoint, it is aesthetically displeasing. The steep slope of the lot, which makes it impossible to put out a lawn chair in the back yard without having it tip over, is an intolerable deficiency. These deficiencies are, objectively assessed, of such magnitude that it would be unconscionable to allow [the builder] ... to successfully assert that the exclusionary clauses inserted by it into the Agreement permit it to vary the construction of the home to the extent it has. In my opinion, the wording of those provisions, when interpreted in the context of the Agreement as a whole, is insufficient to permit it to do so.

The court awarded damages to allow the purchasers to make adjustments to the property necessary to bring their home into reasonable conformity with what they contracted to buy.

7. The decision in *Lattavo* is fairly typical of the approach of courts to exclusion clauses involving the purchase of new homes; see K. Chatzidimos & J. Schwarz, "Exclusion clause interpretations often turn on definition of *fundamental breach*", *Lawyers Weekly*, February 24, 2006. In *Plas-Tex Canada Ltd. v. Dow Chemical Canada Ltd.*, [2005] A.J. No. 1098, 245 D.L.R. (4th) 650, [2005] 7 W.W.R. 419 (C.A.) the principal plaintiff pipeline company purchased polyethylene resin from the defendant petro-

chemical company for use in the natural gas pipelines that were built by it and its subsidiaries. The resin was defective, and although the defendant knew of this before it
sent the first shipment, it gave no warning of the defect. The pipe manufactured with
the defective resin cracked, causing major repair costs, the loss of customers, and a destruction of the plaintiffs' business reputation. The defendant claimed it was protected
because of an exclusion clause in the contract limiting liability to the selling price of
the resin, and excusing it from any responsibility for loss or damage. The trial judge
found the defendant liable in both contract and tort and awarded damages to the plaintiffs. In upholding the decision and ruling that the exclusion clause was of no effect,
Picard J.A. in the Alberta Court of Appeal wrote (at paras. 52-55):

> The cases of *Olshaski Farms Ltd. v. Skene Farm Equipment Ltd.* (1987),
> 49 Alta. L.R. (2d) 249 (Q.B.), *Bryandrew Holdings Ltd. v. Sifton Properties
> Ltd.* (1994), 38 R.P.R (2d) 95 (Ont. Gen. Div.), and *Atlas Supply Co. of Can-
> ada Ltd. v. Yarmouth Equipment Ltd.* (1991), 103 N.S.R. (2d) 1 (C.A.), …
> provide … some guidance on what constitutes "unconscionability". The courts
> in those cases concluded that if a defendant (a) knew of a possible risk associ-
> ated with its product, (b) failed to disclose important assumptions within its
> knowledge thereby preventing the other party from properly measuring the
> consequences and risks they were undertaking, and (c) deliberately withheld
> information and induced the claimant to enter the agreement on the basis that
> the other party had "scientifically done their homework", this would prohibit
> the defendant from relying on the limited liability clauses in the contract.

> These cases reinforce the principle that unconscionability should be used
> sparingly to avoid an exclusionary clause. However, such cases also establish
> that a party to a contract will not be permitted to engage in unconscionable
> conduct secure in the knowledge that no liability can be imposed upon it be-
> cause of an exclusionary clause.

> In this case, Dow [the defendant] knew that defects in its product would
> cause the pipe manufactured from it to fail. Further, it knew that the respon-
> dents and others would be burying the pipe in order to supply natural gas all
> over rural Alberta. Common sense says that anyone would know that cracking
> of such pipe could result in potential danger to property and persons. Dow was
> aware of all this before it made the first commercial shipment. … Moreover,
> by the time it signed the contract … it had significantly more detailed informa-
> tion about the nature of the defect and the pipe's propensity for early failure.
> … Rather than disclosing this knowledge to [the plaintiffs] … using the pipe
> made from the resin, Dow chose to protect itself from liability by inserting li-
> ability-limiting clauses in its contract …

The *Plas-Tex Canada Ltd.* decision is an example of a case in which a court used the
concept of unconscionability to protect a commercial entity.

If, by accident, the document that one party wants the other to sign, and which in
the usual course the other party would have signed, is not signed, the terms of the
document do not become part of the contract. This result follows from the rules
governing signed documents. The following extract from a case in which the
document mistakenly remained unsigned illustrates this point, and discusses the
unrealistic nature of the traditional legal analysis of formation of a contract of adhesion.

McCUTCHEON v. DAVID MACBRAYNE LTD.

[1964] 1 All E.R. 430, [1964] 1 W.L.R. 125
(H.L., Lords Reid, Hodson, Guest, Devlin, Pearce)

[Only the judgment of Lord Devlin is reproduced. This was his last judgment in the House of Lords. The other lords agreed in the result in separate judgments.]

LORD DEVLIN: — [1] My Lords, when a person in the Isle of Islay wishes to send goods to the mainland he goes into the office of MacBrayne (the respondents) in Port Askaig which is conveniently combined with the local Post Office. There he is presented with a document headed "Conditions" containing three or four thousand words of small print divided into 27 paragraphs. Beneath them there is a space for the sender's signature which he puts below his statement in quite legible print that he thereby agrees to ship on the conditions stated above. The appellant, Mr. McCutcheon, described the negotiations which preceded the making of this formidable contract in the following terms:

Q. Tell us about that document; how did you come to sign it?

A. You just walk in the office and the document is filled up ready and all you have to do is to sign your name and go out.

Q. Did you ever read the conditions?

A. No.

Q. Did you know what was in them?

A. No.

[2]   There are many other passages in which Mr. McCutcheon and his brother-in-law, Mr. McSporran, endeavour more or less successfully to appease the forensic astonishment aroused by this statement. People shipping calves, Mr. McCutcheon said (he was dealing with an occasion when he had shipped 36 calves), had not much time to give to the reading. Asked to deal with another occasion when he was unhampered by livestock, he said that people generally just tried to be in time for the boat's sailing; it would, he thought, take half a day to read and understand the conditions and then he would miss the boat. In another part of his evidence he went so far as to say that if everybody took time to read the document, "MacBrayne's office would be packed out the door." Mr. McSporran evidently thought the whole matter rather academic because, as he pointed out, there was no other way to send a car.

[3]   There came a day, October 8, 1960, when one of the respondents' vessels was negligently sailed into a rock and sank. She had on board a car belonging to Mr. McCutcheon which he had got Mr. McSporran to ship for him, and the car was a total loss. It would be a strangely generous set of conditions in which the persistent reader, after wading through the verbiage, could not find something to protect the carrier against "any loss . . . wheresoever or whensoever occurring"; and condition 19 by itself is enough to absolve the respondents several times over for all their negligence. It is conceded that if the form had been signed as usual, the appellant would have had no case. But, by a stroke of ill luck for the respondents, it was upon this day of all days that they omitted to get Mr. McSporran to sign the conditions. What difference does that make?

[4]   If it were possible for your Lordships to escape from the world of make-believe which the law has created into the real world in which transactions of this sort are actually done, the answer would be short and simple. It should make no difference whatever. This sort of document is not meant to be read, still less to be understood. Its signature is in truth about as significant as a handshake that marks the formal conclusion of a bargain. . . .

[5]   It seems to me that when a party assents to a document forming the whole or a part of his contract, he is bound by the terms of the document, read or unread, signed or unsigned, simply because they are in the contract; and it is unnecessary and possibly misleading to say that he is bound by them because he represents to the other party that he has made himself acquainted with them. But if there be an estoppel of this sort, its effect is, in my opinion, limited to the contract in relation to which the representation is made; and it cannot (unless of course there be something else on which the estoppel is founded besides the mere receipt of the document) assist the other party in relation to other transactions. The respondents in the present case have quite failed to prove that the appellant made himself acquainted with the conditions they had introduced into previous dealings. He is not estopped from saying that, for good reasons or bad, he signed the previous contracts without the slightest idea of what was in them. If that is so, previous dealings are no evidence of knowledge and so are of little or no use to the respondents in this case.

[6]   I say "of little or no use" because the appellant did admit that he knew that there were some conditions, though he did not know what they were. He certainly did not know that they were conditions which exempted the respondents from liability for their own negligence, though I suppose, if he had thought about them at all, he would have known that they probably exempted the respondents from the strict liability of a carrier. Most people know that carriers exact some conditions and it does not matter in this case whether Mr. McCutcheon's knowledge was general knowledge of this sort or was derived from previous dealings. Your Lordships can therefore leave previous dealings out of it [and] ask yourselves simply what is the position of a man who, with that amount of general knowledge, apparently makes a contract into which no conditions are expressly inserted?

[7]   The answer must surely be that either he does not make a contract at all because the parties are not *ad idem*, or he makes the contract without the conditions. You cannot have a contract subject to uncommunicated conditions the terms of which are known only to one side. . .

A TENTATIVE SOLUTION

The original justification for the doctrine of fundamental breach and for the offer-and-acceptance games played by the courts in the ticket cases was that these devices gave the courts a method for protecting the reasonable expectations of those who had relied on a certain appearance to the transaction. When it turned out that this appearance was not coincident with the legal relations created by the posted signs or the signed contract, and the courts had a motive for interference, these devices gave them a useful tool. Like the judicial use of the law of misrepresentations, warranties and negligent misrepresentation, the offer and acceptance analysis of cases like *Heffron v. Imperial Parking* and *Thornton v. Shoe Lane*, the doctrine of fundamental breach became a "peg" on which counsel and the courts could hang arguments.

The problems that those cases created arose because the theory of the law used by the judges prevented them from talking openly about what they were doing or what concerned them. So long as the contracts in the ticket cases were analyzed under the rules of offer and acceptance, the courts did not discuss the expectations of the party who had simply never thought about who would bear the risk of loss in any circumstance that might arise. Nor could they talk about the different expectations that, if the party had thought about it, he or she might have had with respect to the loss of his or her car (which could be insured against) and personal injury (which, apart from health insurance and, possibly, some disability insurance, could not be insured against). There is a close analogy to the problem of the "Battle of the Forms" studied in Chapter 3: the law is projected on to facts which do not support it.

With the signed contract, the problems become worse. The ritual incantation of the words of Scrutton L.J. in *L'Estrange v. Graucob* (supplemented, if necessary, by the equally ritualistic incantation of the parol evidence rule) meant that the court did not discuss either the expectations of the parties or the possible unfairness in the standard form of the transaction, which denied any effective remedy to the consumer.

When the document that would have governed the transaction is unsigned, there is, as Lord Devlin said in *McCutcheon v. MacBrayne*, no basis for making the party who would have borne the risk had it been signed bear it in the circumstances that occurred. Had the document represented a bargain expressing or reflecting the expectations of each party, signing may be irrelevant: the terms are part of the deal because they are known and expected to cover the allocation of the risk of loss.

If judges are prepared to discuss openly the issues that are the reason for concern, then the law is transformed and a variety of better solutions may appear. The following extract discusses both the history of the courts' treatment of the problem of the standard-form contract and a solution to that problem.

LLEWELLYN, THE COMMON-LAW TRADITION

(New York: Little Brown and Company, 1960)
(At pp. 362-71)

[Footnotes omitted.]

[1]   I know of few "private" law problems which remotely rival the importance, economic, governmental, or "law"-legal, of the form-pad agreement; and I know of none which has been either more disturbing to life or more baffling to lawyers.

[2]   The impetus to the form-pad is clear, for any business unit: by standardizing terms, and by standardizing even the spot on the form where any individually dickered term appears, one saves all the time and skill otherwise needed to dig out and record the meaning of variant language; one makes check-up, totaling, follow-through, etc., into routine operations; one has duplicates (in many colors) available for the administration of a multi-department business; and so on more. The content of the standardized terms accumulates experience, it avoids or reduces legal risks and also confers all kinds of operating leeways and advantages, all without need of

either consulting counsel from instance to instance or of bargaining with the other parties. Not to be overlooked, either, is the tailoring of the crude misfitting hand-me-down pattern of the "general law" "in the absence of agreement" to the particular detailed working needs of your own line of business — whether apartment rentals, stock brokerage, international grain trade, installment selling of appliances, flour milling, sugar beet raising, or insurance. It would be a heart-warming scene, a triumph of private attention to what is essentially private self-government in the lesser transactions of life or in those areas too specialized for the blunt, slow tools of the legislature — if only all businessmen and all their lawyers would be reasonable.

[3]   But power, like greed, if it does not always corrupt, goes easily to the head. So that the form-agreements tend either at once or over the years, and often by whole lines of trade, into a massive and almost terrifying jug-handled character; the one party lays his head into the mouth of a lion — either, and mostly, without reading the fine print, or occasionally in hope and expectation (not infrequently solid) that it will be a sweet and gentle lion. The more familiar instances, perhaps, are the United Realtors' Standard Lease, almost any bank's collateral note or agreement, almost any installment sale form, an accident insurance policy, a steamship ticket, a beet sugar refinery contract with a farmer or a flour miller's with its customer; or, on a lesser scale, the standard non-warranty given by seed companies or auto manufacturers. In regard to such, one notes four things: (1) sometimes language which seems at first sight horrifying may have good human and economic stimulus; thus, suits for loss of crop before a farmer jury are pretty terrible things to face for the price of a few bags of seed; and (2) there are crooked claims and there are irrationally unreasonable ones — each with its jury risk — as well as solid ones; and only a clause which in law bars the claim absolutely can free an outfit like an insurance company to deal fairly though "in its discretion" with the latter class. On the other hand, (3) boiler-plate clauses can and often do run far beyond any such need or excuse, sometimes (. . . distressingly today in, e.g., the cheap furniture business) involving flagrant trickery; and (4) not all "dominant" parties are nice lions, and even nice lions can make mistakes.

[4]   There is a fifth and no less vital thing to note: Where the form is drawn with a touch of . . . "gentlemanly restraint," or where, as with the overseas grain contracts or the Pacific Coast dried fruit contracts or the Worth Street Rules on textiles, two-fisted bargainers on either side have worked out in the form a balanced code to govern the particular line or trade or industry, there is every reason for a court to assume both fairness and wisdom in the terms, and to seek in first instance to learn, understand, and fit both its own thinking and its action into the whole design. Contracts of this kind (so long as reasonable in the net) are a road to better than official-legal regulation of our economic life; indeed, they tend to lead into the setting up of their own quick, cheap, expert tribunals. . . .

[5]   Such is the background of a phenomenon which has been gaining in importance for more than a century, its well-done pieces tending, as stated, to slide off out of court or "legal" notice because of dispute avoidance, ready adjustment, or arbitration. For the work of official law that has been unfortunate. It has tended to keep out of the familiar law books, where they might stir imitation and imagination of other lawyers, the balanced type of boiler-plate. It has tended also to keep away from the appellate courts enough contact with the balanced type of form to let that

type grow into a recognized pattern and a welcomed standard against which hog-drafting can be spotted, measured, and damned, so that the two different approaches and technique-lines of construction which are needed could be made articulate and reserved each to its appropriate sphere. Instead, the material which has come into court and into the American books has been in the main the jug-handled, mess-making stuff. What, then, of that?

[6]   For the courts, the story is quick to tell, though the cases must run into the thousands, and with no reckonability anywhere in sight. Unpredictably, they read the document for what it says, drop a word about freedom of contract, or about opportunity to read or improvident use of the pen, or about powerlessness of the court to do more than regret, or the like, and proceed to spit the victim for the barbecue. With equal unpredictability, they see the lopsided document as indecent, and evade it:

> A court can "construe" language into patently not meaning what the language is patently trying to say. It can find inconsistencies between clauses and throw out the troublesome one. It can even reject a clause as counter to the whole purpose of the transaction. It can reject enforcement by one side for want of "mutuality," though allowing enforcement by the weaker side because "consideration" in some other sense is present. Indeed, the law of agreeing can be subjected to divers modes of employment, to make the whole bargain or a particular clause stick or not stick according to the status of the party claiming under it: as when, in the interest of the lesser party, the whole contract is conditioned on some presupposition which is held to have failed. The difficulty with these techniques of ours is threefold. First, since they all rest on the admission that the clauses in question are permissible in purpose and content, they invite the draftsman to recur to the attack. Give him time, and he will make the grade. Second, since they do not face the issue, they fail to accumulate either experience or authority in the needed direction: that of marking out for any given type of transaction what the *minimum decencies* are which a court will insist upon as essential to an enforceable bargain of a given type, or as being inherent in a bargain of that type. Third, since they purport to construe, and do not really construe, nor are intended to, but are instead tools of intentional and creative misconstruction, they seriously embarrass later efforts at true construction, later efforts to get at the true meaning of those wholly legitimate contracts and clauses which call for their meaning to be got at instead of avoided. The net effect is unnecessary confusion and unpredictability, together with inadequate remedy, and evil persisting that calls for remedy. Covert tools are never reliable tools.

[7]   It is plain that the effect of such work on "Words and Phrases" and the like can be pretty awful. Above all, the sound impulse for fairness — better, against outrage — fails to *cumulate* into any effective or standard techniques, except in a very few areas such as life and fire insurance. Moreover, such techniques as the above are, for the most part (the "repugnancy" idea is a striking exception), mere dodge or artifice, ready to prove embarrassing if taken seriously tomorrow in a case of a different flavor. Thus, knocking out an auto manufacturer's enforcement of a power-clause in an agency contract on the ground that the bargain lacks consideration or "mutuality" can lead (and has) to conferring at-will termination power on the same manufacturer, so to speak by operation of court. . . .

[8]   At best, however, in our system an approach by statute seems to me dubious, uncertain, and likely to be both awkward in manner and deficient or spotty in scope. And the true answer to the whole problem seems, amusingly, to be one which could occur to any court or any lawyer, at any time, as readily as to a scholar who had spent a lifetime on the subject — though I doubt if it could occur

to anyone without the inquiry and analysis in depth which we owe to the scholarly work.

[9]   The answer, I suggest, is this: Instead of thinking about "assent" to boiler-plate clauses, we can recognize that so far as concerns the specific, there is no assent at all. What has in fact been assented to, specifically, are the few dickered terms, and the broad type of the transaction, and but one thing more. That one thing more is a blanket assent (not a specific assent) to any not unreasonable or indecent terms the seller may have on his form, which do not alter or eviscerate the reasonable meaning of the dickered terms. The fine print which has not been read has no business to cut under the reasonable meaning of those dickered terms which constitute the dominant and only real expression of agreement, but much of it commonly belongs in.

[10]   The queer thing is that where the transaction occurs without the fine print present, courts do not find this general line of approach too hard to understand: thus in the cases . . . in regard to what kind of policy an oral contract for insurance contemplates; nor can I see a court having trouble, where a short memo agrees in due course to sign "our standard contract," in rejecting an outrageous form as not being fairly within the reasonable meaning of the term. The clearest case to see is the handing over of a blank check: no court, judging as between the parties, would fail to reach for the circumstances, in determining whether the amount filled in had gone beyond the reasonable.

[11]   Why, then, can we not face the fact where boiler-plate is present? There has been an arm's-length deal, with dickered terms. There has been accompanying that basic deal another which, if not on any fiduciary basis, at least involves a plain expression of confidence, asked and accepted, with a corresponding limit on the powers granted: the boiler-plate is assented to en bloc, "unsight, unseen," on the implicit assumption and to the full extent that (1) it does not alter or impair the fair meaning of the dickered terms when read alone, and (2) that its terms are neither in the particular nor in the net manifestly unreasonable and unfair. Such is the reality, and I see nothing in the way of a court's operating on that basis, to truly effectuate the only intention which can in reason be worked out as common to the two parties, granted good faith. And if the boiler-plate party is not playing in good faith, there is law enough to bar that fact from benefiting it. We had a hundred years of sales law in which any sales transaction with explicit words resulted in two several contracts for the one consideration: that of sale, and the collateral one of warranty. The idea is applicable here, for better reason: any contract with boiler-plate results in *two* several contracts: the *dickered* deal, and the collateral one of *supplementary* boiler-plate.

[12]   Rooted in sense, history, and simplicity, it is an answer which could occur to anyone.

———————————

The following case illustrates one attempt to arrive at the solution that Llewellyn suggests.

TILDEN RENT-A-CAR CO. v. CLENDENNING

(1978), 18 O.R. (2d) 601, 83 D.L.R. (3d) 400
(C.A., Dubin, Lacourcière and Zuber JJ.A.)

[The defendant arrived at Vancouver Airport and went to the Tilden Rent-A-Car counter to rent a car. He was asked by the Tilden clerk if he wanted "additional coverage" and he replied that he did. A contract was presented for his signature. He signed the contract in the presence of the Tilden clerk and returned the contract to her. She placed his copy in an envelope and gave it to him with the car keys. The defendant did not read a copy of the contract then (and this fact was obvious to the clerk) nor had he done so before. The defendant had an accident with the rented car. As a result of the accident, he was charged in Vancouver with impaired driving. At the later civil trial, he testified that, on the advice of a Vancouver lawyer, he pleaded guilty to the criminal charge, but he testified at the civil trial that he was not actually impaired. Tilden sued in Ontario for the damage to the car, relying on a clause in the agreement that denied insurance coverage to the driver if he consumed any alcohol.

The trial judge in Ontario accepted the defendant's claim that he had at all times been in complete control of the car and that he had not been impaired. The judge held, however, that he was bound by *L'Estrange v. Graucob* so that the defendant's signature would have bound him to the terms of the contract but for the fact that Tilden was held to have misrepresented the terms of the contract. On this ground the trial judge dismissed Tilden's claim for the value of the car. Tilden appealed.]

DUBIN J.A.: — **[1]** . . . The issue on the appeal is whether the defendant is liable for the damage caused to the automobile while being driven by him by reason of the exclusionary provisions which appear in the contract.

[2] On the front of the contract are two relevant clauses set forth in box form. They are as follows:

15. COLLISION DAMAGE WAIVER BY CUSTOMERS INITIALS "J.C." *In consideration of the payment of $2.00 per day customers liability for damage to rented vehicle including wind shield is limited to NIL.* But notwithstanding payment of said fee, customer shall be fully liable for all collision damage if vehicle is used, operated or driven in violation of any of the provisions of this rental agreement or off highways serviced by federal, provincial, or municipal governments, and for all damages to vehicle by striking overhead objects.

16. I, the undersigned have read and received a copy of above and reverse side of this contract.

Signature of customer or employee of customer "John T. Clendenning"

(Emphasis added.)

[3] On the back of the contract in particularly small type and so faint in the customer's copy as to be hardly legible, there are a series of conditions, the relevant ones being as follows:

6. The customer agrees not to use the vehicle in violation of any law, ordinance, rule or regulation of any public authority.

7. The customer agrees that the vehicle will not be operated:

(a) By any person who has drunk or consumed any intoxicating liquor, whatever be the quantity, or who is under the influence of drugs or narcotics . . .

[4]   A witness called on behalf of the plaintiff gave evidence as to the instructions given to its employees as to what was to be said by them to their customers about the conditions in the contract. He stated that unless inquiries were made, nothing was said by its clerks to the customer with respect to the exclusionary conditions. He went on to state that if inquiries were made, the clerks were instructed to advise the customer that by the payment of the $2 additional fee the customer had complete coverage "unless he were intoxicated, or unless he committed an offence under the *Criminal Code* such as intoxication."

[5]   Mr. Clendenning acknowledged that he had assumed, either by what had been told to him in the past or otherwise, that he would not be responsible for any damage to the vehicle on payment of the extra premium unless such damage was caused by reason of his being so intoxicated as to be incapable of the proper control of the vehicle, a provision with which he was familiar as being a statutory provision in his own insurance contract.

[6]   The provisions fastening liability for damage to the vehicle on the hirer, as contained in the clauses hereinbefore referred to, are completely inconsistent with the express terms which purport to provide complete coverage for damage to the vehicle in exchange for the additional premium. It is to be noted, for example, that if the driver of the vehicle exceeded the speed limit even by one mile per hour, or parked the vehicle in a no parking area, or even had one glass of wine or one bottle of beer, the contract purports to make the hirer completely responsible for all damage to the vehicle. Indeed, if the vehicle at the time of any damage to it was being driven off a federal, provincial or municipal highway, such as a shopping plaza, for instance, the hirer purportedly would be responsible for all damage to the vehicle.

[7]   Mr. Clendenning stated that if he had known of the full terms of the written instrument, he would not have entered into such a contract. Having regard to the findings made by the trial judge, it is apparent that Mr. Clendenning had not in fact acquiesced to such terms.

[8]   It was urged that the rights of the parties were governed by what has come to be known as "the rule in *L'Estrange v. F. Graucob Ltd.*". . .

[9]   *Consensus ad idem* is as much a part of the law of written contracts as it is of oral contracts. The signature to a contract is only one way of manifesting assent to contractual terms. However, in the case of *L'Estrange v. F. Graucob Ltd.* there was in fact no *consensus ad idem*. Miss L'Estrange was a proprietor of a cafe. Two salesmen of the defendant company persuaded her to order a cigarette machine to be sold to her by their employer. They produced an order form which Miss L'Estrange signed without reading all of its terms. Amongst the many clauses in the document signed by her, there was included a paragraph, with respect to which she was completely unaware, which stated "any express or implied condition, statement, or warranty, statutory or otherwise not stated herein is hereby excluded." In her action against the company she alleged that the article sold to her was unfit for the purposes for which it was sold and contrary to *The Sale of Goods Act*. The company successfully defended on the basis of that exemption clause.

[10] Although the subject of critical analysis by learned authors . . . the case has survived, and it is now said that it applies to all contracts irrespective of the circumstances under which they are entered into, if they are signed by the party who seeks to escape their provisions.

[11] Thus, it was submitted that the ticket cases, which in the circumstances of this case would afford a ready defence for the hirer of the automobile, are not applicable.

[12] As is pointed out in Waddams, *The Law of Contracts* [(2nd ed.) (1984)], at 191:

> From the 19th century until recent times an extraordinary status has been accorded to the signed document that will be seen in retrospect, it is suggested, to have been excessive.

[13] The justification for the rule in *L'Estrange v. F. Graucob Ltd.* appears to have been founded upon the objective theory of contracts by which means parties are bound to a contract in writing by measuring their conduct by outward appearance rather than what the parties inwardly meant to decide. This, in turn, stems from the classic statement of Blackburn J. in *Smith v. Hughes* (1871), L.R. 6 Q.B. 597 at 607:

> I apprehend that if one of the parties intends to make a contract on one set of terms, and the other intends to make a contract on another set of terms, or, as it is sometimes expressed, if the parties are not *ad idem*, there is no contract, unless the circumstances are such as to preclude one of the parties from denying that he has agreed to the terms of the other. . . . *If, whatever a man's real intention may be, he so conducts himself that a reasonable man would believe that he was assenting to the terms proposed by the other party, and that other party upon that belief enters into the contract with him, the man thus conducting himself would be equally bound as if he had intended to agree to the other party's terms.*

(Emphasis added.)

[14] Even accepting the objective theory to determine whether Mr. Clendenning had entered into a contract which included all the terms of the written instrument, it is to be observed that an essential part of that test is whether the other party entered into the contract in the belief that Mr. Clendenning was assenting to all such terms. In the instant case, it was apparent to the employee of Tilden-Rent-A-Car that Mr. Clendenning had not in fact read the document in its entirety before he signed it. It follows under such circumstances that Tilden-Rent-A-Car cannot rely on provisions of the contract which it had no reason to believe were being assented to by the other contracting party.

[15] As stated in Waddams, *The Law of Contracts*, at 191:

> One who signs a written document cannot complain if the other party reasonably relies on the signature as a manifestation of assent to the contents, or ascribes to words he uses their reasonable meaning. But the other side of the same coin is that only a reasonable expectation will be protected. If the party seeking to enforce the document knew or had reason to know of the other's mistake the document should not be enforced.

In ordinary commercial practice where there is frequently a sense of formality in the transaction, and where there is a full opportunity for the parties to consider the terms of the proposed contract submitted for signature, it might well be safe to assume that the party who attaches his signature to the contract intends by so doing to acknowledge his acquiescence to its terms, and that the other party entered into the contract upon that belief. This can hardly be said, however, where the contract is entered into in circumstances such as were present in this case.

[16] A transaction, such as this one, is invariably carried out in a hurried, informal manner. The speed with which the transaction is completed is said to be one of the attractive features of the services provided.

[17] The clauses relied on in this case, as I have already stated, are inconsistent with the overall purpose for which the contract is entered into by the hirer. Under such circumstances, something more should be done by the party submitting the contract for signature than merely handing it over to be signed. . . .

[18] In modern commercial practice, many standard-form printed documents are signed without being read or understood. In many cases the parties seeking to rely on the terms of the contract know or ought to know that the signature of a party to the contract does not represent the true intention of the signer, and that the party signing is unaware of the stringent and onerous provisions which the standard form contains. Under such circumstances, I am of the opinion that the party seeking to rely on such terms should not be able to do so in the absence of first having taken reasonable measures to draw such terms to the attention of the other party, and, in the absence of such reasonable measures, it is not necessary for the party denying knowledge of such terms to prove either fraud, misrepresentation or *non est factum*.

[19] In the case at bar, Tilden Rent-A-Car took no steps to alert Mr. Clendenning of the onerous provisions in the standard form of contract presented by it. The clerk could not help but have known that Mr. Clendenning had not in fact read the contract before signing it. Indeed the form of the contract itself with the important provisions on the reverse side and in very small type would discourage even the most cautious customer from endeavouring to read and understand it. Mr. Clendenning was in fact unaware of the exempting provisions. Under such circumstances, it was not open to Tilden Rent-A-Car to rely on those clauses, and it was not incumbent on Mr. Clendenning to establish fraud, misrepresentation or *non est factum*. Having paid the premium, he was not liable for any damage to the vehicle while being driven by him.

[20] As Lord Denning stated in *Neuchatel Asphalt Co. Ltd. v. Barnett*, [1957] 1 W.L.R. 356, at 360, "We do not allow printed forms to be made a trap for the unwary."

[21] In this case the trial judge held that "the rule in *L'Estrange v. Graucob*" governed. He dismissed the action, however, on the ground that Tilden Rent-A-Car had by their prior oral representations misrepresented the terms of the contract. He imputed into the contract the assumption of Mr. Clendenning that by the payment of the premium he was "provided full non-deductible coverage unless at the time of the damage he was operating the automobile while under the influence of intoxicating liquor to such an extent as to be for the time incapable of the proper control of the automobile." Having found that Mr. Clendenning had not breached such a provision, the action was dismissed.

[22] For the reasons already expressed, I do not think that in the circumstances of this case "the rule in *L'Estrange v. Graucob*" governed, and it was not incumbent upon Mr. Clendenning to prove misrepresentation.

[23] In any event, if "the rule in *L'Estrange v. Graucob*" were applicable, it was in error, in my respectful opinion, to impute into the contract a provision which Tilden Rent-A-Car had not in fact represented as being a term of the contract. . . .

[24] Under such circumstances, absent the exclusionary provisions of the contract, the defendant was entitled to the benefit of the contract in the manner provided without the exclusionary provisions, and the action, therefore, had to fail.

[25] In the result, therefore, I would dismiss the appeal with costs.

LACOURCIÈRE J.A. (dissenting): — **[26]** I have had the advantage of reading the reasons for judgment prepared for release by my brother Dubin, which relieves me of the obligation of setting out the facts in this appeal, which are not really in dispute, or the relevant clauses of the contract. In my view the printing is not difficult to read, and the presence of conditions on the reverse side of the signed contract is brought to the signatory's attention in a very clear way.

[27] It is not in dispute that the respondent violated two conditions of the contract: he drove the company's vehicle into a post, after drinking an unrecalled quantity of alcohol between 11:30 p.m. and 2 a.m. He was given a breathalyzer test, indicating a police officer's belief, on reasonable and probable grounds, that he had committed an offence of driving a motor vehicle while his ability to drive was impaired by alcohol or after having consumed alcohol in such quantity that the proportion of alcohol in his blood exceeded the penal limit. On the advice of counsel he pleaded guilty to a charge of impaired driving. I have set this out only to show that the respondent's violation of the contractual conditions was not a mere technical breach of an admittedly strict clause.

[28] In the wisdom of the common law there has been a traditional distinction with respect to standard-form contracts between the position of person who signed the contract and the one who did not do so. In the absence of duress, fraud or misrepresentation — and subject to the defence of *non est factum* — the former was bound by the printed conditions, even if he or she did not read them: *L'Estrange v. F. Graucob Ltd.* . . .

[29] The traditional attitude, with which I respectfully agree, has been for Judges to avoid the difficult task of deciding the issue of "reasonableness" of clauses in businesses which compete freely in the market place for consumer support. . . .

[30] In this contract of bailment of a vehicle for a fixed remuneration, the customer is normally bound to take reasonable care of the vehicle, and is liable for damages caused by his negligence. This is subject to collision insurance: the customer is responsible for the deductible amount, $100 or $200 depending on location. By the payment of an additional premium, this liability of the customer is eliminated with this proviso:

> . . . notwithstanding payment of said fee, customer shall be fully liable for all collision damage if vehicle is used, operated or driven in violation of any of the provisions of this rental agreement or off highways serviced by federal, provincial, or municipal governments, and for all damages to vehicle by striking overhead objects.

[31] The clause is undoubtedly a strict one. It is not for a court to nullify its effect by branding it unfair, unreasonable and oppressive. It may be perfectly sound and reasonable from an insurance risk viewpoint, and may indeed be necessary in the competitive business of car rentals, where rates are calculated on the basis of the whole contract. On this point, see the majority judgment delivered by Lord Wilberforce in *New Zealand Shipping Co. Ltd. and A.M. Satterthwaite & Co. Ltd.*, [1975] A.C. 154 at 169, where it was held that the court must give effect to the clear intent of a commercial document.

[32] I am of the view that, even if the respondent's signature is not conclusive, the terms of the contract are not unusual, oppressive or unreasonable and are binding on the respondent. I would therefore allow the appeal with costs, set aside the judgment below and in lieu thereof substitute a judgment for the amount of the agreed damages and costs.

NOTES AND QUESTIONS

1. The decision to give Mr. Clendenning the benefit of his expectation can be justified if Tilden had no reasonable basis for a belief that Mr. Clendenning's signature indicated his acceptance of the risk of loss the contract placed upon him. If one considers, however, what risks of loss Mr. Clendenning should be forced to bear simply because he should have never expected not to bear them, then the issue becomes more complex. One could argue, for example, that a person who knows the extent of the standard collision coverage under any Canadian automobile insurance policy cannot reasonably claim that he or she expected the risk to be shifted to the car rental company under the terms of a standard car rental agreement. One could, perhaps, also say that car rental corporations are entitled to expect that the customer knows what anyone renting a car in Canada would generally know.

    This analysis points to a number of serious problems:

    (a) there are clear efficiency gains in the rule of *L'Estrange v. Graucob*: the mass-production of standardized contracts is greatly facilitated;

    (b) the rule threatens the basic premise that the courts are concerned with in enforcing contracts: *viz.*, that people not be caught by unfair surprise, where the word "unfair" permits the court to consider how much surprise is unfair;

    (c) if courts consider the individualized subjective expectations (and the consequent surprise when they are not met), the process of deciding what to do in each case will become very much more complex and expensive, and the job of the solicitor who has to draft a standard form for his or her client will be correspondingly much more difficult.

    None of these problems is, alone or in combination with the others, sufficient to justify the rule in *L'Estrange v. Graucob*. What these problems illustrate is that we have to remember that the business of enforcing contracts, especially when we do not have a background of a relatively standard pattern of trade practice shared by both parties, is a complex process in which it is not always easy to be certain that we have reached a satisfactory result.

2. How would a court be likely to deal with a clause that significantly limits the rights of a purchaser on a website in a lengthy multi-screen consumer contract that a consumer did not read, but entered into by clicking "I have read and accept these terms." Consider how the Court dealt with the unread jurisdiction clause in *Rudder v. Microsoft*, *supra*, Chapter 3.

3. If the statement of Lacourcière J.A. that the car rental business is a competitive market is correct, does it follow that the clause in question is the result of competitive pressures? What conditions would have to exist before it could be assumed that the clause

in the Tilden contract was the product of competitive pressures? Because individual consumers often have difficulty in understanding terms and assessing their significance, it is rare to have "term" competition, even in highly competitive consumer markets. Car rental companies vigorously compete in areas of price, service, car quality and location, but not in regard to terms. Similarly, banks lending to individuals may compete on interest rate, or even on "approachability", but only rarely on the terms of the loan.

4. The judgment of the majority of the Court of Appeal supports the idea that the function of the law of contracts is to protect the reasonable expectations of the parties. There are, however, considerable problems in discovering what these expectations might be, even in a case as superficially simple as *Tilden v. Clendenning*. Dubin J.A., in ¶ 5, mentions that Mr. Clendenning knew that his own car insurance would not have extended to protect him if he were driving while impaired and had an accident. Under the standard automobile insurance policy in Ontario (and in all the other provinces of Canada except Quebec), an owner has no insurance coverage if he or she is impaired when the accident happens. The insurer may have to indemnify any third parties who are injured, but is then entitled to recover the amount it has paid from the driver. See, *e.g.*, the *Insurance Act*, R.S.O. 1990, c. I.8, s. 258(4) and s. 258(13). A claim under any collision coverage would similarly be denied. Even if we know what Mr. Clendenning's "reasonable expectations" were when he took out insurance coverage from Tilden, another Tilden customer may have quite different expectations.

5. *Tilden v. Clendenning* raises an important point about the process of adjudication. If the courts do not *talk* about what is relevant, counsel cannot know what facts the courts will consider (though, of course, good counsel may have an idea of what facts will move the court one way or the other) and evidence on those facts may not be introduced. Part of the problem is that a person in the position of Mr. Clendenning is not likely to know very much about the terms of his or her insurance policy, though most people may know some of the serious consequences of driving while impaired.

6. It is important to be clear about the possible differences between the points of view of Dubin J.A. in *Tilden v. Clendenning* and in the Llewellyn extract, *supra*. The distinction between the objective and subjective views of contract has been considered throughout these materials. If a party knew what the other expected there is a strong pressure to hold the first party to the expectations of the other. If there is no actual knowledge, the courts are left with what may well be a very difficult decision, one which may well disappoint one party's actual expectations. A focus on *reasonable expectations* forces one to consider what a person in the situation of the party *should* have expected. A focus on the question whether the contract or its terms *were reasonable* has a different slant and suggests that different evidence might be relevant.

7. In *Crocker v. Sundance Northwest Resorts Ltd.*, [1988] S.C.J. No. 6 [1988] 1 S.C.R. 1186, 51 D.L.R. (4th) 321, a man who was rendered a quadriplegic as a result of injuries suffered in an accident during a promotional competition involving sledding down a steep ski hill run in an inner tube sued the resort that operated the hill. Prior to participating in the event, the man had signed an entry form and waiver without reading it and paid the entry fee. In upholding the trial decision that allowed the man to recover 75 per cent of his damages, Wilson J. wrote (at paras. 36 and 37):

> Sundance correctly points out that a contractual waiver clause can serve as a full defence to a claim in tort. In *Dyck v. Manitoba Snowmobile Association Inc.*, [1985] 1 S.C.R. 589, the plaintiff took part in a snowmobile race. The plaintiff collided with Wood, an association official, who following usual practice had signalled the end of the race by moving to the middle of the track. The collision caused the plaintiff to strike the outside wall of the track. The plaintiff was injured and sued the Association in tort. This Court agreed with the courts below that, while the Association had been negligent, it was exonerated from liability by the waiver clause in the entry form.

Sundance argues that the situation in the present appeal is not dissimilar to that in *Dyck* and that the waiver signed by Crocker should relieve Sundance of liability for its negligent conduct. In my view this is not the case. There is a very significant difference between *Dyck* and the present appeal which, in my view, renders the reasoning in *Dyck* inapplicable here. In *Dyck* the plaintiff had read the rules of the Association that purported to release the Association from liability for injuries suffered in the Association's races. The plaintiff in *Dyck* signed the waiver in full knowledge of the Association's intention to exempt itself from liability. Not so here. As already mentioned, the trial judge found that the waiver provision in the entry form was not drawn to the plaintiff's attention, that he had not read it, and, indeed, did not know of its existence. He thought he was simply signing an entry form. In these circumstances Sundance cannot rely upon the waiver clause in the entry form.

8.   In *Shelanu Inc. v. Print Three Franchising Corp.*, [2003] O.J. No. 1919, 64 O.R. (3d) 533, 226 D.L.R. (4th) 577 (C.A.), the Ontario Court of Appeal considered a franchise agreement that contained three exclusionary clauses: paragraph 20, which provided that delay exercising a right was not a waiver; paragraph 26, which provided that there was no waiver or amendment to the agreement unless signed by all parties; and paragraph 27, which was an entire agreement clause providing that the written agreement constituted the entire agreement between the parties with respect to all matters. The Court of Appeal concluded that, as a matter of interpretation, none of the clauses was applicable to the case, but Weiler J.A. also made the following comments about the effect of exclusion clauses:

> [35] In *Guarantee Co. of North America v. Gordon Capital Corp.*, [1993] 3 S.C.R 423, 178 D.L.R. (4th) 1, the Supreme Court of Canada ". . . interpreted *Hunter Engineering* in such a way as to indicate that there was little distinction between the approaches of Dickson C.J. and Wilson J." respecting the enforceability of exclusion clauses ... I agree. At para. 52 of the reasons in *Gordon Capital, supra*, Iacobucci and Bastarache JJ. stated:
>
>> The only limitation placed upon enforcing the contract as written . . . would be to refuse to enforce an exclusion of liability in circumstances where to do so would be unconscionable, according to Dickson C.J., or unfair, unreasonable or otherwise contrary to public policy, according to Wilson J.
>
> . . .
>
> *(iii) Discretion not to enforce the exclusion clauses*
>
> [53] In view of my conclusion above, it is not strictly necessary for me to address the enforceability of the exclusion clauses. However, given the trial judge's conclusion and the extent of argument on the question of whether he erred in refusing to give effect to the clauses, I will consider this issue.
>
> [54] ... Where the parties have, by their subsequent course of conduct, amended the written agreement so that it no longer represents the intention of the parties, the court will refuse to enforce the written agreement. This is so even in the face of a clause requiring changes to the agreement to be in writing. See *Colautti Construction Ltd. v. City of Ottawa* (1984), 46 O.R. (2d) 236, 9 D.L.R. (4th) 265 (C.A.), *per* Cory J.A.
>
> [55] On appeal, the appellant has conceded the existence of the oral agreement and its terms but asks this court to enforce the written agreement instead. That submission, in effect, asks this court not to give effect to the intention of the parties. Such a submission is contrary to the classical theory of contract interpretation which emphasizes that courts should ascertain and give effect to the intention of the parties: R. Sullivan, "Contract Interpretation in Practice and Theory" (2000) 13 S.C.L.R. (2d) 369.

[56] Sullivan states, at p. 378, that, "if a conflict arises between the intention of the parties as inferred from the totality of the evidence on the one hand and the meaning of the text on the other, intention should win." Professor Waddams has also argued that if a party knows or has reason to know that a written contract on which that party relies does not represent the intention of the other party, it should not be enforced. See S.M. Waddams, *The Law of Contracts*, 3rd ed. (Toronto: Canada Law Book, 1993) at paras. 328-29.

[57] The rationale of Sullivan and Waddams is similar, namely, that in addition to certainty, legal values such as fairness, equity and justice underlie contractual interpretation and enforcement. Before the court allows the coercive power of the state to be used to serve the private interests of a party to a contract, the court will want to ensure that the contract does not offend these legal values.

[58] ...[T]he agreement that we are dealing with is a franchise agreement. A franchise agreement is a type of contract of adhesion, that is, a type of contract whose main provisions are presented on a "take it or leave it basis". In such situations, the case for holding that an exclusion clause represents the intention of the signer and that the signer should be bound by it is weaker because there is usually an inherent inequality of bargaining power between the parties. See Waddams, *supra*, at para. 342. Examples of cases involving contracts of adhesion where this court has refused to apply an exclusion clause because it did not accord with the intention or reasonable expectations of the parties include: ... *Solway v. Davis Moving & Storage Inc.* (2002), 62 O.R. (3d) 522, [2002] O.J. No. 4760 (QL) (C.A.) at para. 21; and ... *Mellco Developments Ltd. v. Portage la Prairie (City)*, [2002] M.J. No. 381 (QL), 222 D.L.R. (4th) 67 (C.A.).

[59] Enforcing an exclusion clause that is contrary to the reasonable expectation and understanding of the parties in these circumstances would not be fair or reasonable and would also come within the exception enunciated in *Gordon Capital, supra*.

[60] I would hold that even if the exclusion clauses applied, the trial judge was entitled to refuse to enforce paras. 20, 26, and 27 of the agreement.

The context in which *Tilden v. Clendenning* was signed was characterized by a supplier to consumers, offering its customers a mass-produced, standard form. The following case illustrates the very different considerations which will be relevant in a negotiated, bilateral agreement that is "custom-made" for a particular relation.

978011 ONTARIO LTD. v. CORNELL ENGINEERING CO. LTD.

[2001] O.J. No. 1446, 53 O.R. (3d) 783, 198 D.L.R. (4th) 615
(C.A., Weiler, Rosenberg and MacPherson JJ.A.)

The judgment of the court was delivered by **WEILER J.A.**: —

Overview

[1] The respondent, Cornell Engineering Company Limited ("Cornell"), unilaterally terminated its contract (hereinafter called the Services Agreement) with the appellant, 978011 Ontario Ltd., for the services of Glenn Macdonald ("Macdonald"). The appellant brought an action to enforce the clause in the contract that provided for compensation upon unilateral termination. In the alternative, the ap-

pellant claimed damages at common law for the wrongful dismissal of Macdonald.
Robert Stevens, who signed the Services Agreement on behalf of the respondent,
did not read the termination clause before signing it. Stevens and his partner,
Remzi Bimboga, are the sole shareholders, officers and directors of the respondent. The trial judge held that, in the circumstances under which the Services
Agreement was signed, Macdonald owed a duty to bring the termination clause in
the agreement to Stevens' attention before Stevens signed the contract. The trial
judge purported to rectify the Services Agreement by striking out the termination
clause. After striking out the termination clause, the trial judge dismissed the appellant's action in its entirety.

[2]   The appellant submits that Macdonald did not conceal the termination clause
from Stevens and that he had no duty to draw the termination clause to the attention of Stevens simply because outside of the business relationship Macdonald and
Stevens maintained a personal relationship as friends. The appellant further submits that the doctrine of rectification does not apply when, as here, the mistake is
unilaterally Stevens' and the contract is no longer capable of performance.

[3]   For the reasons that follow, I would agree with the appellant that Macdonald
had no duty to draw the termination clause to Stevens' attention. I say this for two
reasons. First, although there was a relationship of trust between Stevens and
Macdonald, it was one in which Stevens acted as a mentor and was in a position of
ascendancy, not dependency, with respect to Macdonald. Second, Macdonald discharged his duty, if one existed, when he advised Stevens to read the contract. If
Stevens had followed Macdonald's advice he would have had the means to ascertain the terms of the clearly visible termination clause.

[4]   The trial judge also erred when he purported to rectify the contract by striking out the termination clause. In order for the remedy of rectification to apply,
there must be a mutual intention between the parties concerning what would happen in the event Cornell unilaterally terminated the Services Agreement. There is
no evidence that such a mutual intention existed. The parties had never discussed
what was to happen in the event Cornell unilaterally terminated the Services
Agreement. Even if the doctrine of rectification were applicable to a unilateral
mistake when the contract is no longer capable of performance, it would be inappropriate to apply it in this case.

The Facts

The parties

[5]   Macdonald, aged 41, is a qualified professional engineer with aspirations to
own a business. He is the sole shareholder, director and officer of the appellant
corporation.

[6]   Bimboga is also 41 years of age. He studied and worked abroad and emi-
grated from Turkey to Canada in 1985. Around this time, he met Stevens and they
went into business together. Because of his uneasiness with the English language,
he relied on Stevens' articulateness, knowledge and familiarity with the Canadian
business scene. Stevens took care of "external" matters while Bimboga concentrated on the "internal" and production side of the business.

[7]   Stevens is 70 years of age and a very experienced businessperson. He holds a Masters Degree in Business Administration from Harvard University. Prior to purchasing Cornell in 1990, he was the owner of Beatty Brothers, an appliance manufacturer. He also was the Vice-Chair and a member of the Board of Directors of General Steelwares, a company which had $600 million in annual sales. As Vice-Chair, the presidents of the six divisions of General Steelwares reported to him. He is knowledgeable and experienced in matters of contract negotiation and formation.

[8]   Stevens was a friend of Macdonald's family for many years and had acted as a mentor to Macdonald on business matters since January 1992, providing business and career advice to him. Macdonald valued their relationship and respected Stevens. He did not question Stevens or his expertise on business matters and looked up to him as a role model.

[9]   Cornell was incorporated in Ontario in 1945 and carried on the business of stamping metal to be used in the manufacturing of household appliances. Stevens and Bimboga purchased Cornell in 1990 and were the sole shareholders, officers and directors of Cornell. Stevens owned 51 per cent of the Cornell shares and Bimboga owned the remaining 49 per cent. Stevens and Bimboga had financed the total purchase price of Cornell in 1990.

Events leading up to the signing of the Services Agreement

[10]   In or about 1992, Bimboga developed health problems and decided to sell his shares in Cornell. There was a Shareholders Agreement between Stevens and Bimboga containing a buy-sell clause. This clause required Stevens to sell his shares unless a purchaser could be found for Bimboga's interest. It was in Stevens' interest to find a purchaser for Bimboga's shares.

[11]   In June 1992, Macdonald sought Stevens' personal advice regarding the purchase of another company that Macdonald was in the process of negotiating. During the meeting, Macdonald began to consider the opportunity of working for Stevens and to learn more about the business as an employee.

[12]   By letter dated June 23, 1992, Macdonald raised the possibility of working under Stevens at Cornell. He stated that he could not "imagine a more exciting or rewarding opportunity", that he would "never let Stevens down", and that he would "love to give [Stevens] a chance to pass on some of [his] expertise to someone who is willing, eager, and more than capable to sop it up like a dry sponge. I would love to be that sponge".

[13]   As a result of this letter, Stevens met with Macdonald on June 26, 1992. After Macdonald indicated he would be interested in working for Cornell, Stevens suggested that Macdonald might want to buy Bimboga's interest. Stevens also suggested that, when he retired, Macdonald might acquire his majority interest as well.

[14]   Over the next several months, Stevens and Macdonald discussed the possible terms for Macdonald to purchase Bimboga's interest in Cornell. Initially, Stevens advised that the price of Bimboga's shares was $1,000,000. Then Stevens advised that Bimboga had changed his mind and did not want to sell his shares. A few weeks later, Stevens told Macdonald that Bimboga would sell his shares for $1,150,000. Later, he again told Macdonald that Bimboga had changed his mind.

[15] In September 1992, Stevens told Macdonald that Bimboga would sell his shares for $1,450,000. Macdonald did not ask why the price kept increasing. (Bimboga testified that his asking price for his shares was always $1,450,000. Stevens testified that it was his negotiating style to advise Macdonald that the shares were not for sale.)

[16] Macdonald was to make a first payment of $650,000 for Bimboga's shares in January 1995. Cornell was to provide financing for $150,000, leaving Macdonald to obtain financing for the remaining $500,000. During a two-year period Macdonald also had to satisfy Bimboga that he had the ability and experience to take over Bimboga's role as president of Cornell.

[17] On October 5, 1992, Stevens advised Macdonald that Bimboga had agreed to the flexible closing date and to pay a salary of $55,000. As a result of the agreement, Macdonald declined a salary of $135,000 per year as President of Don Park and did not pursue further interviews for a position at Noranda. Macdonald began work at Cornell on January 4, 1993.

The Services Agreement

[18] Stevens arranged for Macdonald to meet with Cornell's accountant on February 17, 1993. The accountant advised that it would be beneficial to both Cornell and Macdonald for his services to be provided to Cornell through the appellant corporation, pursuant to a written Services Agreement. Stevens asked Macdonald to prepare a written agreement.

[19] Macdonald had not previously prepared such an agreement. He obtained a copy of an 11-page printed contract for the provision of engineering services from his professional association as a guide. He prepared two copies of the printed agreement on which he made a number of revisions to the standard form document — striking out some of the clauses and attaching labels over the deleted clauses on which he had typed other terms. The amendments to the first page of the document described the services to be performed for Cornell over a period of two years for an annual fee of $55,000.

[20] Macdonald struck out the termination provisions in the printed contract and opposite them inserted the following clause in slightly larger type:

> 1.7 Without the mutual consent of the Client and the Engineer, should either this contract or the agreement to purchase 49 per cent of Cornell Engineering Company Ltd. by Glenn Macdonald at the completion of this contract, be terminated or changed, the following terms shall be honoured:
>
> (a) the engineer and Glenn Macdonald shall be released from all conditions and commitments associated with both this contract and the agreement to purchase 49 per cent of Cornell Engineering Company Ltd.
>
> (b) the client shall pay compensation to the Engineer at a rate equal to two times the total remuneration already paid to the Engineer to date.

There had been no prior discussion between the parties as to what would occur if Macdonald's employment was terminated and he did not purchase the shares of Cornell.

[21] On March 3, 1993, Macdonald presented two copies of the Services Agreement to Stevens at his office and asked that Stevens read the agreement. Macdonald was anticipating that Stevens would need time to review the 11-page contract and would likely suggest some amendments. In his evidence-in-chief, Stevens testified that he asked Macdonald, "Does this cover what you want, what you want to do?" to which Macdonald replied, "yes". In cross-examination, Stevens testified that he asked Macdonald, "Is this agreeable to you?" to which Macdonald responded, "Is this agreeable to you?" Stevens then told Macdonald, "It looks like you've covered everything you wanted."

[22] Stevens acknowledged that he knew it was important to read a document before execution, because once signed one would be bound by the document whether it had been read or not. He admitted that he read and agreed with the terms described on the first page of the Services Agreement and specifically agreed to the provisions regarding the performance of the described services over a two-year period at the rate of $55,000 per year.

[23] There was no pressure on Stevens to sign the Services Agreement. Because Stevens was in a position of ascendancy, Macdonald testified that he did not consider it appropriate to demand that Stevens read the Agreement before signing it.

Performance of the Services Agreement

[24] From January 4, 1993 to July 4, 1994, Macdonald provided the services referred to in the Services Agreement and the appellant rendered monthly invoices. On August 26, 1993, Macdonald, Stevens and Bimboga reviewed a third and final draft of an agreement containing the terms of the share purchase upon which they had all agreed (the "Skeleton Agreement"). The substantive provisions of the Skeleton Agreement were as follows:

- Cornell shall redeem all shares owned by Bimboga and re-issue shares to Macdonald on a pro-rata basis as he pays for them.

- The price paid by Macdonald to Bimboga for his share interest shall be $1,450,000.00 payable in the following way:

  (a) $500,000.00 payable on January 4, 1995,

  (b) $300,000.00 payable on January 6, 1997,

  (c) $650,000.00 payable on January 8, 1999.

- Macdonald may pay Bimboga the $300,000.00 sum prior to January 6, 1997.

- Interest shall be calculated monthly on the unpaid portion of the $300,000.00 at a rate of prime plus 1 per cent and paid by Macdonald to Bimboga on January 5, 1996 and January 6, 1997.

- The closing date may be earlier than January 4, 1995 should it be agreed by Stevens, Bimboga, and Macdonald.

- Bimboga shall be available for a period of three months after the closing date to assist in the daily operations of Cornell.

[25] When Macdonald reviewed the draft documentation prepared by Cornell's solicitors, he advised Stevens that it was not satisfactory. Stevens advised Macdonald that revisions to the draft should be deferred until Macdonald had obtained financing for the share purchase.

[26] Macdonald made extensive efforts to obtain financing for the purchase of Bimboga's shares. By July 1994, about 18 months into the Services Agreement, these efforts had not been successful. Macdonald admitted that there was no point in continuing the Services Agreement if he could not obtain financing but he still hoped to do so.

[27] On July 4, 1994, Bimboga requested a meeting during which he and Stevens told Macdonald that they would not pay for services rendered during the month of June 1994 and would not pay any future remuneration. They also demanded that Macdonald sign the share purchase documentation in the form prepared by Cornell's solicitors and immediately deliver a $60,000 deposit to Bimboga. Macdonald was told that unless he agreed to those demands, "the deal was dead." Macdonald requested an opportunity to speak to a financial or legal advisor.

[28] On July 5, 1994, after meeting with his advisors, Macdonald advised Bimboga and Stevens that he was not prepared to work without remuneration but would provide a $60,000 deposit to be placed in trust upon signing a mutually acceptable share purchase agreement. Bimboga, however, continued to demand that he be paid $60,000 immediately or he would sue Macdonald for the salary already paid, legal costs and "suffering".

[29] Shortly before trial, Macdonald received payment from Cornell for services rendered in June.

. . .

[WEILER J.A.'s summary and extensive quotation from the trial judge's reasons are omitted. The trial judge held that, in the circumstances under which the agreement was signed, Macdonald owed a duty to bring the termination clause to Stevens' attention before he signed the contract. The basis for the trial judge's conclusion was that since Stevens was Macdonald's mentor and owed the latter a fiduciary duty, Macdonald owed Stevens a reciprocal duty, though it was not a fiduciary one. The trial judge purported to rectify the agreement by striking out the termination clause. He then dismissed the action. **WEILER J.A.** referred particularly to the trial judge's reasons at (1998), 41 B.L.R. (2d) 219 at pp. 238-41, 41 C.C.E.L. (2d) 118 (Ont. Gen. Div.).]

The Law

[31] The law to be applied to this case is not really in issue. A succinct formulation of the law is found in *Can-Dive Services Ltd. v. Pacific Coast Energy Corp.* (2000), 134 B.C.A.C. 19, by Southin J.A. at para. 137, in which she quotes J. Story, *Commentaries on Equity Jurisprudence, as Administered in England and America*, 13th ed. (Boston, Little, Brown, 1886), vol. 1, paras. 147-55. Story states that a unilateral mistake as to a material term of a contract will afford a ground of relief in equity where the mistake operates as a fraud or surprise upon the ignorant party. However, Story adds at para. 147:

> But in all such cases the ground of relief is not the mistake or ignorance of material facts alone, but the unconscientious advantage taken of the party by the concealment of them. For if the parties act fairly, and it is not a case where one is bound to communicate the facts to the other upon the ground of confidence or otherwise, there the court will not interfere. . . .

[32] This quote encapsulates the fact that we have a judicial system that emphasizes individual responsibility and self-reliance. Generally, parties negotiating a contract expect that each will act entirely in the party's own interests. Absent a special relationship, the common law in Canada has yet to recognize that in the negotiation of a contract, there is a duty to have regard to the other person's interests, namely, to act in good faith: see *Bell v. Lever Brothers Ltd.*, [1932] A.C. 161, [1931] All E.R. Rep. 1 (H.L.), and more recently, *Martel Building Ltd. v. Canada*, [2000] 2 S.C.R. 860, 2000 S.C.C. 60 at para. 73. In keeping with the principle of self-reliance imposed by law on each party to a contract, the failure to read a contract before signing it is not a legally acceptable basis for refusing to abide by it. Nor is the fact that the clause was not subject to negotiations sufficient in itself: see *Fraser Jewellers (1982) Ltd. v. Dominion Electric Protection Co. Ltd.* (1997), 34 O.R. (3d) 1 at p. 10, 148 D.L.R. (4th) 496 (C.A.); *L'Estrange v. Graucob (F.) Ltd.*, [1934] 2 K.B. 394 at p. 403, [1934] All E.R. Rep. 16.

[33] The law does, however, regulate contractual conduct between individuals through the imposition of three types of standards: unconscionability, good faith and the fiduciary standard. All three standards are points on a continuum in which the law acknowledges a limitation on the principle of self-reliance and imposes an obligation to respect the interests of the other. They are defined by P. Finn, "The Fiduciary Principle", in T. Youdan, ed., *Equity, Fiduciaries and Trusts* (Scarborough, Ont.: Carswell, 1989), 1 at 4 as follows:

> "Unconscionability" accepts that one party is entitled as of course to act self-interestedly in his actions towards the other. Yet in deference to that other's interests, it then proscribes excessively self-interested or exploitative conduct. "Good faith", while permitting a party to act self-interestedly, nonetheless qualifies this by positively requiring that party, in his decision and action, to have regard to the legitimate interests therein of the other.[1] The "fiduciary" standard[2] for its part enjoins one party to act in the interests of the other — to act selflessly and with undivided loyalty. There is, in other words, a progression from the first to the third: from selfish behaviour to selfless behaviour. Much the most contentious of the trio is the second, "good faith". It often goes unacknowledged. It does embody characteristics to be found in the other two.

[34] The circumstances where the law requires more than self-interested dealing on the part of a party share certain characteristics. First, one party relies on the other for information necessary to make an informed choice and, second, the party in possession of the information has an opportunity, by withholding (or conceal-

---

[1] At pp. 11-12, Finn, *supra*, gives examples of relationships where a duty of good faith has been imposed. These include an applicant applying for insurance; a doctor counselling a patient on a proposed treatment; the possessor of superior information dealing with one to whom that information is not reasonably accessible. The duty of good faith requires the person exercising a power or discretion to have regard to the other person's interests but this does not necessarily mean that the other person's interests are paramount; see *Freedman v. Mason*, [1958] S.C.R. 483, 14 D.L.R. (2d) 529; The Hon. Justice Charles D. Gonthier, "Liberty, Equality, Fraternity: The Forgotten Leg of the Trilogy, or Fraternity: The Unspoken Third Pillar of Democracy" (2000), 45 *McGill L.J.* 567 at pp. 583-84, subtitled "Good Faith in Contracts".

[2] Well-known categories of fiduciary relationships that come to my mind here include solicitor-client, trustee and *cestui que trust*, parents and children under age, adults and "ancient" parents, and relationships where one of the parties has some known infirmity. Before enforcing a contract in these relationships, a court will want assurance that in entering into the contract the ascendant party acted only with regard to the dependent party's interests.

ing) information, to bring about the choice made by the other party. See Finn, *supra*, at pp. 17-18[3] and Waddams, *The Law of Contracts*, 3d ed. (Toronto: Canada Law Book, 1993), at para. 438. If one party to a contract relies on the other for information, that reliance must be justified in the circumstances. Finn, *supra*, suggests at p. 20 that the following five factors are indicative of situations where reliance is justified:

(1)   A past course of dealing between the parties in which reliance for advice, etc., has been an accepted feature;

(2)   The explicit assumption by one party of advisory responsibilities;

(3)   The relative positions of the parties particularly in their access to information and in their understanding of the possible demands of the dealing;

(4)   The manner in which the parties were brought together, and the expectation that could create in the relying party; and

(5)   [W]hether "trust and confidence" knowingly [has] been reposed by one party in the other.

[35]   The presence of one of these elements alone will not necessarily suffice to justify the imposition of a duty in law on the other. Dependence, influence, vulnerability, trust and confidence are of importance only to the extent that they evidence a relationship suggesting an entitlement not to be self-reliant: see Finn, *supra*, at p. 47. While the relationship may be the foundation for the entitlement, in and of itself, the relationship does not create the entitlement. The entitlement arises either because one party has no ability to readily inform himself or herself by accessing important information or because one party has an inability to appreciate the significance of the information. That inability may be due to a cognitive disability or it may arise out of the circumstances created by the other party. To determine whether the entitlement is created, regard must be had to all the circumstances.

Issue on Appeal

[36]   The trial judge found that prior to signing the contract, Stevens was entitled to expect that Macdonald would specifically tell him about the termination clause because they had a fiduciary-type of relationship. Was he correct? The answer to this question requires a more detailed examination of the facts and the trial judge's findings.

Analysis

[37]   The trial judge found that a special relationship existed between Macdonald and Stevens based on the following factors: Stevens had previously advised Macdonald about career prospects; they were working towards a partnership and partners owed one another a fiduciary duty. Despite these findings, the trial judge found at para. 65, "Macdonald had no obligation to actively advance or protect Stevens' interests during their negotiations." Therefore, the relationship was not a fiduciary one.

---

3   Although Finn's comments are directed to the circumstances in which a fiduciary relationship will be found, I am of the opinion that they are equally applicable to the circumstances in which a lesser duty of good faith will be imposed.

[38] However, based upon Stevens' complete trust in Macdonald, the trial judge found that Macdonald had an obligation to act in good faith towards Stevens. He went on to hold that this obligation to act in good faith required Macdonald to disclose the existence of the termination clause to Stevens, and that Stevens should not be held responsible for his own negligence in failing to read the agreement because he had trusted Macdonald and relied on him to prepare the Services Agreement.

[39] I respectfully disagree that Stevens was justified in law in relying on Macdonald to bring the termination clause to his attention. In reaching his conclusion, the trial judge relied on Finn, *supra*, and Waddams, *supra*. I will also follow the indicia used by these authors as a guide in my conclusion.

(1) *Past course of dealing*

[40] When Stevens signed the Services Agreement, he did so on behalf of Cornell. Although Stevens and Macdonald were friends and Stevens acted as a mentor in advising Macdonald on his career, Macdonald had no prior dealing and no relationship with Bimboga, the other person affected by the Agreement. The undisputed purpose of the Services Agreement was to facilitate the transfer of Bimboga's shares in Cornell to Macdonald. Macdonald was at the mercy of Bimboga's discretion in the sense that even if he raised the money for the first payment towards the purchase of Bimboga's shares, Bimboga still had to be satisfied of Macdonald's ability to run the company before transferring his shares. Without the termination clause, Macdonald had no protection from Bimboga.

[41] It is also important to recall that Macdonald turned down a salary of $135,000 as President of Don Park for an indefinite period in return for a two-year employee position for $55,000. In this context, the termination clause in the Services Agreement, although one-sided, was not unreasonable. Furthermore, by entering into the Services Agreement, Macdonald was potentially relinquishing his common law protection from wrongful dismissal. In these circumstances, the inclusion of a termination clause in the agreement was not unusual.

[42] At para. 58, the trial judge considered *Hartog v. Colin & Shields*, [1939] 3 All E.R. 566 (K.B.) and *Stepps Investments Ltd. v. Security Capital Corp.* (1976), 14 O.R. (2d) 259, 73 D.L.R. (3d) 351 (H.C.J.) and concluded that there is no material distinction in principle between those cases and the present one. In both *Hartog*, *supra*, and *Stepps Investments*, *supra*, the parties had specifically discussed and agreed to a term of a contract that was then unilaterally changed without notice to the other party.

[43] It appears that the trial judge was of the opinion that since Macdonald had already started work for Cornell, all of the terms of his employment had been agreed upon and therefore the termination clause was a unilateral change to the oral agreement. Technically, the parties to the oral contract were not the same as the parties to the written contract. The oral contract was entered into by Macdonald personally, the written contract was entered into by the appellant corporation. More importantly, there was no discussion, and no prior agreement between any of the parties regarding termination.

[44] Upon seeing the 11-page agreement, Stevens must have known from the length of the document that it contained terms other than the few that had been agreed upon orally. The terms that had been agreed upon orally, namely, compensation of $55,000 per annum, at the rate of 1/12 per month, and the duration of the agreement, two years, were all on the first page which Stevens read.

(2) *Explicit assumption by one party of advisory responsibilities*

[45] It was Stevens who explicitly assumed advisory responsibilities and it was Stevens who was in a position to influence Macdonald.

(3) *Relative positions of the parties, particularly in their access to information and in their understanding of the possible demands of the dealing*

[46] Macdonald intended to leave the agreement with Stevens to read and in fact advised him to read it. Stevens and Bimboga would have had ready access to the necessary information had it not been for Stevens' precipitous act in deciding to sign the agreement after reading only the first page. Macdonald did nothing to pressure Stevens to sign the agreement without reading it.

[47] The Agreement was easy to read with clear headings including the heading "Termination" in bold. The changes to the standard form were easy to detect. After the heading "Termination" there is a line drawn through the remainder of the pre-printed portion that remains visible on the right-hand side. The amendment that is typed in is located on the opposite side and stands in slightly larger type than the pre-printed font and is clearly worded. Stevens could readily have accessed the information concerning the termination clause by simply reading the Services Agreement.

[48] In *Stepps, supra*,[4] part of the rationale for the decision of Grange J.A., that there was a duty on the party making a change to the agreement to draw it to the attention of the other side, was that the significance of the change was not easy to detect. That is not the situation here. Nor is this a case where a party has accepted a standard form contract containing onerous and verbose provisions in small type and in circumstances where it could not reasonably be expected for the signing party to read to the contract: see *Tilden Rent-A-Car Co. v. Clendenning* (1978), 18 O.R. (2d) 601, 83 D.L.R. (3d) 400 (C.A.). In this case, Stevens, an experienced person in signing contracts, had the opportunity to examine the documents, and was encouraged to do so. The clause is plainly visible, clearly worded and capable of being detected as in *Downtown King West Development Corp. v. Massey Ferguson Industries Ltd.* (1996), 28 O.R. (3d) 327, 133 D.L.R. (4th) 550 (C.A.), leave to appeal to the S.C.C. refused (1996), 96 O.A.C. 233; *Craven v. Strand Holidays (Canada) Ltd.* (1982), 40 O.R. (2d) 186, 142 D.L.R. (3d) 31 (C.A.). Ste-

---

4   The facts in *Stepps, supra*, are complex, but can be simplified in the following way: The parties had negotiated and agreed that the defendant would purchase certain shares from the plaintiff 10 days after the closing of another agreement between the defendant and a third party. The agreement between the defendant and the third party did not close. However, a new agreement between the defendant and the third party was entered into. The defendant then entered into negotiations again with the plaintiff and a document was executed that had the effect of making their arrangement no longer conditional on the closing of the third party agreement. The significance of this change, which was not easy to detect, was not brought to the attention of the defendant or his solicitor.

vens' failure to act reasonably in the circumstances should not exonerate Cornell from the terms of the contract.

(4) *The manner in which the parties were brought together and the expectation that could be created in the relying party*

[49] The negotiations for the sale of Bimboga's shares, carried out through Stevens, involved the use of a negotiation "tactic". Stevens represented that the sale was on, then off, then on again, returning each time to Macdonald with an increase in the purchase price. In acting in this manner Stevens did not have regard for Macdonald's interests and therefore this conduct would not require Macdonald to have regard for Stevens' interests. The negotiating tactic that Stevens implemented indicates a commercial arm's-length approach to business dealings with Macdonald. The actions of Stevens do not suggest that he, on behalf of Cornell, was a "relying party" on Macdonald.

[50] In deciding what the expectations of the parties were at the time the contract was signed, the court is entitled to have regard to the parties' actions after the signing of the contract: *Montreal Trust Co. of Canada v. Birmingham Lodge Ltd.* (1995), 24 O.R. (3d) 97 at p. 108, 125 D.L.R. (4th) 193 (C.A.). When Cornell withheld payment to Macdonald under the Services Agreement in June 1994, the trial judge found that Stevens, "supported or at least acquiesced in, and associated himself with Bimboga's threats to cause Cornell to discontinue the payments". Both before and after the signing of the contract, Stevens' actions do not give rise to a reasonable expectation that Macdonald would have regard for his interests.

(5) *Whether trust or confidence has knowingly been reposed by one party in the other*

[51] The trial judge found that Stevens trusted Macdonald completely and Macdonald knew this. He found in effect that Macdonald took advantage of that trust. The trial judge appears to conclude that Macdonald took advantage of this "special relationship" without adequate consideration of all the circumstances. As Finn, *supra*, indicates, the presence of trust and confidence may be the foundation for a reasonable expectation that one party should have regard to the interests of the other but it, alone, will not create that obligation. Stevens was in an advisory position to Macdonald, it was not the other way around. Quite apart from advancing Macdonald's interests, when their interests did not coincide, Stevens appears to have had no regard for Macdonald's interests in his dealings with him. As a sophisticated and experienced businessperson, Stevens had the cognitive ability to appreciate the significance of the document he was signing. That ability was not impaired as a result of any act by Macdonald.

[52] Having regard to all of the circumstances, Stevens was not justified in law in expecting that he would not be bound by the termination clause in the Services Agreement when he signed the agreement without reading it.

(6) *Is rectification applicable?*

[53] Before the remedy of rectification can be obtained an applicant must establish: (a) that the written document in issue does not reflect the true agreement of the parties, and (b) that the parties shared a common, continuing intention up to the time of signing the document concerning a matter that is not reflected in the agreement: *Can-*

Dive Services Ltd. v. Pacific Coast Energy Corp., *supra*, at para. 159; *H.F. Clarke Ltd. v. Thermidaire Corp.*, [1973] 2 O.R. 57 at pp. 64-65, 33 D.L.R. (3d) 13 (C.A.) (revd on other grounds, [1976] 1 S.C.R. 319); *Pointe Anne Quarries Ltd. v. "M.F. Whalen" (The)* (1921), 63 S.C.R. 109 at pp. 126-27, 63 D.L.R. 545.

[54] In order for the trial judge to apply the doctrine of rectification, he not only had to find that the Services Agreement did not represent the common intention of the parties, he had to be positively satisfied as to what their common intention was. In the absence of any common intention as to what was to happen in the event that the Services Agreement was unilaterally terminated, rectification is simply inapplicable. Prior to the signing of the Services Agreement, there was never any common intention or understanding as to what was to happen in the event that Cornell unilaterally terminated Macdonald because there was never any discussion about it beforehand. The trial judge accepted Stevens' evidence that he would not have signed the agreement had he known of the termination clause. There is no evidence, however, that Macdonald would have signed the Services Agreement without the termination clause.

[55] In view of my conclusion, it is unnecessary for me to deal with the other issues raised by the appellant.

Conclusion

[56] I would allow the appeal, set aside the judgment of the trial judge and grant judgment in accordance with the termination clause in the Services Agreement with costs here and at trial to the appellant.

Appeal allowed.

NOTES

1. In para. 32 of her reasons, Weiler J.A. says:

> . . . Absent a special relationship, the common law in Canada has yet to recognize that in the negotiation of a contract, there is a duty to have regard to the other person's interests, namely, to act in good faith: see *Bell v. Lever Brothers Ltd.*, [1932] A.C. 161, [1931] All E.R. Rep. 1 (H.L.), and more recently, *Martel Building Ltd. v. Canada*, [2000] 2 S.C.R. 860, 2000 S.C.C. 60 at para. 73. . . .

Weiler J.A. suggests that a duty to act in good faith requires one to have regard to the "other person's interests". This view of what a duty to behave in good faith — whether in the negotiation, performance or enforcement of a contract — entails may explain why Canadian courts have such trouble with the concept. It is true that some duties, principally fiduciary duties, require a person to have regard, even an exclusive regard for another's interests, but a duty to behave in good faith, *i.e.*, to behave decently (or even honourably) requires one to have regard for another's interests only in the sense that good behaviour, like good manners, involves treating others with dignity, honesty and fairness. In this sense a duty to act in "good faith" does not require one to subordinate one's own interests to those of another or to compromise in any way one's ability to pursue one's interests. There is no incompatibility between good faith and a hard-nosed attitude to the achievement of one's goals.

A duty to act in good faith may be contrasted with a duty to act reasonably. Such a duty is frequently accepted by contracting parties: a landlord may require the tenant to get its permission to assign the lease, but agree that the permission "may not be unreasonably withheld"; a person may have a right to back out of a transaction "if there are reasonable grounds for believing that" there is, for example, a material adverse environmental risk. The obligation to act reasonably requires a person to meet a standard of behaviour that can be objectively assessed; it prevents a person from acting on a whim. Such duty will clearly limit a person's freedom of action, but it does not normally require the person to have regard to the other party's interests.

If good faith is understood as requiring no more than decent behaviour, it is hard to understand how any social, commercial or legal relations could function if there has been no such willing acceptance of such a standard by the parties. The duty to act in good faith is not something imposed by the courts that is external to the parties' relation: it is something that inheres in their relation, the recognition of which gives life to it and without which it could not achieve whatever goal the parties have for it.

This view of good faith does not mean that the result in *Cornell Engineering* is inconsistent with the recognition of such a duty: behaving decently may require no more than that one give a person who has been asked to sign a contract an opportunity to read it. If the person does not, good faith does not require one to insist that he or she read it or that its terms must be explained. Of course, if a fiduciary duty is owed or if there are special reasons for concern — situations that will be explored later in this chapter — much more may have to be done before the person's signature on the document will bind him or her.

It is unfortunate that Canadian courts have taken such a narrow view of what an obligation to behave in good faith entails. Their statements do not reflect what they actually do, and are contrary to what those engaged in any kind of contractual relation typically expect of each other.

Despite some confusing statements from the Canadian courts, it is clear that on a certain level it would be hard to imagine a law of contracts that did not incorporate the concepts of concepts of good faith and reasonableness as pervasive aspects of the law. Their relevance at this point is that they set standards of conduct by which the actions of a party to a contract can be assessed. As such a standard, good faith incorporates honesty and fair dealing or, as has been said, it denotes the absence of bad faith.

2.   In *Transpacific Sale v. Sprott Securities Ltd.*, [2003] O.J. No. 3900, 67 O.R. (3d) 368 (C.A.) a relatively sophisticated investor signed a subscription agreement to purchase shares in a company whose shares were not publically traded without fully reading the document, and listed his occupation as "janitor". The company went bankrupt, and the investor sued the brokerage firm that arranged the investment. Conk J.A. considered the effect of his having signed the agreement without having read it, and of his having listed his occupation as janitor (at paras. 52-55).

> Abrams [the investor] made a deliberate decision, motivated by his admitted desire to avoid the legal consequences of the subscription agreements, not to read them in their entirety. By signing them, however, he represented or acknowledged to Sprott [the brokerage firm] and the applicable offering company that he was capable of evaluating the merits and risks of the Investments, that he was financially able to bear the economic risk of the Investments and … that he was aware that he might not be able to sell the securities for "an indefinite period of time". By the terms of the agreements, Abrams' statements were expressed to be made with the intention that they be relied upon by Sprott and the offering companies, and that they would survive the closing of the transactions concerning the Investments.

> Abrams also sought to qualify his obligations under the agreements by inserting the word "janitor" below his signatures in several places in the agreements, a description of his position which he knew to be false, with the subsequently asserted intention of signalling to the appellants [the brokerage firm] that he did not intend to be bound by the agreements notwithstanding his representations to the contrary in both documents.

> Abrams' approach to the signing of the subscription agreements is most troubling. His conduct is contrary to the normal practices and requirements of ordinary commerce, upon which reasonable people are entitled to rely. I also

agree with the appellants' submission that Abrams' conduct, if condoned, could be viewed as calling into question the utility and efficacy of written agreements in consumer securities transactions. Abrams' conduct cannot be condoned....

This court has recognized the general proposition that the deliberate tactic of not reading a commercial agreement before signing it will not relieve the signatory from his or her obligations under the agreement. As stated by Robins J.A. in *Fraser Jewellers (1982) Ltd. v. Dominion Electric Protection Co.* (1997), 34 O.R. (3d) 1, 148 D.L.R. (4th) 496 (C.A.), at p. 10 O.R.:

> As a general proposition, in the absence of fraud or misrepresentation, a person is bound by an agreement to which he has put his signature whether he has read its contents or has chosen to leave them unread: Cheshire, Fifoot & Furmston's, *Law of Contract*, 13th ed. (1996) at p. 168. Failure to read a contract before signing it is not a legally acceptable basis for refusing to abide by it. A businessman executing an agreement on behalf of a company must be presumed to be aware of its terms and to have intended that the company would be bound by them. The fact that [the signatory] chose not to read the contract can place him in no better position than a person who has. Nor is the fact that the clause is in a standard pre-printed form and was not a subject of negotiations sufficient in itself to vitiate the clause. ...

> That general proposition, however, is not determinative of whether the appellants are entitled in this case to rely on Abrams' written representations, thereby escaping all liability to him. In my opinion, the trial judge correctly found that the appellants are precluded from doing so. ...

The Court of Appeal accepted that the broker had failed adequately to advise the investor of the risks inherent in this type of investment, and upheld the decision of the trial judge to award the investor 50 per cent of his losses, accepting that his "contributory negligence" was to be taken into account, with Cronk J.A. concluding (at paras. 58-61):

> Unlike the facts in *Fraser Jewellers*, the relationship between the appellants and Abrams gave rise to a duty of care owed to Abrams... as recognized by this court in *Cornell Engineering* [53 O.R. (3d) 783], at p. 795 O.R., contracting parties are obliged to respect the interests of the other where: "First, one party relies on the other for information necessary to make an informed choice and, second, the party in possession of the information has an opportunity, by withholding (or concealing) information, to bring about the choice made by the other party." Although the trial judge found that Abrams did not repose trust and confidence in Spork sufficient to create a fiduciary relationship between them, he expressly held that Abrams was entitled to and did rely on Spork to provide information to him concerning the Investments. He further held that, without that information, Abrams was not in a position to make an informed decision about whether to invest in the special warrants and special shares. It is significant in that regard that Spork was bound under the professional standards of conduct set out in the [Canadian Securities Institute, *Conduct and Practices*] *Handbook* to "display absolute trustworthiness since the client's interests must be the foremost consideration in all business dealings".

REVIEW PROBLEMS

1. Review the cases in this section and in the previous sections from the perspective of the drafter of a contract. Consider the following questions.

    (a) You are asked to draft a notice to be displayed on the wall at the entrance to a squash court in an apartment building limiting the owner's liability. What guidance do you get from the cases as to the location, size and contents of the notice?

(b) You are asked why lawyers tend to use convoluted and lengthy clauses in contracts. Give an explanation. What would you say to a client who asked for a short, simple agreement that he could understand?

(c) What incentive does the doctrine of fundamental breach give to the drafter of contracts? Is it desirable that the law provide such an incentive?

(d) Draft a set of instructions to be given to the clerks who work at the desks where people come to rent cars. If your client wants to use the kind of clause found in *Tilden v. Clendenning*, will the problems in drafting the instructions lead you to suggest that some other kind of clause should be used? Make a set of notes to remind yourself of the factors you should keep in mind as you draft the instructions. What dangers do you have to guard against?

(e) You are asked to advise a client whose business is the conversion of oil furnaces to natural gas. In the course of removal of the old furnace and oil tank, soot and oil can be expected to be spread about on nearby carpeting and furniture. Of course, damage can be minimized by proper covering of the floor and furniture. Your client has asked you to draft a clause to be included in its standard form to avoid liability for damage caused by soot and oil. Advise the client as to what kind of clause will be most effective.

2. You act for a firm that supplies security services. Over the years the firm has developed a standard-form contract that contains the usual boiler-plate exclusions of liability. The firm's customers are large commercial and industrial enterprises. A significant number of customers are beginning to ask, "How is it that you purport to provide a security service, yet your contract suggests that you are not even prepared to do that?" In addition, the client's marketing staff are finding it increasingly hard to sell what looks to some potential customers like little more than an expensive gimmick. (The firm's customers actually read the contract and consider carefully what level of protection the service will provide.) You have been asked to redraft the standard-form contract to be used by the firm. Outline the provisions you think might resolve your client's problems and any other steps that the firm might take to deal with them.

3. You act for an airline. The standard airline ticket strictly limits liability for the loss of a passenger's baggage. The standard home owner's or tenant's "package policy" of insurance offers baggage insurance. A typical "plain-language" policy reads, "We insure your personal property . . . while it is temporarily removed from your premises anywhere in the world." Does the existence of the insurance background, which passengers may or may not know about, provide you with any solution to the problem of whether your client should continue to exclude liability or not? If so, what should it do about the passenger who loses her luggage and complains vociferously?

4. You act for a client who is planning to open an aerobic exercise studio. Prepare a standard-form contract to protect your client from the risk of liability arising from a heart-attack and other similar causes suffered by a member/customer during an exercise class. Prepare a memorandum explaining what risks can and cannot be avoided by the use of the contract you have drafted. Describe what other steps, if any, should be taken by your client to reduce the risk of exposure. Keep in mind that, while insurance is probably available at the beginning of your client's enterprise, it is very likely to be cancelled if your client ever has a large claim, and it is certain to be cancelled if it has more than one. Once cancelled, it is very unlikely that any more insurance can be obtained, and, without insurance, your client is out of business.

THE PROTECTION OF OTHER INTERESTS

Control Based on Notions of Egalitarianism

The previous section considered judicial devices which, when they were not per-verted to serve other purposes, are used to protect the reasonable expectations that have been created by the contract in the mind of one of the parties. A major justifi-cation for the enforcement of an exemption clause, or the refusal to enforce the clause, is the belief of the courts, articulated or not, that the enforcement of the contract in a particular way would defeat the expectations of one side, and that in the circumstances these expectations are worthy of protection.

In this section, the focus shifts to cases in which there is less concern about the parties' reasonable expectations. The judicial control is asserted regardless of the parties' expectations or how carefully those expectations might have been stated in the contract. There are some arrangements that parties to a contract are simply not to be permitted to make. In studying the judicially developed doctrines that allow a court to interfere with a contract, regardless of the expectations of the parties or the clarity of the contract, it is necessary carefully to consider the basis for and the justification of the courts' interference. This type of judicial control obviously runs counter to the values of freedom of contract that are an important underlying as-sumption in the law. The theoretical, political, practical and philosophical implica-tions of this type of judicial control over freedom of contract need to be carefully considered.

The cases in this section are not a representative sample of all cases where the kind of peremptory judicial control over freedom of contract can be found. There are cases which on any functional basis would be regarded as contracts cases, but which are often put into special categories, and which will not be examined in this section. One large category consists of mortgage contracts. For centuries courts of equity have policed the power of persons who lend money on the security of land. The courts have limited the power of lenders on the security of land to take the land in satisfaction of a default in repayment of the debt, regardless of the explicit-ness of the borrower's understanding of and the contract terms giving the lender the right to do so. The control of lenders was an early exercise of the power of the court of equity. Equity's intervention led to the creation of the borrower's so-called "equity of redemption". Even though the contract gave no right to redeem, and the common-law courts would have enforced the lender's right to take the land, the "equity of redemption" gave a borrower who defaulted extra time to pay before the land was forever forfeited. The power of the court to control the lender's right is so well settled that the borrower's equity of redemption has be-come a well-established property right. The justification for the interference of equity is that "necessitous men are not, truly speaking, free men, but, to answer a present exigency will submit to any terms that the crafty may impose on them" (Lord Nottingham in *Vernon v. Bethell* (1762), 2 Eden. 113, 28 E.R. 838).

The views of Lord Nottingham about the judicial protection of a borrower whose loan is secured on real property in a mortgage case may be contrasted with the views about the general importance of enforcing contracts "freely entered into" of Jessel M.R. (regarded as one of the great equity judges of the nineteenth cen-tury) in 1875 in *Printing and Numerical Registering Co.* quoted at the very begin-ning of this chapter, and of Scrutton L.J. in 1934 in *L'Estrange v. Graucob*.

The development of a generalized law of contracts during the period from about 1820 to 1900 from disparate bits of law, mortgages, insurance, the law merchant and the common law forms of action was a selective process that, as we have seen, chose to regard certain areas of law as outside the contracts' canon. We have looked at other aspects of the development of classical contract theory, for example, the doctrine of consideration, such as the rule of *Stilk v. Myrick*. Significant portions of the classical doctrine of contract law are quite sterile; they have been slowly modified in the period since 1945.

What is often regarded as the "modern law of contracts" is generally (though, of course, not always) characterized by a concern for reasonableness and fairness. In some respects this more recent approach is similar to the more flexible judicial approaches of the eighteenth century; in the nineteenth century for a range of philosophical, political and economic reasons, judges and academics wanted to deny the existence of judicial discretion to control freedom of contract, though in some defined areas, like the law of mortgages, the courts continued to recognize a judicial authority to decline to enforce contracts on the grounds of unfairness.

As the cases in the preceding sections illustrate, the proper exercise of a judicial power to control contracts may not be an easy task; it is made more difficult if underlying issues of poverty, relative weakness in bargaining power and "craftiness" are not openly discussed. The rule of law approach to the doctrine of fundamental breach applied in commercial cases like Lord Denning's 1970 judgment in *Harbutt's Plasticine* was not a monument to modern philanthropy, but to muddled thinking. The development of the doctrine was caused by the belief that the enforcement of contracts was a comparatively simple process calling for the application of relatively simple rules with only minimal knowledge of the factual background of the deal. Fortunately, the law has developed a more sophisticated and useful approach to dealing with problems of exemption and limitation clauses, as reflected in more recent Canadian decisions like *Hunter Engineering v. Syncrude Canada*.

The focus here is on the judicially developed power to refuse to enforce a contract on the terms agreed to. There are, however, also many important examples of legislation that restrict freedom of contract, such as minimum wage legislation and rent control schemes. This type of legislation is often enacted with a view to promoting a more egalitarian or just society, and in preventing exploitation of those with limited market power. Such statutory control is in some contexts extensive and capable of transforming the relation into one where the power of the parties to bargain is reduced to little more than the power to consent to enter into a relation, almost all the terms of which are already set. Automobile, life, and fire insurance contracts, some contracts of employment, residential tenancies and many contracts for transportation are almost completely governed by legislation and regulations. This list does not include contracts such as those for telephone and cable television service, which arise out of statutory monopolies and are almost entirely controlled by legislation.

Penalties and Forfeitures

An important feature of the ticket cases and those in which the courts invoked the doctrine of fundamental breach was that one side was attempting to reduce the level of performance below that to which it would otherwise have been held, *i.e.* to limit or completely exclude its contractual obligations.

Conversely, in the event that one party fails to perform, the other party may seek to impose on the party in breach a liability to pay damages specified at a high amount. Thus, a contract may specify that, in the event of breach by the seller of its obligation to deliver the goods, the seller shall pay damages of $10,000 for each day's delay. Depending on the nature of the contract, such a stipulation could be regarded as exorbitant. For centuries the courts have asserted an equitable jurisdiction to control such clauses. A sum stipulated as payment on breach may, if it is regarded by the court as excessive, be characterized as a "penalty" and not be enforced, leaving the victim of the breach to collect damages based on ordinary principles.

A variation on this method of controlling the other party is the stipulation that a large deposit shall be paid by the purchaser at the time of the formation of the contract, and in the event of a breach by the purchaser, that the deposit shall be forfeited to the vendor. Excessive deposits and forfeitures have, like penalties, come under the protection of the courts of equity. However, if a court views a clause as reasonable, it will be given effect.

In *Dunlop Tyre Co. v. New Garage and Motor Co.*, [1915] A.C. 79 (H.L.), Lord Dunedin stated the principle to govern the court's treatment of penalties:

> I do not think it advisable to attempt any detailed review of the various cases, but I shall content myself with stating succinctly the various propositions which I think are deducible from the decisions which rank as authoritative:
>
> 1.   Though the parties to a contract who use the words "penalty" or "liquidated damages" may prima facie be supposed to mean what they say, yet the expression used is not conclusive. The court must find out whether the payment stipulated is in truth a penalty or liquidated damages. This doctrine may be said to be found passim in nearly every case.
>
> 2.   The essence of a penalty is a payment of money stipulated as *in terrorem* of the offending party; the essence of liquidated damages is a genuine covenanted pre-estimate of damage.
>
> 3.   The question whether a sum stipulated is penalty or liquidated damages is a question of construction to be decided upon the terms and inherent circumstances of each particular contract, judged of as at the time of the making of the contract, not as at the time of the breach.
>
> 4.   To assist this task of construction various tests have been suggested, which if applicable to the case under consideration may prove helpful, or even conclusive. Such are:
>
>   (a)   It will be held to be penalty if the sum stipulated for is extravagant and unconscionable in amount in comparison with the greatest loss that could conceivably be proved to have followed from the breach.
>
>   (b)   It will be held to be a penalty if the breach consists only in not paying a sum of money, and the sum stipulated is a sum greater than the sum which ought to have been paid. . . .
>
>   (c)   There is a presumption (but no more) that it is penalty when "a single lump sum is made payable by way of compensation, on the occurrence of one or more or all of several events, some of which may occasion serious and others but trifling damage" . . . .
>
>   On the other hand:
>
>   (d)   It is no obstacle to the sum stipulated being a genuine pre-estimate of damage, that the consequences of the breach are such as to make precise

pre-estimation almost an impossibility. On the contrary, that is just the situation when it is probable that pre-estimated damage was the true bargain between the parties.

Traditionally there was a clear judicial distinction in the treatment of "penalty clauses" (being viewed as unenforceable), and "liquidated damages clauses" (which were enforceable). The issue of whether a clause was "penal" was, however, a legal conclusion and not dependent on the language used by the drafters of a contract. In everyday parlance, and sometimes in legal documents, both types of clauses are referred to loosely as "penalty clauses". What was critical to their legal enforceability was their ultimate legal characterization by a court, not how the parties referred to these clauses. More recently, some decisions have tended to focus not on the legal characterization of the clause, but on the underlying issue of whether the clause is "unconscionable".

It is important here, as it was in the earlier cases in this chapter, to consider the guidance the courts give to the drafter. As you read the cases, consider how much guidance is given by the courts.

ELSLEY v. J.G. COLLINS INSURANCE AGENCIES LTD

[1978] S.C.J. No. 47, [1978] 2 S.C.R. 916, 83 D.L.R. (3d) 1
(S.C.C., Laskin C.J.C., Martland, Ritchie, Pigeon, Dickson, Beetz and Pratte JJ.)

The judgment of the court was given by **DICKSON J.**:

[1]   The question for decision in this case is whether a restrictive covenant contained in a certain contract of employment, to which I will shortly refer, is valid.

[2]   The facts are, to all intents, undisputed. On April 24, 1956, an agreement was entered into for the purchase by the Collins company of the general insurance business of a competitor, D.C. Elsley Limited. The price was $46,137. The life insurance business and the real estate business conducted by the Elsley company were not included. The agreement contained a covenant on the part of the vendor that it would not, for a period of ten years, carry on or be engaged in the business of a general insurance agency within the City of Niagara Falls . . . and that the vendor would pay the purchaser $1,000 for each and every breach. The parties entered into a further agreement on May 1, 1956, whereby Elsley was employed as interim manager of the combined general insurance businesses. . . .

[3]   The interim management agreement was short-lived. It was replaced by an agreement of May 30, 1956, by which Elsley undertook to serve as manager of the Collins company's general insurance business in the greater Niagara Falls area, devoting all necessary time and attention to such employment, subject to the proviso that he might supervise the Elsley company in its real estate and life insurance business. The agreement commenced June 1, 1956, and was stated to continue in force from year to year until terminated by either party upon three months' notice. As things developed, it continued until May 1973.

[4]   Clause 3 of the management agreement contains the covenant which gave rise to the present proceedings. It reads:

3.   Subject to the restrictive covenants contained in the Agreement made between the Parties dated May 1, 1956, in consideration of the employment, the Manager shall not, while in the employ of the company or of its successors and assigns, whether in the capacity in which he is now or in any other capacity, or during the period of five years next after he shall, whether by reason of dismissal, retirement or otherwise, have ceased to be so employed, directly or indirectly, and whether as principal, agent, director of a company, traveller, servant or otherwise, carry on or be engaged or concerned or take part in the business of a general insurance agent within the corporate limits of the City of Niagara Falls, the Township of Stamford and the Village of Chippawa, all in the County of Welland; and in the event of his failing to observe or perform the said agreement, he shall pay to the said Company, its successors or assigns, or other the person or persons entitled for the time being to the benefit of the said agreement, the sum of One Thousand Dollars ($1,000.00) as and for liquidated damages, and the said Mrs Elsley, wife of the Manager, by her signature hereto, agrees to observe and be bound by the aforesaid covenant.

[5]   . . . To return to the narrative, Elsley managed the combined general insurance business for 17 years, from June 1, 1956, until May 31, 1973, at which time he gave proper notice of termination of employment. During the 17-year period Elsley dealt with customers of the agency to the almost total exclusion of Collins. To them Elsley was the business, Collins little more than a name. Elsley met the customers, telephoned them frequently, placed their insurance policies and answered their queries. Such were the findings of the trial Judge. People became accustomed to doing business with him on a personal basis and he looked after their insurance needs. He served not only customers of the business he formerly owned, but also Collins' customers.

[6]   From 1956 to 1973 the business bore the name "Collins & Elsley Insurance Agencies." During that period, as a convenience, many policy-holders paid their premiums at the office of D.C. Elsley Limited, the real estate office of Elsley, because a large part of the business purchased by Collins from Elsley came from the area in which this office was located. As general manager of the combined businesses, Elsley, of course, had access to all policy-holder records; he was familiar with the nature and extent of coverage and the premium paid by each policy-holder. He had knowledge of the insurable assets, financial credit, likes and dislikes and idiosyncrasies of each customer, in a recurring and confidential relationship not unlike that of lawyer/client or doctor/patient. It was only natural that policy-holders would follow him if he made a change.

[7]   Following termination of his employment with Collins, Elsley commenced his own general insurance business under D.C. Elsley Limited. He took with him two insurance salesmen and an insurance clerk formerly employed by Collins and Elsley agency. A large number of former clients of the agency transferred their business. Exhibit 10 comprised a list of approximately two hundred former clients who had advised Collins they were transferring their insurance business to Elsley. . . .

[**DICKSON J.** held that in this case a covenant against non-solicitation would not have been adequate to protect the employer Collins' proprietary interest. Only the restrictive covenant prohibiting Elsley from soliciting customers *and* from establishing a business or working for others could effectively prevent Elsley's appropriating Collins' trade connection through his acquaintance with Collins' customers.]

[8] The damage issue is one of some importance and difficulty. It subsumes two questions: (i) the right of a plaintiff enforcing a restrictive covenant to claim both an injunction and damages (ii) whether the quantum is, or is limited to, the amount stipulated as liquidated damages in the covenant. In other words, can Collins claim *any* damages; and if so, is the amount limited to $1,000? I would answer both of these questions in the affirmative.

[9] . . . In the recent case in this court, *H.F. Clarke Ltd. v. Thermidaire Corp. Ltd.* [[1976] 1 S.C.R. 319, 54 D.L.R. (3d) 385], the claim was for damages for breach of a restrictive covenant contained in a distributorship agreement. The question of injunction was not in issue. The agreement provided that the defaulting party would be required to pay as liquidated damages the gross profit realized from the sale of competitive products. The issue was whether the plaintiff could recover this amount or only provable damages. A majority of the court held in favour of the latter disposition.

[10] . . . It should be remembered that if a plaintiff is entitled to an injunction to restrain breach of a restrictive covenant, he is entitled to prevent the entire breach, not just part of it. Thus, for any part not restrained, he may be entitled to unliquidated damages in equity. There would be no double recovery provided the damages were not referable to any period during which breach was restrained by the injunction. This right to damages would not be based on the liquidated damages clause, but on the right under section 21 [of the *Judicature Act* R.S.O. 1970, c. 228] to damages in equity in substitution for an injunction in respect of the period of breach prior to the granting of the injunction. A plaintiff, of course, cannot delay seeking an injunction in order to inflate his damages. He would not be entitled to damages past the time when he should have sought the injunction.

[11] How then should the measure of such damages be determined? It will generally be appropriate to adopt in equity rules similar to those applicable at law . . . This is so not because the Court is obliged to apply analogous legal criteria, but because the amount of compensation which would satisfy the loss suffered, and which the Court considers it just and equitable be paid, usually happens to be equivalent to the amount of legal damages which would be appropriate. The award is still governed, however, by general equitable considerations which would not apply if the plaintiff were seeking damages at law rather than in equity. These considerations might serve, for example, to reduce the amount, due to such factors as delay or acquiescence. In addition, if the parties have agreed on a set amount of damages at law, or a maximum amount, it would be unconscionable, in my opinion, to allow recovery of a greater amount of damages in equity.

[12] In this case of a gross underestimate of damages, as presumably in the present case, the plaintiff may receive an amount equivalent to the liquidated damages sum, plus an injunction, and therefore appear to have double relief. But such is not the case. The injunction relates to the latter part of the period in respect of which the restrictive covenant imposes restraint, the damages (not exceeding the stipulated liquidated damages) relate to the period prior to the granting of the injunction and are in substitution for injunctive relief during that period.

[13] The matter of the right of a plaintiff to recover legal damages for actual loss sustained where a lesser stipulated amount is mentioned was considered in the House of Lords decision in *Cellulose Acetate Silk Co., Ltd. v. Widnes Foundry*

(1925), Ltd., [1933] A.C. 20. The amount stipulated was £20 for each week of delay in the erection of an acetone recovery plant. The contractors were 30 weeks late. The actual loss suffered was £5,850. The case is of interest in two respects. First, the recovery was limited to £600, the agreed damages. Second, Lord Atkin, delivering judgment, said that he found it unnecessary to consider what would be the position if the stipulated £20 per week were a penalty, adding, at 26:

> It was argued by the appellants that if this were a penalty they would have an option either to sue for the penalty or for damages for breach of the promise as to time of delivery. I desire to leave open the question whether, where a penalty is plainly less in amount than the prospective damages, there is any legal objection to suing on it, or in a suitable case ignoring it and suing for damages.

[14] There is authority indicating that a penalty clause is ineffective even where it is less than the actual loss suffered . . . The result would be that actual damages could be recovered which exceeded the amount stipulated as a penalty. To that extent, the proposition appears to me to be contrary to principle and productive of injustice. The foundation of relief in equity against penalties is expressed in Story, *Equity Jurisprudence* (14th ed.) at s. 1728, as follows:

> Where a penalty or forfeiture is designed merely as a security to enforce the principal obligation, it is as much against conscience to allow any party to pervert it to a different and oppressive purpose as it would be to allow him to substitute another for the principal obligation.

[15] The operation of this relief in the face of contrary agreement by the party is also explained in this section:

> If it be said that it is his own folly to have made such a stipulation, it may equally well be said that the folly of one man cannot authorize gross oppression on the other side.

[16] It is now evident that the power to strike down a penalty clause is a blatant interference with freedom of contract and is designed for the sole purpose of providing relief against oppression for the party having to pay the stipulated sum. It has no place where there is no oppression. If the actual loss turns out to exceed the penalty, the normal rules of enforcement of contract should apply to allow recovery of only the agreed sum. The party imposing the penalty should not be able to obtain the benefit of whatever intimidating force the penalty clause may have in inducing performance, and then ignore the clause when it turns out to be to his advantage to do so. A penalty clause should function as a limitation on the damages recoverable, while still being ineffective to increase damages above the actual loss sustained when such loss is less than the stipulated amount . . . Of course, if an agreed sum is a valid liquidated damages clause, the plaintiff is entitled at law to recover this sum regardless of the actual loss sustained.

[17] In the context of the present discussion of the measure of damages, the result is that an agreed sum payable on breach represents the maximum amount recoverable whether the sum is a penalty or a valid liquidated damages clause. . . .

[18] To summarize:

1. Where a fixed sum is stipulated as and for liquidated damages upon a breach, the covenantee must elect with respect to that breach between these liquidated damages and an injunction.

2.   If he elects to take the liquidated damages stipulated he may recover that sum irrespective of his actual loss.

3.   Where the stipulated sum is a penalty he may only recover such damages as he can prove, but the amount recoverable may not exceed the sum stipulated.

4.   If he elects to take an injunction and not the liquidated sum stipulated, he may recover damages in equity for the actual loss sustained up to the date of the injunction or, if tardy, up to the date upon which he should have sought the injunction, but in either case, not exceeding the amount stipulated as payable upon a breach.

5.   Where a liquidated damages sum is stipulated as payable for each and every breach, the covenantee may recover this sum in respect of distinct breaches which have occurred and he may also be granted an injunction to restrain future breaches.

Applying these propositions to the present case, in my view the plaintiff was entitled to an injunction and such damages as he could prove to date of trial but not to exceed the sum of $1,000.

[19] I would accordingly dismiss the appeal and direct the payment of such damages, not to exceed $1,000, as the respondent can establish in respect of the period from June 1, 1973, to date of trial, for the loss of commission on all contracts of general insurance sold by Elsley during that period, after taking into account expenses incurred in securing and servicing the contracts. . . .

The following extract discusses some of the economic issues underlying the decision to enforce (or deny effect to) a clause providing for damages payable on breach.

GOETZ AND SCOTT, "LIQUIDATED DAMAGES, PENALTIES AND THE JUST COMPENSATION PRINCIPLE"

(1977), 77 *Colum. L. Rev.* 554, at 558-76 [footnotes omitted]

[1]   [It is our] hypothesis that, absent evidence of process unfairness in bargaining, efficiency will be enhanced by the enforcement of an agreed allocation of risks embodied in a liquidated damage clause. We argue that agreed damage measures and *in terrorem* provisions represent, under many circumstances, the most efficient means by which parties can insure against the otherwise noncompensable consequences of breach. . . .

[2]   . . . Generally, breach will occur where the breaching party anticipates that paying compensation and allocating his resources to alternative uses will make him "better off" than performing his obligation. . . .

[3]   . . . [T]he principle embodied in present law of giving the non-breaching party "just compensation" or quasi-performance leads to one limiting result, in which all the efficiency gains go to the breacher. But the payment of substantial overcompensation, i.e., penalties, is not necessarily incompatible with an equally efficient result in the neighborhood of the other limiting solution . . . where (infinitesimally less than) all of the efficiency gains from breach go to the non-breaching party. Ranging between these extremes, there are an infinite number of other efficient breach solutions where both parties divide the gains from breach . . . all of which embody varying combinations of compensatory and "penalty" damages. Obstinate insistence on the enforcement of certain penalties may result in a failure to exploit potential efficiency gains by inducing the penalized party not to breach. However, the very existence of such unexploited gains acts as an incentive to the holder of the penalty rights to renegotiate the penalty provision [by dividing the potential gain from breach between them]. Hence, the existence of an over-compensation [or penalty] provision is never per se evidence of an efficiency impediment. Absent significant negotiation costs, the pre-stipulation of a penalty still permits alternative post-breach efficient solutions in which the efficiency gains are divided between the breacher and non-breacher in a bargained-for manner.

[4]   Is there, then, no fairness content to the analysis of alternative remedies? Modern contract theory seems primarily concerned with providing a "standard" compensatory rule which supplies an incentive for efficient breaches to be made and resulting gains to be fully exploited. It does not draw upon any obvious principle of fairness in evaluating the post-breach end result. As noted above, the "just compensation" formula gives all of the gains to the breacher. Why should this end result be regarded as any "fairer" than one which splits the gains fifty-fifty or gives them all to the non-breacher? . . . Allocatively, for society, these solutions are indistinguishable; they differ only in terms of wealth transfers, the manner in which the gains from non-performance are distributed between the parties. It seems then that the only appropriate fairness inquiry is one concerned solely with process fairness, the bargaining conditions, and not an examination of end results. . . .

[5]   Optimal systematic rules establishing post-breach compensation may require some limiting assumptions concerning the extent of harm caused by contract breach. These assumptions reduce the direct or administrative costs of implementing the compensation principle through the legal mechanism, but purchase these advantages at the price of breaking the equivalency between the damage rule and the actual subjective harm which is difficult to assess. In assessing damages, two limiting assumptions — valuation and foreseeability — may operate to prevent the recovery of idiosyncratic value. The rule requiring the loss to be foreseeable, designed to control for causation and remoteness, can be overcome in some circumstances by pre-contract disclosure of the causal relation between the loss and the breach and of the parameters of reasonable foresight. The requirement of valuation, given the existence of a market, is a more rigid barrier to the recovery of subjective losses. First, the "value" of a promised performance is generally limited to "the amount of money that can be obtained in exchange for it in some market." Second, where the exchange value is conceded to be inadequate, and "value to the owner" is substituted, any "fanciful or sentimental" value will be excluded on the grounds that such losses are too speculative and uncertain. Together, these valuation and certainty limitations may well preclude the non-breacher's recovery of idiosyncratic value.

[6]   [T]he promisee who places a higher subjective value on performance [than is recognized by standard damage measures may want] to provide for that idiosyncratic valuation at the time of contracting unless satisfactory post-breach cover is really achievable at market terms. One method of covering in advance for this

idiosyncratic value would be for the promisee to secure the performance to the extent necessary by proposing a liquidated damages clause to the prospective promisor. In addition, the compensation limitation affects the entire continuum of cases where the losses upon breach are uncertain or difficult to establish. Parties to contracts within this range will be particularly induced to negotiate liquidated damage agreements because the uncertainty in damage recovery increases the probability of error in enforcing the compensation standard. Clearly, these agreements will not necessarily approximate provable damages.

[7]   [I]t might be argued that the costly [effects, in some cases, resulting from the law's refusal to enforce penalties are] exceeded by the savings on the more numerous cases where process unfairness infected the agreement and it was unnecessary to actually prove the unfairness of the bargaining, a costly procedure. However, a more significant aggregate cost is produced over the entire range of cases where true losses from breach are uncertain to some degree. Here the efficiency incentives identified earlier induce negotiated damage agreements. But the current penalty rule imposes additional transaction costs on all of these cases, by inducing the party who regrets the initial allocation to litigate on whether the *ex ante* agreement sufficiently mirrors the anticipated losses. The actuality — or even the mere threat — of such post-breach attacks increases the transaction costs of contracting even in those cases where no disproportion between agreed and anticipated damages is ultimately discovered by the court.

NOTES

1.   Goetz and Scott assume that breach generally will occur when the breaching party expects that by breaching and paying damages it will be better off than it will be by performing the contract. (This is the familiar "efficient breach" argument developed by Posner in Chapter 1.) But suppose that a party breaches because it believes that it is entitled to do so, and that therefore no damages will be payable. Does the argument that a provision for liquidated damages should be enforced apply in that case?

2.   Another basic assumption of the article is that "[t]here is no reason to presume that liquidated damages provisions are more susceptible to duress and other bargaining aberrations than other contractual allocations of risk." Is this true? A party who agrees to a contract term requiring him to perform expects to do so, and considers carefully the cost of performance. What do you think of an argument that a party agreeing to a liquidated damages clause may believe that it will never be relevant, and therefore will not consider its impact with the same care.

3.   Parties may have very different, personal or subjective reasons for wanting a particular clause in a contract — as (at least from the theoretical point of view) Mr. and Mrs. Peevyhouse had in *Peevyhouse v. Garland Coal*. Would a liquidated damages clause in that situation have effectively protected their interests?

4.   It is also difficult to foresee all of the events that may lead to breach or termination, and it is correspondingly difficult to determine, during the bargaining, what will trigger the liquidated damages clause.

5.   In its 1978 decision in *Elsley*, the Supreme Court seems to indicate that in a commercial contract, the courts should enforce a clause stipulating the amount of damages in the absence of it being established that such a clause is "oppressive" or "unconscionable". This is a narrower approach to judicial discretion than was articulated in some earlier cases like *H.F. Clarke Ltd. v. Thermidaire Corp. Ltd.*, [1976] 1 S.C.R. 319. The Supreme Court did not cite any law and economics analysis in this 1978 decision, and that type of analysis was still in its relative infancy at that time. Since Goetz and Scott's article was published in 1977, there is now a much larger law and economics

literature on this and other subjects. That literature generally favours a narrow approach to judicial discretion in this area.

Do you think that the Supreme Court was aware of the law and economics literature in 1978? If a similar case came before a Canadian court today, should counsel cite law and economics literature?

The next two cases deal with the problem of deposits — money paid by the purchaser which the vendor claims to be forfeited on breach by the purchaser.

LOZCAL HOLDINGS LTD. v. BRASSOS DEVELOPMENT LTD.

[1980] A.J. No. 857, 12 Alta. L.R. (2d) 227, 111 D.L.R. (3d) 598
(C.A., McGillivray C.J.A., Clement and Morrow JJ.A.)

The judgment of the court was delivered by **McGILLIVRAY C.J.A.**:

[1]   The issue in this case is the effect of the phrase "as liquidated damages" as the same appears in a real estate offer and acceptance form.

[2]   The respondent made an offer to purchase the land in question for $67,000, and with that offer he paid a $2,500 "deposit herewith as an indication of good faith in making this offer" and he agreed to pay the balance of $64,500 on conveyance, the same to be before 1st June 1978. The appellant accepted the offer.

[3]   The respondent-purchaser then repudiated the agreement and the appellant accepted the repudiation, advising that he would resell and hold the purchaser liable for damages. The property was then resold without the payment of further commission for $60,000. The vendor claims damages for his loss, being the difference between the original sale price of $67,000, less commission, and $60,000 . . .

[4]   In my opinion, it is clear that, without more, the vendor would be entitled to retain the deposit on his accepting the purchaser's repudiation of the contract, and this even if he re-sold the land at an increased price. If he sold the land at a loss, he would be entitled to recover that loss, less the amount of the deposit, for which he would be obliged to give credit. . . .

[5]   A genuine deposit ordinarily has nothing to do with damages, except that credit must be given for the amount of the deposit in calculating damages.

[6]   It is then necessary to consider the nature of liquidated damages. Liquidated damages in a proper case are a genuine pre-estimate agreed upon by the parties as to damages in the event of a breach of contract. . . .

[7]   It seems clear that the designation of a sum, whether it be called "penalty," whether it be called "liquidated damages," or whether it is spoken of as being "forfeited," does not relieve the court of determining whether it is intended to represent a genuine pre-estimate of damages or a penalty, or whether it is intended as a limitation on the depositor's liability. . . . [T]he question is one of construction, to be decided upon the terms and inherent circumstances of each particular contract, judged as at the time of making the contract.

[8]   Frequently a sum is designated as liquidated damages in an attempt to curtail the court's right to relieve from forfeiture. So, in this case, had the deposit been, say, $30,000, a court would undoubtedly, because of its size, treat it as a part-payment, notwithstanding the contractual provision that it would be forfeited "as liquidated damages" and the court would relieve against forfeiture.

[9] In the case at bar, because of the size of the deposit in relation to the magnitude of the transaction, it was no doubt a genuine deposit made, as the offer says, "as an indication of good faith in making the offer."

[10] It seems to me that because it is in the nature of a genuine deposit, that the court can say it was not intended as a genuine pre-estimate of damages at all. Then, the question arises as to whether the intention of the parties, looked at in the light of the terms and inherent circumstances of the contract, was to seek to limit the vendor's damage, in the event of a breach of the contract, to the deposit paid. Certainly . . . the parties may, by their contract, govern the arrangements between them, and if they provide that the vendor's damages in the event of breach by the purchaser were to be limited to the deposit paid, it would have been competent for them to do so. The question here is whether they have done this by providing that the deposit shall be "forfeited as liquidated damages."

[11] In my view, if the intention were to limit the purchaser's liability, that could have been easily said, and the court should not import into the words "as liquidated damages" (particularly when they appear in a printed form), any such intention. It seems to me that very much more express language is required. . . .

[12] In the case at bar . . . [damages] might or might not exceed $2,500. No reason appears for a deviation of the ordinary rule that actual damages suffered by the vendor are recoverable. It is true that a particular purchaser might stipulate that he was not to be liable for damages beyond the deposit, but that may be simply but clearly stated, and to my mind, the use of the phrase "liquidated damages" would convey no such meaning to the ordinary citizen. . . .

[13] In my opinion, the vendor in this case is not limited in the recovery of damages by the phrase "the deposit shall be subsequently forfeited as liquidated damages."

[14] One further matter should be mentioned. It has been urged by the appellant that as the contract was terminated by the repudiation of the respondent, the contract was at an end, and the respondent could not rely, then, on a term of the contract, even if that term meant that the appellant could not recover more than the amount of the deposit by way of damages. I think this argument is unsound in the light of the decision of the House of Lords in *Photo Production Ltd. v. Securicor Tpt. Ltd.*, [1980] 1 All E.R. 556. Lord Wilberforce in that case said this:

> Damages, in such cases [where contracts were terminated] are then claimed under the contract, so what reason in principle could there be for disregarding what the contract itself said about damages — whether it "liquidates" them, or limits them, or excludes them?

[15] The report then refers to Lord Diplock's judgment as follows:

> [Lord Diplock concurring, said that] the "rule of law" theory which the Court of Appeal has adopted in the last decade to defeat exclusion clauses is at first sight attractive in the simplicity of its logic. A fundamental breach is one which entitles the party not in default . . . to terminate the contract. On his doing so the contract comes

to an end. The exclusion clause is part of the contract, so it comes to an end too; the party in default can no longer rely on it.

His Lordship then rejected this theory... [The Court of Appeal allowed the appeal, and awarded judgment in favour of the appellant-purchaser.]

QUESTION

What is the significance of the fact that in *Lozcal* the clause which the buyer sought to take advantage of appeared on a "printed form", doubtless provided by the buyer's real estate agent? Why do you think the clause was drafted the way it was? Even if the clause was on a printed form, was it a part of the "dickered deal"?

STOCKLOSER v. JOHNSON

[1954] 1 Q.B. 476, [1954] 1 All E.R. 630
(C.A., Romer, Somervell and Denning L.JJ.)

[The plaintiff agreed to purchase a quarry and equipment from the defendant for a total purchase price of £14,000; each party had legal advice prior to signing. The contract provided that the payment of the purchase price should be made by an initial payment (treated as a "deposit") at time of signing of £3,000, and the balance by instalments over three years. The contract provided that if the purchaser defaulted in making any payment for 28 days, the vendor should be entitled to rescind the contract, keep all of the payments already made and retake possession of the equipment and quarry. After operating the quarry for about a year and a half and making instalment payments totalling £3,500, the plaintiff defaulted and the defendant retook possession. The plaintiff sued for the return of all of the £6,500 paid. The trial judge allowed the plaintiff's claim in respect of the £3,500 in instalments paid. The defendant appealed and the plaintiff cross-appealed.]

DENNING L.J.: — [1] There was acute contest as to the proper legal principles to apply in this case. On the one hand, Mr. Neil Lawson urged us to hold that the buyer was entitled to recover the instalments at law. He said that the forfeiture clause should be ignored because it was of a penal character; and once it was ignored, it meant that the buyer was left with a simple right to repayment of his money on the lines of *Dies v. British and International Mining and Finance Corporation* [*supra*, Chapter 4] subject only to a cross-claim for damages. In asking us to ignore the forfeiture clause, Mr. Lawson [counsel for the plaintiff] relied on the familiar tests which are used to distinguish between penalties and liquidated damages, and said that these tests had been applied in cases for the repayment of money . . . There is, I think, a plain distinction between penalty cases, strictly so called, and cases like the present.

[2]   It is this: when one party seeks to exact a penalty from the other, he is seeking to exact payment of an extravagant sum either by action at law or by appropriating to himself moneys belonging to the other party . . . The claimant invariably relies, like Shylock, on the letter of the contract to support his demand, but the courts decline to give him their aid because they will not assist him in an act of oppression. . . .

[3]   In the present case, however, the seller is not seeking to exact a penalty. He only wants to keep money which already belongs to him. The money was handed to him in part payment of the purchase price and, as soon as it was paid, it be-

longed to him absolutely. He did not obtain it by extortion or oppression or anything of that sort, and there is an express clause — a forfeiture clause, if you please — permitting him to keep it. It is not the case of a seller seeking to enforce a penalty, but a buyer seeking restitution of money paid. If the buyer is to recover it, he must, I think, have recourse to somewhat different principles from those applicable to penalties, strictly so called.

[4]   On the other hand, Mr. Beney [counsel for the defendant] urged us to hold that the buyer could only recover the money if he was able and willing to perform the contract, and for this purpose he ought to pay or offer to pay the instalments which were in arrears and be willing to pay the future instalments as they became due. . . . I think that this contention goes too far in the opposite direction. If the buyer was seeking to re-establish the contract, he would of course have to pay up the arrears and to show himself willing to perform the contract in the future, just as a lessee, who has suffered a forfeiture, has to do when he seeks to re-establish the lease. So, also, if the buyer were seeking specific performance he would have to show himself able and willing to perform his part. But the buyer's object here is not to re-establish the contract. It is to get his money back, and to do this I do not think that it is necessary for him to go so far as to show that he is ready and willing to perform the contract.

[5]   I reject, therefore, the arguments of counsel at each extreme. It seems to me that the cases show the law to be this: (1) *When there is no forfeiture clause.* If money is handed over in part payment of the purchase price, and then the buyer makes default as to the balance, then, so long as the seller keeps the contract open and available for performance, the buyer cannot recover the money; but once the seller rescinds the contract or treats it as at an end owing to the buyer's default, then the buyer is entitled to recover his money by action at law, subject to a cross-claim by the seller for damages . . . (2) *But when there is a forfeiture clause or the money is expressly paid as a deposit (which is equivalent to a forfeiture clause),* then the buyer who is in default cannot recover the money at law at all. He may, however, have a remedy in equity, for, despite the express stipulation in the contract, equity can relieve the buyer from forfeiture of the money and order the seller to repay it on such terms as the court thinks fit.

[6]   The difficulty is to know what are the circumstances which give rise to this equity, but I must say that I agree with all that Somervell L.J. has said about it, differing herein from the view of Romer L.J. Two things are necessary: first, the forfeiture clause must be of a penal nature, in this sense, that the sum forfeited must be out of all proportion to the damage, and secondly, it must be unconscionable for the seller to retain the money. . . .

[7]   These illustrations convince me that in a proper case there is an equity of restitution which a party in default does not lose simply because he is not able and willing to perform the contract. Nay, that is the very reason why he needs the equity. The equity operates, not because of the plaintiff's default, but because it is in the particular case unconscionable for the seller to retain the money. In short, he ought not unjustly to enrich himself at the plaintiff's expense. This equity of restitution is to be tested, I think, not at the time of the contract, but by the conditions existing when it is invoked. Suppose, for instance, that in the instance of the necklace, the first instalment was only 5 per cent of the price; and the buyer made default on the second instalment. There would be no equity by which he could ask

for the first instalment to be repaid to him any more than he could claim repayment of a deposit. But it is very different after 90 per cent has been paid. Again, delay may be very material. . . .

[8]   Applying these principles to the present case, even if one regards the forfeiture clause as of a penal nature — as the judge did and I am prepared to do — nevertheless I do not think that it was unconscionable for the seller to retain the money. The buyer seems to have gambled on the royalties being higher than they were. He thought that they would go a long way to enable him to pay the instalments; but owning to bad weather they turned out to be smaller than he had hoped and he could not find the additional amount necessary to pay the instalments. The judge summarized the position neatly when he said that the purchaser "is in the position of a gambler who has lost his stake and is now saying that it is for the court of equity to get it back for him." He said, "if it is a question of what is unconscionable, or, to use a word with a less legal flavour, unfair, I can see nothing whatever unfair in the defendant retaining the money." With that finding of the judge I entirely agree and think that it disposes of the purchaser's claim to restitution. . . .

ROMER L.J.: — [9] . . . Pausing then at this point, it appears to me that the cases establish that if a purchaser defaults in punctual payment of instalments of purchase-money the court will, in a proper case, relieve the purchaser from his contractual liability to forfeit instalments (apart from the deposit) already paid to the extent of giving him further chance and further time to pay the money which is in arrears if he is able and willing to do so; but the cases do not, in my judgment, show that the court will relieve such a purchaser to any further extent than this. . . .

[10]   There is, in my judgment, nothing inequitable per se in a vendor, whose conduct is not open to criticism in other respects, insisting upon his contractual right to retain instalments of purchase-money already paid. In my judgment, there is no sufficient ground for interfering with the contractual rights of a vendor under forfeiture clauses of the nature which are now under consideration, while the contract is still subsisting, beyond giving a purchaser who is in default, but who is able and willing to proceed with the contract, a further opportunity of doing so; and no relief of any other nature can properly be given, in the absence of some special circumstances such as fraud, sharp practice or other unconscionable conduct of the vendor, to a purchaser after the vendor has rescinded the contract.

[11]   My brother Denning in his judgment has referred to the hypothetical case which was suggested during the argument of a purchaser who buys a pearl necklace on terms that the purchase price is to be payable by instalments and that the vendor is to be entitled to get the necklace back and retain all previous payments if the purchaser makes default in the punctual payment of any instalment, even the final one. It would certainly seem hard that the purchaser should lose both the necklace and all previous instalments owing to his inability to pay the last one. But that is the bargain into which the purchaser freely entered and the risk which he voluntarily accepted. The court would doubtless, as I have already indicated, give him further time to find the money if he could establish some probability of his being able to do so, but I do not know why it should interfere further; nor would it be easy to determine at what point in his failure to pay the agreed instalments the suggested equity would arise. In any event I venture to suggest that it is extremely unlikely that such a case would occur in practice; for a purchaser who had paid,

say, nine-tenths of the agreed price for the necklace would have little difficulty in borrowing the remaining one-tenth on the security of his interest therein. . . .

[**SOMERVELL L.J.** gave a judgment to the same effect as **DENNING L.J.**, dismissing the plaintiff's claim for return of the instalments.]

The following decision returns to the issue of stipulated remedy and penalty clauses, though taking a more flexible approach than some of the older cases.

PEACHTREE II ASSOCIATES — DALLAS L.P. v. 857486 ONTARIO LTD.

[2005] O.J. No. 2749, 76 O.R. (3d) 362, 256 D.L.R. (4th) 490
(C.A., Feldman, MacPherson and Sharpe JJ.A.)

[Leave to appeal to S.C.C. dismissed 19 January 2006]

[The parties entered into agreements to purchase and operate two rental properties. The respondents were passive investors who became limited partners in the ventures, which were arranged to provide them with significant income tax deductions. They provided the appellant with promissory notes to secure their obligation to reimburse the appellant for certain fees and advances. The agreement contained a stipulated remedy provision which stated that in the event the appellant defaulted on its obligations, the promissory notes were to be deemed paid, and the respondents discharged from any obligations owing. The respondents alleged that the appellant failed to live up to its obligations under the agreements. They served a series of notices to that effect, and the appellant failed to remedy the alleged defaults. The agreements provided for arbitration of disputes. The respondents issued claims for a declaration deeming the promissory notes paid in full, or in the alternative damages on the basis of the appellant's alleged default. The arbitrator found that the appellant was in serious default of its obligations. The arbitrator was prepared to assume that the deemed payment of the promissory notes was analogous to a payment of damages by the appellant and concluded that it could be regarded as a "penalty". However, he found that the stipulated remedy clause should be enforced and that the appellant was not entitled to relief from forfeiture. The appellant's appeal to the Superior Court was dismissed, with the judge rejecting the argument that the arbitrator was required in law to restrict the respondents to their remedy in damages after having found that the stipulated remedy clause "could be a penalty". The judge held that the arbitrator had the discretion to decide whether or not the clause should be enforced even if it were a penalty. The appellant appealed to the Court of Appeal.]

The judgment of the court was given by **SHARPE J.A.**: —

Analysis

[19] The appellant submits that the arbitrator found that the stipulated remedy clause was a "penalty", and that, having done so, the arbitrator was required to apply a simple, black-letter common law rule that precludes enforcement of penalty clauses. The appellant further submits that the appeal judge erred in finding that the arbitrator had the discretion to enforce what he had found to be a penalty clause.

[20] In my view, the applicable legal and equitable principles are considerably more nuanced than is suggested by the appellant's argument. I do not agree that the arbitrator found the stipulated remedy clause to fall into the category of penalties that contract law does not enforce. I also consider the applicable legal and equitable principles to be sufficiently flexible to support the enforcement of the clause at issue in this case on the basis of the relief from forfeiture doctrine.

[21] To understand the law's treatment of stipulated remedy clauses as it pertains to this case, we must turn to history and to the two great streams of our legal tradition, common law and equity. Although those two streams were joined well over a century ago, as this case demonstrates, we continue to encounter issues of confluence and the reconciliation of doctrines derived from one tradition with those derived from the other.

[22] The courts of common law and equity adopted similar but distinctive rules with respect to stipulated remedy clauses that had penal consequences. The courts of common law dealt with attempts to enforce the payment of penalties while the courts of equity dealt with pleas for relief from penal forfeitures. In the oft-quoted words of Lord Dunedin in *Dunlop Pneumatic Tyre Co. Ltd. v. New Garage & Motor Co. Ltd.*, [1915] A.C. 79, 23 C.L.T. 106 (H.L.), at pp. 86-87 A.C., "The essence of a penalty is a payment of money stipulated as in terrorem of the offending party ..." On the other hand, a forfeiture is the loss, by reason of some specified conduct, of a right, property, or money, often held as security or part payment of the obligation being enforced under the threat of forfeiture. Like promises to pay a penalty, forfeitures often have penal consequences as the right or property forfeited by the defaulting party may bear no relation to the loss suffered by the innocent party.

[23] There is a venerable common law rule to the effect that the courts will not require a party to pay a genuine or true penalty on grounds of public policy. The parallel, but distinctive, equitable rule is to the effect that penal forfeitures will be relieved against where their enforcement would be inequitable and unconscionable.

[24] While both doctrines have the effect of relieving the breaching party of the penal consequences of stipulated remedy clauses, in their traditional formulations they bear significant differences. The common law penalty rule involves an assessment of the stipulated remedy clause only at the time the contract is formed. If the stipulated remedy represents a genuine attempt to estimate the damages the innocent party would suffer in the event of a breach, it will be enforced. On the other hand, again to quote Lord Dunedin from *Dunlop*, *supra*, "[i]t will be held to be a penalty if the sum stipulated for is extravagant and unconscionable in amount in comparison with the greatest loss that could be conceivably be proved to have followed from the breach". Laskin C.J.C. adopted a virtually identical formulation (taken from *Snell's Principles of Equity*, 27th ed. (London: Sweet & Maxwell, 1973) at p. 535) in *H.F. Clarke Ltd. v. Thermidore Corp. Ltd.* ... Although the common law defined penalties in terms of unconscionability, that assessment is to be made at the time the contract was formed. The common law doctrine did not include any discretion to be exercised in the light of circumstances that may exist at the time of breach.

[25] Equity, on the other hand, considers the enforceability of forfeitures at the time of breach rather than at the time the contract was entered. Equity also looks

beyond the question of whether or not the stipulated remedy has penal consequences to consider whether it is unconscionable for the innocent party to retain
the right, property, or money forfeited. As explained by Denning L.J. in *Stockloser
v. Johnson,* [1954] 1 All E.R. 630, [1954] 1 Q.B. 476 (C.A.), at p. 638 All E.R.:
"Two things are necessary: first, the forfeiture clause must be of a penal nature, in
the sense that the sum forfeited must be out of all proportion to the damage; and,
secondly, it must be unconscionable for the seller to retain the money."

[26] Against this general background, I cannot agree with the appellant's contention that the arbitrator and the appeal judge erred by refusing to strike down the
stipulated remedy clause as an unenforceable penalty. The central pillar of the
appellant's argument, as I understand it, is that there is an iron-clad rule to the
effect that all stipulated remedy clauses, whether penalties or forfeitures, assessed
at the date of the contract as having penal consequences will not be enforced. In
my view, that proposition does not represent an accurate statement of the law. Not
all stipulated remedy clauses having penal consequences are unenforceable. In
particular, the equitable doctrine of relief from forfeiture enforces such penalty
clauses, where they are in the form of a forfeiture, where it is not unconscionable
to do so.

[27] The proposition advanced by the appellant has been explicitly rejected in the
case law. For example, in *Dimensional Investments Ltd. v. Canada,* [1968] S.C.R.
93, 64 D.L.R. (2d) 632, the Supreme Court of Canada dealt with a contract to purchase lands that provided for installment payments. If the purchaser defaulted, the
contract terminated, and the vendor could retain all installments. This amounted to
a penalty as it bore no relation to the damages suffered. The court adopted the approach taken in *Stockloser*, *supra*, and enforced the term, holding at p. 100 S.C.R.
that "even if [the impugned stipulated remedy clause] had been found to impose a
penalty rather than a genuine pre-estimate of damage, it does not follow" that the
clause would not be enforced.

[28] *Else (1982) Ltd. v. Parkland Holdings Ltd.*, [1993] E.W.J. No. 4674 (C.A.)
involved an agreement that required the purchaser of shares to make certain payments in default of which the vendor would recover shares held in escrow and
would be permitted to retain half of the substantial payments that had already been
made for the shares. This was a penal provision, as the amount forfeited bore no
relation to the damages suffered, yet it was enforced. The purchaser made essentially the same argument as that advanced by the appellant in the case [at] bar. The
English Court of Appeal, at para. 23, flatly rejected the submission that all stipulated remedy clauses having penal consequences are unenforceable as being inconsistent with the doctrine of relief from forfeiture: "[I]t has never been held or even
argued, so far as the law reports indicate, that forfeiture clauses which foreseeably
at the time of the contract involved penal consequences are unenforceable and
should therefore be disregarded for that reason alone."

[29] On these authorities, if the appellant's case, properly considered, amounts to a
request for relief from forfeiture, the appeal must fail as the findings of the arbitrator in that regard are not attacked and, in any event, appear to me to be unim-
peachable. I pause here to note that it is with some reluctance that I frame the issue
in terms of a choice between common law and equity. In doing so, I do not wish to
be taken as encouraging the perpetuation of what very well may amount to an out-
dated distinction between the common law's treatment of penalty clauses and the
equitable doctrine of relief from forfeiture. However, as I am satisfied that the

appeal fails even on the terms of these traditional categories, it is unnecessary to go further. Moreover, as I will explain, my analysis is driven in large part by considerations that would tend to favour, whenever possible, the equitable approach as the dominant one.

[30] Should the impugned clause in the present case be assessed from the perspective of the common law rule against penalty clauses or does the appellant's case amount to a request for relief from forfeiture? For the following reasons, I consider that the appellant's case amounts to a request for relief from forfeiture.

[31] First, it seems to me more apt to describe deeming the notes paid as being a forfeiture rather than the payment of a penalty. A penalty is the payment of a sum as a consequence of breach. By the terms of the clause at issue here, the appellant pays nothing on account of its breach. Rather the appellant forfeits the right to enforce the notes. Admittedly, in the case at bar, we are to some extent looking at two sides of the same coin, but as I shall explain, there is good authority to the effect that courts should, if at all possible, avoid classifying contractual clauses as penalties and, when faced with a choice between considering stipulated remedies as penalties or forfeitures, favour the latter.

[32] Second, I agree with Professor Waddams' observation in *The Law of Damages*, looseleaf (Aurora: Canada Law Book Inc., 1991) at para. 8.310 that as there is often little to distinguish between the two types of clauses and that there is much to be said for assimilating both under unconscionability. The effect of assimilation would be "to provide a more rational framework for the decisions of both forfeitures and penalties". Unconscionability is also the direction suggested by the dictum of Dickson J. in *Elsley v. J.G. Collins Insurance Agencies Ltd.*, [1978] 2 S.C.R. 916, 83 D.L.R. (3d) 1, at p. 937 S.C.R.: "It is now evident that the power to strike down a penalty clause is a blatant interference with freedom of contract and is designed for the sole purpose of providing relief against oppression for the party having to pay the stipulated sum." As pointed out by the [Superior Court] ... judge, this would also appear to be the direction of s. 98 of the *Courts of Justice Act*, R.S.O. 1990, c. C.43: "A court may grant relief against penalties and forfeitures, on such terms as to compensation or otherwise, as are considered just." All of this suggests to me that courts should, whenever possible, favour analysis on the basis of equitable principles and unconscionability over the strict common law rule pertaining to penalty clauses.

[33] Third, there is good authority for the proposition that the strict rule of the common law refusing to enforce penalty clauses should not be extended. The English Court of Appeal has stated in *Else, supra*, at para. 30 (*per* Evans L.J.) that "in modern conditions the courts should not seek to extend the common law rule" and at para. 58 (per Hoffman L.J.) "the penalty doctrine, being an inroad upon freedom of contract which is inflexible compared with the equitable rules of relief against forfeiture, ought not to be extended". A similar view was expressed by Diplock L.J. in *Robophone Facilities Ltd. v. Blank*, [1966] 1 W.L.R. 1428, [1966] All E.R. 128 (C.A.), at p. 1447 W.L.R., stating that courts should not be "astute to descry 'a penalty clause' in every provision of a contract which stipulates a sum to be payable by one party to the other in the event of a breach by the former".

[34] This is closely related to the fourth factor, namely, the policy of upholding freedom of contract. Judicial enthusiasm for the refusal to enforce penalty clauses has waned in the face of a rising recognition of the advantages of allowing parties

to define for themselves the consequences of breach. As I have already noted, in *Elsley*, *supra*, Dickson J. labelled the penalty clause doctrine as "a blatant interference with freedom of contract", a sentiment echoed by the English Court of Appeal in *Else*. The arguments favouring the enforcement of stipulated remedy clauses on this score are recognized by Fridman, *The Law of Contract in Canada*, 4th ed. (Toronto: Carswell, 1999) at p. 817 and are especially well put by Waddams, *supra*, at para. 8.330:

> It is useful to remember that the jurisdiction to strike down penalty clauses represents an exception to a general principle of freedom of contract. The force of the general principle should not be underestimated. There are strong arguments for enabling parties to set their own value on performance. The power to do so gives flexibility to the contracting process; it enables the promisor to offer an assurance of performance while limiting liability for consequential damages and thereby making the cost of breach predictable. It enables the promisee to avoid the cost of securing compensation by litigation and the risks of undercompensation that may be caused by the legal restrictions on damages, such as remoteness, certainty of proof, mitigation, and failure to recognize intangible losses; it reduces the cost to the parties and to the state of settling a dispute after breach; it enables the promisee to purchase insurance against default from the party in the best position to provide it at the lowest cost. A further point is that the striking down of the clause may represent an injustice to the promisee for the price of performance will have been agreed in the light of all the promisor's obligations, including the promise to pay an agreed sum on breach; if that promise is struck down, the promisee does not receive what has been paid for. …

[35] Taking all of these factors into account, I conclude that the appellant's contention that the stipulated remedy clause should not be enforced, properly considered, amounts to a request for relief from forfeiture. As there is no basis upon which I would interfere with the arbitrator's treatment of relief from forfeiture, it follows that the appeal must be dismissed.

[36] My conclusion with respect to relief from forfeiture makes it unnecessary for me to consider the point dealt with by the appeal judge, namely, whether there is a residual discretion to enforce a payment that would be a penalty under the common law rule, and I leave that question to another day.

Conclusion

[37] For these reasons, I would dismiss the appeal. The respondents are entitled to their costs of the appeals fixed at $40,000, inclusive of disbursements and GST.

Appeal dismissed.

NOTES, PROBLEMS AND QUESTIONS

1. In *Elsley*, Dickson J. rationalized the result of the earlier Supreme Court decision *H.F. Clarke Ltd. v. Thermidaire Corporation Ltd.*, [1976] 1 S.C.R. 319, 54 D.L.R. (3d) 385, by saying that *Clarke* was a case of oppression. He also suggested that where the clause sets an amount that is *less* than the actual damages, the clause is enforceable. Does this mean that such a clause *cannot* give rise to oppression? What is the difference between a clause establishing a small amount payable on breach and an exemption clause? Notice that McGillivray C.J.A. in *Lozcal* drew attention to the exemption clause decision in *Photo Production v. Securicor*.

2. The question of the enforcement of a liquidated damages clause is said in *Lozcal* to be a question of the intention of the parties. Is there any evidence of the intention of the parties in that case? What would you think that parties to an agreement to sell land ex-

pect from a clause providing for forfeiture of a deposit on breach by the purchaser? A survey of house purchasers conducted in the late 1970's (though never published) indicated that many people expect that the damages should be the amount of the deposit, and no more. This fact raises again the question whether the law has any business in giving disappointed promisees any more as damages than they actually expect: a "deemed" expectation is not good enough.

3.   Imagine that you are asked to consider *Lozcal* and, in the light of that decision, to redraft the standard agreement of purchase and sale for the local real estate board. What clause would you recommend to the board?

4.   Any feelings of sympathy that one might have that the purchaser in *Stockloser v. Johnson* was badly treated have to be balanced against the fact that the property was income producing. The purchaser, presumably, made the deal because he hoped to be able to finance the purchase out of the cash-flow of the business, and he in fact had about £3,000 in revenue in the year of possession. Forcing the vendor to give back the payments on his re-possessing the land would not deal very well with the issues arising on breach by the purchaser. The purchaser did not, for example, offer to refund the vendor any gains he had made while he operated the quarry. (The fact that he breached the contract may indicate that the income was less than his expenses.)

   Should the position be any different in principle if there is a forfeiture of payments clause for a non-income producing asset like a family car?

5.   There are statutory provisions dealing with the issue of the vendor's or creditor's right to repossess chattels. A creditor who takes security in consumer goods may lose its right to re-possess for non-payment after a significant proportion of the purchase price has been paid by the consumer. See, for example, the *Personal Property Security Acts* of British Columbia, Alberta, Saskatchewan, Manitoba and Ontario. The creditor is, of course, entitled to sue for the deficiency, *i.e.*, the difference between the purchase price and financing charges and what has been paid. Similar limitations on the rights of mortgagees exist in the prairie provinces. See, for example, *Law of Property Act*, R.S.A. 2000, c. L-7, s. 40.

   What factors would motivate a legislature to enact such remedies to protect consumers who default in payments on contracts with forfeiture clauses?

6.   An agreement provides that the defendant is to lease 150 parking spaces for 10 years in a parking garage that the defendant is to erect. The plaintiff will rent out these spaces to tenants in its adjacent building. The plaintiff will pay $100 per month for each parking space. The agreement requires that all parking places should be available by April 1, 2002. Should the following clause be subject to whatever controls are placed on "penalty clauses"?

>   The parties agree that in the event all of the parking spaces have not been provided by 1 April 2002, the [defendant] shall pay the plaintiff $20.00 per month per parking space until each and every one of the parking spaces shall have been provided.

   Are there other facts that you would like to know before answering this question? See *Graham v. Wagman* (1978), 21 O.R. (2d) 1, 89 D.L.R. (3d) 282 (C.A).

7.   Do you agree with the proposition that "in general, parties are free to enter into a contract containing whatever terms they wish regarding the establishment of primary rights, but except within narrow limits they are not free to determine what remedial rights will be provided?" (Calamari and Perillo, *The Law of Contracts* (St. Paul: West Publishing, 1970) at 336.

8.   If the parties are free to agree that all disputes must be submitted to arbitration before a party can resort to litigation, can they restrict the power of the arbitrator to give particular remedies?

9.   Consider the following problems:

(a) Builder agrees to construct a house for Owner for $40,000. The date of completion is 1 October. The contract provides that if the house is completed before that date, Owner will pay a bonus of $10,000. The time allowed for completion is reasonable and a fair price would be $50,000.

(b) Contractor agrees with the provincial government to build a bridge on a new highway. The government is concerned that all work be completed on time and that, for example, the opening of the highway (which is planned to take place before the next provincial election) not be delayed because one bridge is unfinished. The contract provides that Contractor shall pay $1,000 per day for every day's delay. Assume that (i) Contractor is ten days late in completing the bridge; (ii) Contractor is fifty days late; or (iii) Contractor abandons the bridge, which is finished by another company one hundred days late.

Are the provisions of these contracts enforceable? How may the government ensure that the bridge is completed on time?

UNCONSCIONABILITY

At various points in this study of contract law, consideration has been given to how the courts will respond to unfairness. The courts may, for example, relieve a party of the consequences of an improvident bargain by finding that there was no consideration for the party's promise (see, for example, the opinions of the Court of Appeal — apart from that of Lord Denning — in *D. & C. Builders Ltd. v. Rees*, *supra*, Chapter 2). In some cases, the courts may provide relief by the manipulation of the rules of offer and acceptance, *e.g.*, Lord Denning in *Thornton v. Shoe Lane Parking*. Those methods of controlling unfairness, being covert methods, were often unsatisfactory. The major debate over the continued existence and function of the doctrine of fundamental breach is whether it should be replaced by a general doctrine of unconscionability. Similarly, the issues raised in cases like *Clarke v. Thermidaire* about forfeiture and penalty clauses were "re-phrased" in more recent cases like *Elsley v. Collins*, *Stockloser v. Johnson* and *Peachtree II* as questions of unconscionability. The following cases are ones in which the courts explicitly recognize unconscionability and unfairness as the ground for relief. As you read the cases, there are a number of questions to consider:

(a) What, precisely, is the basis for the court's interference with the contract?

(b) What factors are important in moving the court to interfere?

(c) What limits are set on the parties' freedom of contract?

(d) What are the effects of judicial interference in this case or others in similar situations?

The cases on unconscionability also raise some important questions about the process of judicial decision-making and institutional design. In all areas of law, there is an interrelation between the application of legal rules and the facts presented to the court. A court can apply a particular rule only if the party seeking to invoke that rule has established the facts that justify the application of that rule.

In general, the development of contract law has been characterized by the expansion of those facts which are legally relevant. There is, however, a limit to the range of facts that the court can be asked to consider. The limit is reached when the burden of fact presentation on the parties becomes more than they can fairly be asked to bear. If the range of facts considered (or, what amounts to the same thing, the range of facts the court thinks it should consider) becomes very large, then a number of things start to happen:

(a) It becomes harder for the court to accurately ascertain the facts, and the chance of getting the facts wrong increases;

(b) an increasingly large burden is placed on the parties;

(c) courts are tempted to find facts on their own and, if they succumb to the temptation, the whole process of adjudication is compromised, for the facts the court discovers for itself may not have been the subject of challenge or argument by the parties; and

(d) courts begin to make decisions that should, perhaps, be made by different institutions in society, institutions that may have better access to facts, that are answerable to the legislature or to the democratic process itself.

Some of these issues were considered in the examination of the cases in which the courts made explicit reference to the criterion of reasonableness. Arguably the central function of the law of contracts is to protect the reasonable expectations of the parties. However, the determination of what the reasonable expectations of the parties are is not always easy, and the institutional process within which the judges must function imposes constraints on the extent to which the courts may "individualize" the application of a legal rule.

One of the central challenges for counsel in dealing with cases that raise unconscionability issues is deciding what facts will be relevant to the court, and then proving them.

The Judicial Development of Unconscionability

There is a long history of at least some judicial power to protect weaker parties from the consequences of agreements made with those who have taken unfair advantage of their economically stronger position or more sophisticated knowledge. It is not the mere fact that one party is stronger or more knowledgeable than the other, it's the fact that an unfair advantage was taken of that position.

The pattern disclosed by an examination of the situations where the law's concern was expressed illustrates the way in which the modern law of contracts has evolved. First, the pattern discloses very different attitudes in the common law courts and the court of chancery. Second, the early development is characterized by isolated examples, both at common law and in equity, where concern was expressed. The early development of the modern law of mortgages was, for example, motivated by the concerns of the court of equity for the position of the mortgagor — almost always the weaker party — faced with the loss of his or her property for non-payment of the mortgage when the mortgagee could be adequately protected in other ways. The modern "equity of redemption" is the legacy of these early concerns of the chancellors.. While mortgagors were protected, no attempt was made to generalize a doctrine of unconscionability to protect all those exposed to the unfairness in other contractual relations.

While the courts of common law typically took a strict view of contractual undertakings, there were situations in which they were prepared to set aside a contract under circumstances which today would be characterized as unconscionable. The courts of common law would, for example, sometimes decline to enforce covenants in "restraint of trade", that is, if one party agreed to restrict his or her future right to contract with others. The principal focus of the common law was on "non-competition clauses", *i.e.*, an undertaking by an employee that he or she would not compete with his or her employer after his or her employment ended. The courts' concern was that the employee might be unable to earn a living if the clause was so wide as to prevent his or her taking any job. Tindal C.J. in *Horner v. Graves* (1831), 7 Bing. 735, 131 E.R. 284 at p. 287, stated the law's position as follows:

> [W]hatever restraint is larger than the necessary protection of the party [seeking to enforce the covenant] can be of no benefit to either, it can only be oppressive; and if it is oppressive, it is, in the eye of the law, unreasonable. Whatever is injurious to the interest of the public is void on the grounds of public policy.

Restraint of trade is more fully discussed later in this chapter. In general, however, the common law rules were relatively narrow and mechanical, with little judicial discretion to refuse to enforce an unfair agreement. In a sense, the common law could afford to adopt this attitude for there was the moderating influence or power of the court of equity.

Apart from equity's historical concern for mortgagors, the chancellors would also provide relief if a person who owed another a special duty, particularly a fiduciary duty, took advantage of his position *vis-à-vis* the beneficiary of the duty. The relations protected by equity in this way included that of trustee and beneficiary, solicitor and client, parent and child (or adult child and aged parent) and even doctor and patient. This focus on relations led to a partial generalization, *viz.*, that a contract was liable to be set aside where there was "undue influence".

There was an important distinction between relief at common law and in equity which showed itself in the form of the remedy. Tindal C.J. in *Horner v. Graves* said the contract, if the protection sought was too wide, was void as against public policy. A void contract is treated as if it had never existed — that was, for example, the consequence of the mistake analysis of Lord Atkin in *Bell v. Lever Brothers*, or the result of a successful plea of *non est factum*. Equitable relief, even for blatant and obvious wrongs like deceit or breach of trust, took the form of rescission, *i.e.*, a declaration of the court that the contract was to be set aside. This declaration made the contract voidable, not void. As between the parties, it might not matter much whether the contract was void or voidable — the result was that the contract could not be sued on and any benefits conferred under it had to be returned — but a void contract was a threat to third parties who, as in the case of *non est factum*, would acquire no rights under the impugned agreement.

While the old distinctions between the courts of common law and equity no longer exist, it remains important to consider whether a challenge to a transaction on the grounds to be examined leads (or should lead) to the transaction being held to be void or voidable.

By the 1960's, Canadian courts had begun to develop a more generalized concept of unconscionability, one that did not depend on any special relation, but simply did depend on two factors: (i) a transaction that was improvident or grossly one-sided from the point of view of the person seeking relief; and (ii) unfairness in the process by which the contract was made. In *Morrison v. Coast Finance Ltd.* (1965), 55 D.L.R. (2d) 710, 54 W.W.R. 257 (B.C.C.A.), the British Columbia Court of Appeal set aside a mortgage given by the plaintiff, a 79-year-old woman, to provide security for a loan made by the defendant to two men whom she scarcely knew. As part of the transaction, the two men promised to make the pay-

ments required under the mortgage but, of course, they never did. As the defendant
knew, the transaction provided no benefits to the plaintiff. Davey J.A. said (p. 713,
D.L.R.):

> The equitable principles relating to undue influence and relief against unconscion-
> able bargains are closely related, but the doctrines are separate and distinct. The
> finding here against undue influence does not conclude the question whether the ap-
> pellant is entitled to relief against an unconscionable transaction. A plea of undue in-
> fluence attacks the sufficiency of consent; a plea that a bargain is unconscionable in-
> vokes relief against an unfair advantage gained by an unconscientious use of power
> by a stronger party against a weaker. On such a claim the material ingredients are
> proof of inequality in the position of the parties arising out of the ignorance, need or
> distress of the weaker, which left him in the power of the stronger, and proof of sub-
> stantial unfairness of the bargain obtained by the stronger. On proof of those circum-
> stances, it creates a presumption of fraud which the stronger must repel by proving
> that the bargain was fair, just and reasonable. . . .

The relief provided by the Court of Appeal was not to set the whole transaction
aside, but to set the mortgage aside without requiring the plaintiff to repay any of
the money secured, on the condition that she assign to the defendant the promises
given to the plaintiff by the two men to whom the defendant had advanced its
money.

In *Harry v. Kreutziger* (1978), 95 D.L.R. (3d) 231, 9 B.C.L.R. 116 (C.A.), the
British Columbia Court of Appeal set aside a contract for the sale of a fishing boat
by the plaintiff to the defendant. The plaintiff, described as "an inarticulate retiring
person, an Indian of Grade V education and partially deaf", agreed to sell his fishing boat to the defendant for $4,500. The defendant, a man of much greater busi-
ness experience, knew that the boat was substantially more valuable because it had
a fishing licence attached to it. The trial judge had refused to give the plaintiff
relief. This decision was reversed in the Court of Appeal. Lambert J.A. said (p.
241, D.L.R.):

> In my opinion, questions as to whether use of power was unconscionable, an advan-
> tage was unfair or very unfair, a consideration was grossly inadequate, or bargaining
> power was grievously impaired . . . are really aspects of one question. That single
> question is whether the transaction, seen as a whole, is sufficiently divergent from
> community standards of commercial morality that it should be rescinded. To my
> mind, the framing of the question in that way prevents the real issue from being ob-
> scured by an isolated consideration of a number of separate questions; as, for exam-
> ple, a consideration of whether the consideration was grossly inadequate, rather than
> merely inadequate, separate from the consideration of whether bargaining power was
> grievously impaired, or merely badly impaired. Such consideration of separate ques-
> tions produced by the application of a synthetic rule tends to obscure rather than aid
> the process of decision.

> . . .

> In my opinion, it is also appropriate to seek guidance as to community standards of
> commercial morality from legislation that embodies those standards in law.

Lambert J.A. considered a number of cases, including *Morrison v. Coast Finance
supra*, and the *Trade Practices Act*, S.B.C. 1974, c. 96, and the *Consumer Protection Act*, S.B.C. 1977, c. 6, and concluded:

> In my opinion, the whole circumstances of the bargain reveal such a marked depar-
> ture from community standards of commercial morality that the contract of purchase
> and sale should be rescinded.

The next case, *Lloyd's Bank v. Bundy*, considers some of the common themes developed in distinct pockets of law by the courts of common law and equity to protect those who are vulnerable. The judgement of Lord Denning, one of his most famous, provides a foundation for the modern study of the judicial doctrine of unconscionability.   *protecting the vulnerable*

LLOYDS BANK v. BUNDY

[1975] Q.B. 326, [1974] 3 All E.R. 757
(C.A., Lord Denning M.R., Cairns L.J. and Sir Eric Sachs)

LORD DENNING M.R.: — **[1]** Broadchalke is one of the most pleasing villages in England. Old Herbert Bundy was a farmer there. His home was at Yew Tree Farm. It went back for 300 years. His family had been there for generations. It was his only asset. But he did a very foolish thing. He mortgaged it to the bank. Up to the very hilt. Not to borrow money for himself, but for the sake of his son. Now the bank have come down on him. They have foreclosed. They want to get him out of Yew Tree Farm and to sell it. They have brought this action against him for possession. Going out means ruin for him. He was granted legal aid. His lawyers put in a defence. They said that when he executed the charge to the bank he did not know what he was doing; or at any rate the circumstances were such that he ought not to be bound by it. At the trial his plight was plain. The judge was sorry for him. He said he was a "poor old gentleman." He was so obviously incapacitated that the judge admitted his proof in evidence. He had a heart attack in the witness box. Yet the judge felt he could do nothing for him. There is nothing, he said, "which takes this out of the vast range of commercial transactions." He ordered Herbert Bundy to give up possession of Yew Tree Farm to the bank.

[2] Now there is an appeal to this court. The ground is that the circumstances were so exceptional that Herbert Bundy should not be held bound.

[3] 1. *The events before December 1969*. Herbert Bundy had only one son, Michael Bundy. He had great faith in him. They were both customers of Lloyds Bank at the Salisbury branch. They had been customers for many years. The son formed a company called MJB Plant Hire Ltd. It hired out earth-moving machinery and so forth. The company banked at Lloyds too at the same branch.

[4] In 1961 the son's company was in difficulties. The father on 19th September 1966 guaranteed the company's overdraft for £1,500 and charged Yew Tree Farm to the bank to secure the £1,500. Afterwards the son's company got further into difficulties. The overdraft ran into thousands. In May 1967 the assistant bank manager, Mr. Bennett, told the son the bank must have further security. The son said his father would give it. So Mr. Bennett and the son went together to see the father. Mr. Bennett produced the papers. He suggested that the father should sign a further guarantee for £5,000 and to execute a further charge for £6,000. The father said that he would help his son as far as he possibly could. Mr. Bennett did not ask the father to sign the papers there and then. He left them with the father so that he could consider them overnight and take advice on them. The father showed them to his solicitor, Mr. Trethowan, who lived in the same village. The solicitor told the father the £5,000 was the utmost that he could sink in his son's affairs. The house was worth about £10,000 and this was half his assets. On that advice the father on 27th May 1969 did execute the further guarantee and the charge, and Mr.

Bennett witnessed it. So at the end of May 1967 the father had charged the house
to secure £7,500.

[5]   2. *The events of December 1969*. During the next six months the affairs of
the son and company went from bad to worse. The bank had granted the son's
company an overdraft up to a limit of £10,000, but this was not enough to meet the
outgoings. The son's company drew cheques which the bank returned unpaid. The
bank were anxious. By this time Mr. Bennett had left to go to another branch. He
was succeeded by a new assistant manager, Mr. Head. In November 1969 Mr.
Head saw the son and told him that the account was unsatisfactory and that he considered that the company might have to cease operations. The son suggested that
the difficulty was only temporary and that his father would be prepared to provide
further money if necessary.

[6]   On 17th December 1969 there came the occasion which, in the judge's
words, was important and disastrous for the father. The son took Mr. Head to see
his father. Mr. Head had never met the father before. This was his first visit. He
went prepared. He took with him a form of guarantee and a form of charge filled in
with the father's name ready for signature. There was a family gathering. The father and mother were there. The son and the son's wife. Mr. Head said that the
bank had given serious thought whether they could continue to support the son's
company. But that the bank were prepared to do so in this way. (i) The bank would
continue to allow the company to draw money on overdraft up to the existing level
of £10,000, but would require the company to pay ten per cent of its incomings
into a separate account. So that 10 per cent would not go to reduce the overdraft.
Mr. Head said that this would have the effect "of reducing the level of borrowing."
In other words, the bank was cutting down the overdraft. (ii) The bank would require the father to give a guarantee of the company's account in a sum of £11,000
and to give the bank a further charge on the house of £3,500, so as to bring the
total charge to £11,000. The house was only worth about £10,000, so this charge
for £11,000 would sweep up all that the father had.

[7]   On hearing the proposal, the father said that Michael was his only son and
that he was 100 per cent behind him. Mr. Head produced the forms that had already been filled in. The father signed them and Mr. Head witnessed them there
and then. On this occasion, Mr. Head, unlike Mr. Bennett, did not leave the forms
with the father; nor did the father have any independent advice.

[8]   It is important to notice the state of mind of Mr. Head and of the father Mr.
Head said in evidence:

> [The father] asked me what in my opinion Company was doing wrong and Com-
> pany's position. I told him. I did not explain Company's accounts very fully as I had
> only just taken over . . . [The son] said Company had a number of bad debts. I
> wasn't entirely satisfied with this. I thought the trouble was more deep-seated . . . I
> thought there was no conflict of interest. I would think the [father] relied on me im-
> plicitly to advise him about the transaction as Bank Manager . . . I knew he had no
> other assets except Yew Tree Cottage.

[9]   The father said in evidence:

> Always thought Mr. Head was genuine. I have always trusted him . . . No discussion
> how business was doing that I can remember. I simply sat back and did what they
> said. . .

[10] The solicitor, Mr. Trethowan, said of the father:

> [The father] is straightforward. Agrees with anyone . . . Doubt if he understood all that Mr. Head explained to him.

[11] So the father signed the papers. Mr. Head witnessed them and took them away. The father had charged the whole of his remaining asset, leaving himself with nothing. The son and his company gained a respite. But only for a short time. Five months later, in May 1970, a receiving order was made against the son. Thereupon the bank stopped all overdraft facilities for the company. It ceased to trade. The father's solicitor, Mr. Trethowan, at once went to see Mr. Head. He said he was concerned that the father had signed the guarantee.

[12] In due course the bank insisted on the sale of the house. In December 1971 they agreed to sell it for £7,500 with vacant possession. The family were very disappointed with this figure. It was, they said, worth much more. Estate agents were called to say so. But the judge held that it was a valid sale and that the bank can take all the proceeds. The sale has not been completed, because the father is still in possession. The bank have brought these proceedings to evict the father.

[13] 3. *The general rule*. Now let me say at once that in the vast majority of cases a customer who signs a bank guarantee or a charge cannot get out of it. No bargain will be upset which is the result of the ordinary interplay of forces. There are many hard cases which are caught by this rule. Take the case of a poor man who is homeless. He agrees to pay a high rent to a landlord just to get a roof over his head. The common law will not interfere. It is left to Parliament. Next take the case of a borrower in urgent need of money. He borrows it from the bank at high interest and it is guaranteed by a friend. The guarantor gives his bond and gets nothing in return. The common law will not interfere. Parliament has intervened to prevent moneylenders charging excessive interest. But it has never interfered with banks.

[14] Yet there are exceptions to this general rule. There are cases in our books in which the courts will set aside a contract, or a transfer of property, when the parties have not met on equal terms, when the one is so strong in bargaining power and the other so weak that, as a matter of common fairness, it is not right that the strong should be allowed to push the weak to the wall. Hitherto those exceptional cases have been treated each as a separate category in itself. But I think the time has come when we should seek to find a principle to unite them. I put on one side contracts or transactions which are voidable for fraud or misrepresentation or mistake. All those are governed by settled principles. I go only to those where there has been inequality of bargaining power, such as to merit the intervention of the court.

[15] 4. *The categories*. The first category is that of "duress of goods." A typical case is when a man is in a strong bargaining position by being in possession of the goods of another by virtue of a legal right, such as, by way of pawn or pledge or taken in distress. The owner is in a weak position because he is in urgent need of the goods. The stronger demands of the weaker more than is justly due, and he pays it in order to get the goods. Such a transaction is voidable. He can recover the excess . . . To which may be added the cases of "colore officii," where a man is in a strong bargaining position by virtue of his official position or public profession. He relies on it so as to gain from the weaker — who is urgently in need — more

strength of one v. urgent need of other

than is justly due . . . In such cases the stronger may make his claim in good faith honestly believing that he is entitled to make his demand. He may not be guilty of any fraud or misrepresentation. The inequality of bargaining power — the strength of the one versus the urgent need of the other — renders the transaction voidable and the money paid to be recovered back. . . .

[16] The second category is that of the "unconscionable transaction." A man is so placed as to be in need of special care and protection and yet his weakness is exploited by another far stronger than himself so as to get his property at a gross undervalue. The typical case is that of the "expectant heir." But it applies to all cases where a man comes into property, or is expected to come into it, and then being in urgent need another gives him ready cash for it, greatly below its true worth, and so gets the property transferred to him . . . Even though there be no evidence of fraud or misrepresentation, nevertheless the transaction will be set aside. . . . This second category is said to extend to all cases where an unfair advantage has been gained by an unconscientious use of power by a stronger party against a weaker: see the cases cited in 17 Halsbury's Laws of England 3rd p. 682 and in Canada, *Morrison v. Coast Finance Ltd.* (1965), 54 W.W.R. 257, 55 D.L.R. (2d) 710, and *Knupp v. Bell* (1968), 67 D.L.R. (2d) 256.

[17] The third category is that of "undue influence" usually so called. These are divided into two classes as stated by Cotton L.J. in *Allcard v. Skinner* (1887), 36 Ch.D. 145, 171. The first are these where the stronger has been guilty of some fraud or wrongful act — expressly so as to gain some gift or advantage from the weaker. The second are those where the stronger has not been guilty of any wrongful act, but has, through the relationship which existed between him and the weaker, gained some gift or advantage for himself. Sometimes the relationship is such as to raise a presumption of undue influence, such as parent over child, solicitor over client, doctor over patient, spiritual adviser over follower. At other times a relationship of confidence must be proved to exist. But to all of them the general principle obtains which was stated by Lord Chelmsford L.C. in *Tate v. Williamson* (1866), 2 Ch. App. 55, 61:

> Wherever the persons stand in such a relation that, while it continues, confidence is necessarily reposed by one, and the influence which naturally grows out of that confidence is possessed by the other, and this confidence is abused, or the influence is exerted to obtain an advantage at the expense of the confiding party, the person so availing himself of his position will not be permitted to retain the advantage, although the transaction could not have been impeached if no such confidential relation had existed.

[18] The fourth category is that of "undue pressure." The most apposite of that is *Williams v. Bayley* (1866), L.R. 1 H.L. 200, where a son forged his father's name to a promissory note, and, by means of it, raised money from the bank of which they were both customers. The bank said to the father, in effect: "Take your choice — give us security for your son's debt. If you do take that on yourself, then it will all go smoothly; if you do not, we shall be bound to exercise pressure." Thereupon the father charged his property to the bank with payment of the note. The House of Lords held that the charge was invalid because of undue pressure exerted by the bank. Lord Westbury said: A contract to give security for the debt of another, which is a contract without consideration, is, above all things, a contract that should be based upon the free and voluntary agency of the individual who enters into it.

free agency to sign K

[19] Other instances of undue pressure are where one party stipulates for an unfair advantage to which the other has no option but to submit. As where an employer — the stronger party — had employed a builder — the weaker party — to do work for him. When the builder asked for payment of sums properly due (so as to pay his workmen) the employer refused to pay unless he was given some added advantage. Stuart V.C. said:

> Where an agreement, hard and inequitable in itself, has been exacted under circumstances of pressure on the part of the person who exacts it this Court will set it aside.

[20] See . . . *D & C Builders Ltd. v. Rees.*

[21] The fifth category is that of salvage agreements. When a vessel is in danger of sinking and seeks help, the rescuer is in a strong bargaining position. The vessel in distress is in urgent need. The parties cannot be truly said to be on equal terms. The Court of Admiralty have always recognised that fact. The fundamental rule is:

rule:
> If the parties have made an agreement, the Court will enforce it, unless it be manifestly unfair and unjust; but if it be manifestly unfair and unjust, the Court will disregard it and decree what is fair and just.

[22] See . . . *The Port Caledonia and The Anna*, [1903] P. 184, when the rescuer refused to help with a rope unless he was paid £1,000.

[23] 5. *The general principles*. Gathering all together, I would suggest that through all these instances there runs a single thread. They rest on "inequality of bargaining power." By virtue of it, the English law gives relief to one who, without independent advice, enters into a contract on terms which are very unfair or transfers property for a consideration which is grossly inadequate, when his bargaining power is grievously impaired by reason of his own needs or desires, or by his own ignorance or infirmity, coupled with undue influences or pressures brought to bear on him by or for the benefit of the other. When I use the word "undue" I do not mean to suggest that the principle depends on proof of any wrongdoing. The one who stipulates for an unfair advantage may be moved solely by his own self-interest, unconscious of the distress he is bringing to the other. I have also avoided any reference to the will of the one being "dominated" or "overcome" by the other. One who is in extreme need may knowingly consent to a most improvident bargain, solely to relieve the straits in which he finds himself. Again, I do not mean to suggest that every transaction is saved by independent advice. But the absence of it may be fatal. With these explanations, I hope this principle will be found to reconcile the cases. Applying it to the present case, I would notice these points. *law protects weak*

[24] (1) The consideration moving from the bank was grossly inadequate. The son's company was in serious difficulty. The overdraft was at its limit of £10,000. The bank considered that their existing security was insufficient. In order to get further security, they asked the father to charge the house — his sole asset — to the uttermost. It was worth £10,000. The charge was for £11,000. That was for the benefit of the bank. But not at all for the benefit of the father, or indeed for the company. The bank did not promise to continue the overdraft or to increase it. On the contrary, they required the overdraft to be reduced. All that the company gained was a short respite from impending doom.

[25] (2) The relationship between the bank and the father was one of trust and confidence. The bank knew that the father relied on them implicitly to advise him about the transaction. The father trusted the bank. This gave the bank much influence on the father. Yet the bank failed in that trust. They allowed the father to charge the house to his ruin.

[26] (3) The relationship between the father and the son was one where the father's natural affection had much influence on him.

[27] (4) He would naturally desire to accede to his son's request. He trusted his son. There was a conflict of interest between the bank and the father. Yet the bank did not realise it. Nor did they suggest that the father should get independent advice. If the father had gone to his solicitor — or to any man of business — there is no doubt that any one of them would say: "You must not enter into this transaction. You are giving up your house, your sole remaining asset, for no benefit to you. The company is in such a parlous state that you must not do it."

[28] These considerations seem to me to bring this case within the principles I have stated. But, in case that principle is wrong, I would also say that the case falls within the category of undue influence of the second class stated by Cotton L.J. in *Allcard v. Skinner*. I have no doubt that the assistant bank manager acted in the utmost good faith and was straightforward and genuine. Indeed the father said so. But beyond doubt he was acting in the interests of the bank — to get further security for a bad debt. There was such a relationship of trust and confidence between them that the bank ought not to have swept up his sole remaining asset into their hands — for nothing — without his having independent advice. I would therefore allow this appeal.

SIR ERIC SACHS: — **[29]** At trial in the county court a number of complex defences were raised, ranging from *non est factum*, through undue influence and absence of consideration to negligence in, and improper exercise of, the bank's duty when contracting for the sale of the relevant property. It is thus at the outset appropriate to record that in this court no challenge has been offered to any of the conclusions of the learned county court judge on law or on fact save as regards one aspect of one of the defences — appropriately pleaded as undue influence. As regards that defence, however, it is clear that he vitally misapprehended the law and the points to be considered and that moreover he apparently fell into error — as his own notes disclose — on an important fact touching that issue. In the result this court is thus faced with a task that is far from being easy.

[30] The first and most troublesome issue which here falls for consideration is whether on the particular and somewhat unusual facts of the case the bank was, when obtaining his signatures on 17th December 1969, in a relationship with the defendant that entailed a duty on their part of what can for convenience be called fiduciary care. (The phrase "fiduciary care" is used to avoid the confusion with the common-law duty of care — a different field of our jurisprudence.)

[31] As was pointed out in *Tufton v. Sperni*, [1952] 2 T.L.R. 516, 522, the relationships which result in such a duty must not be circumscribed by reference to defined limits; it is necessary to

> refute the suggestion that, to create the relationship of confidence, the person owing a duty must be found clothed in the recognizable garb of a guardian trustee, solicitor, priest, doctor, manager, or the like.

× facts imp

[32] Everything depends on the particular facts, and such a relationship has been held to exist in unusual circumstances as between purchaser and vendor, as between great uncle and adult nephew, and in other widely differing sets of circumstances. Moreover, it is neither feasible nor desirable to attempt closely to define the relationship, or its characteristics, or the demarcation line showing the exact transition point where a relationship that does not entail that duty passes into one that does. . . .

duty in relshp.

[33] On the other hand, whilst disclaiming any intention of seeking to catalogue the elements of such a special relationship, it is perhaps of a little assistance to note some of those which have in the past frequently been found to exist where the court had been led to decide that this relationship existed as between adults of sound mind. Such cases tend to arise where someone relies on the guidance or advice of another, where the other is aware of that reliance and where the person on whom reliance is placed obtains, or may well obtain, a benefit from the transaction or has some other interest in it being concluded. In addition, there must, of course, be shown to exist a vital element which in this judgment will for convenience be referred to as confidentiality. It is this element which is so impossible to define and which is a matter for the judgment of the court on the facts of any particular case.

[34] [Confidentiality], a relatively little used word, is being here adopted, albeit with some hesitation, to avoid the possible confusion that can arise through referring to "confidence." Reliance on advice can in many circumstances be said to import that type of confidence which only results in a common law duty to take care — a duty which may co-exist with but is not coterminous with that of fiduciary care. "Confidentiality" is intended to convey that extra quality in the relevant confidence that is implicit in the phrase "confidential relationship" . . . and may perhaps have something in common with "confiding" and also "confidant" when, for instance, referring to someone's "man of affairs." It imports some quality beyond that inherent in the confidence that can well exist between trustworthy persons who in business affairs deal with each other at arm's length. It is one of the features of this element that once it exists, influence naturally grows out of it. . . .

[35] It was inevitably conceded on behalf of the bank that the relevant relationship can arise as between banker and customer. Equally, it was inevitably conceded on behalf of the defendant that in the normal course of transactions by which a customer guarantees a third party's obligations, the relationship does not arise. The onus of proof lies on the customer who alleges that in any individual case the line has been crossed and the relationship has arisen.

[36] Before proceeding to examine the position further, it is as well to dispose of some points on which confusion is apt to arise. Of these the first is one which plainly led to misapprehension on the part of the learned county court judge. Undue influence is a phrase which is commonly regarded — even in the eyes of a number of lawyers — as relating solely to occasions when the will of one person has become so dominated by that of another that, to use the learned county court judge's words, "the person acts as the mere puppet of the dominator." Such occasions, of course, fall within what Cotton L.J. in *Allcard v. Skinner* described as the first class of cases to which the doctrine on undue influence applies. There is, however, a second class of such cases. This is referred to by Cotton L.J. as follows:

In the second class of cases the Court interferes, not on the ground that any wrongful act has in fact been committed by the donee, but on the ground of public policy, and to prevent the relations which existed between the parties and the influence arising therefrom being abused.

[37] It is thus to be emphasised that as regards the second class the exercise of the court's jurisdiction to set aside the relevant transaction does not depend on proof of one party being "able to dominate the other as though a puppet" (to use the words again adopted by the learned county court judge when testing whether the defence was established) nor any wrongful intention on the part of the person who gains a benefit from it, but on the concept that once the special relationship has been shown to exist, no benefit can be retained from the transaction unless it has been positively established that the duty of fiduciary care has been entirely fulfilled. To this second class, however, the learned judge never averted and plainly never directed his mind. It is also to be noted that what constitutes fulfilment of that duty (the second issue in the case now under consideration) depends again on the facts before the court. It may in the particular circumstances entail that the person in whom confidence has been reposed should insist on independent advice being obtained or ensuring in one way or another that the person being asked to execute a document is not insufficiently informed of some factor which could affect his judgment. The duty has been well stated as being one to ensure that the person liable to be influenced has formed "an independent *and informed* judgment," or to use the phraseology of Lord Evershed M.R. in *Zamet v. Hyman*, [1961] 3 All E.R. 933, 938, "after full, free *and informed* thought." (The italics in each case are mine.) As to the difficulties in which a person may be placed and as to what he should do when there is a conflict of interest between him and the person asked to execute a document, see *Bank of Montreal v. Stuart*, [1911] A.C. 120, 139.

free informed thought [handwritten margin note]

[38] Stress was placed in argument for the bank on the effect of the word "abused" as it appears in the above cited passage in the judgment of Cotton L.J. and in other judgments and textbooks. As regards the second class of undue influence, however, that word in the context means no more than that once the existence of a special relationship has been established, then any possible use of the relevant influence is, irrespective of the intentions of the persons possessing it, regarded in relation to the transaction under consideration as an abuse — unless and until the duty of fiduciary care has been shown to be fulfilled or the transaction is shown to be truly for the benefit of the person influenced. This approach is a matter of public policy.

[39] One further point on which potential confusion emerged in the course of the helpful addresses of counsel stemmed from submissions to the effect that Mr. Head, the assistant bank manager, should be cleared of all blame in the matter. When one has to deal with claims of breach of either common-law or fiduciary care, it is not unusual to find that counsel for a big corporation tends to try and focus the attention of the court on the responsibility of the employee who deals with the particular matter rather than on that of the corporation as an entity. What we are concerned with in the present case is whether the element of confidentiality has been established as against the bank; Mr. Head's part in the affair is but one link in a chain of events. Moreover, when it comes to a question of the relevant knowledge which will have to be discussed later in this judgment, it is the knowl-

edge of the bank and not merely the personal knowledge of Mr. Head that has to be examined.

[40] Having discussed the nature of the issues to which the learned county court judge should have directed his mind, it is now convenient to turn to the evidence relating to the first of them — whether the special relationship has here been shown to exist at the material time.

[41] Counsel for the bank stressed the paucity of the evidence given by the defendant as to any reliance placed by him on the bank's advice — and, a fortiori, as to its quality. In cases of the type under consideration the paucity, or sometimes absence, of such evidence may well occur; moreover such evidence, if adduced, can be suspect. In the present case it is manifest that at the date of the trial the defendant's recollection of what happened was so minimal as to be unreliable, though not the slightest attack was made on his honesty. Indeed, his condition at trial was such that his sketchy proof was admitted into evidence. The learned judge's references to him as "poor old Mr. Bundy" and to his "obvious incapacity" are in point on this aspect of the matter. It is not surprising in such a case for the result to depend on the success of the cross-examination of some witness called for the party against whom the special relationship is pleaded.

[42] Prime reliance was accordingly placed by counsel for the defendant on answers given by Mr. Head when under cross-examination by junior counsel for the defendant. In the forefront came an answer which, unfortunately, was misapprehended by the learned judge, who thus came to make a vitally erroneous entry in his notebook. That answer as amended, after trial and judgment, in the notes before us, with the assent of the judge, is agreed to have been: "I would think the defendant relied on me implicitly to advise him about the transaction as Bank Manager." It is to be observed that in the judge's original note there is to be found the following, which was erased when the above quoted answer was substituted: Q. "Defendant relied on you to advise *Company* as to the position in the transaction?" A. "No." (The italicising of the word "Company" is mine — to emphasise the distinction between the answer as noted and the answer not agreed to have been given.)

[43] In the face of that vital answer, counsel for the bank found it necessary to submit that the words "as bank manager" were intended to confine the reliance to the explaining of the legal effect of the document and the sums involved as opposed to more general advice as a confidant. I reject that submission. Taking Mr. Head's evidence as a whole, it seems plain that the defendant was, for instance, worried about, considered material, and asked questions about the company's affairs and the state of its accounts; and was thus seeking and being given advice on the viability of the company as a factor to be taken into account. (The vital bearing of this factor on the wisdom of the transaction is discussed later in this judgment.) Moreover, the answer to the judge followed immediately after: "Q. Conflict of interest?" "A. No, it didn't occur to me at that time. I always thought there was no conflict of interest." That question and answer (which was in itself immediately preceded by questions on the company's viability) do more than merely indicate a failure on the part of Mr. Head to understand the position; they indicate that at that stage of the cross-examination the questions being addressed to Mr. Head related to the wider issue of the wisdom of the transaction.

[44] Moreover, what happened on 17th December 1969 has to be assessed in the light of the general background of the existence of the long-standing relations between the Bundy family and the bank. It not infrequently occurs in provincial and country branches of great banks that a relationship is built up over the years, and in due course the senior officials may become trusted counsellors of customers of whose affairs they have an intimate knowledge. Confidential trust is placed in them because of a combination of status, goodwill and knowledge. Mr. Head was the last of a relevant chain of those who over the years had earned or inherited, such trust whilst becoming familiar with the finance and business of the Bundys and the relevant company; he had taken over the accounts from Mr. Bennett (a former assistant manager at Salisbury) of whom the defendant said: "I always trusted him."

[45] The fact that the defendant may later have referred to Mr. Head as being "straight" is not inconsistent with this view — see also the statement of Mr. Trethowan, that: "Defendant is straightforward. Agrees with anyone." Indeed more than one passage in the defendant's evidence is consistent with Mr. Head's vital answer as to the implicit reliance placed on his advice.

[46] It is, of course, plain that when Mr. Head was asking the defendant to sign the documents, the bank would derive benefit from the signature, that there was a conflict of interest as between the bank and the defendant, that the bank gave him advice, that he relied on that advice, and that the bank knew of the reliance. The further question is whether on the evidence concerning the matters already recited there was also established that element of confidentiality which has been discussed. In my judgment it is thus established. Moreover reinforcement for that view can be derived from some of the material which it is more convenient to examine in greater detail when considering what the resulting duty of fiduciary care entailed.

[47] What was required to be done on the bank's behalf once the existence of that duty is shown to have been established? The situation of the defendant in his sitting-room at Yew Tree Farm can be stated as follows. He was faced by three persons anxious for him to sign. There was his son Michael, the overdraft of whose company had been, as is shown by the correspondence, escalating rapidly; whose influence over his father was observed by the judge — and can hardly not have been realised by the bank; and whose ability to overcome the difficulties of his company was plainly doubtful, indeed its troubles were known to Mr. Head to be "deep-seated." There was Mr. Head, on behalf of the bank, coming with the documents designed to protect the bank's interest already substantially made out and in his pocket. There was Michael's wife asking Mr. Head to help her husband.

[48] The documents which the defendant was being asked to sign could result, if the company's troubles continued, in the defendant's sole asset being sold, the proceeds all going to the bank, and his being left penniless in his old age. That he could thus be rendered penniless was known to the bank — and in particular to Mr. Head. That the company might come to a bad end quite soon with these results was not exactly difficult to deduce (less than four months later, on 3rd April 1970, the bank were insisting that Yew Tree Farm be sold).

[49] The situation was thus one which to any reasonably sensible person, who gave it but a moment's thought, cried aloud the defendant's need for careful independent advice. Over and above the need any man has for counsel when asked to risk his last penny on even an apparently reasonable project, was the need here for informed advice as to whether there was any real chance of the company's affairs becoming viable if the documents were signed. If not, there arose questions such as, what is the use of taking the risk of becoming penniless without benefiting any-one but the bank; is it not better both for you and your son that you, at any rate, should still have some money when the crash comes; and should not the bank at least bind itself to hold its hand for some given period? The answers to such questions could only be given in the light of a worthwhile appraisement of the company's affairs — without which the defendant could not come to an *informed judgment* as to the wisdom of what he was doing.

[50] No such advice to get an independent opinion was given; on the contrary, Mr. Head chose to give his own views on the company's affairs and to take this course, though he had at trial to admit: "I did not explain the company's affairs very fully as I had only just taken over." (Another answer that escaped entry in the learned judge's original notes.)

[51] On the above recited facts, the breach of the duty to take fiduciary care is manifest. It is not necessary for the defendant to rely on another factor tending to show such a breach. The bank knew full well that the defendant had a well-known solicitor of standing. Mr. Trethowan, who usually advised him on important matters, including the previous charge signed in May 1969, only seven months earlier. Indeed, on that occasion the bank seems very properly to have taken steps which either ensured that Mr. Trethowan's advice was obtained or at least assumed it was being obtained. It is no answer that Mr. Head, relatively a newcomer to the Bundy accounts at the Salisbury branch, may not personally have known these matters; it is the bank's knowledge that is material. Incidentally, Mr. Head discussed the relevant accounts with his manager.

[52] The existence of the duty and its breach having thus been established, there remains the submission urged by counsel for the bank that whatever independent advice had been obtained the defendant would have been so obstinately determined to help his son that the documents would anyway have been signed. The point fails for more than one reason, of which it is sufficient to mention two. First, on a question of fact it ignores the point that the independent advice might well have been to the effect that it would benefit the son better in the event of an almost inevitable crash if his father had some money left after it occurred — advice which could have affected the mind of the defendant. Secondly, once the relevant duty is established, it is contrary to public policy that benefit of the transaction be retained by the person under the duty unless he positively shows that the duty of fiduciary care has been fulfilled: there is normally no room for debate on the issue as to what would have happened had the care been taken. It follows that the county court judgment cannot stand. The learned judge having failed to direct his mind to a crucial issue and to important evidence supporting the defendant's case thereon, at the very least the latter is entitled to an order for a new trial. That would produce as an outcome of this appeal a prolongation of uncertainties affecting others beside the defendant, who still resides at Yew Tree Farm, and could hardly be called desirable even if one left out of account the latter's health and financial position. In my judgment, however, a breach by the bank of their duty to take fiduciary care has, on the evidence, as a whole been so affirmatively established that this

court can and should make an order setting aside the guarantee and the charge of 17th December 1969.   conflict of interest → not aware

[53] I would add that Mr. Head, was of course, not guilty of any intentional wrongful act. In essence what happened was that having gone to Yew Tree Farm "in the interests of the bank" (as counsel for the bank stressed more than once), he failed to apprehend that there was a conflict of interest as between the bank and the defendant, that he should have insisted on the obvious need for independent advice. In addition, it was unfortunate that he was — through some absence of relevant information from Mr. Bennett (who had previously dealt with the relevant accounts) — not aware of the way Mr. Trethowan had come to advise the defendant as regards the May 1969 guarantee and charge. Though I have not founded any part of this judgment on that facet of the case, I am yet inclined to view the bank's failure to suggest that Mr. Trethowan be consulted when they were pursuing their quest for the defendant's signature in such a potentially disastrous situation, as open to criticism and as something that might of itself have led to an adverse decision against the bank in this particular case.

[54] The conclusion that the defendant has established that as between himself and the bank the relevant transaction fell within the second category of undue influence cases referred to by Cotton L.J. in *Allcard v. Skinner* is one reached on the single issue pursued on behalf of the defendant in this court. On that issue we have had the benefit of cogent and helpful submissions on matter plainly raised in the pleadings. As regards the wider areas covered in masterly survey in the judgment of Lord Denning M.R., but not raised *arguendo*, I do not venture to express an opinion — though having some sympathy with the views that the courts should be able to give relief to a party who has been subject to undue pressure as defined in the concluding passage of his judgment on that point.

[55] There remains to mention that counsel for the bank whilst conceding that the relevant special relationship could arise as between banker and customer, urged in somewhat doom-laden terms that a decision taken against the bank on the facts of this particular case would seriously affect banking practice. With all respect to that submission, it seems necessary to point out that nothing in this judgment affects the duties of a bank in the normal case where it is obtaining a guarantee, and in accordance with standard practice explains to the person about to sign its legal effect and the sums involved. When, however, a bank, as in this case, goes further and advises on more general matters germane to the wisdom of the transaction, that indicates that it may — not necessarily must — be crossing the line into the area of confidentiality so that the court may then have to examine all the facts, including, of course, the history leading up to the transaction, to ascertain whether or not that line has, as here, been crossed. It would indeed be rather odd if a bank which vis-à-vis a customer attained a special relationship in some ways akin to that of a "man of affairs" — something which can be a matter of pride and enhance his local reputation — should not where a conflict of interest has arisen as between itself and the person advised be under the resulting duty now under discussion. Once, as was inevitably conceded, it is possible for a bank to be under that duty, it is, as in the present case, simply a question for meticulous examination" of the particular facts to see whether that duty has arisen. On the special facts here it did arise and it has been broken. . . .

[**CAIRNS L.J.** agreed with **SIR ERIC SACHS**.]

QUESTIONS AND NOTES

1. It is not clear from the report what happened to Mr. Bundy. The early charges, total-ling £7,500, were apparently still valid, and the Bank would eventually be entitled to obtain this amount, but since these charges were probably worth less than the market value of the house, the Bank would not have the same right to immediate sale and pos-session of the house that it was trying to exercise.

2. What was the most important fact in Lord Denning's analysis; in Sir Eric Sachs's?

3. Consider how Lord Denning derived the principle of "inequality of bargaining power". Was this process legitimate? Is the process normal in the development of the common law? Does it pose risks to the process of adjudication? Does it pose the dan-ger of affecting retroactively the rights of parties who may have conducted themselves in accordance with what they believed the law to be? Are the issues raised by its use beyond the competence of a court?

4. Notice the range of facts considered by Sir Eric Sachs. He said:

    > It not infrequently occurs in provincial and country branches of great banks that a relationship is built up over the years, and in due course the senior offi-cials may become trusted counsellors of customers of whose affairs they have an intimate knowledge. Confidential trust is placed in them because of a com-bination of status, goodwill and knowledge.

    There was no evidence that this fact was proved to the court. Sir Eric Sachs, presuma-bly, took judicial notice of it. It is probably true, but its truth was not tested in the normal way. Is this practice appropriate in the judicial process?
    You are counsel to a person in the position of Mr. Bundy. How will you show the court that banks invite trust and confidence? Will you put in photographs of marble banking halls and copies of bank advertising?
    As counsel for the bank, how will you meet such tactics? Can you argue that banks do not invite trust?

5. The development of the doctrine of unconscionability by Canadian courts now brings within that doctrine (and the tests for its applicability) a number of what were before disparate pockets of the law. The control of the parties' (or one party's) power to stipulate the remedy payable on breach is one example (see, *e.g.*, the decision of the Ontario Court of Appeal in *Peachtree II, supra*); the control over clauses allocating the risks of loss is another (see, *e.g.*, *Hunter Engineering*).

6. The Alberta *Guarantees Acknowledgment Act*, R.S.A. 2000, c. G-11, provides in s. 3 that a person must attend before a notary to acknowledge his guarantee before it is en-forceable against him. Do you think that this provision is likely to do much to deal with the problems of guarantees?   *who benefits?*

7. Contracts of guarantee have always caused difficulties for two reasons:

    (a) the person giving the guarantee is often not the person directly benefiting from it; and

    (b) when the creditor calls on the guarantee, the debtor will usually be insolvent and the guarantor may well be facing personal bankruptcy. At that point he or she has a strong incentive to fight the creditor in court because otherwise everything is lost, and (who knows?), perhaps the guarantee will be set aside.

    The test of unconscionability used by Lord Denning M.R. and the very different test developed by Sir Eric Sachs are tailor-made for use by guarantors.
    Consider also the incentives that operate on bank employees. Bank employees have incentives to make loans, and banks will compete for the chance to lend to a prospec-tive borrower — recall the desire of the Toronto-Dominion Bank to lend to a subsidi-ary so as to get some business from its parent, as illustrated by *Toronto-Dominion Bank v. Leigh Instruments Ltd. (Trustee of)* (1999), 45 O.R. (3d) 417, 178 D.L.R.

(4th) 634 (C.A.), which led the bank to accept the latter's letter of comfort, reproduced in Chapter 2, and the evidence of the desire of the large commercial banks to lend to Enron. When a loan shows signs of turning bad — euphemistically referred to as a "special loan" — banks and their employees have incentives to collect. (These incentives sometimes lead bank employees to do things that get the bank into even more problems. In *Murano v. Bank of Montreal* (1998), 41 O.R. (3d) 222, 163 D.L.R. (4th) 21 (C.A.), the bank was made liable for about $4 million in damages as a result of not giving its customer adequate notice before a receiver was appointed. In *Royal Bank of Canada v. W. Got & Associates Electric Ltd.*, [1999] 3 S.C.R. 408, 178 D.L.R. (4th) 385 (noted in Chapter 1), the bank was held liable for punitive damages for not being forthright in the affidavit submitted in support of its application for the appointment of a receiver of its customer's business.)

It may be that Mr. Head, the Lloyds Bank employee in *Lloyds Bank v. Bundy*, was under strong pressure from his superiors at the bank to get security for the loan to Mr. Bundy's son. Mr. Head would presumably get no "credit" for making the loan, but only for enforcing it. Not even the principal debtor, the son, got much benefit from the final charge, only a short (and unspecified) extension of time to pay the demand loan.

8. In *Manulife Bank of Canada v. Conlin*, [1996] 3 S.C.R. 415, 139 D.L.R. (4th) 426, the Supreme Court of Canada refused to enforce a guarantee signed by the mortgagor's husband because the bank failed to have him acknowledge his obligation on a renewal of the mortgage after he and his wife had separated. It is reasonably certain that the interpretation of the guarantee by the Court — there was a very strong dissent — caught most institutional creditors by surprise: it represented a very technical approach to guarantees. Like all guarantees given by the principal shareholder of a corporation and his or her spouse, the bank's standard guarantee provided that (i) the guarantor was liable, not just as a guarantor but as a "principal debtor", and (ii) the guarantor would not be released if the mortgage was renewed. Clause 7 of the guarantee dealt with this last point and provided (at para. 17, in language which gives a flavour of a standard bank guarantee):

> PROVIDED that no extension of time given by the Mortgagee to the Mortgagor, or anyone claiming under it, or any other dealing by the Mortgagee with the owner of the equity of redemption of said lands, shall in any way affect or prejudice the rights of the Mortgagee against the Mortgagor or any other person liable for the payment of the monies hereby secured, and that this Mortgage may be renewed by an agreement in writing for any term with or without an increased rate of interest, or amended from time to time as to any of its terms including without limitation increasing the interest rate or principal amount notwithstanding that there may be subsequent encumbrances. And it shall not be necessary to register any such agreement in order to retain the priority of this Mortgage so altered over any instrument delivered or registered subsequent to this Mortgage.

The Court narrowly construed the provision that the guarantor was a principal debtor, not (only) a surety, and that the guarantee was to remain in force "notwithstanding the giving of time for payment of this mortgage" or a renewal. Cory J. outlined his "principles of interpretation" and said:

> [7] In many if not most cases of guarantees a contract of adhesion is involved. That is to say the document is drawn by the lending institution on a standard form. The borrower and the guarantor have little or no part in the negotiation of the agreement. They have no choice but to comply with its terms if the loan is to be granted. Often the guarantors are family members with limited commercial experience. As a matter of accommodation for a family member or friend they sign the guarantee. Many guarantors are unsophisticated and vulnerable. Yet the guarantee extended as a favour may result in a financial tragedy for the guarantor. If the submissions of the bank are accepted, it will mean in effect that a guarantor, without the benefit of notice or any further consid-

eration, will be bound indefinitely to further mortgages signed by the mortgagor at varying rates of interest and terms. The guarantor is without any control over the situation. . . .

[8] In my view, it is eminently fair that if there is any ambiguity in the terms used in the guarantee, the words of the documents should be construed against the party which drew it, by applying the *contra proferentem* rule. This is a sensible and satisfactory way of approaching the situation since the lending institutions that normally draft these agreements can readily amend their documents to ensure that they are free from ambiguity. . . .

Why wouldn't all these arguments apply to insureds like Mr. and Mrs. Scott, in *Scott v. Wawanesa*, when they claimed to be entitled to an indemnity when their house burnt down?

9. You are counsel to a bank. You have been asked to draft a set of instructions (to be included in the bank's manual of standard-form letters and operating guidelines for managers and loan officers) to reflect the decision of the English Court of Appeal in *Lloyds Bank v. Bundy*. Draft the requested instructions.

10. In the years following *Lloyds Bank v. Bundy* there were many cases in which guarantors sought to escape their obligations by alleging either that the loan agreement or guarantee was unconscionable or that there had been a breach of a fiduciary obligation.

    In the typical small business situation the business will be financed by a bank loan. This loan will be secured on all the assets of the business: the land, buildings, equipment, inventory and accounts receivable. In addition, the bank will almost always require the personal guarantee — and the standard bank guarantee is a pretty fearsome document, honed to fine effectiveness — of the owner and security over his or her property. It is common for spouses to own the family home in joint tenancy (and even if they did not, family legislation of many provinces gives both spouses rights in the matrimonial home). From the bank's point of view, the security that the owner of the business can provide is not worth very much if his or her spouse does not also guarantee the loans and join in the security agreement. As a matter of practice when a small business collapses, the assets of the owner and his or her spouse (or parent) will go to the bank, just as Lloyds Bank claimed "Yew Tree Farm". When the bank threatens to sue on the spouse's (usually the wife's) personal guarantee and to take the family home, the spouse has little to lose by alleging that the guarantee and security are unenforceable. In this sense, and except for the fact that it was the debtor's father and not his wife who was threatened by the bank, *Lloyds Bank v. Bundy* is a typical hard case.

11. While *Lloyds Bank v. Bundy* is a "famous" case, it has not been extensively applied by Canadian courts. Some Canadian courts held that banks owed fiduciary or other onerous duties to their customers or guarantors, and a number of guarantees were held to be unenforceable on that basis. The pattern was, however, not even, but it did encourage the banks to require those signing guarantees to obtain "independent legal advice".

    It is common now for banks and other lenders to require spouses and other non-business guarantors to get a certificate of "independent legal advice". Such a certificate is often contained on a standard letter drafted by the bank, to be signed by the guarantor and her solicitor. The letter will usually state that the transaction has been fully explained by the solicitor and is understood by the guarantor. What kinds of issues are raised by this practice? What would you, as a solicitor, have to do to feel confident that you had properly discharged your obligation to your client? What options, practically speaking, does a wife who is asked by her husband to sign a guarantee have? What will happen if she refuses? Can you advise her that she should not sign, and at the same time respond adequately to her needs? How do you protect yourself from the risk of liability to either the bank or your client?

"CONDUCT AND ETHICS: INDEPENDENT LEGAL ADVICE NEVER ROUTINE"

Ontario Lawyers Gazette, Vol. 1, No.1 (1997), pp. 7-9

[1]   For many lawyers, independent legal advice is viewed as a routine task that takes less than 30 minutes and results in a bill of about $50. The person seeking the advice isn't really seen to be a client, which gives lawyers an excuse to do the kind of work they would never dream of doing for their regular clients.

[2]   But such attitudes consistently get lawyers into trouble. Independent legal advice that is rushed and fails to ensure that the client truly understands the transaction in question serves no one, including the lawyer giving the advice.

[3]   Lawyers who fail to follow certain rules when giving independent legal advice — even if the client has already made a decision and wants it rubber stamped — could find themselves making a claim to the Lawyers' Professional Indemnity Company if the transaction doesn't work out as the client had planned.

[4]   By treating independent legal advice more seriously, lawyers are protecting clients from a potentially troublesome situation and themselves from higher insurance premiums. Independent legal advice is given in situations where a conflict of interest could arise if a party to a transaction doesn't obtain an opinion from a lawyer who's not involved in the matter. Giving inadequate independent legal advice can be as problematic as failing to send a client to another lawyer.

[5]   Some of the relatively common situations that call for independent legal advice are:

In a matrimonial dispute, where both spouses consult the same lawyer during the drawing up of a separation agreement. Where beneficiaries to an estate are involved in a disagreement. Where a lending institution has a fiduciary relation with a borrower or a risky investment is being considered. Situations involving the elderly, the infirm, the uneducated and unrepresented parties.

[6]   When sending a party on for independent legal advice, it's not adequate to refer them to an associate or partner. In fact, the Ontario Court of Appeal prohibited this in *Bertolo v. Bank of Montreal* (1987), 57 O.R. (2d) 577. It's best to provide the person with a list of a few names of lawyers practising in the relevant area of law.

[7]   Various lawyers have written extensively on independent legal advice and how it should be given. They all say that merely asking the client if he or she understands the document in question is not sufficient to satisfy the minimum requirements of independent legal advice.

[8]   It's advised that in addition to ensuring that the client understands the nature and effect of the document, the lawyer should be aware of all of the relevant circumstances surrounding the transaction and be able to explain them to the client; be aware of the client's financial situation to determine what impact the transaction will have on the client; and be competent in the area of law in question.

[9]   When determining the amount of financial information that needs to be obtained before giving advice, the lawyer should consider the client's age; the level of sophistication and experience of the client; the nature of the transaction; the

relationship of the parties involved; the degree of risk to the client; the lawyer's previous experience with the client; the motivation of the client and others involved in the transaction; and the bargaining power between the parties.

[10] Language is important. If the lawyer is not proficient in the language of the client, an interpreter is necessary to ensure the client fully understands the transaction. The interpreter must be a neutral party. A family member should never be asked to interpret during the giving of independent legal advice because the reliability of his or her interpretation can later be called into question.

[11] In all cases, regardless of a language barrier, information should be relayed to clients in a simple and understandable manner. Before the document is signed, clients should be able to explain, in their own words, their understanding of the transaction.

[12] It's important to be satisfied that the client is exercising free will and judgment. There are a number of relationships that could lead to a presumption of undue influence. While there is no presumption of undue influence in situations involving an employer and employee, or a husband and wife, it doesn't mean that it can't be proven. If a lawyer is not convinced that the client is exercising free will and judgment, the certificate of independent legal advice probably shouldn't be signed — even if that goes against the client's wishes. In cases where a lawyer advises against the signing of the documents in question but agrees to sign the certificate of independent legal advice because the client wishes to proceed, a witness should be present while the lawyer explains the advice. The client, preferably with the witness present, should sign an acknowledgment stating that the document is being signed against the lawyer's advice.

[13] A retainer to provide independent legal advice shouldn't be accepted if issues are involved beyond the lawyer's experience and understanding — for example, if general accounting advice is needed.

Independent Legal Advice Procedure

[14] When giving independent legal advice, a number of steps should be followed:

Open a file. You should be certain that copies of all of the documents signed by the client are included in the file. Other material that should be placed in the file include your notes on the factual background of the matter, the financial disclosure given, and the details of what occurred in the interview. Confirm advice given to the client in writing. Carefully docket time spent on the file. Carefully review the certificate of legal advice that's presented by the client. In some situations, it may be preferable for you to write a letter outlining the independent legal advice that was given, rather than signing the certificate. Accept payment from the client — not from someone with an interest that's contrary to that of the client.

The following decision of the Ontario Court of Appeal gives some direction on what a bank should do in order to ensure that it has an enforceable guarantee. The Supreme Court gave leave to appeal on 7 December 2000, but the parties thoughtlessly filed a notice of discontinuance on 2 August 2001, presumably because they had reached a settlement.

BANK OF MONTREAL v. DUGUID

[2000] O.J. No. 1356, 47 O.R. (3d) 737, 185 D.L.R. (4th) 458
(C.A., McMurtry C.J.O., Osborne A.C.J.O. and Feldman J.A.)

[The facts are taken from the judgment of **FELDMAN J.A.** (dissenting)]

[30] The Bank of Montreal appeals from the judgment of Day J. [reported (1997), 32 B.L.R. (2d) 35] dismissing its action against Mrs. Duguid to enforce a promissory note which she executed as co-signor of a loan made by the Bank to her husband. Since that time, Mr. and Mrs. Duguid have separated. Mr. Duguid went through bankruptcy without repaying the Bank. The Bank's appeal seeks judgment against Mrs. Duguid for the amount of $87,243.84 U.S. together with interest from August 21, 1996 at the rate of 1 per cent per cent per annum above the Bank's prime interest rate per annum in effect from time to time.

Facts and Findings of the Trial Judge

[31] In 1989, Mr. Duguid, a school principal, together with a colleague, applied to the Bank for an investment loan for participation in Mountainside LaCosta Limited Partnership, a tax-driven condominium investment in San Diego, California. The Bank was providing financing on the project to qualified investors based solely on the ability of the investor to repay the loan. Although the Bank had investigated the financial viability of the condominium project, the Bank was not relying on the project's viability or value and was taking no security on the loans.

[32] The Bank was not prepared to extend the investment loan of $76,095 U.S. to Mr. Duguid and his associate based only on their combined income and assets. Mr. Duguid therefore asked his wife, a real estate agent, to fax her financial information to the Bank. She did so, following which the Bank was prepared to extend the loan, if Mrs. Duguid was also on the covenant.

[33] Although the Bank officer signed the documents executed by the Duguids as witness, and testified that they had attended her office for that purpose, the Duguids both testified that they signed the documents at home in their kitchen, and not in front of the Bank officer. The trial judge accepted and found that the documents were executed by the Duguids in their kitchen at home and that the Bank officer did not witness their signatures.

[34] It was the written policy of the Bank for this project that it suggest to investors that they obtain independent legal or financial advice. Again, the Bank officer who purported to witness the signatures of the Duguids also testified that she would have advised them to obtain the independent advice, although she had no specific recollection of the closing. Having rejected her evidence, the trial judge found that the Bank did not suggest to Mr. or Mrs. Duguid that either of them obtain independent legal or financial advice.

[35] The trial judge found that the Bank had concerns about the investment arising from the investigation of the financial viability of the project which it had undertaken for the purpose of deciding whether to extend loans to investors. The Bank nonetheless proceeded to grant financing to qualified investors because it wanted to retain the goodwill of the project promoters for future business. However, the Bank made no disclosure to Mrs. Duguid of any of its information or concerns.

[36] It was pointed out by counsel for the appellant that in making his findings, the trial judge erred by referring to an internal document of the Bank which related to a proposal by four specific investors, not including Mr. Duguid. However, it is clear from all of the evidence including other memoranda filed as exhibits, that the Bank considered the project to be a highly speculative investment and noted the high vacancy rate.

[37] The trial judge found that the Bank's knowledge of the problems with the project made it aware that the transaction was disadvantageous to Mr. and Mrs. Duguid. He held that the Bank therefore had a minimum obligation to impart its information about the project to the co-signor, Mrs. Duguid, as it was requiring her to underwrite the risk. He also held that the Bank had a further minimum obligation, because of its specific policy for this investment, to insist that Mrs. Duguid obtain independent legal or financial advice. Because the Bank did neither, the trial judge dismissed its action.

OSBORNE A.C.J.O. (**MCMURTRY C.J.O.** concurring): —

Overview

[1] I have had the advantage of reading the reasons of Feldman J.A., who would dismiss the Bank's appeal but not for the reasons of the trial judge. I agree with Feldman J.A. that the Bank, in these circumstances, was not required to tell its customers (specifically, Mrs. Duguid, a co-signer) of its views on the quality of the investment. I also agree that the Bank's failure to follow its internal policies (specifically, advising Mrs. Duguid to get independent legal or financial advice) is not a basis upon which to dismiss the Bank's action on the note. I cannot, however, agree with my colleague's conclusions on the issue of presumed undue influence.

[2] Mrs. Duguid alleges that the guarantee was procured by the undue influence of her husband; however, she does not seek any relief as against her husband, who is now bankrupt. Rather, she now seeks to set aside the transaction as against a third party, the Bank. The question, then, is in what circumstances a party can set aside a transaction on the ground of undue influence as against a third party to the alleged wrongdoing.

[3] In my view, the relationship between Mr. and Mrs. Duguid in respect of their financial affairs was not a relationship that would trigger a presumption of undue influence when Mrs. Duguid, at her husband's request, co-signed a promissory note (prepared by the Bank). In any case, having regard to the trial evidence, it seems to me that if a presumption of undue influence was established, the presumption was rebutted. Thus, I think that the Bank's appeal should be allowed.

Analysis

[4] As a general proposition, a party may set aside a transaction where that party was induced to enter into the transaction by another's undue influence. Thus, where a husband induces his wife to enter into a transaction by means of undue influence, the wife will be entitled to set aside the transaction as against her husband.

[5] As Feldman J.A. has noted, the House of Lords reviewed the doctrine of undue influence in *Barclays Bank plc v. O'Brien*, [1993] 4 All E.R. 417, [1993] 3 W.L.R. 786. The facts of *O'Brien* are somewhat similar to the facts of this case.

Mr. O'Brien was a shareholder in a company with an unsecured overdraft. He sought an increase to the company's overdraft limit to be secured by a second charge over the matrimonial home owned jointly by him and his wife. The Bank agreed to grant the increase and prepared the necessary documents, which Mr. O'Brien signed. The following day, Mr. O'Brien brought his wife to the Bank so that she could sign. No one explained the transaction or the documents to her or suggested that she receive independent legal advice. Mrs. O'Brien simply signed the documents. Eventually, the company failed and the Bank sought to realize on its security.

[6]   Mrs. O'Brien defended the Bank's action on the ground that she had been induced to sign the agreement by her husband's undue influence. The trial judge found that there was no undue influence and ruled in favour of the Bank. The Court of Appeal granted the wife's appeal, finding that married women providing security for their husbands' debts constituted a specially protected class, requiring the Bank to ensure that the wife received independent legal advice. The House of Lords dismissed the Bank's appeal. While undue influence was not an issue directly before the House of Lords, Lord Browne-Wilkinson reviewed the law regarding undue influence, and noted that there were two different categories of undue influence — actual and presumed. He set out the following classification [at p. 423]:

> *Class 1: actual undue influence*. In these cases it is necessary for the claimant to prove affirmatively that the wrongdoer exerted undue influence on the complainant to enter into the particular transaction which is impugned.
>
> *Class 2: presumed undue influence*. In these cases the complainant only has to show, in the first instance, that there was a relationship of trust and confidence between the complainant and wrongdoer of such a nature that it is fair to presume that the wrongdoer abused that relationship in procuring the complainant to enter into the impugned transaction . . . once a confidential relationship has been proved, the burden shifts to the wrongdoer to prove that the complainant entered into the impugned transaction freely, for example by showing that the complainant had independent advice. Such a confidential relationship may be established in two ways, viz:
>
> *Class 2A*: Certain relationships (for example solicitor and client, medical advisor and patient) as a matter of law raise the presumption that undue influence has been exercised.
>
> *Class 2B*: Even if there is no relationship falling within class 2A, if the complainant proves the de facto existence of a relationship under which the complainant generally reposed trust and confidence in the wrongdoer, the existence of such a relationship raises the presumption of undue influence. In a class 2B case therefore . . . the complainant will succeed in setting aside the impugned transaction merely by proof that the complainant reposed trust and confidence in the wrongdoer. . . .

[7]   Lord Browne-Wilkinson then considered whether the specific relationship of husband and wife, without more, gave rise to a class 2A presumption of undue influence. He found that it did not. However, noting the continued existence of relationships where the wife is still subjected to, and yields to, influence by her husband, he concluded at p. 424 that:

> . . . in any particular case a wife may well be able to demonstrate that de facto she did leave decisions on financial affairs to her husband thereby bringing herself within class 2B . . . Thus, in those cases which still occur where the wife relies in all financial matters on her husband and simply does what he suggests, a presumption

of undue influence within class 2B can be established solely from proof of such trust and influence without proof of actual undue influence.

In my view, it is clear from *O'Brien* that a wife seeking to set aside a transaction on account of undue influence may raise a class 2B presumption of undue influence by demonstrating that her relationship with her husband was one in which she relied on her husband so that it would be reasonable to presume that the transaction in question was procured by the undue influence of her husband. In *O'Brien*, Lord Browne-Wilkinson rejected at p. 428 a "special equity" theory based on the fact of marriage (or cohabitation) that would allow wives to set aside a transaction where they acted as surety for their husbands' debts:

> Should wives (and perhaps others) be accorded special rights in relation to surety transactions by the recognition of a special equity applicable only to such persons engaged in such transactions? Or should they enjoy only the same protection as they would enjoy in relation to their other dealings? *In my judgment, the special equity theory should be rejected. . . . to require the creditor to prove knowledge and understanding by the wife in all cases is to reintroduce by the back door either a presumption of undue influence of class 2A (which has been decisively rejected). . . .* (Emphasis added)

Lord Browne-Wilkinson concluded that it was "not necessary to have recourse to a special equity theory for the proper protection of the legitimate interests of wives," since the combination of the class 2B presumption and the doctrine of constructive notice provided ample protection for such interests.

. . .

[9]   The principles of undue influence outlined in *O'Brien* were affirmed by the Supreme Court of Canada in *Gold v. Rosenberg*, [1997] 3 S.C.R. 767, 152 D.L.R. (4th) 385. *Gold v. Rosenberg* did not concern undue influence or the presumption of undue influence; nor did the Supreme Court of Canada consider Lord Browne-Wilkinson's statement on that issue. In *Gold v. Rosenberg*, a testator left his estate to his son, Rosenberg, and grandson, Gold, as executors and equal beneficiaries. The assets of the estate were held by two companies. Both Rosenberg and Gold were directors of the companies; however, only Rosenberg was involved in the estate's business. Rosenberg arranged a bank loan to a business of his own, secured by a guarantee from one of the estate companies, and supported by a mortgage over the estate company's assets. Gold signed a directors' resolution authorizing the guarantee, and the law firm acting for both parties gave an opinion that the guarantee was valid. Subsequently, Gold brought an action against Rosenberg, the bank, and the law firm, alleging that he had been misled. The trial judge held the bank and law firm liable, finding that the bank had knowingly assisted in a breach of trust. An appeal by the bank was allowed by this court, and a further appeal to the Supreme Court of Canada was dismissed. Sopinka J. referred to *O'Brien* when he considered the bank's duty to enquire. He said, at pp. 799-801:

> In certain circumstances, a third party in the position of the bank will not have discharged its duty to inquire unless the guarantor has been advised to obtain independent legal advice. In certain cases, the law imposes on a creditor a duty to inquire when the transaction is clearly detrimental to the person offering security and the relationship between that person and the principal debtor is particularly close. In such circumstances, the law presumes undue influence on the part of the principal debtor. The clearest type of relationship giving rise to this presumption is that of husband and wife. Iacobucci J. cites *Barclays Bank plc v. O'Brien* . . . in which the House of

[handwritten margin note: ie. principal vs. creditor]

Lords extended this presumption to include cohabitees. Lord Browne-Wilkinson held that when a creditor is approached by cohabitees, one the principal debtor and the other the surety, and the proposed transaction is clearly to the disadvantage of the surety, it will be under a duty to inquire. A creditor can discharge this duty by explaining to the surety in a meeting not attended by the principal debtor the amount of her potential liability and the risks involved and advising her to take independent advice. . . .

When setting out the strict requirements of a separate meeting with the surety, however, Lord Browne-Wilkinson spoke of "the emotional pressure of cohabitation" (p. 431). Elsewhere, he spoke of how "the sexual and emotional ties between the [married] parties provide a ready weapon for undue influence" (p. 424). When a bank is presented with such a relationship, it should recognize the risk of undue influence (assuming that the transaction is on its face detrimental to the party offering security). But by the same logic, a relationship that is more distant will raise less suspicion of undue influence, even if the transaction is apparently unfavourable to the guarantor. Consequently, less may be required to satisfy an honest and reasonable person that the surety or guarantor is aware of the legal implications of the proposed transaction.

[10] While Sopinka J.'s statement that the law presumes undue influence "when the transaction is clearly detrimental to the person offering security and the relationship between that person and the principal debtor is particularly close" might seem to establish a different test from the one set out in . . . *O'Brien*, it should be viewed in its context. Furthermore, had Sopinka J. intended to depart from, or change, the law pertaining to undue influence as set out in *Geffen*, *supra*, it seems to me that he would have stated his intention to do so.

[11] The issues in *Gold v. Rosenberg* were whether the Bank had notice of Rosenberg's wrongdoing such that Gold could set aside the transaction, and the Bank's duty to inquire. As I have noted, *Gold v. Rosenberg* was not a case where the presence of undue influence was an issue. In *Gold*, Sopinka J. referred to *O'Brien* for the proposition that, in certain circumstances, a third party will owe a duty to inquire whether a guarantor had received independent legal advice. It should be noted that in the end, Sopinka J. concluded that the respondent bank did not owe Gold a duty to advise him to obtain legal advice. In reaching this conclusion, he noted that Gold had "three years of university education in which he had taken courses in business, economics and accounting," and had some business experience. Whether the Bank owed a duty to inquire in this case is one of the issues that arises in this appeal, and it is to this issue that I now turn.

[12] The duty to inquire about the prospect of undue influence in the context of the circumstances in which a third party will be subject to a complainant's equity to set aside a transaction procured by undue influence was central to the House of Lords' decision in *CIBC Mortgages plc v. Pitt*, [1993] 4 All E.R. 433, a companion decision to *O'Brien*. In *Pitt*, the Bank agreed to grant a loan to Mr. Pitt on the security of the matrimonial home. Both Mr. and Mrs. Pitt signed the loan agreement; however, Mrs. Pitt did not read the documents before signing or receive any independent legal advice, nor did any Bank employee suggest that she do so. When Mr. Pitt was unable to keep up the mortgage payments, the Bank sought possession of the house. Mrs. Pitt defended the application on the grounds that she had been induced to sign the agreement by misrepresentation and undue influence on the part of her husband. The trial judge allowed the Bank's application, and Mrs. Pitt's appeal was dismissed. On further appeal, the House of Lords found that there was actual undue influence; however, the Bank was not affected by it as there was nothing to put the Bank on inquiry. In determining what would put the Bank on inquiry, Lord Browne-Wilkinson found that a complainant will be able to set aside a transaction where he or she can establish either (a) that the wrongdoer acted as a third party's agent in procuring the transaction, or (b) that the third party had actual or constructive notice of the wrongdoing.

[13] As noted by Feldman J.A., the cases in which the wrongdoer will be found to have acted as the third party's agent will arise rarely. It is not argued in this case that the Bank had actual notice of the alleged undue influence. Therefore, it is necessary to consider when a third party, such as the Bank, will have constructive notice of a party's equity to set aside a transaction.

[14] The House of Lords considered this question in *O'Brien*. Lord Browne-Wilkinson stated at p. 429 that:

> . . . a creditor is put on inquiry when a wife offers to stand surety for her husband's debt by the combination of two factors: (a) the transaction is on its face not to the financial advantage of the wife; and (b) there is a substantial risk in transactions of that kind that, in procuring the wife to act as surety, the husband has committed a legal or equitable wrong that entitles the wife to set aside the transaction.

In such circumstances, the creditor will be put on inquiry and will be taken to have constructive notice of the complainant's rights *unless* the creditor has taken reasonable steps to satisfy himself that the complainant's agreement was properly obtained.   *(was agreement properly obtained?)*

[15] Lord Browne-Wilkinson's statement regarding constructive notice was accepted by the Supreme Court of Canada in *Gold v. Rosenberg*. In the course of his majority reasons, Sopinka J. commented generally on the duty owed by the Bank to Gold. He cited *O'Brien* at p. 800 for the proposition that "when a creditor is approached by cohabitees, one the principal debtor and the other the surety, and the proposed transaction is clearly to the disadvantage of the surety, it will be under a duty to inquire." In such circumstances, a creditor is required to explain to the surety in the absence of the principal debtor the amount of the sureties and the risks involved, and to advise the surety to obtain independent advice. However, a transaction is not automatically vitiated merely by the failure of a creditor to satisfy these requirements. The surety must establish her legal entitlement to set aside the transaction. If she is successful, the creditor's failure to satisfy its duty to inquire will prevent the creditor from avoiding the rights of the surety.

[16] The case law, then, establishes that a wife may set aside a transaction where she can establish that the transaction was actually procured by undue influence (class 1 — actual undue influence) or where she can raise a presumption of undue influence by demonstrating that *de facto* she left decisions on financial affairs to her husband (class 2B — presumed undue influence). A third party, such as a bank, will be bound by the wife's equity to set aside the transaction where it has constructive notice of the wrongdoing, that is of undue influence or the real prospect of undue influence. Constructive notice may be established by a close relationship between the parties — such as husband and wife — coupled with a manifestly disadvantageous transaction. However, it must be noted that the mere fact of a close relationship does not give rise to a presumption of undue influence. Rather,

a spouse must establish in each case that the relationship was on in which he or she "generally reposed trust and confidence in the wrongdoer".

[17] Applying these principles to this case, it is clear that the Bank is fixed with constructive notice of any wrongdoing between the parties. The existence of a marital relationship is marked by the characteristics of trust and confidence, which create an increased risk of undue influence. Further, as found by the trial judge, the transaction was to the material disadvantage of Mrs. Duguid. Accordingly, the Bank was subject to a duty to inquire. The Bank's failure to discharge the duty to inquire (to determine if there was undue influence) by advising Mrs. Duguid to obtain independent legal advice precludes the Bank from setting aside the finding of constructive notice of the potential for undue influence.

[18] However, the transaction is not vitiated by the mere fact that the Bank had constructive notice of Mrs. Duguid's rights, if any, and failed to take reasonable steps to ensure that her consent was voluntary and informed. Rather, these facts only mean that Mrs. Duguid may set aside the transaction as against the Bank if, and only if, the transaction was procured by undue influence. Since there is no evidence of actual undue influence, the issue is whether there is a basis in the evidence to presume undue influence.

[19] I am unable to agree with my colleague's conclusion that the transaction was procured by undue influence. Feldman J.A. states in her reasons, correctly in my view, that "this is not a situation where the wife put her trust and confidence in the husband for financial matters in the classic sense . . .". Feldman J.A. presumes undue influence on the basis that Mrs. Duguid's concerns about her relationship with her husband provided "a ready weapon" for undue influence. I see a number of problems with this approach. First, Mrs. Duguid must establish that she did in fact repose trust and confidence in her husband. This burden may be met by showing that she left decisions on financial affairs to him. In my opinion, there is little or no evidence that Mrs. Duguid reposed trust and confidence in her husband. Indeed, as I have said, in respect of her financial affairs Feldman J.A. finds that this was not a situation where the "classic" requirements for presuming undue influence were made out.

[20] In my opinion, there is ample evidence that Mrs. Duguid did not repose trust and confidence in her husband in the manner required for a presumption of undue influence. In the circumstances, I will limit my references to the evidence to highlight that part of it that is, in my view, of significance on the presumed undue influence issue.

[21] This was a tax-driven real estate investment by Mr. Duguid, a school principal, and another school principal. Mrs. Duguid was a real estate agent. A short time before she signed the promissory note, the Bank took the position that the income and net worth of Mr. Duguid and his associate were not sufficient. As a result of the Bank's position, Mr. Duguid asked Mrs. Duguid to send an income and net worth statement to the Bank and she did so. Thus, the Bank's request that Mrs. Duguid sign the note did not come out of the blue. Finally, this was not the first time that Mr. Duguid and his associate had made an investment of this type. Mrs. Duguid knew that. These and other features of the evidence support the conclusion that she did not repose trust and confidence in her husband when it came to her, or their, financial affairs.

[22] Moreover, it is clear from the authorities to which I have referred that the mere fact that a close relationship may give rise to "ready weapons for undue influence" is not sufficient to establish the presumption. If that was not the case, every close relationship would give rise to a presumption of undue influence. This would have the very result that Lord Browne-Wilkinson cautioned against in *O'Brien* — it would reintroduce a class 2A presumption of undue influence for every husband and wife relationship (or any other close relationship, for that matter).

[23] There is nothing to suggest that Mr. and Mrs. Duguid had a relationship that would give rise to a finding of presumed undue influence. At trial, Mrs. Duguid testified that she signed the documents because she was not in a stage of her marriage where she would question anything. However, this statement must be viewed in the context of the remainder of her testimony. She testified that she was not aware that her marriage was in a precarious state, and that while she and her husband were "in a valley at that point in time," she did not think that the marriage would end.

[24] Given that there was no actual undue influence and no basis upon which to presume undue influence, Mrs. Duguid has no equity to set aside the transaction as against the Bank. However, assuming that undue influence can be presumed, the inquiry must continue. The presumption of undue influence may be rebutted. . . . Typically, proof that the complainant received, or was advised to receive, independent legal advice will rebut the presumption. . . .

[25] In my view, evidence that the surety obtained, or was advised to obtain, independent legal advice is not the only way to rebut the presumption of undue influence. While *Cheshire, Fifoot and Furmston's Law of Contract*, 13th ed. (London: Butterworths, 1996) notes the significance of independent legal advice, the authors state at p. 329 that "the Privy Council has emphasized that if evidence is given of circumstances sufficient to show that the contract was the act of a free and independent mind, the transaction will be valid even though no external advice was given." Such circumstances might include commercial knowledge, experience, general sophistication or independence: see M.H. Ogilvie, "No Special Tenderness for Sexually Contracted Debt? Undue Influence and the Lending Banker" (1996) *Can. Bus. L.J.* 365 at p. 388.

. . .

[28] Even if undue influence may be presumed, in my view, the presumption is rebutted in the circumstances of this case. Those features of the evidence that demonstrate that Mr. and Mrs. Duguid's relationship was not one giving rise to a presumption of undue influence also serve to rebut any presumption that might arise. To repeat, Mrs. Duguid was a real estate agent. As such, it is likely that she knew about the risks involved in her husband's investment, and almost certain that she would have understood the significance of co-signing his promissory note. In addition, I think that it is significant that Mrs. Duguid did not plead, or contend at trial, that her husband procured her signature by exercising actual undue influence. Nor did she defend the Bank's action on the basis of presumed undue influence. Furthermore, in oral argument of this appeal, Mrs. Duguid did not rely on undue influence, actual or presumed. Undue influence, as a live issue, only arose when the court sought written submissions on that issue.

Disposition

[29] For these reasons, I would allow the appeal, set aside the judgment of Day J. and in its place grant judgment in favour of the Bank. In light of the Bank's conduct as referred to by my colleague, I would not grant costs, here or below.

FELDMAN J.A. (dissenting):

. . .

[38] With respect to the trial judge, I do not agree with these legal conclusions. First, unless it is established that the Bank owes a fiduciary duty to the customer, it has no obligation to provide the customer with either its information or its concerns about the viability of the investment for which the funds are borrowed: *Bertolo v. Bank of Montreal* (1986), 57 O.R. (2d) 577 at pp. 583-84, 33 D.L.R. (4th) 610 (C.A.). . . . Second, the fact that a bank does not comply with its own internal lending practices does not, by itself, render its loan unenforceable or give the borrower a right of recourse. . . .

Undue Influence and Independent Legal Advice

[39] However, that does not end the matter. The trial judge indicated at the opening of his reasons for judgment that Mrs. Duguid was defending the action "on the basis that she did not receive and was entitled to independent legal advice and/or independent financial advice". He stated that the Bank relied on the decision of this court in *Bank of Montreal v. Featherstone* (1989), 68 O.R. (2d) 541 at p. 547, where the court states:

> In the absence of any evidence of undue influence, fraud or misrepresentation or any evidence supporting a defence of *non est factum*, the failure of the bank to ensure that the spouse obtained independent legal advice before signing the guarantee may not be fatal to the claim of the bank.

[40] This remains an accurate statement of the law. However, since *Featherstone*, in two seminal decisions, *Barclays Bank plc v. O'Brien*, [*supra*], together with a companion decision, *CIBC Mortgages plc v. Pitt*, [1993] 4 All E.R. 433, the House of Lords has elucidated and clarified the concept of undue influence within certain defined relationships such as marriage and or other co-habitation relationships, as well as the circumstances where lenders must address the issue of independent legal advice in the context of loans to be guaranteed or co-signed by people in such relationships. Furthermore, in its decision in *Gold v. Rosenberg*, [*supra*], the Supreme Court of Canada adopted the principles articulated by the House of Lords. The result is that there is now a clear procedure which lenders may follow to protect themselves when making a loan to one co-habitee which is to be co-signed or guaranteed by the other, where the lender has constructive notice of actual or presumed undue influence by one over the other.

[41] In *Barclays Bank*, the bank agreed to increase the overdraft limit for Mr. O'Brien's business on the basis of his guarantee secured by a second mortgage on the matrimonial home. Although the bank branch was supposed to ensure that the parties understood what they were signing and to suggest that they speak to their solicitors, in fact no explanation was given to Mrs. O'Brien and she signed the documents without reading them or seeking legal advice. Eventually, the bank called on the husband's guarantee and sought to enforce its security on the home. Mrs. O'Brien defended the action on the basis that she was induced to enter the transaction by her husband's undue influence and misrepresentation as to the extent of the liability.

husband-wife debate

[42] In approaching the issues raised by this case, Lord Browne-Wilkinson first recognized the competing policy considerations involved. On one side he noted the recognition by society of equality of the sexes and the concomitant equality of partners within a marriage or co-habitation relationship, as well as the prevalence of joint ownership of the matrimonial home and the need to be able to obtain a loan based on the security of that home without the bank being unwilling to risk lending on that security because of the spectre of the defence of undue influence. On the other side, he noted that despite society's recognition of equality of the sexes, there are still many marriages where the wife is willing to follow the husband's advice and where wives are subjected to and yield to undue influence by their husbands. In those circumstances, Lord Browne-Wilkinson concluded at p. 422 that, "Such wives can reasonably look to the law for some protection when their husbands have abused the trust and confidence reposed in them." Significantly, Lord Browne-Wilkinson concluded the judgment at p. 431 by extending the same protection of the law to all co-habitees:

> I have hitherto dealt only with the position where a wife stands surety for her husband's debts. But in my judgment the same principles are applicable to all other cases where there is an emotional relationship between cohabitees. The "tenderness" shown by the law to married women is not based on the marriage ceremony but reflects the underlying risk of one cohabitee exploiting the emotional involvement and trust of the other. Now that unmarried cohabitation, whether heterosexual or homosexual, is widespread in our society, the law should recognise this. Legal wives are not the only group which are now exposed to the emotional pressure of cohabitation. Therefore if, but only if, the creditor is aware that the surety is cohabiting with the principal debtor, in my judgment the same principles should apply to them as apply to husband and wife.

[43] Lord Browne-Wilkinson set out the law of undue influence, first, as between the parties in the relationship and, then, as it affects a third party in the transaction who was not involved in the undue influence which induced it. He began at p. 423 with the following basic proposition:

> A person who has been induced to enter into a transaction by the undue influence of another (the wrongdoer) is entitled to set that transaction aside as against the wrongdoer. Such undue influence is either actual or presumed.

[44] In the case of actual undue influence, the claimant must prove affirmatively that the wrongdoer exerted undue influence to induce the transaction. In the case of presumed undue influence, the claimant must show only that there existed a relationship of trust and confidence such that it is fair to presume that the wrongdoer abused that relationship to procure the transaction. The onus then shifts to the wrongdoer to prove that the complainant in fact entered into the transaction freely. One way to rebut the presumption is to demonstrate that the complainant received independent legal advice.

burden of proof

[45] Presumed undue influence may arise in two classes of relationships. The first, class 2(A), are relationships which, in and of themselves raise a presumption, such as solicitor and client or medical adviser and patient. In those the onus is immediately on the wrongdoer to disprove undue influence. The second, class 2(B), are relationships where the complainant can show that *de facto*, she reposed trust and confidence in the wrongdoer. Once that is shown, then the onus shifts to the wrongdoer to disprove undue influence. Lord Browne-Wilkinson pointed out that in . . . *Bank of Montreal v. Stuart*, [1911] A.C. 120, 80 L.J.P.C. 75 (P.C.), it was established that the relationship of husband and wife did not, as a matter of law, raise a presumption of undue influence within the first category (class 2(A)). However, he noted that in any particular case, it is open to a wife (and ultimately to any cohabitee) to demonstrate that *de facto* she did leave decisions on financial matters to her husband and reposed trust and confidence in him (class 2(B)), so that undue influence is presumed without proof of actual undue influence.

[46] He then explained his approval of this legal result in the following way at p. 424:

> In my judgment this special tenderness of treatment afforded to wives by the courts is properly attributable to two factors. First, many cases may well fall into the class 2B category of undue influence because the wife demonstrates that she placed trust and confidence in her husband in relation to her financial affairs and therefore raises a presumption of undue influence. Second, the sexual and emotional ties between the parties provide a ready weapon for undue influence: a wife's true wishes can easily be overborne because of her fear of destroying or damaging the wider relationship between her and her husband if she opposes his wishes.
>
> *For myself, I accept that the risk of undue influence affecting a voluntary disposition by a wife in favour of a husband is greater than in the ordinary run of cases where no sexual or emotional ties affect the free exercise of the individual's will.* (Emphasis added)

. . .

[48] In *Barclays Bank*, Lord Browne-Wilkinson then discussed the effect on a creditor bank of undue influence between a husband and wife, and in particular, under what circumstances a wife may be able to set aside her guarantee, grant of security or covenant given to a bank.

[49] The court set out two circumstances. The first is where the husband is the agent of the bank. Such cases are rare, but where that is the case, the bank is fixed with the wrongdoing of its agent.

[50] The other is where the bank has either actual or constructive notice of the undue influence and, therefore, of the wife's equity to set aside the transaction. The bank will be put on constructive notice of the risk of undue influence when a wife agrees to guarantee or co-sign for her husband's debts where there is the combination of two factors: (1) the transaction on its face, is not to the financial advantage of the wife; and (2) "there is a substantial risk in transactions of that kind that, in procuring the wife to act as surety, the husband has committed a legal or equitable wrong that entitles the wife to set aside the transaction" (p. 429).

[51] When the bank sees those two circumstances, it will be fixed with constructive notice of any undue influence by the husband, whether actual or presumed, which may have existed, unless it takes reasonable steps to satisfy itself that the wife's participation in the transaction was properly obtained. Otherwise the bank will retain constructive notice of the wife's rights and will take subject to them. Lord Browne-Wilkinson then set out a suggested procedure which a bank may follow which he referred to as "reasonable steps" to protect itself from being fixed with constructive notice: the bank must (1) meet with the wife privately, (2) tell her of the extent of her liability, (3) warn her of the risk, and (4) urge her to obtain

independent legal advice. Furthermore, where the bank has specific information which may make undue influence not only possible, but probable, in those circumstances, it must go further and insist that she obtain independent legal advice.

[52] Lord Browne-Wilkinson recognized that his formulation of the constructive notice doctrine, that is, requiring no actual knowledge by the bank in any particular case of the circumstances which would raise the 2(B) presumption, but only a recognition of the risk or possibility of undue influence because of the relationship and the disadvantageous transaction, is an extension of the law of constructive notice. However, he was satisfied that knowledge of the *possibility* of influence is enough to put a third party on inquiry.

[53] In my view, this reasoning and result accord with common sense and commercial reality. They result in a rule which applies in easily identifiable circumstances, and which is not onerous for the bank. It obviates any need for a bank, when extending a loan to one co-habitee but guaranteed or secured by both, to have to make personal inquiries as to the nature of the relationship between the parties or the extent of the literacy or sophistication of the party who is guaranteeing or co-signing the loan. Nor is the bank required (in the case where it has no specific knowledge) to ensure that that party actually obtains the independent advice, but only to urge the party to do so. Unless the bank learns of anything more which would again put it on notice, it can proceed to lend and rely on the covenant or security it receives, if it has taken the reasonable steps set out above.

[54] And of what benefit are these reasonable steps on the part of the bank to the party who is co-signing or guaranteeing the loan? If there is pressure from the relationship partner to sign, whether subtle or not, the fact that the guarantor or co-signor is called to a meeting without the principal debtor, at the behest of the bank, and is told that she or he should obtain independent advice, may give that party the ability and excuse to seek and even rely and act on that advice, without appearing to betray the partner who is exerting the pressure. Of course, the independent advice provides the guarantor or co-signor with specific information about the obligation which she or he may or may not have already had or understood.

[55] In the companion case to *Barclays Bank*, the court made it clear that a precondition to the application of the constructive notice doctrine is the existence of a manifestly disadvantageous transaction for one of the parties in the relationship. There is therefore no constructive notice to the bank of any risk of undue influence where a loan is made to a husband and wife (or other parties in a relevant relationship) for their joint benefit, because in that circumstance, there is no apparent financial disadvantage for the co-signor: *CIBC Mortgages plc v. Pitt, supra*. Again this makes commercial sense. Where parties are jointly seeking a loan such as a mortgage to purchase a home, there should be no impediment to obtaining the funds from the lender on the security of the home, and no hesitation on the part of the lender as to the enforceability of such a loan against both parties.

[56] In applying these principles to the facts in the *Barclays Bank* case, the House of Lords held that because the Bank failed to take the reasonable steps, i.e., to meet with Mrs. O'Brien, to explain the extent of her liability and risk and to urge her to obtain independent legal advice before pledging security on her home in respect of the line of credit for her husband's business, the Bank was fixed with constructive notice of her husband's wrongful misrepresentation to her of the

amount at risk. As a result, Mrs. O'Brien was entitled to set aside the mortgage as against the bank.

[57]   This newly articulated approach to the role of and need for independent legal advice was recognized in 1997 as the law in this country by the Supreme Court of Canada in *Gold v. Rosenberg, supra.* [Feldman J.A. then set out the same quote from Sopinka J. in *Gold*, as Osborne A.C.J.O , *supra* ¶ 9] . . .

[58]   To be clear, a bank is fixed with constructive notice of the risk of undue influence where (1) the transaction is not financially advantageous to the guarantor or co-signor, and (2) the parties are in a relationship which raises the suspicion of undue influence, such as husband and wife or other co-habitees, unless the bank takes reasonable steps to satisfy itself that the co-signature is given freely. However, the surety obligation remains valid and enforceable by the bank even where it did not take the reasonable steps to provide information and advice to the surety, where there was no undue influence, whether actual or presumed, no misrepresentation or other legal wrong by the principal debtor. In other words, the mere failure by the bank to take those steps does not vitiate the guarantee or co-signature on the covenant. That is the result, however, where it transpires that the transaction as between the husband and wife (or other relevant parties) is tainted by undue influence, whether actual or presumed, by misrepresentation or by other legal wrong.

Application of the Law to this Case

[59]   Turning to the case before this court, the first issue is, was the Bank on constructive notice of the possibility of undue influence by Mr. Duguid? It is clear that the transaction was not financially advantageous for Mrs. Duguid. Not only was the Bank aware that there were problems with the viability of the underlying security and therefore its potential to generate income, but also, the Bank knew that Mr. Duguid was not financially able to carry the loan from his own income and assets. Furthermore, the investment belonged to the husband. He would obtain the tax advantage and any increase in the value of the underlying realty. The fact that the loan was not to the financial advantage of Mrs. Duguid, together with the husband and wife relationship, put the Bank on notice of the risk of undue influence. However, the Bank did not take the reasonable steps (or do anything at all) to satisfy itself that Mrs. Duguid's participation was properly obtained.

[60]   Although these events occurred before the decision in *Barclays Bank*, there is no hardship on the Bank in this case because it intended to advise Mrs. Duguid to obtain independent legal advice in accordance with its written policy for this project loan. Ironically, the Bank believed that it had advised Mrs. Duguid to obtain independent legal advice because of the signature of the Bank officer who purported to witness the documents. The trial judge found that it had not. The Bank is therefore fixed with constructive notice of any undue influence, whether actual or presumed, or misrepresentation by the husband.

[61]   The next issue is, was there evidence led at trial of a relationship between Mr. and Mrs. Duguid giving rise to a presumption of undue influence? In my view, there is substantial evidence of presumed undue influence by Mr. Duguid.

[62]   It is clear from the course of the analysis of presumed undue influence by Lord Browne-Wilkinson that he recognized two aspects of the relationship between co-habitees which raise the risk of undue influence. The first is the concept of trust and confidence in financial matters which one of the parties, traditionally a wife, may repose in the other, therefore leaving the financial decisions to the other. The second is the pressure or tension within the relationship created by the sexual and emotional ties. Such pressure can take many forms, including creating a fear in one partner that failure to co-operate in financial matters will damage the relationship, obliging that partner to bow to the will of the other and to sign whatever is requested.

[63] In fact, these two aspects of the marriage and co-habitation relationships are related, as both arise from the classic underlying basis of the relationship, love and affection together with emotional and sometimes financial dependence.

[64] It is important, I believe, to examine the first aspect closely in that context because I perceive that there may exist a misconception of the basis for the belief that traditionally wives often deferred to their husbands on family financial matters. It is certainly an out-dated notion in today's society that women cannot or do not understand financial matters and, more specifically, that they do not understand that when they sign a document, they are committing themselves to its contents.

[65] Therefore, if a wife is asked by her husband to sign a note or guarantee to the bank for his loan, and she does so because she has always reposed trust and confidence in him, she agrees to sign because she has confidence that her husband would not be asking her unless he believed that in the end it would not be detrimental to her and he would ultimately protect her. That is the trust and confidence she reposes in him arising out of their relationship. She knows that he will not get the money he needs unless she signs, but believes that he would not be asking her to take a risk now unless he was convinced there really was no risk for her.

[66] Furthermore, in the context of the relationship, a co-habitee may well feel that it would be perceived as a breach of that trust for her to question whether it would be in her best interests to sign or for her to suggest that she should independently see a lawyer. In other words, the "trust and confidence in financial matters" aspect of the relationship is an example or manifestation of the sexual and emotional ties within a marriage or cohabitation relationship while the relationship remains strong. The second aspect recognized by Lord Browne-Wilkinson, sexual and emotional pressure to go along with the other party's wishes, is also based on the emotional bond of the relationship, but may be more likely to arise when the relationship is undergoing strain and may be in peril.

[67] Clearly this was not a situation where Mrs. Duguid put her trust and confidence in her husband for financial matters in the classic sense. However, it is the second type of situation described by Lord Browne-Wilkinson at p. 424 and referred to by Sopinka J. at p. 800, where the sexual and emotional ties "provide a ready weapon for undue influence": the wife feared destroying or damaging the relationship between herself and her husband if she opposed his wishes. The marriage was foundering, and the husband knew it, yet he asked his wife to co-sign for his loan.

[68] The trial judge found that Mrs. Duguid signed the loan documents at the request of her husband and while she was alone with him in their kitchen. At the time, their marriage was "at a low ebb . . ., and she just signed the documentation without giving consideration to its contents in order to maintain some level of

tranquillity". In her evidence, Mrs. Duguid testified that her husband said she had to sign the promissory note, she signed it, and went out the door. She said that at that time there were problems in her marriage, that her marriage was not going well and therefore she was "walking on eggshells". She testified that she signed because she was not "making waves" at that time. She said that she was not in a stage of her 22-year marriage where she would question anything. Mr. Duguid, who testified on behalf of the Bank, acknowledged that there were difficulties in the marriage at the time they signed the promissory note.

[69] Mr. Duguid also testified that he induced his wife to co-sign for the loan by telling her that he hoped the investment would make enough to help finance their sons' education. However, he did not put the investment into joint names nor secure it in any way for the benefit of their three sons. It was listed as his asset in his later bankruptcy. Counsel for the Bank submitted that Mr. Duguid's stated intention to use the profits from the investment for their sons' education showed that the transaction was not disadvantageous to Mrs. Duguid. Of course his statement to her turned out to be false; because the investment belonged solely to Mr. Duguid, had there been any profits, they would have belonged only to him to be used at his sole discretion. Whether or not this amounted to a misrepresentation in law, had Mrs. Duguid had independent advice, one of the issues she could have discussed with a lawyer was how to ensure that the profits would be legally secured for their sons' education.

[70] The fact that Mrs. Duguid was a real estate agent neither negates nor rebuts the presumption of undue influence by her husband arising out of their relationship. It does not speak to the circumstances under which she signed the note, her fear regarding the status of her relationship with her husband at that time and his knowledge that there were difficulties in the marriage when he asked her to sign the note. Furthermore, there was no evidence of her level of legal knowledge including whether her obligation on the note would survive their separation or divorce, the consequences if her husband were to become bankrupt, or the non-binding nature of his representation that the profits from the investment would be used for their sons' education. These are matters about which a lawyer could give accurate information and independent, objective advice.

Conclusion

[71] As in *Barclays Bank*, the Bank of Montreal in this case was on constructive notice of the possibility of undue influence and consequently of Mrs. Duguid's equity to set aside the transaction. The Bank remained on notice because it failed to take reasonable steps at the time to satisfy itself that she was entering into the obligation freely. As Mrs. Duguid established presumed undue influence arising out of the circumstances of the marital relationship when she signed the note (class 2(B)), the onus was therefore on the Bank seeking to uphold the transaction to rebut the presumption of undue influence by proving that Mrs. Duguid co-signed the loan freely, for example, by showing that she received independent legal advice. That onus was not met. The Bank therefore cannot enforce the promissory note against Mrs. Duguid.

[72] Accordingly, I would dismiss the appeal with costs.

NOTES AND QUESTIONS

1. Surely those who co-habit are "co-habitants" or even "co-habiters", not "co-habitees".

2. Had Feldman J.A.'s judgment been the majority judgment, the obligations on banks *vis-à-vis* those who guarantee the loans of others would have been more extensive than those which now lie on banks. The bench was a strong one and each judgment makes very good arguments. For some curious reason, the Ontario Court of Appeal has had the principal role in developing the law in this area. While one might speculate that a female judge might have sympathy for a female guarantor — and it is a fact that in almost all of the cases dealing with spousal guarantees, the guarantor has been female — Feldman J.A. has very extensive experience in commercial and banking cases and speculation that the guarantor's sex made any difference to the conclusion Feldman J.A. came to would be no more than that.

3. In *Royal Bank of Scotland v. Etridge (No. 2)*, [2001] 4 All E .R. 449 (H.L.), the House of Lords considered eight separate actions involving spousal guarantees. In the course of its judgment dealing with the eight appeals, the Law Lords provided detailed guidelines for both banks and solicitors in advising people who were in the same position as Mrs. Duguid. The rules stated by the House of Lords are not directly applicable in Canada because the practice of solicitors differs in Canada and England, but they provide a useful supplement to (and largely correspond with) the advice given by the Law Society of Upper Canada. Is it consistent with the role of judges and the process of adjudication for a court to perform such a rule-making function?
    The rules developed by the House of Lords can be summarized:

    1. In the ordinary course, a wife's guarantee of her husband's business debts is not to be regarded as a transaction which, failing proof to the contrary, was procured by the husband's undue influence.

    2. Where the wife proposes to charge (or mortgage) the matrimonial home, (i) the bank is put on inquiry because the transaction is, on its face, not the advantage of the wife (the House disapproved of the phrase, "manifest disadvantage") and there is a substantial risk that the husband may have committed an equitable wrong; (ii) where the bank is put on inquiry, it need do no more than take reasonable steps to satisfy itself that the wife has understood the transaction and has entered it with her eyes open; it would be reasonable for the bank to rely on confirmation from a solicitor that the wife understands the transaction unless it knows that the solicitor has not advised the wife or that she has not received appropriate advice; (iii) when giving a wife advice the solicitor is acting exclusively for her, and must follow certain steps to make sure that she understands the transaction; (iv) it is not for the solicitor to veto the transaction by refusing to provide confirmation to the bank; (v) the solicitor may act for the husband or the bank, as well as for the wife; (vi) for future transactions, a bank should take certain prescribed steps once it has been put on inquiry and is looking for protection on the ground that the wife has been advised by a solicitor: (a) the bank should communicate directly with the wife, telling her that it will need confirmation from a solicitor; (b) she should be told that she needs to see a solicitor so that she will be unable to claim later on that she is not bound by what she has signed; (c) she should be asked to nominate a solicitor who may also be her husband's, though she should be asked if she would like to be represented separately; (d) the bank should not proceed with the transaction until it has received an appropriate response directly from the wife; (e) if the bank is unwilling to explain the financial circumstances to the wife, it has to provide the solicitor with the necessary information and get its customer's consent to the disclosure; (f) if the bank has any concerns about the wife's being improperly influenced by her husband, the bank must inform the solicitor; and (g) the bank should obtain confirmation from the wife's solicitor. A bank must always take reasonable steps to bring home to the individual guarantor the risks that he or she is running by signing a guarantee.

4.   It is worth noting that the way in which the Supreme Court of Canada grants leave makes it virtually impossible for it to consider the wide range of facts that were dealt with by the House of Lords in eight separate actions in *Royal Bank of Scotland v. Etridge (No. 2)*.

5.   What advice would you have given Mrs. Duguid if she had come to see you before signing the promissory note? Would you inquire into her satisfaction with her marriage and its stability? Do you think that she would have signed the note regardless of any advice you might have given her?

6.   A number of Canadian jurisdictions have statutory provisions that allow courts to control certain classes of contracts if they are unfair or unconscionable. For example, the *Consumer Protection Act, 2002*, S.O. 2002, c. 30, Sched. A and other provincial legislation, deal with "unfair" business practices. Such practices are defined to include false, misleading and "unconscionable" consumer representations. The remedies provided include rescission, damages and criminal penalties.

The *Unconscionable Transactions Relief Act*, R.S.O. 1990, c. U.2, and similar legislation (in every province except British Columbia) authorizes courts to grant relief from "harsh and unconscionable" loans. How often would you expect the jurisdiction under the act to be invoked?

The Ontario *Consumer Protection Act, 2002* provides certain protections for consumers, for example, allowing for a 10-day "cooling-off period" (giving the consumer the right to cancel without penalty) for purchasers in some "direct sales" (door-to-door sales), and provides for compulsory warranties when goods are sold to a consumer.

The *Bank Act*, S.C. 1991, c. 46, s. 450, and the *Cost of Borrowing (Banks) Regulations*, SOR/2001-101, require disclosure of the costs of borrowing by consumers (those not borrowing for business purposes).

The *Competition Act*, R.S.C. 1985, c. C-34 (as am. by the *Competition Tribunal Act*, R.S.C. 1985, c. 19 (2nd Supp.)), controls fraudulent and misleading advertising as well as certain other kinds of objectionable commercial conduct by making such behaviour a criminal offence.

7.   A.A. Leff in "Unconscionability and the Code — The Emperor's New Clause" (1967), 115 *U. Pa. L. Rev.* 485, 486-87, distinguishes two kinds of unconscionability:

> [T]o make a contract one needs (i) parties with capacity, (ii) manifested assent, and (iii) consideration. This is all very simple. If these criteria are met, a party to the resulting nexus who has made promises is obligated to carry them out, unless he can maintain successfully one of the standard contract-law defenses, such as fraud, duress, mistake, impossibility or illegality. These defenses' might be classified in diverse ways to serve various analytical purposes. For our particular needs, however, there is a simple way of grouping them which is signally illuminating: some of these defenses have to do with the process of contracting and others have to do with the resulting contract. When fraud and duress are involved, for instance, the focus of attention is on what took place between the parties at the making of the contract. With illegality, on the other hand, the material question is instead the content of the contract once made. The law may legitimately be interested both in the way agreements come about and in what they provide. A "Contract" gotten at gunpoint may be avoided; a classic dicker over Dobbin may come to naught if horse-owning is illegal.

Leff's analysis has been widely adopted. It is now common to refer to evils in the bargaining process as "procedural unconscionability" and to evils in the resulting contract as "substantive unconscionability." An example of the latter is provided by the next case. The legislation invoked is similar to Canadian statutes like Ontario's *Business Practices Act* and the *Unconscionable Transactions Relief Act*.

M.J. Trebilcock in "An Economic Approach to the Doctrine of Unconscionability" in Reiter and Swan (eds.) *Studies in Contract Law* (Toronto: Butterworths, 1980) says (at 420):

> [T]he concept of substantive unfairness, in the sense of a judicially perceived non-equivalence in the values exchanged by contracting parties, poses real conceptual difficulties following a determination of (1) no abnormal market power and (2) no aberrations in the process of contract formation. Almost by definition, the outcome of such a process cannot be unfair. Moreover, in determining whether the values exchanged are reasonably equivalent, the court has little option but to identify some significantly more satisfactory choice that was open in the market and use this as a benchmark.

Would a legal system that accepted this view of the problem and judicial response to it be satisfactory? What challenges would a lawyer or judge in litigation face if this view is adopted? Are there any alternatives to Trebilcock's view? If so, would their adoption facilitate or render more complex the work of judges and lawyers?

exploitatn of power

8.   Rick Bigwood, "Contracts by Unfair Advantage: From Exploitation to Transactional Neglect" (2005), 25 *Oxford J. Legal Stud.* 65, argues that courts assert that they are preventing "exploitation" by one party to a contract when they invoke unconscionability or similar doctrines, but that they often are protecting against what he refers to as "transactional neglect". That is, the courts will give relief if a party to a contract fails to take reasonable precautions against the risk that the other party will be exploited by someone else or by the circumstances, if the situation is one where the stronger party should reasonably have known that exploitation was possible. That is, exploitation by the stronger party is not necessary (though it is sufficient); rather, "passive exploitation" or "transactional neglect" will suffice for judicial action. Do you agree?

KRONMAN, "CONTRACT LAW AND DISTRIBUTIVE JUSTICE"

(1980), 89 *Yale L.J.* 472 at 472-75

[1]   Among contract scholars, there is nearly universal agreement that the law of contracts, the tangled mass of legal rules that regulate the process of private exchange, has three legitimate functions: first to specify which agreements are legally binding and which are not; second, to define the rights and duties created by enforceable but otherwise ambiguous agreements; and finally, to indicate the consequences of an unexcused breach. Beyond this, however, it has sometimes been suggested that the law of contracts should also be used as an instrument of distributive justice and that those responsible for choosing or designing rules of contract law — courts and legislatures — should do so with an eye to their distributional effects in a self-conscious effort to achieve a fair division of wealth among the members of society.

[2]   There are, in fact, many rules of contract law that are deliberately intended to promote a distributional end of some sort. Obvious examples include: usury laws limiting the interest that can be charged on loans; implied, but nevertheless non-disclaimable, warranties of quality or habitability; and minimum wage laws. The object of each of these rules is to shift wealth from one group — lenders, sellers, landlords, employers — to another — borrowers, buyers, tenants, workers — presumably in accordance with some principle of distributive justice, by altering the terms on which individuals are allowed to contract. Can legal rules of this sort be defended? More generally, is it ever appropriate to use the law of contracts — understood in the broad sense in which I have been using the term — as an instrument of redistribution, or should the legal rules that govern the process of private exchange be fashioned without regard to their impact on the distribution of wealth in society?

[3]   Libertarians, who deny that the state is ever justified in forcibly redistributing wealth from one individual or group to another, answer this question in the negative. Surprisingly, many liberals, who believe that at least some compulsory redistribution of wealth is morally acceptable, even required, give the same answer. The libertarian's opposition to the use of contract law as a mechanism for redistribution derives from his general belief that the compulsory transfer of wealth is theft, regardless of how it is accomplished. By contrast, liberals who oppose the use of contract law as a redistributive device do so because they believe that distributional objectives (whose basic legitimacy they accept) are always better achieved through the tax system than through the detailed regulation of individual transactions.

[4]   Thus, despite their fundamentally different views regarding the moral legitimacy of forced redistribution, liberals and libertarians often find themselves defending a similar conception of contract law. While lawyers and philosophers in both camps approvingly describe the role that contract law plays in reducing the cost of the exchange process itself and emphasize the importance of protecting those engaged in the process against threats of physical violence and other unacceptable forms of coercion, there also appears to be widespread agreement, on both sides, that the legal rules regulating voluntary exchanges between individuals should not be selected or designed with an eye to their distributional consequences. It is tempting to conclude that this conception of contract law, which I shall call the non-distributive conception, must be correct if those with such sharply divergent views on the most basic questions of distributive justice agree on its soundness.

[5]   In this article, I argue that the non-distributive conception of contract law cannot be supported on either liberal or libertarian grounds, and defend the view that rules of contract law should be used to implement distributional goals whenever alternative ways of doing so are likely to be more costly or intrusive. …I examine the libertarian theory of contractual exchange and argue, against the standard libertarian view, that considerations of distributive justice not only *ought* to be taken into account in designing rules for exchange, but *must* be taken into account if the law of contracts is to have even minimum moral acceptability. My aim here is to show that the idea of voluntary agreement — an idea central to the libertarian theory of justice in exchange — cannot be understood except as a distributional concept, and to demonstrate that the notion of individual liberty, taken by itself, offers no guidance in determining which of the many forms of advantage-taking possible in exchange relations render an agreement involuntary and therefore unenforceable on libertarian grounds. Having established this general point, I propose a simple test, similar in form to Rawls's difference principle, for deciding which kinds of advantage-taking should be permitted and which should not, and argue that this test is the one libertarians ought to accept as being most compatible with the moral premises of libertarianism itself.

[6]   In the second part of the article, I challenge the standard liberal preference for taxation as a method of redistribution. The choice of a redistributive method involves moral issues as well as questions of expediency. In my view, however, a blanket preference for taxation is not justified by considerations of either sort.

There is no reason to think that taxation is always the most neutral and least intrusive way of redistributing wealth, nor is there reason to think it is always the most efficient means of achieving a given distributive goal. Which method of redistribution has these desirable properties will depend, in any particular case, on circumstantial factors; neither method is inherently superior to the other. And while any redistributive scheme is bound to involve a conflict between distributive justice and individual liberty, the existence of this conflict, although it raises serious difficulties for liberal theory in general, does not provide a reason for adopting a non-distributive conception of contract law.

[7]   There are important but different lessons to be learned from both the liberal and libertarian opposition to using the law of contracts for distributive purposes, and I shall attempt to clarify these in the course of my argument. However, while both views contribute to our understanding of the difficulties involved in treating the law of contracts as a mechanism for redistributing wealth, neither view justifies the claim, implicit in the writings of liberals and libertarians alike, that there is something *morally* wrong with using contract law in this way.

QUESTIONS

1.   What are the social, economic and legal costs of judicial "interference" in the enforcement of contracts as written?

2.   Are these costs justified in terms of the benefits that they can be expected to yield? What alternatives are there?

3.   You are counsel in the policy division of the provincial Ministry of the Attorney-General. The Women's League, a well-known activist feminist organization, has proposed that legislation be enacted to prohibit the giving of guarantees by one spouse of the business liabilities of the other. You are asked for your comments on the proposal.

Restraints in the Interest of Freedom of Contract

Early on in the history of capitalism, it became apparent that some individuals would enter into contracts that greatly restrict the operation of a free market place. Individuals were prepared to enter into contracts that would eliminate their possibility of entering into future contracts with others; individuals could be taken out of the market for so long that their productive capacities would be significantly reduced, or they might be tempted to sell themselves into servitude. If the courts enforced such contracts "in restraint of trade", they would contribute to the undermining of the operation of a free market, and might weaken freedom and capitalism.

Whether one accepts that people are unable to perceive their own best long-term interests, or that, as noted above, "necessitous men are not, truly speaking, free men" (*Vernon v. Bethell* (1762), 2 Eden. 110 at p. 113, 28 E.R. 838), controls on the freedom of people to contract were imposed by the common law from an early date. Courts asserted this control by striking down covenants that produced an unacceptable "restraint of trade".

In all commercial societies (and that category includes much of the African, American, Asiatic and European world) there were constant tendencies on the part of merchants to create monopolies. Sometimes the state encouraged monopolies (as with the Spanish trade to America, the Venetian trade to the Levant, and the

English Crown's grant to the Hudson Bay Company), but it was also recognized that monopolies could also have undesirable effects.

The history of controls on certain undesirable contracts in the common law goes back several centuries. Many of the common-law rules remain relevant today. More recently, legislation has also come to play a significant role. While the role of legislation will not be explored here, it is sufficient to mention that the *Competition Act*, R.S.C. 1985, c. C-34 (as am. by the *Competition Tribunal Act*, R.S.C. 1985, c. 19 (2nd Supp.)), contains prohibitions on contracts in unreasonable restraint of trade.

Common-law controls centred on one particular form of contract: covenants in restraint of trade. A covenant in restraint of trade is a clause in a contract (of any kind) that limits competition. A promise by an employee not to compete with his employer on leaving his employment, or a promise by the vendor of a business not to compete with the purchaser is a covenant in restraint of trade. The basic position of the common law was that such clauses were prima facie unenforceable, unless they could be shown to be justifiable in the circumstances.

The cases that follow explore briefly the content of the common-law rules regarding such clauses. The first case deals with the issue in the context of a contract of employment.

LYONS v. MULTARI

[2000] O.J. No. 3462, 50 O.R. (3d) 526, 3 C.C.E.L. (3d) 34
(C.A., Austin, Goudge and MacPherson JJ.A.)

[leave to appeal to S.C.C. dismissed 3 May 2001]

MacPHERSON J.A.: —

Introduction

[1]   This appeal calls for striking a proper balance, in a professional employment context, between competing values — on the one side, the sanctity of a clear contract between equals, set against, on the other side, the law's long-standing aversion to contracts that attempt to restrict competition generally. Moreover, the appeal calls for a consideration of the relationship between non-solicitation and non-competition clauses in a professional employment context.

A. Factual background

1.   *The parties and the events*

[2]   In the spring of 1993, Dr. Joseph Multari was completing his specialization training in oral surgery at Dalhousie University in Halifax, Nova Scotia. For family and professional reasons, he decided that he wanted to practise his profession in Windsor, Ontario.

[3]   At the same time, Dr. Bernard Lyons, who had practised oral surgery in Windsor for almost a quarter century, was looking for a new associate dentist because his previous associate had decided to move to Thunder Bay.

[4]　Dr. Lyons and Dr. Multari met in April and June 1993. Following relatively short negotiations, they agreed to work together. Dr. Lyons continued as the principal dentist in his practice; Dr. Multari became his associate.

[5]　The two dentists signed a short handwritten contract of less than a page on June 17, 1993. There were only three provisions in the contract. The first provision dealt with Dr. Multari's remuneration and the third provision required him to give six months' notice if he decided to leave Dr. Lyons' practice. It is common ground on this appeal that both dentists complied with these provisions.

[6]　The second provision was a non-competition clause that limited where Dr. Multari could practise his profession if he chose to leave Dr. Lyons' office. The entirety of this non-competition clause was: "Protective Covenant. 3 yrs. — 5 mi.".

[7]　Dr. Multari worked with Dr. Lyons for about 17 months. On January 18, 1995, he gave his six months' notice. On July 18, he began to work part-time in a dental office located more than five miles from Dr. Lyons' office.

[8]　On January 2, 1996, Dr. Multari and Dr. Paul George opened an oral surgery practice in Windsor. It is common ground that this practice was in competition, in a legal sense, with Dr. Lyons' oral surgery practice. Moreover, there is no dispute that Dr. Multari opened his new practice less than six months after he had left Dr. Lyons' practice and that Dr. Multari's new office was located 3.7 miles from Dr. Lyons' office. In short, Dr. Multari breached the second term of the contract he had signed.

[9]　Dr. Lyons launched an action against Dr. Multari, seeking damages for breach of contract. Dr. Multari defended the action and counterclaimed, stating that Dr. Lyons had interfered with his practice during the six-month notice period, thus causing him to lose income.

2.　*The Trial Judgment*

[MACPHERSON J.A. summarized the findings of the trial judge. The trial judge (i) held that Dr. Multari understood what the restrictive covenant meant; (ii) held that the protection from competition provided by the covenant was a "proprietary interest" of Dr. Lyons; (iii) held that the covenant was reasonable; (iv) considered evidence that Dr. Lyons lost almost $120,000 in the first year after Mr. Multari left, but discounted this figure by 40 per cent to take account of contingencies; and (v) held that any damages for the second and third years of the restriction were "too remote". The trial judge rejected the counter-claim.]

. . .

[MACPHERSON J.A. continued:]

[16]　Dr. Multari appeals the trial judge's decision. He does not assert that the trial judge erred in finding that the restrictive covenant was clear and that Dr. Multari understood its meaning and effect. However, he contends that the trial judge erred in two respects: first, in finding that the restrictive covenant was valid and enforceable; and second, in his assessment of damages. Dr. Multari does not appeal the trial judge's dismissal of his counterclaim.

[17] Dr. Lyons cross-appeals the trial judge's decision respecting damages. He contends that the trial judge erred in his treatment of contingencies and in his refusal to award any damages for the second and third years of Dr. Multari's breach of the restrictive covenant.

B. Issues

[18] The appeal . . . raise[s] the following issues:. . .

1. Did the trial judge err in concluding that Dr. Lyons had a proprietary interest in the dentists who referred patients to his specialized oral surgery practice?

2. Did the trial judge err in concluding that the restrictive covenant was not overbroad and did not restrict competition generally?

3. Did the trial judge err in concluding that Dr. Multari's breach of the restrictive covenant caused financial injury to Dr. Lyons entitling him to damages? . . .

(a)   *The restrictive covenant*

[19] The general rule in most common law jurisdictions is that non-competition clauses in employment contracts are void. This proposition, and the rationale for it, were succinctly stated by Lord Macnaghten in the leading English case, *Nordenfelt v. Maxim Nordenfelt Guns & Ammunition Co.*, [1894] A.C. 535 at p. 565, [1891-94] All E.R. Rep. 1 (H.L.):

> The public have an interest in every person's carrying on his trade freely: so has the individual. All interference with individual liberty of action in trading, and all restraints of trade themselves, if there is nothing more, are contrary to public policy, and therefore void. That is the general rule.

[20] This general rule is not without exception. In *Nordenfelt*, Lord Macnaghten went on to say that for a restraint on trade to be valid it must be reasonable in the interests of the contracting parties and also reasonable in the public interest.

[21] The position in Canada is similar. The leading Canadian case dealing with non-competition clauses in an employment context is *Elsley v. J.G. Collins Insurance Agencies Ltd.*, [1978] 2 S.C.R. 916, 83 D.L.R. (3d) 1.[5] In *Elsley*, Dickson J. began his analysis by recognizing that such clauses presented a collision between two long-standing common law principles — discouraging restraints on trade and respecting freedom of contract. Dickson J. explained, at p. 923:

> The principles to be applied in considering restrictive covenants of employment are well-established . . . A covenant in restraint of trade is enforceable only if it is reasonable between the parties and with reference to the public interest. As in many of the cases which come before the courts, competing demands must be weighed. There

---

5   A non-competition clause usually arises in one of two contexts: first, in the sale of a business where the purchaser wants to ensure that the vendor will not set up a new rival business; and, second, in an employment relationship where an employer will try to guard against an employee leaving his business to establish, or work for, a rival business. Mr. Elsley was subject to both types of clauses. He sold his insurance business; part of the contract of sale was a ten-year non-competition clause. However, the purchaser rehired Elsley as the manager of the new business; part of the employment contract was a non-competition clause prohibiting Elsley from becoming a general insurance agent in Niagara Falls, Stamford and Chippawa for five years after his employment ceased. The litigation in *Elsley* involved the second of these clauses. Hence it is the leading case dealing with restrictive covenants in an employment context.

is an important public interest in discouraging restraints on trade, and maintaining free and open competition unencumbered by the fetters of restrictive covenants. On the other hand, the courts have been disinclined to restrict the right to contract, particularly when that right has been exercised by knowledgeable persons of equal bargaining power.

[22] In *Elsley,* Dickson J. said that a proper reconciliation of these conflicting principles was anchored in the notion of reasonableness, which could only be determined "upon an overall assessment, of the clause, the agreement within which it is found, and all of the surrounding circumstances" (at p. 924).

[23] Importantly, Dickson J. then set out the factors that require special attention when considering a restrictive covenant in an employment contract. In his view, there are three such factors: first, whether the employer has a proprietary interest entitled to protection; second, whether the temporal or spatial features of the clause are too broad; and, third, whether the covenant is unenforceable as being against competition generally, and not limited to proscribing solicitation of clients of the former employee (at p. 925). I will consider these factors in turn as they apply to the restrictive covenant involving Dr. Lyons and Dr. Multari.

(i) *Proprietary interest*

[24] The appellant contends that Dr. Lyons had no proprietary interest in the dentists who referred patients to his specialized oral surgery practice. He points out that Dr. Lyons stated during his testimony that the dentists who referred patients to him changed over time. Some dentists referred patients to him regularly, others commenced referrals at a certain point, and still others ceased making referrals. The appellant asserts that this evolving group of referring dentists was insufficient to establish a proprietary interest.

[25] I disagree with this submission for several reasons. First, there is case law supporting the proposition that employers in the professions have a proprietary interest in their client base: see, for example, *Gordon v. Ferguson* (1961), 30 D.L.R. (2d) 420 (N.S.S.C.) with respect to physicians; *Friesen v. McKague* (1992), 96 D.L.R. (4th) 341, [1993] 1 W.W.R. 627 (Man. C.A.) with respect to veterinarians; and *Simoni v. Sugarman,* [2000] N.J. No. 28 (T.D.) with respect to podiatrists.

[26] Second, I am attracted to the trial judge's analysis on this point. He described Dr. Lyons' practice as one in which long years of service in Windsor had resulted in a core group of dentists who by custom made referrals to him. He characterized these customary referrals as goodwill and concluded that they qualified as a proprietary interest capable of legal protection. In my view, this reasoning is sound, and the finding of a proprietary interest was clearly open to him on the evidence.

[27] Third, the appellant's position that there is *no* proprietary interest in the referring dentists is undercut by this paragraph in his factum:

> 35. Since Lyons had no special arrangement with the dentists whereby they would refer exclusively to himself, it seems apparent that he can claim "goodwill" only in those dentists who referred regularly and on a continuous basis to him, for he could not be said to have goodwill in dentists who had referred to him one time only, or on a few occasions, or who no longer referred to him. Goodwill connotes regular continuance of patronage.

[28] It seems to me that in this paragraph the appellant recognizes that there are *some* referring dentists (those who make regular referrals to Dr. Lyons) who do ground a claim in goodwill and proprietary interest. Once it is conceded that Dr. Lyons has a proprietary interest in *some* of his referring dentists, it becomes necessary to move to the second and third inquiries mandated by *Elsley*, namely, the temporal and spatial limits of the covenant, and whether the covenant goes too far by restricting competition generally.

(ii)   *Temporal and spatial limits of the covenant*

[29] The appellant does not assert that if the restrictive covenant complies with the first and third components of the *Elsley* test, it would nevertheless fail under the second component of the test relating to its temporal and spatial limits. In my view, such an assertion could not succeed. The case law is replete with covenants similar to the five-mile/three-year covenant in issue in this appeal. Indeed, in *Elsley* the Supreme Court of Canada upheld a restrictive covenant that was both broader (it prohibited competition in three communities, not just part of one community) and longer (five years, not three) than the Lyons/Multari covenant.

(iii)   *Non-competition versus non-solicitation*

[30] It is quite common for employers to insist that their employees sign a contract containing a non-solicitation clause. This type of provision prohibits a departing employee from soliciting the customers of his or her previous employer.

[31] The non-competition clause is a more drastic weapon in an employer's arsenal. Its focus is much broader than an attempt to protect the employer's client or customer base; it extends to an attempt to keep the former employee out of the business. Usually, non-competition clauses are limited in terms of space and time.

[32] Dr. Lyons chose the more drastic weapon in his dealings with Dr. Multari. The covenant he chose, and to which Dr. Multari agreed, was a non-competition covenant with spatial (five miles) and temporal (three years) limits.

[33] An important question in the case law relates to the relationship between non-solicitation and non-competition clauses. Generally speaking, the courts will not enforce a non-competition clause if a non-solicitation clause would adequately protect an employer's interests. In *Elsley*, Dickson J. framed the inquiry in this fashion, at p. 925:

> The next and crucial question is whether the covenant is unenforceable as being against competition generally, and not limited to proscribing solicitation of clients of the former employer.

[34] Dickson J. continued, at p. 926:

> Whether a [non-competition] restriction is reasonably required for the protection of the covenantee can only be decided by considering the nature of the covenantee's business and the nature and character of the employment. Admittedly, an employer could not have a proprietary interest in people who were not actual or potential customers. Nevertheless, *in exceptional cases*, of which I think this is one, the nature of the employment may justify a covenant prohibiting an employee not only from soliciting customers, but also from establishing his own business or working for others so as to be likely to appropriate the employer's trade connection through his acquaintance with the employer's customers. This may indeed be the only effective covenant

to protect the proprietary interest of the employer. A simple non-solicitation clause would not suffice. (Emphasis added)

[35] The question to be addressed in this appeal is whether this is one of those "exceptional cases" where "a simple non-solicitation clause would not suffice".

[36] There are factors in favour of the broad non-competition clause. First, in *Elsley* Dickson J. said that "the courts have been disinclined to restrict the right to contract, particularly when that right has been exercised by knowledgeable persons of equal bargaining power" (at p. 923). I have no hesitation saying that the relationship between Dr. Lyons and Dr. Multari was one between equals. Although Dr. Lyons had practised oral surgery in Windsor for almost 25 years whereas Dr. Multari was just embarking on his career, the reality is that Dr. Multari was a highly educated man with many employment options open to him. Indeed, he chose an association with Dr. Lyons over one with Dr. Silverman, another oral surgeon in Windsor.

[37] Second, there is no question that, in many respects, Dr. Lyons treated Dr. Multari well during their association. Dr. Lyons took steps to introduce Dr. Multari to his referring dentists, he encouraged the dentists to refer patients to Dr. Multari, his receptionist identified both doctors when she answered the telephone and he was instrumental in obtaining hospital privileges for Dr. Multari. All of this meant that, as he started his career as an oral surgeon, Dr. Multari had a steady flow of patients and, not inconsequentially, a substantial income (approximately $200,000 per year).

[38] In spite of these factors, in my view the non-competition clause in this appeal does not come within the category of "exceptional cases" as explained by Dickson J. in *Elsley*. I reach this conclusion for several reasons.

[39] First, although Dr. Lyons had some proprietary interest in some regular referring dentists, he had *no* proprietary interest in Windsor dentists who had never referred patients to him in the past or who stopped referring patients to him before Dr. Multari's arrival. As Dickson J. expressed it in *Elsley*: "Admittedly, an employer could not have a proprietary interest in people who were not actual or potential customers" (at p. 926).

[40] Second, although it is true that Dr. Lyons treated Dr. Multari well during their association, it must be said that this worked as much to Dr. Lyons' benefit as to Dr. Multari's. Dr. Lyons paid Dr. Multari a generous base salary. However, for fees above a certain amount, Dr. Multari received a percentage and Dr. Lyons kept the rest. The reality is that both Dr. Multari and Dr. Lyons made a great deal of money because of their association.

[41] Third, the role of Dr. Multari in Dr. Lyons' oral surgery practice was that of a normal associate. It did not even come close to the special role Mr. Elsley played in the insurance business in Elsley.

[42] Mr. Elsley managed the agency's insurance business for 17 years. Dickson J. described his role in this fashion, at p. 920:

> During the seventeen-year period Elsley dealt with the customers of the agency to the almost total exclusion of Collins. *To them Elsley was the business*, Collins little more than a name. Elsley met the customers, telephoned them frequently, placed their insurance policies and answered their queries. (Emphasis added)

[43] This description does not apply to Dr. Multari. He did not manage the practice; Dr. Lyons did. Dr. Multari was a junior associate dentist who worked for Dr. Lyons for less than two years, a far cry from 17 years. Dr. Multari dealt with some patients. However, the records of the practice during the relevant two years establish that in every respect, including billings, Dr. Lyons was the dominant figure. Dr. Multari simply handled the patients who were referred to him. On a monthly basis, he received a printout of his patients and the dentists who referred them. However, he was not the front man, or principal contact person, for communication with those dentists. That role, which had been played for almost a quarter century by Dr. Lyons, continued to be played by Dr. Lyons after Dr. Multari's arrival.

[44] In *Friesen v. McKague, supra,* Scott C.J.M. stated that a non-competition clause should be enforced "where the nature of the employment will likely cause customers to perceive an individual employee as the personification of the company or employer" (at p. 346). In my view, that description does not fit Dr. Multari as he embarked upon his career as an oral surgeon. In the eyes of referring dentists, the personification of Dr. Lyons' practice was the same person it had been for almost 25 years — Dr. Lyons.

[45] Fourth, in *Elsley,* Dickson J. stated, at p. 924:

> Although blanket restraints on freedom to compete are generally held unenforceable, the courts have recognized and afforded reasonable protection to trade secrets, confidential information, and trade connections of the employer.

[46] The broad non-competition clause in this appeal cannot be enforced on the basis that it was required to protect confidential information. When he departed, Dr. Multari took no trade secrets or confidential information with him. He never saw a list of Dr. Lyons' patients and referring dentists. He did know, of course, the names of the referring dentists of patients he had treated personally. However, a simple non-solicitation covenant would have prevented him from soliciting those dentists.

[47] Fifth, and admittedly a minor point, there is some evidence in the record that the practice in the dental profession with respect to restrictive covenants did not uniformly accord with Dr. Lyons' practice. When Dr. Multari was negotiating in Windsor in 1993 with a second oral surgeon, Dr. Silverman, the proposed Silverman-Multari contract had a non-solicitation, not a non-competition, clause. Moreover, the non-solicitation clause was not an absolute one; it would have permitted Dr. Multari to solicit patients with whom he had developed relationships during his association with Dr. Silverman.

[48] For all of these reasons, I conclude that Dr. Lyons' non-competition clause is unenforceable. His legitimate interest in protecting his own referring dentists and patients could have been protected by a non-solicitation clause. An established professional person or firm — be it in the field of dentistry, medicine, engineering, architecture, law or other professions — will constantly seek to recruit entry level associates to the practice. Such recruitment is good for the established person or firm and for the young associate.

[49] It is natural that many of those relationships will end after a few years. Sometimes the firm will terminate the relationship; in other cases the associate will decide to move on. For professional and personal reasons, many associates will want to continue to work in the same community after they have left their original employer. There is nothing wrong with such a preference. However, the employer has a legitimate interest to protect — namely, its clients. In my view, in the circumstances of this case, a proper balancing of the interests of the employer and the departing employee is struck by the line drawn in *Elsley*. As a general rule, non-solicitation clauses are permissible; "in exceptional cases" only, non-competition clauses will be upheld.

[50] In my view, this is not an exceptional case. Indeed, the Lyons-Multari relationship strikes me as the norm in a professional setting. Accordingly, the non-competition covenant is unenforceable.

. . .

[57] The appeal is allowed. The plaintiff's action against the defendant is dismissed. The appellant is entitled to his costs of the appeal and of the action.

Appeal allowed.

QUESTIONS, NOTES AND PROBLEMS

1. As noted in *Lyons v. Multari*, the courts give closer scrutiny to non-competition clauses in employment contracts than to similar clauses in contracts selling a business. The Supreme Court of Canada in *Doerner v. Bliss & Laughlin Industries Inc.*, [1980] 2 S.C.R. 865 at pp. 872-73, 117 D.L.R. (3d) 547, explained (*per* McIntyre J.):

    The general principles governing cases of this nature are well settled. While, generally speaking, covenants in restraint of trade have been considered contrary to public policy and unenforceable, certain exceptions have been recognized. Covenants which restrain competition by an employee with his former employer, and those restraining a vendor of a business from competing with his purchaser, form two exceptions to the general rule where the restraint imposed is reasonable considering the interest of the respective parties and also the interest of the public. It is recognized that the public has an interest in the continued provision of goods and services resulting from the employment of skills acquired by employees in the course of their employment and, as well, an interest in the continuation of the trade or business. Covenants which seek to interfere with such activity are to that extent injurious to the public interest. On the other hand, it is said that it is also in the public interest that a person who has built up a valuable business should be able to sell it and be competent in law to bind himself to refrain from competition with the business he has sold, so that a purchaser will be encouraged to acquire and thus maintain the business in active operation for the general public benefit, as well as his own profit.

    A distinction also has been recognized between a covenant given by the vendor of a business to protect his purchaser, and one given by an employee terminating his employment to protect his employer from competition. This latter type of covenant, it has been said, may well arise from dealings between unequals and thus be oppressive to an employee. It may be acceptable, however, where the purpose of the covenant is not to prohibit the employee from exploiting the skills he has acquired in his past employment, but to protect the former employer against competition where the scope and nature of the employee's work and his contact with clients and customers of his former employer is such that he could readily do harm to his employer.

2. If the Court in *Lyons* had refused to give effect to a non-competition clause, should it have also ordered a reference to determine the reduction in base salary or other benefit provided to Dr. Multari that Dr. Lyons would have insisted on as the price for getting less protection than he had expected? In other words, if the court reduces the value of

the goodwill of the plaintiff, should the plaintiff be compensated for this loss? How would such a reduction be determined? Can it be denied on principle (as opposed to being denied on the simple ground that it might be impossible to calculate)?

3. Consider the problems of drafting clauses designed to restrict competition. What factors must you keep in mind if you are acting for the employer or purchaser? For the employee or vendor? Does the likely effect on the price or salary paid in each case give you any useful guidance?

    Draft a clause to give the purchaser of a law practice as much protection as you think she can get. The price paid for a law practice is generally two to three years' "purchase" (that is, the net, or sometimes the gross, annual income multiplied by two or three). What further facts do you need to know before you can feel confident that you can do a good job for your client? What guidance does the method of calculating the price give you? Is the factor implicit in the price paid for a law practice relevant in the sale of any other kind of business, or in the salary (or other benefits) paid to a senior employee?

4. The choice as to what point of temporal reference a court is to use to determine an issue is complex but important. Similar issues arose in dealing with foreseeability of loss in damage assessments in cases like *Hadley v. Baxendale,* and in the conflicting approaches of Dickson C.J.C. and Wilson J. in *Hunter Engineering v. Syncrude.* The date for determining the enforceability of a non-competition clause raises the problem again.

    Is the determination of "reasonableness between the parties" to be made at the time the contract is made on an *ex ante* — before breach — basis, or on an *ex post* — after breach — basis? Diplock L.J., for example, in *Gledhow Autoparts v. Delaney,* [1965] 3 All E.R. 288, [1965] 1 W.L.R. 1366 (C.A.), said (p. 295, All E.R.):

    > It is natural . . . to look at what in fact happened under the agreement; but the question of the validity of the covenant in restraint of trade has to be determined at the date at which the agreement was entered into and has to be determined in the light of what may happen under the agreement. . . . A covenant of this kind is invalid *ab initio* or valid *ab initio.* There cannot come a moment at which it passes from the class of the invalid to that of valid covenants.

    Can a valid agreement become invalid? Should the same rules apply to non-competition clauses in employment agreements and those in asset or share purchase and sale agreements? The former agreement is a relational one, while the latter is likely to be close to the discrete end of the spectrum. Notice that the issue of timing bears directly on the purpose of the clause and on the ability of the drafter of a contract to foresee what may happen when the clause has to be relied on.

5. As a practical matter, solicitors recognize that non-competition clauses in employment agreements are far more open to challenge than similar clauses in asset or share purchase agreements: the public policy issues in the two situations are very different. It is nevertheless important to consider not just the public policy issue, but the issue of fairness. In *Friesen v. McKague* (1993), 96 D.L.R. (4th) 341, [1993] 3 W.W.R. 627 (Man. C.A.), the defendant was a veterinarian who had been employed by the plaintiff. He entered into a five-year non-competition clause after advice from his (lawyer) wife. The trial judge had given summary judgment in favour of the plaintiff and enjoined the defendant from acting in breach of the non-competition clause. On appeal it was held that the restriction was reasonable and, since the defendant had legal advice, should not be interpreted against the plaintiff.

    It is important to remember that courts can seldom consider one purpose to the exclusion of another or others: every decision will be a compromise between two or more goals.

6. Sometimes the direct enforcement of a non-competition clause can be avoided. In *Burgess v. Industrial Frictions and Supply Co.,* [1987] 4 W.W.R. 182 (B.C.C.A.), the plaintiff had been a major shareholder, director and officer of the defendant corpora-

tion. In 1978, he retired and sold his shares to the defendant. In the agreement for the sale of his shares, the defendant promised to pay $300,000, conditional, as provided by cl. 3 of the agreement, on the plaintiff's continuously acting and conducting himself as a fiduciary of the defendant. By cl. 10 of the agreement, the plaintiff agreed to a five-year non-competition clause. In 1984, the plaintiff went to work for the major competitor of the defendant. The defendant refused to pay the next annual instalment due under the agreement. In an action for the instalment, a majority of the Court held that there was no inconsistency between cls. 3 and 10, and that the former did not involve a prohibition, merely a "disincentive" to competition. The majority of the Court also held that, if cl. 3 was in restraint of trade, it was reasonable. Anderson J.A. dissented on the ground that the plaintiff could not be required to give up the whole purchase price of his shares, and be prevented from working for a competitor.

There is no indication from the judgment that the plaintiff argued that cl. 3 was in the nature of a penalty or a forfeiture clause, indirectly enforcing (by means of a very powerful disincentive!) the non-competition clause. The result of the decision is that the defendant was able to keep about 40 per cent of the purchase price without showing any loss arising from the plaintiff's actions, and without having to justify either its enrichment or the satisfaction of the normal tests for the enforceability of a penalty, forfeiture or non-competition clause.

7.   Decisions limiting the power of corporations to act in restraint of trade can have far reaching implications. For example in *Esso Petroleum Co. v. Harper's Garage (Stourport) Ltd.*, [1968] A.C. 269, [1967] 1 All E.R. 699 (H.L.), the House of Lords held that Esso Petroleum was acting in restraint of trade by requiring independent gas stations to sell only its products for 21 years. The House of Lords, however, accepted that a five-year agreement would be enforceable. The decision had major implications for the gasoline market in the United Kingdom: the major oil companies, like Esso, simply bought up gas stations until there were almost no independents left.

8.   Is there a limit to how far the courts should go in achieving distributional goals, or does the limit arise from the kind of problem that the law has to deal with? In other words, is it more justifiable for the courts to impose non-delegable duties of care on a builder (for example, *Fraser-Reid v. Droumtsekas*) than it is to restrict the freedom of large multinational oil producers to run their business as they see fit? Is it merely a matter of the size of the body being controlled, or is it that the builder has virtually no alternative strategies open to it to avoid the impact of the courts' decision, while the oil producer has a wide range of alternatives open to it (and nearly unlimited assets to pursue them)?

9.   The enforcement of the controls on anti-competitive behaviour in Canada through the *Competition Act* may involve investigations by the Competition Bureau and, in some cases, a determination by the Competition Tribunal that there is an objectionable course of conduct by the members of the industry.

10.   Your client is a licensed real estate broker with an office just outside a major metropolitan centre. She wants to join a multiple-listing service ("MLS") operated by the Real Estate Board of the area. The bylaws of the MLS provide that anyone wanting to join must have an office in the metropolitan area, be approved as a new member by all of the existing members, and pay a fee so large that it can be recovered only by operating within the MLS framework. It is also clear that only by operating in the MLS system can a broker in the area or close to it be successful. Is there any way by which your client can compel the board to accept her for membership? Should there be a way?

11.   For many corporations today, particularly those in the high-tech area, a significant part of their corporate assets lies in the brains of their employees. The programmer employed by a software developer may be the most important asset of the corporation. The traditional assets employed by a corporation to earn income — its land, its buildings and its intellectual property — can be used exclusively by the corporation and simultaneously denied to its competition: they are owned. The employee cannot be

owned but can, perhaps, be discouraged from leaving his or her employment by carefully drafted non-competition and non-solicitation clauses in an employment contract. The imposition on an employee of fiduciary obligations, *i.e.*, the obligation to respect and protect his or her employer's confidential information, may also be an important supplement to the terms of any employment contract.

The employer of an employee with a readily marketable "knowledge asset" faces two problems if the employee leaves. The first is competition from the employee who goes into business for himself or herself. In that situation a non-competition or non-solicitation clause is likely to be the principal method to prevent unfair competition. Such clauses may limit but will not prevent all competition, for the employee cannot be completely prevented from using what is his or her knowledge. The second problem arises if the employee leaves to work for a competitor. The imposition on the employee and on the new employer of the duties based on the employee's fiduciary obligation will be the simultaneous protection from some kinds of competition and a disincentive to the new employer to employ the employee.

Another aspect of the employment contract is the increasing use of the tort of wrongful interference with economic relations to discourage new employers from enticing employees to leave their present employment. In *Ernst & Young v. Stuart & Arthur Andersen & Co.* (1994), 92 B.C.L.R. (2d) 335, [1994] 8 W.W.R. 431 (C.A.), the plaintiff was successful in a claim against the defendant partnership for damages for wrongfully inducing the individual defendant to breach his partnership agreement. The tort of wrongful interference with contractual relations or economic relations is very broad and no satisfactory limits have yet been established. The requirements are:

(a)   a valid and enforceable contract existed between the plaintiff and the third party;

(b)   the defendant had knowledge that the third party had a contract with the plaintiff;

(c)   the defendant intended to induce the third party to breach its contract with the plaintiff;

(d)   the defendant successfully persuaded the third party to breach its contract with the plaintiff; and

(e)   the plaintiff suffered loss as a result of the breach.

The employer who actively solicits an employee who is working for a competitor now faces obvious problems. Even the position of the new employer who does not solicit but who is approached by a person seeking a job is not without problems. That employer has to worry about wrongfully inducing the breach of the existing employment contract and about the risk that the employee will come with knowledge that he or she may not lawfully disclose to it because its disclosure would be in breach of the employee's fiduciary obligation to his or her former employer.

The disputes that can now arise over the termination of one employment relation and the creation of another centre on property-type problems. The first employer wants to deny anyone else the benefits of the investment that it has made in the employee and to assert that, in effect, it "owns" the employee's knowledge. The second employer is faced with the risk that it may get an "asset", *i.e.* its new employee and his or her knowledge, in which someone else has what amounts to a proprietary claim and which it cannot safely use for its benefit. In the negotiations with the employee, the second employer will be concerned to establish that the employee is able to show that he or she has "clear title" to his or her knowledge, *i.e.* that the employee can freely use what he or she knows to the benefit of the new employer. In some areas where an employee's knowledge is crucial — software development, for example — it may be very difficult for the employee to give the new employer a great deal of comfort.

In some cases, the first employer may obtain an injunction to prevent a former employee from working for a new employer in violation of a non-competition clause; see e.g., *Towers, Perrin, Forster & Crosby, Inc. v. Cantin* (1999), 46 O.R. (3d) 180 (S.C.J.).

12. In *RBC Dominion Securities Inc. v. Merrill Lynch Canada Inc.*, [2003] B.C.J. No. 2700, 44 B.L.R. (3d) 72 (S.C.); additional reasons (2004), 50 B.L.R. (3d) 308 (B.C.S.C.) Merrill Lynch secretly solicited and co-ordinated the mass departure of almost all of RBC's staff from its office in Cranbrook, British Columbia, including the branch manager and most of the staff of investment advisors. The departing staff contacted clients before and immediately after their departure in a campaign to move their book of business to Merrill Lynch. The branch manager only told RBC of the mass departure the day that the staff left the employment of RBC. According to industry practice, RBC did not require non-competition covenants from staff. The industry-wide expectation was that departing key employees need give no notice and could carry away much of their book of business to the employer's detriment. RBC brought an action against Merrill Lynch for inducing breach of the employees' contracts of employment. Holmes J. concluded that none of the departing employees was sufficiently senior to have a fiduciary duty to RBC, but concluded that the branch manager and his staff breached their duty of "good faith" towards their employer, and imposed liability on the manager and investment advisors, as well as ordering Merrill Lynch to pay $250,000 in punitive damages. The secret use of RBC's client records by its key employees prior to and immediately after their departure breached their duty of good faith. As Merrill Lynch induced the employee's breach of their good faith obligations, it was liable along with them for RBC's losses arising from their breach. In regard to the duty of good faith, Holmes J. wrote (at paras. 35-36, 126 and 128):

> Every employee, whether or not in a fiduciary relationship to the employer, owes a duty of fidelity or good faith to the employer which is not limited to current employment. This general duty includes a duty not to compete unfairly against the employer during or after the employment arrangement, and in turn a duty not to make use of the employer's confidential information and material to compete with the employer. ... However, unless bound by a non-competition clause in the employment contract, an employee is entitled to compete fairly with the employer.
>
> A former employee is more restricted if he or she stands in a fiduciary relationship to the employer. Like a non-fiduciary employee, he or she may compete fairly against the former employer. ...
>
> ...
>
> [The branch manager's] duty of good faith ... also required him to keep his regional manager fully and promptly advised of all significant information relating to the operation of the branch, particularly as to events with the obvious potential of damaging or destroying the very viability of the branch. He was in serious breach of that duty from, at the latest, June, 2000, when he personally visited Merrill Lynch's operations and arranged for others to do likewise, and encouraged or acquiesced in [Merrill Lynch's] mass recruiting efforts.
>
> ...
>
> In all these circumstances, it is difficult to conceive of a more fundamental breach of the duty of good faith as branch manager.

While it remains common for investment advisors (stockbrokers) to change employers without notice and to immediately solicit their former clients, this decision sets some limits to the practice, and in particular restricts the use of records of the original employer.

13. In *BMO Nesbitt Burns Inc. v. Wellington West Capital Inc.*, [2005] O.J. No. 3566, 77 O.R. (3d) 161, 257 D.L.R. (4th) 122 (C.A.), a case with facts somewhat similar to those of *RBC v. Merrill Lynch*, the Ontario Court of Appeal held that, in response to a claim for punitive damages brought by the plaintiff, the defendant could plead that the plaintiff's practices were no better and that the kind of conduct which the plaintiff alleged should be discouraged by punitive damages was endemic in the brokerage in-

dustry. In other words, it is a defence to a claim for punitive damages that the pot should not call the kettle black!

14. As in the financial services industry, law firms will develop very close relations with their clients, usually, but by no means always, corporations. These "firm clients" will, in turn, develop very close relations with the individual lawyers with whom they are in close contact and these relations may, over the years, be passed from lawyer to lawyer within the firm; as one lawyer retires from practice, he or she will bring less senior lawyers along to provide services to the firm's clients. Law firms do not, as general practice, have non-competition or non-solicitation clauses in their employment contracts or partnership agreements because the fiduciary duties that an individual lawyer would owe his or her clients would trump any attempted restriction on his or her ability to work for (or to continue to work for) a client. There are, however, real concerns about potential (or actual) conflicts of interest when a lawyer leaves one firm to go to work for another and these conflicts may prevent a lawyer who changes firms from continuing to represent his or her client. The more serious problem is actually the reverse of this: unless the lawyer's new firm takes immediate and careful steps, that firm may be prevented from acting for clients that it may have represented for years. See *Skye Properties Ltd. v. Wu*, [2003] O.J. No. 3481, 247 D.L.R. (4th) 151 (S.C.J.) for an extreme case. See also discussion of Kim Alexander-Cook, "Advertising, Competition and Restraint of Trade", Chapter 7 in K. Lysyk, L. Sossin & J. Hoskins, eds., *Barristers & Solicitors in Practice* (LexisNexis Canada, 2005) para. 14.3.

Draft the following documents:

(a) instructions from the CEO to middle managers advising them how to conduct negotiations with prospective employees who may be subject to fiduciary obligations to former employers;

(b) a letter to be sent by the new employer in response to an inquiry about an advertised job-opening from a person known to be working for a competitor;

(c) a letter offering employment to a person known to be working for a competitor; and

(d) instructions to the new employee on his or her starting to work dealing with the required treatment of information that is possibly subject to the fiduciary obligation owed to the employee's former employer.

———————

The issues raised in the restraint of trade cases are related to the general issue of unconscionability. An important distinction between the restraint of trade cases and the typical unconscionability cases is that the latter tend to focus exclusively on the relation between the parties, while the former are also concerned with broader market issues and social values. At base, however, the two concerns are similar. The next case makes the connection between unconscionability and restraint of trade explicit and, in doing so, raises the problem of determining what the factual underpinning of any decision that an agreement is unconscionable should be.

A. SCHROEDER MUSIC PUBLISHING CO. LTD. v. MACAULAY

[1974] 3 All E.R. 616, [1974] 1 W.L.R. 1308
(H.L., Viscount Dilhorne, Lords Reid, Diplock, Simon and Kilbrandon)

[The parties entered into an agreement in 1966. The respondent was then 21 years old and an aspiring composer and songwriter; he had written a few songs, but none had been published. The appellant was a music publisher and a subsidiary of an American corporation with worldwide connections. The composer signed the appellant's standard-form contract for composers of music and song-writers. At the time of signing, the composer was aware of the terms and wished to get a different kind of contract, but agreed to sign this one. The contract (in cls. 1 and 9(a)) provided for a five-year term, during which time the composer would give his services exclusively to the publisher (cl. 2). The composer was paid £50 on the signing of the agreement. This payment was an advance on royalties (cl. 8). As royalties were earned, the publisher would pay the composer another £50, and so on. If the royalties paid to the composer during the first five-year term of the agreement exceeded £5,000, the publisher could renew the agreement for another five-year term (cl. 9(a)). The publisher could cancel the agreement at any time on giving notice, but there was no power in the composer to cancel (cl. 9(b)).

The composer was required to give the publisher all of his compositions (cl. 10(a)) and was required to indemnify the publisher if any problems with copyright arose (cl. 10(b)). The publisher could assign the contract without the composer's consent, but he could not do so without the publisher's consent (cl. 16). The composer brought an action for a declaration that the agreement was contrary to public policy and was void. The trial judge made the declaration sought, a decision upheld by the Court of Appeal; the publisher appealed to the House of Lords.]

LORD REID, after stating the facts, continued: —

[1] It is not disputed that the validity of the agreement must be determined as at the date when it was signed and it is therefore unnecessary to deal with the reasons why the respondent now wishes to be freed from it. The law with regard to the validity of agreements in restraint of trade was fully considered by this House in *Esso Petroleum Co. Ltd. v. Harper's Garage* [[1968] A.C. 269, [1967] 1 All E.R. 699 (H.L.)] and I do not intend to restate the principles there set out or to add to or modify what I said myself. I think that in a case like the present case two questions must be considered. Are the terms of the agreement so restrictive that either they cannot be justified at all or that they must be justified by the party seeking to enforce the agreement? Then, if there is room for justification, has that party proved justification normally by shewing that the restrictions were no more than what was reasonably required to protect his legitimate interests. In this case evidence on the second question was scanty and I turn first to the terms of the agreement. . . .

[2] [The agreement] was to last for five years in any event and for ten years if the royalties for the first five years exceeded £5,000. There is little evidence about this extension. Five thousand pounds in five years appears to represent a very modest success, and so if the respondent's work became well known and popular he would be tied by the agreement for ten years. The duration of an agreement in restraint of trade is a factor of great importance in determining whether the restrictions in the agreement can be justified, but there was no evidence as to why so long a period was necessary to protect the appellants' interest. Clause 2 requires the respondent to give the exclusive services to and obey all lawful orders of the appellants. It is not very clear what this means. Read in conjunction with cl. 2(c) it probably does not prevent him from doing non-musical work so long as that does not interfere with his obligations to the appellants. I do not attach importance to this clause as being at all unduly restrictive. Clause 3 is of importance but I shall return to it later. Clauses 5 to 8 deal with remuneration. Some parts are not very clear but it was not argued that this was an unreasonable basis for the remuneration of a composer unknown when the agreement was made. Clause 9(b) entitles the appellants to terminate the agreement but there is no corresponding provision in favour of the respondent. I shall have to deal with this later. Clause 10(b) could be rather oppressive but no serious objection was taken to it . . . . Clause 16 appears to me to be important. There may sometimes be room for an argument that although on a strict literal construction restrictions could be enforced oppressively, one is entitled to have regard to the fact that a large organisation could not afford to act oppressively without damaging the goodwill of its business. But the power to assign leaves no room for that argument. We cannot assume that an assignee would always act reasonably.

[3]   The public interest requires in the interest both of the public and of the individual that everyone should be free so far as practicable to earn a livelihood and to give to the public the fruits of his particular abilities. The main question to be considered is whether and how far the operation of the terms of this agreement is likely to conflict with this objective. The respondent is bound to assign to the appellants during a long period the fruits of his musical talent. But what are the appellants bound to do with those fruits? Under the contract nothing. If they do use the songs which the respondent composes they must pay in terms of the contract. But they need not do so. As has been said, they may put them in a drawer and leave them there. No doubt the expectation was that if the songs were of value they would be published to the advantage of both parties. But if for any reason the appellants chose not to publish them the respondent would get no remuneration and he could not do anything. Inevitably the respondent must take the risk of misjudgment of the merits of his work by the appellants. But that is not the only reason which might cause the appellants not to publish. There is no evidence about this so we must do the best we can with common knowledge. It does not seem fanciful and it was not argued that it is fanciful to suppose that purely commercial consideration might cause a publisher to refrain from publishing and promoting promising material. He might think it likely to be more profitable to promote work by other composers with whom he had agreements and unwise or too expensive to try to publish and popularise the respondent's work in addition. And there is always the possibility that less legitimate reasons might influence a decision not to publish the respondent's work.

[4]   It was argued that there must be read into this agreement an obligation on the publisher to act in good faith. I take that to mean that he would be in breach of contract if by reason of some oblique or malicious motive he refrained from publishing work which he would otherwise have published. I very much doubt this but even if it were so it would make little difference. Such a case would seldom occur and then would be difficult to prove.

[5]   I agree with the appellants' argument to this extent. I do not think that a publisher could reasonably be expected to enter into any positive commitment to publish future work by an unknown composer. Possibly there might be some general undertaking to use his best endeavours to promote the composer's work. But that would probably have to be in such general terms as to be of little use to the composer.

[6]   But if no satisfactory positive undertaking by the publisher can be devised, it appears to me to be an unreasonable restraint to tie the composer for this period of

years so that his work will be sterilised and he can earn nothing from his abilities as a composer if the publisher chooses not to publish. If there had been in cl. 9 any provision entitling the composer to terminate the agreement, in such an event the case might have had a very different appearance. But as the agreement stands not only is the composer tied but he cannot recover the copyright of the work which the publisher refuses to publish.

[7] It was strenuously argued that the agreement is in standard form, that it has stood the test of time, and that there is no indication that it ever causes injustice. Reference was made to passages in the speeches of Lord Pearce and Lord Wilberforce in the *Esso* case with which I wholly agree. Lord Pearce said: "It is important that the court, in weighing the question of reasonableness, should give full weight to commercial practices and to the generality of contracts made freely by parties bargaining on equal terms." Later Lord Wilberforce said:

> The development of the law does seem to show, however, that judges have been able to dispense from the necessity of justification under a public policy test of reasonableness such contracts or provisions of contracts as, under contemporary conditions, may be found to have passed into the accepted and normal currency of commercial or contractual or conveyancing relations. That such contracts have done so may be taken to show with at least strong prima facie force that, moulded under the pressures of negotiation, competition and public opinion, they have assumed a form which satisfies the test of public policy as understood by the courts at the time, or, regarding the matter from the point of view of the trade, that the trade in question has assumed such a form that for its health or expansion it requires a degree of regulation.

[8] But those passages refer to contracts "made freely by parties bargaining on equal terms" or "moulded under the pressures of negotiation, competition and public opinion." I do not find from any evidence in this case, nor does it seem probable, that this form of contract made between a publisher and an unknown composer has been moulded by any pressure of negotiation. Indeed, it appears that established composers who can bargain on equal terms can and do make their own contracts.

[9] Any contract by which a person engages to give his exclusive services to another for a period necessarily involves extensive restriction during that period of the common-law right to exercise any lawful activity he chooses in such manner as he thinks best. Normally the doctrine of restraint of trade has no application to such restrictions: they require no justification. But if contractual restrictions appear to be unnecessary or to be reasonably capable of enforcement in an oppressive manner, then they must be justified before they can be enforced.

[10] In the present case the respondent assigned to the appellants "the full copyright for the whole world" in every musical composition "composed created or conceived" by him alone or in collaboration with any other person during a period of five or it might be ten years. He received no payment (apart from an initial £50) unless his work was published and the appellants need not publish unless they chose to do so. And if they did not publish he had no right to terminate the agreement or to have any copyrights reassigned to him. I need not consider whether in any circumstances it would be possible to justify such a one-sided agreement. It is sufficient to say that such evidence as there is falls far short of justification. It must therefore follow that the agreement so far as unperformed is unenforceable.

[11] I would dismiss this appeal.

LORD DIPLOCK: — **[12]** My Lords, the contract under consideration in this appeal is one whereby the respondent accepted restrictions on the way in which he would exploit his earning power as a songwriter for the next ten years. Because this can be classified as a contract in restraint of trade the restrictions that the respondent accepted fell within one of those limited categories of contractual promises in respect of which the courts still retain the power to relieve the promisor of his legal duty to fulfil them. In order to determine whether this case is one in which that power ought to be exercised, what your Lordships have in fact been doing has been to assess the relative bargaining power of the publisher and the songwriter at the time the contract was made and to decide whether the publisher had used his superior bargaining power to exact from the songwriter promises that were unfairly onerous to him. Your Lordships have not been concerned to enquire whether the public have in fact been deprived of the fruit of the songwriter's talents by reason of the restrictions, not to assess the likelihood that they would be so deprived in the future if the contract were permitted to run its full course.

[13] It is, in my view, salutary to acknowledge that in refusing to enforce provisions of a contract whereby one party agrees for the benefit of the other party to exploit or to refrain from exploiting his own earning-power, the public policy which the court is implementing is not some 19th-century economic theory about the benefit to the general public of freedom of trade, but the protection of those whose bargaining power is weak against being forced by those whose bargaining power is stronger to enter into bargains that are unconscionable. Under the influence of Bentham and of laissez-faire the courts in the 19th century abandoned the practice of applying the public policy against unconscionable bargains to contracts generally, as they had formerly done to any contract considered to be usurious; but the policy survived in its application to penalty clauses and to relief against forfeiture and also to the special category of contracts in restraint of trade. If one looks at the reasoning of 19th-century judges in cases about contracts in restraint of trade one finds lip service paid to current economic theories, but if one looks at what they said in the light of what they did one finds that they struck down a bargain if they thought it was unconscionable as between the parties to it, and upheld it if they thought that it was not.

[14] So I would hold that the question to be answered as respects a contract in restraint of trade of the kind with which this appeal is concerned is: was the bargain fair? The test of fairness is, no doubt, whether the restrictions are both reasonably necessary for the protection of the legitimate interests of the promisee and commensurate with the benefits secured to the promisor under the contract. For the purpose of this test all the provisions of the contract must be taken into consideration.

[15] My Lords, the provisions of the contract have already been sufficiently stated by my noble and learned friend, Lord Reid. I agree with his analysis of them and with his conclusion that the contract is unenforceable. It does not satisfy the test of fairness as I have endeavoured to state it. I will accordingly content myself with adding some observations directed to the argument that because the contract was in a "standard form" in common use between music publishers and songwriters, the restraints that it imposes on the songwriter's liberty to exploit his talents must be presumed to be fair and reasonable.

[16] Standard forms of contracts are of two kinds. The first, of very ancient origin, are those which set out the terms on which mercantile transactions of common occurrence are to be carried out. Examples are bills of lading, charterparties, policies of insurance, contracts of sale in the commodity markets. The standard clauses in these contracts have been settled over the years by negotiation by representatives of the commercial interests involved and have been widely adopted because experience has shown that they facilitate the conduct of trade. Contracts of these kinds affect not only the actual parties to them but also others who may have a commercial interest in the transactions to which they relate, as buyers or sellers, charterers or shipowners, insurers or bankers. If fairness or reasonableness were relevant to their enforceability the fact that they are widely used by parties whose bargaining power is fairly matched would raise a strong presumption that their terms are fair and reasonable.

[17] The same presumption, however, does not apply to the other kind of standard form of contract. This is of comparatively modern origin. It is the result of the concentration of particular kinds of business in relatively few hands. The ticket cases in the 19th century provide what are probably the first examples. The terms of this kind of standard form of contract have not been the subject of negotiation between the parties to it, or approved by any organisation representing the interests of the weaker party. They have been dictated by that party whose bargaining power, either exercised alone or in conjunction with others providing similar goods or services, enables him to say: "If you want these goods or services at all, these are the only terms on which they are obtainable. Take it or leave it."

[18] To be in a position to adopt this attitude towards a party desirous of entering into a contract to obtain goods or services provides a classic instance of superior bargaining power. It is not without significance that on the evidence in the present case, music publishers in negotiating with song-writers whose success has been already established do not insist on adhering to a contract in the standard form they offered to the respondent. The fact that the appellants' bargaining power *vis-a-vis* the respondent was strong enough to enable them to adopt this take-it-or-leave it attitude raises no presumption that they used it to drive an unconscionable bargain with him, but in the field of restraint of trade it calls for vigilance on the part of the court to see that they did not.

[**VISCOUNT DILHORNE** agreed with **LORD REID**; **LORDS SIMON** and **KILBRANDON** agreed with **LORDS REID** and **DIPLOCK**.]

QUESTIONS AND NOTES

1. Lord Diplock divides standard form contracts into two classes. Was there any evidence concerning the validity of his classification? Does his classification bind future courts? Is it correct? Do the extracts from Kessler, Macneil and Havighurst at the beginning of this chapter support Lord Diplock's conclusions?

2. You are the new solicitor to the Schroeder company (your predecessor having been dismissed after the decision in the case just reproduced). The president of the company has asked you whether, in the light of the decision of the House of Lords, it is necessary to renegotiate the many contracts that are outstanding with composers. She wants to know if the contracts have to be modified so that a similar result will not occur in the future. What advice will you give her? The president has also asked you to redraft the contract to be used by Schroeder to give the company as much protection

as it needs (or as much as it can have). What terms would you recommend for inclusion in the new contract?

3.   Would counsel for Schroeder have weakened or strengthened the company's case by showing that the contract used was essentially standard throughout the music-publishing industry?

4.   Professor Trebilcock, in "Economic Analysis of Unconscionability" in Reiter and Swan (eds.) *Studies in Contract Law* (Toronto: Butterworths, 1980) criticizes two aspects of the decision in *Schroeder v. Macaulay*. First, the mere fact that there are standard forms in use in an industry is not evidence of "cartelization". Second, the music publishing business is highly competitive.

He concludes by saying: "In short, to attempt comprehensive wage rate regulation and control over employment of factors by judicial fiat in an industry like the music publishing industry, with many firms and substantial product differentiation, would make the acknowledged problems of public-utility regulation look easy. But anything short of this is like squeezing putty." He argues that while the decision may help Schroeder, who has become a successful composer, this will come at the expense of future unknown composers who may find that publishing companies will offer them lower royalties, or require them to pay part of the promotion costs, or in some other way give them a lower return.

The argument of Trebilcock suggests that the role of the courts in controlling unconscionability should be limited to those cases in which there may be said to be procedural unconscionability. The courts have no role in problems of substantive unconscionability.

His argument would seem to be premised on the music industry being a competitive, stable industry. In fact, between 1966, when Macaulay made his contract, and 1974, when the House of Lords decided the case, it would appear that the industry expanded greatly and became more concentrated and more profitable. If this is correct, what would this say about Trebilcock's argument?

Barry Reiter, in "The Control of Contract Power" (1981), 1 *Oxford J. of Legal Stud.* 347 at 362-74, makes a different argument, which can be summarized as follows: It is a waste of scarce social resources to argue that the problem of unconscionability should be dealt with only by the legislature. It cannot be argued that courts do not make difficult and complex value judgments, or that useful rules do not arise from such judgments. It is inevitable that courts *must* take sides on the issues submitted to them for decision. Whether the court decides in favour of Macaulay or the Schroeder Music Publishing Company, it has made a value judgment, and such a judgment necessarily involves the consideration of what should be done in the circumstances of that case.

Are the positions of Trebilcock and Reiter reconcilable?

5.   In *Panayiotou v. Sony Music Ltd.* (1994), 13 Tr.L. 532 (Ch. Div.), the popular singer George Michael sought a declaration that his 1988 exclusive recording contract with Sony was unenforceable as an unreasonable restraint of trade.

An exclusive agreement had been negotiated between the parties in 1984. In 1988, Michael claimed that the 1984 agreement was invalid as a restraint of trade, but did not bring the matter to court; rather the parties entered into the new exclusive agreement that was the subject of the 1994 trial. The 1988 agreement had more favourable terms for Michael than the 1984 agreement, though the 1988 agreement could be extended by Sony for up to 15 years. In upholding the validity of the 1988 agreement, the Court emphasized that it was a compromise agreement, observing that there is "a clear public interest in upholding genuine and proper compromises". The Court received considerable evidence about the highly competitive nature of the recording industry, and distinguished *Schroeder* by concluding that the 1988 agreement was not "oppressive" or the product of "lack of competition". Included in the Court's consideration was the fact that Michael had experienced counsel representing him when the 1988 agreement was negotiated.

For a further discussion, see Nigel Palmer, "Implications of the George Michael Case" (1994), 138 *Solic. J.* 772; and Alan Coulthard, "*George Michael v. Sony Music*: A Challenge to Artistic Freedom" (1995), 58 *Mod. L. Rev.* 731.

6.   In the professional sports industry in North America it was very common until about 1970 for athletes to sign long-term contracts giving their exclusive playing rights to one club, unless that club decided to trade the player. The clubs argued that long-term contracts were necessary because of the large investments they made in developing athletes in the minor leagues.

As the sports industry became much more profitable, the long-term exclusive contracts disappeared, and "free agency" became more common. These developments were a result of unionization, application of anti-trust laws and civil litigation.

Sports and entertainment law is now an important, complex area of practice. It has many elements, including taxation and intellectual property, as well as contract law. See, e.g., John Barnes, *Sports and the Law in Canada,* 3rd ed. (Toronto: Butterworths, 1996); and Jacqueline L. King, *Entertainment Law in Canada* (Toronto: Butterworths, 2000).

The Protection of Relations

The classical model of contracting and the legal analysis which is based upon it is premised on a discrete or transactional model of contracting; the parties come together for one deal and then go their separate ways. This approach tends to focus on the situation at the time of the making of the deal. However, as illustrated by many cases in this book, difficult problems of unfairness can arise when the terms of a relation, *i.e.*, the framework for future co-operation, operate in ways that one party, at least, may not have expected.

The House of Lords had to deal with this kind of relational problem in *Schroeder v. Macaulay*. That Court saw only one possibility: the contract was either valid or void. As you would quickly realize if you drafted the standard contract for a music publisher (who may receive solicitations to publish songs or music from hundreds of aspiring musicians, of whom only a tiny proportion will ultimately be successful) the House of Lords gave no guidance at all at that stage of the relation. The problem is not (or should not be) the initial validity of the contract but the possibility that the power given by the terms of the contract to one side may be abused. This problem is raised in the following case.

McKINLAY MOTORS LTD. v. HONDA CANADA INC.

[1989] N.J. No. 332, 46 B.L.R. 62
(Nfld. S.C. T.D., Wells J.)

WELLS J.: — **[1]** The plaintiff, to which I shall refer as "McKinlay", is a Newfoundland company incorporated in 1953. The McKinlay family has been engaged in automobile sales and service in St. John's since 1919.

[2]   The defendant is the Canadian subsidiary of Honda of Japan, an automobile, motorcycle and power products manufacturer. Honda Canada Inc., to which I shall refer as "Honda", distributes that company's products in Canada by means of uniform authorized dealer agreements.

[3]   The issues between the parties arose because of Honda's termination of the McKinlay dealership on April 6, 1984, to be effective on September 30, 1984. McKinlay claims that the terminations were improper, and that they were in breach of the agreements between the parties, and that there was bad faith on the part of Honda, prior to the terminations.

The History

[4]   McKinlay was founded by the late Joseph McKinlay, and after his death the company was carried on by his three sons: Alexander, Robert, and Douglas.

[5]   Over the years the company represented various automobile manufacturers. These changed from time to time as they merged or ceased to make cars, or as McKinlay chose to sell other products, until by 1974 the company represented Renault.

[6]   McKinlay learned that Honda had begun the manufacture of a small car named the Civic, and that it intended to sell the car in Canada. In October 1974, Honda and McKinlay entered into a dealership agreement. Shortly afterward, McKinlay relinquished the Renault dealership in order to sell and service Hondas exclusively.

[7]   At first, the Civic was largely unknown and sales were slow. However, by 1979, Honda had gained wide market acceptance. That process was accelerated by the introductions of the Accord and Prelude in 1977-1978. These cars appealed to different segments of the market, and sales increased until the demand became greater than the number of cars available to supply it.

[8]   In 1979 Honda decided to update its dealer agreements. New and identical forms were prepared for the Civic, Accord, and Prelude. Agreements were not negotiated with dealers, although a dealer association had some minor input. Essentially, they were Honda documents, incorporating the terms and conditions which Honda required. They were presented to prospective dealers on a take-it or leave-it basis, to be executed after the dealer had obtained independent legal advice.

[9]   On November 30, 1979, McKinlay executed three identical agreements, which as a package comprised application forms in the case of the Accord and Prelude, and dealer agreements and standard provisions in respect of all three models. At a later date, a fourth agreement for the sale of power products was executed by the parties and terminated by Honda on April 6, 1984. However, I am only concerned with the automobile agreements. These identical agreements, taken together, comprised the entire agreement between the parties, and I shall refer to them collectively as "the agreement". . . . [**WELLS J.** summarized the scope of the agreements.]

[10]   From 1974 to 1982, the relationship between Honda and McKinlay was good, and there is no evidence of complaints by Honda or any major disagreements. In fact, in 1981, the company received a written commendation from Mr. Fujie, the President of Honda Canada.

Service

[11]   It was part of the agreement that McKinlay would service Honda vehicles and keep on hand a sufficient volume of parts. . . .

[12] I am persuaded to that view, not only by the McKinlay evidence, but by the Honda evidence, that "service" was not a factor in the McKinlay termination.

Premises

[13] [Honda maintained that the plaintiff's premises were inadequate. The judge discussed the plaintiff's premises, the efforts of Honda to have the plaintiff improve them, and the problem caused to the plaintiff by the limitation on sales of Honda cars imposed by the Japanese manufacturers in response to the Canadian government, which limited its access to funds to finance the renovation of the premises. When notice of termination was eventually given, on April 6th, 1984, the premises were essentially as they had been in 1974.]

The Allocation System

[14] After becoming a Honda dealer, McKinlay successfully marketed the Civic, and later the Accord and Prelude. In 1981 and 1982, it sold 342 and 371 cars respectively.

[15] Under s. 6 of the standard provisions of the agreement, dealers requested product from Honda and allocations were made at Honda's discretion, by the use of a mathematical formula. The formula was unilaterally imposed and administered by Honda, but it was based on dealer performance, and as long as the formula was adhered to, dealers knew approximately what allocations to expect.

[16] Section 6.01, 6.02 and 6.03 say as follows:

6.01 All orders for Products shall be submitted in writing by the Dealer to Honda on such forms as Honda may supply, or pursuant to the procedures set forth in connection therewith in the Dealer Bulletins in effect at the time such orders are accepted by Honda. Orders for Products shall be placed with Honda from time to time in accordance with the policies of Honda and are subject to acceptance by Honda which may be in whole or in part. All orders submitted by the Dealer shall be binding upon the Dealer unless and until they are rejected in writing by Honda, provided however that in the event of a partial acceptance by Honda it is understood that the Dealer shall no longer be bound in respect of the part of the order not accepted.

6.02 Honda will endeavour to the extent practicable considering all relevant factors, to deliver new Products to the Dealer that are ordered by the Dealer and required in the fulfilment of the Dealer's responsibilities under this Agreement. The Dealer acknowledges that Honda has a commensurate obligation to endeavour to deliver Honda Products to other Honda Dealers that are required by them to fulfil their responsibilities under their Dealer Agreements with Honda.

Because of the number of factors that affect the distribution of the Products and the relevance thereof at any time, Honda necessarily reserves to itself discretion in applying such factors and in processing orders of Honda Products from its Dealers. The judgment and decisions of Honda, therefore, shall be final in all matters relating to the distribution and delivery of Products to the Dealer.

6.03 Honda shall not be liable for failure to process or for any delay in processing orders for any Products where such failure or delay is due, in whole or in part, to any labour, material, transportation or utility shortage or curtailment, to governmental regulations, to discontinuance of sale by Honda of the Products ordered, to any labour trouble in the plants of Honda Motor or its suppliers, to any curtailment of production due to economic or trade conditions, or where such failure or delay is due to any cause beyond the control or without the fault or negligence of Honda.

[17] In the fall of 1981, the import restrictions began. They took the form of a voluntary decision by the Japanese auto manufacturers to limit entry of their products into Canada in the hope of avoiding regulations. The voluntary restrictions caused each manufacturer to compete vigorously to obtain the largest possible percentage of the total number of cars allocated into Canada. These percentages were based on the manufacturers' performance in the Canadian market, so that it became very important to sell cars quickly and keep inventories low.

[18] When sales were made promptly, the manufacturer was rewarded by a greater share of the agreed import allocation. This competition caused Honda to exert considerable pressure on its dealers to sell cars quickly. To further that objective, it changed the dealer allocation system in 1982.

[19] Until a modification occurred in the fall of 1982, cars were allocated to dealers by the Honda zone office, which took the total number of cars expected to enter the zone, added the number of cars in dealer inventory, and took a percentage of the total to allocate to each dealership based on its previous year's sales. The system ensured that cars were allocated to dealers on the basis of zone performance, and the dealer's percentage of it. When the allocation was made, the number of cars which a dealer had in inventory was deducted from the total number allocated. That system ensured that a dealer could expect a comparable number of cars to be allocated to him each year, depending of course on the total numbers entering the zone, and his own performance.

[20] To understand what happened to McKinlay it is necessary to examine the changes to the system which were introduced by Honda in the fall of 1982. The system was changed in the following way: the expected allocation to the zone was considered in isolation, without adding the number of cars already in the zone inventory, for purposes of calculation. The zone management took the dealer's percentage of zone sales for the previous half year and applied that percentage directly to the expected zone allocation. From the number obtained, the zone then deducted the number of cars showing in the dealer's inventory, so that the number of cars allocated to that dealer was reduced by that amount.

[21] In successive half years based on monthly sales and month-end inventories, the same calculation was made, each time with the cars in inventory being deducted. It is obvious that most dealers at the end of each month would have some cars in inventory; therefore, the allocation system usually resulted in a downward spiral in the number of cars allocated to a dealer. Because the numbers entering the zone were not affected by individual dealer allocations, it meant that an increasing number of cars became available to Honda to allocate solely at its discretion.

[22] I am satisfied that the operation of the allocation system as modified in the fall of 1982 not only permitted, but virtually ensured, that dealers would for the most part receive increasingly fewer cars under the mathematical formula.

[23] It was Honda's evidence that it needed a greater discretion in order to allocate more cars to major market dealers, i.e., to dealerships which served populations of 100,000 or more. These areas included Halifax, St. John's, Moncton, and Saint John. The stated objective of Honda in concentrating on major markets was to attempt to become No. 1 in Japanese sales in each major market.

[24] The operation of the modified allocation system resulted in McKinlay experiencing what was called at trial "the downward allocation spiral", and becoming more and more dependent in 1983 and 1984 on the discretion of zone management, which could allocate or withhold cars at will.

[25] Although it was a major market dealer, the allocation to McKinlay fell from 340 in 1982, to 276 in 1983, and 126 for the nine-month period in 1984.

[26] The built-in problem of the downward spiral was worsened in the McKinlay case because cars had to be transported by ship from the auto-port in Dartmouth to St. John's. That meant, in contrast to Halifax where cars could be delivered quickly, that cars forwarded to St. John's took several days to arrive because of delays at dockside, loading and unloading, and sea time. Honda also had to compete with other manufacturers for space on the ship, so that many times cars destined for McKinlay had not arrived in time for dealer preparation and sale before month's end, but nevertheless they showed on Honda's books as being unsold and in dealer inventory, thereby further decreasing McKinlay's allocation.

[27] Honda said that it made adjustments to compensate for these factors, but I have not found confirmation of that statement in the statistical evidence.

[28] I am satisfied that the downward spiral experienced by McKinlay was greater than that experienced by other major market dealers in the zone, and, as a result, McKinlay became increasingly dependent on the discretionary allocation by zone management. Honda says that the allocation system and its 1982 modification was explained to the dealers. However, it is doubtful if the dealers at that time understood the full implications of the modification and that its operation would result in a growing measure of discretion by the zone to allocate cars as it saw fit.

The Parties' Relationship

[29] Early in 1983, the relationship between the parties was adversely affected by McKinlay's delay of the renovations. At the same time, Honda began to use the new system to allocate fewer cars to McKinlay, and I am satisfied that these two matters were related.

[30] McKinlay did not commence the renovations, and Mr. Patriquin became increasingly dissatisfied with McKinlay's failure to do so. Mr. Patriquin, in May 1983, recommended termination of the McKinlay dealership. Mr. Robinson did not agree at that time; however, nothing occurred to change Mr. Patriquin's view of the situation, and we know that the number of cars being allocated to McKinlay by the zone was being substantially reduced.

[31] Obviously, the fewer the cars that McKinlay received, the more its management questioned the financial viability of expansion, and McKinlay did not begin the expansion as quickly as it otherwise would have. The company was in a very difficult position. In 1982, it had spent $160,000 to acquire land and $17,917 to improve the parking lot. It knew that it would have to spend as much as $500,000 in total to complete the project, while at the same time the viability of the dealership was being threatened because of the decreased allocation of cars.

[32] As a result, while McKinlay slowed its efforts to finance and obtain a construction contract, Mr. Patriquin was assiduously working to persuade his superiors to terminate the McKinlay dealership. By April 6, 1984, he had succeeded in

persuading Mr. Robinson that McKinlay was not representing Honda properly. His arguments were that sales were declining, that they had not begun the renovations, that they were not properly handling their service and warranty arrangements, and that they generally lacked good management. It was demonstrated at trial that some of the internal information given to head office by zone management was factually incorrect. In any event, as a result of the representations by Mr. Patriquin, Honda, through its vice-president of sales, Mr. Robinson, gave notice of termination to McKinlay on April 6, 1984. It was given pursuant to s. 23 of the dealer standard provisions, to be effective September 30, 1984. By coincidence, the termination was received in the same month that McKinlay concluded financing arrangements with the bank.

[33] Despite vigorous protests by McKinlay and pleas for reconsideration, the Honda decision was final, and the dealership concluded on September 30, 1984.

[34] Various reasons for the termination were argued, but I am satisfied on the evidence that the termination was because, in Mr. Patriquin's opinion, McKinlay was not moving quickly enough to expand and renovate the premises, coupled with his belief that the dealership was in a poor location and that Honda could be better served by a younger and more vigorous dealer located on auto row with modern premises designed to accommodate Honda's needs in the 1980s and beyond. These beliefs on the part of Mr. Patriquin were the major and motivating causes of the termination.

The Claim

[35] The McKinlay claim is twofold. First, it says that Honda wrongly exercised its right to terminate the agreement. It says that by giving a notice period of almost 6 months, instead of 30 days as stipulated in subs. 23.01, Honda placed itself in breach of the agreement, and that by reason of that breach it is entitled to damages from Honda.

[36] Secondly, and in the alternative, McKinlay says that Honda acted in bad faith in its allocation of cars to McKinlay in the years 1983 and 1984 and that the act of bad faith, itself, constituted a breach of the agreement, for which Honda is liable in damages.

[37] Honda says that it had a right under subs. 23.01 to terminate the contract at will, such termination to be effective 30 days after the date of mailing of the notice by Honda. It further says that there was no breach by reason of its giving a notice of almost 6 months, because McKinlay could have rejected that notice period had it chosen to do so. It could have insisted on 30 days, as it was entitled to do under subs. 23.01, and that, in fact, McKinlay waived the 30-day requirement in favour of the longer notice.

[38] On the second issue, Honda denies that it at any time acted in bad faith in the allocation of cars.

Breaches of the Agreement

[39] Section 23 deals with termination. Subsection 23.01 says:

Termination by Honda or the Dealer

Either Honda or the Dealer may terminate this Agreement at will by serving written notice of termination on the other. Such termination shall become effective thirty (30) days after the date of mailing of the said notice by Honda or the Dealer as the case may be.

[40] Subsection 23.02 deals with termination for cause, and subs. 23.03 with automatic termination. Neither of these subsections is applicable to this case, and Honda did not rely on them.

[41] Section 6.01 of the agreement requires termination to be made under s. 23 of the dealer standard provisions. Subsection 25.05 provides that the agreement may not be varied, modified or amended, except by an instrument duly executed by both parties. McKinlay argued that to extend the notice beyond 30 days was a unilateral modification of the agreement, and as such was in itself a breach.

[42] I am not persuaded that that is so. The entire agreement, and the law as submitted in argument, has led me to the conclusion that Honda had the right under the agreement to terminate "at will", and that it did so. McKinlay had the option to insist on 30 days notice, but it did not do so. No doubt Honda gave the longer notice period to give itself sufficient time to arrange for a new dealer and have that dealer prepare to commence operations. By the same token, it seems likely that McKinlay acquiesced in the longer period of notice in order to give itself planning and reorganization time, and to allow its business to continue more or less intact, until a new dealership could be arranged.

[43] In my view, having availed of the longer notice period, McKinlay cannot now say that Honda was in breach by granting it . . .

[44] I find, therefore, that the termination of all four agreements on April 6, 1984, were valid, and were not in themselves breaches of these agreements. It follows, therefore, that liability does not attach to Honda by reason of them.

Bad Faith

[45] McKinlay says that, prior to the terminations, Honda acted in bad faith in its allocation of cars to the dealership and that such bad faith was itself a breach of the agreement.

[46] McKinlay had always sold the cars allocated to it during the 10-year life of the dealership. Its largest allocation was in 1982, when it sold approximately 371 cars. It is interesting to compare the McKinlay sales with those of the new dealership which has been operating since October 1, 1984. The published figures, up to and including 1988, show that the new dealer, with whom and with whose premises and location Honda is satisfied, has not yet equalled the McKinlay sales figure of 371 units in 1982. That is so, despite the fact that larger numbers of cars have become available since 1984 because of new Honda plants in Canada and the United States.

[47] I have found that poor sales performance was not a genuine factor in the termination. On a balance of probabilities, the major reason for the termination was the dissatisfaction of Honda's zone management with the physical premises and the location of the dealership. Had McKinlay moved swiftly in 1982 and early in 1983 to expand and renovate the dealership according to Honda's wishes, the termination may not have taken place. Nevertheless, I believe that zone management wanted to change both the premises and the dealer, and what they felt was undue delay on McKinlay's part provided them with justification, in their minds, for attempting to bring about that change.

[48] The allocation system, as mentioned in the fall of 1982, was explained as a mathematical process based on sales performance; however, in reality, it was much more than that. It was a system which set out to impose competition between dealers for the available cars. It had a downward spiral mechanism built into it, whereby cars remaining in inventory at month's end cumulatively affected the supply of cars to that dealer for the future. It lacked a mathematical formula whereby a dealer could by his sales performance increase his allocation.

[49] Expressed another way, it was a mechanism which inevitably brought an allocation down by reason of cars left in inventory, but even a nil inventory at month's end could not make the allocation rise. The only method by which a dealer's allocation could rise was if Honda exercised its discretion to allocate more cars to the dealer. That was so because the operation of the mathematical formula could only lower, not raise, the allocation. In my view, the formula had in 1983 become a device which masked the full extent of the zone's discretion to allocate.

[50] The net result of the operation of the system was that in practice Honda had an unfettered discretion, despite the formula, to determine dealer allocations. As could be expected, the system resulted in a large and steadily increasing number of discretionary cars.

[51] McKinlay had sold 371 cars in 1982, yet because of the way that Honda exercised its discretion, McKinlay was allocated only 276 cars in 1983, a substantial decrease.

[52] In 1984, prior to termination, the decrease was proportionally of the same order. These decreases must be considered in the light of two factors which ought to have worked in the opposite way. Firstly, St. John's was by definition a major market area, which was supposed to receive a proportionally greater share of cars than smaller dealership areas. Secondly, the total number of Honda cars entering the Atlantic zone did not appreciably decrease with import restrictions. It is interesting to note that of the major market areas in the Atlantic zone, only one was allocated more cars in 1983 than it had been in 1982, but no other major market dealer received the large reduction which did McKinlay.

[53] I would have had little difficulty on the basis of the undisputed numbers alone in finding that there was an unexplained peculiarity in the way in which Honda exercised its discretion in the McKinlay allocations of 1983 and 1984. However, I have had the benefit of the evidence of Mr. George Backman, the former district sales manager for the zone from 1977 until May 1982. His evidence was that when Mr. Patriquin became zone manager in 1981, he visited the McKinlay dealership and formed a bad impression of it. He came to the conclusion that Honda ought to obtain a new and more aggressive dealer, with a new location and more "pizzazz".

[54] It was Mr. Backman's opinion that the system was being deliberately operated to the disadvantage of McKinlay. When he tried to take steps to treat McKinlay more fairly, especially on the shipping of product from the auto-port, he

said that Mr. Patriquin told him not to worry about it, and went on to say, "if we put enough thorns in their side, they may give up the dealership," or words to that effect.

[55] That evidence, coupled with the serious and otherwise unexplained decline in the number of cars allocated, and the undisputed efforts by Mr. Patriquin to persuade his superiors to terminate McKinlay, has simply persuaded me that Honda acted in bad faith in the exercise of its discretion to allocate cars to McKinlay in the years 1983 and 1984.

[56] I am satisfied that had good faith and fairness been exercised in the allocations, McKinlay would have proceeded much more quickly with the renovations and expansion. In the circumstances, their delay is understandable. The expenses of operating their business had remained the same, but the reduced allocation of cars threatened the financial viability of the company itself. To have borrowed and invested up to $500,000 under these circumstances could have been an imprudent business decision. The problem was explained to Honda many times, and I can find no evidence of bad faith on McKinlays part.

[57] For the reasons given, I find that Honda acted in bad faith under the agreement. It is obviously an implied term of any such agreement that the parties act toward each other in their business dealings in good faith. I find, therefore, that the use of the allocation system in respect of McKinlay in 1983 and 1984 was not in good faith and was sufficiently serious to constitute a breach of the agreement and entitle McKinlay to judgment and damages on that portion of its claim.

Damages

[58] Since Honda is liable for a breach of the agreement which occurred prior to the termination, McKinlay's claim for damages must be limited to proven losses arising directly from that breach. Specifically, damages must be assessed on the basis of gross profit lost by reason of the unwarranted under-allocation of cars in 1983 and 1984.

[59] It is impossible on the evidence precisely to determine the number of vehicles involved or to calculate damages with complete accuracy. The evidence is that McKinlay received an average gross profit of $693 from each car sold. I am of the view that on an allocation of cars, fairly arrived at, McKinlay would have been allocated and thus been able to sell approximately the same number of cars in 1983 as it had been allocated in 1982, or 64 additional units. On the same basis, to September 30, 1984, in proportion, McKinlay should have received 255 cars, that is, 129 more than it did. The total of those two figures is 193, which multiplied by $693 gives $133,749 as being, on a balance of probabilities, the gross profit lost.

[60] In respect of the other items of damage claimed, I find that the construction of the parking lot at 57 LeMarchant Road was an improvement to the McKinlay premises, the value of which they retain, and from which they are benefiting in their new dealership. The McKinlay claim for the value of that work is dismissed, as well as their claim for legal and survey fees and their claim for the reduced valuation of the plaintiffs' business as a result of the termination.

[61] On the matter of inventory, McKinlay neglected to pursue to a conclusion its right to return parts to Honda after the termination and, in fact, used most of these parts after 1984. Having elected to deal with the parts issue in that way, McKinlay

cannot now seek to obtain payment from Honda for those parts still in its possession. The parts inventory claim is, therefore, dismissed.

[62] McKinlay, in argument, abandoned its claim for general damages but allowed its claim for punitive damages to remain. It was within the contractual right of Honda to terminate the agreement at will, and it did so, and in my opinion an award by way of punitive damages would be inappropriate in the circumstances.

[63] The plaintiff shall have judgment in the amount of $133,749, interest to the date of judgment, and costs to be taxed.

NOTES AND QUESTIONS

1. What interest of the plaintiff was protected by the award of damages in *McKinlay v. Honda*?

2. The judgment of Wells J. did not depend on a finding or claim that the agreement or agreements were unfair or unconscionable when made, nor did the court find that the agreement was in any sense "void" or unenforceable; the judge, nevertheless, asserted a power to ensure that Honda conducted itself decently, *i.e.*, in good faith, during the relation.

    Richard Potter, "Case Comment: *McKinlay Motors Ltd. v. Honda Canada Inc.*" (1990), 46 B.L.R. 111, argues (at p. 111) that the case "represents the possible emergence of a major new contractual principle in Canada, that of good faith". Wells J. cites no authority for his general principle of good faith, though there is an emerging body of literature and jurisprudence on the subject of good faith in Canadian contract law. See, *e.g.*, Belobaba, "Good Faith in Canadian Contract Law" in Law Society of Upper Canada, *Commercial Law: Recent Developments and Emerging Trends* (Don Mills, Ont.: R. de Boo, 1985), p. 73; Reiter, "Good Faith in Contracts" (1983), 17 *Val. U. L. Rev.* 704; David Stack, "The Two Standards of Good Faith in Canadian Contract Law" (1999), 62(1) *Sask. L. Rev.* 201-223; and John D. McCamus, "Abuse of Discretion, Failure to Co-operate and Evasion of Duty: Unpacking the Common Law Duty of Good Faith in Contractual Performance" (2004), 29 *Advocates Q.* 72.

3. The courts have held, without much difficulty, that any relation that does not have a fixed term may be terminated on reasonable notice. (That position underlies the whole law of wrongful dismissal.) See, *e.g.*, *Hillis Oil & Sales Ltd. v. Wynn's Canada Ltd.*, [1986] 1 S.C.R. 57 at p. 67, 25 D.L.R. (4th) 649 at pp. 665-66, *Scapillati v. A. Potvin Construction Ltd.* (1999), 44 O.R. (3d) 737, 175 D.L.R. (4th) 169 (C.A.) and *Marbry v. Avrecan International Inc.* (1999), 67 B.C.L.R. (3d) 102, 171 D.L.R. (4th) 436, [1999] 10 W.W.R. 429 (C.A.). Wells J. does not deny that Honda may terminate the dealership, only that it may not terminate the contract *while it is an ongoing relation* without accepting certain obligations, obligations that Honda probably did not expect and which it almost certainly assumed that it did not have.

4. The relations of automobile manufacturers and their dealers have caused problems for a long time. As *McKinlay v. Honda* illustrates, the dealers are very much at the mercy of the manufacturer, which may, as Honda did, leave the dealer with a very large investment but without a way to earn income from it. The judgment gives one dealer a remedy because the manufacturer was held to have behaved badly. The judgment does not deal with the larger issue of unconscionability or the power of the court to limit the right of the manufacturer to terminate the relation.

5. You are corporate counsel to a Canadian automobile manufacturer. Draft the instructions that you would send to those in the corporate organization who might be considering terminating or "disciplining" a franchisee so that the risks created by *McKinlay v. Honda* may be minimized.

6. A corporation is a form of relational contract organized in a particular way. A corporation differs from a contract principally in the provision of a governance structure — in the form of a board of directors and annual shareholder meetings. A governance structure permits the corporation to make decisions in response to changing circumstances. The basic principle underlying corporate governance is that it is "democratic": its powers are subject to democratic control through the power of the shareholders to elect the board of directors, though of course those who own more shares have more votes, and can control the company.

As in any human relation, the power conferred on those who manage or those who have control of the corporation may be abused. The *Canada Business Corporations Act*, R.S.C. 1985, c. C-44, and the corporation statutes of the common law provinces permit an action by a "complainant" — defined as including a shareholder, a security holder, director, officer or creditor — to seek relief under the "oppression remedy". The *CBCA*, for example, provides:

241.(1) A complainant may apply to a court for an order under this section.

(2) If, on an application under subsection (1), the court is satisfied that in respect of a corporation or any of its affiliates

(*a*) any act or omission of the corporation or any of its affiliates effects a result,

(*b*) the business or affairs of the corporation or any of its affiliates are or have been carried on or conducted in a manner, or

(*c*) the powers of the directors of the corporation or any of its affiliates are or have been exercised in a manner

that is oppressive or unfairly prejudicial to or that unfairly disregards the interests of any security holder, creditor, director or officer, the court may make an order to rectify the matters complained of.

(3) In connection with an application under this section, the court may make any interim or final order it thinks fit including, without limiting the generality of the foregoing,

(*a*) an order restraining the conduct complained of;

. . .

(*c*) an order to regulate a corporation's affairs by amending the articles or by-laws or creating or amending a unanimous shareholder agreement;

. . .

(*h*) an order varying or setting aside a transaction or contract to which a corporation is a party and compensating the corporation or any other party to the transaction or contract;

The "oppression" remedy of s. 241 exists to deal with the problems that may arise when the powers of a corporation are abused, *i.e.*, when there is conduct by the corporation "that is oppressive or unfairly prejudicial to or that unfairly disregards the interests of" the complainant. The range of remedies open to the court is nearly unlimited: the court has the option to reverse or change a decision of the board of directors, the majority shareholders, force the purchase of the complainant's shares, re-write the by-laws, set aside a contract, *etc*.

The power of the court under the oppression remedy can be contrasted with the general inability of a court when reviewing the exercise of a power *given by contract* to deal with the same kind of management problems or to do more than hold the contract invalid, or require notice of termination.

The difference in the courts' power in the two situations is all the more striking when it is remembered that at the beginning of a relation, the parties have a wide freedom to arrange their relation through contract, as a partnership or as a corporation — any one of these could also be referred to as a "joint venture". These devices are largely functional substitutes; either one will work as a framework for the arrangement. The choice will often be made for tax reasons or because the more formal structures permit some flexibility through a management structure.

7.   *McKinlay Motors* introduces the notion that a relation created by contract has some kind of integrity that must be protected. Macneil, in *The New Social Contract* (1980), maintains that one of the basic contract "norms" (one of the values that the law must recognize) is "role integrity". Parties have expectations arising out of the relation that is created by the deal they have made. The relation they create may require that one put significant trust in the other, or that each must trust the other, and they must be sure that the trust will not be abused. Not all contracts, of course, create a significant degree of trust: there is no reason for not expecting each of the parties to look out for its own interest, and "the devil take the hindmost". Other relations, especially a fiduciary relation like that of lawyer and client, may even require that one party put the interest of the other ahead of its own; the law will protect the expectations created by this trust.

We have already seen the notion of role integrity being used as a criterion for decision. In *Lloyds Bank v. Bundy* (*supra*), Sir Eric Sachs stressed the notion of "fiduciary care", that the bank's principal mistake was not considering the interest of Herbert Bundy as well as its own. As we have seen, he justified this decision by reference to the role played by English country banks in the affairs of their customers.

The relation of agency is a central type of business relation that typically entails fiduciary obligations. The individual merchant (or sole proprietor) must, if he or she is not to do everything himself or herself, employ agents in his or her business. In the simplest case, the agents he or she employs may be the members of his or her family. Any employee who makes deals on behalf of the merchant will be the latter's agent. When communications were slow, the merchant would often have to place great trust in and grant wide discretion to the agents who represented his or her interests in distant places.

The agency relation is at the heart of the partnership arrangement, a business relation that can be regarded as one step up from the individual acting on his own behalf. Each partner, unless the partners make different arrangements (which may or may not affect third parties), is an agent of the firm, *i.e.*, of all the other partners, so that each partner is liable for all the debts of the firm. The degree of trust required in this situation is obvious.

In the most fully developed form of the business association, the modern corporation, the idea of fiduciary obligation is fundamental: directors owe a fiduciary obligation to the corporation, as do the officers and all employees. Outside the business context, it is also important to note that solicitors owe such a duty to their clients.

The development of the notion of fiduciary obligations is one of the most significant achievements of the Court of Chancery, and even though that court may be no more, it remains true that "the categories of fiduciary relations are never closed". The essence of a fiduciary relation is that one party has (or does) put his trust in the integrity of the other. In other words, it is a relation of dependence of one on the integrity of the other. In some cases, like *Lac Minerals*, *supra*, Chapter 3, the courts may impose fiduciary obligations on those in contractual or quasi-contractual relations in order to prevent bad faith dealings; see *e.g.*, L.I. Rotman, "Developments in Fiduciary and Trust Law: The 1998-99 Term" (2000), 11 S.C.L.R. (2d) 483-515.

There can be serious problems with the sale and control of franchises. The position of franchisees, like car dealerships, is in some respects not much better than that of consumers. Many franchises are bought by relatively inexperienced individuals who would not have gone into business for themselves had it not been for the support and advice of the franchisor.

A franchisor has to have fairly draconian powers to ensure that the franchisee, for example, the operator of a "Tim Hortons" coffee shop, keeps the premises clean and meets the obligations undertaken in the advertising campaigns carried out by the franchisor. This power can easily be abused. The franchisee often makes a large investment in the business, and serious problems of unconscionable behaviour arise if the franchisor can appropriate or neutralize this investment.

The Alberta *Franchises Act*, R.S.A. 2000, c. F-23, subjects the sale of franchises to some of the same disclosure requirements as the securities industry, as the purchase of a franchise is, from many points of view, an investment much like the purchase of a security. In Ontario, the *Arthur Wishart Act (Franchise Disclosure), 2000*, S.O. 2000, c. 3, also imposes obligations of disclosure on franchisors at the time an agreement is made. Both statutes also impose on "each party a duty of fair dealing in its performance and enforcement" of obligations under the franchise agreement (s. 3 of the Ontario Act, and s. 7 of the Alberta statute). Statutory remedies include rescission and damages.

Historically, the courts gave only very limited protections to franchisees, though as in other areas the law has developed to provide more protection for the vulnerable. In *Jirna Ltd. v. Mister Donut of Canada Ltd.*, [1973] S.C.J. No. 129, [1975] 1 S.C.R. 2, 40 D.L.R. (3d) 303 the plaintiff was a franchisee of the defendant. The franchise agreement provided that the franchisee had to buy its supplies from the franchisor or suppliers approved by it. The agreement also provided that the parties were independent contractors and that no partnership, joint venture or agency relation was intended. The trial judge held that the franchisor, by taking secret kickbacks from the suppliers from whom the franchisees were bound to obtain their supplies, had breached a duty owed to the franchisees. The Court of Appeal and the Supreme Court held that a fiduciary duty was excluded by the terms of the agreement. The Supreme Court held that the franchisee's claim could only succeed if the franchisor had been guilty of fraud and that fraud had not been established. When the case was decided, the result was widely seen as important for the franchising industry, the inference being that denying franchisors their right to make money from secret kickbacks would be to interfere with their entitlement under the franchise. It is an indication that Canadian law has changed since 1975 that, while *Jirna* has never been said to have been wrongly decided, the secret kickbacks that were paid to the franchisor in that case would now almost certainly (and apart altogether from the legislated requirements of good faith conduct) be held to breach any franchise agreement. The following case is an example of this change.

SHELANU INC. v. PRINT THREE FRANCHISING CORP.

[2003] O.J. No. 1919, 64 O.R. (3d) 533, 226 D.L.R. (4th) 577
(C.A., Weiler, Austin, Laskin JJ.A.)

[In 1987, BCD Print Inc. ("BCD"), a company owned by Brian Deslauriers, purchased a copy and print store franchise from the defendant Print Three Franchising Corporation ("Print Three") for one store in Toronto, and in 1989, Deslauriers and his wife purchased the shares of the plaintiff Shelanu Inc. ("Shelanu"), which had outlets at two other nearby locations. The franchise agreement for Print Three Outlets provided for the payment of royalties to Print Three, with royalty rebates depending upon the volume of sales. In the early 1990's, two of the locations were closed without written formalities. In January 1995, pursuant to an oral agreement with Print Three, the BCD franchise was cancelled, and Shelanu began reporting its sales as a single franchise, which entitled it to a greater royalty rebate under the franchise agreement than was the case when sales were divided between BCD and Shelanu.

By letter on May 2, 1997, Shelanu purported to terminate the franchise agreement, and in August 1997, it sued Print Three for damages, alleging that the franchisor had breached the agreement in various ways. The trial judge held that the 1995 oral agreement was enforceable. He held that Print Three had breached its contractual obligations and a duty of good faith in four respects, including by allowing the establishment of a Le Print Express franchise, a new franchise concept that would operate in competition with Shelanu's existing franchise operation. The trial judge held that the breach entitled Shelanu to terminate the franchise agreement, and assessed damages. Print Three appealed. The Court of Appeal allowed the appeal. Only a portion of the judgment dealing with the nature of the duty of good faith and one of the factual issues is reproduced.]

WEILER J.A.: —

2. *The Duty of Good Faith and Fiduciary Duty*

[63] The trial judge found that the appellant owed the respondent a duty of good faith either under the *Arthur Wishart Act* … or at common law. Having regard to my conclusions regarding good faith, set out below, it is unnecessary to decide whether the *Arthur Wishart Act*, which applies to existing franchises, is applicable in this case where the acts in issue took place prior to the coming into force of the Act.

A. *Circumstances giving rise to a duty of good faith*

[64] In *Wallace v. United Grain Growers Ltd. (c.o.b. Public Press)*, [1997] 3 S.C.R. 701, 152 D.L.R. (4th) 1, the majority of the Supreme Court was prepared to recognize a good faith obligation in employment contracts. Indeed, at paras. 91-95, Iacobucci J. held that contracts of employment have unique characteristics that set them apart from ordinary commercial contracts. He described three special characteristics of employment contracts: (1) the formation of the contract is not the result of the exercise of bargaining power between two equals; (2) the person in the weaker position is unable to achieve more favourable contractual terms because of, for example, that person's inability to access information; (3) the power imbalance continues to affect other facets of the relationship after the contract has been entered into.

[65] In some instances a duty of good faith may arise ordinarily out of the nature of the relationship, or the circumstances created by the other party: see *978011 Ontario Ltd. v. Cornell Engineering Co.* (2001), 53 O.R. (3d) 783, 198 D.L.R. (4th) 615 (C.A.) at para. 35.

[66] The relative position of the parties as outlined by Iacobucci J. in *Wallace* also exists in the typical franchisor-franchisee relationship. First, it is unusual for a franchisee to be in the position of being equal in bargaining power to the franchisor: See *Kentucky Fried Chicken Canada, a Division of Pepsi-Cola Canada Ltd.*

v. Scott's Food Services Inc. (1998), 41 B.L.R. (2d) 42, 114 O.A.C. 357 (C.A.), per Goudge J.A. at para. 16; *Machias v. Mr. Submarine Ltd.*, [2002] O.J. No. 1261 (QL), 24 B.L.R. (3d) 228 (S.C.J.) at para. 109. The second characteristic, inability to negotiate more favourable terms, is met by the fact that a franchise agreement is a contract of adhesion. As I have indicated, a contract of adhesion is a contract in which the essential clauses were not freely negotiated but were drawn up by one of the parties on its behalf and imposed on the other. Further, insofar as access to information is concerned, the franchisee is dependent on the franchisor for information about the franchise, its location and projected cash flow, and is typically required to take a training program devised by the franchisor. The third characteristic, namely that the relationship continues to be affected by the power imbalance, is also met by the fact the franchisee is required to submit to inspections of its premises and audits of its books on demand, to comply with operation bulletins, and, often is dependent on, or required to buy, equipment or product from the franchisor. It is hardly surprising, therefore, that a number of courts, including the Manitoba Court of Appeal in *Imasco Retail Inc. (c.o.b. Shoppers Drug Mart) v. Blanaru*, [1995] 9 W.W.R. 44, 104 Man. R. (2d) 286 (Q.B.), affd (1996), [1997] 2 W.W.R. 295, 113 Man. R. (2d) 269 (C.A.) have recognized that a duty of good faith exists at common law in the context of a franchisor-franchisee relationship.

B. *Whether the trial judge held Print Three to a fiduciary duty*

[67] The appellant submits that the trial judge held Print Three to a higher standard than that imposed by the duty of good faith, namely, the duty of a fiduciary. The appellant's submission that the trial judge applied a fiduciary standard to Print Three rests on the trial judge's comment that the relationship of franchisor to franchisee is akin to a partnership. The appellant states partners owe each other a fiduciary duty and that this is the standard that he applied to Print Three's relationship with Shelanu.

[68] The imposition of a duty of good faith and a fiduciary duty are closely related. As stated in *Cornell, supra*, at para. 33 they, along with the standard of unconscionability:

> [a]re points on a continuum in which the law acknowledges a limitation on the principle of self-reliance and imposes an obligation to respect the interests of the other. They are defined by P. Finn, "The Fiduciary Principle" in T. Youdan, ed., *Equity, Fiduciaries and Trusts*, (1989), 1 at 4 as follows:
>
>> "Unconscionability" accepts that one party is entitled as of course to act self-interestedly in his actions towards the other. Yet in deference to that other's interests, it then proscribes excessively self-interested or exploitative conduct. "Good faith," while permitting a party to act self-interestedly, nonetheless qualifies this by positively requiring that party, in his decision and action, to have regard to the legitimate interests therein of the other. The "fiduciary" standard for its part enjoins one party to act in the interests of the other — to act selflessly and with undivided loyalty. There is, in other words, a progression from the first to the third: from selfish behaviour to selfless behaviour. Much the most contentious of the trio is the second, "good faith." It often goes unacknowledged. It does embody characteristics to be found in the other two [footnotes omitted].

[69] There is at least one important difference between the duty of good faith and a fiduciary duty. If, for example, A owes a fiduciary duty to B, A must act only in accordance with B's interests when A exercises its powers or exercises a discretion arising out of the relationship. … If, on the other hand, A owes a duty of good faith to B, A must give consideration to B's interests as well as to its own interests before exercising its power. Thus, if A owes a duty of good faith to B, so long as A deals honestly and reasonably with B, B's interests are not necessarily paramount. …

[70] The trial judge recognized that the relationship between a franchisor and a franchisee would not normally be characterized as a fiduciary one in accordance with *Jirna Ltd. v. Mister Donut of Canada Ltd.*, [1972] 1 O.R. 251, 22 D.L.R. (3d) 639 (C.A.), affd [1975] 1 S.C.R. 2, 40 D.L.R. (3d) 303. I do not agree that it logically follows from the trial judge's reference to partners that he applied the fiduciary standard in this case. At a later point in his reasons, the trial judge reiterated that a franchise relationship was akin to that of a partnership and, accordingly, like a partnership required mutual respect. … that parties to a contract are required to exercise their rights under that agreement honestly, fairly, and in good faith, and that, when a party acts contrary to community standards of honesty and reasonableness or fairness, he acts in bad faith. The trial judge well knew the distinction between a duty of good faith and a fiduciary duty and did not hold Print Three to a fiduciary duty.

[71] Moreover, the fact that contractual terms are ultimately complied with, does not mean that there has been no breach of the duty of good faith.

C. *Breaches of Print Three's obligations as found by the trial judge*

[72] The trial judge found that Print Three breached its duty of good faith towards Shelanu in four respects. The specific breaches found by the trial judge are. …

> — Print Three's establishment of the Le Print Express system, "not only would but did take work and customers from existing Print Three franchises". As a consequence he held that, ". . . the establishment of such an enterprise by the very person who owned and controlled the defendant was fundamentally at odds with the defendant's obligations, including the obligation to deal in good faith, to its franchisees."

[73] [T]he trial judge … did not award separate damages for breach of the duty of good faith. No damages were awarded for the establishment of the Le Print Express franchise. The breaches, including his finding respecting the establishment of the Le Print Express franchise, led the trial judge to conclude that Print Three did not intend to honour or be bound by the commitments it had made to its franchisees and that, as a result, Shelanu should be discharged from any further obligation under the contract.

[74] Whether or not a party under a duty of good faith has breached that duty will depend on all the circumstances of the case, including whether the party subject to a duty of good faith conducted itself fairly …

3. *Breaches of Print Three's Obligations to Shelanu*

…

C. *Le Print Express*

(i) *Facts and finding of the trial judge*

[99] Around October 1990, the appellant set up a business initially known as Print Three Express that subsequently became known as Le Print Express. The trial judge found that these outlets were to be smaller than Print Three franchises in order to target individuals and small businesses. The cost to purchase these franchises was lower than the cost to purchase a Print Three franchise and some financing was also offered to potential Le Print Express franchisees. Shelanu complained that the establishment of the Le Print Express concept involved the franchisor in a business that competed with existing Print Three franchises. Brian Deslauriers testified that Le Print Express offered the same kinds of products and services that were, to a large extent, offered by Print Three. In support of his evidence he produced a flyer from the Le Print Express at the Eaton Centre that had been faxed to Shelanu. He further testified that contrary to his understanding that the Le Print Express operations were to be small, occupying 200 square feet, the Eaton operation was three to four times this size and had the same kind of equipment and capabilities as Shelanu. The same personnel and staff who operated and marketed Print Three franchises also handled the requirements of the new franchise. The trial judge held:

> It seems to me to be intrinsically troublesome for a franchisor to develop a concept for a new franchise operation that will operate in competition with its existing franchise operation. Even though Le Print Express franchisees were directed at a specific segment of the industry, I am satisfied that they not only would, but did, take work and customers from existing Print Three franchisees. As a consequence, in my view, the establishment of such an enterprise by the very person who owned and controlled the defendant was fundamentally at odds with the defendant's obligations, including the obligation to deal in good faith, to its franchisees. The defendant could not properly and fairly institute this new concept without at least obtaining the agreement of the existing Print Three franchisees to this crucial change to their contractual relationship which, of course, the defendant made no attempt to do. The establishment of the Le Print Express franchises fundamentally altered the nature of the Print Three franchise network and impacted directly on the business environment in which the Print Three franchisees operated.

(ii) Argument and analysis

[100]   The appellant challenges the trial judge's finding of fact that Le Print Express competed with Shelanu's business as well as his conclusion that the establishment of this business took work and customers from Print Three franchisees and Shelanu in particular. The appellant emphasizes that, while there may have been some overlap of services, Le Print Express was in a different business sector than Print Three.

...

[102]   The franchise agreement is silent as to whether the franchisor can engage in a similar business during the term of the agreement. ... Print Three did, however, agree not to take any action that would be likely to injure the goodwill or reputation associated with the Print Three trademark, logo or mark.

[103]   Print Three targeted corporate accounts, whereas Le Print Express did small copying jobs for individuals and small businesses. None of the Le Print Express franchises was established within Shelanu's exclusive territory; the three Le Print Express locations were the Eaton Centre, Union Station, and Scotia Bank Plaza. Shelanu did not complain about Le Print Express for almost seven years after it was established and Shelanu presented no evidence that it lost income as a result of competition from Le Print Express. The trial judge's reasons do not address these considerations.

[104]   The trial judge also rejected a number of Shelanu's submissions that would have affected its claim respecting Le Print Express. Shelanu's statement of claim claimed damages for misrepresentation on the basis that the franchise agreement contained representations that Print Three was an expanding organization; it had a commitment to continue to introduce leading edge technologies and systems in document reproduction technology; it would continue to develop the credibility and presence of the Print Three name and logo; and it would continue to improve and modify the know-how it had developed. The trial judge held that the failure of these representations to materialize were not breaches of the franchise agreement but goals that had not been achieved. In other words, they were not representations of fact.

[105]   On the issue of technology, the trial judge described the contribution of Print Three as the bare minimum a franchisee ought to expect in return for royalty payments and held that ". . . in the end result, I am not satisfied on the evidence that the failures of the defendant [Print Three] on this issue were so great as to constitute a breach of its obligations under the franchise agreement." The trial judge noted that the evidence in this case was like that in *Khagen Investments Ltd. v. 710497 Ontario Ltd.*, [1999] O.J. No. 2152 (QL), 98 O.T.C. 241 (S.C.J.), in that there was no evidence as to the standard of service given to other franchisees or whether provision of the same level of service to other franchisees resulted in their failure. ...

[106]   Brian Deslauriers testified that the number of Print Three franchises declined after Le Print Express was created. The trial judge held that, on balance, the reduction in the number of Print Three franchises was largely the result of prevailing economic conditions. By implication, therefore, the establishment of Le Print Express did not contribute to the decline in the number of Print Three franchises.

[107]   I would therefore, hold that the appellant has met the high standard required to overturn a trial judge's finding of fact that Le Print Express competed with Shelanu and took business from it. My reasons for doing so may be summarized as follows: (1) the different nature of the business engaged in by Le Print Express; (2) Shelanu's delay in complaining about the establishment of that business; (3) the lack of evidence before the trial judge as to Shelanu's consequential loss of income; (4) the trial judge's findings that there had been no misrepresentation concerning what Print Three was to provide in exchange for royalty payments and that Print Three had done the minimum required to discharge those obligations; and (5) the trial judge's finding that the decline in Print Three franchises was primarily due to prevailing economic conditions. The finding that Print Three breached "reasonable commercial standards" must also fail for the same reasons.

[108]   Inasmuch as I have not upheld the trial judge's finding of fact in respect of Le Print Express, I would not uphold his conclusion that the establishment of Le Print Express was a breach of Print Three's duty of good faith.

NOTES AND QUESTIONS

1.   In para. 69 in *Shelanu* Weiler J.A. cited the Supreme Court of Canada decision in *Wallace v. United Grain Growers Ltd.*, [1997] S.C.J. No. 94, [1997] 3 S.C.R. 701 as establishing a "good faith obligation in employment contracts." *Wallace* was studied in Chapter 1, and it is interesting to recall that the Court, speaking through Iacobucci J., specifically rejected the argument that an employer owes its employees a duty of good faith in making the *decision to dismiss*. He said (para. 76):

A requirement of "good faith" reasons for dismissal would, in effect, ... deprive employers of the ability to determine the composition of their workforce. In the context of the accepted theories on the employment relationship, such a law would, in my opinion, be overly intrusive and inconsistent with established principles of employment law, and more appropriately, should be left to legislative enactment rather than judicial pronouncement.

Justice Weiler referred only to para. 95, where Iacobucci J. articulated a narrower "obligation of good faith and fair dealing in *the manner of dismissal*, the breach of which will be compensated for by adding to the length of the notice period". One can ask whether this represents a deliberate extension of *Wallace*, or whether courts will return at some point to this distinction to narrow the scope of the still-developing doctrines of good faith in performance (or termination) of contracts.

2. Until recently there was not much litigation involving disgruntled franchisees, and the reported cases were often at the interlocutory stage, when the franchisee has gone to court to get an interlocutory injunction to prevent termination and loss of supplies and goodwill: see, *e.g.*, *Prairie Hospitality Consultants Ltd. v. Renard International Hospitality Consultants Ltd.* [1980] B.C.J. No. 2177, 118 D.L.R. (3d) 121 (S.C.).

3. More recently, there has been more litigation by dissatisfied franchisees, and there is likely to be more in the future, with franchisees forming groups to strengthen their negotiation and litigation position. See, *e.g.*, *1490664 Ontario Ltd. v. Dig This Garden Retailers Ltd.*, [2005] O.J. No. 3040, 256 D.L.R. (4th) 451 (C.A.), where a franchisee was able to obtain rescission of the franchise agreement, the return of money paid to the franchisor and damages for breach of the disclosure requirements of the Ontario *Arthur Wishart Act (Franchise Disclosure), 2000.*

4. In *Country Style Food Services Inc. v. 1304271 Ontario Ltd.*, [2005] O.J. No. 2730, 200 O.A.C. 172, 7 B.L.R. (4th) 171 (C.A.) the Ontario Court of Appeal upheld a trial decision that found a franchisor liable to a franchisee for losses arising due to changes in the layout of the mall where the coffee shop was located. Prior to the construction of the mall, the franchisee had entered into a franchise agreement and a sub-lease with Country Style, the franchisor. A site plan prepared by the landlord, setting out the proposed design of the mall, was attached to the sub-lease lease. As construction began, the landlord unilaterally changed the site plan for the mall, without notice to the franchisee or Country Style. The franchisee claimed that the new plan would negatively affect its business by making it harder for cars to have access from the main streets. Country Style informed the franchisee that it was going to take legal action against the landlord. When the franchisee ceased to make rent payments, Country Style terminated the sub-lease with the franchisee and commenced an action against it. The trial judge found that the change to the site plan constituted negligent misrepresentation by the landlord. At trial, Country Style took the position with the franchisee that the landlord's actions were not wrongful, but took the contrary position in a third party action against the landlord, seeking contribution and indemnity from the landlord, as well as a declaration that the landlord's actions constituted a fundamental breach of the lease. Country Style's action against the franchisee was dismissed; the franchisee was awarded damages of $400,000 against Country Style and the landlord, jointly and severally.

The Court of Appeal upheld the trial judge's conclusion that the landlord negligently misrepresented and Country Style innocently misrepresented the mall development to the franchisee, and the award of $400,000 in damages. The appeal court also upheld the finding that Country Style breached its duty of good faith owed to the franchisee by failing to protect its interest as against the landlord. However, the appeal court concluded that the trial judge erred in finding the landlord liable to indemnify Country Style. Country Style was estopped by its conduct from claiming against the landlord, as its position against the landlord was fundamentally inconsistent with its pleaded position against the franchisee. In the Court of Appeal, Cronk J.A. wrote:

[96] In *Shelanu*, at para. 74, this Court stated regarding the duty of good faith owed by a franchisor to its franchisees:

> Whether or not a party under a duty of good faith has breached that duty will depend on all the circumstances of the case, including whether the party subject to a duty of good faith conducted itself fairly throughout the process [citations omitted].

[97] The trial judge was mindful of a franchisor's obligations of good faith and fair dealing in relation to its franchisees. She correctly observed, "The relationship of franchisor to franchisee is a complex one. The franchisor's duty of care, the duty to act in good faith, while not elevated to the status of a fiduciary, speaks to concepts of loyalty, respect and fair dealing." I agree.

[98] In this case, the trial judge made the following findings of fact:

> Initially, both Country Style and the franchisee articulated a firm resolve against the landlord's unilateral changes to the site plan. In fact, Country Style wrote to the landlord on July 9, 1999, demanding that all construction and addition to the development be completed according to the site plan. ... But, this occurred at the embryonic stage of the development; and Country Style never followed through on its threats to commence legal action ...

> It appears that somehow the franchisor changed its position in midstream and decided to side with the landlord. In my view, in its dealings with the franchisee, Country Style resembled a wolf dressed in sheep's clothing. Its actions displayed a superficial seductiveness. It says it remained supportive of the franchisee and open to all eventualities. At the same time, it asserts that "it was not incumbent on or the responsibility of Country Style to gather evidence on behalf of the franchisee". Maybe not, but its actions displayed a perplexing array of contradictory messages. In the end, it failed to support the franchisee and it attempted to walk the fence between the franchisee and the landlord.

Indeed, the totality of the evidence propels the conclusion that Country Style turned its back on the franchisee when the latter needed it most. For whatever reason, it did not deal with its own franchisee in good faith.

[99] These findings were grounded in the evidence. Although Country Style initially objected to the Landlord's construction activities and its planned redesign of the Development, it took no legal steps to halt either, instead asserting in its defence to the Franchisees' counterclaim that these activities did not occasion any damages to the Franchisees. I agree with Country Style that it was not legally obliged to commence injunction proceedings against the Landlord. But, here, Mesic [a principal of the franchisee] testified, and the trial judge accepted, that when he complained to Country Style about the Landlord's activities, a Country Style senior executive agreed that the Landlord was "wrong" and assured Mesic that Country Style would take legal action against the Landlord. The trial judge found as a fact that Country Style "never followed through on its threats to commence legal action" against the Landlord. This was correct in the sense that Country Style took no legal steps to prevent the construction or the completion of the redesign or to protect the Franchisees' interests. Its Third Party Action against the Landlord was confined to Country Style's own claim for contribution and indemnity from the Landlord.

[100] Moreover, in the Third Party Action, Country Style took a position diametrically opposed to that advanced in its defence to the counterclaim, by pleading that the redesign of the Development was detrimental to the Overlea Franchise business and that the redesign was a breach of the Headlease. Yet it did not amend its defence to the counterclaim or alter its pleaded position at

trial so as to relieve the Franchisees from any part of their burden of proving damages as a result of the Landlord's conduct. To the contrary, it aggressively supported the Landlord in resisting the Franchisees' claim that the redesign of the Development, as reflected in the changes to the Site Plan, damaged the …Franchise.

[101] The structure of the tripartite leasing arrangement in this case placed Country Style, as the party in a direct contractual relationship with the Landlord, in the best legal and business position to influence the Landlord regarding the redesign of the Development and to hold the Landlord to its obligations under the Headlease. When litigation ensued, Country Style sought to advance its own interests by denying the Franchisees' claims, supporting the Landlord's position in its pleadings and at trial, and confining the Third Party Action to a recovery claim that, if successful, would benefit only Country Style. These actions do not enjoy the hallmarks of fair dealing; nor do they support the conclusion that Country Style's conduct was influenced by the interests of the most vulnerable of the involved parties, the Franchisees.

[102] Nor is it any response to the finding of breach of good faith to argue, as Country Style does, that it was legally entitled to evict the Franchisees upon their non-payment of rent and related charges or that, for a time, it agreed to forbear on the enforcement of its rights under the Franchise Agreement and the Sublease. The question is what Country Style did in relation to the Landlord given the emergent dispute. In that respect, apart from its early protestations to the Landlord, Country Style's actions were self-interested.

Preservation of the Social Values of Contracts

The materials in this chapter (and indeed throughout this book) demonstrate the need to view a contract as a social institution, and the importance of considering the social context of a contract. It is easy to think that only those values that attracted the interest of classical economists (efficiency, creation of viable markets, freeing "private" initiative) are relevant in a contractual setting. It is, however, clear that there are a range of social values that can operate as limitations on — or are of more importance than — the classical economists' "contract values".

The following decision articulates a view of contracts as a social institution, and recognizes the importance of a broad range of social and economic interests in the development of the law of contracts.

HENNINGSEN v. BLOOMFIELD MOTORS, INC.

161 A.2d 69
(N.J. Sup. Ct. 1960)

I

The opinion of the court was delivered by **FRANCIS J.**: — [1] Plaintiff Claus H. Henningsen purchased a Plymouth automobile, manufactured by defendant Chrysler Corporation, from defendant Bloomfield Motors, Inc. His wife, plaintiff Helen Henningsen, was injured while driving it and instituted suit against both defendants to recover damages on account of her injuries. Her husband joined in the action seeking compensation for his consequential losses. The complaint was predicated upon breach of express and implied warranties and upon negligence. At the trial the negligence counts were dismissed by the court and the cause was submitted to the jury for determination solely on the issues of implied warranty of merchantability. Verdicts were returned against both defendants and in favor of the plaintiffs. Defendants appealed and plaintiffs cross-appealed from the dismissal of their negligence claim. The matter was certified by this court prior to consideration in the Appellate Division.

[2]   The facts are not complicated, but a general outline of them is necessary to an understanding of the case.

[3]   On May 7, 1955 Mr. and Mrs Henningsen visited the place of business of Bloomfield Motors, Inc., an authorized De Soto and Plymouth dealer, to look at a Plymouth. They wanted to buy a car and were considering a Ford or a Chevrolet as well as a Plymouth. They were shown a Plymouth which appealed to them and the purchase followed. The record indicates that Mr. Henningsen intended the car as a Mother's Day gift to his wife. He said the intention was communicated to the dealer. When the purchase order or contract was prepared and presented, the husband executed it alone. His wife did not join as a party.

[4]   The purchase order was a printed form of one page. On the front it contained blanks to be filled in with a description of the automobile to be sold, the various accessories to be included, and the details of the financing. The particular car selected was described as a 1955 Plymouth, Plaza "6," Club Sedan. The type used in the printed parts of the form became smaller in size, different in style, and less readable toward the bottom where the line for the purchaser's signature was placed. The smallest type on the page appears in the two paragraphs, one of two and one-quarter lines and the second of one and one-half lines, on which great stress is laid by the defense in the case. These two paragraphs are the least legible and the most difficult to read in the instrument, but they are most important in the evaluation of the rights of the contesting parties. They do not attract attention and there is nothing about the format which would draw the reader's eye to them. In fact, a studied and concentrated effort would have to be made to read them. De-emphasis seems the motive rather than emphasis. More particularly, most of the printing in the body of the order appears to be 12-point block type, and easy to read. In the short paragraphs under discussion, however, the type appears to be six-point script and the print is solid, that is, the lines are very close together.

[5]   The two paragraphs are:

> The front and back of this Order comprise the entire agreement affecting this purchase and no other agreement or understanding of any nature concerning same has been made or entered into, or will be recognized. I hereby certify that no credit has been extended to me for the purchase of this motor vehicle except as appears in writing on the face of this agreement.

> I have read the matter printed on the back hereof and agree to it as a part of this order the same as if it were printed above my signature. I certify that I am 21 years of age, or older, and hereby acknowledge receipt of a copy of this order.

[6]   On the right side of the form, immediately below these clauses and immediately above the signature line, and in 12-point block type, the following appears:

CASH OR CERTIFIED CHECK ONLY ON DELIVERY.

[7]   On the left side, just opposite and in the same style type as the two quoted clauses, but in eight-point size, this statement is set out:

> This agreement shall not become binding upon the Dealer until approved by an officer of the company.

The two latter statements are in the interest of the dealer and obviously an effort is made to draw attention to them.

[8]   The testimony of Claus Henningsen justifies the conclusion that he did not read the two fine-print paragraphs referring to the back of the purchase contract. And it is uncontradicted that no one made any reference to them, or called them to his attention. With respect to the matter appearing on the back, it is likewise un-contradicted that he did not read it and that no one called it to his attention.

[9]   The reverse side of the contract contains 8 1/2 inches of fine print. It is not as small, however, as the two critical paragraphs described above. The page is headed "Conditions" and contains ten separate paragraphs consisting of 65 lines in all. The paragraphs do not have headnotes or margin notes denoting their particular subject as in the case of the "Owner Service Certificate" to be referred to later. In the seventh paragraph, about two-thirds of the way down the page, the warranty, which is the focal point of the case, is set forth. It is as follows:

> 7.   It is expressly agreed that there are no warranties, express or implied, *made* by either the dealer or the manufacturer on the motor vehicle, chassis, of parts furnished hereunder except as follows.
>
> The manufacturer warrants each new motor vehicle (including original equipment placed thereon by the manufacturer except tires), chassis or parts manufactured by it to be free from defects in material or workmanship under normal use and service. Its obligation under this warranty being limited to making good at its factory any part or parts thereof which shall, within ninety (90) days after delivery of such vehicle *to the original purchaser* or before such vehicle has been driven 4,000 miles, whichever event shall first occur, be returned to it with transportation charges prepaid and which its examination shall disclose to its satisfaction to have been thus defective; *this warranty being expressly in lieu of all other warranties expressed or implied, and all other obligations or liabilities on its part,* and it neither assumes nor author-izes any other person to assume for it any other liability in connection with the sale of its vehicles. (Emphasis ours.)

[10]   After the contract had been executed, plaintiffs were told the car had to be serviced and that it would be ready in two days. According to the dealer's president, a number of cars were on hand at the time; they had come in from the factory about three or four weeks earlier and at least some of them, including the one selected by the Henningsens, were kept in the back of the shop for display purposes. When sold, plaintiffs' vehicle was not "a serviced car, ready to go." The testimony shows that Chrysler Corporation sends from the factory to the dealer a "New Car Preparation Service Guide" with each new automobile. The guide contains detailed instructions as to what has to be done to prepare the car for delivery. The dealer is told to "Use this form as a guide to inspect and prepare this new Plymouth for delivery." It specifies 66 separate items to be checked, tested, tightened or adjusted in the course of the servicing, but dismantling the vehicle or checking all of its internal parts is not prescribed. The guide also calls for delivery of the Owner Service Certificate with the car.

[11]   This certificate, which at least by inference is authorized by Chrysler, was in the car when released to Claus Henningsen on May 9, 1955. It was not made part of the purchase contract, nor was it shown to him prior to the consummation of that agreement. The only reference to it therein is that the dealer "agrees to promptly perform and fulfill all terms and conditions of the owner service policy." The certificate contains a warranty entitled "Automobile Manufacturers Associa-

tion Uniform Warranty." The provisions thereof are the same as those set forth on the reverse side of the purchase order, except that an additional paragraph is added by which the dealer extends that warranty to the purchaser in the same manner as if the word "Dealer" appeared instead of the word "Manufacturer".

[12]   The new Plymouth was turned over to the Henningsens on May 9, 1955. No proof was adduced by the dealer to show precisely what was done in the way of mechanical or road testing beyond testimony that the manufacturer's instructions were probably followed. Mr. Henningsen drove it from the dealer's place of business in Bloomfield to their home in Keansburg. On the trip nothing unusual appeared in the way in which it operated. Thereafter, it was used for short trips on paved streets about the town. It had no servicing and no mishaps of any kind before the event of May 19. That day, Mrs. Henningsen drove to Asbury Park. On the way down and in returning the car performed in normal fashion until the accident occurred. She was proceeding north on Route 36 in Highlands, New Jersey, at 20-22 miles per hour. The highway was paved and smooth, and contained two lanes for northbound travel. She was riding in the right-hand lane. Suddenly she heard a loud noise "from the bottom, by the hood." It "felt as if something cracked." The steering wheel spun in her hands; the car veered sharply to the right and crashed into a highway sign and a brick wall. No other vehicle was in any way involved. A bus operator driving in the left-hand lane testified that he observed plaintiffs' car approaching in normal fashion in the opposite direction; "all of a sudden [it] veered at 90 degrees . . . and right into this wall." As a result of the impact, the front of the car was so badly damaged that it was impossible to determine if any of the parts of the steering wheel mechanism or workmanship or assembly were defective or improper prior to the accident. The condition was such that the collision insurance carrier, after inspection, declared the vehicle a total loss. It had 468 miles on the speedometer at the time.

[13]   The insurance carrier's inspector and appraiser of damaged cars, with 11 years of experience, advanced the opinion, based on the history and his examination, that something definitely went "wrong from the steering wheel down to the front wheels" and that the untoward happening must have been due to mechanical defect or failure; "something down there had to drop off or break loose to cause the car" to act in the manner described.

[14]   As has been indicated, the trial court felt that the proof was not sufficient to make out a prima facie case as to the negligence of either the manufacturer or the dealer. The case was given to the jury, therefore, solely on the warranty theory, with results favorable to the plaintiffs against both defendants.

II

[15]   *The effect of the disclaimer and limitation of liability clauses on the implied warranty of merchantability.* Judicial notice may be taken of the fact that automobile manufacturers, including Chrysler Corporation, undertake large-scale advertising programs over television, radio, in newspapers, magazines and all media of communication in order to persuade the public to buy their products. As has been observed above, a number of jurisdictions, conscious of modern marketing practices, have declared that when a manufacturer engages in advertising in order to bring his goods and their quality to the attention of the public and thus to create consumer demand, the representations made constitute an express warranty run-

ning directly to a buyer who purchases in reliance thereon. The fact that the sale is consummated with an independent dealer does not obviate that warranty. . . .

[16] In view of the cases in various jurisdictions suggesting the conclusion which we have now reached with respect to the implied warranty of merchantability, it becomes apparent that manufacturers who enter into promotional activities to stimulate consumer buying may incur warranty obligations of either or both the express or implied character. These developments in the law inevitably suggest the inference that the form of express warranty made part of the Henningsen purchase contract was devised for general use in the automobile industry as a possible means of avoiding the consequences of the growing judicial acceptance of the thesis that the described express or implied warranties run directly to the consumer.

[17] In the light of these matters, what effect should be given to the express warranty in question which seeks to limit the manufacturer's liability to replacement of defective parts, and which disclaims all other warranties, express or implied? In assessing its significance we must keep in mind the general principle that, in the absence of fraud, one who does not choose to read a contract before signing it, cannot later relieve himself of its burdens . . . and in applying that principle, the basic tenet of freedom of competent parties to contract is a factor of importance. But in the framework of modern commercial life and business practices, such rules cannot be applied on a strict, doctrinal basis. The conflicting interests of the buyer and seller must be evaluated realistically and justly, giving due weight to the social policy evinced by the Uniform Sales Act, the progressive decisions of the courts engaged in administering it, the mass-production methods of manufacture and distribution to the public, and the bargaining position occupied by the ordinary consumer in such an economy. This history of the law shows that legal doctrines, as first expounded, often prove to be inadequate under the impact of later experience. In such case, the need for justice has stimulated the necessary qualifications or adjustments. . . .

[18] In these times, an automobile is almost as much a servant of convenience for the ordinary person as a household utensil. For a multitude of other persons it is a necessity. Crowded highways and filled parking lots are a commonplace of our existence. There is no need to look any farther than the daily newspaper to be convinced that when an automobile is defective, it has great potentiality for harm.

[19] No one spoke more graphically on this subject than Justice Cardozo in the landmark case of *MacPherson v. Buick Motor Co.* 217 N.Y. 382, 111 N.E. 1050, 1053, L.R.A. 1916F, 696 (Ct. App. 1916):

> Beyond all question, the nature of an automobile gives warning of probable danger if its construction is defective. This automobile was designed to go 50 miles per hour. Unless its wheels were sound and strong, injury was almost certain. It was as much a thing of danger as a defective engine for a railroad . . . The dealer was indeed the one person of whom it might be said with some approach to certainty that by him the car would not be used . . . Precedents drawn from the days of travel by stage-coach do not fit the conditions of travel today. The principle that the danger must be imminent does not change. But the things subject to the principle do change. They are whatever the needs of life in a developing civilization require them to be.

[20] In the 44 years that have intervened since that utterance, the average car has been constructed for almost double the speed mentioned; 60 miles per hour is permitted on our parkways. The number of automobiles in use has multiplied

many times and the hazard to the user and the public has increased proportionately. The Legislature has intervened in the public interest, not only to regulate the manner of operation on the highway but also to require periodic inspection of motor vehicles and to impose a duty on manufacturers to adopt certain safety devices and methods in their construction. R.S. 39:3-43 et seq., N.J.S.A. It is apparent that the public has an interest not only in the safe manufacture of automobiles, but also, as shown by the Sales Act, in protecting the rights and remedies of purchasers, so far as it can be accomplished consistently with our system of free enterprise. In a society such as ours, where the automobile is a common and necessary adjunct of daily life, and where its use is so fraught with danger to the driver, passengers, and the public, the manufacturer is under a special obligation in connection with the construction, promotion and sale of his cars. Consequently, the courts must examine purchase agreements closely to see if consumer and public interests are treated fairly.

[21] What influence should these circumstances have on the restrictive effect of Chrysler's express warranty in the framework of the purchase contract? As we have said, warranties originated in the law to safeguard the buyer and not to limit the liability of the seller or manufacturer. It seems obvious in this instance that the motive was to avoid the warranty obligations which are normally incidental to such sales. The language gave little and withdrew much. In return for the delusive remedy of replacement of defective parts at the factory, the buyer is said to have accepted the exclusion of the maker's liability for personal injuries arising from the breach of the warranty, and to have agreed to the elimination of any other express or implied warranty. An instinctively felt sense of justice cries out against such a sharp bargain. But does the doctrine that a person is bound by his signed agreement, in the absence of fraud, stand in the way of any relief?

[22] In the modern consideration of problems such as this, Corbin suggests that practically all judges are "chancellors" and cannot fail to be influenced by any equitable doctrines that are available. And he opines that "there is sufficient flexibility in the concepts of fraud, duress, misrepresentation and undue influence, not to mention differences in economic bargaining power" to enable the courts to avoid enforcement of unconscionable provisions in long printed standardized contracts. 1 *Corbin on Contracts* (1950) section 128, p. 188. Freedom of contract is not such an immutable doctrine as to admit of no qualification in the area in which we are concerned. As Chief Justice Hughes said in his dissent in *Morehead v. People of State of New York ex rel. Tipaldo*, 298 U.S. 587, 627, 56 S. Ct. 918, 930, 80 L.Ed. 1347, 1364 (1936):

> We have had frequent occasion to consider the limitations on liberty of contract. While it is highly important to preserve that liberty from arbitrary and capricious interference, it is also necessary to prevent its abuse, as otherwise it could be used to override all public interests and thus in the end destroy the very freedom of opportunity which it is designed to safeguard.

[23] That sentiment was echoed by Justice Frankfurter in his dissent in *United States v. Bethlehem Steel Corp.*, 315 U.S. 289, 326, 62 S. Ct. 581, 599, 86 L.Ed. 855, 876 (1942):

> It is said that familiar principles would be outraged if Bethlehem were denied recovery on these contracts. But is there any principle which is more familiar or more firmly embedded in the history of Anglo-American law than the basic doctrine that

the courts will not permit themselves to be used as instruments of inequity and injustice? Does any principle in our law have more universal application than the doctrine that courts will not enforce transactions in which the relative positions of the parties are such that one has unconscionably taken advantage of the necessities of the other?

These principles are not foreign to the law of contracts. Fraud and physical duress are not the only grounds upon which courts refuse to enforce contracts. The law is not so primitive that it sanctions every injustice except brute force and downright fraud. More specifically, the courts generally refuse to lend themselves to the enforcement of a "bargain" in which one party has unjustly taken advantage of the economic necessities of the other.

[24] The traditional contract is the result of free bargaining of parties who are brought together by the play of the market, and who meet each other on a footing of approximate economic equality. In such a society there is no danger that freedom of contract will be a threat to the social order as a whole. But in present-day commercial life the standardized mass contract has appeared. It is used primarily by enterprises with strong bargaining power and position. "The weaker party, in need of the goods or services, is frequently not in a position to shop around for better terms, either because the author of the standard contract has a monopoly (natural or artificial) or because all competitors use the same clauses. His contractual intention is but a subjection more or less voluntary to terms dictated by the stronger party, terms whose consequences are often understood in a vague way, if at all." Kessler, "Contracts of Adhesion — Some Thoughts About Freedom of Contract" 43 *Col. L. Rev.* 629, 632 (1943); Ehrenzweig "Adhesion Contracts in the Conflict of Laws" 53 *Col. L. Rev.*, 1072, 1075, 1089 (1953). Such standardized contracts have been described as those in which one predominant party will dictate its law to an undetermined multiple rather than to an individual. They are said to resemble a law rather than a meeting of the minds. *Siegelman v. Cunard White Star*, 221 F .2d 189, 206 (2d Cir. 1955).

[25] Vold, in the recent revision of his *Law of Sales* (2d ed. 1959) at page 447, wrote of this type of contract and its effect upon the ordinary buyer:

In recent times the marketing process has been getting more highly organized than ever before. Business units have been expanding on a scale never before known. The standardized contract with its broad disclaimer clauses is drawn by legal advisers of sellers widely organized in trade associations. It is encountered on every hand. Extreme inequality of bargaining between buyer and seller in this respect is now often conspicuous. Many buyers no longer have any real choice in the matter. They must often accept what they can get though accompanied by broad disclaimers. The terms of these disclaimers deprive them of all substantial protection with regard to the quality of the goods. In effect, this is by force of contract between very unequal parties. It throws the risk of defective articles on the most dependent party. He has the least individual power to avoid the presence of defects. He also has the least individual ability to bear their disastrous consequences.

[26] The warranty before us is a standardized form designed for mass use. It is imposed upon the automobile consumer. He takes it or leaves it, and he must take it to buy an automobile. No bargaining is engaged in with respect to it. In fact, the dealer through whom it comes to the buyer is without authority to alter it; his function is ministerial — simply to deliver it.

[27] The form warranty is not only standard with Chrysler but, as mentioned above, it is the uniform warranty of the Automobile Manufacturers Association.

Members of the Association are: General Motors, Inc., Ford, Chrysler, Stude-baker-Packard, American Motors, (Rambler), Willys Motors, Checker Motors Corp., and International Harvester Company. *Automobile Facts and Figures* (1958 ed., Automobile Manufacturers Association) 69. Of these companies, the "Big Three" (General Motors, Ford, and Chrysler) represented 93.5% of the passenger-car production for 1958 and the independents 6.5%. Standard & Poor (*Industrial Surveys, Autos, Basic Analysis*, June 25, 1959) 4109. And for the same year the "Big Three" had 86.72% of the total passenger vehicle registrations. *Automotive News*, 1959 *Almanac* (Slocum Publishing Co., Inc.) p. 25.

[28] The gross inequality of bargaining position occupied by the consumer in the automobile industry is thus apparent. There is no competition among the car mak-ers in the area of the express warranty. Where can the buyer go to negotiate for better protection? Such control and limitation of his remedies are inimical to the public welfare and, at the very least, call for great care by the courts to avoid injus-tice through application of strict common-law principles of freedom of contract. Because there is no competition among the motor vehicle manufacturers with re-spect to the scope of protection guaranteed to the buyer, there is no incentive on their part to stimulate goodwill in that field of public relations. Thus, there is lack-ing a factor existing in more competitive fields, one which tends to guarantee the safe construction of the article sold. Since all competitors operate in the same way, the urge to be careful is not so pressing. See "Warranties of Kind and Quality," 57 *Yale L.J.* 1389, 1400 (1948).

[29] Although the courts, with few exceptions, have been most sensitive to prob-lems presented by contracts resulting from gross disparity in buyer-seller bargain-ing positions, they have not articulated a general principle condemning, as op-posed to public policy, the imposition on the buyer of a skeleton warranty as a means of limiting the responsibility of the manufacturer. They have endeavored thus far to avoid a drastic departure from age-old tenets of freedom of contract by adopting doctrines of strict construction, and notice and knowledgeable assent by the buyer to the attempted exculpation of the seller. 1 *Corbin, supra*, 337; 2 Harper and James, *supra*, 1590; Prosser, "Warranty of Merchantable Quality," 27 *Minn. L. Rev.* 117, 159 (1932). Accordingly to be found in the cases are statements that dis-claimers and the consequent limitation of liability will not be given effect if un-fairly procured". . . .

[30] Basically, the reason a contracting party offering services of a public or quasi-public nature has been held to the requirements of fair dealing, and, when it attempts to limit its liability, of securing the understanding consent of the patron or consumer, is because members of the public generally have no other means of ful-filling the specific need represented by the contract. Having in mind the situation in the automobile industry as detailed above, and particularly the fact that the lim-ited warranty extended by the manufacturers is a uniform one, there would appear to be no just reason why the principles of all of the cases set forth should not chart the course to be taken here.

[31] It is undisputed that the president of the dealer with whom Henningsen dealt did not specifically call attention to the warranty on the back of the purchase order. The form and the arrangement of its face, as described above, certainly would cause the minds of reasonable men to differ as to whether notice of a yielding of basic rights stemming from the relationship with the manufacturer was adequately

given. The words "warranty" or "limited warranty" did not even appear in the fine print above the place for signature, and a jury might well find that the type of print itself was such as to promote lack of attention rather than sharp scrutiny. The inference from the facts is that Chrysler placed the method of communicating its warranty to the purchaser in the hands of the dealer. If either one or both of them wished to make certain that Henningsen became aware of that agreement and its purported implications, neither the form of the document nor the method of expressing the precise nature of the obligation intended to be assumed would have presented any difficulty.

[32] But there is more than this. Assuming that a jury might find that the fine print referred to reasonably served the objective of directing a buyer's attention to the warranty on the reverse side, and, therefore, that he should be charged with awareness of its language, can it be said that an ordinary layman would realize what he was relinquishing in return for what he was being granted? Under the law, breach of warranty against defective parts or workmanship which caused personal injuries would entitle a buyer to damages even if due care were used in the manufacturing process. Because of the great potential for harm if the vehicle was defective, that right is the most important and fundamental one arising from the relationship. Difficulties so frequently encountered in establishing negligence in manufacture in the ordinary case make this manifest. 2 Harper and James, *supra*, sections 28.14, 28.15; Prosser, *supra*, 506. Any ordinary layman of reasonable intelligence, looking at the phraseology, might well conclude that Chrysler was agreeing to replace defective parts and perhaps replace anything that went wrong because of defective workmanship during the first 90 days or 4,000 miles of operation, but that he would not be entitled to a new car. It is not unreasonable to believe that the entire scheme being conveyed was a proposed remedy for physical deficiencies in the car. *In the context* of this warranty, only the abandonment of all sense of justice would permit us to hold that, as a matter of law, the phrase "its obligation under this warranty being limited to making good at its factory any part or parts thereof" signifies to an ordinary reasonable person that he is relinquishing any personal injury claim that might flow from the use of a defective automobile. Such claims are nowhere mentioned. The draftsmanship is reflective of the care and skill of the Automobile Manufacturers Association in undertaking to avoid warranty obligations without drawing too much attention to its effort in that regard. No one can doubt that if the will to do so were present, the ability to inform the buying public of the intention to disclaim liability for injury claims arising from breach of warranty would present no problem.

[33] In this connection, attention is drawn to the Plymouth Owner Certificate mentioned earlier. Obviously, Chrysler is aware of it because the New Car Preparation Service Guide sent from the factory to the dealer directs that it be given to the purchaser. That certificate contains a paragraph called "Explanation of Warranty". Its entire tenor relates to replacement of defective parts. There is nothing about it to stimulate the idea that the intention of the warranty is to exclude personal injury claims. . . .

[34] The task of the judiciary is to administer the spirit as well as the letter of the law. On issues such as the present one, part of that burden is to protect the ordinary man against the loss of important rights through what, in effect, is the unilateral act of the manufacturer. The status of the automobile industry is unique.

Manufacturers are few in number and strong in bargaining position. In the matter of warranties on the sale of their products, the Automotive Manufacturers Association has enabled them to present a united front. From the standpoint of the purchaser, there can be no arm's-length negotiating on the subject. Because his capacity for bargaining is so grossly unequal, the inexorable conclusion which follows is that he is not permitted to bargain at all. He must take or leave the automobile on the warranty terms dictated by the maker. He cannot turn to a competitor for better security.

[35] Public policy is a term not easily defined. Its significance varies as the habits and needs of a people may vary. It is not static and the field of application is an ever-increasing one. A contract, or a particular provision therein, valid in one era may be wholly opposed to the public policy of another. . . .

[36] Courts keep in mind the principle that the best interests of society demand that persons should not be unnecessarily restricted in their freedom to contract. But they do not hesitate to declare void as against public policy contractual provisions which clearly tend to the injury of the public in some way. . . .

[37] Public policy at a given time finds expression in the Constitution, the statutory law and in judicial decisions. In the area of sale of goods, the legislative will has imposed an implied warranty of merchantability as a general incident of sale of an automobile by description. The warranty does not depend upon the affirmative intention of the parties. It is a child of the law; it annexes itself to the contract because of the very nature of the transaction . . . The judicial process has recognized a right to recover damages for personal injuries arising from a breach of that warranty. The disclaimer of the implied warranty and exclusion of all obligations except those specifically assumed by the express warranty signify a studied effort to frustrate that protection. True, the Sales Act authorizes agreements between buyer and seller qualifying the warranty obligations. But quite obviously the Legislature contemplated lawful stipulations (which are determined by the circumstances of a particular case) arrived at freely by parties of relatively equal bargaining strength. The lawmakers did not authorize the automobile manufacturer to use its grossly disproportionate bargaining power to relieve itself from liability and to impose on the ordinary buyer, who in effect has no real freedom of choice, the grave danger of injury to himself and others that attends the sale of such a dangerous instrumentality as a defectively made automobile. In the framework of this case, illuminated as it is by the facts and the many decisions noted, we are of the opinion that Chrysler's attempted disclaimer of an implied warranty of merchantability and of the obligations arising therefrom is so inimical to the public good as to compel an adjudication of its invalidity. See 57 *Yale L.J. supra*, at pp. 1400-04; proposed Uniform Commercial Code, 1958 Official Text, section 202.

QUESTIONS AND NOTES

1. Notice that the Court in *Henningsen* provides a much more detailed discussion of the lack of term competition and the effects of market concentration than Lord Diplock did in *Schroeder v. Macaulay.*

2. To what extent is the issue in *Henningsen* the same as that in *Fraser-Reid v. Droumtsekas* (*supra*, Chapter 5) or in *Thornton v. Shoe Lane* (*supra*)?

3.   Where do the values that Francis J. uses as the basis for his decision in *Henningsen* come from? Is he justified in drawing the conclusions he does from the values he finds (or holds)?

4.   As discussed in Chapter 5, many Canadian jurisdictions now have legislation which provides that any purported waiver by a consumer of the implied warranties and conditions of the *Sale of Goods Act* is invalid: see. *e.g.*, Ontario *Consumer Protection Act, 2002*, S.O. 2002, c. 30, Sched. A, s. 9(3). Are there other doctrinal differences in how a Canadian court might deal with the issues in *Henningsen*?

The development of the law of contracts has always been, whether it was openly admitted by the courts or not, concerned with the implementation of public policy, *i.e.*, the values that Canadian society recognizes and wants to forward. The cases examined in this chapter have been presented to illustrate how, working towards this goal and within the framework of the legal process, the courts can move from a narrow focus on the parties' agreement and what particular terms they might have assented to a wider focus on what kinds of agreements they think people should make.

When the courts' concern shifts from a contract to a relation and to what is necessary to maintain that relation's integrity, the courts are necessarily broadening the scope of their inquiry, the range of facts that they have to consider and the kind of legal principle that they will apply.

Modern human rights legislation fits with this development. That legislation prohibits various kinds of contractual provisions (or behaviour in the contractual context) that violate the values declared by the legislation. For example, one may not refuse to rent accommodation to, employ (or fire) a person or deny a person services on grounds considered to be objectionable.

A person's right to earn his or her living as a lawyer is protected by the requirement that, before he or she can be expelled from the Law Society, a hearing must be held at which the rules of natural justice must be observed. These rules require notice of the allegations against the member, an opportunity to answer the allegations and that the decision be made by an impartial body. These very concerns were expressed well over a century ago in *Dawkins v. Antrobus* (1879), 17 Ch. Div. 615 (C.A.). In that case a member of a London club was expelled and he sought a declaration from the Court that the expulsion was unlawful. Brett L.J. in the Court of Appeal, said (at 630):

> The only question which a Court can properly consider is whether the members of the club, under such circumstances, have acted *ultra vires* or not, and it seems to me the only questions which a Court can properly entertain for that purpose are, whether anything has been done which is contrary to natural justice, although it is within the rules of the club—in other words, whether the rules of the club are contrary to natural justice . . . .

It is oddly inconsistent with (i) the open recognition by the Supreme Court of the importance of a job to a person's life, sense of worth and well-being, (ii) the widespread imposition of restrictions on what is the same as dismissal, *viz.*, expulsion from a body like a Law Society, and (iii) the kind of control readily asserted by Brett L.J., that the Supreme Court would deny that an employer owes its employees a duty of good faith in deciding whether to dismiss an the employment relation (para. 76 in *Wallace v. United Grain Growers*, Chapter 1). Yet, even as the Supreme Court held that there is "no good faith obligation in employment contracts", other courts were protecting employees' rights to be fairly treated, to have proper performance evaluations and, if cause for dismissal was alleged, to know what the allegations were in order to be given an effective opportunity to answer them and to have the decision made by a person whose mind was not already made up: see, *e.g.*, *Shah v. Xerox Canada Ltd.* (2000), 49 C.C.E.L. (2d) 166 (Ont. C.A.).

The role that natural justice can (and could) play in contractual relations is a reflection of two concerns. The first is the concern that the power that one party has in a relation, particularly one that has a significant temporal dimension, may be abused. The second (which is an aspect of the first) is that the possibility of an individual earning a livelihood can often depend on his or her membership in an association. The right of a lawyer to earn his or her livelihood through the practice of law is protected by the requirement that each provincial law society may impose sanctions which might limit or deny the lawyer the right to practise only after a hearing which has met the standards of natural justice. The right of a member of a real estate board to the benefits of membership will be as important to that member as the right of any lawyer to practise. If the right of an English gentleman to natural justice in the decision to expel him from his club will be protected by requiring the club to follow the rules of natural justice, it is equally justifiable and necessary that members of associations be protected in the same way.

Lawyers consulted by clients who have run afoul of the rules of their association sometimes respond by seeking judicial review; see *e.g.*, *Pestell v. Kitchener-Waterloo Real Estate Board Inc.* (1981), 131 D.L.R. (3d) 88 (H.C.J.). That remedy is only available when the association has a statutory basis. When the association is created by contract, as is a real estate board, equivalent protection can be found in the ability of the courts to require the association to follow the rules of natural justice when any member threatened with discipline, either by seeking injunctive relief or iun an action for damages.

The issues that have just been raised can now be expanded even further. In Macneil's analysis of contract, he presents the institution of contract as part of a spectrum of consensual arrangements that can, if pushed to the limit, include not only the nation-state but the entire world. In other words, there is no logical place to stop and say, "Up to here we are in the domain of private arrangements and beyond this point we are in the realm of the state and public arrangements." The difficulty of making this statement justifiable or of defending the drawing of any line anywhere is illustrated by the following extract. We cannot explore here the issues raised by the transformation of an arrangement which, when we started to examine it, appeared to be the paradigm of the private arrangement — the one in which society had only a concern that people be free to make whatever deals seemed good to them — into one that has many if not most of the hallmarks of a political society. Such an arrangement presents problems of decision-making by democratic processes, the extent of the society's rule-making powers, and the sanctions for breach of the rules.

GEIS, "RESIDENTIAL PRIVATE GOVERNMENTS AND THE LAW"

(1981), 67 *A.B.A.J.* 1418

[1]   High land costs and the growing use of flexible zoning techniques by local governments are powerful inspiration for real estate developers to keep trying to squeeze more housing onto less land. One result has been the explosive growth

during the 1970s in the number of projects served by community facilities owned or managed by condominium, co-operative, and homeowner associations.

[2] For many years community associations have been operating private systems of roads, utilities, parks, open space, and recreational amenities that are indistinguishable from public facilities run by departments of municipal or county governments. The functional distinctions between these "residential private governments" and units of local government are hazy, to say the least. All members of these community associations are bound together by contract in a network of reciprocal obligations that can only be characterized as a private constitution for a quasi-government. They elect directors to govern their community facilities. These elected representatives have the power to assess the members for the purpose of paying the common expenses of the community, and the assessments are secured by liens on all of the real estate in the community. The quasi-government even can adopt rules and regulations controlling nuisances in the public areas and can enforce sanctions for violations.

[3] The legal differences between municipal bodies and community associations are rooted in the mode of their creation. Municipal bodies are publicly created, and exercise enumerated statutory powers, while community association regimes are privately created and exercise general powers derived from the law of contract and real property, including condominium statutes and local ordinances. From this premise flows a truism so natural that it has escaped close analysis: because community associations essentially are creatures of private contract rather than of public law, real estate developers are able, within broad limits, to act as framers of private constitutions that govern the quasi-political rights of their customers.

[4] Last April, in *Ball v. James*, 101 S.Ct. 1811, (1981) a narrow majority of the Supreme Court wrestled again with the subtle distinction between exercising property rights and wielding sovereignty. By a vote of five to four the court held that the constitutional requirement of "one man, one vote" did not apply to an Arizona water district that generated and sold electricity to half the population of the state and distributed water in central Arizona. The court upheld a state law under which directors of the district were elected by a vote of property owners weighted according to the amount of property owned. The weighted-voting formula was no different in principle from the formula that governs the way in which condominium association directors must be elected under the condominium laws of most states: each owner votes in proportion to the percentage ownership interest in the common elements allocated to him by the condominium declaration.

[5] The rationale of the *Ball* case was that the water district did not administer the "normal functions of government" such as imposing taxes, maintaining roads, and passing laws. Condominium associations in many states now must surely wonder what side of the sovereignty line they are treading.

[6] The solution to the continuing identity crisis of community associations lies in a searching examination of the laws underlying all multiple-ownership real estate regimes. The emphasis must be shifted from the present preoccupation with the real and imagined conflicts between developers and consumers and focused instead on those problems that are inherent to the daily government of all common interest housing communities. The real estate communities operated by condominium, co-operative, and homeowner associations must be viewed as specific forms

of a more generalized phenomenon and must be subjected to a scrutiny that cuts through the legal niceties that have restricted legislative attention to the condominium form.

[7]   A thoughtful study might demonstrate, for example, that the real need is for a new species of not-for-profit corporation act, modeled on municipal corporation enabling acts, to furnish the organizational structure and operating guidelines for all community associations, irrespective of the form of organization of the real estate titles in the regime.

[8]   Most important, more support must be given to the National Conference of Commissioners on Uniform State Laws in its efforts to bring some semblance of order to the patchwork of state laws that confuse the real issues in this field. The conference already has promulgated a *Uniform Condominium Act*, a *Uniform Planned Community Act* governing homeowner association regimes, and recently has finished work on a *Model Real Estate Co-operative Act*. In coming years the conference, it is hoped, will start work on a Uniform Multiple Ownership Act that at last will put all the pieces together and bring order and rationality to this troubled corner of the law.

While the focus of this book has been principally on private contracts and contracts between individuals or merchants, wider concerns are never far away. One of the odd features of the law of contracts is that the problems and the solutions developed for them have relevance in many situations that appear to be far removed from private negotiations, performance and enforcement. Contract principles are relevant in both international law and aboriginal law when treaties, their making, amending and enforcement are in issue. Indeed, in Canada many aspects of constitution making and, for example, the possible separation of Quebec can be analyzed in contractual terms.

CHAPTER SEVEN

ILLEGALITY

INTRODUCTION

The issues in this chapter can be seen as a natural progression from the issues raised in the earlier chapters. In Chapters 5 and 6 the focus was on the judicial control of contracts on various grounds. In most of the situations, the parties could have achieved all, or most, of their objectives by making some change in the words used or by restraining their self-interest. Only occasionally — in the cases on non-delegable duties of care or restraint of trade — would the parties run up against judicially imposed limits on what they wanted to do. Even in those cases, the imposition of the legal limits on freedom of contract could sometimes be justified on the ground that the acquiescence of one party may not have been entirely voluntary. In this chapter the focus is on the problems that arise when a contract is contrary to some rule of law, or to the provisions of some statute.

These three chapters can be seen as presenting a spectrum of techniques of legal control over contracts. At one end, with the cases discussed in Chapter 5, the courts' concern was usually only with determining the terms of the contract. Control was exercised only by indirect (and frequently erratic) methods, for example, by the parol evidence rule, or by the imposition of duties arising from the courts' perception of how risks should be allocated if the parties had made no effort to allocate them. It was implicit in those cases (at least for commercial contracts) that, if the parties had clearly wanted to do so, they could have avoided, for example, the responsibility for a warranty. In the cases on mistake there was no effort at control: the courts were only doing what was necessary to sort out the problem that the parties' inability to foresee the future had created.

In Chapter 6 the focus was on more explicit examples of control. Control was exercised to protect one party's reasonable expectations, to impose some kind of basic fairness in the exchange process, or to preserve the institution of contract itself.

In Chapters 5 and 6 the control that was exercised was, in general, responsive to what might be called "contract values". When the control was justifiable, it enhanced the effectiveness of the contract as a social mechanism of fair exchange. Control in the interests of fairness or to protect the integrity of a relation makes the whole enterprise of contracting more effective and more likely to achieve the values that society seeks to advance. In this chapter the focus is on problems that arise when there is a direct attempt to control or prohibit certain transactions, but no clear specification of what happens if a transaction occurs. All too often, the control is likely to frustrate the achievement of contract values, and provides perverse or random incentives to the parties.

The problems that the law has to deal with arise from the fact that generally legislation does not deal with the consequences of any contract that might involve the violation of the statute. It may not be sufficient to say that a contract entered into in violation of a statute or some rule of public policy is "invalid" or "void" if one party is, as a result of that decision, significantly enriched at the other's expense. Courts are, moreover, aware of the risk that holding a contract to be invalid just because it violates some statutory provision may impose on one party what amounts to a sanction for breach that may be out of all proportion to the "offence".

The general rule is that an illegal contract is unenforceable. There are two problems with this simple statement. What does it mean to say that a contract is "illegal"? And what does it mean to say, in this context, that a contract is "unenforceable"?

Some situations are easy to deal with. A contract to sell heroin is a violation of the *Controlled Drugs and Substances Act*, S.C. 1996, c. 19. Both parties to the contract commit a criminal offence by entering into it. A civil court will take no role in enforcing such a contract or in providing relief if the contract is partially performed. Many situations, however, are more complicated, since the illegality involves much less serious offences and may only apply to one party.

Suppose, for example, that a person who is not a member of a provincial law society offers legal advice relating to the incorporation of a business. Suppose also that the advice is accurate and useful. Suppose that the person sues for the promised (and reasonable) fee.

The *Law Society Act*, R.S.O. 1990, c. L.8, provides:

> 50(1) Except where otherwise provided by law,
>
> (a) no person other than a member [of the Law Society] whose rights and privileges are not suspended, shall act as a barrister or solicitor or hold themself [*sic*] out as or represent themself to be a barrister or solicitor or practise as a barrister or solicitor. . . .
>
> 50.1(1) Every person who contravenes section 50 is guilty of an offence and on conviction is liable to a fine of not more than $10,000.

The *Solicitors Act*, R.S.O. 1990, c. S.15, provides:

> 1. If a person, unless a party to the proceeding, commences, prosecutes or defends in his or her own name, or that of any other person, any action or proceeding without having been admitted and enrolled as a solicitor, he or she is incapable of recovering any fee, reward or disbursements on account thereof, and is guilty of a contempt of the court in which such proceeding was commenced, carried on or defended, and is punishable accordingly.

The *Solicitors Act* does not deal with the particular situation that has been supposed: giving advice would not be doing anything in an "action or proceeding". Notice, however, that the section states what "unenforceable" means: the person cannot recover anything in respect of his or her fee or for the disbursements made on the other's behalf. Such precision in the legislation making a contract illegal is unusual.

The *Law Society Act* makes it an offence for a person (i) to act as a lawyer; (ii) to hold out or to represent him or herself to be a lawyer; or (iii) to practise as a lawyer. The giving of legal advice by a person who is not a lawyer (leaving aside for the moment the awkward problem of knowing what constitutes "acting" as a lawyer — non-lawyers might have fun with that concept!) may then attract a quasi-criminal sanction. Does it follow from the fact that the conduct is illegal that the promise by the client to pay is unenforceable as an illegal contract? Assuming that the service provided was in all respects good quality work — much of the work done on behalf of corporations is not rocket science — should the law condone the enrichment of the client at the expense of the "lawyer"? Notice that denying recovery of the fee is less Draconian that denying recovery of amounts paid to someone else on the "client's" behalf. The client may benefit from the disbursement whether or not the person making the payment was a lawyer. If, on the other hand, we permit the unlicensed "lawyer" to sue, are we not at least indirectly encouraging conduct that is illegal?

What if the performance of a contract either involves conduct that is illegal only in some technical sense (perhaps notification had not been given to some public official) or that any criminal sanction is trivial, and that the benefit conferred by the plaintiff is very substantial. Is it fair or good social policy to increase, in effect, the penalty by denying any right to recover on the promise to pay? Can one infer from the fact that the legislature saw fit to impose only a mild sanction that it is proper to ignore the fact that what the plaintiff did was illegal and to allow recovery of the amount promised by the other party? The chances of there being a technical violation of some statute (or, more probably, of some regulation) in the performance of a contract are not negligible in our society.

As the risk of violation of technical regulation increases, there are also increasingly concerns about the prevention of unjust enrichment. If the unenforceability of the contract is clearly required by the legislation, then presumably the enrichment is not unjust: the legislature must have intended the defendant to keep the benefit, regardless of the enrichment involved. However, if it is less clear that the legislature expects the contract to be unenforceable, there are concerns about unjust enrichment. The following cases explore some of these issues.

Keep these questions in mind as you read the cases:

1. If a regulation governing a particular contract is violated, should executory contracts be treated differently from executed contracts?

2. When a statute is the basis for the determination that the contract is illegal, to what extent is the choice of the remedy dependent on the legislative intent? (Remember that in the absence of explicit words, it may be very difficult, if not impossible, to know what the legislature really intended.)

3. In the case of executed or partly executed contracts, when will the courts' use of quasi-contractual or restitutionary remedies be justified?

4. Is the making of the contract itself an illegal act, or could the contract have been performed in a lawful manner?

5. Are both parties equally at fault? If they are not, what effect does this fact have on the court's approach to the remedy?

6. In what circumstances may a court sever the illegal part of the contract and enforce the legal part?

As was the case in other areas, there is an evolution of law in regard to illegal contracts, moving from a fairly clear but narrow rule, to a situation of greater flexibility and fairness, but with correspondingly less certainty.

CONTRACTS CONTRARY TO PUBLIC POLICY

Courts have distinguished between two situations of illegality: contracts that are contrary to judicially defined "public policy", known as "common law illegality", and those that are contrary to statute.

The courts have an inherent power to prevent an abuse of their process and refuse to give effect to contracts that are illegal. What this means is that they may refuse to hear a case that presents a "scandalous" claim. This power is separate from and more extensive than that expressed, for example, in rule 25.11 of the Ontario *Rules of Civil Procedure*, R.R.O. 1990, Reg. 194, and in the rules of other provinces. (Rule 25.11 permits a court to strike out a pleading on the ground that, *inter alia*, it "is scandalous, frivolous or vexatious" or "an abuse of the process of the court".) The courts' inherent power is more extensive because in cases of illegality the courts may exercise their power to refuse enforcement regardless of what the parties might want or how they plead their cases.

The courts have long exercised an inherent power to refuse to give relief when a contract is considered "contrary to public policy", or contrary to "public morals" (*contra bonos mores*), even if the contract is not strictly illegal. In *Pearce v. Brooks* (1866), L.R. 1 Ex. 213, the plaintiff sought to recover for the hire of a carriage he had let to the defendant. The plaintiff knew that the defendant was a prostitute, and that she intended to use the carriage in her business. On these facts the plaintiff was denied the right to recover the amount of the hire for the carriage on the ground that such a contract was contrary to public policy, even though prostitution was not a crime.

There are obvious problems with this line of argument. What about the claim of the person who sells food to the prostitute or rents her accommodation? What about the claim of the person who sells her clothes or make-up? There are cases on these issues, and the courts have generally taken the view that a prostitute has to live, and that to deny sellers generally the right to recover would be undesirable, for who then would sell to a person from whom no payment could be collected by action? On the other hand, the law creates some risk, so that the person who deals with a prostitute, for example to rent her a room, may perhaps require cash in advance. Even if the person renting the carriage to a prostitute could not recover what the prostitute had promised to pay, the courts will not allow the prostitute to recover what has been paid if the carriage is not delivered. This result is justified by the maxim, *in pari delicto potior est conditio defendentis*, *i.e.*, when the parties are equally guilty, the defendant's position is stronger. The effect of this maxim is that the plaintiff will be unable to show that the loss it has suffered should be shifted to the defendant. Like many Latin maxims, it obscures the important questions: When will the parties be regarded as equally guilty? Does the nature of the plaintiff's claim not matter at all?

The court could do what it did in *Pearce v. Brooks* because the plaintiff had to have the court's assistance in enforcing his claim against the defendant and because the plaintiff knew that the defendant intended to use the carriage for an "immoral purpose". (It was not necessary to find that the plaintiff expected to be paid from the proceeds of prostitution, though this probably was the case.)

The importance of the public-policy argument is that it illustrates the power of the court to refuse to enforce a contract where enforcement would be "scandalous" or give the appearance that the courts were, even indirectly, enforcing an "immoral contract". Other clear examples of contracts that the courts would never enforce include contracts to commit crimes or torts, or to undermine the administration of justice. Contracts that to the knowledge of both parties involve deliberate schemes of income tax evasion are also likely to be unenforceable. Similarly, a contract whose principal purpose was to defraud a third person would not be enforced.

Indeed, courts have refused to enforce a provision in a partnership agreement that in the event of the insolvency of one partner, the other partner may buy the interest of the other at the lesser of the book value or the fair market value. Even if the agreement is made when both parties are solvent and without any dishonest intent, it is contrary to public policy as a "fraud upon the bankruptcy law". While the parties' intent may not have been dishonest and the agreement freely entered into, it is not enforceable against the trustee in bankruptcy; see *Canadian Imperial Bank of Commerce v. Bramalea Inc.* (1995), 33 O.R. (3d) 692, 44 B.L.R. (2d) 188 (Gen. Div.).

In the category of agreements undermining the administration of justice, an agreement that may hinder the prosecution of a serious offence is unenforceable, and may well constitute the criminal offence of obstruction of justice. Hence an agreement by the relatives of an embezzler that they will repay the bank where he worked the amount that he embezzled in return for the bank's promise not to contact the police and prosecute is unenforceable: *Jones v. Merionethshire Permanent Benefit Building Society*, [1892] 1 Ch. 173 (C.A.). On the other hand, if the offence involved is quite minor, such as a violation of regulations governing motor vehicles, and the agreement not to facilitate a prosecution is part of a compromise of a civil action, the agreement may be valid: see, *e.g.*, *Morgan v. Fee*, [1908] O.J. No. 6, 18 O.L.R. 30 (Div. Ct.).

The boundaries of judicially defined "public policy" have shifted over the years. Until a few decades ago, Canadian courts were unwilling to enforce any agreements between unmarried cohabitants about their rights and obligations towards one another, as such agreements were viewed as "immoral" and contrary to public policy. In recent years, agreements between unmarried cohabitants have become common, if not expected. Even in the absence of an agreement, relief for unjust enrichment has been imposed on the unmarried person who gains from the domestic contributions of a partner. On the other hand, Canadian courts in the first half of the twentieth century were quite willing to enforce covenants that required discrimination on the basis of race, religion or gender, but would now view them as contrary to public policy (as well as to human rights legislation).

Surrogate motherhood contracts are typically made between a fertile woman and a married couple with a fertile husband and an infertile wife. The fertile woman agrees to be artificially inseminated with the semen of the husband, and to surrender the child to the couple for adoption. These arrangements may be informal and may not involve the exchange of money, but increasingly in North America commercial surrogate motherhood is a significant "industry". Lawyers, especially in the United States, are involved as brokers and negotiators in the making of formal surrogate motherhood contracts. While the courts have not ruled on the enforceability of all of the clauses of these contracts, some American courts have ruled that these contracts are not contrary to public policy and have considered the contractual intent of the parties when deciding how to resolve disputes that may arise after a child is born; see, *e.g.*, *Johnson v. Calvert*, 19 Cal. Rptr.2d 494 (1993). In other states, however, such agreements are considered void as contrary to public policy; see *Re Baby M.*, 537 A.2d 1227 (N.J. 1988). In Canada, the *Royal Commission on New Reproductive Technologies* (1993) argued that surrogate motherhood agreements that involve payment of fees are not compatible with "Canadian values". In 2004, Parliament enacted the *Assisted Human Reproduction Act*, S.C. 2004, c. 2, with s. 6(1) creating an offence for any person to "pay consideration to a female person to be a surrogate mother, offer to pay such consideration or advertise that it will be paid". However, the statute goes on to provide in s. 6(5) that: "This section does not affect the validity under provincial law of any agreement under which a person agrees to be a surrogate mother." Do you think that such agreements should be regarded as unenforceable for being contrary to public policy by Canadian courts? If the couple makes the payment and the woman then refuses to give them the child, should they be able to obtain restitution for the money paid? A.H. Young, "New Reproductive Technologies in Canada and the United States: Same Problems, Different Discourses" (1998), 12 *Temple Inter. & Comp. L.J.* 43, argues that if such contracts are unenforceable but not illegal, this will give the commissioning couple and the professionals involved "a significant incentive . . . to treat the gestational mother very well" (at 84).

The limited response of the Parliament of Canada in part reflects the division of constitutional authority between the federal and provincial governments in Canada. It also illustrates the challenges faced by courts when a particular kind of transaction violates criminal or regulatory law, but there is not a clear provision about the effect of such a law for civil purposes; that issue is considered in the following sections of this chapter. An important factor in any proposal to enact legislation would be whether it might not do more harm than good. The response, "there ought to be a law . . ." sometimes fails to consider whether the criminalization of an activity will simply drive it underground where there are no controls and, when agreements have to be made, legal advice is unavailable.

STATUTORY ILLEGALITY

In addition to the common law power to declare unenforceable a contract that is contrary to public policy, there is a related judicial power to deal with statutory illegality. In Canada, a contract to commit a crime necessarily involves breach of a statute, the *Criminal Code*, R.S.C. 1985, c. C-46, since the person paying to have a crime committed is a "party" to the offence (s. 21 of the *Code*). A contract to commit a crime could be included in the category of contracts contrary to public policy on the ground that the principal objection to its enforcement is the scandalous aspect of enforcement, though statutory illegality is generally considered a distinct reason for not enforcing a contract. In the end, nothing much turns on the classification: in both situations the courts have the power to consider on their own motion the existence of some kind of illegality and the questions that were raised earlier in this section then become relevant. The difficult issues generally do not arise in situations where there is a violation of a criminal statute — though the section of the *Criminal Code* dealing with a "criminal rate" of interest has caused serious problems with many common commercial agreements — but rather where there is a violation of a regulatory or administrative statute.

A classic statement on the effect of illegality arising from breach of statute is the 1775 decision in *Holman v. Johnson* (1775), 1 Cowp. 341, 98 E.R. 1120, (K.B.), where Lord Mansfield said (p. 1121 E.R.):

> The objection, that a contract is immoral or illegal as between plaintiff and defendant, sounds at all times very ill in the mouth of the defendant. It is not for his sake, however, that the objection is ever allowed; but it is founded in general principles of

policy, which the defendant has the advantage of, contrary to the real justice, as between him and the plaintiff, by accident, if I may so say. The principle of public policy is this; *ex dolo malo non oritur actio* [no action can arise out of a fraudulent act]. No court will lend its aid to a man who founds his cause of action upon an immoral or an illegal act. If, from the plaintiff's own stating or otherwise, the cause of action appears to arise *ex turpi causa* [from a disgraceful matter], or the transgression of a positive law of this country, there the court says he has no right to be assisted. It is upon that ground the court goes; not for the sake of the defendant, but because they will not lend their aid to such a plaintiff. So if the plaintiff and defendant were to change sides, and the defendant was to bring his action against the plaintiff, the latter would then have the advantage of it; for where both are equally in fault, *potior est conditio defendentis*.

This passage was, for example, quoted and relied upon by the court in *Rogers v. Leonard* (1973), 1 O.R. (2d) 57, 39 D.L.R. (3d) 349 (H.C.J.). That case illustrates the problems of an unthinking application of Lord Mansfield's statement. The parties, an American purchaser and a Canadian vendor, signed an agreement to sell a summer vacation cottage on a Sunday. At that time, the *Lord's Day Act*, R.S.C. 1970, c. L-13, provided:

> 4. It is not lawful for any person on the Lord's Day, except as provided herein . . . to sell or offer for sale or purchase any goods, chattels, or other personal property, or any real estate, or to carry on or transact any business of his ordinary calling, or in connection with such calling, or for gain to do, or employ any other person to do, on that day, any work, business, or labour.

The purchasers were unaware of the legislation, but the vendor admitted that she knew of the statute. She was prepared to ignore it, she said, because she was "dealing with friends". The purchasers went into possession after the agreement was signed, but the vendor refused to close the transaction. When the plaintiffs sued, the trial judge, Haines J., rejected the argument of the plaintiff that s. 4 was intended to protect purchasers from those engaged in the business of selling land on Sundays. He held that s. 4 was "dictated by considerations of public policy". On this basis, he held that the agreement was "illegal and void" and that no action could be brought to enforce the contract to sell the land or to seek damages for the failure to perform. The court also rejected a claim by the purchasers for compensation for money that they had spent in fixing the cottage. Haines J. said (pp. 69-70 O.R.):

> As a general rule a party may not invoke the aid of the courts to recover property transferred or money expended pursuant to an illegal transaction, the legal maxim being *in pari delicto potior est conditio defendentis*. While there are exceptions to this rule, I cannot see that the plaintiffs, who are not among a class for whose benefit the statute was passed, and who to succeed would be forced to rely on the illegal contract, fall within these exceptions. . . .

> I must therefore dismiss the plaintiff's action for damages and for recovery of the sum [for expenditures on the cottage]. . . . I do so with regret, as the plaintiffs have at all times proceeded in good faith and with a genuine intent to comply with all laws. The defendant on the other hand, knowingly breached the *Lord's Day Act*, only to rely on her own illegal breach. . . . While the defendant is entitled at law to succeed on the basis of the technical defences set out, her actions throughout have been characterized by gross bad faith, and in view of this I dismiss the plaintiffs' action without costs.

Haines J. held that, in view of the fact that the contract was void, the defendant was entitled to an order for possession, but dismissed her claim for occupation rent.

Given the knowledge of the vendor of the illegality and the ignorance of the purchasers of that fact, does the decision discourage or encourage people to break the law? For whose benefit was the *Lord's Day Act* passed?

Suppose that instead of an agreement of purchase and sale being made on a Sunday, the parties had actually executed a conveyance (remember that they had no legal advice) and the Rogerses had gone into possession. A year later, the Rogerses decide to sell to a third party (whose lawyer fails to notice the problem created by the Sunday conveyance) and three years later Leonard sues to recover possession from this party. Should she succeed?

The *Lord's Day Act* has been repealed as a result of litigation brought under the *Canadian Charter of Rights and Freedoms* on the basis that it violates freedom of religion; see *R. v. Big M Drug Mart Ltd.*, [1985] 1 S.C.R. 295, 18 D.L.R. (4th) 321. The concerns that led to legislation like the *Lord's Day Act* are now no longer widely accepted and commercial transactions of all kinds take place on Sunday, although there is provincial legislation in some provinces that regulates employment and retail selling that attempts to promote Sunday as a "common day of rest" with more opportunities for family activities. The provinces where Sunday shopping remains at least partly illegal are still wrestling with the problem of permitting Sunday shopping and with the concomitant problems of drawing lines between lawful (drug stores) and unlawful (supermarkets) shopping.

In *Sidmay Ltd. v. Wehttam Investments Ltd.*, [1967] 1 O.R. 508, 61 D.L.R. (2d) 358 (affirmed, [1968] S.C.R. 828, 69 D.L.R. (2d) 336) the Ontario Court of Appeal had to deal with the problem created by the fact that a lender was not properly registered as a "loan company" under the *Loan and Trust Corporations Act*, R.S.O. 1960, c. 222, s. 133. The plaintiff mortgagor, had borrowed money from the defendant mortgagee, on a mortgage. The mortgage was executed by the plaintiff and registered. The amount of the mortgage ($308,250) was duly advanced to the plaintiff on its direction. The plaintiff sought a declaration that the mortgage was void on the sole ground that the mortgagee was not registered under the Act.

The trial judge, Grant J., made the declaration. The defendant appealed. In the Court of Appeal, Kelly J.A. described what the effects of the trial judge's decisions would be. He said (p. 512 O.R.):

> The decision under appeal has had a drastic and perhaps unexpected result for Wehttam, but it need hardly be emphasized that the effect of that decision if upheld will be to hamper seriously a large part of the conveyancing work in Ontario. A solicitor in examining a title to land derived from a mortgagee corporation not registered under the Act could not safely pass the title until exhaustive inquiries had been made to discover not only the nature of the transaction which gave rise to the mortgage, but the general conduct of the business of the corporate mortgagee: and to accept the title he would be bound to satisfy himself that despite the particular mortgage, considered in concert with other mortgage transactions in which the corporation had engaged, the corporate mortgagee had not been at the particular time undertaking or transacting the business of a loan corporation, something that no examination of the records of any one registry office, no matter how exhaustive, would conclusively disclose.
>
> Granted that the effect which a decision of this Court may have on others than the parties to the action is not a valid ground for tempering the judgment of the Court, yet the unfavourable consequences which will result from the universal appli-

cation of the principle under which the impugned mortgage was declared null and void demand that, in the public interest, this Court, unless compelled to do so by authorities which are so clear and unambiguous that they defy distinction, should not arrive at a conclusion the effect of which will interfere with the rights and remedies accorded to parties by the ordinary law of contract, particularly when such interference will have such an impact upon a substantial area of the financial life of the community. . . .

Kelly J.A. dealt with the argument that the mortgage was unenforceable because the mortgage was not registered by saying (pp. 524-25 O.R.):

> In my opinion, the words used by the Legislature in framing s. 133, even when read without the assistance of the realization of the overall purpose of the legislature in enacting the statute in which they appear, would not extend to make illegal an otherwise legal transaction merely because at the time of making the loan the lender was contravening the prohibition with respect to undertaking or transacting the business of a loan company. . . .

> Even if I had been satisfied that Wehttam had been at the relevant times operating a business in contravention of s. 133(l), in my opinion this would not have served to make illegal the mortgage transaction in question. I have come to this conclusion for two principal reasons: first, I find in the Act itself indications of precise and deliberate avoidance of any reference to interference with contractual obligations incurred in the course of a prohibited business. It is not without significance that s. 133(3) which specifically creates a punishable offence, carefully avoids the imposition of any penalty on the corporation which transacts the business and imposes the burden of the offence on the promoter, organizer, manager, director, officer, collector, agent, employee or person who undertakes or transacts the business of the corporation. This is completely consistent with the overriding intention of the Act to afford every possible protection to the funds of the depositors and a reluctance to place any burden on the corporation which would adversely affect those funds. Second, the underlying purpose of the Act to afford greater security to the depositors, creditors and security holders of the corporation would be defeated if its assets become depleted by the inability to recover from the borrower the money lent on the security of real estate.

> To permit a borrower to retain the amount of the loan made to it from the funds entrusted to such corporation for investment would produce exactly the opposite of the result sought to be obtained by the Act; and again, to rely on the provisions of s. 133, dealing with the transaction of business, to nullify a particular contract, appears to me to be so out of keeping with the intention of the legislature as to compel the adoption of any alternative construction which will preserve the legality of the borrower's undertaking to repay the money received by him as the result of his request for an advance to him by way of loan. It is my opinion that this statute, read as a whole, must be interpreted as indicating an intention not to affect the validity of any contractual obligation arising from a loan made on the security of real estate even if that loan were made in the course of a business, the transaction of which by an unregistered corporation is prohibited. . . .

Wells J.A. agreed with Kelly J.A.; Laskin J.A. wrote a separate concurring judgment. Like Kelly J.A., he held that holding the mortgage to be unenforceable would harm those, such as the depositors and other investors in the mortgagee, for whose protection the legislation had been enacted.

QUESTIONS AND PROBLEMS

1. It is argued, and *Sidmay v. Wehttam* would be a good illustration of the argument, that it would, in general, be preferable to have a right to claim on a restitutionary basis in

all cases of illegality. Does this shift in focus help avoid the problems of illegal contracts? When would one know that any enrichment was or was not unjust?

2. Insurer, a New York-based insurance corporation, decides to sell insurance in Canada. It employs a general agent to look after the requirements of setting up the business. The agent fails to obtain the required licences to carry on an insurance business. It is an offence in Ontario to carry on the business of insurance without a licence. A loss has occurred and a claim has been made, at which point all the facts come to light. The insured sues for the amount of the loss; the insurer defends on the ground that the contract was illegal. What result?

    With the same facts as the preceding question, Insurer claims the premium due under a policy from an insured who defends on the ground that the contract is illegal. What result?

There have been many cases since *Sidmay v. Wehttam* in which the same approach has been taken and courts are now very unlikely to adopt the brutally pointless approach of Haines J. in *Rogers v. Leonard*.

The recognition that poor people had serious problems with money-lenders has led over the years to a significant amount of legislation. At the provincial level the protection of borrowers has taken the form of mandatory disclosure rules (*e.g.*, the provisions of the various provincial *Consumer Protection Acts*) and relief for unconscionable transactions, e.g., the *Unconscionable Transactions Relief Act*, R.S.O. 1990, c. U.2). The regulation of interest is a matter reserved to the Parliament of Canada under the *Constitution Act, 1867* (U.K.), 30 & 31 Vict., c. 3. The modern expression of the concern that poor people not be victimized by loan sharks is the following section of the *Criminal Code*:

347(1) Notwithstanding any Act of Parliament, every one who

    (a)   enters into an agreement or arrangement to receive interest at a criminal rate, or

    (b)   receives a payment or partial payment of interest at a criminal rate,

is guilty of

    (c)   an indictable offence and liable to imprisonment for a term not exceeding five years, or

    (d)   an offence punishable on summary conviction and is liable to a fine not exceeding twenty-five thousand dollars or to imprisonment for a term not exceeding six months or to both.

    (2) In this section,

"credit advanced" means the aggregate of the money and the monetary value of any goods, services or benefits actually advanced or to be advanced under an agreement or arrangement . . . ;

"criminal rate" means an effective annual rate of interest calculated in accordance with generally accepted actuarial practices and principles that exceeds sixty per cent on the credit advanced under an agreement or arrangement;

. . .

"interest" means the aggregate of all charges and expenses, whether in the form of a fee, fine, penalty, commission or other similar charge or expense or in any other form, paid or payable for the advancing of credit under an agreement or arrangement, by or on behalf of the person to whom the credit is or is to be advanced, irrespective of the person to whom any such charges and expenses are or are to be paid or payable. . . .

The extent to which the poor and weak are at the mercy of those who lend them money is a serious problem, and is the stuff of stories, plays and songs, but the extent to which the law can really help them is a matter of considerable dispute. There are examples where the law probably was instrumental in preventing some of the worst problems, *e.g.*, the development of the "equity of redemption" to protect mortgagors. The doctrine of unconscionability, as illustrated by the cases examined in Chapter 6, offers another example.

Section 347 was intended to deal with the problem of "loan sharking". Whether the legislative efforts have had any effect on the mischief that s. 347 was intended to control is certainly open to doubt. What is clear is that the section has caused problems in many cases where neither of the parties fits the standard model of the poverty-stricken victim or the evil moneylender.

TRANSPORT NORTH AMERICAN EXPRESS INC. v. NEW SOLUTIONS FINANCIAL CORP.

[2004] S.C.J. No. 9, [2004] 1 S.C.R 249, 235 D.L.R. (4th) 335
(S.C.C., Iacobucci, Major, Bastarache, Arbour, LeBel, Deschamps and Fish JJ.)

ARBOUR J.:—

I. Overview

[1]   In March 2000, the appellant, New Solutions Financial Corp. ("New Solutions"), and the respondent, Transport North American Express Inc. ("TNAE"), entered into a credit agreement pursuant to which New Solutions advanced TNAE the sum of $500,000. In addition to various other fees and charges, the agreement provided for interest to be paid at the rate of four percent per month, calculated daily and payable monthly in arrears. By all accounts, the various payments called for by the agreement constituted a "criminal rate" of interest as defined in s. 347 of the *Criminal Code*, R.S.C. 1985, c. C-46 (the "*Code*"). The payments soon became too onerous for TNAE to meet, and the company applied to the Ontario Superior Court of Justice for a declaration that the agreement contained an illegally high rate of interest and should not be enforced.

[2]   The application judge, Cullity J., ruled that he was not confined to the so-called "blue-pencil" approach to severance in dealing with the statutory illegality of the contract, whereby only discrete illegal promises could be excised. Using "notional severance", he read down the offending interest rate so the contract provided for the maximum legal rate of interest. ...

[3]   Upon appeal to the Court of Appeal for Ontario, Rosenberg J.A., for the majority, concluded that the doctrine of severance only permits the striking of distinct promises from a contract: (2002), 60 O.R. (3d) 97. He reversed the application judge's finding that notional severance was an available remedial instrument. Rosenberg J.A. found that it was appropriate to strike out or blue-pencil the provision calling for interest at four percent per month, calculated daily and payable monthly in arrears, leaving the balance of the agreement to be enforced in accordance with its terms. Sharpe J.A., agreeing with the reasons of Cullity J., dissented.

[4]   There is broad consensus that the traditional rule that contracts in violation of statutory enactments are void *ab initio* is not the approach courts should necessarily take in cases of statutory illegality involving s. 347 of the *Code*. Instead, judicial discretion should be employed in cases in which s. 347 has been violated in order to provide remedies that are tailored to the contractual context involved. The primary issue in this appeal by New Solutions is whether notional severance, as formulated and applied by Cullity J., is valid in Canadian law and applicable here.

[5]   Given the desirability of remedial flexibility in cases of statutory illegality arising in connection with s. 347 of the *Code*, the evolving nature of the law regarding statutory illegality generally and the sound policy basis in which the concept is rooted, I find that notional severance is available as a matter of law as a remedy in cases arising under s. 347.

[6]   A spectrum of remedies is available to judges in dealing with contracts that violate s. 347 of the *Code*. The remedial discretion this spectrum affords is necessary to cope with the various contexts in which s. 347 illegality can arise. At one end of the spectrum are contracts so objectionable that their illegality will taint the entire contract. For example, exploitive loan-sharking arrangements and contracts that have a criminal object should be declared void *ab initio*. At the other end of the spectrum are contracts that, although they do contravene a statutory enactment, are otherwise unobjectionable. Contracts of this nature will often attract the application of the doctrine of severance. The agreement in this case is an example of such a contract. In each case, the determination of where along the spectrum a given case lies, and the remedial consequences flowing therefrom, will hinge on a careful consideration of the specific contractual context and the illegality involved.

[7]   The application judge in this case found that (i) the agreement between New Solutions and TNAE only inadvertently violated s. 347; (ii) the parties were experienced in commercial matters and negotiated at arm's length; (iii) there was no evidence that they did not have equal bargaining power; and (iv) they each had the benefit of independent legal advice in the course of the negotiations leading to the agreement. Consequently, the application of notional severance to the agreement between New Solutions and TNAE in this case by Cullity J. was appropriate. I would allow the appeal.

II. Facts

[8]   For the relevant time period, TNAE was in the business of expedited freight trucking. Ken and Karen Dragosits were shareholders in TNAE and actively involved in the operation of its business. Prior to the end of 1999, other shareholders held a 50 percent interest in TNAE. A corporation connected to these other shareholders provided TNAE the funds needed for the firm's working capital. A demand was made by this other corporation for the repayment of the funds owed to it by TNAE. The Dragosits and TNAE decided to search out a source for the means to repay the indebtedness.

[9]   The Dragosits sought financing from BDO Capital, now the appellant, New Solutions, to enable TNAE to repay its indebtedness and for the other shareholders in TNAE to be bought out. The parties eventually entered into an agreement that contained a high rate of interest and also significant other fees and charges. The

costly nature of the loan for TNAE no doubt reflected the high risk New Solutions was taking on in making the funds available.

[10] Before arriving at their agreement, New Solutions expressed interest in acquiring a 30 percent equity interest in TNAE in conjunction with the contemplated credit facility. The Dragosits resisted this as they wished to be the sole shareholders of TNAE. In lieu of surrendering an equity interest, they agreed that New Solutions would receive a "royalty payment" of $160,000, payable in eight quarterly installments, to reflect the approximate value of a 30 percent equity interest in TNAE.

[11] In the negotiations leading up to the agreement, each party had the benefit of independent legal advice. On March 6, 2000, a commitment letter in respect of the proposed credit facility was signed by the Dragosits and provided for the following payments:

(a) interest at four percent per month calculated daily, payable monthly in arrears;

(b) a monthly monitoring fee of $750;

(c) a one percent standby fee;

(d) royalty payments of $160,000 in eight quarterly installments;

(e) payment of legal and other fees; and

(f) a commitment fee of $5,000.

With the exception of the standby fee, all these payments were found by Cullity J. and by Rosenberg J.A. to constitute "interest" under s. 347(2) of the *Code*. Presumably, the standby fee was not included in the calculation of the effective interest rate because no standby fees were charged since the full credit facility of $500,000 was drawn upon.

[12] By March 30, 2000, the parties had, in addition to the commitment letter, executed an accounts receivable factoring agreement, a promissory note and a general security agreement. The Dragosits also each executed personal guarantees of the indebtedness for up to $500,000 plus interest at the rate of 30 percent per annum. From the outset, the parties had agreed to depart from the terms of the accounts receivable factoring agreement. On March 28, 2000, the solicitor for New Solutions wrote to the solicitor for TNAE and the Dragosits, confirming that the parties had agreed on March 27 that they would not strictly follow the terms of the accounts receivable factoring agreement unless New Solutions elected to exercise its rights under it. Instead, the understanding was that TNAE would borrow the full $500,000 from New Solutions and pay the interest, fees and royalties as set out in the commitment letter. According to Cullity J., "the concept of a factoring of receivables was put aside and replaced by a revolving credit facility" (para. 5).

[13] The principal amount of $500,000 was advanced by New Solutions. At the outset, TNAE paid interest at the rate of four percent per month, calculated daily and payable monthly in arrears, as well as the other fees and charges, in general accordance with the terms of the commitment letter.

[14] The various payments eventually became onerous, and TNAE sought legal advice regarding the repayment of the borrowed funds. TNAE then applied to the Ontario Superior Court of Justice for a declaration that the agreement contained an interest component that contravened s. 347 of the *Code*. It also sought an order that interest previously paid be returned.

[15] On the basis of actuarial evidence, Cullity J. found that the effective interest rate on the loan, if it was repaid in full within two years, was 90.9 percent per annum. In itself, the promise to pay interest at four percent per month calculated daily, payable monthly in arrears, amounted to an effective annual interest rate of 60.1 percent. The remaining payments amounted to an effective annual interest rate of 30.8 percent.

[16] New Solutions originally denied that the agreement violated the *Code* but sought severance and rectification if it did. Cullity J. found that the agreement was in contravention of s. 347(1)(*a*) and applied "notional severance" to reduce the effective annual interest rate to 60 percent so the agreement would comply with s. 347. The Court of Appeal allowed TNAE's appeal; it struck out the clause providing for interest at a rate of four percent per month calculated daily and payable monthly in arrears, and left in place the other payments, which amounted to an effective annual rate of 30.8 percent when computed as interest as *per* s. 347(2). New Solutions seeks the restoration of the decision of the application judge. ...

. . .

IV. *Issue*

[18] Are judges in Canada permitted by law to exercise remedial discretion to partially enforce a contract contravening s. 347 of the *Code* by reading down interest rate provisions to avoid what would otherwise be illegality?

V. *Analysis*

A. *Illegality of the Contract*

[19] The definition of "interest" in s. 347(2) is broad: see *Garland v. Consumers' Gas Co.*, [1998] 3 S.C.R. 112, at para. 28. The various payments made by TNAE, with the exception of any portion of the payments relating to the repayment of principal, satisfy the definition of "interest" as defined in s. 347(2). This includes the "royalty payments". I agree with the courts below that the payments made by TNAE to New Solutions cumulatively amount to an interest rate in excess of that permitted by the *Code*.

B. *The Doctrine of Illegality*

[20] The Federal Court of Appeal's decision in *Still v. M.N.R.*, [1998] 1 F.C. 549, provides a useful summary of the development of the doctrine of illegality, including a discussion of the development and evolution of the doctrine's common law and statutory branches. In addressing the current state of the doctrine of illegality, Robertson J.A. remarked, at para. 12:

> Law reform agencies have been quick to conclude that the law of illegality is in an unsatisfactory state ... . There is a plethora of conflicting decisions and great uncertainty as to the principles which should be guiding the courts. Arguably, so many exceptions have been grafted on to the common law rule that illegal contracts are void *ab initio* that the validity of the rule itself is brought into question.

In light of the excellent treatment of the doctrine's history by Robertson J.A. in *Still v. M.N.R.*, there would be little benefit to fully retracing the doctrine's history here. Instead, given the evolving nature of this area of law, a very brief survey of some of the existing case law on the application of the doctrine of illegality will provide sufficient context for the finding in this case that notional severance is available as a discretionary remedy in cases where s. 347 has been violated.

[21] The historical common law approach to contractual illegality is reflected in the following passage of Parke B. in *Cope v. Rowlands* (1836), 2 M. & W. 149, 150 E.R. 707 (Ex. Ct.), at p. 710:

> [W]here the contract which the plaintiff seeks to enforce, be it express or implied, is expressly or by implication forbidden by the common or statute law, no court will lend its assistance to give it effect. It is equally clear that a contract is void if prohibited by a statute, though the statute inflicts a penalty only, because such a penalty implies a prohibition.

In *Cope v. Rowlands*, the question surrounded whether an unlicensed broker could recover for the work that he had done for the defendant. The court concluded that the legal requirement (under threat of penalty) that brokers be licensed by the city of London implied a prohibition on work being done by unlicensed brokers. As a consequence, the contract was held to be void *ab initio* and the unlicensed broker was unable to enforce his claim for payment for the work that had been done. The Court of Appeal for Ontario denied recovery in a similar case involving an electrician seeking to recover for work done without possessing the appropriate class of licence: see *Kocotis v. D'Angelo* (1957), 13 D.L.R. (2d) 69.

[22] The historical common law approach that contracts illegal under statute are void *ab initio* has been applied by this Court : see, e.g., *Bank of Toronto v. Perkins* (1883), 8 S.C.R. 603, and more recently, *Neider v. Carda of Peace River District Ltd.*, [1972] S.C.R. 678. However, some time ago Canadian courts began to develop a more flexible approach to statutory illegality in contract, often severing the illegal provisions and enforcing the remainder. For example, in one of the earliest cases dealing with the application of s. 347 of the *Code*, *Mira Design Co. v. Seascape Holdings Ltd.*, [1982] 4 W.W.R. 97 (B.C.S.C.), Huddart L.J.S.C. held that although the interest provisions of a mortgage were unenforceable, exceeding as they did the maximum effective interest rate permitted under s. 305.1 of the *Code* (the predecessor to s. 347), the contract as a whole should not be held to be void *ab initio*. Her reasoning, at p. 104, was that although the section makes it an offence to receive interest at an illegal rate, the section did not seek to make associated collateral agreements (such as for the transfer of the real estate or the payment of the principal amount owing on the mortgage) void *ab initio*:

> Most Canadians would agree that the purpose of the Criminal Code is to protect the public by providing for the punishment of behaviour that Parliament considers to be against the public interest. The purpose of s. 305.1 [now s. 347] is to punish everyone who enters into an agreement or arrangement to receive interest at a criminal rate. It does not expressly prohibit such behaviour, nor does it declare such an agreement or arrangement to be void. The penalty is severe, and designed to deter persons from making such agreements. It replaces the Small Loans Act, which included a prohibition of such agreements and gave the court the power to reconstruct them. It is designed to protect borrowers. There is no penalty imposed on a person who makes an agreement to pay, or pays, interest at a criminal rate. It is not designed to prevent persons from entering into lending transactions per se.

[23] The same approach was taken by the Court of Appeal for Ontario in *William E. Thomson Associates Inc. v. Carpenter* (1989), 61 D.L.R. (4th) 1. Having considered s. 347 of the *Code*, the court in that case concluded that where an interest rate provided for in an agreement exceeds the 60 percent statutory maximum, the interest rate provision of the contract may be severed without declaring the whole contract void.

[24] In *Thomson*, at p. 8, Blair J.A. considered the following four factors in deciding between partial enforcement and declaring a contract void *ab initio*: (i) whether the purpose or the policy of s. 347 would be subverted by severance; (ii) whether the parties entered into the agreement for an illegal purpose or with an evil intention; (iii) the relative bargaining positions of the parties and their conduct in reaching the agreement; and (iv) whether the debtor would be given an unjustified windfall. He did not foreclose the possibility of applying other considerations in other cases, however, and remarked (at p. 12) that whether "a contract tainted by illegality is completely unenforceable depends upon all the circumstances surrounding the contract and the balancing of the considerations discussed above and, in appropriate cases, other considerations".

[25] In *Trillium Computer Resources Inc. v. Taiwan Connection Inc.* (1993), 11 B.L.R. (2d) 1 (Ont. Ct. (Gen. Div.)), aff'd (1994), 11 B.L.R. (2d) 1 (Ont. Div. Ct.), Conant J. entered summary judgment in favour of the plaintiff who had paid $8,000 interest in consideration of credit extended by the defendant for eight days. In a brief judgment and without addressing the authorities on this point, Conant J. stated, at p. 2:

> I am satisfied that an interest rate of over 3,000 % per annum, whether it be for credit and/or compensation for damages and other matters suffered by the Defendant, is a flagrant breach of s. 347 of the *Criminal Code* of Canada. This, in my view, is illegal and shall be returned to the Plaintiff *less the maximum rate of 60% per annum allowed under the Code*. [Emphasis added.]

This approach is similar to the one applied by Cullity J. and endorsed by Sharpe J.A. (in dissent at the Court of Appeal) in the present case.

[26] In *Milani v. Banks* (1997), 145 D.L.R. (4th) 55, the Court of Appeal for Ontario applied the contextual approach endorsed by Blair J.A. in *Thomson, supra*. This case involved a $32,000 loan with a term of 30 days. The contract provided for $3,000 to be kept by the creditor in respect of the costs associated with the loan, and an 18 percent annualized interest rate to be paid on the full principal amount. McKinlay J.A. for the court held, at pp. 59-60 that:

> In this case, the appellant takes the position that the only offensive part of the loan was the $3,000 charge for "fees", and that if the agreement were left intact apart from that provision, the result would be a fair one in the circumstances. I am inclined to agree with that position. ...
>
> ...
>
> I consider this case to be one strongly favouring the position of the appellant. She is clearly not entitled to the $3,000 fee, but I would strike only that provision, and leave the loan otherwise intact as a $32,000 loan with interest at 18% per annum for a thirty day term.

The approach taken by McKinlay J.A. in *Milani* is reflected in the path taken by Rosenberg J.A. at the Court of Appeal for Ontario in the case at bar. McKinlay J.A. severed one of the "interest" terms (actually attributable to "costs") from the loan so that the interest rate would be legal, just as Rosenberg J.A. in this case severed the promise to pay interest at four percent per month, calculated daily, payable monthly in arrears, thereby leaving the other charges to amount, cumulatively, to a permissible rate of interest under s. 347.

C. *The Problematic Nature of the Blue-Pencil Test*

[27] The blue-pencil approach is understood both as a test of the availability of severance to remedy contractual illegality and also as a technique for effecting severance. The blue-pencil approach as a test of the appropriateness of severance requires a consideration of whether an illegal contract can be rendered legal by striking out (i.e., by drawing a line through) the illegal promises in the agreement. The resulting set of legal terms should retain the core of the agreement. If the nature or core of the agreement is disturbed, then on this test the illegal clause in the contract is not a candidate for severance and the entire contract is void. The blue-pencil approach as a *technique* of effecting severance involves the actual excision of the provisions leading to the illegality, leaving those promises untainted by the illegality to be enforced.

[28] The use of the blue-pencil approach to sever one or more provisions from a contract alters the terms of the agreement between the parties. The only agreement that one can say with certainty the parties would have agreed to is the one that they actually entered into. The insistence in the case law that the blue-pencil test derives its validity from refusing to change or add words or provisions to the contract is unconvincing. It is doubtful, for example, that the lenders in cases such as *Thomson*, *supra*, or *Mira Design*, *supra*, would have entered into the agreements at issue had they been aware *ex ante* that they would only be entitled to the return of the principal advanced. The change effected by the blue-pencil technique will often fundamentally alter the consideration associated with the bargain and do violence to the intention of the parties. Indeed, in many cases, the application of the blue-pencil approach will provide for an interest-free loan where the parties demonstrated in the agreement a clear intention to charge and pay considerable interest.

[29] The blue-pencil test was developed in cases where the courts were considering instruments under seal, where the form of the deed governed and where the intention of the parties was irrelevant. It was therefore important that what remained after severance would be a valid deed:

> In the deed form was everything; the actual intention of the parties was immaterial. It was, therefore, natural that in considering the possibility of severance of promises in a deed, the court should be concerned to see that what was left remained a valid deed; there could be no question of implying a promise to take effect if part of the original bargain was illegal. This is the historical origin of what was later called the 'blue-pencil test'.
>
> (N.S. Marsh, "The Severance of Illegality in Contract" (1948), 64 *L.Q.R.* 230 and 347, at pp. 351-52)

Historically, courts were not concerned with the intention of the parties. The artificiality of the blue-pencil test arises from the common law constraints imposed on courts unaided by principles of equity.

[30] Courts inescapably make a new bargain for the parties when they use the blue-pencil approach. As Cullity J. remarked, at paras. 35-36:

> The blue-pencil test is, I believe, a relic of a bygone era when the attitude of courts of common law — unassisted by principles of equity — towards the interpre-

tation and enforcement of contracts was more rigid than is the case at the present time. At an early stage in the development of the law relating to illegal promises, severance was held to be justified on the basis of the blue-pencil test alone. As the reasoning in *Milani* and *William E. Thomson* demonstrates, we have moved a long way beyond that mechanical approach. Enforcement may be refused in the exercise of the kind of discretionary judgment I have mentioned even where blue-pencil severance is possible.

> *Despite repeated statements in the cases that the court will not make a new agreement for the parties, that is, of course, exactly what it does whenever severance is permitted in cases like William E. Thomson and Milani.* [Emphasis added.]

I am in complete agreement with the conclusion that when a court employs the blue-pencil test, it is making a new agreement for the parties. Indeed, all forms of severance alter the terms of the original agreement.

[31] I also agree with the view of Rosenberg J.A. at the Court of Appeal in the present case, at para. 33, that severance lies along a spectrum of available remedies. Depending on the circumstances, the court may exercise its discretion to find the whole agreement unenforceable or sever only the provision(s) that put the effective interest rate over 60 percent:

> [A] judge has discretion to apply the doctrine of severance to an agreement that offends the criminal interest rate provisions of the Code. This discretion gives rise to a *spectrum of available remedies.* Where the loan transaction resembles a traditional loan sharking arrangement, the court may refuse to apply the doctrine of severance and hold the entire loan agreement unenforceable, including the obligation to repay the principal. While this remedy leaves the borrower with a windfall, this result may be justified in some cases by the need to denounce such usurious practices. See *C.A.P.S. International Inc. v. Kotello*, [2002] M.J. No. 205 [(QL)] (Q.B.). At the other end of the spectrum, in the case of a good faith commercial transaction where the equities favour the lender and severance does not undermine the policy of the legislation, *the court may sever only those provisions of the loan agreement that put the effective interest rate over 60 per cent*, leaving intact the borrower's obligation to repay the principal and pay some interest. See *e.g.*, *Milani*, *supra*. Closer to the centre of the spectrum lies a case like *Terracan* [*Capital Corp. v. Pine Projects Ltd.* (1993), 100 D.L.R. (4th) 431 (B.C.C.A.)], where the court severed all the interest provisions but upheld the debtor's obligation to repay the principal. [Emphasis added.]

This statement of the remedial discretion of a judge in a case involving a violation of s. 347 of the *Code* takes into account the seriousness of the illegality involved in any given case, the identity and nature of the parties and the broader contractual context.

[32] If the case is an appropriate one for the court to sever only those provisions of the loan agreement that put the effective interest rate over 60 percent, and if it is conceded, as it must be, that such a rewording alters the agreement of the parties, the question becomes only a choice of the appropriate technique of severance. The preferred severance technique is the one that, in light of the particular contractual context involved, would most appropriately cure the illegality while remaining otherwise as close as possible to the intentions of the parties expressed in the agreement. The blue-pencil technique may not necessarily achieve that result.

[33] The blue-pencil test is imperfect because it involves mechanically removing illegal provisions from a contract, the effects of which are apt to be somewhat arbitrary. The results may be arbitrary in the sense that they will be dependent upon accidents of drafting and the form of expression of the agreement, rather than the substance of the bargain or consideration involved. For example, if the effective interest rate of the total interest obligation (as defined in s. 347(2)) in the agreement between New Solutions and TNAE were only 0.1 percent lower, then the excision of the various charges, fees and royalty payment provisions using the blue-pencil technique would have resulted in a legally valid agreement bearing an effective annual rate of interest of 60 percent. Although the results obtained from the blue-pencil approach will in many cases be sensible and may often be desirable, due to its artificiality, the application of the blue-pencil approach will sometimes be inappropriate.

[34] Section 347 of the *Code* invites difficulties with arbitrariness by imposing a bright line of 60 percent as demarcating legal interest from illegal interest. This legislatively mandated bright line distinguishes s. 347 cases from those involving provisions, for example, in restraint of trade, where there is no bright line. The interaction of the blue-pencil test with the bright line separating illegal interest from legal interest leads to erratic results. Consider the following three substantively equivalent contracts. Assume for each contract that each party was commercially sophisticated, of equivalent bargaining power and in receipt of independent legal advice. Assume also that neither party was aware the interest payable was prohibited by the *Code*. The three contracts lead to dramatically different results when the blue-pencil test is applied.

[35] First, consider the result obtained using the blue-pencil approach in the case at bar. Accepted actuarial evidence showed that the contract between TNAE and New Solutions providing for interest at four percent per month, calculated daily, payable monthly in arrears, represented an effective interest rate of 60.1 percent per annum; other fees and charges reflected a further 30.8 percent interest per annum, resulting in a total rate of 90.9 percent. The application of the blue-pencil test required that, at the very least, the 60.1 percent interest provision be struck from the contract since, standing alone, it violated s. 347. After considering the equities of the contractual context, Rosenberg J.A. concluded that TNAE should have to repay the principal and at least some interest. Consequently, the provision calling for 60.1 percent effective annual interest was struck from the contract, and TNAE was held accountable for repaying the principal plus the other fees and charges, amounting to an effective annual interest rate of 30.8 percent.

[36] Second, consider a contract that provides for 60.0 percent interest in one provision and 30.9 percent interest in the remaining provisions. This contract would result in the same 90.9 percent per annum rate of interest payable overall. Given the equities of the contractual context as found in the courts below, the application of the blue-pencil test would result in the other fees and charges being struck from the contract and the 60.0 percent interest payment obligation surviving.

[37] Finally, consider what the result would be under the blue-pencil approach if there were only one interest provision, and that this provision called for an effective annual interest rate of 90.9 percent, which would also involve exactly the same amount of consideration passing from borrower to the lender as under the previous two contracts. The blue-pencil test would require that the entire interest obligation be severed from the contract, since it alone would violate s. 347. This would result in no interest being payable under the contract. It is possible, in this last example, that the illegality of the rate would be so apparent that courts would

be justified in reducing to zero such a blatantly illegal rate. On the other hand, if the criminal rate was arrived at inadvertently — or under a misapprehension of the law — as assumed for the comparison of these three contracts, the obligation to repay at least some interest should be upheld. In that case, the maximum permissible rate would best reflect the intention of the parties, while curing the illegality.

[38] This demonstrates that, at least in the case of contracts in violation of s. 347 of the *Code*, the results associated with the application of the blue-pencil approach are overly dependent upon the form of the contract, rather than its substance. In these three similar contracts, the borrower must pay 30.8 percent interest, 60.0 percent interest, or no interest, depending on otherwise insignificant differences in drafting. Results this erratic and sensitive to the form of contractual expression are undesirable, and can be avoided through the use of notional severance in cases where considerations flowing from the broad contractual context favour the lender.

[39] There is little danger that abuses of this remedial flexibility would surreptitiously creep past trial judges. On the contrary, judges are apt to be quite suspicious, and rightly so, of credit arrangements which provide for effective annual rates of interest in excess of 60 percent per annum. Using notional severance to read down interest provisions to be just within the legal limit would not find application in traditional loan-sharking transactions. It would be available as a remedy where a court recognizes the commercial sophistication and professional advice received by both parties, concludes that the violation of s. 347 by the parties was unintentional, and considers it equitable to give effect to the highest legal interest obligation available. In such cases, there is no reason, in my view, to prefer the blue-pencil approach as more likely to deter criminal interest rates. I will return to this point below.

[40] Thus, the appropriate approach is to vest the greatest possible amount of remedial discretion in judges in courts of first instance. The spectrum of available remedies runs from a court holding contracts in violation of s. 347 void *ab initio*, in the most egregious and abusive cases, according to the criteria identified in *Thomson, supra*, to notional severance. In the determination of where along the spectrum a particular contract lies, the considerations identified in *Thomson* by Blair J.A. should be referred to and analysed carefully. Although Blair J.A. was considering the desirability of severing illegal interest from principal, the same factors are helpful in determining whether to reduce illegal interest to a legal level.

D. *Application of the Revised Approach*

[41] Finding, as I do, that the maximum level of remedial flexibility should be vested in judges and available for application by them subject to a careful analysis of the factors identified in *Thomson*, I will apply this approach to the facts of the case at bar.

[42] As outlined above, in *Thomson*, Blair J.A. identified four considerations relevant to the determination of whether public policy ought to allow an otherwise illegal agreement to be partially enforced rather than being declared void *ab initio* in the face of illegality in the contract:

1. whether the purpose or policy of s. 347 would be subverted by severance;

2. whether the parties entered into the agreement for an illegal purpose or with an evil intention;

3.   the relative bargaining positions of the parties and their conduct in reaching the agreement;

4.   the potential for the debtor to enjoy an unjustified windfall.

[43] The first factor — whether the policy behind s. 347 would be subverted here by partial enforcement — is related to the concerns expressed by Rosenberg J.A. in this case that civil remedies should not frustrate the deterrence purpose of the criminal prohibition. In this regard, it is important to identify the policy purpose underlying s. 347. Ostensibly, it was intended to curb loan-sharking activity. It is difficult to pinpoint the precise rationale behind the provision, however, because the legislative record yields few clues. According to Professor Ziegel:

> On July 22nd, 1980, only a day after its first reading, the House of Commons gave second and third reading to Bill C-44, "An Act to amend the Small Loans Act and to provide for its repeal and to amend the Criminal Code". The Bill was not debated and its adoption had the unanimous support of all three political parties. Any public discussion of the merits of the Bill was effectively forestalled by the haste with which it was rushed through the House. This failure to give interested parties an opportunity to study and comment on the Bill would be serious enough if the Bill only dealt with minor technical matters. But it does not. The Bill deals with questions of major social, economic, and legal importance which warranted careful examination. Even if one accepts the soundness of the objectives of the Bill, it does not follow that its technical implementation is equally unobjectionable or that the same goals could not have been realized in a less controversial manner. In the writer's view, the Bill is open to objections on both counts and may generate as many new problems as it was designed to resolve.

> (J.S. Ziegel, "Bill C-44: Repeal of the Small Loans Act and Enactment of a New Usury Law" (1981), 59 *Can. Bar Rev.* 188, at p. 188)

As was stated by this Court in *Garland, supra*, at para. 25:

> The ostensible purpose of s. 347 was to aid in the prosecution of loan sharks. See *House of Commons Debates*, 1st Sess., 32nd Parl., vol. III, July 21, 1980, at p. 3146; *Thomson, supra*, at p. 549. However, it is clear from the language of the statute — e.g., its reference to insurance and overdraft charges, official fees, and property taxes in mortgage transactions — that s. 347 was designed to have a much wider reach, and in fact the section has most often been applied to commercial transactions which bear no relation to traditional loan-sharking arrangements. Although s. 347 is a criminal provision, the great majority of cases in which it arises are not criminal prosecutions. Rather, like the case at bar, they are civil actions in which a borrower has asserted the common-law doctrine of illegality in an effort to avoid or recover an interest payment, or to render an agreement unenforceable. For this reason, the provision has attracted criticism from some commercial lawyers and academics, and calls have repeatedly been made for its amendment or repeal. ... Nevertheless, it is now well settled that s. 347 applies to a very broad range of commercial and consumer transactions involving the advancement of credit, including secured and unsecured loans, mortgages and commercial financing agreements.

Since it is very difficult to identify the policy objective behind s. 347 of the *Code* beyond the prevention of loan-sharking, violations of the section that clearly do not involve loan-sharking should be approached cautiously, keeping in mind that there is no need to deter, through the criminal law, effective interest rates of up to 60 percent per year. Given that this was a commercial transaction engaged in by experienced and independently advised commercial parties, it is difficult to see why the choice of a 30.8 percent rather than 60 percent rate better fosters compliance with s. 347(1)(*a*) of the *Code*.

[44] The second factor is whether the agreement was entered into for an illegal purpose or with an evil intention. There is no evidence on the record to suggest that New Solutions has been charged with violating s. 347(1)(*a*). Absent a criminal conviction, New Solutions has the benefit of the presumption of innocence. Concerns with specific and general deterrence are best addressed by the criminal law. A prosecution under s. 347 of the *Code* cannot be initiated without the consent of the Attorney General. This suggests that even a criminal remedy is not always appropriate for an infringement of s. 347, let alone a civil remedy seeking to promote the criminal law objective of deterrence. Cullity J. found that the parties were unaware that the agreement contravened s. 347, their intent being only to provide the means by which TNAE could buy out its remaining shareholders and acquire commercially necessary working capital. It was a contract entered into for ordinary commercial purposes. There was nothing inherently illegal or evil about this intention. The worst that could be said is that TNAE was a high-risk debtor for New Solutions to lend to (even with the personal guarantees of the Dragosits), the corporation's needs were high relative to its value, and it needed the money on relatively short notice. This second consideration militates in favour of a flexible remedy.

[45] The third factor concerns the relative bargaining positions of the parties and their conduct in reaching the agreement. Each party had independent legal advice. Each party was commercially experienced. The Dragosits and TNAE knew what they were getting into, as did New Solutions. The one failing seems to be that neither side realized that their agreement would contravene s. 347 of the *Code*. This third consideration, too, favours a flexible remedy.

[46] Finally, any potential for an unjustified windfall in this case arises from TNAE possibly not having to repay the principal and interest, or from TNAE possibly not having to pay a commercially appropriate rate of interest on the loan. Given that each party had independent advice and knew precisely the obligations that they were taking on, my conclusion is that the equities of the situation favour New Solutions. This is in accord with the findings by both the lower courts in this case.

[47] New Solutions should be repaid the principal, with the highest amount of interest legally allowable, namely 60 percent. This represents a reduction from the interest rate of 90.9 percent that the contract provided for, but, given s. 347 of the *Code*, is the most that New Solutions can legally receive. This no more rewrites the contract than enforcing only the other obligations, which cumulatively amount to "interest" at 30.8 percent.

[48] My colleague, Bastarache J., refers to clause 9.1 of the accounts receivable factoring agreement (para. 68), arguing it supports the blue-pencil approach to severance. I agree that by clause 9.1 the parties expressed a preference for the use of severance to give full effect to the valid provisions of that agreement. I have two responses to the view, however, that the clause calls for the use of the blue-pencil approach to severance rather than notional severance. First, from the outset the parties agreed not to strictly abide by the terms of the accounts receivable factoring agreement. Therefore, I question whether it is appropriate to refer to clause 9.1 of this agreement. Second, accepting for the sake of argument that the factoring agreement is relevant, the use of notional severance is not foreclosed by the intent underlying the inclusion of clause 9.1 in the factoring agreement. The genuine intent underlying clause 9.1 was to preserve as much of the agreement as possible should any part of it be deemed to be invalid. In light of the analysis above, the part of the agreement that is invalid is the obligation to pay an effective interest rate in excess of 60 percent per annum. Therefore, notional severance is the most appropriate remedy to apply here, since it gives the greatest possible legal effect to the valid aspects of the agreement, which is in concert with the intention underlying clause 9.1.

VI. Conclusion

[49] For the foregoing reasons I would allow the appeal, set aside the order of the Court of Appeal and restore the order of Cullity J. I would award costs to the appellant in this Court and in the Court of Appeal.

[Deschamps and Fish JJ. dissented on the ground that the well-established "blue-pencil" remedy applied in the Court of Appeal respects the trial judge's findings of fact and achieves an equitable result consistent with established principle. They rejected the use of the doctrine of "notional severance". Unlike notional severance, "blue-pencil" severance does not do violence to the policy purposes of s. 347 of the *Code* or require a judicial re-writing of the interest clause agreed to, as such, by the parties. It appears neither "artificial" nor "arbitrary" to sever the criminal rate of interest agreed to as interest and to leave intact the distinct and separate charges not agreed to as interest, and not considered to be interest by either party. This solution still leaves the appellant with a return of slightly more than 30 percent per annum. The effect of the trial judge's decision was to stretch the principles of equity in an inappropriate way and to send the wrong message to those who lend money at a criminally prohibited rate to "willing" borrowers who cannot otherwise obtain a loan. They should not be encouraged to believe that if their illegal arrangement is subjected to judicial scrutiny, they will nonetheless recover the highest rate they could legally have charged — and thus suffer no pecuniary disadvantage for having violated s. 347 of the *Code*.

Bastarache J. also dissented and rejected the adoption of the remedy of "notional severance". He said:

[52] ... There is a fundamental difference between striking out offending sections of a contract and rewriting a central provision. Although both approaches interfere in some way with the intent of the parties, the added flexibility of the rewriting approach comes at a considerable cost [and] it is not supported by any principle of contract law. On the contrary, the severance doctrine is a long-standing one. ...

[59] ... [T]he availability of "notional severance" as a remedy creates greater uncertainty in the law. ... [U]nder notional severance, courts will be permitted to literally add new words to the parties' agreement. By doing so, courts will be substituting their intentions for those of the parties.]

NOTES

1. Section 347 of the *Criminal Code* causes banks and other lenders serious problems. For example, what is "interest"? If a person invests money in a corporation, it may not be entirely clear if he is making the investment as a shareholder or as a lender, and indeed the investment may well have elements of each type. It will be important to determine if the investor takes the risk of loss as well as the chance of gain. It will be equally important whether the payment of a return on the investment is paid out of net earnings or gross earnings. In other words, the more the arrangement looks like an equity investment, the less the likelihood that the return will be held to be interest and, of course, the converse applies if the investment looks like a loan.

2.   It is a feature of most commercial or residential mortgage lending that the borrower pays the lender's legal costs and other charges. If the loan is outstanding for a short time or is not fully drawn down, then the problems in *William E. Thomson v. Carpenter* arise. In *Aectra Refining and Marketing Inc. v. Lincoln Capital Funding Corp.* (1991), 6 O.R. (3d) 146, 85 D.L.R. (4th) 595 (Gen. Div.), a loan agreement provided for the payment by the borrower of a number of lump sums, initial fees, etc., and annual interest of 16 per cent. The borrower went into default and subsequently went into receivership. In order to gain priority in an insolvency situation, a lender with a claim against the borrower with lower security than the lender on the loan in question alleged that the interest payable on the loan exceeded the criminal rate, and that the loan was illegal. The judge held that the interest was not criminal. The lender never agreed to receive interest at more than the criminal rate, even though it asserted rights that could have led, retrospectively, to such a return. The decision of Borins J. is typical of the decision in which the court does what it can to uphold the contract as legal. Note that s. 347, states in clauses (1)(a) and (b) that the lender can neither *agree to nor receive* interest at more than the criminal rate.

3.   In *Garland v. Consumers' Gas Co.*, [1998] 3 S.C.R. 112, 165 D.L.R. (4th) 385, the Supreme Court of Canada considered a preliminary motion in a class action law suit dealing with utility bills that included a "due date" for the payment of current charges, and provided that customers who did not pay by the due date incurred a late payment penalty ("LPP"), calculated at five per cent of the unpaid charges for that month. The LPP was a one-time penalty that did not compound or increase over time. It was implemented following a series of rate hearings conducted by the Ontario Energy Board. The Board accepted that the primary purpose of the LPP was to encourage customers to pay their bills promptly, thereby reducing the cost to the utility of carrying accounts receivable. The Board recognized that if a bill is paid very soon after the due date, the penalty could represent a very high rate of interest, but it noted that customers could avoid such a charge by paying their bills on time.

      Garland commenced an action on behalf of a large number of the respondent's customers alleging that the LPP violated s. 347 of the *Criminal Code* because — for a significant number of customers each month — it constituted interest at a rate exceeding 60 per cent per year. Actuarial evidence showed that under the normal billing plan, the LPP gave rise to an interest rate exceeding 60 per cent per annum for customers who paid within 37 days after the due date. Evidence also indicated that while many of the customers paid late, most paid only a few days late.

      The majority of the Supreme Court of Canada held that the utility was violating s. 347 and remitted the case for a class action remedy hearing. The utility, which had the approval of the Ontario Energy Board, and the support of all of the lower courts, was surprised at the result.

      Major J., writing for a majority of the Court, held that, for the purposes of s. 347, "interest" is an extremely comprehensive term which expressly includes charges or expenses "in the form of a . . . penalty". However, not every charge or expense will be subject to the criminal interest rate provision. In order to constitute "interest" under s. 347, a charge — whatever its form — must be "paid or payable for the advancing of credit under an agreement or arrangement". Under s-s. 347(2), "credit advanced" encompasses not only "the money" advanced under an agreement or arrangement, but also "the monetary value of any goods, services or benefits" that may be so advanced. Major J. concluded that the most plausible interpretation of s-s. 347(2) is that an "advance" of "the monetary value of any goods, services or benefits" means a deferral of payment for such items. The utility provided services to its customers, for which a specified amount of money was payable each month on a certain date. The deferral of that payment past the due date constituted "credit advanced" within the meaning of ss. 347(2).

      While it was clear that the utility neither encouraged late payments nor sought to profit from them, under the terms of the agreement customers were permitted to defer their payment, albeit for a price. That is an arrangement for the advancing of credit under the broad language adopted in s. 347. On the facts of this case, a penalty incurred, pursuant to the terms of a standing arrangement between the parties, for the deferral of payment of a specified amount of money owing for goods, services or benefits was an "interest" charge within the meaning of s. 347 and was subject to the prohibitions against requiring or receiving interest at a criminal rate.

The arrangement between the utility and its customers did not, on its face, require the payment of interest at a criminal rate. Whether an interest payment violates the provision is determined as of the time the payment is received. For the purposes of para. 347(1)(b), the effective annual rate of interest arising from a payment is calculated over the period during which credit is actually outstanding. There is no violation of para. 347(1)(b) where a payment of interest at a criminal rate arises from a voluntary act of the debtor, that is, an act wholly within the control of the debtor and not compelled by the lender or by the occurrence of a determining event set out in the agreement. The actuarial evidence showed that if a regular billing customer waited 38 days or longer to pay, the annual interest rate represented by the five per cent charge dropped below the criminal threshold of 60 per cent per annum. While customers could delay their payment of the LPP beyond 38 days, there was no "invitation" to do so, and the Court felt that it would be "disingenuous" to conclude that customers actually perceived themselves to be at liberty to wait that long, citing the statistical evidence showing that many customers actually paid within the 38 days, actually paying the "criminal rate of interest".

Bastarache J., in his dissent, concluded that s. 347 was not applicable since the LPP did not involve a sum "paid or payable for the advancing of credit", but was rather intended to deter late payment. He noted that the case involved a provincially regulated utility and that it is "inappropriate and unwarranted" to invoke federal criminal law to limit how a regulator functions in this regard.

Once the issue of the violation of s. 347 of the *Criminal Code* was resolved, litigation began over whether the class should receive restitution for all of the LLP payments made prior to Consumers' Gas having ceased to collect the payments in 1998, due to the Supreme Court of Canada decision interpreting s. 347. The issue of the restitution for past payments was also litigated to the Supreme Court of Canada, which rendered a decision on this question in *Garland v. Consumers' Gas*, [2004] S.C.J. No. 21, [2004] 1 S.C.R. 629, 237 D.L.R. (4th) 385. Iacobucci J., writing for a unanimous Court, gave the claimants a limited restitutionary claim, ordering Consumers' Gas to repay LPPs collected from the class in excess of the interest limit stipulated in s. 347 of the *Code* after the action was commenced in 1994 in an amount to be determined by the trial judge.

The Court observed that the test for unjust enrichment has three elements: (1) an enrichment of the defendant; (2) a corresponding deprivation of the plaintiff; and (3) an absence of juristic reason for the enrichment. The proper approach to the juristic reason analysis is in two parts. The plaintiff must show that no juristic reason from an established category exists to deny recovery. The established categories include a contract, a disposition of law, a donative intent, and other valid common law, equitable or statutory obligations. If there is no juristic reason from an established category, then the plaintiff has made out a *prima facie* case. The *prima facie* case is rebuttable, however, where the defendant can show that there is another reason to deny recovery. Courts should have regard at this point to two factors: the reasonable expectations of the parties and public policy considerations.

Consumers' Gas received the monies represented by the LPPs and had that money available for use in the carrying on of its business. The transfer of those funds clearly constituted a benefit to the company, and it was accepted by the parties in this case that the second prong of the test — deprivation — had been satisfied. With respect to the third prong, the only possible juristic reason from an established category that could have justified the enrichment was the existence of the Ontario Energy Board orders creating the LPPs under the "disposition of law" category. The OEB orders, however, did not constitute a juristic reason for the enrichment because they were inoperative to the extent of their conflict with s. 347 of the *Criminal Code*. Garland thus made out a *prima facie* case for unjust enrichment.

Consumers' Gas reliance on the OEB orders was, however, relevant when determining the reasonable expectations of the parties at the rebuttal stage of the juristic reason analysis, even though it did not provide a defence if the respondent was charged under s. 347 of the *Code*. An overriding public policy consideration in this case was the fact that the LPPs were collected in contravention of the *Criminal Code*. As a matter of public policy, criminals should not be permitted to keep the proceeds of their crime. In weighing these considerations, the Supreme Court accepted that the reliance of Consumers' Gas on the inoperative OEB orders from 1981 to 1994, prior to the commencement of the action, provided a juristic reason for the enrichment. However, after the action was commenced and Consumers' Gas was put on notice that there was a serious possibility its LPPs violated the *Criminal Code*, it was no longer reasonable to rely on the OEB rate orders to authorize the LPPs.

What is also curious when the reasons for judgment in *Transport North American Express* and *Garland v. Consumers' Gas* are compared is that Iacobucci J., in holding that there has been unjust enrichment and that the "change of position" defence is not available, says (at para. 64) that Consumers' Gas was a "wrongdoer", even though it was doing what it was authorized to do by the Ontario Energy Board. Yet in the former case, in spite of the fact that the agreement was clearly in violation of s. 347, Arbour J. appears almost anxious to give the lender as much as it can lawfully collect.

At the date of writing (April 2006), the actual amount that must be repaid has not been settled. The argument of Consumers' Gas (now Enbridge Gas Distribution Inc.) is that the concept of notional severance in *Transport North American Express* applies (with the result that the plaintiffs' victory may be pyrrhic). The parties brought a motion in the Supreme Court asking it to provide specific guidance, but the Court declined to do so.

The application of the concept of notional severance to non-competition clauses was rejected in *Globex Foreign Exchange Corp. v. Kelcher*, [2005] A.J. No. 1654, 10 B.L.R. (4th) 229, (C.A.).

4.   The problems of s. 347 are potentially very serious for a large number of financial products. A participation mortgage is a mortgage in which the mortgagee does not (or may not) receive interest but instead gets a share in the amount, if any, by which the property appreciates in value. There is nothing wrong with such a mortgage and from the point of view of the borrower, it may be far preferable to a conventional one. In *677950 Ontario Ltd. v. Artell Developments Ltd.* (1992), 93 D.L.R. (4th) 334, 24 R.P.R. (2d) 113 (Ont. C.A.), affirmed, [1993] 2 S.C.R. 443, 32 R.P.R. (2d) 286, the plaintiff corporation (and its owner, Horvat) agreed to purchase property for $2.2 million and expected to sell it at a profit of about $3.2 million. To finance the purchase, the plaintiff borrowed money from the defendant and the plaintiff undertook to pay the defendant one-half of the net profit on the resale (about $1.3 million). The plaintiff sued for a declaration that the mortgage was void. The defendant sued to enforce the mortgage. The trial judge gave judgment for the defendant on the ground that the bonus was a "collateral arrangement for profit sharing". The Court of Appeal and the Supreme Court held that the arrangement was caught by s. 347. The actual interest rate earned on the mortgage in question was about 1,400 per cent.

Many financial products are similar to participation mortgages: the lender gets, not interest, but a chance at a gain. A convertible debenture is a debenture, *i.e.*, a debt instrument issued by a corporation, that is convertible into shares. The expectation of both parties is that the corporation will not have to pay the loan, but will redeem it by shares. For the deal to be attractive to the investor, the value of the shares has to be such that it will be adequately compensated for the risk. If the value of the shares increases to an extent that the actual return enjoyed by the investor exceeds 60 per cent per annum, it may be that the transaction is caught by s. 347.

Many other more or less exotic financial products such as derivatives and swaps are similarly threatened. One argument made to defend the validity of, for example, a debenture that comes with a share warrant, *i.e.*, a right to buy shares at a fixed price, is that the section is not relevant if the warrant, *i.e.*, the interest component of the transaction, can be separately priced, as a warrant can be. It may well be that a court would be strongly moved to recognize the transaction as valid — it is about as far as one can get from the image of the poverty-stricken debtor and the loan shark — but the Supreme Court in *Degelder Construction Co. v. Dancorp Developments Ltd.*, [1998] S.C.J. No. 75 [1998] 3 S.C.R. 90, 165 D.L.R. (4th) 417 said that para. 347(1)(*b*) should be widely construed, *i.e.*, to catch as many transactions as possible. It has been held that, if the borrower has the option of choosing how to be paid, its election of a return that is greater than 60 per cent will not make the loan illegal. But with a convertible debenture or other similar financial product, the person choosing to exercise his or her rights of conversion or purchase is the *lender*.

The fact is that s. 347 is (and was) an unwieldy solution to the problem of loansharking. There have been very few prosecutions under it — a prosecution can only be brought with the consent of the provincial Attorney General — and no evidence that it has actually put loan-sharks out of business, let alone behind bars. Such lenders are, in any case, unlikely to use the courts to enforce their debts: they have much more unpleasant and effective remedies that, of course, are very likely to involve independently criminal actions. What the section has done is to make many perfectly reasonable, fair and useful transactions subject to attack and, as a direct result, it has given a lot of work to lawyers.

The particular point that will lead to high legal fees is that the law firm acting for the corporation will have to give a "transaction opinion", *i.e.*, a statement to the borrower or in a prospectus or offering memorandum that a transaction like the convertible debentures already mentioned, is "valid and enforceable in accordance with its terms". The firm faced with a decision like that in *Degelder Construction* has to worry whether it can give a "clean" opinion or one qualified by, for example, a statement that the "interest" provisions may not be enforceable. Such a qualified opinion gives little comfort to the investor.

A private Bill introduced in the Senate, *inter alia*, to exempt large commercial transactions from the scope of s. 347 passed in the Senate but died in the House of Commons when Parliament was dissolved in the fall of 2005.

5. The problems of drafting around the problems of s. 347 of the *Criminal Code* are not easy and no law firm seems to have come up with a formula that has won widespread approval. A court faced with the prospect of making unenforceable a sophisticated financial product like a convertible debenture may be moved to uphold a clause that seeks to limit the lender's payment to an amount that is less than the criminal interest rate.

As the following Small Claims Court decision illustrates, however, there are situations in which low-income borrowers have benefited from s. 347 of the *Criminal Code*. This decision was one of a number in which the Deputy Judge limited the claims of payday lenders.

AFFORDABLE PAYDAY LOANS v. JEVON FIRTH

[2005] O.J. No. 1232 (Ont. Sm. Cl. Ct.)

G.C. HOUSE DEPUTY J.:—

...

[4]   The Plaintiff, Affordable Payday Loans is engaged in the business of lending money on a short-term basis to consumers. Mr. Firth is one of these borrowers. On the 1st day of February, 2002 (sic), the Defendant completed a credit application. On January 31st of January, 2003, Mr. Firth executed a document purporting to be a promissory note (sic) set out as follows:

"AFFORDABLE PAYDAY LOANS — PROMISSORY NOTE

For value received the undersigned promises to pay Affordable Payday Loans the sum of 587.20 on or before the 28 day of February, 2003.

The total charges paid as due shall be $22.00 per $100.00 advanced. (2% interest per pay period and $20.00 Administration and Verification fee + GST).

In the event that ant [*sic*] cheque for payment is not honoured or negotiable by my financial institution, for any reason whatsoever, I further understand and hereby agree to pay $75.00 as liquidated damages and not as a penalty.

Upon failure to make full payment by the specified date, should this note be turned over for collection/legal action, I understand and agree to pay an additional $190.00 in costs as liquidated damages and not as a penalty.

I agree to provide my current address and phone number to Affordable Payday Loans until this note is paid in full. Should any mail addressed to me be returned, or my phone number is disconnected for any reason, I agree to pay a locate fee of $150.00.

I agree to allow Affordable Payday Loans to obtain and share my personal records and credit information regarding this pay advance.

Signed this 31 day of Jan. 2003 in the City of Ottawa.

"Original signed"　　　　"Original signed"

-----------------　　　　------------------

Witness Signature　　　Borrower Signature

[address and phone number omitted]

[5]　　Though not critically important, the document is not a promissory not[e] and falls far short of the definition as set out in the *Bills of Exchange Act*. It contains five (5) conditions under which the loan shall be made, three of which are penal and are triggered by a default in payment on the due date which was the 28th of February, 2003. In my view the charges of $75.00, $190 and most particularly $150.00 are clearly penal and cannot be considered as simply "liquidated".

[6]　　The other document is a statement of account, which sets out as follows:

"AFFORDABLE PAYDAY LOANS INC.

69 MONTREAL ROAD

OTTAWA, ONTARIO K1L 6E8

STATEMENT OF ACCOUNT JEVON FIRTH

AS AT NOVEMBER 30, 2004

NSF LOAN REPAYMENT DATED JANUARY 31, 2003	$ 587.20
NSF CHARGE PURSUANT TO LOAN AGREEMENT	$ 75.00
LIQUIDATED DAMAGES PER PROMISSORY NOTE	$ 190.00
LOCATE FEE PER PROMISSORY NOTE	$ 150.00

INTEREST AT 4% PER MONTH (48% PER ANNUM) ON $587.20 $ 494.211 FROM FEBRUARY 28, 2003 TO NOVEMBER 30, 2004 (640 DAYS)

TOTAL OWING　　　　　　　　　　　　　　　　$1,496.41"

[7] Curiously, the Plaintiff has included in the debt a claim for pre-judgment interest for a period of 640 days at forty-eight per cent (48%) per annum. As indicated, default occurred on the 28th of February 2003, the claim having been issued on the 2nd of December 2004. Since pre-judgment interest is discretionary, it will be dealt with later on in this disposition. There is no correspondence in the file relating to demands for payment from the Defendant.

THE INTEREST

[8] The documents reveal that a gross amount was to be repaid by the Defendant in the amount of $587.20. The amount actually advanced to Mr. Firth is not disclosed, and one would necessarily have to work backwards to ascertain the fee charged, the difference presumably being the sum received by the Defendant. (Using the fee of $105.89 and the amount of $481.31) advanced to the Defendant for a period of 28 days, … would be 286.79% per annum. Factoring the penalty charges the calculation would be 1362% per annum.

THE LAW

...

[10] Historically, and subsequent to the passage of section 347 of the *Criminal Code*, there appears to be a plethora of reported cases with each dealing with its particular set of facts. Remedies varied and were dependent upon a number of factors.

...

[12] In *Transport North American Express Inc. v. New Solutions Financial Corporation*, [2004] 1 S.C.R. 249, the Supreme Court of Canada considered and dealt with a matter involving a usurious claim and as well in its decision defined what remedies should be available to the parties. A brief summary of the facts indicated that the parties entered into a loan agreement which called for interest payments on the principal, a royalty fee, a monitoring fee, a commitment fee, and other legal expenses and administrative costs. There was a consensus of the Trial and Appeal Courts, affirmed by a majority in the Highest Court that the cumulative effect of the additional payments when the interest calculation was made, showed clearly a rate per annum in excess of the 60 per cent per annum permitted under section 347 of the Code. It appears that the major issue to be decided was one of remedy. In this instance and on the facts, the Court found that the parties to this transaction were experienced in commercial matters and in fact the violation as to the rate of interest was inadvertent. Resultantly, the Court applied a remedy which it called notional severance and in effect struck the claim for interest but allowed a sum equal to 60 per cent being the maximum allowable under section 347 of the Code. It appears that the important factors in allowing this relief was the good faith intention of the parties, their experience in commercial matters and the inadvertence. As well, there was not indication of unequal bargaining power.

Arbour, J. stated, drawing from *Garland v. Consumers' Gas* (1998), 165 D.L.R. (4th) 385 (S.C.C.) [paraphrase]:

"Notional severance is available as a remedy in cases arising under s. 347 of the Code. The application of notional [severance] was appropriate in this case because the agreement only inadvertently violated s. 347; the parties were experienced in commercial matters and had negotiated at arm's length; there was no evidence that the parties did not have equal bargaining power, and the parties had the benefit of independent legal advice. The creditor should be repaid the principal together with the highest amount of interest legally allowable, being 60 per cent. This notional severance did not rewrite the contract any more than enforcing only the other payments, which amounted to "interest" at 30.8 per cent."

Bastarache, J., in a dissenting opinion expressed [paraphrase]:

"There is a fundamental difference between striking out offending sections of a contract and rewriting a central provision of a contract ... the rewriting approach comes at a considerable cost and is not supported by any principle of contract law. The notional severance or rewriting approach is inconsistent with the notional severance of the kind ordered by the application judge is to effect a substantial innovation in the common law doctrine of severance to the benefit of those who *prima facie* stand in violation of the criminal law. The finding that there was no ... intent ... should not obscure the analysis. Knowledge is not a requirement under s. 347 of the Code."

[13] Although bound by the decision in *New Solutions*, my concern not is that lenders can seek the refuge of notional severance knowing that perhaps the only consequence of a usurious challenge would be to reduce the relief to an interest rate permitted by law and up to 60 per cent per annum.

[14] The facts of the case at bar differ from those in New Solutions, as the Court found, in assessing the competence and good faith intentions of the parties, that bargaining power was not considered a factor in the decision. However, under the present circumstances, in my view, bargaining power is a critical component to be considered in order to arrive at a just disposition. The ingredients of bargaining power were canvassed in *Morrison v. Coast Finance* (1965), 55 D.L.R. (2d) 710, wherein the Court of Appeal of British Columbia set out as follows [paraphrase]:

"Whether the appellant was entitled to relief against the transaction if it appeared unconscionable when viewed as a whole. On such a claim the ingredients are: 1) proof of inequality in the position of the parties arising out of ignorance, need or distress of the weaker, leaving him in the power of the stronger, and 2) proof of substantial unfairness of the bargain thus obtained by the stronger. Proof of these circumstances having been made here, there arose a presumption of fraud which Defendants as the stronger parties could not rebut, being unable to show that the bargain as a whole was fair, just and reasonable, with no advantage taken. This was not a simple loan transaction, but an outreaching one in which Defendants knowingly advanced their own interest at the cost of the gullible Plaintiff's folly."

CONCLUSIONS

1) Having reviewed the salient features of this transaction which are principally the documents *supra*, this Court is satisfied that the Plaintiff, Affordable Payday Loans, engaged in a loan transaction which seriously violated the provisions of s. 347 of the *Criminal Code* of Canada having charged a rate of interest that exceeded the highest rate permitted under said Code, which is 60 per cent per annum.

2) Accordingly and having regard to the law to which I have referred, the facts of this case and the others which form part of this disposition, differ radically from those in New Solutions, in that I find that the transgression was intentional on the part of the Plaintiff and there was a palpable imbalance in bargaining power. Affordable Payday Loans engaged in an organized, consistent and concerted pattern of conduct designed to exploit the vulnerable.

3) Resultantly, this Court finds that given the findings in the previous paragraph, the Plaintiff should not be entitled to any equitable relief and this is not a mat-

ter where notional severance should be applied in this or any of the actions cited.

[15] There will be Judgment for the Plaintiff in the principal amount of $481.31, plus the disbursement for the issuance of the claim, effective as of the date of the release of this disposition. There shall be no pre-judgment interest for the reasons expressed above. Judgments will be allowed in the remaining actions on a similar basis.

[16] The intention of s. 347 of the Code was to prevent loan sharking. Even in isolation such a finding in this case might be appropriate. Having said that, I have attached as a schedule to this Judgment, copies of the statements of account for the balance of the actions above referenced. I have reviewed each file and find an identical pattern of conduct on the part of the plaintiff, Affordable Payday Loans. These are files presently awaiting process by the Small Claims Court. My analysis reveals, in each case, a violation of s. 347 of the *Criminal Code* as the rates of interest charged [were] usurious.

[17] I am therefore requesting that a copy of this Judgment be referred to the Ministry of Corporate and Consumer Affairs to allow it an opportunity to review these matters and take whatever action it deems necessary. As well, a copy should go to the Attorney General of the Province of Ontario. …

QUESTION

There is no easy solution to the problem of the pay-day loan industry. The rate charged to Firth was very high. However, the costs of lending to this market are high, in terms of both administrative costs and the costs of defaults. There is clearly a demand for this type of loan, and if it is not available from legal lenders, borrowers are more likely to be driven to seek short-term loans from criminal loan sharks. What legal solution would you like to see?

AVOIDING THE CONSEQUENCES OF ILLEGALITY

The consequences of illegality are often so serious that (as in a case such as *Sidmay* and some of the other cases we have looked at) the courts may have a strong incentive to find some way out of the difficulties Lord Mansfield has created for them. The following cases illustrate some of these techniques.

ARCHBOLDS (FREIGHTAGE) LTD. v. S. SPANGLETT, LTD.

[1961] 1 Q.B. 374, [1961] 1 All E.R. 417
(C.A., Pearce, Sellers and Devlin L.JJ.)

[The defendant was a furniture manufacturer. It had trucks that it used to carry its goods. Its trucks were not licensed to carry goods for others. A load of whisky was carried for the plaintiff by one of the defendant's trucks. This arrangement was made by one Field, on behalf of the plaintiff. The load was stolen through the negligence of the defendant's driver, Randall. The plaintiff sued for damages. The illegality of the contract was raised as a defence. The trial judge held that the plaintiff did not know that the contract of carriage would be carried out by means of an unlicensed truck and allowed the claim. The defendant appealed.]

DEVLIN L.J.: — **[1]** The effect of illegality upon a contract may be threefold. If at the time of making the contract there is an intent to perform it in an unlawful way, the contract, although it remains alive, is unenforceable at the suit of the party having that intent; if the intent is held in common, it is not enforceable at all. Another effect of illegality is to prevent a plaintiff from recovering under a contract if in order to prove his rights under it he has to rely upon his own illegal act; he may not do that even though he can show that at the time of making the contract he had no intent to break the law and that at the time of performance he did not know that what he was doing was illegal. The third effect of illegality is to avoid the contract ab initio and that arises if the making of the contract is expressly or impliedly prohibited by statute or is otherwise contrary to public policy.

[2]   The defendants do not seek to bring this case under either of the first two heads. They cannot themselves enforce the contract because they intended to perform it unlawfully with a van that they knew was not properly licensed for the purpose: but that does not prevent the plaintiffs, who had no such intent and were not privy to it, from enforcing the contract. Nor can it be said that the plaintiffs committed any illegal act. To load a vehicle is not to use it on the road, which is what is forbidden: no doubt loading would be enough to constitute aiding and abetting if the plaintiffs knew of the defendants' purpose (*National Coal Board v. Gamble*, [1959] 1 Q.B. 11), but they did not.

[3]   So what the defendants say is that the contract is prohibited by the *Road and Rail Traffic Act, 1933*, section 1. In order to see whether the contract falls within the prohibition it is necessary to ascertain the exact terms of the contract and the exact terms of the prohibition. For reasons which I shall explain later, I shall begin by ascertaining the latter. Section 1 of the act provides that no person shall use a goods vehicle on a road for the carriage of goods for hire or reward except under a licence. Section 2 provides for various classes of licences, "A," "B" and "C". It is agreed that the carriage of the goods which were the subject-matter of this contract required an "A" licence. The fact that the van had a "C" licence does not therefore help one way or the other; and it is admitted that the defendants' use of this van for the carriage of these goods was prohibited. As I have noted, the plaintiffs are not to be treated as using the van because they supplied the load. Section 1(3) provides that the driver of the vehicle or, if he is an agent or servant, his principal, shall be deemed to be the person by whom the vehicle is being used.

[4]   The statute does not expressly prohibit the making of any contract. The question is therefore whether a prohibition arises as a matter of necessary implication. It follows from the decision of this court in *Nash v. Stevenson Transport Ltd.*, [1936] 2 K.B. 128, that a contract for the use of unlicensed vehicles is prohibited. In that case the plaintiff held "A" licences which the defendant wanted to purchase. But the act of 1933 provides that licences may not be transferred or assigned, and it was therefore agreed that the defendant should run the vehicles in the plaintiff's name so that they might obtain the benefit of his licences. It was held by the court that that was an illegal agreement because the defendant was the person who was using the vehicles and the plaintiff the person who was licensed to use them; thus the user was not the licensee. In the present case there was no contract for the use of the vehicle.

[5]   On the other hand, it does not follow that because it is an offence for one party to enter into a contract, the contract itself is void. In *In re Mahmoud and Ispahani*, [1921] 2 K.B. 716, 730, Scrutton L.J. said: "In *Bloxsome v. Williams* (1824), 3 B. & C. 232, the position was that the defendant, a horse dealer, was prohibited from trading on Sunday, but there was nothing illegal in another person

making a contract with a horse dealer, except that if he knew that the person with whom he was dealing was a horse dealer and was guilty of breaking the law he might be aiding and abetting him to break the law. But merely to make a contract with a horse dealer, without knowing he was a horse dealer, was not illegal."

[6]   The general considerations which arise on this question were examined at length in *St. John Shipping Corporation v. Joseph Rank Ltd.*, [1957] 1 Q.B. 267, 285 . . . Fundamentally they are the same as those that arise on the construction of every statute; one must have regard to the language used and to the scope and purpose of the statute. I think that the purpose of this statute is sufficiently served by the penalties prescribed for the offender: the avoidance of the contract would cause grave inconvenience and injury to innocent members of the public without furthering the object of the statute. Moreover, the value of the relief given to the wrongdoer if he could escape what would otherwise have been his legal obligation might, as it would in this case, greatly outweigh the punishment that could be imposed upon him, and thus undo the penal effect of the statute.

[7]   I conclude, therefore, that this contract was not illegal for the reason that the statute does not prohibit the making of a contract for the carriage of goods in unlicensed vehicles and this contract belongs to this class. I am able, therefore, to arrive at my judgment without an examination of the exact terms of the contract. It would have been natural to have begun by looking at the contract; I have not done so because it is doubtful whether the state of the pleadings permits a thorough examination. But as [the] argument [of counsel for the defendant] before us turned upon its terms, I think that I should deal with them. . . .

[8]   So the correct line of inquiry into the terms of the contract in this case should have been not as to whether it provided for performance by a specified vehicle or by any vehicle that the defendants chose to nominate, but as to whether the defendants warranted or agreed that the vehicle which was to do the work, whether a specified vehicle or any other, was legally fit for the service which it had to undertake, that is, that it had an "A" licence.

[9]   I think there is much to be said for the argument that in a case of this sort there is, unless the circumstances exclude it, an implied warranty that the van is properly licensed for the service for which it is required. It would be unreasonable to expect a man when he is getting into a taxicab to ask for an express warranty from the driver that his cab was licensed; the answer, if it took any intelligible form at all, would be to the effect that it would not be on the streets if it were not. The same applies to a person who delivers goods for carriage by a particular vehicle; he cannot be expected to examine the road licence to see if it is in order. But the issue of warranty was not raised in the pleadings or at the trial and so I think it is preferable to decide this case on the broad ground which Pearce L.J. has adopted and with which, for the reasons I have given, I agree.

[10]   There are many pitfalls in this branch of the law. If, for example, Mr. Field had observed that the van had a "C" licence and said nothing, he might be said to have accepted a mode of performance different from that contracted for and so varied the contract and turned it into an illegal one: see *St. John Shipping Corporation v. Joseph Rank Ltd.*, [1957] 1 Q.B. 267, 283, 284, where that sort of point was considered. Or, to take another example, if a statute prohibits the sale of goods to an alien, a warranty by the buyer that he is not an alien will not save the contract. That is because the terms of the prohibition expressly forbid a sale to an alien: consequently, the question to be asked in order to see whether the contract

comes within the prohibition is whether the buyer is in fact an alien, not whether he represented himself as one. *In re Mahmoud*, [1921] 2 K.B. 716, is that sort of case. The statute forbade the buying and selling of certain goods between unlicensed persons. The buyer falsely represented himself as having a licence. It is not said that he so warranted but, if he had, it could have made no difference. Once the fact was established that he was an unlicensed person the contract was brought within the category of those that were prohibited. *Strongman v. Sincock*, [1955] 2 Q.B. 525 exemplifies another sort of difficulty. It was an action brought by a builder against a building owner to recover the price of building work done. The statute forbade the execution of building operations without a licence. The building owner expressly undertook to obtain the necessary licence and failed to do so; and it was held that the builder could not recover. The builder, I dare say, might have contended that, having regard to the undertaking, the contract he made was for licensed operations and therefore legal. But unfortunately he had himself performed it illegally by building without a licence and he could not recover without relying on his illegal act because he was suing for money for work done. The undertaking might make the contract legal but not the operations. All these cases are distinguishable from the present one, where the contract is not within the prohibition and the plaintiffs themselves committed no illegal act and did not aid or abet the defendants. Apart from the pleading point, it might not matter if the last two cases were not distinguishable, since the plaintiffs could obtain damages for breach of the warranty as in *Strongman v. Sincock*.

QUESTIONS AND NOTES

1.   To what extent can the device of the (implied) warranty of legality be used as a general remedy for the problems created by the existence of an illegal contract? Can one now use *Hedley Byrne v. Heller & Partners*, [1964] A.C. 465 (H.L.) and the remedy of the negligent misstatement? (*Archbolds* was decided before *Hedley Byrne*.)

2.   Should it be relevant that the defendant's insurance coverage probably only applied when it was acting lawfully?

3.   One device sometimes used by the courts to avoid the consequences of illegality is to allow the plaintiff to sue on some ground other than the contract. Thus, in *Bowmakers, Ltd. v. Barnet Instruments Ltd.*, [1945] K.B. 65, [1944] 2 All E.R. 579, goods were sold to the defendant under hire-purchase agreements. These agreements were illegal under regulations issued during the Second World War. When the defendant refused to pay on the ground that the contracts were illegal, the plaintiff was held to be able to sue for conversion, relying on its ownership of the goods. The availability of such an alternative device is often mere good fortune: there will be many cases in which restitutionary grounds for relief will not be available.

4.   Courts have sometimes allowed an unlicensed tradesman to sue for the value of the materials supplied, even if he cannot sue for his labour: *Monticchio v. Torcema Construction Ltd.* (1979), 26 O.R. (2d) 305, 102 D.L.R. (3d) 462 (H.C.J.). Such a case suggests that the courts are moving away from the more rigid view found in *Kocotis v. D'Angelo*, [1958] O.R. 104, 13 D.L.R. (2d) 69 (C.A.), where an unlicensed tradesman was held to be unable to sue on the contract of labour. In the latter case, Schroeder J.A. dissented on the ground that the denial of the plaintiff's remedy did not follow from the fact that the plaintiff was unlicensed. The legislature did not specify that that consequence should follow, and that the contract should be regarded as illegal.

5.   It is apparent that judicial attitudes still vary, and that courts are not moving uniformly toward restricting the scope of illegality. In *Communities Economic Development Fund v. Canadian Pickles Corp.*, [1991] 3 S.C.R. 388, 85 D.L.R. (4th) 88, the plain-

tiff, the "Fund", was a corporation established under the *Communities Economic De-velopment Fund Act*, R.S.M. 1987, c. C155. It lent $150,000 to one defendant, the "Corporation". The individual defendant, the "Guarantor", was a director and counsel to the Corporation, and one of three guarantors who gave the Fund a guarantee of the Corporation's obligation to the Fund. The Corporation at the date of trial had assets of about $12,000 and owed the Fund about $180,000. The Guarantor was, apparently, the only party with any assets.

At trial, the loan was held to be *ultra vires* the Fund under the legislation and to be unenforceable — the Fund was by its statute confined to lending only to corporations doing business in remote or isolated communities, and the Corporation was not such a corporation. The trial judge held that the guarantee was, however, enforceable because the Guarantor had encouraged the Fund to lend the money and because he, as a share-holder and director of the Corporation, had benefited from the loan. The Manitoba Court of Appeal allowed the Guarantor's appeal on the ground that the loan, being *ultra vires*, was a nullity and that, in consequence, the Guarantor could not be liable un-der a guarantee of a loan that was invalid from the moment of its making. The Court of Appeal rejected, on the facts, the argument that the Guarantor had encouraged the Fund to make the loan.

The Fund appealed to the Supreme Court, which, in a judgment by Iacobucci J., dismissed the appeal, holding that the guarantee violated the statute and was therefore unenforceable. The basis for the judgment in the Supreme Court was that it was neces-sary to recognize the limits set by the legislation on the activities of the Fund. This justified making the loan unrecoverable. The Guarantor was also released on the ground that the language of the guarantee did not specifically deal with *ultra vires* loans and did not then apply in the circumstances.

The basis for the decision of the Supreme Court on the validity of the loan was that the legislation should be interpreted so as to limit the plaintiff's powers to those that it was authorized to exercise under the legislation. The reason for this conclusion was that the Fund was authorized to make loans only to enterprises in remote or isolated communities, and the place where the defendant had its business was neither remote nor isolated. The loan was, therefore, made in violation of the limits on the Fund un-der the legislation. On the liability under the guarantee, Iacobucci J. held that the wording of the guarantee did not specifically cover the exact situation — the mak-ing of an *ultra vires* loan — that had occurred and, accordingly, the guarantee did not apply.

Consider whether enforcement or a refusal to enforce would be more likely to co-incide with the legislative purpose. What was the effect of the decision on the position of the Fund?

Some recent decisions reflect a more purposive approach to contracts that violate statutory provisions, including greater concern about issues of unjust enrichment.

JOHNSON v. LAZZARINO

[1998] O.J. No. 1941, 39 O.R. (3d) 724, affirmed [1999] O.J. No. 143,
43 O.R. (3d) 253n
(Ont. Gen. Div., Sharpe J.; C.A., Doherty, Abella and O'Connor JJ.A.)

SHARPE J.: — **[1]** The plaintiff is a chartered accountant. On February 27, 1996, the defendant, Toronto Supermarket Products Limited ("TSPL") entered into a written agreement, engaging the plaintiff to prepare amended financial statements and corporate income tax returns for the years 1994 and 1995 to reflect certain research and development expenditures. The agreement provided for a retainer of $5,000, but specified that the fees for the service to be provided by the plaintiff were to be "an amount equal to 30 per cent of the investment tax credit received related to Research and Development Expenditures". The retainer was refundable in the event no income tax credit was received.

[2]   It is not disputed that as a result of the work done by the plaintiff, TSPL received a benefit of $278,883. The plaintiff claims 30 per cent of that amount or $83,664.90, plus GST, less the $5,000 retainer, for a balance due of $84,521.44.

[3]   It is common ground that the sole issue arising on this motion by the plaintiff for summary judgment against TSPL is whether the contingency fee arrangement is enforceable. TSPL submits that it is not, as at the time the agreement was made, the Rules of Professional Conduct of the Institute of Chartered Accountants of Ontario ("ICAO") provided as follows:

> Rule 215. A member engaged in the practice of public accounting shall not offer or agree to render any professional service for a fee contingent on the results of such service, nor shall the member represent that he or she does any professional service without fee except services of charitable, benevolent or similar nature.

This rule was amended by the ICAO on June 10, 1996 to permit chartered accountants to enter into contingency fee arrangements in certain circumstances. It is common ground between the parties that the arrangement in the case at bar would comply with the amended Rule. There is also evidence before me that this change to the rules was being discussed at the time the parties entered their arrangement.

[4]   The defendant submits that as the contingency fee contract was forbidden by the ICAO Rules of Professional Conduct, it is void and unenforceable at the suit of the plaintiff. In my view, this argument cannot be accepted.

[5]   The common law doctrine of illegality of contracts has evolved significantly in recent years. In my view, the fact that a contract that renders a member liable to professional discipline by the ICAO does not necessarily render the contract unenforceable at the suit of the member in a court of law.

[6]   In *Still v. M.N.R.*, [1998] 1 F.C. 549, 154 D.L.R. (4th) 229 the Federal Court of Appeal undertook a detailed analysis of the common law doctrine of illegality. Robertson J.A. identified two models, namely, the "classical model" and the "modern approach". Under the classical model, a statutory prohibition rendered the contract illegal and void *ab initio* and unenforceable. The modern approach is to examine the statutory provision, to analyze its purpose and to determine whether enforceability of the contract is affected. Robertson J.A., having reviewed the authorities, rejected the classical model in favour of the modern approach and concluded as follows at p. 249:

> Professor Waddams [*The Law of Contracts*, 3rd ed. (1993)] suggests that where a statute prohibits the formation of a contract the courts should be free to decide the consequences (at 372). I agree. If legislatures do not wish to spell out in detail the contractual consequences flowing from a breach of a statutory prohibition, and are content to impose only a penalty or administrative sanction, then it is entirely within a court's jurisdiction to determine, in effect, whether other sanctions should be imposed. As the doctrine of illegality is not a creature of statute, but of judicial creation, it is incumbent on the present judiciary to ensure that its premises accord with contemporary values.

[7]   In *Beer v. Townsgate I Ltd.* (1997), 36 O.R. (3d) 136, 152 D.L.R. (4th) 671, the Ontario Court of Appeal adopted a similar approach, summarized in the following statement of Brooke J.A., at p. 144:

If a statute does not expressly deprive a party of his or her rights under the contract, the question is whether, having regard to the purpose of the Act, and the circumstances under which the contract was made, and to be performed, it would be contrary to public policy to enforce it because of illegality. . . .

[8] I turn, accordingly, to a consideration of the purpose of the statutory prohibition at issue here. The ICAO is established by *An Act to Reconstitute the Institute of Chartered Accountants of Ontario*, S.O. 1956, c. 7. The objects of the ICAO are specified in s. 3, namely:

   (a)   to promote and increase the knowledge, skill and proficiency of its members and students-in-accounts;

   (b)   to regulate the discipline and professional conduct of its members and students-in-accounts;

   (c)   to promote and protect the welfare and interest of the Institute and the accounting profession.

The Act provides that the affairs of the ICAO are to be managed by the council and that the council is authorized to pass by-laws to carry out the objects of the ICAO. The power to enact by-laws includes providing for the exercise of disciplinary authority and providing Rules of Professional Conduct. The by-laws of the ICAO make it clear that where a member violates the Rules of Professional Conduct, the member is subject to the ICAO's disciplinary authority.

[9] It is apparent from its terms that Rule 215, as it existed at the relevant time, did not explicitly purport to render contingency fee contracts unenforceable at common law. The purpose and effect of Rule 215 and the by-laws of the ICAO is to provide that members who violate the rule are liable to disciplinary sanctions. Those sanctions do not include making contracts unenforceable. Indeed, it is difficult to see how the ICAO would have that power. Moreover, the authority to enforce the Rules of Professional Conduct is vested in the ICAO itself. It is not for this court to engage in the discipline of chartered accountants for breach of those Rules, yet that would be the effect of depriving the plaintiff of the right to sue on this agreement.

[10] From a contractual perspective, it would be patently unjust to deny the plaintiff the right to recover the fee the parties stipulated in the circumstances of the present case. The parties bargained this arrangement at arm's length. There is no suggestion that unfair advantage was taken of the defendant. The contract has been fully performed and TSPL has received a very significant benefit. There is nothing about the contract that renders it inherently wrong or contrary to public policy. The fact that the ICAO has changed the Rule to permit such contracts demonstrates that, even from the perspective of the ICAO, contingency fee arrangements are not inherently wrong.

[11] I conclude, accordingly, that the plaintiff is entitled to enforce the contract against TSPL despite Rule 215 of the Rules of Professional Conduct of the ICAO. The plaintiff is entitled to summary judgment against TSPL for $84,521.44. . . .

[The decision of Sharpe J. was affirmed in a brief decision in the Ontario Court of Appeal (1999), 43 O.R. (3d) 253*n* (C.A.), where Doherty, Abella and O'Connor JJ.A. endorsed the record:]

[1] We agree with the analysis of Sharpe J. The Rule in question was intended to regulate the professional conduct of members of the Institute of Chartered Accountants of Ontario by prohibiting contingency fees. It did not provide that contracts entered into in contravention of the Rule were void or otherwise unenforceable.

[2]   The professional consequences to the respondent flowing from his alleged breach of that Rule are for the Institute. The effect, if any, of the breach of that Rule on the validity of the contract made between the parties is for the court to determine applying judge-made rules applicable to allegations that a contract is void for illegality.

[3]   As Sharpe J. observes, this court favours an approach which looks to the purpose animating the statute which is said to have been violated, and the circumstances under which the particular contract was made and then asks whether it would be contrary to public policy to enforce the contract: *Beer v. Townsgate I Ltd.* (1997), 36 O.R. (3d) 136, 152 D.L.R. (4th) 671 (C.A.). In this case, the alleged breach of the Rule had no impact on the creation of the contract, caused no harm to the appellants, and did not affect the performance of the contract. Indeed, by the time payment was due under the contract, the rules had been amended so as to permit contingency fees like that contemplated in this agreement.

[4]   To give effect to the appellant's argument would be to sanction to unjust enrichment of the appellant without in any way furthering the regulatory purposes of the Rule. In our view, that would not be good public policy.

NOTE

The issue of the legality and enforceability of contingency fee arrangements that was addressed in *Johnson v. Lazzarino* was of special interest to lawyers in Ontario. Contingency fees are legal and commonly used in many parts of North America, especially in tort cases. Such arrangements are lawful in Manitoba (from 1890), Quebec (1968), Alberta (1969), Nova Scotia (1972), New Brunswick (1973), Saskatchewan (1975), Prince Edward Island (1977), British Columbia (1979), Northwest Territories (1979) and Yukon Territory (1980). Since 2002, the Ontario *Solicitors Act*, R.S.O. 1990, c. S.15 has also allowed contingency fees. Even before the Act was amended, the courts were sympathetic to lawyers charging contingency fees, as without them certain types of litigation could never be undertaken by claimants with limited means: see *McIntyre Estate v. Ontario (Attorney General)*, [2002] O.J. No. 3417, 61 O.R. (3d) 257, 218 D.L.R. (4th) 193 (C.A.). On the other hand, both legislation and case law recognize the need for judges to ensure that contingency fees are not unreasonable.

CHAPTER EIGHT

CONTRACTS: POSTSCRIPT AND PRELUDE

Throughout this book we have attempted to demonstrate the dynamic nature of contracts and of contract law. Both are being employed to control and shape relations unheard of only a few years ago. The stress of change has caused much tearing at the seams: long-established doctrine is being successfully challenged. Judges are more willing to consider the economic and social implications of their decisions. Narrow doctrinal categories are giving way to broader approaches that are premised on the protection of interests that arise out of contractual relations, and take greater account of principles of reasonable reliance, fundamental fairness and good faith. The process continues and must be welcomed if the law is to retain its legitimacy in intervening in our affairs.

The materials in this book were designed to assist law students in understanding the present law, and in coping with these future developments. The article that follows was written by a famous Contracts professor for an audience of American law teachers quite a few years ago, but it still offers important insights about the way in which contract law is evolving, and the role of a first-year Contracts course in legal education. Many of the themes he identifies are addressed in this book.

I. MACNEIL, "WHITHER CONTRACTS"
(1969), 21 *J. of Leg. Ed.* 403

[1]   Two preliminary questions require answering before determination of the optimum content of any law school course of particular name: (1) Is there any such thing? (2) If there is, is it significant enough to future lawyers to justify spending law school time on it?

[2]   In [any consideration of the study of the law of] contracts the first question is, therefore: Is there such a thing as contracts? My friends teaching such courses as Contracts 201 (Sales), Contracts 202 (Negotiable Instruments), Contracts 307 (Creditors' Rights), Contracts 312 (Labor Law), Contracts 313 (Corporations) and Contracts 319 (Trade Regulation) delight in telling me that there is no such thing as contracts. There are, they say, sales contracts, negotiable instruments, secured transactions and bankruptcy, collective bargaining agreements, insurance contracts, real estate transactions . . . and a host of other contract-types, but contracts-in-gross there ain't. Having earlier rejected childhood beliefs in the higher abstractions of Samuel Williston's metaphysics, I almost came to believe them. But a personal vested economic interest in the existence of contracts-in-gross caused me to search further. Since you too share that vested interest you will be pleased to know that I have reached the conclusion that contracts exists.

[3]   In view of the large number of books on your desks with the unmodified word "contracts" on the spine, some of you will doubtless be inclined to think that the foregoing paragraph is an overt manifestation of the departure of its author from reality. The accuracy of that reflection I am not qualified to debate. I should warn you, however, that I do not propose to maintain that there is such a thing as contracts simply because large numbers of distinguished legal scholars have organized their work as if there is, nor even because the word "contracts" is an important organizing-indexing tool for a large amount of judicial doctrine and to a considerable extent for statutes and administrative law. To do so would raise similar doubts about my mental stability among the many who believe, "that there is no such thing as a 'law of contracts' applicable to all consensual transactions, but rather a variety of transaction-types for which the courts and legislatures are developing sets of specialized rules and exceptions as the need arises."

[4]   Accepting *arguendo* that there is no such thing as a "law of contracts" necessitates looking to something besides the law to support a belief that there is such a thing as contracts. The only place to turn is to the human behavior which in common usage is called contractual. Upon doing this one finds that a vast variety of behavior is encompassed, from a child's purchase of a nickel candy bar to an arrangement to build an SST for the government, from a purchase of stock on a stock exchange where neither buyer nor seller ever see each other, to the continuing close relationship found between employer and employee. Is it possible to find common elements in that array of behavior, or is the ordinary use of the word "contracts" itself a generalization with no basis in behavior? Happily for our future as first-year contracts teachers, there are common elements in contractual behavior, in fact at least five of them.

[5]   First, every time a relationship seems properly to enjoy the label "contracts" there is, or has been some co-operation between or among the people connected with it. While this observation distinguishes contracts from behavior like murder, solo fast driving, and solitary sunbathing, it does not distinguish it from the building of dams by the Army engineers, the collection of taxes, or necking in the moonlight. In short, there is a great deal of behavior which would not normally be called contractual. And so a search for other elements is necessary.

[6]   The second common element jumps to the fore, more obviously, indeed, than the first: economic exchange. While borderlines may give us trouble, whenever behavior occurs which we are sure we can call contractual there is always an element of economic exchange in it.

[7]   Before examining other elements common to contracts, it is probably desirable to examine briefly the apparent conflict between the presence of economic exchange and the notion that contractual behavior is co-operative behavior. We do, after all, think of economic exchange as being extremely individualistic and selfish, rather than co-operative. Looked at historically or anthropologically, it is readily seen that where tradition and custom dominate production and distribution of goods and services the society in question is generally less individualistic and more common in structure, operation, and attitudes than are the societies in which exchange dominates. And in [the twentieth] century a decline in individualism has paralleled a decline in the significance of exchange as the dominant social mechanism, whether one looks at the modern Western welfare state in its many varieties or at frankly socialistic states. (Conversely, the . . . recent innovations in Russia and Eastern Europe which increase the use of market mechanisms have been hailed, in the Western press at least, as evidence of increasing individualism in those countries.) Moreover, our thinking on this score is also influenced by the deification of exchange by nineteenth (and twentieth) century laissez faire political economists, and the countervailing consignment of exchange to the works of the devil by Karl Marx and at least some of his successors.

[8] Easy to escape in view of the foregoing is the fact that exchange represents a species of human co-operation. In the first place it is a kind of social behavior — the true lone wolf has no one with whom to exchange goods or services. Nor, of course, can the true lone wolf participate in the specialization of labor which both causes and is caused by exchange. Moreover, exchange involves a *mutual* goal of the parties, namely, the reciprocal transfer of values. And this is true however strongly the "economic man" — the "as-much-as-possible-for-as-little-as-possible-in-return-man" — may dominate the motivations of both parties to an exchange.

[9] The core of co-operation which is involved in the immediate exchange of existing goods tends to expand if the exchange is extended over time. Whether he likes it or not a customer who enters a contract to purchase goods in the future enables the seller to plan his activities with a degree of assurance which he otherwise would probably have lacked. The customer is thereby co-operating in the seller's production or acquisition of the goods in a manner which would not have occurred had the customer simply purchased goods already produced. Requirements and output contracts are prime examples of this. They provide a framework for co-operation in the production of goods in some (but not all) respects not unlike that which would occur if the buyer and seller were to merge their corporate identities. Other contracts which simply expand the time for exchange perform similar co-operative functions.

[10] Continuing exchange relationships also are very likely to involve varying degrees of mutual social contracts. These contracts inevitably lead to co-operative behavior, whether or not it is motivated by heavily economic exchange. Employment relationships are one of the more obvious examples of this kind of contractual behavior. In such contracts the co-operative behavior which in the quick one-shot exchange is obscured by selfish economic motives bursts into view as a panoply of continual co-operative behavior. This co-operation is motivated not only by economic exchange motives, but also by social exchange motives and by whatever altruistic or other internal motives cause men to "get along together."

[11] A third element in contractual behavior is that it involves mutual planning for the future. At the very least each party must decide that he wants what the other proposes to give and is willing to give what the other wants in return. Since in some exchanges this happens very quickly it is easy to overlook the element of mutuality in the planning of the parties for the future. But in the contract which more clearly involves more than an immediate exchange of existing goods, this mutual planning becomes obvious. (Man being a talkative animal, such planning is to a considerable extent verbalized in some way.) We have, however, all too often obscured the fact that it is mutual planning of the relationship which is occurring by our focus on assent and its binding (or non-binding) nature in terms of legal sanctions. This focus may make practical sense in quick exchanges, but its value diminishes in the case of continuing relationships. We have further obscured the fact that it is planning we are talking about by our emphasis on such legal concepts as consideration, mutuality, the sanctity of written verbalizations of plans,

etc. Nevertheless, it is mutual planning for the future which is so involved in such matters.

[12] The fourth element in contractual behavior is that potential sanctions external to the "contract" itself are incorporated or added to give reinforcement to the relationship. We are perhaps inclined to think of these sanctions as being legal sanctions, but they are, of course, not so limited, and non-legal sanctions, e.g. business ostracism, are not only significant, but often more significant, than legal sanctions.

[13] The fifth element of contractual behavior is that like all social behavior it is subject to social control and social manipulation which may or may not take into account the interest and desire of those engaging in the behavior. I am tempted to add a sixth common element, but it is not quite as universal among contractual relationships as the others. A great many contracts, however, acquire the characteristics of property, and in particular the characteristic of alienability. This is bound to happen in a market-credit economy, since the contractual relationship very commonly acquires an economic value of its own and tends to be treated like any other economic value owned by someone.

[14] There are thus, it seems to me, five basic elements of contracts: (1) co-operation; (2) economic exchange; (3) planning for the future; (4) potential external sanctions; and (5) social control and manipulation. There is also a sixth which is equally basic whenever it is present, the property characteristics of contracts. These conclusions, however, answer only the first of the two preliminary questions posed at the beginning of this paper, namely whether there is any such thing as contracts. The affirmative answer simply brings on the second question: Is contracts a significant enough social phenomenon to justify spending law school time on it?

[15] Given our heavy reliance on a market economy it is not necessary to justify teaching courses relating to important types of exchange relationships, such as distribution of goods and services, collective bargaining, insurance, trade regulation, corporate finance, credit transactions, government contracts, etc. And conceivably a first-year law school course could be justified which is no more than a collection of important and representative contract areas, simply to introduce those areas. A strong argument could be made for at least that much of a "contracts" course on the ground that the subsequent curriculum is heavily elective, and that it is desirable for lawyers to be aware of the extent to which economic exchange transactions permeate our economic, social and legal life.

[16] But can we go farther and justify a course which explores the behavioral elements common to all of contracting? Is it worthwhile to attempt to examine the legal significance of these elements and the varying ways they affect and are affected by the legal system? Since these questions are answered affirmatively in practically every law school curriculum in the United States a great many people may feel that the discussion can stop at this point. But as noted above I agreed not to base my arguments on the position that there is a "law of contracts" in the Willistonian (or perhaps even a Corbinian) sense. Is there, then, any justification for a generalizing first-year course in contracts if we abandon, ex hypothesi, a belief in a "law of contracts"?

[17] I am not convinced that the disappearance of a generalized course in contracts from the law school curriculum would be a disaster on the scale of Waterloo.

Nor do I think the Western world would collapse if the generalized concept of contracts ceased altogether to be a way of organizing statutes, judicial decisions, administrative action, textbooks, legal digests, etc. I do think, however, that we would lose some of our understanding of the functions and techniques of contracting and of contract law in the various transaction-type areas themselves. In short, recognition that the various transaction-types do have common elements of behavior can lead lawyers, judges, legislators, administrators and even law teachers to a better grasp of and better dealing with each transaction-type itself. To the extent that this is true a generalized contracts course becomes justified, not on the ground that there is a "law of contracts" but on the ground that the common elements in contracts-in-gross present problems and challenges for the legal system which widely cut across transaction-type lines.

[18] All right, you say, prove it. It is, of course, impossible to prove it to a group like this or in a paper like this. All that can be done is to present some of the significant challenges to the legal system and to lawyers which do cut across the transaction-types. They are set out below not in order of significance, but following generally the order in which the common elements have been presented above.

[19] *Co-operation.* The fact that contracts are fundamentally mechanisms of co-operation, and only mechanisms of conflict when things have gone wrong, presents the legal system with special problems. In the first place, contracts get along very well without the law most of the time, or at least without its active intervention. The law thus has to deal largely with pathological cases. This in itself would not be so very troublesome except for the feedback of precedent: the rule of the pathological case governs the healthy contract too. To the extent that contractual behavior is influenced by the law this feedback can have very significant effect on all contractual behavior. At least two primary problems arise from this. First, the law arising from sick cases is not necessarily the optimum law for healthy cases. Second, the legal system has only limited techniques and abilities to deal with contracts-in-conflict, and must define the contractual relationship quite specifically in order to do so. In contracts-in-cooperation, however, the most important single ingredient often is an unspecific general willingness to co-operate to achieve mutual success in the relationship. The legal system is thus often in the position not unlike that of a scientist who has to dry out a jellyfish before his instruments of examination can be used on it.

[20] *Economic exchange.* Many of the consequences of the fact that contracts is a mechanism of economic exchange can better be considered subsequently. Three might, however, be noted at this point. First, the overall impact on the legal system of the exchange-credit economy is something of which no lawyer can afford to be unaware of — so too of the impact of the legal system on the exchange-credit economy. Second, exchange-credit is only one of the two major ways in which societies answer basic economic problems, the other being socialist mechanisms which do not depend upon exchange, e.g. public schools, taxation for defense, etc. A lawyer needs to be aware of the similarities and differences between exchange mechanisms and socialist mechanisms and of their legal significance in view of the importance of both in our society. Third, and closely related to the foregoing, a profitable study can be made of the borderlines between exchange and other kinds of relationships. We have been doing this for years in contract courses with respect to family gifts and the doctrine of consideration. But there are borderline areas of far more social significance, e.g. forced exchanges, such as condemnation of prop-

erty, the duty to bargain in good faith in the NLRA, duties to enter contracts under the various civil rights laws.

[21] *Planning for the future.* This aspect of contractual behavior is extremely and directly significant to the practicing lawyer irrespective of the nature of the transaction-type with which he is dealing. First, he must be aware of the fact that the primary purpose of the planning of the parties is to achieve a workable operating relationship for the future. Second, as an expert in verbalizing, in questioning, in anticipating problems, etc. the lawyer may be called upon to assist the parties in planning a workable operating relationship. Third, the lawyer as legal technician has two important further planning roles: (a) planning for trouble between the parties, e.g. thinking about and preparing for such things as risks of non-performance, changed circumstances, liquidated damages, arbitration, etc.; (b) planning both to avoid illegality, e.g. . . . to utilize the law affirmatively, e.g. qualifying the transaction for beneficial tax treatment.

[22] *Potential external sanctions.* A lawyer needs to know at least the following generalities about this aspect of contracts-in-gross: The most important support for contractual relationships is not a sanction at all, but a continuation of the exchange motivations which led the parties to enter the relationship in the first place. These motivations may continue in effect even after one party has fully performed while the other has not. The motivation causing the debtor in such a case to perform may well be his desire to enter other exchange relationships with the same creditor. Also of great importance are internal command and habit. For example, it simply never dawns on many people not to pay their department store bills on time, or if it does dawn on them the thought is put aside immediately as immoral or otherwise unthinkable. The lawyer needs to know also that informal social and community sanctions are extremely important. So too are non-legal but more formalized community sanctions, as for example, trade association penalties, or mediation or arbitration (even when these are of no legal force). Legal sanctions are but a last resort, however important they may become when in fact resorted to.

[23] Since, when the last resort is reached, the lawyer is practically always involved, it is essential for him to have some understanding of what it is. The kind of development found in the first chapter of Fuller and Braucher, *Basic Contract Law* (1964) is a proper and very desirable foundation for thinking about contract remedies relating to any transaction-type.

[24] *Social control and manipulation.* The most obvious example of social control and manipulation of contractual behavior is the one most observed, most noted and the nature of which as a social control is most overlooked. That is the fact that the legal system enforces contracts at all. Its doing so, of course, represents a conscious or unconscious policy of reinforcing market mechanisms by the law, a policy which goes far beyond simply protecting the changes in property interests which may have been effectuated in a completed contract. This policy is what Macaulay has called the market goals of contract law and policy. One of the most important pedagogical aims of a course in contracts should be to bring home to the student the fact that these market goals themselves constitute social control and manipulation, the social value of which in particular instances must be weighed against competing goals.

[25] The competing non-market goals of legal policy in contractual relationships are bifurcated rather than unitary. Since contract, especially when reinforced by legal sanctions reflecting market goal policy, can be a wild and dangerous animal, it is often necessary to control it by limiting its power. Such control can be achieved in numerous ways, some obvious and some not so obvious. For example, certain transaction types or certain contractual provisions may be made illegal in a criminal sense, or may be stripped of legal enforcement. These limitations are obvious enough. Less obvious, however, may be such things as rules of interpretation which may subtly prevent certain types of parties from effectively creating particularly undesirable contractual provisions. Moreover, the limited nature of contract remedies themselves represents an extremely important limitation on the market goal policy — the law does not, for example, consider that goal sufficiently important to make a breach of contract an economic crime punishable criminally.

[26] Limitation on contract power, however, is not the only social alternative to the market goal policy. The contracts of its citizens are far too valuable and important in a market society for the society to refrain from using them affirmatively for its own purposes. There is thus affirmative social manipulation and exploitation of "private" contracts which is an extremely important goal competing not only with market goals, but often with limitation-of-power goals as well. In the heyday of laissez faire this type of manipulation and exploitation was somewhat limited in scope, taxation of certain kinds of contractual relationships and subsidies being the most obvious examples. In the modern mixed economy, however, social manipulation and exploitation of contractual relationships abound. Not only has transaction-type taxation, notably the sales tax and the income tax, increased vastly in importance, but many kinds of social goals are being achieved by other kinds of required (or societally encouraged) appurtenances to contractual relationships. Nowhere is this more evident than in employment relationships with such imposed appurtenances as Social Security, unemployment insurance, workmen's compensation, health and safety requirements, etc. But employment is by no means the only example, it is merely one of the areas where the process started early. A more recent entry into the field is the vast amount of legal manipulation of contractual relationships to try to solve racial and religious discrimination problems. Although the focus thus far in the civil rights area has been on preventing refusal to contract, certainly more and more it will also be on preventing discrimination within established contractual relationships, e.g. preventing price discrimination by supermarkets in the ghetto or racial discrimination in employee promotion.

[27] Thus, throughout contractual relationships three competing social policies are found: market goals, limitation of contract power and affirmative manipulation and social exploitation. The interplay of these policies cuts across transaction-type lines in such a way that study of them in some transaction-types should aid considerably in understanding them in other types of transactions.

[28] *Property characteristics of contracts.* Just as society in general may exploit contracts made between its citizens, so too may individual third parties seek to take advantage of them. This is, of course, inevitable in any society in which contracts become a significant form of wealth. At least as long as there is significant market for the subject matter of a contract there may be third party interests of one kind or another. And since markets are available in a great many transaction-types, such legal matters as assignability, third-party beneficiaries, etc. are also a proper subject of a generalized contracts course.

[29] To summarize the answer to the second question which started this paper, all five (or six) of the common elements of contractual relations do present to the legal system and to lawyers problems and challenges which cut across transaction-type

boundaries. These problems and challenges could be studied in separate transaction-type courses, and it would even be possible to demonstrate in such courses something of their universality. Nevertheless, their great social and practical-lawyer significance call for a unitary contracts course as the most effective way possible to present the elements and their legal ramifications to the students. In the remainder of the paper I propose to set out some thoughts about the content and structure of a course built around these basic elements.

[30] *Contents and structure of a unitary contracts course built on the common contract elements.* This is not the proper place to develop a thesis that present generalized contract legal doctrine is vastly deficient as a useful organization of the social and legal problems inherent in contractual relationships. And it certainly is not the place to undertake the task of revamping contracts doctrine to present a theoretical model which corresponds to the basic elements in contractual relationships. And even more it is not the place to try to reconcile such a model with the actual outcome of cases, with legislation and administrative law, with business and other social practice, etc. It is, however, an appropriate place to suggest what should be included in a generalized contracts course in order to bring into the open and to develop the common elements of contractual relationships and the common problems and challenges presented to the legal system by them. So too, the basic organization of the teaching materials is a proper subject for consideration.

[31] The reader who has troubled to arrive at this point will already have inferred some of the purposes and goals of a contracts course built on the common contract elements. Nevertheless, it is appropriate to summarize them at this point:

1. To perform its share (or more) of the development goals of all first-year courses: learning to read (and write) and developing other communication skills; developing an increased capacity for sustained rational thought; increasing perception of human values and of how to achieve them; developing a workable sense of justice; developing understanding of decision-making and engaging in vicarious practice in human problem-solving; sharpening abilities to use legal tools such as statutes and precedent.

2. Broadening perception of the significance, consequences, roles and limitations of contractual relations in our society.

3. Acquiring some information about and some understanding of specific and important contractual transaction types, e.g., collective bargaining agreements, consumer purchases, franchise agreements, insurance, etc.

4. Developing a general understanding of the interplay of contractual relationships with the legal system, and specific comprehension of contractual legal problems such as dispute settlement, limitations on legal remedies and their effectiveness, those caused by incomplete and flexible planning, by the need of the legal system to reduce co-operative ongoing relationships to relatively rigid verbalizations in order to be able to cope with conflicts, by specific social limitations and exploitations of contractual relationships, etc.

5. Developing an understanding of the role of the lawyer in contractual relationships generally, and specifically with respect to the response of the legal system to contractual relationships.

6. Acquiring elemental skills in the "lawyering" of contracts from negotiation and drafting to advocacy and judging in appellate litigation, to legislating, etc.

[32] Goals such as the foregoing may look very nice in a law school catalogue or sound good in a teacher's introductory lecture, but we all know that we are lucky to achieve much of anything we set out to do in the classroom. It would perhaps therefore be better to call them directions, rather than goals. And so the question is, if we set out with these directions in mind, what goes into the contracts course and how does it go in?

[33] First, the areas of human behavior from which materials are selected are as broad as the common elements of contractual behavior. This broad area of selection encompasses not only most of the traditional contract areas, but gives full weight to continuing economic exchange relationships which have tended to drop out of contracts courses, e.g. collective bargaining and other aspects of employment relationships, mediation, arbitration. Perhaps even more important is that it brings into the contracts fold all of the black sheep transaction-types which have tended to slip away as the academic shepherds of contracts have sought to avoid the doctrinal stresses which otherwise would have been caused by legislative, administrative and sometimes judicial regulation. With the return of such transaction-types comes the regulation as an integral part of the contractual relationship. [Insurance statutes, union legislation and] Workmen's Compensation, all seem to be as much a proper study of contracts as is the mailbox rule. Indeed, they are considerably more so since they have some current significance — a comment which brings me to the next point.

[34] Second, the subject matter of the materials selected should have some present or future topical significance. This is important to the achievement of almost all the goals enumerated above. Dead problems, however fascinating intellectually, simply do not achieve most of those goals, unless enough history is reincarnated with them so that the student can see them with the full flavor of the social and economic background of their day. This is a pretty tricky thing to pull off with an 1854 English case concerning the well known carriers trading under the name of Pickford & Co. who evidently did not use printed shipping forms. I shall be the first to agree that it is not always easy to tell when a problem is dead and when it is still topically significant — certainly its absence from current reported appellate cases does not conclusively demonstrate its topical demise. Nevertheless, the difficulty does not justify failure to make an attempt. Moreover, I suspect that there would be considerable agreement about what was and what was not topical if a representative group of contracts teachers were to survey current casebooks.

[35] Third, non-legal as well as legal aspects of contractual relationships should be considered. I have in mind in part, but only in part, the sort of formal sociological studies which have been done by Stewart Macaulay and others. In addition to such studies, however, legal materials themselves can often yield a great deal of enlightenment on non-legal aspects of contractual relations. For example, cases, while the "spawn of trouble," often nevertheless yield much information about the way people "really" conduct themselves in the real world, even when there is no trouble. Moreover, there is much to be found with respect to "real life" in journals, etc. dealing with areas of contracts such as collective bargaining agreements, government contracts, etc. Nor, in spite of my own relative lack of success in digging out much, am I yet convinced that business school libraries, for example, do not have something for us. And certainly, such genuinely negotiated form contracts as those of the American Institute of Architects are goldmines of information about how the parties plan many of the things which have to be done in connection with

the construction of buildings. In short, I do not think that it is either necessary or desirable to wait until the legal sociologists have progressed further before making more diligent efforts to work in considerably more information on contracting in contrast to that on contract law and litigation.

[36] Fourth, since it is impossible to study the elements of contractual behavior with any degree of breadth without going heavily into areas regulated by statute and administrative law, a considerable volume of statutory law and administrative regulation and decisions will inevitably be included. This, plus the fact that even the traditional area of contract doctrine has now been invaded by the UCC will help the contracts course do its bit towards remedying the present absurdity of a common-law first-year curriculum in an age of legislative and administrative legal dominance. In addition, such important dispute settling mechanisms as arbitration require treatment with more care than is now generally devoted to them — perhaps even as much as we now devote to some of the topically insignificant aspects of the doctrine of consideration. Thus, if the course is broadened as is herein suggested, there will inevitably be a marked reduction in reliance on appellate cases and especially on common law appellate cases, with corresponding increases in other types of legal materials.

[37] Fifth, it is apparent that a traditional doctrinal organization of the materials, with chapter headings such as consideration or offer and acceptance, puts nearly insurmountable hurdles in the way of achieving the goals of the course. For one thing, that kind of organization simply does not fit the functional legal problems created by contracts. For another, it causes students to see contracts backwards. They tend to see contractual relations as extrapolations of legal doctrines, rather than see legal doctrines as a response to contractual relations. Whatever validity this approach may have with respect to non-market policies in contract law, it is extremely misleading with respect to market policies, the very area with which traditional doctrines are most at home. The organization should, therefore, be based on assessments of the most effective way of accomplishing those goals, rather than doctrinally.

[38] It is not meant to suggest that even the more abstract legal doctrines can be ignored (except insofar as they have nothing to do with significant modern problems). For example, the doctrine of consideration would be dealt with as it arises in the legal responses to various problems, e.g. in the mutuality questions arising in output and requirements contracts and franchise agreements, in the duress problems arising out of adjustments in existing contracts, in the problems arising from unconscionable contracts, in dealing with the revocation of offers, etc. On the other hand, whether it would be dealt with at all in respect to family gifts would depend upon an assessment of the current importance of the revocability of family gift promises. Or such cases might be included for contrasting the utilization of the consideration doctrines with the handling of similar transactions under the Internal Revenue Code (the latter being a significant and lively current problem).

[39] The foregoing paragraphs outline some of the principles which I think should be applied in order to get into the contracts course what is necessary in order to move it in the direction of the goals argued for earlier. Obviously, however, as soon as we take off from the doctrinal organizations now available, the door is open to a host of possible organizations, selections of topic areas, emphases on types of materials, etc. I am doubtless falling down on the job assigned by the esoteric title which we chose for this panel in failing to be more specific as to

the measure of the "mix." My justification is that until someone has in fact attempted to make a mix along the foregoing lines there is not much sense in guessing at the proportions with which he would come up.

NOTE

Re-read the Introduction to this book, and reflect on how your understanding of the ideas discussed there has changed since you first read it.

INDEX

1096 Index

Ticket cases — *cont'd*
- conflicting principles, 847-850
- whether terms reasonably brought to attention of party, 847-850
- exemption clause, 851
- imposing terms of contract, 846
- internet licence agreement, 859-860
- parking lot exemption cases, 853-859
- bailment, contract of, 855, 858-859
- fundamental breach, 856
- plain language drafting, 859
- reasonable notice of exemption, whether, 857-858
- reasonable notice of conditions, 848, 850, 851-852

U

Unconscionability
- bank guarantee: foundation of judicial doctrine, 943-956, 957
- breach of duty to take fiduciary care, 953-954
- general rule of enforceability, 945-946
- exceptions, 945-946
- inequality of bargaining power, 947-948, 955
- unconscionable transaction, 946
- bank guarantee: issues in enforcement, 959-977
- independent legal advice, need for, 961, 963, 964, 967, 968-974
- rules developed by House of Lords, 975-976
- statutory provisions, 976
- undue influence, presumption of, 961, 962-966, 969-970
- constructive notice of wrongdoing between spouses, 965, 966, 968-969, 971, 972, 974
- rebutted, 961, 966-967
- criterion of reasonableness, 940
- distributive justice, 977-979
- domestic contracts, 808
- expansion of, 939-940
- failure to acknowledge obligation on renewal, 956-957
- independent legal advice, need for, 958-959, 968-977
- procedure, 958-959
- rules developed by House of Lords, 975-976
- undue influence and, 961, 963, 964, 967, 968-974
- judicial development, 940-957
- covenants in restraint of trade, 940-941
- equitable principles, 941, 942
- factors considered by Canadian courts, 941-942
- improvident or grossly one-sided transaction, 941, 942
- unfairness, 941, 942
- fiduciary duty, 941
- undue influence, 941
- void or voidable, 941

- public policy, implementation of, 1029-1032
- relations, protection of, 999-1019
- abuse of power given by contract, whether, 999-1010
- bad faith, issue of, 1005-1007, 1008
- corporations and oppression remedy, 1009-1010
- franchises, 1010-1019
- changes, franchisor's liability for, 1017-1019
- disclosure requirements, 1011
- duty of good faith and fiduciary duty by franchisor, 1011-1015, 1016-1017
- breaches of obligations, 1014-1015
- limited protection for franchisees, 1011
- relation having integrity warranting protection, 1010
- restraints in interest of freedom of contract, 979-999
- connection between unconscionability and restraint of trade, 992-99
- standard form contracts, use of, 995, 996-997, 998
- not evidence of "cartelization", 998
- contract of employment, 980-989
- non-competition clauses, 982-983, 986-987
- non-competition clauses vs. non-solicitation clauses, 984-985
- reasonableness between parties, 988
- temporal and special limits, 984, 988
- corporations, power of, 989-992
- generally, 979-980
- social values of contracts, preservation of, 1019-1032
- contracts as social institution, 1019
- effect of disclaimer and limitation of liability clauses, 1022-1024
- inequality in bargaining position and standardized warranty, 1024-1027
- spirit of law, 1027-1028

Uniform Commercial Code (UCC)
- battle of forms, 548
- exclusive dealing, 279-281
- frustration: delay or non-delivery, 811-812
- organization, 65
- purpose, 64

Uniform Law Conference of Canada, 66

Unjust enrichment and part performance
- inequitable contract not enforced, 247-249
- part performance exception, 239-240
- *quantum meruit*, 240
- restitutionary remedy, 238

W

Warranties. *See* **Misrepresentations and warranties**

Writing requirement. *See* **Statute of Frauds**